Understanding Abnormal Behavior

Understanding Abnormal Behavior

Third Edition

David Sue

Western Washington
University

Derald Sue

California State University,
Hayward

Stanley Sue

University of California,
Los Angeles

Houghton Mifflin Company   Boston
Dallas   Geneva, Illinois   Palo Alto
Princeton, New Jersey

Cover design by Peter Good

Cover illustration by Janet Cummings Good

Chapter opening photos by Ralph Mercer

All other credits appear on p. C-1, which constitutes an extension of the copyright page.

Library of Congress Catalog Card Number: 89-080968

ISBN: 0-395-43262-6

To our parents, Tom and Lucy Sue, who never suspected they would produce three psychologists, and to our wives and families, who provided the emotional support that enabled us to complete this edition

Contents

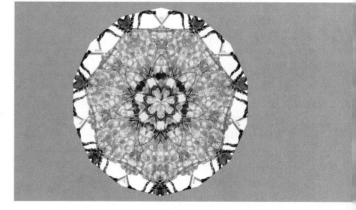

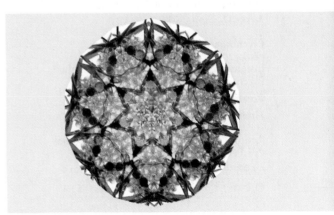

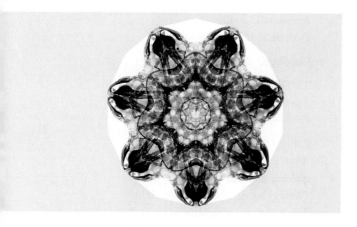

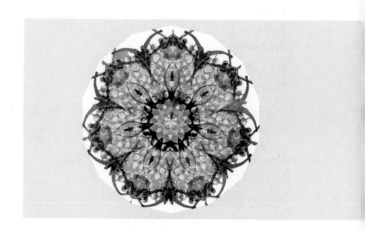

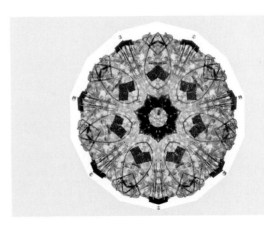

Focus Boxes

Preface

In writing and then twice revising this book we have sought to lead students to a fuller understanding of abnormal behavior and the ways that psychologists study and attempt to treat it. In pursuing this goal, we have been guided by three major objectives.

1. To produce a book based solidly on good scholarship
2. To offer a balanced presentation of the field, as free of theoretical bias as we can make it, which examines abnormal psychology as both a scientific and clinical endeavor
3. To make our book accessible and stimulating to a wide range of students

The comments we have received from many students and instructors suggest that we have met our objectives in the past. The third edition, we believe, builds on this achievement and surpasses it.

OUR APPROACH

The text covers the major categories of disorders listed in the revised third edition of the *Diagnostic and Statistical Manual of Mental Disorders* (DSM-III-R). The DSM nosological system has generated much controversy, which we discuss as we examine the system's strengths and weaknesses.

Of course, no useful text is merely a reiteration of DSM. We take an eclectic, multicultural approach to the field, drawing on important contributions from various disciplines and theoretical stances. We believe that different combinations of life experiences and constitutional factors influence behavioral disorders, and we project this view throughout the text. For example, an analysis of schizophrenia would be incomplete if both psychosocial and psychophysiological factors were not discussed; we cover both extensively. We also believe that cross-cultural comparisons of abnormal behavior and treatment methods can greatly enhance our understanding of behavioral disorders, so we pay special attention to cultural phenomena.

As psychologists we know that learning is enhanced whenever material is presented in a lively and engaging manner. We accomplish this by bridging the abstract to the concrete, blending case vignettes and clients' descriptions of their experiences with research-based explanations. Controversial topics are highlighted and explored in depth. Among these are

- The relationship between stress and illness and the mind's role in healing (Chapter 8)
- Crack and cocaine use (Chapter 10)
- Suicide among college students (Chapter 13)
- Cultural bias in psychotherapy (Chapter 19)
- Sexual intimacy in therapist-client relationships (Chapter 21)

Complex material is presented with clarifying examples. The intriguing cluster of symptoms known as borderline personality disorder emerges from ambiguity as two therapists, practiced in treating the disorder, describe their experiences in detail (pp. 237-238). The fine distinctions between organic mental syndromes and disorders are made plain in a few sentences (p. 422). In making these and other connections, we try to encourage students to think critically about the knowledge they acquire in the hope that they will develop an appreciation of the study of abnormal behavior rather than merely assimilate a collection of facts and theories.

Contributing to the strength of the third edition are a number of features popularized in one or both of the previous two editions. Among these is the extended case study of Steven V., a unique device that translates theory into reality by interpreting the problems of a troubled college student through different theoretical perspectives. The case appears in four chapters, reflecting many of the issues presented in the text, such as the relationship between theoretical stances and the way therapists diagnose and treat mental illness. Steven's background and clinical history are described in Chapter 1. He is viewed from the biogenic, psychoanalytic, and humanistic-existential perspectives in Chapter 2 and from the behavioral and family systems perspectives in Chapter 3. The case culminates in Chapter 19, where Steven's therapist discusses his mental state, treatment, and prognosis from a systematic eclectic perspective. Other helpful features appearing in the previous edition include

- A chapter outline on the first page of every chapter
- Focus boxes highlighting high-interest topics
- Key terms with definitions listed at the end of each chapter, plus a glossary at the back of the book that defines all key terms
- Chapter summaries reinforcing important concepts and ideas
- Discussions of treatment approaches in each of the chapters on disorders as well as in a separate chapter
- Separate chapters on suicide and mental retardation
- Two chapters devoted to schizophrenia

NEW TO THE THIRD EDITION

In this edition, we have both updated the material examined in the previous two editions and presented the latest trends in research, including expanded coverage of

- Cognitive behavioral viewpoint
- Object relations theory
- Biochemical explanations for many of the disorders
- Expressed emotion in schizophrenia
- Brain-imaging techniques, such as magnetic resonance imaging

We have written a *new chapter on legal and ethical issues* and have also introduced two unique features—*"First Person" mini-essays* and *disorder charts* illustrating the DSM-III-R diagnostic criteria for each group of disorders. Further, the book is now presented in *full color* throughout.

The chapter on legal and ethical issues examines legal definitions of insanity, confidentiality in psychotherapy, deinstitutionalization, and therapist-client relationships. In view of the growing interest in these topics, the social dilemmas they present, and their implications for research and practice, we believe these concerns need extensive discussion.

The "First Person" mini-essays are written by mental health practitioners, who describe their personal experiences assessing and treating clients. In many abnormal psychology courses, instructors invite guest lecturers to speak, suggest additional readings to supplement course materials, and provide personal accounts of their experiences in the mental health field. The "First Person" mini-essays simulate these functions. For example, read the essay by J. Richard Woy, a practicing therapist and consultant, who writes about some of his experiences with treatment approaches used prior to the widespread use of psychotropic drugs (p. 506). By incorporating this feature into the text, we provide students with an opportunity to see theoretical constructs directly applied in actual settings—in other words, to see psychology at work and to deepen their sense of clinical reality.

Because students are sometimes confused by the presentation of so many categories and subcategories of disorders, we have introduced fifteen disorder charts, presented with the disorders they illustrate. The disorder charts (see p. 146, for example) facilitate the student's conceptual grasp of the structural relationships between disorders. In addition, instructors may find that the charts make it easier to organize lectures on specific disorders.

Among the new topics in the third edition are AIDS and dementia, a discussion of the psychology of women from a feminist perspective, copycat suicides, patients' rights, multicultural criteria for defining abnormal behavior, stress inoculation training, childhood depression, and the fragile X syndrome. We also augment our discussion of autism with a Focus box on the original "Rain Man."

We have also made a few organizational changes in the third edition, as we note below.

ORGANIZATION OF THE TEXT

The third edition is organized into six major sections. Part One (Chapters 1 through 5) provides a context for viewing abnormal behavior and treatment by introducing students to historical contributions (Chapter 1) and to the diverse theoretical perspectives that are currently used to explain deviant behaviors. These theoretical perspectives are categorized into biogenic and psychogenic models, which are presented in Chapter 2, and behavioral and family systems models, which are presented in Chapter 3. Chapter 4 discusses classification and assessment, and the section ends with Chapter 5, an examination of research methods that psychologists use in studying abnormal behavior.

The bulk of the text, the thirteen chapters in Parts Two through Five, presents the major disorders covered in DSM-III-R. In each chapter, symptoms are presented first, followed by diagnosis, theoretical perspectives, etiology, and treatment.

Part Two contains three chapters that deal with anxiety and stress. Anxiety disorders are discussed in Chapter 6, somatoform and dissociative disorders in Chapter 7, and stress and psychophysiological disorders in Chapter 8. Although the separate chapter on stress that appeared in the second edition has been eliminated in this revision, much of the chapter's content as well as new material has been integrated into Chapters 6 and 8. We believe this change has the advantage of showing how stress affects specific disorders.

Part Three includes three chapters dealing with personality and impulse control disorders (Chapter 9), substance abuse (Chapter 10), and psychosexual disorders and dysfunctions (Chapter 11). We have grouped these topics together because they pose such acute social and clinical dilemmas. Chapter 9 includes a substantive discussion of antisocial personality disorder, but it also examines the other personality disorders in greater depth than many other texts. We have added to this chapter a discussion of impulse control disorders, including compulsive gambling and pyromania, because of growing concern over their effects. Chapter 10 explores alcohol and drug abuse, the personal and social devastation they cause, and treatment approaches. Chapter 11 includes discussions of the latest research on sexual disorders and dysfunctions, the elimination of homosexuality as a category in DSM-III-R, and the effects of aging on sexual activity.

Part Four contains four chapters that deal with mood disorders, suicide, and schizophrenia. Although mood disturbances can vary in degree of severity, we chose to devote a substantial part of Chapter 12 to the more severe depressive and bipolar disorders. Suicide (Chapter 13) is included in Part Four because of its relationship to depression. We present two chapters (14 and 15) on schizophrenia because the topic is so complex and the research on it so voluminous. In addition, particular attention is paid to the relationship between genetic factors, physiological factors, and environmental conditions in schizophrenia and certain mood disorders.

Part Five encompasses organic and developmental problems. One chapter is devoted to each of the following topics: organic brain disorders (Chapter 16), disorders of childhood and adolescence (Chapter 17), and mental retardation (Chapter 18). Although organic brain dysfunctions can occur at any age, we have focused on those associated with the aging process. Also note that eating disorders, previously discussed in the psychophysiological disorders chapter (Chapter 8), are now presented in Chapter 17.

Part Six comprises three chapters. The first two (Chapters 19 and 20) examine treatment and community intervention. Although the therapies used to treat specific disorders are discussed in the chapters on disorders, the different approaches can be more easily contrasted in a separate chapter. The chapter on community psychology (Chapter 20) explores the argument that community and institutional forces have a major impact on emotional well-being and that community interventions can be used to promote mental health. The final chapter (Chapter 21), as we have already mentioned, deals with legal and ethical issues. Because of the growing concern over such matters as the insanity defense, patients' rights, confidentiality, and mental health practices in general, we believe it is important to understand the issues and controversies surrounding these topics.

ANCILLARIES

The text is accompanied by a wide-range of ancillary items. We enthusiastically thank Richard L. Leavy of Ohio Wesleyan University, who substantially revised the *Instructor's Manual*, *Test Bank* (completely new), and a student *Study Guide*.

For each chapter of the text, the *Instructor's Manual* includes an extended chapter outline, a set of learning objectives, discussion topics, classroom exercises, handouts, and a list of supplementary readings and audiovisual resources. The chapter outlines are available on disk in a generic ASCII-code format known as *LectureBank* that allows instructors to use standard word-processing software to integrate their own lecture notes and ideas into the text outlines.

The *Test Bank* includes seventy multiple-choice questions per chapter. For each question, the corresponding learning objective, text page number, question type (fact/conceptual or application), and page number are provided. *MicroTest*, the computerized version, allows instructors to generate exams and integrate their own test questions with those on disk.

The *Study Guide* provides a complete review of each chapter in the text through the use of chapter outlines, learning objectives, a fill-in-the-blank-review of key terms, and multiple-choice questions. The answers to the test questions include an explanation of each incorrect answer as well as the right answer; we know of no other study guide in abnormal psychology that contains this valuable pedagogical device.

We find it particularly valuable that the same set of learning objectives is used throughout the *Instructor's Manual, Test Bank,* and *Study Guide,* thus helping to make these three items an integrated package.

A videocassette containing short films on topics in abnormal psychology, including biological bases of disorders, schizophrenia, and depression, is also available to adopters of this text.

ACKNOWLEDGMENTS

The publication of a textbook results from the efforts of many people, and we are particularly grateful for the assistance provided by the following colleagues and reviewers, who guided us on the third edition:

Ileana Arias
University of Georgia

David H. Barlow
State University of New York at Albany

James Bartee
Pacific University

Robert A. Brown
University of Maryland

James F. Calhoun
University of Georgia

Rita Yopp Cohen
University of Maryland

Lorry J. Cology
Owens Technical College

Michael E. Connor
California State University at Long Beach

Robert D. Coursey
University of Maryland

Ian M. Evans
State University of New York at Binghamton

Kenneth France
Shippensburg University

Alan J. Fridlund
University of California at Santa Barbara

Stuart Golann
University of Massachusetts at Amherst

Gary S. Goldstein
University of New Hampshire at Manchester

Albert Gorman
Suffolk County Community College

John A. Greaves
Jefferson State Junior College

Wendy S. Grolnick
New York University

Elaine Heiby
University of Hawaii

Bruce Hinrichs
Lakewood Community College

William L. Hoover
Suffolk County Community College

Sandra Guest Houston
University of Central Florida

Richard L. Leavy
Ohio Wesleyan University

Mark F. Lenzenweger
Cornell University

Arnold LeUnes
Texas A&M University

Susan A. Locke
Baruch College

José Lopez
University of California at Los Angeles

Dikran J. Martin
College of Marin

Francis A. Martin
Belmont College

Gregory A. Miller
University of Illinois at Urbana-Champaign

William J. Ray
Pennsylvania State University

Duane H. Reeder
Glendale Community College

Robert W. Reiber
John Jay College, CUNY

Esther Rothblum
University of Vermont

Robert F. Sabalis
University of South Carolina

Herb Severson
Oregon Research Institute

For contributing "First Person" mini-essays we are indebted to Mary Kay Barbieri, Eugene Givens, III, Margaret Hamilton, Mary Ann Mayer, Eddy Regnier, Susan Safranski, Jes Sellers, Edward Spauster, Leslie Sue, Merryl Maleska Wilbur, Normund Wong, and J. Richard Woy.

Finally, it has been our pleasure to work with the highly competent professional staff at Houghton Mifflin.

David Sue
Derald Sue
Stanley Sue

Understanding Abnormal Behavior

PART 1

The Study of Abnormal Psychology

chapter 1
Abnormal Behavior

The study of abnormal psychology is a journey into known and unknown territories of the mind. To help you understand the scope and dynamics of this field, we would like to start by introducing you to Steven V. Steve is a 21-year-old college student who exemplifies many of the issues we discuss in this text. We begin his story in the office of his therapist.

The therapist could feel himself becoming tense, apprehensive, uncertain: How should he interpret the threat? How should he act on it? One wheel of his swivel chair squealed sharply, breaking the silence, as he backed it away from his client, Steven V.

Eighteen months earlier, Steve's woman friend, Linda, had broken off her relationship with Steve. Steve had fallen into a crippling depression. During the past few weeks, however, with the encouragement of the therapist, Steve had begun to open up—to express his innermost feelings. His depression had lifted, but it was replaced by a deep anger and hostility toward Linda. In today's session, Steve had become increasingly loud and agitated as he recounted his complaints against Linda. Minutes ago, with his hands clenched into fists, his knuckles white, he had abruptly lowered his voice and looked his therapist in the eye.

"She doesn't deserve to live," Steve had said. "I swear, I'm going to kill her."

Until this session, the therapist had not believed Steve was dangerous. Now he wondered whether Steve could be the one client in ten thousand to act out such a threat. Should Linda, or the police, be told of what Steve had said?

Steven V. had a long psychiatric history, beginning well before he first sought help from the therapist at the University Psychological Services Center. (In fact, his parents wanted their son to continue seeing a private therapist, but Steve stopped therapy during his junior year at the university.) Steve had actually been in and out of psychotherapy since kindergarten; while in high school, he was hospitalized twice for depression. His case records, nearly two inches thick, contained a number of diagnoses, including labels such as *schizoid personality, paranoid schizophrenia,* and *manic–depressive psychosis.* Although his present therapist did not find these labels particularly helpful, Steve's clinical history did provide some clues to the causes of his problems.

Steven V. was born in a suburb of San Francisco, California, the only child of an extremely wealthy couple. His father was a prominent businessman who worked long hours and traveled frequently. On those rare occasions when he was at home, Mr. V. was often preoccupied with business matters and held himself quite aloof from his son. The few interactions they had were characterized by his constant ridicule and criticism of Steve. Mr. V. was greatly disappointed that his son seemed so timid, weak, and withdrawn. Steve was extremely bright and did well in school, but Mr. V. felt he lacked the "toughness" needed to survive and prosper in today's world. Once, when Steve was about ten years old, he came home from school with a bloody nose and bruised face, crying and complaining of being picked on by his schoolmates. His father showed no sympathy but instead berated Steve for losing the fight. In his father's presence, Steve usually felt worthless, humiliated, and fearful of doing or saying the wrong thing.

Mrs. V. was very active in civic and social affairs, and she too spent relatively little time with her son. Although she treated Steve more warmly and lovingly than his father did, she seldom came to Steve's defense when Mr. V.

bullied him. She generally allowed her husband to make family decisions.

When Steve was a child, his mother had been quite affectionate at times. She had often allowed Steve to sleep with her, in her bed, when her husband was away on business trips. She usually dressed minimally on these occasions and was very demonstrative—holding, stroking, and kissing Steve. This behavior had continued until Steve was twelve, when his mother abruptly refused to let Steve into her bed. The sudden withdrawal of this privilege had confused and angered Steve, who was not certain what he had done wrong. He knew, though, that his mother had been quite upset when she awoke one night to find him masturbating next to her.

Most of the time, however, Steve's parents seemed to live separately from one another and from their son. Steve was raised, in effect, by a full-time maid. He rarely had playmates of his own age. His birthdays were celebrated with a cake and candles, but the only celebrants were Steve and his mother. By age ten, Steve had learned to keep himself occupied by playing "mind games," letting his imagination carry him off on flights of fantasy. He frequently imagined himself as a powerful figure—Superman, Batman, or Zorro. His fantasies were often extremely violent, and his foes were vanquished only after much blood had been spilled.

As Steve grew older, his fantasies and heroes became increasingly menacing and evil. When he was fifteen, he obtained a pornographic videotape that he viewed repeatedly on a video player in his room. Often, Steve would masturbate as he watched scenes of women being sexually violated. The more violent the acts against the women, the more aroused he became. Steve now recalls that he spent much of his spare time between the ages of fifteen and seventeen watching X-rated videotapes or violent movies like *The Texas Chainsaw Massacre,* in which a madman saws and hacks women to pieces. Steve always identified with the character perpetrating the outrage; at times, he imagined his parents as the victims.

At about age sixteen, Steve became convinced that external forces were controlling his mind and behavior and were drawing him into his fantasies. He was often filled with guilt and anxiety after one of his "mind games." Although he was strongly attracted to his fantasy world, he also felt that something was wrong with it and with him. After seeing the movie *The Exorcist*, he became convinced that he was possessed by the devil.

Until this time, Steve had been a quiet, withdrawn person. In kindergarten the school psychologist had diagnosed his condition as *autistic-like*, because Steve seldom spoke, seemed unresponsive to the environment, and was socially isolated. His parents had immediately hired a prominent child psychiatrist to work with Steve. The psychiatrist had assured them that Steve was not autistic but would need intensive treatment for several years. And throughout these years of treatment, Steve never acted out any of his fantasies. But with the development of his interest in the occult and in demonic possession, he became outgoing, flamboyant, and even exhibitionistic. He read extensively about Satanism, joined a "Church of Satan" in San Francisco, and took to wearing a black cape on weekend journeys into that city. Against his will, he was hospitalized twice by his parents with diagnoses of, respectively, manic–depressive disorder and schizophrenia in remission.

Steve was twenty-one years old when he met Linda at an orientation session for first-year university students. Linda struck him as different from the other women students: unpretentious, open, and friendly. He quickly became obsessed with their relationship. But although Linda dated Steve frequently over the next few months, she did not seem to reciprocate his intense feelings. She took part in several extracurricular activities, including the student newspaper and student government, and her willingness to be apart from him confused and frustrated Steve. When her friends were around, Linda seemed almost oblivious to Steve's existence. In private, however, she was warm, affectionate, and intimate. She would not allow sexual intercourse, but she and Steve did engage in heavy petting.

Even while he and Linda were dating, Steve grew increasingly insecure about their relationship. He felt slighted by Linda's friends and began to believe she disliked him. Several times he accused her of plotting against him and deliberately making him feel inadequate. Linda continually denied these allegations. Finally (on one occasion), feeling frightened and intimidated by Steve, she acquiesced to having sex with him. Unfortunately, in that instance Steve could not maintain an erection. When he blamed her for this "failure" and became verbally and physically abusive, Linda put an end to their relationship and refused to see him again.

During the next year and a half, Steve suffered from severe bouts of depression and twice attempted suicide by drug overdose. For the past six months, up to the time of his threat, he had been seeing a therapist regularly at the University Psychological Services Center.

What do you make of Steven V.? His behavior is certainly beyond almost anyone's definition of normal. But is he a dangerous person from whom society must be protected? Is he a pathetic figure, doomed to fail in relationships with others as he did with Linda? Or is his major problem simply a lack of social skills that, once learned, will enable him to interact comfortably and confidently with other people?

In a sense, the purpose of this book, *Understanding Abnormal Behavior,* is to help you answer such questions. But at this point these questions are premature. Let's first examine some basic aspects of the study of abnormal behavior, including a bit of its history. Then, at the end of this chapter, we'll again discuss the case of Steven V. and its place in this book.

THE CONCERNS OF ABNORMAL PSYCHOLOGY

Abnormal psychology is the scientific study whose objectives are to describe, explain, predict, and control behaviors that are considered strange or unusual. Its subject matter ranges from the bizarre and spectacular to the more commonplace—from the violent homicides and "perverted" sexual acts that are widely reported by the news media to such unsensational (but more prevalent) behaviors as stuttering, depression, ulcers, and anxiety about examinations.

Describing Abnormal Behavior

The description of a particular case of abnormal behavior must be based on systematic observations by an attentive professional. These observations, usually paired with the results of psychological tests and with the person's psychological history, become the raw material for a **psychodiagnosis,** an attempt to describe, assess, and systematically draw inferences about an individual's psychological disorder.

Diagnosis is obviously an important early step in the treatment process. But a diagnosis that is not developed with great care can end up as nothing more than a label that tends to hinder rather than aid treatment. Such labels present two major problems. First, a term such as *manic-depressive* (which was used to describe Steven V.) can cover a wide range of behaviors. But this label may mean different things to different psychologists. So a label may be too general—it may describe something other than a client's specific behaviors. Second, a person's (especially a young person's) psychological problems are likely to change over time. A previous diagnosis can quickly become obsolete, a label that no longer describes that person. To guard against these prob-

lems, sensitive therapists ensure that labels, either old or new, are not used to substitute for careful investigation of a client's condition.

Explaining Abnormal Behavior

To explain abnormal behavior, the psychologist must identify its causes and determine how they led to the described behavior. This information, in turn, bears heavily on how a program of treatment is chosen.

As you will see in later chapters, explanations of abnormal behavior do vary, depending on the psychologist's theoretical orientation. For example, Steve's therapist might stress his client's loneliness, lack of self-esteem, and feelings of worthlessness brought about by his parents' actions—primarily his father's—and his lack of companions of his own age. To make up for what was missing from his life (the therapist might contend), Steve created a fantasy world in which he could feel powerful, freely express his anger toward his parents, and experience a sense of self-worth. But when Steve became disturbed by his own anger and hatred toward his parents, he protected himself by adopting the belief that these

During a therapy session, the therapist not only hears about the client's problems, but also carefully observes the client's behavior and emotional reactions. These observations can help to form the basis of a psycho-diagnosis.

feelings were implanted by a demon and beyond his (Steve's) control.

Explanations offered by other psychologists might be more biological in nature, emphasizing genetics or a biochemical imbalance. Still other psychologists might focus on Steve's inadequate interpersonal skills: he cannot make friends or develop meaningful relationships because he has never learned how to act around others. And still others might see and treat Steve's behavior as resulting from a combination of these causes.

Predicting Abnormal Behavior

If a therapist can correctly identify the source of a client's difficulty, he or she should be able to predict the kinds of problems the client will face during therapy and the symptoms the client will display. And the therapist *should* try to predict the process, in order to prepare the client for potential problems. But therapists have difficulty predicting the future course of many disorders. Even an experienced professional finds it hard to foretell how a particular client will behave.

For example, consider Steve's threat to kill Linda. Was it an empty threat—just Steve's way of venting his anger—or was it serious? Research shows that mental health professionals do a poor job of answering such questions; they tend to greatly overpredict violence.

Steve's threat raises another significant issue—that of the legal and ethical responsibilities of the therapist. Psychologists routinely grapple with questions of social responsibility. In particular, should Steve's therapist make the threat known? And if he does, how will it affect the therapeutic process? These issues are discussed more fully in Chapter 21.

In a landmark legal case (*Tarasoff* v. *Regents of the University of California,* 1974), the California Supreme Court ruled that, if a therapist hears a client threaten someone and does not inform the threatened person, and if the threat is carried out, then the injured person has the right to sue the therapist. Naturally, no therapist wants a client to hurt or kill anyone. But the ruling has unpleasant implications for the confidentiality of the client-therapist relationship. As one therapist remarked, "No one wants a shrink who's a fink."

Controlling Abnormal Behavior

Abnormal behavior may be controlled through **therapy,** a program of systematic intervention whose purpose is to modify a client's behavioral, affective (emotional), or cognitive state. For example, many therapists would believe that allowing Steve to vent his anger at Linda would reduce the chances of his harming her. Others might also recommend family therapy, or social skills training, or medication. As we have noted, the treatment for abnormal behavior generally follows from its explanation. Just as there are many ways to explain abnormal behaviors, many ways have been proposed to control them.

DEFINING ABNORMAL BEHAVIOR

Implicit in our discussion so far is the one overriding concern of abnormal psychology: abnormal behavior itself. But what exactly is abnormal behavior, and how do psychologists recognize it?

We shall examine four types of criteria that may be used to define or characterize behaviors as abnormal. Two of them—statistical criteria and criteria for ideal mental health—define abnormal behavior as, essentially, deviations from what is considered normal. The third considers multicultural factors in defining abnormality. The fourth type—consisting of the practical criteria—takes account of the effect of the behavior on the person exhibiting it or on others.

Statistical Criteria

Statistical criteria equate normality with those behaviors that occur most frequently in the population. Then abnormality is defined in terms of those behaviors that occur least frequently. For example, data on IQs may be accumulated and an average calculated. Then IQ scores near that average are considered normal, and relatively large deviations from the norm (in either direction) are considered abnormal. In spite of the word *statistical,* however, these criteria need not be quantitative in nature: People who talk to themselves, undress in public, or laugh uncontrollably for no apparent reason are considered abnormal

What is abnormal behavior? The question is as old as humanity itself, and an absolute answer to it cannot be given. Although specific criteria for defining abnormality have been proposed, they still cannot account for all differences in behavior or establish whether seemingly odd behavior is truly "abnormal."

use a statistical definition, the dominant or most powerful group generally determines what constitutes normality and abnormality.

In addition, the statistical criteria do not provide any basis for distinguishing between desirable and undesirable deviations from the norm. An IQ of 100 is considered normal or average. But what constitutes an abnormal deviation from this average? More important, is abnormality defined in only one direction or in both? An IQ of 55 would be considered abnormal by most people; but should people with IQ scores of 145 or higher also be considered abnormal? How does one evaluate such personality traits as assertiveness and dependence in terms of statistical criteria?

Two other central problems also arise. First, people who strike out in new directions—artistically, politically, or intellectually—may be seen as candidates for psychotherapy simply because they do not conform to normative behavior. Second, statistical criteria may "define" quite widely distributed but undesirable characteristics, such as anxiety, as normal.

In spite of these weaknesses, statistical criteria remain among the most widely used determinants of normality and abnormality. Not only do they underlie the layperson's evaluation of behaviors, but they are the most frequently used criteria in psychology. Many psychological tests and much diagnosis and classification of behavior disorders are based in part on statistical criteria.

Criteria for Ideal Mental Health

The concept of ideal mental health has been proposed as a criterion of normality by humanistic psychologists Carl Rogers and Abraham Maslow. Deviations from the ideal are taken to indicate varying degrees of abnormality.

Such criteria stress the importance of attaining some positive goal. Maslow and his followers suggest *self-actualization* or *creativity*. Psychoanalytically oriented psychologists have used the concept *consciousness* (awareness of motivations and behaviors) and *balance of psychic forces* as criteria for normality. Aspects of maturity such as *competence*, *autonomy*, and *resistance to stress* have also been proposed. But using any of these constructs as the sole criterion for defining normality leads to a number of problems.

according to these criteria simply because most people do not behave in that way.

Statistical criteria may seem adequate in some specific instances, but they have many problems. For one thing, they fail to take into account differences in place, community standards, and cultural values. For example, some lifestyles that are acceptable in San Francisco and New York may be judged abnormal by community standards in other parts of the nation. Likewise, if deviations from the majority are considered abnormal, then many ethnic and racial minorities that show strong subcultural differences from the majority must be classified as abnormal. When we

Mother Teresa and the Reverend Martin Luther King, Jr. are perceived by many to be self-actualized people, who have made extensive commitments and contributions to society—Mother Teresa to the poor in India and other Third World countries, providing shelter and medical care; Reverend King to the Civil Rights movement in the United States.

First, which particular goal or ideal should be used? The answer depends largely on the particular theoretical frame of reference or values embraced by those proposing the criterion. Second, most of these goals are vague; they lack clarity and precision. If resistance to stress is the goal, is a healthy person only someone who can always adapt? Recent experiences with prisoners of war indicate that, under repeated stress, many eventually break down. Should we label them as unhealthy? Third, ideal criteria exclude too many people: most individuals would be considered mentally unhealthy by these definitions.

Multicultural Criteria

The traditional view of abnormal psychology has been based on the assumption that a fixed set of mental disorders exists, whose obvious manifestations cut across cultures (Draguns, 1985; D. W. Sue & D. Sue, in press; Triandis, 1983). This psychiatric tradition dates back to Emil Kraepelin (to be discussed shortly), who felt that depression, sociopathic behav-

ior, and especially schizophrenia were universal disorders that appeared in all cultures and societies. Early research supported the belief that these disorders occurred worldwide, had similar processes, and were more similar than dissimilar (Wittkower & Rin, 1965). Such **cultural universality** has led to the belief that a disorder such as depression would be similar in origin, process, and manifestation in Asian, Black, Hispanic, or White clients. As a result, no modifications in diagnosis and treatment need be made; Western concepts of normality and abnormality could be considered universal and equally applicable across cultures.

At the other extreme were social scientists who stressed **cultural relativism**. This concept arose from anthropological tradition and stressed the importance of diversity in symptom manifestation of psychopathology. Deviant behavior was seen to reflect the lifestyle, cultural values, and world views of the afflicted peoples. For example, a body of research supports the conclusion that "acting-out" behaviors associated with mental disorders are much higher in the United States than in Asia, and even Asian Americans in the United States are less likely to express symptoms via "acting out" (Leong, 1986). Researchers have proposed that Asian cultural values (restraint of feelings, emphasis on self-control, and need for subtlety in approaching problems) all contribute to their restraint. Furthermore, cultures seem to vary in what they consider to be normal or abnormal behavior. In some societies and cultural groups, hallucinating is considered normal in specific situations. Yet in the United States, hallucinating is generally perceived to be a manifestation of pathology.

Which of these views is correct? Are the criteria used to determine normality and abnormality culturally universal or specific? Few mental health professionals today would embrace the extreme of either position, although most would gravitate toward one or the other. Proponents of cultural universality focus on the disorder and minimize cultural factors, while proponents of cultural relativism focus on the culture and on how the disorder is manifested within it. Both views have validity. It would be naive to believe that there are *no* disorders that cut across different cultures and share universal characteristics (World Health Organization, 1975). For example, even though hallucinating may be viewed as normal in one culture, proponents of cultural universality would argue that it still represents a breakdown in biological–cognitive processes. Likewise, it would be equally naive to believe that the relative frequencies and manner of symptom formation for various disorders do *not* reflect dominant cultural values and the lifestyles of a society. A more fruitful approach to studying multicultural criteria of abnormality would be to explore two questions: First, what is universal in human behavior that is also relevant to understanding psychopathology? Second, what is the relationship between (1) cultural norms, values, and attitudes to (2) the incidence and manifestation of behavior disorders? These are important questions that we hope you will constantly ask as we continue our journey into the field of abnormal psychology.

Practical Criteria

Practical, or clinical, criteria are subject to many of the same criticisms as other criteria. Nonetheless, according to Buss (1966), they are often the basis on which people who are labeled *abnormal* or *unhealthy* come to the attention of psychologists or other mental health specialists. Moreover, clinicians often must act primarily on the basis of pragmatic manifestations. The practical criteria for abnormality include subjective discomfort, bizarreness, and inefficiency.

Discomfort Most people who see clinicians are suffering physical or psychological discomfort. Many physical reactions stem from a strong psychological component; among them are such disorders as asthma, hypertension, and ulcers, as well as such physical symptoms as fatigue, nausea, pain, and heart palpitations. Discomfort can also be manifested in extreme or prolonged emotional reactions, of which anxiety and depression are the most significant. Of course, it is normal for a person to feel depressed after suffering a loss or a disappointment. But if the reaction is so intense, exaggerated, and prolonged that it interferes with the capacity of the individual to function adequately, it is likely to be considered abnormal.

Bizarreness As a practical criterion for abnormality, bizarreness is closely related to statistical criteria. Bizarre or unusual behavior is an abnormal deviation from an accepted standard of behavior (such as an antisocial act) or a false perception of reality (such as a *hallucination*). This criterion is very subjective; it depends on the individual and, as we have just seen, on the particular culture.

Certain sexual behaviors, delinquency, and homicide are examples of acts that our society considers abnormal. But social norms are far from static, and behavioral standards cannot be considered absolute. Changes in our attitudes toward human sexuality provide a prime example. During the Victorian era, women wore six to eight undergarments to make sure every part of the body, from the neck down, was covered. Exposing an ankle was roughly equivalent to wearing a topless bathing suit today (Kirkpatrick, 1975). Taboos against publicly recognizing sexuality dictated that words be chosen carefully to avoid any sexual connotation. Victorians said "limb" instead of "leg," because the word *leg* was considered too erotic. (Even pianos and tables were said to have limbs.) People who did not adhere to these strict codes of conduct were considered immoral or even perverted.

Nowadays, however, magazines and films openly exhibit the naked human body, and topless *and* bottomless nightclub entertainment is hardly newsworthy. Various sex acts are explicitly portrayed in X-rated movies. More and more, homosexuals "come out" publicly, professing their sexual orientation without shame, guilt, or much fear of public reaction. In fact, homosexuality is no longer classed as a mental disorder by the American Psychiatric Association. Women are freer to question traditional sex roles and to act more assertively in initiating sex. Such changes in behavioral standards make it difficult to subscribe to absolute standards of normality. (Another example, pointing up a different type of danger inherent in applying absolute standards of normality, appears in Focus 1.1.)

Nevertheless, some behaviors can usually be judged abnormal without hesitation. Among these are hallucinations, delusions, and severe disorientation. **Hallucinations** are false impressions that involve the senses. People who have hallucinations (they may be pleasant or unpleasant) may hear, feel, or see things that are not really there: voices accusing them of vile deeds, insects crawling on their bodies, or monstrous apparitions. **Delusions** are false beliefs steadfastly held by the individual despite contradictory objective evidence. A delusion of *grandeur* is a belief that one is an exalted personage, such as Jesus Christ or Joan of Arc; a delusion of *persecution* is a belief that one is controlled by others or is the victim of a conspiracy. The following example of a delusionary system involving both grandiosity and persecution is reported by Schroth and Sue (1975, p. 291):

A young schizophrenic believed that there was an elaborate plot to kill him because he was, in truth, Jesus Christ. The plotters had discovered his true identity and were themselves agents of Israel. He believed he was sent to earth to save humanity from Communist and Jewish foolishness. He said God had told him personally of his role but requested him to maintain secrecy while saving the world. Somehow the word got out, even to his relatives, who had been corrupted by his enemies, and they were trying to keep him in the hospital.

Disorientation is confusion with regard to identity, place, or time. People who are disoriented may not know who they are, where they are, or what historical era they are living in.

Inefficiency In everyday life, people are expected to fulfill various roles—as students or teachers, as workers and caretakers, as parents, lovers, and marital partners. Emotional problems sometimes interfere with the performance of these roles, and the resulting role *inefficiency* may be used as an indicator of abnormality.

One way to assess efficiency (or inefficiency) is to compare an individual's performance with the *requirements* of the role. Another, related means is to compare the individual's *performance* to his or her *potential*. An individual with an IQ of 150 who is failing in school can be labeled inefficient. (The label *underachiever* is often hung on students who possess high intelligence but obtain poor grades in school.) Similarly, a productive worker who suddenly becomes unproductive may be experiencing emotional stress. The major weakness of this approach is that it is difficult to assess potential accurately. How do we know whether a person is performing at his or her peak? To answer such questions, psychologists, educators, and the business sector have relied heavily on testing. Tests of specific abilities and of intelligence are attempts to assess potential and to predict performance in schools or jobs.

The Concept of Multiple Perspectives

Different definitions of abnormality carry different implications, and there is no easy consensus on a best definition. All the criteria we have discussed have shortcomings. Some are more precise than others in specifying what behaviors are or are not to be considered abnormal; some seem to fit our beliefs about abnormality better than others; all are sensitive to such variables as psychological orientation and societal and individual value systems.

Perhaps, then, abnormality should not be viewed from a single perspective or measured in accordance with a single criterion. Two researchers (Strupp & Hadley, 1977), working together, have proposed a three-part method that can be used to define normality and abnormality. They identify three vantage points from which to judge a person's mental health: (1) that of society, (2) that of the individual, and (3) that of the mental health professional. Each "judge" operates from a different perspective, perhaps using different criteria. At times, three people taking these viewpoints would agree that a person is either mentally disturbed or mentally healthy. At other times, they might disagree. Nonetheless, using multiple criteria would alleviate the problems inherent in imposing a single criterion.

We must give two important points careful consideration as we assess the value of the multiple-perspectives concept. First, a person who feels subjectively contented—mentally sound—may be perceived as unhealthy from a societal perspective. For example, people who commit antisocial acts such as rape, murder, or robbery may not feel remorseful but may be quite contented with their acts. Likewise, an artist living a very unconventional lifestyle may be judged maladapted from society's perspective; but from that individual's perspective and the perspective of many health professionals, he or she is intact and sound.

Second, a judgment must be recognized as stemming from one of the three vantage points. Otherwise, even greater confusion could result.

A truly adequate understanding of mental illness and health could be reached through comprehensive evaluation from all points of view. It may not be enough to rely solely on the judgments of mental health professionals, who are not immune to biases and shortcomings.

A Definition of Abnormal Behavior

Thus we may define **abnormal behavior** as behavior that departs from some norm and that harms the affected individual or others. This definition encompasses—or at least allows room for—the various criteria and perspectives on behavior. It also accurately implies that no precise, universally acknowledged line delineates normal behavior from abnormal behavior.

Somewhat more loosely, we shall speak of *mentally disturbed* people as those individuals who display abnormal behavior. And by a *mental disorder* or *mental disturbance* we mean some recognizable pattern of abnormal behavior.

THE INCIDENCE OF ABNORMAL BEHAVIOR

A student once asked one of us (the authors), "How crazy is this nation?" Well, put in somewhat more scientific terms, this question has occupied psychologists for some time. Psychiatric epidemiology provides insights into factors that contribute to the occurrence of specific mental disorders. From this information, we can find out how frequent or infrequent various disturbances occur in the population, how the prevalence of disorders vary by sex and age, and whether current mental health practices are sufficient and effective (Watkins & Peterson, 1986).

Current Research into the Epidemiology of Mental Disorders

An early but highly regarded and frequently cited study, the Midtown Manhattan Study, was performed in 1950 (Srole et al., 1962). Fifteen hundred New Yorkers were interviewed and rated on their psychological health impairment. The results were startling: Approximately 25 percent of the subjects showed severe impairment. About 55 percent were mildly impaired. And only 20 percent (one in five) were rated unimpaired.

Some social commentators contend that our mental health has deteriorated since the Midtown Manhattan Study was conducted. They point to such "evidence" as the mushrooming of cults, a revival of belief in the supernatural, the incidence of mass and serial murders, and attempts at political assassination. To ascertain whether the population's mental health was deteriorating, a similar study was carried out in the 1970s (Srole & Fisher, 1980). The investigators found no support for this contention. But neither did they find any evidence that the mental health of Americans had improved in the intervening decades!

According to research done in 1984, almost one out of every five Americans suffers from some kind of mental disorder. This incidence rate was about the same in 1950. What is alarming, though, is that fewer than one-third of those suffering from a mental disorder are receiving mental health services.

A number of other studies have found equally disheartening tendencies (Dohrenwend & Dohrenwend, 1982; Dohrenwend et al., 1980; Mechanic, 1978; and Regier et al., 1978). These studies estimate that some 25 to 40 million Americans, or approximately 15 percent of the population, suffer from emotional disorders that could be considered serious. Counting both severe and milder disturbances, estimates are that 44 million Americans suffer from symptoms of depression, 20 million have drug-related problems, 4 to 9 million suffer from some form of phobic or anxiety disturbance, 6 million are mentally retarded, and 2 million suffer from schizophrenia. In addition, some 25,000 to 60,000 people commit suicide each year, and another 200,000 attempt it. These estimates do not include such disorders as child abuse, sexual dysfunctions, and pathological expressions of violence, which could increase the total substantially. For example, every year 20,000 murders are committed in the United States; an average of 10 Americans out of every 100,000 will be murdered (Thiers, 1988). Crime statistics also show that 456,000 acts of family violence are reported each year in the United States, and that figure probably grossly underestimates the number of acts committed, because many such acts go unreported.

Perhaps the most thorough and comprehensive study on the incidence of mental disorders in the U.S. adult population (eighteen years and older) was conducted by the National Institute of Mental Health (Eaton et al., 1984; Freedman, 1984; Myers et al., 1984; Regier et al., 1984; Robbins et al., 1984). The NIMH epidemiological study included data collection at three major cities: New Haven, Baltimore, and St. Louis. The study has several features that distinguishes it from others. It included a large sample of approximately 20,000 subjects, and it used the categories in the Diagnostic and Statistical Manual of the American Psychiatric Association (DSM-III) in the construction of the research instruments.

Like the previous studies cited, a high rate of disorders was reported by subjects. Approximately 29 to 38 percent (percentage range accounts for variations in the three cities) of the sample reported they experienced at least one DSM-III disorder! Alcohol abuse or dependence was the most prevalent disorder (11 to 16 percent), and phobic disorders were a clear second (8 to 23 percent) followed by several other disturbances with averages of greater than 5 percent (depressive episodes, drug abuse, and dependence). Schizophrenia, often one of the most severe mental disturbances, affects 1 percent of the population, or approximately 1.4 million Americans. Researchers also found that although men and women were equally likely to suffer from mental disorders, they differ in the kinds of disorders they experience. For example, alcohol abuse or dependence occurs in 24 percent of men and only 4 percent of women; men are more likely to abuse drugs; and depression and anxiety are more likely to occur in women. Age was also an important factor. Alcoholism and depression are most prominent in the 25- to 44-year-old age group; drug dependence in the 18 to 24 age group); and cognitive impairment occurred more often in people age 65 and older. Phobias, however, were equally represented at all ages.

These epidemiological findings are disturbing, to say the least. Clearly, mental disturbances are widespread, and many of us are currently suffering from them. What is even more disturbing is that the study reveals that less than one-third of people suffering from a DSM-III disorder are receiving mental health services!

The Psychologically Oriented Society

Afflicted people and their families and friends pay a huge price in human suffering. In addition, the U.S. public spends increasing amounts each year in either direct or indirect expenses for mental health care. In 1974 we spent $40 billion, of which nearly 40 percent went for direct care, including therapy and hospitalization (Levine & Willner, 1976). And as Americans have become more oriented toward understanding behaviors and motives of the self and others, their demand for various forms of mental health treatment has increased. This demand is evident in the following statistics:

◆ The proportion of Americans seeking mental health consultation increased from 4 to 14 percent between 1957 and 1976. Among the college-educated, the increase has been even greater—from 9 to 21 percent.

◆ Mental health professionals seem to believe in what they do, as they are the heaviest consumers of therapy. Seventy-four percent have been in treatment, one-third have been treated more than once, and the average time spent in treatment was 4½ years.

◆ More than 5 million people have taken part in encounter or sensitivity groups in the past fifteen years; over a million have been taught Transcendental Meditation (TM); over a million have participated in marriage enrichment programs; and countless millions have entered nonprofessional therapeutic programs for drug, alcohol, smoking, and weight control (Zilbergeld, 1983).

Focus 1.2 examines some of the beliefs that underlie this enthusiasm for psychological therapy and self-enhancement.

Stereotypes About the Mentally Disturbed

Despite our "psychology-mindedness" and our belief in the efficacy of various therapies, we Americans tend to regard the mentally disturbed with suspicion. Are most of them really maniacs who at any moment may be seized by uncontrollable urges to murder, rape, or maim? Such portrayals seem to emerge from the news media and the entertainment industry, but they are rarely accurate. Like other minority groups in America, the mentally disturbed are the subject of rampant stereotyping and popular misconceptions. It is worthwhile, at this point, to dispel the most common of these misconceptions, or myths.

Myth: "Mentally disturbed people can always be recognized by their consistently deviant abnormal behavior."

Reality: Mentally disturbed people are not always distinguishable from others on the basis of consistently unusual behaviors. Even in an outpatient clinic or a psychiatric ward, it is often difficult to distinguish the patients from the staff on the basis of behavior alone. There are two main reasons for this difficulty. First, as already noted, no sharp dividing line usually exists between "normal" and "abnormal" behaviors. Rather, the spectrum of behaviors is continuous, ranging from abnormal to normal. Depending on the situational context and the perspective of the person judging the behavior, many behaviors

could be considered either normal or deviant. Second, even when people are suffering from some form of emotional disturbance, that experience may not always be detectable in their behavior.

Myth: "The mentally disturbed have inherited their disorders. If one member of a family has an emotional breakdown, other members will probably suffer a similar fate."

Reality: The belief that insanity runs in certain families has caused misery and undue anxiety for many people. Except for *certain forms* of mental retardation, schizophrenia, and depression, heredity does not seem to play a significant role in most mental disorders, although the data are far from conclusive. Evidence suggests that, even though heredity may predispose an individual to certain disorders, environmental factors are extremely important. In families where many members suffer from mental disorders, a stress-producing environment is usually acting on the family predisposition. If the environment is benign, however, or predisposed individuals modify a stressful environment, psychopathology may never occur.

Myth: "The mentally disturbed can never be cured and will never be able to function normally or hold jobs in the community."

Reality: This erroneous belief has caused great distress to many people who have at some time been labeled mentally ill. Former mental patients have endured social discrimination and have been denied employment because of the public perception that "once insane, always insane." Unfortunately, this myth may keep former mental patients or those currently experiencing emotional problems from seeking help. Although most people don't hesitate to consult a doctor, dentist, or lawyer for help, many who need mental health services feel fearful and anxious about the social stigma attached to being labeled "mentally ill." However, according to several studies (World Health Organization, 1973a; U.S. Department of Health and Human Services, 1985), nearly three-fourths of clients with severe disorders who are hospitalized improve and go on to lead productive lives. Many recovered mental patients make excellent employees, and employers frequently report that they outperform other workers in attendance and punctuality. Some famous examples of

FOCUS 1.2

The Psychologizing of America

In his book *The Shrinking of America* (1983), psychologist Bernie Zilbergeld contends that Americans seem to have set out to psychologize almost every aspect of their lives. A main theme of Zilbergeld's is that our national history and cultural values have prepared us for this psychology-minded orientation. He notes that our culture is strongly committed to the following propositions:

- We are endowed with an unalienable right to the pursuit of happiness.
- We have a duty to better ourselves.
- Individual freedom is important.
- There are no limits to what we can do in life.

- We are highly malleable.
- Solutions to an individual's problems do exist, and finding a cure is possible.

Accepting these basic tenets, thousands of people each year try to banish all conceivable forms of failure and misfortune from their lives. They spend millions of dollars and countless hours of effort in attempts to improve their behavior, attitudes, personality, and moods. Zilbergeld argues that the following beliefs underlie what he calls our "therapeutic sensibility":

1. *The world is best understood in psychological terms*. It appears that psychology has become the most important way of understand-

ing our internal and external world. When we think of ourselves or others, we often think of psychological characteristics—anxiety, insecurity, passivity, depression, paranoia, hostility, and unconscious processes. When some important person is assassinated or a bizarre killing is reported, the media call on mental health experts to analyze the slayer's state of mind. On radio and television programs and in newspaper columns, mental health professionals dispense advice to callers or readers. High on the best-seller lists are many self-help psychology books.

2. *There is much more to behavior than meets the eye*. Unconscious processes and hidden meanings have become important in our belief sys-

recoveries from mental illnesses are President Abraham Lincoln, philosopher William James, Senator Thomas Eagleton, singer Rosemary Clooney, and golfer Bert Yancy (DHHS, 1985).

Myth: "People become mentally disturbed because they are weak-willed. To avoid emotional disorders or cure oneself of them, one need only exercise will power."

Reality: These statements show that the speaker does not understand the nature of mental disorders. Needing help to resolve difficulties does not indicate a lack of will power. In fact, recognizing one's own need for help may be seen as a sign of strength rather than a sign of weakness. Many problems in living stem from situations that are not under the individual's immediate control, such as the death of a loved one or the loss of a job. Other problems stem from lifelong patterns of faulty learning; it is naive to expect a simple exercise of will to override years of experience.

Myth: "The mentally disturbed person is unstable and potentially dangerous."

Reality: This misconception has been perpetuated by the mass media. Many murderers on television are labeled "psychopathic," and the news media concentrate on the occasional mental patient who kills. But the thousands of mental patients who do not commit crimes, do not harm others, and do not get into trouble with the law are not news. An important study of the issue does not support the notion that mental patients are seriously dangerous (Rabkin, 1979). Unfortunately, the myth persists.

The Mental Health Professions

The traditional therapy fields have grown along with the demand for mental health treatment. In 1968 there were 12,000 clinical psychologists in America; today there are over 40,000. We now have some 280,000 professional therapists (primarily in clinical

tem. Such thinking was popularized through the writings of Sigmund Freud, who claimed that hidden purposes lay behind nearly all human behavior: A desire for bananas, hot dogs, or carrots may represent unfulfilled sexual cravings. A person's charity work may be an expression of repressed hostility. Illness may be a result of the need to be loved and cared for. As a result of this emphasis, insight into one's own motives and behaviors has become highly valued.

3. *People are not OK.* In general, mental health professionals tend to focus on pathology rather than on healthy characteristics. People are often described in terms of their inadequacies or deficiencies. A large portion of the public seems to have accepted a fantasy model of well-being and mental health that none of us can attain.

4. *Individuals need to be liberated.* People are basically good, creative, and aspiring, but their nature has been blocked, inhibited, distorted, or repressed by the traditions and institutions of society. Excessive guilt may be caused by religious teachings, confining family ties, or rigid sex roles. We need to liberate ourselves in order to be whole, free, and well.

5. *Everyone needs and can benefit from therapy.* The number of people who sought some form of counseling or therapy increased threefold between 1957 and 1976, and the trend seems to be continuing. When other forms of treatment such as encounter groups, Weight Watchers, EST (Earhardt Seminar Training), and TM (transcendental meditation) are included, it becomes obvious that this belief has been widely taken to heart.

6. *The therapist is an expert and knows best.* Ours is a highly credentialed society, and the title "therapist" evokes the image of a person with much wisdom and knowledge. However, even though therapy is supposed to free the client and allow him or her to advance and grow, therapists may inadvertently foster reliance on their "expert" judgment.

Zilbergeld may be correct in asserting that "psychological man reigns supreme." To the question, "Whatever became of sin?" he answers, "It was psychologized away."

psychology, counseling psychology, psychiatry, psychoanalysis, social work, and marriage and family counseling). As one writer observed, there are more professional therapists than librarians, firefighters, or mail carriers, and twice as many therapists as dentists and pharmacists (Zilbergeld, 1983). Table 1.1 lists the qualifications, training, and functions of the people who work within these specialties and, in the process, clarifies the distinctions among them.

HISTORICAL PERSPECTIVE ON ABNORMAL BEHAVIOR

In this section and the next, we briefly review the historical development of Western thought concerning abnormality. This task is extremely difficult, for several reasons. First, the information and data we have are necessarily incomplete. We lack specific facts about our historical past and must piece them together. Often these gaps in our knowledge lead us to

mistaken conclusions until other information is uncovered. For example, disagreements now exist over the psychiatric interpretation of witchcraft. Second, historical interpretation depends on the perspective of the researcher. For example, an anthropological approach to the study of history may be different from a psychological one. Even within each discipline, one's biases and point of view may affect how an interpretation is made. Even with these limitations in mind, it appears that many current attitudes toward abnormal behavior, as well as modern ideas about its causes and treatment, have been influenced by early beliefs. In fact, some psychologists contend that modern societies have, in essence, adopted more sophisticated versions of earlier concepts. For example, the use of electroconvulsive therapy to treat depression is in some ways similar to ancient practices of exorcism in which the body was physically assaulted. The Greek physician Hippocrates, 2,500 years ago, believed that many abnormal behaviors were caused by imbalances and disorders in the brain

TABLE 1.1 | Mental Health Professionals

Occupation	Qualifications	Training	Functions
Clinical psychologist	Ph.D. or Psy.D. (Doctor of Psychology) in psychology	Coursework in psychopathology, personality, diagnosis, psychological testing, psychotherapy, and human physiology. Doctoral dissertation in candidate's area of specialization and usually a one-year internship at a psychiatric hospital or mental health agency.	Study, assessment, treatment, and prevention of abnormal behavior in disturbed people. Work settings include hospitals, clinics, private practice, academia, private agencies or local, state, and national agencies. All work sites may include therapy, teaching, and/or research.
Counseling psychologist	Ph.D. or Psy.D.	Similar to clinical psychologists.	Although similar to clinical psychologists, counseling psychologists are usually more concerned with the study of life problems in relatively normal people. More likely to be found in educational settings than in hospitals and clinics.
Psychiatrist	M.D.	Four years of medical school and an additional three to four years of training in psychiatry.	Medical specialists in mental health care, psychiatrists are the only mental health providers who may prescribe drugs in the treatment of mental disorders.

and the body, a belief shared by many contemporary psychologists.

Most ideas about abnormal behavior are firmly rooted in the system of beliefs that is operative in a given society at a given time. Perhaps for that reason, change—especially in the form of new ideas—does not come quickly or easily. People who dare to voice ideas that differ from the prevalent beliefs of their time are often made outcasts; in some periods, some were even executed. Yet in spite of the difficulties, we have evolved a humanistic and scientific explanation of abnormal behavior. It remains to be seen whether such an explanation will still be thought valid in decades to come. [Much of this history section is based on discussions of deviant behavior by Zilboorg and Henry (1941), Hunter and Macalpine (1963), Alexander and Selesnick (1966), Spanos (1978), and Neugebauer (1979).]

Prehistoric and Ancient Beliefs

Prehistoric societies some half a million years ago did not distinguish sharply between mental and physical disorders. Abnormal behaviors, from simple headaches to convulsive attacks, were attributed to evil spirits that inhabited or controlled the afflicted person's body. According to historians, these ancient peoples attributed many forms of illness to demonic possession, to sorcery, or to the behest of an offended ancestral spirit. Within this system of belief, called **demonology**, the victim was usually held at least partly responsible for the misfortune.

It has been suggested that Stone Age cave dwellers may have treated behavior disorders with a surgical method called **trephining**, in which part of the skull was chipped away to provide an opening through which the evil spirit could escape. People may have

TABLE 1.1 | **Mental Health Professionals** (*continued*)

Occupation	Qualifications	Training	Functions
Psychoanalyst	M.D. or Ph.D. degree (usually).	Intensive training in the theory and practice of psychoanalysis at an institute devoted to the field. Also includes the individual's own analysis by an experienced analyst.	The practice of psychoanalysis.
Psychiatric nurse	R.N. in nursing. Advanced degrees such as M.A. or Ph.D. is possible in this field as well.	Specialized training in the care and treatment of psychiatric patients is stressed.	Usually works as part of a psychiatric team in the diagnosis and treatment of mental disorders. Settings are psychiatric facilities and hospitals.
Psychiatric social worker	Master's degree in social work (may also obtain D.S.W. (Doctor of Social Work).	Graduate program in social work with a one-year internship in a social service agency or mental health agency.	Traditionally, have worked in family counseling services or community agencies, where they specialize in intake, take psychiatric histories, and deal with other agencies. May engage in private practice.
Marriage and family counselor	Usually a master's degree in counseling.	Graduate coursework in counseling with many hours of supervised clinical experience.	Works with married couples and families in coping with relationship issues. Work settings include mental health agencies, public welfare agencies, and private practice.

believed that when the evil spirit left the person would return to his or her normal state. Surprisingly, some trephined skulls have been found to have healed over, indicating that some patients survived this extremely crude operation. As pointed out earlier, however, disputes often arise from the interpretation of historical data: a different explanation of trephining is that it was used to remove bone splinters and blood clots resulting from blows to the head in fights between men (Maher & Maher, 1985). This explanation is consistent with findings that most trephined skulls were men, and many had fractures (suggesting a vigorous blow).

Another treatment method, used by the early Greeks, Chinese, Hebrews, and Egyptians, is called **exorcism**. In an exorcism, elaborate prayers, noises, emetics (drugs that induce vomiting), and such extreme measures as flogging and starvation were mar-

shaled to cast the evil spirit out of the afflicted person's body.

Naturalistic Explanations (Greco-Roman Thought)

In the ancient world, then, both physical and mental illness was thought to be supernatural in origin. But with the flowering of Greek civilization and its continuation into the era of Roman rule (500 B.C.– A.D. 500), naturalistic explanations gradually became distinct from supernatural ones. Early thinkers, such as Hippocrates (460–370 B.C.), a physician who is often called the father of medicine, actively questioned prevailing superstitious beliefs, proposing much more rational and scientific explanations for mental disorders.

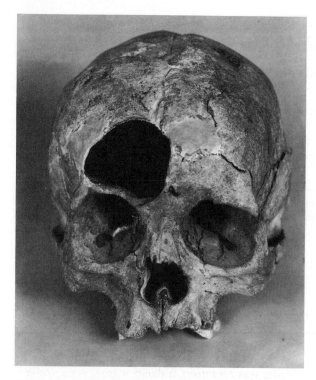

There are two theories about trephining. The most widely accepted postulates that trephining was a form of surgery that enabled an evil spirit to leave the body. The other theory rejects this idea, proposing instead that trephined skulls were actually wounds received when one person clubbed another over the head during a fight.

The beliefs of many thinkers of this era were based on incorrect assumptions. However, they all relied heavily on observations and explanations, which form the foundation of the scientific method. Also, they denied the intervention of demons in the development of abnormality and instead stressed organic causes, so the treatment they prescribed for mental disorders tended to be more humane than previous treatments.

Hippocrates believed that, because the brain was the central organ of intellectual activity, deviant behavior was caused by **brain pathology**—that is, a dysfunction or disease of the brain. He also considered heredity and environment important factors in psychopathology. He classified mental illnesses into three categories—mania, melancholia, and phrenitis (brain fever)—and for each category gave detailed clinical descriptions of such disorders as paranoia, alcoholic delirium, and epilepsy. Many of his descriptions of symptoms are still used today, eloquent testimony to his keen powers of observation.

To treat melancholia, Hippocrates recommended tranquility, moderate exercise, a careful diet, abstinence from sexual activity, and bloodletting if necessary. His belief in environmental influences on behavior sometimes led him to separate disturbed patients from their families. He seems to have gained insight into a theory popular among psychologists today, the theory that the family constellation often fosters deviant behavior in its own members.

Other thinkers who contributed to the organic explanation of behavior were the philosopher Plato and Galen, a Greek physician who practiced in Rome. Plato (429–347 B.C.) carried on the thinking of Hippocrates; he insisted that the mentally disturbed be the responsibility of the family and not be punished for their behavior. Galen (A.D. 129–199) made major contributions through his scientific examination of the nervous system and his explanation of the role of the brain and central nervous system in mental functioning. His greatest contribution may have been his codification of all medical knowledge from Hippocrates to his own.

Reversion to Superstition (the Middle Ages)

With the collapse of the Roman Empire and the rise of Christianity, rational and scientific thought gave way to a reemphasis on the supernatural. Religious dogma included beliefs in nature as a reflection of divine will, as beyond human reason, and earthly life as prelude to the "true" life (after death). Scientific inquiry—attempts to understand, classify, explain, and control nature—was less important than accepting it as a manifestation of God's will. Early Christianity did little to promote science and in many ways actively discouraged it. The Church demanded uncompromising adherence to its tenets. Christian fervor brought with it the concepts of heresy and punishment; certain truths were deemed sacred, and those who challenged them were denounced as heretics. Scientific thought that was in conflict with Church doctrine was not tolerated. Because of this atmosphere, rationalism and the scholarly scientific works went underground for many years, preserved mainly by Arab scholars and European monks. Natural and supernatural explanations of illness became fused.

People came to believe that many illnesses, although having natural causes, were the result of supernatural forces. In many cases, the mentally ill were treated gently and with compassion in monasteries and at shrines where they were prayed over and allowed to rest. In other cases, treatment could be quite brutal, especially if illnesses were believed to be due to God's wrath. Relief could come only through atonement or repentance. Because illness was perceived as punishment for sin, the sick person was assumed to be guilty of wrongdoing.

In primitive societies, mental illness was attributed to the demonic possession of a person's soul. During the Greco-Roman period, demonology gave rise to more naturalistic explanations. However, these views were repressed during the Dark and Middle Ages, when mental illness was again believed to be caused by supernatural forces.

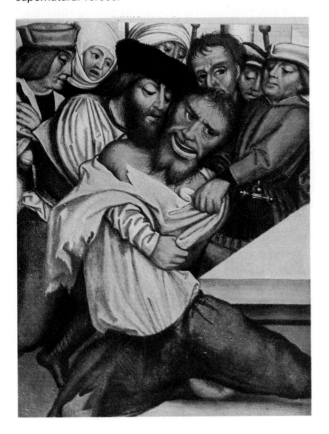

In some cases, treatment of the mentally ill during this period consisted of torturous exorcistic procedures seen as appropriate to combat Satan and eject him from the possessed person's body. Prayers, curses, obscene epithets, and the sprinkling of holy water—as well as such drastic and painful "therapy" as flogging, starving, and immersion in hot water—were used to drive out the devil. The humane treatments that Hippocrates had advocated centuries earlier were challenged severely. A time of trouble for everyone, the Dark Ages (A.D. 400–900) were especially bleak for the mentally ill.

Mass Madness (Thirteenth Century)

Belief in the power of the supernatural became so prevalent and intense that it frequently affected whole populations. Early in the thirteenth century beginning in Italy, large numbers of people were affected by various forms of group hysteria, or **mass madness.** One of the better known manifestations of this disorder was *tarantism,* a dance mania characterized by wild raving, jumping, dancing, and convulsions. The hysteria was most prevalent during the height of the summer and was attributed to the sting of a tarantula. A victim would leap up and run out into the street or marketplace, jumping and raving, to be joined by others who believed they had also been bitten. The mania, which started in Italy, soon spread throughout the rest of Europe, where it became known as *St. Vitus's Dance.*

Another form of mass madness was *lycanthropy,* a mental disorder in which victims imagine themselves to be wolves and imitate wolves' actions. (Motion pictures about *werewolves*—people who assume the physical characteristics of wolves during the full moon—are modern reflections of this delusion.)

How can these phenomena be explained? Stress and fear is often associated with outbreaks of mass hysteria. For example, there was enormous social unrest during the thirteenth century. The bubonic plague had decimated half the population of Europe. War, famine, and pestilence were rampant, and the social order of the times was crumbling.

A more recent example was evident in the small town of Berry, Alabama, where elementary school children became ill. It began when a fifth-grader came to school with a rash and began scratching vigorously and uncontrollably. Other classmates began to scratch at an imaginary itch. The incident resulted in over 150 schoolchildren afflicted with a frenzy of scratching, fainting, vomiting, numbness, crying, and screaming. Medical authorities concluded after months of study that the culprit could not be an infectious disease or food poisoning. Rather, the symptom pattern, onset, and manifestation suggested mass hysteria (Kramer, 1983).

Witchcraft (Fifteenth Through Seventeenth Centuries)

During the fifteenth and sixteenth centuries, the authority of Church was increasingly challenged by social and religious reformers. Reformers, such as Martin Luther, attacked the corruption and abuses of the clergy, precipitating the Protestant Reformation of the sixteenth century. Church officials saw such protests as insurrection and felt their power threatened. According to the Church, Satan himself fostered these attacks. By doing battle with Satan and with people supposedly influenced or possessed by Satan, the Church actively endorsed an already popular belief in demonic possession and witches.

To counter the threat, Pope Innocent VIII issued a papal bull (decree) in 1484 calling on the clergy to identify and exterminate witches. Means of detecting witches were publicized. For example, red spots on the skin (birthmarks) were supposedly made by the claw of the devil in sealing a blood pact, and thus were damning evidence of a contract with Satan. Such birth defects as the club foot and the cleft palate also aroused suspicion.

The Church initially recognized two forms of demonic possession: unwilling and willing. God let the devil seize an unwilling victim as punishment for a sinful life. A willing person, who made a blood pact with the devil in exchange for supernatural powers, was able to assume animal form and to cause such disasters as floods, pestilence, storms, crop failures, and sexual impotence. Although an unwilling victim of possession was at first treated with more sympathy than one who willingly conspired with the devil, this distinction soon evaporated.

People whose actions were interpreted as peculiar were often suspected of witchcraft. It was acceptable to use torture to obtain confessions from suspected witches, and many victims confessed because they preferred death to prolonged agony. Thousands of innocent men, women, and even children were beheaded, burned alive, or mutilated.

Witch hunts also occurred in colonial America. The witchcraft trials of 1692 in Salem, Massachusetts, were the most infamous. Authorities there acted on statements taken from children who may have been influenced by the sensational stories told by an old West Indian servant. Several hundred people were accused, many were imprisoned and tortured, and twenty were killed. It has been estimated that some 20,000 people were killed as witches in Scotland alone, and that well over 100,000 were executed as witches during the middle of the fifteenth to the end of the seventeenth century.

It would seem reasonable to assume that the mentally ill would be especially prone to being perceived as witches. Indeed, most psychiatric historians argue that mental disorders were at the roots of witchcraft persecutions (Alexander & Selesnick, 1966; Deutsch, 1949; Zilboorg & Henry, 1941). However, Spanos (1978) in a comprehensive critical analysis concludes that very little support can be found to indicate that accused witches were insane.

The Rise of Humanism (the Renaissance)

A resurgence of rational and scientific inquiry during the Renaissance (fifteenth and seventeenth centuries) led to great advances in science and **humanism,** a philosophical movement that emphasizes human welfare and the worth and uniqueness of the individual. Until this time, most asylums were at best custodial centers where the mentally disturbed were chained, caged, starved, whipped, and even exhibited to the public for a small fee, much like animals in a zoo. But if people were "mentally ill," not possessed, then they should be treated as though they were sick. A number of new methods for treating the mentally ill reflected this humanistic spirit.

In 1563 Johann Weyer (1515–1588), a German physician, published a revolutionary book that challenged the foundation of witchcraft. Weyer asserted that many people who were tortured, imprisoned, and burned as witches were mentally disturbed, not possessed by demons. The emotional agonies he was made to endure for committing this heresy are well documented. His book was severely criticized and banned by both Church and state, but it proved to be a forerunner of the humanitarian perspective on mental illness. Others eventually followed his lead.

The Reform Movement (Eighteenth and Nineteenth Centuries)

In France, Philippe Pinel (1745–1826), a physician, was put in charge of La Bicêtre, a hospital for insane men in Paris. Pinel instituted what came to be known as the **moral treatment movement.** He ordered that inmates' chains be removed, replaced dungeons with sunny rooms, encouraged exercise out of doors on hospital grounds, and treated patients with kindness and reason. Surprising many disbelievers, the freed patients did not become violent; instead, this humane treatment seemed to foster recovery and improved behavior. Pinel later instituted similar equally successful reforms at La Salpêtrière, a large mental hospital for women in Paris.

In England William Tuke (1732–1822), a prominent Quaker tea merchant, established a retreat at York for the "moral treatment" of mental patients. At this pleasant country estate, the patients worked, prayed, rested, and talked out their problems—all in an atmosphere of kindness quite unlike that of the lunatic asylums of the time.

The American Reformers In the United States, three individuals made important contributions to the moral-treatment movement: Benjamin Rush, Dorothea Dix, and Clifford Beers. Benjamin Rush (1745–1813), widely acclaimed as the father of U.S. psychiatry, attempted to train physicians to treat mental patients and to introduce more humane treatment policies into mental hospitals. He insisted that patients be accorded respect and dignity and that they be gainfully employed while hospitalized, an idea that anticipated the modern concept of work therapy. Yet Rush was not unaffected by the established practices and beliefs of his times: his theories were influenced by astrology, and his remedies included bloodletting and purgatives.

As skeptics look on, Philippe Pinel orders the chains removed from the inmates of La Bicêtre. Jean-Baptiste Pussin, an untrained ward superintendent, actually abolished the chaining of inmates. Pinel introduced even more radical changes, such as talking with patients to give them comfort and advice.

Dorothea Dix (1802–1887), a New England schoolteacher, was the preeminent American social reformer of the nineteenth century. While teaching Sunday school to female prisoners, she became familiar with the deplorable conditions in which jailed mental patients were forced to live. (Prisons and poorhouses were commonly used to incarcerate these patients.) For the next forty years, Dix worked tirelessly for the mentally ill. She campaigned for reform legislation and funds to establish suitable mental hospitals and asylums. She raised millions of dollars, established more than thirty modern mental hospitals, and greatly improved conditions in countless others. But the struggle for reform was far from over. The large hospitals that replaced jails and poorhouses had better physical facilities, but the humanistic, personal concern of the moral treatment movement was lacking.

That movement was given further impetus in 1908 with the publication of *A Mind That Found Itself,* a book by Clifford Beers (1876–1943) about his own mental collapse. His book describes the terrible treatment he and other patients experienced in three mental institutions, where they were beaten, choked, spat on, and straitjacketed. His vivid account aroused great public sympathy and attracted the interest and support of the psychiatric establishment, including such eminent figures as psychologist-philosopher William James. Beers founded the National Committee for Mental Hygiene, an organization dedicated to educating the public about mental illness and about the need to treat the mentally ill rather than punish them for their unusual behaviors.

It would be naive to believe that these reforms have totally eliminated inhumane treatment of the mentally disturbed. Books like Mary Jane Ward's *The Snake Pit* (1946) and films like Frederick Wiseman's *Titicut Follies* continue to document harsh treatment of mental patients. Even the severest critic of the mental health system, however, would have to admit that conditions and treatment for the mentally ill have improved in this century.

CAUSES: TWO VIEWPOINTS

Paralleling the rise of humanism in the treatment of mental illness was an expanding inquiry into its causes. Two main schools of thought emerged. The

Dorothea Dix was an exceptional contributor to the social reform movements of the nineteenth century— an era when women were discouraged from political participation.

organic viewpoint holds that mental disorders are the result of physiological damage or disease, whereas the psychological viewpoint stresses an emotional basis for mental illness.

The Organic Viewpoint

Hippocrates' suggestion of an organic explanation for abnormal behavior was ignored during the Middle Ages but was revived after the Renaissance. However, not until the nineteenth century did the organic or **biogenic view** become important. The ideas of Wilhelm Griesinger (1817–1868), a German psychiatrist who believed that all mental disorders had physiological causes, received considerable attention. Emil Kraepelin (1856–1926), a follower of Griesinger, observed that certain symptoms tend to occur regularly in clusters, called **syndromes;** he believed that each cluster of symptoms represented a mental disorder with its own unique—and clearly specifiable—

cause, course, and outcome. He attributed all disorders to one of four organic causes: metabolic disturbance, endocrine difficulty, brain disease, or heredity. In his *Textbook of Psychiatry* (1923 [1983]), Kraepelin outlined a system for classifying mental illnesses on the basis of their organic causes. That system is still the basis for the diagnostic categories in the *Diagnostic and Statistical Manual of Mental Disorders* (DSM), the classification system of the American Psychiatric Association.

The acceptance of organic causation for mental disorders was accelerated by medical breakthroughs in the study of the nervous system. The effects of brain pathology, such as cerebral arteriosclerosis, on mental retardation, senile psychoses, and certain other psychoses led many scientists to suspect or advocate organic factors as the sole cause of all mental illness.

The organic point of view gained even greater strength with the discovery of the organic basis of general *paresis,* a progressively degenerative and irreversible physical and mental disorder. Several breakthroughs had led scientists to suspect that the deterioration of mental and physical abilities exhibited by certain mental patients might actually be caused by an organic disease. The work of Louis Pasteur (1822–1895) established the germ theory of disease (invasion of the body by parasites). Then in 1897 Richard von Krafft-Ebing (1840–1902), a German neurologist, inoculated paretic patients with pus from syphilitic sores; when the patients failed to develop the secondary symptoms of syphilis, Krafft-Ebing concluded that the subjects had been previously infected by that disease. Finally, in 1905 a German zoologist, Fritz Schaudinn (1871–1906), isolated the microorganism that causes syphilis and thus paresis. These discoveries convinced many scientists that every mental disorder might eventually be linked to an organic cause.

The Psychological Viewpoint

Some scientists noted, however, that certain types of emotional disorders were not associated with any organic pathology in the patient. Such observations led to another view, stressing psychological factors rather than organic factors as the cause of many disorders. For example, the inability to attain personal goals and resolve interpersonal conflicts could lead to intense feelings of frustration, depression, failure, anger, and consequent disturbed behavior.

Mesmerism and Hypnotism The unique and exotic techniques of Friedrich Anton Mesmer (1734–1815), an Austrian physician who practiced in Paris, presented an early challenge to the organic point of view. It is important to note, however, that Mesmer was really an anomaly and not part of the mainstream scientific thinking. Mesmer developed a highly controversial treatment that came to be called *mesmerism* and was the forerunner of the modern practice of hypnotism.

Mesmer performed his most miraculous cures in the treatment of *hysteria*—the appearance of symptoms such as blindness, deafness, loss of bodily feeling, and paralysis that seem to have no organic basis. According to Mesmer, hysteria was a manifestation of the body's need for a redistribution of the magnetic fluid that determined a person's mental and physical health. His techniques for curing this illness involved inducing a sleeplike state, during which his patients became highly susceptible to suggestion. During this state, their symptoms often disappeared.

Mesmer's dramatic and theatrical techniques earned him censure as well as fame. A committee of prominent thinkers, including U.S. ambassador Benjamin Franklin, investigated Mesmer and declared him a fraud. He was finally forced to leave Paris.

Although Mesmer's basic assumptions were discredited, the power of suggestion proved to be a strong therapeutic technique in the treatment of hysteria. The cures he effected stimulated scientific interest in, and much bitter debate about, the view that mental disorders are **psychogenic** in nature—that is, caused by psychological and emotional rather than organic factors.

An English physician, James Braid (1795–1860), renamed mesmerism *neurohypnotism* (later shortened to **hypnotism**) because he believed the technique induced sleep by producing paralysis of the eyelid muscles. (The Latin word *hypnos* means "sleep.") Braid's trance-inducing technique of having a subject gaze steadily at an object has now become almost a standard procedure in hypnosis.

The Nancy School About ten years after Mesmer died, a number of researchers began to experiment actively with hypnosis. Jean-Martin Charcot (1825–1893), a neurosurgeon at La Salpêtrière Hospital in Paris and the leading neurologist of his time, was among them. His initial experiments with hypnosis led him to abandon it in favor of more traditional methods of treating hysteria, which he claimed was caused by organic damage to the nervous system. However, other experimenters had more positive results using hypnosis, which convinced him to try it again. His subsequent use of the technique in the study of hysteria did much to legitimize the application of hypnosis in medicine.

The experimenters most instrumental in Charcot's conversion were two physicians practicing in the city of Nancy, in eastern France. First working separately, Ambroise-Auguste Liébeault (1823–1904) and Hippolyte-Marie Bernheim (1840–1919) later came together to work as a team. As a result of their experiments, they hypothesized that hysteria was a form of self-hypnosis. The results they obtained in treating patients attracted other scientists, who collectively became known as the "Nancy school." In treating hysterical patients under hypnosis, they were often able to *remove* symptoms of paralysis, deafness, blindness, and anesthesia. Likewise, they were able to *produce* these symptoms in normal subjects through hypnosis. Their work demonstrated impressively that suggestion could cause certain forms of mental illness; that is, symptoms of mental and physical disorders could have a psychological rather than an organic explanation. This conclusion represented a major breakthrough in the conceptualization of mental disorders.

Breuer and Freud   The idea that psychological processes could produce mental and physical disturbances began to gain credence among several physicians who were using hypnosis. Among them was the Viennese doctor Josef Breuer (1842–1925). He discovered accidentally that, after one of his female patients spoke quite freely about her past traumatic experiences while in a trance, many of her symptoms abated or disappeared. He achieved even greater success when the patient recalled previously forgotten memories and relived their emotional aspects. This latter technique became known as the **cathartic method.** It foreshadowed psychoanalysis, one of the major theories of psychopathology, whose founder, Sigmund Freud (1856–1939), was influenced by Charcot and was a colleague of Breuer. Freud's theories have had a great and lasting influence in the field of abnormal psychology.

WHAT LIES AHEAD IN THIS TEXT

The first part of this text is intended to acquaint you with the study of abnormal psychology. In Chapter 1, we have marked out the boundaries of our subject and surveyed its historical antecedents. In Chapters 2 and 3, we discuss several explanations of abnormal behavior, including those that have their roots in the organic and psychological views of mental disorder. Chapter 4 examines the contemporary means by which abnormal behavior is classified and individual problems are assessed. Then, to help you understand and evaluate the psychological research cited and described in this text, Chapter 5 explains the use of scientific methods in abnormal psychology.

The next four parts of this book cover specific disorders. Part 2 contains four chapters on disorders that are characterized predominantly by anxiety and stress. In Part 3, we examine disorders commonly associated with social problems: alcohol and drug abuse, psychosexual problems, and faulty interpersonal relationships. Part 4 covers disorders that often have an exceptional impact on individual functioning, those that used to be labeled psychotic disorders—schizophrenia and the affective disorders. Suicide, too, is discussed in Part 4. Part 5 is devoted primarily to organic brain dysfunction and mental retardation.

Finally, in Part 6, we discuss and evaluate the major approaches to therapy, as well as community psychology, a field that seeks to identify and implement ways to prevent disorders from occurring. Our final chapter ends with a discussion of some of the major legal and ethical issues raised in our study of abnormal psychology.

In Chapters 2 and 3, we discuss the case of Steven V. Gradually, we uncover more and more of his past. You will be able to take part in searching through the details of Steve's life for clues to his current condition. Then, in Chapter 20, we discuss a therapeutic approach to Steve's problems. There you will also see how Steve's therapist solved the dilemma brought about by Steve's threat against Linda.

Steve's behaviors are, by any definition, abnormal. But Steve does not suffer from every mental disorder known to psychology. His problems are different from those faced, for example, by the mentally retarded child, by the 80-pound teenager suffering from anorexia nervosa, or by the older person deteriorating from Alzheimer's disease. Why spend so much time with Steven V.?

FOCUS 1.3

"I Have It Too": The Medical Student Syndrome

Medical students probably caught it first. As they read about physical disorders and listened to lecturers describe illnesses, some students began to imagine that they themselves had one disorder or another. "Diarrhea? Fatigue? Trouble sleeping? That's me!" In this way, a cluster of symptoms—no matter how mild or how briefly experienced—can lead some people to suspect that they were very sick.

Students who take a course that examines psychopathology may be equally prone to believe they have a mental disorder that is described in their text. It is possible, of course, that some of these students do suffer from a disorder and would benefit from counseling or therapy. Most, however, are merely experiencing an exaggerated sense of their susceptibility to disorders. In one study, it was found that one of every five individuals responded *yes* to the question "Have you ever felt

that you were going to have a nervous breakdown?" Of course, most of those people never suffered an actual breakdown (U.S. Department of Health, Education and Welfare, 1971).

Two influences in particular may make us susceptible to these imagined disorders. One is the universality of the human experience. All of us have experienced misfortunes in life. We can all remember and relate to feelings of anxiety, unhappiness, guilt, lack of self-confidence, and even thoughts of suicide. In most cases, however, these feelings are normal reactions to stressful situations, not symptoms of pathology. Depression that follows the loss of a loved one, or anxiety prior to giving a speech to a large audience, may be perfectly normal and appropriate. The second influence is our tendency to compare our own functioning with our *perceptions* of how other people are functioning. The

outward behaviors of fellow students may lead us to conclude that they experience few difficulties in life, are self-assured and confident, and are invulnerable to mental disturbance. If we were privy to their inner thoughts and feelings, however, we might be surprised to find that they share our apprehension and insecurities.

If you see yourself anywhere in the pages of this book, we hope you will take the time to discuss the matter with a friend or with one of your professors. You may be responding to pressures that you have not encountered before—a heavy course load, for example—and to which you have not yet adjusted. Other people can help point out these pressures to you. However, if your discussion *supports* your suspicion that you have a problem, then by all means consider getting a professional evaluation.

There are two good reasons to dwell on Steve. The first is to emphasize the fact that abnormal behavior is nonetheless human behavior. We hope that Steve will become, for you, a real, live human being rather than some specimen exhibiting strange behavior. (Steve is actually a composite character based on various clients whom we, the authors, have treated.)

Second, through Steve's psychological history we can examine a variety of concerns and issues that arise in virtually every case of abnormal behavior. What are the most important features of the behavior? Would all psychologists diagnose a given condition similarly? What kind of treatment, in what setting, would promise the best results? And so on. Steve's case provides a format for discussing such questions more explicitly and concretely than we could in the more conventional textbook discourse.

We would like to close this chapter with a word of caution. To be human is to encounter difficulties and problems in life. A course in abnormal psychology dwells on human problems, and many of these problems are familiar to us all. As a result, we may be prone to the "medical student syndrome" (see Focus 1.3): reading about a disorder may lead us to suspect we *have* the disorder or that a friend or relative has it. This reaction to the study of abnormal behavior is common, but one that it pays to guard against.

SUMMARY

1. The objectives of abnormal psychology are to describe, explain, predict, and control behaviors that

are strange or unusual. Various criteria may be used to define such behaviors. Statistical criteria define abnormality in terms of those behaviors that occur least frequently in the population. Ideal mental health criteria characterize abnormality as an inability to attain some positive goal. The multicultural criteria stress cultural influences in the process and manifestation of a disorder. The various practical criteria define abnormality on the basis of discomfort, either physical or psychological, suffered by the affected individual; the bizarreness of the person's actions; or his or her inefficiency in filling life roles. It may be that a single criterion or viewpoint is not sufficient but that abnormality should be defined from the combined vantage points of society, the individual, and the mental health professional.

2. Mental health problems are widespread in the United States, and more and more Americans are seeking professional help. The result has been a gigantic growth in the number of mental health professionals practicing in the United States. These professionals include clinical psychologists, counseling psychologists, psychiatrists, psychoanalysts, psychiatric social workers, and marriage and family counselors.

3. Many of our current concepts of mental illness have their roots in past beliefs and practices. Ancient people believed in demonology and attributed abnormal behaviors to evil spirits that inhabited the victim's body. Treatment consisted of trephining or exorcism. Rational and scientific explanations of abnormality emerged during the Greco-Roman era. Especially influential was the thinking of Hippocrates, who believed that abnormal behavior was due to brain pathology. However, with the collapse of the Roman Empire and the increased influence of the Church and its emphasis on divine will and the hereafter, rationalist thought was suppressed and belief in the supernatural began to flourish again. During the Middle Ages, famine, pestilence, and dynastic wars caused enormous social upheaval. Forms of mass hysteria affected groups of people. In the fifteenth century, the Church endorsed witch hunts both in response to fear generated by social unrest and as a way to deal with those opposing its authority. Among the numerous men, women, and children who were tortured and killed as witches were some whom we would today call mentally ill. The Renaissance brought a return to rational and scientific inquiry along with a heightened interest in humanitarian methods of treating the mentally ill.

4. In the nineteenth and twentieth centuries, major medical breakthroughs fostered a belief in the organic roots of mental illness. The discovery of the microorganism that caused general paresis was especially important in this regard. Scientists believed that they would eventually find organic causes for all mental disorders. Mesmerism and later hypnosis supported another view, however. The uncovering of a relationship between hypnosis and hysteria corroborated the belief that psychological processes could produce emotional disturbances.

KEY TERMS

abnormal behavior Behavior that departs from some norm and that harms the affected individual or others

abnormal psychology The scientific study whose objectives are to describe, explain, predict, and control behaviors that are considered strange or unusual

biogenic view The belief or theory that mental disorders have a physical or physiological basis

brain pathology Dysfunction or disease of the brain

cathartic method The therapeutic use of verbal expression to release pent-up emotional conflicts

cultural relativism The belief that lifestyles, cultural values, and world views affect the expression and determination of deviant behavior

cultural universality The belief that many behavior disorders cut across lifestyles, cultural norms, and world views

exorcism Ritual in which prayer, noise, emetics, and extreme measures such as flogging and starvation, were used to cast evil spirits out of an afflicted person's body

humanism An emphasis on human welfare and on the worth and uniqueness of the individual

mass madness Group hysteria

moral treatment movement A shift to more humane treatment of the mentally disturbed; its initiation is generally attributed to Philippe Pinel

psychodiagnosis An attempt to describe, assess, and systematically draw inferences about an individual's psychological disorder

psychogenic view The belief or theory that mental disorders are caused by psychological and emotional factors

syndrome A cluster of symptoms that tend to occur together and are believed to indicate a particular disorder

therapy A program of systematic intervention whose purpose is to modify a client's behavioral, affective, or cognitive state

trephining An ancient surgical technique in which part of the skull was chipped away to provide an opening through which evil spirits could escape

chapter 2
Biogenic and Psychogenic Models of Abnormal Behavior

I n Chapter 1, we described the rise of humanism in society's attitude toward mental disorders. As rational thought replaced superstition in the eighteenth and nineteenth centuries, the mentally disturbed were increasingly regarded as unfortunate human beings who deserved respectful and humane treatment, not as monsters inhabited by the devil.

This humanistic view gave rise, in the late nineteenth and early twentieth centuries, to two differing schools of thought about the causes of mental disorders. According to one group of thinkers, mental disorders are *biogenic*—that is, caused by biological problems. The disturbed individual, this group contended, is displaying symptoms of physical disease or damage. A second group of theorists found organic explanations inadequate. These thinkers believed that abnormal behavior is essentially *psychogenic*, rooted not in cells and tissues but in the invisible complexities of the human mind.

In this chapter, we trace the evolution of these two schools of thought and bring them up to date. We begin with the biogenic perspective and then examine three psychogenic perspectives: the psychoanalytic theory first articulated by Sigmund Freud and the more recent humanistic and existential perspectives. Later, in Chapter 3, we discuss two additional perspectives on abnormal behavior, the behavioral and family systems theories.

The five theories we examine are by no means the only possible explanations of abnormal behavior. One survey identified more than 130 such theories in the United States alone (National Institute of Mental Health, 1975). However, many are variants of the more basic theories discussed here and others have never gained widespread acceptance.

To help bring the major theories to life, and to show how they may be applied to individual problems, in Chapters 2 and 3 we continue to explore the case of Steven V. Immediately after our discussion of each major approach, we examine Steve's problems through the eyes and insights of a hypothetical follower of that approach.

Let's begin by clarifying two terms that we use frequently. The first is **psychopathology,** which clinical psychologists use as a synonym for abnormal behavior. The second is model, a term that requires a more elaborate explanation.

MODELS IN THE STUDY OF PSYCHOPATHOLOGY

When they need to discuss a phenomenon that is difficult to describe or explain, scientists often make use of an analogy, in which they liken the phenomenon to something more concrete. A **model** is such an analogy, and it is most often used to describe something that cannot be observed directly. In an analogy, terms, concepts, or principles are borrowed from one field and applied to another. The person who likens the heart to a pump or the eye to a camera is making use of a model.

When psychologists speak of deviant behavior as "mental illness" or refer to their "patients," they are borrowing the terminology of medicine and, in essence, applying a *medical model* of abnormal behavior. They may also describe certain external symptoms as being visible signs of deep underlying conflict. Again, the medical analogy is clear: just as fevers, rashes, perspiration, or infections may be symptoms of a bacterial or viral invasion of the body, bizarre behavior may be a symptom of a mind "invaded" by unresolved conflicts. Psychologists have used models extensively to help them conceptualize the causes of abnormal behavior, ask probing questions, determine what information or data are relevant, and interpret data. Each model is a means of viewing abnormal behavior, and it generally embodies a particular

theoretical approach. Hence we tend to use the terms *model, theory, viewpoint,* and *perspective* somewhat interchangeably.

Every model, however apt, is limited in its usefulness. None provides all the answers. The complexity of human behavior and our relatively shallow understanding of it prevent psychologists from developing *the* definitive model. Most theorists do not believe that the models they construct will correspond in every respect to the phenomenon they are studying. Rather, they are used as a way to visualize psychopathology as if it truly worked in the manner described by the models. (Millon, 1973).

In reality, most practicing clinicians do not adhere rigidly to any one model. In a survey of clinical psychologists, 64 percent identified their approach as **eclectic** (Garfield & Kurtz, 1976, 1977). These therapists remain open to all perspectives; they borrow diagnostic techniques and treatment strategies from all approaches and use them selectively with clients. To the eclectic therapist, the important question is always "What theories will work best with this particular client, in what setting, and with what expected therapeutic outcome?"

To be sure, the eclectic approach has disadvantages (Brammer & Shostrom, 1984; Norcross & Prochaska, 1988). Because often it is not rooted in a carefully constructed system of concepts and assumptions, the eclectic approach may result in uncritical picking and choosing: one therapeutic technique from Column A, another from Column B, and so on down the menu of theories. Furthermore, any novel mixture of concepts and techniques necessarily lacks a substantial base of research to prove how effective it is; essentially, it is educated guesswork. And finally, therapists who do not associate themselves with a traditional theory of psychopathology may be especially prone to embrace the fad therapy of the moment.

Despite these potential shortcomings, eclecticism is inevitable, because we have no single "true" model of abnormal behavior. In fact, most psychologists see considerable value in an eclectic approach (discussed more fully in Chapter 19). They recognize that different models of psychopathology do not completely contradict each other on every point. Rather, the elements of various models can complement each other to produce a broad and detailed explanation of a person's condition.

THE BIOGENIC MODEL

The idea that mental disorders are caused by organic problems was proposed by Hippocrates around 400 B.C., but this organic viewpoint was not generally accepted until the late eighteenth and early nineteenth centuries. The contributions of Wilhelm Griesinger, Emil Kraepelin, and other pioneers; Pasteur's formulation of the germ theory of disease; and Fritz Schaudinn's discovery of the microorganism that caused general paresis all reinforced the belief that abnormal behavior is symptomatic of organic disease. And if every mental disorder has a physiological source, it should also have an organic cure. This reasoning is the essence of the **biogenic model** of psychopathology.

In the first half of the twentieth century, researchers and physicians supporting the biogenic viewpoint, developed new ways to treat mental disorders. Some treatments were more successful than others. For example, in 1938 Ugo Cerletti and Lucio Bini, two Italian psychiatrists (Andreasen, 1984), administered the first electroshock treatment to a schizophrenic patient. They decided on this course of treatment when they discovered that certain symptoms of schizophrenia disappeared after convulsive seizures from grand mal epilepsy. Cerletti decided to use electric currents to induce seizures after discovering that agitated pigs in a slaughterhouse could be stupefied by electric shocks before slaughter. This treatment was the forerunner of electroconvulsive therapy (ECT), discussed in Chapter 19. Although ECT is still used today—with depressed patients rather than schizophrenics—it is a controversial treatment, and its use has declined drastically in recent years (Fink, 1979).

The biological model has been heavily influenced by the neurosciences, a group of subfields focusing on brain structure, function, and pathology. Advances in the neurosciences have lent support to the belief that if anatomical and biochemical abnormalities underlie mental disorders, then pharmacological treatments can be developed. Proponents of this view (Andreasen, 1984) point to Parkinson's disease as an example. In 1917 James Parkinson described a disorder that he called "shaking palsy" because one of its symptoms was tremors, especially hand tremors. When it was discovered that the disorder was caused by an insufficient amount of dopamine, the drug L-

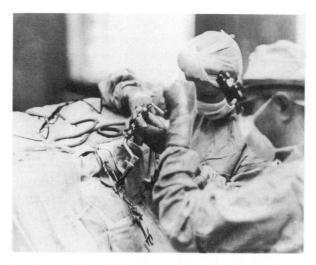

During a prefrontal lobotomy, surgeons used a drill to open the skull. Because of severe side-effects, lobotomies have rarely been used since the 1950s.

dopa was developed to treat the disease. (Parkinson's disease is discussed more fully in Chapter 16.)

There are, of course, many biological causes for psychological disorders. Damage to the nervous system is one: as Schaudinn demonstrated, general paresis results from brain damage caused by parasitic microorganisms. Tumors, strokes, excessive intake of alcohol or drugs, and external trauma (such as a blow to the head) have also been linked to cognitive, emotional, and behavioral pathology. However, two specific biological sources deserve special attention here, for they have given rise to important modern biogenic theories of psychopathology. These causes are body chemistry and heredity.

Biochemical Theories

Most physiological and mental processes, from sleeping and digestion to reading and thinking, involve chemical actions within the body. Thus it seems likely that body chemistry has considerable effect on behavior. The basic premise of the biochemical theories is that chemical imbalances underlie mental disorders. Support for these theories has been provided by research into anxiety disorders, mood disorders (both depression and bipolar disorder, or manic depression), and schizophrenia (McGeer & McGeer, 1980).

Differential Effects of Drugs The search for chemical causes and cures for mental disorders accelerated tremendously in the early 1950s with the discovery that different tranquilizers have different effects on mental disorders (National Institute of Mental Health, 1970; Snyder, 1980). These drugs can act like "bloodhounds" in leading us to specific problem areas in an individual's biochemical system (Sahakian, 1979). For example, some drugs, such as diazepam (Valium) and chlordiazepoxide (Librium), dramatically decrease anxiety in milder disorders but do nothing for schizophrenia, even though schizophrenics commonly exhibit anxiety. Certain other drugs (the phenothiazines) affect schizophrenics but not individuals with phobias or panic disorder.

Such findings also seem to indicate that the milder disturbances are totally different from the more severe (psychotic) disorders (Snyder et al., 1974; Snyder, 1980). They cast doubt on the assumption that mental disorders exist on a continuum from the mildest to the most severe.

Nevertheless, the fact is that a number of different mental disturbances respond to specific medications. According to some psychologists, a sophisticated understanding of drug therapy should be part of every clinician's repertoire of treatment strategies (Wender & Klein, 1981; Andreasen, 1984). The success of drug treatments, they say, points to the effectiveness of medication in normalizing deep abnormality and relieving symptoms. Drugs don't provide a permanent cure, but then, neither does traditional psychotherapy, in most cases. The discoveries that antipsychotic drugs have beneficial effects on schizophrenics, that lithium is useful in controlling affective disorders, and that tricyclic and monoamine oxidase inhibitors alleviate symptoms of severely depressed patients have led some psychiatrists to systematically seek "the right drug for the right patient."

We have already discussed the finding that insufficient dopamine is a possible cause of Parkinson's disease. Ironically, an *excess* of dopamine has been implicated in the development of schizophrenia (Cooper et al., 1986). Dopamine is a neurotransmitter, one of many responsible for the transmission of information from nerve cell to nerve cell, and controls the level of nerve cell activity. In the past few decades, increasing numbers of neuroregulators have been associated with abnormal behaviors. The dopamine hypothesis—discussed more fully in Chapter 15— proposes that schizophrenics may have too many postsynaptic dopamine receptors, or that their receptors may be supersensitive to dopamine.

Of course, no single hypothesis can provide a completely satisfactory explanation of all abnormal behavior. Researchers should instead expect to find hundreds—or perhaps thousands—of pieces in the biochemical puzzle.

Genetic Explanations

Clearly, genetics also play an important part in the development of certain abnormal conditions. For instance, past research has shown that "nervousness" can be inherited in animals by breeding generations of dogs that were either fearful or friendly (Murphree & Dykman, 1965). Evidence supports the contention that autonomic nervous system (ANS) reactivity may be inherited in humans as well; that is, a person may be born with an ANS that makes an unusually strong response to stimuli (Andreasen, 1984). Recent studies (Neale & Oltmanns, 1980; Paykel, 1982; Cloninger et al., 1986) now implicate heredity as a causal factor in alcoholism, schizophrenia, and depression. But to show that a particular disorder is inherited, researchers must show that it is caused by biological rather than environmental factors, that closer genetic relationships produce greater similarity of the disorder in human beings, and that people with these problems have similar biological and behavioral patterns (Gottesman & Shields, 1972).

Biological inheritance is transmitted by the genes. A person's genetic makeup is called his or her **genotype;** interaction between the genotype and the environment results in the person's **phenotype,** or physical and behavioral characteristics. However, at times it is difficult to determine which influence predominates. For example, characteristics such as eye color are determined solely by the coding of the genes (genotype). But other physical characteristics, such as height, are determined partly by the genetic code and partly by environmental factors. Undernourished children may become grownups who are shorter than the height they were genetically capable of reaching. On the other hand, even the most effective nutrition cannot spur people to grow taller than their "programmed" height limit.

Twin Studies As is detailed more fully in Chapter 15, one of the most useful procedures for studying the contributions of heredity is to compare the degree of similarity between identical twins and same-sex nonidentical twins. Identical or **monozygotic (MZ) twins** are derived from a single egg; they have the same genetic makeup. It can be assumed that differences between MZ twins are due to their environment. **Dizygotic (DZ) twins,** derived from two eggs, do not share the same genes.

Many studies of human twins indicate that MZ twins tend to be more alike on autonomic (that part of the nervous system concerned with involuntary bodily functions and changes) measures than DZ twins (Cohen et al., 1972; Kringlen, 1964; Lader & Wing, 1966; and Pogue-Geile & Rose, 1985). A study of anxiety reactions among seventeen pairs of MZ twins and twenty-eight pairs of DZ twins also found strong evidence for an inherited component to anxiety reactions (Slater & Shields, 1969). In 65 percent of the cases where one MZ twin received a diagnosis of marked anxiety, the other twin received the same diagnosis. By contrast, both DZ twins received a diagnosis of marked anxiety in only 13 percent of the cases.

Although twin studies seem to strongly implicate heredity, most are based on an examination of only a few pairs of twins. Thus we must be cautious in interpreting their implications. Furthermore, these results do not explain why, in 35 percent of the MZ cases, one identical twin became disordered and the other did not. It seems, however, that interactions between heredity and environment can either facilitate or retard the manifestation of disorders. For example, a person with an inherited predisposition to anxiety may be born into a benign environment, peopled with supportive parents and friends, that retards anxiety development.

Overall, it is clear that heredity influences autonomic reactions, that heredity contributes to the development of anxiety reactions, and that individual exposure to the environment can moderate the effects of an inherited predisposition to anxiety.

Correlation Studies   There also appears to be a strong correlation between (1) genetic inheritance and (2) the development of bipolar disorder, some forms of schizophrenia, and certain kinds of mental retardation. Down syndrome, for example, is a result of chromosomal aberrations. Except in specific cases, however, the exact influence of genes is difficult to ascertain. Because law and basic morality prohibit selective breeding of humans, we rely on correlation

Clearly, genetics play an important role in the development of some disorders—schizophrenia, for example. A useful way to separate the effects of heredity from environmental factors is to conduct research on twins, especially identical twins who have the same genetic makeup.

studies in seeking the relationship between heredity and mental disorders. But such studies are really just comparisons of existing frequencies of mental disorders in various populations; no matter how strong the correlations they reveal, they do not demonstrate cause-and-effect relationships. For that reason, they must be interpreted cautiously.

Criticisms of the Biogenic Model

The biogenic model of abnormal behavior, which drifted out of favor when psychoanalysis was at the peak of its influence in the 1940s, has regained its popularity. But the biogenic model of mental disorders has some major shortcomings.

First, one of its basic tenets is that abnormal behavior results from an underlying physical condition, such as damage to the brain or malfunction of neural processes. It implies that treatment should be aimed at controlling the underlying disease by changing the individual's biochemistry or removing toxic substances. This approach ignores the many empirical findings that emphasize the importance of environmental factors. It doesn't acknowledge the interpersonal and social causes of abnormal behavior. Nor does it adequately account for more complex abnormal behavior for which no organic etiology, or cause, can be found. For example, the American Psychiatric Association recognizes five categories of schizophrenia. One of the categories, the "undifferentiated" type, is a grab-bag classification that includes schizophrenics who show atypical as well as traditional symptoms. Biochemical treatment has mixed and uneven effects on these patients.

Second, the biogenic model implicitly assumes a correspondence between organic dysfunction and mental dysfunction. Environmental or cultural influences are thought to have minimal impact. But rarely are the equations of human behavior so uncomplicated. More often there are a multitude of causes behind any human behavior, and environmental factors seem to play as important a role as any other. Increasingly, mental health research has focused on the **diathesis-stress theory,** originally proposed by Meehl (1962) and developed further by Rosenthal (1970). The diathesis-stress theory holds that it is not a particular abnormality that is inherited but rather a *predisposition to develop illness* (diathesis). Certain environmental forces, called *stressors,* may activate the predisposition, resulting in a disorder. Alternatively, in a benign and supportive environment, the abnormality may never materialize.

A third shortcoming, related to the preceding one, is revealed by our accumulating knowledge that biochemical changes often occur *because of* environmental forces. We know, for example, that stress-produced fear and anger cause the secretion of adrenalin and noradrenalin. Similarly, excess amounts of chemicals such as dopamine in schizophrenics could tend to *result from the disorder* rather than to cause it.

Last, wholesale adoption of the biogenic model could foster helplessness in the patient by eliminating patient responsibility in the treatment process. The patient might be seen—both by the therapist and by him- or herself—as a passive participant, to be treated only with appropriate drugs and medical interventions. For patients who are already suffering from feelings of helplessness or loss of control, such an approach could be devastating.

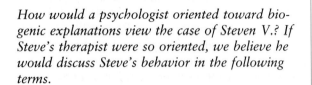

A BIOGENIC VIEW OF STEVEN V.

How would a psychologist oriented toward biogenic explanations view the case of Steven V.? If Steve's therapist were so oriented, we believe he would discuss Steve's behavior in the following terms.

Before I interpret the symptoms displayed by Steven V. and speculate on what they mean, I must stress my belief that many "mental disorders" have a strong biological basis. I do accept the importance of environmental influences; but, in my view, the biological bases of abnormality are too often overlooked by psychologists. This seems clearly to be the case with Steven V.

Much of Steve's medical history is missing from his case records, along with important information about his biological and developmental milestones. We do not have the data necessary to chart a family tree, which would show whether other members of his family have suffered from a similar disorder. This lack of information about possible inherited tendencies in Steve's current behavior pattern is a serious shortcoming.

At age fifteen, Steve was given a diagnosis of bipolar affective disorder (formerly called *manic-depressive psychosis*). Pharmacological treatment was moderately effective in controlling his symptoms. After Steve's condition became stabilized, lithium carbonate treatment was instituted for a period of time, and Steve was free of symptoms during that period. Unfortunately, Steve apparently disliked taking medication and did so only sporadically.

In any case, there is evidence to document and support a diagnosis of bipolar affective disorder. Steve displays the behaviors associated with this disorder, ranging from manic episodes (elevated mood characterized by expansiveness, hyperactivity, flight of ideas, and inflated self-esteem) to depressive episodes (depressed mood characterized by loss of interest, feelings of worthlessness, and thoughts of death or suicide). These symptoms are not of recent origin but probably were evident very early in his life. Steve's first contact with a mental health professional was with the school psychologist in kindergarten, who described him as "autistic-like." I believe the child psychiatrist whom Steve subsequently visited was correct in saying Steve was not autistic. The chief symptoms described in his early years and used to indicate autism (social isolation and unresponsiveness) are similar to those of depression. I suspect Steve was experiencing a major depressive episode, and it may not have been his first. Unfortunately, we do not have access to Steve's pediatrician, who may have observed even earlier signs of bipolar disorder. What we do have, however, are several statements from his parents indicating that "even at birth, Steve did not respond in a normal way."

Thus the following conclusions can be drawn: Steve's disorder was evident early in his life. In spite of a shortage of information, there is some indication that other relatives may have suffered from a similar disorder. The most defensible diagnosis is bipolar affective disorder. In the past, the most effective way to treat the disorder was through drug therapy.

These conclusions strongly support a biological interpretation of the patient's psychopathology. Heredity seems to have played a part; we have some evidence that relatives may have suffered a similar disorder. The precise biological mechanism that triggered the disorder is probably within one of the two major classes of neurotransmitters (catecholamines and indoleamines). If this diagnosis is accurate, the patient should resume taking medication. Of course, stressful life events may also be contributing to Steve's emotional problems, and I intend to continue psychotherapy with him. But I believe that many of Steve's depressive episodes would have occurred regardless of *psychological* intervention. And they will probably continue to occur unless Steve controls his biological problem with medication. I am not an M.D. and therefore cannot prescribe drugs, so I have arranged for

Steve to visit a physician at the college medical center. Only when Steve's organic problem is under control can I or any other therapist begin to make headway with Steve's problems in relating to other people.

THE PSYCHOANALYTIC MODEL

The **psychoanalytic model** of abnormal behavior has two main distinguishing features. First, this approach places strong emphasis on childhood experiences in explaining adult behavior. Psychoanalysts view disorders in adults as the result of traumas or anxieties experienced in childhood. Second, the psychoanalytic model holds that many of these childhood-based anxieties operate unconsciously; because they are too threatening for the adult individual to face, they are repressed through mental defense mechanisms. As a result, people exhibit symptoms they are unable to understand. To eliminate the symptoms, the therapist must make the patient aware of these unconscious anxieties or conflicts.

The early development of psychoanalytic theory is generally credited to Sigmund Freud (1938, 1949), a Viennese neurologist. Before he developed the technique of psychoanalysis, Freud had already made significant contributions in neurology. He was acquainted with the methods of the "Nancy school"

Sigmund Freud (1856-1939) began his career as a neurologist. He became increasingly intrigued with the relationship between illness and mental processes when he worked with Josef Breuer, who successfully used hypnotism to treat hysterical patients.

(see Chapter 1) and had worked with Josef Breuer, a colleague who was successfully using hypnosis to treat hysterical patients (those who exhibited physical symptoms for which no organic cause could be found). This background led his creative and tenacious mind into the field of psychiatry. During his clinical work, Freud became convinced that powerful mental processes could remain hidden from consciousness and could cause abnormal behaviors. He believed the therapist's role was to help the patient achieve insight into these unconscious processes. Although he originally relied on hypnosis for this purpose, Freud soon dropped it in favor of other techniques. He felt that cures were more likely to be permanent if patients became aware of their problems without the aid of hypnosis. This view eventually led Freud to his formulation of psychoanalysis.

Although critics have vehemently attacked the psychoanalytic view on the grounds that it is not a scientific theory, it has undoubtedly had a profound impact on Western thought. Not only is it an extremely popular explanation of abnormal behavior among the lay public, but many other theories of psychopathology are derivatives of, or reactions to, its basic tenets. "Slips of the tongue" or pen, the dynamic workings of the unconscious, the importance of childhood experiences, "defense mechanisms," and countless other concepts and terms that permeate our thinking and language have their roots in the work of Sigmund Freud.

Personality Structure

Freud believed that the personality is composed of three major components and that all behavior is a product of their interaction. He called these mental structures the *id*, the *ego,* and the *superego.* The *id* is the original component of the personality present at birth from which the ego and superego eventually develop. It is impulsive, subjective and pleasure seeking; it is completely selfish and seeks immediate gratification of instinctual needs. The ego comes into existence because the human personality must be able to cope with the external world if it is to survive. Although the id operates from the **pleasure principle,** the *ego* is influenced by the **reality principle;** it represents the realistic and rational part of the mind. Its decisions are dictated by realistic considerations rather than moral judgment. Moral judgments and

moralistic considerations are the domain of the *superego.* It is composed of the *conscience,* which instills guilt feelings about engaging in immoral or unethical behavior, and the ego *ideal,* which rewards altruistic or moral behavior with feelings of pride.

Take the case of a young soldier who has been raised to respect and value human life. He may find the act of killing abhorrent even in a war. However, witnessing the death of several of his closest friends in bloody hand-to-hand combat may cause the soldier to feel severe conflict. Filled with anger and a desire to avenge the death of his friends (id impulses), he may also feel guilty about having these thoughts (superego versus id). Now suppose he suddenly encounters a new situation: He spots an enemy soldier aiming a rifle at him from behind a tree. Here the soldier experiences a conflict between superego and ego. His superego tells him not to kill because it is "bad" (a moralistic consideration), whereas his ego tells him to defend himself (a realistic consideration).

Instincts

Instincts are the energy system from which the personality operates. Instincts give rise to our thoughts and actions and fuel their expression. Freud postulated the existence of two groups of instincts: the *life instincts* and the *death instincts.* The life instincts, also referred to by the Greek term *eros,* consist of self-preservation and sexual drives. Freud focused mainly on the latter as the most important human motivation. The manifestation of sexual instincts, called the *libido,* plays a central role in his theory of abnormal behavior.

During his later years Freud became convinced that there was a second group of instincts. He termed these the *death instincts* (collectively called *thanatos,* the ancient Greek word for death). The death instincts function in opposition to the life instincts, and are manifested in the form of aggression and hostility.

Freud emphasized sex and aggression as the dominant human instincts because he recognized that the society of his times placed strong prohibitions on these drives and that, as a result, people were taught to inhibit them. A profound need to express one's instincts is often frightening and can lead one to deny their existence. Indeed, Freud felt that even though most impulses are hidden from consciousness, they nonetheless determine human actions.

Psychosexual Stages

According to psychoanalytic theory, all human beings develop through a sequence of five stages. Each **psychosexual stage** brings a unique challenge. If unfavorable circumstances prevail, the personality may be drastically affected. Because Freud stressed the importance of early childhood experiences, he saw the human personality as largely determined in the first five years of life—during the **oral, anal,** and **phallic stages.** The last two psychosexual stages are the **latency** and **genital stages.**

Oral Stage   The first year of life is characterized by a focus of instincts on the *oral* cavity. For infants, the mouth is not only the primary source of pleasurable sensations, as in sucking and feeding, but also the mechanism with which they can respond to and deal with the outside world.

The importance of the oral stage for later development lies in how much *fixation* occurs during that stage. (Fixation is the arresting of emotional development at a particular psychosexual stage.) If the infant is traumatized (harmed) in some way during this period, much fixation can occur; that is, some

of the infant's instinctual energy becomes trapped and doesn't move on to more mature stages. Consequently, the personality of such an adult retains strong features of the oral stage. Passivity, helplessness, obesity, chronic smoking, and alcoholism may all be characteristics of an oral personality.

Anal Stage   Toward the end of the first year of life, the *anal* region becomes the zone of pleasurable sensations, and the second psychosexual stage begins. During the anal stage, parents demand that the child control what is a normal biological and innate urge—evacuation of feces. Toilet training is rarely achieved smoothly, and the child may react in ways that may manifest themselves in later adulthood as passive-aggressive or obsessive-compulsive styles.

Phallic Stage   During the third and fourth years of life, the genitals (the boy's penis and the girl's clitoris) become the focus of pleasurable sensations. In both sexes, incestuous feelings for the opposite-sex parent become very strong. Freud concentrated on male development and used the term **Oedipus complex** to describe male sexuality at the phallic stage. The term is taken from the ancient Greek myth

During the oral stage, the first stage of psychosexual development, the infant not only receives nourishment but also derives pleasure from sucking and being close to its mother. Later, during the anal stage, toilet training can be a time of intense emotional conflict between parent and child, or it can be a time of cooperation.

During the latency stage, sexuality is repressed and activities that develop the child's skills and enhance his or her ability to deal with the world are the primary focus. Sexual urges reemerge during the genital stage, which is characterized by rapid physical and emotional changes in the child.

According to psychoanalytic theory, the resolution of the Oedipus complex—the central issue of the phallic stage—occurs when a young boy begins to identify with his father, adopting many of his characteristics, values, and mannerisms.

in which Oedipus killed his father and married his mother (both unwittingly).

In essence, the Oedipus complex is a *conflict: a wish* for a form of sexual possession of the mother (for her warmth, nurturance, and so on) countered by a *fear* of reprisal from a powerful rival for the mother's affection, the father. (**Castration anxiety** is the young boy's fear that the father will punish him for his forbidden desires by cutting off the guilty organ, his penis.)

For the girl, according to Freud, the phallic stage is characterized by **penis envy**, the girl's desire to have a penis. Because she lacks the valued organ, the girl believes castration has already taken place, as a punishment by the mother. The child sees her mother as a hostile rival in competition for the father's penis. As in the Oedipus complex, the conflict becomes very intense for the girl. She resolves it in the same way

and for the same reasons as the boy resolves his conflict—by identifying with the same-sex parent.

The phallic stage of development is crucial to sexual identity in later adult life. According to psychoanalytic theory, if incomplete resolution occurs, impotence, frigidity, promiscuity, and homosexuality may result. Because this stage is characterized by development of the superego, anxiety disorders and personality disorders have their roots in this stage.

Latency Stage Freud believed that the years from age six to twelve (*latency* stage) were generally devoid of sexual motivations. Developmental skills, activities, and interests are the primary concern during this latency stage. Sexuality is repressed because of strong social taboos against its expression. Children of this age may become upset on encountering overt sexual displays.

Genital Stage   The reawakening of sexual urges during puberty and adolescence ushers in the *genital* stage. Physiological and physical changes occur that drastically affect heterosexual relationships. The first relationship is generally *narcissistic* in nature: affection is directed toward one's own body. True heterosexual love does not develop until the emotional investment can be transferred to a member of the opposite sex. That is, intense interest in one's own body and concern with its health indicate a "self" orientation rather than the "other" orientation needed for interpersonal relationships.

Freud believed that a person who could transcend the various fixations would develop into a normal, healthy individual. Heterosexual interests, stability, vocational planning, marriage, and other social activities would become a person's prime concern during this stage.

Anxiety and Psychopathology

Anxiety is at the root of Freud's theory of psychopathology. The three-part personality structure that Freud postulated can produce a number of conflict situations. Freud identified three types of anxiety (shown diagrammatically in Figure 2.1). *Realistic anxiety* occurs when there is potential danger from the external environment. For example, when you smell smoke in a building, your ego warns you to take action to protect yourself from physical harm. *Moralistic anxiety* results when someone does not live up to his or her own moral standards or engages in unethical conduct. In this case, the ego warns of possible retaliation from the superego. *Neurotic anxiety* often results when id impulses seem to be getting out of hand, bursting through ego controls. In all these cases, anxiety is a signal that something bad is about to happen and that appropriate steps should be taken to reduce the anxiety.

Although Freud dealt with all three types of anxiety, he concentrated mainly on neurotic anxiety. We shall do the same, although much of our discussion applies to the other two types as well. Current changes in the third edition, revised, of the *Diagnostic and Statistical Manual* (DSM-III-R) of the American Psychiatric Association have replaced the traditional subcategories of neurotic behavior with other, more refined concepts, but we use the term *neurotic* because of its importance to Freud's theory.

Figure 2.1   Three Types of Anxiety
Freud believed that people suffer from three types of anxiety, arising from conflicts involving the id, ego, and superego. Each type of anxiety is, in essence, a signal of impending danger.

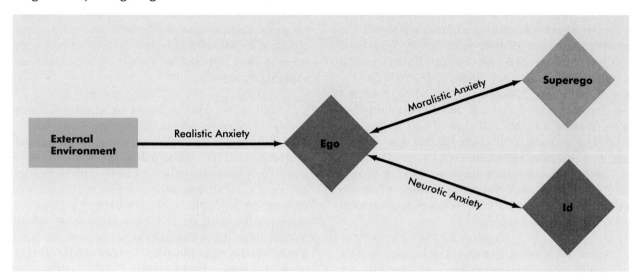

Defense Mechanisms

Neurotic behavior develops from the threat of overwhelming anxiety, which may lead to full-scale panic. To forestall this panic, the ego often resorts to **defense mechanisms** to reduce anxiety. These mechanisms are ways of preventing awareness of anxiety-arousing impulses and thoughts. Defense mechanisms have three characteristics in common: they protect the individual from anxiety, they operate unconsciously, and they distort reality.

All individuals make use of strategies to reduce anxiety. The defense mechanisms discussed here are considered maladaptive, however, when they become the predominant means of coping with stress and when they interfere with one's ability to handle life's everyday demands.

Repression   Repression is the blocking of forbidden or dangerous desires and thoughts to keep them from entering one's consciousness. According to Freud, it is the most basic defense mechanism and is generally the first used. However, simply forcing this material into what Freud called the *unconscious* does not solve the problem. Unconscious material continually seeks consciousness, which means the ego must constantly expend energy to keep it hidden. This draining of psychic energy leaves the person less energy to use for more adaptive functions. Moreover, unconscious material often tends to increase in energy and strength.

According to Freud, unconscious material can become conscious in two ways: by overpowering the forces of repression, or by circumventing them. The former results in a break with reality (psychotic episode), and the latter occurs during states of ego weakness when the ego's guard is relaxed. For example, when you are asleep or very tired, your ego defenses are weakened and unconscious impulses often surface. Dreams and slips of the tongue and pen express unconscious material that has escaped during a period of ego weakness.

As well as preventing dangerous and unacceptable desires from reaching consciousness, repression expels painful or traumatic memories from consciousness. Here is a case example.

> Mr. X was a 35-year-old veteran who complained of listlessness, occasional anxiety, and inability to taste the flavor of foods. In addition, he complained of numbness throughout his body and a ringing in his ear that correlated with certain mood states. For example, a high pitch meant he was angry, and a low pitch meant he would become elated. A thorough neurological exam revealed no significant organic problem, so he was referred to the psychology service for further evaluation. Subsequent interviews revealed a strange obsession on the part of Mr. X. For the past two months he had found himself drawn to reading the obituary column of the local newspaper, although he found such activity extremely frightening. He could not make sense of his obsession, nor could he ever recall anything related to this preoccupation. Under hypnosis, Mr. X was finally able to recall that as an adolescent he had broken into several cemeteries and had dug up graves as a prank. One night he broke into a coffin containing the body of a young female and found himself sexually aroused by the body. The thought of being sexually attracted to a corpse was so abhorrent to him that he . . . repressed the entire memory from consciousness. However, his repressive mechanisms were beginning to fail. (Schroth & Sue, 1975, pp. 253–254)

Reaction Formation   In **reaction formation,** dangerous impulses are repressed and then converted to their direct opposite. Feelings of hate may be converted to superficial love, sexual desires to rigid morality, and pessimism to optimism. The extremely overprotective mother who is afraid to let her seven-year-old child play anywhere but in the back yard, may be masking unconscious resentment and hostility toward an unwanted child who has tied her down for years. Because mothers are supposed to love their children, she cannot admit these feelings and converts them to their opposite by showering the child with superficial attention.

Projection   The defensive reaction in which people rid themselves of threatening desires or thoughts by attributing them to others is called **projection.** Projection can be manifested in two ways. First, a person may blame his or her mistakes or shortcomings on some external source. A worker may mask unpleasant feelings of inadequacy by blaming his or her poor performance on the incompetence of fellow workers. Second, in extreme cases a person may form a **delusional system,** in which the person believes that enemies are disrupting his or her life.

Rationalization Rationalization is a common defense in which a person gives well thought-out and socially acceptable reasons for certain behavior—but these reasons do not happen to be the real ones. For example, a student may explain flunking a test as follows: "I'm not interested in the course and don't really need it to graduate. Besides, I find the teacher extremely dull." These may be plausible and rational statements. However, the student has failed to mention the fact that she did not try hard because she was afraid the course was too difficult for her to pass. In essence, rationalization helps people justify their behavior and softens disappointments connected with unattainable goals.

It can be very difficult for rationalizer and listener alike to tell the difference between objective truths and rationalizations. People who rationalize fequently become upset when their reasons are questioned. They never tire of dredging up justifications. A common example of rationalization is the myriad of reasons that smokers can generate to justify their habit.

Displacement Displacement is the directing of an emotion such as hostility or anxiety toward a substitute target. For example, a meek clerk who is constantly belittled by his boss may build up tremendous resentment. If he were to express this anger openly at work, he might be fired. Instead, he snaps at family members or teases the dog at home. Commonly referred to as *scapegoating,* displacement occurs when the expression of feelings toward their real source is too threatening. Displacement is generally directed toward a less powerful object (human or pet). Prejudice and discrimination against certain identifiable groups may be partly explained as displacement.

Displacement can also be self-directed; that is, people may unconsciously turn their anger in on themselves. In most cases, such people have inhibited personalities and can be described as passive. They let others take advantage of them and then build up a great deal of resentment. On the subconscious level, these people castigate themselves for not being able to stand up to others. A poor self-image begins to form, accompanied by self-hatred that is manifested in self-recriminations and strong guilt feelings. Some clinicians feel that people who are depressed harbor a great deal of hostility that needs to be expressed.

Psychoanalytically oriented therapists believe that a strong relationship exists between depression and aggression.

Undoing In most cases, **undoing** can be viewed as a symbolic attempt to right a wrong or negate some disapproved thought, impulse, or act. It tends to be ritualistic and repetitive. In Shakespeare's play, Lady Macbeth goaded her husband into slaying the king, and then tried to cleanse herself of sin by constantly going through the motions of washing her hands. More commonplace examples of this defense mechanism may be seen in the superstitious behaviors people engage in to ward off bad luck and to maximize good luck—for example, knocking on wood. Some clinicians believe that compulsive behaviors are associated with undoing.

Regression Regression is a retreat to an earlier developmental level that demands less mature responses and aspirations. Freud believed that a person using this defense generally moves back to his or her most fixated psychosexual stage. Whether this interpretation is true or not, many people, when faced with severe stress, often resort to immature or infantile behavior. They seem to want to remove themselves from the threatening situation by regressing to a stage in which they were allowed to be dependent, helpless, and irresponsible.

Examples of regression may be found everywhere, from the child who reverts to infantile behavior, such as thumb sucking or bed wetting, when a sibling is born, to the dignified college president who whoops it up at a reunion with college classmates. However, regression becomes extremely pathological when the person begins to live in the state to which he or she has regressed and cannot function as a mature individual. In severe forms, the individual loses contact with reality. Certain forms of schizophrenia, such as *catatonia,* represent the ultimate in regression from the psychoanalytic perspective. Here the person withdraws completely into his or her own world and becomes mute and deaf. The catatonic frequently assumes rigid postures—often the fetal position—for long periods of time.

As we noted earlier, all people use defense mechanisms to some extent. However, persons with emotional disorders are likely to overuse them. The difference is one of degree, not of kind.

Psychoanalytic Therapy

Besides occurring in the natural states of sleep and excessive fatigue, ego weakness can be externally induced. To rid people of maladaptive behaviors, **psychoanalytic therapy,** better known as **psychoanalysis,** induces ego weakness through such techniques as hypnosis and *projective tests,* in which such ambiguous stimuli as ink blots, word associations, or pictures provoke revealing verbal responses. These techniques give the therapist (called a *psychoanalyst* or just an *analyst*) some access to unconscious material. This material is used to help patients achieve insight into their own inner motivations and desires. The basic premise of psychoanalysis is that a cure can be effected only in this way. (Psychoanalytic methods are discussed in Chapter 19.)

Carl Jung (1875-1961) proposed the collective unconscious to represent the cumulative experience that all humans share. Unlike Freud's psychoanalysis, Jung's theory took an optimistic view of human beings.

Neo-Freudian Perspectives

Freud's psychoanalytic movement attracted many followers. Some of Freud's disciples, however, came to disagree with his insistence that the sex instinct is the major determinant of behavior. Many of his most gifted adherents broke with him and formulated coherent psychological models of their own. These thinkers have since become known as **neo-Freudians** (or post-Freudians) because, despite their new ideas, they remained strongly influenced by Freud's constructs. For example, nearly all of them continued to believe in the power of the unconscious, in the use of "talking" methods of psychotherapy that rely heavily on the patient's introspection, in the three-part structure of personality, and in the one-to-one analyst-patient approach to therapy.

The major differences between the various neo-Freudian theories and psychoanalytic theory lie in the emphasis that the neo-Freudians placed on four areas:

1. Freedom of choice and the importance of future goals
2. Consciousness and ego autonomy
3. The influence of social forces on psychological functioning
4. Importance of significant others (object relations)
5. The need to treat the seriously disturbed individual

Let us look at each of these areas in greater detail.

Choice and Future Goals Two of the first pupils to break with Freud were Alfred Adler (1870–1937) and Carl Jung (1875–1961). Adler developed his own approach, called *individual psychology.* He contended that human beings are much less at the mercy of instinctual unconscious motivations than Freud had indicated. Adler deemphasized biological drives and stressed social drives instead. Psychologically healthy people, Adler believed, have some freedom of choice in their actions; their behavior is directed toward goals they value and is guided in part by their vision of what they want their future to become. Adler thought psychopathology resulted from inappropriate child-rearing practices, and he thought therapists should focus on the social context of their patients' lives.

Like Adler, Carl Jung believed human beings are goal directed and future oriented and that these characteristics help guide behavior. Although he shared Freud's premise that the unconscious is a powerful force, Jung was more optimistic in outlook. He asserted that the unconscious is composed of two parts: the individual unconscious, as in the Freudian theory, and the collective unconscious. The **collective unconscious** contains positive attributes and spiritual elements; it is a kind of storehouse of religious and aesthetic values derived from the cumulative experience of the human species. In addition, Jung viewed the id as a creative force and not a regressive one that needed to be controlled.

More than any other prominent psychologist, Jung was a student of history. His writings on mythology, religion, folklore, ancient symbols and rituals, dreams, and visions have had a great impact on art, literature, and sociology. In addition, his concepts of introversion and extroversion have permeated psychological thinking. Jung's work continues to be popular among college students.

Ego Autonomy Whereas Adler and Jung moved contemporary psychoanalytic theory toward a more optimistic, less deterministic, and less biological orientation, others, such as Heinz Hartmann (1894–1970), Freud's daughter Anna Freud (1895–1982), and Erik Erikson (born 1902), emphasized the role, operation, and importance of the ego. Thus they and their followers are often called *ego psychologists*. Ego psychologists accept Freud's three-part division of the personality, but they believe the ego is an autonomous component. The ego is not at the mercy of the id; it is able to be creative while remaining independent of the sexual and aggressive drives.

In his book *Ego Psychology and the Problems of Adaptation* (1958), Hartmann argued persuasively that the ego is independent from the id, that it is a creative force, and that the manifestations of memory, perception and learning are not simple manifestations of id impulses. Like Hartmann, Anna Freud focused on ego functions as the executive of the personality that part that controls the gateways to action by mediating id, superego, and environmental demands. Her major contributions were made in the study of ego defenses and the pioneering psychoanalytic treatment of children.

Erik Erikson (1902-1982) studied with Anna Freud (Freud's daughter). He formulated an important theory of psychosocial ego development from infancy to late adulthood.

Erik Erikson is perhaps the most influential of the ego theorists. His outstanding contribution was formulating the stages of ego development from infancy to late adulthood—one of the first truly developmental examinations of personality structures and processes. His analyses of identity crises in youth are held in especially high regard. Unlike Freud, Erikson considered personality to be flexible and capable of growth and change throughout the adult years. He believed, in other words, that we need not remain imprisoned in our past.

Social Forces A third major influence in contemporary psychoanalytic theory came from thinkers such as Erich Fromm (1900–1980), Karen Horney (1885–1952), and Harry Stack Sullivan (1892–1949). Despite considerable differences among their ideas, all three agreed on the primary role of interpersonal relationships in the development of the personality.

Although Erich Fromm drew heavily on psychoanalytic concepts, his major themes emphasize

FOCUS 2.1 *Cults: Escape from Freedom?*

What do the followers of Bhagwan Shree Rajneesh and Rev. Sun Myung Moon, the Hare Krishnas, and the members of an estimated 2,500 additional cults in the United States have in common? If Erich Fromm were alive today, he might well view young people's joining of cults as an "escape from freedom." Confronted with the many choices of life and the need to establish greater independence and individual identity, some young people have found only unbearable insecurity and loneliness. Cult membership has often been their answer.

A recent analysis of cult followers that reiterates Fromm's escape-

from-freedom theme is Saul V. Levine's *Radical Departures: Desperate Detours to Growing Up* (1984). Levine's study of cults began in the 1960s. He studied more than a thousand individuals belonging to fifteen different groups—drug groups, religious cults, political organizations, and therapy groups. To augment this broad perspective, Levine concentrated on nine young men and women as they journeyed into and out of communal groups.

Levine did not find the typical group member to be a loner, a failure, a substance abuser, or a misfit. Nor did he find that members were controlled, duped, or held captive.

Group members by and large showed no serious signs of pathology, came from pleasant homes, were raised by concerned parents, were well off financially, and had much to look forward to. These "radical departers," as Levine prefers to call the group members, are generally between eighteen and twenty-six years old, unmarried, affluent, well educated, white, and from intact families.

Levine's findings seem to make the radical departer's sudden leave-taking from the family strange and puzzling. He believes that joining a cult may represent a desperate attempt to avoid choice and responsi-

Karen Horney (1885-1952), one of the first feminist psychologists, developed a theory of personality development and pathology based on the social relationship between parent and child.

the social and interpersonal aspects of psychological development. According to Fromm, people have become separated from nature and have lost a sense of community. In his book *Escape from Freedom* (1941), Fromm points out that the price of greater freedom and individuation is loneliness. Thus people attempt to *escape* freedom, which has become a negative condition (see Focus 2.1). To find meaning in their lonely lives, they have two choices: unite in a spirit of love and shared work or seek security through submission and conformity. The former leads to the development of a better society; the latter may lead to behavior disorders.

Karen Horney argued that the cause of behavior pathology is *basic anxiety*, a disturbance of the child's security resulting from parental rejection or overprotection. This interpersonal childhood disturbance may lead to the development of a need to move *closer to* people, a need to move *away from* people, or a need to move *against* people. Neurotic behavior then results from this need.

Horney is also considered by many to be the first feminist psychologist. She rejected Freud's concept of penis envy, denying that feminine psychology

bility. To understand the framework of his analysis, we need to recognize the pressures that adolescents experience as they enter adulthood.

In our middle-class culture, we stress the importance of children growing up, separating from their parents, and establishing their own independence and identity. As children become teenagers, their parents begin to relinquish control, allowing them greater freedom and decision-making power. Parents make it clear that adult responsibilities loom ahead. Young adults must think about college, make career choices, leave home. Not only do adolescents feel a sense of loss and loneliness as this occurs; they also grope with identity issues. In the normal course of growing up, they seek intimacy with friends and lovers. But radical departers seem to have been unable to form satisfactory relationships with others or to commit themselves to a value system. Separation from parents then involves pain, and cults seem to offer a magical solution: separation without accompanying pain. Submission and conformity to a group bring temporary security. For as long as this commitment lasts, the struggle to form an independent self is given up in favor of a flawless "group self." Radical departers, then, are escaping from freedom—making a temporary retreat from growing up.

Levine does not believe, however, that joining a cult is wholly negative. He observes, for example, that more than 90 percent of radical departers return home within two years and that virtually all eventually abandon their groups. A radical departure thus may represent a rehearsal for separation from the parents. Levine also argues that joining a cult and voluntarily separating can be a therapeutic process. He warns against "deprogramming," which involves kidnapping the member and then systematically assailing the values and beliefs the group has instilled. Deprogramming interferes with the natural and normal departure process.

had anything to do with either male or female anatomy. (See Focus 2.2.) She also rejected the concept of psychopathology as a sexual-aggressive conflict resulting from an Oedipus or Electra complex.

Harry Stack Sullivan's major contribution was his interpersonal theory of psychological disorders. Sullivan believed that the individual's psychological functions could be understood only in the context of his or her social relationships. We say considerably more about Sullivan and his interpersonal theory in Chapter 3.

Object Relations   One contemporary trend in the psychodynamic perspective has been the contributions of the object relations theorists. The technical term **object relations** is roughly equivalent to "past interpersonal relationships." It refers to how people develop patterns of living from their early relations with significant others, particularly their mothers.

In the 1930s, Melanie Klein (1975) and Harry Guntrip (1968) began to formulate object relations theory. These researchers theorized that small children may identify with and incorporate the symbolic representation of important figures. As adults, the object or symbol may influence the way they experience, behave, or interpret events. Because stable personality characteristics tend to develop quite early, the goal of therapy is to understand how these childhood patterns are repeated in many variations in adult life. For example, a young boy who has been neglected and unloved by his mother (object) may experience severe unmet needs for nurturance. The relationship he forms with his mother (constant seeking to be taken care of and loved) forms the core of his relationship with women. When he grows up, his distorted idealized representation of nurturing women is at odds with the real women he meets. When he marries, he may be disappointed by the discrepancy between his wife and the distorted image of the ideal woman. As a result, he may go through numerous divorces and relationships.

Additional contributions to object relations theory are attributed to Margaret Mahler (Mahler et al., 1975, 1979). She concentrated on the psychological aspects of how a child separates him- or herself from the mother. Although the newborn seems to possess little differentiation between its own existence

FOCUS 2.2   *The Psychology of Women: A Feminist Viewpoint*

Freud's theory of female sexuality and personality has drawn heavy criticisms from feminists over many years. Phallic-stage dynamics, penis envy, unfavorable comparisons of the clitoris to the penis, the woman's need for a male child as penis substitute, and the belief that penetration is necessary for the woman's sexual satisfaction all rest on assumptions that are biologically questionable and that fail to take into consideration social forces shaping women's behavior. At face value, the theory seems to depreciate female sexuality while legitimizing male sexuality.

One of the earliest psychoanalytic critics of the penis envy notion was Karen Horney, who argued persuasively that psychoanalysis was a creation of male bias and that almost all those who had developed Freud's ideas were men (1965). Horney felt that the desire to be a man did not reflect penis envy, but reflected the sociocultural devaluation of women. She called for anthropological studies in other cultures to investigate whether penis envy was universal, and whether social conditioning and sex-limited roles might not account for this phenomenon. For example, the well-known anthropologist, Margaret Mead (1949) provided a vivid description of the traditional emotional characteristics of men and women in three societies of New Guinea. Among the Arapesh, both men and women display emotional characteristics that in our society would be considered distinctly feminine. Both sexes are trained to be unaggressive, cooperative, kind, noncompetitive, and responsive to the needs of other people. The river-dwelling Mundugumur, however, present a sharp contrast. In their society, both men and women are violent, combative, ruthless, and competitive; fighting has become a way of life with them, in which they take great delight.

Perhaps the most interesting pattern is that of the lakeshore community of the Tchambuli, in whom sex role stereotypes typical of our culture seem completely reversed. The women hold the positions of power and are responsible for the fishing and manufacturing of the tribe's chief article of trade. The men are engaged predominantly in the arts and have become skilled in dancing, carving, and painting. Tchambuli women are described as impersonal, practical, and efficient, while the men are reported to be humanistically oriented, artistic, timid, and submissive. Interestingly enough, in the Tchambuli society the "masculine" man and the "effeminate" woman are considered to be deviants!

---

and that of the mother, the process of *separation and individuation* in the development of the child is crucial for further growth. Many factors may disrupt the differentiation process, but how the mother and other significant figures in the child's life handle the situation is very important.

Two other individuals important to object relations theory are Otto Kernberg and Heinz Kohut. Kernberg (1980) is especially known for his studies of the borderline personality (discussed more fully in Chapter 9). He observed many clients who seemed to have difficulty in establishing stable relationships. These individuals often appeared to have internalized but nonintegrated pathological objects in their past. Because they have been unable to synthesize contradiction self-images and object images, these people find it difficult to form consistent relationships with others (object constancy).

Heinz Kohut (Kohut & Wolf, 1978), however, emphasized emotional support of the child by the parents. If a child's emotional needs are not met, then the child's psyche may be damaged. The result may be a *narcissistic personality* (also discussed further in Chapter 9), a constant and exaggerated need to satisfy the self.

It is important to note that the object relations movement differs from traditional psychodynamic theory in several ways. First, it deemphasizes the id and ego and instead concentrates on the significant early figures of the child; especially important is the mother. Second, biological factors are downplayed in favor of interpersonal or social forces. Third, while it does stress the importance of early childhood experiences, object relations approaches are strongly centered on discovering current and consistent patterns of behavior and thinking in the here and now.

Modern feminist psychologists (Chesler, 1972; Williams, 1977; Chodorow, 1978; Holroyd, 1980) have not limited their criticisms to psychoanalytic theory alone, but have taken the mental health profession to task for implicitly and explicitly accepting sex role stereotypes. They point out several sociocultural factors (rather than inferior biology) that contribute to the denigration of women. First, images of women throughout history have been unflattering or fearful. Women were portrayed as seductress-enchantresses or as powerful mother goddesses. In most cases, women were perceived as evil, lustful, and depraved, needing to be controlled, subordinated, and devalued. Such images justified men's need to control them (women were burned as witches), to treat them as property, and to exclude them from positions of power (Williams, 1977). Second, socialization was seen as one way to "keep them in their place." From the time of birth, boys are taught to be clever, independent, brave, rational, and assertive while girls are taught to be docile, kind, dependent, emotional, and nurturant. Sex roles for adults also parallel those taught to children. Men are supposed to be providers, strong, independent, competitive, and rational beings. Women are supposed to be emotional, irrational, weak, and passive. No wonder women may regard the man's role highly.

Feminist psychologists believe that the role ascribed to women is not only less desirable in our society but also has drastic implications for their mental health. Feminist thinking recognizes that women's sex roles may make them "sick," particularly when the role of wife or mother is at odds with their needs. Furthermore, one early study (Broverman, et al., 1972) found that clinicians often viewed behaviors associated with the male role to be an ideal standard of mental health but that the female one (weakness, irrationality, submission to authority, and dependency) was equated with unhealthiness.

In 1975, the American Psychological Association's *Report on Sex Bias and Sex-Role Stereotyping in Psychotherapeutic Practice* engaged in a comprehensive study of the research literature on this topic, surveyed women psychologists, and obtained case studies of such practices. They concluded that strong therapy bias in the area of fostering traditional sex roles, devaluating of women, sexist use of psychoanalytic concepts, and responding to women as sex objects (including seduction of women in therapy) were present. The subjugation of women in our society, and not inferior biological makeup or intrapsychic dynamics, may account for much of the differences we see between men and women.

Treatment of the Seriously Disturbed During the 1950s and 1960s, a number of psychoanalysts admitted that classical psychoanalysis had certain inherent weaknesses. For example, Freud disqualified from psychoanalysis a large percentage of the population that he considered "analytically unfit." That is, they did not have sufficient contact with reality or possess characteristics which would make psychoanalyes suitable for them. Very seriously disturbed people, particularly schizophrenics, were viewed as unfit because they did not respond to the "verbal interpretive" techniques advocated by Freud. In addition, certain narcissistic neurotic patients were too isolated (not psychologically minded) to respond to verbal therapy.

Under the rubric of modern psychoanalysis, Hyman Spotnitz (1963, 1968, 1976) and his colleagues have introduced new treatment techniques that do not require the patient to be emotionally or intellectually capable of understanding interpretations. These techniques, are, in essence, reflection or mirroring in which the analyst actively provides feedback to the patient. The patient is then helped to resolve conflicts by experiencing the conflicts rather than understanding them. Although Spotnitz's work is not well known outside the psychoanalytic movement, it has become an important contribution to contemporary psychoanalysis.

Criticisms of the Psychoanalytic Model

Psychoanalytic theory has had a tremendous impact on the field of psychology. Psychoanalysis and its variations are very widely employed. Nonetheless, the usefulness of the psychoanalytic view in explaining and treating behavior disorders has been challenged. Two major criticisms are often leveled at psychoanalysis (Hall & Lindzey, 1970), as follows.

First, the empirical procedures by which Freud validated his hypotheses have grave shortcomings. His observations about human behavior were often made under uncontrolled conditions. For example, he relied heavily on case studies and on his own self-analysis as a basis for formulating theory. His patients, from whom he drew conclusions about universal aspects of personality dynamics and behavior, tended to represent a narrow spectrum of people. Although case studies are often a rich source of clinical data, the fact that Freud did not keep verbatim notes means his recollections were subject to distortions and omissions. Furthermore, he seldom checked the accuracy of the material related by his patients through any form of external corroboration (relatives, friends, test data, documents, or medical records). Using such private and uncontrolled methods of inquiry as a basis for theory is fraught with hazards.

Freud failed to make explicit the line of reasoning by which he drew inferences and conclusions. In his numerous writings, he presented the end results of his thinking without giving the original data on which they were based, his method of analysis, or any systematic presentation of his empirical findings. It is difficult, if not impossible, to replicate many of Freud's investigations. Thus the reliability of his observations is impossible to evaluate. Did he really find a relationship between alcoholism and orality, between obsessive-compulsive behavior and anality, and between hysteria and phallic fixation? Did he read into his cases only what he wanted to find? How much was he influenced by his own personal biases and needs? Freud's reluctance to follow the conventions of full scientific reporting leaves many people skeptical about his concepts and explanations.

Much of psychoanalytic theory, then, cannot be empirically validated. A "good" theory should clearly and precisely explain phenomena, specifying the relationship between events and forces. It should also be capable of predicting what will happen, given certain conditions. Psychoanalysis falls short on both scores. The vagueness with which certain relationships are presented makes them virtually useless. What exactly is the relationship between the superego and the Oedipus complex? How intense must an

experience be to become traumatic? Exactly how strong must instinctual forces be to overcome the ego? Not only does psychoanalytic theory lack specificity, but it cannot adequately predict what will happen. For example, the concept of a death instinct can be used to explain certain events, such as suicides and wars, after the fact. Yet such a vague concept helps us little in understanding or predicting such events.

A second criticism of psychoanalysis is that there is a wide range of disturbed people to which it cannot be applied. Individuals who have speech disturbances or are inarticulate (talking is important in therapy); people who have urgent, immediate problems (classical psychoanalysis requires much time); and people who are too young or too old may not profit from psychoanalysis (Fenichel, 1945). Research studies have shown that psychoanalytic therapy is best suited to well-educated people of the middle and upper socioeconomic classes who exhibit anxiety disorders rather than psychotic behavior. It is more limited in therapeutic value with people of lower socioeconomic levels and with people who are less verbal, less intelligent, and more severely disturbed (Sloane et al., 1975).

A PSYCHOANALYTIC VIEW OF STEVEN V.

Let us hypothesize again. Suppose Steven V.'s therapist had a psychoanalytic orientation. Here is what we believe he (or she) might have to say about this patient.

In Steve's case records, I see many possible explanations for his continuing problems. I will focus on four areas that I find particularly important: Steve's early childhood experiences; his repression of conflicts, intense feelings, and other impulses; the oedipal dynamics that seem to be at work; and the unconscious symbolism behind his relationship with Linda.

Steve did not receive the love and care, at crucial psychosexual stages, that a child needs in order to develop into a healthy adult. He was neglected, understimulated, and left on his own. The result was that he felt unloved and rejected. We have evidence that he was prone to "accidents"—being hit on the head by a swing, burning himself severely on an electric range, numerous falls. I believe these were not really accidents. They represented Steve's unconscious attempts to gain attention and to test his parents' love for him. Furthermore, I believe his proneness to accidents was the forerunner of his attempts at suicide, a reflection of the death instinct and a desire to punish himself. Although Steve may not have been conscious of his feelings or able to verbalize them, it is obvious that he was deeply affected by his parents' negative attitudes. It must be an awful experience for a young child to believe he or she is unloved. For many of us, it is easier to deny or repress this belief than to face up to it.

Steve may have been the victim of marital unhappiness between his mother and father. The records indicate that they lived rather separate lives and that Mr. V. kept several mistresses whom he saw on his frequent "business trips." In one therapy session, when Mrs. V. was seen alone, she stated that she knew of her husband's extramarital affairs but never confronted him about them. Apparently she was fearful of his dominating and abusive manner at home, and she avoided potential conflicts by playing a passive role. When Mr. V. belittled Steve, she chose not to intervene; but secretly she identified with her son's predicament. Unable to form an intimate relationship with her husband, she became physically seductive toward Steve. As you recall, Mrs. V. frequently caressed and kissed her son and even had him sleep with her. To a youngster still groping his way through oedipal conflicts, nothing could have been more damaging. Steve's sexual feelings toward the mother were no doubt intensified by her actions.

Mr. V.'s verbal abuse of Steve also aggravated Steve's problems. One of his father's common remarks to Steve was "You've got no balls." Abuse such as this deepened and prolonged Steve's oedipal feelings of rivalry with and fear of his father. Steve's oedipal conflict was never adequately resolved. His continued feelings of inadequacy and anger, and his sexual drives as

well, have remained repressed and are expressed symbolically.

Repressed anger is certainly present in both Steve's fantasies and his behavior. His violent "mind games" and his preference for sadistic pornographic films are an indirect expression of anger at his father, whom he continues to see as a powerful feared rival (he has failed to identify with his father in resolution of the oedipal conflict), and at his mother, who never came to his defense and suddenly withdrew his "bed privileges" when she became aware of Steve's sexual excitement. There also appears to be a strong relationship between anger and depression. Steve's periodic bouts of depression are probably the result of anger turned inward. His frequent accidents, his episodic depression, and his attempts at suicide are classic manifestations of the death instinct.

Steve's early childhood experiences continue to affect his behavior with women. Note the similarities between his woman friend, Linda, and his mother. Linda is described as being active in student affairs; the mother was always involved with civic activities. Linda seemed oblivious to Steve's existence in the presence of others, and he felt slighted by her friends; his mother seems never to have introduced Steve to her friends and relatives. Linda was "warm, affectionate, and intimate" in private; the mother, when "alone with Steve," was quite affectionate. Linda would consent to "heavy petting" but drew the line short of intercourse; the mother suddenly withdrew "bed privileges" when Steve showed incestuous sexual interest. It is clear that Steve continues to search for a "mother figure" and unconsciously selects women who are most like his mother. His impotence with Linda is additional evidence that Steve unconsciously views her as his mother. (In our society, incest is an unthinkable act.)

If Steve is to become a healthier individual, he must commit himself to intensive, long-term therapy aimed at helping him gain insight into his deep conflicts and repressed experiences. Resolving past traumas, overcoming resistance, and working through a transference relationship with the therapist will be crucial components of his therapy.

FOCUS 2.3   *The Healthy Personality*

One major contribution by humanistic psychologists has been their optimistic perception of people. Rather than focusing on pathology, they have stressed our assets and strengths. Psychologist Abraham Maslow has identified characteristics of mental health in well-known figures, including Thomas Jefferson, Albert Einstein, and Eleanor Roosevelt. Other studies have provided additional information about healthy individuals. Here are some of the traits that are most prominent in the healthy personality—traits that, according to humanists, distinguish human beings from other species.

1. *An ability to accept oneself, others, and nature* Self-actualizers accept their shortcomings and are not ashamed of being what they are. They have a positive self-concept and feel they are making contributions to the world. They are also receptive to others—even others who are different.

2. *An adequate perception of and comfortable attitude toward reality* Self-actualizers prefer to cope with unpleasant realities rather than to avoid or deny them. They waste little time in feeling sorry for themselves. They base decisions on how things really are rather than on how they wish they were.

3. *Spontaneity* Healthy individuals are relatively spontaneous in behavior, thoughts, and inner impulses. They tend to behave naturally.

4. *Focus on external problems* Most healthy people tend to focus on external problems rather than worrying about themselves or their personal problems and concerns. For example, Maslow's subjects were concerned with the major world issues of the day and were also interested in developing a philosophy of life. Not overly self-conscious, they could devote their attention to a task that seemed particularly appropriate for them.

HUMANISTIC AND EXISTENTIAL APPROACHES

The humanistic and existential approaches evolved as a reaction to the determinism of other behavioral models. For example, many proponents of these approaches were disturbed that Freudian psychology did not focus on the inner world of the client but rather categorized the client according to a set of preconceived diagnoses (May, 1967). Psychoanalysts, these critics said, described clients in terms of blocked instinctual forces and psychic complexes that made them victims of some mechanistic and deterministic personality structure.

It is important to note that the humanistic and existential perspectives cannot be classified as a single school of thought. But they do share a set of assumptions that distinguish them from other approaches or viewpoints.

First, both perspectives view an individual's reality as a product of that person's unique perceptions of the world. How the individual experiences the world determines his or her behavior. Hence, to understand why a person behaves as he or she does, the psychologist must reconstruct the world from that individual's vantage point. Moreover, the subjective universe of this person—how he or she construes events—is more important than the events themselves. Second, both humanistic and existential theorists stress the ability of individuals to make free choices and to be responsible for their own decisions. Third, these theorists believe in the "wholeness" or integrity of the person. Attempts to reduce human beings to a set of formulas, to explain us simply by measuring our responses to certain stimuli, are viewed as pointless. And last, according to the humanistic and existential perspectives, people have the ability to become what they want, to fulfill their capacities, and to lead the lives best suited to themselves.

The Humanistic Perspective

The psychoanalytic view of personality strongly emphasizes unconscious determinants of behavior. And, if unconscious forces determine behavior, then free choice is not really available. As we have noted, a number of theorists take issue with these concepts, placing greater emphasis on people's conscious experiences and their ability to choose among alternatives.

5. *A need for privacy* Self-actualizers seem to enjoy solitude and privacy more than others. Other people may perceive them as being somewhat aloof, reserved, and unruffled by events that disturb most people. But although they do need time to be by themselves, they also appreciate other people and enjoy being around them.

6. *Independence from the environment* Mentally healthy people remain relatively stable and secure in spite of harsh environmental conditions. They can maintain happiness in circumstances that might upset others. In other words, they are able to withstand severe forms of stress such as economic deprivation, the loss of a loved one, or physical hardships.

7. *A continued freshness of appreciation* Self-actualizers have the capacity to appreciate again and again the basic joys of nature. They have an ability to see uniqueness and wonder in many apparently commonplace experiences. In essence, the mentally healthy person is creative, open, and possesses a strong feeling of "belongingness" with all humanity.

In evaluating these traits, however, we must bear two cautions in mind. First, in almost all cases where criteria for mental health are used (as here), the issue of values and subjectivism arises. The fact that the researchers and their subjects do not represent a cross section of socioeconomic classes or subcultures in our society may re-

sult in overgeneralizations. Second, as noted in Chapter 1, mental health can be viewed from several perspectives. For example, one healthy trait is spontaneity—the uninhibited expression of thoughts and feelings. Yet various cultural groups value restraint with regard to feelings and discourage their direct expression.

SOURCES: Maslow, 1954; Rogers, 1961; Jahoda, 1958; Sibler et al., 1961; Coelho et al., 1963; Wild, 1965; Barron, 1963; Korchin & Ruff, 1964; and Ruff & Korchin, 1964.

Carl Rogers (1902–1987) is perhaps the best known of the humanistic psychologists. Rogers's theory of personality (1959) reflects his concern with human welfare and his deep conviction that humanity is basically "good," forward-moving, and trustworthy. One of the major contributions of the **humanistic perspective** has been this positive view of the individual.

Besides being concerned with treating the mentally ill, psychologists such as Rogers (1961) and Abraham Maslow (1954) have focused on improving the mental health of the person who is considered normal. This focus has led humanistic psychologists and others to explore the characteristics of the healthy personality. (See Focus 2.3.)

The Actualizing Tendency Instead of concentrating exclusively on behavior disorders, the humanistic approach is concerned with helping people *actualize* their potential and with bettering the state of humanity. The quintessence of humanistic psychological theory is the concept of **self-actualization.** This term, popularized by Maslow, implies that people are motivated not only to fill their biological needs (for food, warmth, and sex) but also to cultivate,

maintain, and enhance the **self.** The self is one's image of oneself, the part one refers to as "I" or "me."

The humanistic psychologist believes that all people are born with an inherent tendency to become actualized or fulfilled. This tendency can be defined as the impetus to achieve one's inherent potential as a fully functioning person. As one psychologist has pointed out, the actualizing tendency can be viewed as fulfilling a grand design or a genetic blueprint (Maddi, 1972). This thrust of life that pushes people forward is manifested in such qualities as curiosity, creativity, and joy of discovery. According to Rogers (1961), this inherent force is common to all living organisms; its psychological manifestation is *self-actualization* (Maslow, 1954; Rogers, 1959). How one views the self, how others relate to the self, and what values are attached to the self constitute one's **self-concept.**

During the course of their development, children increase their awareness of the world and gain experience in it. From various encounters they learn of two needs that affect the self-concept: the need for *positive regard* (how they think others perceive them) and the need for *positive self-regard* (how they perceive themselves). All people are sensitive to and

Abraham Maslow (1908-1970) proposed that people are motivated toward self-actualization once more basic needs are met. He based his ideas on his study of self-actualized, healthy people such as Einstein, Spinoza, and Eleanor Roosevelt.

influenced by others' opinions and reactions; group or peer pressure can be extremely powerful. People need positive feedback from others and feel frustration when they are looked on with disapproval. Each person also needs to approve of his or her self and feels distress when that need goes unmet. Both needs define how the actualizing tendency will be expressed.

Development of Abnormal Behavior   Rogers believes that, if people were left unencumbered by societal restrictions and allowed to grow and develop freely, the result would be self-actualized, fully functioning people. In such a case, the self-concept and the actualizing tendency would be congruent.

However, society frequently imposes *conditions of worth* on its members. These conditions are standards by which people determine whether they have worth.

They are transmitted via *conditional positive regard.* That is, significant others (parents, peers, friends, spouse, and so forth) in a person's life accept some but not all of that person's actions, feelings, and attitudes. The person's self-concept becomes defined as having worth only when others approve. But this reliance on others forces the individual to develop a distorted self-concept that is inconsistent with his or her self-actualizing potential, inhibiting that person from being self-actualized (see Focus 2.4). A state of disharmony or *incongruence* is said to exist between the person's inherent potential and his or her self-concept (as determined by significant others).

According to Rogers, behavior disorders are a result of this state of incongruence. The developing child who attempts to become what others wish is at odds with what he or she wants or was meant to be. This conflict forms the basis of abnormal behavior.

Rogers believed that fully functioning people have been *allowed to grow* toward their potential. The environmental condition most suitable for this growth is called *unconditional positive regard* (Rogers, 1951). In essence, people who are significant figures in someone's life value and respect that person *as a person.* Giving unconditional positive regard is valuing and loving regardless of behavior. People may disapprove of someone's actions, but they still respect, love, and care for that someone. The assumption that humans need unconditional positive regard has many implications for child rearing and psychotherapy. For parents, it means creating an open and accepting environment for the child. For the therapist, it means fostering conditions that will allow clients to grow and fulfill their potential; this approach has become known as *nondirective* or *person-centered* therapy.

Person-Centered Therapy   Carl Rogers emphasized that therapist attitudes are more important than specific counseling techniques. The therapist needs a strong positive regard for the client's ability to deal constructively with all aspects of life. The more willing the therapist is to rely on the client's strengths and potential, the more likely the client is to discover such strengths and potential. The therapist cannot help the client by explaining the client's behavior or by prescribing actions. Therapy techniques involve expressing and communicating respect, understanding, and acceptance. The therapist tries to understand the client's internal frame of reference by thinking,

FOCUS 2.4   *The Case of Bill M.*

Bill M. was a nineteen-year-old college sophomore. All through high school and in his freshman year at college, his grades were straight A's. Many students would have been elated to have his fine record, but Bill was depressed and unhappy; he felt life had no meaning.

Bill's parents had always praised his intellectual accomplishments, and they presented him with gifts whenever he excelled in school. To some degree of awareness, Bill felt his worth as a person was dependent on earning good grades. Attempting to please his parents, who unwittingly imposed these conditions of worth, Bill denied his own hopes, aspirations, and feelings. His prime objective was to remain a straight-A student. Although he had originally loved the excitement of learning, achieving, and mastering new knowledge, he now became cautious and obsessed with "safety." As his string of perfect grades became longer and longer, safety (not risking a B grade) became more and more important. He began to choose safe and easy topics for essays, to enroll in very easy courses, and to take "incompletes" or withdraw when courses appeared tough. Bill's fear of receiving any grade less than an A prompted defensive maneuvers that denied and blocked his actualizing tendency.

---

feeling, and exploring with him or her. Indeed, Rogers shuns the term *patient* because it denotes a helpless and disabled person in need of help to "cure" the disorder. The therapist needs to avoid seeing the person as "sick," which is why Rogers moved to the term *client*. In his later years, he dropped the description of his therapy as *client centered* to *person centered*. He believed that the term "person" was broader and more holistic than "client." Instead of a client-to-helper relationship, Rogers prefers a person-to-person relationship.

The way the person-centered therapist most commonly communicates understanding of the client's subjective world, is through *reflecting feelings*. In "saying back" to the client what he or she understood the client to say, the therapist provides a "mirror" for the client. The client can then actively evaluate thoughts and feelings with less distortion. Even in very strained situations, the person-centered therapist relies on reflection of feelings and on acceptance in working with the client. The following dialogue between client (S) and counselor (C), transcribed by Rogers, (1951, pp. 211–213) illustrates the technique:

S: (Silent for two minutes. Then begins to talk in hard, flat voice, quite unlike her usual tone. Does not look at counselor. There is much repetition but the following excerpts give the major thoughts.) You feel I want to come, but I don't! I'm not coming anymore.

Carl Rogers (1902-1987) believed people need both positive regard from others and positive self-regard. When positive regard is given unconditionally, a person can develop freely and become self-actualized.

It doesn't do any good. I don't like you. I hate you! I wish you never were born.

C: You just hate me very bitterly.

S: I think I'll throw you in the lake. I'll cut you up! You think people like you, but they don't. . . . I wish you were dead.

C: You detest me and you'd really like to get rid of me.

S: You think my father did bad things to me, but he didn't! You think he wasn't a good man, but he was. You think I want intercourse, but I don't.

C: You feel I absolutely misrepresent all your thoughts.

You might well sense a lack of direction here and wonder where this conversation is leading. The therapist, as you can see, is not steering this exchange but is using a standard technique of humanistic therapy, the understated reflection of the client's feelings. It is the client who will ultimately move on his or her own in the direction of health; the client, that is, *wants* to be healthy.

The Existential Perspective

The **existential approach** is really not a systematized school of thought but a set of attitudes. It shares with humanistic psychology an emphasis on individual uniqueness, a quest for meaning in life and for freedom and responsibility, a phenomenological approach to understanding the person, and a belief that the individual has positive attributes that will eventually be expressed unless they are distorted by the environment.

The existential and humanistic approaches differ from one another in several dimensions. First, existentialism is less optimistic than humanism; it focuses on the irrationality, difficulties, and suffering encountered in life. Although humanism allows the clear possibility of self-fulfillment and freedom, existentialism deals with human alienation from the social and spiritual structures that no longer provide meaning in an increasingly technological and impersonal world. Second, humanists focus on the individual. Humanistic therapists attempt to reconstruct the subjective world of their clients through empathy. Although phenomenology is also stressed among existentialists, the perspective is slightly different. The individual must be viewed within the context of the human condition, and moral, philosophical, and ethical considerations are part of the relationship. Last, humanism stresses individual responsibility; that is, the individual is ultimately responsible for what he or she becomes. Existentialism also stresses individual responsibility but it stresses responsibility to others as well. Self-fulfillment is not enough.

Roots of Existentialism Existential psychology has its roots in the nineteenth and twentieth century and is an outgrowth of the European existential thought of Kierkegaard, Heidegger, and Sartre. Some Europeans who have made important contributions to existential psychology are Viktor Frankl, J. H. van den Berg, and R. D. Laing. Frankl developed his system of logotherapy (from the Greek word *logos*, meaning *word* or *thought*) as a direct result of experiences suffered in a Nazi concentration camp. Not only did he witness horrible atrocities, but he also observed prisoners who were able to transcend pain, torture, and suffering. Those who transcended the camp experience were generally able to find spiritual meaning in life. They exhibited a "will to meaning," a capacity to find reasons for their existence.

Psychologist Rollo May was especially influential in developing an existential perspective in the United States (May et al., 1958; May, 1958, 1961). He, like his European counterparts, stressed that rapidly accelerating technology, a reliance on science to solve pressing human problems, increasing urbanization, and emphasis on naturalistic rather than religious or spiritual explanations of human nature have led to great personal confusion and strain. Both literature and the media have explored this theme in books like *Future Shock* (Alvin Toffler) and *The Stranger* (Albert Camus), and in movies such as *Star Wars, Making Mr. Right,* and *Short Circuit.* Technology and all the accoutrements of a modern society have reduced people to "cogs in the machine." Such rapid and dehumanizing change has led to a questioning of old values, of the meaning of life, and of basic human nature.

Indeed, many therapists *have* observed an increase in the number of patients complaining about the meaninglessness of life and reporting a sense of emptiness. Such symptoms as loneliness, alienation, isolation, detachment, and depersonalization have increased. Many psychotherapists find American psychology's naturalistic view of people inadequate for

Existentialism is less positive than humanism, focusing on the difficulties of being in this world instead of the possibilities. The goal of existential therapy is to help the client come to terms with a world from which he or she feels estranged, to become aware of his or her potential for growth, and ultimately to create a meaningful life.

helping patients or clients. They feel that essential human characteristics—awareness of self (existence) and self-directed, goal-oriented striving (becoming)—have been ignored. Many find that the concepts underlying existential analysis fill this void.

Existential Concepts   Three concepts are essential to existential thought: being, nonbeing, and being-in-the-world.

1. *Being* The distinctive character of human existence is that human beings are aware of themselves and their experience of being (existence) at a particular point in time and space. Because people are *conscious* of their existence, existentialists say, they are *responsible* for it and are capable of *choosing* their direction. They are *free,* and such factors as heredity, environment, and culture are merely excuses for not experiencing the process of "becoming"—attaining their potential.

2. *Nonbeing* Most people also know that at some future time they will cease to exist (not be). Awareness of eventual nonbeing or nonexistence is necessary to fully understand and experience being. Death gives life reality because it is an absolute fact that must be confronted. Impending nonbeing is the source of anxiety, aggression, and hostility. Because

the threat is always present, the anxiety it produces is considered normal. This anxiety is frequently called *existential anxiety* because it represents a conflict between being and nonbeing. When a person cannot accept this condition without repression, that person's choices become restricted and his or her actualization of potentials is thwarted.

3. *Being-in-the-World* We are all "beings in the world." The "world" can be described as the structure of meaningful relationships in which all people must function. One major problem caused by the complexity of contemporary society is that many people have lost their world. This loss is reflected in alienation—estrangement from other human beings or from the natural world. The French writer Albert Camus brilliantly portrays this modern predicament in his novel *The Stranger* (1946, p. 85):

> [The modern human is] a man who is a stranger in his world, a stranger to other people to whom he speaks or pretends to love; he moves about in a state of homelessness, vagueness, and haze as though he has no direct connection with his world but were in a foreign country where he does not know the language and has no hope of learning it, and is always doomed to wander in quiet despair, incommunicado, homeless, a stranger.

Development of Abnormal Behavior Abnormal behavior, say the existentialists, results from conflicts between people's essential nature and the demands they make on themselves or others make on them. The more alienated a person becomes from his or her total being, the fewer alternatives are available: Behavior becomes increasingly stereotyped, inhibited, conforming, and morally rigid. The potential for disturbance is ever present.

Anxiety stems from two main sources: the threat of imminent nonbeing, of losing oneself to nothingness, and the inability to relate to all the ways of our world. When these two conflicts (nonbeing and being-in-the-world) are not confronted and adequately resolved, crippling anxiety results. This anxiety leaves one with a sense of living a meaningless life; ultimately, it causes despair.

Existential Therapy The goal of the existential approach to therapy is to help the individual become aware of his or her own potential for growth, for choice, and for finding meaning in life. The existential approach is not a fixed system of therapy or a set of techniques; it is a means of understanding and illuminating the patient's being-in-the-world through exploration by therapist and patient together. People who are being helped are not placed in theoretical categories, because categories are inconsistent with the existential situation. Therapy techniques are de-emphasized in favor of the therapist's ability to see the patient's "reality" from the patient's perspective. In fact, because techniques must evolve from an understanding of the patient, the approach used may be derived from almost any school of therapy.

May (1961)* lists six characteristics of existential therapy:

1. Techniques vary from patient to patient; the goal is to illuminate the person's being-in-the-world.

2. Although therapists use terms such as *transference, repression,* and *resistance,* they always relate these psychoanalytic concepts to the existential situation of the patient's immediate life.

3. Therapists emphasize that the patient is not a subject but an "existential partner" with the therapist in a genuine encounter.

* From May, Rollo, *Existential Psychology.* Copyright © 1961 by Rollo May. Used by permission of Random House, Inc.

4. The therapist attempts to avoid behavior that would impede or terminate the genuine quality of the relationship. A full encounter with a person can create anxiety even within the therapist. Overreliance on therapy techniques permits a therapist to avoid the full encounter and is therefore undesirable.

5. Therapy is aimed at having the patient experience and become aware of the fact that his or her existence is redefined at each moment.

6. For the patient, increased awareness of potentialities and the possibility of commitment will enable the patient to make decisions and to implement actions.

These characteristics of existential psychotherapy may seem excessively vague and insubstantial. Nowhere is there any systematic explication of existential therapy and its procedures and techniques. Indeed, there *is* no single existential therapy. Instead, the therapy springs from a collaborative and shared venture between therapist and patient. Both are open to experience, are honest with each other, and act as authentically as possible. What matters is what the therapist *is,* rather than what he or she does. The therapist's task is to understand the private meaning of the patient's existence (being-in-the-world), and the patient's task is to be responsible for accepting his or her existential being. Each client is the author of his or her world and is responsible for his or her life and future.

Criticisms of the Humanistic and Existential Approaches

Many psychologists have criticized the formulations of the humanistic and existential perspectives (Holt, 1962; Millon, 1973; Smith, 1950). Although these phenomenological approaches have been extremely creative in describing the human condition, they have been less successful in constructing theory. Moreover, they are not suited to scientific or experimental investigation. The emphases on subjective understanding rather than prediction and control, on intuition and empathy rather than objective investigation, and on the individual rather than the more general case, all tend to hinder empirical study.

Carl Rogers has certainly expressed many of his ideas as researchable propositions, but it is difficult to verify scientifically the humanistic concept of people as rational, inherently good, and moving toward self-fulfillment. The existential perspective can be similarly criticized for its lack of scientific grounding and for its reliance on the unique experiences of individuals to describe the inner world. Nevertheless, the existential concepts of freedom, choice, responsibility, being, and nonbeing have had a profound influence on contemporary thought beyond the field of psychology.

Another major criticism leveled at the humanistic and existential approaches is that they do not work well with severely disturbed clients. They seem to be most effective with intelligent, well-educated, and relatively "normal" individuals who may be suffering adjustment difficulties. In fact, Carl Rogers's person-centered counseling originated from his work with college students who were bright, articulate, and psychology-minded—what some psychologists described as the "worried well." This limitation, along with the occasional vagueness of humanistic and existential thought, has made it difficult to apply these ideas broadly to abnormal psychology.

◈ A HUMANISTIC-EXISTENTIAL VIEW OF STEVEN V.

A therapist who strongly endorses the humanistic or existential approach would see Steven V. quite differently from the way a psychoanalyst or a proponent of the biogenic model would see Steve. If Steve's therapist were so oriented, we believe he or she would consider the case of Steven V. very much as follows.

I must begin by stressing a point that is likely to be underemphasized by many other psychologists. Steven V. is not merely the sum of the voluminous case records I have before me. Steve is a flesh-and-blood person, alive, organic, and moving, with thoughts, feelings, and emotions. How could anyone hope to understand Steve by reading a pile of material that is static and inorganic and occasionally seeks to pigeonhole him into diagnostic categories? To classify Steve as

schizophrenic, manic-depressive, or suicidal does not help me understand him. Indeed, such labels might serve as barriers to the development of a therapeutic relationship with him.

I intend to develop such a relationship with Steve, to engage him in a dialogue that will require no pretenses or self-justifications, and to travel with him on a journey whose destination neither of us will know until we get there. What makes me so sure that such a journey will be worthwhile? Almost everything I know of Steve, I learned from Steve himself. Here, for example, is an entry from Steve's diary, written when he was in his junior year in high school.

> Seems like I can't do anything right. Why does he always pick on me? Came home with top scores on my SAT. Mother was impressed. Showed Dad. Wouldn't even look up from his newspaper. All he's interested in is the *Wall Street Journal*. Make money, that's the goal!!
>
> Tried to tell him at dinner again. Got top score, Dad!! Don't you care?? Of course not! Said he expected it from me. Said he wanted me to do better next time. Said I should sit up and not slurp my soup. . . . Said I should learn better table manners. . . . Said I was an *asshole!!!* I am an asshole, I am, I am, who am I? Who cares?

There are strong feelings and emotions in this passage. Steve is deeply hurt by his father, he is angry at his father, and he seems to be seeking approval and validation from his father; he is also grappling with identity issues. These themes, but especially that of seeking approval from his father, are sounded throughout Steve's diary. His self-image and self-esteem seem to depend on his father's reaction to him. He clings to this perception of himself because he is afraid that without it he would not know who he is. This is illustrated in his questions: "Who am I? Who cares?" Until Steve knows who he is, he cannot understand what he might become. Now here is another diary entry, this one during his senior year in high school:

> Hello diary! Another do-nothing day! Parents won't let me do anything. Maybe I should jack off. . . . Got another good porno tape. This room's like a prison. Hello walls. . . . hello desk . . . hello fly . . . hello hell! Ha, that's a good one . . .

Every day's the same.
When you're in the well!
Every day's a game.
When you're in hell!

This passage reveals another aspect of what is happening with Steve. He feels trapped, immobilized, lonely, and unable to change his life. He has never recognized or accepted the responsibility of making choices. He externalizes his problems and views himself as a passive victim. In this way Steve evades responsibility for choosing and protects himself by staying in the safe, known environment of his room.

Steve needs to realize that he is responsible for his own actions, that he cannot find his identity in others. He needs to get in touch with, and express directly, his feelings of anxiety, guilt, shame, and anger. And he needs to be open to new experiences. All this can be accomplished through a free, open, and unstructured relationship.

SUMMARY

1. Psychologists use theories, or models, to explain behavior. Each model is built around its own set of assumptions. The model one adopts determines not only how one explains abnormal behavior but also what treatment methods one is likely to consider using. Most clinicians, however, take an eclectic approach, blending and using components of various models.

2. Biogenic models cite various organic causes of psychopathology. Damage to the nervous system is one such cause. Another is biochemical imbalances; several types of disturbances have been found to respond to drugs. In addition, a good deal of biochemical research has focused on identifying the role of neuroregulators in abnormal behavior. Still another biogenic theory cites heredity in mental disorders: correlations have been found between genetic inheritance and certain psychopathologies.

3. Psychoanalytic theory emphasizes past experiences and the role of the unconscious in determining present behavior. Sigmund Freud, the founder of psychoanalysis, believed personality has three components: the id, which represents the impulsive, selfish, pleasure-seeking part of the person; the ego,

which represents the rational part; and the superego, which represents society's values and ideals. Each component checks and balances the others. The life instincts and the death instincts are the energy system from which the personality operates. These instincts manifest themselves in various ways during the five different periods of life, or psychosexual stages, through which people pass: the oral, anal, phallic, latency, and genital stages. Each stage poses unique challenges that, if not adequately resolved, can result in maladaptive adult behaviors.

4. According to Freud, neurotic behavior results from the threat that unconscious thoughts will attain consciousness. To repress forbidden thoughts and impulses, the ego uses defense mechanisms: repression, reaction formation, projection, rationalization, displacement, undoing, and regression. Psychoanalytic techniques induce an ego weakness that allows access to unconscious material, which the therapist uses to help the patient achieve insight into his or her unconscious.

5. Neo-Freudians have adapted traditional psychoanalytic theory. While accepting basic psychodynamic tenets, they differ along several dimensions. First, they place greater emphasis on freedom of choice and the importance of future goals. Second, they see consciousness and ego autonomy as equally important to id processes. Third, they recognized the influence of social forces as important. Fourth, they highlight important people or object relations in the past. And, last, they give increasing attention to adapting psychoanalytic techniques in working with seriously disturbed people.

6. Advocates of the humanistic approaches see people as capable of making free choices and fulfilling their potential. This viewpoint emphasizes conscious rather than unconscious processes. Perhaps the best-known humanistic formulation is Carl Rogers's person-centered approach. Rogers believes that people are motivated not only to meet their biological needs but also to grow and to enhance the self, to become actualized or fulfilled. Behavior disorders result when a person is forced to develop a self-concept that is at odds with his or her actualizing tendency. In person-centered therapy, the therapist projects a strong belief in the ability of the client to deal with life, to grow, and to reach his or her potential.

7. Existentialists believe that rapidly accelerating technology and an emphasis on naturalistic rather

than spiritual explanations of the world have led to much personal trauma. Loneliness, alienation, isolation, and depersonalization have all been increased in contemporary times, as a direct result of society's treating people like objects. Existentialists see behavior disorders as a product of the conflict between people's essential natures and the demands made on them by themselves and others. Three concepts essential to existentialism are *being* (human awareness of existence), *nonbeing* (human awareness of death), and *being-in-the-world* (existing in a social context). Existential therapy is an unstructured collaborative venture between therapist and patient; its objective is to illuminate the patient's being-in-the-world.

KEY TERMS

biogenic model The theory or expectation that every mental disorder has an organic basis and cure

collective unconscious A term devised by Jung that refers to ancient, primordial memories common to all humanity

defense mechanism In psychoanalytic theory, the unconscious and automatic means by which the ego is protected from anxiety-provoking conflicts

diathesis-stress theory The theory that a predisposition to develop mental illness is inherited and that this predisposition may or may not be activated by environmental factors

dizygotic (DZ) twins (fraternal) Twins from two separate eggs; such twins share about 50 percent of the same genes

eclectic approach An openness to all models of abnormal behavior, along with a willingness to borrow and integrate techniques from all approaches and to use them selectively with clients

existential approach The belief that contemporary society has a dehumanizing effect and that mental disorders result from a conflict between essential human nature and the demands made on people by themselves and others

genotype The genetic component of a trait or characteristic

humanistic perspective The optimistic viewpoint that people are born with the ability to fulfill their potential and that abnormal behavior results from disharmony between the person's potential and self-concept

model An analogy, most often used to describe or explain something that cannot be directly observed

monozygotic (MZ) twins (identical) Genetically identical twins who developed from one fertilized egg

neo-Freudians Psychologists whose ideas are strongly influenced by Freud's psychoanalytic model but who have modified that model in various ways

object relations Past interpersonal relations that shape and affect the individual's current interactions with people

phenotype The observable results of the interaction of the genotype and the environment

pleasure principle The impulsive, pleasure-seeking aspect of our being usually associated with the id, which seeks immediate gratification regardless of moral or realistic concerns

psychoanalysis Therapy based on the Freudian view that unconscious conflicts must be aired and understood by the patient if abnormal behavior is to be eliminated

psychoanalytic model The view that adult disorders arise from the unconscious operation of repressed anxieties originally experienced during childhood

psychopathology Abnormal behavior

psychosexual stages In psychoanalytic theory, human personality develops through a sequence of stages during the first five years of life: oral, anal, phallic, latency and genital

reality principle In Freudian theory, awareness of the demands of the environment and adjustment of behavior to meet these demands; acts to modify the pleasure principle and is part of the ego structure

self-actualization An inherent tendency in people to strive toward the realization of their full potential

self-concept An individual's assessment of his or her own value and worth

chapter 3
Behavioral and Family Systems Models of Psychopathology

This is the second of two chapters concerned with models of abnormal behavior. Recall that such models are idealized constructs or analogies; their purpose is to provide insight into the causes of abnormal behavior and thus to suggest methods of treatment. In Chapter 2, we discussed the biogenic model and three psychogenic models. The biogenic model of abnormal behavior emphasizes an organic basis for mental disorders and, therefore, medical therapies. The psychogenic models look to the mind, or psyche, for both causes and treatment.

The models discussed in this chapter focus more on the environment or cognitive processes than on the intrapsychic inner life of the individual. The behavioral models hold that all behavior and cognitions—normal and abnormal—are learned through interaction between the person and the environment. The mentally disturbed person either has learned the wrong behaviors and thoughts or has not learned the right ones. Therapy should be directed toward helping the client replace inappropriate behaviors or learn appropriate ones.

The **family systems model** of abnormal behavior concentrates on a particular part of the total environment. According to its proponents, individual identity and the quality of our relationships with others are largely the result of our family experiences. When psychopathology occurs, the therapist must look to the family for causes and for possible approaches to treatment.

BEHAVIORAL MODELS OF PSYCHOPATHOLOGY

The behaviorist approach to psychology was suggested in 1913 by John B. Watson (1878–1958), in a lecture delivered at Columbia University. Watson said that if psychology were ever to become a science, it must be limited to the study of directly observable and measurable events. Furthermore, he declared that there was no place in psychology for the subjective study of mind, emotions, and thought processes. (In this, Watson's view contrasted with the intrapsychic approach of Freud.) The single goal of the science of psychology, Watson said, should be the prediction and control of human *behavior.*

At the time, several scientists were doing laboratory experiments on *conditioning,* or basic learning processes. Watson saw such experimentation as a proper part of the science of psychology, and he viewed these investigators' results as closely related to the study of behavior. Watson himself began to experiment with conditioning, and learning became the primary focus of behaviorism.

The **behavioral models** of psychopathology are thus concerned with the role of learning in abnormal behavior. The differences among them lie mainly in their explanations of how learning occurs. Although some models disagree, they generally tend to complement each other. That is, each of the four models discussed here is, for the most part, applied to a different type of behavior.

The Classical Conditioning Model

Principles of Classical Conditioning Early in the twentieth century, Ivan Pavlov (1849–1936), a Russian physiologist, discovered an associative learning process that is known as **classical conditioning** or **respondent.** This process involves the involuntary responses (such as reflexes, emotional reactions, and sexual arousal), which are controlled by the autonomic nervous system.

Pavlov's discovery was accidental. He was measuring dogs' salivation as part of a study of their digestive processes when he discovered that the dogs would begin to salivate at the sight of an assistant carrying their food. The dogs' salivation in response to a stimulus other than food placed in their mouths puzzled Pavlov and led to his formulation of classical conditioning. He reasoned that food is an **unconditioned stimulus** (UCS) that, in the mouth, automatically elicits salivation; this salivation is an unlearned or **unconditioned response** (UCR) to the food. Pavlov then presented a previously *neutral* stimulus (one that does not initially elicit salivation, such as the sound of a bell) to the dogs just before presenting the food. He found that, after a number of repetitions, the sound of the bell alone elicited salivation. This learning process is based on association: the neutral stimulus acquires some of the properties of the unconditioned stimulus when they are repeatedly paired together. When the bell alone can provoke this response, it is called a **conditioned stimulus** (CS), and the salivation it elicits is termed a **conditioned response** (CR). Each time the conditioned stimulus is paired with the unconditioned stimulus, the conditioned response is said to be *reinforced,* or strengthened. Pavlov's conditioning process is illustrated in Figure 3.1.

Ivan Pavlov (1849-1936), a Russian physiologist, discovered the associative learning process we know as classical conditioning, while he was studying salivation in dogs. Pavlov won the Nobel Prize in physiology and medicine in 1904 for his work on the principal digestive glands.

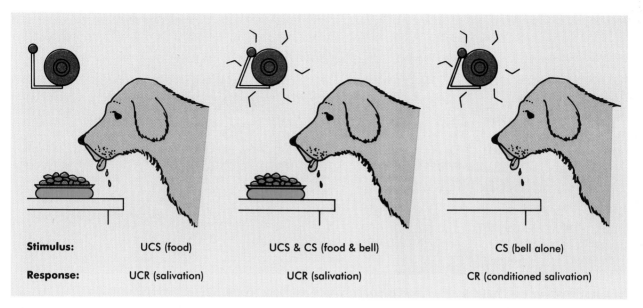

Stimulus: UCS (food)   UCS & CS (food & bell)   CS (bell alone)

Response: UCR (salivation)   UCR (salivation)   CR (conditioned salivation)

Figure 3.1   A Basic Classical Conditioning Process
Dogs normally salivate when food is provided (left drawing). With his laboratory
dogs, Ivan Pavlov paired the ringing of a bell with the presentation of food
(middle drawing). Eventually, the dogs would salivate to the ringing of the bell
alone, when no food was near (right drawing).

Pavlov also discovered other principles governing classical conditioning. If he presented the bell many times without following it with the food, the animals would gradually salivate less and less in response to the bell. This process, by which a response is eliminated when it is not reinforced, is called **extinction.** Pavlov also observed that the dogs salivated when he presented stimuli that were similar to the original conditioned stimulus. For example, a bell with a somewhat different tone might elicit salivation. This process is called **generalization.** The reverse of generalization, **stimulus discrimination,** is learning *not* to respond to a stimulus that is different from the conditioned stimulus.

Classical Conditioning in Psychopathology
A **phobia** is an exaggerated, seemingly illogical fear of a particular object or class of objects. (Phobias are discussed in greater detail in Chapter 6.) In an important study, John B. Watson and his associate Rosalie Rayner (1920) used classical conditioning to induce a phobia in a child. Watson had theorized that infants are born with only a few emotional response patterns (fear, rage, and love), and he hypothesized that there must be some "simple method"

by which other stimuli also elicit these emotions. This method could, he thought, be association. Watson and Rayner decided to test the hypothesis on an eight-month-old infant named Albert.

They observed the child for any signs of fear when they confronted him suddenly with a series of different stimuli, including a white rat. "At no time did this infant ever show fear in any situation. . . . The infant practically never cried" (Watson & Rayner, 1920, p. 66). They did, however, elicit a fear response in Albert by striking a suspended steel bar with a hammer. They then attempted to generate a fear response toward a previously neutral stimulus (the white rat) by coupling it with the fear-producing stimulus (the loud sound). They presented the white rat to Albert and, as he began to reach for it, made the frightening sound. Albert soon displayed fear whenever they presented the white rat. This fear also generalized to other stimuli with furry characteristics—a rabbit, a sealskin coat, a Santa Claus beard, cotton wool, and Watson's hair—items that Albert had not feared before.

Watson and Rayner considered their experiment a successful demonstration of a process by which conditioned fears can be produced. Today, however,

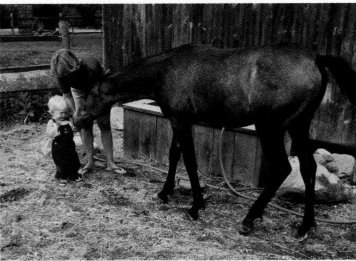

Most behaviorists believe that fear of animals is not an innate response, but a conditioned one. The young girl on the left is obviously not afraid of snakes (unconditioned response), while the young boy on the right exhibits a conditioned fear of horses.

conditioning fear in humans would be considered highly unethical.

Although the case of Little Albert is often cited as evidence that fear can be conditioned, one scholar has cast doubt on the conclusions drawn from this study (Harris, 1979). Harris compared several articles written by Watson on "Little Albert" and found that misinterpretations could be made on the basis of the separate reports, especially with regard to the number of pairings of the UCS and the CS. Harris believes there is little evidence for the view that Albert developed a phobia. He also believes that Watson's work contained methodological flaws that make it difficult to draw *any* conclusions from the study. However, it must also be noted that Albert still displayed an emotional reaction to the white rat approximately one month after the conditioning trials.

Other studies and observations provide some support for the idea that fears and sexual attractions may be acquired through classical conditioning. In studies of phobic patients, approximately 50 percent recalled frightening experiences in the development of their excessive fears (Ost & Hugdahl, 1981; Rimm et al., 1977). The relationship between the development of a phobia and a traumatic event is illustrated in the case of a seventy-year-old woman who developed an extreme fear of dogs after being attacked by a Saint Bernard. She was bitten repeatedly on the head, stomach, and buttocks. After this event, she experienced terror when she saw any dog and she went so far as to curtail her shopping trips because of this fear (Thyer, 1981).

Sexual deviations and preferences may also be learned through an association process. A mild sexual response to women's shoes was produced in male graduate students by pairing the shoes with slides of nude females. Through association, the shoes acquired some of the properties of the sexual stimuli (Rachman, 1966).

Therapy Based on Classical Conditioning The various processes involved in classical conditioning can be used to treat behavior problems. For example, two researchers used conditioning to design an electrical device for treating **enuresis,** or bedwetting (Mowrer & Mowrer, 1938). The device is a special pad, placed under the child's bed sheet, which causes a bell to ring when it is wet. The bell is an unconditioned stimulus that causes the child to awaken (the unconditioned response). After it is paired with the ringing of the bell a number of times, the distended bladder (the urge to urinate) serves as a conditioned stimulus. This CS becomes a signal to wake up or tighten the sphincter muscle to prevent urination: a conditioned response. This conditioning apparatus has been used quite successfully for a number of years.

Fears and sexual response patterns acquired through classical conditioning can be removed through extinction—that is, by repeatedly presenting the conditioned stimulus *without* the unconditioned stimulus. Because it is no longer paired with the UCS, the CS gradually loses its acquired properties. The seventy-year-old woman with the fear of dogs was gradually and systematically exposed to dogs under safe conditions over a period of time until her fear had completely faded away. The male students' sexual response to women's shoes gradually disappeared when the shoes were no longer paired with slides showing nude women.

Just as it is possible to create a phobia by repeatedly pairing a neutral stimulus with an unpleasant stimulus, it is also possible to eliminate a phobia through a slightly different procedure, called **counterconditioning**. In this case, the negative stimulus for the undesirable response is paired with a pleasant stimulus until its negative aspects are lost. A three-year-old boy, Peter, who feared rabbits, was treated for his phobia with this method. Peter was given his favorite food to eat while the therapist gradually introduced a rabbit at distances that were not unduly disturbing. The positive aspects of the food eventually overcame the negative (fear-arousing) aspects of the rabbit (Jones, 1924). In the case of a 5½-year-old boy with an extreme fear of the dark, the positive effects of a fictional character were employed. The child was especially interested in the cartoon character Batman, so he was asked to imagine that he and his hero were working together on a secret project. While imagining scenes involving himself and Batman, the child was able to tolerate more and more time alone in the dark, until his fear was entirely lost (Jackson & King, 1981).

In a process called *systematic desensitization*, Joseph Wolpe (1958, 1973) used relaxation, assertion, and sexual arousal as anxiety-inhibiting responses to fearful situations. As we discuss more fully in Chapter 19, this therapeutic technique relies on the inhibition or reduction of anxiety (avoidance behavior) when the conditions that provoke it are paired with positive stimuli. In a study of phobias associated with high places and loud noises, an Air Force veteran was successfully treated with this technique (Rimm & Lefebvre, 1981). While in a state of relaxation, the man was instructed to imagine fearful scenes related to his phobia. Through repeated visualization, the man's fears gradually diminished, and he began to feel relatively at ease in the previously fear-producing situations.

In the foregoing cases, the capacity of a conditioned stimulus to elicit anxiety was eliminated by associating the CS with a positive response. A reverse process can be employed to reduce the *attractiveness* of a conditioned stimulus. Repeated association of an established behavior pattern with aversive stimuli results in an avoidance behavior. To eliminate or suppress temper tantrums in a 5-year-old psychotic boy, Rolider and Van Houten (1985) successfully associated punishment (isolating the child in a corner or firm verbalizations) with the boy's inappropriate behavior, to reduce the behavior. This procedure might also be useful in treating problems such as the consumption of alcohol, cigarette smoking, and deviant sexual patterns. To reduce the attractiveness of these behaviors, the therapist associates them with negative responses. For example, an individual who wants to quit smoking might be asked to imagine feeling sick when picking up a cigarette. The therapist might say,

> As you pick up the cigarette, you feel your stomach churning. When you place the cigarette to your lips, you feel vomit entering your throat. You swallow it back down. Lighting the cigarette causes vomit to stream into your mouth. You swallow it back down and take a puff. Vomit spills out of your mouth and nose. It soils your clothes. The smell is terrible. You put out the cigarette, take a shower, and feel relieved.

This use of the imagination to associate a negative quality with a bad habit, called *covert sensitization,* was developed by Joseph Cautela (1966).

The principles of classical conditioning can also be used to produce or strengthen a nondeviant sexual pattern. In *orgasmic reconditioning*, a weak sexual response to an appropriate stimulus is made stronger by pairing it consistently with sexual arousal and orgasm. For people who are sexually excited by inappropriate stimuli, such as children, sexually arousing procedures can be used to increase the sexual attractiveness of adult partners (Leonard & Hayes, 1983).

The Operant Conditioning Model

An **operant behavior** is a voluntary and controllable behavior, such as walking or thinking, that "operates" on an individual's environment. Suppose you are in an extremely warm room. It would be very difficult for you to consciously control your sweating—to "will" your body not to perspire. You could, however, decide to change your environment by simply walking out of the uncomfortably warm room.

Most human behavior is operant in nature. The concept of **operant conditioning** was first formulated by Edward Thorndike (1874–1949), although he used the term *instrumental conditioning*. In working with cats, Thorndike observed that they would repeat certain behaviors when those behaviors were associated with positive consequences. Likewise, if the consequences were unpleasant, the behaviors would

In operant conditioning, positive consequences increase the likelihood and frequency of a desired response. This is particularly important in a classroom setting where a child knows that appropriate behavior will be rewarded and inappropriate behavior will be punished.

be discouraged and reduced. This principle became known as the **law of effect.** Some fifty years later, B. F. Skinner (born 1904) started a revolution in the field by innovatively applying Thorndike's law of effect, which he renamed *reinforcement*.

This type of learning differs from classical conditioning primarily in two ways. First, classical conditioning is involved in the development of involuntary behaviors such as fear, whereas operant conditioning is related to voluntary behaviors. (However, as Focus 3.1 notes, this distinction may not be an absolute one.)

Second, as we discussed earlier, behaviors based in *classical* conditioning are controlled by stimuli, or events *preceding* the response: Salivation occurs only when it is preceded by a UCS (food in the mouth) or a CS (the thought of a sizzling, juicy steak covered with mushrooms). In *operant* conditioning, however, behaviors are controlled by events that *follow* them. Positive consequences increase the likelihood and frequency of a response. But when the consequences are negative, the behavior is less likely to be repeated. For example, a student is likely to raise his or her hand in class often if the teacher recognizes the student, smiles, and seems genuinely interested in the student's comments. However, if the instructor frowns, looks disgusted, or yawns, the student's hand-raising behavior will probably become less frequent.

Principles of Operant Conditioning

The principles of operant conditioning are statements about the relationships between behavior and consequences (also called *contingencies*). Let us look at some of the most basic of these principles.

Reinforcement Anything that increases the frequency or magnitude of the behavior it follows is called a *reinforcer*. A positive reinforcer does so by providing a positive or wanted or pleasant consequence; it may be tangible (money, food, sexual activity) or social (attention, praise, a smile).

Whether a consequence is a reinforcer depends only on its effect. Certain consequences that are aversive to most people can function as reinforcement to others. One study of classroom behavior recorded the number of times schoolchildren left their seats, and the number of teacher reprimands (Madsen et al., 1970). To assess the relationship between these two variables, teachers were asked to triple the frequency of reprimands. Amazingly, the out-of-seat

There has been considerable controversy over the distinction between operant and classical conditioning. At one time some psychologists thought operant procedures were effective only on voluntary behaviors (walking, talking, and so on), which are controlled by the central nervous system, and that only classical conditioning procedures were capable of modifying "involuntary" processes, which are controlled by the autonomic nervous system. In the past, the autonomic nervous system, which controls skin temperature, heart rate, and blood pressure, has been considered beyond conscious control and not amenable to change through reinforcement. Recent studies, however, indicate that operant procedures using **biofeedback** (giving people information about minute changes in their bodily processes) can influence such involuntary processes as irregular heartbeats (Bleecker & Engel, 1973), blood pressure (Miller, 1974), skin temperature (Green et al., 1970), and cranial blood volume pulse (Bild & Adams, 1980). The results of these studies may lead to a redefinition of the distinction between operant and classical conditioning. Because certain autonomic processes can be controlled through reinforcement, it is possible that many psychophysiological reactions are learned through this procedure. This research also suggests that disorders such as diarrhea, asthma, and hypertension may be treatable with operant principles.

Biofeedback procedures are not a panacea for all problems involving the autonomic nervous system. This form of treatment has clearly helped with migraine headaches and certain forms of seizures, but results with cardiovascular and other conditions have been mixed (Rimm & Masters, 1979).

behaviors increased. The greater the number of commands to sit down, the more often children stood up! In this situation, reprimands functioned as a reinforcer, that is, they increased the frequency of the response.

A **negative reinforcer** increases the frequency of a behavior by removing an aversive (unpleasant or punishing) event. Suppose around dinner time a small child wants a cookie. The mother, afraid that the cookie will spoil the child's appetite, says no. Out of frustration and anger, the child throws a temper tantrum (which is aversive to the mother). Because the mother is fearful that the child will be injured, she gives in and grants the child's demand. Although it is easy for us to see that the mother has positively reinforced the child's tantrum behavior, it is more difficult to see that the mother has been negatively reinforced. Once the child gets the cookie, the aversive behavior ends (removal of aversive stimulus) and the mother is negatively reinforced (the probability of her giving in increases).

Punishment A **punishment** is either the removal of a positive reinforcer or the presentation of an aversive stimulus. Both reduce the probability of the response. Note that negative reinforcement increases the probability. In the first kind of punishment, privileges such as use of the car, television viewing, or access to games may be withdrawn after an inappropriate action is performed. This is often referred to as *response cost*. The second kind of punishment involves the presentation of an aversive consequence such as a reprimand or a spanking.

Extinction You have already seen how extinction works in classical conditioning: after the conditioned stimulus is presented repeatedly without the unconditioned stimulus, the conditioned response disappears. In operant conditioning, **extinction** is the process of eliminating a behavior through nonreinforcement. When the reinforcement for a behavior is discontinued, the behavior usually disappears.

These four basic components of operant conditioning are listed and distinguished in Table 3.1. In addition, you should be aware of two more concepts that are important in the operant conditioning model; (1) discriminative stimulus and (2) shaping.

Discriminative Stimulus A cue that is usually present when reinforcement occurs is known as a **discriminative stimulus**. For example, through experience people learn that success is more likely when

TABLE 3.1 | **Increasing and Decreasing the Frequency of Behavior Through Operant Conditioning**

These increase *the frequency of a behavior*	These decrease *the frequency of a behavior*
Positive Reinforcement: Presentation of a positive reinforcer	*Punishment:* Presentation of an aversive stimulus or removal of a positive reinforcer
Negative Reinforcement: Removal of an aversive event	*Extinction:* Removal of a positive reinforcer

they address a request to a person who is smiling than when they approach one who looks angry. Most people are more likely to cross a street when the light is green than when it is red because of the consequences associated with the color of the light. In other words, the smile and the green light indicate that reinforcement is likely to follow.

Shaping **Shaping** is the process of developing a new or complex behavior by reinforcing successive behaviors that increasingly approximate the final goal desired by the experimenter. Many responses are very complex and do not usually occur spontaneously. In these cases, the experimenter can break down a response into a series of small steps and can reinforce each step.

Operant Conditioning in Psychopathology Studies have demonstrated a relationship between environmental reinforcers and certain abnormal behaviors. For example, self-injurious behavior, such as head banging, is a dramatic form of psychopathology that is often reported in psychotic and mentally retarded children. It has been hypothesized that some forms of head banging may be linked to reinforcing features in the environment (Schaefer, 1970). To test this hypothesis, a self-injurious behavior (head hitting) was shaped in two monkeys through successive approximations. First the raising of the animal's paw was reinforced, then holding the paw over the head, and finally bringing the paw down on the head. This sequence of behaviors was shaped in about sixteen minutes in both monkeys. The discriminative stimulus for reinforcement comprised the words "Poor boy! Don't do that! You'll hurt yourself." Head hitting occurred whenever these words were spoken by the experimenter, because they had been associated with reinforcement (bananas). It

seems clear from these findings that self-injurious behaviors can be developed and maintained through reinforcement.

In another instance, an unusually large number of mentally retarded children were engaging in head banging at one institution—a hospital. The superintendent of the hospital became alarmed at the number of children displaying self-injurious behavior and discovered the following sequence of events. As soon as the children began to hit their heads against the wall, the nurses rushed over to comfort them and provided candy. In other words, the nurses were offering rewards contingent on head banging; the candy and attention were serving as positive reinforcers for that behavior! Furthermore, the mere sight of candy functioned as a discriminative stimulus: Children immediately began their head-banging behavior whenever a nurse appeared with candy (Schaefer & Martin, 1969).

Although positive reinforcement can account for some forms of self-injurious behaviors, in some instances other variables seem more important (Carr, 1977). Negative reinforcement, for example, can also strengthen and maintain unhealthy behaviors. Consider a student who has enrolled in a class in which the instructor requires oral reports. The thought of doing an oral presentation in front of a class produces feelings of anxiety, sweating, an upset stomach, and trembling in the student. Having these feelings is aversive. To stop the unpleasant reaction, the student switches to another section whose instructor does not require oral presentations. The student's behavior is reinforced by escape from aversive feelings, and such avoidance responses to situations involving "stage fright" will increase in frequency.

A type of research that lends itself to study of the relationship between environmental contingencies and problem behaviors is called the *single-subject experiment.* This research strategy is discussed in Chapter 5, but the steps involved can be demonstrated with the case of Mary, a nine-year-old who had received diagnoses of mental deficiency, autism, and childhood psychosis. Her problem behaviors involved hitting, slapping, pulling hair, tantrums, and spitting. During the *baseline period* (a typical sample period in the child's waking state), the frequency of these behaviors was recorded. Next, during the *intervention phase* (when the experimenter actively intervenes), Mary received praise and a favorite food if she displayed none of the aggressive behaviors during a specified period, as measured by a timer. If any of the target behaviors occurred during the period, the timer was reset. During this phase, there was a 60 percent drop in the problem behaviors. To make certain that the experimental manipulation was responsible for this reduction, the baseline conditions were reinstated, and Mary was treated as in the baseline period. During this *reversal phase* (reinstilling original baseline condition), her aggressive behaviors returned to preintervention levels. When the experimental procedures were again employed, her problem behaviors plummeted to very low levels (Luiselli & Slocumb, 1983). Behaviorists believe that such results clearly indicate the influence of environmental factors in producing and maintaining problem behaviors.

Therapy Based on Operant Conditioning In later chapters on specific psychological disorders, and in Chapter 19 on treatment approaches, we discuss a variety of ways in which operant conditioning has been applied to the treatment of abnormal behaviors. Here we intend only to illustrate the use of the basic principles in treatment procedures.

In one case, an eleven-year-old child was suffering delusions (recall from Chapter 1 that delusions are false beliefs held in spite of contrary evidence). The child's delusional statements were reduced when experimenters ignored any statements that stemmed from delusions and fantasies. Appropriate statements increased when *positive reinforcement* was given every time they were made. Overall, the percentage of appropriate verbalizations in the child was increased significantly (Varni et al., 1978).

Negative reinforcement in the form of reduced nagging was used to increase the duration of speech in a withdrawn psychotic patient. When the patient spoke only briefly, he was told to speak for longer periods of time. If he did not comply within three seconds, nagging would begin. To avoid this aversive consequence, the patient spoke for longer periods (Fichter et al., 1976).

A fourteen-year-old retarded boy was subject to severe tantrums that caused substantial damage in his home. As operant punishment, the boy was required to perform about one hour of cleanup work, repairing any damage he had done, after every tantrum. The frequency of tantrums dropped from an average of one per week to none during the final three months of treatment (Altman & Krupsaw, 1983).

Two psychologists used **extinction** to eliminate a case of operant vomiting. An eleven-year-old boy was vomiting from two to ten times a day. Physical examinations and tests revealed no organic problem. However, sympathetic attention by family members and assistance in cleaning up consistently followed the vomiting episodes. The psychologists felt that the behavior was being maintained by this social attention. Family members were trained to ignore the vomiting and were told not to help the child clean up. Eventually the vomiting ceased (Munford & Pally, 1979).

Autistic children are profoundly disturbed; they generally give few vocal responses and show little or no social interaction with peers. Two experimenters (Hingtgen & Trost, 1966) were able to *shape* vocal and physical responses in two pairs of autistic children. The experimenters initially rewarded the children for any sound—even a cough, sneeze, or yell. After this, they gave reinforcement only for recognizable syllables. To shape physical contact, they first rewarded the children for physical closeness, then for accidental physical contact, and finally for actual hand-to-body contact. To pair physical contact with vocalizations, they gave reinforcement after one child had touched the other and had made a vocal response. They obtained the final goal of vocal response-and physical interaction by reinforcing the children only after *both* had touched each other with their hands and *both* had made vocal responses.

The Observational Learning Model

The traditional behavioral theories of learning—classical conditioning and operant conditioning—require that the individual actually perform behaviors in order

Observational learning is based on the theory that behavior can be learned by observing it. Research indicates that a direct relationship exists between actual aggression and violence viewed on television. But as this photograph shows, observational learning can also be positive.

to learn them. **Observational learning** theory suggests that an individual can acquire new behaviors by simply watching them performed (Bandura, 1969; Bandura & Walters, 1963). The process of learning by observing models (and later imitating them) is called *vicarious conditioning* or **modeling.** Direct reinforcement for imitation of the model is not necessary, although reinforcers are necessary to *maintain* behaviors learned in this manner. Observational learning can involve both respondent and operant behaviors, and its discovery has had such an impact in psychology that it has been proposed as a third form of learning.

Vicarious Classical Conditioning You would probably not be surprised to hear that an eight-year-old boy who has never left his hometown of Seattle is afraid of snakes, elephants, and monsters, none of which he has ever met. Some of these fears can be explained by the phenomenon of *generalization:* The boy perhaps generalized fears of animals he had encountered, or had been warned about, to creatures he had never seen. However, people may also acquire

fears by seeing others exhibit fear or arousal (through vicarious classical conditioning).

In one study, subjects watched a person go through a classical conditioning procedure in which a neutral stimulus was presented and followed by an electric shock (Berger, 1962). The model displayed pain cues (grimaces and jerks) in response to the shock (UCS). The observers, whose emotional reactions were monitored, also developed responses to the conditioned stimulus, although they never received a shock.

Vicarious Operant Conditioning Operant behavior can also be learned through modeling. Some of the most compelling research in this area has examined the acquisition of aggressive behaviors in children.

The finding that symbolic representations of aggressive action in films and television can increase aggression in children has alarmed parents, educators, and researchers. Heavy viewing of aggressive programs, including cartoon shows, on television appears to be related to overt aggression in preschool children (Singer & Singer, 1983). The National Institute of Mental Health also found a relationship between the viewing of violent fare on television and aggressive behavior in children (Pearl et al., 1982). In a long-term study, L. D. Eron (1963) surveyed hundreds of third-grade students to assess their television-viewing habits and found that children who preferred violent programs were more likely than children who preferred nonviolent fare to be rated aggressive by peers. A follow-up study of this same sample of children ten years later (when the subjects were approximately nineteen years old) again found a correlation between preference for violent programs and aggressiveness ratings (Eron et al., 1972).

Although these studies were correlational, the link between modeled television violence and aggressive behavior has also been demonstrated experimentally. In one study, children were exposed to either a violent television program or a sports show involving track events. When the researchers later observed both groups of children playing, they saw significantly more aggression among the children who had watched the violent scenes (Liebert & Baron, 1972).

Observational learning does not, however, have to be negative. Prosocial behaviors such as cooperation, empathy, friendliness, and delay of gratification can be increased through appropriate modeling (Rubinstein, 1983).

Observational Learning in Psychopathology and Therapy Observational learning approaches, like those emphasizing classical and operant conditioning, assume that abnormal behaviors are learned in the same manner as normal behaviors; exposure to disturbed models is likely to produce disturbed behaviors. For example, when monkeys watched other monkeys respond with fear to an unfamiliar object, they learned to respond in a similar manner (Cook et al., 1986). Observational learning can have four possible effects on the observers (Spiegler, 1983): (1) new behaviors can be acquired by watching a model; (2) a model may serve to elicit particular behaviors by providing observers with cues to engage in those behaviors; (3) behaviors that are inhibited because of anxiety or other negative reactions may be performed after they are observed; and (4) a behavior may become inhibited in the observer if the model's similar behavior resulted in aversive consequences.

Observational learning has also been used in eliminating problem behaviors. For example, a 48-year-old man had been claustrophobic for over thirty years. His extreme fear of confinement probably originated when, as a child, he suffered a severe asthmatic attack while playing underneath his home (which was built on stilts). Being in elevators, sleeping bags, boats, or shower stalls provoked strong anxiety reactions. The client's fear had generalized to the point where he was afraid of being under bed covers or of enduring any kind of oral or nasal constriction, such as wearing a scarf over his mouth. He was also unable to work beneath his automobile, and he had resigned from membership in a volunteer fire department, an activity he valued highly, because he could not tolerate wearing an oxygen mask. Two psychologists treated this client using *participant modeling,* in which the therapist demonstrates the behaviors that the client is to perform. The thirteen-week treatment program involved the therapists' demonstrating tasks such as wearing a handkerchief over the mouth and then having the client perform the same task. At the end of the program, the client had progressed to the point where he could wear a surgical mask and lie in a zipped-up sleeping bag (Speltz & Bernstein, 1979).

The Cognitive Behavioral Model

The cognitive behavioral perspective probably originated with the Stoic philosopher Epictetus, who noted, "Men are disturbed not by events, but by the views they take of them." The cognitive viewpoint is based on the assumption that people actually create their own problems (and symptoms as well) by the way they interpret events and situations. For example, one person who fails to be hired for a job may become severely depressed, blaming himself for the failure. Another might only become mildly irritated, believing her failure to get the job had nothing to do with personal inadequacy. In both cases the situation (not being hired for a job) is identical, but the response is very different. Why is this so? To explain this phenomenon, we have to look at *mediating processes*—thoughts, perceptions, and self-evaluations that determine the reactions and behaviors of people.

Traditionally, behaviorists have dismissed events that cannot be observed and have not considered internal mediating processes significant in modifying behavior. By the mid-1970s, however, cognitive-behavioral and cognitive approaches became popular and prevalent. At that time three theories were solidly formulated: George Kelly's (1955) personal construct approach, Albert Ellis's (1962) rational-emotive therapy, and Aaron T. Beck's (1963, 1970) cognitive therapy. That number has increased to at least twenty (Mahoney & Lyddon, 1988). All are based on the premise that the way an individual perceives, anticipates, or evaluates an event—rather than the event itself—has the greatest impact on that individual's behavior. Further, cognitive theories argue that modifying thoughts and feelings is essential to changing behavior. Think back to the two job hunters. The assumptions and expectations of each individual could not have been further apart. One blamed himself, and was overcome with feelings of worthlessness; the other recognized that not every person is right for every job (or vice versa), and left the situation with her self-esteem intact. How people label a situation and how they interpret events profoundly affects their emotional reactions and behavior. How a person interprets events is a function of his or her **schema**—underlying assumptions held by the person and heavily influenced by experiences, values, and perceived capabilities.

Albert Ellis (b. 1913) believes that psychological problems occur because of irrational thought processes. In his rational-emotive therapy, the therapist disputes the client's irrational beliefs and helps the client to replace them with more reasonable ideas.

In many respects, the cognitive-behavioral model resembles the psychogenic models examined in Chapter 2. However, this approach shares many characteristics evinced by the traditional behavioral models. They emphasize learned cognitions that occur within people as they interact with internally generated stimuli and external events. Great stress is placed on altering behavior, childhood experiences are deemphasized, and insight into a problem is not considered necessary to alleviate it (Beck, 1970; Rimm & Masters, 1979). In addition, successful treatment is measured by changes in overt behavior and experimental methodology is relied on to validate techniques.

Do mediating processes affect an individual's behaviors? Velten (1968) asked subjects to read statements to themselves. Some statements were positive ("I really feel good"); others were negative ("I have too many bad things in my life"). Velten found that subjects' moods varied directly with the type of statement they had read. In a similar experiment, it was found that college students who read negative sentences ("My grades may not be good enough this semester" or "I might flunk out of school") experi-

enced more emotional arousal than subjects who read neutral statements (Rimm & Litvak, 1969). In addition, test-anxious individuals and some people suffering phobic anxieties report having disruptive thoughts in the fear-producing situation (Meichenbaum, 1972; Rimm et al., 1977). These studies all support the view that internal processes—at least in the form of verbal self-statements—contribute to one's emotional state and thus to one's pattern of behavior.

Cognitive therapy is generally aimed at modifying the client's perception or evaluation of events and situations. To give some indication of the direction taken by therapists, let's look at several types of cognitive behavioral approaches.

Attacking Irrational Beliefs The therapeutic system called **rational-emotive therapy** (**RET**), identified with Albert Ellis (1962, 1971), strongly emphasizes cognitive variables. According to Ellis, psychological problems are produced by irrational thought patterns that stem from the individual's belief system. Unpleasant emotional responses that lead to anger, unhappiness, depression, fear, and anxiety result from one's thoughts about an event rather than from the event itself (see Focus 3.2). A student who becomes depressed when he or she fails in a dating situation develops the depression not because of the failure but because of an irrational belief regarding the failure. An appropriate emotional response in such an unsuccessful dating situation might be frustration and temporary disappointment, but a more severe depression develops only if the student adds irrational thoughts, such as "Because this person turned me down, I am worthless . . . I will never succeed with anyone of the opposite sex . . . I am a total failure."

These thoughts continually sustain and regenerate the negative emotions. If the student were to eradicate the irrational self-statements, the negative emotional reaction would also fade away. The rational-emotive therapist asks the student to discriminate between the real event and the unrealistic assumptions. "Not succeeding with the opposite sex is frustrating," the therapist might point out, "but the conclusion that you are a worthless failure and will never succeed does not follow. The idea that you will always fail in future encounters is an irrational belief that is producing your depression."

FOCUS 3.2 — Some Common Irrational Assumptions

Rational-emotive therapy (RET) is based on the principle that psychological problems are produced by irrational assumptions such as those listed here. Making such irrational assumptions, RET advocates contend, results in anger, fear, anxiety, or depression.

1. It is necessary to be loved or approved by virtually every significant other.

2. One should be thoroughly competent, adequate, and achieving in all possible respects if one is to consider oneself worthwhile.

3. Certain people are bad, wicked, or villainous, and they should be severely blamed and punished for their villainy.

4. It is awful and catastrophic when things are not the way one would like them to be.

5. Human unhappiness is externally caused, and people have little or no ability to control their sorrows and disturbed behavior.

6. If something is or may be dangerous or fearsome, a person should be terribly concerned about it and should constantly dwell on the possibility of its occurring.

7. It is easier to avoid than to face certain responsibilities and difficulties in your life.

8. Each person should be dependent on others; people need someone stronger than themselves to rely on.

9. A person's past history is the all-important determinant of his or her present behavior. Because something once strongly affected a person's life, it should have a similar effect indefinitely in the future.

10. People should become emotionally involved in other people's problems and disturbances.

SOURCE: Adapted from A. Ellis, 1962.

Once the student understands and accepts this interpretation, he or she is trained to eliminate such thoughts and to replace them with more reasonable notions. The student is also assigned "homework" tasks, such as asking others out on dates. It is emphasized that failure is possible until the student develops more social skills or meets more compatible dating partners. However, he or she is to consider these unsuccessful ventures as part of the learning experience—perhaps unpleasant, but necessary.

Ellis (1957) claims a 90 percent success rate using RET, with an average of 27 therapy sessions. Other studies (Meichenbaum et al., 1971; Beck, 1985) have also reported success. However, most of the experimental support for RET has involved treatment of mild fears in college students; there are few controlled studies involving clinical populations.

Coping Strategies One prominent cognitive theorist, Donald H. Meichenbaum (1976), suggests that therapists not only should deal with clients' specific problems but also should teach them cognitive and behavioral skills—**coping strategies**—that can be applied in a variety of stressful situations. He has developed a training program that can be useful in "inoculating" clients against future problems and in facilitating the development of self-control. His program involves determining his clients' thought patterns and strategies in stressful situations and teaching them more productive self-statements. Table 3.2 gives some examples of coping self-statements designed to be used in a variety of situations.

Learning to replace irrational self-statements with more productive ones allows the client both to adopt problem-solving strategies when faced with a problem and to self-reinforce the appropriate use of these strategies. The program has been used successfully with schizophrenics, who were trained to monitor their own behavior and thinking and to be sensitive to cues from others that they were displaying psychotic symptoms. With this internal approach, the schizophrenics were able to improve their performance in reducing "sick talk," in proverb abstraction, and in inkblot tests. The self-statements included

TABLE 3.2 | **Examples of Coping Self-Statements**

Preparing for a Stressful Situation

What is it you have to do?
You can develop a plan to deal with it.
Just think about what you can do about it. That's better than getting anxious.
No negative self-statements; just think rationally.
Don't worry; worry won't help anything.
Maybe what you think is anxiety is eagerness to confront it.

Confronting and Handling a Stressful Situation

Just "psych" yourself up—you can meet this challenge.
One step at a time; you can handle the situation.
Don't think about fear; just think about what you have to do. Stay relevant.
This anxiety is what the therapist said you would feel. It's a reminder to use your coping exercises.
This tenseness can be an ally, a cue to cope.
Relax; you're in control. Take a slow deep breath.
Ah, good.

Coping with the Feeling of Being Overwhelmed

When fear comes, just pause.
Keep the focus on the present; what is it you have to do?

Coping with the Feeling of Being Overwhelmed (continued)

Label your fear from 0 to 10 and watch it change.
You should expect your fear to rise.
Don't try to eliminate fear totally; just keep it manageable.
You can convince yourself to do it. You can reason your fear away.
It will be over shortly.
It's not the worst thing that can happen.
Just think about something else.
Do something that will prevent you from thinking about fear.
Describe what is around you. That way you won't think about worrying.

Reinforcing Self-Statements

It worked; you did it.
Wait until you tell your therapist about this.
It wasn't as bad as you expected.
You made more out of the fear than it was worth.
Your damn ideas—that's the problem. When you control them, you control your fear.
It's getting better each time you use the procedures.
You can be pleased with the progress you're making.
You did it!

SOURCE: D. H. Meichenbaum, 1976.

comments such as "Be relevant," "Be coherent," "Make myself understood," and "Give healthy talk" (Meichenbaum, 1977).

Meichenbaum (1985) developed a more sophisticated approach to teaching coping strategies that he calls *stress inoculation training* (SIT). While similar to many cognitive strategies in basic assumption and practice, it is aimed at teaching clients both cognitive and physical skills in dealing with *future* problems. SIT operates like its medical counterpart, which relies on vaccines to defend the body against future disease. SIT is used to prepare people to deal with anticipated stresses, anxieties, tensions, or a wide variety of potentially traumatic or debilitating situations. Thus, it is both proactive and future oriented. SIT is based on the premise that self-statements influence attitudes and feelings. The idea is not to judge the statements in terms of rationality or irrationality but to train individuals to test their own assumptions and, in

doing so, transform them into more positive self-statements. Three phases can be identified in SIT as follows.

1. The first phase is educational and conceptual in nature. The client and therapist form a collaborative team in which a rational dialogue is established. The therapist explains to the client how a concern or problem may have a number of causes. One of the more important, however, is the client's own attitudes and perceptions. The client is taught relaxation techniques to help reduce stress, and coping skills to help alter his or her negative cognitions.

2. The second phase encompasses skill acquisition (behavioral rehearsal) and cognitive skills in self-awareness. This training may involve seeking new information, planning for escape routes, changing negative self-statements and behavioral efforts of relaxation, assertion, and self-reward. The first phase tends to be more conceptual and abstract in nature;

the second phase personalizes the analysis and puts it into actual practice.

3. The last stage involves refining, applying, and transferring coping skills. In sessions with the therapist, skills are rehearsed via role playing, simulations, and imagery. The client practices these strategies outside of the sessions and reports back to the therapist. The attempt here is to have these coping skills become natural (or second nature) to the client. If therapy is successful, the client can now generalize to other problematic situations in which these functional and adaptive skills might also be used.

So far, SIT has been shown to be effective with test anxiety (Deffenbacher & Hahnloser, 1981); social phobias (Butler et al., 1984); anxiety disorders (Clark et al., 1985); occupational stress (Sharp & Forman, 1985); and medical problems such as headaches, back pain, and Type A behavior (Moses & Hollandsworth, 1985; Turner, 1982; Anderson et al., 1981).

Cognitive Restructuring All cognitive theorists emphasize the importance of **cognitive restructuring** in their therapeutic approaches. The assumption is that an individual's cognitive system can be changed directly and this change will result in an altered and more appropriate set of rational behaviors. Among those most noted for this orientation is Aaron Beck (Beck, 1967, 1976). Beck contends that specific emotions such as depression are a product of situational interpretations made by the person. He tries to help clients identify the ways in which they distort their own thinking. Typical distortions include dichotomous reasoning (things are all good or all bad, with no in-between), overgeneralization (if my husband leaves me, I'm totally alone), magnification (perceiving things as worse than they are), and faulty reasoning.

In his approach to cognitive restructuring, Beck first attempts to understand what the client is thinking. Faulty reasoning and irrational ideas are then identified; and the client is assisted in recognizing these debilitating thinking patterns. This may be done by challenging the person's ideas and supplying another frame of reference (restructuring the cognition) from which to view the situation. The last step involves feedback to see whether the changes developed in the client's reasoning more accurately reflect the situation.

Donald H. Meichenbaum (b. 1940) suggests that problematic behavior, especially stress-related behavior, can be changed for the better if the person learns new behavior strategies and uses more productive self-statements.

Beck focuses on cognition and thinking, whereas Ellis and Meichenbaum focus on internal mediating processes. Indeed, Meichenbaum (1985) coined the phrase "cognitive-semantic" to describe Beck's approach because of its emphasis on ideas and words. Both Ellis and Meichenbaum focus more on how internal cognitive processes operate to produce the thoughts and language we use.

Although more evaluative research must be conducted before the cognitive learning approach can be evaluated, this approach, with its emphasis on the powerful influence of internal mediating processes, seems to offer an exciting new direction for behaviorists. One proponent goes so far as to speculate that psychology is undergoing a "revolution" in that cognitive and behavioral approaches are being integrated, with the acceptance of many psychologists (Mahoney, 1977).

Criticisms of the Behavioral Models

Behavioral approaches to psychopathology are a strong force in psychology today. The behaviorist perspectives have had tremendous impact in the areas of etiology and therapy. Some of these contributions have been

- To question the adequacy of the organic model of psychological disorders
- To stress the importance of external influences on behavior
- To require strict adherence to scientific methodology
- To encourage continuing evaluation of the techniques employed by psychologists

These features endow behaviorism with a degree of effectiveness and accountability that is lacking in the insight-oriented perspectives.

However, a strict behaviorist orientation excludes from consideration the inner determinants of behavior. This exclusion has been criticized, as has the behaviorists' extension to human beings of results obtained from animal studies. A lack of attention to human values in relation to behavior has also led to the charge that the behaviorist perspective is mechanistic, viewing people as "empty organisms" (Hayes & Zettle, 1979, p. 5). Some critics complain that behaviorists are not open minded and that they tend to dismiss out of hand the advances and data accumulated by other approaches to therapy (Hayes & Zettle, 1979; Lazarus, 1977). Criticism that behavioral approaches ignore the inner life of the person are less applicable to the cognitive schools. Although they do not emphasize the importance of intrapsychic dynamics, they do stress the importance of cognitions. Yet many theorists and practitioners find it hard to believe that clients can help themselves by simply changing their thinking.

There is, in fact, a movement among some therapists to seek the best ideas and techniques from all the psychotherapies. They feel that both psychoanalysts and behavior therapists could offer a more complete form of psychotherapy if they listened more carefully to each other and borrowed useful ideas from one another (Wachtel, 1977). Cognitive learning theorists are now stressing the importance of internal mediating processes (the individual's perception of events), which has always been emphasized by humanistic psychologists.

It is clear from recent writings and research publications that a major evolution, or revolution, is occurring in behaviorism. This movement may lead to an integration of some of the currently contrasting views on treatment and psychopathology, in line with the eclectic approach discussed in Chapter 2. However, such integration is a long way off, and there are still strong fundamental differences among the major schools of psychotherapy.

A BEHAVIORAL VIEW OF STEVEN V.

In the previous chapter we included three possible treatment approaches to the case of Steven V., as a therapist might apply them. Now suppose that Steve's therapist is strongly oriented toward the behavioral models. He or she would then discuss Steve's problems, we believe, in terms very much like the following. (Before going on, you may find it useful to refresh your memory by rereading the discussion of Steve's case at the beginning of Chapter 1.)

Let me start by drawing an analogy between behavior and music. In music, all the songs a performer has learned to sing or play are said to make up the performer's *repertoire*. Quite similarly, all the behaviors an individual knows—all the responses the person has learned to make in each given situation—constitute the person's *behavioral repertoire*.

The roots of Steve's problems can be traced to his behavioral repertoire. Many of the behaviors he has learned are inappropriate (much like songs that nobody wants to hear), and his repertoire lacks useful, productive behaviors.

Many of Steve's troubles stem from his deficiency in, or lack of, social skills. He has had little practice in social relationships, and so has difficulty distinguishing between appropriate behavior and inappropriate behavior. You can see evidence of these problems in his withdrawn behavior when he is in the company of relatives or his parents' friends and when Linda's friends are around. Steve himself reports that he feels apprehensive and anxious in the company of others (for example, Linda's friends) and finds himself with no idea of what to do or say. While others seem to have no difficulty making "small talk," Steve remains silent. When he does speak, his statements are usually perfunctory, brief, and inappropriate. I think this deficiency stems from Steve's early social isolation, which prevented him from developing interpersonal skills, and from his lack of good role models. His parents seldom interacted with one another or with Steve. Recall that Mr. V.'s manner of relating to his son was generally antagonistic; he did not model effective and appropriate skills.

I am also interested in exploring Steve's bouts of depression, but I need to know several things: First, through what specific behaviors is Steve's depression made manifest? Does he withdraw from social contact? Lose his appetite? Weep? Make negative statements? If we are to help Steve change his behavior, we must know what behavior we are talking about. Too often terms such as *depression, passivity,* and *anxiety* are used without a common referent. For example, when a client calls himself "shy," we must be sure that both therapist and client understand the term in the same way.

Second, what situations tend to elicit his depression? If the events share common characteristics, then we may be able to control or alter them to Steve's advantage. Again, it appears that Steve experiences depression when he believes himself to be worthless: when rejected by his woman friend, when belittled by his father, and on becoming impotent in his first sexual encounter. Steve may be able to master such situations by developing more effective behaviors. He might benefit, for example, from learning to respond to his father's bullying by telling his father how hurt and angry he feels when antagonized. A behavioral program designed to enhance Steve's sexual functioning could also prove helpful in combatting his depression. And Steve must learn to challenge his own irrational beliefs—for example, the belief that his father's failure to acknowledge Steve's academic achievements is somehow Steve's fault.

Heterosexual anxiety and impotence also need to be addressed. I believe Steve has a condi-

tioned or learned anxiety toward women and especially toward sexual intercourse. This anxiety not only blocks his ability to relate to members of the opposite sex but also directly affects his autonomic nervous system, so that his sexual arousal is impaired. We must teach Steve through classical conditioning how to subtract anxiety from the sexual encounter. Counterconditioning techniques seem to offer promise in treating Steve's impotence; relaxation could be used as a response that is antagonistic to his anxiety about sexual intercourse.

I have purposefully saved the discussion of Steve's delusional system for last. Perhaps you find it difficult to imagine a behavioral analysis of delusions. But I am not concerned with the phenomena of Steve's imagination; my concern is with the behaviors that are alleged to express a delusional system. Many people display inappropriate behaviors that are considered aversive, odd, or unusual but that may be somehow reinforced. Steve's repeated assertion that he is controlled by demonic forces and his continual thinking about Satanism disturb many people. But the people who call him crazy and are occasionally frightened by him may actually be reinforcing these behaviors. When Steve behaves in this way, he garners much attention from his parents, peers, and onlookers. Fully seven pages of a ten-page psychological report, prepared by a therapist two years ago, are devoted to Steve's delusional system. I submit that the therapist found the topic fascinating and spent a lot of time talking with Steve about his delusions. He thus *reinforced* the client's verbal behavior! I am not the only behaviorist who contends that psychoanalytically oriented therapists make this mistake. Many behavioral therapists believe, for example, that psychoanalysts elicit so much sexual material from their clients precisely because they unwittingly reinforce this concentration on sex. Is it possible that Steve's verbal and other behavioral evocations of Satanism would diminish if people ignored them? It is more than possible.

In sum, modeling, role playing, and assertiveness training could be used to enhance Steve's social skills. I would use cognitive strategies and teach him behaviors through which he may more adequately control his environment in order to

FOCUS 3.3 — Can Psychopathology Serve a Family Function?

Family systems practitioners commonly observe that when two siblings are raised under the same pathological influences, one may be normal but the other quite disturbed. Common sense would lead us to expect that all the siblings should be affected equally by pathological family dynamics. Why aren't they? Could it be that the family systems approach is misguided and that influences outside the family are more powerful shapers of behavior?

Actually, family systems theorists can account for this perplexing situation. According to family systems theory, each family has a wholeness or unity greater than the sum of its parts. An individual child may develop pathological symptoms not from internal conflict, but from the unhealthy values and pressures of family life. Some theorists assert that this pathological behavior may actually serve a family function. Scottish psychiatrist R. D. Laing (1965) has applied the term *mystifi-cation* to this phenomenon. Deviances in a family, Laing contends, have meaning and purpose in the context of family interactions. A family member's "madness" may actually preserve the fragile equilibrium of the family. For example, a husband and wife who are experiencing marital discord may avoid potentially damaging conflicts in their marriage by "forcing" one of their children to play the "sick role." In this way, attention is diverted from the parents' unhappi-

combat his depression. His heterosexual anxiety and impotence would be treated via counterconditioning methods and relaxation training. Finally, the use of extinction strategies might reduce his excessive concern with Satanism.

THE FAMILY SYSTEMS MODEL OF PSYCHOPATHOLOGY

The biogenic and psychogenic approaches to psychopathology focus on the individual. Even the behavioral schools of thought, though they are concerned with external determinants of behavior, are mainly involved with assessing and altering individual behavior. Given the American emphasis on individual achievement and responsibility—our "rugged individualism"—it is not surprising that these approaches have been very popular in the United States.

The family systems model of psychopathology does not isolate the individual as other theories do. As the term *family systems* indicates, this viewpoint holds that all members of a family are enmeshed in a network of interdependent roles, statuses, values, and norms. What one member does directly affects the entire family system. Correspondingly, people typically behave in ways that reflect family influences.

Thus the **family systems model** concentrates on the influence of the family on individual behavior.

We can identify three distinct characteristics of the family systems approach (Robinson, 1975). First, personality development is ruled largely by the attributes of the family, especially the way parents behave toward and around their children. Second, abnormal behavior in the individual is usually a reflection or "symptom" of unhealthy family dynamics and, more specifically, of poor communication among family members. Third, the therapist must focus on the family system, not solely on the individual, and must strive to involve the entire family in therapy (see Focus 3.3).

Development of Personality and Identity Within the Family

One of the earliest individuals to emphasize the importance of family influences was American psychiatrist Harry Stack Sullivan (1892–1949). Sullivan started out with a strong psychoanalytic orientation but eventually broadened his focus to include interpersonal relations. He proposed that our concepts of self, identity, and self-esteem are formed through our interactions with "significant others," typically parents, siblings, and peers (Sullivan, 1953). Parents, of

ness and unfulfilled needs. Identifying one member of the family as the problem seems to relieve the entire family system. Parents can avoid their marital conflicts, and siblings can pursue their own development.

Some family systems theorists also assert that if the identified patient is treated *individually* and gets better, another family member may show stronger signs of pathology. This tendency to regain a kind of family equilibrium has been called *family homeostasis*. Many families exist in a closed system: An accepted state of equilibrium or balance has been attained, and change is unwelcome. When a child is treated outside the system and improvement occurs, it unbalances the system. The husband and wife just described can no longer use their "sick" child as an excuse to avoid marital conflicts. To restore balance to the system, the child may be forced to play the sick role again; the family may go to great lengths to undermine the child's treatment and consequent improvement! If this approach does not work, another sibling may begin to exhibit symptoms that represent family pathology. Or the husband and wife may begin to express their conflicts with each other in other unhealthy ways, creating an atmosphere of strife and discord.

If such analyses are accurate, an individual's pathological behavior can serve a function in the family. This phenomenon certainly dramatizes the assertion of family therapists that treating one individual in an unhealthy family system is unproductive. The entire family should be the focus of treatment.

course, have the major share of responsibility for socializing the child. If parents behave toward the child as though he or she is worthwhile, the child is likely to develop a positive self-image and sense of self-worth. This sense of self, in turn, provides the emotional resilience that all people need if they are to persevere through defeats, conflicts, and the many other stressors that day-to-day life serves up. Those parents who do not see their child as a worthwhile person, and who belittle or antagonize the child, may cause the child to develop a negative self-image, to make self-statements such as "I am worthless"; "If I try, I'll only fail."

Another neo-Freudian, Erik Erikson, also stressed child-parent relationships. He pointed out that parental love and attention are important in the child's development of a sense of trust (Erikson, 1968). We all need a few people on whom we can rely and confide in with confidence. Without this trust, we are likely to see the world as dangerous, hostile, and threatening. As a result, we may shun close personal relationships and avoid even casual social interactions. How trust develops in a child depends very much on the parents, as is illustrated in the following case.

Jonathan R. first came to the attention of juvenile authorities at the age of thirteen, when he was picked up for vandalism and repeated truancy from school. At age fifteen, he was arrested again, this time for shoplifting and assaulting a clerk. At first Jonathan refused to give his name or cooperate with the police in any way. Finally, when the prospect of incarceration was raised, he relented, giving his name and the names of his parents. He was referred to a child welfare agency.

The social worker assigned to the case found Jonathan guarded, openly hostile, and suspicious of her. He responded noncommittally, disclosed a minimum of information about himself, and would not submit to any diagnostic tests until told their purpose. When a psychiatric evaluation was ordered by the court, he refused to say anything to the examining psychiatrist. During the administration of psychological tests, Jonathan appeared apprehensive and frequently stated that he knew "what you're trying to do."

A workup of Jonathan's family revealed an unemployed father who himself had numerous run-ins with the law, a mother who worked as a clerk, and two younger brothers who also attended school sporadically. The family atmosphere appeared to be extremely defensive in that all members perceived the outside world as hostile. This was demonstrated during the social worker's first visit to Jonathan's home. When she rang the doorbell, the social worker heard noises behind the door—and the sounds of people scurrying around. After a few moments, she rang the bell again. This time she noticed curtains moving slightly as though someone were peeking at her. When she called out, asking whether anyone was home, a male voice from behind the door asked her what she wanted. She said she was the social worker *who had called earlier.* The voice asked if she had identification. She pushed her business card through the mail slot, and the man asked for further identification. At this point, the social worker became angry and threatened to leave, informing the man that he and his family would then have to visit the agency. At that point, she was allowed into the home.

As the social worker became familiar with the family, it became increasingly clear to her that many of Jonathan's problems stemmed from his pathological family identity and upbringing. The father in particular raised his children to trust no one. The parents had no identifiable friends, kept primarily to themselves, and seldom ventured out of their home.

Jonathan manifested many of the behavioral characteristics of the family. His mistrust of people, tendency to be a loner, and inability to form close relationships with others were clearly evident during the time he spent at juvenile hall. When other boys made efforts to include him in their activities, he rebuffed them. In group therapy, Jonathan usually contributed only statements indicating that "You've got to look out for number one!" and "You can't trust no one."

As the case of Jonathan R. illustrates, personality and identity depend heavily on the attitudes of parents toward their children, the values they instill, and the models they provide.

Family Dynamics

By **family dynamics** we mean the day-to-day "operation" of the family system, including communication among its members. Inconsistent communication or distorted patterns of operation can cause children to develop a misconception of reality.

Early theorists proposed that psychopathology (especially schizophrenia) was the result of inconsistency in family communications (Bateson et al., 1956; Weakland 1960). Most communications occur at two levels—verbal and nonverbal. The verbal content of a message can be enhanced or negated by its nonverbal content. For example, a father who insists, "I'm *not* angry!"—while raises his voice, clenches his fists, and pounds the table—is physically contradicting his

verbal message. Inconsistency may also result when family members continually disqualify one another's messages. For example, a mother who tells her child one thing may have her message negated by the father: "Your mother doesn't know what she's talking about." Such contradictions create a *double bind* within the child, which may result in an inability to communicate, social withdrawal, and eventually schizophrenia (Abels, 1975, 1976; Bateson, 1978; Nichols, 1984; Smith, 1972). The process is discussed in greater detail in Chapter 15. Although the double-bind theory was very popular in the 1950s and 1960s, it has since fallen into disrepute. As a specific explanation of schizophrenia, it has been found seriously lacking. However, faulty and/or distorted communications continue to be strongly emphasized in family system approaches.

Communication Approaches   Among those who have emphasized the importance of clear and direct communications for healthy family system development is Virginia Satir (Satir, 1967; Bandler & Grinder, 1979). Her *conjoint family therapeutic approach* stresses the importance of teaching message-sending and message-receiving skills to family members. Like other family therapists, Satir believes that the identified patient is really a reflection of the family system gone awry. Problematic behaviors or symptoms always involve at least two people: the "feeder" and the one "fed." Satir strongly believes that the family is truly an individualized system of feeders and those fed, directors and the directed, supporters and the supported.

Satir believes that group or family communication takes place at two levels: the literal and the *metacommunicative.* The second level can best be described as *the message about the message,* because it reflects the sender's feelings about and intentions toward the receiver. When the metacommunication contradicts the literal meaning and allows no opportunity or receptivity for clarification, it can be considered dysfunctional. Pathological family systems are often the result of dysfunctional communication patterns.

The goal of family therapy is to teach families and its members healthy communication patterns. Satir considers communication training to be a central feature in therapy. She believes that the effective

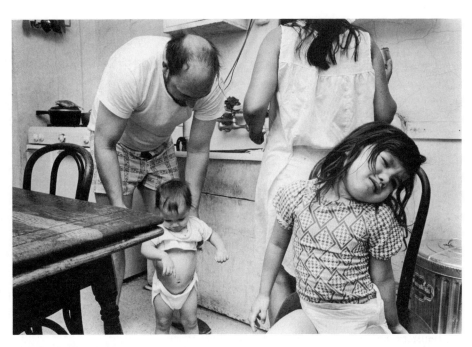

Family interaction patterns can exert tremendous influence on a child's personality development, determining the child's sense of self-worth and acquisition of appropriate social skills. A chaotic family life can foster psychological problems in a child.

communicator firmly states his or her case, clarifies and qualifies meaning, and asks for and considers feedback. Ineffective or dysfunctional communicators are vague and send incomplete and inconsistent messages.

Strategic Approaches The term *strategic* as applied to family therapy grew out of the ideas of Don Jackson and Jay Haley (Haley, 1977). Therapy is conceived as a power struggle between client and therapist. The crucial issue is one of control. According to this viewpoint, the identified patient is in control, making others around him or her feel helpless. The role of the therapist is to reestablish boundaries and restructure the family system (Haley, 1980). To shift the balance of power, the therapist must devise strategies to effect (hence the term *strategic*) change. The word *change* best summarizes the work of the strategic group. The group's general approach is to define the family problem (noting that the problem is a family problem and not only that of the symptomatic individual), determine what the family has done about it (what has and hasn't worked), establish family goals (not those of the therapist),

and construct strategic interventions that disrupt the patterns that sustain the problem.

Structural Approaches In the structural family approach advocated by Salvatore Minuchin (1974), pathology is seen simply as a result of a system of relationships that need to be strategically changed or restructured. Most family problems arise because members are either too involved or too little involved with each other. The following case study illustrates how family members may be too enmeshed with one another, thereby supporting a pathology within the family.

Mario C., a former marine sergeant, ran his family like a military unit. His wife catered to his every wish and forced her four children (two boys, ages twelve and sixteen; two girls, ages thirteen and fifteen) to be equally obedient. All had to rise at 6 A.M. The girls would help their mother cook breakfast while Mr. C. and his sons went through a 45-minute exercise routine. He inspected each child's bed, making sure it was properly made. When a bed did not meet his standards, Mr. C. ripped off all the bedding and forced the offending child to remake the bed completely.

On one occasion the oldest son became angry and said other children did not live the way they did. Mr. C. struck his son, knocking him to the floor. For nearly half an hour, Mr. C. gave the boy a stern lecture about other families that had lost the values of love and respect for one another; divorce and juvenile delinquency were the result. He, however, ran a good family and was teaching his children to respect their parents. At the end of the lecture, Mr. C. ordered his son to do fifty pushups and one hundred situps as punishment.

On the rare occasions when the children complained to their mother, Mrs. C. staunchly defended her husband. She pointed out that Mr. C. worked hard for a living, that he was teaching them good survival skills, that he knew how the world worked, and that there was nothing wrong with him. It would benefit them, she said, to be more like their father.

The dynamics of the C. family are typical of an unbalanced relationship. Here the husband exhibits a serious pathology that dominates the family, and the wife supports the husband's interpretation of reality. Suggestions that something may be wrong within the family are flatly denied. As a result, the children are daily subjected to a deviant picture of reality. Among children from such a background, the risk of psychopathology is relatively high. Minuchin would say that the therapeutic task with this family is to restructure the power and rules of the family with the ultimate goal of balancing enmeshment and detachment.

Criticisms of the Family Systems Model

The family systems approach has added an important social dimension to our understanding of abnormal behavior, and there is no denying that we are social creatures. In fact, much evidence shows that unhealthy family relationships can contribute to the development of disorders. But the family systems model is subject to a number of criticisms. For one thing, both its basic tenets and its specific applications are difficult to study and quantify. As you will see in Chapter 15, the double-bind hypothesis is very controversial, and the controversy intensifies when the

hypothesis is applied to the acquisition of severe disorders like schizophrenia. For example, it is often difficult to obtain agreement among psychologists on whether a double bind actually exists within a given family. Then there is the fact that not all siblings raised in a pathological family environment become disturbed. It seems that factors beyond family life may be equally influential in mental health.

As we have stated frequently, a psychologist who places too much emphasis on any one model may overlook the influence of factors that are not included in that model. But exclusive emphasis on the family systems model may have particularly unpleasant consequences. Too often, psychologists have pointed an accusing finger at the parents of children who suffer from certain disorders, despite an abundance of evidence that parental influence may not be a factor in those disorders. The parents are then burdened with guilt over a situation they could not have controlled. (We discuss this problem in greater detail when we examine childhood and adolescent disorders in Chapter 17.)

A FAMILY SYSTEMS VIEW OF STEVEN V.

What if Steven V.'s therapist were a proponent of the family systems model? We believe he or she would view Steve and his family very much as follows.

Officially, only Steve is my client. In reality, however, Steve's father and mother are also suffering, and their pathological symptoms are reflected in Steve. My attempts to help Steve must therefore focus on the entire family. It is obvious that the relationship between Steve and his father, that between Steve and his mother, and that between his father and mother are unhealthy. Let me comment briefly on each of these relationships.

Relationship Between Steve and His Father If we accept that a person's identity, self-concept, and feelings of self-worth are based on how significant others treat the person, it is not hard to see why Steve has very low self-esteem. It appears that he could do nothing right in his father's eyes. Mr. V. constantly derogated his son, seldom praised him, and always focused on Steve's inadequacies and mistakes. Steve's case records are filled with examples of this negative interaction:

- Steve had many medical problems as a young child. He was prone to ear infections and colds, had multiple allergies, and seemed to contract an unusual number of childhood illnesses. He also seemed accident prone and one time suffered a near-fatal injury when he walked into a playground swing. Instead of expressing concern and sympathy when his son was ill or got hurt, Mr. V. became irritated and angry at Steve. He teased him, called him a "weakling," and blamed him for the illness or injury.

- At school Steve was frequently the butt of his classmates' pranks and was constantly teased and beaten by them. His father's reaction to these incidents was to call his son a "sissy," someone who was unmasculine and "didn't have the guts to defend himself."

- Even when Steve had successes (academically he was outstanding), Mr. V. did not praise him but instead emphasized that Steve could do better still. Early in his life his father labeled him a "bookworm," a social isolate who would "never amount to anything."

As a result of this consistently negative interaction, Steve's self-concept is negative. He sees himself as inadequate and ineffectual. For this reason he withdraws from social interactions, neglects to learn new behaviors, and has a fatalistic outlook on life.

Relationship Between Steve and His Mother

This relationship is more complicated than that between father and son. On the surface it appears that his mother was affectionate, warm, and loving toward Steve. But much of this behavior seems to have been stimulated by, or to have arisen out of, the mother's unfulfilled needs. We have considerable evidence that the mother continually gave inconsistent messages to Steve. I submit that Mrs. V. actually had a deep-seated hostility toward her son but masked it in socially appropriate ways. For example, Steve's childhood illnesses seemed to upset Mrs. V. quite a bit—not out of concern for her child, but because these illnesses interfered with her own social plans. She sent double messages to Steve: on the one hand, "I'm worried about you. Are you okay?" and, on the other, "Why did you have to get sick? Now I can't go to the theater this evening." One message is "I love and care about you," and the other is "I don't love you." Consider the confusing double bind Steve experiences. If he responds to the first message, he must deceive himself into believing his mother loves him—a distortion of reality. If he responds to the second and more accurate message, he must acknowledge that he is unloved. He's damned if he does and damned if he doesn't. Other examples of double messages can be seen in the mother's alternately seductive and withdrawing behavior toward Steve. Mrs. V. was physically seductive in having him sleep with her when she was scantily clothed, but she withdrew and punished him when he became sexually aroused.

Relationship Between Husband and Wife

Mr. and Mrs. V. had a relationship that we can characterize as isolative. Each seemed to live a separate life, even when they were together in the same house. Both had unfulfilled needs, and both denied and avoided interactions and conflicts with one another. Publicly they maintained the façade of the ideal family, but privately they seemed to care little for one another. Neither wanted to confront their unfulfilling relationship: The wife knew of the husband's extramarital affairs but pretended she didn't, and the husband knew of his wife's unhappiness but never mentioned it. To avoid dealing with their marital disappointments, the parents made Steve their scapegoat. As long as Steve was the "identified patient" and was seen as "the problem," Mr. and Mrs. V. could continue in their mutual self-deception that all was well between them.

TABLE 3.3 | A Comparison of the Most Influential Models of Psychopathology

	Biogenic	**Psychoanalytic**	**Humanistic**
Motivation for Behavior	State of biological integrity and health	Unconscious influences	Self-actualization
Basis for Assessment	Medical tests, self-reports, and observable behaviors	Indirect data, oral self-reports	Subjective data, oral self-reports
Theoretical Foundation	Animal and human research, case studies, and other research methods	Case studies, correlational methods	Case studies, correlational and experimental methods
Source of Abnormal Behavior	Biological trauma, heredity, biochemical imbalances	Internal: early childhood experiences	Internal: incongruence between self and experiences
Treatment	Biological interventions (drugs, ECT, surgery, diet)	Dream analysis, free association, transference; locating unconscious conflict from early childhood; resolving the problem and reintegrating the personality	Nondirective reflection, no interpretation; providing unconditional positive regard; increasing congruence between self and experience

Even though Steve does not live at home while college is in session, his psychological roots remain there, and his parents are still enormously influential in his life. It would therefore be most desirable to include the entire family in a program of therapy.

A FINAL NOTE ABOUT THE MODELS OF PSYCHOPATHOLOGY

Table 3.3 compares the models of psychopathology that we have discussed in Chapter 2 and this chapter. Each model has devout supporters who, in turn, are influenced by the model they support. But even though theory building and the testing of hypotheses are critical to psychology as a science, it seems evident that we can best understand abnormal behavior only by integrating the various approaches. We are all biological, psychological, *and* social beings. To neglect any one of these aspects of human life would be to deny an important part of our existence.

SUMMARY

1. Behaviorism evolved in the early twentieth century, at a time when the existing theories of psychology emphasized the subjective analysis of the inner—and unobservable—workings of the mind. John B. Watson proposed that psychology's goal

TABLE 3.3 | A Comparison of the Most Influential Models of Psychopathology *(continued)*

Existential	Traditional Behavioral	Cognitive Behavioral	Family Systems
Capacity for self-awareness; freedom to decide one's fate; search for meaning in a meaningless world	External influences	Interaction of external and cognitive influences	Interaction with significant others
Subjective data, oral self-reports, experiential encounter	Observable, objective data, overt behaviors	Self-statements, alterations in overt behaviors	Observation of family dynamics
An approach to understanding the human condition rather than a firm theoretical model	Animal research, case studies, experimental methods	Human research, case studies, experimental methods	Case studies, social psychological studies, experimental methods
Failure to actualize human potential; avoidance of choice and responsibility	External: learning maladaptive responses or not acquiring appropriate responses	Internal: learned pattern of irrational or negative self-statements	External: faulty family interactions (family pathology and inconsistent communication patterns)
Provide conditions for maximizing self-awareness and growth, to enable clients to be free and responsible	Direct modification of the problem behavior; analysis of the environmental factors controlling the behavior and alteration of the contingencies	Understanding relationship between self-statements and problem behavior; modification of internal dialogue	Family therapy involving strategies aimed at treating the entire family, not just the identified patient

should be the prediction and control of human behavior and that, as a science, psychology should be limited to observable and measurable events. Traditional behaviorists are concerned primarily with the influence of environmental factors on behavior through the processes of learning.

2. The traditional behavioral models of psychopathology hold that abnormal behaviors are acquired through association (classical conditioning) or reinforcement (operant conditioning). Negative emotional responses such as anxiety can be learned through classical conditioning: a formerly neutral stimulus evokes a negative response after it has been presented along with a stimulus that already evokes that response. Negative voluntary behaviors may be learned through operant conditioning if those behaviors are reinforced (rewarded) when they occur.

3. Some psychologists assert that the acquisition of many complex behaviors cannot be explained solely by classical or operant conditioning. These behaviors may, however, be acquired through observational learning, in which a person learns behaviors by observing them in other people, who act as models, and then imitating them. Pathological behavior results when inappropriate behavior is imitated or when normal behavior is inappropriately applied.

4. Cognitive behaviorism developed partly as a reaction to the criticism that traditional behaviorists ignore the influence of thought processes on behavior. According to the cognitive behavioral model, perceptions of events are mediated by thoughts and feelings, and the perception may have a greater influence on behavior than the event itself. Despite this emphasis on cognition, the cognitive behavioral model shares

many characteristics with the traditional behavioral models. Cognitive therapeutic approaches, such as rational-emotive therapy and use of coping strategies, stress inoculation training, and cognitive restructuring are generally aimed at normalizing the client's perception of events.

5. The family systems model asserts that family interactions guide an individual's development of personal identity as well as his or her sense of reality. Abnormal behavior is viewed as the result of distortion or faulty communication or unbalanced structural relationships within the family. Children who receive faulty messages from parents, or who are subjected to structurally abnormal family constellations, may develop behavioral and emotional problems. Therapeutic techniques generally focus on the family as a whole, rather than on one disturbed individual.

KEY TERMS

behavioral models Theories of psychopathology that are concerned with the role of learning in abnormal behavior

classical (respondent) conditioning A principle of learning, applying to involuntary behaviors, in which responses to new stimuli are learned through association

cognitive behavioral model A principle of learning holding that conscious thought mediates, or modifies, an individual's behavior in response to a stimulus

cognitive restructuring An attempt to alter problematic cognitions by replacing them with more rational and positive thoughts

conditioned response (CR) In classical conditioning, the response made to a previously neutral stimulus

conditioned stimulus (CS) In classical conditioning, a previously neutral stimulus

counterconditioning A therapeutic means of eliminating anxiety by gradually pairing the fear-producing stimulus with a pleasant stimulus

covert sensitization The use of imagination to associate a negative quality with a bad habit

discriminative stimulus A cue that is usually present when reinforcement occurs

extinction In classical and operant conditioning, the process by which a response is gradually eliminated by not being reinforced

family dynamics The day-to-day "operation" of the family system

family systems model A model of psychopathology that emphasizes the influence of the family on individual behavior

generalization Responding in a similar manner to different stimuli which share common characteristics

law of effect An increase in behaviors associated with positive consequences and a reduction when associated with unpleasant ones.

modeling The process of learning by observing models

negative reinforcer Increases the frequency of a behavior by removing an adverse event

observational learning theory A theory of learning that holds that people can learn new behaviors by watching other people perform those behaviors and then imitating them

operant behavior A voluntary and controllable behavior that "operates" on an individual's environment

operant conditioning A theory of learning, applying primarily to voluntary behaviors, that holds that these behaviors are controlled by the consequences that follow them

punishment Either the removal of a positive reinforcer or the presentation of an adversive stimulus

rationale-emotive therapy (RET) The system of therapy developed by Albert Ellis, which stresses cognitive variables as the basis for treating psychological problems; believed to be the result of irrational thought patterns

reinforcement In operant conditioning, a consequence that increases the frequency or magnitude of the behavior it follows; may be positive or negative

schema The underlying assumptions held by a person that are influenced by experiences, values, and perceived capabilities and by how he or she interprets events

shaping A systematic but incremental method of rewarding similar behavior with the purpose of attaining a desired but more complex one

stimulus discrimination Being able to differentiate differences between similar stimuli

unconditioned response In classical conditioning, the response first made to the unconditioned stimulus

unconditioned stimulus In classical conditioning, the stimulus that elicits an unconditioned response

chapter 4
Classification and Assessment of Abnormal Behavior

We noted in Chapter 1 that a psychodiagnosis, which involves describing and drawing inferences about an individual's psychological state, is often an early step in the treatment process. It is for many psychotherapists the basis on which a program of therapy is first formulated. This diagnosis is developed by *assessing* the patient's condition—that is, by obtaining and evaluating as much information as possible about the patient. Among the assessment tools available to the clinician are observation, conversations and interviews, a variety of psychological tests, and the reports of the patient and his or her relatives and friends. When the data gathered from all sources are combined and analyzed, the therapist can gain a good picture of the patient's behavior and mental state.

In most cases, the information-gathering process results in a rather bulky file on the patient. The information needs to be sorted and integrated—boiled down to its essentials and categorized on the basis of similarities or relatedness.

This *classification* of behaviors or of information about behaviors performs several functions. First, it helps to clarify the therapist's "picture" of the client's mental state; once the data are organized, they are easier to analyze. Second, if the classification scheme is an effective one, it can lead the therapist to possible treatment programs. Third, the names of the categories within a classification scheme provide concise descriptions of or referents to symptoms and disorders; these descriptions are useful in communications among psychologists, including the reporting of research findings, to the extent that each name means the same thing to all those who use the scheme. Finally, using a classification scheme standardizes psychological assessment procedures. That is, if particular information is required for classification, therapists tend to use the assessment techniques that provide that information. Thus classification may affect the entire psychodiagnostic process, as well as the therapy that follows it.

In this chapter, we examine the most-used diagnostic classification system and assessment methods and discuss some of the issues involved in their use.

In an 1883 publication, the psychiatrist Emil Kraepelin (1856–1926) proposed that mental disorders could be directly linked to organic brain disorders, and further proposed a diagnostic classification system for disorders. Kraepelin is also noted for being a pioneer in experimental abnormal psychology. He established his own laboratory where he conducted research on mental illness.

THE CLASSIFICATION OF ABNORMAL BEHAVIOR

The goal of having a **classification system** for abnormal behaviors is to provide distinct categories, indicators, and nomenclature for different patterns of behavior, thought processes, and emotional disturbances. Thus the pattern that is classified as, say, *paranoid schizophrenia* should be clearly different from the pattern named *borderline personality*. At the same time, the categories should be constructed in such a way as to accommodate wide variation in these patterns. That is, the clinician should be able to categorize paranoid schizophrenic behavior as such, even when the patient does not show the "perfect" or "textbook" paranoid schizophrenic pattern.

Problems with Early Diagnostic Classification Systems

As indicated in Chapter 1, the first effective classification scheme for mental disorders was devised by Emil Kraepelin toward the end of the nineteenth century. Kraepelin held the organic view of psychopathology, and his system had a distinctly biogenic slant. Classification was based on the patient's symptoms, as in medicine. It was hoped that disorders (similar groups of symptoms) would have a common **etiology** (cause or origin), would require similar treatments, would respond to those treatments similarly, and would progress similarly if left untreated.

Many of these same expectations were held for the first edition of the *Diagnostic and Statistical Manual of Mental Disorders* (DSM-I), published by the American Psychiatric Association in 1952 and based on Kraepelin's system. However, these expectations were not realized in DSM-I. The DSM was revised in 1968 (DSM-II), 1980 (DSM-III), and 1987 (DSM-III-R). Each revision was made to increase the reliability, validity, and usefulness of the classification scheme (Spitzer & Williams, 1987). Reliability and validity are crucial to any diagnostic scheme and, in fact, to any scientific construct.

Reliability   The **reliability** of a procedure or test is the degree to which it yields the same result repeatedly, under the same circumstances. The greater the difference between repeated trials, the lower the reliability.

A variety of techniques may be used to test the reliability of a diagnostic classification system (Anastasi, 1982). One technique of particular interest to psychologists is the extent to which different clinicians using the system agree on the diagnosis for a particular patient. Early studies of the DSM that compared the diagnoses of pairs of clinicians found poor agreement between the members of each pair (Ash, 1949; Schmidt & Fonda, 1956). The greatest disagreement was found in *specific* categories, even though, in about 80 percent of the pairs, both clinicians agreed on which *general* category (organic, psychotic, or personality disturbance) a particular disorder belonged in. As a rule, reliability is higher for broad rather than for fine distinctions (Phares, 1984). Unfortunately, reliability in making broad categorizations is not very helpful in making specific diagnoses.

In other reliability studies, the same information was presented to clinicians on two occasions or at different times. These studies showed that the clinicians' later diagnoses often did not agree with their earlier ones (Beck, 1962; Wilson & Meyer, 1962). Thus even a single clinician's diagnosis was not very reliable over time.

Much unreliability of early DSM editions can be attributed to the diagnostic categories themselves. Three sources of diagnostic error have been identified: Of the errors, 5 percent were attributable to the patients, who gave different material to different interviewers. Nearly one-third (32.5 percent) of the errors were due to inconsistencies among diagnosticians in interview techniques, in interpreting similar data, and in judging the importance of symptoms. Most significantly, however, 62.5 percent of the errors derived from inadequacies of the diagnostic system (Ward et al., 1962). It was simply not clear which behavior patterns belonged in which categories.

Validity The **validity** of a procedure or test is the degree to which it actually performs the function it was designed to perform. With respect to diagnosis, a classification scheme that is supposed to distinguish depression from anxiety, say, should not misclassify an anxiety disorder as depression.

Many critics questioned the validity and usefulness of psychiatric classification (Ferster, 1965; Jones et al., 1965; Kanfer & Phillips, 1969; Ullmann & Krasner, 1965). They claimed that DSM did not adequately convey information about underlying causes, processes, treatment, and prognosis. (A **prog-**nosis is a prediction of the future course of an untreated disorder.)

The problem arose because early versions of DSM were strongly influenced by the biogenic model of mental illness, in which etiology is supposed to be a basis of classification. With the exception of the categories of organic mental disorders (brain damage), which may parallel diseases, most other DSM categories were purely descriptive. Kraepelin's attempt to develop a classification system that would identify causes and differential treatment was not successful, especially in the case of functional disorders (that is, where the physical causes are unknown).

The Current System: DSM-III-R

The problems of the 1952 and 1968 DSM editions led to the 1980 version, DSM-III. And in 1987, DSM-III itself was revised (DSM-III-R) to take into account new research findings (Spitzer & Williams, 1987). Although Kraepelin's concepts still underlie some of its categories, DSM-III and DSM-III-R contain substantial revisions. For example, to improve reliability the exact criteria to be used in making a diagnosis are specified. Clinical usefulness and suitability for research studies were also considered. DSM-III-R is intended to be atheoretical and descriptive, making it more useful to clinicians of varying orientations. The newest version is undergoing extensive field testing. Studies suggest that reliability of diagnosis is higher in DSM-III (and presumably DSM-III-R) than in DSM-I or DSM-II (Millon, 1983; Spitzer, 1981b; Spitzer & Forman, 1979).

DSM-III-R recommends that the individual's mental state be examined and evaluated with regard to five factors or dimensions (called *axes* in the manual). The five-axis evaluation is intended to provide more comprehensive and useful information than previous systems (Millon, 1983; Spitzer & Williams, 1987). Axes I, II, and III deal with the individual's present condition. Axes IV and V provide additional information about the person's life situation and probable degree of success in coping.

◆ *Axis I—Clinical Syndrome* Any mental disorder (except those included on Axis II) listed in the manual are indicated on Axis I—clinical syndrome.

◆ *Axis II—Personality or Specific Developmental Disorders* Patients may also have personality disorders, or, in the case of children, developmental disorders; these are specified, also from a list. They may be present with, or without, a mental disorder from Axis I.

◆ *Axis III—Physical Disorders* Listed in Axis III are any physical or medical problems that accompany the mental disorder. This axis was included because physical disorders can be relevant to understanding and treating the person.

◆ *Axis IV—Psychosocial Stressors* The severity of stressors experienced by the patient during the preceding one-year period is rated on a seven-point scale from *none* to *catastrophic* (the higher the score, the greater the stress). This information can provide insight into the causes or prognosis of the disorder.

◆ *Axis V—Highest Level of Adaptive Functioning* The patient's highest level of functioning during the past year and current level of functioning are rated on a ninety-point scale from absent (score of 90) or minimal symptoms to extreme level of disturbance (score of 1). This information, too, may be significant in judging treatment needs and prognosis (American Psychiatric Association, 1987).

Table 4.1 lists the disorders (categories) that are included in DSM-III-R. Focus 4.1 provides an example of the diagnoses that result from the five-axis evaluation.

DSM-III-R Mental Disorders

The task of making a diagnosis of mental disorder involves the classification of individuals on Axes I and II. Most clients have a disorder that is listed under either Axis I or Axis II. Sometimes, clients may be diagnosed as having disorders in both axes. Listed under Axis II are the personality disorders and some of the specific developmental disorders included in the category of "disorders usually first evident in infancy, childhood, or adolescence." The following are the broad categories of mental disorders discussed in this book:

Disorders Usually First Evident in Infancy, Childhood, or Adolescence Included in the category of disorders that begin before maturity is a variety of problems. The problems involve impairment in cognitive and intellectual functioning, language or motor deficiencies, disruptive behaviors, poor social skills, anxiety, eating disorders, and so on (see Chapter 17).

Organic Mental Syndromes and Disorders The essential feature of the organic mental disorders is a psychological or behavioral abnormality that is associated with a transient or permanent, identifiable dysfunction of the brain. Included in this category are cognitive, emotional, and behavioral problems that arise from head injuries, ingestion of toxic or intoxicating substances, brain degeneration or disease, and so on (see Chapter 16).

Psychoactive Substance Use Disorders Psychoactive substances, such as alcohol, amphetamines, marijuana, cocaine, and nicotine, are those that affect the central nervous system. Whenever use of these substances continues despite social, occupational, psychological, or physical problems, it is considered a mental disorder. Individuals with substance use disorders are often unable to control intake and have a persistent desire to use the substance (see Chapter 10).

Schizophrenia The disorder known as schizophrenia is marked by severe impairment in thinking and perception. Speech may be incoherent, and the person often has delusions (false belief systems), hallucinations (such as hearing imaginary voices), and inappropriate affect. The disturbance seriously disrupts social, occupational, and recreational functioning (see Chapters 14 and 15).

Mood Disorders A separate class of disorders is composed of disturbances in mood or affect. The mood may be one of serious depression, in which the person shows marked sadness, diminished interest, and loss of energy. Extreme elation or mania is also included in these disorders. People with mania frequently have grandiosity, decreased need for sleep, flight of ideas, and impairment in functioning. Severity of mood disorders can vary, and sometimes, in bipolar conditions, both depression and mania are exhibited (see Chapter 12).

An Example of Classification Using DSM-III-R

The Client: Mark is a 56-year-old machine operator who was referred for treatment by his supervisor. The supervisor noted that Mark's performance at work had deteriorated during the past four months. Mark was frequently absent from work, had difficulty getting along with others, and often had a strong odor of liquor on his breath after his lunch break. The supervisor knew Mark was a heavy drinker and suspected that Mark's performance was affected by alcohol consumption. In truth, Mark could not stay away from drinking. He consumed alcohol every day; during weekends, he averaged about 16 ounces of Scotch per day. Although he had been a heavy drinker for thirty years, his consumption had increased after his wife divorced him six months ago. She claimed she could no longer tolerate his drinking, extreme jealousy, and unwarranted suspicions concerning her marital fidelity. Co-workers avoided Mark because he was a cold, unemotional person who distrusted others.

During interviews with the therapist, Mark revealed very little about himself. He blamed others for his drinking problems: If his wife had been faithful or if others were not out to get him, he would drink less. Mark appeared to overreact to any perceived criticisms of himself. A medical examination revealed that Mark was developing cirrhosis of the liver as a result of his chronic and heavy drinking.

The Evaluation: Mark's heavy use of alcohol, which interfered with his functioning, resulted in an *alcohol abuse* diagnosis on Axis I. Mark also exhibited a personality disorder, which was diagnosed as *paranoid personality* on Axis II because of his suspiciousness, hypervigilance, and other behaviors. Cirrhosis of the liver was noted on Axis III. Primarily because of

Mark's divorce, a rating of 4 (severe) was given to him on Axis IV to indicate the level of psychosocial stressors. Finally, on Axis V, Mark was given a 54 on the Global Assessment of Functioning scale (GAF), used in Axis V to rate his current level of functioning, mainly because he was exhibiting moderate difficulty at work. His highest rating on the GAF was 70 for past level of functioning, since the symptoms were mild before his divorce.

Mark's diagnosis, then, was as follows:

Axis I—Syndrome: alcohol abuse

Axis II—Personality disorder: paranoid personality

Axis III—Physical disorder: cirrhosis

Axis IV—Stressors: divorce, 4 (severe and predominantly enduring circumstance)

Axis V—Current GAF, 54; Highest GAF past year: 70

Anxiety Disorders Anxiety is the predominant symptom, in anxiety disorders, and avoidance behaviors are almost always present. For example, in phobias people fear an object or situation and avoid encountering the feared object. In other anxiety disorders, the people may not know the reasons for their extreme feelings or anxiety or may exhibit obsessions (recurrent thoughts) or compulsions (repetitive behaviors), which, when not performed, cause marked distress (see Chapter 6).

Somatoform Disorders Symptoms of a physical disorder in which no demonstrable organic cause is observed and in which psychological factors are linked to the symptoms are usually classified as

somatoform disorders. Individuals with these disorders usually complain of bodily problems or dysfunctions, are preoccupied with beliefs of having a disease or health problem, or experience pain. Yet the symptoms may be inconsistent with anatomical structures, and the discrepancy casts doubt on the organic or physical basis for the symptoms (see Chapter 7).

Dissociative Disorders The essential feature of these disorders is a disturbance or alteration in memory, identity, or consciousness. The disturbance may be reflected in people who cannot remember who they are, who assume new identities, who have two or more distinct personalities, or who experience

TABLE 4.1 | **DSM-III-R Classification: Categories for Axes I and II (abbreviated)**

DISORDERS USUALLY FIRST EVIDENT IN INFANCY, CHILDHOOD, OR ADOLESCENCE

Developmental Disorders

Mental Retardation

Mild mental retardation
Moderate mental retardation
Severe mental retardation
Profound mental retardation
Unspecified mental retardation

Pervasive Developmental Disorders

Autistic disorder
Pervasive developmental
    disorder NOS[a]

Specific Developmental Disorders

Academic skills disorders
    Developmental arithmetic
        disorder
    Developmental expressive
        writing disorder
    Developmental reading
        disorder
Language and speech disorders
    Developmental articulation
        disorder
    Developmental expressive
        language disorder
    Developmental receptive
        language disorder
Motor skills disorder
    Developmental coordination
        disorder
    Specific developmental
        disorder NOS

Other Developmental Disorders

Developmental disorder NOS
    (*Note:* Developmental disor-
    ders are coded on Axis II.)

Disruptive Behavior Disorders

Attention-deficit hyperactivity
    disorder
Conduct disorder
    Group type
    Solitary aggressive type
    Undifferentiated type
Oppositional defiant disorder

Anxiety Disorders of Childhood or Adolescence

Separation anxiety disorder
Avoidant disorder of childhood
    or adolescence
Overanxious disorder

Eating Disorders

Anorexia nervosa
Bulimia nervosa
Pica
Rumination disorder of infancy
Eating disorder NOS

Gender Identity Disorders

Gender identity disorder of
    childhood
Transsexualism
Gender identity disorder of
    adolescence or adulthood,
    nontranssexual type
Gender identity disorder NOS

Tic Disorders

Tourette's disorder
Chronic motor or vocal tic
    disorder
Transient tic disorder
Tic disorder NOS

Elimination Disorders

Functional encopresis
Functional enuresis

Speech Disorders Not Elsewhere Classified

Cluttering
Stuttering

Other Disorders of Infancy, Childhood, or Adolescence

Elective mutism
Identity disorder
Reactive attachment disorder of
    infancy or early childhood
Stereotype/habit disorder
Undifferentiated attention-
    deficit disorder

ORGANIC MENTAL DISORDERS

Dementias Arising in the Senium and Presenium

Primary degenerative dementia
    of the Alzheimer type,
    senile onset
    With delirium
    With delusions
    With depression
    Uncomplicated
Primary degenerative dementia
    of the Alzheimer type,
    presenile onset
Multi-infarct dementia
Senile dementia NOS
Presenile dementia NOS

Psychoactive Substance-Induced Organic Mental Disorders

Alcohol
    Intoxication
    Idiosyncratic intoxication
    Uncomplicated alcohol
        withdrawal
    Withdrawal delirium
    Hallucinosis
    Amnestic disorder
    Dementia associated with
        alcoholism
Amphetamine or similarly acting
    sympathomimetic
    Intoxication
    Withdrawal
    Delirium
    Delusional disorder
Caffeine
    Intoxication
Cannabis
    Intoxication
    Delusional Disorder
Cocaine
    Intoxication
    Withdrawal
    Delirium
    Delusional disorder
Hallucinogen
    Hallucinosis
    Delusional disorder
    Mood disorder
    Posthallucinogen perception
        disorder
Inhalant
    Intoxication
Nicotine
    Withdrawal
Opioid
    Intoxication
    Withdrawal

Phencyclidine (PCP) or similarly
    acting arylcyclohexylamine
    Intoxication
    Delirium
    Delusional disorder
    Mood disorder
    Organic mental disorder NOS
Sedative, hypnotic, or anxiolytic
    Intoxication
    Uncomplicated sedative,
        hypnotic, or anxiolytic
        withdrawal
    Withdrawal delirium
    Amnestic disorder
Other or unspecified psycho-
    active substance
    Intoxication
    Withdrawal
    Delirium
    Dementia
    Amnestic disorder
    Delusional disorder
    Hallucinosis
    Mood disorder
    Anxiety disorder
    Personality disorder
    Organic mental disorder NOS

Organic Mental Disorders associated with Axis III physical disorders or conditions, or whose etiology is unknown

Delirium
Dementia
Amnestic disorder
Organic delusional disorder
Organic hallucinosis
Organic mood disorder
Organic anxiety disorder
Organic personality disorder
Organic mental disorder NOS

TABLE 4.1 │ **DSM-III-R Classification: Categories for Axes I and II (abbreviated)** *(continued)*

PSYCHOACTIVE SUBSTANCE USE DISORDERS

Alcohol
  Dependence
  Abuse
Amphetamine or similarly acting
    sympathomimetic
  Dependence
  Abuse
Cannabis
  Dependence
  Abuse
Cocaine
  Dependence
  Abuse
Hallucinogen
  Dependence
  Abuse
Inhalant
  Dependence
  Abuse
Nicotine
  Dependence
Opioid
  Dependence
  Abuse
Phencyclidine (PCP) or similarly
    acting arylcyclohexylamine
  Dependence
  Abuse
Sedative, hypnotic, or anxiolytic
  Dependence
  Abuse
Polysubstance dependence
Psychoactive substance
    dependence NOS
Psychoactive substance abuse
    NOS

SCHIZOPHRENIA

Schizophrenia
  Catatonic
  Disorganized
  Paranoid
  Undifferentiated
  Residual

DELUSIONAL (PARANOID) DISORDER

Delusional (paranoid) disorder

PSYCHOTIC DISORDERS NOT ELSEWHERE CLASSIFIED

Brief reactive psychosis
Schizophreniform disorder
Schizoaffective disorder
Induced psychotic disorder
Psychotic disorder NOS (atypical
    psychosis)

MOOD DISORDERS

Bipolar Disorders

Bipolar disorder
  Mixed
  Manic
  Depressed
Cyclothymia
Bipolar disorder NOS

Depressive Disorders

Major depression
  Single episode
  Recurrent
Dysthymia
Depressive disorder NOS

ANXIETY DISORDERS

Panic disorder
  With agoraphobia
  Without agoraphobia
Agoraphobia without history of
    panic disorder
Social phobia
Simple phobia
Obsessive-compulsive disorder
Posttraumatic stress disorder
Generalized anxiety disorder
Anxiety disorder NOS

SOMATOFORM DISORDERS

Body dysmorphic disorder
Conversion disorder
Hypochondriasis
Somatization disorder
Somatoform pain disorder
Undifferentiated somatoform
    disorder
Somatoform disorder NOS

DISSOCIATIVE DISORDERS

Multiple personality disorder
Psychogenic fugue
Psychogenic amnesia
Depersonalization disorder
Dissociative disorder NOS

SEXUAL DISORDERS
Paraphilias

Exhibitionism
Fetishism
Frotteurism
Pedophilia
Sexual masochism
Sexual sadism
Transvestic fetishism
Voyeurism
Paraphilia NOS

Sexual Dysfunctions

Sexual desire disorders
  Hypoactive sexual desire
      disorder
  Sexual aversion disorder
Sexual arousal disorders
  Female sexual arousal
      disorder
  Male erectile disorder
Orgasm disorders
  Inhibited female orgasm
  Inhibited male orgasm
  Premature ejaculation
Sexual pain disorders
  Dyspareunia
  Vaginismus
Sexual dysfunction NOS

Other Sexual Disorders

Sexual disorder NOS

IMPULSE CONTROL DISORDERS NOT ELSEWHERE CLASSIFIED

Intermittent explosive disorder
Kleptomania
Pathological gambling
Pyromania
Trichotillomania
Impulse control disorder NOS

ADJUSTMENT DISORDER

Adjustment disorder
  With anxious mood
  With depressed mood
  With disturbance of conduct
  With mixed disturbance of
      emotions and conduct
  With mixed emotional
      features
  With physical complaints
  With withdrawal
  With work (or academic)
      inhibition
Adjustment disorder NOS

PSYCHOLOGICAL FACTORS AFFECTING PHYSICAL CONDITION

Psychological factors affecting
    physical condition

PERSONALITY DISORDERS

Paranoid
Schizoid
Schizotypal
Antisocial
Borderline
Histrionic
Narcissistic
Avoidant
Dependent
Obsessive compulsive
Passive aggressive
Personality disorder NOS
    (Note: Personality disorders
are coded on Axis II.)

SOURCE: Reprinted with permission from the Diagnostic and Statistical Manual of Mental Disorders, Third Edition, R. Copyright 1987 American Psychiatric Association.
[a]NOS = Not otherwise specified.

feelings of depersonalization in which the sense of reality is lost (see Chapter 7).

Sexual Disorders Two main groups of disturbances are included in sexual disorders: paraphilias and sexual dysfunctions. Paraphilias are characterized by intense sexual arousal and fantasies involving nonhuman objects, suffering or humiliation of oneself or one's partner, or children or nonconsenting people. They are considered disorders only if the person has acted on the fantasies or is markedly distressed by them. Sexual dysfunctions may involve inhibitions in sexual desires, inhibited orgasms, premature ejaculations among males, or recurrent pain during the process of sexual intercourse (see Chapter 11).

There is a fine line between mental disorders and extreme but normal behavior. Shy children could easily be diagnosed as disordered, when instead their social development may simply be delayed.

Impulse Control Disorders Not Elsewhere Classified A separate class of disorders involves the failure to resist an impulse or temptation to perform some act that is harmful to the individual or others. Included are disorders involving loss of control of impulses over aggression, stealing, gambling, fire setting, and hair pulling. Disorders of impulse control that are listed under other disorders (such as drug use or paraphilias) are not classified in this group of disorders (see Chapter 9).

Psychological Factors Affecting Physical Condition Certain disorders have two features: (1) the presence of environmental stimuli (such as stressors) and (2) a reaction to the stimuli in which demonstrable organic pathology or a known pathophysiologic process occurs. For example, a stressor may result in migraine headaches, acne, gastric ulcers, nausea, or obesity (see Chapter 8).

Personality Disorders Whenever personality traits are inflexible and maladaptive and significantly impair functioning or subjective distress, a diagnosis of personality disorder is likely. The patterns of these disorders are usually evident by adolescence. They typically involve odd or eccentric behaviors, excessive dramatic and emotional behaviors, or anxious and fearful behaviors (see Chapter 9).

Evaluation of DSM-III-R

It is too soon to provide a comprehensive evaluation of DSM-III-R, because it was so recently developed. Extensive research needs to be conducted on its reliability and validity with different populations; and the social and research consequences of its use need to be studied. Although many sections of DSM-III-R are basically unchanged from those of DSM-III, more substantive changes have been made for certain disorders, such as personality disorders (Morey, 1988). Unlike DSM-III, DSM-III-R does note that caution should be exercised in making diagnoses for people from groups who differ culturally in values and behaviors from those in Western societies.

Most objections have been directed to DSM-III (and appear to also apply to DSM-III-R). For example, many clinicians and researchers feel that DSM-III and III-R have a strong medical orientation, even though more than half the disorders listed are not attributable

Gender Bias in DSM?

From its very inception, DSM-III has encountered a great deal of criticism. One criticism has focused on gender issues. Kaplan (1983) has argued that some diagnostic categories in the DSM-III are biased in favor of masculine traits. These biases tend to view certain behaviors of women as being unhealthy or disturbed, biases that were denied by those who helped to formulate DSM-III (Williams & Spitzer, 1983).

The revised 1987 version of the diagnostic system, DSM-III-R, has also encountered much criticism over sex bias (Holden, 1986), particularly in the proposal to establish the diagnostic categories of self-defeating personality disorder and late luteal phase dysphoric disorder. The essential feature of self-defeating personality disorder is a pervasive pattern of self-defeating behavior, in which the person avoids or undermines pleasurable encounters and is

drawn to situations in which he or she will experience suffering. Critics were concerned that this category of disorders might unfairly be applied to battered women. The women could be diagnosed as having a mental disorder when they were actually victims of abuse. Furthermore, women are often socialized into the roles of being more nurturant, deferential, and willing to delay gratification. These behaviors could be interpreted as being masochistic—a sign of a mental disorder (Caplan, 1984; D. Franklin, 1987). Late luteal phase dysphoric disorder, better known as premenstrual syndrome (PMS), is also a hotly debated category. According to DSM-III-R, the diagnosis involves symptoms such as marked changes in mood, persistent anger, depression or irritability often accompanied by complaints of breast tenderness, water retention, and bodily aches. These symptoms occur in a cyclical

pattern a week before menses and remit a few days afterward. Although critics of this category acknowledge that many women have some of these symptoms, they feel that PMS should be treated strictly as a physical or gynecological disorder. Labeling it as a psychiatric disorder would stigmatize women as being emotional and controlled by "raging hormones." It also suggests that being a woman is per se a risk factor in developing psychiatric disorders (Holden, 1986). Because of the controversial nature of these categories and the serious objections raised, these categories were placed in the appendix rather than in the body of DSM-III-R. These disorders were considered as proposed categories in need of further study (see Chapter 9 of this book, on personality disorders).

to known or presumed organic causes and should not be considered biogenic in nature (Schacht, 1985; Schacht, & Nathan, 1977). Some psychologists believe that the medical emphasis of DSM-III is in part a response to psychiatrists' need to define abnormality more strongly within their profession. A survey of psychotherapists who are psychologists rather than psychiatrists indicated that there was little enthusiasm for DSM-III (Smith & Kraft, 1983). Most of the respondents rejected the notion that mental disorders form a subset of medical disorders. They preferred a social and interpersonal, rather than a medical, approach to mental disorder. However, no such alternative to DSM enjoys widespread use at present.

Other psychologists question the usefulness of the DSM-III-R classification scheme for research. Some of the categories were created out of compro-

mises between conflicting views or were rooted in practical considerations such as ease of application and acceptability to practitioners. Schacht (1985) believes that political and practical aspects of DSM are inseparable from scientific considerations. For example, certain diagnostic categories in DSM have been characterized as being sexist (see Focus 9.1 in Chapter 9). In other words, specific behaviors sometimes seen among women may be inappropriately interpreted as signs of mental disorders (D. Franklin, 1987; M. Kaplan, 1983). (See Focus 4.2) Some researchers (Persons, 1986) have argued that the study of the symptoms of a disorder is more valuable than research on diagnosed disorders, because many patients may be misdiagnosed. Furthermore, by placing patients in diagnosed categories, important information regarding the severity of symptoms is lost.

For these reasons, the DSM (in *any* revision) may be difficult to use for scientific purposes (Zubin, 1978).

Millon (1983) has tried to clarify the intent of DSM-III and to respond to critics. He noted that the classification system was not intended to imply that all mental disorders have an organic basis. To Millon, the important question is whether the DSM revised editions are a substantial improvement over past systems. He believes they are. Millon also points out that constructing a diagnostic classification system is an ongoing process, requiring continual revision and improvement. So the limitations in the usefulness of DSM-III-R partly reflect holes in our knowledge of psychopathology (Goldman & Foreman, 1988).

As noted earlier, research suggests that DSM-III and III-R yield greater reliability in diagnosis than previous versions. In fact, one would expect better reliability on logical grounds alone. DSM-III-R specifies the criteria for rendering a diagnosis much more clearly than DSM-II, and in much greater detail. By specifying its criteria and including such measures as age of onset of the disorder and the number of symptoms required for each diagnosis, DSM-III-R eliminates much of the guesswork and ambiguity that plagued earlier versions of DSM. Whether such criteria are better able to distinguish disorders—to provide greater validity—remains to be determined. We should note, however, that improved reliability is one prerequisite for improved validity.

An Alternative Approach: Behavioral Classification

Some alternatives to the traditional (DSM) classification and diagnostic procedures have gained support; the most developed ones are behavioral. Behavioral approaches tend to examine the interactions between a person's behaviors and situation (Phares, 1984). In their classification scheme, Goldfried and Davison (1976) categorize deviant behaviors according to the variables that are maintaining these behaviors (see Table 4.2). They use five categories to classify disorders. The first involves *stimulus control:* either (1) different stimuli do not produce different (and appropriate) behaviors, or (2) particular stimuli produce inappropriate behaviors. For example, a child may learn to be physically aggressive while playing football and then bring such behavior into the classroom. The change of stimuli (playing field to classroom) fails to change the child's behavior. Or a stimulus or situation, such as the classroom, may elicit a strong and inappropriate emotional response, such as fear.

The second category comprises deficiencies in the range of skills required for day-to-day living. When one or more of these skills are lacking in an individual, he or she is said to exhibit a "deficient behavioral repertoire."

The third category involves *aversive behaviors—* those that are unpleasant, irritating, or harmful to others.

Difficulties with *incentive systems*, or reinforcers for appropriate behavior, are included in the fourth category. As Table 4.2 indicates, these difficulties are of four types: the reinforcers may be defective or weak, they may themselves be inappropriate, some reinforcers may be missing, or various reinforcers may conflict with each other.

Finally, the fifth category involves *aversive self-reinforcement* or the absence of positive reinforcement. People who have unrealistically high standards of behavior, for instance, may be very critical of their own performance. As a result, they may fail to appreciate their accomplishments and become depressed or feel inadequate.

Obviously, an individual may manifest problems that can be classified in several of these categories. Nevertheless, because this system emphasizes the variables that maintain behavioral patterns, it lets the therapist isolate those variables for treatment purposes (Goldfried & Davison, 1976).

Evidence shows that the behavioral classification approach is superior to DSM in reliability and validity (Bellack & Hersen, 1980). However, many clinicians and therapists prefer a psychodynamic (rather than a purely behavioral) approach to mental disorder and thus to assessment and classification as well.

Objections to Classification

Diagnostic classification has been criticized on the grounds that it fosters belief in an erroneous all-or-nothing quality of psychopathology. As we noted in Chapter 1, behaviors lie on a spectrum from normality to abnormality. To place a diagnostic label on someone categorizes that person as "abnormal" and im-

TABLE 4.2 | A Behavioral Approach to Classification

I. Difficulties in Stimulus Control of Behavior

Environmental stimuli may fail to control maladaptive instrumental behavior or some stimuli may elicit maladaptive emotional reactions.

    A. Defective stimulus control. The individual possesses an adequate behavioral repertoire but is unable to respond to socially appropriate discriminative stimuli.

    B. Inappropriate stimulus control. The individual has intensive aversive emotional reactions that are elicited by objectively innocuous cues.

II. Deficient Behavioral Repertoires

The individual lacks social skills needed to effectively cope with situational demands.

III. Aversive Behavioral Repertoires

Maladaptive behavior patterns that are aversive to other people are included here.

IV. Difficulties with Incentive Systems (reinforcers)

Deviant behaviors that are functionally tied to reinforcing consequences would be placed in this category.

    A. Defective incentive system in individual. The person's behavior is not under the control of social stimuli that are reinforcing to most people.

    B. Inappropriate incentive system in the individual. This category includes individuals for whom the incentive system itself is maladaptive. Those things reinforcing are harmful and/or culturally disapproved.

    C. Absence of incentives in environment. The person's environment is lacking in reinforcement.

    D. Conflicting incentives in environment. In this category are maladaptive behavior patterns stemming from conflicting environmental consequences.

V. Aversive Self-Reinforcing Systems

It is assumed that cognitive processes can maintain behavior so that the presence or absence of self-reinforcement influences behaviors and emotions.

SOURCE: Goldfreid & Davison, 1976.

plies that he or she is qualitatively different from normal. Many psychologists now perceive that, for many disorders, the differences between normal and abnormal are differences of degree, not of kind (Persons, 1986).

In Chapter 1, we also touched on two problems that can arise when a diagnosis becomes a label. Here are three more:

1. *A label can cause people to interpret all activities of the affected individual as pathological.* A young psychology intern, training in the psychiatric ward of a VA hospital, talked very openly about his feelings of inadequacy. Most people have such feelings, but his openness gave him the reputation of being anxious. On the basis of this prejudgment and label, his supervisor became concerned about the young intern's competence and watched him very closely. One of the supervisor's chief complaints about the intern was that his anxiety prevented him from acquiring sufficient information during interviews with patients. Frustrated by his inability to shake this impression from the supervisor's mind, the intern took copious notes on all his patients. When he was next scheduled to present a case to his supervisor, the young intern prepared thoroughly and memorized details of the patient's life. He displayed a remarkable knowledge of the patient's life history to his supervisor that day, but the supervisor's response was not at all what he expected. The supervisor felt that the intern's anxiety had caused him to become so compulsive in obtaining information from patients that he was not listening to their feelings! Thus a label can predispose the observer to distort even contradictory evidence to fit into the frame of reference suggested by the label.

2. *A label may lead others to treat a person differently even when he or she is perfectly normal.* A study by Rosenthal and Jacobson (1968) has shown

FOCUS 4.3 — Sanity or Insanity: The Consequences of Labeling?

Can sane people be diagnosed as disturbed? To find out, psychologist D. L. Rosenhan (1973) sent eight experimenters as pseudopatients to different psychiatric hospitals. Their assignment was first to simulate psychiatric symptoms so as to gain admission into psychiatric wards and, once there, to behave in a normal manner. Rosenhan wanted the pseudopatients to record their experiences as patients without hospital staff members becoming aware of the experiment.

Several interesting and provocative findings emerged. First, no one on the ward staff in the hospitals ever detected the fact that the pseudopatients were normal—despite the fact that many *patients* suspected the pseudopatients were not crazy but were merely "checking up on the hospital." In fact, the pseudopatients' length of hospitalization ranged from seven to fifty-two days. Second, nearly all the pseudopatients were initially diagnosed as schizophrenic. And many of their normal behaviors on the ward were subsequently interpreted as manifestations of schizophrenia; one example was "excessive note taking." Third, the staff failed to interact much with patients, who were treated as powerless, irresponsible individuals.

Rosenhan concludes that it is difficult to distinguish the sane from the insane in mental hospitals, that the labels applied to patients often outlive their usefulness, and that the hospital environment is harsh and frequently maintains maladaptive behaviors. His study has generated a great deal of controversy (Millon, 1975; Weiner, 1975). One critic argues that, because patients did report abnormal symptoms at the time of hospital admission, it is understandable that they were hospitalized (Spitzer, 1975). And, although the pseudopatients were not detected by the staff, they were all released within sixty days. All were said to be "in remission."

---

how responses to a label can cause differential treatment. They randomly assigned schoolchildren to either of two groups. Teachers were told that tests of one group indicated that they were potential intellectual "bloomers" (gaining in competence and maturity); the other group was not given this label. After a one-year interval, children from both groups were retested (they had also been tested the year before). Children identified as bloomers showed dramatic gains in IQ. How did this occur? Many have speculated that the label led teachers to have higher intellectual expectations for the "bloomers" and thus to treat them differently. Even though there was no significant difference in IQ between the two groups to begin with, differences *were* present by the end of the year. The Rosenthal and Jacobson study has been criticized on the basis of its methodology and statistical analysis. Nevertheless, other studies have yielded similar results (Rappaport & Cleary, 1980).

3. *A label may lead those who are labeled to believe that they do indeed possess such characteristics. In these cases, the label becomes a self-fulfilling prophecy.* In the Rosenthal and Jacobson study just cited, the label not only caused teachers to behave differently but also affected the children. It is possible that when people are constantly told by others that they are stupid or smart, they may come to believe such labels. For example, if people ascribe certain stereotypical traits to a racial minority or an ethnic group, then it is reasonable to believe that they will behave differently toward that group and cause cognitive and behavioral changes among members of that group. Rosenhan (1973) has shown how people labeled mentally ill can become trapped by this label. Rosenhan's most renowned research study is discussed in Focus 4.3. Another case of labeling is presented in the First Person narrative. The narrative raises the question of what would have happened to a boy's self-image had the initial labels of his adjustment persisted.

THE ASSESSMENT OF ABNORMAL BEHAVIOR

Assessment is the process of gathering information and drawing conclusions about the traits, skills,

Eddy Regnier

FIRST PERSON

Early in my training, when I was learning about psychological assessment tools, diagnostic criteria, and nomenclature, I became aware of the limitations of methodology. This discovery occurred because of a case I had as a graduate student. During my graduate training, I worked with a ten-year-old boy who as an infant and a child had been through the most horrendous experiences. He had, perhaps for years, been sexually assaulted by his father in a dark, confined space. Furthermore, he had watched an older sibling being similarly abused.

I met Steven (not his real name) after he had been hospitalized for a year. When I was assigned to be his primary therapist, he had already undergone a variety of psychological tests that included behavioral observations, intelligence tests and projectives, such as the Rorschach, Thematic Apperception, and Harris-Goodenough Draw-A-Person tests. The results of these tests suggested that Steven was intellectually below average and functioning emotionally in the pervasive developmental disorder range, which is characterized by impaired social interactions and communication skills.

My supervisors cautioned me against getting too attached to Steven, probably because they thought he was unlikely to ever improve. He had not shown any social response during the year he had been hospitalized, and held himself aloof from everyday affairs. Although he ate and slept, he refused all overtures of friendship by the staff and the other boys on the ward. Their attempts to involve him in games and activities actually seemed to frighten him. He had an odd quality about him, and drove most people away.

At our first meeting, I was immediately drawn to his eyes. They had the distant, faraway expression of a person who had been in hell. I believe he thought that at any moment he would be returned to the fiendish world he had come from. My first goal was to reevaluate his intellectual and emotional functioning. But I didn't know how to engage him sufficiently to get a true sample of his abilities. Usually a psychologist has only a limited amount of time to complete such an evaluation. In this instance, because I was a student and also seeing Steven for therapy, that time was extended.

I thought how frightening it must be for a baby to be born into a violent world of bright lights, sensations, and rapid change and wondered whether it was equally difficult for Steven to re-engage our world. I spent as much time with him as I could, and slowly he began to trust me. As he opened up to me, we started to communicate through a game we developed, which can be described as "Draw what you are feeling." This game involved his drawing a picture, usually a family scene; I would then try to guess what was happening in it. To shape his drawings to more closely approximate the themes (sexual and physical abuse) I thought he was trying to convey, I made wild guesses about what was going on in his pictures to encourage him to reveal much more of what he had experienced. Responding to my incorrect guesses, Steven added more detail to his pictures, thus clarifying his experiences. I was eventually able to complete an evaluation using standard psychological tools, and discovered that Steven had above-normal intellectual functioning.

By today's standards, Steven would have been diagnosed as posttraumatic stress disordered, because his traumatic experiences were so far outside the range of usual human experience. A person experiencing such traumatic events may show such symptoms as depression and anxiety, poor social interactions, and somatic changes. So it isn't hard to understand how Steven could have been misdiagnosed.

Once Steven was correctly diagnosed and given appropriate therapy, he began to get better. I have watched him grow from a terrified little boy into a wonderful, bright adolescent. He's lost that sad look in his eyes, and I'm grateful that I've had the chance to play a small part in his development.

Dr. Eddy Regnier is director of the day treatment program at the Fuller Mental Health Center in Boston, Massachusetts.

abilities, emotional functioning, and psychological problems of the individual, generally for use in developing a diagnosis. Assessment tools are necessary to the study and practice of mental health. Without them, data could not be collected, and psychologists could not conduct meaningful research, develop theories, or engage in psychotherapy. Data collection necessarily involves the use of tools to systematically record the observations, behaviors, or self-reports of individuals. Four principal means of assessment are available to clinicians: observations, interviews, psychological tests, and neurological tests.

Observations

Observations of overt behavior provide the most basic method of assessing abnormal behavior; indeed, observation is the most basic tool in all of science. Research methods are examined in Chapter 5; we concentrate here on clinical observations. These can be either controlled or naturalistic. *Controlled* observations are made in a laboratory, clinic, or other contrived setting. *Naturalistic* observations, which are much more characteristic of the clinician's work, are made in a natural setting—a schoolroom, an office, a hospital ward, or a home—rather than in a laboratory.

Observations of behavior are usually made in conjunction with an interview, although verbal interaction is not necessary. A trained clinical psychologist watches for external signs or cues and expressive behaviors that may have diagnostic significance (Kleinmuntz, 1967). The client's general mode of dress (neat, conventional, sloppy, flashy), significant scars or tattoos, and even the type of jewelry worn may be correlated with personality traits or perhaps with pathology. Likewise, people's expressive behaviors, such as body posture, facial expression, body type, language and verbal patterns, handwriting, and self-expression through graphic art, may all reveal certain characteristics of their lives. Here is an example:

> Margaret is a 37-year-old depressive patient who was seen by one of the authors in a hospital psychiatric ward. She had recently been admitted for treatment.
>
> It was obvious from even a casual glance that Margaret had not taken care of herself for weeks. Her

face and hands were dirty. Her long hair, which had originally been done up in a bun, had shaken partially loose on one side of her head and now hung down her left shoulder. Her beat-up tennis shoes were only halfway on her stockingless feet. Her unkempt and disheveled appearance and her stooped body posture would lead one to believe she was much older than her actual age.

> When first interviewed, she sat as though she did not have the strength to straighten her body. She avoided eye contact with the interviewer and stared at the floor. When asked questions, she usually responded in short phrases: "Yes," "No," "I don't know," "I don't care." There were long pauses between the questions and her answers. Each response seemingly took great effort on her part.

Some psychologists rely on trained raters, or on parents, teachers, or other third parties, to make the observations and gather information for assessment and evaluation. Others prefer their own observations to those of a third party. In observational strategies, two problems may occur (Sundberg et al., 1983). First, observers must check the validity of their own interpretations of the patient's behaviors. This is particularly important when the patient is from a culture different from that of the observer. Second, if the patient is aware of being observed, he or she may behave differently, a phenomenon called **reactivity**. Observers must try to minimize the impact of their observations on the patient's behaviors.

Interviews

The clinical interview is a time-honored tradition as a means of psychological assessment. It provides the opportunity for observation of the subject as well as for collection of data about the person's life situation and personality. Verbal and nonverbal behaviors, as well as the content (what the client is saying) and process (how the client is communicating; for example, with anxiety, hesitation, or anger) of communications are important to analyze (Reiser, 1988).

Depending on the particular disciplinary training of the interviewer, the frame of reference for the interview and its emphasis may vary considerably. (This variability has been a source of inconsistency and error in the assessment of clients.) Psychiatrists, being trained in medicine, may be much more interested in biological or physical variables. Social workers may be more concerned with life history data and the socioeconomic environment of the client. Clinical psychologists may be most interested in establishing rapport with clients as a form of therapy.

Likewise, variations within the discipline of psychology affect the interview. Because of their strong belief in the unconscious origin of behavior, psychoanalysts may be more interested in psychodynamic processes than in the surface content of the client's words. They are also more likely to pay particular attention to life history variables and dreams. Behaviorists are more likely to concentrate on current environmental conditions as related to the client's behavior. However, it should be noted that, in practice, different mental health practitioners can also exhibit a great deal of similarity in style.

Standardization Interviews vary in the degree to which they are structured and consistently conducted in the same manner. In some, the patient is given considerable freedom about what to say and when to say it. The clinician does little to interfere with conversation or direct its flow. Psychoanalysts, who use free association, and Rogerians, who carry on nondirective therapy, tend to conduct highly unstructured interviews. Behaviorists tend to use more structured interviews.

The most highly structured interview is the formal standardized interview. The questions are usually arranged as a checklist, complete with scales for rating answers. The interviewer uses the checklist to ask the same set of questions of each interviewee, so that errors are minimized.

Errors In the field of mental health, straightforward questions do not always yield usable or accurate information. Believing personal information to be private, patients may refuse to reveal it, may distort it, or may lie about themselves. Furthermore, many patients may not be able to articulate their inner thoughts and feelings. The interview should therefore be considered a measurement device that is fallible and subject to error (Wiens, 1983).

Three sources of interviewing errors were summarized by Kleinmuntz (1967). One is the interview process itself and the relationship between the interviewer and interviewee. If either the client or the clinician does not respect the other, or if one or the

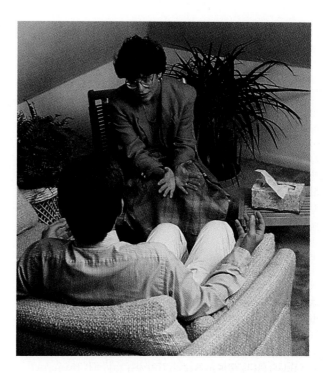

During the clinical interview the therapist can observe and gather information about the client. Moreover, the client can use the interview to gather important information about the therapist, such as his or her training, theoretical orientation, licensure status, and overall manner and style.

other is not feeling well, information exchange may be blocked. A second source of error may be intense anxiety or preoccupation on the part of the interviewee; his or her revelations may be inconsistent or inaccurate. Third, the interviewer may be a source of error. A clinician's unique style, degree of experience, and theoretical orientation definitely will affect the interview.

Psychological Tests

Psychological tests have been used to assess maladaptive behavior, development of social skills, intellectual abilities, vocational interests, and brain damage. Tests have also been constructed for the purpose of understanding personality dynamics and conflicts. They vary in form (that is, they may be oral or written and may be administered to groups or to individuals), structure, degree of objectivity, and content. Most do, however, share two characteristics: First, they provide a standard situation in which certain kinds of responses are elicited. The same instructions are given to all who take the same test, the same scoring is applied, and similar environmental conditions are maintained to ensure that the responses of each test taker are due to his or her unique attributes rather than due to differences in situations. Second, by comparing them with norms, the therapist uses these responses to make inferences about the underlying traits of the person. For instance, a person who answers yes to questions such as "Is someone trying to control your mind?" more frequently than most other people answer yes might be assumed to be responding in a manner similar to diagnosed paranoids.

In the remainder of this section, we examine two different types of personality tests (projective and objective) and tests of intelligence and brain damage.

Projective Personality Tests A **projective personality test** is one in which the test taker is presented with ambiguous stimuli, such as inkblots, pictures, or incomplete sentences, and is asked to respond to them. The stimuli are generally novel, and the test is relatively unstructured. Conventional or stereotyped patterns of response usually do not fit the stimuli. The person must "project" his or her attitudes, motives, and other personality characteristics into the situation. The nature of the appraisal is generally well disguised: subjects are often unaware of the true nature or purpose of the test and usually do not recognize the significance of their responses.

No matter which form of test is used, the goal of projective testing is to get a multifaceted view of the total functioning person, rather than a view of a single facet or dimension of personality. We shall concentrate on inkblot descriptions and storytelling because they are both popular and typical of projective tests.

The **Rorschach technique** was devised by Swiss psychiatrist Hermann Rorschach in 1921 for personality appraisal. A Rorschach test consists of ten cards displaying symmetrical inkblot designs. The cards are presented one at a time to subjects, who are asked (1) what they see in the blots and (2) what characteristics of the blots make them see that. Inkblots are considered appropriate stimuli because they are ambiguous, are nonthreatening, and do not elicit learned responses.

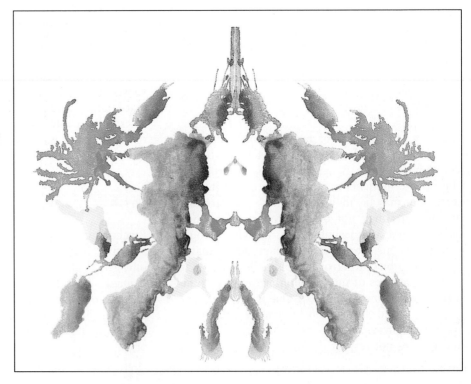

The Rorschach technique uses a number of cards, with each showing a symmetrical inkblot design. The earlier cards in the set are black and white, while the later cards are more colorful. A client's responses to the inkblots are interpreted according to assessment guidelines and can be compared by the therapist to the responses that other clients have made.

What people see in the blots, whether they focus on large areas or details, whether they respond to color, and whether their perceptions suggest movement are assumed to be symbolic of inner promptings, motivations, and conflicts. Subjects react in a personal and "unlearned" fashion, because there are no right or wrong answers. These reactions are interpreted by the psychologist. Both the basic premise of the Rorschach test and the psychologist's interpretation of the symbolism within the patient's responses are strongly psychoanalytic. For example, seeing eyes or buttocks may imply paranoid tendencies; fierce animals imply aggressive tendencies; blood, strong uncontrolled emotions; food, dependency needs; and masks, avoidance of personal exposure (Klopfer & Davidson, 1962).

There are actually a variety of approaches to the interpretation and scoring of Rorschach responses. The most extensive and recent is that of Exner (1983), whose scoring system is based on reviews of research findings and studies of the Rorschach technique. Exner thinks of the Rorschach as a problem-solving task; test takers are presented with ambiguous stimuli that they interpret according to their preferred mode of perceptual-cognitive processing. Because it relies on research findings and develops of normative data, Exner's system will most likely become standard for scoring the Rorschach (Weiss, 1988).

The **Thematic Apperception Test** (TAT) was first developed by Henry Murray in 1935 (Murray & Morgan, 1938). Like the Rorschach, the TAT taps underlying motives, drives, and personality processes through projection. However, most clinicians agree that the TAT is best at uncovering aspects of interpersonal relationships. It consists of thirty picture cards, each typically depicting two human figures. Their poses and actions are vague and ambiguous enough to be open to different interpretations. Some cards are designated for specific age levels or for a single sex, and some are appropriate for all groups.

Generally, twenty TAT cards are shown to the subject, one at a time, with instructions to tell a story about each picture. Typically, the tester says, "I am going to show you some pictures. Tell me a story about what is going on in each one, what led up to it, and what its outcome will be." The entire story is recorded verbatim. There is usually no limit on time or the length of the stories.

The subject's responses are interpreted by a trained clinician, either subjectively or by using a

In the Thematic Apperception Test, clients tell a story about each of a series of pictures they are shown. These pictures—often depicting one, two, or three people doing something—are less ambiguous than Rorschach inkblots.

formal scoring system. Both usually take into account the style of the story (length, organization, and so on); recurring themes, such as retribution, failure, parental domination, aggression, and sexual concerns; the outcome of the story in relationship to the plot; primary and secondary identification (the choice of hero or secondary person of importance); and the handling of authority figures and sex relationships. The purpose is to gain insight into the subject's conflicts and worries as well as clues about his or her core personality structure.

Other types of projective tests are briefly described in Focus 4.4.

The analysis and interpretation of responses to projective tests are subject to wide variation. Clinicians given the same data frequently disagree with one another about scoring. Much of this disparity is due to the fact that clinicians differ in orientation, skills, and personal style. But, as noted earlier, the demonstrably low reliability and validity of these instruments means that they should be used with caution and in conjunction with other assessment measures (Weiss, 1988). And even when projective tests exhibit reliability, they may still have low validity. For example, many clinicians may agree that certain specific responses to the Rorschach inkblots indicate repressed anger. The fact that many clinicians agree makes the test reliable, but those specific responses could indicate something other than repressed anger. Some have warned that illusory correlations may exist and that clinicians may erroneously link a patient's response to the existence of a syndrome (Chapman & Chapman, 1967).

Objective Personality Inventories　Unlike projective tests, **objective personality tests** supply the test taker with a list of alternatives from which an answer is selected. The "questions" are usually self-descriptive statements with which subjects are asked to either agree or disagree. Because a predetermined score is assigned to each possible answer, human judgmental factors in scoring and interpretation are minimized. In addition, subjects' responses and scores can be compared readily.

Perhaps the most widely used personality inventory is the **Minnesota Multiphasic Personality Inventory,** or MMPI (Hathaway & McKinley, 1943). This test consists of 566 statements; subjects are asked to indicate whether each statement is true or false as it applies to them. There is also a "cannot say" alternative, but using this category is strongly discouraged because too many such responses can invalidate the test.

The test taker's MMPI results are rated on ten clinical scales and three validity scales. The clinical scales were constructed by analyzing the responses of different types of diagnosed psychiatric patients (and the responses of normal subjects) to the 566 test items to determine what kinds of responses each of the various types of psychiatric patients usually made. Table 4.3 shows the possible responses to ten sample items and the kinds of responses that contribute to a high rating on each scale. The validity scales assess the degree of candor, confusion, and falsification. They help the clinician detect potential faking or special circumstances that may affect the outcome of other scales.

A basic assumption of the MMPI is that people whose MMPI answers are similar to those of diagnosed patients are likely to behave similarly to those patients. However, single-scale interpretations are fraught with hazards. Although a person with a high rating on Scale 6 may be labeled paranoid, many

TABLE 4.3 | **The Ten MMPI Clinical Scales and Sample MMPI Test Items** The answers shown on the grid contribute to high ratings on the related clinical scales. Item 9 illustrates a male's response.

Ten MMPI Clinical Scales with Simplified Descriptions	Sample Items									
	I like mechanics magazines.	I have a good appetite.	I wake up fresh and rested most mornings.	I think I would like the work of a librarian.	I am easily awakened by noise.	I like to read newspaper articles on crime.	My hands and feet are usually warm.	My daily life is full of things that keep me interested.	I am about as able to work as I ever was.	There seems to be a lump in my throat much of the time.
1. Hypochondriasis (Hs)—Individuals showing excessive worry about health with reports of obscure pains.		NO	NO					NO	NO	
2. Depression (D)—People suffering from chronic depression, feelings of uselessness, and inability to face the future.		NO			YES			NO	NO	
3. Hysteria (Hy)—Individuals who react to stress by developing physical symptoms (paralysis, cramps, headaches, etc.)		NO	NO			NO	NO	NO	NO	YES
4. Psychopathic Deviate (Pd)—People who show irresponsibility, disregard social conventions, and lack deep emotional responses.								NO		
5. Paranoia (Pa)—People who are suspicious, sensitive, and feel persecuted.										
6. Psychasthenia (Pt)—People troubled with fears (phobias) and compulsive tendencies.							NO	NO		YES
7. Schizophrenia (Sc)—People with bizarre and unusual thoughts or behavior.								NO		
8. Hypomania (Ma)—People who are physically and mentally overactive and who shift rapidly in ideas and actions.										
9. Masculinity-Femininity (Mf)—People tending to identify with the opposite sex rather than their own.	NO			YES						
10. Social Introversion (Si)—People who tend to withdraw from social contacts and responsibilities.										

SOURCE: Summarized from Dahlstrom & Welsh, 1965.

"paranoids" are not detected by this scale. Interpretation of the MMPI scales can be quite complicated and requires special training. Generally, multiple-scale interpretations (pattern analysis) and characteristics associated with the patterns are examined. The MMPI should be used by clinicians who have mastered its intricacies and who understand relevant statistical concepts (Newmark, 1985).

A number of criticisms have been leveled against personality inventories:

1. The fixed number of alternatives offered to subjects can limit them in presenting a true picture of themselves. Being asked to answer true or false to the statement "I am suspicious of people" does not permit an individual to qualify the item in any way.

2. Although some personality tests are devised to measure "normal" psychological traits, most clinicians tend to be most alert to responses that may signal pathology. Thus the best the subject can do is avoid a "bad" score.

3. Many individuals are able to fake their scores in a direction they see as desirable (for example, to secure a psychiatric discharge from the army or to get a job). Even the MMPI, which has controls to detect faking, can sometimes be "psyched out."

4. A subject's unique response style may distort the results. For example, many people have a pressing need to present themselves in a favorable light, and this may cause them to give answers that are socially acceptable but inaccurate.

5. Interpretations of responses of people from different cultural groups may not be accurate if norms for these groups have not been developed.

Despite these objections, personality inventories are used widely. Some, like the MMPI, have been extensively researched and their validity in many cases has been established. In general, inventories are easier to administer than projective tests, are inexpensive, and can be scored without much difficulty. (In fact, some inventories are now scored and interpreted by computer.) These features make the use of objective personality inventories desirable, especially in the busy clinic or hospital environment.

Moreover, although progress has been agonizingly slow, the predictive ability and validity of personality assessment have been improved. **Psychometrics**—the techniques used in making mental measurements—are becoming increasingly sophisticated. Further refinement will be achieved when situational variables that help determine behaviors can be taken into account and when fluctuations in mood and other more stable personality processes can be measured.

Intelligence Tests Intelligence testing has two primary diagnostic functions and one secondary function. First, it is used to obtain an estimate of a person's current level of cognitive functioning, called the **intelligence quotient** (IQ). An IQ indicates an individual's level of performance relative to the performance level of others of the same age. As such, it is a significant aid in predicting school performance and detecting mental retardation. (Through statistical procedures, IQ test results are converted into numbers such that 100 is the mean, or average, score. An IQ score of about 130 indicates performance exceeding that of 95 percent of all same-aged peers.) Second, intelligence testing is used to assess intellectual deterioration in organic or functional psychotic disorders. Third, an individually administered intelligence test may yield additional useful data for the clinician. The therapist may also find important observations of how the subject approached the task (systematic versus disorganized), handled failure (depression, frustration, or anger), and persisted (or gave up) in the task.

The two most widely used intelligence tests are the Wechsler scales (Wechsler, 1981) and the Stanford-Binet scales (Terman & Merrill, 1960). The **Wechsler Adult Intelligence Scale** (the WAIS and its revised version WAIS-R) is limited to ages sixteen and older, though two other forms are appropriate for ages six to sixteen (WISC-R) and four to six (WPPSI). The WAIS-R consists of six verbal and five performance scales, which yield verbal and performance IQ scores. These scores are combined to present a total IQ score. (Table 4.4 shows subtest items similar to those used in the WAIS-R.)

The **Stanford-Binet Scale** is used for people ages two and older. Much more complicated in administration and scoring, and not standardized on an adult population, the Stanford-Binet requires considerable skill in its use. The test procedure is designed to establish a basal age (the subject passes all subtests for that age) and a ceiling age (the subject fails all subtests for that age), from which an IQ is calculated. In general, the WISC-R is preferred over the Stanford-Binet for school-age children (LaGreca & Stringer, 1985). It is easier to administer, and yields scores on different cognitive skills (such as verbal and performance subtests).

IQ testing (and some other standardized testing) has come under attack by many ethnic groups. There are three major issues. First, some investigators believe that IQ tests have been popularized as a means of measuring innate intelligence, when in truth the tests largely reflect cultural and social factors (Garcia, 1981; Williams, 1974). In that case, the tests may bestow an unfair advantage on members of the groups whose culture they reflect. Second, and related to the first point, is the issue of the predictive validity of IQ tests. That is, do IQ test scores accurately predict the future behaviors or achievements of different cultural groups? Proponents and critics disagree on this point (Anastasi, 1982). Third, there has been disagreement over criterion variables (in essence, what is actually being predicted by IQ tests). For example, two investigators may be interested in the ability of IQ tests to predict future success. The first may try to find a correlation between test scores and grades subsequently received in school. The second investigator may argue that grades are a poor indicator of success—that leadership skills and ability to work with people are better indicators of success.

One finding is clear: reliance on IQ scores has resulted in discriminatory actions. In California, for example, black children were disproportionately assigned to classes for the educable mentally retarded on the basis of IQ results. Mercer (1979) has argued that all cultural groups have the same average intellectual potential. On a given IQ test, members of a cultural minority may score low, not because of mental retardation, but because they are less familiar with the tasks required on such tests. She has developed the System of Multicultural Pluralistic Assessment, through which performance on the WISC-R is assessed in relation to that of groups with similar social and cultural backgrounds. In other words, a person is compared with others who have similar backgrounds, rather than with others from different backgrounds. This assessment procedure results in fewer children who represent ethnic minorities being assigned to classes for the mentally retarded.

Intelligence tests provide valuable information about intellectual functioning and can help psychologists to assess mental retardation and intellectual deterioration. Although many of these tests have been severely criticized as being culturally biased, they can be beneficial tools, if used appropriately.

The Kaufman Assessment Battery for Children (K-ABC) An increasingly popular means of evaluating the intelligence and achievement of children aged two and one-half to twelve and one-half years is the Kaufman Assessment Battery for Children (K-ABC). Based on theories of mental processing developed by neuropsychologists and cognitive psychologists, the K-ABC is intended for use with both the general population and special populations. For example, the assessment battery has been employed with children who have hearing or speech impairments and who have learning disabilities. However, because of its reliance on visual stimuli, the K-ABC is unsuitable for the visually impaired (Kaufman et al., 1985).

TABLE 4.4 | Simulated Items for the Wechsler Adult Intelligence Scale—Revised (WAIS—R)

Information

1. How many nickels make a dime?
2. What is steam made of?
3. What is pepper?

Comprehension

1. Why do some people save sales receipts?
2. Why is copper often used in electrical wire?

Arithmetic (all calculated "in the head")

1. Sue had 2 pieces of candy and Joe gave her 4 more. How many pieces of candy did Sue have altogether?
2. If 2 pencils cost 15¢, how much will a dozen pencils cost?

Similarities

In what way are the following alike?

1. lion/tiger
2. saw/hammer
3. circle/square

Vocabulary

What is the meaning of the following words?

1. chair
2. mountain
3. guilt
4. building
5. foreboding
6. prevaricate
7. plethora

SOURCE: Wechsler Adult Intelligence Scale—Revised. Copyright © 1981, 1955 by The Psychological Corporation. Reproduced by permission. All rights reserved.

The K-ABC can also be used with exceptional children and members of ethnic minority groups. Its applicability to diverse groups has been attributed to measures that (1) are less culturally dependent than those found on traditional tests and (2) focus on the process used to solve problems rather than on the specific content of test items. Verbal performance and nonverbal performance are assessed, and children are administered a wide variety of tasks, such as copying a sequence of hand movements performed by the examiner, recalling numbers, assembling triangles to match a model, and demonstrating reading comprehension. For certain language-disordered children or those who do not speak English, nonverbal performance can be used to estimate intellectual functioning.

A Spanish-language version of the K-ABC is available, and norms for Black and Hispanic children have been developed. Interestingly, differences in performance between white and ethnic minority children are much lower on the K-ABC than on traditional IQ tests. Kaufman and Kaufman (1983) and Kaufman et al. (1985) report that the K-ABC has high reliability and validity. This approach offers promise in the effort to devise more culturally unbiased tests of intelligence. Further research on the K-ABC is needed in order to more fully assess its strengths and limitations.

Tests for Brain Damage Clinical psychologists, and especially those who work in a hospital setting, are concerned with the detection and assessment of damage to the central nervous system (**organicity**). Identifying organic brain damage can sometimes be aided by the use of individual intelligence tests such as the WAIS. Discrepancy between an individual's verbal and performance scores or the pattern of scores on the individual subtests often suggests possible organicity. For example, a difference of twenty points between verbal and performance scores indicates the possibility of brain damage. Subtests that measure verbal concept formation or abstracting ability (comparison and comprehension) can also reveal brain damage. Because impaired abstract thinking may be characteristic of organicity, a lower score on this scale (when accompanied by other signs) must be investigated.

One of the routine means of assessing organicity is the **Bender-Gestalt Visual-Motor Test,** shown in Figure 4.1, developed by Bender (1938). Nine geometric designs, each drawn in black on a piece of white cardboard, are presented one at a time to the subject, who is asked to copy them on a piece of paper. Certain errors in the copies are characteristic of neurological impairment. Among these are rotation of figures, perseveration (continuation of a pattern to an exceptional degree), fragmentation, oversimplification, inability to copy angles, and reversals.

The **Halstead-Reitan Neuropsychological Test Battery,** developed by Reitan from the earlier work of Halstead, has been used successfully in differentiating patients with brain damage from those without brain damage and in providing valuable information about the type and location of the damage (Boll, 1983). The full battery consists of eleven tests, although several are often omitted. Patients are presented with a series of tasks that assess sensorimotor, cognitive, and perceptual functioning, including abstract concept formation, memory and attention, and auditory perception. The full battery takes over 6 hours to administer, so it is a relatively expensive and time-consuming assessment tool.

A less costly test for organicity is the **Luria-Nebraska Neuropsychological Battery,** which requires about two and one-half hours to administer and is more standardized in content, administration, and scoring. Developed by Golden and his colleagues, this battery includes twelve scales that assess motor functions, rhythm, tactile functions, visual functions, receptive and expressive speech, memory, writing, intellectual processes, and other functions (Golden, 1981). Validation data indicate that the battery is highly successful in screening for brain damage and

quite accurate in pinpointing damaged areas (Anastasi, 1982). A children's version has been developed. Although the battery has been shown to differentiate brain-damaged from normal children, its ability to discriminate between different types of learning disabilities has been questioned (Morgan & Brown, 1988).

Neurological Tests

In addition to psychological tests, a variety of neurological medical procedures are available for diagnosing of brain damage. For example, brain x-rays can often detect tumors. A more sophisticated procedure, **computerized axial tomography (CAT scan),** involves the repeated scanning of different areas of the brain with beams of x-rays. With the assistance of a computer, a three-dimensional image of the structure of the brain emerges, and the results of the CAT scan provide a detailed view of brain deterioration or abnormality. More recently, **positron emission tomography (PET scan)** has been developed to study the physiological and biochemical processes of the brain, rather than the anatomical structures that result from the CAT scan. In PET scans, a radioactive substance is injected into the patient's bloodstream.

Figure 4.1 The Nine Bender Designs
The figures presented to subjects are shown on the left. The distorted figures drawn by subjects are possibly indicative of organicity (brain damage) and are shown on the right. SOURCE: The American Orthopsychiatric Association, 1938.

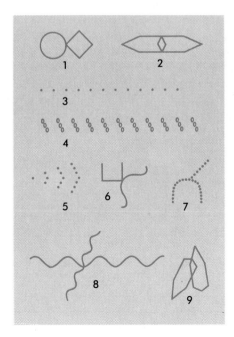 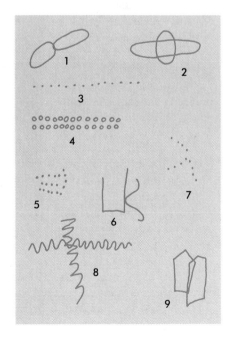

The scanner detects the substance as it is metabolized in the brain. Information can then be gained about brain functioning. A widely used examination involves the **electroencephalograph (EEG)**, in which electrodes are attached to the skull. The electrical activity (brain waves) is recorded from the electrodes, and abnormalities in the activity can provide information as to the presence of tumors or other brain conditions. Finally, in **magnetic resonance imaging (MRI)**, an amazingly clear "picture" of the brain and

Recent neurological tests have dramatically improved our ability to study the brain and to assess brain damage. In magnetic resonance imaging, radio waves are used to produce detailed pictures of a person's brain.

plaints of clients. Clients were given a computer interview in which various questions were presented. They were told to answer the questions by pressing the keyboard keys that corresponded to their feelings. Depending on their answers, additional questions were asked in order to refine their responses. Clients were also interviewed by practitioners and given psychological tests, so that the results of the computer interview could be compared with the results of more traditional forms of assessment. The researchers were encouraged by the results. There was a high agreement between both forms of assessment. Furthermore,

clients had little difficulty mastering the keyboard, and many found it easier to answer questions on the computer than to respond to interviewer questions. However, most preferred to see the clinician.

Although some studies have provided positive results, critics are concerned about the proliferation of computer assessment techniques and the scarceness of research to establish their validity (Matarazzo, 1986). Extensive computer assessment is not justified until concerns over validity, use and abuse of test results, and ethical issues such as privacy are addressed. Assessment is an intimate and important process

that often requires extensive training, flexibility, and human judgment that can be provided by trained clinicians. Individual differences between clients may not be fully appreciated by computer software. Also, popularizing computer assessment presents the risk that untrained individuals, or even clients themselves, may not be aware of the limits of this form of assessment, and may misinterpret the meaning of the findings. Clearly research into computer assessment should be strongly encouraged and computer applications should be guided by both research and consideration of social and ethical consequences.

---

its tissues are obtained. By creating a magnetic field around the patient and using radio waves, abnormalities in the brain can be detected. These neurological techniques, coupled with psychological tests, are increasing our diagnostic accuracy and understanding of brain functioning and disorders.

The Ethics of Assessment

In recent years, a strong antitesting movement has developed in America. Issues such as the confidentiality of client's records, invasion of privacy, client welfare, cultural bias, and unethical practices have increasingly been raised (Bersoff, 1981). In assessing and treating emotionally disturbed people, the clinical psychologist must often ask embarrassing questions or use tests that may be construed as invasions of privacy. In many cases, the clinician may not know beforehand whether the results of the tests will prove beneficial to the client. Yet to exclude testing because it may offend the client or place him or her in an uncomfortable position could ultimately deprive the client of its long-range benefits.

Some people strongly criticize tests on the grounds that they can have undesirable social consequences. They ask, "Who will use the test results, and for

what purpose is the test employed?" Test results may be used to the client's detriment in some instances. Tests may also be insufficiently accurate to avoid serious misdiagnosis and the consequences of misdiagnosis. Note the fears and concerns over the possible widespread use of tests to detect antibodies to the HIV virus (AIDS) and drug abuse, as well as the use of the polygraph in job settings.

Psychological testing has ethical, legal, and societal implications that go beyond the field of psychology. Psychologists should be aware of these implications and should guard against the misuse of test results. They should also carefully weigh the consequences of permitting such considerations to interfere with devising, improving, and applying tests that will benefit their patients. The mental health professions and the general public are increasingly aware of the need to guard against possible abuses and to continually refine and improve classification systems and assessment procedures.

As indicated in Focus 4.5, more sophisticated use of computers in the mental health professions may be likely in the near future (Sundberg et al., 1983). At least one clinician has predicted that assessment and psychological testing will be applied more and more broadly as computerization spreads (Cummings, 1984).

SUMMARY

1. The psychiatric classification manuals DSM-I and DSM-II were based to a large extent on the biogenic model of mental illness. They assumed that people classified in a psychodiagnostic category show similar symptoms that stem from a common etiology, should be treated in a certain manner, and have similar prognoses. Critics questioned the reliability and validity of DSM-I and -II. In the current version, DSM-III-R, detailed diagnostic criteria are given; as a result, its reliability appears to be higher than that of the previous manuals. Furthermore, data are collected on 5 axes so that much more information about the patient is systematically examined. General objections to classification are primarily based on the problems involved in labeling.

2. Clinicians primarily use three methods of assessment: observations, interviews, and psychological tests. Observations of external signs and expressive behaviors are often made during an interview and can have diagnostic significance. Interviews, the oldest form of psychological assessment, involve a face-to-face conversation after which the interviewer differentially weighs and interprets verbal information obtained from the interviewee. Psychological tests provide a more formalized means of obtaining information. Most testing situations have two characteristics in common. They provide a standard situation in which certain responses are elicited. And responses from subjects are measured and used to make inferences about underlying traits. In personality testing, projective techniques or personality inventories may be used. In the former, the stimuli are ambiguous; in the latter, the stimuli are much more structured. Two of the most widely used projective techniques are the Rorschach inkblot technique and the Thematic Apperception Test (TAT). Unlike projective tests, objective personality inventories, such as the Minnesota Multiphasic Personality Inventory (MMPI), supply the test taker with a list of alternatives from which to select an answer. Intelligence testing can be used to obtain an estimate of a person's current level of cognitive functioning and to assess intellectual deterioration. Behavioral observations of how a person takes the test are additional sources of information about personality attributes. The WAIS, Stanford-Binet, and Bender-Gestalt tests can be used to assess brain damage, as can various strictly neurological tests, such as those that use computer-generated analyses (for example, CAT and PET scans).

3. In addition to issues involving reliability and validity, a number of ethical questions have been raised about classifying and assessing people through tests. These include questions about confidentiality, privacy, and cultural bias. Concerned with these issues, psychologists have sought to improve classification and assessment procedures and to define the appropriate conditions for testing and diagnosis. In spite of the problems and criticisms, classification and assessment are necessary to psychological research and practice.

KEY TERMS

assessment With regard to psychopathology, the process of gathering information and drawing conclusions about the traits, skills, abilities, emotional functioning, and psychological problems of an individual

classification system With regard to psychopathology, a system of distinct categories, indicators, and nomenclature for different patterns of behavior, thought processes, and emotional disturbances

etiology The causes or origins of a disorder

objective personality test An inventory of personality attributes in which the test taker either agrees or disagrees with specific self-descriptive statements; administration, scoring, and interpretation are largely independent of the test giver's subjectivity

organicity Brain damage or deterioration

prognosis A prediction of the future course of an untreated disorder

projective personality test A personality assessment technique in which the test taker is presented with ambiguous stimuli and is asked to respond to them in some way

psychological test Any test instrument used to assess personality, maladaptive behavior, development of social skills, intellectual abilities, vocational interests, or brain damage

psychometrics Mental measurement, including its study and techniques

reliability The degree to which a procedure or test yields the same result repeatedly, under the same circumstances

reactivity A situation in which people who know they are being observed or assessed change the way they respond

validity The degree to which a procedure or test actually performs the function that it was designed to perform

chapter 5
The Scientific Method in Abnormal Psychology

Scientists who work in the field of abnormal psychology seek, as their primary goal, to understand abnormal behavior and to use that understanding to describe, explain, predict, and control such behavior. In this chapter, we are concerned with the means scientists use to add to their knowledge of psychopathology.

Historically, two approaches have been used. The first (and earliest) is called the "armchair approach." It consists of personally observing behavior and events, followed by drawing conclusions from these observations, on the basis of the observer's speculations.

The problem with this approach stems from the multitude of variables that are at work in any situation involving human behavior. The armchair researcher does not control any of these variables. Instead, he or she must decide, after the fact, which variable is primarily responsible for the observed behavior, and which variable is cause and which is effect. Those decisions are much influenced by the researcher's own experience, attitudes, and convictions; another researcher might well choose some other variable (or variables) as being paramount. Furthermore, it is extremely difficult—often impossible—to duplicate the observed situation and behavior exactly, with the result that the original observer's conclusions cannot easily be tested and either verified or shown to be erroneous.

Despite these problems, armchair speculation has been a useful means of generating hypotheses about abnormal behavior. (A **hypothesis** is a conjectural statement, usually describing a relationship between variables.) However, as we previously noted, armchair speculation does not provide a way of testing hypotheses.

The second approach has come to be called the **scientific method**; this method of inquiry provides for the systematic collection of data through controlled observation and for testing the hypotheses based on those data. The *systematic* and *controlled* collection of data ensures that situations and events (including experiments) are open to replication—that is, to repeated demonstration. The testing of hypotheses ensures against biased or subjective conclusions.

Of these two, the scientific approach is better for discovering the facts of and relationships in abnormal psychology. In fact, the remainder of this chapter is a discussion of the characteristics of the scientific method and its techniques, as applied to studying psychopathology. However, two points need to be emphasized before we move on to these topics.

The first point concerns the "purity" of the scientific method as we know it. This approach has been developed and refined over the years, by people who were—and people who are—influenced by the beliefs, values, and cultural forces of their times. In other words, the concept that has been accepted as "the scientific method" in each time and place has been partly determined by the values people held in that time and place (Sarason, 1984). Thus neither the scientific method as we now know it nor the results we achieve with that method should be viewed as perfect or ultimate (Bergin, 1980; Kilbourne & Richardson, 1984). As our values change, so do our constructs. What is more important is that we remain open to differing viewpoints and alternative realities and that we continue to improve our methodology and techniques.

The second point we want to emphasize concerns the substantial "nonscientific" component in the work of most practicing counselors and clinicians. Ideally, psychotherapy should be based on empirical knowledge, and its practitioners should be able to consult and make use of a full body of literature that reports scientifically conducted research. This state of affairs would allow the clinician to move beyond armchair

speculation and the trial-and-error application of techniques, to the integrated and rational application of principles. Unfortunately, the results provided by researchers have not yet caught up with our needs; moreover, much psychological research is not easily put into practice. So therapists must often rely on their own personal experiences, creativity, and convictions in treating clients—must, in fact, become armchair researchers.

CHARACTERISTICS OF THE SCIENTIFIC METHOD

Perhaps the unique and most general characteristic of scientific inquiry is its potential for self-correction. Under ideal conditions, data and conclusions are freely exchanged and experiments are replicable, so that all are subject to discussion, testing, verification, and modification. As a result, the knowledge that is developed is as free as possible from the scientist's personal beliefs, perceptions, biases, values, attitudes, and emotions.

Four additional, and more specific, characteristics of the scientific method have been identified: (1) the use of conceptual schemes and theoretical structures, (2) the testing of hypotheses and theories, (3) the control of extraneous variables, and (4) the avoidance of metaphysical explanations (Kerlinger, 1971). We shall examine each of these in turn.

Use of Conceptual Schemes and Theoretical Structures

At any given time, there is an existing body of knowledge (and beliefs) about each area of science. The bits of information that compose this knowledge are very much like the pieces of a jigsaw puzzle. Each bit or piece must be scrutinized to determine where it fits into the overall picture. In the case of a science, the "overall picture" is a *conceptual* scheme or framework—a broad, general explanation that organizes known facts and relationships. There may be more than one such conceptual scheme at any one time; for example, there are several viewpoints on the origins of abnormal behavior.

The conceptual scheme itself is sometimes called a *theory*. But more often a **theory** is a substructure consisting of a group of principles and hypotheses that together explain a particular aspect of the area of inquiry. Like the conceptual scheme, the theory is a means of organizing available information (generally, more detailed information). It also provides a framework for speculating on (and then verifying) the nature of yet-undiscovered facts and principles through the formulation (and then the testing) of hypotheses. And theory serves to provide direction for scientific research by pointing up existing gaps in current knowledge.

Testing of Theories and Hypotheses

Theories, then, are explanations, and hypotheses are specific conjectures that form part of those explanations. Examples of hypotheses are statements such as "Frustration leads to aggression" and "Electroconvulsive shock therapy reduces the symptoms of depression." Although most hypotheses focus on the existence of a relationship between variables, a *null hypothesis* states that the variables are unrelated. For example, if a researcher says that ECT does not affect depression, he or she is advancing a null hypothesis. A theory is tested when any of its hypotheses is tested; a theory is confirmed only when *all* of its hypotheses have been verified. Obviously, confirmation of a theory is difficult, and most theories are continually revised or replaced by better ones, in accordance with research findings.

Scientific testing can proceed only when the relationship expressed in a hypothesis is clearly and systematically stated and when the variables of concern are measurable. Suppose scientists are interested in testing the hypothesis that frustration leads to aggression. How can they measure the variables *frustration* and *aggression,* when each scientist may define these terms differently? In such cases, psychologists often resort to **operational definitions,** which describe concepts in terms of the operations used to measure them. For example, *aggression* may be operationalized as "the number of times the subject strikes a large inflated doll," and *frustration* may be

When conducting experiments, researchers often observe and record behavior. In some cases, they may sit behind a one-way mirror to note how a person performs a given task.

defined as "physically preventing the person from reaching a desirable goal."

Control of Extraneous Variables

The scientific method requires the systematic investigation of relationships, and that includes eliminating the possible effects of variables that are *not* under investigation. If scientists were interested in studying the relationship between alcoholism and hallucination, for example, they would certainly avoid including psychotic subjects, who might be hallucinating for reasons that have nothing to do with their alcoholic condition. Psychosis in subjects would introduce an *extraneous variable,* one that is not going to be tested or observed but that may affect the outcome of the study.

In psychological studies, an extraneous variable can be controlled in three ways. If possible, the variable is *eliminated* from the study (for example, by excluding psychotic subjects). Or the extraneous variable may be *randomized* (included randomly in all groups studied, so that its effects are canceled out). Finally, the extraneous variable may be *included* in the study for investigation as a second *variable*. In this case, the variable is no longer extraneous, because it is being investigated or tested. The important point is that such control provides reliability and enhances confidence in the results of a scientific investigation.

Avoidance of Untestable Metaphysical Explanations

Science does not involve itself with metaphysical or supernatural explanations because they cannot be tested. To say that we have become ill because of bad luck, that God is punishing poor people for their past sins, or that all human beings are evil is to make a metaphysical statement. Such explanations have been labeled *parascientific* (apart from, or outside, the realm of science), if they cannot be subjected to the scientific method. Belief in the occult, for example, rests on currently untestable private convictions. For parascientists, reality is based on a kind of evidence that is alien to science (McNeil, 1974).

Let us now examine the major techniques of scientific research.

EXPERIMENTS

The **experiment** is perhaps the best tool for testing cause-and-effect relationships. In its simplest form, the experiment involves

1. An **experimental hypothesis,** which is the prediction concerning how an independent variable affects a dependent variable in an experiment

2. An **independent variable** (the possible cause), which the experimenter manipulates so as to determine its effect on a dependent variable

3. A **dependent variable** that, according to the hypothesis, is somehow controlled by the independent variable

As we noted, the experimenter is also concerned with controlling extraneous variables.

Let us clarify these concepts with an example:

Melinda N. was a 19-year-old sophomore who sought help from a university psychology clinic for test anxiety. She indicated that she always became highly anxious before and during class examinations and felt that the anxiety interfered with her ability to perform. Melinda was so anxious that she could not concentrate on test questions, would feel inferior to classmates, and would waste a great deal of time by looking at her wrist watch, which made her feel even more anxious. The therapist felt that Melinda was intelligent but was unable to perform better because of irrational or exaggerated thoughts about her presumed inferiority and because of her self-preoccupation, which interfered with the ability to concentrate on the task. For five sessions, he conducted a treatment approach using a self-coping cognitive approach in which he tried to help Melinda to replace the self-preoccupation and exaggerated thoughts with more task-related thoughts and behaviors during examinations.

Is the self-coping cognitive treatment used by Melinda's therapist effective in helping students to overcome anxiety and poor test performance? Crowley et al. (1986) conducted an experiment to test the hypothesis that cognitive treatment is effective in lowering anxiety and in improving the examination performance of anxious students. They also wanted to test whether treatment was more effective when the treatment is administered for six hours on one day or for two hours a week over a three-week period.

To begin the experiment, the investigators had to identify test-anxious students. They administered the Achievement Anxiety Test (AAT), which measures the presence of anxiety that interferes with performance, to hundreds of students. Students who scored high on the AAT were considered to be test anxious and participated in the actual experiment. These students were then randomly assigned to an experimental group or the control group.

The Experimental Group

An *experimental group* is one that is subjected to the independent variable. In the study by Crowley and her colleagues, two experimental groups were created: one exposed to cognitive treatment for six hours on one day, and the other exposed for six hours distributed over a period of three weeks. Thus the experimental groups received the same treatment; however, the treatment was either a one-day intensive experience or a less intensive experience for a longer period of time. Treatment involved teaching the students to (1) identify their thoughts and worries about examinations, (2) separate truth from exaggerated concerns about their performance, and (3) replace irrational, non-task-related thoughts and behaviors with coping/task-related thoughts and behaviors.

Because the investigators were interested in how treatment affects level of anxiety and ability to perform in test situations, the *dependent variables* included two measures of anxiety and a problem-solving measure that assessed students' ability to perform on a multiple-choice test. These dependent measures were administered twice: *Pretesting* occurred before treatment, and *posttesting* occurred three weeks after pretesting, when treatment for both experimental groups was concluded. In this way, it was possible to evaluate how much improvement was made on the measures after treatment.

The Control Group

If students in the two experimental groups show a reduction of anxiety and improvement on the multiple-choice test from pre- to posttesting, can we conclude that cognitive treatment is an effective form of therapy? No. An alternative explanation is that students may have shown less anxiety and better performance at posttesting simply because they had been given the measures previously at pretesting. That is, the improvement may have been caused by familiarity with the measures. The use of a *control group* enables one to evaluate the validity of this alternative explanation.

A control group is a group that is similar in every way to the experimental group *except for* the manipulation of the independent variable. Crowley and her colleagues used a control group composed of highly anxious students, who, like the experimental groups, were administered pre- and posttests, but did not participate in the cognitive therapy sessions (the independent variable). Results indicated that both

experimental groups showed greater improvement in anxiety and test performance than did the control group. Therefore, the experiment confirmed the hypothesis that cognitive treatment is effective. Both experimental groups performed equally well, so there appeared to be no advantage to intensive versus distributed treatment sessions.

The Placebo Group

You should note that the results of the experiment on cognitive therapy may also be challenged for another reason. For example, what if the students in the treated, experimental groups improved not because of cognitive therapy per se but because they had faith or an expectancy that they would improve? Some researchers have found that if subjects expect to improve from treatment, this expectancy—rather than specific treatment—itself is responsible for the outcome.

One method to induce an expectancy in students without using the specific treatment is to have a *placebo control group*. For example, in the study on the effect of cognitive therapy on test anxiety, the experimenters could have told students in the placebo control group that they would receive an antianxiety drug that would help reduce their anxiety. In actuality, they would be given an inert drug or placebo (such as a sugar pill) that could have no chemical impact on their anxiety. If the cognitive therapy groups improved more than the placebo control group, then one can be more confident that therapy, rather than expectancy, was responsible for the results.

Extraneous Variables and Validity

In an experiment, the control group and the experimental group must be as similar as possible. This can be achieved by matching the characteristics of both groups. If Crowley and her colleagues had used males in their experimental groups and females in the control group, the experimenters would not know whether the results were due to differences in anxiety or differences between males and females. Or, if experimental group members were significantly younger than control group members, how would the experimenter know whether the results were due to the effects of age? These questions deal with the **internal validity** of the experiment, or the extent to which changes in the dependent variable (the variable being controlled by the independent variable) are actually brought about by the independent variable (the variable being manipulated). Achieving internal validity is essentially a problem of controlling extraneous variables (variables that are not going to be tested).

One of the best ways to control extraneous variables in an experiment is to randomly assign participants to the groups (Hersen & Bellack, 1984), as was done in the study by Crowley and her colleagues. Random assignment increases the chances that the groups are similar in all characteristics and that differences between the experimental and control groups are not caused by these characteristics. The **external validity** of an experiment is the generalizability or representativeness of the results it yields. To the extent that the results can be generalized to different populations, the experiment has external validity.

Quasi-Experimental Design

Sometimes it is not possible to randomly assign individuals to the experimental and control groups. In clinical settings, patients may be assigned to treatment or control conditions in accordance with clinic practices. In such situations, where researchers cannot exert the control possible in true experiments, a **quasi-experimental design**, which attempts to compensate for the lack of random assignment, is created. Because researchers can never be sure that the nonrandomly assigned patients in the experimental and control groups have similar characteristics, techniques must be used to discover if the groups differ in some important way and to eliminate the possibility that treatment effects are confounded with these differences. To make this determination, the two groups may be pretested on certain characteristics to see whether they are equivalent. For example, in the clinical setting, researchers may want to assess if the two groups initially differ in demographic characteristics or severity of disturbance. If the groups are similar in these variables, then these variables are unlikely to be confused with treatment effects. If the groups are dissimilar, an attempt must be made to take into consideration the possible influence of these

variables. Sometimes statistical procedures can be used to control for this influence.

So research is a complicated process, often requiring a series of systematic procedures to test hypotheses and alternative explanations.

CORRELATIONS

A **correlation** is a measure of the extent to which variations in one variable are accompanied by variations in a second variable. It is expressed as a statistically derived *correlation coefficient*, symbolized by the symbol r, which has a numerical value between -1 and $+1$.

The greater the value of r, positive *or* negative, the stronger the relationship. Thus the correlation expressed by $r = 0.88$ is much stronger than that expressed by $r = 0.15$. (The correlation expressed by $r = -0.88$ is also much stronger than that expressed by $r = 0.15$.) A correlation coefficient of $r = +1.00$ indicates a *perfect positive correlation* between two variables. We all know, for instance, that the taller people are, the more they are likely to weigh. If there were a perfect positive correlation between height and weight, then one of these variables could be predicted on the basis of the other, and the relationship between them would be expressed as $r = +1.00$. This does not happen to be the case, however; perfect correlations are rare in the field of abnormal psychology.

The absence of a relationship (or correlation) between two variables is signified by $r = 0$. For example, no relationship whatsoever has been found between the number of lumps on a person's head and that person's character traits; thus these two variables have a correlation coefficient of 0.

A negative correlation coefficient indicates an *inverse* relationship, meaning that an increase in one of the two variables is generally accompanied by a decrease in the other. For example, depression and activity level are often inversely related—the *more* depressed a person is, the *lower* his or her activity level. A correlation coefficient of -1.00 indicates a *perfect negative correlation* between two variables.

The correlation coefficient r is computed with a statistical formula. The data for the computation are

Depression is often inversely related to activity level. The more depressed a person is, the less likely he or she is to engage in any activities, particularly physical ones. It is not surprising then that research continues to show that jogging or other aerobic activity helps to reduce depression.

obtained by measuring the two variables in a sample of the population of interest. Note that there is no manipulation of a variable, as there is in experimentation; existing values of the variables are simply measured. However, as in experimentation, researchers try to reduce the effect of extraneous variables, primarily by randomization and the use of large samples. They may also calculate a *level of significance* α (alpha) for the computed value of *r*, to determine how likely it is that the relationship it indicates is due to chance. When α = 0.05, for example, the result (the correlation) could have occurred by chance in only 5 of 100 studies. In practice, when α = 0.05 or lower, the finding is considered statistically significant and is usually presumed to be true, rather than an accidental (chance) finding.

Figure 5.1 shows various possible results of correlation studies and the correlation coefficients they would produce. Each plotted point represents a measurement of variable *X* and of variable *Y* in a single individual.

Correlational techniques are extremely useful research tools, especially when experimentation would be difficult or inadvisable, or when past events are being investigated. But extreme care must be taken in interpreting a correlation, because *correlation does not necessarily imply a cause-and-effect relationship.* The following example illustrates the problems that can arise in inferring a cause-and-effect relationship from a correlation. Several years ago, a newspaper story announced a significant negative correlation between smoking and academic grades. How should such a relationship be interpreted? One might conclude that *smoking causes poor grades;* however, a case can also be made that *poor grades cause increased smoking.* In other words, we cannot determine the *direction* of causality, or if there is any causality at all. For it is entirely possible that some third variable is causing both poor grades and smoking. Perhaps, if teachers prefer that students do not smoke, they may unconsciously assign lower grades to those who do. Or high-strung students may tend both to smoke more and to have poor study habits that adversely affect their grades (Ruch & Zimbardo, 1971).

Such third-variable possibilities in correlations are endless. Consider the following actual observations. What third-variable explanations can you suggest for them?

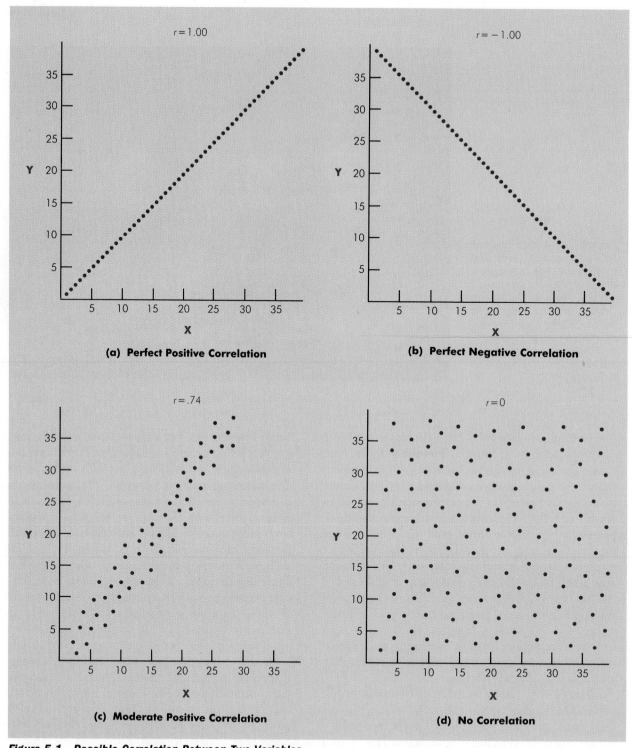

Figure 5.1 *Possible Correlation Between Two Variables*
The more closely the data points approximate a straight line, the greater the magnitude of the correlation coefficient r. The slope of the regression line rising from left to right in example (a) indicates a positive perfect correlation between two variables, whereas example (b) reveals a negative correlation. Example (c) shows a lower positive correlation. Example (d) shows no relationship whatsoever.

1. The number of storks nesting on rooftops in certain New England communities is positively correlated with the human birthrate.

2. The number of violent crimes committed in a community is positively correlated with the number of churches in the community.

3. The number of traffic fatalities and indices of progress in third world countries are negatively correlated.

In summary, correlations indicate the degree to which two variables are related. However, even when the variables are highly related caution must be exercised in interpreting causality. The two variables may not be causally related, or both may be influenced by a third variable. Even if they are causally related, the direction of causality may be unclear.

ANALOGUE STUDIES

For a variety of reasons, researchers may be unable to devise certain studies on mental disorders or on the effects of treatment. First, not enough subjects may be found for a particular study. For example, it may be difficult to find patients with a rare type of mental disorder. Second, ethical, moral, or legal standards may prevent certain studies from being conducted. For example, a researcher might be interested in the effects of intense stress such as the effects of torture on psychological adjustment, but it is unethical to torture people. Third, studying real-life situations is not only difficult but also frequently unmanageable, because researchers have a hard time controlling extraneous variables.

In such cases, researchers may resort to **analogue studies**—research that attempts to replicate or simulate, under controlled conditions, a situation that occurs in real life. Here are some examples of analogue studies:

1. To study the possible effects of a new form of treatment on patients with anxiety disorders, the researcher may use students who have high test anxiety rather than patients with anxiety disorders.

2. To test the hypothesis that human depression is caused by continual encounters with events that one cannot control, the researcher may expose rats to uncontrollable aversive stimuli and examine the increase of depressive-like behaviors (such as lack of motivation, inability to learn, and general apathy) in these animals.

3. To test the hypothesis that sexual sadism is influenced by watching sexually violent film and television programs, an experimenter exposes normal subjects to either violent or nonviolent sexual programs. The subjects then complete a questionnaire assessing their attitudes and values toward women and their likelihood of engaging in violent behaviors with women.

Obviously, each example is only an approximation of real life. Students with high test anxiety may not be equivalent to individuals with anxiety disorders; findings based on rats may not be applicable to humans; and exposure to one violent sexual film and the use of a questionnaire may not be sufficient to allow a researcher to draw the conclusion that sexual sadism is caused by long-term exposure to such films. To the extent that the research is not applicable to the population or phenomena of interest, then it lacks external validity. However, analogue studies give researchers insight into the processes that might be involved in abnormal behaviors and treatment. Analogue studies are devised by the experimenter, who can thus control extraneous factors, which enhances the internal validity of such studies. Researchers use their judgment in trying to balance the problems in internal and external validity.

FIELD STUDIES

In some cases, analogue studies would be too contrived to accurately represent the real-life situation. Investigators may then resort to the **field study,** in which behaviors and events are observed and recorded in the natural environment. The subjects of a field study are most often the members of a given social unit—a group, institution, or community. However, the investigation may also be limited to a single individual; single-subject studies are discussed in the next section.

Such data collection techniques as questionnaires, interviews, and the analysis of existing records may be used in field studies, but the primary technique is observation. The observers must be highly trained, with enough self-discipline to avoid disrupting or

The cataclysmic earthquake that destroyed large sections of Mexico City in September 1985 provided a unique opportunity for scientists to use field study techniques to evaluate the psychological and social effects that a major disaster can have on a population.

modifying the behavior processes that they are observing and recording. The observers in one study also had to be careful not to disclose the fact that they were indeed observers:

> In 1954 several psychologists became intrigued by the beliefs of a certain Ms. Kreech, who claimed she received messages from superior beings inhabiting a planet called Clarion. These beings, who had visited Earth in flying saucers, noticed fault lines in Earth's crust that indicated a forthcoming catastrophe. They claimed that a cataclysmic flood would strike Earth in December 1954. Kreech gathered about her a group of dedicated believers, and together they went into seclusion to prepare for the terrible event. Their preparation included group indoctrination meetings, during which members explored the meanings of their mystical experiences and dreams. When no flood appeared by December 21, many of the followers left. The most dedicated followers, however, persisted in their beliefs and even recruited new members.
>
> Several psychologists and their students, pretending to be believers, joined the group and diligently observed the believers and their attitudes. The results of their study were published in the book *When Prophecy Fails* (Festinger et al., 1957).

The field study may be used to examine mass behavior after events of major consequence, such as wars, floods, and earthquakes (see Focus 5.1). It may also be applied to the study of personal crises, as in military combat, major surgery, terminal disease, or the loss of loved ones.

Although field studies offer a more realistic investigative environment than other types of research, they suffer from certain limitations. First, as with other nonexperimental research, it is hard to determine the direction of causality because the data are correlational. Second, in real-life situations so many variables are at work that it is impossible to control—and sometimes even to distinguish—them all. As a result, they may contaminate the findings. Third, observers can never be absolutely sure that their presence did not influence the interactions they observed.

SINGLE-SUBJECT STUDIES

Most scientists advocate the study of large groups of people in order to uncover the basic principles governing behavior. This approach, called the **nomothetic orientation,** is concerned with formulating general laws or principles while deemphasizing individual variations or differences. Experiments and correlational studies are nomothetic in nature. Other scientists advocate the in-depth study of one person. This approach, exemplified by the single-subject study, has been called the **idiographic orientation.** Ever since Allport (1937) argued for making a distinction between these two study methods, much debate has boiled over which method is more fruitful in studying psychopathology (Beck, 1953; Eysenck, 1954).

Although the idiographic method has many limitations, especially its lack of generality, it has proved very valuable in applied clinical work (Maher, 1966). Furthermore, the argument over which method is more fruitful is not productive, because both approaches are needed in studying abnormal behavior. The nomothetic approach seems appropriate for laboratory scientists, whereas the idiographic approach seems appropriate for their clinical counterparts, the psychotherapists, who daily face the pressures of treating disturbed individuals.

There are two types of single-subject studies: the *case study* and the *single-subject experiment.* Both techniques may be used to examine a rare or unusual phenomenon, to demonstrate a novel diagnostic or treatment procedure, to disprove an assumption, to generate future hypotheses on which to base controlled research, and to collect comprehensive information for a better understanding of the individual (Garfield, 1974).

The Case Study

Physicians have used the case study extensively in describing and treating medical disease. In psychology, the **case study** is based on clinical data (observations, psychological tests, and historical and biographical information on the subject) and thus lacks the control and objectivity of many other methods. It serves as the primary source of data where systematic experimental procedures are not feasible (Millon & Diesenhaus, 1972). It is especially valuable for studying rare phenomena. Case studies can also be helpful in analyzing the course of a disorder or responding to treatment over time (Kratochwill et al., 1984).

An interesting case study is that by Thigpen and Cleckley (1957), who describe in detail a very rare but classic multiple personality disorder. (This case is also discussed in Chapter 7.) Eve White was a 25-year-old woman who sought therapy because of severe headaches and blackouts. Many of her symptoms seemed related to her marital conflicts and forced separation from her four-year-old daughter. Eve seemed to be a demure, reserved, and retiring person until one day, during an interview, she was seized by a sudden pain.

After a tense moment of silence, her hands dropped. There was a quick, restless smile, and in a bright voice that sparkled, she said, "Hi there, Doc." . . . There was in the newcomer a childishly daredevil, erotically mischievous glance, a face marvelously free from the habitual signs of care, seriousness, and underlying distress, so long familiar in her predecessor. This new and apparently carefree girl spoke casually of Eve White and her problems, always using *she* or *her* in every reference, always respecting the strict boundaries of a separate identity. When asked her own name she immediately replied, "Oh, I'm Eve Black." (Thigpen & Cleckley, 1957, p. 137)

After months of therapy, two more personalities emerged, making a total of four. This case was popularized in the film *The Three Faces of Eve,* in which Eve was portrayed by actress Joanne Woodward. Less widely known is that in 1977, a woman called Chris Sizemore revealed in a book that she was "Eve" (Sizemore & Pittillo, 1977). The book described her bouts with over twenty separate personalities. At times, a different personality, lasting from one to several days, would emerge after a brief headache. In 1982, Sizemore discussed her experiences at the annual convention of the American Psychological Association and met with several psychologists (Suinn, 1984). She felt that perhaps the occurrence of the personalities was a coping mechanism to deal with unbearable conflicts and problems that confronted her. She also believed that recovery was facilitated by psychotherapy and by her eventual ability to accept herself as she was. When asked how she knew her current personality (as Chris Sizemore) was the final one, Sizemore indicated that she had experienced a headache and contacted her therapist. The therapist provided reassurance by telling her to simply "take an aspirin." Sizemore reported that no

FOCUS 5.1

*Field Study of a Natural Disaster:
The Mt. St. Helens Eruption and Ashfall*

Mt. St. Helens, a volcanic peak located near Seattle, Washington, erupted on Sunday morning, May 18, 1980. Several local residents were killed, and the force of the explosion and the subsequent lava flow caused miles and miles of destruction to vegetation and wildlife. In addition, the disaster sent tons and tons of ashes throughout Washington, Oregon, and Idaho. In many communities, the ashfall was so heavy that it blotted out the sun, leaving residents in total darkness.

The Mt. St. Helens eruption and the people it affected provided a natural setting for the study of stress reactions to catastrophic events. Two researchers conducted a field study of the disaster to evaluate what DSM-III-R now calls post-

traumatic stress disorder (Adams & Adams, 1984). Studies generally support the belief that severe stress can result in psychological disturbances, but the Mt. St. Helens disaster provided a unique opportunity to address two questions: Does such stress cause long-term psychological disturbances in relatively normal people? Do the symptoms disappear as quickly as the environmental stressor? To answer these questions, the investigators used the following procedure.

1. They selected for study a single social unit—Othello, Washington, a town of approximately 5,000 people. They identified the characteristics of its population and its community help-giving networks, from which data were collected.

2. They developed a conceptual model in which, according to theory, a stressor (here, the Mt. St. Helens disaster) is seen as creating a two-part stress reaction. One part is associated with physiological responses, and the second with psychoemotional responses; both are believed to be manifested in overt behavior.

3. They divided the observable behaviors and/or consequences into five categories and selected operational definitions for each, as shown in the table.

4. They established postdisaster (experimental) and predisaster (control) time periods in which they could measure and compare behaviors. First, the researchers took the postdisaster period as the seven-

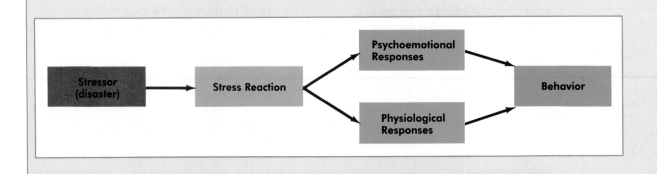

other personality emerged after the headache (Suinn, 1984).

The Single-Subject Experiment

The **single-subject experiment** differs from the case study in that the former is actually an experiment in

which some aspect of the person's own behavior is taken as the control or baseline from which to compare. An interesting type of single-subject experiment is the **multiple-baseline design,** which involves measuring changes (or the lack of change) in several related behaviors over a given period of time. The experimenter first makes a careful record of each behavior to establish multiple baselines (Risley &

month period following the disaster. Then, to eliminate (control) the effect of seasonal fluctuations on the measured behaviors, they took, as the predisaster period, the identical seven-month period of the *preceding year*.

5. The results revealed that cases of mental illness increased by nearly 236 percent, psychosomatic illness by 219 percent, and stress-aggravated illness by 198 percent. The researchers concluded that a disaster of this sort is likely to increase physical and psychosomatic illness, alcohol-related problems, aggression and violence, and family stress. They cautioned, however, that although they were able to control for seasonal variations, such variables as economic factors also need to be considered.

In any case, this particular field study is a prime example of the application of the scientific method: the formulation of hypotheses (here, as questions), identification of the unit of study, development of a conceptual scheme to guide the research, control of variables to the greatest extent possible, provision of an objective measurement scheme, reporting of the results, and critical analysis of the findings.

Behaviors/Consequences	Operational Definitions
Increased susceptibility to illness and a greater frequency of psychosomatic illnesses and illnesses aggravated by stress	Total patient contacts at medical clinic; hospital emergency room visits; psychosomatic problems diagnosed; employee sick leave and vacation time used; average patient census at hospital; death rate; absenteeism; welfare caseloads; diagnoses of illness aggravated by stress; mental illness diagnoses
Marital and family problems	Divorces filed; child-abuse investigations; police calls for domestic violence; juvenile court referrals
Alcohol abuse	Clients served in community alcohol program; citations issued for driving while intoxicated; other alcohol-related tickets or arrests; rate of auto accidents; police "breathalyzer" tests for intoxication
Aggression and violence	Police calls; criminal bookings; criminal cases opened in Superior Court
Adjustment problems	Psychiatric commitment investigations; District and Superior Court caseloads; mental health appointments; crisis-line calls

Baer, 1970). Once this task is completed, the experimenter applies a modification to one of the behaviors until a change occurs. Then the experimenter applies the same modification to the second behavior, to the third, and successively to all the others being measured. If in all cases the behavior changes when the experimenter applies the modification, a strong inference of causal relationship can be made.

Schmidt (1974) used the multiple-baseline design to gauge his success in treating an eighteen-year-old client who wanted to increase her verbal skills. After determining that three types of behavior were related to verbal skills (frequency of verbal statements, loudness of voice, and number of times conversations are initiated), Schmidt had the client count the frequencies of all three behaviors for one week. During that week, the mean baselines were found to be 1.0 times per day for the number of times she spoke at work, 0.8 times per day for speaking loudly, and 0.4 times per day for initiating conversations. These figures reveal an extremely withdrawn individual.

At the beginning of the second week, Schmidt told the client that any time she spoke with someone at work that day (Behavior A), she would be allowed two minutes with Schmidt to discuss anything she wanted. Her mean frequency for speaking at work increased to 8.2, whereas speaking loudly increased slightly and initiating conversations remained the same (see Figure 5.2). At the beginning of the third week, he told her she could have one minute per day

with him for each time she engaged in either speaking at work or speaking loudly (Behaviors A and B). The frequencies of these behaviors increased to 15.8 and 5.2 times per day, respectively; the third behavior remained the same. The fourth week, Schmidt told his client she could have one minute per day for each time she engaged in any of the three verbal behaviors. The mean frequencies for speaking at work, speaking loudly, and initiating conversations became 14.6 (down an insignificant amount), 12.2, and 7.4 times per day, respectively.

Because each behavior changed successively with the introduction of the same technique, we can be fairly certain that "talking to the counselor" caused

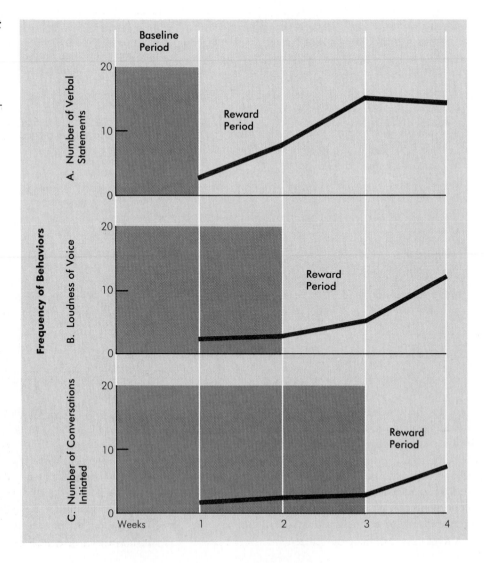

Figure 5.2   A Single-Subject Experiment with Three Baseline Variables
The first week was the baseline period. Behavior A was treated during the second week, behaviors A and B during the third week, and all three behaviors during the fourth week. SOURCE: Schmidt, 1974.

the behavior changes. Of course, such a technique only worked because the client obviously found talking to the counselor highly desirable or reinforcing. If that had not been the case, another change-inducing reward would have had to be found. Many researchers use a **reversal design** (sometimes called an ABAB design) to demonstrate the effect of a treatment. A baseline for the frequency of a behavior is established. Then, a treatment such as a reward is introduced. As in Schmidt's study, we would expect an increase in the behavior. Next, the treatment is withdrawn and reinstated again. If the treatment affects the behavior, the behavior should vary according to the presence or absence of treatment.

EPIDEMIOLOGICAL AND OTHER FORMS OF RESEARCH

In the field of abnormal and clinical psychology, different types of research are frequently employed, using experimental, correlational, case study, or field observation strategies. Some of these are listed here:

Survey research   Collecting data from all or part of a population to assess the relative incidence, distribution, and interrelationships of naturally occurring phenomena. Surveys are frequently conducted by epidemiologists.

Longitudinal research   Observing and evaluating people's behaviors over a long period of time so that the course of a disorder or the effects of some factor such as a prevention program can be assessed over time.

Historical research   Reconstructing the past by reviewing and evaluating evidence available from historical documents (see Focus 5.2 for a revealing look at some of this research).

Twin studies   Focusing on twins as a population of interest, since twins are genetically similar. Twin studies are often used to evaluate the influence of heredity and environment.

Treatment outcome studies   Evaluating the effectiveness of treatment in alleviating mental disorders. Outcome is concerned with answering the question of whether treatment is effective.

Treatment process studies   Analyzing how therapist, client, or situational factors influence each other during the course of treatment. Process research focuses on how or why treatment is effective.

Program evaluation   Analyzing the effectiveness of intervention or prevention programs.

These types of research frequently use experimental, correlational, and single-subject methodologies. For instance, survey researchers often collect data and then correlate certain variables such as social class and adjustment, in order to discover the relationship between variables. Researchers may also combine elements in different types of research. For example, an investigator may want to be conducting treatment outcome studies but use surveys and longitudinal studies.

One of the more important types of research is **epidemiological research** which examines the rate and distribution of mental disorders in the population. This type of research is used to determine the extent of mental disturbance that is found in a targeted population and the factors influencing the rate of mental disturbance. Two methods, prevalence and

Historical researchers spend hours poring over original documents and records, systematically reconstructing some moment in the past in a detailed and accurate manner. Usually, the researcher is trying to prove some hypothesis, so any conclusions reached must be defensible.

FOCUS 5.2 — *Historical Research: Minorities and Pathology*

When we seriously study the "scientific" literature of the past relating to people who are culturally different from the dominant social group, we are immediately impressed with how often minority groups and pathology are implicitly equated (Sue, 1981). For example, the historical use of science in the investigation of racial differences seems to be linked with white supremacist notions. A. Thomas and Sillen (1972) refer to this as "scientific racism" and cite several historical examples to support their contention:

1. In 1840, fabricated census figures were used to support the notion that black people living under "unnatural" conditions of freedom were prone to anxiety.

2. Mental health for blacks was taken to consist of contentment with subservience.

3. It was assumed that psychologically normal blacks were faithful to their "masters," and happy-go-lucky.

4. Influential medical journals presented as facts what were really fantasies supporting the belief that the anatomical, neurological, or endocrinological attributes of blacks were always inferior to those of whites.

5. The black person's brain was assumed to be smaller and less developed.

6. Blacks were thought to be less prone to mental illness "because their minds were so simple."

7. The dreams of blacks were judged juvenile in character and not as complex as those of whites.

Furthermore, the belief that various human groups exist at different stages of biological evolution was accepted by the respected psychologist G. Stanley Hall (1904). He explicitly stated that Africans, Indians, and Chinese were members of "adolescent races" and in a stage of incomplete development. In most cases, the evidence used to support these conclusions was fabricated, extremely flimsy, or distorted to fit the belief in nonwhite inferiority (A. Thomas & Sillen, 1972). For example, Gossett (1963) reports how, when one particular study in 1895 revealed that the sensory per-

---

incidence, are used to describe the rates. First, the *prevalence rate* tells us how many individuals in a targeted population have a particular disorder. This figure is determined for a specified time period. For example, in Chapter 1, we discussed a major epidemiological study (Myers et al., 1984) in which the prevalence of schizophrenia (the type of disorder) for adults aged 18 or older in the United States (the population) was determined to be nearly 1 percent over a six-month period. Determining the prevalence rate is especially important in the planning of treatment services, because mental health workers need to know the percentage of people who are likely to be afflicted with disorders (Bromet, 1984).

Second, the *incidence rate* tells us how many *new* cases of a disorder appear in an identified population within a specified time period. The inci-

dence rate is likely to be lower than the prevalence rate, because incidence involves only new cases, while prevalence includes new and existing cases during the specified time period. Incidence rates are important for examining etiologic hypotheses about the risk for a disorder. For example, if we find that new cases of a disorder are more likely to appear in a population that is exposed to a particular stressor than in another population not exposed to the stressor, we can hypothesize that the stress causes the disorder. Epidemiological research, then, is important not only in describing the distribution of disorders but also in analyzing the possible factors that contribute to disorders. Focus 5.3 compares the prevalence rates of disorders in the United States and China and some problems that must be considered in conducting epidemiological research.

ception of Native Americans was superior to that of blacks, and that of blacks to that of whites, the results were used to support a belief in the mental superiority of whites. "Their reactions were slower because they belonged to a more deliberate and reflective race than did the members of the other two groups" (p. 364). The belief that blacks are "born athletes" (as opposed, for example, to being "born" scientists or heads of state) derives from this tradition. The fact that Hall was a well-respected psychologist often referred to as "the father of child study," and first president of the American Psychological Association (APA), did not prevent him from inheriting the racial biases of his times.

In psychological literature, the portrayal of the culturally different has generally taken the form of stereotyping them as "deficient" in certain "desirable" attributes. For example, de Gobineau's *Essay on the Inequality of the Human Races* (1915) and Darwin's *On The Origin of the Species by Means of Natural Selection* (1859) were used to support the genetic intellectual superiority of whites and the genetic inferiority of the "lower races." Galton (1869) wrote explicitly that African "Negros" were "half-witted men" who made "childish, stupid and simpleton-like mistakes," and Jews were deemed inferior physically and mentally and fit only for a parasitical existence on other nations. Using the Binet scales in testing Spanish, Indian, Mexican American, and black families, Terman (1916) concluded that these people were uneducable.

That the genetic deficiency model still exists can be seen in the writing of Shuey (1966), Jensen (1969), Hernstein (1982), and Shockley (1972). These writers have adopted the position that genes play a predominant role in the determination of intelligence. While heredity plays a role in intelligence, the central issues are whether racial differences or IQ can be attributed to heredity and what policy implications are proposed. For example, Shockley (1972) has expressed fears that the accumulation of genes for weak or low intelligence in the black population will seriously affect overall intelligence in the general population. Thus he advocates that people with low IQs should not be allowed to bear children; they should be sterilized. Such ideas have generated considerable anger and controversy.

ETHICAL ISSUES IN RESEARCH

Although research is primarily a scientific endeavor, it has also raised ethical issues. Consider the following examples:

1. In order to study the effects of a new drug in treating schizophrenia, a researcher needs an experimental group that receives the drug treatment and a control group that receives no treatment. Is it ethical to withhold treatment from a control group of schizophrenics, who need treatment, in order to test the effectiveness of the drug?

2. To study the way depressed individuals respond to negative feedback, an investigator deceives depressed people into believing that they performed poorly on a task. Is the deception ethical?

3. A researcher is interested in developing a new assessment tool to uncover personal conflicts. The assessment tool asks people to disclose information about their sexual conduct and private thoughts and feelings—information that may cause embarrassment and discomfort. Does the assessment measure invade the subjects' privacy?

4. A researcher hypothesizes that alcoholics cannot stop drinking after having one alcoholic drink. He arranges for alcoholic patients to have one drink and then examines how strongly they are motivated to receive additional drinks. Is it ethical and detrimental for alcoholics to be given alcohol as a part of an experiment?

5. An investigator believes that people who are exposed to inescapable stress are likely to develop feelings of helplessness and depression. Because the

FOCUS 5.3

Do Americans Have Higher Rates of Mental Disturbance than Chinese?

The prevalence rate of mental disorders in the mainland of China appears to be much lower than in the United States (see *Chinese Journal of Neurology and Psychology,* 1986). A major epidemiological study of mental disorders in China was conducted with the assistance of U.S. investigators including the director of mental health for the World Health Organization. The results revealed that the prevalence of most disorders was much lower than that in the United States. For example, nearly 1 percent of the U.S. population was diagnosed as having schizophrenia (Myers et al., 1984), about two times the proportion in China. Americans were also far more likely than the Chinese to have other forms of mental disturbance. Do the findings mean that Americans are more disturbed?

Americans may in fact be more prone to mental illness, but an alternative explanation is that the different prevalence rates are the result of methodological and conceptual differences between the two studies that yielded the different results.

Bromet (1984) has suggested that two major sources of error must be controlled, especially in cross-cultural comparisons: *sample characteristics* and *case* identification. If samples from the two populations were not comparable, that might account for the different rates. For example, the Chinese study included people fifteen years of age and older while the U.S. sample targeted people aged eighteen and older. Social class and rural-urban differences were also apparent. With respect to case identification, one requirement of an epidemiological study is that cases of a disorder be correctly identified. In cross-cultural or cross-national research, this task is extremely difficult. We do not know if the same procedures and assumptions were used in the two populations. The criteria used to define whether a person has a particular mental disorder may have varied from study to study. Furthermore, respondents might have differed in their willingness to report or show symptoms of mental disorders. Some studies have shown that Chinese may not as readily report psychological symptoms as Americans (Sue & Morishima, 1982). Even more problematic is the possibility that different cultures express the same mental disorders in different ways. For example, Chinese are more likely than Americans to show somatic complaints when they are depressed. These factors are important to consider before the conclusion can be drawn that one population is more disturbed than another. Although it may be true that Chinese are less prone to mental disturbance, much more research needs to be conducted before this conclusion can be accepted.

investigator does not want to subject human beings to inescapable stress, the experiment is conducted with dogs, which are given painful and inescapable electric shocks. Is it ethical to cause pain to animals as part of a study?

These examples raise a number of ethical concerns about how research is conducted and whether it has, or should have, limits. How can the rights of humans (or even of other animals) be protected without impeding valuable experimentation? There is no question that in order to understand psychopathology and to devise effective treatment and prevention interventions, experimenters may have to occasionally devise investigations that cause pain and involve deception. In order to study human behavior, infliction of pain may occur (e.g., surgical implants may cause pain or shocks may be used to induce stress); and deception is sometimes necessary in order to conceal the true nature of a study. However, the research must be consistent with certain principles of conduct, intended to protect subjects as well as to enable researchers to contribute to the long-term welfare of human beings (and other animals).

The American Psychological Association (1985) has adopted the principle that the prospective scientific, applied, or educational value of the proposed

If research is to be conducted ethically, then certain guidelines must be agreed upon by the scientific community and must be followed. To ensure respectful treatment of research subjects, an investigator must carefully explain all features of the research to a prospective participant, especially those features that might influence willingness to participate.

research must outweigh the risk or discomfort to its subjects. Certain guidelines have been used to protect participants. Subjects should be fully informed of the procedures and risks involved in the research and should give their consent to participate. Deception may be used only when alternative means are not possible to use, and participants should be provided with a sufficient explanation of the study as soon as possible. They should be free to withdraw from a study at any time. Furthermore, all participants must be treated with dignity, and research procedures must minimize pain, discomfort, embarrassment, and so on. If undesirable consequences to participants are found, the researcher has the responsibility to detect and remedy these consequences. Finally, unless otherwise agreed on in advance, information obtained from participants is confidential.

Recent concern has also been expressed by animal rights groups over the use of animals in psychological research (Bales, 1988). The American Psychological Association principles state that psychologists should make every effort to minimize discomfort, illness, and pain of animals. Only when alternative procedures are unavailable and the goal is justified by the potential value to humans of the research, should researchers be allowed to consider subjecting animals to discomfort or pain. Animals should be treated in a humane fashion.

Researchers usually submit their research plans to review boards from their institutions (e.g., a university review board). If the review boards feel that the research is unethical, careless, or inhumane, the research is not approved. Although instances can be found of unethical or questionable conduct on the part of researchers, particularly in the past, the principles adopted by the American Psychological Association have now minimized such conduct.

SUMMARY

1. The scientific method provides for the systematic and controlled collection of data and the formulation of objective hypotheses based on those data. The characteristics of the scientific method include self-correction, the use of conceptual schemes and theoretical structures, the testing of theories and hypotheses, the control of variables, and the avoidance of metaphysical explanations.

2. The experiment is the most powerful research tool we have for determining and testing cause-and-effect relationships. In its simplest form, an experiment involves an experimental hypothesis, an independent variable, and a dependent variable. The independent variable is manipulated for the experimental group of subjects. Extraneous variables are typically controlled through the use of control groups (of subjects), randomization procedures, or matching of subjects in experimental and control groups.

3. A correlation is a measure of the degree to which two variables are related. It is expressed as a correlation coefficient, a numerical value between -1 and $+1$, symbolized by r. Correlational techniques provide less precision, control, and generality than experiments, and they cannot be taken to imply cause-and-effect relationships.

4. In the study of abnormal behavior, an analogue study is used to create a situation as close to real life as possible. It permits the study of phenomena under controlled conditions.

5. The field study relies primarily on naturalistic observations. In this technique, the psychologist enters a situation as unobtrusively as possible in order to observe and record behavior as it occurs naturally.

6. Rather than studying large groups of people, many scientists advocate the in-depth study of one individual. Two types of single-subject techniques are the case study and the single-subject experiment. The case study is especially appropriate when a phenomenon is so rare that it is impractical to try to study more than one instance of it. Single-subject experiments differ from case studies in that they rely on experimental procedures; some aspect of the person's own behavior is taken as the control.

7. A particularly important type of research in abnormal psychology is epidemiological research, which examines the rate and distribution of mental disorders in a population. It can also provide insight into what groups are at risk for mental disturbance and what factors may influence disturbance.

8. The scientific method has weaknesses and limitations. Like other tools, it is subject to misuse and misunderstanding, both of which can give rise to moral and ethical concerns. Such concerns have led to the development of guidelines from the American Psychological Association for ethical conduct and of ways to deal with violations within the mental health professions.

KEY TERMS

analogue study An investigation that attempts to replicate or simulate, as closely as possible, a situation under controlled conditions that occurs in real life.

case study Intensive study of one individual that relies on observation, psychological tests, and historical and biographical data

correlation The degree to which two variables covary or are associated with each other in a population

dependent variable Attitudes or behaviors that are expected to change as a result of the manipulation of the independent variable in a psychological experiment

epidemiological research The study of the rate and distribution of mental disorders in a population

experiment A technique of scientific inquiry in which an independent variable is manipulated, the changes in a dependent variable are measured, and extraneous variables are controlled to the extent possible

experimental hypothesis A prediction that is made concerning how an independent variable affects a dependent variable in an experiment

external validity The degree to which the results of an experiment may be generalized

field study An investigative technique in which behaviors are observed and recorded in the natural environment

hypothesis A conjectural statement that describes a relationship between variables

independent variable The variable or condition that is manipulated by the experimenter and tested for its effects on the dependent variable

internal validity In an experiment, the extent to which changes in the dependent variable are actually brought about by the independent variable (rather than extraneously)

operational definition Describing concepts in terms of the operations used to measure them

quasi-experimental design A research design patterned after a true experiment but lacking the random assignment of individuals to experimental and control groups

reversal (ABAB) design An experiment in which behaviors are measured at four times: (A) before the independent variable or treatment is introduced; (B) after the independent variable is introduced; (A) after the independent variable is withdrawn; and (B) after the reintroduction of the independent variable

scientific method A method of inquiry that provides for the systematic collection of data through controlled observation and for the testing of hypotheses based on those data

single-subject experiment An experiment performed on a single individual in which some aspect of that individual's own behavior is used as the control

theory A group of principles and hypotheses that together explain some aspect of a particular area of inquiry

PART 2

Anxiety
and Stress

chapter 6
Anxiety Disorders

The disorders discussed in this chapter are all characterized by **anxiety**, or feelings of fear and apprehension. These disorders can produce seemingly illogical—and often restrictive—patterns of behavior, as illustrated in the following examples:

A 33-year-old woman has been experiencing periods of intense anxiety since adolescence. At the age of twenty-three, she reported her first full-blown panic attack. The attacks have been overwhelming and produce feelings of terror. She feels "out of control." Her heart pounds, and she has difficulty breathing. These episodes have been increasing in frequency. She has started to avoid shopping malls and people (George et al., 1987).

A 26-year-old man has an eleven-year history of obsessional thoughts involving similarities and differences. When reading, he often wonders if he has seen a particular word recently. To alleviate his anxiety over this, he spends hours going through newspapers and magazines in an attempt to locate the word. If two trees appear similar, he feels compelled to compare the texture and odor of their leaves, their bark, and the shape of their branches to find out if they are the same or different (Junginger & Turner, 1987).

Anxiety is a fundamental human emotion that was recognized as long as 5,000 years ago. Everyone has experienced it, and all of us will continue to experience it throughout our lives. (Focus 6.1 examines

FOCUS 6.1 — *Anxiety and Fear: Do We Need Them?*

Fear and anxiety have unpleasant effects, can lead to psychomotor and intellectual errors, can impair psychological functioning, and can disturb concentration and memory. Yet some evidence that anxiety may serve an adaptive or stimulating purpose (Antonovsky, 1979; Epstein, 1972; R. S. Lazarus, 1966; Rachman, 1974). It is important that organisms be able to assess a dangerous situation rapidly and take immediate action. When a dangerous threat appears, the organism becomes aroused (via fear or aggression) in preparation for flight or attack. If too much time elapses between assessing a threat and taking action, the organism's survival is jeopardized.

Thus fear and anxiety can serve to arouse a person in preparation for constructive action. Indeed, the

absence of appropriate fear can foster careless behavior in dangerous situations. Smith (1949) found that inexperienced combat soldiers displayed little fear and often engaged in careless behavior that placed their lives in jeopardy. After exposure to combat, they were more fearful but also more vigilant and careful. Janis (1971) found that moderate anticipatory fear about realistic threats is necessary for the development of coping behavior. He divided patients about to undergo major surgery into three groups on the basis of the degree of fear they expressed. After the operation, the highly fearful group displayed considerable pain and discomfort; the moderately fearful group coped better and displayed less pain; and the fearless patients suffered excessive postoperative anger, resentment,

discomfort, and pain. Janis believes the moderately fearful patients were able to rehearse mentally what was about to happen and what was to follow and thus reduced both novelty and surprise. The highly fearful group tended to become defensive and preoccupied with their problem. The fearless group did not have realistic expectations about what was to occur and responded negatively.

Thus moderate fear levels can enhance vigilance and aid in a realistic appraisal of what is to come, both of which help the individual develop the coping responses necessary for survival. Functional fear appeals have been used in advertising campaigns to encourage people to stop smoking cigarettes, to use safety belts, and to have regular health checkups.

---

the possible adaptive function anxiety serves.) Many observers regard anxiety as a basic condition of modern existence. The British poet W. H. Auden, for instance, called the twentieth century "the age of anxiety." However, "reasonable doses" of anxiety act as a safeguard to keep us from ignoring danger and have an adaptive function. Only when overwhelming anxiety disrupts social functioning or produces significant distress is an anxiety disorder indicated, as illustrated in the following case.

> I've always been tense from as far back as I can remember. But lately it's getting worse. Sometimes I think I'm going crazy—especially at . . . night. I can't sleep for fear of what has to be done the next day. Should I go to my psych class tomorrow, or skip it and study for my stat exam? If I skip it, maybe the prof will throw a pop quiz. He's known for that, you

know. These attacks are frightful. I had another one last week. It was horrible. I thought I would die. My roommate didn't know what to do. By the time it was over, my blouse was completely drenched. My roommate was so scared she called you. I was so embarrassed afterward. I think she [the roommate] wants to move out. I don't blame her.

MANIFESTATIONS OF ANXIETY

Anxiety is manifested in three ways: *cognitively* (in a person's thoughts), *behaviorally* (in a person's actions), and *somatically* (in physiological or biological reactions).

Cognitive manifestations of anxiety may vary from mild worry to panic. Severe attacks can bring a conviction of impending doom (the end of the

Evidence suggests that anxiety may serve an adaptive purpose and that moderate levels of fear about realistic threats may play a role in the development of coping behaviors. Functional fear appeals have been used in advertising campaigns to encourage people to stop smoking, use seat belts, and as shown in this photo, to think about the effects of drinking and driving.

world or death), a preoccupation with unknown dangers, or fears of losing control over bodily functions. In one study, patients suffering from *panic disorder* had such terrifying cognitions as dying of suffocation and physical catastrophe befalling a family member. Individuals with *generalized anxiety disorder* tended to have milder anxiety-evoking thoughts dealing with themes such as misfortune, financial concerns, academic and social performance, and rejection (Lindsay et al., 1987). These apprehensions are out of proportion to the actual situation.

Behavioral manifestations of anxiety involve avoidance of anxiety-provoking situations. A student with an extreme fear of public speaking will avoid classes in which class presentations are necessary. Individuals who have panic attacks may stay at home rather than risk the possibility of experiencing anxiety in public. Possible somatic changes include shallow breathing, mouth dryness, cold hands and feet, diarrhea, frequent urination, fainting, heart palpitations, elevated blood pressure, increased perspiration, muscular tenseness (especially in the head, neck, shoulders, and chest), and indigestion.

The anxiety disorders do not involve a loss of contact with reality: people suffering from them can usually go about most of the day-to-day business of living. Although these people are aware of the illogical and self-defeating nature of some of their behaviors, they seem incapable of controlling them. In severe cases, the disturbed individuals may spend great amounts of time dealing with their debilitating fears—but to no avail. This preoccupation may, in turn, lead to emotional stress and turmoil, maladaptive behaviors, and disruptions in interpersonal relationships.

Until recently the anxiety disorders were classified as *neuroses,* along with the dissociative and somatoform disorders described in Chapter 7. The term *neurosis* had been associated with anxiety by Sigmund Freud, and it was applied to these three diverse classes of disorders because they were all believed to be based in, or characterized by, anxiety. But when the authors of DSM-III examined these disorders, they encountered two problems. First, anxiety is present in many mental illnesses that had *not* been classified as neuroses; and, although anxiety was assumed to underlie certain neurotic disorders, it was not always a visible symptom of those disorders. As a result, anxiety was not an effective indicator of the very disorders it was supposed to characterize. Second, the disorders that were classified as neuroses seemed too disparate to be placed in a single category; they included such problems as *multiple personality, amnesias,* and *hypochondriasis,* as well as the phobias and other specific anxiety disorders.

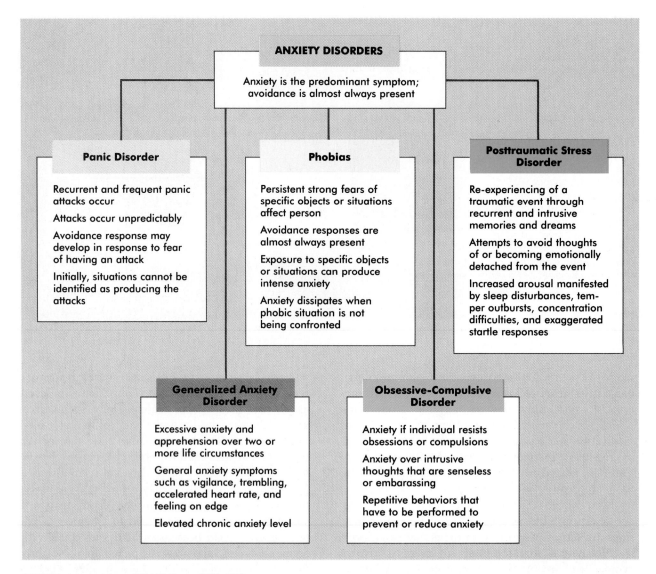

ANXIETY DISORDERS

Anxiety is the predominant symptom; avoidance is almost always present

Panic Disorder

Recurrent and frequent panic attacks occur

Attacks occur unpredictably

Avoidance response may develop in response to fear of having an attack

Initially, situations cannot be identified as producing the attacks

Phobias

Persistent strong fears of specific objects or situations affect person

Avoidance responses are almost always present

Exposure to specific objects or situations can produce intense anxiety

Anxiety dissipates when phobic situation is not being confronted

Posttraumatic Stress Disorder

Re-experiencing of a traumatic event through recurrent and intrusive memories and dreams

Attempts to avoid thoughts of or becoming emotionally detached from the event

Increased arousal manifested by sleep disturbances, temper outbursts, concentration difficulties, and exaggerated startle responses

Generalized Anxiety Disorder

Excessive anxiety and apprehension over two or more life circumstances

General anxiety symptoms such as vigilance, trembling, accelerated heart rate, and feeling on edge

Elevated chronic anxiety level

Obsessive-Compulsive Disorder

Anxiety if individual resists obsessions or compulsions

Anxiety over intrusive thoughts that are senseless or embarassing

Repetitive behaviors that have to be performed to prevent or reduce anxiety

SOURCE: Adapted from DSM-III-R, pp. 235–253.

After much discussion among mental health professionals, the former neuroses were reclassified as anxiety disorders, dissociative disorders, or somatoform disorders. A diagnosis of anxiety disorder is not made if anxiety is found to accompany some other disorder. Thus the word **neurosis** no longer signifies a particular category of disorders. However, it is still used in a general sense to refer to the less severe mental illnesses.

To be included as an **anxiety disorder,** one of the following criteria must be met. The anxiety may itself be the major disturbance, as in *panic disorder* and *generalized anxiety disorder*; it may be manifested only when the affected individual encounters particular situations, as in the *phobias*; or the anxiety may result from an attempt to master other symptoms, as in *obsessive-compulsive disorder*. In this chapter, we discuss all four of these major groups of anxiety disorders, which are shown in the disorders chart on p. 146. In addition, we discuss *posttraumatic stress disorder,* a disorder characterized by the extraordinary stress experienced in combat situations or natural catastrophes.

PANIC DISORDER AND GENERALIZED ANXIETY DISORDER

The predominant characteristic of both panic disorder and generalized anxiety disorder is unfocused, or *free-floating,* anxiety. That is, the affected individual is fearful and apprehensive but often does not know exactly what he or she is afraid of. (The First Person narrative in this chapter describes a college senior's attempt to come to grips with his anxiety and its underlying causes.)

Panic Disorder

Panic disorder is characterized by severe and frightening episodes of apprehension and feelings of impending doom. These attacks are often described as horrible and can last from a few minutes to several hours. The anxiety associated with his disorder is much greater than is found in generalized anxiety disorder.

One 25-year-old woman described her feelings in the following way: "It could not be worse if I were hanging by my fingertips from the wing of an airplane in flight. The feeling of impending doom was just as real and frightening" (Fishman & Sheehan, 1985, p. 26). The attacks are especially feared because they often occur unpredictably and without warning. "They would start just out of nowhere with this explosive anxiety or panic, fast heartbeat—just uncontrollable shaking and wanting to clutch up and not move" (Pasnau, 1984, p. 7). A variety of physical symptoms such as sweating, choking, and heart palpitations are reported during the panic attacks (Balon et al., 1988). Four attacks must occur within a four-week period for the diagnosis to be made (DSM-III-R). In a substantial number of such cases, people develop *agoraphobia*, or anxiety about leaving the home, caused by fear of having an attack in a public place.

The Scream, *by Edvard Munch, depicts some of the symptoms that accompany anxiety. The swirling colors of the background evoke a feeling of uncontrollable disorder that cannot be escaped. The subject, clutching his head, seems terrorized by something, which must be in his own mind, for the scene is otherwise peaceful.*

Such cases are diagnosed as panic disorder with agoraphobia. The following case seems typical:

Lois R. was 16 when she had her first panic attack. She felt as if she was going to die. "My heart was beating so fast that I thought I was having a heart attack, my mouth was very dry, I couldn't think. . . ."

That was only the start. At school she began running to the nurse's office several times a week, in terror and asking for help. She lived in fear of attacks and of being where she could not cope with them. She stopped riding in elevators. She was afraid to go anywhere in a car. Open spaces seemed threatening, especially if she was alone.

Jes Sellers

FIRST PERSON

Anxiety is universal. It strikes the Wall Street broker trading shares moments before the final bell ends business for the day, the sprinter in the block trying to concentrate before the starting gun, and the high school student taking a college entrance exam.

As a counseling psychologist in a university counseling center, I frequently talk to students who are feeling anxious over the everyday experiences that mark each generation's passage from childhood into adulthood—intimate relationships beginning or dissolving, parents divorcing and remarrying, fear of failure (and sometimes success), and ever-present money worries. These issues and others often arouse acute anxiety and stress, which can usually be relieved by a supportive word from me or a friend. But I also talk with students whose anxieties threaten the very independence associated with adulthood. In Jason's case (not his real name), his very independence seemed to have

been assaulted by growing helplessness and perpetual self-doubt.

When Jason came to see me, he wasn't sure he needed counseling. He just felt "lazy" and uninspired. His senior research project was past due, and he "just couldn't seem to get started," although he'd compiled all the data. As he continued to meet with me, some interesting things happened. Instead of discovering he was lazy, he realized that he was afraid of completing the project report. He revealed that he had become frightened of other things as well—driving his car, walking to class alone, and even getting out of bed in the morning. In the initial phase of our work together, I instructed him on relaxation techniques, such as meditation and progressive relaxation training, which involves tensing and relaxing groups of muscles to create emotional calm. I also helped him understand the role of his negative, self-defeating thoughts in arousing anxiety. Although these approaches were helpful, he seemed most curious about how his childhood experiences related to his most current dilemma. For example, he remembered growing up afraid that his father would die of a heart attack if he let his father down in school and sports. He also remembered his older brother's auto accident, in which a passenger was killed. He wondered if his mother's nightly cocktails before dinner may have

been a sign of a real drinking problem, long overlooked by everyone else in the family. He wondered how these and many other memories affected his ability to manage anxieties and fears as an adult.

As months passed, Jason gained some important insights into his past experiences. He realized that while his parents supported him financially they did not help him develop his confidence during times of distress and fear. He recognized that he had to learn how to cope on his own, using skills, insights, and self-empathy.

I learned a lot as well. Using empathy helped me realize that fear and anxiety can be overwhelming and incapacitating. It was painful for me to watch Jason struggle, but I couldn't escape my responsibility to listen intently and with concern. I also adapted my therapeutic style as a result of working with him. I became more understanding, more flexible, and more respectful of the role of insight into past family interactions and their significance in the developing person. Growing and developing isn't just the client's experience, it's the therapist's experience as well.

Dr. Jes Sellers is a counseling psychologist and director of the University Counseling Services at Case Western Reserve University in Cleveland, Ohio.

For the next 39 years fear plagued her. It sometimes waned but never left. She saw many doctors: a family physician who thought she was having a nervous breakdown and tried to cure her by making her sleep for a week; a psychiatrist who prescribed Valium and other tranquilizers, plus sleeping pills, over a 10-year period; a psychologist who hypnotized her to

bring her back to her childhood. "It was expensive," she says, "and it didn't help" (*Novato* [California] *Independent Journal,* July 6, 1984, p. C3).

Individuals with panic disorder report periods of relatively low anxiety alternating with intense panic attacks, although there may be apprehension over having another panic attack. The majority of panic attack patients report a disturbed childhood environment; most indicate that they first experienced panic attacks after some form of separation, such as leaving home or the loss or threatened loss of a loved one (Raskin et al., 1982; Roy-Byrne et al., 1986).

For men, the *lifetime prevalence rate* (whether the individual had the disorder at any time in his or her life) for panic disorder is approximately 0.9 percent. For women, it is approximately 1.9 percent (Robins et al., 1984). However, it is quite probable that future studies will report a higher prevalence of the disorder. This is because the category of panic disorder has been expanded to encompass most cases of agoraphobia.

Panic attacks appear to be fairly common. In one study of college students, over one-third reported having had a panic attack during a one-year period (Norton et al., 1985). Kayton et al., (1987) found that 36 percent of 195 medical patients also have experienced at least one panic attack (Kayton et al., 1987). Although panic attacks appear common, only a small percentage of them develop into panic disorder. The predisposing conditions that make some people more vulnerable to developing the disorder still need to be identified.

Generalized Anxiety Disorder

Generalized anxiety disorder (GAD) is characterized by persistent high levels of anxiety, **hypervigilance** (overalertness), and physiological symptoms, even in situations where no realistic danger is present. Afflicted people may have difficulty sleeping, are easily startled, and are continually "on edge." The inability to discover the "real" source of their fears maintains the level of anxiety and occasionally causes even more acute attacks of anxiety.

Such people often feel apprehension or worry over life situations (such as the ability to do well in a job or in school, acceptance by others, or worry over misfortune befalling someone loved). The following case illustrates a generalized anxiety disorder:

Joanne W. was known by her college friends as a worrier. She was apprehensive about anything and everything: failing in school, making friends, eating the right foods, maintaining her health, and being liked. Because of her concerns, Joanne was constantly

Anxiety that arises unpredictably and without warning creates feelings of helplessness and frustration. The unexpected nature of anxiety may increase arousal and result in a panic attack.

tense. She often felt short of breath, which was accompanied by a fast heart rate and trembling. Joanne also had difficulty making decisions. Her insecurity was so great that even the most common decisions—what clothes to wear, what to order at a restaurant, which movies to see—became major problems. At night Joanne reviewed and re-reviewed every real and imaginary mistake she had made during the day or might make in the future. This produced another problem, sleeplessness.

To meet the criteria for making a diagnosis of generalized anxiety disorder, symptoms must be present for six months. The anxiety may be so great that the individual may also experience panic attacks and depression (DSM-III-R).

Etiology of Panic Disorder and Generalized Anxiety Disorder

In our discussions of the causes and origins of mental disorders in this chapter and ensuing chapters, we must distinguish among the viewpoints that derive from the various models of psychopathology. Here we'll examine the etiology of unfocused anxiety disorders from the psychoanalytic, learning, cognitive-behavioral, and biological perspectives.

Psychoanalytic Perspective The psychoanalytic view stresses the importance of internal conflicts (rather than external stimuli) in the origin of panic disorder and generalized anxiety disorder. Because the problem originates in sexual and aggressive impulses that are seeking expression, anxiety is always present. When a forbidden impulse threatens to disturb the ego's integrity, an intense anxiety reaction occurs. Because this conflict is unconscious, the individual does not know the source of the anxiety.

The defense against this unfocused anxiety is generally considered to be poorly organized and less effective than those mounted against other anxiety disorders. In a phobia, for example, the conflict between id impulses and ego is displaced onto a specific external stimulus that can be controlled simply through avoidance. But the person with generalized anxiety disorder has only one defense—to try to repress the impulses. When that defense weakens, panic attacks may occur.

Learning Perspective The behaviorists believe that anxiety is a learned response to stimuli. Wolpe (1982) argues that so-called free-floating anxiety stems from classical conditioning to an omnipresent stimulus, such as light or shade contrasts, size, or the passage of time. Wolpe also prefers the term *pervasive* to *free-floating*, because the latter implies the lack of an external source for the anxiety.

Wolpe suggests that two factors may be involved in producing pervasive anxiety. One is the intensity of the unconditioned stimulus; an intense UCS may produce conditioning to more of the stimulus elements than are present at the time of conditioning. The

second factor is the lack of a distinct environmental stimulus during conditioning. Wolpe presents a case study involving a patient whose pervasive anxiety developed after a guilt-ridden sexual experience that took place in the dark and evoked a great deal of emotional turmoil. This person developed anxiety in many situations in which sexual cues and darkness were present.

Although classical conditioning to an often-present stimulus may account for some cases of panic and generalized anxiety disorder, it is difficult to believe that all cases develop in this manner.

Cognitive Behavioral Perspective Cognitive behavioral theorists emphasize cognitions, not conditioning, in the development of anxiety disorders. Because an external source of anxiety often cannot be identified, it is possible that thoughts may function as *internal triggers* for panic attacks. Some theorists (Clark, 1986; Hibbert, 1984) believe that the cognitions and somatic symptoms can best be viewed as a positive feedback loop which results in increasingly higher levels of anxiety. In other words, a person may become aware of a bodily sensation, such as a racing heart. Anxiety develops when the sensation is interpreted as signaling a dreadful event. This belief produces even greater physical reactions. Figure 6.1 illustrates this configuration. If the positive feedback loop continues, a panic attack may ensue. Although this pattern begins with the perception of bodily sensations, some research also indicates that panic attacks may begin with anxiety-provoking thoughts.

To support this hypothesized relationship between cognitions and anxiety, a researcher must be able to (1) find that thoughts precede or contribute to panic attacks and (2) demonstrate that cognitions influence the severity of somatic symptoms. Some

Figure 6.1 Positive Feedback Loop Between Cognitions and Somatic Symptoms

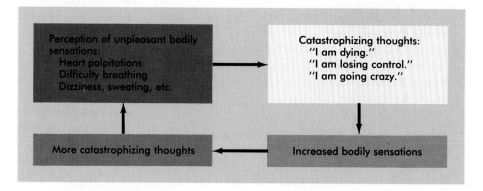

Perception of unpleasant bodily sensations:
Heart palpitations
Difficulty breathing
Dizziness, sweating, etc.

Catastrophizing thoughts:
"I am dying."
"I am losing control."
"I am going crazy."

More catastrophizing thoughts

Increased bodily sensations

research supports the cognitive hypothesis. Cognitions preceding or accompanying panic attacks in patients have been reported by George and his colleagues (1987) and by Rachman and his colleagues (1988). The cognitions included thoughts of being "out of control," "passing out," or "acting foolish." These thoughts resulted in increases in anxiety.

Cognitions or appraisal (interpretation) can have an influence on somatic symptoms. Significant increases in cardiovascular activity were found in a group of college students who were asked to focus on negative thoughts such as "My mind is racing," "I'm so worried. I can't concentrate on anything," or "It's frightening how tense I feel." In contrast, concentrating on neutral statements had little effect on somatic responses (York et al., 1987). Although disturbing thoughts can increase cardiovascular activity, can they precipitate a panic attack? In some cases, the answer appears to be yes. A 25-year-old woman with a nine-year history of panic attacks received two types of feedback, accurate and false. When accurate feedback of her resting heart rate was given, no changes in physiological functioning were observed. However, within 20 seconds of receiving inaccurate feedback indicating an increase in heart rate, her heart rate increased 50 beats per minute over baseline. During this period, the patient reported having a severe panic attack (Margraf et al., 1987). Similar results were found in another group of patients with panic disorder. Of particular interest is the finding that false feedback indicating arousal produced significantly greater increases in physiological measures in people who had histories of panic than in people who had no such history (Ehlers et al., 1988).

Although the search for cognitive factors is promising, certain issues must be addressed. First, although the majority of patients report that panic attacks are accompanied by cognitions, a substantial percentage report not being aware of any thoughts during these episodes (Rachman et al., 1987). "Noncognitive" panic attacks present a problem for cognitive theorists. Second, it is unclear why individuals with GAD and panic disorder are so prone to having thoughts of catastrophe.

Biological Perspective Biological factors associated with GAD have not been widely investigated. Panic disorder, however, has received a great deal of attention. Although the precise mechanism triggering panic disorder has not been identified, several explanations have been offered to support a biological model. Klein (1981) believes that people who experience panic have a specific biological dysfunction that predisposes them to this disorder. It is hypothesized that the dysfunction involves the receptors monitoring the amount of oxygen in the blood. They give the incorrect message that there is insufficient oxygen, triggering fears of suffocation (Fishman & Sheehan, 1985). To determine if some people have a predisposition to panic attacks, biological challenge tests have been used. This procedure involves administering a biological agent to people who have panic attacks and to others who do not have such attacks. It is expected that only people who are biologically susceptible will show a response.

Biological Challenge Tests The majority of people with panic disorder will have a panic attack when given sodium lactate (Stewart et al., 1988; Klein, 1984). It is assumed that a biological sensitivity to lactate produces feelings of alarm. In addition, antidepressants have been found to block both spontaneous and lactate-induced panic attacks (Aronson, 1987). Presumably medication raises the threshold for attacks in susceptible individuals. Although these results support a biological model, some findings are contradictory. For example, some "normal" subjects infused with sodium lactate will also experience panic attacks (Balon et al., 1985). In another study, desensitization was found to be effective in blocking panic attacks in a person who had a panic disorder. Before desensitization, the subject responded to lactate infusions with a panic attack (Guttmacher & Nelles, 1984), but successfully inhibited a lactate-induced panic attack after desensitization. Expectations may also affect the results of biological challenge tests. For example, instructions given before lactate infusion seem to influence the way subjects respond to the substance. Those who expect pleasant sensations show less anxiety than those who expect unpleasant bodily sensations (Van Der Molen et al., 1986). Although the research seems to support a biological mechanism in panic disorder, cognitive factors also play a role.

Genetic Studies Genetic studies are difficult to interpret for several reasons. First, research conducted before 1980 used DSM-II diagnostic criteria. Whether these findings still apply to the current definitions of generalized anxiety disorder and panic disorder is uncertain. Second, adoption studies have not been reported, so that environmental influences cannot be eliminated. Nevertheless, several studies do support a genetic influence. Higher **concordance rates** (percentages of relatives sharing the same disorder) for panic disorder have been found for monozygotic (MZ) twins versus dizygotic (DZ) twins (Torgersen, 1983). A lifetime risk of 41 percent has been found in first-degree relatives (parents and siblings) of individuals with panic disorder (Crowe et al., 1983). In general, available data support a genetic predisposition for panic disorder.

Fewer genetic studies have been done on generalized anxiety disorder than on panic disorder. The strategy used to study GAD has been to examine the distribution of anxiety disorders among family members of people with the disorder and compare it with control group members. There is less support for the role of genetic factors in generalized anxiety disorder than for panic disorder (Crowe et al., 1983; Torgersen, 1983).

Treatment of Panic Disorder and Generalized Anxiety Disorder

The anxiety disorders have received increasing attention from researchers over the past few years. An issue of particular concern is whether or not some types of anxiety disorders (in particular, panic disorder and generalized anxiety disorder) are really distinct disorders, each requiring special treatment. Because this question has not been resolved, we discuss their treatments separately here.

Panic Disorder Treatments for panic disorder can generally be divided into two approaches: biological (via medication) and psychotherapeutic. Both antidepressants and tranquilizers have been used for medication. Although there is considerable controversy about how antidepressants work against panic attacks, these drugs do seem to reduce not only depression but also extreme fears (Mavissakalian, 1987a; Klein, 1984). Success has been reported in treating panic disorder with a particular antidepressant, imipramine (Garakani et al., 1984; Pohl et al., 1984).

In a study of ten patients with panic disorder, who were treated with imipramine, Garakani and his colleagues found that nearly all improved. However, four patients discontinued the medication because of its side effects, and the researchers based their report of success on the self-reports of the patients' self-reports. Moreover, altered patterns of exposure to anxiety-producing situations may have affected the results. Antidepressants may be successful because they make it easier for patients to confront fearful stimuli. Aronson (1987) concludes that imipramine only blocks panic attacks and that patients still must learn to overcome avoidance responses through exposure.

Other medications, such as alprazolam (Fyer et al., 1987) and verapamil (Klein & Uhde, 1988), have been also proved effective in treating panic disorder. That so many different medications have been used successfully raises questions about the biological nature of panic disorder. It is possible that there are several different forms of the disorder which would help explain the successful use of so many different medications.

The application of behavioral techniques to panic disorder is still quite limited, probably because the disorder is considered biological. However, several behavioral strategies have been used in treating panic disorder. Ost (1987b) compared the relative effectiveness of (1) standard relaxation training with (2) applied relaxation, working with fourteen patients who had panic disorders. Both groups were taught relaxation techniques, but the applied relaxation group was also taught to recognize the beginning signs of anxiety and to respond to them rapidly. They also practiced relaxation methods in different anxiety-evoking situations. Although both procedures improved symptoms, the applied relaxation was much more effective. All patients in the applied relaxation group were panic free at posttreatment and during the nineteen-month follow-up. In the progressive relaxation group, two of the seven had panic attacks after treatment and three had attacks during the follow-up period. Applied relaxation also effectively reduced depressive and general anxiety symptoms.

Although applied relaxation is a promising technique, many researchers still conclude that panic disorder patients need treatment specifically aimed at cognitions (Butler & Mathews, 1983). One approach is cognitive restructuring (Hibbert, 1984). In this psychotherapeutic treatment, the therapist helps the patient identify anxiety-arousing thoughts, examine the basis for these thoughts, and change them into more realistic thoughts. Combining cognitive restructuring with muscle relaxation or biofeedback training has been suggested to produce an even more effective treatment package (Barlow et al., 1984).

Generalized Anxiety Disorder In general, psychological treatment for generalized anxiety disorder is similar to that for panic disorder. Treatment that deals with the three response systems (cognitive, physiological, and behavioral) appears to be more effective in treating GAD than therapy relying on only a single technique such as relaxation training. Butler et al. (1987) reported a highly effective treatment that includes identifying and altering anxiety-evoking thoughts, developing coping strategies, relaxation training, and gradual self-exposure to anxiety-evoking situations. Highly significant changes were reported in anxiety, depression, and avoidance responses. Behavioral treatment for generalized anxiety disorder appears to be a viable option to medication.

Benzodiazepines (Valium and Librium) have been used successfully to treat generalized anxiety disorder. However, tolerance and dependence are a problem (Committee on the Review of Medicines, 1980). Lindsay et al. (1987) compared the relative effectiveness of anxiety management training to treatment with benzodiazepines for a group of GAD patients. At first, the benzodiazepines seemed more effective, but as the study progressed the anxiety management group began to show more improvement. In general, it appears that medication can help reduce anxiety in people who have GAD, but that psychological intervention is also necessary to reduce their avoidance responses.

PHOBIAS

The word *phobia* comes from the Greek word that means *fear*. A **phobia** is a strong, persistent, and unwarranted fear of some specific object or situation. Nearly anything can become the focus of this intense fear. In fact, there is even a fear of phobias, called *phobophobia* (see Table 6.1). Phobias are the most common mental disorder in the United States and affect over 15 million individuals (National Institute of Mental Health, 1986).

DSM-III-R includes three subcategories of phobias: agoraphobia, which is a single irrational fear that may be manifested in different ways; the social phobias, which generally involve social situations; and the simple phobias, which include most of the fears listed in Table 6.1.

TABLE 6.1 | Phobias and Their Objects

Acrophobia—fear of heights	*Microphobia*—fear of germs
Agoraphobia—fear of open spaces	*Monophobia*—fear of being alone
Ailurophobia—fear of cats	*Mysophobia*—fear of contamination or germs
Algophobia—fear of pain	
Arachnophobia—fear of spiders	*Nyctophobia*—fear of the dark
Astrapophobia—fear of storms, thunder, and lightning	*Ochlophobia*—fear of crowds
Aviophobia—fear of airplanes	*Pathophobia*—fear of disease
Brontophobia—fear of thunder	*Phobophobia*—fear of phobias
Claustrophobia—fear of closed spaces	*Pyrophobia*—fear of fire
Dementophobia—fear of insanity	*Syphilophobia*—fear of syphilis
Genitophobia—fear of genitals	*Topophobia*—fear of performing
Hematophobia—fear of blood	*Xenophobia*—fear of strangers
	Zoophobia—fear of animals or some particular animal

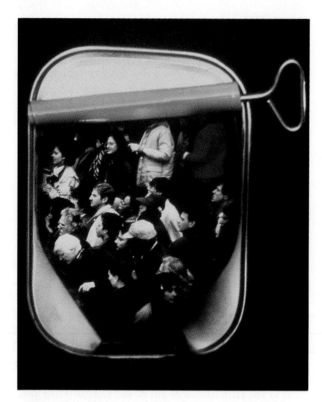

Agoraphobics may suffer extreme anxiety or panic attacks when they are outside, alone, or in a crowd. Many agoraphobics can recall the situation that triggered the disorder.

Agoraphobia

Agoraphobia is an intense fear of being in public places where escape or help may not be readily available. It often arises from a fear that frightening physical symptoms will occur that will incapacitate or cause the person to behave in an embarrassing manner (fainting, losing control over bodily functions, displaying excessive fear in public). Anxiety over showing these symptoms can prevent people from leaving their homes. Agoraphobia has a lifetime prevalence rate of approximately 2.7 percent for males and 8.0 percent for females (Robins et al., 1984). Although this is not the most common phobia, people who have this disorder account for the large majority of phobics who are seen for treatment (Michelson, 1987).

Many people report having panic attacks before developing agoraphobia (Franklin, 1987) as illustrated in the following case:

The patient was a 28-year-old woman whose attacks of anxiety were triggered by the terrifying sensation of impending death. This feeling was so horrifying that she would clutch passers-by and beg them for help. These episodes were acutely embarrassing to her, because no physical illness could be found. In an interview, it was discovered that her anxiety attacks occurred in situations where she felt trapped, such as in a crowded restaurant. Finally, her fear of experiencing these symptoms in public reached the point where she was unwilling to leave her home unless accompanied by her husband.

The precise relationship between agoraphobia and panic disorder is not clear. One might be a variant of the other. If an agoraphobic meets the criteria for a panic disorder (four panic attacks within a four-week period), the appropriate diagnosis would be panic disorder with agoraphobia.

A nationwide survey of over 900 agoraphobics revealed that nearly 75 percent of those surveyed could recall an event that precipitated the disorder. In 38 percent of the cases, this event was a traumatic experience; in 23 percent it was the death of a family member or friend; in 13 percent, a personal illness; in 8 percent, giving birth; and in 4 percent, marital difficulties. The situations most likely to produce attacks involve being trapped, having to wait in line, being far away from home, and having domestic arguments. But most of those surveyed feel less anxious when they are accompanied by a spouse or friend or when they have easy access to an exit (Thorpe & Burns, 1983).

There is increased interest in examining the role of cognitions in agoraphobia. Like depressed clients, people with panic disorders or agoraphobia display perception of personal helplessness (Ganellen, 1988). It is possible that agoraphobics misinterpret events or elevate them to catastrophes. In a study of the sixty patients with agoraphobia, J. A. Franklin (1987) found the following pattern:

- *Some physical or psychological stressor*
- *Altered physical sensations* (increased heart rate, overbreathing, and so forth)

◆ *Faulty appraisal* (incorrectly interpreting the symptoms as representing a severe physical problem such as a heart attack or loss of control)

◆ *Avoidance* (Although the attacks were described as highly aversive, believing that it represented a pathological outcome intensified the fear.) This led to avoidance of the situation associated with the fear.

Not everyone who experiences physical sensation develops anxiety attacks. Reiss et al. (1986) contend that people react differently to physical symptoms or sensations. They developed the Anxiety Sensitivity Inventory (ASI) to investigate this phenomenon. The ASI measures a person's reaction to anxiety symptoms. People who score high on the test agreed with such statements as "When I notice that my heart is beating rapidly, I worry that I might be having a heart attack." People with low anxiety sensitivity only interpreted the sensation as being unpleasant. Reiss and his colleagues did find that agoraphobics scored higher on the ASI than people who had other anxiety disorders. Similar results were obtained by McNally and Lorenz (1987). It is too early to tell whether anxiety sensitivity or faulty appraisal act as predisposing factors in the development of panic disorders and agoraphobia, or whether they are the result of having the disorders. However, there is increasing support for the role of cognitions in the etiology of anxiety disorders.

Social Phobias

A **social phobia** is an intense fear of being scrutinized. The most common forms include extreme fear of public speaking, of eating in restaurants, of using public restrooms, or of performing in public. There is no fear when the person engages in any of these activities in private. The person's fear stems from anxiety that, in the company of others, he or she will perform one of these activities in a manner that is embarrassing or humiliating, as indicated in the following case example:

A 21-year-old man was so anxious when using public toilet facilities that he would search for an isolated restroom when he needed to urinate. Even when he was alone in the restroom, urination was difficult; it became impossible when another man entered. His anticipatory anxiety eventually became so great that he severely restricted his intake of liquids during the day.

One common type of social phobia is an irrational fear of public speaking. For some people, the anxiety felt before a public speaking engagement is so overwhelming that they are unable to deliver their prepared talk.

FOCUS 6.2 *When Is a Fear a Phobia?*

Social fears are common. In one study, 40 percent of college and high school students were found to suffer from social fears (Zimbardo, 1977). These students displayed excessive self-consciousness and concern about what others thought, along with such physiological reactions as increased pulse rate, blushing, and perspiration.

Social phobias, however, are considered to be relatively uncommon. But when is a fear extreme enough considered a phobia? According to DSM-III-R, several elements must be present for the diagnosis of phobia: (1) a persistent and irrational fear with a compelling desire to avoid the situation, (2) anxiety in the presence of the phobic stimulus, and (3) significant distress because the person recognizes that the fear is excessive.

Are these criteria fulfilled in the case of a student with public speaking anxiety who drops out of classes where oral participation is required, or in the case of a student with heterosexual anxiety who will not talk to people of the opposite sex even when he or she strongly wants to do so? The subjective nature of the criteria makes that question difficult to answer. Exactly how "com-pelling" must the fear be, and how much distress is "significant"? Even the usually very specific DSM-III-R is less than clear on this issue. DSM-III-R gives public speaking anxiety as an example of a social phobia. But later (p. 242) says that "avoidance of certain social situations that are normally a source of some distress, which is common in many individuals with 'normal' fear of public speaking, does not justify a diagnosis of social phobia." So the question still remains: When does a "normal" fear become "abnormal"?

As is true of other phobics, socially phobic people usually realize that their behavior and fears are irrational, but this understanding does not reduce the distress they feel. The six-month prevalence rate (whether the person had the disorder within the last six months) for social phobia is approximately 1.3 percent for males and 2.1 percent for females (Myers et al. 1984). Social phobias tend to begin during adolescence (Ost, 1987a). Social phobias are relatively rare, with the exception of public speaking, but anxiety in social situations is fairly common. Focus 6.2 explores the difference between the two.

Socially phobic (and anxious) people are concerned that their nervousness and anxiety will be detected by others. However, researchers have found that other people often do not detect behavioral signs of anxiety in highly socially anxious subjects (McEwan & Devins, 1983). Socially anxious individuals apparently are more aware of their anxiety than are other people.

Simple Phobias

A **simple phobia** is an extreme fear of a specific object (such as snakes) or situation (such as being in an enclosed place). In a sense, the simple phobias provide a catchall category for irrational fears that are neither agoraphobia nor social phobias. The only similarity among the various simple phobias is the existence of an irrational fear. The most common of these fears involve small animals, heights, the dark, and lightning; others involve death, exams, deep water, and being mentally ill (Kirkpatrick, 1984). Unusual and uncommon simple phobias have involved bathwater running down the drain (after pulling out the plug, the affected person would dash out of the bathroom with great anxiety); snow (the fear developed after the man got stuck in a snowstorm and arrived too late to talk to his dying father); and a woman who was terrified of three-legged stools (Adler et al., 1984).

The following report of a fairly common simple phobia demonstrates one treatment method as well:

Ms. B, a 23-year-old woman, complained of a phobia of spiders that had not changed for as long as she could remember. She had no history of any other psychiatric symptoms. In treatment, when initially approached with a closed glass jar containing spiders, she breathed heavily, wept tears, and rated her subjective distress as 70 to 80. She suddenly began scratching the back of her hand, stating she felt as though spiders were crawling under her skin, although she knew this was not the case. The sensation lasted only a few seconds and did not recur. Her total treatment consisted of four 1-hour sessions distributed over the span of a month. At completion she had lost all fear of spiders and became able to let them crawl freely about her arms, legs, and face as well as inside her clothing with no distress whatever. She remained free of fear at 1-year follow-up, expressing disbelief that she had allowed such a "silly fear" to dominate her life for so long. (Curtis, 1981, p. 1095)

Simple phobias are more prevalent in women than in men and are rarely incapacitating. The degree to which they interfere with daily life depends on how easy it is to avoid the feared object or situation. Simple phobias often begin during childhood. In a study of 370 phobic patients (Ost, 1987a), retrospective data revealed that animal phobias tend to have the earliest onset age (7 years), followed by blood phobia (9 years), dental phobia (12 years), and claustrophobia (20 years).

Fears are quite common in children and involve themes such as injury and death, being in the dark, traffic accident, not being able to breathe, and looking foolish (Ollendick et al., 1985). These fears very seldom remain to become phobias; most are lost as the child gets older. Even in phobic children, most recover without treatment. However, phobias that begin during later adolescence or adulthood tend to persist if they are not treated.

Etiology of Phobias

How do such strong and "irrational" fears develop? Both psychological and biological explanations have been proposed. In this section, we will examine the psychoanalytic, behavioral, and biological views of the etiology of phobias.

Psychoanalytic Perspective According to the psychoanalytic viewpoint, phobias are symptomatic of unconscious sexual or aggressive conflicts that are displaced (or shifted) from their original internal source to an external object or situation. The phobia is less threatening to the person than is recognition of the underlying unconscious impulse. A fear of knives, for example, may represent castration fears produced by an unresolved Oedipus complex or aggressive conflicts. Agoraphobics may develop their

Simple phobias, unlike agoraphobia or social phobia, do not interfere greatly with daily life. Many people, for example, are scared of flying. They cannot board a plane or even think about flying without being overwhelmed by fear that the plane will crash and they will die in it.

fear of leaving home because they unconsciously fear they may act out unacceptable sexual desires. The presence of a friend or spouse lowers anxiety because it provides some protection against the agoraphobic's impulses.

In this sense, phobias represent a compromise between the ego and the impulses that seek gratification. The person blocks from consciousness the real source of anxiety and is able to avoid the dangerous impulse that the phobia represents.

Psychoanalysts believe the level of phobic fear indicates the strength of the underlying conflict. This formulation, presented by Freud in 1909, was based on his analysis of a fear of horses displayed by a five-year-old boy named Hans (Freud, [1909] 1959). Freud believed that the phobia represented a symptomatic or displaced fear arising from the Oedipus complex. The factors involved were the boy's incestuous attraction to his mother, hostility toward his father because of the father's sexual privileges, and castration fear (fear of retribution by his father). Freud became convinced that all these elements were present in the phobic boy.

At the age of three, Hans had displayed an interest in his penis (which he called his "widdler"); he would examine animate and inanimate objects for the presence of a penis. One day as he was fondling himself, his mother threatened to have a physician cut off his penis. "And then what will you widdle with?" (Freud, 1909, p. 151). Hans enjoyed having his mother bathe him and especially wanted her to touch his penis. Freud interpreted these events to indicate that Hans was aware of pleasurable sensations in his penis and that he knew it could be "cut off" if he did not behave. Wanting his mother to handle his genitals indicated Hans's increasing sexual interest in her.

Hans's fear that horses would bite him developed after he saw a horse-drawn van overturn. According to Freud, little Hans's sexual jealousy of his father and the hostility it aroused in Hans produced anxiety because he believed his father could retaliate by castrating him. This unconscious threat was so unbearable that the fear was displaced to the idea that horses "will bite me." Freud concluded that phobias were adaptive because they prevented the surfacing of more traumatic unconscious conflicts.

Although Freud's formulation has clinical appeal, it has problems. According to the psychoanalytic

perspective, if the phobia is only a symptom of an underlying unconscious conflict, treatment directed to that symptom—the feared object or situation—should be ineffective, or leave the patient defenseless and subject to overwhelming anxiety, or lead to the development of a new symptom. But the evidence does not support the view that eliminating the phobia is ineffective (Rachman & Wilson, 1980).

Classical Conditioning Perspective   The behavioral position regarding the origin of phobias—that they are conditioned responses—is based primarily on Watson's conditioning experiment with Little Albert (see Chapter 3). However, the use of classical conditioning principles to produce intense fears in humans was demonstrated more recently (Campbell et al., 1964). This experiment, however, has been *severely* criticized on several ethical grounds. In the experiment, a traumatic conditioning procedure was used to establish fear of a tone in five alcoholic patients. The unconditioned stimulus was a drug (scoline) that paralyzes the skeletal musculature. The drug makes breathing very difficult, although the patient is still conscious and aware of what is happening. The experimenters sounded a tone at the first signs of paralysis. The paralysis produced an inability to breathe for 90 to 130 seconds, which resulted in feelings of utter terror on the part of the subjects. All the subjects thought they were going to die. This conditioned emotional reaction was highly resistant to extinction.

Although some phobias may result from a traumatic event or from classical conditioning, the experimental data do not entirely support this view. English (1929) was unable to replicate the results of Watson and Rayner's experiment when he tried to establish a conditioned fear in a 14-month-old girl by presenting a painted wooden duck while banging a steel bar behind her. Conditioning did not take place (although the noise upset teachers and students throughout the building). Bregman (1934) was also unable to condition fifteen infants aged 8 to 16 months to fear wooden blocks and triangles by using a loud electric bell as the unconditioned stimulus. However, perhaps these experiments didn't replicate Watson and Rayner's experiment because it's more difficult to establish a fear response to inanimate objects than to animate stimuli, or because the experimenters didn't use an unconditioned stimulus that was strong enough.

In three studies (Ost, 1987a; Ost & Hugdahl, 1981; Rimm et al., 1977) on the acquisition of phobias, more patients attributed their disorders to direct (classical) conditioning experiences than to any other factor (Table 6.2). Ost and Hugdahl (1981) found that agoraphobics were the most likely to attribute their disorder to direct conditioning experiences followed by claustrophobics and people with dental phobia. Phobias caused by indirect (or observational) conditioning experiences involved cognitive and subjective factors more than physiological ones. These findings suggest the role of cognitive, behavioral, and physiological factors may vary according to the type of phobia.

There is some clinical and survey support for the classical conditioning perspective on phobias. However, a substantial percentage of surveyed patients report something other than a direct conditioning experience as the "key" to their phobias. And, in the Rimm et al. (1977) study, 36 percent could not recall how their fear was acquired. Moreover, the classical conditioning perspective does not explain why only a small percentage of people exposed to potential conditioning experiences actually develop phobias.

Observational Learning and Operant Conditioning Perspectives Emotional conditioning can be developed through modeling or through observational learning. An observer who watched while a model exhibited pain cues in response to an auditory stimulus (a buzzer) gradually developed an emotional reaction to the sound (Bandura & Rosenthal, 1966). The buzzer, formerly a neutral stimulus, became a conditioned stimulus for the observer. In a clinical (rather than an experimental) example involving modeling, several people who had seen the horror film *The Exorcist* had to be treated for a variety of anxiety reactions (Bozzuto, 1975).

Table 6.2 shows that only a small proportion of surveyed patients indicated that they acquired phobias through vicarious (indirect) conditioning, or modeling. If information or instruction received is also considered as leading to observational learning, this means of acquisition would account for about 20 to 25 percent of the phobias. (One interpretation of the high prevalence of anxiety reactions among close relatives of phobics involves modeling as a cause, rather than genetics.) However, the data shown in Table 6.2 are based on patients' recollections of past events, and such data are subject to a variety of errors.

The observational learning perspective seems to have the same problem as classical conditioning with regard to the etiology of phobias. It's not enough, by itself, to explain why only some people develop phobias after exposure to a vicarious experience.

Some theorists have suggested that phobias may be learned through reinforcement (operant conditioning). For example, a child who is reinforced—perhaps by being held and comforted—after making statements about fears tends to increase such verbalizations of fears. However, in light of the aversive nature of phobias and the distress they produce, such reinforcement is not likely to be a major factor in their development.

Biological Perspective If a higher-than-average prevalence of a disorder is found in close relatives, or if identical twins (who share the same genetic

TABLE 6.2 | Means of Acquiring Phobias, as Reported by Patients (in percentages)

Means of Acquisition	Study		
	Ost and Hugdahl (1981)	Rimm et al. (1977)	Ost (1987a)
Direct conditioning	57.5	44.4	64
Indirect conditioning	17	8.3	14
Information/instruction	10.4	11.1	6
No recall	15.1	36.1	16

makeup) show a higher concordance rate for the disorder than fraternal twins (who have different genetic makeups), a case can be made for the role of genetic factors in the disorder. Harris and her colleagues (1983) found that the prevalence of reported anxiety disorders for *first-degree relatives* (parents and siblings) of agoraphobic patients was more than twice that for first-degree relatives of a control group (32 percent versus 15 percent). These findings can be interpreted as supporting the view that agoraphobia is a familial disorder. However, as we noted earlier, an alternative explanation for such results is that they are due to modeling.

Evidence for the direct genetic transmission of specific anxiety disorders is not strong. More support exists for the view that constitutional or physiological factors may *predispose* individuals to develop fear reactions. It is possible that a certain level of autonomic nervous system (ANS) reactivity is inherited; then people born with high ANS reactivity respond more strongly to stimuli, and their chances of developing an anxiety disorder are increased. In support of this possibility, researchers found that people who had high resting arousal levels showed easier conditioning to certain stimuli than did people with low resting arousal levels (Hugdahl et al., 1971).

A different biological approach to the development of fear reactions is that of **preparedness** (Seligman, 1971). Proponents of this position argue that fears develop nonrandomly. In particular, they believe that it is easier for humans to learn fears to which we are physiologically predisposed. Such quickly aroused (or "prepared") fears may have been necessary to the survival of pretechnological humanity in the natural environment.

Several predictions can be made from the preparedness hypothesis:

1. Certain classes of stimuli (those dangerous to pretechnical humans such as snakes and other animals) should be more easily conditioned.

2. Onset of phobias should be sudden rather than gradual since the organism is biologically prepared to respond to certain stimuli.

3. The phobia should be resistant to extinction.

One proponent of this view notes that it is rare to encounter phobias about automobiles or electrical appliances: Presumably, this is because pretechnical

humans did not have an innate phobic response to these items (McConaghy, 1983). DeSilva (1988) wanted to see whether the preparedness theory applied to non-Western populations. Records of eighty-eight phobic patients treated in Sri Lanka were examined and rated in terms of "preparedness" (objects or situations dangerous to pretechnical humanity under most circumstances). Most of the phobias were rated as "prepared." However, in conflict with the preparedness theory, no association was found between the type of phobia and sudden or gradual onset.

The combination of classical conditioning and prepared learning is a promising area for further research. But it is difficult to believe that many (or even most) phobias stem from prepared fears, simply because they just do not fit into that model. It would be difficult, for example, to explain the survival value of such social phobias as the fear of using public restrooms and of eating in public, of agoraphobia, and of many simple phobias. In addition, prepared fears appear to have variable age of onset and are among the most easy to eliminate.

Treatment of Phobias

We begin our discussion of how phobias are treated with agoraphobia, the disorder on which most treatment effort has been focused.

Agoraphobia The primary treatment approaches for agoraphobia are medical, behavioral, and a combination of the two. A number of studies have shown that antidepressants such as imipramine not only help reduce depression but also the extreme fear displayed by agoraphobics (Garakani et al., 1984; Mavissakalian et al., 1983). But less positive results with imipramine were reported when the antidepressant was compared with a placebo and exposure to the feared object; these researchers concluded that the effective component was exposure (Marks et al., 1983; Lelliott et al., 1987). Significant improvement was also found in twenty agoraphobic patients who received a placebo rather than imipramine (Mavissakalian, 1987).

Methodological flaws tend to hamper the evaluation of drugs in treating agoraphobia, because (1) most studies rely only on self-reports as measures of success, (2) control groups are generally not employed, and (3) patients are often encouraged to expose themselves to the fear-producing situation while they are receiving medication. One study was designed specifically to separate and compare the contributions of drugs and exposure in the treatment of agoraphobics. The patients were randomly assigned to treatment with imipramine alone, imipramine plus exposure, or placebo plus exposure. An important element in the study was control of the possible effects of exposure on the drug-only group: patients in this group were told not to enter fear-arousing situations until the medication had a chance to build up (some six or eight weeks). Results were measured via self-reports and behavioral and physiological scales. Both exposure groups showed significant improvement according to all three measures. The imipramine-only patients showed no improvement on any of the measures, although they did show a significant reduction of depressed mood. Imipramine plus exposure showed a slight advantage over placebo plus exposure in reducing phobic anxiety (Telch, 1982).

Agoraphobics treated with imipramine seem to require behavioral treatment as well, to reduce anxiety and avoidance of the feared situation. Because 60-70 percent of agoraphobics can be successfully treated by exposure methods alone, medication is not necessary as a treatment for most individuals with this disorder (Mavissakalian et al., 1983).

The behavioral treatment of agoraphobia (and other phobias) has centered on **exposure therapy**. In this technique, the patient is gradually introduced to increasingly difficult encounters with the feared situation (Ghosh & Marks, 1987). An agoraphobic might, for example, be asked to take longer and longer walks outside the home with the therapist. The earliest of these encounters may often be only imagined or visualized by the patient, at the therapist's request. After the fear is reduced, relapse training is conducted to anticipate and deal with setbacks.

Exposure therapy has been successful in significantly reducing fears and panic attacks in agoraphobic patients. Exposure, especially with appropriate modifications, seems to be a viable treatment for agoraphobia. Follow-up studies at periods ranging from four to seven years after exposure treatment show little evidence of relapse (Marks, 1987). However, even though significant improvements occur, most patients still retain mild to moderate symptoms (Michelson et al., 1988).

To increase the effectiveness of behavioral treatment of agoraphobia, therapists increasingly emphasize multiple treatment methods. Exposure treatment tends to ignore the cognitive, although some studies show that cognitions and expectations are important in such treatment. Agoraphobics who have high expectancy (have been told that the procedure is an effective treatment) were able to travel about twice as far from home as those with low expectancy (being told that the procedure is merely for the purposes of assessment). Both groups had received ten *in vivo* exposure sessions. Thus, expectancy may mediate exposure to feared situations.

Marchione et al. (1987) also contend that adding cognitive therapy to exposure therapy can increase the effectiveness of both. They assigned agoraphobic patients to (1) a *gradual exposure-only* group, or (2) a gradual exposure plus cognitive therapy group. The cognitive component included the monitoring and recording of automatic thoughts, understanding their relationship to phobic behavior, generating alternative rational responses, developing problem-solving skills, and learning relapse prevention. Both approaches were successful in treating agoraphobia, but the inclusion of cognitive therapy increased the potency of the exposure treatment. More researchers are stressing the importance of assessing and directly altering different response systems to increase the effectiveness of treating agoraphobia.

Social and Simple Phobias The treatment of choice for the social and simple phobias is also behavioral, but a number of different behavioral techniques appear to be beneficial. For example, **systematic desensitization** has been used as a treatment for phobias. Wolpe (1958, 1973), who introduced the treatment, taught phobics a response (relaxation) that is incompatible with fear, by repeatedly pairing relaxation with visualizations of the feared stimulus. Systematic desensitization has been demonstrated to be effective with both simple and social phobias (Hekmat et al., 1984).

Modeling therapy procedures have also been highly effective in treating certain phobias. When modeling is used as therapy, the phobic person observes a fearless model in the act of coping with, or responding appropriately in, the fear-producing situation. Some researchers feel that modeling is a unique therapeutic approach in its own right, whereas others feel that it is a type of exposure treatment.

Graduated exposure has been used successfully to treat a variety of phobias such as fear of heights (Marshall, 1988) and flying (Walder et al., 1987). As with agoraphobia, it appears that graduated exposure is more effective if combined with other techniques such as coping skills (Hayes & Marshall, 1984) and anxiety management (Butler et al., 1984). There is also increased interest in assessing cognitions and using cognitive treatment strategies. Walder and his colleagues found that people with dental phobias had such anxiety-provoking thoughts as "The dentist is going to hit a nerve." Feelings of anxiety were related

to thoughts of losing control. These researchers suggest that treatment procedures be developed to enhance control over both behavior and cognitions.

The behavioral approaches just mentioned have all demonstrated reasonably good results in treating a variety of phobias. McCann et al. (1987) compared the effectiveness of systematic desensitization, behavioral rehearsal (exposure and practice), and cognitive restructuring in treating individuals with severe interpersonal anxiety. All the treatments successfully reduced social fears. Although few differences appeared among the three treatment groups, cognitive restructuring (identifying anxiety-inducing thoughts and replacing them with positive coping statements) had a more significant impact on the cognitive measures of anxiety, while behavioral rehearsal had greater impact on behavioral measures. The researchers believe that the results are consistent with the three-part model of anxiety, in which there is some overlap but also some independence among the three dimensions (cognitive, behavioral, and biological). A multimodal treatment strategy seems to be the most effective (Mattick & Peters, 1988).

Although cognitive-behavioral approaches are effective in treating phobias, interpersonal factors such as positive regard are also important. In one study, phobics received treatment involving both exposure and cognitive intervention. Everyone improved, but those who rated their therapist more favorably during the initial session reported more improvement. Bennun and Shindler (1988) believe the effectiveness of behavior therapy could be improved by paying attention to interpersonal variables.

Modeling therapy has proven effective in treating both simple and social phobias. Watching a fear-producing act being successfully performed (like the act being performed by the man in this photo) can help a person overcome his or her own fear of the behavior.

OBSESSIVE-COMPULSIVE DISORDER

Obsessive-compulsive disorder is an anxiety disorder that is characterized by intrusive and uncontrollable thoughts or the need to perform specific acts repeatedly, or both. Obsessive-compulsive disorder is highly distressing because it involves a lack of voluntary control over one's own thoughts and actions. The inability to rid oneself of uncontrollable, alien, and often unacceptable thoughts, or to keep from performing ritualistic acts over and over again, arouses intense anxiety. In one study of obsessive-compulsives, 70 percent indicated that their rituals were distressing to both themselves and their families, 78 percent considered their rituals absurd, and over 50 percent attempted to resist carrying out the rituals (Stern & Cobb, 1978). But failure to engage in ritual acts often resulted in mounting anxiety and tension.

Some features of obsessive-compulsive disorder are obvious in the following case:

> A 24-year-old single man felt compelled to ruminate practically all his waking hours. He had a seven-year history of obsessional ruminations, had been out of work for three years, and was living with his parents. Ruminations usually involved worrying in case he had made a mistake in the course of performing some quite trivial action. Anxiety and doubt would be evoked by mundane activities, such as turning a light switch, changing direction when walking or going from one room to another. For example, when driving his car and taking a right turn at a traffic light, he would start thinking, "What would happen if I had turned left?" His ruminations would only come to an end once he had gone through all the possible alternative routes in his head. The degree of doubt felt by this patient was so strong that at times, when switching on a light, he would not trust his perception, and wondering if he had made a mistake, he would attempt to trace the wiring behind the wall in order to try to follow where the current went back to the switch, thus convincing himself that the bulb was actually illuminated.
>
> If necessary, his ruminations could be postponed for some hours but as long as they remained "unresolved" he would feel subjectively anxious. As a child, he remembered checking his schoolbooks and homework excessively. Later, mental checks replaced physical ones because they were quicker and unobtrusive. He reached university, but his obsessions had greatly multiplied by then. Yet he qualified as an engineer and started work. The necessity to take responsibility and make decisions caused a significant deterioration and eventually forced him to abandon the job. His basic fear was that of making a mistake and appearing foolish in front of others. At the time of his admission to hospital, he was thinking of hypothetical solutions to hypothetical errors following almost every activity he did. (Robertson et al., 1983, p. 352)

The disturbed individual may be plagued by either obsessions (which involve thoughts) or compulsions (which involve acts) or by both. Or, as in this case, one symptom may be replaced by the other at different stages of the disorder. Obsessive-compulsive people

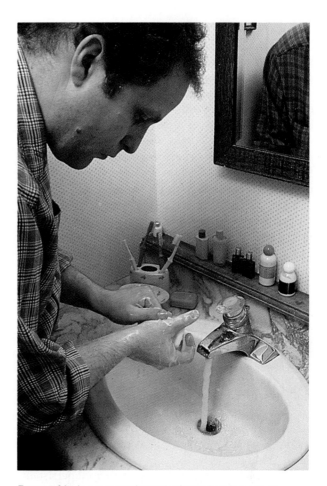

Fears of being contaminated trigger handwashing, which may last several hours a day. Unless this behavior is performed in a specific manner, intense anxiety occurs.

are highly secretive about their disorders and seldom become totally disabled. The approximate lifetime prevalence for the disorder for males is 1.9 percent and in women is 3.0 percent (Robins et al., 1984).

Obsessions

An **obsession** is an intrusive, uncontrollable, and persistent thought. The person may realize that the thought is irrational, but can't keep it from arising over and over again.

Sanavio (1988) found four factors associated with obsessional characteristics in both normal populations and in obsessive-compulsives:

1. *Impaired control over mental processes* This factor includes the inability to stop thinking of something such as thoughts of death of a loved one, catastrophic results from minor errors made, worry about hurting someone unintentionally, thoughts of obscene and dirty words or actions, or severe doubt over the correctness of a decision.

2. *Urges and worries over the possible loss of control over motor behaviors* Associated with this factor are impulses such as shouting obscene words in a church or classroom, throwing oneself in front of a car, killing or injuring others, performing inappropriate sexual acts in public, and feeling compelled to make stereotyped gestures or to perform activities in a certain way.

3. *Contamination* This factor involves worry, concern, and anxiety over being contaminated, including concern regarding contact with germs, diseases, dirty objects, animals, strangers, public lavatories, public telephones, library books, money, or bodily secretions. This factor was often associated with compulsions of washing and cleaning.

4. *Checking behaviors* Checking behaviors included: worry that doors, windows, or that drawers are not properly shut, that gas, water faucets, or lights have not been turned off, and subsequently feeling a need to "check" to determine that it had been "done properly."

Although most of us have experienced persistent thoughts—for instance, a song or tune that keeps running through one's mind—clinical forms are stronger and more intrusive. They create great distress and/or interfere with social or occupational activities. Many people who suffer from this disorder become partially incapacitated. Howard Hughes, a spectacularly successful businessman, pilot, and movie producer, withdrew so completely from the public that his only communication with the outside world was through telephones and intermediaries. His seclusiveness was connected to his obsessional fear of germ contamination.

> He took to refusing to shake hands with people and covering his hands with the ubiquitous sheets of Kleenex when he had to hold a glass or open a door. He forbade aides to eat onions, garlic, Roquefort dressing or other "breath destroyers." He considered air conditioners deadly germ collectors; he is said to have taken to sitting naked in darkened, sweltering hotel rooms, surrounded by crinkled

Kleenex and covered only with a few sheets over his privates. (*Newsweek,* April 19, 1976, p. 31)

Covering his hands with Kleenex as a defense against germs indicates that Hughes had also developed compulsions. In addition, he was preoccupied with the care of women's breasts. If women were passengers in his car, he would instruct his chauffeur to slow down when going over bumps in the road. Otherwise, he felt, the stress on the breasts would cause tissue breakdown and sagging; he was very concerned about preventing this.

Do "normal" people have intrusive, unacceptable thoughts, and impulses? Several studies (Edwards & Dickerson, 1987; Rachman & DeSilva, 1978; Salkovskis & Harrison, 1984; Sanavio, 1988) have found that over 80 percent of normal samples report the existence of unpleasant intrusive thoughts and impulses. Apparently, a considerable majority of the "normal" population have obsessive symptoms. But are obsessions reported by patients different from those reported by normal individuals?

Rachman and DeSilva (1978) printed the obsessions of individuals with and without obsessive-compulsive disorder on cards, mixed them up, and gave them to six expert judges to re-sort into normal and clinical obsessional thoughts. On the whole, the judges were not very accurate in identifying the clinical obsessions. They were somewhat more successful in identifying "normal" obsessions or impulses (such as the impulse to buy unwanted things). Obsessions reported by obsessive-compulsive patients and by normal populations overlap considerably. Rachman and DeSilva did find some differences, however. Obsessive patients reported that their obsessions lasted longer, were more intense, produced more discomfort, and were more difficult to dismiss. The mere existence of obsessive-compulsive symptoms for diagnostic purposes may not be very meaningful, because these symptoms are also reported in "normal" populations.

Compulsions

A **compulsion** is a behavior performed in a stereotyped manner. Distress or anxiety occurs if it is not performed or if it is not done "correctly." Compulsions are usually, but not always, associated with obsessions. Mild forms include such behaviors as refusing to walk under a ladder or to step on cracks in sidewalks, throwing salt over your shoulder, and knocking on wood. In the severe compulsive state, the behaviors become stereotyped and rigid; if they are not performed in a certain manner or a specific number of times, the compulsive individual is flooded with anxiety. To the compulsive, these behaviors often seem to have magical qualities, as though their correct performance warded off danger. The following case, known to us (the authors) and mentioned at the beginning of this chapter, is fairly typical:

A 15-year-old boy had a two-year history of compulsive behaviors, involving sixteen repetitions of the following behaviors: opening and closing a door, touching glasses before drinking from them, walking around each tree in front of his house before going to school. These compulsive acts produced a great deal of discomfort in the boy. His schoolmates ridiculed

him, and his parents were upset because his rituals prevented him from reaching school at the appropriate time. An interview with the boy revealed that his compulsive behaviors were associated with the onset of masturbation, an act that the boy considered "dirty," although he was unable to refrain from it. It was when he began to masturbate that the first of his compulsive behaviors (touching a glass sixteen times before drinking from it) developed.

Table 6.3 contains additional examples of obsessions and compulsions.

Etiology of Obsessive-Compulsive Disorder

The causes of obsessive-compulsive disorder remain unclear. In fact, therapists still argue about whether obsessions elevate or reduce anxiety. We'll examine

TABLE 6.3 | Clinical Examples of Obsessions and Compulsions

| Patient | | Duration of Obsession | |
Age	Sex	in Years	Content of Obsession
21	M	6	Teeth are decaying, particles between teeth
42	M	16	Women's buttocks, own eye movements
55	F	35	Fetuses lying in the street, killing babies, people buried alive
24	M	16	Worry about whether he has touched vomit
21	F	9	Strangling people
52	F	18	Contracting venereal disease

| Patient | | Duration of Compulsions | |
Age	Sex	in Years	Compulsive Rituals
47	F	23	Handwashing and housecleaning. Contact with dirt, toilet, or floor triggers about 100 hand-washings per day.
20	F	13	Severe checking ritual; checks 160 times to see if window is closed. Also compelled to read the license number of cars and the numbers on manhole covers.
21	M	2	Intense fear of contamination after touching library books, money. Washes hands 25 times a day and ruminates about how many people had handled the objects before him.

SOURCE: Compiled from Boersma et al., 1976; Rachman et al., 1973; Roper et al., 1975; Stern et al., 1973; and Shahar & Marks, 1980.

three theories that have been advanced to explain obsessive-compulsive behavior: the substitution, anxiety reduction, and superstition hypotheses. Then we'll discuss some biological explanations for the disorder.

Substitution Hypothesis   The *substitution hypothesis* is psychoanalytic in nature. Freud ([1909] 1949) believed that obsessions represent the substitution or replacement of an original conflict (usually sexual in nature) with an associated idea that is less threatening. He found support for his notion in the case histories of some of his patients. One, a girl, had disturbing obsessions about stealing or counterfeiting money, thoughts that were absurd and untrue. During analysis, Freud discovered that these obsessions reflected anxiety that stemmed from guilt about masturbation. When the patient was kept under constant observation, which prevented her from masturbating, the obsessional thoughts ceased.

The dynamics of obsession have been described as involving "the intrusion of the unwelcome thought [that] 'seeks' to prevent anxiety by serving as a more tolerable substitute for a subjectively less welcome thought or impulse" (Laughlin, 1967, p. 311). Freud's patient found thoughts involving stealing less disturbing than masturbation. Her displacement of that feeling to a substitute action prevented her ego defenses from being overwhelmed.

Several other psychoanalytic defense mechanisms are considered prominent in obsessive-compulsive behaviors. For example, *undoing* is canceling or atoning for forbidden impulses by engaging in repetitive, ritualistic activities. Washing one's hands may symbolically represent cleansing oneself of unconscious wishes. However, because the original conflict remains, one is compelled to perform the act of atonement over and over again. *Reaction formation* provides a degree of comfort because it counterbalances forbidden desires with diametrically opposed behaviors. To negate problems stemming from the anal psychosexual stage (characteristic of obsessive-compulsives), such as the impulse to be messy, patients tend toward excessive cleanliness and orderliness. Obsessive-compulsives may also employ the defense of *isolation,* which allows the separation of a thought or action from its effect. Aloofness, intellectualization, and detachment reduce the anxiety produced by patently aggressive or sexual thoughts.

The Anxiety Reduction Hypothesis   Proponents of the *anxiety reduction hypothesis* maintain that obsessive-compulsive behaviors develop because they reduce anxiety. A distracting thought or action recurs more often if it reduces anxiety. For example, many college students may develop mild forms of compulsive behavior during intense exam periods, such as final examinations. During this stressful and anxiety-filled time, students may find themselves engaging in escape activities, such as daydreaming, straightening up their rooms, or eating five or more times a day, all of which serve to shield them from thoughts of the upcoming tests. If the stress lasts a long time, a compulsive behavior may develop.

Although the anxiety reduction hypothesis is popular among learning theorists, it has not been very helpful in explaining how a behavior, such as handwashing that goes on for hours, can originate. Maher (1966) suggests that a compulsion is acquired through operant conditioning. For example, a person who has developed a compulsion for handwashing might have been reinforced in the past by parents for cleanliness, and therefore he or she considers handwashing desirable. When a transgression occurs, performing a socially learned anxiety-reducing response reduces the transgressor's feeling of guilt. Because this response is reinforcing, the person uses it whenever he or she feels anxiety or some other negative emotion. Unfortunately, this formulation does not explain why childhood anxiety-reducing behaviors are displayed by some adults and not by others. Neither does it explain why some compulsives perform acts that certainly were not endorsed by parents or otherwise socially reinforced—for example, walking around every tree in the back yard before performing a task.

Researchers have sought support for the anxiety reduction hypothesis with a specific sample of patients: obsessive washers and checkers. If the hypothesis is correct, touching a contaminated item should increase anxiety, and performing the compulsive act should reduce anxiety (Carr, 1974; Hodgson & Rachman, 1972; Roper & Rachman, 1976). Carr found that compulsive acts were performed when there were high levels of autonomic activity and that the performance of these acts reduced the person's arousal levels to those of a resting state.

In some cases, it does appear that the compulsive acts may continue because they reduce anxiety. However, the anxiety reduction hypothesis does not explain how these behaviors originate. In addition, many obsessional ruminations involve disease, insanity, mutilation or death—events that one would expect to elevate anxiety. As yet we can only speculate about the reinforcements associated with them.

The Superstition Hypothesis

According to the *superstition hypothesis,* a chance association of a behavior with a reinforcer is responsible for continuation of the behavior. According to some theorists, this is the mechanism by which superstitions are formed. Skinner's (1948) classic example of the causation of superstitious behavior involved reinforcing pigeons (with food) at regular intervals, regardless of their behavior. Each pigeon began to display unique head or body movements, presumably because these happened to be the behaviors the birds were engaged in when they were given food.

Many obsessive-compulsive rituals may be reinforced by chance when a positive outcome follows performance of a certain behavior (O'Leary & Wilson, 1975). A student may take exams with only one special pencil or pen that he or she associates with past success. Athletes have been reported to continue wearing the same dirty uniform as long as a winning streak lasts. Even though there is no actual relationship between these behaviors and a favorable or unfavorable outcome, the obsessive-compulsive may behave as though such a relationship existed. Anxiety develops if these rituals are not observed, because the person feels they are necessary to produce a positive outcome.

Although the hypothesis that obsessive-compulsive disorders are produced by the chance association of a behavior with a reinforcer is plausible, the proponents of the hypothesis have not specified the conditions under which "superstitious" behavior develops. Furthermore, the hypothesis does not explain the development of powerful and intrusive thoughts or rituals.

Biogenic Models

Biological explanations of obsessive-compulsive behaviors are based on data relating to brain structure, genetic studies, and biochemical abnormalities. Differences in brain activity have been found among people who have obsessive-compulsive disorder, severe depression, and those with no psychiatric disorders. Obsessive-compulsives show increased metabolic activity in the frontal lobe of the left hemisphere. Perhaps this area of the brain, the left orbital gyrus, is associated with obsessive-compulsive behaviors (Bower, 1987). It is not clear, however, whether metabolic changes reflect the *cause* of obsessive-compulsive disorder or its *effects*, or a combination of the two.

Some researchers (Comings & Comings, 1987) believe that some obsessive-compulsive behaviors are caused by genetic factors. Family and twin studies support this theory. In a carefully controlled study, McKeon and Murray (1987) found that the relatives of obsessive-compulsives were twice as likely to have a "neurotic" disorder than relatives of the matched control group. However, both groups had a similar number of relatives with obsessive compulsive disorder. These researchers concluded that a "neurotic tendency" may be inherited, and that whether or not an obsessive-compulsive disorder develops depends on life events or personality factors.

Because medications such as clomipramine and fluoxetine that increase the amount of serotonin in the brain have been effective in treating individuals with obsessive-compulsive disorder, researchers have hypothesized that the disorder is the result of a serotonin deficiency (Perse et al., 1987). Although most studies using medication have methodological flaws—including reliance on clinical reports, small sample size, failure to include control and placebo groups, and differences in dosage levels—a small body of methodologically sound literature supports the serotonin involvement in obsessive-compulsive disorder (Turner et al., 1985).

Treatment of Obsessive-Compulsive Disorder

The primary modes of treatment for obsessive-compulsive disorder are either biological or behavioral in nature. Behavioral therapies have been used successfully for a number of years, but treatment via medication has recently enjoyed increased attention.

Biological Treatments

Because obsessive-compulsive disorder is classified as an anxiety disorder, minor tranquilizers might be thought helpful. However, these drugs have not proved capable of decreasing to any extent the frequency of obsessive thoughts or compulsive rituals in patients. They *are* occasionally used to reduce tension in patients who are about to participate in psychotherapy (Ananth, 1976).

Antidepressant drugs have also been tried, with mixed results. A review of nineteen studies led to the conclusion that antidepressants were a beneficial part of the treatment for obsessive-compulsive disorder if the patient showed signs of depression. In these cases, the drugs not only alleviated depression but also decreased ritualistic behavior (Marks, 1983). Fluvoxamine, which increases the serotonin level in the brain, has been reported to successfully treat patients with obsessive-compulsive disorder (Perse et al., 1987; Price et al., 1987). Although certain medications can be useful in treating this disorder, the reason for their effectiveness is not known.

Behavioral Treatments   One of the earliest behavioral treatments for obsessive-compulsive patients was systematic desensitization. The purpose of this relaxation treatment was to break the bond that had formed between the conditioned stimulus (for example, germs or dirt) and anxiety. It was believed that, if anxiety was no longer generated by contact with the conditioned stimulus, the compulsive rituals would disappear.

Wolpe (1973) successfully used the method to treat an 18-year-old male with a severe handwashing compulsion. The disorder involved a fear of contaminating others with urine. After urinating, the patient felt compelled to spend 45 minutes cleaning his genitalia, two hours washing his hands, and four hours showering. If other "contamination" occurred, he would spend additional time on these rituals. These behaviors presumably developed as a result of his having shared a bed with his sister until he was fifteen years old and his sister was seventeen. He reported having had erotic responses and feeling guilty and ashamed. This developed into a revulsion toward his own urine. Treatment involved placing the young man in a state of relaxation and then asking him to imagine low-anxiety scenes (such as an unknown man touching a trough of water containing one drop of urine). As the patient's anxiety gradually dissipated, Wolpe gradually increased the imaginary concentration of urine. In addition, a real bottle of urine was presented at a distance and moved closer to the patient in gradual steps.

Finally Wolpe could apply drops of diluted urine to the back of the patient's hand without evoking anxiety. A follow-up four years later revealed complete remission of the compulsive behaviors.

Even though impressive results may be obtained in specific cases, systematic desensitization has been successful only about 50 percent of the time it has been used with obsessive-compulsives. In general, systematic desensitization is viewed as more promising when symptoms are of recent onset (Foa & Tillmanns, 1980).

The treatment of choice for obsessive-compulsive disorder is the combination of flooding and *response prevention*. This approach typically requires fewer therapy sessions than systematic desensitization, and the results have been consistently impressive (Moergen et al., 1987). Meyer et al., (1974) were the first to treat obsessive compulsives with this two-stage program. **Flooding** is a technique that involves continued *in vivo* (actual) or imagined exposure to a fear-arousing situation (always involves high anxiety) In the flooding segment, they repeatedly exposed patients to the anxiety-producing stimulus; in the response prevention stage, they blocked patients' performance of rituals. As an example, consider a man who fears that he will develop a fatal infection from contact with germs. The flooding stage could involve exposing the patient to something he perceives as containing deadly germs (perhaps dirt, a newspaper, or leftover food). The man would be required to touch the items at first, and later to smear them over his body. Once he was properly "contaminated," the client would not be allowed to cleanse himself by engaging in his compulsive ritual (such as repeated handwashing). Instead, in this response prevention stage, he would be required to remain "contaminated" until his anxiety had extinguished.

In this approach, the flooding is used to extinguish anxiety as a response to the conditioned stimulus, and the response prevention further extinguishes anxiety and helps eliminate the avoidance behavior (the ritual). The treatment is more effective if the exposure occurs *in vivo* (that is, in actuality) rather than in the imagination (Marks, 1976). In addition, *in vivo* exposure plus imagined exposure is significantly better than using *in vivo* exposure alone (Foa et al., 1980).

POSTTRAUMATIC STRESS DISORDER

Posttraumatic stress disorder (PTSD) is an anxiety disorder that develops in response to a "psychologically distressing event that is outside of the range of usual human experience." These events often involve a threat to one's life or to a spouse or family member. Examples include being abducted and threatened (Saigh, 1987), traumatic accidents and natural disasters (Malloy et al., 1983), rape and incest (Kilpatrick et al., 1985), concentration camp experience (Kinzie et al., 1984), and child abuse (Eth & Pynoos, 1985). These events produce feelings of terror and helplessness. Symptoms of posttraumatic stress disorder include reexperiencing of the event in dreams or intrusive memories. One veteran reported continued disturbing thoughts of a Viet Cong soldier whom he had taken prisoner. Later, he saw the prisoner pushed out of a helicopter in flight. Because Mr. B had captured the prisoner, he felt responsible for the death (Hendin et al., 1981) and continued to reexperience this episode. Many rape victims often report intrusive memories of the attack (Kilpatrick et al., 1985). As a defense against these thoughts, people who have this disorder may withdraw emotionally and may avoid anything that might remind them of the events. Concentration camp survivors who developed posttraumatic stress disorder often displayed emotional numbness and avoided talking about their experiences in the camp. One man said flatly, "What is there to say? There was just killing and death" (Kinzie et al., 1984, p. 646). Avoidance is only partially successful, however. Certain stimuli, such as helicopters for combat veterans, would bring back the intrusive memories (Mooney, 1988). In addition, posttraumatic stress disorder is associated with heightened autonomic arousal indicated in sleep disturbances, hypervigilance, and loss of control over aggression.

Although posttraumatic stress disorder clearly exists, many questions regarding diagnosis, etiology, and treatment remain open. In diagnosing the disorder, subjective judgment still plays a big role. For example, what constitutes a "psychologically traumatic event?" Although examples are given in DSM-III-R, it is not clear what specific situations can produce the disorder. Little is said about subjective perception of the event. The degree of trauma often

The intense terror and fear associated with combat may result in posttraumatic stress disorder. Recurrent and disturbing recollections of the event may occur.

depends on the way the individual views the event (Janoff-Bulman, 1985). Figley (1985) poses the following questions: Among people who are exposed to a psychologically traumatic event, which ones will develop posttraumatic stress disorder? Is this condition lifelong or curable? Among those who develop PTSD, how many will show the reaction immediately and how many after a period of time? Can we determine who has PTSD and who is malingering? In one study (Sparr & Pankratz, 1983), five men who met the DSM-III criteria for PTSD (complained of reexperiencing the trauma, sleep disturbances, and concentration difficulties and were emotionally constricted) were later found to be feigning.

More research is necessary to answer questions about diagnosing posttraumatic stress disorder. Malloy et al., (1983) point out that diagnoses that are based on self-report measures often have problems with reliability and validity. Instead, they recommend using a three-part assessment package that incorporates behavioral, physiological, and self-report measures. All three were used in a study of three groups

Posttraumatic stress is not isolated to combat situations. Any catastrophic event that is deeply traumatic, such as an earthquake or plane crash, can trigger a stress reaction in people experiencing or even observing the event.

of veterans: (1) those with PTSD, (2) those without PTSD, and (3) those with psychiatric disorders other than PTSD. These groups were exposed to both audiovisual combat stimuli (helicopters flying, soldiers disembarking from a helicopter, and sounds of machine gun fire) and neutral stimuli (couple departing from a house, people walking around a mall, and crowd sounds). Veterans with posttraumatic stress disorder differed from the comparison groups only when exposed to the combat stimuli. To the latter, they displayed a greater physiological response (increased heart rate), greater behavioral avoidance

(pressed a button to terminate the stimuli), and reported higher levels of fear and anxiety. Symptoms of PTSD appear to be specific to the traumatic situation and not merely increased arousal. The three part assessment promises to increase diagnostic reliability and validity and also to furnish more information about the symptoms of this disorder.

Etiology and Treatment of Posttraumatic Stress Disorder

Because a traumatic event precipitates the disorder, several researchers (Keane et al., 1985; Kilpatrick et al., 1985; Kolb, 1987) believe that classical conditioning is involved. People who have PTSD often show reactions to stimuli present at the time of the trauma (darkness, time of day, smell of diesel fuel, propeller noises, and so on). Extinction does not occur, because the individual avoids thinking about the situation. However, as we indicated in our discussion of phobias, the classical conditioning model is insufficient. Not everyone who is exposed to a traumatic event develops posttraumatic stress disorder. Other factors such as the person's individual characteristics, his or her perception of the event, and the existence of support groups also have an influence (see Figure 6.2). According to this model, the degree of trauma is one variable in developing PTSD but the person's own coping styles and a supportive recovery environment can reduce its effects. One study showed that war veterans who developed PTSD were more likely to have sustained injuries, came closer to their own death, felt more guilty about their role in the event, and perceived less support from their families (Solkoff et al., 1986). Incest victims who were able to "make sense" of their victimization showed better adjustment than those who were unable to redefine the event (Janoff-Bulman, 1985).

One treatment for posttraumatic stress disorder involves the use of support groups. People share their experiences in a supportive environment within which they can seek to find meaning in their experience. Extinction procedures have also been successful. A six-year-old boy with PTSD that developed after being involved in a bomb blast and seeing injured people was successfully treated through relaxation techniques and imaginal flooding. The boy was asked

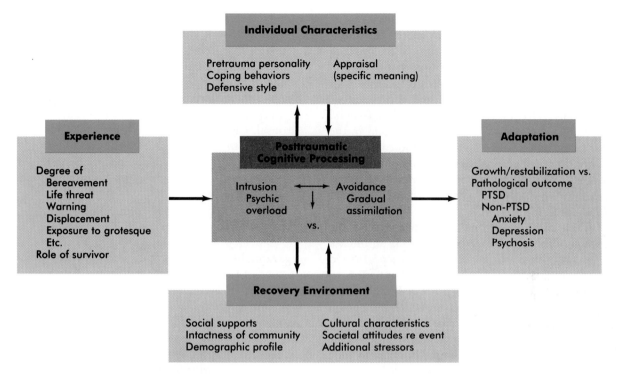

Figure 6.2 Processing a Catastrophic Event: A Working Model
SOURCE: From Green, Wilson & Lindy, 1985.

to imagine scenes of injured people, the smell of smoke, and shouts of individuals. This procedure markedly reduced his symptoms (Saigh, 1986).

Cognitive behavioral approaches have also been developed for working with posttraumatic stress disorder. Symptoms of PTSD are caused by the person seeing the world as an unpredictable or uncontrollable place to live in. Strategies include allowing the person to (1) redefine the event to gain a sense of consistency in the world (by comparing oneself with those who are less fortunate, considering possible benefits from the experience, and so on), (2) finding meaning and purpose in the experience, (3) changing behaviors to help prevent the event from recurring, and (4) seeking social support (Janoff-Bulman, 1985). Because the category for PTSD was created only recently (with DSM-III), there is not enough research at this point to determine how effective therapy is for this disorder.

SUMMARY

1. The anxiety disorders are all characterized by anxiety—by feelings of fear and apprehension. The anxiety may be the major disturbance (as it is in panic disorder and generalized anxiety disorder), may arise when the individual confronts a feared object or situation (as in the phobias), may result from an attempt to master the symptoms (as in obsessive-compulsive disorder), or may occur during intrusive memories of a traumatic event (as in posttraumatic stress disorder).

2. Anxiety is an emotion that all of us experience. It appears in our cognitions or thoughts, in motor (physical) behaviors, in physical reactions, and in affective or emotional reactions. The means of assessing anxiety include self-reports, observations of motor or behavioral reactions, and physiological measures.

3. Panic disorder and generalized anxiety disorder (GAD) are characterized by direct and unfocused anxiety. Panic disorder is marked by episodes of extreme anxiety and feelings of impending doom. Generalized anxiety disorder involves chronically high levels of anxiety, hypervigilance, and apprehension. Psychoanalysts feel that these disorders are unfocused because they stem from conflicts that remain in the person's unconscious. Behaviorists believe the disorders are the result of conditioning to an omnipresent stimulus. Both drug therapy and behavioral therapies, as well as psychoanalysis, have been used to treat these disorders.

4. Phobias are strong fears that exceed the demands of the situation. Agoraphobia is an intense fear of being in public places; it can keep afflicted people from leaving the home, because attempts to do so may produce panic attacks. Social phobias are irrational fears about situations in which the person can be observed by others. The anxiety generally stems from the possibility of appearing foolish or making mistakes in public. Simple phobias include all the irrational fears that are not classed as social phobias or agoraphobia. Commonly feared objects in simple phobias include small animals, heights, and the dark. In the psychoanalytic view, phobias represent unconscious conflicts that are displaced onto an external object. In the classical conditioning view, phobias are based on an association between some aversive event and a conditioned stimulus. Biological explanations are based on genetic influences or on the concept of preparedness to develop certain fears. The most effective treatments for phobics seem to be medicinal (via antidepressants) and behavioral (via exposure and flooding, systematic desensitization, and modeling).

5. Obsessive-compulsive disorder involves involuntary, intrusive, and uncontrollable thoughts or actions. Most obsessive-compulsives are aware that their distressing behaviors are irrational. Obsessions (which involve thoughts) and compulsions (which involve actions) may occur together or separately. Freud believed that this disorder represented the substitution of a threatening conflict with a behavior or thought that was less threatening. According to the anxiety reduction hypothesis, obsessions and compulsions develop because they reduce anxiety. The superstition hypothesis holds that the disorder stems from the chance association of a behavior with

a reinforcer. The most commonly used treatments are behavioral: systematic desensitization or flooding plus response prevention.

6. Posttraumatic stress disorder involves exposure to a traumatic event resulting in intrusive memories of the occurrence, attempts to forget or repress the memories, emotional withdrawal, and increased arousal. Classical conditioning principles have been used to both explain and treat the condition.

KEY TERMS

agoraphobia An intense fear of being in public places or of being alone where help may not be available; in extreme cases, a fear of leaving one's home

anxiety Feelings of fear and apprehension

anxiety disorders Disorders (panic disorders, generalized anxiety disorders, phobias, and obsessive-compulsive disorders) whose major characteristic is irrational feelings of fear and apprehension

compulsion A behavior performed in a stereotypical manner

exposure therapy Gradual exposure to a feared situation

flooding A therapeutic technique that involves continued *in vivo* (actual) or imagined exposure to a fear-arousing situation (always involves high anxiety)

generalized anxiety disorder (GAD) Disorder characterized by persistent high levels of anxiety in situations where no real danger is present

graduated exposure Gradual exposure to a feared situation

hypervigilance Overalertness and arousal. Often a characteristic of the anxiety disorders

modeling therapy A therapeutic approach to phobias in which the phobic individual observes a fearless model coping with the fear-producing situation

neurosis Formerly a category of mental disorders including what are presently called the "anxiety, dissociative, and somatoform disorders"; now generally used to denote any less severe mental disorder

obsession An intrusive, uncontrollable, and persistent thought

obsessive-compulsive disorder Anxiety disorder characterized by intrusive and uncontrollable thoughts, or the need to perform specific acts repeatedly, or both

panic disorder Anxiety disorder characterized by severe and frightening episodes of apprehension and feelings of impending doom

phobia A strong, persistent, and unwarranted fear of a specific object or situation

posttraumatic stress disorder An anxiety disorder that develops in response to an event that is "outside the range of normal human experience." It is characterized by intrusive memories of the traumatic event, emotional withdrawal, and increased arousal levels

simple phobia An extreme fear of a specific object or situation; a phobia that is not classed as either agoraphobia or a social phobia

social phobia An intense fear of being scrutinized

systematic desensitization A therapy in which relaxation is used to eliminate the anxiety associated with phobias and other fear-evoking situations

chapter 7
Dissociative Disorders and Somatoform Disorders

I n 1978, at the age of twenty-three, Billy Milligan became the first person in the United States to be acquitted of a major crime because of having a *multiple personality* disorder. He was tried for rape, was found not guilty by reason of insanity, and was sent to a psychiatric hospital for therapy. Milligan had raped several women near the Ohio State University campus. He first claimed not to remember these attacks, then later suggested that it was his lesbian personality, Adelena, who had committed the acts (Keyes, 1982).

The Milligan case raises several issues concerning the diagnosis of mental disorders and the appropriateness of the insanity plea (discussed in more detail in Chapter 21). The prosecution and some mental health professionals felt that Milligan was deceiving the court about having different personalities; a number of inconsistencies were found in his testimony. However, with the help of psychiatrist Cornelia Wilbur, a specialist in multiple personality, the defense convinced the judge that Milligan actually suffered from the disorder and that his present personality was not responsible for the rapes. Milligan also showed some of the childhood background typically found multiple-personality cases. His stepfather had abused him sexually and had once buried him in the ground with only a length of pipe left open to the air. Incidents like these were thought to have precipitated the disorder.

Milligan was ordered to be confined to mental institutions for an open-ended period, to be released only when he was judged sane. He escaped from a psychiatric hospital in Columbus, Ohio, on July 4, 1986, and lived for a time in Bellingham, Washington, under the name of Christopher Carr. He was questioned by the local police about the disappearance of a university student who lived in the same apartment house (Milligan had sold the student's car after the disappearance). In a bizarre incident, the police chief received a late night call from an individual claiming to be a professor of law at Western Washington University. He threatened to bring a lawsuit against the police department unless they dropped the investigation of Christopher Carr. The police suspect that the call was made by Milligan. Milligan was apprehended in Florida and was returned to Ohio to face charges of unlawful flight to avoid confinement. His "friend" is still missing (Communication from Dean Kahn, *Bellingham Herald*, July 26, 1988).

Even if Milligan did have multiple personality, questions remain about the appropriate treatment or punishment for people who are found "not guilty by reason of insanity." When and how can the public be reasonably certain that such a person will not be involved in a major crime in the future?

Multiple personality is one of four **dissociative disorders**—mental disorders in which a person's identity and consciousness are altered or disrupted. These and the **somatoform disorders,** which involve physical symptoms or complaints that have no physiological basis, are the subjects of this chapter. Both the dissociative disorders and the somatoform disorders, like the anxiety disorders discussed in Chapter 6, were classified as neuroses in DSM-II but were later accorded separate diagnostic categories in DSM-III and DSM-III-R. Both occur as a result of some psychological conflict or need.

The symptoms of the dissociative disorders and the somatoform disorders, such as memory disturbance or hysterical blindness, generally become known through self-reports. There is, then, the possibility of faking, as was suspected in the case of Billy Milligan's multiple personality. However, the fact remains that in genuine cases such symptoms are produced "involuntarily" or unconsciously. This situation, however, leads to a paradox: A person *does* suffer memory disturbance in psychogenic amnesia, yet that memory must exist somewhere in the neurons and synapses of the brain. Similarly, a person *does* "lose" his or her sight in hysterical blindness, yet physiologically the eyes are perfectly capable of seeing. What exactly has happened? The dissociative disorders and the somatoform disorders are among the most puzzling of all disorders.

DISSOCIATIVE DISORDERS

The dissociative disorders, *psychogenic amnesia, psychogenic fugue, depersonalization disorder,* and *multiple personality,* are shown in the disorders chart on p. 178. Each involves some sort of dissociation, or separation, of a part of the person's consciousness or identity from the central identity. These disorders are highly publicized and sensationalized, although all except depersonalization seem to be relatively uncommon. However, reports of one dissociative disorder—multiple personality—have increased dramatically. Kluft (1985) estimates that well over 1,000 patients are currently being treated for this disorder. Reasons for this increase are discussed later in the chapter.

Psychogenic Amnesia

Amnesia is the partial or total loss of memory, due to either organic or psychological causes. **Psychogenic amnesia** is the psychologically based inability to recall personally significant information. This disorder usually occurs suddenly after a traumatic event. The disturbed person may forget his or her name, address, friends, relatives, and so on, but remembers the necessities of daily life—how to read, write, and drive, for example. The disorder is rare and occurs more frequently in young women (DSM-III-R).

There are four types of psychogenic amnesia which vary in terms of the degree and type of memory loss reported. The most common, **localized amnesia,** involves the failure to recall all events of a particular short period of time. Most often, this "lost" period includes an event that was highly painful or disturbing to the afflicted individual, as illustrated in the following cases.

An 18-year-old woman who survived a dramatic fire claimed not to remember it or the death of her child and husband in the fire. She claimed that her relatives were lying about there having been a fire. She became extremely agitated and emotional several hours later, when her memory abruptly returned.

A 4-year-old boy whose mother was murdered in his presence was found mopping up her blood. During interviews with a psychiatrist, however, he denied any memory of the incident.

Selective amnesia involves the failure to remember only some details of an incident. For example, a man remembered having an automobile accident but could not recall the fact that his child had died in the crash. Selective amnesia is often claimed by people who are involved in violent criminal offenses. Many murderers report remembering arguments but don't remember killing someone. In fact, 30 to 65 percent of individuals who are charged or convicted of homicide claim amnesia as a defense (Schacter, 1986).

In **generalized amnesia,** the person cannot remember anything about his or her past life. For example, in 1980 a woman was discovered partly clothed, poorly fed, and disoriented, wandering through a park in Florida. She claimed to have no knowledge of her past. Her parents identified her when she appeared on the *Good Morning, America* television news program. She seemed perplexed and confused while being interviewed on the program and did not recognize her parents when they arrived to get her. The woman still cannot remember her past. Psychologists theorized that an extremely traumatic incident was responsible for this massive memory blockage.

In another case, the traumatic event associated with generalized amnesia was discovered through hypnosis:

A 27-year-old man found lying in the middle of a busy intersection was brought to a hospital. He appeared agitated and said, "I wanted to get run over." He claimed not to know his personal identity or anything about his past. He only remembered being brought to the hospital by the police. The inability to remember was highly distressful to him. Psychological tests using the TAT and the Rorschach inkblot test revealed primarily anxiety-arousing, violent, and sex-

Psychogenic amnesia generally occurs after a traumatic event. People suffering from this disorder can usually perform the skills they've acquired over a lifetime, such as driving a car and reading, but they forget more personal information, such as who they are.

ual themes. The clinician hypothesized that a violent incident involving sex might underlie the amnesia. Under hypnosis the patient's memory returned, and he remembered being sodomized by two men. He had repressed the painful experience (Kaszniak et al., 1988).

Finally, **continuous amnesia,** the least common form of psychogenic amnesia, is the inability to recall any events that have occurred from a specific time in the past, up to the present time. The individual remains

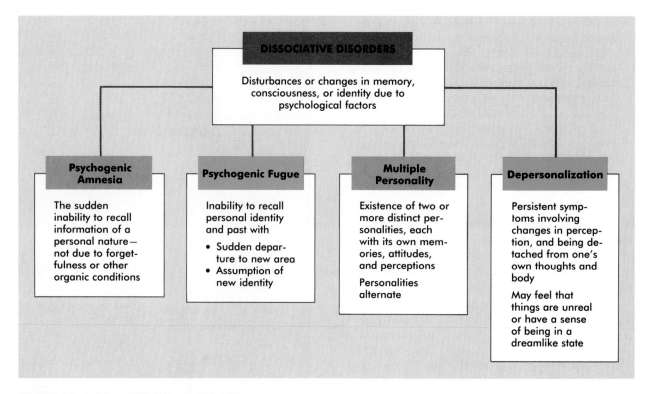

SOURCE: Adapted from DSM-III-R, pp. 269–277.

alert and attentive but forgets each successive event after it occurs (Aalpoel & Lewis, 1984).

Psychologists are uncertain about the processes involved in psychogenic amnesia, but they believe it results from the person's repression of a traumatic event or from some process closely related to repression. For example, **posthypnotic amnesia,** in which the subject cannot recall events that occurred during hypnosis, is somewhat similar to psychogenic amnesia. In both cases, the lost material can sometimes be retrieved with professional help. However, there is one important difference. In posthypnotic amnesia, the hypnotist *suggests* what is to be forgotten, whereas in psychogenic amnesia both the source and the content of the amnesia are unknown (Sarbin & Cole, 1979). Because of this difference, experiments to study amnesia are difficult to design. Therefore, information on psychogenic amnesia has been gathered primarily through case studies.

Psychogenic Fugue

Psychogenic fugue (also called *fugue state*) is psychogenic amnesia accompanied by flight. The affected individual moves to a new area and establishes a new identity. Most cases involve only short periods away from home and an incomplete change of identity. However, there are exceptions:

A 38-year-old man who had been missing for a year was living in another state when relatives saw his photograph printed in a newspaper. The man had established a new identity and was spearheading a charitable drive in his new home state; the newspaper article praised him for his energy and leadership. When confronted by his relatives, the man initially denied knowing them. The relatives were certain of their identification but also puzzled by his outgoing personality. The person they knew had always been shy and retiring.

In some cases, a patient reports multiple fugue episodes, as here:

> E. F. was a 46-year-old man who described twelve to fifteen episodes of "going blank" during the previous five years. He said that these episodes lasted 2 to 36 hours, and that, in "coming round," his feet were often sore, he was a long way from home, and he had no idea of the time or what had been happening during the previous hours. For example, he found himself on one occasion near the Thames, ten miles from his home, with his clothes sopping wet. Marital and legal difficulties were believed to be contributing factors in the episodes of fugue (Kopelman, 1987, p. 438).

As with psychogenic amnesia, recovery from fugue state is usually abrupt and complete.

Depersonalization Disorder

Depersonalization disorder is perhaps the most common dissociative disorder. It is characterized by feelings of unreality concerning the self and the environment. At one time or another, most young adults have experienced some of the symptoms typical of depersonalization disorder: perceptions that the body is distorted or the environment has somehow changed, feelings of living out a dream, or minor losses of control (Aalpoel & Lewis, 1984). But episodes of depersonalization can be fairly intense, and they can produce great anxiety because the people who suffer from them consider them unnatural.

A 20-year-old college student became alarmed when she suddenly perceived subtle changes in her appearance. The reflections she saw in mirrors did not seem to be hers. She became even more disturbed when her room, her friends, and the campus also seemed to take on a slightly distorted appearance. The world around her felt unreal and was no longer predictable. During the day prior to the sudden appearance of the symptoms, the woman had been greatly distressed by the low grades she received on several important exams. When she finally sought help at the university clinic, her major concern was that she was going insane.

Like other dissociative disorders, depersonalization can be precipitated by physical or psychological stress. People who have the disorder are generally able to

Psychogenic fugue and psychogenic amnesia are similar disorders, except that a person experiencing a fugue literally walks away from his or her life and assumes an entirely different identity.

function with minimal impairment of work or social activities. However, the anxiety that is generated and the fear of losing one's mind can be terribly disruptive.

Multiple Personality

Multiple personality is a dramatic disorder in which two or more relatively independent personalities exist in one person. The relationship among the personalities is often complex. Only one personality is evident at any one time, and the alternation of personalities usually produces periods of amnesia in the personality that has been displaced. However, one or several personalities may be aware of the existence of the others. The personalities involved are usually quite different from one another; in some cases, they are direct opposites. The following case illustrates the vast differences that can exist among personalities.

A 28-year-old female has a total of sixteen personalities. Three major personalities are usually present sometime during each day.

Margaret is the core personality and is described as having good social skills but tends not to be assertive. She has a good sense of humor and puts on a "good front" to prevent the detection of the other personalities. She is left-handed.

Rachel is sixteen years old. She engages in antisocial behaviors involving activities such as prostitution and aggression. She has a sarcastic sense of humor and appears when there is a need to fight back. She is right-handed.

Dee is eight years old. She speaks and behaves like a child. She appears to have "taken the pain" whenever the personalities have been abused. She holds the memories of sexual abuse. She is ambidextrous (Dick-Barnes et al., 1987).

In cases where one personality is that of a child (like Dee), that part of the personality may be aware only of events that took place at an early age. For example, one woman's "child" personality was confused about being in an adult body and had never heard of *Sesame Street*, Burger King, or Sprite (they did not exist when she was a child). She wanted to see her childhood friends and return to elementary school (Davidson et al., 1987).

Multiple personality is much more prevalent in females, who often report having experienced childhood physical or sexual abuse (Coons & Bradley, 1985; Kluft, 1987). Conversion symptoms (loss of physical or sensory function with no physical basis), depression, and anxiety are common in these people (Bliss, 1980; Coons, 1986).

In the best-known case of multiple personality (discussed briefly in Chapter 4), Eve White—described as sad, conservative, dignified, and passive—alternated with Eve Black, who was flirtatious, light-hearted, and sexy (Thigpen & Cleckley, 1957). During therapy a third personality, Jane, emerged. And Jane was subsequently replaced by an even more mature personality, Evelyn.

Although it is widely reported that Eve was successfully treated, she recently wrote a book indicating that during therapy she actually had more than the four personalities reported by her therapists, and that an additional eighteen personalities emerged after she completed psychotherapy. With further treatment and the support of her family, she feels that she became an integrated personality at the age of forty-eight (Sizemore & Pittillo, 1977).

A large number of personalities was reported in the highly publicized case of the "sixteen selves of Sybil," although three personalities were generally dominant (Schreiber, 1973). Each personality had its own distinctive style, mannerisms, facial expressions, and skills. Two of the personalities were male (both were carpenters). Kluft (1987) reports that a person with this disorder typically has thirteen to fourteen personalities.

Psychological and physiological tests have been used to attempt to confirm the existence of distinct personalities in multiple-personality disorders. An attempt to validate the existence of multiple personalities is discussed in Focus 7.1.

Diagnostic Controversy We noted earlier that multiple personality is among the less common dissociative disorders, but there is some question about how rare it really is. Hundreds of cases of multiple personality have been reported in recent years (Fagan & McMahon, 1984); one clinician alone reported over 130 cases (Kluft, 1982). The identification of multiple personality in children has also increased. Fagan and McMahon (1984) diagnosed eleven childhood cases in eighteen months and believe that thousands of children may have this disorder.

Fagan and McMahon feel that parents, teachers, and mental health professionals should be aware of the signs of multiple personality in children, including trance states and confusion about time, place, or person; responding to more than one name; marked and rapid shifts in personality; forgetting recent events; extreme or odd variation in skills such as handwriting, in food preferences, and in artistic abilities; varying responses to discipline; self-injurious behavior; multiple physical complaints and hysteric symptoms such as sleepwalking, sudden blindness, or loss of sensation; and reports of hearing voices, losing track of time, or being innocent when punished. The more such symptoms the child displays, the more likely that the diagnosis of incipient multiple personality is appropriate.

Some clinicians believe that multiple-personality disorder is relatively common but that the condition is underreported because of misdiagnosis. For example, in a study of 100 people diagnosed with this disorder, Putnam and his colleagues (1986) found that nearly seven years elapsed from the initial assessment of symptoms before an accurate diagnosis was made. The patients received an average of four prior psychiatric or neurological diagnoses.

Misdiagnosis is illustrated in the case of a 37-year-old man who reported having experienced symptoms of dissociation since age six. He reported having a history of blackouts, amnesia for certain acts, and behavior and personality changes. He received several diagnoses, including undifferentiated schizophrenia, organic brain syndrome, schizoid personality, and seizure disorder (Salley, 1988). People with multiple personality have also been diagnosed as having bipolar disorder and major depression with psychotic features. They commonly complained about "hearing voices arguing," "hearing voices commenting on my actions," "experiencing feelings that don't seem to be coming from me," and feelings of depression (Kluft, 1987). Since changes in mood and memory and hearing voices are symptoms of multiple personality as well as schizophrenia, a differential diagnosis may be difficult to make.

Of course, misdiagnosis works both ways: other disorders may be diagnosed as multiple personality. In addition, it is possible that some researchers, in

In multiple personality disorder, only one personality is evident at any one time, even though the different personalities may be aware of what is happening. It has been hypothesized that the personalities evolve as a coping mechanism in response to some kind of severe abuse or trauma, usually experienced in childhood.

FOCUS 7.1   *A Study of Multiple Personality*

A. M. Ludwig and his colleagues (1972) performed an elaborate study to clarify the processes underlying multiple personalities. The specific questions that the study addressed were

1. What functions do the alternating personalities perform for the individual, and under what conditions do they emerge?
2. In what areas is each personality dependent or independent from the others?
3. If one personality is amnesiac concerning the behavior of another, is this amnesia total or does some transfer of learning occur?

The patient involved in the study was a 27-year-old man who complained of headaches and lapses of memory. During these episodes, the patient referred to himself as Usoffa Abdulla or Son of Omega and became highly violent toward others. Hypnosis was used to elicit each of his four different personalities for interviewing and testing.

Jonah ("The Square") was the primary personality. Jonah was unaware of the existence of the others and was described as shy, retiring, sensitive, polite, and passive. He was anxious and frightened during interviews.

Sammy ("The Lawyer") represented the intellectual and rational side. He enjoyed gaining knowledge and debating; he emerged every time Jonah ended up in jail. He was aware of the other personalities, and he could coexist in consciousness with Jonah.

King Young ("The Lover") was only indirectly aware of the other personalities and appeared whenever shy Jonah was encountering difficulties interacting with a woman. He was a ladies' man and a glib talker. During interviews, he radiated charm and smiled frequently, especially if women were present. (Jonah's mother used to dress him in girl's clothes, which created confusion in Jonah about his sexual identity. King Young had appeared to set Jonah straight.)

Usoffa Abdulla ("The Warrior") was aware of Jonah but only indirectly aware of the others. His role was to protect and watch over "defenseless" Jonah. He appeared at the first sign of physical danger and left after the problem was (often violently) resolved. He was a cold, angry, and belligerent person whom Ludwig and his associates described as "a formidable and scary person to interview." Usoffa first appeared at age ten when a group of boys were beating Jonah. When Jonah lost consciousness, Usoffa emerged

---

their enthusiasm, are labeling people as multiple personalities who are not (such labels are called *false positives*). For example, Bliss and his colleagues (1983) reported that approximately 60 percent of a group of schizophrenics with auditory hallucinations showed evidence of multiple personality. It is difficult to believe that such a large percentage could be misdiagnosed and may reflect the researchers' bias. Other researchers suggest that the sudden increase in reports of multiple personality disorder may be an artifact of the procedures used in investigating this disorder (see Focus 7.2). Whether the increase in cases is the result of more accurate diagnosis, false positives, an artifact, or an actual increase in the incidence of the disorder is still unknown.

Etiology of Dissociative Disorders

The diagnosis and etiology of dissociative disorders are subject to a great deal of conjecture. Diagnosis is difficult because it depends heavily on patients' self-reports. Feigning or faking is always a possibility. One man charged with driving under the influence of alcohol said that he had been in a fugue state. In a study of accused murderers who claimed amnesia for the act, almost all who submitted to polygraph tests or sodium amytal appeared to be lying (Bradford & Smith, 1979). Coons and Bradley (1985) also discovered that a person diagnosed as a multiple personality was feigning the disorder. Differentiating between genuine cases of dissociative disorders and

and was so violent that he nearly killed several of the boys.

Clinical tests were conducted, and physiological and neurological measures were obtained on each of the personalities.

Clinical Tests   Objective psychological tests, including the MMPI, the Adjective Check List, and the McDougall Scale of Emotions, revealed consistent differences in personality among the four entities. An IQ was determined for each personality (all four scored in the low normal range), and they responded with similar answers to test questions.

Learning and Memory Tasks Paired learning tasks were used to assess the transfer of learning among the personalities, and different paired associations were administered to each personality. When mistakes were corrected by the experimenter, material learned by one personality facilitated learn-

ing by the following personalities. However, when corrective feedback by the experimenter was eliminated, there was no transfer effect.

Two standard forms of the logical memory task were presented to the personalities in two different orders. The experimenter read stories of paragraph length and asked each personality to recall as many details as possible. Again, transfer of learning occurred from one personality to another.

Physiological Measures   Each personality was asked to supply words of personal emotional significance. Two words were selected for each personality and interspersed with twelve neutral words to make a standard list of twenty words. Each personality's galvanic skin response (GSR) was measured after he heard each of the twenty words. Jonah responded to the emotional words of all his alternating personalities, although they responded only to their own words and exhib-

ited little response to the words supplied by the other personalities. It is interesting to note that Jonah's response to emotional words supplied by his alternative personalities was greater than his response to his own.

Neurological Examinations   Electroencephalograms (measures of brain wave activity), obtained for each personality, revealed significant differences. In addition, meticulous neurological examinations were performed on each of the personalities. Unlike the other personalities, "The Warrior" had a markedly reduced sense of pain. He displayed a hysterical conversion reaction (*hypalgesia*) indicating that portions of his body were immune to pain.

faked ones is difficult. Even expert judges cannot distinguish between genuine inability to recall and subjects who simulate amnesia (Schacter, 1986). Researchers have found that recollections obtained under hypnosis are often inaccurate and distorted, and that the information retrieved can alter waking memories (Nash et al., 1986; Sheehan et al., 1984).

It was hoped that objective measures such as electroencephalogram (EEG) readings could indicate the presence of multiple personality (Ludwig et al., 1972). However, in a study of two multiple personalities, the researchers concluded that EEG differences among the different personalities reflect differences in concentration, mood changes, and degree of muscle tension rather than some inherent difference between

the brains of people with multiple personality and those of normal people (Coon et al., 1982). Although the clinical evidence supports the existence of dissociative disorders, reliable methods to determine their validity do not currently exist.

We shall examine the etiology of dissociative disorders from the psychoanalytic perspective and from the learning perspectives, but it is important to realize that neither provides completely satisfactory explanations. As indicated earlier, the dissociative disorders are not well understood.

Psychoanalytic Perspective   In the psychoanalytic view, the dissociative disorders involve the person's use of repression to block from consciousness

FOCUS 7.2   Are Therapists Creating Multiple Personalities in Their Patients?

The term *iatrogenic* refers to conditions or disorders produced by a physician or therapist through mechanisms such as selective attention, reinforcement, and expectations (demand characteristics) that are placed on the patient. Could some or even most cases of multiple personality be the result of these factors? Is this a possible explanation for the sudden increase in the reported number of individuals with this disorder? Spanos and his colleagues (1985) believe that this is a distinct possibility: the methods used in investigating multiple personality may encourage the "appearance" of this phenomenon. From a social psychological perspective, the following elements are generally present:

1. *A well-known role* The characteristics of multiple personality are well known through the mass media. The disorder has been portrayed in newspapers, books, television, talk shows, and movies. The public is aware that symptoms of multiple personality include periods of amnesia and personality changes.

2. *A mechanism by which the disorder can be produced* In nearly all cases, hypnosis is used to investigate this phenomenon. Questions are often posed to "parts" of the person of which he or she might not be aware. Hypnosis then provides a vehicle for and "legitimizes" the appearance of another personality.

3. *Encouragement of the different "personalities"* Because the disorder is rare, people who report multiple personalities often achieve a "special patient" status. Therapists become highly attentive to the patients. Coons (1986) found this to be a major problem and warned against reinforcing a patient for being a multiple personality.

4. *Solidifying the roles* Hypnosis is used to contact the different personalities. Patients give names to the personalities. The history, feelings, and experiences of each personality are obtained.

Can characteristics of multiple personality be obtained through the use of social psychological principles? Spanos and his colleagues (1985) reasoned that whether or not symptoms of multiple personality were reported would depend on situational cues. To test out their hypothesis, a group of college students

were given the following information. The subjects were told that they were to play the role of an accused murderer who had to go through a psychiatric evaluation. Men received the name of Harry Hodgins, women were named Betty Hodgins. They were told nothing about what behaviors to display and there was no mention of multiple personality. All subjects were asked about the crime, their interpersonal relationships, their childhood, and their relationship with their parents. The subjects were assigned to one of three groups that varied in terms of the amount of cues for eliciting symptoms of multiple personality and whether or not hypnosis was employed.

Group A These subjects were hypnotized and then told the following: "I've talked a bit to Harry (Betty) but I think perhaps there might be another part of Harry (Betty) that I haven't talked to, another part that maybe feels somewhat differently from the part I've talked to. And I would like to communicate with that other part. Would you talk to me, Part, by say-

unpleasant or traumatic events (Kopelman, 1987). When complete repression of these impulses is not possible, because of the strength of the impulses or the weakness of the ego, dissociation or separation of certain mental processes may occur. In psychogenic amnesia and fugue, for example, large parts of the individual's personal identity are no longer available to conscious awareness. This process protects the individual from painful memories or conflicts (Paley, 1988).

The dissociation process is carried out to an extreme in multiple personality. In this case, the splits in mental processes become so extreme that more or less independent identities are formed, each with its own unique set of memories. Conflicts within the personality structure are responsible for this process. Equally strong and opposing personality components (stemming from the superego and the id) render the ego incapable of controlling all incompatible elements. A compromise solution is then reached in

ing, 'I'm here'?" After the subjects responded, the "psychiatrist" further asked, "Part, are you the same thing as Harry (or Betty) or are you different in any way?" Questions were then asked about the "part" regarding name, identity, and other personal information.

Group B These subjects were also hypnotized but received less direct information about the hidden part. They were told that individuals often block certain feelings or thoughts from the conscious mind, and that under hypnosis it is possible to get behind the wall and to contact a different part. The subjects were told that when the "psychiatrist" placed his hand on a subject's shoulder, he would be in contact with that person's other part. After placing his hand on a subject's shoulder, the psychiatrist asked the part about name, identity, and other personal information.

Group C Subjects in Group C were not hypnotized but received the same information as in Group B. However, references to contacting the part by placing the hand on the shoulder were not included.

During the second session, the subjects in Groups A and B were hypnotized again. In those who exhibited a second personality, the "parts" were contacted and asked to complete two tests—the sentence completion and semantic differential tests. The individuals were then "awakened" and asked to complete the same tests again. Individuals in Group C and those not exhibiting a "second personality" completed the tests just once.

Over 80 percent of subjects in Group A, which received the most specific cues for multiple personality, indicated having a different personality and referred to their primary identity in the third person. They demonstrated "spontaneous amnesia" for the other personality when they existed as Harry or Betty. The other personality made statements such as "I'm inside of Harry. I control Harry's outer feelings" or "I've always been with Betty since I can remember. She doesn't know I'm here, but I know I'm here." The psychological tests (often used in working with multiple personalities) revealed distinct personalities. Approximately one-third of the subjects in Group B displayed a different personality, while none in the control group did.

Spanos and his colleagues demonstrated that the ability to elicit a "different personality" depended on the number of cues available to the subjects and whether or not a means (hypnosis) was provided for the "emergence" of the personality. The subjects who reported "another personality" obviously knew the characteristics of a multiple personality (amnesia for the actions of the other personality, and so on). They were also able to respond on tests in a manner that indicated different personality patterns. The results of this study raise several questions. Is the sudden increase in multiple personalities due merely to iatrogenic factors? In other words, is the therapist creating the disorders? Additionally, how can we investigate this phenomenon without inducing reports of multiple personality? Certain therapists report having dealt with more than fifty people with multiple personality (Allison & Schwartz, 1980; Bliss, 1980; Braun, 1984; Kluft, 1987). Are these therapists merely more accurate in diagnosing the disorder, or could their methods of investigation actually result in reports of these conditions in their patients?

which the different parts of the personality are alternately allowed expression and repressed. Because intense anxiety and disorganization would occur if these personality factions were allowed to coexist, each is sealed off from the other.

The split in personality may develop as a result of traumatic early experiences combined with an inability to escape them. From case histories, we have learned about some of the conditions that may produce a dissociative reaction. In the case of Sybil, for example, Sybil's mother severely abused her. Dr. Wilbur, Sybil's psychiatrist, speculated that "by dividing into different selves [which were] defenses against an intolerable and dangerous reality, Sybil had found a [design] for survival" (Schreiber, 1973, p. 158). The majority of people with multiple personalities do report a history of physical or sexual abuse during childhood (Fagan & McMahon, 1984;

Rosenbaum & Weaver, 1980). However, in addition to traumatic childhood events, the person must have the capacity to dissociate, or to separate certain memories or mental processes. A person's susceptibility to hypnotism may be a characteristic of the dissociation process, and in fact people who have multiple personalities appear to be very receptive to hypnotic suggestion. Those people might escape unpleasant experiences through self-hypnosis—by entering into a hypnotic state. (Bliss, 1980; Sakheim et al., 1988). According to Kluft (1987), the four factors necessary in the development of multiple personality are

1. The capacity to dissociate (whether this is produced by traumatic events or is innate is not known)
2. Exposure to overwhelming stress, such as physical or sexual abuse
3. Walling off or encapsulation of the experience
4. Development of different memory systems

If a supportive environment does not develop, multiple personality results from these factors.

Learning Perspective Learning theorists suggest that the avoidance of stress by indirect means is the main factor to consider in explaining dissociative disorders. For example, psychogenic amnesia and fugue patients are often people who are ill equipped to handle emotional conflicts. Their way of fleeing stressful situations is to forget or block out disturbing thoughts. These people typically have much to gain and little to lose from their dissociative symptoms.

Behavioral explanations of multiple personality include the additional factors of role playing and selective attention. Each of us exhibits behaviors that are appropriate to particular situations but that may be quite different from one another. For example, you wear different clothes and display different styles or mannerisms depending on whether you are scrubbing a floor, going shopping, working, or socializing. In multiple personality, role playing may be combined with selective attention to certain cues. The person responds to only certain environmental stimuli and then behaves in a manner that would be appropriate only if those stimuli were present.

Treatment of Dissociative Disorders

A variety of treatments for the dissociative disorders have been developed that range from supportive counseling to the use of hypnosis and personality reconstruction. Multiple personality has received the most attention by psychotherapists.

Psychogenic Amnesia and Psychogenic Fugue The symptoms of psychogenic amnesia and fugue tend to remit, or abate, spontaneously. Moreover, patients typically complain of psychological symptoms other than the amnesia, perhaps because the amnesia interferes only minimally with their day-to-day functioning. As a result, usually little therapeutic intervention is directed specifically toward the amnesia. Instead, therapists provide supportive counseling for clients with amnesia.

It has been noted, however, that depression is often associated with fugue state and that stress is often associated with both fugue and psychogenic amnesia (Sackeim & Vingiano, 1984). A reasonable therapeutic approach is then to treat these dissociative disorders indirectly by alleviating the depression (with antidepressants or cognitive behavior therapy) and the stress (via stress management techniques).

Depersonalization Disorder Depersonalization is also subject to spontaneous remission, but at a much slower rate than psychogenic amnesia and fugue. Treatment generally concentrates on the feelings of anxiety or depression, or the fear of going insane.

Occasionally a behavioral approach has been tried. For example, behavior therapy was successfully used to treat depersonalization disorder in a fifteen-year-old girl who had blackouts that she described as "floating in and out." These episodes were associated with headaches and feelings of detachment, but neurological and physical examinations revealed no organic cause. Treatment involved getting increased attention from her family and reinforcement from them when the frequency of blackouts was reduced, training in appropriate responses to stressful situations, and self-reinforcement (Dollinger, 1983).

Multiple Personality The mental health literature contains more information on the treatment of *multiple personality* than on the other three dissociative disorders combined.

Treatment for multiple personality is not always successful. Jonah, discussed in Focus 7.1, was never successfully integrated into one, "whole" personality. As discussed in Chapter 5, Chris Sizemore (of *The Three Faces of Eve*) developed additional personalities after therapy but has now recovered. She is a writer, lecturer, and artist. Sybil also had a positive outcome—she has become a college professor. Success, however, may be difficult to achieve in many cases. Coons conducted a follow-up study of twenty patients with multiple-personality disorder. Each patient was studied for about 39 months after their initial assessment. Nine patients achieved partial or full recovery but this was maintained by only five patients—the others dissociated again. Over one-third were unable to work because of the disorder (Coons, 1986).

Patients with multiple personality are difficult to work with. Coons found that 75 percent of the therapists indicated that they had feelings of exasperation, 58 percent anger, and 50 percent emotional exhaustion during the course of therapy. One or more of the personalities might resist treatment. A thirty-year-old woman physician abruptly got up in the middle of a session and remarked, "You can analyse HER, but I'm leaving" (p. 723). More positive outcomes have been reported when therapists are experienced in working with multiple personalities and when therapy continues even after the personality has become fused (Kluft, 1987).

The most widely reported approaches to multiple personality combine *psychotherapy* and *hypnosis*. One suggested procedure begins with hypnosis. With the patient in a hypnotic state, the different personalities are asked to emerge and introduce themselves to the patient, to make the patient aware of their existence. Then they are asked to help the patient recall the traumatic experiences or memories that originally triggered the development of new personalities. An important part of this recalling step is to experience the emotions associated with the traumatic memories. The therapist then explains to the patient that these additional personalities used to serve a

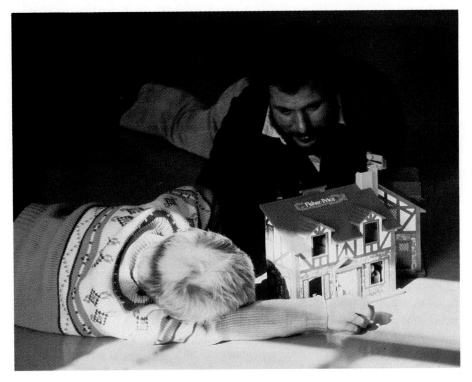

Family therapy and play therapy are two treatments advocated for children with multiple personality. The most important aspect of play therapy seems to be a supportive, nonthreatening environment in which the child can explore all of his or her personalities.

purpose, but that alternative coping strategies are available now. The final steps involve piecing together the events and memories of the personalities and integrating them, and continuing therapy to help the patient adjust to the new self (Bliss, 1980; Sakheim et al., 1988).

Behavioral therapy has also been used successfully in some cases of multiple personality. Here is an example:

> A 51-year-old male, diagnosed as a schizophrenic with multiple personalities, was treated through selective reinforcement. The reinforcement consisted of material and social rewards; the patient received reinforcement only when he displayed his "healthiest" personality. Eventually his other two personalities were completely eliminated, and the patient was discharged (Kohlenberg, 1973).

As illustrated in this case, reinforcement can dramatically increase the frequency with which a specific personality appears.

A number of clinicians advocate the use of family therapy in treating multiple personalities. In one case, the therapist regarded a female client's symptoms as signifying an imbalanced family situation; he found an unusually strong, dependent, and emotional attachment between the client and her mother. He believed the girl was part of an emotional triangle with her mother and father, and he interpreted her transformations to different personalities as an attempt to include the father in her family life. As the client gradually became somewhat detached from her mother, her relationship with her father improved, and the family system became more balanced. The multiple personalities appeared less frequently as the client accepted more responsibility for her actions (Beal, 1978).

Fagan and McMahon (1984) also recommend family therapy for children displaying multiple personalities. In addition, for the child client they suggest play therapy, in which games and fantasy are used to explore the child's other personalities in a non-threatening manner. Particularly intriguing is their method of fusing the child's different personalities by having them hug each other repeatedly, a little harder each time, until they become one.

SOMATOFORM DISORDERS

The **somatoform disorders,** shown in the disorders chart on p. 190 involve complaints of physical symptoms that closely mimic authentic medical conditions. Although there is no actual physiological basis for the complaints, the symptoms are not considered voluntary or under conscious control. The patient believes that the symptoms are real and are indications of a physical problem.

The somatoform disorders include the following:

◆ *Somatization disorder,* characterized by multiple physical complaints and an early onset of the condition

◆ *Conversion disorder,* characterized by the loss or alteration of physical functioning

◆ *Somatoform pain disorder,* or *psychalgia,* in which pain is the main complaint

◆ *Hypochondriasis,* characterized by fear of and complaints of bodily disease

◆ *Body dysmorphic disorder,* characterized by preoccupation with an imagined defect in a normal-appearing individual.

Before we discuss the somatoform disorders individually, we should note that they are wholly different from the **factitious disorders.** The latter are mental disorders in which the symptoms of physical or mental illnesses are deliberately induced or simulated (see Focus 7.3). Individuals with somatoform disorders believe that a physical condition actually exists.

Somatization Disorder

An individual with **somatization disorder** (also known as *Briquet's syndrome)* chronically complains of bodily symptoms that have no physical basis.

> A 29-year-old married mother, admitted via the emergency room complaining of acute right flank pain [pain in her right side], revealed only right flank [side] tenderness on examination. Because of [her] history of a very brief admission to another hospital for a "kinked right ureter" [tube conducting urine from kidney to bladder] around the time of her first child's birth, she was hospitalized on a medical floor with a

FOCUS 7.3 — *Factitious Disorders*

A most remarkable type of mental disorder is illustrated in the following case.

> The woman had an FUO (a fever of unknown origin) and nothing seemed to help. For two-and-a-half months, specialists at two hospitals studied her x-rays and blood tests, prescribed penicillin and a variety of other antibiotics, and had no success at all—until doctors at Massachusetts General tried a massive dose of skepticism. She was whisked off for x-rays and her belongings searched, and in her purse was found the source of her baffling sickness: three used syringes and a cup with traces of spittle. She had been injecting herself with traces of spittle. (Adler & Gosnell, 1979, p. 65)

A recent survey by the National Institute of Health suggests that the problem deserves more attention. Of 343 FUOs recorded over sixteen years, thirty-two patients (nearly 10 percent) were found to be faking their fevers. Among them was a 25-year-old practical nurse who underwent exploratory surgery four times before it was discovered she was injecting herself with fecal matter (Adler & Gosnell, 1979). Others have "spit up blood from a rubber pouch hidden in the mouth, caused genital bleeding by use of sharp objects, [and] injected themselves with insulin, sputum, or bacteria" (Lipsitt, 1983).

These cases illustrate a group of mental disorders, termed **factitious disorders** in DSM-III-R, in which people voluntarily simulate physical or mental conditions or voluntarily induce an actual physical condition. (This practice differs from **malingering,** which involves the simulation of a disorder so as to achieve some goal—such as feigning sickness to collect insurance.) In factitious disorders, the purpose of the simulated or induced illness is much less apparent, and complex psychological variables are assumed to be involved. The person has a compulsive quality in the need to simulate illness. According to DSM-III-R, "a diagnosis of a factitious disorder always implies a psychopathology, most often a severe personality disturbance." Because this diagnostic category is relatively new, little information is available on prevalence, age at onset, or familial pattern.

provisional diagnosis of ureteral colic [pain in ureter]. In 16 days of hospitalization, all diagnostic tests were normal, and despite complaints of poor appetite, nausea, severe pain, and insomnia, no definitive organic diagnosis could be supported, even with consultations with a surgeon, a gynecologist, a gastroenterologist, and an internist. Her medical intern began to doubt her stories of pain although he could elicit tenderness on examination; she did not look distressed or depressed. . . .

In subsequent post-discharge interviews, she spent most of the time complaining about pain and discouragement about her unaltered condition. She later returned to see the surgeon, who thought she had a retrocecal appendix and scheduled her for surgery three days hence. . . . Following surgery, she called to say she had immediately developed joint pains. . . . After a few psychiatric interviews . . . she recalled how, in her childhood, her parents used to argue but would be harmonious and caring when she was sick or hurt. She remembered how she always had to take care of everyone: mother who got sick; father who was partially disabled; husband who was moody; children who needed mothering. Now she was working in a nursery school. She began to recognize resentment of the demands upon her. . . . She saw that being sick might have been the only acceptable way for her to express her feelings. . . . She saw similarities in the ways both she and her mother "used" illness to achieve their aims. (Lipsitt, 1974, pp. 134–136)

This case illustrates several characteristics of somatization disorder. The woman complains about a number of concurrent physical symptoms. In DSM-III-R, complaints of at least thirteen physical symptoms must be involved for a diagnosis of somatization disorder. People who have somatization disorder

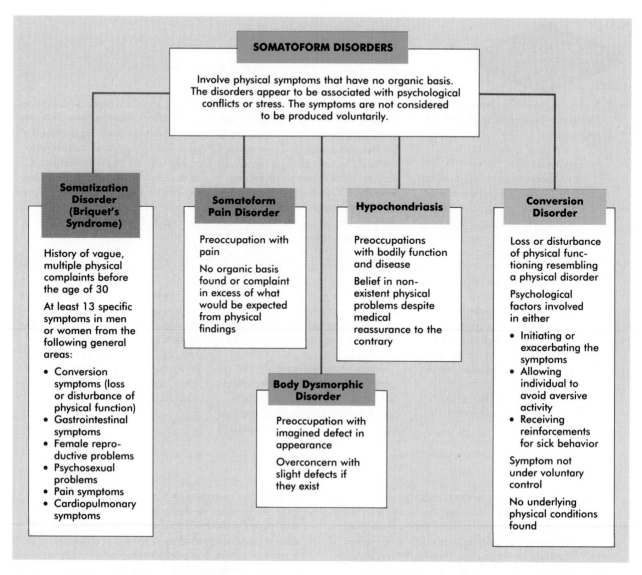

SOURCE: Adapted from DSM-III-R, pp. 255–267.

commonly report abdominal gas, nausea, diarrhea, feeling sickly, abdominal pain, dizziness, pain in the extremities, and vomiting (Swartz et al., 1986). They tend to constantly "shop around" for doctors and often have unnecessary operations. Psychiatric interviews typically reveal psychological conflicts that may be involved in the disorder. Anxiety and depression are common complications of somatization disorder (Gordon et al., 1986).

Historically, somatization disorder (or *hysteria*, as it was called) has been reported primarily in women; it is estimated that 1 percent of all females suffer from the disorder (Swartz et al., 1986). However, accurate data on its prevalence are difficult to obtain because until DSM-III was published, somatization disorder and conversion disorder were grouped together in prevalence studies. This disorder is rarely diagnosed in males (Kroll et al., 1979).

Conversion Disorder

In **conversion disorder**, also known as *conversion reaction*, there is significant physical impairment without an underlying organic cause.

It is often difficult to distinguish between actual physical disorders and conversion reactions. However, conversion disorder usually involves either the senses or motor functions that are controlled by the voluntary (rather than the autonomic) nervous system, and there is seldom any actual organic damage. For example, a person with hysterical paralysis of the legs rarely shows the atrophy of the lower limbs that occurs when there is an underlying organic cause (though in some persistent cases, disuse *can* result in atrophy).

Some symptoms, such as glove anesthesia (the loss of feeling in the hand, ending in a straight line at the wrist) are easily diagnosed as conversion disorder because the area of sensory loss does not correspond to the distribution of nerves in the body. Others may require extensive neurological and physical examinations to rule out a true medical disorder before a diagnosis of conversion disorder can be made. However, the art of medical diagnosis is limited, and the possibility that a condition is actually a physical illness should always be considered (Hyler & Spitzer, 1978). In fact, in a follow-up of patients originally diagnosed as suffering from conversion disorders, about half were found to have actual physical conditions, such as multiple sclerosis or colitis (Slater, 1975).

Discriminating between people who are faking and those with conversion disorder is difficult. For example, subjects asked to simulate a hearing loss can produce response patterns highly similar to individuals with hearing loss due to conversion disorder (Aplin & Kane, 1985).

Conversion disorders are not considered to be under voluntary control. However, psychological factors are considered important with regard to either the timing of a conflict or the immediate function that episodes may serve. Both are illustrated in the following case:

The patient, a 42-year-old white, married male, was admitted in a wheelchair to the Psychiatry Service of the Veterans Administration Center, Jackson, Missis-sippi. When admitted, he was bent forward at the waist (45-degree angle) and unable to straighten his body or move his legs. For the past 15 years, he had consistently complained of lumbosacral [lower back] pain. On two occasions (12 and 5 years prior to admission) he underwent orthopedic surgery; however, complaints of pain persisted. In the last 5 years the patient had numerous episodes of being totally unable to walk. These episodes, referred to by the patient as "drawing over," typically lasted 10–14 days and occurred every 4–6 weeks. The patient was frequently hospitalized and treated with heat applications and muscle relaxants. Five years prior to this admission the patient had retired on Social Security benefits and assumed all household duties, as his wife was compelled to support the family.

Orthopedic and neurological examinations failed to reveal contributory causes. An assessment of the patient's family life revealed that there were numerous stresses coinciding with the onset of "drawing over" episodes. Included were the patient's recent discharge from the National Guard after 20 years of service, difficulties with his son and youngest daughter, and "guilt" feelings about the role reversal he and his wife had assumed. Moreover, it was clear that the patient received considerable social reinforcement from family members when he presented symptoms of "illness" (e.g., receiving breakfast in bed and being relieved of household chores) (Kallman et al., 1975, pp. 411–412).

Other factors involved in conversion disorders include having had an actual physical condition, exposure to people who had physical disorders, and extreme psychosocial stress (such as combat).

In a study of the prevalence and type of conversion symptoms in forty male patients at a Veterans Administration (VA) hospital, it was found that the most common were *paresis* (muscle paralysis), *anesthesia* (loss of bodily sensation), *paresthesia* (prickling or tingling sensations), and dizziness (Watson & Buranen, 1979). Conversion reactions were also diagnosed in fifteen children, of whom nine were girls. Their most common problems involved the function of the legs (paralysis and flexing or walking difficulties), whereas problems involving vision and speech accounted for only three cases. Twelve of the fifteen children had had psychological problems in the past (Regan & LaBarbera, 1984).

There seems to be a contradiction between some of the physical evidence and the belief that conversion disorders are involuntary rather than faked. For example, sophisticated visual tests on a sixteen-year-old girl who reported tunnel vision showed that she made significantly more "seeing" errors than would be predicted by chance. To explain this result, the researchers hypothesized that the girl could indeed see peripherally but chose, either consciously or unconsciously, to deny it (Sackeim et al., 1979). Hypnotically induced blindness may shed light on the processes involved.

Somatoform Pain Disorder

Somatoform pain disorder is characterized by reports of severe pain that may (1) have no physiological or neurological basis, (2) be greatly in excess of that expected with an existing physical condition, or (3) linger long after a physical injury has healed (Fordyce, 1988). The disorder occurs more frequently in women than in men. As with the other somatoform disorders, psychological conflicts are involved. People who have psychogenic pain disorder make frequent visits to physicians and may become drug or medication abusers.

Pain is an extremely complex phenomenon involving both psychological and physiological factors (Elliot & Jay, 1987). Typically, pain behaviors result from *nocioception* (sensations from pain receptors), and cognitive factors such as the expectations of experiencing pain while engaging in certain activities (such as exercising or working). If a painful experience is expected, fewer activities are attempted (Fordyce, 1988). Whether avoidance is exhibited depends on the following factors (Philips, 1987): (1) the current pain level, which fluctuates; (2) environmental rewards for avoidance; and (3) cognitions involving expectations, memories, and self-efficacy beliefs (the view that one can successfully perform a certain activity)—see Figure 7.1. Avoidance reduces feelings of self-control and increases expectancies of pain. This "self-defeating cycle" between behavior and the cognitions may play the greatest role in maintaining avoidance.

Hypochondriasis

The primary characteristic of **hypochondriasis** is a persistent preoccupation with one's health and physical condition, even in the face of physical evaluations that reveal no organic problems. People with this disorder are hypersensitive to bodily functioning and processes. They regard symptoms such as chest pain or headaches as evidence of an underlying disease, and they seek repeated reassurance from medical professionals, friends, and family members (Salkovskis & Warwick, 1986).

Figure 7.1 *Avoidance Behavior and Its Role in Sustaining Chronic Pain*
SOURCE: Philips, 1987.

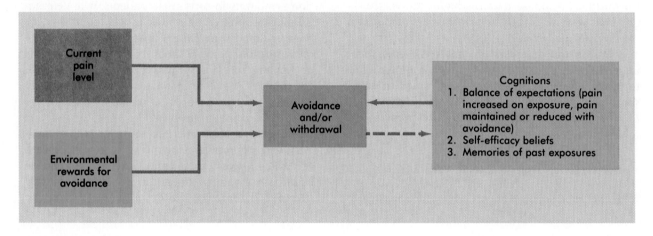

B. is a 26-year-old married manual worker. He developed headaches while on holiday abroad, probably due to excess exposure to direct sunlight. These persisted, and he also developed precordial [chest] pain associated with a range of other bodily symptoms, particularly dizziness, breathlessness, and weakness. Physical investigations by a number of physicians including cardiologists and neurologists revealed no physical basis for his symptoms, and he was referred to the department of clinical psychology after a further series of tests (including brain scans), which were carried out with the explicit purpose of reassuring him. He was on sick leave from work, spent much of his time in a prone position, and frequently called the emergency services. He also asked his wife constantly for reassurance, to take his pulse and not to leave him alone in the house. At referral he complained that the doctors were missing something and was eager for more tests to be carried out. The most probable causes of his symptoms were identified by the patient as heart disease, a brain tumour or some other cancer. (Salkovskis & Warwick, 1986, p. 599)

A study of forty-five hypochondriacs (twenty-eight females and seventeen males) found that fear, anxiety, and depression were common complaints. Each patient feared that he or she had an undetected physical illness; anxiety was increased by the expectation that the disorder was progressive and terminal. As a group, the subjects also felt that previous physical examinations had been inaccurate (Kellner, 1982).

In his review of hypochondriacs, Kellner (1985) found several predisposing factors. These factors included a history of physical illness, parental attention on somatic symptoms, low pain threshold, and/or greater sensitivity to somatic cues. Hypochondriasis, therefore, might develop in predisposed people in the following manner: an anxiety- or stress-arousing event, the perception of somatic symptoms, and the fear that sensations reflect a disease process, resulting in even greater attention to somatic cues. Kellner feels that reassurance by physicians only temporarily reduces anxiety because the patients continue to experience bodily symptoms that they interpret as symptoms of an undiagnosed condition.

Body Dysmorphic Disorder

Body dysmorphic disorder involves a "preoccupation with some imagined defect in appearance in a normal-

Hypochondriasis involves a preoccupation with physical symptoms and frequent visits to the doctor in an effort to identify a physical problem. If no readily discernible cause for the physical complaint can be found, a diagnosis of hypochondriasis may be made inappropriately.

appearing person" (DSM-III-R). Concern over facial features such as spots, excessive hair, or shape of the face, eyes, or nose are the most common. As with the other somatoform disorders, individuals with body dysmorphic disorder seek medical attention—often from dermatologists and/or plastic surgeons. They are also likely to undergo multiple medical procedures. One patient had surgery to increase the size of her breasts, later had them reduced because they were "too large," and then requested to change her breast size again (Turner et al., 1984).

People with body dysmorphic disorder show evidence of emotional problems, have a minimal degree of "disfigurement," and make frequent requests for additional operations regardless of the outcome of previous treatment. They may have a body image disorder similar to that found in anorexia (Conant et al., 1988). Only a small percentage of individuals who seek cosmetic surgery have body dysmorphic disorder. Although the belief in the "defect" is strong, it is not severe enough to be delusional.

Etiology of Somatoform Disorders

Most etiological theories tend to focus on what they consider to be the "primary" cause of somatoform disorders. In reading the theoretical perspectives that follow, consider how they might fit into the diathesis-stress model presented in Figure 7.2. What advantages do you feel this model may have over single-focus explanations?

Psychoanalytic Perspective Sigmund Freud believed that hysterical reactions (psychogenic complaints of pain, illness, or loss of physical function) were caused by the repression of some type of conflict, usually sexual in nature. To protect the individual from intense anxiety, this conflict is *converted* into some physical symptom (Breuer & Freud, [1895] 1957). For example, in the case of a 31-year-old female who developed visual problems with no physical basis, therapy revealed the woman had, as a child, witnessed her parents engaging in sexual intercourse. The severe anxiety associated with this traumatic scene was later converted into visual difficulties (Grinker & Robbins, 1954).

The psychoanalytic view suggests that two mechanisms produce and then sustain somatoform symptoms. The first provides a *primary gain* for the person by protecting him or her from the anxiety associated

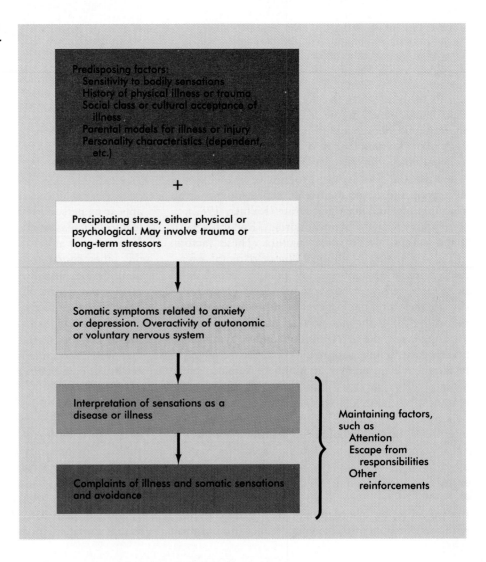

Figure 7.2   Diathesis-Stress Model for Somatoform Disorders SOURCE: Adapted from Kellner, 1985.

Predisposing factors:
 Sensitivity to bodily sensations
 History of physical illness or trauma
 Social class or cultural acceptance of illness
 Parental models for illness or injury
 Personality characteristics (dependent, etc.)

+

Precipitating stress, either physical or psychological. May involve trauma or long-term stressors

Somatic symptoms related to anxiety or depression. Overactivity of autonomic or voluntary nervous system

Interpretation of sensations as a disease or illness

Complaints of illness and somatic sensations and avoidance

Maintaining factors, such as
 Attention
 Escape from responsibilities
 Other reinforcements

with the unacceptable desire or conflict; the need for protection gives rise to the conversion. Then a *secondary gain* accrues when the person's dependency needs are fulfilled through attention and sympathy. Consider the case of an 82-year-old man who reported the sudden onset of diffuse right abdominal pain in March 1977. No abnormal signs were found at that time. In August 1977, he was rehospitalized for the same complaint. Again nothing physical was found. In an analysis of the case, Weddington (1979) noted that the patient's symptom first developed near the twelfth anniversary of his wife's death. His second hospitalization took place near the anniversary of his mother's death, which had occurred when he was twelve. Weddington hypothesized that the painful memories were converted to a physical symptom and that the care and attention bestowed by the hospital staff fulfilled the patient's dependency needs.

Learning Perspective Learning theorists generally contend that people with somatoform disorders assume the "sick role" because it is reinforcing and because it allows them to escape unpleasant circumstances or avoid responsibilities. Among 180 subjects, Moss (1986) found that parental modeling and reinforcement of illness behaviors were influential in determining people's current reactions to illness.

Fordyce (1982, 1988) analyzes psychogenic pain from the operant perspective. He points out that the only available data concerning the pain (or any other somatoform symptoms) are the subjective reports from the afflicted people and that the medical profession is highly sensitive to pain cues. Physicians and nurses are trained to be attentive to reports of pain. Medication is given quickly to patients suffering pain. In addition, exercise and physical therapy programs are set up so that exertion continues only until pain or fatigue is felt. All these practices serve to reinforce the expression of pain.

Fordyce says that psychogenic pain is often under the influence of these and other external (or environmental) variables. He cites several studies that support his contention. For example, when chronic pain patients were asked to perform physical therapy exercises until "the pain becomes too great," approximately half the time they stopped after multiples of five exercises! This neatness led to the suspicion that something other than pain was controlling their behavior. When pain patients exercised on bicycles arranged so that they received no feedback regarding their performance, their tolerance for exercise did not differ from that of nonpain patients. But when performance feedback was available, the pain patients performed significantly worse. Clearly, the pain patients' tolerance depended on more than their internal bodily sensations.

The importance of reinforcement was indicated in a study of male pain patients. Men who had supportive wives (attentive to pain cues) reported significantly greater pain when their wives were present than when the wives were absent. The reverse was true of patients with wives who were nonsupportive. In this case, reports of pain were greater when the spouse was absent.

Sociocultural Perspective Hysteria (conversion disorder) was originally perceived as a problem that afflicted only women. (The word *hysteria* is derived from the ancient Greek word for "uterus.") Hippocrates believed that a shift or movement of the uterus resulted in complaints involving breathing difficulties, anesthesia, and seizures. The movement was presumed to be due to the uterus "wanting a child." Although Freud was among the first to indicate that hysteria could also occur in men, the majority of his patients were women. Satow (1979) has argued that hysteria was more prevalent in women when social mores did not provide them with appropriate channels for the expression of aggression or sexuality. Hollender (1980) also stresses the importance of societal restrictions in producing hysterical symptoms in women and suggests the case of Anna O. as an example:

Anna O., a patient of Freud and Breuer, was a 20-year-old woman who developed a variety of symptoms including dissociation, muscle rigidity, and insensitivity to feeling. Freud and Breuer both believed that these symptoms were the result of intrapsychic conflicts. They did not consider the impact of social roles on abnormal behavior.

According to Hollender, Anna O. was highly intelligent, but her educational and intellectual opportunities were severely restricted because she was a woman. She was described as "bubbling over with intellectual vitality" by Breuer. As Hollender points out, "Not only was Anna O., as a female, relegated to an inferior position in her family with future prospects limited to that of becoming a wife and mother, but at the age of 21 she was suddenly called on to assume the onerous chore of nursing her father" (Hollender, 1980, p. 798). He suggests that many of her symptoms were produced to relieve the guilt she felt because of her resentment of this duty—as well as to maintain her intellectually stimulating contact with Breuer. After treatment, Anna was supposedly cured. However, Anna O. remained severely disturbed and received additional treatment at an institution. Later, she headed a home for orphans, was involved in social work, and became recognized as a feminist leader. Interestingly, Ellenberger (1972) found that the cathartic treatment was unsuccessful and that Anna O. remained severely disturbed and required further treatment.

Satow believes that, as societal restrictions on women are loosened, the incidence of somatoform disorders among females should be decline. However, the diagnostic criteria involved in some of these disorders tend to ensure the overrepresentation of women.

Biological Perspective Some physical complaints may have more than a merely imaginary basis. Researchers have found that hypochondriac patients were more alert to internal processes than phobic people; they were better at estimating their own heart rates when exposed to short films (Tyrer et al., 1980). It has been hypothesized that "people who continually report being bothered by pain and bodily sensations [hypochondriacs] may have a higher-than-normal arousal level, which results in increased perception of internal stimuli" (Hanback & Revelle, 1978, p. 523). College students who are predisposed to attending to somatic symptoms rate the sensations they experience more negatively than those who attend less to bodily symptoms (Ahles et al., 1987). Innate factors may account for greater sensitivity to pain and bodily functions.

The role of biological factors in the etiology of somatoform disorders is less evident than in the more severe disorders (psychoses). In a study involving 15,909 pairs of twins, researchers analyzed the concordance rate for anxiety, somatoform disorders, and dissociative disorders. The concordance rate for identical twins was one and one-half times as high as that for fraternal twins. But the researchers concluded that environmental factors could account for this difference and that heredity plays a minimal role in the development of these disorders (Pollin et al., 1969).

Treatment of Somatoform Disorders

Somatoform disorders have been treated with psychoanalytic approaches, cognitive and operant techniques, and family therapy. The learning approaches have received the greatest amount of attention.

Psychoanalytic Treatment The earliest treatment for somatoform disorders was *psychoanalysis*. Over the years Freud (1905) and Freud and Breuer (1895) reported numerous cases of "hysterical" patients who, like Anna O., would probably now be classified as showing a conversion reaction or a somatization disorder. Freud believed that the crucial element in treating hysterical patients via psychoanalysis was to help them *relive* the actual feelings associated with the repressed traumatic event—and not simply to help them remember the details of the experience. Once the emotions connected with the traumatic situation were experienced, the symptoms would disappear.

Although Freud eventually dropped hypnosis from his psychoanalytic repertoire, many of his disciples continued to find it beneficial, and variations of it became known as *hypnotherapy*. Bliss (1984) was a modern advocate of hypnotherapy as treatment for somatization disorder and conversion symptoms. In essence, Bliss argued that people afflicted with a somatoform disorder engage in involuntary self-hypnosis as a defense, much as multiple-personality patients do. Hypnotherapy involves bringing repressed conflicts to consciousness, mastering these traumas, and developing coping skills that are more adaptive than self-hypnosis.

Behavioral Treatment Although psychoanalytic treatments are most often associated with certain somatoform disorders, several behavioral methods appear worth investigating.

Individuals with hypochondriasis have been treated with a variety of approaches, including exposure and response prevention. The approach generally involves extinction and nonreinforcement of complaints of bodily symptoms. For example, one group of seventeen patients was forced to confront their fears by visiting hospitals, reading literature about their feared illness, and writing down extensive information about the illness. Some were asked to try to "bring forth a heart attack." Reassurance seeking was banned; relatives were taught not to reinforce the behavior. If a patient said, "My heart has a pain. I think it might be a heart attack," relatives were instructed to ignore the statements. Under this program, the patients improved significantly. However, seven of the patients were found to still have concerns about illness or disease at a five-year follow-up (Warwick & Marks, 1988).

Some researchers suggest that a cognitive-behavioral approach might be valuable in dealing with somatoform disorders. Salkovskis & Warwick (1986) compared the effectiveness of operant and cognitive treatments. Eighty-one patients with chronic low back pain were randomly assigned to one of three groups:

1. An operant-behavioral group that focused on changing social and environmental reinforcers (patients' spouses were instructed to reinforce exercising and well behaviors, and to ignore complaints of pain)
2. A cognitive-behavioral group that focused on modifying patients' cognitions about pain (patients identified negative thoughts associated with pain and practiced more adaptive ones)
3. A waiting list control group

Both the operant-behavioral and cognitive-behavioral treatments significantly reduced physical and psychosocial disability, although the operant-behavioral approach showed the greatest improvement. Interestingly, a twelve-month follow-up revealed that the cognitive-behavioral group eventually improved as much as the operant-behavioral group. Patients in the cognitive-behavioral group were more satisfied with their treatment. They rated the therapy as more helpful and the therapist as warmer (Turner & Clancy, 1988).

Future behavioral treatments will probably include more complete treatment packages. Most somatoform disorders are characterized by sensitivity to somatic symptoms, reinforcement for "sick" behaviors, and concern about disease and the inability to perform activities. Use of operant or cognitive approaches alone may not be enough. A combination of relaxation training to reduce somatic sensations, changing environmental rewards, and altering cognitions may be most successful in treating somatoform disorders.

Freud dropped hypnosis as a treatment for hysteria because he believed the patient must reexperience the traumatic event; hypnosis actually prevented this reliving. Some modern treatments for somatization and conversion disorders are beginning to rely on hypnosis once again, based upon the belief that these disorders are induced by self-hypnosis.

Family Systems Treatment The role of the family in maintaining somatoform symptoms has also been recognized by promoters of family therapy for the disorder. Chronic pain is often used to gain rewards (such as attention) and to disclaim responsibility for certain behaviors (such as anger) within the family system. Thus family therapy is recommended as an important part of the treatment for somatoform disorders (Hudgens, 1979).

Research has indicated that, in families of somatization disorder patients, a disproportionately high number of female relatives also have somatization disorder, and a large number of male relatives are labeled either antisocial personalities or alcoholics

(Arkonac & Guze, 1963; Bohman et al., 1984). It is certainly not necessary to have multiple cases of psychiatric disorders in a family before considering family therapy, but these research findings strongly suggest that the entire family be drawn into the treatment process. The therapy could then be used to place the identified patient's disorder in proper perspective, to teach the family adaptive ways of supporting each other, and to prepare family members to deal with anticipated (and predicted) problems.

SUMMARY

1. The dissociative disorders (which are considered relatively rare) involve an alteration or disruption of the person's identity or consciousness. Psychogenic amnesia and psychogenic fugue involve a selective form of forgetting in which the person loses memory of information that is of personal significance. Depersonalization disorder is characterized by feelings of unreality—distorted perceptions of oneself and one's environment. Multiple personality involves the alternation of two or more relatively independent personalities in one individual.

2. Psychoanalytic perspectives on the etiology of dissociative disorders attribute them to the repression of certain impulses that are seeking expression. Learning explanations suggest that avoiding stress by indirect means is the main causal factor. Psychogenic amnesia and psychogenic fugue tend to be short-lived and to remit spontaneously; behavioral therapy has also been used successfully. Multiple personality has most often been treated with a combination of psychotherapy and hypnosis, as well as with behavioral and family therapies. In most cases, the therapist attempts to fuse the several personalities.

3. Somatoform disorders involve complaints about physical symptoms that mimic actual medical conditions but for which no organic basis can be found. Instead, psychological factors are directly involved in the initiation and exacerbation of the problem. Somatization disorder, or Briquet's syndrome, is characterized by chronic multiple complaints, dramatic presentation of the symptoms, and early onset. Conversion disorder involves such problems as the loss of sight, paralysis, or some other physical impairment with no organic cause. Somatoform pain disorder is a condition in which reported severe pain has a psychological rather than a physical basis. Hypochondriasis involves a persistent preoccupation with bodily functioning and disease. Body dysmorphic disorder is preoccupation with an imagined bodily defect in a normal-appearing individual.

4. The psychoanalytic perspective holds that somatoform disorders are caused by the repression of sexual conflicts and their conversion into physical symptoms. Learning theorists contend that the role of "being sick" is reinforcing and allows the individual to escape from unpleasant circumstances or avoid responsibilities. Furthermore, psychogenic pain is often reinforced by the external environment. From the sociocultural perspective, the somatoform disorders are seen to result from the societal restrictions placed on women, who are affected to a much greater degree than men by these disorders. Psychoanalytic treatment emphasizes the reliving of emotions associated with the repressed traumatic event. Other treatment approaches involve the reinforcement of only "healthy" behaviors rather than the pain or disability. If possible, treatment is administered within the family system.

KEY TERMS

amnesia The partial or total loss of memory due to either organic or psychological causes

body dysmorphic disorder A somatoform disorder that involves preoccupation with an imagined physical defect

continuous amnesia The inability to recall past and present events; each new event is forgotten after it occurs

conversion disorder A somatoform disorder in which there is significant impairment of sensory or motor function without an underlying physical cause (also known as *conversion reaction*)

depersonalization disorder A dissociative disorder in which there are feelings of unreality or distortion concerning the self or the environment

dissociative disorders Mental disorders characterized by the alteration or disruption of the person's identity or consciousness; include psychogenic amnesia, psychogenic fugue, depersonalization disorder, and multiple-personality disorder

factitious disorders Deliberately self-induced or simulated physical or mental condition

generalized amnesia The inability to recall the entire past, due to some psychosocial stress

hypochondriasis A somatoform disorder characterized by a persistent and strong preoccupation with one's health and physical condition even in the face of physical evaluations that reveal no organic problems

localized amnesia The most common type of amnesia; the inability to recall all events during a specific period

malingering Faking an illness to obtain a goal

multiple personality A dissociative disorder in which two or more relatively distinct personalities exist in one individual

posthypnotic amnesia The inability to recall information as a result of a suggestion made during a hypnotic state

psychogenic amnesia A dissociative disorder characterized by the inability to recall information of personal significance, usually after a traumatic event

psychogenic fugue A dissociative disorder in which psychogenic amnesia is accompanied by flight from familiar surroundings; also called *fugue state*

selective amnesia The inability to recall only some aspects of a situation due to some psychosocial stress

somatization disorder A somatoform disorder in which the person chronically complains of a number of physical symptoms for which no physiological basis can be found; also called *Briquet's syndrome*

somatoform disorders Mental disorders that involve complaints of physical symptoms that closely mimic authentic medical conditions but have no physical basis; include somatization disorder, conversion disorder, somatoform pain disorder, and hypochondriasis

somatoform pain disorder A somatoform disorder characterized by pain that has primarily a psychological, rather than a physical, basis; also called *psychalgia*

chapter 8
Psychological Factors in Physical Disorders

Can people "worry themselves to death"? Medical evidence suggests that they can. Stress and anxiety appear to have at least some role in what is called the **sudden death syndrome**—deaths that often seem to have no specific physical basis.

A study of 170 cases of sudden death reported in newspaper articles indicated that most were preceded by an intense emotional event (such as the loss of significant others) or by the person's experience or perception of helplessness (Engel, 1971). One article reported the case of a 61-year-old woman who had taken her ailing 71-year-old sister to the hospital. After hearing that her sister had died, the younger woman developed an irregular heartbeat and also died. Her sister's death seems to have created severe emotional distress, which in turn produced the physical symptoms that led to her death.

Emotional factors are also implicated in the following case:

A 22-year-old woman pleaded to be admitted to a hospital. She reported that she and her two sisters had been cursed by a midwife. The midwife said that one sister would die before her sixteenth birthday (one sister did die in an automobile accident before her sixteenth birthday); another would die before becoming twenty-one (the second sister died on the evening of her twenty-first birthday); and the last would die before her twenty-third birthday. This last, surviving sister was only a few days away from her birthday and was obviously frightened. She was admitted into the hospital but was found dead the next morning. (Seligman, 1975)

Each year, about half a million people in the United States get up feeling fine, but later on in the day they collapse and die. Sudden death is the leading cause of death in industrialized countries. Most people who die this way are discovered to have coronary heart disease such as narrowing of the arteries or evidence of past heart attacks. Approximately 10 percent who succumb have normal hearts and cardiac vessels (Natelson, 1981). Many cases appear to be the result of *ventricular fibrillation* (rapid, ineffective contractions of the heart) that may have been triggered by a strong emotional stress (Lane & Schwartz, 1987). Physiological response to stress may also take the form of **bradycardia** (slowing of the heartbeat), **tachycardia** (speeding up of the heartbeat), or **arrhythmia** (irregular heartbeat, as in the case of the 61-year-old woman described earlier).

Death from bradycardia, in particular, may result from feelings of helplessness. The following case indicates the impact of this emotion on heart rate:

The patient was lying very stiffly in bed, staring at the ceiling. He was a 56-year-old man who had suffered an anterior myocardial infarction [heart attack] some 2 1/2 days ago. He lay there with bloodshot eyes, unshaven, and as we walked into the room, he made eye contact first with me and then with the intern who had just left his side. The terror in his eyes was reflected in those of the intern. The patient had a heart rate of forty-eight that was clearly a sinus bradycardia. I put my hands on his wrist, which had the effect of both confirming the pulse and making some physical contact with him, and I asked what was wrong. "I am very tired," he said. "I haven't slept in two and one-half days, because I'm sure that if I fall asleep, I won't wake up."

I discussed with him the fact that we had been at fault for not making it clear that he was being very carefully monitored, so that we would be aware of any problem that might develop. I informed him further that his prognosis was improving rapidly. As I spoke, his pulse became fuller. (Shine, 1984, p. 27)

In this case, the patient's physiological response was counteracted by the physician's assurance that his

situation was not hopeless—in essence, by removing the source of stress.

Certainly, the sudden death syndrome is an extreme example of the power of anxiety and stress to affect physiological processes. But the examples cited here and in Focus 8.1 are convincing proof that feelings and emotional states can have an impact on physical well-being. In DSM-I and II, physical disorders that stem from psychological problems, such as asthma, ulcers, hypertension, and headaches, were called *psychosomatic disorders*, partly to distinguish them from conditions that were considered strictly organic in nature. However, mental health professionals now recognize that almost any physical disorder can have a strong psychological component or basis.

Previously, the psychosomatic disorders were considered a separate class of disorders. However, DSM-III-R does not categorize them as such. Instead, it contains a category called psychological factors affecting physical condition. Psychological factors are listed on Axis I; the physical disorders themselves are listed on Axis III. This classification method acknowledges the belief that both physical and psychological factors—both body and mind—are involved in all human processes. And the term *psychosomatic disorder* has been replaced with **psychophysiological disorder**, meaning *any* physical disorder that has a strong psychological basis.

The psychophysiological disorders should not be confused with the conversion disorders discussed in Chapter 7. The conversion disorders do involve reported physical symptoms, such as loss of feeling, blindness, and paralysis, but they do not involve any physical pathology or process; they are considered essentially psychological in nature. By contrast, most psychophysiological disorders involve actual tissue damage (such as an ulcer) or physiological dysfunction (as in asthma or migraine headaches). Both medical treatment and psychotherapy are usually required.

The relative contributions of physical and psychological factors in a physical disorder may vary greatly. DSM-III-R suggests that psychological factors should be suspected when evidence shows that environmental stressors preceded the onset or worsening of the disorder. Although stressors are often difficult to detect, repeated association between stressors and

FOCUS 8.1

The Hmong Sudden Death Syndrome

Vang Xiong is a former Hmong (Laotian) soldier who, with his wife and child, was resettled in Chicago in 1980. The change from his familiar rural surroundings and farm life to an unfamiliar urban area must have produced a severe "culture shock." In addition, Vang vividly remembered seeing people killed during his escape from Laos, and he expressed feelings of guilt about having to leave his brothers and sisters behind in that country. He reported having problems almost immediately.

[He] could not sleep the first night in the apartment, nor the second, nor the third. After three nights of sleeping very little, Vang came to see his resettlement worker, a young bilingual Hmong man named Moua Lee. Vang told Moua that the first night he woke suddenly, short of breath, from a dream in which a cat was sitting on his chest. The second night, the room suddenly grew darker, and a figure, like a large black dog, came to his bed and sat on his chest. He could not push the dog off and he grew quickly and dangerously short of breath. The third night, a tall, white-skinned female spirit came into his bedroom from the kitchen and lay on top of him. Her weight made it increasingly difficult for him to breathe, and as he grew frantic and tried to call out he could manage but a whisper. He attempted to turn onto his side, but found he was pinned down. After 15 minutes, the spirit left him, and he awoke, screaming. (Tobin & Friedman, 1983, p. 440)

About forty of the Laotian refugees who settled in the United States have died from the "Hmong sudden death syndrome." All the reports were the same: A person in apparently good health went to sleep and died in his or her sleep. In many cases, the victim displayed labored breathing, screams, and frantic movements before death occurred. The Center for Disease Control conducted an investigation of these mysterious deaths, but no medical cause has yet been found (Center for Disease Control, 1981). Some consider the deaths to represent an extreme and very specific example of the impact of psychological stress on physical health.

Vang was one of the lucky victims of the syndrome—he survived it. He went for treatment to a Hmong woman, a Mrs. Thor, who is highly respected in Chicago's Hmong community as a shaman. She interpreted his problem as being caused by unhappy spirits and performed the ceremonies that are required to release them. After that, Vang reported, he had no more problems with nightmares or with his breathing during sleep.

---

the disorder or its symptoms should increase the suspicion that a psychological component is involved.

In this chapter, we first consider three models that help explain the impact of stress on physical health. Second, we examine the evidence indicating a connection between stress and the onset and course of cancer. Finally, we discuss several of the more prevalent psychophysiological disorders: coronary heart disease, hypertension (high blood pressure), ulcers, headaches, and asthma.

Before we turn to these disorders, however, we should emphasize that the change from the "psycho-somatic" to the "psychophysiological" view is more than a change in terminology. It represents an enlarging and redirecting of efforts to control disease. The new field of **behavioral medicine** is an important product of this redirection. The field of behavioral medicine, which includes a number of disciplines concerned with illness, deals with the following factors (Gentry, 1984):

1. *Etiology* Involves the study of how stress, lifestyle, and personality characteristics interact to affect susceptibility to illness

2. *Host resistance* Determining the effects of such factors as social and economic support, cognitive style, and personality in reducing the impact of stress

3. *Disease mechanisms* Determining how stress changes physiology in such a way as to produce problems such as gastrointestinal disorders and cardiovascular disease

4. *Patient decision making* The process by which patients make decisions about their health practices

5. *Compliance* The development of programs to increase patients' cooperation in taking medications, exercising, and participating in other therapies and preventive measures

6. *Intervention* Educational and behavioral therapies aimed at altering unhealthy lifestyles and indirectly reducing illnesses or illness-inducing behavior

MODELS FOR UNDERSTANDING STRESS

Stress is an internal response to an external stimulus or situation (**stressor**). But something that disturbs one person does not necessarily disturb someone else. Moreover, different people react differently to the same stressors. Many people who are exposed to stressors, even traumatic ones, are eventually able to get on with their lives. Other people show intense and relatively long-lasting psychological symptoms. What accounts for this difference?

The three stress models discussed in this section seek to explain (1) the development and differential effects of stress, (2) the apparent ability of relatively weak stressors to result in strong stress reactions, and (3) the ability some people have to cope more "easily" with stress.

The General Adaptation Model

Being alive means you are constantly exposed to stressors: illness, marriage, divorce, the death of someone you love, hunting for and keeping a job, aging, retiring, even schoolwork. Most people can cope with most of the stressors they encounter, provided those stressors are not excessively severe and do not "gang up" on the individual. But when someone is confronted with excessive external demands—stressors—his or her coping behaviors may fail and the person may resort to inappropriate means of dealing with them. The result may be psychophysiological symptoms, apathy, anxiety, panic, stupor, depression, violence, and even death.

There are, in general, three kinds of stressors:

- *Biological stressors* such as infection, physical trauma, disease, malnutrition, and fatigue
- *Psychological stressors* such as threats of physical harm, attacks on self-esteem, and guilt-inducing attacks on one's belief system
- *Social stressors* such as crowding, excessive noise, economic pressures, and war

A helpful model for understanding the body's physical reaction to biological stressors was proposed by Hans Selye (1956, 1982). He identified three stages in the **general adaptation syndrome (GAS):** (1) the alarm stage, (2) the stage of resistance, and (3) the stage of exhaustion.

Selye describes the first stage as a "call to arms" of your body's defenses when it is invaded or assaulted biologically. During this *alarm stage*, your body reacts immediately to the assault (with rapid heartbeat, loss of muscle tone, and decreased temperature and blood pressure), followed by a rebound reaction in which your adrenal cortex enlarges and your adrenals secrete corticoid hormones. If exposure to the stressor continues, the *adaptation or resistance stage* ensues. Now your body mobilizes itself to defend, destroy, or coexist with the injury or disease. Either you improve or the symptoms of illness disappear. At the same time, however, there is a decrease in your body's resistance to most other assaults. That is, you may become susceptible to other infections or illnesses. If the stressor continues to tax your body's finite resistive resources, the symptoms may reappear as you become exhausted (hence the name *exhaustion stage*). If stress continues unabated, death may result.

Biological Consequences of Stress Although Selye developed his model as a means of describing physical responses to biological stressors, continuing research now indicates that psychological and social stressors have similar effects. In fact, sustained stress—resulting from psychological or social stressors—may not only make the person more susceptible to illness, but may actually alter the course of a disease. For example, it has been documented that recently bereaved widows are three to twelve times more likely to die than are married women; that tax accountants are most susceptible to heart attacks around April 15; that people living in high-noise areas near airports

High-pressure jobs, such as that of an air traffic controller, are likely to be stressful and produce physical and psychological symptoms. But the amount of stress needed to negatively affect an individual varies from person to person. In fact, some people seem to deal efficiently with a great deal of stress, while others find it difficult to cope with even small amounts.

have more hypertension and medical complaints than other people; and that air traffic controllers suffer four times more as much hypertension as the general population (Wilding, 1984). The common factor in all these groups is *stress*.

For years scientists were skeptical about the supposed effects of stress on the body and dismissed any relationship between the two as folklore. However, we now know that stress affects the immune system, heart function, hormone levels, the nervous system, and metabolic rates. Bodily "wear and tear" due to stress can contribute to diseases such as hypertension, ulcers, chronic pain, heart attacks, cancer, and the common cold.

Psychological Consequences of Stress Most of us maintain certain levels of psychological adjustment that vary little over time. When we encounter a crisis that cannot be resolved through our customary method of coping, our behaviors can become disorganized and ineffective in solving problems.

Brady (1975) has described stages in crisis decompensation that parallel the three stages of Selye's general adaptation syndrome. (**Decompensation** is

the loss of the ability to deal successfully with stress, resulting in more primitive means of coping.) During the impact of a crisis (the first stage), the person experiences a sense of confusion and upset. He or she is bewildered and wonders what is happening, why it is happening, and how a situation so far beyond his or her experience can be resolved. Feelings of panic are not unusual. This disequilibrium is followed by a period of attempted resolution (the second stage) during which all resources are mobilized to deal with the situation. In the case of a divorce, the person may seek out friends for emotional support or validation. In the case of a disaster, the person may selectively perceive the situation in a more favorable light ("We've lost our home and all our possessions, but we're lucky to be alive. We can always rebuild."). When people cope successfully, they are likely to resume functioning once more at the precrisis level and, in some cases, move into a growth adjustment phase. There are some indications that the experience of coping with and mastering a personal crisis or disaster may even enhance a person's psychological well-being (Taylor, 1983). If coping is ineffective, however, the person is likely to move into a decompensated adjustment phase (the third stage). This phase may be characterized by withdrawal, depression, guilt, apathy, anxiety, anger, or any number of physical illnesses.

The Life Change Model

Holmes and Holmes (1970) accepted the GAS model for the physical and psychological reactions to stressors. They noted, though, that the events that led to stress reactions need not be of crisis proportions; seemingly small, everyday events could also create stress. They hypothesized that any life change, even positive ones, can have a detrimental impact on health. Their work led to the formulation of the **life change model,** which assumes that all changes in a person's life—large or small, desirable or undesirable—can act as stressors. And the accumulation of small changes is thought to be as powerful as a major stressor. Consider the following case:

Janet M., a college freshman, had always been a top-notch student in her small-town high school and had been valedictorian of her graduating class. Her SAT test scores placed her in the ninety-fifth percentile of all students taking the exam. Her social life was in high gear from the moment she arrived on the Berkeley campus. Yet Janet was suffering. It started with a cold that she seemed unable to shake. During her first quarter, she was hospitalized once with the "flu" and then three weeks later for "exhaustion." In high school Janet had appeared vivacious, outgoing, and relaxed; at Berkeley she became increasingly tense, anxious, and depressed.

What was happening to Janet is often seen, to various degrees, among entering college students. Going to college is a major life change for students and may result in stress. Most students are able to cope with the demands, but others need direct help. In Janet's case, all the classic symptoms of stress were present. No single stressor was responsible; rather, a series of life changes had a cumulative impact. An examination of Janet's intake interview notes at the counseling center revealed the following stressors:

1. Change from a relatively conservative small-town environment to a more permissive atmosphere on a liberal campus

2. Change from being the top student in her high school class to being slightly above average at Berkeley

3. Change in living accommodations, from a home with a private room to a dormitory with a roommate

4. Change from being completely dependent on family finances to having to work part-time for her education

5. Change from having a steady boyfriend in her home town to being unpaired

6. Change in family stability (her father recently lost his job, and her parents seem headed for divorce)

7. Change in food intake from home-cooked meals to dormitory food and quick snacks

Although each of these changes may seem small and relatively insignificant by itself, their cumulative impact was anything but insignificant.

To measure the impact of life changes, Holmes and Rahe (1967) devised the Social Readjustment Rating Scale (SRRS). People rated forty-three events in terms of the amount of readjustment required. For example, the death of a spouse was noted as requiring the greatest adjustment, while the least stressful event was a minor law violation. Each life event was given a numerical value that corresponds to its strength as a stressor (Wyler et al., 1971). These "stress potential" values are referred to as *life change units* (LCUs). The investigators found that 93 percent of health problems (infections, allergies, bone and muscle injuries, and psychosomatic illness) hit patients who, during the previous year, had been exposed to events whose LCU values totaled 150 or more. Although a minor life change was not sufficient to constitute a serious stressor, the cumulative impact of many events could be considered a crisis. Particularly revealing was the finding that exposure to a greater number of LCUs increased the chances of illness. Of those exposed to mild crises (150 to 199 LCUs), 37 percent reported illness; to moderate crises (200 to 299 LCUs), 51 percent; and to major crises (more than 300 LCUs), 79 percent.

Other studies not only support these findings but also indicate that when the life crisis is more severe, more serious illnesses also result. A high life change score was likely to be associated with the

Changes in a person's life can be stressful. Research has found, however, that undesirable life changes, such as loss of a spouse, are more likely to produce anxiety, depression, and physical symptoms in people than are positive life changes, such as graduating from college and beginning a new phase in life.

more severe chronic diseases (leukemia, cancer, and cardiac attack). Constant stress and the activity of coping may lower a person's resistance to disease; when that happens, illness may result (Masuda & Holmes, 1976; Rahe, 1968).

Although research does support the view that life changes can have a cumulative effect on mental and physical health, it has not supported the hypothesis that *any* life change will increase stress. Only undesirable life changes were associated with negative emotions such as anxiety, depression, or physical symptoms (Sarason et al., 1978). Thus in most cases, negative life changes seem to be more detrimental than positive life changes.

Clearly, stressful life events *do* play some part in producing of physical and psychological illnesses, for many people. Yet it is too soon to say that one is caused by the other. Most studies that have been cited are retrospective and correlational in nature, so no cause-and-effect relationship can be inferred. In addition, the data used in the studies depend on (1) people's perceptions of health and illness, (2) their recollections and reports of illness (both psychological and physical), and (3) their health histories over a defined period of time (Mechanic, 1974). Further-

more, the illnesses of many people do not seem to be preceded by identifiable stressors, and some who undergo stress don't seem to get sick. Finally, evidence now shows (1) that positive and negative life events do not have equal effects and (2) that personal interpretations or characteristics modify the impact of life changes (Lazarus, 1983; Kobasa et al., 1979; Sarason et al., 1978). Obviously, further investigation of the relationship between life changes and illness is needed.

The Transaction Model

The GAS model is concerned with the process by which the body reacts to stressors, and the life change model is concerned with external events that cause stress as a response. But neither model considers the person's subjective definition or interpretation of stressful events or life changes. Apparently a number of processes intervene between the stressor and the development of stress. In particular, the thoughts we have about impending threats (stressors), the emotions we attach to them, and the actions we take to avoid them can either increase or decrease the impact of stressors. In his classic book *Psychological Stress and the Coping Process* (1969), Lazarus formulated a **transaction model of stress**. He noted that stress resides neither in the person alone nor in the situation alone, but is a transaction between the two. Let us use an example to illustrate this point:

On the morning of August 16, 1984, Mrs. Marva B. discovered a small lump near the left side of her right breast. She immediately contacted her doctor and made an appointment to see him. After examining her, the physician stated that the lump could be a cyst or a tumor. He recommended a biopsy, which revealed that the tumor was malignant.

Mrs. B. accepted the news with some trepidation but went about her life with minimal disruption. When she was questioned about the way in which she was handling the situation, she replied, in essence, that there is no denying that this is a serious illness, and there is great ambiguity in the prognosis; but people are successfully treated for cancer, she planned to undergo treatment, and she would not give up.

Unlike Mrs. B., many patients would have been horrified at even the thought of having cancer. The news that the tumor was malignant would have been viewed as a catastrophe. Thoughts of dying would have arisen; all hope might have been abandoned. This sort of reaction differs from Mrs. B.'s in how the individual *perceives and copes with* the stressor via internal processes.

The impact of stressors can be reduced or increased depending on the way the situation is interpreted. A person who develops cognitive adaptation may reduce susceptibility to illness or limit its course.

One dominant theme threads its way through each of the models discussed—no one factor is enough to cause illness. Rather, illness results from a complex interaction of psychosocial, physiological, and cognitive stressors. Figure 8.1 illustrates this interaction.

STRESS AND THE IMMUNE SYSTEM

We have already indicated a relationship between stress and illness. How do emotional and psychological states influence the disease process? Consider the following case:

Anne was an unhappy and passive individual who always acceded to the wishes and demands of her husband. She had difficulty expressing strong emotions, especially anger, and often repressed her feelings. She had few friends and, other than her husband, had no one to talk to. She was also depressed and felt a pervasive sense of hopelessness about her life. During a routine physical exam, her doctor discovered a lump in her left breast. The results of a biopsy revealed that the tumor was malignant.

Could Anne's personality or emotional state have contributed to the formation or the growth of the malignant tumor? If so, how? Could she now alter the course of her disease by changing her emotional state? That such questions are being asked represent a profound change in the way in which physical illness is being conceptualized.

The view that diseases other than traditional psychophysiological disorders are strictly organic appears too simplistic. Many theorists now believe that most diseases are caused by an interaction of social,

Figure 8.1 *Interaction Among Psychosocial, Physiological, and Cognitive Stressors*
SOURCE: Adapted from Rahe & Arthur, 1978.

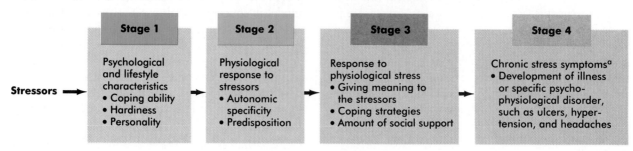

[a]This stage occurs only if the person has been unable to respond successfully to stressors.

psychological, and biological factors. This relationship has been found in a number of diseases. The recurrence of herpes symptoms, for example, appears to be influenced by emotional factors. In one study (McLarnon & Kaloupek, 1988), people with herpes reported their moods and thoughts daily on a questionnaire. New lesions developed in participants who reported higher anxiety four days before lesions appeared. Stress has also been implicated in the etiology and course of mononucleosis, colds, and ulcerative gingivitis (inflammation of gums and tissues in the mouth) (Jemmott & Locke, 1984). Even in a disease process such as Acquired Immune Deficiency Syndrome (AIDS), the great variations found in the clinical course may be due partly to psychological variables (Kiecolt-Glaser & Glaser, 1988).

The Immune System

We know that stress is related to illness, but what is their precise relationship? How does stress affect health? Stress, itself, does not appear to cause infections but may decrease the immune system's efficiency, thereby increasing a person's susceptibility to disease. This connection has received the greatest amount of attention.

As mentioned earlier, stress results in physiological changes in the body. Part of the stress response involves the release of several neurohormones (catecholamines, corticosteroids, and endorphins). These substances impair the functioning of the immune system. *Corticosteroids*, for example, have very strong immunosuppressive actions and are often used to suppress immunity caused by allergic reactions. Endorphins also seem to decrease the efficiency of natural killer cells in tumor-fighting ability (Ornstein & Sobel, 1987).

The white blood cells in your immune system help to maintain health by recognizing and destroying pathogens such as bacteria, viruses, fungi, and tumors. In an intact system, over a thousand billion white blood cells are based in the lymph system or circulate through the bloodstream. There are two major classes of white blood cells, lymphocytes and phagocytes. *Lymphocytes* are comprised of B-cells (produce antibodies against invaders), T-cells (detect and destroy foreign cells), and natural killer (NK) cells (early detection system to prevent the growth of tumors). *Phagocytes* are also attracted to and destroy invaders

(Maier & Landenslager, 1985). A deficient immune system may fail to detect invaders or to produce antibodies. Its killing ability may be impaired, or its blood cells may be unable to multiply. Because of the weakening in defenses, infections and diseases are more likely to develop or worsen.

Decreased Immunological Functioning as a Function of Stress Impaired immunological functioning has been associated with a variety of social and psychological stressors. Divorced or separated men, for example, tend to have poorer immunological functioning than do married men. And happily married men tend to have stronger immune systems than men who are experiencing marital problems (Kiecolt-Glaser et al., 1987). The quality of social relationships may affect our vulnerability to illnesses.

Bereavement (loss of a spouse) has also been found to weaken the immune system. The lymphocyte responsiveness of men who were married to women with terminal breast cancer was measured one month before their wives' death and again afterward. The second measurement showed a drop in immune response. The decrease in efficiency continued for approximately two months, after which the immune functioning gradually increased (Schleifer et al., 1983). Similar results have also been reported in recently widowed women. Women whose husbands had died show a lower NK cell responsiveness than a group of nonbereaved women (Irwin et al., 1987). Although these stressors are associated with a decrease in immune response, not everyone was equally affected. As indicated in our discussion of the transaction model, the person's perception or interpretation of the event is important. In the case of separated and divorced men, men who were preoccupied with thoughts of their former partner demonstrated a lower level of immune functioning (Kiecolt-Glaser et al., 1987). How a person interprets an event can influence its impact.

Mediating the Effects of Stressors

It is clear from the studies cited earlier that not everyone who faces stressful events develops an illness. This fact suggests that certain factors may mediate the effects of a stressor. In this section, we discuss certain factors that mitigate stress.

Control or the perception of control over one's environment and its stressors appears to lessen the effects of stress. People in low-stress, low-control jobs may experience greater levels of stress than do people in high-stress, high-control jobs.

Helplessness or Control Control and the perception of control over the environment and its stressors appear to mitigate the effects of stress. One study of nursing home residents examined the impact of control on the residents' health and emotional states. In the "responsibility induced" group, residents were allowed to make certain decisions, such as how to arrange their rooms, when to see movies, whether or not to accept visitors, or whether to have plants in their room. The "traditional" group was not offered these choices. Movies were seen when scheduled. Nurses arranged rooms and chose and cared for residents' plants. Within a short period, the nurses

rated 71 percent of the "traditional" group as more debilitated and 93 percent of the "responsibility induced" group as improved. Self-report questionnaires also revealed that the responsibility-induced group rated themselves as more active and happier. Mortality rates also differed between the two groups. After 18 months, 15 percent (7 of 47) of those in the responsibility-induced group had died, versus 30 percent (13 of 44) in the traditional group. The reason for the differences in mortality rates is unclear. However, some of the deaths might be associated with a less efficient immune system (Langer & Rodin, 1976; Rodin & Langer, 1977).

A direct relationship between control and the immune system has been found in several studies. In one, ten subjects were placed in two stress situations—one they could control and one they couldn't. In the first situation, subjects could control noise level by pressing buttons in a simple sequence. In the other, subjects could not control the noise level. Blood samples were obtained after each session and analyzed. Epinephrine (a hormone released during stress) levels in the uncontrollable stress situation were significantly higher than those in the controllable one. The subjects also reported a greater sense of helplessness, higher tension, anxiety, and depression during the uncontrollable stress situation (Breier et al., 1987). Although changes in physical functioning occur with stress, can we demonstrate experimentally that control is related to disease?

A study to directly measure the ability to "control" immune functioning was performed. Rats were injected with cancer cells and assigned to one of three situations: (1) an *escapable shock* (pressing a bar would terminate the shock), (2) a *yoked control* (rats in this group would receive the same pattern of shocks as in the escapable condition, but would have no control over it), or (3) a *no-shock* control group. In the controllable shock group, 65 percent of the rats rejected the cancer cells, as opposed to only 27 percent in the yoked group and 55 percent in the no-shock control group. The inability to control a stressor seems to decrease immune system efficiency (Laudenslager et al., 1983; Visintainer et al., 1982).

Hardiness: Personality Characteristics and Mood State Maddi (1972) believes that "hardy" people are more resistant to illnesses. Kobasa and his colleagues (1979) conducted large-scale research on highly stressed executives in various occupations, seeking to identify the traits that distinguish those who handle stress well from those who do not. They found that high-stress executives who reported few illnesses showed three kinds of **hardiness**. In their attitudes toward life, these stress-resistant executives showed an *openness to change*, a feeling of *involvement* or *commitment*, and a *sense of control* over their lives. The most important protective factor correlated with health was attitude toward change (or *challenge*). Those who are open to change are more likely to interpret events to their advantage and to reduce their level of stress.

Suppose two people lost their jobs. The person who is open to change may view this situation as an opportunity to find a new career better suited to his or her abilities. The person who is not open to change, however, is likely to see it as a devastating event and to suffer the emotional and physical consequences of this perception.

What can we conclude about stress and its impact on the immune system? The results of many studies consistently show that both short-term stressors (exams, loss of sleep, emotional state) and long-term stressors (marital problems, divorce, bereavement, care for the chronically ill) impair immune system function. Stress also aggravates and prolongs some viral or bacterial infections. However, evidence suggests that the reduction in immune system efficiency is often relatively small. And finally, attitudes and perceptions influence the impact of stress.

Personality, Mood States, and Cancer

Are certain emotions or personality characteristics involved in either the cause or the course of cancers? Certain researchers believe so. Simonton and his colleagues (1978) believe that certain emotions can inhibit immune system functioning, allowing malignant cells to form. The inability to express emotions or to form lasting interpersonal relationships are hypothesized to be associated with cancer. According to Simonton and his colleagues, positive emotions can enhance immune functioning. Meares (1979) agrees, and says that physicians should take "the big step of attempting to influence cancer growth by psychological means" (p. 978). Many cancer patients also believe that they could control the course, outcome, and recurrence of the cancer. One patient put it this way: "I think that if you feel you are in control

of it [cancer], you can control it up to a point. I absolutely refuse to have any more cancer" (Taylor, 1983, p. 1163). This patient clearly believes that her attitude would have an effect on her cancer. However, this interpretation is still a subject of controversy (see Focus 8.2).

Several problems exist in research investigating the relationship between moods and personality on cancer. First, *cancer* is a general name for a variety of disease processes, each of which may have a varying susceptibility to emotions. Second, cancer develops over a relatively long period of time. Determining a temporal relationship between its occurrence and a specific mood or personality is not possible. Third, most studies examining the relationship between psychological variables and cancer have been retrospective—that is, personality or mood states were assessed after the cancer was diagnosed. The discovery that one has a life-threatening disease can produce a variety of emotional reactions. Instead of being a cause, the emotional state may be the result of knowing that you have a life threatening disease.

Fourth, while it has been shown that injected malignant cells are more likely to grow in stressed versus unstressed mice, the findings do not address the development of "spontaneous" cancers. Would the stressed mice be more likely to develop cancer anyway, without being injected with malignant cells?

The relationship between personality characteristics and cancer is difficult to demonstrate even with well-designed research. Consider the following study: One-hundred-and-sixty women with breast tumors were given a battery of personality tests before being told the results of their biopsies. This was done to control for effects that knowledge of the malignancy would create. Of the women, sixty-nine were found to have a malignant tumor. According to personality measures, the women in this group tended to display extremes in dealing with anger—some were very controlled, others had frequent outbursts (Greer & Morris, 1975). Although this study appeared to control for the impact of knowledge of having a disease on the emotional state, perhaps it did not. Could some of the women in this study have guessed correctly about the results of their biopsies? and if so, how?

Schwartz and Geyer (1984) found that many patients are aware that they have cancer before a formal diagnosis is made. How do they know? Patients may be very attentive to their physicians'

FOCUS 8.2   Do Psychological and Social Factors Contribute to the Development of Cancer?

Are cancers caused by psychological factors, and if so can they be cured by psychological means? To examine the impact of social and psychological factors on patients' ability to fight their disease, Cassileth and his colleagues (1985) studied a group of 204 men and women with advanced cancer and a group of 155 women with breast cancer. The variables they examined included social ties and marital history, job satisfaction, general life satisfaction, and degree of hopelessness and helplessness. These variables were selected because they were considered factors that might influence immune functioning. However, no relationship was found between disease recurrence or length of survival with any of the social or psychological variables. Cassileth and his colleagues concluded that in advanced cancer "the inherent biology of the disease alone determines the prognosis" (p. 1555).

In an editorial accompanying the Cassileth study, deputy editor of the *New England Journal of Medicine* Marcia Angell (1985) asked, "Is cancer more likely in unhappy people? Can people who have cancer improve their chances of survival by learning to enjoy life and to think optimistically?" (p. 1570). Angell answers these questions with a resounding "no!" She points out that most reports indicating the influence of psychological factors on diseases are anecdotal and that few of the studies are "scientifically sound." In addition, the view that psychological states can influence the development of and cause of cancer serves to blame the victims and to further burden them. She concludes by stating that "it is time to acknowledge that our belief in disease as a direct reflection of mental states is largely folklore" (p. 1572).

Angell's comments produced a flurry of letters to the *New England Journal of Medicine*. Williams, Benson, and Follick (1985), each of whom has served as the president of the Society of Behavioral Medicine, commented that the Cassileth study did not rule out the possibility that psychological factors were involved in the initiation of cancer and warns that accepting Angell's views could eliminate research into the biological correlates of mental states. Livnat and Felton (1985) point out that a growing body of scientific literature indicate that biological factors influence a number of physiologic functions. They argue that "Angell urges us to throw out the baby with the bath water" (p. 1357). The American Psychological Association sent a letter to the *New England Journal of Medicine* characterizing Angell's editorial as "inaccurate" (Abeles, 1986). This debate will continue. The results of research, so far, do not allow any conclusions to be reached regarding the relationship of cancer and social or psychological influences.

---

reactions during the examination; physicians may "unwittingly" convey cues that reflect their opinion. These unconscious cues may account for the fact that 75 percent of the women in the study were accurate in predicting whether or not they had the disease before the biopsy results were received. Schwartz and Geyer suggest that emotional expressions such as anger, depression, denial, and hopelessness may reflect the patient's reaction to the anticipated negative diagnosis. Because it is difficult to eliminate patient expectations, the precise relationship that exists between personality and anger is still unclear.

Specific emotional states have been suspected of influencing the onset and course of cancer. Depression (measured by the MMPI) was positively associated with a twenty-year incidence of mortality from cancer (Persky and his colleagues, 1987). People with high depression scores were 1.38 times more likely to develop cancer and 1.96 times more likely to die of cancer as compared with those rated low in depression. This was true even when risk factors such as age, smoking, alcohol intake, occupational status, family history of cancer, and serum cholesterol levels were taken into account. Because the study was prospective (before cancer diagnosed), the possibility that depression resulted from knowledge of having a cancer was eliminated. However, depression was only assessed at the beginning of the study. To demonstrate a relationship of this emotion with cancer, we would have to show that depression was a long-term disorder in these people.

Do stress, emotional difficulties, or personality characteristics increase the chance that a person will develop cancer, or increase the cancer's severity if it does occur? Certain emotions and stressors have been associated with a less efficient immune system. Possibly under these conditions cancer might be more likely to gain a foothold. However, the connection between stress and naturally occurring cancers remains to be demonstrated. Maybe only certain cancers at a certain level of development are influenced by emotional states. Researchers are currently investigating this possibility.

PSYCHOLOGICAL INVOLVEMENT IN SPECIFIC PHYSICAL DISORDERS

Although most research studying the impact of psychological factors on immunological functioning is fairly recent, the mind-body connection between some physical disorders has been extensively studied. In many instances, a relationship has been found between psychological and/or social factors and the origin and organization of these conditions. In addition, particularly stressful occupations have also been linked to the development of certain disorders. The First Person narrative in this chapter examines some of the more stressful aspects of police work.

Coronary Heart Disease

It is estimated that over 600,000 people die of coronary heart disease each year in the United States; of these, more than one-third are people under 65 years old (Fishman, 1982). However, the incidence of this disorder has been diminishing in recent years due to changes in smoking, diet, exercise, and treatment of hypertension (Matarazzo, 1984). **Coronary heart disease (CHD)** is a narrowing of the arteries in or to the heart, which results in the restriction or partial blockage of the flow of blood and oxygen to the heart. Its symptoms may range from chest pain (*angina pectoris*) to heart attack or, in severe cases, cardiac arrest. Cigarette smoking, physical inactivity, obesity, hypertension, and elevated serum cholesterol

have been found to increase the risk of coronary heart disease. However, these factors alone do not seem to be sufficient to cause the disease; studies suggest that other variables are involved as well.

Type A Personality Pattern Friedman and Rosenman (1974) identified a behavior pattern, called Type A behavior, that they believe is associated with increased risk of heart attack. The pattern involves aggressiveness, competitiveness, hostility, time pressure, and constant striving for achievement. In self-reports, Type A people indicate that they are easily aroused to anger and that they experience this emotion intensely and frequently (Levenkron et al., 1983; Stevens et al., 1984). A second behavior pattern, Type B, is characterized as relaxed and not subject to time pressure. Coronary heart disease is more likely in Type A people than in Type B (Suinn, 1977).

Because of their sense of time urgency, Type A people perceive time as passing more quickly, and they work more rapidly than Type B people. On tasks, they try to accomplish as much as possible in the shortest amount of time (Yarnold & Grimm, 1982). Stress has been found to increase blood pressure, and hypertension is a major factor in heart

Although sensitivity to time pressure, hostility, competitiveness, and the inability to relax are some characteristics of type A personalities, only hostility has been directly related to coronary heart disease.

Leslie Sue

FIRST PERSON

Stress and police work go hand in hand. In fact, very few careers cause as much stress as law enforcement. Research shows that police officers spend more time maintaining order than making arrests. Nevertheless, at any moment in an otherwise routine day an officer may confront a life-and-death situation. When an officer stops a vehicle for speeding, for example, he or she has no idea what to expect. The occupant could be a newly licensed teenager, a bank executive hurrying to get home, or a psychopath who has just robbed a local convenience store at gunpoint! It is the uncertainty of what lies ahead and the need to respond to it immediately that leads to stress and its symptoms.

I recall one incident that occurred in 1983. While assigned to the Selma resident agency of the Mobile, Alabama FBI field office as a special agent, I was called to a scene where an armed robbery had just occurred. When I got there, the police had already cordoned off a heavily forested area where the suspect was thought to be hiding. We knew he was armed, but the area had to be searched anyway. It was a stressful situation and I'm sure every officer there was as apprehensive as I was, because we knew we could be wounded or killed. And in fact, during the early morning hours, the suspect was killed in an exchange of gunfire, that began when he resisted arrest.

Police officers must always be mentally and physically prepared to respond quickly to threatening situations. Their lives and the lives of others often depend on quick response. It's not surprising, then, that the stress this causes often manifests itself in a high prevalence of cardiovascular disease, suicide, marital conflict and divorce, alcoholism and drug dependency, and stomach ailments.

There are also other reasons why police work tends to be very stressful. First, police departments are paramilitary organizations, which means they are patterned after military models. This type of organization reduces communication and decision making among the ranks; orders come from top to bottom. Individualism is discouraged. Second, officers are expected to know what to do in every situation, to maintain order even during violent confrontations, to render first aid to the injured, and to use deadly force when appropriate. Third, they are also expected to have strong interpersonal skills, despite the fact that most officers don't receive any training in this area. Fourth, police are often undervalued by the communities they serve and criticized by people who don't fully appreciate or understand the nature of police work.

In recent years, researchers have identified stress as a major occupational hazard in the occupation. Some of the more progressive police agencies have even designed programs to help officers improve their diet and learn stress reduction techniques such as meditation and relaxation. Many organizations also provide counseling services. These efforts have had a positive impact on reducing job stress and burnout, resulting in increased use of such programs. However, stress on the job continues to be a major debilitator in police work.

Dr. Leslie Sue is an associate professor at Vincennes University, where he teaches in the law enforcement program. He is a former special agent with the FBI and police officer.

attacks and strokes, so the constant pressure under which Type A people perform presumably increases the risk of heart attacks (Essau & Jamieson, 1987). Type A people do show increased activation of the sympathetic nervous system, as evidenced by increased pupil size and higher *plasma catecholamine* (hormones released by adrenal gland) levels. This activity increases cholesterol and *serum triglycerides* (fat molecules). These substances tend to be deposited on the arterial walls, narrowing or blocking the arteries and causing CHD.

Although evidence initially suggested that the Type A personality was related to coronary heart disease, recent research suggests something different (Friedman et al., 1984). The picture of a harried businessman, under strict time constraints doing several things at one time, competitive and hostile, is being reexamined. Heckler and his colleagues (1988) reviewed cases of coronary heart disease related to the Type A personality and found that the only significant risk factor was hostility. Similar conclusions have been reached by Williams et al. (1988) and Wood (1986). The Type A behavior pattern apparently includes factors that both are benign and place individuals at risk. If hostility is the key element, programs to help people to slow down and enjoy life may not be very helpful. Williams et al. (1988) found that depression and anxiety, along with anger and hostility, were related to coronary heart disease.

Age also appears to play a role in the relationship between CHD and Type A personality. In a study of 2,289 patients undergoing diagnostic coronary angiography, Type A characteristics were significantly related to CHD. However, the relationship depended on age. Among patients aged forty-five or younger, Type A personalities had more severe coronary arterial disease (CAD) than Type B's; among patients aged forty-six to fifty-four, there was no significant difference between the two groups. But among patients fifty-five years and older, more severe CAD was found among Type B than among Type A personalities. It seems that Type A behavior is involved in the pathogenesis (disease production) of CHD among only the younger age groups. What could account for this relationship? The researchers (Williams et al., 1988) hypothesize that Type A's who develop the disease when relatively young are biologically vulnerable to it, while older Type A's who don't develop CHD at a young age may be biologically hardier than their Type B counterparts. The results of this study and the others discussed earlier illustrate some of the difficulties involved in trying to determine the relationship between psychological variables and coronary heart disease.

Essential Hypertension

On October 19, 1987 (or "Black Monday," the day the stock market dropped 508 points) a 48-year-old stockbroker was wearing a device that measured stress related to the work environment. The instrument measured his pulse every 15 minutes. At the beginning of the day, his pulse was 64 beats per minute and blood pressure was 132/87 (both rates within a normal range). As stock prices fell dramatically, the man's physiological system surged in the other direction. His heart rate increased to 84 beats per minute

and blood pressure hit a dangerous 181/105. His pulse was "pumping adrenalin, flooding his arteries, maybe slowly killing himself in the process." (Tierney, 1988)

This case illustrates the impact of a stressor on blood pressure. Under what conditions will this physiological response, found in all of us, develop into a chronic condition? High blood pressure (the force of blood against the walls of the arteries and veins), or **essential hypertension,** is a common disorder that can lead to heart attacks or serious circulatory problems. In 90 percent of the cases, no organic cause can be determined. Over 10 percent of the U.S. population suffers from this condition—which is defined as 140/90 mm Hg and above (Surwitt et al., 1982). Chronic hypertension may lead to *arteriosclerosis* (narrowing of arteries) and increased risk of strokes and heart attacks.

A number of studies indicate that stressors may be related to hypertension. Living in crowded neighborhoods and being in a stressful occupation are both associated with high blood pressure (Ely & Mostardi, 1986; Fleming et al., 1987). Increases in blood pressure have also been demonstrated experimentally in subjects exposed to stressors. Interestingly, people who indicated that they were feeling a great deal of stress before the experiment showed elevated blood pressure even after the stressor was eliminated, while low-stress people quickly returned to their prestress levels (Pardine & Napoli, 1983). Reducing stress by relaxing, both at home and at work, significantly *lowers* blood pressure (Pickering et al., 1982). Such studies show that stress has a definite impact on blood pressure and support the contention that people who suffer from chronic stress may be at risk for developing hypertension.

Along with exposure to stressors, emotional reactions may also contribute to hypertension. Blood pressure tends to be temporarily higher when people are angry or anxious than when they are relaxed and contented (James et al., 1986). Researchers are trying to identify emotional patterns that produce a chronic elevation. The inability to appropriately express anger may be involved.

In a study of blacks living in Detroit, suppressed hostility, unexpressed anger, and low socioeconomic class were linked to high blood pressure. However, blood pressure could also be elevated by *expressing* anger: The investigators asked people whether they

Environmental conditions, such as crowded neighbor-hoods, have been associated with elevated blood pressure.

would respond to an angry boss by (1) keeping anger in ("just walk away from the situation"); (2) letting anger out ("protest to someone higher up"); or (3) reflection ("talk to the boss about it after he or she has cooled down"). Those who indicated they would choose the reflective response had lower blood pressure than those who responded with anger. Reflective coping was more characteristic of female than of male respondents (Harburg et al., 1979). Other studies have also found sex differences. A significant relationship between suppressed anger and blood pressure exists for white and black men but not for women (Dimsdale et al., 1986).

Ethnic Factors in Hypertension That blacks have higher mean blood pressure levels and higher

rates of hypertension than whites has been taken as evidence of genetic influence. Findings that black men show greater increases in systolic and diastolic blood pressure in reaction to cold stimulation than white men have also been used to support the view that there may be differences in sympathetic nervous system activity between the two groups. Increased awareness and better treatment for the disorder has substantially reduced hypertension among blacks and slightly reduced rates for white women (Foreyt, 1987). However, hypertension is still more prevalent among blacks (Anderson et al., 1988).

Social factors are also involved. Dressler and colleagues (1986) found that the availability of psychosocial resources modified black-white differences in blood pressure. The highest blood pressure was found among blacks with the lowest psychosocial resources. This finding suggests the impact of environmental factors. The degree of genetic contribution to hypertension remains an open question.

Peptic Ulcers

Peptic ulcers, which are essentially open sores within the digestive system, cause 10,000 deaths each year in the United States. One of every ten people is afflicted by this disorder at some point in his or her life (Whitehead et al., 1982).

Tony L. is a hard-working and competitive student. For a period of about a year, he has felt a burning sensation in his stomach. On the day before he is to take his graduate record examinations, he feels an overwhelming pain in his abdomen. He collapses and is taken to a hospital, where examination reveals that he has a duodenal ulcer.

The most common site for ulcers is the small intestine; ulcers located there are called *duodenal ulcers*. A somewhat less common site is the stomach, where they are called *gastric ulcers*. (See Table 8.1 for differences between the two types.) Duodenal ulcers are associated with excessive hydrochloric acid secretion. The pain tends to be rhythmic, occurring when the stomach is empty and diminishing after eating. Gastric ulcers seem to be related to how well the mucous membrane protects the walls of the stomach. Ulcers result from excessive secretion of

TABLE 8.1 | **Some Differences Between Duodenal and Gastric Ulcers**

Duodenal Ulcer	Gastric Ulcer
1. More frequent in young people	More frequent in older people
2. Associated with oversecretion of stomach acid	Associated with normal amounts of stomach acid
3. Occurs in members of higher social classes	Usually occurs in members of lower social classes
4. Associated with intellectually demanding jobs	Associated with jobs involving heavy manual labor
5. Eating relieves symptoms	Eating causes discomfort
6. Occurs mainly in males	Somewhat more common in males than in females

SOURCE: Adapted from Eisenberg, 1978.

stomach acid, insufficient secretion of the mucus that coats and protects the walls of the stomach, or slow or inadequate regeneration of the stomach lining (Salim, 1987). Under psychological stress, these conditions can lead to peptic ulcers.

Weiner and colleagues (1957) examined the proposition that a high level of *pepsinogen* (a digestive system secretion), along with stress, predisposes someone to develop peptic ulcers. From 2,073 newly inducted soldiers, a group of 63 oversecretors of pepsinogen and a group of 57 undersecretors were selected. None of the soldiers in these groups had ulcers at the beginning of their training period. After sixteen weeks of basic training, however, 9 of the oversecretors had developed ulcers, whereas none of the undersecretors displayed this disorder. Although the level of stomach acid is related to the development of peptic ulcers (and possibly to other gastrointestinal disorders), that certainly cannot be the only factor involved, because 86 percent of the oversecretors did not develop ulcers.

Because physical factors cannot fully explain the etiology of ulcers, psychological factors must be examined. Conflicts overdependency and subsequent feelings of guilt and hostility have been suggested as possible contributors. Magni and colleagues (1986) found three distinct personality profiles among 79 ulcer patients: (1) dependent and anxious, (2) neurotic and anxious, and (3) "balanced personality." These ulcer patients, however, did not form a homogeneous group. Most attempts to find a specific personality type associated with this disorder have not been very successful. Instead of looking at personality as a cause, it may be more helpful to identify emotional states that lead to increased gastric activity and ulcer formation. Ulcer patients often report that emotional events preceded the onset of pain (Salim, 1987).

Migraine, Tension, and Cluster Headaches

Headaches are among the most common psychophysiological complaints. Approximately 45 million Americans suffer chronic or recurrent headaches that vary in intensity from dull to excruciating (Clark et al., 1988). It is unclear whether the different forms of headaches (migraine, tension, and cluster) are produced by different psychophysiological mechanisms or if they merely differ in severity. Stress contributes to the initiation of headaches (Gannon et al., 1987).

We discuss migraine, tension, and cluster headaches separately, although the same person can be susceptible to several types of headaches. Furthermore, Blanchard and Andrasik (1982), who analyzed well-designed research studies comparing the different forms of headaches, concluded that, in spite of some apparent differences, there is little support for the view that the forms can be easily distinguished from one another. (Figure 8.2 illustrates some differences among the three types of headaches.)

Migraine Headaches   Dilation of the cerebral blood vessels and spasms in the cranial arteries, resulting in moderate to severe pain, are the distinguishing features of **migraine headache.** Anything that affects the size of these blood vessels, which are connected to sensitive nerves, can produce a headache. Thus certain chemicals, such as sodium nitrate (found in hot dogs), monosodium glutamate (used generously in restaurants that serve Asian food), and tyramine (found in red wines), can produce headaches by

distending blood vessels in sensitive people (Goleman, 1976). Migraine headaches are usually severe, may last from a few hours to several days, and are often accompanied by nausea and vomiting. Women report more migraine episodes than do men (Clark et al., 1988).

Migraine headaches are of two general types: classic and common. The *classic* type begins with an intense constriction of the blood vessels in the brain, dramatically diminishing the supply of blood. Depending on which part of the brain is affected most, the person may show various neurological symptoms, such as distortion of vision, numbness of parts of the

Figure 8.2 *What to Do If Headaches Strike*
SOURCE: From Newsweek on Health, Spring 1988. © 1988 Newsweek, Inc. All rights reserved. Reprinted by permission.

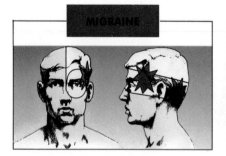
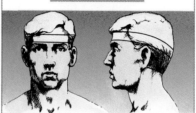
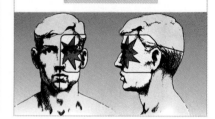

MIGRAINE

Symptoms

Throbbing pain (most severe in red) on one side of the head. Often preceded by an "aura," with glowing spots before the eyes. May cause nausea and aversion to lights, sounds. Often associated with menstruation. Lasts four hours to two days.

Treatment

During attacks: rest in a quiet, dark place. Medications include ergot compounds and nonnarcotic and anti-inflammatory pain relievers. To prevent attacks: beta blockers, tricyclic antidepressants, and anti-inflammatories.

TENSION

Symptoms

Dull, constricting ache on both sides of head rather than piercing pain. Often concentrated in "hatband" region or running into neck and shoulders. Can be intermittent or chronic.

Treatment

During attacks: nonnarcotic pain relievers and muscle relaxants. To prevent attacks: biofeedback, relaxation exercises, and tricyclic antidepressants.

CLUSTER

Symptoms

Intense pain, always on the same side of the head. Eye often teary, nose clogged. Lasts 20 minutes to two hours. Occurs at least once a day for weeks or months, then stops for months or years before recurring.

Treatment

During attacks: ergotlike compounds, oxygen. To prevent attacks: calcium channel blockers, ergotlike compounds, lithium, and steroids.

body, or speech and coordination problems. When the blood vessels then become distended to compensate for the diminished blood supply, severe pain occurs. The nerves become so sensitive that the blood, as it courses through the vessels with each heartbeat, produces a characteristic pulsating or throbbing pain (Goleman, 1976; Walen et al., 1977).

With *common* migraine headaches, the first phase is less severe, and neurological symptoms may not be evident. The pain also appears to be less intense than in classic migraine headaches.

Migraine sufferers have typically been described as being moral, ambitious, perfectionistic, and as having above-average intelligence and a tendency to repress emotions. But in a well-controlled study, migraine sufferers were not found to be especially ambitious or highly desirous of perfection (Henryk-Gutt & Rees, 1973). Although their headaches were precipitated by emotional stress, the sufferers were not generally exposed to more stressors than the controls. It was concluded that migraine patients are congenitally predisposed to headaches. An extensive review of the migraine headache literature also indicated that this problem probably has a hereditary basis, possibly represented by excessive cranial vascular responsiveness (Bakal, 1975).

Tension Headaches Tension headaches were once thought to be produced by prolonged contraction of the scalp and neck muscles, resulting in vascular constriction and steady pain. However, some studies have found a lack of correspondence between reports of pain and muscle tension among people who have tension headaches. Many people show no detectable muscle tension but still reported headaches (Philips, 1983). Friedman (1979) listed some of the complaints of 1,420 people who experienced tension headaches:

◈ "Feeling as if my head is being squeezed in a vise"

◈ "A tight headband that keeps getting tighter"

◈ "Top of the head is blown off"

Psychological factors precipitated the headaches in 77 percent of the cases, and most of the patients were women. Tension headaches are generally not as severe as migraine headaches, and they can usually be relieved with aspirin or other analgesics.

Cluster Headaches Little research has been conducted on cluster headaches, which are often described as excruciating. These headaches tend to occur on one side of the head near the eye, producing tears and a blocked nose. The pain is so great that sufferers may commit violent acts such as banging their heads against the wall (Clark et al., 1988).

Headaches appear to involve a biological predisposition such as greater reactivity of the blood vessels in the brain that respond to physical and psychological stressors. However, the precise mechanism involved is not known. Headache pain is being perceived as more than a function of a physiological factor (muscle tension, dilation of cranial arteries). Cognitive-emotional and pain-motivated behaviors, such as verbal and nonverbal complaints and avoidance, are also being considered (Philips, 1983).

Asthma

Asthma is a respiratory disorder that results from constriction of the airways in the lungs, due to muscle spasms or excessive mucus secretion (Creer, 1982). During asthmatic attacks, breathing becomes very difficult and produces a wheezing sound. The person struggles for breath and may develop acute anxiety, which aggravates the condition.

Asthma appears to have a diurnal variation, with symptoms often being worse during the night and early morning. Asthmatics often report nightmares involving strangling or drowning (Monday et al., 1987). The prevalence of asthma is estimated to be about 5 percent of the population, most of whom are under 17 years of age. As many as 40 percent show substantial or complete remission of symptoms as they grow older (Alexander, 1981).

Pollens or other substances to which an asthmatic person is allergic can produce such attacks, but in some cases psychological factors seem more important. In one study (Fritz et al., 1987), psychological factors such as depression and family conflicts were found to be the main causes in 18 percent of the cases. Asthma attacks can also serve to manipulate family members, as indicated in the following case:

Kathy was a 15-year-old girl whose asthma was diagnosed at age six. . . . Early on, emotional reactions were identified as important triggers to her episodes, along with exercise and infections. . . . Her biologic parents had a stormy relationship that included the father's physical abuse of the mother during their frequent drinking bouts, numerous separations, and financial insecurity. . . . Her asthma also served to interrupt parental fights, and Kathy consciously used her asthma in her role as a peacemaker. . . . The asthmatic symptoms were . . . associated with helplessness and extreme anxiety. (Fritz et al., pp. 253–254)

Although this case illustrates the interplay of psychological factors, physical factors such as infections can also play a major role in asthma. In most cases, however, physical and psychological causes interact. For example, when asthmatic children were exposed to tape recordings of emotional incidents from their earlier life, they displayed a decrease in forced expiratory rates—a response that is related to respiratory attacks (Tal & Miklich, 1976).

Perspectives on Etiology

Why does stress produce a physical disorder in some people but not in others? If a disorder does develop under emotional duress, what determines which psychophysiological illness it will be? Innate, developmental, and acquired characteristics certainly interact, but the nature and contribution of each are not well understood. In this section we discuss different perspectives on etiology—none of which adequately accounts for all the factors involved.

Psychodynamic Perspective Psychoanalysts have developed several formulations to explain physical disorders associated with psychological factors. According to these formulations, each type of psychophysiological disorder is produced by a specific form of unconscious conflict.

Alexander (1950) believes that an early unresolved childhood conflict produces a emotional response that is reactivated in adulthood. For example, the inhibition of aggressive feelings may produce hypertension or other cardiovascular disorders. According to this hypothesis, aggression and dependency needs are the basis for most of the psychophysiological disorders. The expression of dependency needs in-

creases activity of the parasympathetic division of the autonomic nervous system. Chronic activation of this division produces such disorders as peptic ulcers, diarrhea, and colitis. If feelings of anger predominate, the energy-expending sympathetic nervous system is activated, which may result in hypertension, migraine headaches, or arthritis.

A list of the unconscious complexes associated with certain disorders is given in Table 8.2. Although Alexander's theory is impressive in breadth and specificity, his propositions have not been supported experimentally.

Biological Perspective Some evidence points to a genetic base for the development of psychophysiological disorders. For example, ulcers are twice as common in siblings of ulcer victims as in siblings of nonvictims. And people with Type O blood are more likely to develop duodenal ulcers than are those with Type A, B, or AB blood (Eisenberg, 1978). A modest significant correlation on cardiovascular reactivity has been found between monozygotic (identical) twins. Presumably a greater reactivity could contribute to the development of hypertension and CHD (Smith et al., 1987).

In addition, three other biological explanations for psychophysiological disorders have been suggested: somatic weakness, autonomic response specificity, and general adaptation syndrome.

The *somatic weakness hypothesis* is a commonsense explanation for the development of particular psychophysiological disorders. This view suggests that congenital factors or a vulnerability acquired through physical trauma or illness may predispose a particular organ to develop irregularities or become weakened structurally by stressors. Therefore, which particular physiological disorder develops is determined by which system is the "weakest link" in the body. For example, 80 percent of the asthmatics in one study had previous respiratory infections, compared to only 30 percent of the nonasthmatic controls (Rees, 1964). The infection may have weakened the respiratory system and made it more vulnerable to the development of asthma. Logical as it seems, the somatic weakness hypothesis is difficult to validate, because it is not yet possible to measure the relative strengths of the different physical systems in the human body before an organ weakness appears.

TABLE 8.2 | **A Psychodynamic Etiology: The Unconscious Correlates to Certain Physical Disorders**

Disorder	Unconscious Correlates
Peptic ulcer	A conflict over dependency needs produces guilt and hostility. The person unsuccessfully attempts to sublimate these aggressive tendencies through achievement. Unsatisfied oral needs produce over-activity of gastrointestinal function, which produces an ulcer.
Asthma	The person has an unresolved dependency on his or her mother, who is perceived as cold; fears separation; or needs to be protected. The person feels guilty about the dependency needs. Instead of crying, he or she develops a wheeze that can develop into respiratory disorder.
Hypertension	The person experiences a struggle against unconscious hostile impulses and fluctuates from excessive control to outbursts of aggression. Repressing these hostile feelings leads to chronic blood pressure elevation.
Arthritis	The person inhibits hostile impulses or has experienced parental restrictions of freedom of movement. Developing arthritis allows the individual to avoid physically expressing aggression.

SOURCE: Adapted from Alexander, 1950.

Closely related to the somatic weakness hypothesis is the concept of *autonomic response specificity:* Each person has a unique physiological reaction to all types of stressful situations. This specific response is largely inherited, but it can be affected by a previously acquired vulnerability. Moreover, it has been demonstrated experimentally: College students subjected to a variety of stressors (from cold water to tough mathematics problems) tended to show stable and consistent idiosyncratic patterns of autonomic activity in the different stress-producing conditions. That is, a person who showed a rise in blood pressure when reacting to one type of stressor also showed this same reaction to other types of stressors (Lacey et al., 1953). Similar consistency was found in people who suffered migraine headaches, but not in a control group of people who did not get migraines (Cohen et al., 1978). The suggestion that these physiological responses are innate is supported by researchers who observed that distinctive autonomic behavior patterns in infants tended to persist throughout early childhood (Thomas et al., 1968).

The *general adaptation syndrome*, consisting of an alarm stage, a resistance stage, and an exhaustion stage, was discussed earlier in the chapter. According to Selye (1956), continued stress after the final stage may result in *diseases of adaptation* such as ulcers or hypertension. Unfortunately, this formulation is very general and does not explain why these diseases do not occur in all people undergoing long-term stress. Nor does it specify which psychophysiological disorder will develop. Combining this theory with the somatic weakness or autonomic response specificity hypotheses may be one way to deal with such conceptual problems.

The Classical Conditioning Perspective As noted, classical conditioning may be involved in the psychophysiological disorders. The conditioning of neutral stimuli can elicit or activate a physiological response through generalization, as discussed in Chapter 4. Probably, the greater the number of stimuli that can produce a specific physical reaction, the more likely a chronic condition will develop. Psychophysiological reactions can generalize to words or thoughts. For example, the bronchial reactions of forty asthmatic subjects were compared with those of a normal control group. The subjects were told that they were being exposed to different concentrations of substances to which they were allergic, when in fact they were exposed only to neutral saline solution. Nearly half (nineteen) of the asthmatic subjects displayed bronchial constriction (a symptom of asthmatic attacks), and twelve developed full-blown asthmatic attacks. None of the controls showed any of these symptoms (Luparello et al., 1968). The experimenters hypothesized that principles of classical conditioning could account for their finding. The thought of inhaling an allergic substance had become a conditioned stimulus capable of inducing asthmatic symptoms or attacks.

The classical conditioning position alone cannot, however, account for the etiology of the disorders discussed in this section. Physiological reactions must occur before other stimuli can be conditioned to them, or before generalization can occur. Hence classical conditioning may explain the continuation or increased severity of a disorder, but not its origin.

The Operant Conditioning Perspective Although theorists first believed that the autonomic nervous system is not under operant control, recent research shows that involuntary processes such as heart rate, blood pressure, and a variety of other functions can be influenced by reinforcement. These findings have important implications for the origin and the treatment of psychophysiological disorders.

Evidence that operant learning influences visceral (digestive tract) responses supports the possibility that disorders involving the autonomic nervous system can be learned (Miller, 1974). A child who fears school, for example, may show a variety of physiological responses (increase in heart rate, changes in blood pressure, constriction of the bronchioles, and increased gastrointestinal activity). The parents' attention to a particular physical symptom can reinforce the appearance of that symptom. Thus expressing sympathy or allowing a child to stay home to recover from a stomachache might contribute to the development of gastrointestinal disorders such as ulcers, colitis, or diarrhea.

The precise role of operant conditioning in the etiology of the disorders discussed here is still not clear. There is support for the contention that autonomic processes can be altered through reinforcement. But there is also controversy about the magnitude of the changes that are possible and about whether the disorders develop through shaping or through other operant processes.

Sociocultural Perspectives In a study of Japanese in Japan, Hawaii, and California, researchers found that Japanese living in California had the highest mortality rate from coronary heart disease and that those living in Japan had the lowest. This difference was not accounted for by differences in the risk factors for CHD discussed earlier. In trying to determine what was responsible for the variation in mortality rates, the researchers compared Japanese immigrants who had maintained a traditional orientation with those who had acculturated (adopted the habits and attitudes prevalent in their new home). The CHD rate for acculturated Japanese turned out to be five times greater than that for Japanese who had retained their traditional values (Marmot & Syme, 1976). Perhaps breaking close social and community ties, which is part of the acculturation process, caused the acculturated Japanese to become more vulnerable to the disease.

Treatment of Psychophysiological Disorders

Treatment programs for psychophysiological disorders generally consist of both medical treatment for the physical symptoms and conditions and psychological therapy to eliminate stress and anxiety. Behavioral medicine has provided an array of psychological approaches to these disorders, with mainly positive results. Among these are the stress management and anxiety management programs, which usually include either relaxation training or biofeedback. The concept of combined therapies is illustrated in the following case.

Jerry R. is a 33-year-old male who has always taken pride in the vigor with which he attacks everything he does, whether it involves work or social activities. He worries about keeping slim, so he exercises at a health spa three nights a week. He is shocked to discover, during a routine physical examination, that he has borderline high blood pressure. His physician explains that exercise is not enough, particularly when he uses a lot of salt, drinks coffee throughout the day, and overdoes the "drinking with the guys."

Jerry is told that antihypertensive medication is not indicated, primarily because his blood pressure is only mildly elevated at this point. However, he must take steps to reduce his blood pressure, and he is advised to reduce his intake of salt, caffeine, and alcohol. On learning that coronary heart disease runs in Jerry's family, the physician also strongly suggests that Jerry decrease his cholesterol intake by reducing the amounts of eggs, saturated fats (red meat, butter), and whole milk in his diet. He commends Jerry for having given up smoking five months ago.

Finally, Jerry is urged to become active in a stress management program geared toward lowering his blood pressure and preventing coronary heart disease. Although the effectiveness of these programs is somewhat controversial, Jerry's physician feels that Jerry has more to gain than he has to lose by participating in a course of biofeedback and relaxation training.

The success of such combined treatment programs suggests that the psychological approach to the treatment of certain physical disorders is much more than a passing fad (Rees, 1983; Ford et al., 1982; Miller, 1983; Barber, 1984).

In the remainder of this section, we discuss relaxation training and biofeedback, which are emerging as the primary stress management techniques of behavioral medicine. They are used in treating all the psychophysiological disorders described in this chapter.

Relaxation Training Present **relaxation training** programs are typically modeled after Jacobson's (1938, 1967) progressive relaxation training. Imagine that you are a patient who is beginning the training. You are instructed to concentrate on one set of muscles at a time—first tensing them and then relaxing them. First you clench your fists as tight as possible, for approximately ten seconds, and then release them. As you release your tightened muscles, you are asked to focus on the sensation of warmth and looseness in your hands. You practice this tightening and relaxing cycle several times before proceeding to the

next muscle group, in your lower arms. After each muscle group has received individual attention in the form of tensing and relaxing, the trainer asks you to first tighten and then to relax your entire body. The emphasis throughout the procedure is on the contrast between the feelings produced during tensing and those produced during relaxing. For a novice, the entire exercise lasts about thirty minutes.

With practice, you eventually learn to relax the muscles without first having to tense them. You can then use the technique to relax at almost any time during the day, even when only a few moments are available for the exercise.

Biofeedback In **biofeedback training,** the client is taught to control a particular physiological function voluntarily. During training, the client is provided with second-by-second information (feedback) regarding the activity of the organ or function of interest. For someone suffering from high blood pressure, for example, the biofeedback training would focus on developing the ability to lower blood pressure. The feedback might be actual blood pressure readings presented visually on a screen or some auditory representation of blood pressure presented over a set of headphones. The biofeedback device

In biofeedback training, clients can get instant-by-instant information about their heart rate, blood pressure, gastrointestinal activity, muscle tension, or other physical functions. Through operant conditioning techniques, they learn to control their physiological functions.

enables the patient to learn his or her own idiosyncratic method for controlling the particular physiological function. Eventually the patient learns to use that method without benefit of the feedback device.

> A 23-year-old male patient was found to have a resting heart rate that varied between 95 and 120 beats per minute. He reported that his symptoms first appeared during his last year in high school, when his episodes of tachycardia were associated with apprehension over exams. The patient came into treatment concerned that his high heart rate might lead to a serious cardiac condition.
>
> The treatment consisted of eight sessions of biofeedback training. The patient's heart rate was monitored, and he was provided with both a visual and an auditory feedback signal. At the end of the treatment period, his heart rate had stabilized and was within normal limits. One year later, his heart rate averaged 73 beats per minute. The patient reported that he had learned to control his heart rate during stressful situations such as going for a job interview, by both relaxing and concentrating on reducing the heart rate. (Janssen, 1983)

Biofeedback is essentially an operant conditioning technique in which the feedback serves as reinforcement. It has been used to help people lower their heart rate and decrease their blood pressure (Glasgow et al., 1982), reduce muscle tension (Gamble & Elder, 1983), and redirect blood flow (Reading & Mohr, 1976). Patients with duodenal ulcers have been taught to decrease the level of gastric acid secretion by providing feedback on stomach acidity (Welgan, 1974). Biofeedback and verbal reinforcement were used to help asthmatic children control their respiratory functioning (Kahn et al., 1974). In an interesting marriage of operant and classical conditioning techniques, the children were also trained to control bronchial constriction by dilating their bronchi when exposed to previously conditioned stimuli.

The purely biological or purely psychological models are too simplistic. But to merely advocate the diathesis stress model is also insufficient. Certainly both processes (psychological and biological) are involved in all diseases. However, in some disorders, and in some people, biological factors have the primary influence while in others psychological factors predominate. Because so many variables are involved, the question of which person will develop a psychophysiological disorder under what conditions is difficult to answer.

Although much is known about the psychophysiological disorders, a great deal is still to be learned. Psychologists involved in behavioral medicine are seeking to decrease a person's vulnerability to physical problems by suggesting changes in lifestyle, attitudes, and perceptions. Attention is also directed toward altering the course of an illness after it has occurred. The field of behavioral medicine will continue to receive greater attention from psychologists. We are only beginning to understand the relationship between psychological factors and physical illnesses.

SUMMARY

1. The sudden death syndrome is an extreme example of the effect of psychological factors on physical health. In sudden death, stress is thought to produce bradycardia, tachycardia, or arrhythmia, killing susceptible people.

2. Formerly, the term *psychosomatic* was used to categorize a number of specific physical disorders that are produced or aggravated by emotional stress. This usage fostered the incorrect view that only certain physical conditions have significant psychological components. Now, the DSM-III-R category "psychological factors affecting physical condition" recognizes the belief that both physical and psychological factors may be involved in any illness. The field of behavioral medicine represents this new direction in controlling disease.

3. Immunological functioning seems to be affected by physical and psychological stress. A variety of factors such as anxiety, divorce, and bereavement can produce poor immunological responses. Some research supports the suggestion that psychological stress can influence the initiation and course of certain infectious diseases. Stress decreases the ability of animals to reject injected cancer cells. However, whether or not psychological variables influence the development of cancer in humans is not known.

4. Coronary heart disease (CHD) and essential hypertension are the most pervasive cardiovascular disorders. The incidence of CHD is influenced by

social factors, personality, and lifestyle, as well as such risk factors as smoking and inactivity. Hypertension is related to the emotions and how they are expressed, especially anger.

5. Peptic ulcers—duodenal or gastric—afflict 10 percent of all people at some point in their lives. Along with stress, oversecretion of stomach acid and insufficient secretion of protective mucus apparently predispose ulcers.

6. Headaches are among the most common psychophysiological complaints. Migraine headaches involve the constriction and then the dilation of blood vessels in the brain. Tension headaches are thought to be caused by contraction of the neck and scalp muscles, which results in vascular constriction. However, these headaches can occur without tension.

7. Asthma attacks result from constriction of the airways in the lungs. Breathing is extremely difficult during the attacks, and acute anxiety may worsen the situation. Suppressed aggression and conditioning have been suggested as causes.

8. Etiological theories must be able to explain why some people develop a physical disorder under stress, whereas others do not, and what determines which psychophysiological illness develops. According to psychodynamic formulations, the particular illness that is manifested depends on the stage of psychosexual development and the type of unresolved unconscious conflict involved. Biological explanations focus on somatic weakness and response specificity. Learning theorists emphasize the importance of classical and operant conditioning in acquiring or maintaining these disorders.

9. Psychophysiological disorders are generally treated through stress management or anxiety management programs, combined with medical treatment for physical symptoms or conditions. Relaxation training and biofeedback training, which help the client learn to control muscular or organic functioning, are usually a part of such programs.

KEY TERMS

asthma A respiratory disorder characterized by attacks in which breathing becomes extremely difficult due to constriction of the airways in the lungs

behavioral medicine A number of disciplines that study social, psychological, and lifestyle influences on health

biofeedback training A therapeutic technique in which the person is taught to control a particular physiological function such as heart rate or blood pressure

coronary heart disease (CHD) A cardiovascular disease in which the flow of blood and oxygen to the heart is restricted by a narrowing of the arteries in or near the heart

decompensation Loss of the ability to deal successfully with stress, resulting in more primitive means of coping

essential hypertension High blood pressure, usually with no known organic cause

general adaptation syndrome (GAS) A model for understanding the body's physical and psychological reaction to biological stressors

hardiness A concept developed by Kobasa and Maddi that refers to a person's ability to deal well with stress

life change model Hypothesis that all life changes can act as stressors

migraine headache Severe headache resulting from constriction and then dilation of the cerebral blood vessels

peptic ulcer An open sore within the digestive system

psychophysiological disorder A physical disorder that has a strong psychological basis or component

relaxation training A therapeutic technique in which the person acquires the ability to relax the muscles of the body in almost any circumstances

stress A person's internal reaction to an external stimulus (stressor)

stressor A physical or psychological demand placed on a person by some external event or situation

sudden death syndrome Unexpected abrupt death that may be brought on by stress. In most cases, there is an underlying coronary condition.

tension headache A headache that is thought to be produced by prolonged contraction of the scalp and neck muscles

transaction model of stress Hypothesis that a person's perception of a stressor mediates its impact

PART 3

Disorders Involving Conduct

chapter 9
Personality Disorders and Impulse Control Disorders

Although this chapter discusses personality disorders and impulse control disorders, the two are separate and distinct categories in DSM-III-R (American Psychiatric Association, 1987). We are discussing them together because each disorder involves conduct problems that interfere with effective social relationships or that may have detrimental consequences for society.

THE PERSONALITY DISORDERS

Personality disorders are characterized by behavioral patterns that are inflexible and maladaptive. People with these disorders consistently show personality traits that cause personal and social difficulties, distress, or problems functioning. These people also have temperamental deficiencies or aberrations, rigidity in dealing with life problems, and defective perceptions of self and others.

In spite of all this, people with personality disorders can often function well enough to get along without aid from others. For this reason, and because these people rarely seek help from mental health professionals, the incidence of personality disorders has been difficult to ascertain. Available statistics indicate that the personality disorders account for about 5 to 15 percent of admissions to hospitals and outpatient clinics.

FOCUS 9.1   *Self-Defeating and Sadistic Personality Disorders*

Two new personality disorders have been proposed in DSM-III-R (American Psychiatric Association, 1987): self-defeating personality disorder and sadistic personality disorder. The controversy over the two disorders involve whether the two categories actually represent disorders and the consequences of including them in the diagnostic manual. Let us first examine their definitions.

The essential feature of self-defeating personality disorder is a pervasive pattern of self-defeating behavior, in which the person avoids or undermines pleasurable encounters and is drawn to situations in which he or she will experience suffering. Specifically, a person with this disorder may choose people or situations that lead to disappointment, mistreatment, or failure; may reject attempts of others to help; fails to accomplish tasks crucial to achieving personal objectives; and rejects opportunities for pleasure. These behaviors occur whether or not the person is depressed.

Sadistic personality disorder is characterized by a pervasive pattern of cruel, demeaning, and aggressive behavior directed toward other people. The behavior is evident with family members, subordinates, and others but rarely with people in positions of authority or higher status. If the sadistic behavior is directed only toward one person (such as a spouse) or is exhibited for the purpose of sexual gratification (which would then be diagnosed as sexual sadism), the diagnosis would not be made. People with this disorder often come from families in which cruelty was evident or directed toward them as children.

Critics of these two disorders questioned whether these should be

Diagnosing personality disorders is difficult for two primary reasons. First, many people show certain traits that characterize personality disorders—for example, suspiciousness, dependency, sensitivity to rejection, or compulsiveness. In fact, we all exhibit some of these traits, to varying degrees and at various times. In addition, personality patterns may not be stable. Many investigators have consistently argued that personality characteristics vary according to the situation and are not fixed or stable across situations (Mischel, 1968). Second, some symptoms of one personality disorder are also symptomatic of other disorders, so that differential diagnosis is often a problem. Using DSM-III-R criteria, Morey (1988) found that many people diagnosed as having one type of personality disorder also met the criteria for other personality disorders. Moreover, people can have more than one type of personality disorder, so the diagnostic problems for these disorders are formidable.

DSM-III-R asserts that a number of traits, not just one, must be considered in determining whether a disorder exists. For example, to diagnose dependent personality disorder, the clinician must find a constellation of characteristics (such as the inability to make decisions independently and the subordination of one's own needs). Other criteria or factors must also be considered: the personality pattern (1) must characterize the person's current as well as long-term functioning, (2) must not be limited to episodes of illness, and (3) must either significantly impair social or occupational functioning or cause subjective distress. Thus a person who is temporarily dependent because of an illness would not be diagnosed as having a dependent personality.

The signs of a personality disorder usually become evident during adolescence. In some cases, a person with a personality disorder may have had a similar childhood disorder. For example, it is not uncommon to find that a person diagnosed as having *schizoid personality disorder* was previously diagnosed as having *schizoid disorder of childhood.* When the features of certain childhood disorders persist into adulthood (that is, beyond age eighteen), the diagnosis may be changed to a given personality disorder.

In the diagnostic scheme of DSM-III-R, personality disorders are recorded on Axis II. This means that a person may receive diagnoses on both Axis I

considered as disorders. They were concerned that the diagnosis of self-defeating personality disorder might unfairly be applied to battered women. The women could be diagnosed as having a mental disorder when they were actually victims of abuse. And women are often socialized into the roles of being more nurturant, deferential, and willing to delay gratification. These behaviors could be interpreted as being masochistic, a sign of a mental disorder (Caplan, 1984; Franklin, 1987).

Furthermore, feminists charged that sadistic personality disorder, which mainly applies to men, was proposed in an attempt to counterbalance the creation of the category of self-defeating personality disorder, which applied primarily to women (Holden, 1986).

Because of the controversial nature of this category and the serious objections to it, self-defeating personality disorder was included, along with sadistic personality disorder, in the appendix of DSM-III-R. These disorders were considered as proposed categories in need of further study.

These issues regarding the diagnostic system reveal the fact that classification schemes are not simply objective systems, free from socio-political controversies. The allegations over sex bias, compromises made in trying to establish new categories of disorders, and concerns over the social implications of the categories illustrate this point. As noted in Chapter 4, other considerations also entered into the development of DSM-III-R, such as the ease of application and acceptability of the categories to practitioners. Thus classification schemes need continual revision and modification in order to respond to changing scientific and social issues involving validity, utility, and fairness.

and Axis II. For example, a person with a personality disorder may also be diagnosed as schizophrenic or as alcohol dependent. Usually, people with personality disorders are hospitalized only when a second, superimposed disorder so impairs social functioning that they require inpatient care. The rationale for having two axes for mental disorders is that Axis II disorders generally begin in childhood or adolescence and persist in a stable form into adulthood. Axis I disorders usually fail to show this early feature with stable characteristics.

DSM-III-R lists eleven specific personality disorders and groups them into three clusters, depending on whether they may be characterized by (1) odd or eccentric behaviors; (2) dramatic, emotional, or erratic behaviors; or (3) anxious or fearful behaviors. The clustering of these disorders is based more on convenience than on actual similarity of symptoms or etiology. First we will briefly discuss each of the eleven personality disorders. Then we'll discuss one of them—the *antisocial personality disorder*—in more detail, primarily because more information is available regarding this disorder. Two other newly proposed personality disorders are discussed in Focus 9.1.

Disorders Characterized by Odd or Eccentric Behaviors

Three personality disorders are included in this cluster: paranoid personality, schizoid personality, and schizotypal personality. These and two other clusters of personality disorders discussed in this chapter are shown in the disorders chart on p. 232.

Paranoid Personality Disorder People with **paranoid personality disorder** show unwarranted suspiciousness, hypersensitivity, and restricted affect (that is, aloofness and lack of emotion). They tend to be rigid and to be preoccupied with unfounded beliefs that stem from their suspicions and sensitivity. These beliefs are extremely resistant to change. Here is an example:

Ralph and Ann married after knowing each other for two months. The first year of their marriage was relatively happy, although Ralph tended to be domineering and very protective of his wife. Ann had always known that Ralph was a jealous person who demanded a great deal of attention. She was initially

PERSONALITY DISORDERS

Inflexible and maladaptive personality traits that cause significant functional impairment or subjective distress for the individual

Odd, eccentric

Paranoid
Unwarranted suspiciousness, hypersensitivity, and reluctance to confide in others

Schizoid
Socially isolated, emotionally cold, indifferent to others

Schizotypal
Peculiar thoughts and behaviors, poor interpersonal relationships

Dramatic, emotional, erratic

Antisocial
Failure to conform to social or legal codes, lack of anxiety and guilt, irresponsible behaviors

Borderline
Intense fluctuations in mood, self-image, and interpersonal relationships

Histrionic
Self-dramatization, exaggerated emotional expressions, and attention-seeking behaviors

Narcissistic
Exaggerated sense of self-importance, hypersensitivity, and lack of sympathy

Anxious, fearful

Avoidant
Fear of rejection and humiliation, reluctance to enter into social relationships

Dependent
Reliance on others and inability to assume responsibilities

Obsessive-Compulsive
Perfectionism, indecision, devotion to details, and rigidity

Passive-Aggressive
Passive expression of aggression through stubbornness, inefficiency, and procrastination

SOURCE: Adapted from DSM-III-R, pp. 335–358.

pleased that her husband was concerned about how other men looked at her; she felt that it showed Ralph really cared for her. It soon became clear, however, that his jealousy was excessive. One day when she came home from shopping later than usual, Ralph exploded. He demanded an explanation but did not accept Ann's, which was that she stopped to talk with a neighbor. Ralph told her he wanted her to be home when he returned from work—always. Believing him to be in a bad mood, Ann said nothing. Later, she found out that Ralph had called the neighbor to confirm her story.

The situation progressively worsened. Ralph began to leave work early in order to be with his wife. He said that business was slow, and they could spend more time together. Whenever the phone rang, Ralph insisted on answering it himself. Wrong numbers and

male callers took on special significance for him; he felt they must be trying to call Ann. Ann found it difficult to discuss the matter with Ralph. He was always quick to take the offensive, and he expressed very little sympathy or understanding toward her.

Arguments between the two increased. Ann could not convince him that she had no interest in other men. At one point, she threatened to leave him; Ralph told her he would never let her go and threatened her with physical harm. He then produced a diary, which detailed his account of her behaviors. Ann was shocked to find out how many of her behaviors and the behaviors of others Ralph had interpreted as signs of infidelity. Her smiles or remarks to other men on the telephone or in stores were seen as secret messages inviting sexual contact; her neighbor was perceived as acting as a go-between for Ann and other men; dressing in a particularly attractive manner meant that she was going to see another man or that she was flirting with others. After reading the diary, which went back to the day they met, Ann realized that Ralph was disturbed, something she had not been willing to admit to herself before. Failing to convince her husband that he needed professional help, Ann went alone to a psychologist.

Ralph's suspicions regarding his wife's fidelity were obviously unjustified. Nothing that Ann did implicated her with other men. Yet Ralph persisted in his pathological jealousy and suspiciousness, and he took the offensive when she suggested that he was wrong in distrusting her. This behavior pattern, along with Ralph's absence of warmth and tenderness, indicates paranoid personality disorder.

As a follow-up to the case, it is interesting to note that after several weeks of treatment, Ann began to feel stronger in her relationship with Ralph. During one confrontation, in which Ralph objected to her seeing the therapist, Ann asserted that she would continue the treatment. She said that she had always been faithful to him and that his jealousy was driving their marriage apart. In a rare moment, Ralph broke down and started crying. He said he needed her and begged her not to leave him. At this time, Ralph and Ann are each seeing a therapist for individual psychotherapy, and together they see still another therapist for marital therapy.

Schizoid Personality Disorder The **schizoid personality disorder** is marked primarily by social isolation. People with this disorder have a long history of impairment of social functioning. They are often described as being reclusive and withdrawn (Siever, 1981). Many live alone in apartments or furnished rooms and engage in solitary recreational activities such as watching television, reading, or taking walks. Because of a lack of capacity or desire to form social relationships, schizoid people are perceived by others as peculiar and aloof and therefore inadequate as dating or marital partners.

Schizoid people may have to relate to others in certain situations—for example, at work. But these relationships are superficial and frequently awkward. Such people tend to comply with the requests or feelings of others, perhaps in an attempt to avoid extensive involvements, conflicts, and expressions of hostility.

Social isolation can be found even in their marital relationships. Spitzer and co-workers (1981) describe the case of a man who had married primarily to please his parents. After a while, his wife literally forced him to see a therapist because he lacked affection, interest in sex, and willingness to participate in family activities. He was as emotionally unrespon-

We all feel suspicious at one time or another—sometimes reasonably so and sometimes unreasonably. What differentiates normal suspiciousness from that which characterizes paranoid disorder is the degree and intensity of the belief and the rigidity with which it is held.

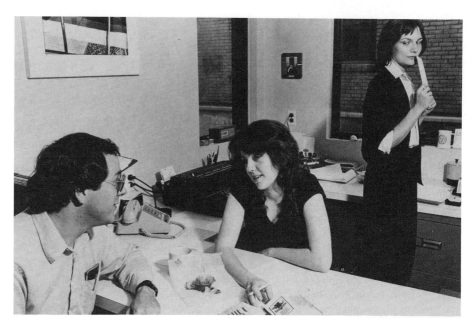

sive to members of his family as he was to his colleagues at work.

The relationship between this disorder and schizophrenia (which is described in Chapter 14) is unclear. One view is that schizoid personality is a beginning stage of schizophrenia. Another is that schizophrenia may develop as a complication of the schizoid personality disorder.

Schizotypal Personality Disorder People who have **schizotypal personality disorder** show oddities in various aspects of their thinking and behavior. Many victims believe they possess magical thinking abilities or special powers ("I can predict what people will say before they say it"). Some are subject to recurrent illusions ("I feel as if my dead father is watching me"). Speech oddities, such as frequent digression or vagueness in conversation, are often apparent.

The peculiarities seen in schizotypal personality disorder stem from distortions or difficulties in cognition (Siever, 1981). That is, these people seem to have problems in thinking and perceiving. People with this disorder often show social isolation, hypersensitivity, and inappropriate affect (emotions). However, it is believed that the disorder is defined primarily by cognitive distortions and that affective and interpersonal problems are secondary.

The woman described in the following case was diagnosed as having schizotypal personality disorder.

The patient is a 32-year-old unmarried, unemployed woman on welfare who complains that she feels "spacey." Her feelings of detachment have gradually become stronger and more uncomfortable. For many hours each day she feels as if she were unreal. She feels especially strange when she looks into a mirror. For many years she has felt able to read people's minds by a "kind of clairvoyance I don't understand." According to her, several people in her family apparently also have this ability. She is preoccupied by the thought that she has some special mission in life, but is not sure what it is; she is not particularly religious. She is very self-conscious in public, often feels that people are paying special attention to her, and sometimes thinks that strangers cross the street to avoid her. She is lonely and isolated and spends much of each day lost in fantasies or watching TV soap operas. She speaks in a vague, abstract, digressive manner, generally just missing the point, but she is never incoherent. She seems shy, suspicious, and afraid she will be criticized. She has no gross loss of reality testing, such as hallucinations or delusions. She has never had treatment for emotional problems. She has had occasional jobs, but drifts away from them because of lack of interest. (Spitzer et al., 1981, pp. 95–96)

As peculiar as this patient's behaviors may seem, they are not serious enough to warrant a diagnosis of schizophrenia. Her belief that she is clairvoyant does not appear to be delusional: it is not firmly held (she admits to being confused about it), and there is no gross loss of contact with reality. Moreover, no previous history of psychosis was found. All these factors point to a personality disorder.

As is true of schizoid personality, many characteristics of schizotypal personality disorder resemble those of schizophrenia (although in less serious form). There does appear to be a hereditary link between the two disorders. Kendler (1988) found a higher risk of schizotypal personality disorder among relatives of schizophrenics than among nonschizophrenic controls. In general, family, twin, and adoption studies support the genetic relationship between schizophrenia and schizotypal personality disorder.

Disorders Characterized by Dramatic, Emotional, or Erratic Behaviors

The group of disorders characterized by dramatic, emotional, or erratic behaviors includes four personality disorders: histrionic, narcissistic, antisocial, and borderline.

Histrionic Personality Disorder A person with **histrionic personality disorder** engages in self-dramatization, the exaggerated expression of emotions, and attention-seeking behaviors. Despite superficial warmth and charm, the histrionic person is typically shallow and egocentric. These behaviors were evident in a woman client seen by one of the authors of this book:

The woman was a 33-year-old real estate agent who entered treatment for problems involving severe depression. She had recently been told by her boyfriend that she was a self-centered and phony person. He found out that she had been dating other men, despite

The symptoms of histrionic personality disorder include exaggerated emotional expression, attention-seeking or manipulative behavior, self-dramatization, egocentrism, and a lack of genuineness. A person must exhibit a combination of these characteristics in order to be diagnosed as histrionic.

their understanding that neither would go out with others. The woman claimed that she never considered her "going out with other men" as actual dating. Once their relationship was broken, her boyfriend refused to communicate with her. The woman then angrily called the boyfriend's employer and told him that unless the boyfriend contacted her, she would commit suicide. He never did call, but instead of attempting suicide she decided to seek psychotherapy.

The woman was attractively dressed for her first therapy session. She wore a tight and clinging sweater. Several times during the session she raised her arms, supposedly to fix her hair, in a very seductive manner. Her conversation was animated and intense: when she was describing the breakup with her boyfriend, she was tearful; later, she raged over the boyfriend's failure to call her and, at one point, called him a "son of a bitch." Near the end of the session, she seemed to be upbeat and cheerful, commenting that the best therapy might be for the therapist to arrange a date for her.

None of the behaviors exhibited by this client would, by itself, warrant a diagnosis of histrionic personality disorder. However, the combination of her subjective distress (or depression), self-dramatization, incessant drawing of attention to herself via

seductive movements, angry outbursts, manipulative suicide gesture, and lack of genuineness points to this disorder (which, in fact, is diagnosed far more frequently among women than among men, perhaps because of sex roles that have traditionally favored emotional expression among women). Millon and Everly (1985) believe that biogenic factors such as autonomic or emotional excitability, and environmental factors such as parental reinforcement of attention-seeking behaviors among children and the existence of histrionic parental models, are important in the disorder.

Narcissistic Personality Disorder The clinical characteristics of **narcissistic personality disorder** involve an exaggerated sense of self-importance. People with this disorder require attention and admiration and have difficulty in accepting personal criticism. In conversations, they talk about themselves and show a lack of interest in others and a lack of empathy. Many have fantasies about power or influence, and they constantly overestimate their talents and importance. Owing to their sense of self-importance, narcissistic people expect to be the superior participants in all relationships. For example, they may be impatient and irate if others arrive late for a meeting, but they may frequently be late themselves and think nothing of it.

One narcissistic client reported, "I was denied promotion to chief executive by my board of directors, although my work was good, because they felt I had poor relations with my employees. When I complained to my wife, she agreed with the board, saying my relations with her and the children were equally bad. I don't understand. I know I'm more competent than all these people" (Masterson, 1981, p. ix). The client was depressed and angry about not being promoted and about the suggestion that he had difficulty in forming social relationships. His wife's confirmation of his problems further enraged him. During therapy, he was competitive and sought to devalue the observations of the therapist.

Narcissistic people may often use denial and devaluation of others to maintain an inflated self-concept (Kernberg, 1975). Denial is also used to ward off feelings of inferiority that may have developed from early childhood (Marmar, 1988). These are the tools with which they take the offensive in response to criticism.

Antisocial Personality Disorder Chronic antisocial behavioral patterns such as irresponsibility, lying, using other people, and aggressive sexual behavior indicate **antisocial personality disorder.** People with this disorder fail to conform to social norms or legal prescriptions but show little guilt for their wrongdoing. Their relationships with others are superficial and fleeting, and little loyalty is involved.

Antisocial personality, which is far more prevalent among men than among women, is the second of the two disorders that we deal with in greater detail later.

Borderline Personality Disorder Contrary to popular belief, **borderline personality disorder** is not a condition that is midway between, or that fluctuates between, neurotic and psychotic disturbances (Gallahorn, 1981). It is a disorder in and of itself, manifested by impulsiveness and by intense fluctuations in mood, self-image, and interpersonal relationships. Borderline people may be quite friendly one day and quite hostile the next day. Although no single feature defines the disorder, its true essence can be captured in the capriciousness of behaviors

and the lability of moods (Millon & Everly, 1985). The First Person narratives in this chapter and the example below illustrate the many facets of borderline personality disorder.

Bryan was a 23-year-old graduate student majoring in sociology at a prestigious university. He was active in student government and was viewed as charismatic, articulate, and sociable. When he met other students for the first time, he could often convince them to participate in the campus activities that interested him. Women were quite attracted to him, because of his charm and self-disclosing nature. They described him as being exciting, intense, and different from other men. Bryan could form close relationships with others very quickly.

Bryan, however, could not maintain his social relationships. Sometimes he would have a brief but intense affair with a woman and then abruptly and angrily ask himself what he ever saw in her. At other times, the woman would reject him after a few dates, because she thought Bryan was moody, self-centered, and demanding. He would often call his friends after midnight, because he felt lonesome, bored, and wanted to talk. He gave little thought to the inconvenience he was causing. Once he organized a group of students to protest the inadequate student parking the university provided. The morning of the planned protest demonstration, he announced that he no longer supported the effort. He said he was not in the right mood for the protest, much to the consternation of his followers, who had spent weeks preparing for the event.

Bryan's intense but brief relationships, the marked and continual shifts in moods, and boredom with others in spite of his need for social contacts all point to borderline personality.

Masterson (1981) believes many clients with borderline personality disorder lack purposefulness. For example, one of his clients reported, "I have such a poor self-image and so little confidence in myself that I can't decide what I want, and when I do decide, I have even more difficulty doing it" (p. ix). Masterson sees this lack as a deficiency in the borderline personality's emotional investment in the self—a lack of directedness in long-term goals.

People with borderline personality may exhibit psychotic symptoms, such as auditory hallucinations (for example, hearing imaginary voices that tell them

Edward Spauster

FIRST PERSON

Growing up, I was always fascinated by the characters I encountered in literature, film, and television. Many seem to live exciting, enviable lives, and all were distinct individuals. Consider Scarlett O'Hara and *Dynasty*'s Alexis Carrington-Colby. Their dramatic, seductive, attention-seeking behaviors (*histrionic* is the clinical term) draw us to them; their lies, exploitation, and lack of true warmth or remorse (antisocial traits) arouse our dislike. Similarly, successful comedy often depends on humorous portrayals of personality extremes. Fonzie's narcissism, Felix Unger's compulsiveness, and Walter Mitty's flights into schizoidal fantasy are all enduring personality traits that actually define the characters who possess them.

As an adult, I continue to be intrigued by personality characteristics and as a psychologist I work with many patients who are considered personality disordered. They are usually quite distinct, occasionally exciting—but rarely enviable. Unable to change their behavior patterns, they repeatedly suffer the painful consequences these patterns produce. This situation is most evident in borderline personality disorder, which is perhaps the most disturbing and most commonly treated character disorder. The following case is fairly typical.

Yolanda was transferred to the acute psychiatric unit after two days in intensive care, where she had been medically treated for an overdose of her antidepressant medication. The history gathered by the treatment team included several years of physical abuse by her parents; three prior suicide attempts; dozens of full and part-time jobs; one marriage and three engagements; two abortions; and a cocaine habit that at times she supported through providing sex to dealers. Yolanda was twenty-four years old.

During her hospitalization, Yolanda showed many sides of herself. Sometimes she was gregarious and quickly made friends with other patients. On other occasions, she grew furious with staff and patients and sought solitude. Once, after a bitter phone conversation with her family, she was found in the bathroom scratching her wrists with an opened paper clip. Her emotions were so intense that she felt lost in them and unbearably empty. In this state, she found physical pain a relief, because it reassured her of her existence.

Yolanda's constellation of symptoms, especially the mood instability, identity disturbance, uncontrolled anger, and self-destructive behaviors are typical of borderline personality disorder. What is it like to work with someone with so many problems? It's often frightening. The reality of Yolanda's life is that she often considers suicide. Because she depends on others to provide boundaries for her emotions and behavior, she is extremely sensitive to the slightest shift in others, including me, her therapist. Her anger, fueled by years of abuse, is always expressed as rage, and frightens both her and others. I've been its target more than once.

At other times, her attachment to me is so strong that she finds her own fragile boundaries breaking down. Soon after revealing to me that she had been sexually abused fifteen years earlier, Yolanda became afraid that I would be killed by her uncle, the abuser. He had silenced Yolanda by threatening to hurt her parents if she told anyone about the abuse. The fear produced by her disclosure was as real in our sessions as it was years ago. She found it very difficult to believe that my bout of flu was not some repercussion for her telling me about the abuse.

Although challenging and exciting, working with borderlines is also tiring. I function best when I limit the number of borderline clients in my practice and have a colleague available for consultation. Maintaining an accepting and consistent therapeutic stance in the face of borderline chaos is not easy, but necessary. A therapeutic relationship that is stable, sets appropriate boundaries, survives in spite of intense emotions, and fosters hope becomes, in a very small way, a break in the pattern. And for disorders of personality, changing patterns is the only way out.

Dr. Edward Spauster is a staff psychologist on the Adult Services Unit at the Holliswood Hospital, a private psychiatric hospital in Queens, New York.

Normund Wong

FIRST PERSON

Is borderline personality disorder one personality or many? I've been practicing psychiatry for over thirty years and spent most of my professional life treating patients with borderline personality disorders, long before the diagnosis became popular and was included in the American Psychiatric Association's Diagnostic and Statistical Manual. In many instances, these patients didn't get better in treatment—but they also didn't get worse. They could function surprisingly well in society and yet present as highly disturbed people in the office of the therapist.

One of the most memorable borderline patients I ever treated was Barbara, who helped me understand borderline pathology and prompted me to begin using the combined individual and group approach that has become a standard treatment modality for borderline patients today.

When I first met Barbara, she was suffering from severe anorexia nervosa, depression, and obsessive-compulsive symptoms. She looked pathetic and physically wasted and had a childlike demeanor. Barbara had been treated by three previous psychiatrists with little success. She was a brilliant but highly eccentric

college student who had been hospitalized several times for suicide attempts, anxiety attacks, and depressions. Over the years she had received major tranquilizers, antidepressants, and electroshock therapy, with little improvement. But her apparent psychological health was so deceiving that she was once placed in psychoanalytic therapy, which was abruptly terminated when she made a serious suicide attempt.

Early in the course of our work, she entertained frequent suicidal thoughts and lamented that she had blown any chances for happiness and success in life. In the beginning, because of her immense anxiety and needs, she wanted to see me daily and often awakened me in the middle of the night with frantic phone calls. As therapy progressed, Barbara revealed tremendous rage and envy at her successful siblings. And her great dependency on me changed to an attitude of pseudoindependence and devaluation. Sometimes she saw me as the "worse therapist" she had ever met; other times I was "the only person in the world" who understood her. She felt she would perish if treatment were stopped. But as we worked together and learned from each other, Barbara began to emerge as an attractive, high-spirited, and forceful woman.

Four years into her individual therapy, which was now twice a week, we decided she would also participate in a psychotherapy group that I led. In her treatment with me, she was hospitalized only once for a brief period; she threatened suicide on many occasions but made no actual attempts; she was no longer anorexic and was off all

antipsychotic medications. But she still lived with her family and had no other significant social relationships. She presented an abrasive and arrogant side to the outside world, and in the office I often felt frustrated and annoyed with her narcissistic traits. How she had changed!

Barbara remained in combined therapy for the next three years working through her impulsive, critical attitude and behavior. Sometimes she threatened to leave the group; at other times the other group members wanted to throw *her* out. But her interpersonal skills and understanding of herself and others vastly improved despite her stormy course. She turned into a very likeable person. She graduated from college, completed graduate school, practiced her profession, and soon thereafter got married. She raised a young daughter and finally seemed content.

We both gained from her therapy; she got better and I reaped the benefits of increased knowledge that has since benefited other patients.

Dr. Normund Wong is a clinical professor of psychiatry at the University of California in San Francisco and director of Research and Group Psychotherapy at the Letterman Army Medical Center. Dr. Wong is also a past director of the Menninger School of Psychiatry.

to commit suicide), but the symptoms are usually transient. Borderline people also usually have an *ego-dystonic* reaction to their hallucinations (Spitzer et al., 1981). That is, they recognize their imaginary voices or other hallucinations as being unacceptable, alien, and distressful. By contrast, in a psychotic disorder the person may not realize that his or her hallucinations are of a pathological nature.

From a psychodynamic perspective, Kernberg (1976) proposes the concept of *object splitting*: for example, borderline people perceive others as all good or all bad at different times. This split results in emotional fluctuations toward others. Although precise figures on the prevalence of the disorder are not available, borderline personality disorder is apparently common (American Psychiatric Association, 1987). Some researchers believe that the prevalence of the disorder is increasing, since our society makes it difficult for people to maintain stable relationships and a sense of identity.

Disorders Characterized by Anxious or Fearful Behaviors

The last cluster of personality disorders, characterized by anxious or fearful behaviors, includes the avoidant, dependent, obsessive-compulsive, and passive-aggressive personalities.

Avoidant Personality Disorder
The essential feature of **avoidant personality disorder** is a hypersensitivity to potential rejection, humiliation, and shame. Avoidant personalities are reluctant to enter into social relationships without a guarantee of uncritical acceptance by others. This reluctance is not derived from a desire to be alone. On the contrary, people with this disorder crave affection and an active social life. They want—but fear—social contacts. Their ambivalence may be reflected in different ways: for example, many avoidants engage in intellectual pursuits, wear fine clothes, or are active in the artistic community (Millon, 1981). Their need for contact and relationships is often woven into their activities. Thus an avoidant person may write poems expressing the plight of the lonely or the need for human intimacy. A primary defense mechanism is fantasy

whereby wishes are fulfilled to an excessive degree in the person's imagination (Millon & Everly, 1985).

People who have avoidant personality disorder are caught in a vicious cycle: because of their concern with rejection, they are constantly alert to signs of derogation or ridicule. This concern, along with many perceived instances of rejection, causes them to avoid others. Their social skills may then become deficient and invite criticism from others. In other words, their very fear of criticism may lead to criticism. Avoidants often feel depressed, anxious, angry at themselves, and inadequate.

Jenny L., an unmarried 27-year-old bank teller, shows several of the features of avoidant personality disorder. Although she functions adequately at work, Jenny is extremely shy, sensitive, and quiet with fellow employees. She perceives others as being insensitive and gross. If the bank manager jokes with other tellers, she feels that the manager prefers them to her.

Jenny has very few hobbies. A great deal of her time is spent watching television and eating chocolates (as a result, she is about 40 pounds overweight). Television romances are her favorite programs; after

People with avoidant personality disorder fear and avoid social contacts because they are hypersensitive to potential rejection. They often have few close friends or confidants.

watching one, she tends to daydream about having an intense romantic relationship.

Jenny L. eventually sought treatment for her depression and loneliness.

Dependent Personality Disorder People who are unwilling to assume responsibility because of an inability to function and to make decisions independently show **dependent personality disorder**. These people lack self-confidence, and they subordinate their needs to those of the people on whom they depend. However, their dependency may go unrecognized or may be misinterpreted by casual observers. For example, a dependent personality may allow his or her spouse to be dominant or abusive for fear that the spouse will otherwise leave.

Friends may perceive dependent personalities as understanding and tolerant, without realizing that they are fearful of taking the initiative because they are afraid of disrupting their relationships. Depression, helplessness, and suppressed anger are often a part of dependent personality disorder. All are evident in the following case.

Jim is 56, a single man who was living with his 78-year-old widowed mother. When his mother recently was hospitalized for cancer, Jim decided to see a therapist. He was distraught and depressed over his mother's condition. Jim indicated that he did not know what to do. His mother had always taken care of him, and, in his view, she always knew best. Even when he was young, his mother had "worn the pants" in the family. The only time he was away from the family was during his six years of military service. He was wounded in the Korean War, was returned to the United States, and spent a few months in a Veterans Administration hospital. He then went to live with his mother. Because of his service-connected injury, Jim was unable to work full time. His mother welcomed him home, and she structured all his activities.

At one point, Jim met and fell in love with a woman, but his mother disapproved of her. During a confrontation between the mother and Jim's woman friend, each demanded that Jim make a commitment to her. This was quite traumatic for Jim. His mother finally grabbed him and yelled that he must tell the other woman to go. Jim tearfully told the woman that he was sorry but she must go, and the woman angrily left.

While Jim was relating his story, it was clear to the therapist that Jim harbored some anger toward his mother, though he overtly denied any feelings of hostility. Also clear were his dependency and his inability to take responsibility. His life had always been structured, by his mother and then by the military. His mother's illness meant that his structured world might crumble.

Obsessive-Compulsive Personality Disorder The person with **obsessive-compulsive personality disorder** shows an inability to express warmth or warm feelings, coupled with excessive perfectionism, stubbornness, indecision, and devotion to details. Many of these traits are found in normal people. Unlike normals, however, obsessive-compulsive personalities show significant impairment in occupational or social functioning. Furthermore, the extent of the character rigidity is greater among people who have this disorder (Weintraub, 1981). Unlike obsessive-compulsive disorder, in which there are specific recurrent thoughts or repetitive behaviors (see Chapter 6), obsessive-compulsive personality disorder involves general traits of perfectionism, inflexibility, and attention to details.

Co-workers may find the compulsive individual too demanding and perfectionistic. Compulsives may actually be ineffective on the job, despite long hours of devotion. Their preoccupation with details, rules, and possible errors leads to indecision and an inability to see "the big picture."

Cecil, a third-year medical student, was referred for therapy by his graduate adviser. The adviser told the therapist that Cecil was in danger of being expelled from medical school because of his inability to get along with patients and with other students. He often berated patients for failing to follow his advice. In one instance, Cecil told a patient with a lung condition to stop smoking. When the patient indicated that he was unable to stop, Cecil angrily told the patient to go for medical treatment elsewhere; the medical center had no place for such a "weak-willed fool."

Cecil's relationships with others were similarly strained. He considered many members of the faculty to be "incompetent old deadwood," and he characterized fellow graduate students as "party-goers."

The graduate adviser told the therapist that Cecil had not been expelled only because several faculty members thought that he was brilliant. Cecil studied and worked sixteen hours a day. He was extremely well read and had an extensive knowledge of medical disorders. Although he was always able to provide a careful and detailed analysis of a patient's condition, it took him a great deal of time to do so. His diagnoses tended to cover every disorder that each patient could conceivably have, on the basis of all possible combinations of symptoms.

Passive-Aggressive Personality Disorder People with **passive-aggressive personality disorder** are extremely resistant to demands for adequate social and occupational performance. Their resistance may be shown in procrastination, stubbornness, and intentional inefficiency, which are all means of passively or indirectly expressing aggression.

> Ryan O. is a 21-year-old college student who visited his university's counseling center at the strong suggestion of his parents. Arriving about 15 minutes late for his first appointment with the counselor, Ryan indicated that his parents felt he should receive help because his grades were so low. The reason for his poor academic performance, he said, was the noisiness of his dormitory; he could not study elsewhere because the "conditions" were not right. For example, studying in the library made him sleepy.
>
> During his interview with the counselor, Ryan said very little. When asked whether he felt he could be helped in counseling, Ryan responded, "Oh, I've heard that therapy can be very effective—for some people." In later visits, Ryan indicated a long-term pattern of resistance: he would procrastinate, dawdle, or rationalize his failure to meet demands or requests from others.

Ryan's tardiness, his blaming others for his poor academic performance, and his reluctance to provide information to the therapist indicate a passive-aggressive personality.

Normal people may resort to passive-aggressive behaviors in situations where direct and assertive responses are punished. However, passive-aggressive personalities repeat such behaviors in a variety of inappropriate situations. Their behaviors are neither flexible nor adaptable (Malinow, 1981).

The Lack of Information on the Personality Disorders

Although personality disorders have generated rich clinical examples and speculations, not much empirical research has been conducted in order to provide definitive insight into the causes of the disorders. Indeed, the prevalence rates of the disorders are not clear. We do know that the sex distribution varies from disorder to disorder. In a study of sex differences, Reich (1987) found that men more often than women were diagnosed as having paranoid, obsessive-compulsive, and antisocial personality disorders. Women were more likely than men to be assigned a diagnosis of histrionic personality disorder. Although the popular belief is that women are more highly represented in the borderline and dependent personality disorders, Reich's study failed to reveal sex differences in these categories. Although these findings need cross-validation, the existence of sex differences in certain personality disorders is widely accepted.

Research on personality disorders has been hindered by some of the problems just mentioned. Diagnosis has been difficult, and many symptoms of one disorder overlap with symptoms of other disorders. The lack of more reliable and valid means of identifying personality disorders makes it very difficult to conduct research studies. Furthermore, researchers are still debating the importance of personality versus situational determinants in behaviors. Finally, while psychodynamic perspectives have guided the formulation of these disorders, many interpretations of their etiology are possible. Genetic, biological, learning, cognitive, humanistic, and systems approaches have also been advanced as important frameworks for understanding these disorders.

Because of the many different theories about how personality characteristics develop and change, many varied treatment approaches have been used. In general, however treatment for personality disorders is not very effective. Many people with these disorders do not seek treatment, often because they don't believe they need it. Many can function in society despite their adjustment problems, so their motivation to change may be weak. Also, because the disorders are characterized by long-term and inflexible personality traits, modifying these traits is not easy.

In the next section, we focus more specifically on antisocial personality disorder, about which much more is known.

ANTISOCIAL PERSONALITY DISORDER

The following case presents an example of antisocial personality disorder:

Roy W. is a seventeen-year-old high school senior who was referred by juvenile court for diagnosis and evaluation. He was arrested for stealing an automobile, something he had also done on several other occasions. The court agreed with Roy's mother that he needed evaluation and perhaps psychotherapy.

During his interview with the psychologist, Roy was articulate, relaxed, and even witty. He said that stealing was wrong but that none of the cars he stole was ever damaged. The last theft occurred because he needed transportation to a beer party (which was located only a mile from his home) and his leg was sore from playing basketball.

When Roy was asked how he got along with girls, he grinned and said that he was very outgoing and could easily "hustle" girls. He then related the following incident: "Let me tell you what happened about three months ago. I was pulling out of the school parking lot real fast and accidentally sideswiped this other car. The girl who was driving it started to scream at me. God, there was only a small dent on her fender! Anyway, we exchanged names and addresses and I apologized for the accident. When I filled out the accident report later, I said that it was *her* car that pulled out from the other side and hit my car. How do you like that? Anyway, when she heard about my claim that it was her fault, she had her old man call me. He said that his daughter had witnesses to the accident and that I could be arrested. Bull, he was just trying to bluff me. But I gave him a sob story—about how my parents were ready to get a divorce, how poor we were, and the trouble I would get into if they found out about the accident. I apologized for lying and told him I could fix the dent. Luckily he never checked with my folks for the real story. Anyway, I went over to look at the girl's car. I really didn't have any idea of how to fix that old heap so I said I had to

wait a couple of weeks to get some tools for the repair job. Meanwhile, I started to talk to the girl. Gave her my sob story, told her how nice I thought her folks and home were. We started to date and I took her out three times. Then one night I laid her. The crummy thing was that she told her folks about it. Can you imagine that? Anyway, her old man called and told me never to get near his precious little thing again. She's actually a slut. At least I didn't have to fix her old heap. I know I shouldn't lie but can you blame me? People make such a big thing out of nothing."

The irresponsibility, disregard for others, and disregard for societal rules and morals evident in this interview indicated to the psychologist that Roy has antisocial personality disorder. Historically, the terms *moral insanity, moral imbecility, moral defect,* and *psychopathic inferiority* have been attached to this condition. An early nineteenth-century British psychiatrist, J. C. Prichard (1837), described it thus:

The moral and active principles of the mind are strongly perverted or depraved; the power of self-government is lost or greatly impaired; and the individual is found to be incapable, not of talking or reasoning upon any subject proposed to him . . . but of conducting himself with decency and propriety in the business of life (p. 15).

Prichard believed that the disorder was reflected not in a loss of intellectual skills but in gross violations of moral and ethical standards.

The diagnosis of antisocial personality (also referred to as *sociopathic* or *psychopathic* personality) has now lost some of its original moral overtones. Nevertheless, people with antisocial personalities do show a disregard for conventional societal rules and morals.

Cleckley's (1976) classic description of the disorder included the following characteristics:

1. *Superficial charm and good intelligence*   Antisocial personalities are often capable in social activities and in manipulating others.

2. *Shallow emotions and lack of empathy, guilt, or remorse*   Absent are genuine feelings of love and loyalty toward others and of concern over the detrimental consequences of the behaviors.

3. *Behaviors are impulsive or seem to be unmotivated*   The actions of antisocial personalities are

not well planned and are often difficult to understand or predict.

4. *Failure to learn from experiences and absence of anxiety* Although the behaviors may be punished, people with antisocial personality repeat the same behaviors and frequently show little anxiety.

5. *Unreliability, insincerity, and untruthfulness* Antisocial personalities are irresponsible and may lie or feign emotional feelings in order to callously manipulate others; their social relationships are usually unstable and short-lived.

Some of these characteristics are apparent in Roy's case. For example, he felt no guilt for his actions or for manipulating the girl and her family. In fact, he was quite proud of his ability to seduce the girl and avoid responsibility for the automobile repair. The ease with which Roy related his story to the psychologist demonstrated his lack of concern for those who were hurt by his behaviors. Roy showed no anxiety during the interview.

DSM-III-R criteria for the disorder differ from Cleckley's description, which is based on clinical observations of various cases. For example, they do not include lack of anxiety, shallow emotions, failure to learn from past experiences, and superficial charm. The DSM-III-R seeks to specify concrete behaviors (cruelty to others, theft, and so forth) that can be used to render a diagnosis, rather than taking a more conceptual and integrated view of the disorder. Criteria include a history before age fifteen of truancy and delinquency and a number of irresponsible and antisocial behaviors since age fifteen, such as poor work history, criminal acts, irresponsibility, and repeated lying. For the diagnosis to be made, the individual must be at least eighteen years of age. Robins (1966) studied the behaviors and symptoms of antisocial adults. The behaviors were consistent with those specified by DSM-III-R. Poor work history, marital problems, financial dependency, arrests, excessive alcohol problems, and school problems were found in the majority of the adults.

The incidence of antisocial personality disorder is estimated to be 3 percent for American men and less than 1 percent for American women (American Psychiatric Association, 1987). However, estimates vary from study to study. The differences may be due to differences in the sampling, diagnostic, and methodological procedures used. Goodwin and Guze (1984) conclude that antisocial personality is fairly common, and probably increasingly so. It is much more frequent in urban than in rural environments, and in lower socioeconomic groups.

A distinction should be made between the behavior patterns associated with antisocial personality disorder and behaviors involving social protest or criminal lifestyles. People who engage in civil disobedience or violate the conventions of society or its laws as a form of protest are not as a rule psychopathic. Such people can be quite capable of forming meaningful interpersonal relationships and of experiencing guilt. They may perceive their violations of rules and norms as acts performed for the greater good. Similarly, engaging in delinquent or adult criminal behavior is not a necessary or sufficient condition for diagnosing antisocial personality. Although many convicted criminals have been found to be psychopathic, many others are not. They may come from a subculture that encourages and reinforces criminal activity; hence, in perpetrating such acts they are adhering to group mores and codes of conduct.

Psychopaths are a difficult population to study because they do not voluntarily seek treatment. Consequently, researchers often seek psychopathic subjects in prison populations, which presumably harbor a relatively large proportion of psychopaths. But now a different problem arises: researchers cannot know whether or not the psychopaths in prison are representative of the nonprison psychopathic population as well.

Using an ingenious research approach, Widom (1977) tried to find a number of noninstitutionalized psychopaths in order to discover whether their characteristics matched those typically found in prison groups. She placed the following advertisement in a major Boston counterculture newspaper:

> *Are You Adventurous?* Psychologist studying adventurous, carefree people who've led exciting, impulsive lives. If you're the kind of person who'd do almost anything for a dare and want to participate in a paid experiment, send name, address, phone, and short biography proving how interesting you are.

Widom reasoned that such an ad might appeal to psychopaths. Of the seventy-three people who responded, twenty-eight met her criteria for antisocial personality and were studied further. On the basis of psychological tests and interviews, Widom concluded that the people she studied did have characteristics similar to those associated with psychopathy. But her respondents tended to have a higher level of education and, although they were often arrested, they were convicted of crimes infrequently.

Explanations of Antisocial Personality Disorder

Antisocial people have an apparent inability to learn from past experience. They continue to engage in antisocial behaviors despite criticism and scorn from others, the disruption of close personal relationships, and their frequent encounters with legal authorities. They often sincerely promise to change their lives and make amends, only to return to antisocial behavior soon after.

Theories of the etiology of antisocial personality vary with theoretical orientation and with the theorist's definition of psychopathy. We'll examine a number of the most frequently cited constructs from the psychoanalytic, family and socialization, and biological perspectives.

Psychoanalytic Theory According to one psychoanalytic approach, the absence of guilt and the frequent violation of moral and ethical standards in psychopaths are the result of faulty superego development (Fenichel, 1945). Id impulses are more likely to be expressed when the weakened superego cannot exert very much influence. People exhibiting antisocial behavior patterns presumably had inadequate identification with their parents. Frustration, rejection, or inconsistent treatment resulted in fixation at an early stage of development.

Family and Socialization Theories A variety of theories emphasize the inability of psychopaths to learn appropriate social and ethical behaviors. The reasons given for this defect, however, are quite diverse. Some theorists believe that relationships within the family—the primary agent of socialization—are paramount in the development of antisocial patterns (McCord & McCord, 1964). Rejection or deprivation by one or both parents may provide little opportunity

to learn socially appropriate behaviors or may diminish the value of people as socially reinforcing agents. Parental separation has been correlated with antisocial personality. Children may have been traumatized or subjected to a hostile environment during the parental separation (Vaillant & Perry, 1985). Millon and Everly (1985) believe that hostility in such families may result in interpersonal hostility among the children. Hence psychopaths may find little satisfaction in close or meaningful relationships with others. Psychopaths do show a significant amount of misperception about people in general (Widom, 1976). The inability to perceive another's viewpoint can create problems in personal interactions.

Note that antisocial personalities can learn and use social skills very effectively (Ullmann & Krasner, 1975), as shown in their adeptness at manipulation and at being charming and sociable. The difficulty is that, in many areas of learning, these people do not pay attention to social stimuli and have different schedules of reinforcement from most other people. Perhaps because they received negative or inconsistent reinforcement from parents or inadequate feedback for behaviors, psychopaths find little reason to attend to social stimuli. Consequently, they feel no concern for others and easily use lying, cheating, and manipulation to their own advantage.

Another explanation is that the child may have modeled the behaviors of a parent who had antisocial tendencies. In one study, researchers examined the past records and statuses of nearly 500 adults who had been seen about thirty years earlier as children in a child guidance clinic. More than 90 of the adults exhibited antisocial tendencies. These subjects were compared with a control group of 100 adults who, as children, had lived in the same geographic area but had never been referred to the clinic. Results indicated that (1) there was little relationship between having antisocial personality as an adult and participation in gangs as a youth; (2) antisocial behavior (theft, aggression, juvenile delinquency, lying) in childhood was a predictor of psychopathy in adults; (3) the adjustment level of fathers, but not that of mothers, was significant—having a father who was antisocial was related to adult psychopathy; and (4) growing up in a single-parent home was not related to psychopathy (Robins, 1966).

The study seems to indicate that antisocial behavior is probably influenced by the presence of an

People with antisocial personalities are often "outsiders," choosing to disregard conventional rules and morals. They are unable to take responsibility or feel guilt for their actions and are incapable of forming lasting relationships. Often called sociopaths or psychopaths, antisocial personalities do not learn from experience.

antisocial father who either serves as a model for such behavior or provides inadequate supervision, inconsistent discipline, or family conflict. The father's influence on antisocial behaviors in children may be a result of traditional sex role training. Males have traditionally received more encouragement to engage in aggressive behaviors than females, and psychopathy is more prevalent among men than among women. If traditional sex roles change, one might reasonably expect psychopathy to increase among females and expect mothers to play a greater role in the development of antisocial behaviors in children.

A disturbed family background or disturbed parental model is neither a necessary nor a sufficient condition for the development of antisocial personality. Indeed, psychopathy probably has multiple causes.

Genetic Factors Throughout history, many people have speculated that some individuals are "born to raise hell." These speculations are difficult to test because of the problems involved in distinguishing between the influences of environment and of heredity on behavior. For example, DSM-III-R notes antisocial personality disorder is five times more common among first-degree biologic relatives of males, and ten times more common among the first-degree

biologic relatives of females with this disorder than among the general population (American Psychiatric Association, 1987). These findings can be used to support an environmental or genetic hypothesis. Within the last decade, however, some interesting research has been conducted on genetic influences in psychopathy.

One strategy has been to compare concordance rates for identical, or monozygotic (MZ), twins with those for fraternal, or dizygotic (DZ), twins. Recall from Chapter 2 that MZ twins share exactly the same genes. But DZ twins share about 50 percent of the same genes; they are genetically no more alike than any two siblings. Most studies show that MZ twins do tend to have a higher concordance rate than DZ twins for psychopathy, delinquency, and criminality (Mednick & Christiansen, 1977); this finding tends to support a genetic basis for these behavior patterns.

Another strategy for studying genetic influence is to note the rate of psychopathy among adopted people with psychopathic biological parents. Because these adoptees were separated from their biological parents early in life, it would have been difficult for them to learn antisocial behaviors from their parents. Results generally show that adoptees whose biological parents were psychopathic have a higher rate of psychopathy than adoptees whose biological parents were nonpsychopathic (Cadoret & Cain, 1981). Even Robins' study (1966), in which the development of antisocial personality was associated with having antisocial fathers, revealed that the association existed even when the people were not reared in the presence of their fathers.

How about the influence of the adoptive parents on psychopathic adoptees? (This influence would be environmental.) Results show that the rate of criminality or psychopathy is higher among the biological parents than among the adoptive parents (Hutchings & Mednick, 1977; Schulsinger, 1972). Again the evidence suggests that antisocial personality patterns are influenced by heredity (Goodwin & Guze, 1984).

However, this evidence should be examined carefully, for several reasons. First, many of the studies do not clearly distinguish between psychopaths and criminals; or, as we noted earlier, they may draw subjects only from criminal populations. Truly representative samples of people with antisocial personality disorder should be investigated. Second, evidence that supports a genetic *basis* for antisocial tendencies does not preclude the environment as a *factor*. Psychopathy is undoubtedly caused by environmental as well as genetic influences. The relative contribution of each factor, as well as the interaction between heredity and environment, should be investigated (Marmar, 1988). Third, studies indicating that genetic factors are significant do not provide much insight into *how* antisocial personality is inherited (into what exactly is transmitted genetically). We need to understand more thoroughly the process that leads to the disorder.

Central Nervous System Abnormality Some early investigators suggested that psychopaths tend to have abnormal brain wave activity (Hill & Watterson, 1942; Knott et al., 1953). In these studies, the brain waves, or electroencephalograms (EEGs), of psychopaths were sometimes found to be similar to those of normal young children. According to one survey, most studies revealed that between 31 and 58 percent of psychopathic people showed some EEG abnormality, frequently in the form of slow-wave (*theta*) activity (Ellingson, 1954). Perhaps brain pathology inhibits the capacity of psychopaths to learn how to avoid punishment and perhaps they are accordingly unable to learn from experience (Hare, 1970). This explanation is plausible, but there is simply not enough evidence to support its acceptance. Many diagnosed psychopaths do not show EEG abnormalities, but nonpsychopathic individuals may show abnormalities in the form of theta-wave activity. In addition, the EEG is an imprecise diagnostic device, and abnormal brain wave activity in psychopaths may be simply correlated with, rather than a cause of, disturbed behavior.

Autonomic Nervous System Abnormalities The inability to learn from experience, absence of anxiety, and thrill-seeking behaviors are prominent features of antisocial personality disorder. Some interesting and promising research has been conducted that points to the involvement of the autonomic nervous system (ANS) in the disorder. Two lines of investigation can be identified, both based on the assumption that psychopaths have ANS deficiencies or abnormalities. The first is based on the premise that ANS abnormalities make antisocial personalities less susceptible to anxiety, and therefore less likely to learn from experiences. People who lack anxiety may fail to learn in situations where aversive stimuli (or punishment) are involved. The second line of research focuses on ANS abnormalities that keep antisocial people emotionally underaroused. Underaroused individuals may then seek excitement and thrills, and fail to conform their behaviors to conventional standards, in order to achieve optimal level of arousal or to avoid boredom. The two concepts—lack of anxiety and underarousal—may, of course, be related, because the underarousal may include underaroused anxiety.

Eysenck (Eysenck, 1957; Eysenck & Rachman, 1965) was among the first to clearly argue the relevance of the ANS in antisocial personality. He felt that temperamental characteristics could help to explain why antisocial personalities fail to become adequately socialized to the rules and norms of society.

Eysenck focused on two personality dimensions, or temperamental characteristics. *Neuroticism* is autonomic instability or emotionality. Very neurotic people have an easily aroused and overactive autonomic nervous system. People who are not neurotic show the opposite characteristics—little anxiety or emotionality. The second personality dimension is *introversion-extroversion*. Introverts are inhibited, less sociable, and quick to learn. Extroverts tend to be impulsive, sociable, uninhibited, and slow to learn.

Heroes and Psychopaths

Lykken (1982) argues that heroes and psychopaths are two sides of the same coin. For example, Lykken notes that Chuck Yeager, a heroic test pilot, once concealed broken ribs that he had suffered in a wild midnight horseback ride, so that he could go aloft in the belly of a B-29, wedge himself in a tiny cockpit of the X-1 rocket plane, and let himself be jettisoned at 26,000 feet altitude, to become the first person to travel faster than the speed of sound. And Ted Bundy was a charming, intelligent, and articulate psychopath who left a coast-to-coast trail of brutal and sadistic murders of young women. Lykken believes that heroes and psychopaths share one characteristic—namely, fearlessness. In an attempt to measure fearlessness, he developed the Activity Preference Questionnaire. The questionnaire instructs respondents to pretend that one or the other situations described must occur, and asks respondents to choose the situation that is the lesser of two evils. Here are some of the items:

1. a. Cleaning up your house after floodwaters have left it filled with mud
   b. Making a parachute jump
2. a. Spending hours fixing a fancy barbecue for some guests, who then eat very little and seem not to like it
   b. Distributing 1,000 handbills in mailboxes from door to door
3. a. Having to walk around all day on a blistered foot
   b. Sleeping out on a camping trip in an area where rattlesnakes have been reported
4. a. Washing a car
   b. Driving a car at 95 miles an hour

The questionnaire items present a frightening or embarrassing situation paired with a situation that is merely onerous. People who are relatively fearless, such as heroes and psychopaths, have a greater tendency than do fearful people to choose the frightening or embarrassing alternative.

What factors influence the probability of becoming a hero rather than a psychopath among those who are relatively fearless? Although very fearless children are difficult to bring up, circumstances and family environment may play crucial roles. Those who have the opportunity to channel their fearlessness into socially approved activities (such as being a test pilot) and who are socialized in families that emphasize warm and loving relationships rather than punishment techniques may be less likely to become psychopaths.

Eysenck hypothesized that temperamental characteristics are inherited and that primary psychopaths are not highly neurotic and are extroverted. They show little anxiety and emotionality, and they are impulsive and uninhibited. They learn slowly, quickly develop reactive inhibition (fatigue in learning), and slowly dissipate that reactive inhibition. The low anxiety and the difficulty in learning become a handicap in developing normal social patterns.

Eysenck argues that psychopaths can learn but that they require more trials or repetitive experiences than others do. Hence antisocial patterns are seen primarily in youth or young adults who have not yet been exposed to enough experiences to learn to control their behaviors.

Fearlessness or Lack of Anxiety Lykken (1982) maintains that because of genetic predisposition,

people vary in level of fearlessness. Antisocial personality develops because of fearlessness or low anxiety levels. People who have high levels of fear avoid risks, stress, and strong stimulation; relatively fearless people seek thrills and adventures. Fearlessness is associated with heroes (such as volunteering for dangerous military action or risking one's life to save others) as well as psychopaths, who may engage in risky criminal activities or impulsively violate norms and rules (see Focus 9.2). His classic research (Lykken, 1957) focused on behaviors of prisoners judged to be primary psychopaths, of prisoners judged to be nonpsychopathic, and of students matched with the prisoners in socioeconomic background, age, and intelligence. He hypothesized that the psychopathic group would show less anxiety and greater deficiencies in avoidance learning. His results generally confirmed these hypotheses. In a classical conditioning

Lykken theorized that people with low anxiety levels are often thrill seekers. The difference between the psychopath who takes risks and the adventurer may largely be a matter of whether the thrill-seeking behaviors are channeled into destructive or constructive acts.

procedure wherein a buzzer (CS) was paired with a shock (US), psychopaths showed less galvanic skin response (GSR), or electrodermal, reactivity than the nonpsychopathic prisoners and the students. (GSR measures sweating, which is presumed to indicate emotional reaction or anxiety.) On the Activities Preference Questionnaire Lykken devised, the psychopaths exhibited less aversion to unpleasant social situations, perhaps reflecting their low anxiety in such situations. In an avoidance learning task, evidence showed that psychopaths were poorer at learning. Given a task in which errors could produce an electric shock, psychopaths made more errors than nonpsychopathic prisoners, who in turn made more errors than the students. Lykken's work suggests that, because psychopaths do not become conditioned so readily as nonpsychopaths, they fail to acquire avoidance behaviors, experience little anticipatory anxiety, and consequently have fewer inhibitions about engaging in antisocial behavior.

Underarousal and Sensation Seeking Lykken's work suggests that psychopaths may have deficiencies in learning because of lower anxiety. Another view is that psychopaths simply have lower levels of ANS reactivity and are underaroused. It takes a more intense stimulus to elicit a reaction in psychopaths than in nonpsychopaths. The lowered levels of reactivity may cause psychopaths to show impulsive, stimulus-seeking behaviors in order to avoid boredom (Quay, 1965). In one study, antisocial preadolescent children were found to exhibit stimulus-seeking behaviors (Whitehill et al., 1976).

In a hypothesis similar to Lykken's concept of fearlessness, Farley (1986) has proposed that people vary in their degree of thrill-seeking behaviors. Those at one end of the thrill-seeking continuum—the "Big T's," are risk takers and adventurers who seek excitement and stimulation. Because of their low levels of CNS or ANS arousal, they need stimulation to maintain a optimal level of arousal. On the other end of the continuum, "Little t's" are people who have high arousal. They seek low levels of stimulation in order to calm their hyped-up nervous systems. In contrast to Big T's, Little t's prefer certainty, predictability, low risk, familiarity, clarity, simplicity, low conflict, and low intensity. Farley speculates that Big T characteristics can lead to constructive or destructive behaviors in mental and physical domains. For constructive behaviors, artists, scientists, and entertainers are included in the mental domain, because they channel their thrill-seeking tendencies into creative mental contributions. In the physical domain, such people become adventurers and physical risk-takers. Big T characteristics can also result in anti-social, destructive tendencies. Criminal masterminds, schemers, and con artists are Big T's who make destructive mental contributions to society. In the physical domain, Big T destructive behaviors include violent delinquents and criminals. Farley (1986) reports that juvenile delinquents are more likely than nondelinquents to be Big T's. In a study of delinquents in prison, Big T's were more likely than Little t's to fight, disobey supervisors, and attempt to escape. Farley believes that we need to direct stimulation-hungry Big T's into constructive rather than destructive mental and physical activities.

Other researchers have found evidence of underarousal as well as lowered levels of anxiety among psychopaths. In a study by Hare (1968), the resting state reactivity and the stress-produced reactivity of primary psychopaths, secondary psychopaths, and nonpsychopaths were determined through cardiac, electrodermal (GSR), and respiratory measures. Hare found that psychopaths demonstrated less autonomic reactivity in both the resting state and in response to stressors than did nonpsychopaths. In other words, it takes a more intense stimulus to elicit a reaction in psychopaths than in nonpsychopaths. Their lowered levels of reactivity may cause psychopaths to engage in impulsive, stimulus-seeking behaviors to avoid boredom (Quay, 1965). In one study, antisocial preadolescent children did show stimulus-seeking behaviors, a finding that tends to support the hypothesis (Whitehill et al., 1976).

If psychopathic learning deficiencies are caused by the absence of anxiety and by lowered autonomic reactivity, is it possible to improve learning by increasing anxiety or arousal ability? Researchers tested the ability of psychopaths and nonpsychopaths to perform an avoidance learning task with electric shock as the unconditioned stimulus, under two conditions. At different times, subjects were administered an injection of adrenalin, which presumably increases arousal, and an injection of a placebo. In the placebo condition, psychopaths made more errors in avoiding the shocks than nonpsychopaths; in the adrenalin condition, however, psychopaths tended to perform better than nonpsychopaths (see Figure 9.1). These findings imply that psychopaths do not react to the same amount of anxiety as do nonpsychopaths

and that their learning improves when their anxiety is increased (Schachter & Latané, 1964).

The *kind* of punishment used in avoidance learning is also an important consideration in evaluating psychopaths' learning deficiencies (Schmauk, 1970). Whereas psychopaths may show learning deficits when faced with physical (electric shock) or social (verbal feedback) punishments, they learn as well as nonpsychopaths when the punishment is material (losing money for an incorrect response). Figure 9.2 charts the results of Schmauk's study of convicted psychopaths.

The *certainty* of punishment may also influence the responsiveness of psychopaths to punishment. Psychopaths and nonpsychopaths do not seem to differ in responding when punishment is a near certainty (Siegel, 1978). When the probability of punishment is highly uncertain, however, psychopaths do not suppress their behaviors. Threats of punishment alone do not seem to be sufficient to discourage psychopaths.

Normal people respond to physical, social, or material punishment, and they are influenced by uncertain as well as certain punishment. The work of Schmauk and Siegel suggests that psychopaths do not respond to the same range of aversive conditions. Hare (1975) has proposed a psychophysiological

Figure 9.1 Anxiety and Avoidance Learning Among Psychopaths and Others
Effects of anxiety-increasing (adrenalin) and placebo injections on the avoidance learning of psychopaths, of a group with mixed characteristics, and a control group. SOURCE: Reprinted from the *1964 Nebraska Symposium on Motivation.*

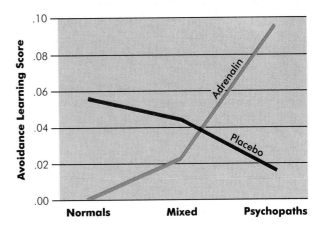

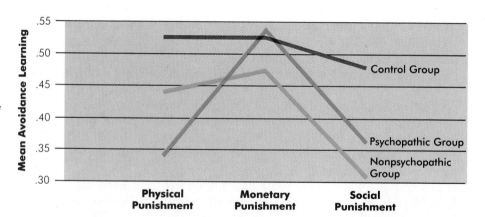

Figure 9.2 Effect of Type of Punishment on Psychopaths and Others
Mean avoidance-learning scores plotted for three types of punishment among three subject groups.
SOURCE: Schmauk, 1970.

model for this lack of responsiveness. He believes that psychopaths tend to lack anxiety, which makes learning difficult for them, and speculates that this lack of anxiety results from a defensive mechanism that reduces the aversiveness of painful stimuli. In other words, psychopaths may develop a psychophysiological ability to reduce the emotional impact (or anxiety-producing effect) of situations—a defense against anxiety and pain.

Hare's hypothesis is interesting but highly speculative. It, along with other hypotheses regarding anxiety, is based on a number of measures that do not always produce the same results. That is, a person may exhibit anxiety according to one measure but not according to another. Furthermore, some measures indicate not only anxiety but also other states, such as general arousal. Obviously, an important goal in research on antisocial personality disorder is to develop a clearer concept of anxiety (and arousal) and a "pure" measure of this reaction.

Reid (1981) agrees that psychophysiological factors may be involved in the disorder. However, he views antisocial personality as a heterogeneous condition, caused by many factors. Diverse groups of factors (or correlates)—familial, biological, social, and developmental—may converge and provide a coherent picture in explaining the disorder.

Treatment of Antisocial Personality Disorder

As you have seen, there is growing evidence that low anxiety and low autonomic reactivity characterize

antisocial personalities. But we still do not know whether these characteristics are due to inherited temperament, an acquired congenital defect, or social and environmental experiences that occur during childhood. The theory that psychopaths have developed a defense against anxiety is intriguing, but the factors behind the development of such a defense have not been pinpointed.

Because people with antisocial personalities feel little anxiety, they are poorly motivated to change themselves; they are also unlikely to see their behaviors as "bad." Thus traditional treatment approaches, which require the cooperation of the client, have not been very effective with psychopaths. For the same reason, relatively little research has been conducted on the efficacy of various treatment approaches. In some cases, tranquilizers (phenothiazines and dilantin) have been helpful in reducing antisocial behavior (Meyer & Osborne, 1982). However, psychopaths are not likely to follow through with the ritual of taking drugs; moreover, drug treatment is effective in only a few cases, and it can result in such side effects as blurred vision, lethargy, and neurological disorders.

It may be that successful treatment can occur only in a setting where behavior can be controlled (Vaillant, 1975). That is, treatment programs may need to provide enough control so that psychopaths cannot avoid confronting their inability to form close and intimate relationships and the effect of their behaviors on others. Such control is possible in prison or hospital environments. Intensive group therapy may then be initiated to help psychopaths in the required confrontation.

Some behavior modification programs have been tried, especially with delinquents who behave in antisocial ways. Money and tokens that can be used to purchase items have been used as rewards for young people who show appropriate behaviors (discussion of personal problems, good study habits, punctuality, and prosocial and nondisruptive behaviors). This use of material rewards has been fairly effective in changing antisocial behaviors (Van Evra, 1983). However, once the young people leave the treatment programs, they are likely to revert to antisocial behavior unless their families and peers help them maintain the appropriate behaviors.

Kazdin (1987) notes that because current treatment programs do not seem very effective, new strategies must be used. They include (1) focusing treatment on antisocial youth who seem amenable to treatment and (2) broadening the base of interventions so that youth and their families and peers are involved. Farley (1986) feels that since antisocial people may seek thrills (Big T's), they may respond to intervention programs that provide the physical and mental stimulation that they need.

IMPULSE CONTROL DISORDERS

The category that includes intermittent explosive disorder, kleptomania, pathological gambling, pyromania, and trichotillomania is a residual category for **impulse control disorders** (loss of control resulting in harm) that are not classified elsewhere. Impulse control behaviors related to sexual conduct or compulsive ingestion of drugs or alcohol, for example, are usually classified under the paraphilias and substance use disorders, respectively. Although not much is known about the etiology of the disorders discussed here, most people have seen films and television programs that depict pathological gamblers, fire setters, or impulsive thieves. Impulse control disorders share three characteristics. First, such people fail to resist an impulse or temptation to perform some act. People with the disorder know that the act is considered wrong by society or is harmful to them. The impulse may or may not be consciously resisted, and its performance may or may not be premeditated. Second, tension or arousal is experienced before the act. Third, after committing the act, a sense of excitement, gratification, or release is felt. Guilt or regret may or

may not follow. Let us briefly examine the five specified disorders, which are shown in the impulse disorders chart on p. 252.

Intermittent Explosive Disorder

People with **intermittent explosive disorder** lose control over their aggressive impulses, which results in serious assaults on others or in the destruction of property. The aggressiveness is grossly out of proportion to any precipitating stress that may have occurred. People with this disorder show no signs of general aggressiveness between episodes and may genuinely feel remorse for their actions. The disorder is apparently rare and believed to be more common among males than females. A patient diagnosed with intermittent explosive disorder described the following incident:

I'm usually a good and safe driver. I'm married and a very successful businessman. My colleagues say that I am a kind and happy-go-lucky person. That's why it's so strange that I lose control of my temper while driving my car. Last week an elderly woman was driving her car very slowly in front of me. I wanted her to speed up so I honked at her. She kept on moving slowly. I became so irritated that I rammed the back of her car and then drove off. Her car was severely damaged—and so was mine—and I could have killed her. After driving for several miles, I was overwhelmed with guilt and disgust with myself. I tried to find the woman, to apologize and pay for damages. But I couldn't find her. There's something wrong with me. Why do I do these things? I've run several people off the road and tried to ram others, if they honk or cut in front of my car. I get so overwhelmed with rage I become a different person. Maybe I should turn myself into the police.

Kleptomania

Kleptomania involves a recurrent failure to resist impulses to steal objects. The objects are not needed for personal use and are not stolen for their monetary value; indeed, people with this disorder usually have enough money to buy the objects, which are typically discarded, given away, or surreptitiously returned. They feel irresistible urges and tension before stealing or shoplifting and then an intense feeling of relief or

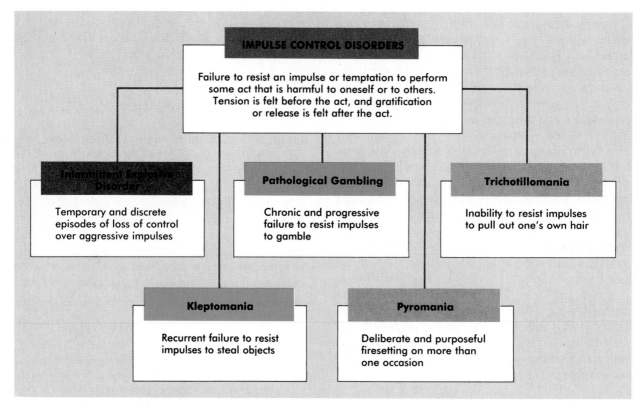

SOURCE: Adapted from DSM-III-R, pp. 321–328.

gratification following the theft. Although theft is common, only a small percentage of thieves fit the criteria for kleptomania, which is believed to be a rare disorder.

> The patient . . . described a special problem that worried her and that she had never disclosed to her husband. Periodically she experienced the urge to walk into one of the more elegant department stores in the city and steal an article of clothing. Over the course of the previous three or four years, she had stolen several blouses, a couple of sweaters, and a skirt. Since her husband's income alone was over $150,000 a year and her investments worth many times that, she recognized the "absurdity" of her acts. She also indicated that what she stole was rarely very expensive and sometimes not even enough to her liking for her to wear. She would become aware of the desire to steal something several days before she actually did it. The thoughts would increasingly occupy her mind until, on impulse, she walked into the store, plucked an item off the rack, and stuffed it into a bag she happened to be carrying or under her coat. Once out the door she felt a sense of relaxation and satisfaction; but at home she experienced anxiety and guilt. (Spitzer et al., 1981, p. 80)

Pathological Gambling

The essential feature of **pathological gambling** is the inability to resist impulses to gamble, despite the detrimental consequences that often accompany the behavior, such as financial ruin, turning to illegal activities to support gambling, disruptions of family or interpersonal relationships, sacrificing obligations and responsibilities, etc. Afflicting about 2 to 3 percent of adults, the disorder is more common among males than females (American Psychiatric Association, 1987). Unlike social gamblers, who may place limits on the amount of money that may be lost or who can avoid gambling, the pathological gambler is preoccupied with gambling for its own sake. He or she may constantly borrow money or engage in illegal activities (such as forgery or theft) in order to continue. The person usually feels tension or restlessness if he or she is unable to gamble. Although the person gambles and shows manic behaviors and a heightened sense of excitement, especially during a winning streak, depression usually follows frequent gambling losses. At such times, the person may try to borrow more money, rationalizing that the "big win" is about to happen, as in the following case.

> Jason L. was a 29-year-old, married salesman. His wife of two years came from a well-to-do family, and Jason increasingly asked his wife's family to help subsidize his business ventures. She was initially impressed with Jason's dreams to "make it big" in his business ventures. However, unknown to his wife, Jason actually needed the money to continue his habit of gambling at a local card house. He was unable to stay away from gambling. When he won, he was ecstatic and would tell his wife that his business ventures were succeeding. Jason would then celebrate by taking her out to the finest restaurants. Unfortunately, he lost money most of the time. He would then beg his wife and her family for more money. After a while, she found out that Jason had no business ventures and that he was simply using the money to continue gambling. She threatened to divorce him if he did not stop gambling. At this point, Jason became infuriated. He claimed that her family looked down on him, so he was gambling in an attempt to get one big win that would let them live in luxury. He also said that he owed thousands of dollars in debts to the card house. Jason's wife indicated that she would take care of the debts but that he must stop gambling. After she gave him the money, Jason promptly lost the money playing cards. His wife then threatened to divorce him unless he entered psychotherapy and ceased his gambling habit. The therapist who saw Jason diagnosed him as a pathological gambler. Although Jason showed some antisocial behaviors, they were confined to his gambling and attempts to get money for gambling.

Pyromania

Pyromania is characterized by deliberate fire setting on more than one occasion. Pyromaniacs have a fascination with fire and with burning objects. They get intense pleasure or relief from setting the fires, watching things burn, or observing firefighters and

Pathological gamblers cannot control their urge to gamble. They often go into debt, turn to illegal activities to support their gambling, and jeopardize their families' security. Even heavy losses cannot deter them from their self-destructive acts.

their efforts to put out fires. Their impulses are driven by this fascination rather than by any motives involving revenge, sabotage, or financial gains for setting fire. Most pyromaniacs have a history of fire setting, beginning in childhood. Although many children may play with fire, they do so without the intense pleasure, lack of concern over the destruction caused by fires, and inability to control the impulse that is seen among pyromaniacs. The prevalence of the disorder is unknown, although it is diagnosed far more frequently among males than females. The case of Kevin, a fourteen-year-old boy, illustrates some of the characteristics associated with pyromania.

Kevin was arrested for the crime of arson in which he had allegedly set a fire that resulted in the destruction of some houses being constructed. Kevin was watching the fire when a witness told firefighters that she had seen Kevin with a gasoline can at the construction site just before the nighttime fire. After arson investigators found the gasoline can (which was later found to have Kevin's fingerprints) and questioned Kevin and his parents, he confessed to the crime. Kevin had a long history of fire setting. When he was about six years of age, he used his father's lighter to burn his sister's doll, which then ignited the window curtain. At age eight, he burned some bushes while he was

Pyromaniacs are fascinated with fire. In fact, it is this fascination with burning objects rather than any motives of revenge that drives them. To be diagnosed as a pyromaniac, a person must feel intense pleasure or relief when setting fires.

camping with his family. Kevin was always playing with matches and lighters. He was also caught setting off a fire alarm at an office building. Kevin's parents reported that he would always become quite excited when hearing the sirens of fire engines. He often asked his parents to follow the fire engines just to see the fires. Although the parents had punished Kevin for playing with fire, he would, without his parents' knowledge, continue burning items. Outside of the fire setting, Kevin had few problems. He was an average student who was quiet and fairly well behaved.

Trichotillomania

Trichotillomania is a disorder characterized by the inability to refrain from pulling one's own hair. The person usually feels a sense of tension before the hair-pulling, and feels release or gratification after the act. Although trichotillomania principally involves the hairs in the scalp, hair from other parts of the body (such as eyelashes, beard, or eyebrows) may be pulled. The hair pulling is not provoked by skin

inflammation, itch, or other physical conditions. Rather, the person simply cannot to resist the impulse. Initially, the hair pulling may not disturb the follicles, and new hairs start to grow. In severe cases, new growth is compromised and permanent balding may occur. One 35-year-old woman entered therapy with one of the authors of this book. She said that she had a compulsion to pull the hairs from her head. When asked to reveal the extent of the hair pulling, the woman took off her wig. She was completely bald except for a few strands of hair at the back of her head. There is no information on the prevalence of the disorder, although it is probably more common than currently believed (American Psychological Association, 1987).

Etiology and Treatment of Impulse Control Disorders

Although some of these disorders such as pathological gambling and pyromania have gained much public attention, not much is actually known about the specific etiologies. In describing the disorders, DSM-III-R notes that little information is available on the causes (American Psychiatric Association, 1987). Furthermore, the characteristics of impulse control disorders seem to be similar to those found in other disorders. First, the disorders have an obsessive-compulsive quality in that the person feels a compulsion to perform certain acts. However, in obsessive-compulsive disorders, the repetitive behaviors seem more purposeful and serve to prevent or produce some future event or situation. Second, the impulse control disorders also have a compulsive feature that is found in substance abusers or addicts who must maintain their habits. The use of substances, however, has a more clear physiological involvement. Third, to some extent, the behaviors of people with impulse control disorders resemble those of people with sexual disorders (such as exhibitionism and fetishism) in that tension, fascination, and release may precede or follow the acts. Indeed, some psychoanalysts link pyromania to sexual release and gratification. The problem is that orgasm and many sexual activities are intrinsically pleasurable or reinforcing, whereas trichotillomania and fire setting are not.

Psychoanalytic explanations for impulse control disorders have been quite varied (see Booth, 1988). Pathological gambling has been likened to masturbation in that masturbation and gambling are both driven by built-up tension and a need to release the tension. Alternatively, pathological gambling has also been attributed to an unconscious need to lose because of underlying guilt. Kleptomania has been seen as an attempt to gain esteem, nourishment, or sexual gratification through stealing. Pyromania has been associated with sexual gratification, attempts to overcome feelings of impotence and inferiority, or unconscious anger toward a parental figure. And trichotillomania has been described as a response to unhealthy parent-child relationships. These psychoanalytic or psychodynamic formulations have been primarily based on clinical case studies rather than on empirical research.

Behaviorists tend to explain impulse control disorders through learning principles such as operant conditioning, classical conditioning, and modeling. For example, pathological gambling has been viewed as being influenced by reinforcement schedules. Re-

searchers have shown that high rates of responding can occur because the positive reinforcement schedule is variable rather than continuous. That is, when people win only occasionally, they may strongly persist in gambling. Initial wins may attract the person to gamble. Then, as wins become less frequent and are quite variable, a high rate of responding is likely. Learning principles can also be used to conceptualize the other disorders. Some researchers have even speculated on the role of physiological factors. Roy and his colleagues (1988) found that compulsive gamblers were more likely than nongamblers to have abnormalities in their noradrenergic system (affecting heart rate and blood pressure), which may indicate a greater sensation- or thrill-seeking drive among pathological gamblers.

The diversity of explanations and the lack of empirical research on impulse control disorders reflect the fact that these disorders have fascinated mental health professionals, and yet the prevalence of such disorders is sufficiently low so that researchers have difficulty studying the disorders. Furthermore, it's very likely that impulse control disorders share similar symptoms (inability to resist an impulse, for example) but lack a common cause. That is, different types of disorders, such as intermittent explosive disorder and kleptomania, may be influenced by quite different factors.

In terms of treatment, a wide variety of approaches has been used, as noted by Booth (1988) in his review of impulse control disorders. In many of the disorders, behavioral and cognitive behavioral methods have been moderately successful. Some patients have been taught to recognize tension states that lead to the behavior, to make self-statements (such as having a kleptomaniac say, "I feel like stealing the item but I'd better not"), rehearse alternative responses (such as having a person with intermittent explosive disorder take a deep breath and relax when tension exists), or associate their behavior with aversive consequences (such as through aversive conditioning). Some insight-oriented approaches have been helpful in treating disorders such as kleptomania, especially with people who feel guilty over the theft. Multimodal approaches (combining techniques) involving family and friends and even organizations (such as Gamblers Anonymous, for pathological gamblers) may be beneficial.

SUMMARY

1. The personality disorders include a diversity of behavioral patterns in people who are typically perceived as being odd, overly sensitive and emotional, hot-tempered, suspicious, moody, or impulsive. DSM-III-R lists eleven specific personality disorders; each causes significant impairment in social or occupational functioning or subjective distress for the person. They are usually manifested in adolescence, continue into adulthood, and involve disturbances in personality characteristics.

2. The main characteristics of antisocial (or psychopathic) personality are selfishness, irresponsibility, lack of guilt and anxiety, failure to learn from experience, superficiality, and impulsiveness. Psychopaths frequently violate the rules, conventions, or laws of society. Most explanations of antisocial personality attribute its development to family and socialization factors, heredity, or ANS abnormalities that result in lowered anxiety or underarousal. Traditional treatment approaches are not particularly effective with psychopaths.

3. The impulse control disorders involve the person's failure to resist a temptation to perform an act. People with such disorders experience tension before the act and a sense of gratification or release afterward. DSM-III-R lists five impulse control disorders: kleptomania, intermittent explosive disorder, pathological gambling, pyromania, and trichotillomania. Although little is known about etiology and effective treatment, the disorders have gained much public attention because of mass media dramatizations of kleptomania, pathological gambling, and pyromania.

KEY TERMS

antisocial personality disorder A personality disorder characterized by failure to conform to social and legal norms, superficial relationships with others, and lack of guilt feelings for wrongdoing

avoidant personality disorder A personality disorder characterized by hypersensitivity to rejection and humiliation and, as a result, reluctance to enter into social relationships

borderline personality disorder A personality disorder characterized by intense fluctuations in mood, self-image, and interpersonal relationships

dependent personality disorder A personality disorder characterized by extreme reliance on others and an unwillingness to assume responsibility

histrionic personality disorder A personality disorder characterized by self-dramatization, the exaggerated expression of emotions, and attention-seeking behaviors

impulse control disorder A disorder in which the person fails to resist an impulse or temptation to perform some act that is harmful to the person or to others

intermittent explosive disorder Loss of control over aggressive impulses, resulting in serious assaults or destruction

kleptomania An impulse control disorder in which the person recurrently fails to resist impulses to steal objects

narcissistic personality disorder A personality disorder characterized by an exaggerated sense of self-importance

obsessive-compulsive personality disorder A personality disorder characterized by inability to express warm feelings, perfectionism, indecision, devotion to details, and a lack of personal warmth

paranoid personality disorder A personality disorder characterized by unwarranted suspiciousness, hypersensitivity, a reluctance to confide in others, and preoccupation with unfounded beliefs

passive-aggressive personality disorder A personality disorder characterized by the passive expression of aggression through stubbornness, inefficiency, procrastination, and, generally, resistance to reasonable demands

pathological gambling An impulse control disorder characterized by an inability to refrain from gambling

personality disorder A behavior pattern characterized by inflexible and maladaptive behaviors

pyromania An impulse control disorder having as its main feature deliberate fire setting on more than one occasion

schizoid personality disorder A personality disorder characterized by social isolation and emotional coldness

schizotypal personality disorder A personality disorder characterized by such oddities of thinking and behavior as recurrent illusions, belief in the possession of magical powers, and digression or vagueness of speech

trichotillomania An impulse control disorder in which the person cannot resist pulling out his or her own hair

chapter 10
Psychoactive Substance Use Disorders

The misuse of psychoactive substances is the nation's foremost public health challenge. The use and abuse of alcohol, cigarettes, illicit drugs (heroin, cocaine, marijuana, etc.), and licit drugs (sedatives and tranquilizers) are by far the largest cause of preventable and premature illness, disability, and death in our society. . . . The 1982 household survey (3) found that almost a third of the household population in the United States age 12 and older had had some experience with illicit drugs. Almost 60 million household residents were current users. . . . Over 20 million had tried cocaine and over 4 million were current users. (Committee on Drug Abuse of the Council on Psychiatric Services, 1987, p. 698)

Throughout history, people have swallowed, sniffed, smoked, or otherwise taken into their bodies a variety of chemical substances for the purpose of altering their moods, levels of consciousness, or behaviors. The widespread use of drugs in our society today is readily apparent in our vast consumption of alcohol, cigarettes, coffee, medically prescribed tranquilizers, and such illegal drugs as cocaine, marijuana, and heroin. Our society is generally permissive (compared to other societies) with regard to the use of such substances. But people and public institutions become concerned when the ingestion of drugs results in (1) the impairment of a person's social or occupational functioning; (2) an inability to abstain from using the drug despite its harmful effects on the body; (3) the user becoming a danger to others; or (4) criminal activities, such as the sale of illegal drugs or robbery

259

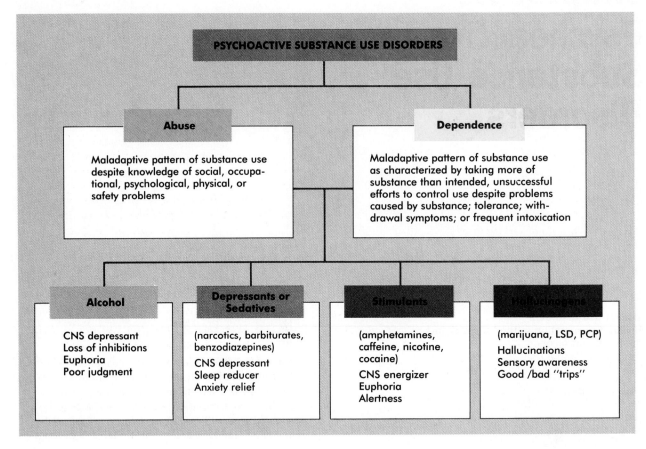

SOURCE: Adapted from DSM-III-R, pp. 165–185.

to support a drug habit. The first two of these problems are directly involved in **psychoactive substance use disorders,** (altering one's psychological state) or maladaptive behavior associated with the pathological use of a substance over a period of at least one month. The other problems arise as concomitants of such use. DSM-III-R distinguishes psychoactive substance use disorders from psychoactive substance-induced organic mental disorders. (See the psychoactive substance use disorders chart on p. 260.) The former term refers to the maladaptive behavior associated with substance use, while the latter term describes the direct acute or chronic effects of such substances on the central nervous system. The distinction is maintained in this chapter. With the exception of alcohol, substance-induced organic mental disorders are not discussed in this chapter.

In DSM-III-R, the substance use disorders are differentiated from each other with regard to the actual substance used, as well as in terms of two patterns of use—substance abuse and substance dependence. **Substance abuse** is a pathological pattern of excessive use in which the person cannot cease or reduce his or her intake of a substance, even though it may be causing physical damage, jeopardizing safety (such as driving a car while intoxicated), or impairing social relationships and occupational functioning. Need for the substance may lead to a preoccupation with its acquisition and use.

To make the diagnosis of **substance dependence,** a therapist must find several of the following symptoms in the client: an inability to cut down or control use, despite knowledge of the harmful effects; a great deal of time spent in activities necessary to obtain the substance, even though important social, occupational, and recreational activities are thereby sacrificed; frequent intoxication; **tolerance** (needing increasing dosages of the substance in order to achieve the desired effect such as a "high"), and **withdrawal symptoms** (physical or emotional symptoms such as shaking, irritability, and inability to concentrate) after reducing or ceasing intake. In general, tolerance and withdrawal symptoms are considered signs of physical dependence, while the other symptoms involve psychological dependence. Because the symptoms of dependence cover a broader range of behavior than those of abuse, people who meet the criteria for both substance dependence and abuse for a particular substance are diagnosed only as dependent and not as abusing.

In this chapter, we first examine the effects, possible causes, and treatment approaches for alcohol use disorders. Then we do the same for disorders involving the use of various other substances.

ALCOHOL USE DISORDERS

Frank is a 42-year-old alcoholic. Before he turned sixteen, he had already tried some liquor, but he did not like the taste at all. Soon after his sixteenth birthday, however, he and some friends "threw" a drinking party. Frank forced himself to drink, and the liquor lost its aversive quality; Frank became drunk and then quite ill. The next day he swore that he would never "touch the stuff again." But over the next three years, he developed a taste for alcohol. Drinking relieved his anxieties and made him feel uninhibited. In college he was proud of the fact that he could drink others "under the table" and then act "normal," even though other students who drank the same amount would either act immaturely or become intoxicated.

Initially, his drinking did not interfere with his school work or social life. Frank was an average student, but he became quite dependent on alcohol to relieve tensions. Before making a presentation in a speech class one day, Frank had a few drinks. He carefully controlled the amount he drank so that he would feel confident but would be able to speak without any telltale signs. He even used a mouthwash so that others would not suspect he had been drinking. After he was successful with the speech, Frank started to drink in the daytime. Social drinking was no longer sufficient; he now had to drink to the point of intoxication. He was careful to ensure that others did not become aware of his drinking, and he believed that he was not an alcoholic.

Frank's preoccupation with alcohol grew; his subsequent inability to control his drinking and his frequent binges made it difficult for him to continue his education. As a result, Frank did not graduate from college. For years he was unable to hold a steady job, because of his frequent absences and ineffectiveness on the job.

On the day after he was arrested for public drunkenness, Frank entered his first treatment program. Depressed over his inability to lead a stable life, he finally admitted he was an alcoholic. For the next five years, he experienced alternating periods of sobriety and drunkenness and was in and out of different treatment programs, including Alcoholics Anonymous. At the age of forty-one, he was brought to a mental hospital for a treatment program aimed at changing his entire lifestyle. The program seems to have been helpful—Frank has currently not had a drink for eleven months.

Problem drinking can develop in many different ways and can begin at almost any age. However, Frank's history is typical in several respects. First, as is true of most people, he initially found the taste of alcohol unpleasant, and, after his first bout of drunkenness, he swore he would never drink again. However, he did return to drinking. Second, heavy drinking served a purpose: it reduced his anxiety, particularly in social settings. Third, Frank took great pains to hide from others the fact that he had been consuming alcohol. Such tactics often fail; friends and colleagues usually smell liquor on the breath or notice the unsteady gait of the problem drinker. Finally, heavy daytime drinking, a preoccupation with alcohol consumption, and the deterioration of social and occupational functioning are also characteristic of the problem drinker.

Alcohol Consumption in the United States

People drink considerable amounts of alcohol in the United States. According to DSM-III-R (American Psychiatric Association, 1987), about 10 percent of adults consume one ounce or more of alcohol a day, 55 percent drink fewer than three alcoholic drinks a week, and 35 percent abstain completely. Most of the alcohol is consumed by a small percentage of people; 50 percent of the total alcohol consumed is drunk by only 10 percent of drinkers. Young adults between the ages of twenty-one and thirty-four drink more than any other group. Males drink two to five times as much as females. It is estimated that 13 percent of the adult population has experienced problems with alcohol abuse or dependence at some time in their lives.

Drinking is widespread among young people. In a national survey of high school seniors, Johnston et al. (1987) found that 91 percent reported using alcohol at some time; 31 percent reported at least one instance of heavy consumption (five or more drinks) during the past two weeks.

Add to these statistics the estimates of the Office of Technical Assessment (1983) on the social, medical, and physical costs of drinking, and you can see how immense the problem really is:

1. An estimated 10 million to 15 million Americans have serious problems directly related to alcohol consumption, and about 35 million people are indirectly affected.

2. Alcoholism may be responsible for up to 15 percent of the nation's health care costs and for significantly lowering the worker productivity at all levels of the economic system. It is estimated that alcoholism costs our society almost $50 billion per year.

3. The life expectancy of an alcoholic is ten to twelve years shorter than average, and alcoholism is related to such health problems as organ damage, brain dysfunction, cardiovascular disease, and mental disorders.

4. Alcoholics have a significantly higher suicide rate than nonalcoholics (up to 58 percent greater in some groups of alcoholics). In addition, alcohol is associated with nearly 55 percent of all automobile accidents (see Focus 10.1), with home and industrial accidents, and with crimes such as assault, rape, and spouse abuse.

5. Alcoholism is estimated to be a factor in up to 40 percent of all problems brought to family courts. It is also known to be a major factor in divorce, and has been associated with family destabilization.

6. Despite the high cost of alcoholism and the wide range of problems associated with alcoholism, an estimated 85 percent of alcoholics never receive any treatment.

Concern has also developed over the children of alcoholic parents. Children who have an alcoholic parent are at risk for social maladjustment, self-depreciation, lower self-esteem, and alcoholism (Berkowitz & Perkins, 1988).

With such grim results, why do people continue to create serious problems for themselves, their families, their employers, and even total strangers on the highways through problem drinking? Before we can explore this question, we need to examine the effects of alcohol.

Alcoholism is often an important factor in divorce and is associated with family destabilization. Women who drink during pregnancy pose a risk to their unborn children who may be born with physical deformities and mental retardation.

The Effects of Alcohol

Alcohol abuse and alcohol dependence are, of course, substance abuse and dependence in which the substance is alcohol. People who have either of these alcohol use disorders are popularly referred to as **alcoholics,** and their disorder is **alcoholism.** Drinking problems can be exhibited in two major ways. First, the person may need to use alcohol daily in order to function; that is, he or she may be unable to abstain.

FOCUS 10.1 *MADD (Mothers Against Drunk Driving)*

On May 3, 1980, a thirteen-year-old girl was walking to a church carnival in Fair Oaks, California. A car suddenly swerved out of control and killed her. Police arrested the vehicle's driver, who was intoxicated. A check of the driver's record revealed that he had a long history of arrests for drunk driving. Only the week before, he had been bailed out of jail after being charged with hit-and-run drunk driving.

Candy Lightner, the mother of the girl, was furious over the death of her daughter and concerned that the driver might not be sent to prison for the crime. At that time the penalties for drunk driving were frequently light, even when injury or death resulted. Lightner wanted to find ways to keep drunk people from driving and to help the victims of drunk drivers and victims' families. She decided to form an organization called Mothers Against Drunk Drivers (MADD).

Initially Lightner was unsuccessful. She wanted to meet with then California Governor Jerry Brown to find a means of dealing with drunk drivers, but the governor declined to see her. Finally, after Lightner began to show up at his office day after day and succeeded in obtaining newspaper publicity for her crusade, Brown took action. He appointed a task force to deal with drunk driving and named her a member.

As a result of the efforts of Lightner and the task force, California eventually passed tough new laws against drunk driving. Lightner's organization has grown as well; MADD now has 320 chapters nationwide and 600,000 volunteers and donors. They have succeeded in convincing most states to enact more severe penalties for drunk driving. In addition, MADD was the most aggressive group lobbying Congress for a law that would force every state to set its minimum drinking age at twenty-one or higher. Such a law was passed by Congress—and signed by President Reagan—in the summer of 1984. Now, any state that does not comply by a certain fixed date can lose millions of dollars in federal highway funds.

Incidentally, the driver responsible for the death of Lightner's daughter did eventually serve twenty-one months in jail (Friedrich, 1985).

Second, the person may be able to abstain from consuming alcohol for certain periods of time but then cannot control or moderate intake once he or she resumes drinking. This person is a "binge" drinker. Both patterns of drinking can result in deteriorating relationships, loss of job, family conflicts, and violence while intoxicated.

Short-Term Effects Alcohol has both short-term and long-term effects and both physiological and psychological effects. Once swallowed, it is absorbed into the blood without digestion. When it reaches the brain, its *short-term physiological effect* is to depress central nervous system functioning. When the alcohol content in the bloodstream (the blood alcohol level) is about 0.1 percent (the equivalent of drinking 5 ounces of whiskey), muscular coordination is impaired. The drinker may have trouble walking a straight line or pronouncing certain words. At the 0.5 percent blood alcohol level, the person may lose consciousness or even die.

The short-term physiological effects of alcohol on a specific person are determined by the individual's body weight, the amount of food present in the stomach, the drinking rate over time, prior drinking experience, heredity, and the personality and culture of the drinker. Table 10.1 shows the effect of alcohol intake on blood alcohol level as a function of body weight.

The *short-term psychological* effects of alcohol include feelings of happiness, loss of inhibitions (because alcohol depresses the inhibitory brain centers), poor judgment, and reduced concentration. Heavy and prolonged drinking often impairs sexual performance and produces a *hangover*.

Long-Term Effects The *long-term psychological* effects of heavy drinking are more serious. In particular, alcoholics who show both abuse and dependence are thought to progress through four stages (Jellinek, 1971). In the *prealcoholic symptomatic phase,* such people begin to drink in social

TABLE 10.1 | **Blood Alcohol Level as a Function of Number of Drinks Consumed and Body Weight**

Body Weight, pounds	Number of Drinks Consumed[a]						
	1	2	3	4	5	6	7
100	.020	.055	.095	.130	.165	.200	.245
120	.015	.045	.075	.105	.135	.165	.195
140	.010	.035	.060	.085	.115	.140	.165
160	.005	.030	.050	.075	.095	.120	.145
180	.0	.025	.045	.065	.085	.105	.125
200	.0	.020	.040	.055	.075	.095	.110
220	.0	.020	.035	.050	.065	.085	.100
240	.0	.015	.035	.045	.060	.075	.090

SOURCE: Adapted from Vogler and Bartz, 1983.

[a]The given blood alcohol levels are those that would exist 1 hour after the start of drinking. Because alcohol is metabolized over time, subtract 0.015 from the given level for each additional hour. For example, a 100-pound person consuming 2 drinks would, after 2 hours, have a blood alcohol level of 0.055 − 0.015 = 0.040. One drink equals 12 ounces of beer, 4 ounces of wine, or 1.25 ounces of liquor.

situations. Because the alcohol relieves tension, the drinkers tend to drink more frequently. Tolerance levels may increase over a period of months or years.

During the *prodromal phase*, drinkers are preoccupied with thoughts of alcohol. They may worry about whether there will be enough alcohol at a party; they may try to drink inconspicuously, or even furtively. They begin to consume large amounts and may "gulp" their drinks. Such drinkers frequently feel guilty; they are somewhat aware that their drinking is excessive. This phase is also characterized by *blackouts*, periods of time for which drinkers have no memory of their activities.

The *crucial phase* occurs when drinkers lose control of their alcohol intake. Once drinking starts, they must continue (or cannot stop) until they become intoxicated. Although it is possible for them to abstain from drinking, they have lost the ability to regulate their drinking after the first drink. They may go on drinking binges that last for days.

The *chronic stage* is the final one in alcohol addiction. Alcohol is consumed frequently, to the point of total intoxication. The alcoholic is now openly drunk in the daytime and constantly concerned with obtaining alcohol. Deterioration in his or her social, familial, and occupational functioning is now evident. The drinker is now living only to drink.

This perspective proposes a biological and developmental process in which alcoholics pass through stages where they cannot control their drinking. As

is discussed later, many investigators have questioned whether alcoholics pass through stages or lose control for biological reasons.

It should also be noted that most investigators, including Jellinek, have formulated their ideas based on research with male alcoholics. Although relatively few studies have examined female alcoholics, the available evidence suggests that gender differences exist. For example, alcoholic women as compared to alcoholic men report more childhood problems, such as having alcoholic parents, unhappy childhoods, and broken homes. Furthermore, women become problem drinkers at a later age than men (Perodeau, 1984). These findings suggest that perspectives based on research with alcoholic men should be carefully scrutinized for their applicability to women.

The *long-term physiological effects* of alcohol consumption include an increase in tolerance as the person becomes used to alcohol, physical discomfort, anxiety, and hallucinations. Chronic alcoholism destroys brain cells and is often accompanied by poor nutritional habits and physical deterioration. Thus, the left brain hemispheres of alcoholics have been found to be less dense than those of a control group of nonalcoholics (Golden et al., 1981). Other direct or indirect consequences generally attributed to chronic alcoholism are such liver diseases as *cirrhosis*, in which an excessive amount of fibrous tissue develops and impedes the circulation of blood; heart failure; hemorrhages of capillaries, particularly those on the sides of the nose, and cancers of the mouth and throat. Alcohol consumption among pregnant women may affect their unborn children: children who suffer *fetal alcohol syndrome* are born mentally retarded and physically deformed.

Interestingly, the *moderate* use of alcohol (one or two drinks a day) in adults has been associated in some studies with lowered risk of heart disease. The precise reasons for this effect are unknown. What is clear, though, is that chronic heavy consumption has serious negative consequences.

Alcohol-Induced Organic Mental Disorders DSM-III-R lists a variety of organic mental disorders attributed to alcohol abuse. Included are alcohol idiosyncratic intoxication, alcohol hallucinosis, alcohol withdrawal, and alcohol amnestic disorder. In these disorders, a psychological or behavioral abnormality is associated with temporary or permanent dysfunction of the brain.

The essential feature of **alcohol idiosyncratic intoxication** is an acute behavior change. After ingesting a relatively small amount of alcohol, the drinker may become hostile, assaultive, depressed, confused, or disoriented, in marked contrast to the behavior the person shows when not drinking. It seems that small amounts of alcohol trigger atypical behaviors in the drinker until the blood alcohol level decreases. Some researchers have speculated that the person with this disorder may have brain damage that, combined with alcohol consumption, results in unusual behavior.

In **alcohol hallucinosis,** stopping or reducing chronic and heavy alcohol intake leads to vivid auditory or visual hallucinations. Often the hallucinations involve voices that accuse the alcoholic person of sins or misdeeds. The drinker may respond to the voices—that is, talk to him- or herself—or may try to ignore them and hide the problem from others.

In **alcohol withdrawal,** if a person who has been drinking for several days ceases or reduces alcohol ingestion he or she may experience tremors of the hands and other parts of the body, nausea and vomiting, weakness, tachycardia (rapid heartbeats), sweating, anxiety, or depression. Hallucinations and sleep disturbances may also occur. If **delirium** (confusion, difficulty in maintaining attention and concentration, and delusions) is also involved, the disorder is called **alcohol-withdrawal delirium.**

Alcohol amnestic disorder, or **Korsakoff's syndrome,** is sometimes found in chronic alcoholics who do not eat a nutritionally adequate diet. The precise etiology of Korsakoff's syndrome is unknown, but the prevailing belief is that nutritional deficiencies, particularly the lack of B-complex vitamins, seriously disrupt brain function and produce brain damage (Redlich & Freedman, 1966). The classic symptoms of Korsakoff's syndrome are the loss of memory for very recent or immediately preceding events (*anterograde amnesia*) and the filling in of memory gaps with false or fanciful accounts (*confabulation*). For example, a patient may be asked what she just saw on television. Rather than report on the football game that was just shown and which she has forgotten, the patient may say that she saw a great adventure movie and then proceed to describe the imaginary movie in detail. When confronted with the fact that she actually saw a football game, the patient may refute it, even if her story is illogical or clearly inaccurate. She may even forget the confabulated story and give another response entirely. Long-term memory is also affected, in that very remote events are remembered better than more recent events. Other symptoms of Korsakoff's syndrome include general confusion, disorientation, and hallucinations.

Alcohol reduces inhibitions and tension because it is a central nervous system depressant. In social situations, which can be anxiety provoking, a person may drink for its relaxing effect. Eventually, over a period of months or years, a person's tolerance level may increase, and alcoholism may develop.

Etiology of Alcohol Use Disorders

Why do some people become dependent on alcohol? Is alcoholism a disease, or is it learned? A number of theories have been propounded in the attempt to answer such questions. Of these, the major types are either biological and physical in perspective (involving genetic or congenital factors) or psychological and cultural (involving personality, sociocultural, or learning factors). Both perspectives may have some validity in explaining alcoholism. The biological-physical theories focus on dependence, or the bodily need for alcohol. The psychological-cultural theories help to explain how drinking patterns develop before actual addiction and why alcoholics who have stopped drinking and no longer have physical cravings may return to drinking.

Investigators have often assumed that the *acquisition* of drinking behavior is the result of psychological factors, whereas the *maintenance* of heavy drinking results from physical dependence on alcohol. That is, one first drinks because of curiosity; exposure to drinking models such as parents, peers, or television characters; and the tension-reducing properties of alcohol. After prolonged consumption, however, the person becomes physically dependent and drinks heavily to satisfy bodily needs. This assumption is overly simplistic. As you will see shortly, the acquisition and maintenance of drinking behavior are both influenced by the complex interaction of psychological and physical factors.

Biological-Physical Explanations

Because alcohol affects metabolic processes and the central nervous system, investigators have explored the possibility that heredity or congenital factors increase susceptibility to addiction. The Research Task Force of the National Institute of Mental Health (1975) suggested that alcoholism "runs in families" and that 20 to 30 percent of the children of alcoholics eventually develop alcoholism. The challenge in these observations is to separate the contributions of genetic and environmental factors, because children share both genetic and environmental influences with their parents. The role of in utero and neonatal influences must also be determined.

Several studies have indicated that children whose parents were alcoholics but who were adopted and reared by nonrelatives are more likely to develop drinking problems than adopted children whose biological parents were not alcoholics (Research Task Force of the National Institute of Mental Health, 1975; Goodwin, 1979). Research comparing the concordance rates for alcoholism among identical (MZ) and fraternal (DZ) twins indicates that, although MZ twins have higher concordance rates, DZ twins also have high rates (Rosenthal, 1971). These findings suggest that both heredity and environmental factors are important. Goodwin (1985) speculates that two types of alcoholism may exist: familial and nonfamilial. *Familial alcoholism* shows a family history of alcoholism, suggesting genetic predisposition. It develops at an early age (usually by the late twenties), is severe, and increases the risk for alcoholism but not other mental disorders. *Nonfamilial alcoholism* does not show these characteristics, and is presumably influenced more by environment.

Finally, there have been attempts to implicate nutritional or vitamin deficiencies, hormonal imbalances, or abnormal bodily processes as causes of alcoholism. No clear-cut evidence has been found to indicate that these congenital factors are important in human alcoholism.

Psychodynamic and Personality Explanations

A number of psychoanalytic explanations have been proposed for alcoholism. Most hold that childhood traumas (such as an overprotecting mother, maternal neglect, or frustration of dependency needs) especially during the oral stage of development, result in the repression of painful conflicts involving dependency needs (Kanas, 1988). During stress or encounters with situations reminiscent of the original conflicts, symptoms such as anxiety, depression, and hostility begin to occur. Alcohol is seen as (1) releasing inhibitions and allowing for the expression of the repressed conflicts or (2) enabling people to obtain oral gratification and to satisfy dependency needs. Most of the psychoanalytic formulations are based on retrospective clinical case studies rather than empirical data, so the validity of the formulations is open to question.

Some researchers believe that certain *personality characteristics* make people vulnerable to alcoholism. These characteristics may predispose people to use alcohol, rather than some other coping strategy, to deal with stressors. Low frustration tolerance, emotional immaturity, feelings of inadequacy, a need for power, and dependent personality characteristics have all been associated with alcoholism or heavy drinking (Jones 1968, 1971; McClelland et al., 1972; Winokur et al., 1970).

Findings regarding a predisposition to drinking are mixed. In one long-term study, researchers found that adolescents reported increased drunkenness when they had (1) lower personal regard for academic achievement; (2) higher tolerance for deviance; (3) more positive reasons, in relation to perceived drawbacks, for drinking; and (4) more positive reasons for drug use (Jessor & Jessor, 1977). Although these four personality characteristics were significantly correlated with being drunk, the correlations were not strong. In another long-term study (of male drinkers only), evidence was found that an unhappy childhood does not cause alcohol abuse, as is popularly believed. Rather, the abuser is unhappy because of heavy drinking (Vaillant & Milofsky, 1982).

In a recent review of research on personality and alcoholism, Nathan (1988) concluded that only two personality characteristics—antisocial behavior and depression—have been associated with drinking problems. Particularly consistent is the relationship between a childhood or adolescent history of antisocial behavior (such as rejection of societal rules) and alcoholism. However, Nathan warns that the role of personality characteristics, including antisocial tendencies and depression, as etiological factors in alcoholism cannot be uncritically accepted. Many alcohol abusers do not show antisocial histories, and many antisocial people do not drink excessively. Furthermore, depression may well be a consequence rather than an antecedent of alcohol abuse (that is, problem drinking may cause people to feel depressed).

Sociocultural Explanations Drinking varies according to sociocultural factors such as sex, age, socioeconomic status, ethnicity, religion, and country. As mentioned previously, males and young adults consume more alcohol than females and older adults, respectively. Interestingly, consumption tends to increase with increasing socioeconomic status, although alcoholism is more frequent in the middle socioeconomic classes (Kanas, 1988). Native Americans and Irish Americans are far more likely to become alcoholics than are Americans of Italian, Hispanic, and Asian backgrounds (Sue & Nakamura, 1984). In terms of religious affiliation, heavier drinking is found among Catholics than among Protestants or Jews. Finally, variations in drinking behavior are found in different countries. In wine countries, such as France and Italy, alcohol consumption is high (Goodwin, 1985). Consumption is low in Israel and mainland China, with the United States ranked in the middle, and the Soviet Union in the lower third of countries. Rates of alcoholism may not correspond to per capita consumption. For example, in Portugal and Italy where per capita consumption is high, the incidence of alcoholism is relatively low (Kanas, 1988). In the United States and the Soviet Union, where consumption is moderate, alcoholism is relatively high. France has high rates of both consumption and alcoholism. Drinking patterns in France are characterized by moderate alcoholic intake throughout the day, and drunkenness is more permissible there than in Italy. In Italy, drinking wine at mealtime is customary but drinking to become intoxicated is discouraged.

These findings suggest that cultural values play an important role in drinking patterns. The values affect not only the amount consumed and the occasions in which drinking takes place but also the given culture's tolerance of alcohol abuse.

Cultural values and behaviors are usually learned within the family and community. A review of the literature on adolescent drinking led researchers to conclude that teenage problem drinkers are exposed first to parents who are themselves heavy drinkers and then to peers who act as models for heavy consumption (Braucht, 1982). The parents not only consumed a great deal of alcohol but also showed inappropriate behaviors such as antisocial tendencies and rejection of their children. When such children loosened their parental ties, they tended to be strongly influenced by peers who were also heavy drinkers.

Learning Explanations Early learning explanations for alcohol abuse and dependence were based on two assumptions: (1) drinking behavior is learned, and (2) alcohol temporarily serves to reduce anxiety and tension. In a classic experiment, an "experimental neurosis" was induced in cats. After the cats were trained to approach and eat food at a food box, they were given an aversive stimulus (an air blast to the face or an electric shock) whenever they approached the food. The cats stopped eating and exhibited "neurotic" symptoms—anxiety, psychophysiological disturbances, and peculiar behaviors. When the cats were given alcohol, however, their symptoms disappeared and they started to eat. As the effects of the alcohol wore off, the symptoms began to reappear (Masserman et al., 1944).

The experimenters also found that these cats now preferred "spiked" milk (milk mixed with alcohol) to milk alone. Once the stressful shocks were terminated and the fear responses extinguished, however, the cats no longer preferred spiked milk. Alcohol apparently reduced the cats' anxieties and was used as long as the anxieties were present. (Note that the cats were placed in an *approach-avoidance* conflict. That is, their desire to approach the food box and eat was in conflict with their desire to avoid the air blast or shock.)

An experimenter wanted to test the hypothesis that alcohol reduces the anxiety of conflict—that it resolves conflicts by increasing approach behaviors or by decreasing avoidance behaviors. He placed rats in a conflict situation and measured the strengths of approach behaviors and avoidance behaviors before and after the use of alcohol (Conger, 1951). He found that the main effect of alcohol was to reduce avoidance behaviors, and concluded that alcohol helps resolve conflicts by reducing fear of the unpleasant or aversive element. Many theorists believe that the anxiety-reducing properties of alcohol are reinforcing and are therefore largely responsible for maintaining the drinking behavior of the alcoholic.

A group of researchers (Marlatt et al., 1973) have challenged the disease concept of alcoholism—the notion that drinking small amounts of alcohol leads, in an alcoholic, to involuntary consumption to the point of intoxication. In their study, alcoholics and social drinkers were recruited to participate in what was described as a "tasting experiment." Both the alcoholics and the social drinkers were divided into four groups:

1. Members of the "told alcohol, given alcohol" group were told that they would be given a drink of alcohol and tonic, and they were actually given such a drink.

2. Members of the "told alcohol, given tonic" group were told that they would receive a drink of alcohol and tonic, but they were actually given only tonic.

3. Members of the "told tonic, given alcohol" group were told that they would receive a drink of

tonic, but they were actually given an alcohol-and-tonic drink.

4. Members of he "told tonic, given tonic" group were told that they would be given tonic, and they were actually given tonic.

The experimenters used a mixture of five parts tonic and one part vodka for their alcohol-and-tonic drink; these proportions made it difficult to tell whether or not the drink contained alcohol. At the beginning of the experiment, the subjects were "primed" with an initial drink—either alcohol and tonic or tonic only, depending on which group they were in. (That is, the *given alcohol* groups were primed with alcohol, and the *given tonic* groups were primed with tonic.) After the primer drink, subjects were given instructions on the kind of drink they would next receive. They were free to sample as much of the drink as they wished, alone and uninterrupted.

If alcoholism is a *condition* in which alcoholics lose control of drinking, then those *given* an alcohol primer should drink more alcohol. Alternatively, if alcoholics *learn* that alcohol reduces anxiety or enhances feelings of well-being, then those *told* that they would receive alcohol (whether or not alcohol was actually given) would drink more because they *expected* alcohol. Subjects who were told they would receive alcohol drank more than those who were told they would receive tonic; and those who actually consumed alcohol did not drink more than those who consumed tonic (Marlatt et al., 1973).

These results suggest that alcoholism is *not* simply a disease in which a person loses control over drinking. The subjects' *expectancy* had a stronger effect than the actual content of their drinks on how much they consumed. In fact, several subjects who were given tonic when they believed they were imbibing alcohol acted as though they were "tipsy" from the drinks!

These experiments on drinking behavior suggest that *psychological factors,* such as tension reduction and expectancy, are important in maintaining drinking behavior. The tension-reducing model, which assumes that alcohol reduces tension and anxiety and that the relief of tension reinforces the drinking response, is difficult to test, and research with alcoholics has produced conflicting findings. In fact, prolonged drinking is often associated with *increased* anxiety and depression (McNamee et al., 1968).

Although alcoholics who have high blood alcohol levels after drinking may show low muscular tension, they tend to report a high degree of distress (Steffen et al., 1974). Although alcohol is a sedative that can reduce anxiety, it is possible that the knowledge that one is drinking alcohol can increase one's level of anxiety (Polivy et al., 1976).

Some evidence suggests that the tension reduction model is too simplistic. Several experiments have shown that situational factors affect the relationship between the effects of alcohol and anxiety. For example, Steele and Josephs (1988) found that alcohol can either increase or decrease anxiety. When confronted with a stressful situation, people who drank alcohol in the experiment experienced anxiety reduction if they were allowed to engage in a distracting activity. However, when faced with a stressor, those who drank and did not have a distracting activity experienced an increase in anxiety. The investigators argued that the distracting activity allowed drinkers to divert attention from the stressor. Without the distraction, drinkers' attention may have focused on the anxiety, which served to magnify their anxiety.

Other studies also point to problems in the tension reduction hypothesis. When a group of subjects expected to receive a painful shock, they did not consume any more alcohol than subjects who expected to receive a nonpainful shock. However, when a social, rather than a physical, source of tension or anxiety was anticipated (for example, when male subjects were told that they would be rated on their personal attractiveness by a group of females), subjects tended to consume more alcohol than a control group that did not expect to be evaluated by others. Thus different types of tension (electric shock versus social evaluation) produced different results (Marlatt, 1975). Marlatt suggests that the type of stressor, the loss of a sense of personal control over situations, and the lack of alternative coping responses influence drinking, as indicated in his analysis of relapse.

Relapse is the resumption of drinking after a period of voluntary abstinence. Many alcoholics who try to stop drinking return to alcohol within a matter of weeks. Reviewing the circumstances leading to the relapse, Marlatt (1978) concluded that feelings of frustration or anger, social pressure to drink, or temptations (such as walking by a bar) are important preconditions for the resumption of drinking. Such

"high-risk" situations make the person vulnerable. If the person has a coping response (a means of resisting social pressure—for instance, by insisting on a soft drink), that response provides an alternative to drinking. Coping responses include assertion (such as saying no when pressured by others to drink), avoidance (such as not walking near a favorite bar), and more satisfactory means of dealing with anger or anxiety. This, in turn, enables the person to feel control over drinking and to continue abstinence. If a person does not have a coping response to the high-risk situation, however, he or she takes that first drink. But why do these cues or preconditions (such as temptations) lead to drinking? One theory is that the cues, in the absence of drinking, lead to feelings of withdrawal. However, relapse can occur without acute withdrawal distress. Niaura and his colleagues (1988) believe that relapse is caused more by anticipated positive feelings over alcohol use than by a motive to avoid withdrawal.

A person can obviously stop drinking after one drink. To explain the full-blown resumption of drinking that occurs with the alcoholic's first drink, Marlatt proposes the notion of an *abstinence violation effect*. That is, once drinking begins, the person senses a loss of personal control. He or she feels weak-willed and guilty and gives up trying to abstain. The abstinence violation effect may also apply to other relapse behaviors, such as overeating, masturbating, and smoking. Treatment to overcome the abstinence violation effect would focus on giving people coping responses for situations in which there is also a high risk of relapse.

Treatment for Alcohol Use Disorders

Although alcoholism and its treatment have been studied for decades, there is no consensus on what is the most effective of the various treatment approaches (Nathan & Wiens, 1983). Many approaches include **detoxification,** in which the alcoholic is eventually allowed no alcohol at all during treatment. If withdrawal symptoms occur, the patient may receive tranquilizers as medication. Individual or group psychotherapy is often initiated after detoxification begins. The alcoholic may also be sent from the hospital to a "halfway house," where support and guidance are available in a community setting.

In this section, we discuss several approaches to the treatment of alcoholism and then review their effectiveness.

Alcoholics Anonymous Alcoholics Anonymous (AA) is a self-help organization composed of alcoholics who want to stop drinking. Perhaps a million or more alcoholics worldwide participate in the AA program, which is completely voluntary. There are no fees; the only membership requirement is the desire to stop drinking. AA assumes that once a person is an alcoholic, he or she is always an alcoholic—an assumption based on the disease model of alcoholism. Members must recognize that they can

Alcoholics Anonymous, a self-help group organized to help people deal with and overcome their addiction, has responded to more than a million people worldwide. Offshoot organizations, such as AlaTeen and Al-Anon, provide support for teenagers and adults living with alcoholics.

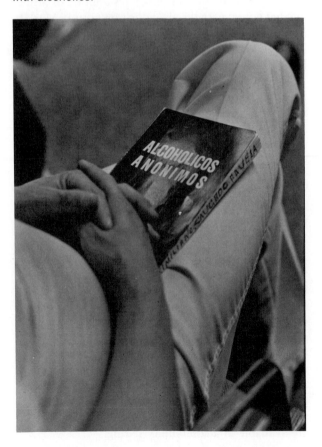

never drink again and must concentrate on abstinence, one day at a time. As a means of helping members to abstain, each is often assigned a sponsor who provides individual support, attention, and help. Fellowship, spiritual awareness, and public self-revelations about past wrongdoings due to alcohol are encouraged during group meetings.

Some people believe that membership in AA is one of the most effective treatments for alcoholism. However, objective outcome studies are difficult to find. Furthermore, it appears that the success rate of AA is not as high as AA members claim it is (Brandsma, 1979). About half the alcoholics who stay in the organization are still abstinent after two years (Alford, 1980). But many drop out of the program and are not counted as failures (when, perhaps, they should be). Thus, although many people are helped by AA, its success rate has not been firmly established. Spinoffs of AA—Al-Anon and AlaTeen—have been helpful in providing support for adults and teenagers living with alcoholics (Kanas, 1988).

Antabuse Some alcohol treatment programs have made use of the chemical *Antabuse* (disulfiram) to produce an aversion to alcohol. If a person consumes alcohol within one to two days after taking Antabuse, he or she suffers a severe reaction, including nausea, vomiting, and discomfort. Antabuse has the effect of blocking the progressive breakdown of alcohol so that excessive acetaldehyde accumulates in the body; and acetaldehyde causes dysphoria. Most alcoholics will not consume alcohol after ingesting Antabuse. Those who do risk not only discomfort but in some cases death.

While clients are taking Antabuse and are abstinent, psychotherapy and other forms of treatment may be used to help them develop coping skills or alternative life patterns. The families of patients may also be encouraged to work at solving the problems created by the drinking. Knowing that alcohol consumption is unlikely during Antabuse treatment, the families do not have to rely solely on the alcoholic's promise to stop drinking—a promise that alcoholics often make but rarely can keep.

The problem with Antabuse treatment is that alcoholic patients may stop taking the drug once they leave the hospital or are no longer being monitored. And some may drink anyway, because they believe the effects of Antabuse have dissipated, because they have forgotten when they last took it, or because they are tempted to drink in spite of the Antabuse.

Cognitive and Behavioral Approaches

Cognitive and behavioral therapists have devised several strategies for treating alcoholics. **Aversion therapy,** which is based on classical conditioning principles, has been used for many years. Aversion therapy is a process by which the sight, smell, or taste of alcohol is paired with a noxious stimulus. For example, alcoholics may be given painful electric shocks while drinking alcohol. Or they may be given *emetics* (agents that induce vomiting) when they get the urge to drink or after smelling or tasting alcohol. After several sessions in which the emetic is used, alcoholics may vomit or feel nauseated whenever they smell, taste, or think about alcohol.

Imagery has been used as part of aversion conditioning in a technique that is also known as **covert sensitization:** alcoholic patients are trained to imagine nausea and vomiting in the presence of alcoholic beverages (Cautela, 1966). In addition, relaxation and systematic desensitization may be used to reduce anxiety. Almost any aversive conditioning procedure may be effective in treating alcoholism if there is also a focus on enhanced social functioning, resistance to stress, and reduction of anxiety (Nathan, 1976). Social learning approaches to treatment have also been used. Cox and Klinger (1988) developed a motivational approach in which alcoholics set important and realistic goals they would like to accomplish. The therapist helps the alcoholics to achieve these goals and to develop a satisfying life without alcohol. Cooper and his colleagues (1988) found that drinking to cope with emotional problems was a strong factor in alcohol abuse. They suggest that alcoholics should find more adaptive ways of coping with negative emotions and stress, through techniques such as stress management and cognitive restructuring.

A great deal of controversy has been generated by the suggestion that it is possible for alcoholics to control their intake and learn to become social drinkers. Proponents of **controlled drinking** assume that, under the right conditions, alcoholics can learn to limit their drinking to appropriate levels. The finding that alcoholics tend to gulp drinks rather than sip them (as social or moderate drinkers do), to consume straight rather than mixed drinks, and to drink many rather than a few drinks gave investigators

clues to the behaviors that require modification. Alcoholics were then trained to drink appropriately. In a setting resembling a bar, they were permitted to order and drink alcohol; but they were administered an aversive stimulus for each inappropriate behavior. For example, if the alcoholics gulped drinks or ordered too many, they would be given painful electric shocks.

One problem with this technique is that patients need to receive periodic retraining or to learn alternative responses to drinking. Otherwise, they tend to revert to their old patterns of consumption on leaving the treatment program (Marlatt, 1983).

Opponents of controlled drinking generally believe that total abstinence should be the goal of treatment, that controlled drinking cannot be maintained over a period of time, and that alcoholism is a genetic-physiological problem. Furthermore, by trying to teach alcoholics that they can resume and control drinking, proponents are unwittingly contributing to the alcoholics' problems. There have even been questions about the validity of the findings in controlled drinking programs (see Focus 10.2).

Multimodal Treatment

In view of the many factors that maintain alcohol consumption, some treatment programs make systematic use of combinations of approaches. For example, alcoholics may be detoxified through Antabuse treatment and simultaneously receive behavioral training (via aversion therapy, biofeedback, or stress management) as well as other forms of therapy.

Other therapies may include combinations of Alcoholics Anonymous, educational training, family therapy, group therapy, and individual psychotherapy. Proponents of multimodal approaches recognize that no single kind of treatment is likely to be totally effective and that successful outcomes often require major changes in the lives of alcoholics. The combination of therapies that works best for a particular person in his or her particular circumstances is obviously the most effective treatment.

Effectiveness of Treatment

With respect to the general effectiveness of the various treatment efforts, Moos and Finney (1983) note that they have indeed helped a number of alcoholics to function normally. Estimates of the proportion of treated alcohol abusers who improve range from 32 to 53

FOCUS 10.2 — The Controlled-Drinking Controversy

In the 1970s, M. B. Sobell and L. C. Sobell (1978) conducted an experiment to determine whether alcoholics could learn to control their drinking. Up to this time, the goal of most treatment programs was total abstinence. The Sobells worked with forty hospitalized male alcoholics. (Other alcoholics in different treatment programs were also studied by the Sobells, but these studies were not part of the controlled-drinking controversy.) Half of the men (the control group) received conventional treatment designed to promote abstinence. The other half (the experimental group) received behavior therapy designed to train them to control, rather than abstain from, drinking. These men participated in therapy sessions in which they saw themselves drinking on videotapes, received electric shocks for inappropriate drinking behaviors (such as ordering drinks too frequently), and learned how to use alternative response in drinking situations. After treatment and for about two additional years, the outcomes for the experimental and control groups were compared. In general, this comparison revealed that the controlled drinkers were functioning better and spent less time in hospitals than the abstaining group.

The controversy started when another group of investigators decided to assess the long-term effects of the treatment and to conduct a follow-up investigation of the patients in the Sobells' experimental group. In addition to raising questions about some of the methods used by the Sobells, the later investigators came to very different conclusions about the success of the controlled-drinking subjects. Using hospital and arrest records and interviews of the subjects, they found that the majority of the controlled drinkers had been hospitalized within one year of the experiment. Only one subject had maintained a pattern of controlled drinking. The majority showed drinking problems (Pendery et al., 1982).

Debates over the effectiveness of various treatment approaches are expected, and they serve to stimulate research. However, when researchers dispute the facts (that is, the outcomes) of a particular study, the situation becomes quite serious and confusing. The controversy over this particular experiment has not yet ended, and it may never be resolved.

---

percent, depending on the criteria that are used to measure improvement. In addition, 10 to 20 percent of alcohol abusers recover "spontaneously," without formal treatment. Moos and Finney note further that "treatment apparently facilitates the recovery process in that treated individuals show higher rates of improvement in many studies than do minimally treated or untreated comparison groups" (p. 1036).

But Moos and Finney (1983, p. 1037) also note that

> Relapse rates during the year after the completion of treatment may be as high as 60% or more. . . . Moreover, researchers have not been very successful in identifying superior treatment methods or in finding treatment approaches that are particularly effective for specific types of patients. Even the idea that more treatment (longer treatment of greater intensity) is better than less treatment has not received

much support. . . . Finally, a large number of persons do not recover "spontaneously," but continue to drink heavily and to incur substantial personal and social costs by doing so.

Such apparently divergent findings indicate that intervention programs and life-context factors can have a powerful impact on the course of alcoholism. By suggesting that this impact can be for better or for worse, they highlight a set of important issues: Why do some alcohol abusers respond positively to an intervention while others show little or no response and quickly resume problem drinking? In what ways do the characteristics of an individual's life context foster or inhibit the recovery process? How do patient, intervention, and life-context factors interrelate to affect recovery and relapse?

Such issues obviously need to be resolved as part of the effort to improve the effectiveness of alcohol treatment programs.

DRUG USE DISORDERS

Miriam K. was a 44-year-old divorced pharmacist. She had been married for over 20 years, but, during the last few years of the marriage, Miriam and her husband had talked about divorce. They had lost interest in each other and pretty much lived their own lives. After their son and daughter left home to attend college, they obtained a divorce.

Although the divorce was relatively amicable, Miriam felt lonesome. With her children at college and her divorce completed, she was very much alone at home. Several of her friends took her along to "singles club" activities to establish some new social relationships. However, Miriam had mixed feelings about men. She was excited about meeting them, but she also felt anxious and inadequate. In addition, Miriam was facing additional responsibilities and demands at work, where a promotion now required that she supervise the operation of three pharmacies.

Although Miriam had occasionally used drugs to calm her nervousness, she now began taking Valium regularly to reduce tension and bring on sleep. Because she worked at pharmacies, she had no trouble in obtaining the drug secretly. Gradually she took more and more. Over the course of several years, her tolerance and intake increased to the point where she was consuming about 75 milligrams a day. This heavy consumption of Valium resulted in a general lethargy, and Miriam was absent from work a great deal. Her employer finally told her that she had to perform better or he would find someone else for her job. Immediately thereafter, Miriam sought help for her dependency on Valium.

In the remainder of this chapter, we discuss a number of additional psychoactive substance use disorders. The substances used include both prescription drugs such as Valium, and also cigarettes, narcotics, and LSD. To differentiate them easily from alcohol, we have lumped them together as "drugs." However, you should realize that alcohol too is a drug—and, in fact, the most widely used drug with potentially harmful effects.

Psychoactive substance use disorders are most prevalent among youths and young adults. Comparing substance use among young adults, Johnston and his colleagues (1987) found a decline in substance use during the past six years. However, changes were slight for alcohol, LSD, and heroin. The use of "crack" cocaine rapidly increased from 1983 to 1986; in 1987, there was a slight decrease. Table 10.2 shows the 1986 prevalence of substance use for people one to nine years beyond high school graduation. Almost 90 percent reported the consumption of alcohol during the past twelve months; the prevalence was 37 percent for marijuana and 20 percent for cocaine. Substance use is, indeed, quite common.

The drugs that we'll discuss can all cause psychological or physical problems; and many can cause legal problems as well. The use of certain substances, except under strict medical supervision, is expressly prohibited by law. Hence the user must obtain them illegally. We'll specifically discuss three classes of drug: depressants (or sedatives), stimulants, and hallucinogens. Each of the drugs within these classes can be the object of an abuse disorder or a dependence disorder. Table 10.3 lists some of these drugs and their effects.

Depressants or Sedatives

Depressants or sedatives cause generalized depression of the central nervous system and a slowing down of

TABLE 10.2 | **1986 Annual Prevalence of Thirteen Types of Drugs Among Respondents One to Nine Years Beyond High School**

Percent Who Used Drugs in Last Twelve Months	
	1986
Marijuana	36.9
LSD	3.1
Cocaine	19.6
"Crack"	3.2
Heroin	0.2
Other Opiates	3.2
Stimulants, Adjusted	10.8
Sedatives	3.1
Barbiturates	2.4
Methaqualone	1.3
Tranquilizers	5.2
Alcohol	88.8
Cigarettes	NA

SOURCE: Adapted from Johnston et al., 1987.
NOTE: Number of respondents = 6,200.

TABLE 10.3 | Drugs and Their Effects

| Drugs | Short-Term Effects[a] | Potential Dependency | |
		Psychological	Physical
Sedatives			
Narcotics (codeine, morphine, heroin, opium, methadone)	Central nervous system (CNS) depressant, pain relief	High	High
Barbiturates (amytal, nembutal, seconal)	CNS depressant, sleep inducer	High	High
Benzodiazepines (Valium)	CNS depressant, anxiety relief	Moderate	Low
Stimulants			
Amphetamines (Benzedrine, Dexedrine, Methedrine)	CNS energizer, euphoria	High	Low
Caffeine	CNS energizer, alertness	Moderate	Low
Nicotine	CNS energizer	High	High
Cocaine	CNS energizer, euphoria	High	Low
Hallucinogens			
Marijuana, hashish	Relaxant, euphoria	Moderate	Low
LSD	Hallucinatory agent	Low	None
PCP	Hallucinatory agent	Moderate	Low

[a]Specific effects often depend on the quality and dosage of the drug as well as on the experience, expectancy, personality, and situation of the person using the drug.

responses. People taking such substances feel calm and relaxed. They may also become sociable and open because of lowered interpersonal inhibitions.

Narcotics The organic **narcotics**—opium and its derivatives morphine, heroin, and codeine—are drugs that depress the central nervous system. They act as sedatives to provide relief from pain, anxiety, and tension. Feelings of euphoria and well-being (and sometimes negative reactions such as nausea) often accompany narcotics use. However, opium and its derivatives (especially heroin) are physiologically addictive. Tolerance for narcotics builds rapidly, and withdrawal symptoms are severe. Opiates such as heroin are usually administered intravenously, fanning the spread of diseases such as AIDS, which can be transmitted through needle sharing (Smith & Landry, 1988).

Because of their strong psychological and physical dependency, narcotics addicts are usually unable to maintain normal relationships with family and friends or to pursue legitimate careers. They live to obtain the drug through any possible means. Nonmedical use of narcotics is illegal, and many addicts have little choice but to turn to criminal activities to obtain the drug and to support their expensive habits.

Barbiturates Synthetic **barbiturates,** or "downers," are powerful depressants of the central nervous system that are commonly used to induce relaxation and sleep. Next to the narcotics, they represent the largest category of illegal drugs, and they are quite dangerous for several reasons. First, psychological and physical dependence can develop. Second, although their legal use is severely restricted, the widespread availability of the drugs makes it difficult to control misuse or abuse. Over 1 million people are now estimated to be barbiturate addicts. Barbiturates are used mostly by middle-aged and older people.

Third, users often experience harmful physical effects. Excessive use of either barbiturates or heroin can be fatal, but the former are the more lethal. Constant heroin use increases the amount of the drug required for a lethal dosage. The lethal dosage of barbiturates *does not* increase with prolonged use, so accidental overdose and death can easily occur. And combining alcohol with barbiturates can be especially dangerous, because alcohol compounds the depressant effects of the barbiturates.

Kelly M., a seventeen-year-old girl from an upper-middle-class background, lived with her divorced mother. Kelly was hospitalized after her mother found her unconscious from an overdose of barbiturates consumed together with alcohol. She survived the overdose and later told the therapist that she had regularly used barbiturates for the past year and a half. The overdose was apparently accidental and not suicidal.

For several weeks following the overdose, Kelly openly discussed her use of barbiturates with the therapist. She had been introduced to the drugs by a boy in school who told her they would help her to relax. Kelly was apparently unhappy over her parents' divorce. She felt her mother did not want her, especially in view of the fact that her mother spent a lot of time away from home building a real estate agency. And, although she enjoyed her occasional visits with her father, Kelly felt extremely uncomfortable in the presence of the woman who lived with him. The barbiturates helped her to relax and relieve her tensions. Arguments with her mother would precipitate heavy use of the drugs. Eventually she became dependent on barbiturates and always spent her allowance to buy them. Her mother reported that she had no knowledge of her daughter's drug use. She did notice, though, that Kelly was increasingly isolated and sleepy.

The therapist informed Kelly of the dangers of barbiturates and of combining them with alcohol. Kelly agreed to undergo treatment, which included the gradual reduction of barbiturate use, and psychotherapy with her mother.

A hazardous practice illustrated in the case of Kelly M. is *polydrug use,* or the use of more than one chemical substance at the same time. This practice can be extremely dangerous. For example, heavy smokers who consume a great deal of alcohol run an increased risk of esophageal cancer. Chemicals may

Heroin is a highly addictive narcotic that is generally taken through hypodermic injection. It acts as a sedative that relieves pain, tension, and anxiety and produces feelings of euphoria and well-being. The dependency is so strong that addicts are often unable to maintain normal social relationships or a legitimate career.

also exhibit a synergistic effect, in which drugs that are taken simultaneously interact to multiply each other's effects. For example, when a large dose of a barbiturate is taken along with alcohol, death may occur because of a synergistic effect that depresses the central nervous system. Furthermore, one of the substances (such as alcohol) may reduce the person's judgment, resulting in excessive (or lethal) use of the other drug. Equally dangerous is the use of one drug to counteract the effect of another. For instance, a person who has taken a stimulant to feel euphoric may later take an excessive amount of a depressant (such as a barbiturate) in an attempt to get some sleep. The result can be an exceedingly harmful physiological reaction.

Benzodiazepines One member of this category of drugs is Valium, which is one of the most widely prescribed drugs in the United States today. As in the case of Miriam K. (described at the beginning of this section), Valium is often used to reduce anxiety and muscle tension. People who take the drug seem less concerned with, and less affected by, their problems. Some side effects may occur, such as drowsiness, skin rash, nausea, and depression, but the greatest danger in using Valium is its abuse. Because life stressors are unavoidable, many people use Valium as their sole means of dealing with stress; then, as tolerance develops, dependence on the drug may also grow.

Stimulants

A **stimulant** is a psychoactive substance that is a central nervous system energizer, inducing elation, grandiosity, hyperactivity, agitation, and appetite suppression.

Amphetamines   The **amphetamines,** also known as "uppers," speed up activity of the central nervous system and bestow on users increased alertness, energy, and sometimes feelings of euphoria and confidence. Amphetamines inhibit appetite and sleep. These stimulants may be physically addictive and become habit forming with a rapid increase in tolerance. "Speed freaks" are those who inject amphetamine into their blood vessels and become extremely hyperactive and euphoric for days. Assaultive, homicidal, and suicidal behaviors can occur during this period of time. Heavy doses can also trigger delusions of persecution, similar to those seen among paranoid schizophrenics. Overdoses are fatal, and brain damage has been observed among chronic abusers. Some people may use amphetamines to get "high" and then use barbiturates to "come down"—an extremely dangerous practice, as we have noted.

Caffeine and Nicotine   Two widely used and legal stimulants are caffeine and nicotine. *Caffeine* is ingested primarily in coffee, chocolate, tea, and cola drinks. It is considered intoxicating to a person when, after the recent ingestion of 250 milligrams (about two cups of coffee) or more of caffeine, the person shows several of the following symptoms: restlessness, nervousness, excitement, insomnia, flushed face, gastrointestinal disturbance, rambling speech, and cardiac arrhythmia. The consequences of caffeine intoxication are usually transitory and relatively minor. In some cases, however, the intoxication is chronic and seriously affects the gastrointestinal or circulatory system.

Nicotine dependence is most commonly associated with cigarette smoking and to a lesser extent, chewing tobacco. The following problems are often seen among those who are nicotine dependent:

- The person's attempts to stop or reduce tobacco use on a permanent basis are unsuccessful.

- Attempts to stop smoking have led to withdrawal symptoms such as tobacco craving, irritability, difficulty in concentrating, and restlessness.

- The person continues to use tobacco despite a serious physical disorder, such as emphysema, that he or she knows is exacerbated by tobacco use.

Focus 10.3 discusses two views on the development and maintenance of smoking behaviors.

Cocaine and Crack   A great deal of publicity and concern have been devoted to the use of **cocaine,** a substance extracted from the coca plant. A number of major-league baseball players, film stars, political figures, and other notables use this drug regularly. Indeed, its use is expanding, particularly among the young and the upwardly mobile. Because of its high cost and euphoria-inducing properties, cocaine is a fashionable drug, especially among middle-class and upper-class professionals.

In the late 1800s, cocaine was heralded as a wonder drug for remedying depression, indigestion, headaches, pain, and other ailments. It was often included in medicines, tonics, and wines; it was even used in cola drinks such as Coca-Cola. However, in the early 1900s, its use was controlled, and the possession of cocaine is now illegal.

Cocaine can be eaten, injected intravenously, or smoked, but it is usually "snorted" (inhaled). Eating does not produce rapid effects, and intravenous use requires injection with a needle, which leaves needle marks and introduces the possibility of infection. When cocaine is inhaled into the nasal cavity, however, the person quickly begins to feel euphoric, stimulated, and confident. Heart rate and blood pressure increase, and (according to users) fatigue and appetite are reduced.

Users may become physiologically and psychologically dependent on cocaine. That is, a user can develop an addiction and be unable to stop using it. Then the constant desire for cocaine can impair social and occupational functioning, and the high cost of the substance can cause users to resort to crime to feed their habit. In addition, side effects can occur. Feelings of depression and gloom may be produced when a cocaine high wears off. Heavy users sometimes report weight loss, paranoia, nervousness, fatigue, and hallucinations. The Committee on Drug Abuse of the Council on Psychiatric Services (1987) also notes that, because cocaine stimulates the sympathetic nervous system, premature ventricular heartbeats and death may occur.

Crack is one of the most talked-about drugs. It is a purified and potent form of cocaine produced by heating cocaine with ether ("freebasing"). Crack is sold as small, solid pieces or "rocks." When it is smoked in a pipe, euphoria is swift and marked, followed by depression. Johnston and his colleagues (1987) found that just over 3 percent of young adults reported using crack during a twelve-month period.

For four reasons, crack is of major concern to society. First, it is inexpensive and readily obtainable, so large segments of the population can have easy access to the substance. Second, the euphoria or high from crack is quite intense and immediate, compared to cocaine sniffing. Thus many people prefer crack. Third, users appear to develop relatively rapid addiction to crack, and they continually seek the substance. Fourth, because of the increasing popularity of the drug and the crimes associated with crack, law enforcement resources have been expended on trying to control its sale, distribution, and use.

Hallucinogens

Hallucinogens are not considered physiologically addictive. Use does not lead to physical dependence (that is, it does not lead to increased tolerance or withdrawal reaction), although psychological dependency may occur. Many people use hallucinogens such as marijuana, LSD, and phencyclidine (PCP) to experience certain illusions, such as more vivid sensory awareness, heightened alertness, or increased insight.

Marijuana The mildest and most commonly used hallucinogen is **marijuana,** also known as "pot" or "grass." This substance is generally smoked in a cigarette, or "joint." About 20 percent of the U.S.

Drug abuse on the job has become a national crisis. It affects worker productivity and safety. Cocaine abuse is particularly problematic. To combat the problem, many companies have initiated drug testing and treatment programs for their employees.

population (including youngsters) have used marijuana, although it is illegal. In a large-scale survey, Mills and Noyes (1984) found that marijuana use by school-age children had declined from 1978 to 1980, but it was still one of the most widely used substances, along with alcohol (see Table 10.4).

The subjective effects of marijuana use include feelings of euphoria, tranquility, and passivity. Once the drug has taken effect, subjective time passes slowly, and some users report increased sensory experiences as well as mild perceptual distortions. One's prior experience with the drug, one's expectancy of its effects, and the setting in which one uses marijuana influence the precise reactions.

FOCUS 10.3 Smoking: Can the Body "Kick the Habit"?

Cigarette smoking is harmful to the body. A U.S. Surgeon General's report has indicated cigarette smoking accounts for one-sixth of deaths in the United States and is the single most preventable cause of death. It also noted that smoking among adults has declined from 50 percent in 1965 to 29 percent in 1988. The decline is especially evident among adults with higher levels of education (Toufexis, 1989).

Many people assume that sufficient will power and motivation on the part of smokers, or legal and social sanctions from nonsmokers (such as prohibiting smoking in public facilities), can reduce or eliminate the smoking habit. Judging from current statistics, however, efforts to motivate smokers to quit, to prohibit smoking in certain areas, and to regulate advertising by the tobacco industry have not been very successful in achieving that goal. Why do smokers continue to smoke? The answer may lie in the physiological effects of smoking. Even though smokers report feeling more relaxed during smoking, cigarettes act as a stimulant. Heart rate, for instance, increases during smoking.

Stanley Schachter, a noted psychologist, argues that people smoke because they are physically addicted to nicotine. In a series of experiments, Schachter (1977) drew two conclusions: First, chronic smokers need their "normal" constant intake of nicotine. When heavy smokers are given low-nicotine cigarettes, they smoke more cigarettes and puff more frequently. Withdrawal symptoms, such as irritability and increased eating, appear when smokers do not receive their "dose" of nicotine. Second, smoking does not reduce anxiety or calm the nerves. But *not smoking* increases anxiety and produces withdrawal reactions. Smokers can tolerate less stress when they are deprived of cigarettes than when they are able to smoke. However, even with cigarettes, smokers do *not* perform better under stress than nonsmokers. Stress seems to deplete body nicotine, so that smoking is necessary to maintain the nicotine level.

If nicotine addiction maintains cigarette smoking, then supplying smokers with nicotine in a nontobacco product may reduce the need to smoke. Some researchers (Hall et al., 1987) have found that giving smokers a nicotine gum was more effective than giving a placebo gum in a stop-smoking program, even if the smokers were not told what substance was in the gum. However, Gottlieb and his colleagues (1987) found that when smokers were led to believe that they had received nicotine gum (whether or not they actually had received it) in a treatment program, they reported less withdrawal symptoms and cigarette consumption in a two-week period than those who were told that they had received no nicotine. Smokers' *belief* about presence of nicotine was more important in treatment than actual *ingestion* of nicotine. This study seems to negate the role of nicotine in treatment and, perhaps, in smoking. However,

TABLE 10.4 | **Percentages of Eighth-, Tenth-, and Twelfth-Grade Students Reporting the Use of Selected Substances**

| Grade | Year | Substance | | | | | | |
		Alcohol	Marijuana	Tranquilizers	Amphetamines	Cocaine	Hallucinogens	Heroin
8	1978	67.2	21.1	4.2	4.8	3.6	2.8	3.6
	1980		15.1	3.8	5.7	4.7	3.6	2.7
10	1978	81.6	42.3	7.7	8.3	9.2	7.6	3.1
	1980		32.4	7.9	10.2	8.1	7.6	3.3
12	1978	87.4	46.6	8.4	8.4	9.0	5.6	1.0
	1980		37.6	7.2	10.0	11.1	7.4	2.4

SOURCE: Mills and Noyes, 1984.

the study only followed the smokers for two weeks, so that the long-term effects of nicotine versus expectancy are unclear.

Without denying the role of nicotine in physical dependence, Lichtenstein (1982) sees the development and maintenance of smoking as a complex process involving a variety of factors. For example, such factors as the availability of cigarettes, curiosity, and smoking models influence the initial use of cigarettes. Then physiological and psychosocial factors such as nicotine addiction and positive consequences maintain smoking. For psychosocial reasons, including health and the expense of smoking materials, the person may try to stop smoking. However, withdrawal symptoms and alcohol consumption (former smokers who drink are often tempted to smoke while consuming alcohol) are powerful factors motivating the resumption of smoking.

Lichtenstein's analysis emphasizes the value of multicomponent programs for the treatment and prevention of smoking. His factors are listed in the following table.

Factors Involved in Smoking Behaviors

Starting (psychosocial factors)	Continuing (physiological and psychosocial factors)	Stopping (psychosocial factors)	Resuming (psychosocial and physiological factors)
Availability	Nicotine	Health	Withdrawal symptoms
Curiosity	Immediate positive consequences	Expense	Stress and frustration
Rebelliousness		Social support	Social pressure
Anticipation of adulthood	Signals (cues) in environs	Self-mastery	Alcohol consumption
Social confidence	Avoiding negative effects (withdrawal)	Aesthetics	Abstinence violation effect
Social pressure/ modeling: peers, siblings, parents, media		Example to others	

SOURCE: Lichtenstein, 1982.

In one experiment, marijuana smokers were given either a marijuana or a placebo cigarette to smoke. Some subjects were told to overcome the drug's effects in performing tasks; others were not told to do so. The researchers wanted to find out whether subjects could control their performance even after marijuana intoxication—that is, whether they could "come down" from a "high" at will. Their results indicated that marijuana intoxication influences the person's ability to estimate time and to remember lists of words. Moreover, motivating subjects to overcome the effects of marijuana improved the subjects' performance at estimating time, but not their ability to remember lists of words (Cappell & Pliner, 1973).

Although much controversy has raged over the effects of marijuana, many states have now decriminalized the possession of small quantities of this substance. Focus 10.4 is a brief report on some of the risks of marijuana smoking.

Lysergic Acid Diethylamide (LSD) LSD or "acid" gained notoriety as a hallucinogen in the mid-1960s. Praised by users as a potent psychedelic, consciousness-expanding drug, LSD produces hallucinations and distorts reality. "Good trips" are experiences of sharpened visual and auditory perception, heightened sensation, convictions that one has achieved profound philosophical insights, and feelings of ecstasy. "Bad trips" include fear and panic from distortions of

FOCUS 10.4   *Marijuana Smoking: Are There Harmful Effects?*

There is growing concern over the potentially harmful physical effects of marijuana (Coates, 1980). Smoking marijuana may cause more serious lung damage than smoking cigarettes. Indeed, smoking four joints a week may be as bad as smoking sixteen cigarettes a day. There is also some evidence that marijuana smoking may temporarily affect the reproductive systems of males and females: heavy marijuana use reduced sperm concentration and sperm motility in males and was associated with failure to ovulate in females. Because these findings are correlational in nature, it cannot be concluded that marijuana smoking *causes* problems in the reproductive system. The results do suggest, however, that much more caution should be exercised in the use of marijuana, in view of the possible consequences.

Fears about marijuana have gone through various fluctuations. In the past (say, the 1920s) the physiological effects of marijuana smoking were greatly exaggerated. More recently (1970s) it was believed that these effects were insignificant. Now researchers are reexamining the latter belief.

The National Academy of Sciences (1982) has taken a dim view of marijuana use. Marijuana smoke can cause serious lung and respiratory problems and can increase the risk of cancer. Furthermore, because the drug affects short-term memory and causes intoxication, people who have recently smoked marijuana may pose a danger while driving a car, operating machinery, or working in occupations that require judgment and decision making (such as air traffic control). Other potential problems include confusion,

flashbacks, and psychotic-like reactions (Committee on Drug Abuse of the Council on Psychiatric Services, 1987).

Coates (1980), however, points out the benefits of marijuana in treating certain physical ailments. For example, open-angle glaucoma, an eye disorder that can lead to blindness, temporarily responds to the drug; patients nauseated by chemotherapy for cancer often find relief with marijuana treatment. Researchers are now experimenting with the use of marijuana for victims of multiple sclerosis and for people afflicted by seizures.

Such findings—and there seem to be new ones almost every week— show how little we know about marijuana and how much we still have to learn.

---

sensory experiences, severe depression, marked confusion and disorientation, and delusions. Some users report "flashbacks" or the recurrence of hallucinations or other sensations days or weeks after taking LSD. Fatigue, stress, or the use of another drug may trigger a flashback.

LSD is considered a *psychotomimetic* drug because, in some cases, it produces reactions that mimic those seen in acute psychotic reactions. It does not produce physical dependence, even in users who have taken the drug hundreds of times. Aside from its psychological effects, no substantial evidence supports the notion that LSD is dangerous in and of itself. Large doses do not cause death, although there are reports of people who have unwittingly committed suicide while under the influence of LSD. Initially researchers believed that LSD caused chromosomal damage and spontaneous abortions, but such events

are probably attributable to impurities in the drug, the use of other drugs, or the unhealthy lifestyles of many users.

Phencyclidine (PCP)   Phencyclidine, also known as PCP, "angel dust," "crystal," "superweed," and "rocket fuel," has emerged as one of the most dangerous of the so-called street drugs. Originally developed for its pain-killing properties, PCP is a hallucinatory drug that causes perceptual distortions, euphoria, nausea, confusion, delusions, and violent psychotic behavior. Reactions to the drug are influenced by dosage, the individual user, and the circumstances in which it is taken. One thing is clear: PCP has in many cases caused aggressive behaviors, violence, or deaths due to the taker's recklessness or delusions of invincibility. The drug is illegal, but it is still widely used, often sprinkled on marijuana and smoked.

Spitzer and co-workers (1981, pp. 229–230) described the effects of PCP on a chronic user. As you will see, one long-term effect may have been a personality change.

The patient is a 20-year-old male who was brought to the hospital, trussed in ropes, by his four brothers. This is his seventh hospitalization in the last two years, each for similar behavior. One of his brothers reports that he "came home crazy" late one night, threw a chair through a window, tore a gas heater off the wall, and ran into the street. The family called the police, who apprehended him shortly thereafter as he stood, naked, directing traffic at a busy intersection. He assaulted the arresting officers, escaped from them, and ran home screaming threats at his family. There his brothers were able to subdue him.

On admission the patient was observed to be agitated, his mood fluctuating between anger and fear. He had slurred speech and staggered when he walked. He remained extremely violent and disorganized for the first several days of his hospitalization, then began having longer and longer lucid intervals, still interspersed with sudden, unpredictable periods in which he displayed great suspiciousness, a fierce expression, slurred speech, and clenched fists.

After calming down, the patient denied ever having been violent or acting in an unusual way ("I'm a peaceable man") and said he could not remember how he got to the hospital. He admitted to using alcohol and marijuana socially, but denied phencyclidine (PCP) use except for once, experimentally, three years previously. Nevertheless, blood and urine tests were positive for phencyclidine, and his brother believes "he gets dusted every day."

According to his family, he was perfectly normal until about three years before. He made above-average grades in school, had a part-time job and a girlfriend, and was of a sunny and outgoing disposition. Then, at age 17, he had his first episode of emotional disturbance. This was of very sudden onset, with symptoms similar to the present episode. He quickly recovered entirely from that first episode, went back to school, and graduated from high school. From subsequent episodes, however, his improvement was less and less encouraging.

After three weeks of the current hospitalization, he is sullen and watchful, quick to remark sarcastically on the smallest infringement of the respect due him. He is mostly quiet and isolated from others, but is easily provoked to fury. His family reports that "This is as good as he gets now." He lives and eats most of his meals at home, and keeps himself physically clean, but mostly lies around the house, will do no housework, and has not held a job for nearly two years. The family does not know how he gets his spending money, or how he spends his time outside the hospital.

Etiology of Drug Use Disorders

Why do people overuse drugs? The answer to this question is complicated by the number of different kinds of drugs that are used and the number of factors that interact to account for the use of any one drug. An explanation of drug abuse must take into account several general observations. First, in the 1960s and 1970s, some researchers had hoped that they could identify a cluster of personality traits that could account for addiction to substances. However, simple attempts to find a common pattern of personality traits that underlie addiction have failed (Platt, 1986). It is highly unlikely that addiction is caused by a single personality type.

Second, physical addiction and the attempt to avoid withdrawal symptoms aren't enough to explain continued narcotics use. Withdrawal reactions have been characterized as being no more agonizing than a bad case of the flu (Ausubel, 1961). We know that heroin addicts who enter the hospital and who don't get any heroin while hospitalized stop having withdrawal symptoms in a week or two. Yet the vast majority who have lost their bodily need for the drug usually return to heroin after hospitalization. Can situational factors explain why they resume heroin use after physical dependence is overcome? Many Vietnam servicemen who were addicted to heroin when they returned to the United States *did* discontinue its use on their return because of such situational factors as the easier access to alcohol and the difficulty of procuring heroin (Pilisuk, 1975).

Third, the conditions that cause a person to try a drug have not been identified (Solomon, 1977). The best predictor of drug sampling is drug availability, but drug use is too widespread and drug addiction too rare for the mere sampling of a drug to be a major cause of subsequent addiction. Solomon suggests that the initial reasons for using drugs are complex, varied, and obscure. Most drug usage is probably reinforcing at the outset—an attempt to solve some social problem, to respond to peer group influences, to relieve unpleasant emotional states, or to become "high." Then, after continued use, the motivation for drug use changes. The user now must cope with drug craving, a fear of withdrawal, and other *acquired* motivations. The addict's desire to maintain social relationships and a certain lifestyle may also be a motivating factor.

In other words, Solomon believes that attempts to find a simple, single-cause explanation for drug addiction are fruitless; addiction is an acquired motivation, much like other acquired motivations such as love or attachment. To explain the process, Solomon (1980) has proposed the *opponent process theory of acquired motivation*, which is summarized in Table 10.5. Consider first the person who has used a drug only a few times. Before taking the drug again, that person, who is not yet addicted, is in a resting state. Then, while ingesting the drug the person experiences a peak state (the rush) and euphoria; in other words, the psychopharmacological properties of the drug make the user feel "high." After the effects subside, there may be mild discomfort ("coming down" from the drug). The person may start to crave the drug in order to combat the discomfort, but the discomfort soon subsides and the person returns to a resting state. The motivation for use is to achieve the high and to avoid the aversiveness of the craving.

For the chronic user, however, the process is somewhat different. During the period before the drug is consumed, this person experiences a craving for the drug. Then, during ingestion of the drug, the experienced user feels only contentment rather than a rush and intense euphoria. And once the effects of

the drug wear off, he or she experiences withdrawal reactions and intense physiological and/or psychological craving, which do not subside until he or she again use the drug. In essence, the motivation for drug use has changed with experience, from positive to aversive control. A new motivation for drug use has been acquired.

Most researchers now agree with Solomon that many factors are involved in substance use. Trying to explain use by posing simple questions (for example, can drug use be explained by personality traits, is addiction a disease or a learned behavior, or is heredity more important than environment?) isn't productive (Sutker & Allain, 1988). Addiction seems to be the product of many interacting factors, and researchers are seeking to understand the various factors that contribute to this interaction.

Treatment for Drug Use Disorders

During the 1970s, a great deal of effort was directed toward the treatment of drug use disorders. An extensive range of therapeutic approaches was studied, including psychoanalytic, behavioral, family, and educational therapy and the residential or therapeutic community approach, in which a number of addicts live together in a drug-free environment and work together to change their attitudes and lifestyles. Treatment concentrated primarily on users of heroin, LSD, and marijuana. Disappointing results with educational "scare tactics" programs and the difficulties involved in measuring progress in the psychoanalytic approach have largely removed these two strategies

---

TABLE 10.5 | **Changes in Affect Before, During, and After Self-Dosing with Opiates (for the First Few Experiences and After Many Experiences)**

| | Affect | |
Period	First Few Experiences	After Many Experiences
Before use	Resting state	Craving
During use	Rush, euphoria	Contentment
After use	Craving; then resting state	Abstinence—agony craving

SOURCE: Solomon, 1980.

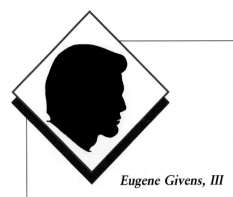

Eugene Givens, III

FIRST PERSON

For nearly ten years, I've served as the clinical director of a residential drug-free treatment program for men and women who have chronically abused or been dependent on opiates (primarily heroin) and other drugs, including alcohol.

As both the treatment program and I matured, we began to focus on the family's contribution to individual dysfunction and on the value of support groups, such as Alcoholics Anonymous, Narcotics Anonymous, Adult Children of Alcoholics and Other Dysfunctions, Overeaters Anonymous, and other groups that focused on mental illness as well as sex and love addiction. We also had to deal with AIDS. It quickly became clear to me that drug and alcohol treatment was no longer our only concern. The early 1980s began to reveal a much more prevalent range of mental health problems than we had ever seen before.

One episode in particular demonstrated the impact that dually-diagnosed residents had on our treatment program. Joan was a slight young woman. Although withdrawn and very quiet in public, in her room she was given to loud outbursts, which could be heard throughout the building. During these outbursts, she was responding to auditory hallucinations. She heard the voices of imaginary people who lived on another planet. The principal characters represented significant people in her life with whom she had extreme conflict.

One afternoon, screams came shrilling from her room. They were so alarming that both staff and residents ran to her room and pushed through the door, only to find her sitting quietly on the edge of her bed knitting an afghan. For nearly four nights following that incident, the male residents couldn't sleep out of fear that Joan would attack them in their sleep. And many of these men had committed capital crimes, including armed assault, manslaughter, and first-degree murder!

It took me a while to understand the source of their fear and prejudice. I began to realize that these men harbored many of the same feelings about mental illness as does the population at large. So, fearing for Joan's safety, I transferred her to another program where I felt she would have a better chance to have both her substance abuse and mental health problems attended to effectively.

The most difficult situation that I have to face as a clinical administrator, a clinician, and as a human being, however, is how to encourage and persuade someone in long-term treatment that treatment and life itself are worth continuing despite test results that reveal the presence of the antibody to the HIV virus (AIDS). I know that drug dependence can be arrested (not "cured") in spite of the fact that our residents, whose average age is thirty, have usually been drug dependent since age fifteen. But helping someone who's just been handed a death sentence fight both drug dependence and AIDS at the same time is a more complicated matter.

Watching men and women such as these scour the obituaries of their hometown newspapers in search of the names of former sexual or needle-sharing partners serves as a chilling reminder of how fragile life really is. It's especially painful since I've come to admire and respect them for engaging in the most valiant struggle I can imagine—the preservation of that life.

Dr. Eugene Givens, III, is the clinical director of the Narcotics Addiction Clinic at Boston City Hospital.

from general use in the 1980s (Braucht et al., 1973; Bratter, 1973). And, although heroin remains the most popular drug to study for treatment purposes, LSD and marijuana have been replaced by cocaine and nicotine. (The First Person narrative in this chapter discussed some of the problems one clinician has encountered as director of a residential drug-free treatment program.)

But how does one even begin to treat a drug user? The answer largely depends on both the individual user and the type of drug being used. The typical treatment program consists of two phases:

(1) immediate removal of the abusive substance and (2) long-term maintenance without it. The immediate removal of the drug usually triggers withdrawal symptoms that are *opposite* in effect to the reactions produced by the drug. For instance, if a person is physically addicted to a CNS depressant such as a barbiturate, he or she experiences drowsiness, decreased respiration, and reduced anxiety on taking the drug. When the depressant is withdrawn, the user experiences symptoms that resemble the effects of a stimulant—agitation, restlessness, increased respiration, and insomnia. Helping someone successfully cope during withdrawal has been a concern of many treatment strategies dealing with various drugs, particularly in treating heroin addicts.

Methadone Treatment for Heroin Addiction

During heroin detoxification (withdrawal), the drug *methadone* is prescribed to decrease the intensity of the withdrawal symptoms. Methadone is a synthetic narcotic chemical that eliminates the craving for heroin without producing euphoria (the "high"). It was originally felt that reformed heroin addicts could then quite easily discontinue the methadone at a later date. Methadone initially seemed to be a simple solution to a major problem, but it has an important drawback: it can itself become addicting. The following case illustrates this problem, as well as other facets of the typical two-phase heroin addiction treatment program.

After several months of denying the seriousness of his heroin habit, Gary B. finally enrolled in a residential treatment program that featured methadone maintenance, peer support, confrontational therapy, and job retraining. At first Gary responded well to the residential program. However, he soon began to feel depressed. He was reassured by the staff that recovering heroin addicts frequently experience depression and that several treatment options existed. A fairly low dose of tricyclic antidepressant medication was prescribed, and Gary also began supportive-expressive (psychodynamic) therapy.

Psychotherapy helped Gary identify the difficult relationships in his life. His dependence on these relationships and his dependence on drugs were examined for parallels. His tendency to deny problems, and to turn to drugs as an escape, was pointed out. The therapy then focused on the generation of suitable alternatives to drugs. He worked

hard during his therapy sessions and made commendable progress.

For the next three months Gary enjoyed his life in a way that previously had been foreign to him. He was hired by a small restaurant to train as a cook. He was entirely satisfied with the direction in which his life had turned, until the day he realized that he was eagerly looking forward to his daily methadone dose. Gary knew of people who had become addicted to methadone, but it was still a shock when it happened to him. He decided almost immediately to terminate his methadone maintenance program. The withdrawal process was physically and mentally painful, and Gary often doubted his ability to function without methadone. But by joining a support group composed of others who were trying to discontinue methadone, he was eventually able to complete methadone withdrawal. Gary had never imagined that the most difficult part of his heroin treatment would be giving up methadone.

Other Drug Use Disorders

Treatment for the use of most other substances follows a very different course from that for the heroin addict, and it seems to be constantly undergoing modification. One technique—used more in the past than now—is covert sensitization, which, as we noted, is often used with alcoholics. One difficulty with this technique is the inability of some patients to generalize the treatment—that is, to pair the learned aversive reaction (nausea and vomiting) with the stimulus (taking a particular drug) once they are outside the clinic or hospital.

Other cognitive-behavioral treatments, based on analyses of why addicts experience relapse, have also been tried. Niaura and his colleagues (1988) believe that certain cues are strongly associated with substance use (smoking while having coffee, drinking alcohol at a party, and so forth). They suggest that addicts be placed in these situations or in the presence of the cues and *prevented* from using the substance. In this way, the consumption response to these cues is extinguished. In order to prevent relapse, some treatment programs help addicts to restructure their thoughts about the pleasant effects of drug use (Cooper et al., 1988). Addicts are taught to substitute negative thoughts for positive ones when tempted to drink. For example, instead of focusing on the euphoria felt from taking cocaine, a person might be taught to say, "I feel an urge to take the substance, but I know that I will feel depressed later on, many of my friends want me to stop taking it, and I may get arrested."

Nowadays most treatment programs are multimodal in nature. For example, in a typical program an amphetamine abuser may initially be admitted to an inpatient facility for approximately thirty days. There he or she receives individual and group therapy, takes part in occupational and recreational therapy, stress management counseling, and perhaps is introduced to a support group modeled after Alcoholics Anonymous. The patient's spouse may also be asked to participate in the group sessions.

Once the patient has successfully completed this inpatient phase, he or she is scheduled for outpatient treatment. As part of this treatment, the patient is asked to agree to unannounced urine screenings to test for the presence of drugs. The patient is encouraged to continue attending the support group, along with his or her spouse, and to become involved in individual outpatient therapy. Family therapy is the treatment of choice for adolescent substance users at this point (Reilly, 1984; Rueger & Liberman, 1984; Haley, 1980), and it is highly recommended for adults. The outpatient program typically continues for about two years.

Cigarette Smoking Behavioral techniques have been used almost exclusively by people who wish to end their addiction to cigarette smoking. Most aversive procedures (such as covert sensitization and shock) have yielded rather disappointing results, but "rapid smoking" appears promising. This technique requires that the client puff a cigarette once every six seconds, until he or she absolutely cannot continue any longer. Its purpose is to pair a highly aversive situation (the feeling of illness that results from extremely rapid smoking) with the act of smoking. This is expected to eliminate or reduce the person's desire to smoke. Although the method has been reasonably effective over both the short and the long term, it is somewhat controversial: the rapid smoking introduces such health hazards as increased heart rate and blood pressure (Lichtenstein & Rodrigues, 1977; Lichtenstein & Glasgow, 1977). It can also aggravate existing cardiovascular problems.

Another noteworthy treatment for cigarette smoking is *nicotine fading* (Foxx & Brown, 1979). In this method, the client attempts to gradually

In spite of strong evidence linking smoking to cancer, lung disease, and heart disease, millions of people continue to smoke. Nicotine addiction is especially difficult to overcome because it has both physiological and psychological components. Many smokers are also drinkers and find it hard to give up one habit without giving up the other.

withdraw from nicotine by progressively changing to cigarette brands that contain less and less nicotine. When clients reach the stage where they are smoking cigarettes that contain only 0.1 milligram of nicotine, their reduced dependence should enable them to stop altogether (Lichtenstein & Danaher, 1976).

SUMMARY

1. Psychoactive substance abuse and dependence are widespread problems that can result in wasted lives, personal misery, crime, the inability to function socially or occupationally, and danger to the substance user and to others. Substance abuse is a pathological pattern of excessive use in which the person is unable to reduce or cease intake, despite knowledge that its use causes social, occupational, psychological, medical, or safety problems. Substance dependence involves not only psychological but also

physical dependence in which tolerance and/or withdrawal symptoms occur.

2. Alcoholism is a major social problem in the United States. The consumption of alcohol results in both long-term and short-term psychological and physiological effects. Chronic consumption can cause a number of organic mental disorders. Some research suggests that heredity may be important, along with environmental factors. Recent experiments indicate the importance of cognitive factors in drinking behavior. The tension reduction hypothesis alone is inadequate to account for alcoholism, because alcohol consumption sometimes results in *increased* feelings of depression or anxiety. Rather, drinking and alcoholism may be closely related to the type of stress anticipated, the perceived benefits of alcohol, the availability of alternative coping responses in a particular situation, and the drinker's genetic or physiological makeup. A variety of treatment approaches have been used, including detoxification, drug therapies, psychotherapy, and behavior modification. Multimodal approaches (the use of several treatment techniques) are probably the most effective. Many alcoholics are helped by treatment, and some achieve abstinence by themselves.

3. Using drugs—depressants, stimulants, and hallucinogens—can result in psychological or physiological problems. There is no single explanation for drug abuse or dependence. In the case of narcotics, both physical and psychological factors are important. According to one theory, drug usage is reinforcing at first because it reduces tension, allows conformity to peer group pressures, and produces feelings of euphoria. After continued use, the person's motivation for using the drug changes: Now the desire to avoid withdrawal symptoms or to maintain social relationships and a particular lifestyle may motivate drug use. The treatment prescribed for drug users depends on the type of drug and on the user. Heroin addicts usually undergo detoxification followed by methadone maintenance and such forms of treatment as residential treatment programs, psychotherapy, cognitive or behavior therapy, and group therapy. Detoxification and occupational, recreational, and family therapies may be suggested for users of other drugs. For addiction to cigarette smoking, aversive procedures, including "rapid smoking" and nicotine fading (the use of brands containing less and less nicotine), have been successful.

KEY TERMS

alcoholics People who abuse and depend on alcohol

alcoholism Substance abuse and dependence in which the substance that is used is alcohol

amphetamines Drugs that speed up central nervous system activity and produce increased alertness, energy, and euphoria, also called "uppers"

aversion therapy A conditioning procedure in which the response to a stimulus is decreased by pairing the stimulus with an aversive stimulus

barbiturate A substance that is a powerful depressant of the central nervous system, capable of inducing psychological and physical dependency

cocaine A drug that induces feelings of euphoria and self-confidence in users; usually inhaled into the nasal cavity

covert sensitization An aversive conditioning technique in which the individual imagines a noxious stimulus in the presence of a behavior

delirium Inability to maintain attention, disorganized thinking, confusion, and disorientation caused by, or presumed to be caused by, an organic factor

detoxification A treatment aimed at removing all alcohol (or other substance) from a user's body and ensuring that none is ingested

hallucinogen A substance that produces hallucinations, vivid sensory awareness, or increased insight

marijuana The mildest and most commonly used hallucinogen; pot

narcotic Opium and its derivatives, which depress the central nervous system, provide relief from pain and anxiety, and are addictive

psychoactive substance use disorder Maladaptive behavior associated with the pathological use of a substance over a period of at least one month

stimulant A psychoactive substance that is a central nervous system energizer, inducing elation, grandiosity, hyperactivity, agitation, and appetite suppression

substance abuse A pathological pattern of excessive use of a substance, in which the person cannot reduce or cease intake despite physical harm or impaired social and occupational functioning

substance dependence A pathological pattern of inability to cut down or control use of a substance, despite knowledge of harmful effects; much time spent in obtaining the substance; frequent intoxication; tolerance and/or withdrawal symptoms

tolerance A condition in which the body requires increasing doses of a substance in order to achieve the desired effect, or a markedly diminished effect is experienced with regular use of the same dose

withdrawal symptoms Physical or emotional symptoms such as shaking or irritability that appear when the intake of a regularly used substance is reduced or halted

chapter 11
Sexual Disorders and Dysfunctions

The following brief cases illustrate the four major groups of sexual disorders described in DSM-III-R: gender identity disorders, paraphilias, sexual dysfunctions, and sexual disorders not otherwise specified.

As a child [although born a male], Murray/Mary had dressed like a girl, played like a girl, and fantasized about "really" being a girl. . . . Her childhood playmates were girls, and she had no interest in boys' games like "ball or bat or dumb marbles." She always went to the ladies' restroom and never learned to urinate while standing. . . . She regrets that, despite sex-reassignment surgery, she will be unable to bear a child by the man she loves. (Sabalis et al., 1974, p. 907)

Mr. A, a 47-year-old man, complained of being unable to obtain sexual satisfaction unless he hurt his wife. His preoccupation with sadistic fantasies made it difficult for him to concentrate, even at work. . . . Every few weeks his cravings would build up to a point where he could not control them. During 25 years of marriage, he had frequently handcuffed his wife, shaved her head, stuck pins in her back and struck her. . . . Ejaculation could not be achieved unless he hurt her. (Berlin & Meinecke, 1981, p. 605)

I haven't had an orgasm during my marriage (twenty-seven years) or with the two other men with whom I had sex besides my husband. I remember an experience when I was fourteen or fifteen . . . I believe I had a mild orgasm. . . . That's the closest I've come to it. I have masturbated occasionally, but nothing happens. I have no idea what would cause me to respond. (Hite, 1976, p. 207)

An unemployed 39-year-old single white male sought treatment to decrease homosexual behavior and to increase heterosexual arousal. . . . Since the age of 12, his masturbatory images had been exclusively homosexual. . . . He claimed his homosexual contacts were not emotionally satisfying, and condemned himself for having "hundreds of partners." He had very strong religious beliefs that homosexuality was wrong. He was steadfast in his desire to decrease homosexual behavior and to develop conventional relationships with women, although he had received extensive therapy over several years aimed primarily at greater "acceptance of himself." (Hayes et al., 1983, p. 385)

As illustrated in the cases above, sexual disorders encompass a wide range of behaviors. In this chapter the disorders will be presented in the following order and include:

♦ The *gender-identity disorders* involve an incongruity or conflict between one's anatomical sex and gender identity (one's psychological feeling of being male or female). Included in this class is the transsexualism illustrated by Murray/Mary.

♦ The *paraphilias* involve sexual urges and fantasies about situations, objects, or people that are not part of the usual arousal pattern that leads to reciprocal and affectionate sexual activity. Included in this category is the sexual sadism Mr. A. shows.

♦ The *sexual dysfunctions* involve problems of inhibited sexual desire, arousal, and response, such as the inhibited orgasm disorder of the married woman in the third description.

♦ The category of *sexual disorder not otherwise specified* includes (1) people who find their sexual orientation to be an "unwanted and persistent source of distress," such as the 39-year-old male just described are classified under this category; (2) people who feel very inadequate about their sexual performance or body shape; (3) people with an unwanted pattern of sexual addiction.

Of all the psychological or psychiatric disorders discussed in this text, sexual disorders present us with the greatest difficulty in distinguishing between "abnormal" (maladaptive) behavior and variances that

are not harmful but reflect personal values and tastes that depart significantly from social norms. The definition of sexual disorders is influenced by both moral and legal judgments. For example, the laws of some states define oral-genital sex as a "crime against nature." This view is reflected in a California statute that was repealed as late as 1976:

> Oral Sex Perversion—Any person participating in an act of copulating the mouth of one person with the sexual organ of another is punishable by incarceration in the state prison for a period not exceeding 15 years, or by imprisonment in the county jail not to exceed one year.

Using a statistical model of normality, it would be difficult to justify the classification of oral sex as a "perversion." The pioneering work of Kinsey and his colleagues revealed that oral sex is widespread, especially among the more highly educated part of the population (Kinsey et al., 1953). Surveys (McBride & Ender, 1977; Young, 1980) have found that most college men and women have engaged in this type of behavior.

Legal decisions on sexuality sometimes reflect past moods and morals or questionable and idiosyncratic views. In 1943, the Minnesota Supreme Court, in the case of *Dittrick v. Brown County,* upheld the conviction of a father of six as a sexual psychopath because he had an "uncontrollable craving for sexual intercourse with his wife." This "craving" amounted to three or four times a week (Kinsey et al., 1953). Conversely, today some researchers currently feel that not having sex often enough indicates a sexual desire disorder.

Ambiguities surround the legal and moral definitions of sexual disorders. Because the behaviors covered in this chapter are so heterogeneous, any classification system will have its share of problems and conflicts. There would be no objection to our considering rape as deviant behavior; it includes the elements of nonconsent, force, and victimization. But sexual arousal to an inanimate object (fetishism), low sexual drive, or sexual identity are not threats to society. Moreover, these problems may not cause distress to people who experience them, and may not result in impaired social or occupational functioning. They are deviant simply because they do not fall within "normal arousal and activity patterns." And they are considered deviant even though what constitutes a normal sexual pattern is a subject of controversy.

Such controversies will become more obvious as we discuss the four groups of sexual disorders in the remainder of this chapter.

GENDER IDENTITY DISORDERS

The **gender identity disorders** (shown in the disorders chart on page 292) are characterized by conflict between the person's anatomical sex and his or her gender identity, or self-identification as male or female. These disorders are relatively rare, and they may appear in adults (as transsexualism and gender identity disorder of adolescence or adulthood, non-

transsexualism type) or in children (as gender identity disorder of childhood).

Transsexualism

In **transsexualism,** the person identifies with the opposite sex. The person's own gender identity thus conflicts with his or her biological sex. The transsexual holds a lifelong conviction that nature has put together a cruel hoax by placing that person in a body of the wrong sex. This feeling produces the person's preoccupation with eliminating the "natural" physical and behavioral sexual characteristics and acquiring those of the opposite sex.

Transsexuals tend to exhibit sex role conflicts at a young age. Early on boys display interests and

One of the treatments advocated for transsexuals is sex reassignment through surgery. Dr. Richard Raskin, a successful ophthalmologist and top-ranked tennis player (left) became Dr. Renee Richards (right).

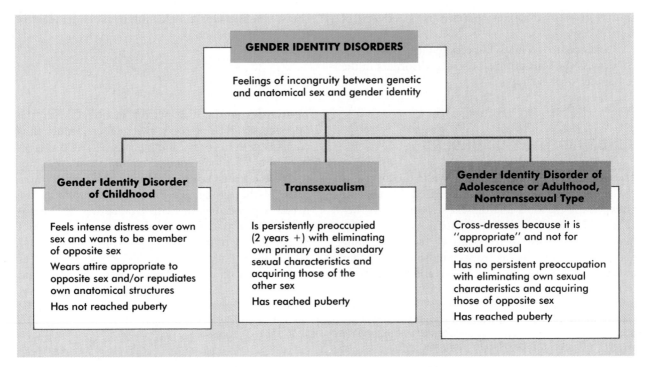

SOURCE: Adapted from DSM-III-R, pp. 71–78.

characteristics that are considered feminine, and they are frequently labeled "sissies" by their male peers. They prefer playing with girls and generally avoid the rough-and-tumble activities in which boys are traditionally encouraged to participate (Sabalis et al., 1974). Female transsexuals report being labeled "tomboys" during their childhood.

Transsexuals may report a variety of sexual interests. Those who are attracted to members of the same sex do not consider themselves to be homosexuals since they feel that they are actually members of the opposite sex.

Transsexualism is more common in males than in females. According to various estimates, there may be as many as 30,000 transsexuals worldwide (Lothstein, 1982).

Childhood Gender Identity Disorder

The **gender identity disorder of childhood** has many of the same characteristics as transsexualism. However, only a small percentage of children with the disorder become transsexuals. This disorder is indicated by the child's strong and persistent desire to be a member of the opposite sex or claims to be a member of the opposite sex. For girls, the gender identity disorder may involve the insistent claim of having a penis and an avid interest in rough-and-tumble play. A boy with this disorder may claim that he will grow up to be a woman, may demonstrate disgust with his penis, and may be exclusively preoccupied with activities considered "feminine." The disorder is much more common in boys than in girls (DSM-III-R).

Boys diagnosed as having gender identity disturbances are more likely than normal boys to play with "feminine" toys. They do not differ from girls in this respect (Rekers & Yates, 1976; Bates et al., 1979). Boys with gender disorders exhibit general personality problems, in addition to their adoption of opposite gender attitudes and behaviors (Bates et al., 1979).

Because most transsexuals report a behavioral pattern (see Table 11.1 for behaviors displayed by boys with opposite sex preferences) similar to that reported by gender disordered boys, the assumption

TABLE 11.1 | **Frequency of Symptoms in 55 Boys with Opposite-Sex Preferences (elicited as part of a structured interview)**

Symptom	Number of Boys			
	Present	Absent	Uncertain	No Data
Feminine dressing	50	2	2	1
Aversion to boys' games	50	1	3	1
Desire to be female	43	6	2	4
Girl playmate preference	42	5	3	5
Doll playing	41	5	4	5
Feminine gestures	40	5	5	5
Wearing lipstick	34	12	3	6

SOURCE: Zuger, 1984.

was that these two disorders were related—that is, having a gender disorder in childhood would lead to the development of transsexualism. This was not found. In a long-term follow up of 55 boys with opposite sex behaviors, nearly two-thirds developed a homosexual pattern. Only one was identified as a transsexual (Zuger, 1984). Early cross-sex behavior appears to be related more to homosexuality than to transsexualism.

Gender Identity Disorder of Adolescence or Adulthood, Nontranssexual Type (GIDAANT)

A new category in DSM-III-R is *gender identity disorder of adolescence or adulthood, nontranssexual type (GIDAANT)*; the criteria for this diagnosis are similar to those for transsexualism. Gender identity conflicts and cross-dressing are present. However, the desire to actually acquire the sexual characteristics of the opposite sex and the desire to eliminate one's primary and secondary sexual characteristics do not exist or are relatively mild.

Little research has been done on this diagnostic category.

Etiology of Gender Identity Disorders

The etiology of the gender identity disorders is unclear, although an interaction between social-psychological and biological variables is probably involved.

Social-Psychological Factors Some researchers have hypothesized that childhood experiences have an influence on the development of gender identity disorders (Bernstein et al., 1981). Factors thought to contribute to these disorders in boys include parental encouragement of feminine behavior and dependency, excessive attention and overprotection by the mother, the absence of an older male as a model, a relatively powerless or absent father figure, a lack of exposure to male playmates, and being encouraged to cross-dress (Rekers & Varni, 1977a; Stoller, 1969). A childhood background that results in other-sex behavior often leads to ostracism and rejection by one's peers; in that case, the only course available to the boy is complete adoption of the already familiar feminine role. However, not all males with gender identity disorders describe their fathers as weak or passive, nor do they all have excessively attentive mothers (Ehrhardt et al., 1979; Sabalis et al., 1977).

Biological Factors Are sexual orientation and sex-typed behaviors substantially determined by neurohormonal factors? Reviewing the research in this area, Ellis and Ames (1987) found some support for this view. For example, female-like sex behaviors are displayed by male rats who were castrated perinatally. In this situation, testosterone is reduced and is unable to effect appropriate neural organization. In human females, early exposure to male hormones has resulted in a more masculine behavior pattern. Thus, it does appear that sex orientation can be influenced by the lack or excess of sex hormones, which seem to affect the brain centers that govern sexual orientation. Not all studies support the biological perspective, however. In one study, children adopted the gender identity of their upbringing, even though it was opposite to their genetic and constitutional makeup (Money et al., 1957). The researchers concluded that gender identity is malleable. Since these children had normal hormone levels, their ability to adopt an opposite sex orientation raises doubt that biology alone determines male-female behaviors. Neurohormonal factors are important but their degree of influence on sexual orientation in humans may be minor (Hurtig & Rosenthal, 1987).

Treatment of Gender Identity Disorders

Most treatment programs for children identified as having a gender identity disorder include separate components for the child and for his or her parents. For the child, treatment begins with sex education. The favorable aspects of the child's physical gender are highlighted, and his or her reasons for avidly pursuing opposite-sex activities are discussed. An attempt is made to correct stereotypes regarding certain roles that are "accepted" for one gender and not for the other. Young boys are always assigned to male therapists, so that positive male identification is facilitated. Meanwhile, the child's parents receive instruction in the behavior modification practice of reinforcing appropriate gender behavior and extinguishing "inappropriate" behavior (Roberto, 1983).

For transsexuals, there was considerable enthusiasm for sex conversion surgery in the 1960s and 1970s, partly because such patients are so extremely resistant to psychotherapy. Most transsexuals regarded therapeutic exploration of their gender conflicts as an obstacle blocking the path to a sex change operation (Lothstein, 1977; Weitz, 1977).

However, some success with behaviorally oriented therapy programs has been reported. These behavioral programs consist of strategies for modifying sex-typed behavior through modeling and behavioral rehearsal. The therapist demonstrates appropriate masculine behavior and mannerisms (modeling) in a number of different situations, and then patients practice their own versions of these behaviors. This is followed by a behavioral procedure that reinforces heterosexual fantasies: electric shock is applied whenever the person reports transsexual fantasies (Barlow et al., 1979; Khanna et al., 1987).

In spite of such gains with psychotherapy and behavioral procedures, sex change operations are indicated for some transsexuals. For men desiring a sex change, the sex conversion operation begins with removal of the penis and testes. Then female genitalia, including a vagina, cervix, and clitoris, are constructed through plastic surgery. The skin of the penis is used in this construction, because the sensory nerve endings that are preserved enable some transsexuals to experience orgasm. The male-to-female operation is nearly perfected and sometimes even fools gynecologists (Stripling, 1986). It costs from $6,000 to $10,000. Women who want to become men generally request operations to remove their breasts, uterus, and ovaries, and some ask for an artificial penis to be constructed. This procedure is much more complicated and expensive than the male-to-female conversion (Fleming et al., 1982).

Society often has difficulty in accepting and understanding people who undergo such extreme operations: A 21-year-old male transsexual who was charged with carrying a concealed weapon was placed in a maximum security prison with several thousand men. This person had already had breast implants and was taking hormones (Blank, 1981). The partners of transsexuals also go through self-doubt. One woman, married to a female transsexual scheduled to undergo the woman-to-man operation, wondered if she might be a lesbian and if her three-year-old son (through artificial insemination) would have gender confusion. Because others react negatively, few transsexuals make their condition public (Stripling, 1986).

A number of postoperative studies of transsexuals have indicated positive outcomes (Pauly, 1968; Fleming et al., 1982). However, many transsexuals remain depressed and suicidal after surgery (Meyer & Peter, 1979; Herschkowitz & Dickes, 1978). Over half the transsexuals in one study who were offered surgery later changed their minds or became ambivalent about having the operations (Kockott & Fahrner, 1987). Doubts about the benefits of sex conversion operations have resulted in a decrease in sex reassignment surgery. Psychotherapy is typically recommended for patients who discover that their problems have not disappeared as a result of the operation (McCauly & Ehrhardt, 1984).

PARAPHILIAS

Paraphilias are sexual disorders in which the person has persistent and strong sexual urges and sexual fantasies regarding (1) nonhuman objects, as in fetishism and transvestic fetishism; (2) real or simulated suffering, as in sadism and masochism; and (3) nonconsenting others, as in exhibitionism, voyeurism, and pedophilia (see the disorders chart on page 296.) The diagnosis is made if the person has either acted on these urges or is severely distressed by them. A person who is highly distressed by paraphiliac urges or fantasies but has not acted on them would be diagnosed as having a mild case of the paraphilia. In addition, according to DSM-III-R this condition must have been present for at least six months.

People in this category often have more than one paraphilia. In one study of sex offenders, researchers found that nearly 50 percent had engaged in a variety of sexually deviant behaviors, averaging between three and four paraphilias, and had committed over 500 deviant acts. For example, of men who reported having committed incest, a substantial number also had molested nonrelatives, exposed themselves, raped adult women, and engaged in voyeurism and frotteurism (rubbing against others for sexual arousal) (Rosenfield, 1985). Paraphilias are much more prevalent in males than females.

Paraphilias Involving Nonhuman Objects

Fetishism is an extremely strong sexual attraction for an inanimate object such as panties, bras, or shoes. The fetish is often employed as a sexual stimulus during masturbation or sexual intercourse.

> Mr. M. met his wife at a local church. Some kissing and petting took place but never any other sexual contact. He had not masturbated before marriage. Although he and his wife loved each other very much, he was unable to have sexual intercourse with her since he could not obtain an erection. However, he had fantasies involving an apron and was able to get an erection while wearing an apron. His wife was described as upset over this discovery but was convinced to accept it. The apron is kept hanging somewhere in the bedroom and it allowed him to consummate the marriage. He remembers being forced to wear an apron by his mother during his childhood years. (Kohon, 1987)

The diagnosis of fetishism is not made if the fetishes only involve articles of clothing used in cross-dressing. Instead, the appropriate diagnosis would be transvestic fetishism.

Most males find the sight of female undergarments sexually arousing and stimulating; again, this does not constitute a fetish. An interest in such inanimate objects as panties, stockings, bras, and shoes becomes a sexual disorder when the person is often sexually aroused to the point of erection in the presence of the fetish item, needs this item for sexual arousal during intercourse, chooses sexual partners on the basis their having the item, or collects these items (Jones et al., 1977). In many cases, the fetish item is enough by itself for complete sexual satisfaction through masturbation, and the person does not seek contact with a partner. As a group, fetishists are not dangerous nor do they tend to commit more serious crimes.

Transvestic Fetishism **Transvestic fetishism** is a disorder in which sexual arousal is obtained through cross-dressing, or the wearing of clothes appropriate to the opposite sex. Several aspects of transvestism are illustrated in the following case study:

> A 26-year-old graduate student referred himself for treatment following an examination failure. He had been cross-dressing since the age of 10 and attributed his exam failure to the excessive amount of time that he spent doing so (four times a week). When he was younger, his cross-dressing had taken the form of masturbating while wearing his mother's high-heeled shoes, but it had gradually expanded to the present stage in which he dressed completely as a woman, masturbating in front of a mirror. At no time had he experienced a desire to obtain a sex-change operation. He had neither homosexual experiences nor homosexual fantasies. Heterosexual contact had been restricted to heavy petting with occasional girlfriends. (Lambley, 1974, p. 101)

Not all people who cross-dress are transvestites; some homosexuals and transsexuals also cross-dress. By contrast to these latter two groups, however, the majority of transvestites are exclusively heterosexual,

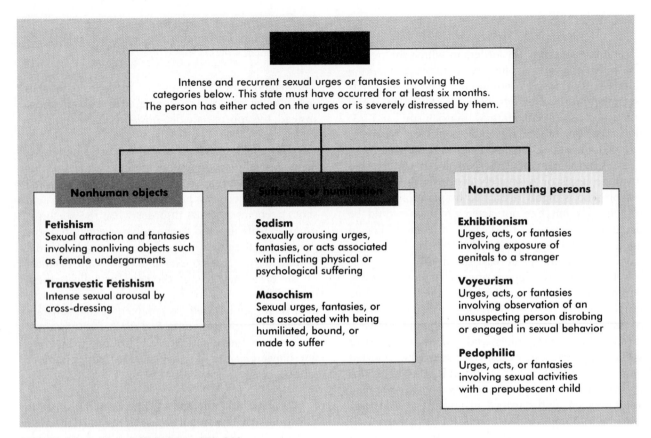

Intense and recurrent sexual urges or fantasies involving the categories below. This state must have occurred for at least six months. The person has either acted on the urges or is severely distressed by them.

Nonhuman objects

Fetishism
Sexual attraction and fantasies involving nonliving objects such as female undergarments

Transvestic Fetishism
Intense sexual arousal by cross-dressing

Suffering or humiliation

Sadism
Sexually arousing urges, fantasies, or acts associated with inflicting physical or psychological suffering

Masochism
Sexual urges, fantasies, or acts associated with being humiliated, bound, or made to suffer

Nonconsenting persons

Exhibitionism
Urges, acts, or fantasies involving exposure of genitals to a stranger

Voyeurism
Urges, acts, or fantasies involving observation of an unsuspecting person disrobing or engaged in sexual behavior

Pedophilia
Urges, acts, or fantasies involving sexual activities with a prepubescent child

SOURCE: Adapted from DSM-III-R, pp. 279–290.

are married, and have fathered or borne children (Benjamin, 1967).

Sexual arousal while cross-dressing is an important criterion in the diagnosis. If arousal is not present or has disappeared over time, then the possibility of a gender identity disorder should be considered. However, this distinction may be difficult to make. Some transsexuals exhibit penile erections in response to descriptions of cross-dressing, which was thought to happen only to transvestites. (Blanchard et al., 1986). So, whether or not sexual arousal occurs in cross-dressing may not serve as a valid distinction between transsexualism and transvestic fetishism.

Male transvestites often wear feminine garments or undergarments during sexual intercourse with their wives, as described by Newman and Stoller (1974, p. 438):

He continued to have sexual intercourse (while clad in a woman's nightgown) with his wife, while imagining that they were no longer man and wife, but rather two women engaged in a lesbian relationship. He especially enjoyed it when she cooperated with his idea and referred to him by his chosen feminine name.

Many transvestites feel that they have alternating masculine and feminine personalities. In a feminine role, they can play out such behavior patterns as buying nightgowns and trying on fashionable clothes. Many transvestites introduce their wives to their female personalities, and urge them to go on shopping trips together as women (Buckner, 1970). Other transvestites cross-dress only for the purposes of sexual arousal and masturbation and do not fantasize themselves as members of the opposite sex.

Paraphilias Involving Nonconsenting Others

Exhibitionism Exhibitionism involves sexual arousal by and intense urges or fantasies about the exposure of one's genitals to strangers. Often the person wants to shock the victim, as this case shows:

> A 19-year-old single white college man reported that he had daily fantasies of exposing and had exposed himself on three occasions. The first occurred when he masturbated in front of the window of his dormitory room, when women would be passing by. The other two acts occurred in his car; in each case he asked young women for directions, and then exposed his penis and masturbated when they approached. He felt a great deal of anxiety in the presence of women and dated infrequently. (Hayes et al., 1983)

Exhibitionism is relatively common. The exhibitionist is almost always male and the victim female. Surveys of selected groups of young women in the United States indicate that between one-third and one-half have been victims of exhibitionists (Cox & McMahon, 1978; Rhoads & Borjes, 1981). Although the majority of women did not report any psychological traumas associated with the episodes, about 40 percent indicated being moderately to severely distressed, and 11 percent felt the incident had negatively affected their attitude toward men (Cox, 1988).

Unlike normal (control) subjects, exhibitionists are sexually aroused by sexually neutral scenes such as women knitting, ironing, or sweeping (Kolarsky & Madlatfousek, 1983). Similar findings were obtained by Fedora and his colleagues (1986), who monitored sexual arousal in exhibitionists, normal control, and nonexhibitionist sex offenders. Only the exhibitionists responded sexually to scenes of fully clothed, erotically neutral females. Fedora hypothesized that exhibitionists may be aroused by female uncooperativeness or neutrality.

The sexual arousal he gets by exposing himself seems to be the main goal of the exhibitionist; most exhibitionists do not want any further contact. However, there may be two types of exhibitionists—those who have been involved with crime and those who have not. The former tend to be sociopathic and

Transvestism is a disorder in which sexual gratification is obtained through cross-dressing. In some cases, makeup may be applied and the individual may attempt to pass as a woman. But in contrast to transsexuals, transvestites do not have a gender conflict.

impulsive, and may be more likely to show aggression (Forgac & Michaels, 1982; Forgac et al., 1984).

Exhibitionists may expect to produce surprise, sexual arousal, or disgust in the victim. The act may involve exposing a limp penis or masturbating an erect penis. In a study of ninety-six exhibitionists, only 50 percent reported that they "almost always" or "always" had erections when exposing, although a large percentage of the men wanted the woman to be impressed with the size of their penis. Fantasies about being watched and admired by female observers were common among exhibitionists. Over two-thirds reported that they would not have sex with the victim even if she were receptive (Langevin et al., 1979).

Most exhibitionists are in their twenties—far from being the "dirty old men" of popular myth. Most are married. Their exhibiting has a compulsive quality to it, and they report that they feel a great deal of anxiety about the act. A typical exposure sequence involves the person first entertaining sexually arousing memories of previous exposures, and then returning to the area where previous exposures took place. Next, the person locates a suitable victim, rehearses the exposure mentally, and finally exposes

Many features of our society, such as topless bars, X-rated movies, or explicitly sexual magazines, are voyeuristic in nature and are accepted, if not approved of, by many people. When voyeurism includes serious risk, is done in socially unacceptable circumstances, or is preferred to coitus, the behavior is abnormal or deviant.

himself. As the person moves through his sequence, his self-control weakens and disappears (Abel et al., 1970).

Voyeurism Voyeurism is sexual gratification obtained by (1) observing the unclothed body of unsuspecting members of the opposite sex, or (2) watching couples engaging in sexual activity. The proliferation of sexually oriented television programs, "romance" paperbacks, explicit sexual magazines, and X-rated movies all point to the voyeuristic nature of our society. Note the increasing number of "night clubs" featuring male exotic dancers and attended by women. This increase may indicate women's increasing interest in men's bodies and their acknowledgment that it is all right to be sexual.

"Peeping," as voyeurism is sometimes termed, is considered deviant when it includes serious risk, is done in socially unacceptable circumstances, or is preferred to coitus. The typical voyeur is not interested in looking at his wife or girlfriend. Observation alone produces sexual arousal and excitement, and the voyeur often masturbates during this surreptitious activity.

The voyeur is like the exhibitionist in that sexual contact is not the goal; viewing an undressed body is the primary motive. However, a voyeur may also exhibit himself or engage in other indirect forms of sexual expression. Because the act is repetitive, arrest is predictable. Usually an accidental witness or the victim notifies the police. It is not uncommon, however, for a potential rapist or burglar who is behaving suspiciously to be arrested as a voyeur.

Pedophilia

Pedophilia is a disorder in which an adult obtains erotic gratification through sexual contact with children. Pedophiliacs may victimize their own children (incest), stepchildren, or those outside the family, according to DSM-III-R, (American Psychiatric Association, 1987). Most pedophiles prefer girls, although a few choose prepubertal boys. Child sexual abuse is common. Between 20 and 30 percent of women reported having had a childhood sexual encounter with an adult man (Herman & Hirschman, 1981; Zverina et al., 1987). And, contrary to the popular view of the pedophile (or child molester) as a stranger, most pedophiles were relatives, friends, or casual acquaintances of their victims (Alter-Reid, 1986).

In most cases of abuse, only one adult and one child are involved, but cases involving several adults or groups of children have recently been reported. For example, a 54-year-old man, a person who had won a community award for his work with youth, was arrested for child molestation involving boys as young as ten years old. The man would encourage and photograph sexual acts between the boys, including mutual masturbation and oral and anal sex. He then would have sex with one of them (Burgess et al., 1984).

A study of 229 convicted child molesters revealed the following information. Nearly a quarter of their victims were under six years of age. Another 25 percent were ages six to ten, and about 50 percent were ages eleven to thirteen. Fondling of the child was the most common sexual behavior, followed by vaginal and oral-genital contact. Bribery was often used to gain cooperation of the victims (Erickson et al., 1988). Pedophiliacs have a recidivism rate of approximately 35 percent, which is the highest among sex offenders (Erickson et al., 1987).

Child victims of sexual abuse show a variety of physical symptoms such as urinary tract infections, poor appetite, and headaches. The psychological symptoms that have been reported include nightmares, difficulty in sleeping, a decline in school performance, acting-out behaviors, and sexually focused behavior. One boy was overheard asking another to take down his pants, which was the request made by the person who had molested him (Burgess et al., 1981). Some child victims show the symptoms of posttraumatic stress disorder. In a sample of sixty-six victims, forty-five reported experiencing flashbacks of the molestation. They also demonstrated diminished responsiveness to their environment, hyperalertness, and jumpiness (Burgess et al., 1984). (The First Person narrative in this chapter discusses some of the problems prosecutors have to deal with when prosecuting cases of child abuse.)

On psychological tests such as the MMPI, child molesters tend to have profiles indicating passive-dependent personality, discomfort in social situations, impulsiveness, and alcoholism (Erickson et al., 1987). Social skills deficits are found among child molesters when compared to control group members. They also

Young children who have been sexually abused often find it difficult to talk about the incident. Especially traumatic for them is having to testify in court against the person who abused them. Prosecutors often prepare their young witnesses by showing them the courtroom before they have to testify in order to make them feel more at ease about the upcoming trial.

display a significantly higher fear of negative evaluation (Overholser & Beck, 1986). Pedophiles display sexual arousal to slides of young children and report fantasies involving children during masturbation (Alford et al., 1987). Over 50 percent of one sample of child molesters reported using "hard core" pornography to excite themselves in preparing to commit an offense (Marshall, 1988).

Paraphilias Involving Pain or Humiliation

Pain and humiliation do not appear to be related to sexual arousal. However, in the following disorders, these factors play a prominent role.

Sadism and Masochism The deviations of **sadism** and **masochism** involve the association of pain

Mary Kay Barbieri

FIRST PERSON

When I first graduated from law school in 1975, I went to work for the King County prosecutor's office in Seattle, Washington. Before that time, cases of child sexual abuse—especially in-family child sexual abuse—were not handled in the criminal justice system. They were treated as "social problems" and handled by Child Protective Services. But around 1975 a movement was afoot to start treating these abuses of children as crimes. Most prosecutors didn't want to handle the cases—they didn't know how to talk to children, they didn't think children could testify in court, and they often didn't believe the children because they didn't understand why they would let the abuse go on so long without telling someone.

I volunteered for all the child sexual abuse cases I could get. I stocked my office with blocks and crayons and big floor cushions and spent hours sitting on the floor with children winning their trust and getting them to tell me about the terrible things that adults had done to them. I was appalled at what I heard from these children. People who were supposed to love or care for them—their parent or stepparent, grandpa or uncle, their teacher

or Cub Scout leader or babysitter—these adults were performing every imaginable kind of sexual act with children. They usually started out by bribing the children and then invariably ended up threatening them to keep them from telling. The most common threats were "If you tell they'll think you're bad and they won't love you," or "If you tell I'll kill your mom." Kids always believed these threats, so usually they only disclosed the sexual abuse inadvertently. Fortunately, the school programs that now educate children about sexual abuse make it more likely that children will disclose abuse sooner.

I learned a lot about bravery from those children. Many of the offenders would plead guilty before trial, but many didn't and then the children would have to go to court and testify. Courtrooms just aren't made for children: they're big and austere and intimidating even for adults. So, a few days before the trial, I would take a child to visit the courtroom when it was not in use. I'd have the child sit in the witness chair and swivel around and try out the microphone. I'd tell the child where the judge sat and what the court reporter did, and I'd prepare the child for the fact that the offender would be in court, too. That was always the hardest part, but by this time the child and I had spent a lot of time together and were friends and I'd say, "Don't worry, you don't have to look at him; just look at me instead." I put children as young as three years old on the witness stand. Yes, those children were brave.

I eventually set up a special unit in the prosecutor's office just to

handle cases of child sexual abuse. The prosecutors were all trained to work with children and to understand the dynamics of child sexual abuse. As often happens when a program is set up to meet a perceived need, the caseload kept increasing and increasing. The unit became a national model, and my career benefited. Eventually I became the chief prosecutor in charge of the whole sixty-attorney prosecutor's office.

But I missed the kids. I'd always been a little envious of the therapists who worked with children. As a prosector my work ended with the trial while the therapists got to go on helping the children. A lot of the process of preparing children for trial is "doing therapy," but I wished that I could be the one to go on working with the child, helping the child to realize that it wasn't his or her fault, and doing the work that needed to be done to keep this experience from haunting the child on into adulthood. Finally I decided that if I wanted to be a therapist, I should become one. I left the practice of law and went to graduate school in clinical and counseling psychology. Now I still get to sit on the floor with blocks and crayons and pillows, and I don't have to stop doing it when the trial is over.

Ms. Mary Kay Barbieri was the former chief prosecutor for the King County prosecutor's office in Seattle, Washington. She is now a practicing therapist, specializing in cases involving child sexual abuse.

and/or humiliation with sexual gratification, respectively. In particular, the sadist obtains sexual gratification by inflicting pain on others; the masochist, by receiving pain, bondage, or humiliation. The word *sadism* was coined from the name of the Marquis de Sade (1740–1814), a French nobleman who wrote extensively about the sexual pleasure he received by inflicting pain on women. The marquis himself was so cruel to his sexual victims that he was declared insane, and jailed for twenty-seven years of his life. The word *masochism* is derived from the name of Leopold von Sacher-Masoch, a nineteenth-century Austrian novelist whose fictional characters obtained sexual satisfaction only when pain was inflicted on them.

Sadistic behavior may range from the pretended or fantasized infliction of pain, through mild to severe cruelty toward partners, to an extremely dangerous pathological form of sadism that may involve mutilation or murder. Because of their passive roles, masochists are not considered dangerous. For some sadists and masochists, coitus becomes unnecessary; pain or humiliation alone is sufficient to produce sexual pleasure.

In a study of 178 sadomasochists (47 women and 131 men), most reported engaging and enjoying both submissive and dominant roles. Only 16 percent were exclusively dominant or submissive. Nearly all engaged in spanking, whippings, and bondage. Approximately 40 percent engaged in behaviors that caused minor pain using ice, hot wax, biting, or face slapping. Less than 18 percent engaged in more harmful procedures such as burning or piercing. Nearly all respondents reported that sadomasochistic (S&M) activities to be more satisfying than "straight" sex (Moser & Levitt, 1987). Most sadomasochists studied don't seek harm or injury but report that they find the sensation of utter helplessness appealing (Baumeister, 1988). S & M activities are often carefully scripted and involve role playing and mutual consent to the activity by the participants (Weinberg, 1987).

Sadomasochistic tendencies may exist to some extent in many people. In a national survey, 10.3 percent of single men reported having obtained sexual pleasure from inflicting or receiving pain (Hunt, 1974). In the same survey, single women were much more likely to report sexual pleasure when receiving pain (10.0 percent) than when inflicting pain (5.2 percent). In addition, fantasies involving sexual abuse, rejection, and forced sex are not uncommon among college students of both sexes (Sue, 1979). Most of these cases involve very mild forms of pain (such as in biting or pinching) that are accepted in our society. Sadomasochistic behavior is considered deviant when pain, either inflicted or received, is necessary for sexual arousal and orgasm.

Some cases of sadomasochism appear to be the result of an early experience associating sexual arousal with pain. One masochistic man reported that as a child he was often "caned" on the buttocks by a school headmaster as his "attractive" wife looked on. He reported, "I got sexual feelings from around the age of twelve, especially if she was watching" (p. 273). He and some of his schoolmates later hired prostitutes to spank them. Later yet, he engaged in self-whipping (Money, 1987). Although the association of pain and sexual arousal can account for some cases of sadomasochistic behaviors, 80 percent of a sample of sadomasochists did not remember a link between physical punishment during childhood and erotic sensations (Weinberg, 1987).

Etiology and Treatment of Paraphilias

All etiological theories for the paraphilias must answer the following questions: (1) What produced the deviant arousal pattern? (2) Why doesn't the person develop a more appropriate outlet for his or her sexual drive? (3) Why is the behavior not deterred by normative and legal prohibitions? (Finkelhor & Araji, 1986). So far, neither the psychoanalytic perspective nor the behavioral perspective has given satisfactory answers, although a number of behavioral strategies have emerged for treating the paraphilias.

Psychoanalytic Perspective   In psychoanalytic theory, all sexual deviations symbolically represent unconscious conflicts that began in early childhood. Castration anxiety is hypothesized to be an important etiological factor underlying transvestic fetishism and exhibitionism, sadism, and masochism. It occurs because the oedipal complex is not fully resolved. Since the boy's incestuous desires are only partially repressed, he fears retribution from his father, in the form of castration. Many sexual deviations are attempts to protect the person from castration anxiety. For example, in transvestic fetishism, acknowledging that women lack a penis raises the fear of castration. To refute this possibility, the male transvestite "restores" the penis to women through cross-dressing. In this manner, he unconsciously represents a "woman who has a penis" and therefore reduces the fear of castration (Shave, 1976). Similarly, an exhibitionist exposes to reassure himself that castration has not occurred. The shock that registers on the faces of others assures him that he still has a penis. A sadist may protect himself from castration anxiety by inflicting pain (power equals penis) while a masochist engages in self-castration through the acceptance of pain. This acceptance limits the power of others to castrate him. Because castration anxiety stems from an unconscious source, the fear is never completely allayed, however, and so the person feels compelled to repeat deviant sexual acts.

The psychoanalytic treatment of sexual deviations involves helping the patient understand the relationship between the deviation and the unconscious conflict that produced it. In the case of the man with a fetish who had to wear an apron before he could engage in sexual intercourse, the therapist used dream analysis and free association to help the patient understand the "roots" of his behavior. The following interpretation was made. The apron was made by his mother from a boiler suit that belonged to his father's mother. Because the patient's relationship with his mother produced castration anxiety, the fetish accomplished two purposes. First, it allowed him to reduce castration anxiety by denying that women do not have penises (the apron symbolized a "penis" that was cut out of the body of another woman). Second, a "penis" (the apron) was returned to him (Kohon, 1987). The psychoanalyst helped the patient bring the conflicts into conscious awareness through interpretation. After this, the patient gains insight into his behavior and is able to work through his problem.

Social Learning Theory   Learning theorists stress the importance of early conditioning experiences that hamper the development of normal sexual patterns in the etiology of sexually deviant behaviors. Masturbating while engaged in sexually deviant fantasies, combined with a lack of social skills, is one type of conditioning experience. For example, one boy developed a fetish for women's panties at age twelve after he became sexually excited watching girls come down a slide with their underpants exposed. He began to masturbate to fantasies of girls with their panties showing and had this fetish for twenty-one years before seeking treatment (Kushner, 1965). In another example, two young men became sexually aroused while urinating in a semiprivate area after they were surprised by women passing by. The accidental association between sexual arousal and exposure resulted in exhibitionism (McGuire et al., 1965). These reports must be interpreted carefully, because they are extracted from case studies and do not originate from controlled research.

Experimental support for the possible role of conditioning in the development of a fetish was demonstrated by Rachman (1966). Three men were shown a picture of a pair of women's black boots and then were shown slides of nude females, which produced sexual arousal (as measured by penile volume). Initially, the picture of boots did not elicit any increases in penile volume. But after slides of boots and nude females were paired several times (classical conditioning), all three subjects developed conditioned sexual arousal at the sight of the boots alone. Although the conditioned responses were weak, they could have been strengthened by masturbating while the boots were shown.

Learning approaches to treating sexual deviations have generally involved one or more of the following elements: (1) weakening or eliminating the sexually inappropriate behaviors through processes such as extinction or aversive conditioning; (2) acquiring, or strengthening of, sexually appropriate behaviors; and (3) developing appropriate social skills. The following case illustrates this multiple approach:

A 27-year-old man with a three-year history of pedophilic activities (fondling and cunnilingus) with four-to-seven-year-old girls was treated through the following procedure. The man first masturbated to orgasm while exposed to stimuli involving adult females. He then masturbated (but not to orgasm) to deviant stimuli. The procedure allowed the strengthening of normal arousal patterns and lessened the ability to achieve an orgasm while exposed to deviant stimuli (extinction). Measurement of penile volume when exposed to the stimuli indicated a sharp decrease to pedophilic stimuli and high arousal to heterosexual stimuli. These changes were maintained over a twelve-month follow-up period. (Alford et al., 1987)

One of the more unique treatments is the *aversive behavior rehearsal* (ABR) program developed by Wickramasekera (1976) for exhibitionism. This "shame aversion" technique uses shame or humiliation as the aversive stimulus. The technique requires that the patient exhibit himself in his usual manner to a preselected audience of females. During the exhibiting act, the patient must verbalize a conversation between himself and his penis. He must talk about what he is feeling emotionally and physically and must explain his fantasies regarding what he supposes the female observers are thinking about him.

The developer of ABR feels that exhibition often occurs when the person is in a hypnotic-like state. At that time, the exhibitionist's fantasies are extremely active and his judgment is impaired. The ABR method forces him to experience and examine his act while fully aware of what he is doing (Kilmann et al., 1982).

The results of behavioral treatment have been generally positive, but the majority of the studies involved single-subject designs. Few control groups were included. Another problem in interpreting the results of these studies becomes apparent when we examine the approaches that were employed. For the most part, several different behavioral techniques were used within each study, so evaluation of a particular technique is impossible.

OTHER SEXUAL DEVIATIONS

Although certain other deviations are not included in DSM-III-R, the magnitude and seriousness of the problems they present warrant discussion.

Rape

Rape is defined by the Federal Bureau of Investigation (FBI) as "carnal knowledge of a female forcibly and against her consent." (Most states also have a criminal offense of statutory rape—sexual intercourse with a girl under a certain age, regardless of consent.)

FBI statistics show that over 87,000 cases of rape were reported in 1985. However, only about 16 percent of reported cases result in a conviction for this crime. Another 4 percent of those charged with rape are convicted of lesser offenses (Rabkin 1979). The low conviction rate and the humiliation and shame involved in a rape trial keep many women from reporting rapes, so the actual prevalence of the crime is probably much higher than reported. Some police officers still feel that the victims are partly to blame because of their manner of dress or behavior and endorse statements such as "Most charges of rape are unfounded" and "Nice women do not get raped" (LeDoux & Hazelwood, 1985). Estimates based on surveys indicate that as many as one of every four women will be a rape victim at some time during her life (Resick, 1983).

One form of rape being reported with increasing frequency is "acquaintance" or "date" rape:

Colleen, twenty-seven, a San Francisco office manager, had been involved with her boyfriend for about a year when it happened. After a cozy dinner at her apartment, he suggested that she go to bed while he did the dishes. But a few moments later he stalked into Colleen's bedroom with a peculiar look on his face, brandishing a butcher knife and strips of cloth. After tying her, spread-eagled, to the bed, the formerly tender lover raped her brutally for three hours. When it was all over, he fell soundly asleep. (Seligmann et al., 1984, p. 91)

It is possible that "date" rapes account for the majority of all rapes. However, the victim may be reluctant to report such an attack; she feels responsible—at least in part—because she made a date with her attacker.

Should intercourse between a dating couple be considered rape, if the woman did not want to engage in that activity? One police official, in reacting to the high number of rapes reported in his community, noted that "We definitely do not have a serious rape problem in this city. The problem is in the classification. If you took all our rapes one by one, you'd see that nine out of ten are a girlfriend-boyfriend thing. These people are known to each other" (Girard, 1984, p. 12). The assumption here is that forced intercourse between acquaintances should not be considered rape. Unfortunately, sexual aggression by men is quite common. Fifteen percent of a sample of college men reported that they did force intercourse at least once or twice. Only 39 percent of the men did not admit to any coerced sex (Rapaport & Burkhart, 1984). In a survey of college students enrolled in 32 universities in the United States, over 50 percent of the women reported being the victims of sexual aggression. Nearly 8 percent of the men admitted committing sexual acts that met the legal definition of rape. Women seldom reported these episodes as rape (Koss et al., 1987). Many universities are conducting workshops for students to help them understand that intercourse without consent during a date or other social activity is rape.

Victims of Rape   Most rape victims are young women in their teens or twenties although victims as young as age five and as old as seventy-three have been reported (Burgess & Holmstrom, 1979b). In about half of all rape cases, the victim is at least acquainted with the rapist and is attacked in the home or in an automobile (Kilpatrick et al., 1979).

Needless to say, rape is highly traumatic. Victims may experience psychological distress, phobic reactions, and sexual dysfunction. In one sample of victims, over 50 percent reported one or more sexual dysfunctions as the result of the rape. Fear of sex and lack of desire or arousal were the most common complaints. Some women recovered quickly but others reported problems years after the episodes (Gilbert & Cunningham, 1986). A one-year follow-up of rape victims found that they were significantly more fearful than control groups. The fears were selective and involved such things as darkness and enclosed places—conditions likely to be associated with rape (Calhoun et al., 1982). Duration and intensity of fear were also found to be related to perceptions of dangerousness. Attacks in circumstances that the woman had defined as "safe" had a greater emotional impact than attacks in places women felt were dangerous. Many women drastically changed their perception of how safe the environment really was (Scheppele & Bart, 1983).

In one survey, about two-thirds of rape victims reported that they could not resume sexual activity for at least six months (Burgess & Holmstrom, 1979b). Their sexual enjoyment was strongly affected. One victim described her attitude toward sex after the rape as follows:

It depends how I relate to the man. If I'm in a position to enjoy it—a 50–50 thing—then I'm ok. But if I'm feeling that I'm only doing this for him and not for my own enjoyment, then I feel like the incident again . . . then sex is bad. (p. 648)

Flashbacks were reported by 50 percent of the sexually active victims. These ranged from fleeting memories that could not be repressed, to reliving of the experience, to associating the present sex partner with the rapist. Sympathetic understanding, nondemanding affection, and a positive attitude from the partner have been found to be beneficial. Hugging and gentle caressing are generally satisfying to the victim even if sexual approaches are aversive (Feldman-Summers et al., 1979).

In light of the severe sexual and psychological problems that a rape victim may experience, the availability of multiple support systems and counseling becomes very important. Most large cities now have rape crisis centers that provide counseling, as well as medical and legal information, to victims. Trained volunteers often accompany the victim to the hospital and to the police station. Women's organizations have made many hospital personnel and police officers more aware of the trauma of rape, and because of this, these individuals have begun to behave more sensitively when dealing with victims.

Etiology   Rape is not specifically listed in DSM-III-R as a mental disorder because the act can have a variety of motivations. In an analysis of 133 rapists, Groth and his colleagues (1977) distinguished the following three motivational types:

1. *Power rapist* This type of rapist (comprising 55 percent of those studied) is primarily attempting to compensate for feelings of personal or sexual inadequacy by trying to intimidate his victims.

2. *Anger rapist* The man in this category (40 percent of those studied) is angry at women in general; the victim is merely a convenient target to direct his rage.

3. *Sadistic rapist* This type (5 percent of those studied) derives satisfaction from inflicting pain on the rape victim and such a man may torture or mutilate her.

Women have made two general responses to the increased incidence of rape: support and care for the victims and prevention. Crisis lines and rape assistance programs are widely publicized in communities. Women's groups have held anti-rape protests, such as the Take Back the Night rally shown in this picture.

These findings tend to support the contention that rape has more to do with power, aggression, and violence than with sex. And, in fact, a study of over 100 rapists indicated that 58 percent showed some sexual dysfunction, such as erectile difficulties, during the attack (Groth & Burgess, 1977).

Although these distinctions are of interest, little empirical research has been done on the importance of aggressive cues in the sexual arousal of rapists until a study performed by Abel et al. (1977). These investigators recorded the degree of penile erection of rapists and nonrapists in response to two-minute audiotapes describing violent and nonviolent sexual scenes. The nonviolent tape described an incident of mutually enjoyable sexual intercourse. The violent tape described a rape in which the man forced himself on an unwilling woman. The rapists were aroused by both tape descriptions, whereas the nonrapists displayed a significantly lesser degree of erection in response to the portrayal of violent sex, preferring the scene involving mutually enjoyable sex. Some rapists also showed strong sexual arousal in response to another tape that was entirely aggressive in content.

Although researchers initially thought that only sadists or rapists would show a sexual arousal pattern

to aggressive sex, later studies show that certain groups of men who are not rapists also respond sexually to aggressive cues. In addition, whether or not the woman displays physical pleasure to the attack also influences sexual responding in men. Here are the results of some of these studies:

1. College men with sadistic tendencies rated slides of women displaying emotional distress (fear, anger, disgust, sadness) as more sexually arousing than did nonsadistic men (Heilbrun & Loftus, 1986).

2. Men who admitted to being more likely to commit rape show more erections when listening to audiotapes of dramatized sex between nonconsenting participants than when listening to scenes between consenting participants. Men who reported that they weren't very likely to rape anyone showed the opposite pattern (Malamuth & Check, 1983).

3. When students were exposed to a situation in which a woman is portrayed as being initially repelled but later responds sexually to rape, males, but not females, became less sensitive to rape victims; viewed the rapist as being less responsible for the act and deserving less punishment; showed desensitization to violent sex; and were more likely to accept rape myths (Donnerstein & Linz, 1986).

FOCUS 11.1 *Is Pornography Harmful?*

The Attorney General's Commission on Pornography (1986) concluded that a causal relationship exists between many forms of pornography and increased violence against women. The same conclusion was reached by the Surgeon General's Workshop on Pornography (Koop, 1987). The latter report indicated that pornography "increases beliefs that less common sexual practices are more common" and may lead men to believe that "coercion and violence are acceptable in sex relations." These views are very different from those of the Commission on Obscenity and Pornography (1970), which found no relationship between exposure to erotic materials and sex crimes. What accounts for the opposing findings? Part of the difference can be attributed to the types of materials that were ex-

amined by each committee. Unlike more recent studies, the 1970 report was based on nonviolent explicit sex. Perhaps not all forms of explicit sex are harmful.

The most important factor may not be the explicitness of the portrayal of sexual activity but the amount of violence and aggression directed toward women. Nonexplicit portrayals of sexual violence on mass media have also been shown to increase men's negative attitudes toward women (Malamuth & Check, 1981). In fact, the Commission on Pornography (1986) concluded that the "slasher films" in which violence is paired with sex are more harmful than other forms of pornography. In one study, the impact of violence or aggression toward women was studied. Male subjects were first angered and then

exposed to films showing, (1) sexual aggression toward women, (2) explicit sex between mutually consenting adults, (3) nonsexual aggression toward women, and (4) nonsexual material. After this exposure, the men were given the opportunity to behave aggressively toward a woman (a confederate of the researcher). The films depicting sexual aggression toward women and nonsexual aggression were associated with high degrees of aggression in male subjects. The men who viewed the films depicting neutral scenes and nonviolent explicit sex displayed low degrees of aggression (Donnerstein et al., 1986). The findings support the belief that it is the violence depicted in pornographic material, and not the degree of sexual explicitness, that influences aggression in males.

Because of these findings, questions are being raised about the effects of media portrayals of violent sex, especially in pornography, on the frequency of rape (see Focus 11.1). Exposure to such materials may affect attitudes, thoughts, and influence patterns of sexual arousal (Malamuth & Briere, 1986).

Incest

Incest is sexual relations between close relatives. Estimates of the incidence of incest range from 48,000 to 250,000 cases per year (Stark, 1984). The most commonly reported incidents of incest involve a father and his daughter or stepdaughter. However, in a survey in which 15 percent of the respondents reported sexual contacts with relatives, the most common incestuous relationship involved siblings (Hunt, 1974). Less than 0.5 percent of the women reported

sexual contact with their fathers. Mother-son incest seems to be rare. In another study, sexual activities between siblings were again found to be relatively frequent: 15 percent of the women and 10 percent of the men reported that they had had sexual involvement with their siblings. In 75 percent of these cases, mutual consent was involved. About half considered the experience positive; the other half, negative (Finkelhor, 1980).

Most research has focused on father-daughter incest. This type of incestuous relationship generally begins when the daughter is between six and eleven years old, and it continues for at least two years (Stark, 1984). Unlike sex between siblings, father-daughter incest is always exploitive. The girl is especially vulnerable because she depends on her father for emotional support. As a result, the daughter victims often feel guilty and powerless. Their problems continue into adulthood and are reflected in their high rates of drug abuse, sexual dysfunction, and psychiatric problems later in life (Emslie & Rosenfeld, 1983; Gartner & Gartner, 1988). Incest victims often have difficulty establishing a trusting relationship with men. Relationships that were forceful, intrusive, or of a long duration are more likely to result in long-lasting negative effects (Herman et al., 1986).

Three types of incestuous fathers have been described (Rist, 1979). The first is a socially isolated man who is highly dependent on his family for interpersonal relationships. His emotional dependency gradually evolves (and expands) into a sexual relationship with his daughter. The second type of incestuous father has a psychopathic personality, and is completely indiscriminate in choosing sexual partners. The third type has pedophilic tendencies and is sexually involved with several children, including his daughter. In addition, incest victims have reported family patterns in which the father is violent and the mother is unusually powerless (Herman & Hirschman, 1981).

Treatment for Incest Offenders and Rapists

Imprisonment has been the main form of treatment for incest offenders and for rapists. In cases of incest, an effort is usually made to keep the family intact, for the benefit of the child. Behavioral treatment for sexual aggressors (rapists and pedophiliacs) generally involve the following steps: (1) assessing sexual preferences through self-report and measuring erectile responses to different sexual stimuli; (2) reducing deviant interests through aversion therapy (the man receives electric shock when deviant stimuli is presented); (3) orgasmic reconditioning or masturbating training to increase sexual arousal to appropriate stimuli; (4) social skills training to increase interpersonal competence; (5) assessing these men after treatment (Marshall et al., 1983). Although treatment is becoming more sophisticated, questions remain about the effectiveness of these programs.

Public revulsion and outrage against incest offenders, pedophiles, and rapists have resulted in a call for severe punishment. A man who had an incestuous relationship with his stepdaughter for seven years was ordered by the judge to receive injections of the hormone progesterone to control his sex drive. This judicial ruling caused an uproar. Some groups felt that the punishment was inadequate, some felt that it would not work, and others indicated that it was "cruel and unusual."

Controversial Treatments Surgical castration has been used to treat sexual offenders in many European countries, but few studies have been made of its effectiveness. An investigation of sex offenders (rapists, heterosexual pedophiles, homosexual pedophiles, bisexual pedophiles, and a sexual murderer) who were surgically castrated reported decrease in sexual intercourse, masturbation, and frequency of sexual fantasies. However, twelve of the thirty-nine were still able to engage in sexual intercourse several years after being castrated. The rapists constituted the group whose members were most likely to remain sexually active (Heim, 1981).

Chemical therapy, usually involving the hormone Depo-Provera, reduces self-reports of sexual urges in pedophiles, but not the ability to show genital arousal. The drugs appear to reduce psychological desire more than actual erection capabilities (Wincze et al., 1986). The effectiveness of biological treatments is not known. Obviously controversy continues over the appropriate treatment for sexual offenders such as incest offenders, pedophiles, and rapists.

SEXUAL DYSFUNCTIONS

In contrast to the paraphilias, which are characterized by sexual arousal as a response to unusual situations, acts, or objects, a **sexual dysfunction** is a disruption of any part of the *normal* sexual response cycle. This normal cycle consists of four stages:

1. The *appetitive* phase is characterized by the person's desire for sexual activity. The dysfunction in which the person lacks sexual desire is called *sexual desire disorder*.

2. The *excitement* phase occurs when the normal male attains erection and the normal female attains vaginal lubrication. Psychologically based difficulties with these physiological changes are termed **inhibited sexual excitement**.

SEXUAL DYSFUNCTIONS

Persistent and recurrent problems in the appetitive, excitement, and orgasm phases of the sexual cycle. Dysfunctions are either psychological or psychophysiological in origin (never primarily physiological).

Sexual desire disorders

Problems during the appetitive phase

Hypoactive Sexual Desire Disorder
Absent or low sexual interest or desire

Sexual Aversion Disorder
Avoidance of and aversion to sexual intercourse

Sexual arousal disorders

Problems involving feelings of sexual pleasure or physiological changes associated with sexual excitement

Female Sexual Arousal Disorder
Inability to attain or maintain physiological response and/or psychological arousal during sexual activity

Male Erectile Disorder
Inability to attain or maintain an erection sufficient for sexual intercourse and/or psychological arousal during sexual activity

Orgasm disorders

Problems with the orgasm phase of the sexual cycle

Inhibited Female Orgasm
Persistent delay or inability to achieve an orgasm after the excitement phase has been reached. The sexual activity must be adequate in focus, intensity, and duration

Inhibited Male Orgasm
Persistent delay or inability to achieve an orgasm after the excitement phase has been reached and the sexual activity has been adequate in focus, intensity, and duration. Usually restricted to the inability to reach orgasm intravaginally

Premature Ejaculation
Ejaculation with minimal sexual stimulation before, during, or shortly after penetration

Sexual pain disorders

Dyspareunia
Genital pain in a man or woman that is not due to a lack of lubrication in the vagina. It occurs either before, during, or after sexual intercourse

Vaginismus
Involuntary spasm of the outer third of the vaginal wall that prevents or interferes with sexual intercourse

SOURCE: Adapted from DSM-III-R, pp. 290–296.

3. The *orgasm* phase is characterized by the release of sexual tension. The inability to achieve an orgasm after entering the excitement phase and receiving adequate sexual stimulation is called *inhibited orgasm.*

4. The *resolution* phase is characterized by relaxation of the body after orgasm. Problems with this last stage are rare.

Other problems that may be involved with the sexual response cycle include *functional dyspareunia,* or pain associated with sexual intercourse but not due to a physical condition; *premature ejaculation* in males; and *functional vaginismus* in females.

Problems occurring during the normal sexual response cycle are fairly common. However, to be diagnosed as a dysfunction, the problem must be "recurrent and persistent." DSM-III-R also requires that such factors as "frequency, chronicity, subjective distress, and effect on other areas of functioning" be considered in the diagnosis. The sexual dysfunctions are shown in the disorders chart on page 308.

Sexual Desire Disorders in Males and Females

Sexual desire disorders involve (1) *hyposexual desire disorder,* characterized by little or no interest in sexual activities either actual or fantasized and (2) *sexual aversion disorder,* characterized by an avoidance and aversion to sexual intercourse. Both of these disorders can be *lifelong* or *acquired* and may be due to psychogenic or a combination of psychogenic and biogenic factors. In the following case relationship problems contributed to the sexual dysfunction:

A 36-year-old woman and her 38-year-old husband were referred by her psychotherapist for sex therapy. The couple had had little or no sexual contact over the preceding three years, and the sexual relationship had been troubled and unsatisfactory since the day they met. . . . Kissing and gentle fondling were enjoyable to both of them, but as their relationship progressed to genital caressing, she became more anxious, despite her being easily orgasic. . . . She explained the difficulty as being due to conflict in the relationship. She saw him as angry, controlling and demanding, and very critical of her. Naturally, she did not

feel loving or sexually receptive. Correspondingly, he felt angry, resentful, and cheated of a "normal sex life." (Golden, 1988, p. 304)

In this case, the woman was diagnosed as having inhibited sexual desire. However, controversy exists over whether sexual desire disorders are labeled correctly. If the woman in the preceding case avoided sexual intercourse because of marital difficulties, is the diagnosis appropriate? And what about cases in which job stress or dual careers interfere with intimacy and sexual interest? According to DSM-III-R, a sexual dysfunction should be diagnosed in such cases because the interpersonal problem is the primary cause of the disturbed functioning. However, many people question the legitimacy of these criteria and the categories

Differences in sexual desire can have a negative impact on a couple's relationship. In this case the man feels pressure to perform sexually; the woman feels neglected because of the lack of sexual interest displayed by her husband.

themselves, challenging the notion that sexual problems stemming from troubled relationships, job dissatisfaction, or academic stress are sufficient to indicate a disorder.

Reports of diminished sexual desire, or a lack of sexual desire, are more common from women than from men. Some clinicians estimate that 40 to 50 percent of all sexual dysfunctions involve deficits in desire (Southern & Gayle, 1982; Stuart et al., 1987). People with sexual desire disorders are often capable of experiencing orgasm. However, they claim to have little interest in, or to derive no pleasure from, sexual activity. Some people may report low sexual desire because of inexperience. Many of these people may not have learned to label or identify their own arousal levels, may not know how to increase their arousal, and may have a limited expectation for their ability to be aroused (LoPiccolo, 1980).

Just as we do not really know what constitutes "normal" sexual desire, we know little about what frequency of sexual fantasies or activities is "normal." Kinsey (1948) found tremendous variation in reported total sexual outlet, or release. One male reported that he had ejaculated only once in thirty years; another claimed to have averaged 30 orgasms per week for thirty years. After analyzing mean frequencies of orgasm from sex surveys, a group of researchers noted that "A total orgasmic outlet of less than once every two weeks is considered one marker of low desire . . . unless extenuating circumstances such as a lack of privacy occur" (Schover et al., 1982, p. 616). However, using some average frequency of sexual activity doesn't seem appropriate for categorizing people as having inhibited sexual desire. Someone may have a high sex drive but not engage in sexual activities; someone else may not have sexual interest or fantasies but may engage in frequent sexual behaviors for the sake of his or her partner (Rosen & Leiblum, 1987). Until we can decide on what a normal range of sexual desire is, we can hardly discover the causes of or developing treatments for sexual desire disorders.

Sexual Arousal Disorders in Males and Females

In men, inhibited sexual excitement takes the form of **erectile dysfunction,** a man's inability to reach or maintain a penile erection sufficient for sexual intercourse. The man may feel fully aroused but can't finish the sex act. *Primary* erectile dysfunction is the diagnosis for a man who has never been able to successfully engage in sexual intercourse. This difficulty often clearly has a psychological origin, because many men with this dysfunction can get an erection and reach orgasm during masturbation and can show erection during the REM (rapid eye movement) phase of sleep. The term *secondary erectile dysfunction* refers to a situation in which the man has had at least one successful instance of sexual intercourse but is currently having erectile difficulty. Failure to achieve an erection and penetration in 25 percent of sexual attempts is sufficient for this diagnosis (Masters & Johnson, 1970). (See Focus 11.2.)

A twenty-year-old college student was suffering from secondary erectile dysfunction. His first episode of erectile difficulty occurred when he attempted sexual intercourse after drinking heavily. Although to a certain extent he attributed the failure to alcohol, he also began to have doubts about his sexual ability. During a subsequent sexual encounter, his anxiety and worry increased. When he failed in this next coital encounter, even though he had not been drinking, his anxiety level rose even more. The client sought therapy after the discovery that he was unable to have an erection even during petting.

The prevalence of erectile dysfunction is difficult to determine because it often goes unreported. Clinicians estimate that approximately 50 percent of men have experienced transient impotence (Kaplan, 1974). Of 448 male sexual dysfunctions treated at the Masters and Johnson sex clinic, 32 were suffering from primary erectile dysfunction and 213 from secondary erectile dysfunction. The number of cases reported may be increasing now, as people feel freer to talk about this problem and as it becomes more acceptable for women to expect greater satisfaction in sexual relationships.

In women, sexual arousal disorder is characterized by a lack of physical signs, such as vaginal lubrication or erection of the nipples, during sexual interactions. The individual may also complain that she derives no sexual pleasure. As with other sexual dysfunctions, this disorder may be lifelong or acquired and is often the result of negative attitudes about sex or early sexual experiences. Receiving negative infor-

FOCUS 11.2 — *Assessment of Erectile Dysfunction*

Although Masters and Johnson (1970) had estimated that only about 5 percent of erectile dysfunctions were due to physical conditions, recent studies have found that in over 30 percent of the cases, biogenic factors may be involved (Slag et al., 1981; Segraves et al., 1983). It is possible that a man may have a minor organic impairment that "makes his erection more vulnerable to being disrupted by psychological, biological, and sexual technique factors" (LoPiccolo & Stock, 1986). However, the technology does not yet exist to accurately assess a "minor" organic impairment.

Distinguishing between erectile dysfunctions that are primarily biogenic or psychogenic has been difficult. For example, one procedure involves the recording of nocturnal penile tumescence (NPT). The reasoning behind this is that men who do not display adequate spontaneous erections during sleep suffer from an organic impairment. Psychological causes are thought to predominate in cases where men show an adequate NPT response. Unfortunately, considerable overlap in NPT scores has been found between samples of diabetic men with erectile difficulties and normal functional controls (LoPiccolo & Stock, 1986). Therefore some people diagnosed as suffering from organic impotence actually have psychological factors as the cause. The reverse could also be true.

Because of the time, expense, and inaccuracies involved with the NPT assessment, other procedures have been suggested. Sakheim et al. (1987) found that the ability to obtain sufficient erections during masturbation to highly erotic videotapes produced as accurate a group assignment between organic and psychogenic impotence as did using the NPT recordings. Individual differences were found with this procedure. Some men showed the greatest sexual arousal by merely watching the videotapes, others by masturbating during the video presentations.

Both the NPT recording and the approach developed by Sakheim and his colleagues are less than perfect. It may be that a combination of the two assessments might result in more accurate distinctions. Differential diagnosis is important because treatment strategies would be different for organic or psychogenic impotence.

---

mation about sex, having been sexually assaulted or molested, and having conflicts with her sexual partner can contribute to the disorder.

> A 38-year-old woman had a satisfying sexual relationship with her husband for many years. Then her husband developed a drinking problem, which created conflict between them. Sexual intercourse started to become aversive to her, and she eventually lost all interest in sex. After her divorce, the woman was disturbed to discover that she was unable to become sexually aroused with other men. A desensitization procedure was used to eliminate her conditioned anxiety toward sexual intercourse. (Wolpe, 1982)

Inhibited Female Orgasm

In **inhibited female orgasm,** the woman is unable to achieve an orgasm with stimulation that is "adequate in focus, intensity, and duration" after entering the excitement phase. However, DSM-III-R includes an exception regarding female orgasm: "Some females are able to experience orgasm during noncoital clitoral stimulation, but are unable to experience it during coitus in the absence of manual clitoral stimulation. In most of these females, this represents a normal variation of the female sexual response" (DSM-III-R, p. 294). Whether the lack of orgasm is categorized as a dysfunction or as a "normal variant" is left to the judgment of the clinician. As is noted in Focus 11.3, the criteria that define adequate functioning during sexual intercourse are quite controversial.

Inhibited female orgasm may be termed *primary,* to indicate that orgasm has never been experienced, or *secondary,* to show that orgasm has occurred in the past. Primary orgasmic dysfunction is considered relatively common in women. Perhaps 8 to 10 percent of all women have never achieved an orgasm by any

FOCUS 11.3   *Sexual Dysfunction or Normal Variant?*

Should women who do not regularly have orgasms during coitus be considered sexually dysfunctional? This question is being debated more frequently as researchers and clinicians alike are discovering that infrequent coital orgasm is a common occurrence in women. Hite (1976) reports that only 30 percent of the women in her study could experience orgasm regularly during sexual intercourse. Similar findings have been reported by Hoch et al. (1981). Hite argues that the prevailing view of orgasm—that it "counts" only during sexual intercourse—is a reflection of our male-dominated society. Kaplan (1974) also denies that women who are otherwise sexually responsive are nonetheless "sick" because they do

not have coital orgasms. She feels that "a woman who is otherwise orgasmic, but does not reach orgasm during coitus, is neither frigid nor sick. This pattern seems to be a normal variant of female sexuality for some women" (p. 83). Hoch goes even further and suggests that the inability to achieve an orgasm without additional stimulation is "not a normal variation of female sexuality but rather normal sexuality for the majority of females" (p. 82).

This controversy has affected sexual therapy. Some sex therapists believe that orgasm during coitus is a justifiable goal for "normal" sexual functioning (Zeiss et al., 1977). Others are satisfied when patients are able to achieve orgasm through

manual stimulation (Schneidman & McGuire, 1976). Regardless of the controversy, however, a reexamination of the "necessity" of coital orgasm for women (and for men?) would seem to be in order. To require that women be able to achieve orgasm during sexual intercourse may be a disservice both to women and to their sex partners.

Male sexual dysfunction is also defined in terms of coital success. Does this mean that men who ejaculate rapidly or not at all during coitus, but who show the normal sexual cycle during masturbation and oral sex, are suffering from sexual problems? Perhaps. But many questions remain concerning the appropriate criteria for sexual dysfunction.

means (Hite, 1976; Kaplan, 1974; Kinsey, 1953). This disorder is not equivalent to primary orgasmic dysfunction in males, who often can achieve orgasm through masturbation or by some other means.

However, Wakefield (1988) argues that inhibited female orgasm actually is rare and exists in less than one percent of women. He points out that many women do not reach orgasm during initial sexual encounters. In addition, they may not have engaged in masturbation. Wakefield believes that the diagnosis of inhibited orgasm should be made only if the woman has had experiences conducive to eliciting orgasmic responses, but still has not had an orgasm.

Inhibited Male Orgasm

Inhibited male orgasm is the inability to ejaculate within the vagina, even with full arousal and penile erection. As noted, men who have this dysfunction can usually ejaculate when masturbating. Inhibited

orgasm in males is relatively rare, and little is known about it (LoPiccolo & Stock, 1986). Treatment is often urged by the partner, who may want to conceive or who may feel (because of the husband's lack of orgasm) that she is not an exciting sexual partner.

An examination of the backgrounds of men who have this dysfunction may reveal either the occurrence of some traumatic event, or a severely restrictive religious background in which sex is considered evil. Masters and Johnson (1970) give an example of a man who discovered his wife engaged in sexual intercourse with another man. Although they remained married, he could no longer ejaculate during intercourse.

Premature Ejaculation

Premature ejaculation is a relatively common sexual problem in males, but sex researchers and therapists offer different definitions of it. Kaplan (1974) defines prematurity as the inability of a man to tolerate high (plateau) levels of sexual excitement without ejaculating reflexively. Kilmann and Auerbach (1979) suggest that ejaculation within five minutes after coital entry is a suitable criterion of premature ejaculation. Masters and Johnson (1970) contend that a male who is unable to delay ejaculation long enough during sexual intercourse to produce an orgasm in the female 50 percent of the time, is a premature ejaculator. The difficulty with the last definition is the possibility that a man may be "premature" with one partner but entirely adequate for another.

Some support has been found for Kaplan's definition. The sexual responsiveness of ten premature ejaculators was compared with that of fourteen normally functioning men, and no differences were found in rate of arousal, degree of arousal, or amount of arousal, either subjectively or physiologically. However, the premature ejaculators did ejaculate at lower levels of arousal. (Spiess et al., 1984).

The inability to satisfy a sexual partner is a source of anguish for many men. In a campus newspaper column at a midwestern college, premature ejaculation was reported as the largest single source of concern in the realm of male sexual dysfunctions (Werner, 1975). In one sample of married men, 38 percent reported problems of too-rapid ejaculation (Nettlebladt & Uddenberg, 1979). And, of the sexually dysfunctional men seeking treatment at a clinic, 29 percent were diagnosed as having premature ejaculation (Hoch et al., 1981).

Functional Vaginismus

Vaginismus is the involuntary muscular constriction of the outer part of the vagina, severely restricting or preventing penile penetration. The prevalence of this dysfunction is not known, but it is considered very rare.

Several causal factors have been identified in vaginismus. Masters and Johnson (1970) found one or more of the following conditions among many women with this dysfunction: (1) a husband or partner who was impotent; (2) rigid religious beliefs about sex; (3) prior sexual trauma, such as rape; (4) prior homosexual identification; and (5) *dyspareunia,* or painful intercourse. A history of incestuous molestation is often found in women with this disorder (LoPiccolo & Stock, 1986).

Etiology and Treatment of Sexual Dysfunctions

Sexual dysfunctions may be due to psychogenic factors alone or a combination of psychological and biogenic causes. They may be mild and transient, or lifelong and chronic. Masters and Johnson (1970) identified some psychological elements in sexual dysfunctions. However, they deemphasized physical factors. Studies now indicate that neurological, vascular, and hormonal factors play a role in many cases of sexual dysfunctions (Sakheim et al., 1987). These physical problems may be relatively minor, but may render sexual functioning more susceptible to psychological or social stresses.

Biological Factors and Treatment Lower levels of testosterone and/or higher levels of estrogens such as prolactin have been associated with lower sexual interest and erectile difficulties in men (Bancroft, 1984). Drugs that suppress testosterone levels appear to decrease sexual desire in men (Wincze et al., 1986).

In addition to the above conditions, certain factors such as hypertensive medication (Rosen et al., 1988), the consumption of alcohol (Malatesta et al.,

William Masters and Virginia Johnson are pioneers in sex research and sex therapy. Their research has contributed much to our current understanding of normal sexual functioning. Many individuals suffering from various sexual dysfunctions have been successfully treated with therapy techniques developed at Masters' and Johnson's clinic.

1979), illnesses, and other physical conditions (Malatesta & Adams, 1984) are associated with sexual dysfunctions. Not everyone who takes hypertensive drugs or is ill has a sexual dysfunction. However, in some people these factors may be enough—in combination with a predisposing personal history or current stress—to produce problems in sexual function. A complete physical workup that includes the medical history, physical exam, and a laboratory evaluation is a necessary first step in assessment before treatment decisions are made.

In women, sexual desire is also influenced by male hormones. The administration of androgens is associated with reports of increased sexual desire in both men and women. (Kaplan, 1974). However, the relationship between hormones and sexual behavior is complex and difficult to understand. People with sexual dysfunctions often have normal testosterone levels.

For some, a lack of sexual desire may be physiological. One group of women reported no feelings of anxiety about, or aversion to, sexual intercourse; but they showed significantly lower sexual arousal than did sexually active women during exposure to erotic stimuli. Moreover, participation in sexual therapy did not increase their responsiveness (Wincze et al., 1978). The researchers concluded that the absence of sexual arousal in these women is biological and the appropriate treatment for this condition is unknown. Hypersensitivity to physical stimulation is another factor that may affect sexual functioning (Assalian, 1988). Men who ejaculate prematurely may have difficulty differentiating between ejaculation and its inevitability once the sympathetic nervous system is triggered.

The amount of blood flowing into the genital area is also associated with orgasmic potential in women and erectile functioning in men. In women, masturbation training and Kegel exercises may increase vascularization of labia, clitoris, and vagina. Vascular problems may also hinder blood flow to the penis and result in erectile difficulties. Vascular surgery to increase blood flow has met with limited success because in most cases the problem is due to arteriosclerosis, which affects a number of the small blood vessels (LoPiccolo & Stock, 1986).

Penile implants have been given to men suffering from organic erectile dysfunction. Although technical success of this procedure is high, problems with the

sexual adjustment often remain as illustrated in the following case:

> Mr. F. was a 54-year-old recovered alcoholic who had received a surgical implant (Scott prosthesis) following a diagnosis of organic impotence. Despite the patient's newfound ability to perform intercourse at will, in the two years following surgery he made infrequent use of the prosthesis. His wife became increasingly distressed by his disinclination to either initiate or respond with any enthusiasm to her overtures for sexual contact. In reviewing the history, it became apparent that his loss of sexual desire had preceded the erectile failure and that the absence of desire appeared to be the primary problem for treatment. Unfortunately, both the urologist and the patient's wife had assumed that once the capacity for intercourse was restored, sexual interest would re-emerge unassisted (Rosen & Leiblum, 1987, p. 153).

Psychological Factors and Behavioral Therapy

Psychological causes for sexual dysfunctions can include historical or predisposing factors, sexual trauma, inadequate or inappropriate sexual experiences, and relationship conflicts.

Predisposing or Historical Factors Early experiences can interact with current problems to produce sexual dysfunctions. Traditional psychoanalysts have stressed the role of *unconscious conflicts*. For example, erectile difficulties and premature ejaculation represent male hostility to women, due to unresolved early developmental conflicts involving the parents. Psychodynamic treatment is directed toward uncovering and resolving the unconscious hostility. The results of this approach have been disappointing (Kaplan, 1974; Kilmann & Auerbach, 1979). It seems plausible, however, that the attitudes parents display toward sex and affection and to each other can influence their children's attitudes. For example, women with sexual desire disorders rated their parents' attitude towards sex more negatively than did women without sexual desire disorders (Stuart et al., 1987). Being raised in a strict religious environment is also associated with sexual dysfunctions in both men and women (Masters & Johnson, 1970). Traumatic sexual experiences involving incestuous molestations during childhood or adolescence or rape are also factors to consider (Burgess & Holmstrom, 1979b; LoPiccolo & Stock, 1986).

Current Factors Factors operating in the present may interact with a predisposing factor to produce a sexual dysfunction. In other cases, current problems may be enough to interfere with sexual function. A relationship problem is often a contributing factor. In a study of fifty-nine women with sexual desire disorders, only eleven had the problem before marriage; the other forty-eight developed it gradually after being married. The women voiced dissatisfaction about their relationship with their husbands, complaining that their spouses did not listen to them. Marital dissatisfaction may have caused them to lose their attraction toward their husbands (Stuart et al., 1987).

Situational or coital anxiety can interrupt sexual functioning in both men and women. Anxieties over sexual overtures were reported by a group of men with psychogenic erectile dysfunction and included a fear of failing sexually, a fear of being seen as being sexually inferior, and anxiety over the size of their genitals. These patients also reported marked increases in subjective anxiety and displayed somatic symptoms such as sweating, trembling, muscle tension, and heart palpitations when asked to imagine engaging in sexual intercourse (Cooper, 1969). In a sample of 275 college men, sexual pressure from a partner was associated with sexual dysfunction. The men most affected were those who identified most heavily with the traditional masculine role (Spencer & Zeiss, 1987).

Factors associated with orgasmic dysfunction in women include having a sexually inexperienced or dysfunctional partner; the crippling fear of performance failure, of anxiety over being able to attain orgasm, of pregnancy, or of venereal disease; an inability to accept the partner, either emotionally or physically; and misinformation or ignorance about sexuality or sexual techniques.

Many approaches have been used in treating sexual dysfunctions, such as desensitization (Wolpe, 1973), graded exercises (Stravynski, 1986), masturbation (Kohlenberg, 1974; Sue, 1978; LoPiccolo & Stock, 1986), sex education training (Kilmann et al., 1986), and the modification of sexual expectations

(Rosen & Leiblum, 1987). Most general treatment approaches include the following components:

- *Education* The therapist replaces sexual myths and misconceptions with accurate information. Discussion involving sexual anatomy and function are also presented.

- *Anxiety reduction* Therapists use procedures such as desensitization or graded approaches to minimize anxiety. Explanations are given of how constantly "observing and evaluating" one's performance can interfere with sexual functioning.

- *Structured behavioral exercises* The therapist gives a series of graded tasks that gradually increase the amount of sexual interaction that takes place. They generally involve having each partner take turns touching and being touched over different parts of the body except for the genital regions. Later the partners fondle the body and genital regions, without making demands for sexual arousal or orgasm. Successful sexual intercourse and orgasm is the final stage of the structured exercises.

- *Communication training* The partners are taught appropriate ways of communicating their sexual wishes to each other and are taught conflict resolution skills.

Specific treatments for the four dysfunctions are discussed below.

Orgasmic Dysfunctions Although the general approach has been successful in treating sexual arousal disorders in women and erectile disorders in men, masturbation appears to be the most effective way for orgasmically dysfunctional women to have an orgasm. The procedure involves education about sexual anatomy, visual and tactile self-exploration, using sexual fantasies and images, and masturbation both individually and with a partner. Success rates of 95 percent have been reported with this procedure for women with primary orgasmic dysfunction (LoPiccolo & Stock, 1986). However, this approach does not necessarily lead to the woman's ability to achieve orgasm during sexual intercourse.

Premature Ejaculation In one technique, the partner stimulates the penis while it's outside the vagina until the man feels the sensation of impending ejaculation. At this point, stimulation is stopped for a short period of time, and then it is continued again. The pattern is repeated until the man can tolerate increasingly greater periods of stimulation before ejaculation (Semans, 1956). Masters and Johnson (1970) and Kaplan (1974) used a similar procedure, called "the squeeze technique." They reported a success rate of nearly 100 percent. The treatment is easily learned.

Although the short-term success rate for treating premature ejaculation is very high, a follow-up period of up to six years found that relapses were very common. (Hawton et al., 1986). More long-term follow-ups of all treatments for the sexual dysfunctions are necessary to judge treatment effectiveness.

Vaginismus The results of treatment for vaginismus have been uniformly positive (Kaplan, 1974; LoPiccolo, 1984; LoPiccolo & Stock, 1986). The involuntary spasms or closure of the vaginal muscle can be deconditioned by first training the woman to relax, to reduce anxiety, and by then inserting successively larger dilators while she is relaxed, until insertion of the penis can occur.

Evaluation of Behavior Therapy Although the initial reports on behavioral treatment for the sexual dysfunctions have been highly positive, later studies have questioned the reports of high success rates (LoPiccolo & Stock, 1986; Malatesta & Adams, 1983). Lower reversal (success) rates than those reported by Masters and Johnson have been found by other researchers (LoPiccolo et al., 1985).

A long-term outcome study of the results of sexual therapy for 140 couples with a variety of sexual dysfunctions came to the following conclusions. Long-term outcome was very good for vaginismus, good for erectile dysfunction, surprisingly poor for premature ejaculation, and very poor for females with sexual desire disorders. Recurrence of the problem during the follow-up period was common (75 percent of the sample had relapses). Some couples were able to eliminate the problem themselves. Discussing the problem with one's partner, practicing exercises learned during therapy, and reading books on human sexuality were reported to be effective strategies. Ignoring the problem or not having sex were ineffective (Hawton et al., 1986). The results of this study indicate that relapse prevention proce-

dures [strategies to be employed when problems recur] should be incorporated in sex therapy programs and that new treatment strategies, especially for the sexual desire disorders, should be developed.

HOMOSEXUALITY

Is homosexuality a mental disorder? The answer the American Psychiatric Association gives to this question depends on whether one consults DSM-I, DSM-II, DSM-III, or DSM-III-R. The changing way homosexuality is conceptualized has been influenced by changes in societal norms and values.

DSM-I and DSM-II classified homosexuality as sexually deviant because sexual behavior was considered normal only if it occurred between two consenting adults of the opposite sex. Two objections were made to this criterion. First, many clinicians felt that heterosexual sexuality shouldn't be the standard to judge other sexual behaviors. Second, many homosexual people argued that they are mentally healthy and that their sexual preference reflects a normal variant of sexual expression. However, some clinicians felt that homosexuality was the result of unhealthy early family relationships. This controversy was aired at a special session of the American Psychiatric Association, held to determine whether the classification of homosexuality as a mental disorder should be retained in the then-current DSM-II (Stoller et al., 1973).

At that meeting, two well-known psychiatrists, Irving Bieber and Charles Socarides, supported the traditional view of homosexuality as a psychosexual disorder resulting from disturbed relationships between parents and their children. They felt this view was supported by studies of homosexuals in treatment and recommended retaining the classification in DSM-II. When that proposal encountered opposition, Bieber suggested that homosexual behavior be reclassified as a category of sexual dysfunction, because "most homosexuals (especially those who are exclusively homosexual) cannot function heterosexually" (Stoller et al., 1973). Many practitioners and clinicians considered this suggestion inappropriate, for several reasons. First, many homosexuals *can* engage in sexual intercourse with members of the opposite sex. Second, heterosexual coitus was still held as the standard on which to judge other sexual behaviors. Third, the issue was considered to be one of sexual preference rather than function.

Because of these reasons, Stoller and his colleagues supported the removal of homosexuality from the DSM-II nomenclature, preferring to consider it a normal variant of human sexual behavior (Stoller et al., 1973). Marmor was especially critical of inferring psychopathology from samples of homosexuals who seek treatment. He remarked, "If our judgment about mental health was based only on those whom we see in our clinical practices, we would have to conclude that all heterosexuals are also mentally ill" (Stoller et al., 1973, p. 1209). From various nonclinical samples of homosexuals, it can be concluded that many are well adjusted (Bell & Weinberg, 1978; Strassberg et al., 1979; Thompson et al., 1971).

After considering the issues, the trustees of the American Psychiatric Association voted, on December 15, 1973, to remove homosexuality from DSM-II (the vote was 13 to 0, with two abstentions). A new category, *sexual orientation disturbance*, was created and applied only to those people who wanted to change from a homosexual to a heterosexual orientation. This change appeared in the seventh printing of DSM-II. The trustees approved the new category because they were swayed by arguments that ho-

mosexuals who wanted to change sexual orientations should be able to seek therapy. Members of the gay community objected to this category, however, because it meant that some homosexuals may be viewed as "sick." DSM-III retained this compromise category, renamed **ego-dystonic homosexuality** (homosexuality that is unacceptable to the ego and is thus a source of distress).

Although DSM-III states explicitly that "homosexuality itself is not considered a mental disorder," it adds that "factors that predispose an individual to ego-dystonic homosexuality are those negative societal attitudes towards homosexuality that have been internalized" (American Psychiatric Association, 1980, p. 282). In other words, pressures to conform to societal standards and the desire to have children and a "socially sanctioned family life" may be incompatible with homosexuality. (See Focus 11.4 for discussion of this issue.) The diagnostic criteria for this disorder included "a persistent pattern of absent or weak heterosexual arousal" that interferes with establishing *desired* heterosexual relationships and a "sustained pattern of homosexual arousal" that the person doesn't want and finds distressing.

However, the diagnosis was inappropriate if a person adjusted to his or her sexual orientation and in cases where people with homosexual inclinations

Homosexuality is controversial in both the mental health community and society at large. Some clinicians still consider it a mental disorder. However, a specific category for homosexuality has been eliminated in the revised DSM-III, which reflects the view that homosexuality is a sexual preference rather than a disorder.

FOCUS 11.4   *Are Children Raised by Homosexuals Confused About Their Gender Identity?*

In the face of strong objections, a growing number of homosexuals and transsexuals are asserting their right to raise children. The objectors argue that homosexuals and transsexuals follow deviant lifestyles and that children living with such parents will adopt their maladaptive orientation. In fact, both social learning and psychoanalytic theorists might predict that such children would be likely to have some form of gender identity problem or other serious confusion.

The development of 21 children (average age, eight years) living with homosexual parents was investigated by Green (1978). The children had lived in these households for an average of four and one-half years. In nearly all cases, the children were aware of their parents' atypical sexual orientation. For example, four girls were living in a transsexual household while their mother underwent androgen hormone treatment and sex conversion surgery. This person became their "father," who then married their "step-mother."

Measures of sexual identity (toy and game preference, peer group composition preference, clothing preference, roles in fantasy games, vocational aspirations, reported romantic crushes, and fantasies) were obtained on all the children. *All of them* displayed heterosexual preferences that were appropriate for their sex. Green cautions that this is a preliminary report and that no control group was present, nor are longer-term effects known. Given these limitations, Green (1978) tentatively suggests that "children being raised by transsexual or homosexual parents do not differ appreciably from children raised in more conventional family settings on macroscopic measures of sexual identity" (p. 696–697).

In another study, ten boys and ten girls between the ages of 5 and 12 who were living with their lesbian mothers were compared with children raised by heterosexual mothers. The two groups of children did not differ with respect to the sex of the first figure they drew, play and sexual preferences, and playroom behavior (Kirkpatrick et al., 1981). However, Green's comments regarding better control and longer-term studies apply to these results as well as to his own. We need more research before we can determine whether gender identity and sex-role development are influenced by homosexual or transsexual parentage.

---

eventually give up the desire to become heterosexual. In addition, DSM-III points out that without intervention the development of heterosexual adjustment in such people is "rare" and that even with therapy the outcome is "disputed."

A major criticism of using ego-dystonic homosexuality as a diagnostic category was the underlying acceptance of heterosexual functioning as the norm. No parallel category exists for a heterosexual who shows a "persistent pattern of absent or weak homosexual arousal" that interferes with "establishing desired homosexual relationships." Spitzer (1981b) acknowledges this criticism, but counters that "there is not a single case in the scientific literature that describes an individual with a sustained pattern of heterosexual arousal who was distressed by being heterosexually aroused and wished to acquire homosexual arousal to initiate or to maintain homosexual relationships." This statement, however, doesn't take into consideration the tremendous amount of prejudice and discrimination that homosexuals face. Heterosexuals who would rather be homosexuals may be intimidated by this societal pressure and may simply not identify themselves. Moreover, in accordance with this bias, a man or woman complaining of weak heterosexual arousal may be labeled as suffering from inhibited sexual desire or arousal.

The fact that nearly all homosexuals go through a period where their homosexuality is ego dystonic made diagnosis difficult. So the diagnosis of ego-dystonic homosexuality was rarely made and was not studied by researchers. These problems proved insurmountable, and so the category was eliminated from DSM-III-R. However, a clinician can still put a patient who would have been diagnosed with ego-dystonic homosexuality according to DSM-III, into a general category—*sexual disorders not otherwise specified*. This move reflects a growing movement to "depathologize" homosexuality and to consider it a matter of sexual preference or choice.

The Question of Choice

In the most comprehensive study of homosexuals to date, researchers analyzed data obtained from four-hour interviews with 979 male and female homosexuals and 477 matched controls (Bell & Weinberg, 1978; Bell et al., 1981). Most homosexuals (both male and female) indicated no regrets at being homosexual, and accepted their sexual orientation. Those who regretted their homosexuality cited, as major problems, the lack of acceptance by society, not being able to have children, and loneliness:

> My regret is not [in] being a homosexual but [in] being a homosexual in this society. . . . I'd like to be a teacher right now. I really would. But I won't go where I have to live a lie and where homosexuals are not accepted or welcome. (Bell & Weinberg, 1978, p. 123)

> The person I love and live with might someday want a child, and I could never give it to her, nor could she to me. This is often important to women. (Bell & Weinberg, 1978, p. 126)

With regard to psychological adjustment, few differences were found between homosexual and heterosexual women. However, homosexual men were more likely than heterosexual men to report feelings of loneliness, depression, and low self-esteem. This difference was accounted for by those relatively few male homosexuals who were dissatisfied with their orientation. Homosexuals who accepted themselves as such did not differ from heterosexuals on psychological adjustment measures.

Like their heterosexual neighbors, homosexual people experienced some problems with sexual functioning: 23 percent of the men reported problems in attaining or maintaining erection (of these problems, about one-fifth were reportedly severe, and the re-

mainder mild); and 28 percent complained of "coming too fast" (again, in about one-fifth this problem was severe). Lack of orgasm was reported by 14 percent of the men and 20 percent of the women.

The researchers found that homosexuals did not differ from heterosexuals in frequency of dating during high school. Most had their first homosexual experience with a friend or acquaintance of about their own age.

Treatment of Homosexuality

A great deal of controversy surrounds the treatment of homosexuality. Some clinicians feel that a homosexual's request for treatment merely reflects societal pressure (Silverstein, 1972; Davison, 1974). Treatment is thus seen as an effort to produce conformity:

> To grow up in a family where the word "homosexual" was whispered, to play in a playground and hear the words "faggot" and "queer," to go to church and hear of "sin" and then to college and hear of "illness," and finally to the counseling center that promises to "cure" is hardly an environment of freedom and voluntary choice. (Silverstein, 1972, p. 4)

When homosexuals present themselves for treatment, therefore, therapists must decide what the appropriate approach should be. The client must first specify whether he or she wants the treatment to focus on eliminating the distress associated with the homosexuality, or on eliminating the homosexual behavior. A homosexual patient seeking to be rid of the ego dystonicity (the distress) would probably receive either supportive counseling, insight-oriented psychotherapy, cognitive-behavioral therapy (examining the irrational beliefs that foster distress), or relaxation training. If the person seeks to change sexual orientation, the therapist must decide whether or not to consider homosexuality a pathological state.

Some clinicians feel that both homosexuals and heterosexuals should have a choice of sexual orientation. To support this philosophy, Masters and Johnson (1979) established a program to help sexually dysfunctional homosexuals change their sexual orientation. Their program is similar to those developed for heterosexuals, and its failure rate is reported to be low. However, the vast majority of homosexuals do not want to change their sexual orientation.

AGING AND SEXUAL ACTIVITY

Sexuality during old age has been the subject of many myths and jokes. In our youth-oriented society, sexual activity is simply not associated with aging. However, a large percentage of older Americans clearly have active sex lives.

In a study of sexual functioning in 60- to 79-year-old married men, a clear relationship was found between the reported frequency of intercourse at younger ages and at present. The most active respondents reported a present frequency of sexual activity that was 61 percent of their frequency level between ages 40 and 59. The respondents that were least active reported a present level of frequency that was only 6 percent of the sexual activity they engaged in between ages 40 and 59. The most active also indicated that they became aroused on seeing women in public situations and in response to visual stimuli. The vast majority (69 percent) felt that sex was important for good health, and most (63 percent) accepted masturbation as an acceptable outlet. Sexual dysfunctions were also more prevalent in this population than in younger groups, and the prevalence was affected by the individuals' prior and present sexual activity levels. Of the least active, 21 percent suffered from premature ejaculation, and 75 percent were either impotent or had erectile difficulties. For the most active group, the corresponding percentages were 8 and 19 percent (Martin, 1981).

Physiologically based changes in patterns of sexual arousal and orgasm have been found in people over age 65 (Masters & Johnson, 1966). For both men and women, sexual arousal takes longer. Erection and vaginal lubrication are slower to occur, and the urgency for orgasm is reduced. However, both men and women are fully capable of sexual satisfaction if no organic conditions interfere.

Sexual activity does, however, appear to play a less important part in the lives of the elderly. They feel that a decline in sexual interest is a natural part of aging, and only 35 percent would seek treatment to obtain greater sexual vigor if this were possible. With or without sex, the elderly men in the Martin (1981) study regarded their marriages as highly successful and their wives as physically attractive; and they themselves were free of performance anxiety.

SUMMARY

1. The gender identity disorders include transsexualism; childhood gender identity disorder; and gender identity of adolescence or adulthood, nontranssexual type. Transsexuals feel a severe psychological conflict between their sexual self-concept on the one hand and their genetic sex on the other. Some transsexuals seek sex conversion surgery, although behavioral therapies are increasingly being used. Gender identity disorders can also occur in childhood. Children with this problem identify with members of the opposite sex, deny their own physical attributes, and often cross-dress. Treatment generally includes the parents and is behavioral in nature.

2. The paraphilias are of three types, characterized by (a) a preference for nonhuman objects for sexual arousal, (b) the association of real or simulated suffering with sexual activity, or (c) repetitive sexual activity with nonconsenting partners. Suggested causes of the paraphilias are unconscious conflicts (the psychodynamic perspective) and conditioning, generally during childhood. Treatments are usually behavioral and are aimed at eliminating the deviant behavior while teaching more appropriate behaviors.

3. Sexual dysfunctions are disruptions of the normal sexual response cycle. They are fairly common in the general population and may affect the person's ability to become sexually aroused or to engage in intercourse. They include the lack of interest in sexual activities, difficulty in achieving sexual arousal, and the inability to achieve an orgasm with adequate sexual stimulation. Other sexual dysfunctions include premature ejaculation in males and vaginismus in females. The etiology often involves a combination of biological, historical, and situational factors. The various treatment programs are generally successful.

4. The category of ego-dystonic homosexuality (homosexuality that is unacceptable to the person) has been eliminated in DSM-III-R. Instead, people who meet the criteria for ego-dystonic homosexuality will now be placed in a more general category: sexual disorders not otherwise specified.

5. Despite myths to the contrary, sexuality extends into old age. However, sexual dysfunction becomes increasingly prevalent with aging, and the frequency of sexual activity typically declines.

KEY TERMS

ego-dystonic homosexuality Homosexuality that is unacceptable to the ego and is thus a source of distress

erectile dysfunction A man's inability to attain or maintain a penile erection sufficient for sexual intercourse

exhibitionism A disorder in which a person gets sexual gratification by exposing his genitals to strangers

fetishism A disorder characterized by an extremely strong sexual attraction for an inanimate object

gender identity disorder A psychological disorder characterized by conflict between a person's anatomical sex and his or her sexual identity

gender identity disorder of childhood In a child, a strong and persistent desire, or claim, to be a member of the opposite sex

incest Sexual relations between close relatives

inhibited orgasm A sexual dysfunction in which the person is unable to achieve orgasm during coitus with adequate stimulation after entering the excitement phase of the sexual response cycle

inhibited sexual excitement A sexual dysfunction characterized by erectile dysfunction in men, or by an inability to attain or sustain arousal in women

masochism A sexual disorder in which erotic or sexual gratification is obtained by receiving pain or punishment

paraphilias Sexual disorders in which unusual or bizarre acts, images, or objects are required for sexual arousal

pedophilia A disorder in which an adult obtains erotic gratification through sexual contact with children

premature ejaculation Ejaculation before penile entry into the vagina or so soon after entry that an unsatisfactory sexual experience results

rape An act of intercourse that is accomplished through force or the threat of force

sadism A sexual disorder in which erotic or sexual gratification is obtained by inflicting pain or humiliation on others

sexual desire disorders Sexual dysfunctions involving a lack of sexual interest as reflected in low levels of both sexual activity and fantasizing or an aversion to sexual intercourse

sexual dysfunction A disruption of any part of the normal sexual response cycle, in a male or female

transsexualism A person's self-identification with the opposite sex

transvestic fetishism A disorder in which the person feels intense sexual interest and urges to cross-dress. Person is highly distressed by these urges or has acted on them

vaginismus Involuntary contraction of the outer part of the vagina, which restricts or prevents penile insertion

voyeurism A disorder in which sexual gratification is obtained by surreptitiously observing nude people or couples engaged in coitus

PART 4

Severe Disorders of Mood and Thought

chapter 12
Mood Disorders

All of us have experienced moods (or affect) involving *depression* or elation at some time during our lives. The loss of a job or the death of a loved one may result in depression: good news may make us *manic* (for example, ecstatic, hyperactive, and brazen). How do we know if these reactions are normal or manifestations of a serious mental disorder? In general, depression or mania that pervades every aspect of a person's life, that persists over along period of time, or that occurs for no apparent reason may be symptomatic of a mood disorder.

Mood disorders are disturbances in emotions that cause subjective discomfort and/or hinder a person's ability to function. Depression and/or mania are central to these disorders. **Depression** is characterized by intense sadness, feelings of futility and worthlessness, and withdrawal from others. **Mania** is characterized by elevated mood, expansiveness, or irritability, often resulting in hyperactivity. Depression is one of the most commonly diagnosed conditions among patients hospitalized for mental disorders and is also quite prevalent in the general population.

In a large-scale survey Myers et al. (1984) found that about 3 percent of the adult male population and 7 percent of the females had experienced a depressive mood disorder over a six-month period. Lifetime prevalence (the proportion of people who develop severe depression at some point in their lives), is as high as 26 percent for women and 12 percent for men (American Psychiatric Association, 1987). Some evidence also suggests that the frequency of depression has increased over the past 50 years (Robins et al., 1984).

Severe depression does not respect socioeconomic status, educational attainments, or personal qualities; it may afflict rich or poor, successful or unsuccessful, highly educated or uneducated. The prevalence of depression is much higher than for mania, which Myers et al. (1984) found to be about 0.6 percent for males and females. The following case illustrates one woman's experience with severe depression:

Amanda is a 39-year-old homemaker with three children, ages 9, 11, and 14. Her husband is the sales manager for an auto agency, and the family does well financially and lives comfortably. For years, family life was stable and no serious problems existed between family members. The family could be described as cohesive and loving. However, Jim began to notice that his wife was becoming more and more unhappy and depressed. She constantly said that her life lacked purpose. Jim would try to reassure her, pointing out that they had a nice home and that she had no reason to be unhappy. He suggested that she find some hobbies or socialize more with their neighbors. But Amanda became progressively more absorbed in her belief that her life was meaningless.

After a while, Amanda no longer bothered to keep the house clean, to cook, or to take care of the children. At first Jim had thought she was merely in a "bad mood" and that it would pass, but as her lethargy deepened, he became increasingly worried. He thought his wife was either sick or no longer loved him and the children. Amanda told him that she was tired, that simple household chores took too much energy. She still loved Jim and the children, but said that she no longer had strong feelings for anything. Amanda did show some guilt about her inability to take care of the children and be a wife, but everything was simply too depressing. Life was no longer important, and she just wanted to be left alone. At that point she began to cry uncontrollably. Nothing Jim said could bring her out of the depression or stop her from crying. He decided that she had to see a physician, and he made an appointment.

The day of the appointment, Jim worked only until noon so that he could go with his wife to the physician's office. On arriving home, he found Amanda nearly unconscious; she had taken a lot of sleeping pills, apparently trying to commit suicide. She was rushed to a hospital where, fortunately, her life was saved. Both the timing of the suicide attempt (just before a scheduled appointment with the physician) and the large number of pills taken convinced hospital staff of her sense of hopelessness and of her need for intensive therapy. Amanda is currently receiving medication and psychotherapy to treat her depression.

In this chapter, we first describe the clinical symptoms of depression and mania, and the two major types of mental disorders—depressive disorders and bipolar disorders. Then we discuss their causes and treatment. In Chapter 13, we examine the very serious problem of suicide—a phenomenon that has been strongly linked to depression.

THE SYMPTOMS OF DEPRESSION AND MANIA

Depression and mania, the two extremes of mood or affect, can be considered the opposite ends of a continuum that extends from deep sadness to wild elation. Of the two, depression is much more prevalent. It appears in 90 percent of all diagnosed cases of mood disorders, and it would be expected to show up in the other 10 percent if they remained untreated.

Clinical Symptoms of Depression

Among the variety of symptoms that depressives may show is a core group of characteristics that identify this disturbance. These characteristics may be organized within the four psychological domains used to describe anxiety: the affective domain, the cognitive domain, the behavioral domain, and the physiological domain. Table 12.1 shows this organization and the core group symptoms.

Affective Symptoms Depressed mood is the most striking symptom of depression. Depressives experience feelings of sadness, dejection, and an excessive and prolonged mourning. Feelings of worthlessness and having lost the joy of living are common. Wild weeping may occur as a general reaction to frustration or anger. Such crying spells do not seem to be directly correlated with a specific situation.

TABLE 12.1 | Symptoms of Depression

Domain	Symptoms
Affective	Sadness, unhappiness, "blue" moods, apathy
Cognitive	Pessimism, ideas of guilt, self-denigration, loss of interest and motivation, decrease in efficiency and concentration, suicidal ideation
Behavioral	Neglect of personal appearance, psychomotor retardation, agitation, suicidal gestures
Physiological	Loss of or increase in appetite, loss of weight or weight gain, constipation, poor sleep, aches and pains, diminished sex drive

SOURCE: Adapted from Mendels, 1970.

To illustrate these affective characteristics, here is a condensed transcript of the words of a patient who has been excessively depressed for nearly six months over the death of her husband in an automobile accident:

> I don't know what to do anymore (weeps) . . . ever since my husband died . . . life. . . . It isn't worth (weeping) . . . worth it. My life is empty. . . . why should I go on? . . . all I do is cry like a baby . . . why can't you help me. . . . All I do now is (weeps) . . . lay in bed and feel miserable. I'm no good. Since he died, I feel totally worthless.

We should note here that severe depressive symptoms often occur as a normal reaction to the death of a loved one. This intensive mourning is thought to have a positive psychological function in helping one to adjust. However, an excessively long period of bereavement accompanied by a preoccupation with feelings of worthlessness, marked functional impairment, and serious psychomotor retardation, can indicate a major mood disorder. DSM-III-R (1987) notes that cultures vary in the normal duration of bereavement but severe, incapacitating depression rarely continues after the first three months.

Cognitive Symptoms Beside general feelings of futility, emptiness, and hopelessness, certain thoughts and ideas are clearly related to depressive reactions. For example, the person feels a profound pessimism about the future. Disinterest, decreased energy, dif-

ficulty in concentration, and loss of motivation make it difficult for the depressed person to cope with everyday situations. Work responsibilities become monumental tasks, and the person avoids them. Self-accusation of incompetence and general self-denigration are common, as are thoughts about suicide.

Depression may be considered to be reflected in a *cognitive triad,* which consists of negative views of the self, of the outside world, and of the future (Beck, 1974). The person has pessimistic beliefs about what he or she can do, about what others can do to help, and about his or her prospects for the future. Some of this triad can be seen in the following self-description of the thoughts and feelings of a severe depressive:

> The gradual progression to this state of semicognizance and quiescence was steady; it is hard to trace. People and things counted less. I ceased to wonder. I asked a member of my family where I was and, having received an answer, accepted it. And usually I remembered it, when I was in a state to remember anything objective. The days dragged; there was no "motive," no drive of any kind. A dull acceptance settled upon me. Nothing interested me. I was very tired and heavy. I refused to do most of the things that were asked of me, and to avoid further disturbance I was put to bed again. (Hillyer, 1964, pp. 158–59)

Ezra Pound, one of the most brilliant poets of the twentieth century, suffered a severe depression when he was in his seventies. He told an interviewer

The single most striking symptom of depression is mood. Feelings of sadness, dejection, and excessive mourning are the predominant moods during depression. Also common are feelings of worthlessness and loss of the joy of living.

bitterly, "I have lived all my life believing that I knew something. And then a strange day came and I realized that I knew nothing, nothing at all. And so words have become empty of meaning. Everything that I touch, I spoil. I have blundered always" (Darrach, 1976, p. 81). Pound stopped writing for years; for days on end, he ceased to speak. For both Hillyer and Pound, motivation, activity, vitality, and optimism had declined drastically.

Behavioral Symptoms The appearance and outward demeanor of a person is often a telltale sign of depression. The person's clothing may be sloppy or dirty; hair may be unkempt and personal cleanliness neglected. A dull, masklike facial expression may become characteristic. Body movements are slow, and new activities are not initiated. Speech is reduced and slow, and the person may respond with short phrases. This slowing down of all bodily movements, expressive gestures, and spontaneous responses is called *psychomotor retardation*. The person often withdraws socially and becomes less productive at work.

By contrast to this typical retarded condition of depressives, however, some may manifest an agitated state and symptoms of restlessness.

Physiological Symptoms The following somatic and related symptoms are frequently found in depressives:

1. Depressed people often experience a *loss of appetite and weight*, although some may actually have increased appetite and gain weight. The loss of appetite often stems from the person's disinterest in eating; food seems tasteless. In severe cases, the weight loss can become life threatening.

2. Depressives may become constipated and may not have bowel movements for days at a time.

3. *Sleep disturbance* is a common complaint. Difficulty in falling asleep, waking up early, waking up erratically during the night, insomnia, and nightmares leave the depressive exhausted and tired during the day. Many depressives dread the arrival of night because it represents a major fatigue-producing battle to fall asleep. (Some show hypersomnia or excessive sleep, however.)

4. In women, depression may *disrupt the normal menstrual cycle*. Usually, the cycle is prolonged, with possible skipping of one or several periods. The volume of menstrual flow may decrease.

5. Many depressives report an *aversion to sexual activity*, and their sexual arousal dramatically declines.

People who have several of these symptoms for a two-week period may be experiencing a major depressive episode. The episode can be mild, moderate, or severe, depending on the degree of impairment and number of symptoms.

Clinical Symptoms of Mania

In mania, the person's mood is elevated, expansive, or irritable. Social and occupational functioning are impaired, as shown in the following case:

Alan was a 43-year-old unmarried computer programmer who had led a relatively quiet life until two weeks before, when he returned to work after a short absence for illness. Alan seemed to be in a particularly good mood. Others in the office noticed that he was unusually happy and energetic, greeting everyone at work. A few days later, during the lunch hour, Alan bought a huge cake and insisted that his fellow workers eat some of it. At first everyone was surprised and amused by his antics. But two colleagues working with him on a special project became increasingly irritated, because Alan didn't put any time into their project. He just insisted that he would finish his part in a few days.

On the day the manager had decided to tell Alan of his colleagues' concern, Alan behaved in a characteristic, delirious, manic way. When he came to work, he immediately jumped on top of a desk and yelled, "Listen, listen! We aren't working on the most important aspects of our data! I know, since I've debugged my mind. Erase, reprogram, you know what I mean. We've got to examine the total picture based on the input!" Alan then spouted profanities and made obscene remarks to several of the secretaries. Onlookers thought that he must have taken drugs. Attempts to calm him down brought angry and vicious denunciations. The manager, who had been summoned, also couldn't calm him. Finally the manager threatened to fire Alan. At this point, Alan called the manager an incompetent fool and stated that he could not be fired. His speech was so rapid and disjointed that it was difficult to understand him. Alan then picked up a chair and said he was going to smash the computers. Several co-workers grabbed him and held him on the floor. Alan was yelling so loud that his voice was quite hoarse, but he continued to shout and struggle. Two police officers were called, and they had to handcuff him to restrain his movements. Within hours, he was taken to a psychiatric hospital for observation.

Manic people like Alan show boundless energy, enthusiasm, and self-assertion. Their mood or *affect* is one of elation or irritability, grandiosity, and exaggeration. Manic patients are often uninhibited, engaging impulsively in sexual activity or abusive discourse. The energy and excitement these patients show may cause them to lose weight or to go without sleep for long periods. If frustrated, they may become profane and quite belligerent.

Cognitive symptoms are generally reflected in the verbal processes of manic patients. For example, their speech is usually quite accelerated and pressured. They may change topics in mid-sentence or utter irrelevant and idiosyncratic phrases. Although much of what they say is understandable to others, the accelerated and disjointed nature of their speech makes it difficult to follow their train of thought. They seem incapable of controlling their attention, as though they are constantly distracted by new and more exciting thoughts and ideas.

In the *behavioral* domain, three levels of manic intensity have been recognized. In the mildest form, *hypomania*, affected people seem to be "high" in mood and overactive in behavior. Their judgment is usually poor, although delusions are rare. They start many projects, but few if any are completed. When they interact with co-workers, hypomanics dominate the conversation and are often grandiose.

Behaviors are more intense in people who suffer from *acute mania*. Overactivity, grandiosity, and irritability are more pronounced; speech may be incoherent; people with acute mania don't tolerate criticisms or restraints imposed by others. The acute manic reaction may develop out of the hypomanic state or may appear suddenly with little warning.

In the most severe form, *delirious mania*, the person is wildly excited, rants, raves (the stereotype of a wild "maniac"), and is constantly agitated and on the move. Hallucinations and delusions often appear, and the person is uncontrollable and frequently dangerous to him- or herself or to others. This disturbance is so severe that physical restraint and medication are frequently necessary. These three levels of intensity roughly correspond to the mild, moderate, and severe degrees of mania outlined in DSM-III-R. The most prominent *physiological* or somatic characteristic is a decreased need for sleep accompanied by high levels of arousal.

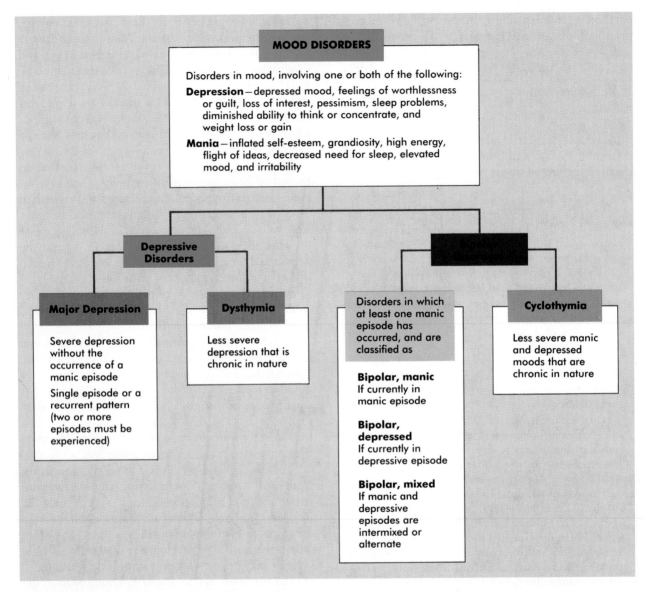

MOOD DISORDERS

Disorders in mood, involving one or both of the following:

Depression—depressed mood, feelings of worthlessness or guilt, loss of interest, pessimism, sleep problems, diminished ability to think or concentrate, and weight loss or gain

Mania—inflated self-esteem, grandiosity, high energy, flight of ideas, decreased need for sleep, elevated mood, and irritability

Depressive Disorders

Major Depression

Severe depression without the occurrence of a manic episode

Single episode or a recurrent pattern (two or more episodes must be experienced)

Dysthymia

Less severe depression that is chronic in nature

Disorders in which at least one manic episode has occurred, and are classified as

Bipolar, manic
If currently in manic episode

Bipolar, depressed
If currently in depressive episode

Bipolar, mixed
If manic and depressive episodes are intermixed or alternate

Cyclothymia

Less severe manic and depressed moods that are chronic in nature

SOURCE: Adapted from DSM-III-R, pp. 213–233.

CLASSIFICATION OF MOOD DISORDERS

Mood disorders are divided into two major categories in DSM-III-R: *depressive* (often referred to as **unipolar**) *disorders* and *bipolar disorders* (see the disorders chart above). Once a depressive or manic episode occurs, the disorder is classified into a category as well as a subcategory. Classification is made if the depressive or manic episode is not associated with organic mood syndromes (such as depression or mania caused by psychoactive substances), with schizophrenia, or normal grieving reactions.

Depressive Disorders

In DSM-III-R, people who experience a major depressive episode and have no history of mania are given the diagnosis of *major depression*. If the episode is the first one, it is classified as a single episode. For people who have had previous episodes, the disorder is considered a recurrent one. About half of those who experience a depressive episode eventually have another episode. In general, the earlier the age of onset, the more likely a recurrence is (Reus, 1988).

Dysthymia is a depressive disorder characterized by poor appetite or overeating, low self-esteem, chronic fatigue, sadness, or sleeping difficulties. It is distinguished from major depression in two ways. First, although the symptoms are similar in both disorders, the degree of impairment is less pronounced in dysthymia. Second, unlike major depression, dysthymia is a chronic condition characterized by mild depression that may last for years. In dysthymia, the depressive symptoms are never absent for more than two months. The mood disturbance is not apparent from a person's usual way of functioning, because he or she is continually depressed. In contrast, major depression affects a usual way of functioning. One study (Myers et al., 1984) has found the prevalence of dysthymia to be higher among women than men. Many researchers believe that the disorder is actually quite common.

Bipolar Disorders

The essential feature of **bipolar disorders** is the occurrence of one or more manic episodes. The term "bipolar" is used because the disorders are usually accompanied by one or more major depressive episodes. If a person is currently experiencing a manic episode, the diagnosis of *bipolar disorder, manic* is given. Cases in which manic but not depressive episodes have occurred are extremely rare; in such cases, a depressive episode will presumably appear at some time. In *bipolar disorder, depressed*, the current episode is one of depression, although one or more manic episodes have been experienced.

Bipolar disorder, mixed is interesting in that the manic and depressive episodes are intermixed or rapidly alternate with only brief intervening "normal" periods. The two phases may also appear irregularly with long periods of relative normality in between. In some cases, there may be no intervening normal mood at all. One manic-depressive patient was reported to demonstrate manic behaviors for almost exactly 24 hours, immediately followed by depressive

behaviors for 24 hours. At the manic extreme, the patient was agitated, demanding, and constantly shouting; the next day, he was almost mute and inactive. The alternating nature of the disorder lasted eleven years (Jenner et al., 1967). Typical manic episodes appear suddenly and last from a few days to months. Depressive episodes tend to last longer. The First Person narrative in this chapter relates the experience one clinician had with a manic-depressive client.

Some people show hypomanic and depressed moods that are not as serious as those found in bipolar or major depressive disorders. If there are many periods of hypomanic and depressed moods and the problem is chronic in nature (that is, lasting for at least two years or one year for children and adolescents), a diagnosis of **cyclothymia** may be given. The diagnosis is not made if during the two-year

This painting by Vincent van Gogh, Portrait of Dr. Gachet, *suggests the extreme melancholy that can characterize the depressive side of manic-depressive disorders.*

Margaret Hamilton

FIRST PERSON

I had been working as a therapist in a community mental health center for two years now. Although I loved the work, by Friday afternoon—after hours of direct service of therapy, meetings and rounds at the hospital—I was ready for some time off. Earlier that day I had received a phone call from a distraught woman about her granddaughter, Patti. Her primary concern was about a change in Patti's behavior, and she asked to be seen at the clinic as soon as possible. I immediately set up an intake appointment late that afternoon. As Patti and her grandmother walked through the door, I was struck by how awkwardly and slowly Patti moved and how disheveled she appeared.

An intake meeting in a community mental health center consists of an initial evaluation and assessment of the client and the situation. Based on this assessment, further plans are made. Patti's history was that of a normal, active, vibrant nineteen-year-old until two months ago, when she began to complain of having no energy and feeling lonely, helpless, and hopeless. It didn't take me long to decide she needed further evaluation for clinical depression. That afternoon, even with all her depressive characteristics, Patti struck me as a delightful, caring, creative person who was suffering from tremendous emotional pain from which she desperately wanted relief. She would do anything to feel better.

After a thorough medical and psychiatric evaluation, Patti was put on antidepressant medication and assigned to me for counseling. After several weeks, Patti began to feel better. The combination of the medication and therapy seemed to be working wonders. She was able to return to work, enjoy her friends again, and even got along well with her grandmother. After several months of steady improvement, Patti decided to stop therapy and her medication. I didn't believe either step to be in her best interest at the time but she told me she hadn't taken her medication in several weeks, and felt better than ever. I knew she wouldn't return to the clinic, and even though I would certainly miss working with her and was skeptical of her perspective that she had no more problems, I said good-bye and wished her well.

Two months after we terminated therapy, I received another frantic call from Patti's grandmother. Patti had spent most of her savings in five days, had flown to Mexico for a day trip but had run out of money, and called her grandmother to wire her more money. According to her grandmother, Patti was very active, sleeping only two to three hours a night, throwing parties, drinking, talking excessively, and making several elaborate plans to purchase a small castle on the Rhine in Germany with her inheritance. I realized that Patti was a manic-depressive, the depression I had seen seven months earlier was a true bipolar disorder. I also realized that as Patti's initial depression lifted and as she began to feel better, no one had identified her mania until she was out of control. I knew that in the early onset of the manic episode the client feels good and sees no need for any medication or help. Now I was acutely aware of just how sick this engaging, delightful young woman was.

The following months weren't easy ones for Patti. She continued in her manic state, trying to escape from the hospital on several occasions, declaring to both patients and staff that she was the director of the psychiatric unit, and even telling her grandmother she had been endowed with special powers from the heavens that would allow her to receive messages via the small radio that she kept in her room. Eventually she stabilized on the medication lithium, used to treat manic depression, and continued therapy.

Eventually, Patti got better. She accepted her disease and realized that even though she would always be a manic-depressive, she could lead a normal, full, and creative life once again.

Dr. Margaret Hamilton is a psychiatric nurse who practices and teaches in the Boston area.

period (or one year for children and adolescents), clear-cut manic or depressive episodes are evident. As in the case of dysthymia, cyclothymia is a persistent, chronic, and low-grade mood disorder, in which the person is never symptom free for more than two months. Cyclothymia is less common than dysthymia and more common than bipolar disorder.

Comparison Between Unipolar and Bipolar Disorders   Several types of evidence seem to support the distinction between unipolar and bipolar disorders (Goodwin & Guze, 1984; Research Task Force of the National Institute of Mental Health, 1975): First, genetic studies reveal that blood relatives of patients with bipolar disorders have a higher incidence of manic disturbances than do relatives of unipolar patients. In addition, stronger evidence of genetic influences exists for bipolar disorders than for unipolar disorders. Second, the age of onset is typically earlier for bipolar disorders (the late twenties) than for unipolar disorders (the mid-thirties). Third, bipolars have retarded depressions (involving a slowing down of movements and speech) and a greater tendency to attempt suicide than unipolars, whose depressive symptoms often include anxiety. And fourth, bipolars respond to lithium, whereas the drug has little effect on unipolars.

Only about 0.4 to 1.2 percent of the adult population have experienced bipolar disorder, whereas about 7 to 18 percent have at some time experienced a major depressive episode (DSM-III-R). Major depression seems to be more common in females than in males (see Focus 12.1), but no apparent sex differential exists in the frequency of bipolar disorders (Weissman & Klerman, 1977).

Other Features of Mood Disorders

Using DSM-III-R, which is more detailed than earlier versions, clinicians can be more specific in diagnosing mood disorders. As mentioned earlier, the disturbance and degree of impairment in major depressive and bipolar disorders can be rated as mild, moderate, or severe. If a patient's disorder is rated as severe, it can be further specified with respect to the presence or absence of *psychotic features*. Psychotic features include delusions, hallucinations, or catatonia (where the patient may assume a position and not move); a **psychosis** is thus a gross impairment in reality testing (an inability to accurately perceive and deal with reality).

One of the more interesting possible features of a psychosis is that for some people moods are accentuated during certain time periods. Lehmann (1985) notes that many depressed people find the morning more depressing than the evening. Many also find winter, when days are shorter and darker, more depressing than summer, when days are longer and brighter. In following DSM-III-R criteria, clinicians indicate whether patients show a *seasonal pattern*. In some cases of recurrent major depression and bipolar disorder, the onset, end, or change of an episode coincides with a particular time (that is, a particular 60-day period) of the year. For example, one man whose wife had died in November had recurrent depressive episodes that began every November for four years. If the seasonal episode (1) appears in three separate years, with two of the years being consecutive, (2) outnumbers any nonseasonal episodes by more than three to one, and (3) is not caused by an obviously season-related stressor (such as being regularly unemployed every winter), then a seasonal pattern exists.

Finally, many clinicians and researchers have distinguished between what were presumed to be psychologically caused (or *exogenous*) depression and biologically caused (or *endogenous*) depression. Many psychologists believed that the former was precipitated by external events, such life stressors as the loss of a job, the death of a loved one, or divorce, whereas the latter was not. The evidence does not seem to support that particular distinction, because in many cases endogenous depression may also be triggered by life stressors (Leff et al., 1970).

However, there does seem to be some difference between the two. What is now called *melancholia* (DSM-III-R), and was called *endogenous depression* in DSM-III, appears to be a more severe disturbance involving a loss of pleasure in all activities, significant weight loss, and excessive guilt. People with this form of depression may also respond better to some types of biological treatment, such as antidepressant drugs and electroconvulsive therapy.

FOCUS 12.1 *Are Women More Likely than Men to Be Depressed?*

Worldwide, depression is far more common among women than among men. According to DSM-III, 18 to 23 percent of females and 8 to 11 percent of males have at some time experienced a major depressive episode. Is this sex difference real and, if so, what accounts for the difference?

Although women are more likely than men to be seen in treatment and to be diagnosed as depressed, this may not mean that women *are* more depressed, for several reasons. First, women may simply be more likely than men to seek treatment when depressed; this tendency

would make the reported depression rate for women higher, even if the actual male and female rates were equal. Second, women may be more willing to report their depression to other people. That is, there may be sex differences in self-report behaviors, rather than in actual depression rates. Third, diagnosticians or the diagnostic system may be biased toward finding depression among women. And fourth, depression in men may take other forms and thus be given other diagnoses, such as substance dependency.

Some clinicians feel that these four possibilities account for only

part of the sex difference in depression, and that women do have higher rates of depression (Radloff & Rae, 1981). The reasons for these differences are unclear, however. Speculation has involved physiological or social psychological factors.

Genetic or hormonal differences between the sexes were once thought to influence depression. However, the failure to find consistent relationships between hormonal changes and depression has led researchers to propose social or psychological factors. One of these is the woman's traditional sex role.

THE ETIOLOGY OF MOOD DISORDERS

Despite increasing evidence for a unipolar-bipolar distinction, little is known about what causes the extreme mood changes in the bipolar disorders. Perhaps the regulatory mechanism for maintaining *homeostasis,* or stability of mood, no longer works. Maybe mania is a way of trying to deal with underlying depression, or perhaps the apparent euphoria, irritability, and overactivity seen in mania are attempts to deny or ward off depression. In any event, much more is known about what causes depression than about what causes the bipolar disorders.

The Causes of Depression

Over the years, a number of different theoretical explanations have been proposed to account for depression. In this section, some of the major theories are discussed.

Psychoanalytic Explanations The psychoanalytic explanation of depression focuses mainly on

two concepts: separation and anger. Separation may occur when a spouse, lover, child, parent, or significant other person dies or leaves for one reason or another. But the loss (separation) need not be physical; it can also be symbolic. For example, the withdrawal of affection or support, or a rejection (a symbolic loss), can induce depression.

In their attempts to distinguish normal grief from depression, Abraham (1948) and Freud ([1917] 1924) postulated several differences between the two. In normal mourning, the loss of a significant other is a *conscious* concern of mourners. They are aware of their own feelings, of what the lost person means to them, and of how the loss may change their lives. This consciousness is in marked contrast to what Freud labeled "neurotic depression," which operates on an *unconscious* level because mourners are not aware of the true loss. The loss is generally symbolic and strikes at their ego. The most common depressive reaction to such a loss is a loss of self-esteem.

Freud believed that depressives are excessively dependent people because they are fixated in the oral stage. As we discussed in Chapter 2, he viewed the mouth as the primary mechanism by which infants

Subservience to men and a lack of occupational opportunities, for example, may produce more depression in women (Bernard, 1976). For the same reason, women may be more likely than men to experience lack of control in life situations. They may then attribute their "helplessness" to an imagined lack of personal worth. Finally, the traditional feminine sex role behaviors (gentleness, emotionality, and self-subordination) may not be so successful in eliciting reinforcement from others as the assertive and more forceful responses typically imputed to males.

In a review of different explanations, Nolen-Hoeksema (1987) concluded that none truly accounts for the observed sex differences in the rates of depression. She hypothesizes that how a person responds to depressed moods contributes to the severity, chronicity, and recurrence of depressive episodes. In her view, women tend to ruminate and amplify their depressive moods, while men dampen or find means to minimize dysphoria.

Egeland and Hostetter (1983) also speculate that responses to depressive moods may affect observed rates of depression. In their study of the Amish, they found that males and females have the same rates for depression. The researchers note that since Amish men do not show alcoholism or antisocial behaviors, their depression cannot be masked. And Amish women, like the men, must work, so engaging in a sick (depressed) role is discouraged. Although role behavior may help to explain some of the differences in rates of depression between men and women, it is not clear if the explanation is enough to account for the vast differences.

relate to the world, so being fixated at this stage fosters dependency. Being passive and having others fill one's needs (being fed, bathed, clothed, cuddled, and so forth) results in emotional dependency that continues into adult life. Thus, for people fixated in the oral stage, self-esteem depends on other important people in the environment. When a significant loss occurs, the self-esteem of the mourner plummets.

Freud also believed that the depressive shows a failure to follow through in the normal mourning process, which he called "mourning work." In the normal course of mourning, there is conscious recall and expression of memories about the lost person in an attempt to undo the loss. In addition, the mourners are flooded with two strong sets of feelings: anger and guilt. The anger, which arises from their sense of being deserted, can be very strong:

After nearly six months of treatment, a young depressive woman finally was able to express her feelings of anger toward her deceased husband. She blamed her husband for his death, even though the circumstances under which he died were not of his making. She expressed feelings of being deserted, left to make it on her own in a cruel world, left to raise her four children alone, left with only minimal life insurance, and left to clean up her husband's business affairs. In therapy, she expressed great bitterness and blame: "He shouldn't have made me so dependent on him! Why didn't he take out more life insurance? Did he think he was indestructible? He should have planned for something like this!"

Mourners may also be flooded with guilt feelings about real or imagined sins committed against the lost person. For example, a father who has just lost a child may think, "My daughter always wanted to go to Disneyland. Why didn't I take her? Now it's too late." These feelings must be resolved through grief. In the attempt to free him- or herself from the lost person, the mourner's emotions become redirected toward new tasks and new relationships.

Because depression cannot always be correlated with the immediate loss of a loved one, Freud used the construct of "symbolic loss" to account for depression that did not result directly from a loss. That is to say, any form of rejection or reproach may be perceived by the depressive as *symbolic* of an earlier loss.

For example, suppose a woman terminates a long-term romance with a potentially depressive man. Although she has not died, her withdrawal of affection may have two effects on this particular partner. First, his fixation at an oral stage predisposes him to perceive the withdrawal as indicating his own worthlessness, so his self-esteem takes a nose dive. Second, the withdrawal may symbolize an earlier traumatic loss that was not fully resolved. For example, it may symbolize to him his early loss of a parent, spouse, or friend.

Psychoanalysis has strongly emphasized the dynamics of anger in explaining depression. Many depressed patients have strong hostile or angry feelings, and some clinicians believe that getting clients to express their anger reduces their depression. Such a belief has led some to speculate that depression is really *anger turned against the self* (Freud, [1917] 1924). Freud suggested that, when a person experiences a loss (symbolic or otherwise), he or she may harbor feelings of resentment and hostility toward the lost person in addition to feelings of love and affection.

The following case exemplifies the concept of anger turned inward:

Ralph was a 20-year-old college junior who first came to the counseling center suffering from depression. A detailed history revealed that Ralph was raised by parents who punished any outward expression of anger or hostility. His mother often reminded him that "Nobody likes a mischievous brat" and that "To keep friends you must behave yourself." As a result he became extremely compliant and conforming, fearful of losing the goodwill of friends and family. In high school and college, Ralph found himself the continual victim of his dormitory peers. He found it difficult to say *no* to them when they asked to borrow his car or to copy his homework. Unable to assert himself, he was often exploited and even mistreated.

Each time such an incident occurred, Ralph denied his anger. Yet he could not completely deny his realization that he was a "doormat" for the rest of the world. Rather than expressing his anger toward others, however, he became angry at himself. Seeing himself as weak-willed and spineless, he developed a negative self-image that resulted in depression. Only when the counselor was able to get Ralph to redirect his anger outward did the depression finally lift.

Learning Explanations Behaviorists also see the separation or loss of a significant other as important in depression. However, behaviorists tend to see the cause as reduced reinforcement rather than as the untestable concept of fixation or symbolic grief. When a loved one is lost, an accustomed level of reinforcement (whether affection, companionship, pleasure, material goods, or services) is immediately withdrawn. No longer can one obtain the support or encouragement of the lost person. When this happens, one's level of activity (talking, expressing ideas, working, joking, engaging in sports, going out on the town, or whatever) is significantly diminished because an important source of reinforcement has disappeared. Thus many behaviorists view depression as a product of inadequate or insufficient reinforcers in a person's life, leading to a reduced frequency of behavior that previously was positively reinforced (Ferster, 1965; Lazarus, 1968; Lewinsohn, 1974a).

As the period of reduced activity (resulting from reduced reinforcement) continues, the person labels him- or herself "depressed." If the new lower level of activity causes others to show sympathy, the depressed person may remain inactive and chronically "depressed." By being sympathetic about the incident (loss), friends, relatives, and even strangers may be reinforcing the depressive's current state of inactivity. (This reinforcement for a lower activity level is known as *secondary gain*.) The depression tends to deepen, and the person disengages still further from the environment and reduces further the chance of obtaining positive reinforcement from normal activity. The result may be continually deepening depression.

Depression has been associated both with low levels of self-reinforcement and with reductions in environmental reinforcements (Heiby, 1983). In other words, when people get less reinforcement from the environment and do not reinforce themselves, they become prone to depression. Depressives may lack the skills required to replace lost environmental reinforcements.

This behavioral concept of depression can be elaborated to cover many situations that may elicit depression (such as failure, loss, change in job status, rejection, and desertion). Lewinsohn's model of depression is perhaps the most comprehensive of the behavioral explanations (Lewinsohn, 1974a, 1974b; Lewinsohn & Graf, 1973; Lewinsohn & Libet, 1972; Lewinsohn et al., 1970). Along with the reinforcement view of depression, Lewinsohn suggests three sets of variables that may enhance or hinder a person's access to positive reinforcement.

First, *the number of events and activities that are potentially reinforcing* to the person is important. This depends very much on individual differences and varies with the biological traits and experiential history of the person. For example, age, sex, or physical attributes may determine the availability of reinforcers. Handsome people are more likely to receive positive attention than those people who look nondescript. Young people are likely to have more social interaction than retirees. A task-oriented person who values intellectual pursuits may not be so responsive as other people to interpersonal or affiliative forms of reinforcement. To such a person, a compliment such as "I like you" may be less effective than "I see you as an extremely competent person."

Second, *the availability of reinforcements in the environment* can also affect the person. Harsh environments, such as regimented institutions or remote isolated places, reduce reinforcements.

Third, *the instrumental behavior of the person*—the number of social skills that can be exercised to bring about reinforcement—is important. Depressed patients lack social behaviors that can elicit positive reinforcements (Lewinsohn et al., 1970). They interact with fewer people, respond less, have very few positive reactions, and initiate less conversation. Depressed people also feel more uncomfortable in social situations (Youngren & Lewinsohn, 1980), and they elicit depression in others (Hammen & Peters, 1978). Further, depressed people seem to be preoccupied with themselves; they tend to talk about themselves (more so than nondepressed people) without being asked to do so (Jacobson & Anderson, 1982). For this reason or others, nondepressed people may not enjoy talking to those who are depressed, and may provide little positive reinforcement to depressives during social interactions. Depressives may even drive others away and thus lose any social reinforcement that others could provide (Coyne, 1976).

A low rate of positive reinforcement in any of these three situations can lead to depression. A beautiful person who begins to age may notice declining interest from possible lovers. A person who has recently lost a loved one through divorce or death and has no other friends or family may receive little or no support. And a young student who lacks social skills in heterosexual relationships may be denied the pleasures of such interactions. Behavioral approaches

Learning theory suggests that depression may be a product of reduced reinforcement in a person's life. The reduced reinforcement leads to reduced activity levels. Unfortunately, consolation and sympathy from others may sometimes serve to reinforce and maintain depressive behaviors.

to treating depression might attempt to intervene in any of these conditions.

Lewinsohn also recognized the important role of other factors in depression. For example, Lewinsohn, Hoberman, and Rosenbaum (1988) found that having a prior depressed mood, encountering stress, and being female (as mentioned previously, women are more likely than men to suffer depression) are associated with the occurrence of depressive episodes.

Cognitive Explanations Some psychologists believe that low self-esteem is the key to depressive reactions. All of us have both negative and positive feelings about what we see as our "self." We like or value certain things about ourselves, and dislike other things. Some people, especially depressed ones, have a generally negative self-concept. Such people perceive themselves as inept, unworthy, and incompetent, regardless of reality. If they do succeed at anything, they are likely to dismiss it as pure luck or to forecast eventual failure. Hence a cognitive interpretation of oneself as unworthy may lead to a host of thinking patterns that reflect self-blame, self-criticism, and exaggerated ideas of duty and responsibility.

One major cognitive theory has been advanced by Beck (1976). According to this theory, depression is a primary disturbance in *thinking* rather than a basic disturbance in *mood*. How you structure and interpret your experiences determines your affective states. If you see a situation as unpleasant, you will feel an unpleasant mood. Depressed patients are said to have *schemas* that set them up for depression. (A **schema** is a pattern of thinking or a cognitive set that determines a person's reactions and responses. In other words, your schema tends to modify, or color, your interpretation of incoming information.)

According to this theory, depressives operate from a "primary triad," which consists of negative views of oneself, one's present experiences, and the future. Four errors in logic typify this negative schema, which leads to depression and is characteristic of depressives:

1. *Arbitrary inference* The depressive tends to draw conclusions that are not supported by evidence. For example, a woman may conclude that "People dislike me" just because no one speaks to her on the bus or in the elevator. A man who invites a woman out to dinner and finds the restaurant closed that evening may see this as evidence of his own unworthiness. In both cases, these people draw erroneous conclusions from the available evidence. Depressives are apparently unwilling or unable to see other, more probable, explanations.

2. *Selected abstraction* The depressive takes a minor incident or detail out of context, and the incidents on which the depressive focuses tend to be trivial. The depressive who is corrected for a minor aspect of his or her work takes the correction as a sign of his or her incompetence or inadequacy—even when the supervisor's overall feedback is highly positive.

3. *Overgeneralization* A depressive tends to draw a sweeping conclusion about his or her ability, performance, or worth from one single experience or incident. A person who is laid off the job because of budgetary cuts may conclude that he or she is worthless. The comments of a student seen by one of the authors at a university psychology clinic provide another illustration of overgeneralization: When he missed breakfast at the dormitory because his alarm clock didn't ring, he concluded, "I don't deserve my

own body because I don't take care of it." Later, when he showed up late for class through no fault of his own, he thought, "What a miserable excuse for a student I am." When a former classmate passed by and smiled, he thought, "I must look awful today or she wouldn't be laughing at me."

4. *Magnification and minimization* The depressive tends to exaggerate (magnify) limitations and difficulties, while playing down (minimizing) accomplishments, achievements, and capabilities. Asked to evaluate his or her strengths and weaknesses, the depressed patient lists shortcomings or unsuccessful attempts endlessly but finds it almost impossible to name any achievements.

All four of these cognitive processes can be seen as results or causes of low self-esteem, which makes the person expect failure and engage in self-criticism that is unrelated to reality. People with low self-esteem must have experienced much disapproval in the past from significant others, such as parents. Their parents or significant others may have responded to them by punishing failures and not rewarding successes or by holding unrealistically high expectations or standards that they could not meet. The following case is an example:

Paul was a 20-year-old college senior majoring in chemistry. He first came to the student psychiatric clinic complaining of headaches and a vague assortment of somatic problems. Throughout the interview, Paul seemed severely depressed and unable to work up enough energy to talk with the therapist. Even though he had maintained a B+ average, he felt like a failure and was uncertain about his future.

His parents had always had high expectations for Paul, their eldest son, and had transmitted these feelings to him from his earliest childhood. His father, a successful thoracic surgeon, had his heart set on Paul's becoming a doctor. The parents saw academic success as very important, and Paul did exceptionally well in school. Although his teachers praised him for being an outstanding student, his parents seemed to take his successes for granted. In fact, they often made such statements as "You can do better." When he failed at something, his parents would make it obvious to him that they not only were disappointed but felt disgraced as well. This pattern of punishment for failures without recognition of successes, combined with his parents' high expectations, led to the development in Paul of an extremely negative self-concept.

Refining his cognitive theory of depression, Beck (1982) has now raised the possibility that personality patterns may also be important: These patterns may influence the kinds of situations or stressors that lead to negative cognitions and, ultimately, to depression.

Although the cognitive explanation of depression has merit, it seems too simple. At times, negative cognitions may be the result of, rather than the cause of, depressed moods, as noted by Hammen (1985). That is, one may first feel depressed and then, as a result, have negative or pessimistic thoughts about the world. Hammen has also found that one's schema tends to mediate the relationship between stress and depression. Stress can lead to depression if one has developed a predisposing schema. Another criticism of cognitive explanations is that many people get depressed, but they do not feel depressed all the time. Yet negative cognitive styles are often hypothesized to be stable or enduring.

Learned Helplessness   A unique and interesting view of depression is that it is **learned helplessness**. This cognitive-learning theory was proposed by Seligman (1975). Its basic assumption is that cognitions and feelings of helplessness are learned. When you see that your actions continually have very little effect on the environment, you develop an expectation of being helpless. When this expectation is borne out in settings that may not be controllable, passivity and finally depression may result.

Your susceptibility to depression, then, depends on your experience with controlling the environment. In his study of helplessness, Seligman discovered strong parallels between the symptoms, etiology, and means of preventing helplessness and those for depression (see Table 12.2). He also noticed similarities in cure; one could say the depression is cured when the person no longer believes he or she is helpless.

To understand this intriguing theory, it is necessary to reconstruct certain laboratory findings about learned helplessness. The first evidence of the phenomenon was obtained accidentally. Dogs that were given inescapable shocks while strapped in a harness showed major differences in their later behavior from dogs who had not received inescapable shocks (Seligman & Maier, 1967; Overmier & Seligman, 1967). When the dogs were placed in a two-compartment box, they were supposed to learn to escape shock in one compartment by jumping over a barrier separating the compartments. When placed in the electrified compartment, dogs that had not been given inescapable shocks would howl, urinate, defecate, thrash, and run about until they accidentally scrambled over the barrier, ending the shock. They soon learned that to avoid the shock they simply had to jump the barrier.

The dogs that had received inescapable shocks earlier, however, reacted quite differently. Although at first they behaved in much the same manner as the dogs that had not received inescapable shocks (howling and running about), most of them soon stopped trying to escape and lay down whimpering, apparently having given up! Regardless of the experimenters' coaxing, pleading, prodding, and offerings of food, these dogs made virtually no attempt to escape on the first or subsequent trials (Seligman,

TABLE 12.2 | Similarities Between Helplessness and Depression

Learned Helplessness		Depression
Symptoms	Passivity	Passivity
	Difficulty learning that response produces relief	Negative cognitive set
	Dissipates in time	Time course
	Lack of aggression	Introjected hostility
	Weight loss, appetite loss	Weight loss, appetite loss
	Social and sexual deficits	Social and sexual deficits
Cause	Learning that responding and reinforcement are independent	Feelings of helplessness
		Belief that responding is useless

SOURCE: Adapted from Seligman, 1975.

1975). These dogs also showed another difference: some that did occasionally jump the barrier in training failed to *learn* or *profit* from this experience.

As research later showed, the dogs' helplessness did not result from the trauma *per se* (the electric shock) but from the experience of *having no control* over shock. The dogs strapped into the harness and given the inescapable shocks could do nothing to prevent them. They had learned that their actions did not matter—and that they were *helpless*. But dogs that had not received inescapable shocks continued trying to escape. The key factor that prevented learned helplessness seemed to be the perception of having control in an aversive situation. The experience of lack of control appears to predispose one to later passivity (Seligman, 1975).

This phenomenon is not unique to animals; studies have documented it in human subjects as well. Loud noise, rather than electric shock, was used with college student subjects in one study (Hiroto, 1974). Uncontrollable noise in one situation resulted in passive acceptance of similar aversive stimuli in later situations: Subjects failed to move their hands back and forth in a shuttle box, which would have turned off the noise. Other subjects, who had no previous experience with uncontrollable noise, learned to control the noise through their own activities.

What does all this have to do with depression? Seligman describes depression as a *belief in one's own helplessness*. Many other investigators have described depression in terms of hopelessness, powerlessness, and helplessness. For example, "The severely depressed patient believes that his skills and plans of action are no longer effective for reaching the goals he has set" (Melges & Bowlby, 1969, p. 693). And, according to Seligman (1975 pp. 55–56), "the expectation that an outcome is independent of responding (1) reduces the motivation to control the outcome; (2) interferes with learning that responding controls the outcome; (3) produces fear for as long as the subject is uncertain of the uncontrollability of the outcome, and then produces depression."

Seligman's theory of learned helplessness was first published in 1975. Three years later, he and his co-workers revised the model to include more cognitive elements (Abramson et al., 1978). Essentially, they believe that human beings who encounter helplessness make causal attributions (that is, they speculate on *why* they are helpless). These attributions can be internal or external, stable or unstable, and

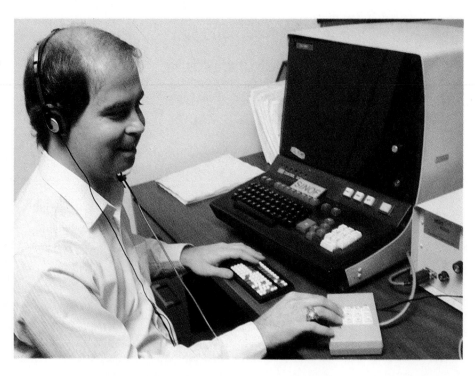

By providing individuals with opportunities to control aspects of their lives, learned helplessness and depression can sometimes be prevented. With the aid of special equipment, this blind person can learn to manipulate and use a computer.

FOCUS 12.2

Attributional Styles: Our Explanations May Influence Our Lives

Martin Seligman's learned helplessness theory has generated considerable research on the role of helplessness in depression. Now Seligman is focusing attention on the role of attributions—how we explain events that happen to us—in our everyday lives. As mentioned in the text, attributions can be global or specific, stable or unstable, and internal or external. Some people tend to have a pessimistic attributional style, explaining bad events (such as failure to pass an examination) in global, stable, and internal terms (such as believing that "I fail in many courses, it always happens to me, and I am dumb"). In fact, the Attributional Style Questionnaire has been developed in which people are given hypothetical situations and are asked to indicate what the cause of each situation is. In this way, people can be rated as to their attri-

butional style. Attributional style is related to a number of characteristics. People who have pessimistic attributional styles receive lower grades in universities, perform worse as sales agents, and have poorer health (Seligman, 1987).

Attributional style can also be reliably determined from a content analysis of verbatim explanations (CAVE), in which the content of an explanation is rated on attributional style. For example, a baseball player who says, "Once in a while I play poorly because of bad breaks, but I always know I'll get my good share of hits," is far more optimistic than one who says, "I'm getting old—my reactions to a pitch have slowed." In an analysis of newspaper quotes from Baseball Hall of Fame players who played during the years between 1900 and 1950, Seligman found that players who had an opti-

mistic attributional style outlived those who were more pessimistic. Zullow and his colleagues (1988) have also noted that when President Lyndon Johnson's press conferences contained optimistic phrases, bold presidential actions were taken in the Vietnam War; when more pessimistic phrases were used, the actions were passive.

The implications are that (1) people vary in their attributional styles, (2) attributional style can be assessed, and (3) attributional style may be related to achievements, health, and other behaviors. Obviously, a causal relationship between attributional style and behavior hasn't been clearly established. But the research suggests that how we explain things may be quite important in our lives.

---

global or specific. For instance, suppose a student in a math course receives the same low grades regardless of how much he or she has studied. The student may attribute the low grades to internal or personal factors ("I don't do well in math because I'm scared of math") or to external factors ("The teacher doesn't like me, so I can't get a good grade"). The attribution can also be stable ("I'm the type of person who can never do well in math") or unstable ("My poor performance is due to my heavy work load"). And the attribution can be global or specific. A global attribution ("I'm a poor student") has broader implications for performance than a specific one ("I'm poor at math but good in other subjects"). Abramson and co-workers believe that a person whose attributions for helplessness are internal, stable, and global is likely to have more pervasive feelings of depression

than someone whose attributions are external, unstable, and specific. More recently, attributions have been found to be associated with many aspects of life, as discussed in Focus 12.2.

The learned helplessness model has generated a great deal of research. There is evidence that depressed people make "depressive" attributions and feel that their lives are less controllable than do nondepressives (Raps et al., 1982). However, as with cognitive theory, there are questions about whether this model, even with its attributional components, can adequately explain depression and about whether attributions result from or are caused by depression. Cognitions and attributions may be important factors in depression, but the disorder is complex; current models tend to include or explain only particular facets of depression (Hammen, 1985). Alloy et al. (1988) also note that the helplessness theory (which they prefer to call the "hopelessness" theory) explains only a certain type of depression. Depression may be a heterogeneous disorder that can be caused by genetic, biochemical, or social factors.

Biological Perspectives on Mood Disorders

Biological approaches to the etiology of mood or affective disorders generally focus on genetic predisposition, physiological dysfunction, or combinations of the two.

Genetic Factors

Mood disorders tend to run in families, and the same type of disorder is generally found among members of the same family (American Psychiatric Association, 1987; Perris, 1966; Winokur et al., 1969). One way to assess the role of heredity is to compare the incidence of mood disorders among the biological and adoptive families of people who were adopted early in life and who had the disorders. If heredity is important, the biological families (which contributed the genetic makeup) should show a high incidence of the disorders. If environment is more important, the adoptive families (which provided the early environment) should show a high incidence. The results of such a comparison indicated that the incidence of mood disorders was higher among the biological families than among the adoptive families; the latter showed an incidence similar to that of the general population (Kety, 1979).

Another way to study the possible genetic transmission of mood disorders is to compare identical (MZ) and fraternal (DZ) twins. Nine such studies of twins have been reported. The concordance rate (the probability of one having the same disorder as the cotwin) for bipolar disorders was 72 percent for MZ twins and 14 percent for DZ twins. By contrast, the concordance rate for unipolar mood disorders was 40 percent for MZ twins and 11 percent for DZ twins (Goodwin & Guze, 1984).

Both of these research approaches (and others as well) consistently turn up evidence of genetic influence on mood disorders. Moreover, the bulk of the research suggests that heredity is a stronger factor in bipolar mood disorders than in unipolar disorders (Reus, 1988).

Egeland and her colleagues (1987) have also provided some evidence of genetic involvement in bipolar disorders. The investigators studied the Amish, a religious community in Pennsylvania. They found a number of people with bipolar disorders, many of whom had the same ancestors. Moreover, by using sophisticated techniques, they found that a gene located on a specific region of a chromosome was associated with mood disorders among the Amish. Such a finding may lead the way for other investigations into the possible genes associated with mood disorders.

Biochemical Factors

But how is heredity involved in the major mood disorders? A growing number of researchers feel that genetic factors influence the amounts of certain substances (the *catecholamines*) found at specific sites in the brain. These substances help transmit nerve impulses from one neuron to another, and are called **neurotransmitters.** They may mediate between active motor behavior and emotions (Weiss et al., 1975; Becker, 1974).

Nerve impulses are transmitted from neuron to neuron across *synapses,* which are junctions where the axon (or transmitting end) of one neuron is next to the dendrites (or receiving end) of the receptor neuron. According to the *catecholamine hypothesis,* or *biogenic amine theory* of mood disorders, depression is caused by a deficit of specific neurotransmitters (*norepinephrine, dopamine,* or *serotonin*) at brain synapses, whereas mania is caused by an oversupply of these substances (Bunney et al., 1979; Schildkraut, 1965).

Two lines of research implicate neurotransmitters in affective disorders: (1) findings that establish a relationship between levels of neurotransmitters and motor activity, and (2) studies of the effects of medication on these neurotransmitters and on mood changes. As noted earlier, depression is characterized by lower motor activity, and mania by overactivity. When rats are put in certain stressful situations—for example, a series of inescapable shocks—the level of norepinephrine in their brains is reduced. The animals then show "depressive" behaviors such as motor passivity and an inability to learn avoidance-escape responses. Giving rats a drug that depletes brain norepinephrine, also results in motor passivity and an inability to learn. But if rats are given a drug that protects against the depletion of norepinephrine and if this drug is administered to rats before an experience with inescapable shock, they become immunized against passivity and poor learning (Weiss et al., 1975).

These findings not only suggest the importance of norepinephrine in depressive behaviors, but also show that environmental stressors produce biochemical and behavioral changes and, conversely, that biochemical changes can produce behavioral effects similar to those of environmental stressors. Even so, no matter how similar they may be in various respects, the behavior of animals is not the same as human behavior. Investigators obviously need a more direct link between the role of neurotransmitters and depressive behaviors in human beings.

Some evidence implicating neurotransmitters in human depression and mania has been obtained accidentally (Goodwin, 1974). For example, it was discovered that when the drug *reserpine* was used in treating hypertension, many patients became depressed. (Reserpine depletes the level of neurotransmitters in the brain.) Similarly, the drug *iproniazid*, given to tubercular patients, elevated the mood of those who were depressed. (Iproniazid inhibits the destruction of brain amines.) Thus mood levels in human beings were found to vary with the level of neurotransmitters in the brain. These variations are consistent with the catecholamine hypothesis.

Some researchers have suggested that the level, or amount, of neurotransmitters present is not the primary factor. They note that, to travel from one neuron to another, an electrical impulse must release neurotransmitters that stimulate the receiving neuron. The problem may not be the amount of neurotransmitter produced or available, but rather a dysfunction in the *reception* of the neurotransmitter by the receiving neuron (Sulser, 1979).

Other findings, of a different sort, have also aroused interest in the biological or physiological processes of depression. For example, depressed adults differ from the nondepressed in sleep patterns, particularly in rapid eye movement (REM) sleep. (There are several stages of sleep, and during REM sleep the eyes move rapidly about, and dreaming occurs.) Depression is linked with a relatively rapid onset of, and an increase in, REM sleep (Goodwin & Guze, 1984). Moreover, reducing the REM sleep of depressives seems to help them (Vogel et al., 1980). Why sleep patterns are linked to depression is unclear.

Considerable interest has also focused on possible abnormalities in neuroendocrine regulation in depressed people. Depressives tend to have high levels of cortisol, a hormone secreted by the adrenal cortex in the brain. Cortisol levels are measured by the *dexamethasone suppression test* (DST). In this test, patients are given dexamethasone, which normally suppresses the cortisol secretion. Studies in different countries show that higher blood levels of cortisol are found in depressives than in normal people (World Health Organization, 1987) and that not suppressing these levels is linked to poorer prognosis for recovery (Reus, 1988). However, it is still unclear whether cortisol helps cause depression or is produced by depression. Furthermore, it's hard to measure cortisol levels accurately, so questions remain over the value of using DST as a tool for assessing depression and prognosis.

Evaluating the Causation Theories

The theories of depression presented in this chapter explain certain aspects of the disturbance, but all have weaknesses. From the psychoanalytic perspective, loss and separation provoke a depressive reaction. But what determines the extent and severity of depression? Fixation at the oral stage, dependency, and symbolic loss are psychoanalytic concepts that are difficult to test. The psychoanalytic assumption that depression may simply be hostility turned inward on the self seems open to question. When some depressed patients experienced success on experimental tasks, their self-esteem and optimism increased (Beck, 1974). If depression is hostility turned inward, why would success alleviate some of its symptoms?

As we have noted, Beck's idea that the tendency to think in negative terms help produce depression, cannot show that a cognitive disturbance *precedes* depression. Maybe a depressed mood or affect *causes* a negative mind set.

Lewinsohn's behavioral theory and Seligman's learned helplessness theory are well grounded in research findings. Lewinsohn's work has mainly shown a relationship between depression and inadequate positive reinforcement. But do these low rates actually cause depression? More research is needed. Seligman has shown that learned helplessness can lead to depressive behaviors. However, this model explains only certain kinds of depression—reactions to uncontrollable environmental stress.

All three of these theories have strengths and weaknesses; in terms of explaining depression, however, no one theory is better than the others.

Endogenous (congenital) factors seem to play a crucial role in mood disorders. Although genetic studies have not been extensive, evidence shows that heredity is involved. The precise genetic mechanisms are not known, but research into biochemical factors or neurotransmitters seems quite promising.

One good way to think about mood disorders is to see them as resulting from an interaction between environmental and biological factors (Kraemer & McKinney, 1979). Thus they range from mild sadness, through normal grief and the specific affective disorders, to the major mood disorders. Milder instances of depression (or, for that matter, mania) may be more externally caused. In mood disorders in the middle of the spectrum, both external and internal factors may be important. In severe disorders, including psychotic forms of the major mood disorders, endogenous factors may become more prominent (Goodwin, 1977).

THE TREATMENT OF MOOD DISORDERS

Biological approaches to the treatment of mood disorders are generally based on the catecholamine hypothesis. That is, treatment consists primarily of a means of controlling the level of neurotransmitters at brain synapses. In addition, psychological treatment seems to offer promise for use with depressives.

Biomedical Treatments for Unipolar Disorders

Biomedical treatments refer to interventions that alter the physical or biochemical state of the patient. They include the use of medication and electroconvulsive therapy.

Medication   The drugs that are primarily used to treat unipolar depression are of two general types; both were introduced in the mid-1950s. The **tricyclic antidepressants** (the first group) are still considered the most effective; about 65 percent of moderately to severely depressed people improve on tricyclics (Klein et al., 1980), which seem to be especially effective in endogenous forms of depression (Georgotas, 1985). These drugs seem to block the re-uptake of norepinephrine. (*Re-uptake* is the process in which a neurotransmitter is taken back into the nerve cells.) When re-uptake is blocked , more norepinephrine is left at the synapses. These higher levels of residual norepinephrine seem to be linked with reduced depressive symptoms.

The **monoamine oxidase (MAO) inhibitors** (the second group of antidepressants) also work by increasing the level of norepinephrine at the brain synapses. However, rather than blocking re-uptake, as the tricyclics do, the MAO inhibitors prevent the MAO enzyme (which is normally found in the body) from breaking down norepinephrine that is already available at the synapse.

Although MAO inhibitors, as well as tricyclics, affect levels of neurotransmitters, there is growing suspicion that the process is more complicated. The drugs may also affect the sensitivity of receptors on the receiving (postsynaptic) neurons.

Currently, MAO inhibitors are usually prescribed for depressed patients who have not responded well to treatment with tricyclics. However, MAO inhibitors have many side effects, including insomnia, irritability, dizziness, constipation, and impotence. But the most serious incompatibility response is the tyramine-cheese reaction. One normal function of the MAO enzyme is to break down tyramine, a substance found in many cheeses, as well as in some beers, wines, pickled products, and chocolate. The MAO inhibitors interfere with this function, of course, so someone who is using one of these drugs must severely restrict his or her intake of tyramine. Failure to do so triggers the tyramine-cheese reaction, which begins with increased blood pressure, vomiting, and muscle twitching and can, if untreated, result in intracranial bleeding followed by death.

Such side effects are a major drawback of the antidepressant drugs. (The tricyclics, too, may cause such reactions as drowsiness, insomnia, agitation, fine tremors, blurred vision, dry mouth, and reduced sexual ability.) Careful monitoring of the patient's reactions is thus absolutely necessary. Another drawback is the fact that the antidepressant drugs are essentially ineffective during the first two weeks of use, which is a serious concern, particularly where suicide is a danger. As mentioned earlier, the effectiveness of antidepressant drugs may be caused by changes in the sensitivity of postsynaptic receptors. These changes in sensitivity seem to require a couple of weeks to develop.

Electroconvulsive Therapy Electroconvulsive therapy (ECT) is generally reserved for severely depressed unipolar patients who have not responded to tricyclics or MAO inhibitors. The procedure is described in Chapter 19; in essence, it consists of applying of a moderate electrical voltage to the person's brain, for up to half a second. The patient's response to the voltage is a convulsion (seizure) lasting for 30 to 40 seconds, followed by a 5- to 30-minute coma.

Most seriously depressed patients show at least a temporary improvement after about four ECT treatments (Campbell, 1981). The ECT mechanism is not fully understood; it may operate on neurotransmitters at the synapses, as do antidepressants. Some of the decrease in symptoms may also be due to the amnesia that develops for a short time after the treatment. One major advantage of ECT is that the response to treatment is relatively fast (Gangadhar et al., 1982). However, common side effects include headaches, confusion, and memory loss. And many patients are terrified of ECT. In about 1 out of 1,000 cases, serious medical complications occur (Goldman, 1988). As noted in Chapter 3, ECT is controversial, and critics have urged that it be banned as a form of treatment.

Focus 12.3 describes a case in which medication was used in combination with ECT to treat a bipolar affective disorder.

Cognitive Behavioral Treatment for Unipolar Disorders

Because the use of antidepressant medication or ECT involves a number of disadvantages, clinicians have sought a therapeutic approach to depression that would either supplement or replace medical treatment. A variety of psychological forms of treatment have been used—psychoanalysis, interpersonal therapies, and family therapies—all with some success (Hirschfeld & Shea, 1985). The most promising replacement is cognitive-behavioral therapy (Kovacs et al., 1981; Williams, 1984b).

As its name implies, cognitive-behavioral therapy combines cognitive and behavioral strategies. The cognitive component involves teaching the patient (1)

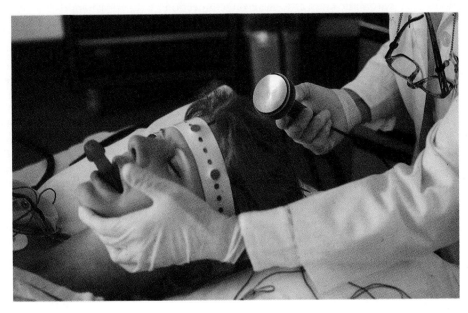

Severely depressed people whose depression cannot be relieved by tricyclics or MAO inhibitors are treated with electroconvulsive therapy. Although most seriously depressed patients show improvement after only a few treatments, negative side effects such as memory loss can result.

FOCUS 12.3 — *I Am Suffering from Depression*

I honestly felt subhuman, lower than the lowest vermin. Furthermore, I was self-deprecatory and could not understand why anyone would want to associate with me, let alone love me. . . . I was also positive that I was going to be fired from the university because of incompetence and that we could become destitute—that we would go broke. . . . I was positive that I was a fraud and phoney and that I didn't deserve my Ph.D. I didn't deserve to have tenure; I didn't deserve to be a Full Professor; I didn't deserve to be Chairman of the Psychology Department. . . . I couldn't understand how I had written the books and journal articles that I had and how they had been accepted for publication. (Endler, 1982, pp. 45–48)

So wrote Dr. Norman Endler, a prominent clinical psychologist, stable family man, and chairman of the psychology department at York University. In a poignant and very explicit book, Endler described his experiences with a bipolar disorder and his reactions to treatment.

Until the spring of 1977, Endler felt fine. He was at the height of his successful career. He was active in sports and was constantly on the move. In retrospect, Endler had realized that he was hypomanic in the fall of 1976, but not until the following April did he became aware that something was wrong. He had difficulty sleeping and had lost his sex drive. "I had gone from being a winner to feeling like a loser. Depression had turned it around for me. From being on top of the world in the fall, I suddenly felt useless, inept, sad, and anxious in the spring" (p. 11).

Endler sought treatment and was administered several drugs that did not prove effective. He was then given electroconvulsive therapy (ECT). Below, Endler describes his reaction to ECT as well as how the treatment was administered.

I was asked to lie down on a cot and was wheeled into the ECT room proper. It was about eight o'clock. A needle was injected into my arm and I was told to count back from 100. I got about as far as 91. The next thing I knew I was in the recovery room and it was about eight-fifteen. I was slightly groggy and tired but not confused. (Endler, 1982, p. 81)

---

to identify negative, self-critical thoughts (cognitions) that occur automatically; (2) to note the connection between negative thoughts and the resulting depression; (3) to carefully examine each negative thought, deciding whether there is any support for it; and (4) to try to replace distorted negative thoughts with more realistic interpretations of each situation (Beck et al., 1979). Cognitive therapists believe that distorted thoughts cause such psychological problems as depression and that changing the former can eliminate the latter.

Patient: Not being loved leads automatically to unhappiness.
Therapist: Not being loved is a "nonevent." How can a nonevent lead automatically to something?
Patient: I just don't believe anyone could be happy without being loved.
Therapist: This is your belief. If you believe something, this belief will dictate your emotional reactions.
Patient: I don't understand that.

Therapist: If you believe something, you're going to act and feel as though it were true, whether it is or not.
Patient: You mean if I believe I'll be unhappy without love, it's only my belief causing my unhappiness?
Therapist: And when you feel unhappy, you probably say to yourself, "See, I was right. If I don't have love, I am bound to be unhappy."
Patient: How can I get out of this trap?
Therapist: You could experiment with your belief about having to be loved. Force yourself to suspend this belief and see what happens. Pay attention to the natural consequences of not being loved, not to the consequences created by your belief. For example, can you picture yourself on a tropical island with all the delicious fruits and other food available?
Patient: Yes, it looks pretty good.
Therapist: Now imagine that there are primitive people on the island. They are friendly and helpful, but they do not love you. None of them loves you.
Patient: I can picture that.
Therapist: How do you feel in your fantasy?

After about seven ECT sessions, his depression lifted dramatically: "My holiday of darkness was over and fall arrived with a bang!" (p. 83).

The next few months were free of depression, and Endler enjoyed everything he did. Later, he realized that he was actually hypomanic during *this* period also. He was a bit euphoric, energetic, and active; he talked incessantly. Then depression struck again. He recognized that he was experiencing the initial signs of depression and again underwent drug treatment and ECT. This time, however, the treatments were ineffective. Slowly, over the course of about two years, his depression was dissipated with the aid of medication.

Endler concludes by offering some advice. First, when people think they are depressed, they should seek treatment immediately. Second, some combinations of such treatments as psychotherapy, antidepressant drugs, and ECT may be effective. Third, the depressive's family can have an important effect on recovery: When a family member becomes severely depressed, existing family conflicts may become exacerbated. A supportive and understanding family can help the depressive survive.

Depression is a common pervasive illness affecting all social classes, but it is eminently treatable. A great deal of heartbreak can be avoided by early detection and treatment. There is nothing to be ashamed of. There is no stigma attached to having an affective disorder. It is unwise to try to hide it and not seek help. I lived to tell and to write about it.

As of this writing . . . I have been symptom-free for almost three years. . . . I am not experiencing an emotional crisis and I hope I never do again. . . . I am reminded of a telephone conversation I had with my wife. . . . I mentioned that I had to do a lot of work to finish the first draft of Chapter 12, the last chapter in this book, before I left Stanford at the end of the month. Beatty said to me, "What's so terrible if you don't finish?" That put it all in perspective for me. I intend to live life to the fullest, but carefully. The sun will rise and shine whether or not I finish things today. But it's nice knowing that I did finish the first draft of this book before I left Stanford! (Endler, 1982, pp. 167–169)

SOURCE: Endler, 1982.

Patient: Relaxed and comfortable.
Therapist: So you can see that it does not necessarily follow that if you aren't loved, you will be unhappy. (Beck et al., 1979, p. 260)

At the outset of the cognitive therapy, the client is usually asked to begin monitoring his or her negative thoughts and listing them on a chart. It is important for the client to include *all* the thoughts and emotions that are associated with each distressing event that takes place each day. (see Figure 12.1).

The client brings the chart to the session each week, and the therapist uses it to demonstrate that the client's distress is being caused by his or her own unnecessarily negative thoughts. The client's own rational alternatives to these thoughts are discussed, and the client makes a conscious effort to adopt those alternatives that seem plausible. The goal of the cognitive part of the therapy is to train the client to automatically substitute logical interpretations for self-denigrating thoughts. Cognitive therapists maintain that, when a patient's thoughts about him- or herself become more consistently positive, the emotions follow suit.

The second part of the cognitive-behavioral approach is behavior therapy. Such treatment is usually indicated in cases of severe depression in which the patient is virtually inactive. One primary assumption underlying this approach is that a depressed person is not doing enough pleasant, rewarding activities. Depressed people tend to withdraw from others when they belittle themselves; then they interpret their self-imposed social isolation as a sign of their being unpopular and inadequate (Lewinsohn, 1977).

To address this problem, depressed patients are asked to keep a daily activity schedule on which they list life events hour by hour and rate the "pleasantness" of each event. When a person is asked to monitor and rate events or activities, activities generally increase in frequency. This, in itself is a worthwhile strategy for severely depressed patients; simply

Date	Situation	Automatic Thoughts	Emotions	Rational Alternative	Emotion
2/9	I sat home all alone on a Fri. night.	Nobody likes me or I would have been asked out.	Depressed	Most people know that I usually work Fri. nights. Maybe nobody knew I had the night off.	Relief, contentment
2/10	I had trouble understanding my reading assignment.	I must be an idiot. This should be an easy subject.	Depressed, anxious.	If I don't understand the material, I bet a number of others don't either.	Calm, determined

Figure 12.1   Daily Cognition Chart for a Typical Depressive Client
SOURCE: Beck, Laude, and Bohnert, 1974.

getting depressed people to engage in more activities increases the chance that they will become involved in some pleasant, reinforcing events. The patient's chart of this information also helps the therapist to spot specific patterns. For instance, a client who insists that he or she does not enjoy anything, may rate as "slightly pleasant" any time spent outdoors. The therapist would point out this pattern and encourage the client to spend more time outdoors (Beck et al., 1979).

Once the severely depressed client becomes more active, he or she may be asked to attend a social skills training program. Improvements in social skills generally help clients become more socially involved and can make that involvement rewarding (Hersen et al., 1980).

Cognitive-behavioral therapy seems very promising as a plausible treatment for depression, although some methodological problems still remain (Kovacs, 1980; Williams, 1984a). Also very interesting at present is the combination of cognitive-behavioral therapy and antidepressant medication. Preliminary findings on such a treatment package have been positive (Roth et al., 1982; Wilson, 1982; Goodwin and Guze, 1984).

Biomedical Treatment for Bipolar Disorders

For bipolar disorders, drugs (especially lithium) are typically used together with psychosocial treatments. Since it was introduced to the United States in 1969, lithium (in the form of lithium carbonate) has been the treatment of choice for bipolar and manic disorders (Fieve et al., 1976). As noted, the manic phase of bipolar disorder seems to be caused by too much neurotransmitter (primarily norepinephrine) at brain synapses. Lithium decreases the total level of neurotransmitters in the synaptic areas by *increasing* the re-uptake of norepinephrine into the nerve cells (Barchas et al., 1977).

The generally positive results achieved with lithium are currently being overshadowed somewhat by reports of distressing side effects (Dubovsky et al., 1982). The earliest danger signals are gastrointestinal complications (such as vomiting and diarrhea), fine tremors, muscular weakness, and frequent urination. The more serious side effects, associated with excessive lithium in the blood, are loss of bladder control, slurred speech, blurred vision, seizures, and abnormal heart rate. Fortunately, accurate measurements of lithium blood levels are easily obtained, and dosages can be adjusted accordingly.

Another problem associated with lithium is lack of patient compliance with the treatment program. For some reason, this problem is consistently worse with bipolar patients taking lithium than with any other group of patients taking any other drug. Bipolar patients often report that they have tried to adjust their lithium dosage, by themselves, so that they will experience the mania but not the depression of bipolar disorder. Unfortunately, lithium levels cannot be manipulated in this manner. When the dosage is decreased, the initial slightly manic state quickly develops into either a severe manic state or depression.

SUMMARY

1. Severe depression is a major component of the mood disorders; it involves affective, cognitive, behavioral, and physiological symptoms. Mania, which may accompany depression in these disorders, is characterized by elation, grandiosity, irritability, and almost boundless energy.

2. In bipolar mood disorders, manic episodes occur, or alternate with depressive episodes. Unipolar disorders (major depression and dysthymic disorder) involve only depression. Psychotic symptoms may also appear in the more severe mood disorders. The depressive disorders are the most common mood disorders; some evidence suggests that they are distinct from the bipolar disorders.

3. Psychological theories of depression have been proposed by adherents of the psychoanalytic, cognitive, and behavioral viewpoints, but each has certain weaknesses. According to the learned helplessness theory of depression, susceptibility to depression depends on the person's experience with controlling the environment. Genetic and biochemical research has demonstrated that heredity plays a role in depression and mania, probably by affecting neurotransmitter levels in the brain.

4. Biological approaches to treating depression focus on increasing the amounts of neurotransmitters available at brain synapses or by affecting the sensitivity of postsynaptic receptors through either medication or electroconvulsive therapy. A cognitive-behavioral treatment for depression seeks to replace negative thoughts with more realistic (or positive) cognitions. The most effective treatment for bipolar disorders is lithium, a drug that lowers the level of synaptic neurotransmitters.

KEY TERMS

bipolar disorder A major mood disorder in which both depression and mania are exhibited, or one in which only mania has been exhibited

cyclothymia A mild and chronic mood disorder characterized by nonpsychotic mood swings

depression An emotional state characterized by intense dysphoria, sadness, feelings of futility and worthlessness, and withdrawal from others

dysthymia A mild and chronic mood disorder characterized by nonpsychotic depression

learned helplessness Acquiring the belief that one is helpless and cannot affect outcomes in one's life

mania An emotional state characterized by great elation, seemingly boundless energy, and irritability

mood disorders Severe disturbances of mood or affect involving depression or mania, or both

neurotransmitters Substances that contribute to the transmission of nerve impulses from one neuron to another

psychosis A severe mental disorder in which there is a loss of contact with reality or a significant distortion of reality

schema A pattern of thinking or a cognitive set that determines (or colors) an individual's reactions and responses

unipolar disorder A major mood disorder in which no mania has been exhibited, only depression

chapter 13
Suicide

Our society views **suicide,** the taking of one's own life, with great confusion. Many segments of the population consider it immoral and provide strong religious sanctions against it (Redestam, 1977). Suicide is both a sin in the canonical law of the Catholic Church and an illegal act according to the secular laws of most countries. Yet in the United States, we are witnessing increased openness in discussing death and dying, the meaning of suicide, and the right to take one's own life. Nonetheless, we find most suicides tragic and baffling.

Late one evening Carl Johnson, M.D., left his downtown office, got into his Mercedes 560 SL, and drove toward his expensive suburban home. He was in no particular hurry because the house would be empty anyway; the year before, his wife had divorced him and with their two children had moved back east to her parents' home. Carl was deeply affected. For the past several months his private practice had declined dramatically. He used to find his work rewarding, but now he found people boring and irritating. The future looked bleak and hopeless. Carl knew he had all the classic symptoms of depression—he was, after all, a psychiatrist. The garage door opened automatically as he rolled up the driveway. Carl parked hurriedly, not even bothering to press the switch that closed the door. Once in the house, he headed directly for the bar in his den; there he got out a bottle of bourbon and three glasses, filled the glasses, and lined them up along the bar. He drank them down, one after the other, in rapid succession. Then Carl sat down at his mahogany desk and unlocked one of the drawers. Taking a loaded .38 caliber revolver from the desk drawer, Dr. Carl Johnson held it to his temple and fired.

In December 1983, Jenny Williams, a 62-year-old housewife, suffered a severe stroke that resulted in crippling paralysis, loss of speech, and an inability to control her basic eliminative functions. Although she had the full support of her husband, two sons, and a daughter, Mrs. Williams was distressed at having to rely on basic life support machinery. Although she couldn't speak, it was clear to her family that she didn't want to live this way and also didn't want to be a burden to others. Over several weeks Mrs. Williams's condition improved moderately, until she could move about, with great effort. But she still could not speak or attend to her own needs. She was discharged from the hospital and was then cared for at home by a part-time nurse and her devoted husband. Two weeks after her discharge, Mrs. Williams took her own life by swallowing a bottle of sleeping pills. Mr. Williams knew of his wife's intention, but he did nothing to prevent her suicide. He didn't have the heart to go against her wishes.

Ten-year-old Tammy Jimenez was the youngest of three children—a loner who had attempted suicide at least twice in the past two years. Tammy's parents always seemed to be bickering about one thing or another and threatening divorce. She and her sisters were constantly abused by their alcoholic father. Finally, in February 1986, Tammy was struck and killed by a truck when she darted out into the highway that passed by her home. The incident was listed as an accident, but her older sister said Tammy had deliberately killed herself. On the morning of her death, an argument with her father had upset and angered her. Her sister said that, seconds before Tammy ran out onto the highway, she had said she was unwanted and would end her own life.

On October 23, 1983, a lone man in a truck containing six tons of explosives drove up to the U.S. Marine barracks in Beirut, Lebanon. The man, believed to be a Shi'ite Muslim terrorist, did not pause when Marine guards signaled him to stop. Instead he drove on through the entrance barricades and set off a blast that killed himself and 240 American soldiers.

Why do people commit suicide? Are such people always mentally disturbed? These questions are difficult to answer, for two important reasons.

First, people who commit suicide—who complete their suicide attempts—can no longer be asked about their motives, frame of mind, and emotional state. We have only indirect information—case records and reports by others—to help us understand what led them to their tragic act. The systematic examination of such information, to understand and explain someone's behavior before his or her death, is called a **psychological autopsy** (Shneidman et al., 1970). (A *medical autopsy* is an examination of a dead body to determine the cause or nature of the biological death.) The *psychological autopsy* is patterned after the medical autopsy; it seeks to make psychological sense of a suicide or homicide. Case histories of victims, interviews with relatives and friends, information obtained from crisis phone calls, and suicide notes are compiled and analyzed in an attempt to uncover some underlying explanation for the act. The psychological autopsy has broader purposes as well. If psychologists can isolate the events and circumstances that lead to suicide and can identify the characteristics of potential suicide victims, they may be able to prevent other people from performing this irreversible act.

Another reason why we do not clearly understand suicide is that no single explanation is sufficient to account for all types of suicide. The examples given at the beginning of this chapter show the diversity of life situations that may result in suicide. Common sense alone should lead you to the conclusion that Jenny Williams's reasons for taking her own life differ from those of the terrorist or of Tammy Jimenez. In seeking to understand why people commit suicide, researchers have focused on events, characteristics, and demographic variables that recur in psychological autopsies and are highly correlated with the act. Our first example, the case of Dr. Carl Johnson, fits a particular profile. Higher suicide rates are associated with divorce and with certain professions (psychiatry in particular), and men are more likely to kill themselves using firearms than by other means. (See Focus 13.1 for other research results.) But the factors that are probably most closely linked with suicide are *hopelessness* and *depression*. We will discuss these next.

HOPELESSNESS AND DEPRESSION

Although it is dangerous to assume that depression causes suicide, a number of studies indicate that the two are very highly correlated. For example, it was found that *suicide wishes* occurred in 74 percent of a group of severely depressed people, compared to only 12 percent in a nondepressed group (Beck, 1967). Of course, a suicide wish is very different from a suicide attempt; yet in another study, 80 percent of the patients admitted to a general hospital because of a *suicide attempt* were found to be depressed at the time of initial observation (Silver et al., 1971). And, again, a study of successful suicides by mental patients in Massachusetts showed that the suicide rate for depressives was thirty-six times higher than that for the general population (Temoche et al., 1964). More recent findings continue to support these statistics (Hawton, 1987). Retrospective studies have also revealed that 80 percent of patients who committed suicide were depressed before they did so (Barraclough et al., 1969). Among children and adolescents as well, depression seems to be highly correlated with suicidal behavior (Kosky, 1983; Rosenthal & Rosenthal, 1984).

Such data can lead to the conclusion that depression plays an important role in suicide. Yet other studies indicate that this role is far from simple. For example, evidence shows that patients *seldom* commit suicide while they are severely depressed (Mendels, 1970). Such patients generally show motor retardation and low energy, which keep them from reaching the level of activity required for suicide. The danger period often comes after some form of treatment, when the depression begins to lift. Energy and motivation increase and patients are more likely to carry out the suicide act. Most suicide attempts occur during weekend furloughs from hospitals or soon after discharge, a fact that supports this contention (Wheat, 1960). The risk of suicide seems to be only about 1 percent during the year in which a depressive episode occurs, but it is about 15 percent after that (Klerman, 1982).

Although depression is undeniably correlated with suicidal thought and behavior, the relationship seems very complex. For example, why do some depressed people commit suicide while others do not?

The answer may be found in the depression, in the factors that contribute to it.

Beck et al., (1985) believe that *hopelessness*, or negative expectations about the future, may be the major catalyst in suicide and could be an even more important factor than depression. Beck conducted a ten-year study of 207 psychiatric patients who expressed suicidal thoughts, but who had no recent history of suicidal attempts. Within seventy-two hours after hospital admission, each patient was measured on three variables: hopelessness, depression, and **suicidal ideation** (thoughts about suicide). During the ten-year time period, fourteen patients committed suicide. The test scores of these people were compared to the others. Researchers found that the people who committed suicide did not differ from the survivors in terms of depression and suicidal ideation. But they did differ in terms of hopelessness. Those who died were more pessimistic about the future than those who survived. The analysis of the depression measure lent even greater support to the notion that the degree of hopelessness felt by people may be the greatest predictor of whether they will commit suicide. Although the overall results obtained by the scale did not predict suicidal risk, the hopelessness item within the measure did. These findings suggest that one should assess every depressed patient's attitude toward his or her future to determine how hopeless each person feels about it.

THE DYNAMICS OF SUICIDE

Some clinicians believe that everyone, at one time or another, has wished to end his or her life. Fortunately, most of us do not act on such wishes, even during extreme distress. But why do some people do so? Because suicide is closely linked to hopelessness and depression, many theories of depression apply to suicide as well. But still the question is not easy to answer. We have already discussed how difficult it is to study this phenomenon. We can never know for certain what causes a person to take his or her life. Yet on a very general level such people do seem to share one common motive: to gain relief from a life situation that is found unbearable.

1. Every 20 to 30 minutes, someone in the United States takes his or her own life. More than 25,000 people kill themselves each year. Suicide is among the top ten causes of death in the industrialized parts of the world; it is the second or third leading cause of death among young people. Some evidence shows that the number of actual suicides is probably 25 to 30 percent higher than that recorded. Many deaths that are officially recorded as accidental, such as single-auto crashes, drownings, or falls from great heights, are actually suicides. According to some estimates, for every person who completes a suicide, eight to ten people make the attempt.

2. Recent reports suggest that about 12,000 children aged five to fourteen are admitted to psychiatric hospitals for suicidal behavior every year, and it is believed that twenty times as many actually try. Suicides among young people aged fifteen to twenty-four have increased by more than 40 percent in the past decade (50 percent for males and 12 percent for females); suicide is now the second leading cause of death for this group.

3. Suicide is the second or third leading cause of death among college students. The suicide rate for college students is twice as high as that for people not in college.

4. The completed suicide rate for men is about three times that for women (although recent findings suggest many more women are now incurring a higher risk); among the elderly, the rate for men is ten times that for women. However, women *attempt* suicide three times as often as men. The suicide rate for black men between the ages of twenty and thirty-five is twice that for white men in the same age group.

5. In terms of marital status, the lowest incidence of suicide is found among people who are married, and the highest among those who are divorced. The suicide rates for single and widowed or divorced men are about twice those for women of similar marital status.

6. Physicians, lawyers, and dentists have higher than average rates of suicide. Among medical professionals, psychiatrists have the highest rate and pediatricians the lowest. Such marked differences raise the question of whether the specialty influences susceptibility or whether

Sociocultural Explanations

Early explanations of suicide emphasized its relationship to various social factors. Rates of suicide have been found to vary with occupation, the size of one's city of residence, socioeconomic status, age, sex, marital status, and race. Higher rates are associated with high- and low-status (as opposed to middle-status) occupations, urban living, middle-aged men, single or divorced people, and the upper and lower socioeconomic classes (Weile, 1960, Hall et al., 1970). In a pioneering work, the French sociologist Emile Durkheim related differences in suicide rates to the impact of social forces on the person (Durkheim, [1897] 1951). He proposed three categories of suicide: egoistic, altruistic, and anomic.

Egoistic suicide results from an inability to integrate oneself with society. A failure to keep close ties with the community deprives the person of the support systems that are necessary for adaptive functioning. Without such support, and unable to function adaptively, the person becomes isolated and alienated from other people (Slater & Depue, 1981).

Altruistic suicide is motivated by the person's desire to further group goals or to achieve some greater good. Someone may give up his or her life for a higher cause (as a religious sacrifice or political protest, for example). Group pressures may make such an act highly acceptable and honored. During World War II, Japanese *kamikaze* pilots voluntarily dove their airplanes into enemy warships "for the Emperor and the glory of Japan." The self-immolation of Buddhist monks during the Vietnam War and the terrorist truck bombing of the Marine barracks in Lebanon also fit this category.

Anomic suicide results when a person's relationship to society is unbalanced in some dramatic way. When a person's horizons are suddenly broadened or constricted by unstable conditions, he or she may not be able to handle the change or cope with the

suicide-prone people choose certain specialties.

7. Suicide is represented proportionately among all socioeconomic levels. Level of wealth does not seem to affect the suicide rate as much as do changes in that level. In the Great Depression of the 1930s, suicide was higher among the suddenly impoverished than among those who had always been poor.

8. Men most frequently choose firearms as the means of suicide; poisoning and asphyxiation via barbiturates are the preferred means for women. The violent means (which men are more likely to choose) are more certain to complete the act; this partially explains the disproportionately greater number of incomplete attempts by women. Among children below the age of fifteen, the most common suicide method tends to be jumping from buildings and running into traffic. Older children try hanging or drug overdoses. Younger children attempt suicide impulsively and thus use more readily available means.

9. Religious affiliation is correlated with suicide rates. Although the U.S. rate is 12.2 per 100,000, in countries where Catholic Church influences are strong—Latin America, Ireland, Spain, Italy—the suicide rate is relatively low (less than 10 per 100,000). Islam, too, condemns suicide, and the suicide rates in Arab countries are correspondingly low. Where church authority is weaker—as for example, in Scandinavian countries, in Czechoslovakia, and in Hungary—higher rates are observed. Indeed, Hungary is the highest, with a rate of 40.7, and Czechoslovakia has a rate of 22.4.

10. Suicide rates tend to decline during wars and natural disasters but increase during periods of shifting norms and values or social unrest, when traditional expectations no longer apply. Sociologists speculate that during wars, people "pull together" and are less concerned with their own difficulties.

11. More than two-thirds of the people who commit suicide communicate their intent to do so within three months of the fatal act. (The belief that people who threaten suicide are not serious about it, or will not actually make such an attempt, is ill founded.) Most people who attempt suicide appear to have been ambivalent about death until the suicide. It has been estimated that fewer than 5 percent unequivocally wish to end their lives.

SOURCES: De Calazaro, 1981; Dublin, 1963; Kosky, 1983; Rosenthal & Rosenthal, 1984; Shneidman, 1976; Shneidman et al., 1970; and Wexler et al., 1978.

---

new status and may choose suicide as an "out." The suicides of people who lost their personal wealth during the Great Depression or who killed themselves after being freed from concentration camps at the end of World War II, are of this type. Similarly, a person who suddenly and unexpectedly acquires great wealth may be prone to suicide.

Psychosocial explanations may be valid to an extent, but attributing suicide to a single sociological factor (economic depression, residence, or occupation) is too simplistic and mechanistic. As we have often noted, correlations do not imply cause-and-effect relationships. Thus, Durkheim's three categories are more descriptive than explanatory. Moreover, purely sociological explanations that take into account only one psychosocial factor—group cohesion, for example—omit the intrapsychic dimension of the person's struggles. They don't explain why only *certain* members of any of the aforementioned groups commit suicide, and others do not.

Intrapsychic Explanations

Early psychological explanations of suicide tended to ignore social factors in favor of intrapsychic ones. In the classical Freudian approach, for example, self-destruction was seen as the result of hostility that is directed inward against the *introjected love object* (the loved one with whom the person has identified). That is, people who kill themselves are really directing anger and the suicidal act against others whom they have incorporated within themselves. If the angry feelings (death instinct) reach murderous proportions, a suicide attempt is the result.

Unfortunately, these ideas are not supported by evidence. Carefully analyzed psychological autopsies indicate that hate and revenge are not the only reasons for suicide; people kill themselves for a number of other psychological reasons, such as shame, guilt, hopelessness, and pain. An analysis of 165 suicide notes that was conducted over a 25-year period

Ernest Hemingway, one of the great authors of the twentieth century (The Old Man and the Sea and The Sun Also Rises are two of his better-known works) committed suicide in 1961 by shooting himself. Although he did not leave a suicide note, many believe this avid sportsman ended his life because of illness and physical decline.

showed that only 24 percent of the suicides expressed hostile or negative feelings toward themselves, whereas 51 percent expressed positive attitudes and another 25 percent were neutral. The investigators concluded that there is not enough evidence to support the belief that hostility is the only cause of suicide (Tuckman et al., 1959).

Biochemical Factors in Suicide

It seems, then, that neither a purely sociological nor a purely psychological perspective is adequate to explain the causes of suicide. Probably both sociological and psychological factors are involved; Focus

13.2 discusses a classification scheme that includes both.

It is also likely that other factors are involved. For example, consistent with the strong evidence that chemical neurotransmitters are associated with depression and mania, similar evidence shows that suicide is influenced by biochemistry. This evidence was discovered in the mid-1970s, when researchers identified a chemical called *5-hydroxyindoleacetic acid* (5HIAA) (Stanley & Mann, 1983; Van Praag, 1983). The spinal fluid of some depressed patients had been found to contain abnormally low amounts of 5HIAA, which is produced when serotonin, a neurotransmitter that affects mood and emotions, is broken down in the body. Moreover, some evidence exists that the serotonin receptors in the brainstem and frontal cortex may be impaired (Mann et al., 1986). Preliminary statistics on low-5HIAA patients indicate that they are more likely than others to commit suicide, more likely to select more violent methods of killing themselves, and more likely to have a history of violence, aggression, and impulsiveness (Edman et al., 1986). Researchers believe that the tendency toward suicide may develop from a combination of aggression and depression.

This discovery may lead to a chemical means of detecting people who are at high risk for attempting suicide. However, researchers in this area caution that social and psychological factors also play a role. If in the future, cerebral serotonin can be detected easily in blood tests, it can be used as a biological marker (a warning sign) of suicide risk (Hawton, 1987). Low 5HIAA content does not cause suicide, but it may make people more vulnerable to environmental stressors (Pines, 1983). And still another caution is in order: this evidence is correlational in nature; it does not indicate whether low 5HIAA is a cause of or a result of particular moods and emotions—or even whether or not the two are directly related.

THE VICTIMS OF SUICIDE

In this section we briefly discuss four groups of people who are especially victimized by suicide: the very young, college students, the elderly—and those who are left behind by suicides.

Suicide Among Children and Adolescents

Suicide among the young is an unmentioned tragedy within our society. We have traditionally avoided the idea that some of our young people find life so painful that they consciously and deliberately take their own lives. As in the case of Tammy Jimenez, it may feel easier to call a suicide "an accident." Yet, as Focus 13.1 shows, as many as 250,000 children aged five to fourteen may attempt suicide each year (Rosenthal & Rosenthal, 1984). The suicide rate for children under fourteen is increasing at an alarming rate, and the rate for adolescents is rising even faster (Kosky, 1983; Cosand et al., 1982). Suicide is now second only to automobile accidents as the leading cause of death among teenagers, and some automobile "accidents" may also really be suicides.

A lack of research on childhood suicide has generally hindered our understanding of why such acts occur. However, two recent studies investigating this phenomenon have helped identify characteristics of suicidal children.

In a retrospective study of admissions to a pediatric hospital emergency room over a seven-year period, researchers identified 505 children and adolescents who had attempted suicide (Garfinkel et al., 1982). This group was compared with a control group of children who were similar in age, sex, and date of admission. Children in the suicidal group had the following characteristics:

1. There were three times as many girls as boys, and the boys who attempted suicide were significantly younger than the girls. The gender rates are consistent with adult rates, but the younger age of the boys is not.

2. The clinical symptoms most often shown by both the children and the adolescents were fluctuating affect and aggressiveness and/or hostility.

3. Most of the suicide attempts (73 percent) occurred at home; 12 percent occurred in public areas, 7 percent at school, and 5 percent at a friend's house. In 87 percent of the attempts, someone else was nearby—generally parents. The fact that most suicide attempts occur at home implies that parents are in the best position to recognize and prevent suicidal behavior.

4. Most of the attempts were made during the winter months, in the evening or afternoon.

5. Drug overdose was the primary means of attempted suicide, accounting for 88 percent of the attempts. Next, in order, were wrist laceration, hanging, and jumping from heights or in front of moving vehicles.

6. Over 77 percent of the attempts were judged to be of low lethality; 21 percent were moderately lethal; and slightly more than 1 percent were highly lethal. Most attempts were judged to have been made in a way that ensured a high likelihood of rescue. These figures lend credence to the belief that most children who attempt suicide do not really want to end their lives.

The researchers found that the families of the suicidal children were under greater economic stress than the families of the control group. The former had twice the rate of paternal unemployment. Maybe parents who are preoccupied with economic concerns are less readily available to support their children in time of need. Furthermore, fewer than half the families of those who attempted suicide were two-parent families. The families of suicide attempters also had higher rates of medical problems, psychiatric illness, and suicide than control group families. The dominant psychiatric problem was alcohol or drug abuse.

In the second study as well, family instability and stress and a chaotic family atmosphere were correlated with suicide attempts (Cosand et al., 1982). Suicidal children seemed to have experienced unpredictable traumatic events and to have suffered the loss of a significant parenting figure before age twelve. Their parents tended to be alcohol or drug abusers who provided poor role models for coping with stress. As in the first study, the child's self-destructive behavior seemed to be a last-ditch attempt to influence or coerce those who threatened his or her psychological well-being. The suicidal children showed considerable anger.

When their problems remain unrecognized and untreated, such children are at great risk of committing suicide. So early detection of their distress signals is vital. Intensive family therapy, including the education of parents with regard to parenting roles, can help. Parents can be taught to recognize the signs of depression, to become aware of their children's after-school activities, and to be cognizant of the role and

FOCUS 13.2 *Suicide Notes*

Suicide notes represent one source of data used in a psychological autopsy. We have already reviewed one frequently cited study (Tuckman et al., 1959) that gave us insights into the emotional state of the suicide victim. Additional studies have found that women are more likely to leave notes than are men; that separated or divorced women left more notes than those who were single; whites left three times more notes than nonwhites; and many notes expressed intense feelings of self-blame, hatred, and vengeance (Cohen & Fiedler, 1974; Farberow & Simon, 1975; Shneidman & Farberow, 1957). One may conclude from these findings that note-writing behavior in suicides is correlated with certain demographic

variables and that the act of writing is apparently an attempt to influence the responses of survivors.

One suggested classification scheme for suicide motives is based in part on information gleaned from suicide notes (Schneidman, 1957). Here are some of the categories, with illustrative suicide notes.

The *egoistic* suicide is the result of an intrapsychic debate, a struggle within the victim's mind. The victim's inner torment may be philosophical or religious in nature. An example:

Mr. Brown:

. . . It seems unnecessary to present a lengthy defense for my suicide, for if I have to be judged, it will not be on this earth.

However, in brief, I find myself a misfit. To me, life is too painful for the meager occasional pleasure to compensate. It all seems so pointless, the daily struggle leading *where?* Several times I have done what, in retrospect, is seen to amount to running away from circumstances. I could do so now—travel, find a new job, even change vocation, but why? It is *Myself* that I have been trying to escape, and this I can do only as I am about to do! Goodbye!

Bill Smith

(Shneidman, 1968, p. 5)

The *dyadic* suicide is interpersonal in nature and is influenced primarily by unfulfilled wishes or needs in-

accessibility of drugs. Finally, in some cases the child may need to be removed from the family (Berman & Bernard, 1982).

More recently, considerable attention has been directed at multiple or so-called *copy-cat suicides* in which youngsters in a particular school or community seem to mimic a previous suicide. For example, within a three-month period in 1985, nine Native American youths ages fourteen to twenty-five killed themselves, all by hanging. They were members of the Shoshone tribe and lived in Wind River, Wyoming. Although many factors may have led to these tragic deaths, suggestion and imitation seemed to have played an especially powerful role. Likewise, in one high school in Omaha, Nebraska, seven students attempted suicide within a very short span of time of each other; three were successful ("Suicide Belt," 1986).

Although imitative suicides may not be as common as the media seem to suggest, research indicates that publicizing the event may have the effect of

glorifying and drawing attention to it. Thus, depressed people may identify with a colorful portrayal, increasing the risk of even more suicides (Gould & Shaffer, 1986; Phillips & Carstensen, 1986). This pattern appears to hold especially true for youngsters who may already be thinking about killing themselves. The stable, well-adjusted teenager does not seem to be at risk in these situations.

Adolescence is often a period of confusing emotions, identity formation, and questioning. It is a difficult and turbulent time for most teenagers, and suicide may seem to be a logical response to the pain and stress of growing up. A suicide occurring in school brings increased risk of other suicides because of its proximity to students' daily life. In such instances, a suicide prevention program should be implemented to let students vent their feelings in an environment equipped to respond appropriately and perhaps even save their lives. One such program is discussed later.

volving a significant other. Frustration, rage, manipulation, and attempts to elicit guilt are common. For example:

Bill,

You have killed me. I hope you are happy in your heart, if you have one which I doubt. Please leave Rover with Mike. Also leave my baby alone. If you don't I'll haunt you the rest of your life and I mean it and I'll do it.

You have been mean and also cruel. God doesn't forget those things and don't forget that. And please no flowers; it won't mean anything. Also keep your money. I want to be buried in Potter's Field in the same casket with Betty. You can do that for me. That's the way we want it. . . .

(Shneidman, 1968, p. 6)

The *ageneratic* suicide is characteristic of the person who has lost the sense of participating in the transgenerational flow of human life—of belonging to "the scheme of things." Alienation, disengagement, and isolation are involved; the feeling and sense are existential.

To the authorities:

Excuse my inability to express myself in English and the trouble caused. I beg you not to lose time in an inquest upon my body. Just simply record and file it because the name and address given on the register are fictitious and I wanted to disappear anonymously. No one expects me here nor will be looking for me. I have informed my relatives in America. *Please do not bury me!* I wish to be *cremated* and the ashes tossed to the winds. In that way I shall return to the noth-

ingness from which I have come into this sad world. This is all I ask of the Americans for all that I have intended to give them with my coming into this country.

Many thanks,

José Marcia

(Shneidman, 1968, p. 8)

Suicide among high-school students is reaching epidemic proportions. One of the dangers parents and teachers need to guard against is copy-cat suicide, a phenomenon in which other students take their lives. To prevent more suicides, schools sometimes initiate programs that help students and faculty cope with their feelings of loss and anger.

Suicide victims often leave notes that can provide clues to their mental state and motivation. These notes and psychological autopsies are sometimes the only way loved ones and mental health professionals can begin to understand the pain and despair underlying the suicide act.

College Student Suicides

When you consider how well endowed college students as a group are—with youth, intelligence, and boundless opportunity—you might wonder whether something about the college situation fosters self-destructive acts among college students because suicide is a high risk for them. Most studies that seek to answer this question have described the characteristics of suicidal students without controlling for the possibility that nonsuicidal students may share the same traits. What is needed is a clear understanding of the characteristics that differentiate suicidal from nonsuicidal students. These characteristics seem to have been pinpointed in several studies where comparison groups were included for controls (Seiden, 1966, 1984a, 1984b; Klagsbrun, 1976).

Characteristics of Student Suicides   At the University of California at Berkeley, a ten-year study found that suicide ranked second only to accidents as the major cause of student deaths (Seiden, 1966, 1984a). Several characteristics of student suicides were distilled from this study. Compared to nonsuicidal students, students who committed suicide

- Tended to be older than the average student by almost four years
- Were significantly overrepresented among postgraduate students
- Were more likely to be men, although the proportion of women suicides was higher than among the general population
- Were more likely to be foreign students and language or literature majors
- As undergraduates, tended to have better academic records, but as postgraduate students were below the graduate grade point average

In addition, more suicides occurred in February and October (near the beginning of a semester) than in the other months of the year. Thus the notion that suicides occur in response to anxiety over final examinations was not supported by the results. In fact, the danger period appeared to be the start, not the finish, of the school semester. Most of the students committed suicide at their campus residence. Suicides seem more frequent at larger universities than at smaller ones, such as community colleges and small liberal arts colleges (Peck & Schrut, 1971). Firearms were the most common means of committing suicide; ingestion of drugs was next. In later studies on other campuses, however, drug overdose was found to be more frequently used than firearms (Klagsbrun, 1976).

Reasons for Student Suicides   These findings suggest explanations for student suicides. First, whereas the ratio of male suicides to female suicides in the general population is 3 to 1, for college students it is 1.5 to 1. In the past, the greater risk of suicide among college women may have resulted from increased conflicting social pressures, which accompany the rapid shift of sex roles among women entering college (Gibbs & Martin, 1964). Whether this now holds true is certainly debatable. It may be that as women's roles and lifestyles become more similar to men, so do their suicide rates.

Second, the fact that undergraduates who commit suicide have better scholastic records than the general college population reveals a painful paradox. By objective standards, suicidal students had done well. However, friends and relatives report that almost all these students were dissatisfied with their academic performance. They were filled with doubts about their own ability to succeed. One explanation for such a feeling is that these students were highly motivated to achieve and had unrealistically high expectations for themselves. For example, at a large eastern university several years ago, an outstanding young woman student, who had consistently made the dean's list and had obtained nearly straight-A grades, leaped to her death from her dormitory room late one winter night. It seemed inconceivable that a student with so much intellectual promise could commit such an act. Interviews with her friends, family, and fiancé indicated that she had been despondent over receiving a B in one of her courses, which spoiled her unbroken string of A's. Seiden (1966, p. 391) describes the psychological dynamics of this situation as follows:

> The internal standards these students applied to themselves were so Olympian, the demands they imposed upon themselves so exacting, that they were destined to suffer frustration and disappointments no matter how well they fared. . . . Whereas they had previously been crackerjack students in high school or junior college, excelling without much difficulty, the precipitous drop in grade points . . . threatened their feelings of self-esteem. Faced with a sudden loss of status, they may have suicided as a response to their egoistic conflict.

Third, and related to the previous explanation, many suicidal students feel overwhelming shame and disgrace because of their sense of failing others. On a particularly lovely June day, Patrick C. Do of Hong Kong, a graduate student at Florida State University, committed suicide after shooting his adviser, Professor James R. Fisher. Observers noted that Do had recently failed to pass a doctoral examination in chemistry (*East-West*, June 16, 1976). We might speculate that Patrick Do could no longer tolerate the experience of failure. He had indeed failed, and he partially blamed his adviser for the outcome. Death seemed the only avenue open.

Foreign students, especially, are under considerable pressure from families and friends to excel and achieve in this country. Their greatest fear is that they may not fulfill the expectations of their families, who may have sacrificed much to finance their educations. The pressures are even stronger for students from cultures in which it is important to bring honor to the family name (Sue, 1975). Academic achievement or occupational success reflects creditably on the whole family, not just on the individual. Conversely, unsatisfactory behaviors such as juvenile delinquency, mental illness, and failure in school shame the family. Faced with such pressures, some foreign students may report only successes to their families and cover up their failures. Needing to constantly reinforce the precariously fabricated image of continuous achievement, and knowing that a day of reckoning will eventually arrive, some students, like Patrick Do, choose suicide. Interestingly, Seiden's study revealed that 17 percent of the Berkeley suicides were Chinese students.

Finally, it is quite possible that the common denominator among suicidal students may simply be *emotional disturbance*. The other factors may all play a part, but psychopathology may predispose students to overreact to them. In fact, some people believe that suicide—any suicide—is simply not the act of a rational person. That is, some deviation within the person's personality causes or predisposes him or her to break with reality. Even the Japanese *kamikaze* pilots and the Shi'ite Muslim terrorist, who sacrificed their lives for a cause, are perceived in such Western

Many find it difficult to understand why members of such a privileged group as college students would commit suicide. Unrealistically high internal expectations, excessive pressure from family and friends to excel, and preexisting emotional problems may be some of the causes.

theories as mentally disturbed. Nevertheless, some psychologists hold firmly to the belief that some suicides may be culturally sanctioned and may represent rational responses to intolerable situations.

Suicide Among the Elderly

Aging inevitably results in generally unwelcome physical changes, such as wrinkling and thickening skin, graying hair, and diminishing physical strength. In addition, the elderly encounter a succession of stressful life changes as the years roll on. Friends and relatives die, social isolation may increase, and the prospect of death becomes more real (Goodstein, 1981). Mandatory retirement rules may lead to the need for financial assistance and the difficulties of living on a fixed and inadequate income. Among the elderly, nearly 30 percent have an annual income of less than $3,200 (Baum & Boxley, 1983). Such conditions make depression one of the most common psychiatric complaints of the elderly. And their depression seems to be involved more with "feeling old" than with their actual age or poor physical health (Baum & Boxley, 1983).

Suicide seems to accompany depression for older people. Their suicide rates (especially for elderly white men) are higher than those for the general population (Pfeiffer, 1977; McIntosh & Santos, 1981). In one study comparing rates of suicide among different racial groups, it was found that the white elderly committed almost 18 percent of all suicides but formed only about 11 percent of the population. However, the suicide rate for elderly white Americans has been declining over the past twenty years (McIntosh & Santos, 1981). Suicide rates for Chinese-Americans, Japanese-Americans, and Filipino-Americans are even higher than the rate for elderly whites. Native Americans and blacks show the lowest rates of suicide among older adults (although both groups are at high risk for suicide during young adulthood).

Of the Asian-American groups, first-generation immigrants were at greatest risk of suicide. One possible explanation for this finding is that the newly arrived Asian-Americans had intended to earn money and then return to their native countries. When they found that they were unable to earn enough either to return home or to bring their families here, they developed feelings of isolation that increased their risk of suicide. This risk has decreased among subsequent generations of Asian-Americans (and, probably, other immigrant groups as well) because of acculturation and the creation of strong family ties.

The Other Victims of Suicide

When a suicide occurs, our thoughts immediately turn to the person who has taken his or her own life. What unbearable pain was he or she suffering, to justify such an end? Yet the true victims of this tragedy are often the family, relatives, and friends who are left behind to face the *meaning* of this act. (see Focus 13.3 for discussion of another possible victim of other people's suicides).

Elisabeth Kübler-Ross, a psychiatrist who has researched and written extensively about death and dying, has outlined a series of reactions people experience when a family member commits suicide. The first of three stages is characterized by shock, denial, and numbness. The act is often incomprehensible to loved ones, who find it difficult to talk about. They tend to avoid using the word *suicide,* and they go through the motions of arranging the funeral as though it had no personal meaning. The depths of pain are too great to be confronted, and family members close themselves off from their feelings. In this state the bereaved person seems detached from others. Kübler-Ross suggests that, at this stage, friends can help most by making themselves available *both day and night.*

In the second stage, family members begin to experience grief. For the spouse especially, anguish is mixed with feelings of anger. He or she now tries to blame someone for something—him- or herself, for example: "Why didn't I see what was happening?" However, such self-blame for the death of one's spouse or child is often only symptomatic of the true source of anger—the person who committed suicide. And eventually that anger and rage toward the deceased is expressed: "How could you desert me and our children? How could you do this to us? Why didn't you have the courage to face life? Damn you, why didn't you tell me you were hurting?"

Kübler-Ross believes that this stage is difficult for family and friends to handle. Most people stay

FOCUS 13.3 — *The Impact of Patient Suicide on Psychologists: Other Victims of Suicide*

We have discussed the tragic consequences of suicide from the perspective of suicide victims and their family and friends. Few of us would think that a mental health professional working with a client might also suffer intensely if that person took his or her own life. After all, aren't psychologists suppose to be able to handle such matters without becoming emotionally involved? Furthermore, aren't suicides rare and unlikely to happen to clients undergoing therapy?

Recently, a nationwide study of 365 psychologists listed in the *National Register of Health Service Providers* was conducted to (a) ascertain the prevalence of client suicides and (b) determine the impact of client suicides on psychologists (Chemtob et al., 1988).

The findings revealed that 22 percent of psychologists had worked with a client who committed suicide. Those psychologists who experienced a client's suicide were asked a number of questions about how it affected their professional practice and personal lives. Many became more sensitive to suicide-related cues, consulted more with their colleagues, and became more aware of forensic-legal issues. Personally, suicides seemed to have major emotional impact on the therapist; they reported increased concerns of death and dying, suffered from intrusive thoughts of suicide, and felt anger and guilt toward their client.

The investigators found that one in five psychologists can expect to have a patient kill him- or herself and that 39 percent of those who lost one patient can expect to lose another. They contend that client suicides should be acknowledged as an occupational hazard because of the impact they have on a therapist's professional and personal life. A large proportion of therapists reported symptoms typical of post-traumatic stress, lasting over six months.

These findings should not be surprising. After all, therapists are just as vulnerable as anyone else. What seem to be needed are resources for psychologists to work through their own experiences of suicide. In addition, training programs in mental health should be initiated to teach trainees and their supervisors how to cope with a client's suicide. The investigators hope that this study will motivate psychology training programs to deal with this issue directly, forcefully, and constructively.

---

away from the parents or spouse of a suicide, whose rage can often make them quite abusive to everyone. It is important, however, that someone listen, act as a sounding board, and bear the brunt of such anger, because it needs to be expressed and is preferable to denial. The family must be helped to experience the pain, rather than postpone or deny it. They need empathic and understanding people, not sedation. Kübler-Ross says that, in suicide, extreme and prolonged grief can be avoided by not fostering denial. The words *suicide, death,* and *dead* should be used directly, without attempts to soften or disguise them (as in "passed away"). Moreover, it is important for older members of the family to see the corpse, to identify it, and to touch it, so that they face the reality of death.

The third and last stage is letting go, or completing "unfinished business." In cases of suicide, there is usually much unfinished business to take care of. A husband may think, "I never told her I loved her" or "There's so much we haven't talked about or shared." It is often helpful for the family to say these things to the suicide victim, either at the funeral or in a role-played situation. Letting go, saying goodbye, and accepting the feelings one has are important therapy for survivors. (The First Person narrative is a sensitive account of one survivor's experience.)

Elisabeth Kübler-Ross is a world-reknowned psychiatrist, author and lecturer, who has researched and written extensively about death and dying. Among her books are Living with Death and Dying, On Children and Death, *and* AIDS: The Ultimate Challenge.

PREVENTING SUICIDE

In almost every case of suicide, there are hints that the act is about to occur. Suicide is irreversible, of course, so preventing it depends very much on early detection and successful intervention. Mental health professionals involved in suicide prevention operate under the assumption that potential victims are ambivalent about the act. That is, the wish to die is strong, but there is also a wish to live. Potential rescuers are trained to exert their efforts to preserve life.

Clues to Suicidal Intent

The prevention of suicide depends very much on the ability to recognize its signs, both demographic and specific. We have already discussed a number of demographic factors, such as the fact that men are three times more likely to kill themselves than are women and the fact that increased age increases the probability of suicide. And, although the popular notion is that frequent suicidal gestures are associated with less serious intent, most suicides do have a history of making suicide threats; to ignore them is extremely dangerous.

General characteristics often help in detecting potential suicides, but individual cases vary from statistical norms. What does one look for in specific instances? Danto (1971) points out that the *seriousness of the intent* is indicated by the amount of detail involved in a suicide threat. A person who provides specific details, such as method, time, and place, is more in risk than one who describes these factors vaguely. Suicidal potential increases if the person has direct access to the means of suicide, such as a loaded pistol. Also, sometimes a suicide may be preceded by a precipitating event. The loss of a loved one, family discord, or chronic or terminal illness may contribute to a person's decision to end his or her life.

A person contemplating suicide may *verbally* communicate the intent. Some people make very direct statements: "I'm going to kill myself," "I want to die," or "If such and such happens, I'll kill myself." Others make indirect threats: "Goodbye," "I've had it," "You'd be better off without me," and "It's too much to put up with." Cues are frequently very subtle:

> A patient says to Nurse Jones, who is leaving on vacation, "Goodbye, Miss Jones, I won't be here when you come back." If some time afterward Nurse Jones, knowing that the patient is not scheduled to be transferred or discharged prior to her return, thinks about that conversation, she may do well to telephone her hospital. (Danto, 1971, p. 20)

As this example illustrates, verbal expressions must be judged within the larger context of recent events and behavioral cues. We have all, at one time or another, made or heard such statements.

Behavioral clues can be communicated directly or indirectly. The most direct clue is a "practice run," an actual suicide attempt. Even if the act is not completed, such a gesture should be taken seriously; it often communicates deep suicidal intent that may be carried out in the future. Indirect behavioral clues can include actions such as putting one's affairs in order, taking a lengthy trip, giving away prized possessions, buying a casket, or making out a will,

Merryl Maleska Wilbur

FIRST PERSON

When I think about it now, from the context of my normal life, what I did that day seems very odd. Wasn't I aware of the passing cars, the curious onlookers who surely must have stared? And what about my father, parked and waiting just up the road—didn't I worry about what he must be feeling and thinking?

But none of this troubled me at the time. All I knew was that my husband had been buried two days earlier and that this day, this Saturday in June, would have been our sixth wedding anniversary. I needed to be near him. If there was any place in the world that I belonged, it was with him. And so I had thrown myself on the upturned dirt that marked his grave and for one sweet, calming hour I had lain there, with my face in the ground, talking to him.

"Why did you do it, Carl? Why did it have to get that bad?" Over and over I asked him that question. "There would have been a way, if you could only have waited. You had no right to just get up and do this."

When my father finally came for me and I had to sit upright and face the blinding light of day, I felt a sudden paralyzing fear. It was as if I had unpeeled layers of my brain and was looking deep inside my own head: I am not going to make it through this. I will go crazy.

I could not know then that exactly one year hence, on the first anniversary of Carl's death, I would drive myself to that same cemetery, stand quietly in front of a newly placed gravestone, and read its inscription aloud to myself; that the tears would come but not in huge engulfing waves; and that when I now asked the question why?, acknowledgment of a universe and a mystery larger than Carl or me would cause me a long moment of philosophical reflection.

Between those points would lie a year counted by its minutes. I got from one point to the other by something that did not feel at all like courage, although people often called me courageous. Instead, it was a simple but pitiless formula that kept me going. I discovered soon enough that, despite that early panic, I really wasn't going to go crazy. Even after an hour of screaming aloud, *I* would always be there in all my alertness and consciousness. Nor could I seem to do what Carl had done. Ending my life by any one of several specific plans was an idea I carried with me at all moments but could never act through. The formula had its own inexorable logic: if I wasn't going to fall apart and if I couldn't kill myself, then what I was left with was having to live.

The choices I made and the things I did that year also seemed to unfold naturally. Like other suicide survivors I met, I found that my guilt was unrelenting. Day after day I put myself on trial, reviewing the minutiae of my life with Carl, searching for ways in which I had hurt him. The feelings of loss, exaggerated not only by what he had meant to me but because of the suddenness with which he had disappeared, came in great swells. In public, I kept my head down, acted by my own laws and instincts, greeting and smiling at no one, and in private I screamed and cried aloud for hours at a time. The way Carl had died, the suicide itself, was so inconceivable that I had a great need to tell the story, to examine it and make it real. With my parents, a new friend who took me into her home, members of a self-help group for suicide survivors, a therapist, colleagues at work, Carl's family— over and over the story I went.

After many months of this, the grief began to change. Although there was no one pivotal moment, a breakthrough occurred as I began to recognize that Carl had done something I could not control. He had acted out of who he was; neither my bad moods or nagging—nor my love—could make him be otherwise. Ironically, the fact that his death was a suicide gave me an unusual opportunity, for it helped me accept an essential human separateness. In giving up responsibility for his life, I also found it less and less astonishing that *I* had my own life and that I could go on without him.

Ms. Merryl Maleska Wilbur is a writer and editor. Her husband, Carl Angiolillo, committed suicide in 1982, after working eight years toward a doctorate degree. He was thirty-three.

depending on the circumstances. In other words, the more unusual or peculiar the situation, the more likely it is that the action is a cue to suicide.

Crisis Intervention

Suicide prevention can occur at several levels, and the mental health profession has now begun to move in several coordinated directions to establish prevention efforts. At the clinical level, attempts are being made to educate staff at mental health institutions and even at schools (Kneisel & Richards, 1988) to recognize conditions and symptoms that indicate potential suicides. For example, a single man over fifty years old, suffering from a sudden acute onset of depression and expressing hopelessness, should be recognized by mental health professionals as being at high risk.

When a psychiatric facility encounters someone who fits a particular risk profile for suicide, *crisis intervention* strategies will most likely be used to abort or ameliorate the processes that could lead to a suicide attempt. Crisis intervention is aimed at providing intensive short-term help to a patient in resolving an immediate life crisis. Unlike traditional psychotherapy, in which sessions are spaced out and treatment is provided on a more leisurely long-term basis, crisis intervention recognizes the immediacy of the patient's state of mind. The patient may be immediately hospitalized, given medical treatment, and seen by a psychiatric team for two to four hours every day until the person is stabilized and the immediate crisis has passed. In these sessions, the team is very active in not only working with the patient, but in taking charge of the person's personal, social, and professional life outside of the psychiatric facility.

After the patient returns to a more stable emotional state and the immediate risk of suicide has passed, the person is then given more traditional forms of treatment, either on an inpatient or outpatient basis. In addition to the intense therapy they receive from the psychiatric team, relatives and friends of the potential suicide will often be enlisted to help monitor the person outside of the hospital. In these cases, the responsible relatives or friends are provided with specific guidelines about how to deal with the patient between treatment team contacts, who to notify should problems arise outside of the hospital, and so forth.

Suicide Prevention Centers

Crisis intervention can be highly successful with potential suicidal patients because they are either already being treated by a therapist or have come to the attention of one through the efforts of concerned family or friends. Many people in acute distress, however, are not formally being treated. Although contact with a mental health agency may be highly desirable, some factors may work against it. Recognizing that suicidal crises may occur at any time and that preventive assistance on a much larger scale may be needed, suicide prevention centers have been established in a number of communities.

The first suicide prevention center (SPC) was established in Los Angeles in 1958 by psychologists Norman L. Farberow and Edwin S. Shneidman. The center first sought patients from the wards of hospitals, but now, owing to its reputation, 99 percent of its contacts are by phone (Farberow, 1970). In the last thirty years, hundreds of suicide prevention centers patterned after the first one have sprung up throughout the United States. These centers are generally adapted to the particular needs of the communities they serve, but they all share certain operational procedures and goals.

Suicide prevention centers typically operate 24 hours a day, seven days a week. Because most suicide contacts are by phone, a well-publicized telephone number is made available for calls at any time of the day or night. Furthermore, many centers provide inpatient or outpatient crisis treatment. If they lack such resources, the centers develop cooperative programs with other community mental health facilities. Most telephone hotlines are staffed by paraprofessionals. All workers are trained in crisis intervention techniques and have been exposed to crisis situations under supervision. Among these techniques are the following (Heilig, 1970):

1. *Maintaining contact and establishing a relationship* The skilled worker who establishes a good relationship with the suicidal caller not only increases the caller's chances of working out an alternative solution but also can exert more influence. Thus it is important for the worker to show interest, concern, and self-assuredness.

2. *Obtaining necessary information* Besides demographic data, the caller's name and address are elicited. This information is very valuable in case an urgent need arises to locate the caller.

3. *Evaluating suicidal potential* The staff person must determine quickly the seriousness of the caller's self-destructive intent. Most centers use lethality rating scales to help the worker determine suicide potential. These usually contain questions on age, sex, onset of symptoms, situational plight, prior suicidal behavior, and the communication qualities of the caller. Staffers also elicit other demographic and specific information that might provide clues to lethality, such as the information discussed in the section on clues to suicidal intent.

4. *Clarifying the nature of the stress and focal problem* The worker must help the caller clarify the exact nature of the stress, recognize that he or she may be under so much duress that his or her thinking may be confused and impaired, and realize that there are other solutions besides suicide. The caller is often disoriented, so it is important that the worker be specific, to help bring the caller back to reality.

5. *Assessing strengths and resources* In working out a therapeutic plan, the worker can often mobilize the caller's strengths or available resources. In their agitated state, suicidal people tend to forget their own strengths. Their feelings of helplessness are so overwhelming that helping them recognize *what they can do* about a situation is important. The worker explores the caller's personal resources (family, friends, co-workers), professional resources (doctors, clergy, therapists, lawyers), and community resources (clinics, hospitals, social agencies).

6. *Recommending and initiating an action plan* Besides being supportive, the worker is highly directive in recommending a course of action. Whether the recommendation entails immediately seeing the person, calling the person's family, or referring the person to a social agency the next day, it is presented as a plan of action and outlined step by step.

This list implies a rigid sequence, but in fact the approach (as well as the order of the steps) is adjusted to fit the needs of the individual caller.

The Effectiveness of Suicide Prevention Centers Today about 200 SPCs function in the United States, as well as numerous "suicide hotlines" in mental health clinics. However, little research has been done on their effectiveness because suicide is a difficult area to research, and many clients of SPCs want to stay anonymous.

Some data are available, however. For example, it is known that 95 percent of callers to SPCs never

Suicide prevention centers (SPC) operate twenty-four hours a day, seven days a week and have well-publicized telephone numbers because most contacts are made by phone. Even though there is controversy about SPC effectiveness, the mental health profession continues to support these centers.

use the service again (Speer 1971). This finding may indicate that the service was so helpful that no further treatment was needed or, just as possibly, that callers do not find SPCs helpful and feel it is useless to call again. Worse yet, they may have killed themselves after the contact. Another study has shown that potential suicides do not perceive contact with an SPC as more helpful than discussion with friends (Speer, 1972). Furthermore, cities with hotline services did not have lower suicide rates than those without such services.

Before you jump to the conclusion that SPCs are ineffective, however, note that the studies cited could have been affected by several factors. For example, cities with and cities without SPCs may differ so much that they are not comparable. Or clients may contact SPCs only when they are in such great distress that they despair of asking friends for help. They may later perceive their contacts with friends as being more beneficial relative to the distress they feel.

Finally, despite the lack of convincing evidence, there is always the possibility that SPCs do help. Because life is precious, the mental health profession continues to support them.

Community Prevention Programs

Suicide prevention programs have recently begun to spring up at work sites and schools. Increasingly, community leaders have recognized that the suicide of a worker or student has dramatic and stressful emotional effects on fellow workers and students who may have known the victim (Calhoun et al., 1982). When a school experiences a suicide, the staff and students quickly learn of the event. This is often followed by emotional upheaval, anxiety, guilt, and severe grieving (Davis, 1985; Praeger & Bernhardt, 1985). Educational institutions now routinely consult mental health professionals after a suicide in order to get help in facilitating the natural grieving process; reducing the secrecy, confusion, and rumors surrounding a suicide; and preventing possible copy-cat suicidal acts.

One particularly interesting and effective form of intervention was developed in response to a particularly violent suicide (Kneisel & Richard, 1988). A fifth- and sixth-grade teacher took her own life by dousing herself with gasoline and igniting herself. Local media coverage was quite intense, and little else was discussed. In responding to this terrible event and the emotional needs of the students, the school assembled a mental health consulting team, comprising of two child psychologists trained in crisis intervention and one representative each of the fire department and mayoral task force. The fire department representative was included because of concern about possible increased risk of firesetting among students. The team worked directly with the school psychologist, who already knew the students and staff. The primary goal of the program was to mitigate the effects of the tragedy by providing survivors with an opportunity to express and understand their reactions to the event. To accomplish this goal, the following activities were undertaken.

1. A faculty meeting was called to give teachers a forum in which they could share feelings and information with one another. This session was only partially successful. It gave the team insight into student concerns but it failed to meet the needs of the faculty.

2. In classroom discussions, children were given an opportunity to express their feelings and concerns, especially those dealing with fears of death, suicide, and fire. They were reassured that the teacher's decision to kill herself was not based on their behavior and her death was not their fault. All questions were answered truthfully and straightforwardly.

3. Throughout this period of intervention, the school psychologist was available for individual sessions with teachers, staff, and students. Some sought individual sessions because they had an especially close relationship to the victim; others sought help because they were already dealing with personal issues of loss, separation, and abandonment. Some students were referred because they were excessively tearful, withdrawn, or distraught; others were seen because they denied the suicide. Many of these individuals were referred for ongoing follow-up treatment.

After these meetings, the team met with the principal to plan follow-up actions. A memorial service was held. Parents were sent letters telling them about the suicide and informing them about mental health resources in the community. And written guidelines for suicide prevention were developed and distributed in the school.

The authors conclude that such an institutional response to a suicide minimizes mental health problems among the survivors, restores equilibrium in the school and community, and represents an effective suicide prevention program.

THE RIGHT TO SUICIDE: MORAL, ETHICAL, AND LEGAL IMPLICATIONS

Doris Portwood believes that elderly and terminally ill people have the right to end their own lives if their continued existence would result in psychological and physical deterioration:

> The choice of suicide is ours to make. It is our life we are giving up, and our death we are arranging. The choice does not infringe on the rights of others. We do not need to explain and excuse. (Portwood, 1978, p. 68)

Portwood contends that these people should be allowed the choice of dying in a dignified manner, particularly if they suffer from a terminal illness or a severely incapacitating illness that would cause misery for their families and friends. Such was the case with Mrs. Jenny Williams (described at the beginning of this chapter), who chose death over life.

As a part of our remarkably successful efforts to prolong life, this society has also begun to prolong the process of dying. And this prolongation has caused many elderly or terminally ill people to fear the medical decision maker who is intent only on keeping them alive, giving no thought to their desires or dignity. They, and many others, find it abhorrent to impose on a dying patient a horrifying array of respirators, breathing tubes, feeding tubes, and repeated violent cardiopulmonary resuscitations—procedures that are often futile and against the wishes of the patient and his or her family. Humane and sensitive physicians, who believe that the resulting quality of life will not merit such heroic measures, but whose training impels them to sustain life, are caught in the middle of this conflict. A civil or criminal lawsuit may be brought against the physician who agrees to allow a patient to die.

More and more people now believe that people ought to have the right to end their own lives, at least in certain circumstances. In cases of obvious terminal illness, when the patient has a short time to live and is suffering unbearable pain, the right-to-die argument seems sensible. In 1976 the California State Assembly became one of the first state legislatures to provide that right to people in such situations. Since then, fifteen states have passed "living will" laws that offer protection against dehumanized dying and confer immunity on physicians and hospital personnel who comply with a patient's wishes.

Advocates of such laws frequently use the terms *quality of life* and *quality of humanness* as the criteria for deciding between life and death. The meanings of these phrases are, however, somewhat indistinct and subjective. At what point do we consider the quality of life sufficiently poor to justify terminating it? Should people who have been severely injured or scarred (through, say, the loss of limbs, paralysis, blindness, or brain injury) be allowed to end their own lives? What about mentally retarded or emotionally disturbed people? It can be argued that their quality of life is equally poor. Moreover, who is to decide that a person is or is not terminally ill? There

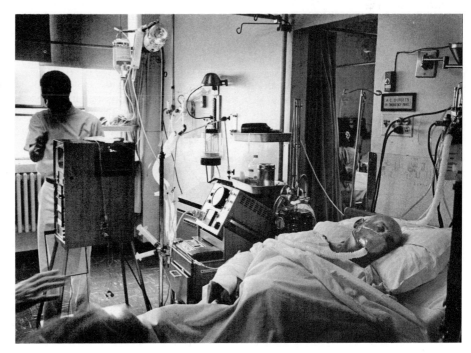

While modern medicine has made incredible advances in prolonging life, many of the procedures simply sustain life without regard to its quality. Many terminally ill or elderly patients, wishing to die with dignity, feel that they have a basic right to refuse treatment and end their own lives. The ethical and legal considerations are complex.

are many recorded cases of "incurable" patients who recovered when new medical techniques arrested, remitted, or cured their illnesses. Such questions cannot be answered easily because they deal with ethics and human values.

Yet the mental health practitioner cannot avoid these questions. Like their medical counterparts, clinicians are trained to save people's lives. They have accepted the philosophical assumption that life is better than death, and that no one has a right to take his or her own life. Strong social, religious, and legal sanctions support this belief. Therapists work not only with terminally ill clients who wish to take their own lives but also with disturbed clients who may have suicidal tendencies. These latter clients are not terminally ill but may be suffering severe emotional or physical pain; their deaths would bring immense pain and suffering to their loved ones. Moreover, most people who attempt suicide do not want to die, are ambivalent about the act, or find that their suicidal urge passes when their life situation improves (Murphy, 1973).

In working with clients who express suicidal wishes, the practicing therapist must confront the following questions (Corey, 1984):

1. Do therapists have a right and responsibility to forcefully protect people from the potential harm that their own decisions may bring?

2. Do therapists have an ethical right to prevent clients from committing suicide when they have clearly chosen death over life?

3. What ethical and legal considerations are involved in right-to-die decisions?

4. Once a therapist determines that a significant risk exists, must some course of action be taken? What are the consequences when a therapist fails to take steps to prevent a suicide?

Of course, these questions would be answered differently by different people. We can, however, directly address one of the issues they raise—the legal implications. According to one observer, no clear constitutional or legal statement gives a person the right to choose death. But the Constitution does seem to provide a basis for the right to refuse treatment, even life-saving treatment (Powell, 1982). Therapists, however, have a responsibility to prevent suicide if they can reasonably anticipate the possibility of self-destruction. Failure to do so can result in legal liability (Schultz, 1982).

Clearly, suicide and suicide prevention involve a number of important social and legal issues, as well as the personal value systems of clients and their families, mental health professionals, and those who devise and enforce our laws. And just as clearly, we need to know much more about the causes of suicide and the detection of people who are at high risk for suicide, as well as the most effective means of intervention. Life is precious, and we need to do everything possible, within reason, to protect it.

SUMMARY

1. Strong social, legal, and religious sanctions against suicide are evidence that this tragic and puzzling act is abhorrent to our society. Although depression and hopelessness are highly correlated with suicidal acts, the complex relationship between those factors and suicide is not simply one of cause and effect.

2. Early explanations of suicide were based on either a sociological or an intrapsychic view. Durkheim identified three categories of suicide on the basis of the nature of the person's relationship to a group: Egoistic suicide results from an inability to integrate oneself with society; altruistic suicide is motivated by the need to further the goals of the group or to achieve a "higher good"; and anomic suicide results when a person's relationship to the group becomes unbalanced in some dramatic fashion. In the psychoanalytic view, self-destruction results when hostility toward another person turns inward. More recent evidence indicates that biochemistry may be involved, but no single explanation seems sufficient to clarify the many facets of suicide.

3. In recent years, childhood and adolescent suicides have increased at an alarming rate. A lack of research has limited our understanding of why children take their own lives. However, the available studies indicate that those who attempt suicide come from families characterized by psychiatric illness (primarily drug and alcohol abuse), suicide, paternal unemployment, and the absence of one parent. Most childhood suicide attempts occur in the home, and drug overdose is the primary means.

4. Suicide among college students is particularly perplexing. Studies indicate that students who commit suicide can be distinguished from their nonsuicidal classmates: They are older and more likely to be postgraduate students, male, language or literature majors, and foreign students. As undergraduates, they have better academic records than their peers. Most college-student suicides occur at the beginning of a semester. They may be related to unrealistically high internal expectations, excessive pressures to excel from family and friends, or simply emotional disturbance.

5. Many people tend to become depressed about "feeling old" as they age. And depressed elderly people often think about suicide.

6. Suicide affects not only the person who commits the act but also the survivors. Loved ones who are left behind frequently respond with denial and shock, followed by grief and anger. The anger may be directed toward the self, but it is usually intended for the person who commits the act. The survivor's grief is resolved if and when he or she is able to "let go" of the deceased.

7. Perhaps the best way to prevent suicide is to recognize its signs and intervene before it occurs. People are more likely to commit suicide if they are older, male, have a history of attempts, describe in detail how the act will be accomplished, and give verbal hints that they are planning self-destruction. Crisis intervention concepts and techniques have been used successfully in treating clients who contemplate suicide. Intensive short-term therapy is used to stabilize the immediate crisis. Suicide prevention centers operate twenty-four hours a day to provide intervention services to all potential suicides, especially those not undergoing treatment. Telephone hotlines are staffed by well-trained paraprofessionals who will work with anyone who is contemplating suicide. In addition, these centers provide preventive education to the public. More and more community intervention programs are directed at organizations that may have experienced a suicide. The focus is not only on preventing future suicides but also on helping friends, family, workers, and others affected by the tragedy.

8. The act of suicide raises moral, ethical, and legal concerns. Do people have a right to take their own lives? This question is difficult to answer in the case of the elderly or of people who are terminally ill and wish to end their suffering. Nevertheless therapists, like physicians, have been trained to preserve life, and they have a legal obligation to do so.

KEY TERMS

altruistic suicide Suicide that is motivated by the need to further group goals or to achieve some greater good

anomic suicide Suicide that results when a person's relationship to society is unbalanced in some dramatic fashion

egoistic suicide Suicide that results from an inability to integrate oneself with society

psychological autopsy A systematic examination of existing information in order to understand and explain a person's behavior before his or her death

suicidal ideation Thoughts about suicide

suicide The taking of one's own life

chapter 14
Schizophrenia: Symptoms and Diagnosis

Schizophrenia is a severely disabling disorder. At times, reality becomes distorted, so the people affected cannot trust their own perceptions and thoughts. Zan Bockes, a woman who completed her undergraduate work between hospitalizations and eventually entered graduate school, gives a personal account of her struggles with schizophrenia:

I'd always been very quiet, somewhat of a "loner," usually energetic, and a good student with a particular interest in literature and creative writing, but the illness began disrupting my school work and job performance when I was 19 years old. . . . I increasingly heard voices (which I'd always called "loud thoughts" or "impulses with words") commanding me to take destructive action. I concluded that other people were putting these "loud thoughts" in my head and controlling my behavior in an effort to ruin my life. I smelled blood and decaying matter where no blood or decaying matter could be found (for example, in the classrooms at school). I had difficulty concentrating, I fantasized excessively, and I had trouble sleeping and eating. When I began responding to the voices' commands by breaking windows in my apartment and starting fires, I was committed with a diagnosis of "chronic hebephrenic schizophrenia." . . .

Over those 5 months, I had to deal with occasional hallucinations, recurrent illusions, increased energy . . . and periods during which I found myself indulging in various paranoid and grandiose thought patterns. Since I had learned to recognize these for what they were and had been able to appreciate the ultimate consequences of reacting to them, I was capable of preventing them from drastically affecting my behavior. . . . I recall one recent example of how I prevented further escalation of some irrational suspicions. In March, I became increasingly uneasy about something which I could not pinpoint, until I was quite fearful that some personal disaster was rapidly approaching. On my way to school one day, three large birds passed over me, stalling briefly in the air above my head. In my class, I noticed that a woman in front of me had a large black bag marked with white letters which read, among other things, "URGENT" and "CONFIDENTIAL." I heard a woman in the hallway say, "You won't go to jail." And my professor said during his lecture, "The choices you make are not inevitable," which angered and frightened me because I misunderstood him to mean, "The choices you make are inevitable." These events loomed in my head, and I interpreted them as warnings of impending disaster. With great difficulty, I suppressed my impulses to cry out and strike the nearby professor, and I tried to concentrate on the lecture. I managed to get through class and then hurried to my favorite isolated place on campus to get better control of myself. . . .

I acknowledge that although I have much control over my behavior, and some control over my thinking, and some control over my feeling, there remain a few things over which I have little or no control—for example, hallucinations. The trick is to realize when or if the hallucinations are truly disrupting my thoughts, feelings, and behaviors, and to take appropriate action before things get out of hand. Gradually I am learning where to draw the line—when medication is helpful and necessary and when I can manage safely without it. . . .

As of yet, I still have a long road ahead of me. There is much that I don't understand about schizophrenia, but I realize I am not alone in my lack of knowledge about the illness. . . . Life puts various limitations on each person, but within those limitations, there is always the freedom to make certain choices—an insight that I find relieving as well as revealing. (Bockes, 1987, pp. 40–42)

These few excerpts from Bockes's account illustrate many features of the schizophrenic disorders, which have been considered disorders of thought or cognition. More specifically, **cognition** consists of the processes of thinking, perceiving, judging, and recognizing. **Schizophrenia** is considered to be a group of disorders characterized by severely impaired cog-

nitive processes, personality disintegration, and social withdrawal. The schizophrenic disorders, shown in the disorders chart on p. 376, are severe disturbances (psychoses) that always involve some disruption of thought processes. People thus affected may lose contact with reality, may see or hear things that are not actually occurring, or may develop false beliefs about themselves or others.

SCHIZOPHRENIA

Schizophrenia has received—and continues to receive—a great deal of attention, for several reasons. First, the disorders are severely disabling and frequently necessitate hospitalization. The financial costs of hospitalization and the psychological costs to patients, families, and friends can be enormous. Second, the lifetime prevalence rate of schizophrenia in the United States is nearly 1 percent, so it affects millions of people directly (it occurs equally among males and females). And third, the causes of these disorders are not well known, and it has been difficult to find effective treatments. Evidence suggests that schizophrenia is a heterogeneous clinical syndrome with different etiologies and outcomes (Carpenter et al., 1988).

In this chapter we discuss the diagnosis and symptoms of schizophrenia, the different types of schizophrenic disorders, and the course of this disorder. Then, in Chapter 15, we examine the etiology and treatment of schizophrenia.

History of the Diagnostic Category

What is schizophrenia? Most clinicians would agree that the symptoms shown by Zan Bockes, which included hearing disembodied voices, smelling nonexistent blood and decaying matter, and disturbed thought processes, are consistent with a diagnosis of schizophrenia. However, the criteria that define this disorder have changed over time. This evolution is important because it has resulted from an improved understanding of the cause of the disorder which directly affects its treatment and outcome.

In 1896 Emil Kraepelin recognized that symptoms such as hallucinations, delusions, and intellectual deterioration were characteristic of a particular

Untitled (pencil, watercolor, and crayon), August Klett (pseudonym, Klotz)

Six of the paintings, etchings, and sketches pictured in this chapter are from the Prinzhorn Collection. Hans Prinzhorn (1886–1933) was a German psychiatrist who also had a degree in art history. During his career he collected about 5,000 pieces of art produced by inmates of psychiatric institutions in Germany, Austria, Switzerland, Italy, and Holland.

The artists were mentally ill patients, with no formal artistic training. They were often diagnosed as schizophrenic and did not express themselves artistically until after the onset of their illness. A remarkable aspect of this art is that it was produced spontaneously, not as part of a therapy program, by people who were living in socially isolated, unstimulating environments (von Baeyer, 1972).

disorder whose onset began at an early age. He called this disorder *dementia praecox* (insanity at an early age). Because he felt that the disorder involved some form of organic deterioration, its outcome was considered to be poor. People who recovered from *dementia praecox* were thought to have been misdiagnosed.

A Swiss psychiatrist, Eugen Bleuler, disagreed with Kraeplin's theory for several reasons. He did not believe that all or even most cases of schizophrenia developed at an early age. He argued that the outcome of schizophrenia did not always involve progressive deterioration, and he believed that *dementia praecox* represented a group of disorders that have different

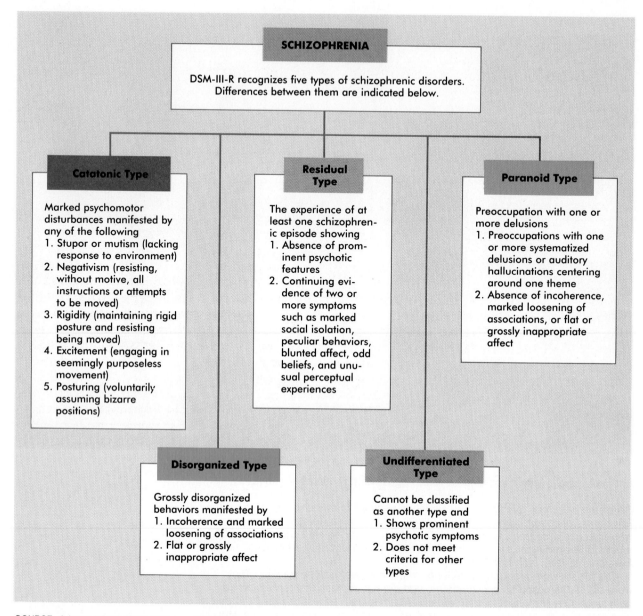

SOURCE: Adapted from DSM-III-R, pp. 187–198.

causes. Bleuler also theorized that environmental factors interacting with a genetic predisposition produced the disorder.

DSM-III-R incorporates some of the views of both Kraepelin and Bleuler. In accord with Kraepelin's standpoint, the condition is described as chronic with a pessimistic view of the outcome. In DSM-III-R, the prognosis for schizophrenia is described thus: "A return to full premorbid [before the illness] functioning in this disorder is not common" (American Psychiatric Association, 1987, p. 191). Bleuler's view of schizophrenia as a group of disorders, rather than a single entity, has also been accepted. There is also some acknowledgment that environmental factors may play a role in the cause and duration of the disorder.

DSM-III-R and the Diagnosis of Schizophrenia

Recall from Chapter 4 the Rosenhan (1973) study in which eight researchers, pretending to be mentally ill, gained admission to psychiatric hospitals. The eight experimenters all told the staff that they heard a voice saying "empty," "hollow," or "thud," auditory hallucinations that had occurred for a period of three weeks. Except for their names, vocations, and occupations, all the other information they provided to the hospital staff was true. All but one of the researchers received a diagnosis of schizophrenia, and that individual was labeled manic-depressive; all were admitted for treatment.

DSM-III-R had not been published at the time of the Rosenhan study, so the pseudopatients were diagnosed according to DSM-II or some other classification scheme. The obvious question is "Would these people have been diagnosed as schizophrenic under the DSM-III-R criteria?" The answer is no, provided that the criteria were followed strictly. Among the requirements that would not have been fulfilled are (1) deterioration from a previous level of functioning and (2) symptoms with a duration of six months or more. In addition, DSM-III-R requires that auditory hallucinations involve "more than one or two words." Actually, the symptoms reported by Rosenhan's pseudopatients do not fully meet the criteria for any of the psychotic disorders. (However, it would have been the duty of any clinician to admit the pseudopatients, for further observation, on the basis of their claims that they heard voices.)

The value of a diagnostic system such as DSM-III-R stems from its consistent and appropriate use—and this has yet to be achieved. In one survey, at a time when DSM-III criteria should have been applied, 301 psychiatrists were asked to "describe the clinical findings that would lead you to a diagnosis of schizophrenia" (Lipkowitz & Idupuganti, 1983). Only one respondent listed all findings necessary for such a diagnosis (symptoms, deterioration, six months' duration, and absence of major organic or affective disorder). Of further interest is the fact that 49 percent said they used only one of the diagnostic criteria, and some used idiosyncratic criteria that are obviously not listed in DSM-III or DSM-III-R, such as the following:

The "smell of schizophrenia"

Patient "doesn't add up"

"Poor ego functions or boundaries"

"Poor eye contact"

"Rapid mood swings"

"Excess religiosity"

The survey results indicate that the DSM-III criteria were not applied at all consistently in diagnosing schizophrenia and that many psychiatrists still use subjective criteria. A hopeful note was the finding that younger psychiatrists tended to use diagnostic criteria that were closer to those of DSM-III.

According to the DSM-III-R criteria, a diagnosis of schizophrenic disorder should be given only if delusions, auditory hallucinations, or marked disturbances in thinking or speech are shown. Furthermore, the patient must have deteriorated from a previous level of functioning with regard to work, interpersonal relationships, self-care, or the like. Evidence should show that the disorder has lasted at least six months at some time in the patient's history and has currently been present for at least two weeks. Organic mental disorders and affective disorders must have been ruled out as causes of the patient's symptoms. (See Table 14.1 for DSM-III-R criteria for schizophrenia.)

The actual DSM-III-R criteria are somewhat more precise and much more extensive than the preceding summary. Although the diagnosis of schizophrenia looks rather straightforward, people disagree over the adequacy of the criteria.

THE SYMPTOMS OF SCHIZOPHRENIA

Schizophrenic disorders are characterized primarily by impaired or disordered thinking. This impairment may be accompanied by disturbances of perception, psychomotor behavior, and affect (mood and emotion). Each of these general categories may be represented in a variety of specific symptoms. The most common symptoms are listed in Focus 14.1 where some related diagnostic problems and issues are also discussed.

TABLE 14.1 | **DSM III-R Criteria for Schizophrenia**

A. Psychotic symptoms in the active phase—either (1), (2), or (3) for at least one week:
   1. Two of the following:
      a. Delusions.
      b. Hallucinations (throughout the day for several days or several times a week for several weeks, each experience lasting longer than a few brief moments.
   2. Bizarre delusions (totally implausible, such as being controlled by a dead person).
   3. Prominent hallucinations of a voice with content having no apparent relation to depression or elation, or a voice keeping up a running commentary on the person's behavior or thought.

B. During the course of the disturbance, functioning in such areas as work, social relations, and self-care has deteriorated markedly from premorbid levels. (In the case of a child or adolescent, failure to reach expected level of social development.)

C. Signs of the disorder must be present for at least six months.

D. Schizoaffective and mood disorders with psychotic features must be ruled out.

E. It cannot be established that an organic factor initiated and maintained the disturbance.

F. If there is a history of autistic disorder, the additional diagnosis of schizophrenia is made only if prominent delusions or hallucinations are also present.

SOURCE: Adapted from DSM-III-R, pp. 187–198.

Thought Disturbances

According to the World Health Organization study cited in Focus 14.1, the most common symptom of schizophrenia is *lack of insight*. During the active phase of their disorder, schizophrenics cannot recognize that their thinking is disturbed. For example, David Zelt, a graduate student in psychology, went through a schizophrenic episode believing that the CIA was listening to and broadcasting his thoughts. He also believed that television stations communicated their views of him through electrical signals. The student did not question these beliefs. One of his therapists noted, "It was impressive to me to find someone with an exhaustive intellectual knowledge about psychosis and still be unable to bring his critical faculties to bear upon the onslaught of ideation" (Zelt, 1981, p. 531). Lack of insight alone, however, is not enough to make a diagnosis since it is also displayed in other disorders. Attempts are being made to identify pathognomonic symptoms—those that are specific only to schizophrenia.

Delusions The disordered thinking of schizophrenics may be exhibited in **delusions**, which are false beliefs that are firmly and consistently held despite disconfirming evidence or logic. However, studies indicate that delusions may differ in strength

and impact on the person's life. An example of a delusion follows:

When first admitted M. wore a piece of cellophane tape over his mouth and could only communicate in writing as he refused to take the cellophane tape off. He explained that he had been saying rude words and generally insulting people, and, although he did not hear himself doing these things, he was aware of the consequences. He dubbed this "saying things without hearing them" and was worried that he might be prosecuted for his behavior. Because of this concern, a lot of his time was spent amassing evidence in his defense about what he had said and the involuntary nature of this speech. (Brett-Jones et al., 1987, p. 262)

M. absolutely believed that he was hurling insults that he was unable to hear, and the presentation of contrary evidence had little effect.

Several types of delusions are listed below:

◆ *Delusions of grandeur* A belief that one is a famous or powerful person (from the present or the past). Schizophrenics may assume the identities of these other people.

◆ *Delusions of bodily disintegration* A belief that one's body is rotting away; for example, that one's vital organs are dissolving and turning to water.

FOCUS 14.1 *Symptoms of Schizophrenia*

The World Health Organization (WHO) conducted a large-scale diagnostic study of schizophrenia to determine its characteristics. Patients from the United States, England, the Soviet Union, China, India, Denmark, Czechoslovakia, Colombia, and Nigeria were included in this *International Pilot Study of Schizophrenia* (World Health Organization, 1973b, 1981). The following symptoms were reported in 50 percent or more of schizophrenic individuals:

These are the symptoms most frequently seen in schizophrenics. For two reasons, however, they are not sufficient to ensure the accurate diagnosis of schizophrenia. First, many of these symptoms also occur in other disorders. Delusions, hallucinations, and lack of insight, for example, may be shown by patients with major affective disorders (Harrow et al., 1982). Second, some of the most frequently observed symptoms, including lack of insight and flat affect, are defined in different ways by different clinicians, so that the symptoms themselves have low reliability in pinpointing schizophrenia.

What is needed for accurate diagnosis is a set of symptoms that are specific to schizophrenia. Unfortunately, these might not be the most common symptoms. An example is neologisms, or made-up words; their appearance in the speech of a patient almost guarantees a diagnosis of schizophrenia in any country in the world (Kaplan & Sadock, 1981). However, they are a fairly rare symptom. Of the common symptoms, the most discriminant—and therefore the most helpful in diagnosing schizophrenia—are auditory hallucinations, voices speaking to the patient, thought alienation, thoughts spoken aloud, and delusions of control.

Symptom	Percentage of Schizophrenics
Lack of insight	97%
Auditory hallucinations	74
Verbal hallucinations	70
Ideas of reference	70
Suspiciousness	66
Flat affect	66
Voices speaking to patient	65
Delusional mood	64
Delusions of persecution	54
Inadequate description of problem	64
Thought alienation	52
Thoughts spoken aloud	50

SOURCE: World Health Organization 1973, 1981.

◆ *Delusions of control* A belief that other people, animals, or objects are trying to influence or take control of one.

◆ *Delusions of nothingness* A belief that nothing really exists. Everything is unreal.

◆ *Delusions of persecution* A belief that others are plotting against, mistreating, or even trying to kill one.

◆ *Delusions of reference* A belief that one is always the center of attention, or that all happenings revolve about oneself. Others are always whispering behind one's back, for example.

◆ *Delusions of sin* A belief that one has committed some great wrong or sin that can never be forgiven.

Delusions may be centered on the schizophrenic's own thoughts. For example, *thought broadcasting* is the belief that one's thoughts are being disseminated to the entire world. *Thought insertion* is the belief that thoughts are being put in one's head by others. And, conversely, *thought withdrawal* is the belief that one's thoughts are being removed from one's mind by other people. Other delusions reported to the authors include a man who believed he derived

Universe Inversion *(crayon), Joseph Schneller (pseu-donym, Joseph Sell)*

was concerned about infecting others with a disease sometimes indicated that her concern could be due to her imagination. At the other extreme, a man who claimed to be in communication with aliens responded, "Absolutely not!" to the suggestion that his imagination was involved.

The *extension* of a delusion is the degree to which it involves other people. One 42-year-old woman complained about being poisoned by her boss, who was using radioactivity near her desk while she was at work. In another case, a 22-year-old man felt persecuted by friends and strangers alike.

Disorganization involves the degree of internal consistency of the delusional system. An example of a consistent belief involved a 48-year-old man who believed that a committee made up of members of his law school class were persecuting him. The persecution involved the committee's hiring of actors to jeer at and insult him. Cameras and monitors were put in his apartment so the committee could alert the actors whenever he left his home. In a case exhibiting inconsistency, a 24-year-old woman claimed that her parents had leukemia, that people were being killed, and that she was being poisoned and turned into a lesbian. She made no attempt to relate these delusional concepts to each other.

The *pressure* of a delusion is the degree to which the person is preoccupied with the belief. For example, one 28-year-old woman was convinced she was the Virgin Mary. Asked how often she thought of herself in that way, she replied, "Oh, it comes to me now and then." At the other extreme, a 56-year-old man, convinced that he was a government double agent, spent all his waking hours trying to recall how and when he first became involved.

This individual variability suggests the need to reconceptualize delusions. Delusions may not always be held firmly or be disruptive. In a study of nine schizophrenic patients, Brett-Jones and his colleagues (1987) found that most were not preoccupied with their delusions. They thought about them "only some of the time." In addition, most indicated that their delusions interfered very little with their daily activities. They responded to contradictory information by ignoring or denying it. They didn't actively test out their beliefs. The researchers, however, warn that we should not automatically view the lack of reality testing as pathological. They point out that the responses shown by the schizophrenics are "little

energy from drinking the blood of raw meat. During group therapy sessions, his participation would be greater if he had recently engaged in this behavior. In another case, a client believed that mental health professionals "sucked" away some of his life force during therapy sessions. He was convinced that he grew smaller after each session.

Although it is commonly believed that delusions are firmly held, the strength actually varies from person to person and even within a single individual (from time to time). In a study of fifty-two delusional patients, researchers identified four qualities of delusions (Kendler et al., 1983).

The *conviction* with which a delusion is held is the degree to which the person is convinced of the delusion. In the study, a 48-year-old woman who

different from the way that most people deal with evidence concerning beliefs or theories that are important to them" (p. 265).

Problems with Verbal Communication

Thought disturbances are also exhibited in unusual patterns of speech or writing.

Loosening of Associations   The **loosening of associations,** or *cognitive slippage,* is the continual shifting of thoughts from topic to topic without any apparent logical or meaningful connection among topics. It may be shown by incoherent speech and bizarre and idiosyncratic responses. In addition, communication may be overgeneralizing or vague, or may be overly concrete (as opposed to abstract). Some of these characteristics are illustrated in the following patient responses to test questions:

> *Q:* Why does a train have an engine?
> *A:* To give it a fantasy of imagination that requires it useless until you produce it.
> *Q:* [What is meant by] "One swallow doesn't make a summer"?
> *A:* That's oriental. When the first bird in the summer swallows the first worm, then she can start to produce eggs. Which do you think came first, the chicken or the egg? I think the egg, definitely. And it was fertilized with the sperm, so the sperm came first, too. Which came first, though, the egg or the sperm? (Harrow et al., 1982, p. 666)

Neologisms   As noted in Focus 14.1, the speech of some schizophrenics contains **neologisms,** which are new words that are typically formed by combining words in common usage. For example, one psychologist asked a patient, "How do you feel today?" The patient responded,

> Yes, sir, it's a good day. Full of rainbows you know. They go along on their merry way without concern for asphyxiation or impurities. Yes sir, like unconcerned flappers of the cosmoblue.

The patient's "cosmoblue" is a neologism, a combination of "cosmos" and "blue," the color of the sky. The response is also *tangential;* rather than answering the question directly, it seems to ramble through a series of asides.

Problems with Attention

Schizophrenics have trouble directing their attention to a particular aspect of their environment and keeping their attention focused on it. In other words, they find it difficult to concentrate and to organize incoming information: "Schizophrenia is frustrating when I can't hold onto my thoughts; when conversation is projected on my mind but won't come out of my mouth; . . . when my eyes and ears drown in a flood of sights and sounds (McGrath, 1987, p. 38).

Schizophrenics appear to be unable to organize speech into a coherent whole, resulting in shifts of thought that are not understandable to the listener.

> *Q:* Can you tell me where you live?
> *A:* I live in Connecticut. We live in a 50-year-old Tudor house. It is a house that is very much a home. It is often hard for people to get to know me. However, there are important clues. The house very much shows my personality. It is comfortable and modest. Also,

Untitled (pencil and watercolor), August Klett

my book collection shows my basic curiosity. (Hoffman et al., 1986, p. 833)

In this case the person shifts back from a discussion of the house to her personality without any logical connection.

Some schizophrenics seem unable to monitor and put forth intelligible speech. Chaika (1985) videotaped a schizophrenic during the active phase of his illness. Later, when the man viewed the tape of himself, he said he never realized he spoke that way. Schizophrenic people seem to lose control of the ability to choose words to reflect what they want to say.

Perceptual Distortion

Schizophrenics often report **hallucinations,** which are sensory perceptions that are not directly attributable to environmental stimuli. They may claim to see people or objects, to hear voices, or to smell peculiar odors that are not really present. (Note the distinction between hallucinations and delusions: hallucinations are false sensory experiences, whereas delusions are false intellectual experiences.)

Hallucinations may involve a single sensory modality or combination of modalities: hearing (*auditory* hallucinations), seeing (*visual* hallucinations), smelling (*olfactory* hallucinations), feeling (*tactile* hallucinations), and tasting (*gustatory* hallucinations). Auditory hallucinations are the most common (Cutting, 1987). Hallucinations sometimes accompany and are related to delusional beliefs. For example, a patient who believed that she had committed an unforgivable sin (delusion of sin) heard imaginary voices (auditory hallucinations) saying that she was evil and worthless. This woman became extremely guilt-ridden, distraught, and eventually suicidal in an attempt to atone for the imagined sin.

Hallucinations are puzzling because they do not seem to be produced by external stimuli. Therefore, researchers have focused on the possible role of internal stimuli. Bick and Kinsbourne (1987) wanted to see if hallucinations are caused by subvocal activity. Eighteen schizophrenics who had reported hearing voices every day for over two years were asked to report the status of their hallucinations under three conditions: (1) eyes closed tightly, (2) mouth open, and (3) fists squeezed tightly. The conditions of eyes shut and tight fists were intended to control for variables such as distraction and facial involvement.

Many people with schizophrenia experience hallucinations, which can involve any of the sensory modalities. During acute stages, an hallucinating person may respond to the hallucinations as if they were real. Evidence suggests, however, that some schizophrenics can exert at least some control over their symptoms.

Among the schizophrenics, most reported that under the "mouth open" condition hallucinations ceased. The other two conditions had little affect on the hallucinations. The researchers also found that non-schizophrenic controls who were hypnotized and told they would hear voices reported that the "mouth open" condition eliminated their hallucinations. Bick and Kinsbourne (1987) conclude that hallucinations involve the following pattern. The patient subvocalizes, listens to the covert speech, and then attributes it to another source.

Delusions and hallucinations can be extremely distressing to schizophrenics as they respond to their internal realities. But are these disturbances recognized as such by the patients themselves? One college student who suffered auditory hallucinations involving messages from radio and television programs asked, "How can I tell when the radio is really on and when it is my imagination?" This question obviously reflects an attempt to discriminate between reality and hallucinations.

During acute stages (when the symptoms are most prominent), the person may be so involved in hallucinations that he or she cannot do anything but respond as though they were real, whether or not they are distinguishable from reality (Larkin, 1979). This may be true with regard to delusions as well. However, as Focus 14.2 suggests, some schizophrenics may be able to break into the process by which hallucinations or delusions are developed, and to actually ward them off.

Motoric Disturbances

The symptoms of schizophrenia that involve motor functions can be quite bizarre. The person may show extreme activity levels (either unusually high or unusually low), peculiar body movements or postures, strange gestures and grimaces, or a combination of these. Like hallucinations, a patient's motoric behaviors may be related to his or her delusions. For example, during a clinical interview one schizophrenic patient kept lowering his chin to his chest and then raising his head again. Asked why he lowered his head in that way, the patient replied that the atmospheric pressure often became too great to bear, and it forced his head down.

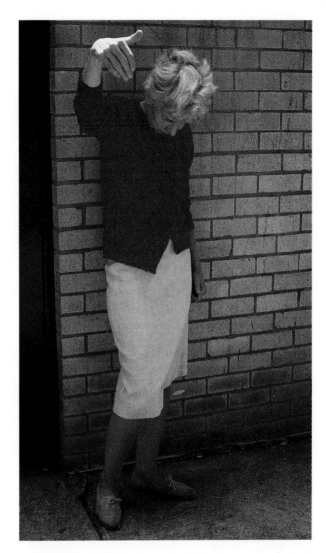

Catatonic schizophrenia is a rare disorder characterized by disturbances in motor activity. Excited catatonics exhibit great agitation and hyperactivity; withdrawn catatonics (like the woman shown in this picture) may exhibit extreme unresponsiveness or adopt strange postures.

Schizophrenics who display extremely high levels of motor activity may move about quickly, swing their arms wildly, talk rapidly and unendingly, or pace constantly. At the other extreme, some patients hardly move at all, staring out into space (or perhaps into themselves) for long periods of time. The inactive patients also tend to show little interest in others, to

FOCUS 14.2   *Can Schizophrenics Control Their Symptoms?*

A 24-year-old man, diagnosed as paranoid schizophrenic, reported that he could sometimes stop or diminish both auditory hallucinations and the belief that he was being persecuted. Two researchers became intrigued by his report and began a study of twenty psychiatric patients, to determine whether and how patients could control their symptoms (Breier & Strauss, 1983). Specifically, they tried to find out whether self-control methods are used by patients, the types of methods employed, and why some patients are unsuccessful in using these methods. They found that most of the patients (seventeen) did try to control their symptoms. The most important factor for success was identifying the feelings and thoughts that occurred before a psychotic episode. One man, for example, learned to be alert to a "high" sensation. If he took no action in response to that feeling, it evolved into psychotic symptoms.

Three general approaches were used by the patients to control their hallucinations or delusions. The first involved self-instruction. One woman would tell herself to "act like an adult" and to "be responsible." Others would actively compare their behavior with that of nearby people or get feedback from such people about their perceptions. The second approach involved reducing activity when the symptoms began to appear. One woman found that she could reduce the severity of her symptoms by isolating herself in the bathroom. Others would stop what they were doing and take a walk or simply relax. The third approach used increasing activity. For example, one patient found that her symptoms would get worse if she remained unoccupied, but she could reduce their severity by keeping busy. Interestingly, the three patients who did not use self-control or were unsuccessful with it had failed to identify the thoughts or

feelings that preceded their symptoms. Similar results were reported by Tarrier (1987). Of those who were able to identify events that precipitated psychotic episodes, 72 percent were able to use coping strategies. Those who used multiple strategies were the most successful at coping.

These studies show that many psychotic patients are aware of the negative nature of their symptoms and take active steps to regulate their psychopathology. It also appears to be easier for patients to break the chain leading to a psychotic episode earlier rather than later in its development—and that the key may be identifying the antecedents to psychotic behavior. These findings have obvious implications for treating schizophrenia and other thought disorders.

---

respond only minimally, and to have few friends. During periods of withdrawal, they are frequently preoccupied with personal fantasies and daydreams.

The assumption and maintenance of an unusual (and often awkward) body position is characteristic of the *catatonic* type of schizophrenia (to be discussed shortly). A catatonic patient may stand for hours at a time, perhaps with one arm stretched out to the side. Or the patient may lie on the floor or sit awkwardly on a chair, staring, aware of what is going on all around, but not responding or moving. If a hospital attendant tries to change the patient's position, the patient may either resist stubbornly or may simply assume and maintain the new position.

Affective Symptoms

The affective symptoms of schizophrenia are usually manifested as either inappropriate emotions or a lack of emotion. Schizophrenic patients may laugh wildly or weep uncontrollably with little relationship to current circumstances; they may display ambivalent feelings and rapid changes of mood for no apparent reason. Some are extremely suspicious of everyone else and react with anger or rage to all personal encounters—including those that are obviously beneficial in nature.

Schizophrenics may express the "wrong" emotions or may express appropriate emotions in an inappropriate way. For example, one patient was severely depressed about the death of her father. While describing the rather gory automobile accident in which her father was killed, however, the patient frequently smiled and giggled about the fact that her father would no longer have to worry about the family's economic situation.

At the opposite end of the emotional spectrum, some schizophrenics may show little or no emotion in situations where one would expect strong reactions. A delusional patient, for instance, might explain in detail how parts of his or her body are rotting away but show absolutely no concern or worry through voice tone or facial expression. This abnormal lack of emotional response, in which no emotion is expressed by any means, is called **flat affect.**

Beiser et al. (1988) reported that over half of the schizophrenic patients they studied showed restricted affect ("expressionless face and voice") whatever the topic of discussion. However, they caution that certain cases of flat affect may not be a symptom of the disorder but the result of institutionalization or antipsychotic medications.

Schizophrenics often show disturbances in their sense of self, and are often perplexed about their identity, as the following quote shows:

> The reflection in the store window—it's me, isn't it? I know it is, but it's hard to tell. Glassy shadows, polished pastels, a jigsaw puzzle of my body, face, and clothes, with pieces disappearing whenever I move. And, if I want to reach out to touch me, I feel nothing but a slippery coldness. Yet I sense that it's me. I just know. (McGrath, 1987, p. 37)

TYPES OF SCHIZOPHRENIA

Five types of schizophrenic disorders are generally recognized: disorganized, catatonic, paranoid, undifferentiated, and residual. These are shown in the disorders chart presented on p. 376. In the past, clinicians had trouble using the available diagnostic schemes to distinguish among these types. However, the authors of DSM-III and DSM-III-R have provided additional criteria and have specified them more precisely. The reliability and validity of these newer criteria have yet to be fully tested.

Disorganized Schizophrenia

Disorganized schizophrenia (formerly called *hebephrenic*) is characterized by severe disintegration and regressive behaviors beginning at an early age. The diagnostic criteria include frequent incoherence of speech, the absence of systematized delusions (delusions are instead fragmented or disorganized), and inappropriate affect (DSM-III-R). People with this disorder act in an absurd, incoherent, or very odd manner that conforms to the stereotype of "crazy" behavior. Their emotional responses to real-life situations are typically flat, but a silly smile and childish

Pablo Picasso painted this portrait in 1910. Picasso was a master of cubism, a style of art characterized by the reduction of forms into geometric shapes. The painting gives a visual impression of the fragmentation and distortion of self felt by some people with schizophrenia. (Note that this painting is not part of the Prinzhorn collection.)

giggle may be shown at inappropriate times. The hallucinations and delusions of disorganized schizophrenics tend to shift from theme to theme rather than remaining centered on a single idea, such as persecution or sin. Because of the severity of the disorder, many people thus affected are unable to care for themselves and are institutionalized.

Disorganized schizophrenics usually exhibit extremely bizarre and seemingly childish behaviors, such as masturbating in public or fantasizing out loud. An example appears in the following excerpt from a clinical interview with a young woman:

> *Therapist:* Do you know why your mother brought you to this clinic?
> *Client:* Well, Mom started yelling at me. She gets too excited about things. People are so excited nowadays. You know what I mean?
> *Therapist:* What did she yell at you about?

Untitled (crayon) Franz Karl Bühler

Client: Just because I smeared some shit on a painting I was doing for school (silly giggle). See, the teacher in art class wanted us to do some finger painting at home. She said that we should be creative. I ran out of paint so I thought I would use some of my shit. After all, it is natural (giggle) and it feels like paint.

Catatonic Schizophrenia

Disturbance in motor activity—either extreme excitement or extreme withdrawal—is the prime characteristic of **catatonic schizophrenia.** This disorder is quite rare nowadays.

Excited catatonics are very agitated and hyperactive. People with this form of the disorder may talk and shout constantly, while at the same time moving or running until they drop from exhaustion. They sleep little and are continually "on the go." Their behavior can become dangerous, however, and violent acts are not uncommon. *Withdrawn catatonics* are extremely unresponsive with respect to motor activity. Such people show prolonged periods of stupor and mutism, despite their awareness of all that is going on around them. Some may adopt and maintain strange postures and refuse to move or change position. Others exhibit a *waxy flexibility,* allowing themselves to be "arranged" in almost any position and then remaining in that position for long periods of time. During periods of extreme withdrawal, catatonic schizophrenics may not eat or control their bladder or bowel functions.

Catatonics may alternate between excited motor activity and withdrawal, as is illustrated in the following case:

A 43-year-old man was admitted to a hospital after his wife became alarmed over his complete inactivity. He had been unemployed for the last two months but had become progressively more uncommunicative for some eight months. A few days before, he had stopped talking altogether, and he now sat in his chair all day with his eyes closed. After about a week in the hospital, a nurse reported that the patient had gotten out of bed and was standing in the hospital's recreation room, giving what appeared to be a lecture to other patients. The ward psychiatrist immediately asked the nurse to bring the patient to his office, where the following conversation took place.

Patient: You wanted to see me, Doctor?

Psychiatrist: Yes. You know you hardly said anything for the past week, and now the nurse says you're interacting with other patients.

Patient: This past week, Doctor, I've been thinking and meditating.

Psychiatrist: About what?

Patient: You see, Doctor, the patient next door always has his television set on. I've been carefully listening to the kinds of programs on television—the walls in the hospital are thin. I'm appalled at the continual outpouring of filth, decadence, sin, immorality, sex, violence. My God! People are so numbed by the stuff that they don't realize the kind of brainwashing that goes on. No wonder we're a sick society. I've decided to counter this trend by informing others of the filth, but it's almost impossible for them to comprehend. If the hospital staff and patients fail to understand, I may start Phase Two of my efforts by breaking the television sets in this hospital!

A few days later the patient attempted to smash the television set in the next room but was restrained by several ward attendants.

Paranoid Schizophrenia

One of the most common forms of schizophrenia is the paranoid type. **Paranoid schizophrenia** is characterized by persistent and *systematized* delusions that are illogical or contradictory. Delusions of persecution are the most common. The deluded individuals believe that others are plotting against them, are talking about them, or are out to harm them in some way. They are constantly suspicious, and their interpretations of the behavior and motives of others are distorted: A friendly, smiling bus driver is seen as someone who is laughing at them derisively; a busy clerk who fails to offer help is part of a plot to mistreat them; a telephone call that was a wrong number is an act of harassment or an attempt to monitor their comings and goings.

Church Light *(watercolor), Konrad Zeuner*

Mr. A, a 37-year-old Mexican-American Vietnam veteran previously treated at several Veterans Administration hospitals with the diagnosis of paranoid schizophrenia, came to the emergency room stating, "My life is in danger." . . . Mr. A told a semicoherent story of international spy intrigue that was built around the release of soldiers still missing in action or held as prisoners of war in Vietnam. He believed he was hunted by Vietnamese agents. . . . Mr. A reported hearing the voices of the men from his company who died. . . . These voices tended to severely criticize and chastise him. He had become so disturbed by these beliefs and auditory hallucinations that he made suicidal efforts to escape the torment. (Glassman et al., 1987, pp. 658–659).

Another common delusion among paranoid schizophrenics involves exaggerated grandiosity and self-importance. Individuals with such delusions of

FOCUS 14.3   *Delusional (Paranoid) Disorder*

Delusional disorder is often confused with schizophrenia. In both, thought processes are disturbed. However, some differences do exist. Delusional disorder involves "nonbizarre" beliefs (situations that could actually occur). Also, except for the delusion, the person's behavior is not odd. With schizophrenics, other disturbances in thoughts and perceptions are involved. People with delusional disorder behave normally when their delusional ideas are not being discussed. Delusional disorder was called *paranoid disorder* in DSM-III. The name of this category was changed because the delusional themes in this disorder involve a variety of beliefs. Some of these specified in DSM-III-R are

- Erotomania (belief that someone is in love with you—usually romanticized rather than sexual love is involved)
- Grandiosity (conviction that you have great, unrecognized talent

or have some special ability or relationship with an important individual)

- Jealousy (conviction that your spouse or partner is being unfaithful)
- Persecution (belief in being conspired or plotted against)
- Somatic complaints (convictions of having body odor, being malformed, or being infested by insects or parasites)

The following case illustrates some features of a delusional disorder.

> Mr. H. . . . was a 55-year-old man who was divorced, unemployed, and living on his own in a two-room flat. He had been referred by his general practitioner for treatment of a "phobia," after complaining that since he had laid an old carpet 6 weeks previously, he had become infested with minuscule insects, which lived under his skin and caused intense itching and burning sensations. He had visited the Casualty and Dermatology Departments of his local hospital three times since then, with complaints of "gritty" sensations in his eyes, and skin rashes showing "samples" of insects for inspection. . . . To escape the insects, he had got rid of the carpet, had his flat fumigated, and got rid of virtually all his furnishings and clothing. (Macaskill, 1987, p. 262)

Lack of feedback may play a role in the development of delusional disorder. In a study of people with this disorder, most were characterized as socially isolated, and nearly half had a physical impairment such as deafness or visual problems (Holden, 1987). A decreased ability to obtain corrective feedback, combined with a preexisting personality type that tends toward suspiciousness, may increase the susceptibility of developing delusional beliefs.

---

grandeur may assume the identities of famous people, living or dead, and genuinely believe in their own great power or fame. (Focus 14.3 describes some other delusional beliefs that characterize this disorder and presents a case study that illustrates one man's experience.)

Undifferentiated and Residual Schizophrenia

Undifferentiated schizophrenia is diagnosed when the person's symptoms are obviously schizophrenic but are mixed or undifferentiated, so that they do not clearly fit into the disorganized, catatonic, or paranoid category. These symptoms may include thought disturbance, delusions, hallucinations, incoherence, and severely impaired behavior. Sometimes the undifferentiated disorder turns out to be an early stage of one of the more specific subtypes.

The diagnosis of **residual schizophrenia** is reserved for people who have experienced at least one episode of schizophrenia in the past but are presently exhibiting no *prominent* signs of the disorders (which may be in remission). These people may show some schizophrenic symptoms, but the symptoms are neither strong enough nor prominent enough to warrant classification as a type of schizophrenia.

Psychotic Disorders Once Considered Schizophrenia

Brief psychotic episodes were considered to represent acute forms of schizophrenia in DSM-II. With DSM-III-R, people who have "schizophrenic" episodes that last fewer than six months are now diagnosed as having either *brief reactive psychosis* (duration up to one month) or *schizophreniform disorder* (duration less than six months). This distinction was made because "There is consistent evidence that people with symptoms similar to those of schizophrenia of less than six months' duration have a better outcome than those with a more prolonged disturbance" (American Psychiatric Association, 1987, p. 207).

Differences between these disorders and schizophrenia are shown in Table 14.2. Although there appear to be distinct differences, the disorders are often highly similar in characteristics. DSM-III-R recommends that the diagnosis for brief reactive psychosis and schizophreniform disorder be "provisional." For example, an initial diagnosis of brief reactive psychosis should change to schizophreniform disorder if it lasts longer than one month and to schizophrenia if it lasts longer than six months. The fact that duration is the only accurate means of distinguishing between the disorders raises questions about the validity of categories.

THE COURSE OF SCHIZOPHRENIA

It is popularly believed that overwhelming stress can cause a well-adjusted and relatively normal person to experience a schizophrenic breakdown. There are, in fact, recorded instances of the sudden onset of schizophrenic behaviors in previously well-functioning people. However, in most cases the person's *premorbid personality* (personality before the onset of major symptoms) shows some impairment. Similarly, most schizophrenics recover gradually rather than suddenly. The typical course of schizophrenia consists of three phases: prodromal, active, and residual.

The *prodromal phase* includes the onset and buildup of schizophrenic symptoms. Social withdrawal and isolation, peculiar behaviors, inappropriate affect, poor communication patterns, and neglect of personal grooming may become evident during this phase. Friends and relatives often consider the person's behavior as odd or peculiar.

Often, psychosocial stressors or excessive demands on a schizophrenic in the prodromal phase result in the onset of prominent psychotic symptoms, or the *active phase* of schizophrenia. The person now shows the full-blown symptoms of schizophrenia—including severe disturbances in thinking, deterioration in social relationships, and flat or markedly inappropriate affect.

TABLE 14.2 | **Comparison of Brief Reactive Psychosis, Schizophreniform Disorders, and Schizophrenia**

	Brief Reactive Psychosis	*Schizophreniform Disorders*	*Schizophrenia*
Duration	Less than one month	Less than six months	Six months or more
Psychosocial stressor	Always present	Usually present	May or may not be present
Symptoms	Emotional turmoil, psychotic symptoms	Emotional turmoil, vivid hallucinations	Emotional reactions variable; psychotic symptoms
Outcome	Return to premorbid level of functioning	Likely to return to earlier, higher level of functioning	Return to earlier, higher level of functioning is uncommon
Familial pattern	No information	Possible increased risk of schizophrenia among family members	Higher prevalence of schizophrenia among family members

FOCUS 14.4 ▷ *Schizophrenia in Developing Countries: Recovery or Misdiagnosis?*

Do people with schizophrenia in developing countries recover more quickly and fully than those in developed countries? If so, why? These questions were examined in a cross-cultural study by the World Health Organization (1973, 1981). Standardized and reliable sets of criteria were used to study schizophrenia in nine different countries. Similar prevalence rates for the disorder were found in the study. However, a follow-up of 1,202 people diagnosed as schizophrenic in the nine countries revealed that patients in India, Colombia, and Nigeria showed more rapid and more complete recovery than those in London, Moscow, or Washington. Over one-third recovered within a short period of time and were still symptom-free after two years. The re-

searchers hypothesized that some cultural difference might be responsible for the observed difference in outcome (Sartorius et al., 1978).

At the present time, reasons for the differences in outcome are unknown. Some have speculated that in developing countries recovered patients are quickly absorbed into the work force and perform whatever tasks are available (Warner, 1986). Researchers in the follow-up study reported difficulty in interviewing recovered patients because they were in the fields. Returning back to work may have helped prevent relapses.

Stevens (1987) believes that the higher recovery rate for schizophrenia found in developing countries is due to misdiagnosis. To support her view, she points out that in the

WHO study, 36 percent of patients in Nigeria and 27 percent in India recovered in less than one month. She conjectures that the illnesses were really either brief reactive psychoses or schizophreniform disorders and not schizophrenia. This explanation is certainly plausible. However, the WHO investigation had found an approximately equal frequency of schizophrenia among the different countries. If misdiagnosis did occur, it must mean that brief reactive psychoses and schizophreniform disorders are more prevalent in developing countries and that schizophrenia occurs less frequently in these countries. Why this would be the case must be examined.

At some later time, the person may enter the *residual phase,* in which the symptoms are no longer prominent. The severity of the symptoms declines, and the individual may show the milder impairment found in the prodromal phase. (At this point, the diagnosis would be residual schizophrenia.) Complete recovery is rare, although long-term studies show that many schizophrenics can lead relatively productive lives. For whatever reason, recovery rates appear higher in developing countries. See Focus 14.4 for a discussion of this phenomenon.

Long-Term Outcome Studies

Ciompi (1980) conducted a 37-year follow-up of 289 schizophrenic patients and found that the long-term

prognosis was favorable in 50 percent of the cases. With advanced age (the average age of the subjects was seventy-five), there was a "pronounced general tendency toward improvement and recovery." More than half the subjects were in good physical condition and were employed either full or part time. Although the majority still had problems with social relationships or independence, most indicated that they felt peaceful and free of conflicts. Ciompi concluded that "Quite contrary to the original—and today still popular—concepts of the nature of schizophrenia, a good majority of definitely 'genuine' schizophrenias (from initial diagnoses) may develop favorably in the long run" (p. 611).

Similar results were obtained in a 22-year follow-up of 502 schizophrenic patients (Huber et al., 1980). Of this group, 22 percent were in complete remission,

FOCUS 14.5   *Discrimination Against the Mentally Ill*

Mental illnesses, especially psychoses such as schizophrenia, are still feared and misunderstood by the public. The resulting discrimination is illustrated by the experiences of a former schizophrenic patient. After he was released from a hospital psychiatric ward, he told his employer about his illness. This marked the beginning of a series of encounters with the general prejudice against former mental patients.

> I was at work only a few days when I was fired but "assured" that I would receive good references. The fact that I had been there for nearly 4 years and [was] a good worker did not matter. (Anonymous, 1981, p. 736)

In applying for a new job, he faced additional problems.

> I also noticed that many job applications would inquire about medical and psychological stability. . . . I learned that honesty is not always the best policy. . . . I am considering graduate school, and there too, questions about past and present psychiatric treatment confront me. . . . The admission forms often request a biographical sketch describing how the student became interested in the field and any personal experiences with psychiatry. This, too, obviously is a Catch-22 position. To admit my personal experiences is to court possible and realistic rejection. I have spoken off the record with an instructor in a well-known school of social work about the situation, and his advice was: "I do not think discussing your hospital experiences would be a plus." [But if] I do not discuss it,

> I would in a way be compromising my principles. (pp. 736–737)

The former patient partly blames the media for this situation:

> Hardly a month goes by that we do not read a lurid news story of "man goes berserk and kills neighbor" or "former mental patient kills wife." . . . The evidence is overwhelming that the majority of mental patients are, as a class, less dangerous than the "average citizen." . . . Psychotherapy and psychotropic drugs have helped thousands of people to continue to go about their daily lives . . . but at times, I am sure they painfully wonder, for what? (p. 737)

---

43 percent showed only residual symptoms, and 35 percent remained unimproved; 87 percent lived in their own homes. Two interesting findings were that the long-term prognosis is unrelated to the original duration of the disorder and that it is more favorable for women than for men.

A criticism that can be leveled against these outcome studies is that they involved patients that were diagnosed according to criteria that preceded DSM-III-R and probably included nonschizophrenic patients who might have a better prognosis. This issue was addressed in a study by Harding et al. (1987), who retrospectively applied DSM-III criteria to schizophrenics who were involved in a 32-year long-term follow-up. These patients from the "back wards" had been ill for an average of sixteen years and had been hospitalized continuously for about six

years. Amazingly, the researchers found that "For one-half to two-thirds of these subjects who retrospectively met the DSM-III criteria for schizophrenia, long-term outcome was neither marginal but an evolution into various degrees of productivity, social involvement, wellness, and competent functioning" (p. 730).

The results of these studies indicate that the long-term outcome for schizophrenics may be more positive than portrayed by Kraepelin or by DSM-III-R. Bleuler might be more correct in indicating a variable outcome for the disorder. The increasing number of studies indicating positive long-term outcome for schizophrenia has prompted Zubin and Ludwig (1983) to comment that there is a "new optimism about this disorder." Unfortunately, this optimism has yet to spread to the general public. (See Focus 14.5.)

Untitled (pencil on cardboard), Berthold L. (or L. Berthold)

SUMMARY

1. Schizophrenia is a group of psychotic disorders characterized by impaired cognitive, affective, and behavioral processes. They are manifested in thought disturbances, including lack of insight, delusions, and loosening of associations; attention problems; perceptual distortion in the form of hallucinations; extremes of motor behavior; and inappropriate affect.

2. The criteria that differentiate schizophrenia, its subtypes, and other psychotic disorders are specified more precisely in DSM-III-R than they have

been in the past. However, the criteria must be applied consistently if they are to be effective.

3. DSM-III-R distinguishes five types of schizophrenia. *Disorganized* schizophrenia is characterized by inappropriate affect and frequent incoherence. Extreme social impairment and severe regressive behaviors are often seen. *Paranoid* schizophrenia is characterized by systematized delusions that are illogical and contradictory. Delusions of persecution or grandeur are common. The major feature of *catatonic* schizophrenia is disturbance of motor activity. Patients show excessive excitement, agitation and hyperactivity, or withdrawn behavior patterns. The *undifferentiated* type includes schizophrenic behavior that cannot be classified as one of the other types. And *residual* schizophrenia is a category for people who have had at least one episode of schizophrenia but are not now showing prominent symptoms. In addition, other severe disorders may include schizophrenia-like symptoms.

4. The typical course of schizophrenia consists of three phases. In the prodromal phase, the symptoms first begin and build. In the active phase, they become quite prominent. And in the residual phase, they decline in severity. Although complete recovery from schizophrenia is uncommon, most schizophrenics recover enough to lead relatively productive lives.

KEY TERMS

catatonic schizophrenia A schizophrenic disorder characterized by disturbance in motor activity—extreme agitation and excitement, or extreme withdrawal and unresponsiveness

cognition The processes of thinking, perceiving, judging, and recognizing

delusional disorder A disorder characterized by persistent, nonbizarre delusions that are not accompanied by other unusual or odd behaviors

delusion A false belief that is firmly and consistently held despite disconfirming evidence or logic

disorganized schizophrenia A schizophrenic disorder characterized by severe disintegration and absurd and incoherent behaviors beginning at an early age

flat affect Abnormal lack of emotional response

hallucinations Sensory perceptions that are not directly attributable to environmental stimuli

loosening of associations Continual shifting from topic to topic without logical or meaningful connection among topics

neologisms New words that are typically formed by combining words in common usage

paranoid schizophrenia A schizophrenic disorder characterized by persistent and systemized delusions

residual schizophrenia A category of schizophrenic disorder reserved for people who have experienced at least one schizophrenic episode but do not now show prominent signs of the disorder

schizophrenia A group of disorders characterized by severe impairment of cognitive processes, personality disintegration, affective disturbances, and social withdrawal

undifferentiated schizophrenia A schizophrenic disorder characterized by mixed or undifferentiated symptoms that do not clearly fit any of the other types of schizophrenia

chapter 15
Schizophrenia: Etiology and Treatment

know I'm a 37-year-old woman, a sculptor, a writer, a worker. I live alone. I know all of this, but, like the reflection in the glass my existence seems undefined—more a mirage that I keep reaching for, but never can touch.

I've been feeling this way for almost a year now, ever since I was diagnosed a paranoid schizophrenic. Sometimes, though, I wonder if I ever knew myself, or merely played the parts that were acceptable, just so that I could fit in somewhere. . . . There are still occasional episodes of hallucinations, delusions, and terrible fears, and I have medication for these times. It relieves my mental stress, but I hate my bodily responses to it and the dulling of my healthy emotions. Therefore, I stop using the drug as soon as the storms in my mind subside. . . .

I've searched, in library books and in articles about schizophrenia, hoping to find other solutions and answers to my whys, how longs, what's the cure. Some of the information is frightening . . . Some of it is confusing . . . Schizophrenia is genetic—no, no, it's surely biochemical—definitely nutritional—sorry, but it's caused by family interactions, maybe stress, etc. Now, with the worship of technological gods, the explanation is that schizophrenia is a brain disease colorfully mapped out by the PET scanner. I suddenly feel that my humanity has been sacrificed to a computer printout, that the researchers have dissected me without realizing that I'm still alive. I'm not comfortable or safe in all their certain uncertainties—I feel they're losing me, the person, more and more.

In the most recently published book I've read, a

doctor writes that psychotherapy is useless with schizophrenia. How could he even suggest that, without knowing me, the one over here in this corner, who finds a lot of support, understanding, and acceptance by my therapist? Marianne is not afraid to travel with me in my fearful times. She listens when I need to release some of the "poisons" in my mind. She offers advice when I'm having difficulty with just daily living. She sees me as a human being and not only a body to shovel pills into or a cerebral mass in some laboratory. Psychotherapy is important to me, and it does help. . . .

I'm hopeful about the ongoing research to find an answer to schizophrenia . . . But I know that I'm the schizophrenic living the experience, and I must look inside myself also for some ways to handle it. I have to be able to see me again as a real person and not a fading reflection. (McGrath, 1987, pp. 37–38)

Mary McGrath thus expressed her frustration in trying to discover the cause of her disorder. Researchers share her frustration. New theories are constantly being espoused. Some are more promising than others. But how do we know which theory, if any, is actually correct? In this chapter, we consider the different causal theories of schizophrenia, examining genetic, physiological, psychological, and environmental explanations. Unfortunately, although a great amount of work has been done, no one theory is universally accepted, and each fails to answer all the questions schizophrenia poses. As you will see in this chapter, methodological flaws and research design limitations restrict the kinds of conclusions that can be drawn about schizophrenia.

We also explore different forms of therapy for schizophrenia. Antipsychotic medications can help treat some symptoms of schizophrenia, but relapse rates remain unacceptably high, and undesirable side effects are reported. As McGrath remarked, her medication kept her "functional," but she also felt "drugged and unreal." Interest in psychotherapy for schizophrenics has revived, especially because most people with this disorder now are only hospitalized temporarily and are then returned to their families. Some new promising approaches are discussed later.

HEREDITY AND SCHIZOPHRENIA

A 13-year-old boy who was having behavioral and academic problems in school, was taking part in a

series of family therapy sessions. Near the end of one session, he suddenly broke down and cried out, "I don't want to be like *her*." He was referring to his mother, who had been receiving treatment for schizophrenia and was taking antipsychotic medication. He had often been frightened by her bizarre behavior, and he was concerned that his friends would "find out" about her condition. But his greatest fear was that he would inherit the disorder. Sobbing, he turned to the therapist and asked, "Am I going to be crazy, too?"

Researchers generally agree that this boy's chances of developing schizophrenia are greater than those of the average person. Why this is so is a subject of controversy; however, some believe the answer lies in heredity. Consider, for example, the following challenge posed by a researcher to his colleagues:

You [are] required to write down a procedure for selecting an individual from the population who would be diagnosed as schizophrenic by a psychiatric staff; you have to wager $1,000 on being right. You may not include in your selection procedure any behavioral fact, such as a symptom or trait, manifested by the individual. (Meehl, 1962, p. 827)

In other words, what procedure would give you the highest probability of selecting a schizophrenic from the general population when you *cannot* consider the person's symptoms or traits? According to Meehl, you should look for someone whose identical twin has already been diagnosed as schizophrenic. This solution reflects the belief that heredity is an important cause in the development of schizophrenia—a belief supported by research (Kendler, 1983; Kendler et al., 1988). However, the degree of influence is still quite controversial.

Problems in Interpreting Genetic Studies

Several factors must be considered when interpreting familial and genetic studies. First, probably several types of schizophrenia exist, each with a different cause or set of causes. For example, a higher risk for developing schizophrenia and related disorders exists for children with schizophrenic parents who do not respond to antipsychotic medication, compared to those who do respond. Second, genetic researchers often do not consider the psychological condition of the nonschizophrenic parent. If the other parent had a similar or related disorder, this could increase genetic risk factors. In one study (Parnas, 1987), the mates of schizophrenics were more likely to have functional psychoses, schizoid, paranoid, or borderline personality disorders, before marriage than mates of nonschizophrenics. Because paternal contributions are not considered, genetic influences based only on the mother's diagnosis may be overestimated. Third, genetic studies are often based on severely and chronically ill schizophrenic patients, among whom genetic influence may be greater. The **concordance rate** (likelihood that family members will exhibit the disorder that is being studied) for schizophrenia was nearly three times higher among the monozygotic twins who were hospitalized for over two years than for those hospitalized less than two years (Gottesman & Shields, 1972). Fourth, researchers differ in their definitions of "concordant." Some define schizophrenia very narrowly and use the same definition to determine concordance. Other investigators consider a number of disorders (schizoid and borderline personality disorders, schizophreniform disorders, and so on) to be concordant. Researchers favoring this view tend to make higher estimates of genetic influence. In this section, we discuss several kinds of research that link heredity to the schizophrenic disorders. Many of them have some of the methodological problems that we have just discussed.

Studies Involving Blood Relatives

Close blood relatives are genetically more similar than distant blood relatives. For example, 50 percent of the genes of two siblings are expected to be the same, whereas a much lower proportion of the genes of two second cousins, say, would be expected to be the same. If schizophrenia has a genetic basis, researchers should find more schizophrenia among close relatives of diagnosed schizophrenics than among more distant relatives.

Table 15.1 suggests that this situation is indeed the case. The data are summarized from several major studies on the prevalence of schizophrenia (Gottesman, 1978). They show that closer blood relatives of diagnosed schizophrenics run a greater risk of developing the disorders. Thus the boy described earlier has a 12 to 13 percent chance of being diagnosed as schizophrenic, but his mother's nieces or nephews have only a 2 to 3 percent chance. (Note that the risk for the general population is 1 percent.)

But the association between relatedness and risk is not as clear as Table 15.1 suggests. Other studies yield different results, showing risks of 1.6 to 3.2 percent of developing the disorder for first-degree relatives—that is, parents and children—of schizophrenics (Abrams & Taylor, 1983; Guze et al., 1983; Tsuang et al., 1980). In fact, one study found no increased risk at all among first-degree relatives (Pope et al., 1982).

What could account for these differences among the various study results? According to one pair of researchers, methodological differences produce these differing results (Abrams & Taylor, 1983). They suggest the following guidelines in evaluating genetic studies of schizophrenia:

1. Do they employ well-defined and restricted criteria for schizophrenia? Many studies, especially those performed before 1972, used very broad definitions that encompassed patients with mood disorders—and the mood disorders do have a strong genetic component (Pope & Lipinski, 1978). This broadness obviously confounded conclusions on the heritability of schizophrenia.

2. Has the individual initially diagnosed as schizophrenic been rediagnosed? This process would test the reliability and validity of the original diagnoses and thus of the studies themselves.

TABLE 15.1	Risk of Schizophrenia Among Blood Relatives of Schizophrenics

Relationship to the Schizophrenic Person	Morbidity Risk (Percent)
Parents	4–5
Children	12–13
Siblings	8–9
Children of two affected parents	36–37
Half-siblings	3–4
Grandchildren	2–3
Cousins	2–3
Nieces and nephews	2–3
Uncles and aunts	2
Grandparents	1–2
No relationship	1

SOURCE: Adapted from Gottesman, 1978.

Identical and fraternal twins are studied to determine the relative importance of genetic factors in schizophrenia and other disorders. Identical twins share the same genes. Thus differences between identical twins can be attributed to differences in their environment rather than in their genetic makeup. Fraternal twins (shown in this photo) share some of the same genes, but no more so than any other pair of siblings.

3. Is the same standardized interview used for both at-risk and control relatives? This standardization would improve confidence in results showing differences between these two groups.

4. Are the raters or interviewers blind to the diagnosis and status of the patients, controls, and their relatives? A rater who knows that he or she is interviewing relatives of a schizophrenic, for example, might be more likely to find pathology. Some evidence shows that studies that do not use blind ratings report higher rates of psychopathology than studies that do (Gottesman & Shields, 1982).

Because most studies of schizophrenia have not been conducted using these guidelines, they must be interpreted very carefully.

However, even if well-designed studies pointed to a relationship between degree of relatedness and schizophrenia, they still would not clearly demonstrate the role of heredity. Why? Simply because closer blood relatives are more likely to share the same environmental factors or stressors, as well as the same genes. To confirm a genetic basis for schizophrenia, research must separate genetic influences from environmental influences.

Twin Studies

We have already described the use of twin studies in seeking to differentiate between the effects of heredity and those of environment. The concept, in somewhat more detail, is this: identical, or monozygotic (MZ), twins are genetically identical, so differences between two MZ twins are presumably caused by differences in their environments. If reared together, MZ twins share the same general environment as well as the same hereditary makeup. But fraternal, or dizygotic (DZ) twins, though born at about the same time, are not more genetically similar than any other two siblings and may be of different sexes. If DZ twins are reared together, they share the same general environment, but their genetic makeup is, on the average, only 50 percent identical.

In a twin study, concordance rates for a particular disorder are measured among groups of MZ and DZ twins. (Recall that a concordance rate is the likelihood that members of a family will exhibit the disorder being studied.) If environmental factors are of major importance, the concordance rates for MZ twins and for DZ twins should not differ much. If genetic factors are of prime importance, however, MZ twins should show a higher concordance rate than DZ twins.

In general, concordance rates for schizophrenia among MZ twins are two to four times higher than among DZ twins. This seems to point to a strong genetic basis for the disorders. However, one study of sixteen pairs of MZ twins found a concordance rate of zero; not one MZ twin of a schizophrenic had the disorder (Tienari, 1963). In fact, concordance rates among MZ twins vary from 0 to 86 percent (Weiner, 1975). How can some twin studies show little or no genetic influence while other studies indicate a strong genetic component in schizophrenia?

Again, methodological differences seem to be involved. Consider Table 15.2, which lists the results of several twin studies performed in Scandinavia. Two percentages are given for most entries in the concordance rate columns. The first (not in parentheses) is the rate according to a narrow definition of schizophrenia. The second (in parentheses) is the rate according to a broad definition, the *schizophrenia spectrum,* which includes latent or borderline schizophrenia, acute schizophrenic reactions, and schizoid and inadequate personality. Note that the Tienari (1963) MZ concordance rate of zero would rise to 19 percent if three twins who showed "borderline" psychotic features were counted. This is true, to varying degrees, of the other studies as well.

The broader definition of schizophrenia was used in most studies that report high concordance rates. Unfortunately, this breadth decreases the diagnostic reliability and validity of twin studies as a whole. In

one study, for example, 25 percent of a normal comparison control group received one of the schizophrenia spectrum diagnoses (Haier et al., 1978). That such a high percentage received this diagnosis is surprising and probably indicated problems in the validity of the assessment.

Even though the high concordance rates reported in many earlier studies have been inflated by using the broad definition of schizophrenia, we can conclude that there is some genetic influence in the disorders—primarily because most studies indicate a greater risk for MZ twins than for DZ twins. This is so whether a strict definition is employed or the schizophrenia spectrum is included. Moreover, it appears that the spectrum disorders are more likely to be found in "at-risk" groups: those whose families include diagnosed schizophrenics.

Adoption Studies

Even with twin studies, it is difficult to separate the effects of heredity from the effects of environment, because twins are usually raised together. Thus, when the child of a schizophrenic parent develops schizophrenia, three explanations are possible: (1) the schizophrenic mother or father may have genetically transmitted schizophrenia to the child; (2) the parent, being disturbed, may have provided a stressful environment for the child; or (3) the child's schizophrenia

TABLE 15.2 | **Concordance Rates Found in Twin Studies in the Scandinavian Countries**

		MZ Pairs		DZ Pairs	
Study	**Country**	**Number of Pairs**	**Concordance Rate (Percent)**	**Number of Pairs**	**Concordance Rate (Percent)**
Tienari (1963)	Finland	16	0 (19)[a]	21	5 (14)
Kringlin (1967)	Norway	55	25 (38)	90	10 (19)
Essen-Moller (1970)	Sweden	7	29 (75)	—	— —
Fischer (1973)	Denmark	21	24 (56)	41	10 (19)
Tienari (1975)	Finland	20	15 —	42	7.5 —

SOURCE: Kringlen, 1980.
[a]The percentages not in parentheses are measured according to a narrow definition of schizophrenia. The percentages in parentheses are concordance rates for the wider schizophrenia spectrum; for example, if one twin has schizophrenia and the other twin has a borderline diagnosis, the pair is considered concordant according to this latter definition.

may have resulted from a combination of genetic factors and a stressful environment.

In an attempt to completely separate the effects of heredity and environment, the incidence of schizophrenia and other disorders was determined for a group of people who were born to schizophrenic mothers but who had no contact with their mothers and had left the maternity hospital within three days of birth (Heston, 1966; Heston & Denny, 1968). This condition eliminated the possibility that contact with the mother increased the chance of developing the disorder. The lives of these people were traced through the records of child care institutions; all had been adopted by two-parent families. A control group, consisting of people born to normal mothers and

One of the problems with studying twins is the difficulty of separating heredity factors from environmental influences. Adoption studies are useful because heredity and environmental factors can be clearly differentiated.

adopted through the same child care institutions, was selected and matched. Information regarding both the at-risk and control groups was collected from many sources (including school records, court records, and interviews). The people themselves were interviewed and given psychological tests. The major results are shown in Table 15.3. Note that five children in the at-risk group were later diagnosed as schizophrenic, compared to none in the control group. These results are highly significant and support a genetic explanation for schizophrenia. The greater incidence of the other disorders such as sociopathic personality among the at-risk group is hard to explain, because those disorders are not part of the schizophrenia spectrum.

The study seems to have been well designed. Its only weaknesses involve the diagnostic criteria, which were described as being based on "generally accepted standards" for schizophrenia, and the fact that the schizophrenic mothers "as a group were biased in the direction of severe, chronic disease." (As discussed earlier, genetic factors seem to play a greater role in the more severe cases of schizophrenia).

Two additional criticisms have been raised, however. First, the schizophrenic mothers received antipsychotic medication during pregnancy, and such drugs present a potential risk to the fetus (Physician's Desk Reference, 1988). Second, most families who adopted the child of a schizophrenic mother knew about the mother's disorder. This knowledge could have influenced the adoptive parents' attitude toward the child (Shean, 1987).

Of special interest is the finding that nearly half of the at-risk group were "notably successful adults."

> The 21 experimental subjects who exhibited no significant psycho-social impairment were not only successful adults but in comparison to the control group were more spontaneous when interviewed and had more colorful life histories. They held the more creative jobs: musician, teacher, home-designer; and followed the more imaginative hobbies: oil painting, music, antique aircraft. Within the experimental group there was much more variability of personality and behaviour in all social dimensions. (Heston, 1966, p. 825)

Sohlberg (1985) reported similar findings that approximately 50 percent of "high risk" children have

TABLE 15.3 | **Comparison of Disorders in People Separated from Schizophrenic Mothers and from Normal Mothers Early in Life**

Characteristic	At-Risk Children	Control
Number of individuals	47	50
Males	30	33
Mean age	35.8	36.3
Ratings of mental health/sickness[a]	65.2	80.1
Number diagnosed as schizophrenic	5	0
Number with mental deficiency (IQ less than 70)	4	0
Number with sociopathic personality	9	2
Number with neurotic personality	13	7
Number spending more than one year in a penal or psychiatric institution	11	2

SOURCE: Heston, 1966.
[a]A lower score indicates greater severity.

"healthy personalities" and are "remarkably invulnerable" to schizophrenia. Being "at risk" doesn't necessarily (or even usually) lead to a negative outcome. Why do some children who have poor familial and/or environmental backgrounds develop so successfully? Perhaps studies of "stress resistant" children will one day answer this question (Garmezy, 1987).

In another study designed to separate hereditary and environmental influences, investigators identified adult schizophrenics who had been adopted in infancy. Then they located both the adoptive parents (the families that had raised the children who became schizophrenic) and the biological parents, who had had minimal contact with their children. If environmental factors play the major role in schizophrenia, the adoptive families should be more disturbed than the biological parents. Conversely, if heredity is more important, biological families should show more disturbance than adoptive families. Interviews with both sets of families showed a greater incidence of the schizophrenia spectrum in the biological family (Kety et al., 1975).

Another group of researchers studied children who had normal biological parents but who were adopted and raised by a parent who later was diagnosed as schizophrenic. If environmental factors are of primary importance, these children should be more likely than others to develop schizophrenia, but no difference was found (Wender et al., 1977). Thus the various adoption studies do indicate that heredity plays a role in the transmission of schizophrenia.

Studies of High-Risk Populations

Perhaps the most comprehensive way to study the etiology of schizophrenia is to monitor a large group of children over a long time, in order to watch the differences between those who eventually develop schizophrenia and those who do not. This sort of developmental study allows the investigator to see how the disorders develop, before the onset of the problem. But because the prevalence of schizophrenia in the general population is only 1 percent, a prohibitively large group would have to be monitored if a random sample of children were chosen. Instead, investigators have chosen subjects from "high-risk" populations; this increases the probability that a smaller group of subjects will include some who develop schizophrenia.

The best-known developmental studies are those by Mednick (1970) and Mednick and Schulsinger (1968), who are still studying about two hundred individuals with schizophrenic mothers (the high-risk group) and about a hundred individuals with non-schizophrenic mothers (the low-risk control group). The researchers intend to study these same groups for a total of twenty-five years. On the basis of existing data, they have predicted the eventual outcome for both high-risk and low-risk subjects (see Figure 15.1). About half the high-risk group may eventually display some form of psychopathology, including but not limited to schizophrenia.

By the time of the first follow-up, twenty members of the high-risk group had already shown psychological problems ranging from theft to psychotic symptoms (Mednick, 1970). Thirteen of these people had been admitted to psychiatric hospitals. Mednick felt that the subjects in this "sick group" were the most likely to have or to develop schizophrenia. But a later follow-up revealed that, of fifteen people who had been diagnosed as schizophrenic, only four came from the sick group (Schulsinger, 1976). The high-risk subjects who became schizophrenic were compared with those who did not; the schizophrenics were more likely to

◆ Have mothers who displayed more severe symptoms of schizophrenia

◆ Have been separated from their parents and placed in children's homes early in their lives

◆ Have had more serious pregnancy or birth complications

◆ Have been characterized by their teachers as extremely aggressive and disruptive

◆ Have a slower autonomic recovery rate (habituate more slowly when exposed to certain stimuli)

Are high-risk children more likely to develop schizophrenia or related disorders if they live with their schizophrenic parents or might they do better when raised in a "healthier" environment? An Israeli research team (Marcus et al., 1987; Ayalon & Mercom, 1985; Nagler et al., 1985; Sohlberg, 1985; and Shotten, 1985) conducted a **prospective study** (a study of subjects before they begin to exhibit signs of illness) on fifty high-risk children (those with schizophrenic

Figure 15.1 Mednick and Schulsinger's Predictions About the Development of Deviance and Schizophrenia in High-Risk and Control Children
SOURCE: Mednick, 1970.

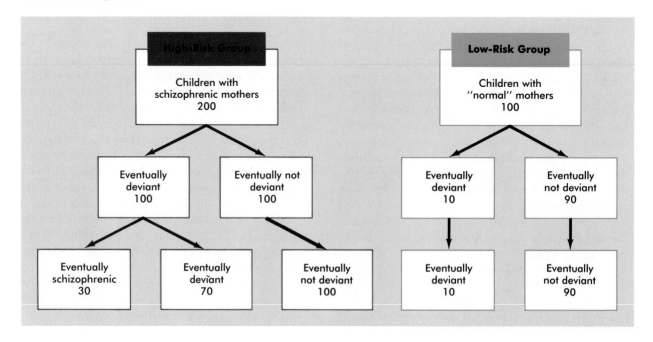

parents). Twenty-five of the children were born and raised in a kibbutz (a collective farm), and the other twenty-five were living in a suburban area with their mentally ill parents. In the kibbutz, all the children lived together. They had regular contact with their parents, but were raised by child care workers.

Researchers wanted to know whether a kibbutz environment would protect the high-risk children from developing schizophrenia. A control group comprising fifty low-risk children of mentally healthy parents—twenty-five living in the kibbutz and the other twenty-five living in town—were included in the study. Neuropsychological, observational, perceptual-motor, psychophysiological and behavioral measures were regularly used. By the time the high-risk subjects reached their twenties, nine individuals had received a diagnosis from the schizophrenic spectrum. Surprisingly, only three came from the group living in town with their parents. The other six came from the group raised in kibbutz. None of the control group was diagnosed as being schizophrenic (see Table 15.4 for a breakdown of the different disorders). Is it possible that the kibbutz is more pathogenic (illness producing) than living with a schizophrenic parent? The finding is surprising and is yet to be explained.

The same researchers found a variety of differences between the high-risk and control children. The former were more likely to be described as withdrawn, poorer in social relationships, behaving in antisocial ways, uncooperative and incapable of relating to the interviewers, poor at school work, having problems with mood, accident prone, and functioning at lower perceptual-motor levels. However, the two groups of children overlapped considerably. Deficiencies were only shown by about half of the at-risk children. The other half appear to show "healthy" development.

Could the mass of data be organized to help predict which children would most probably develop a schizophrenia spectrum disorder? Marcus and his colleagues (1987) said yes: "Of the nine cases who received DSM-III diagnoses within the schizophrenia spectrum, seven followed the 'worst' developmental course: they had a schizophrenic parent, showed signs of neurobehavioral dysfunction, had stressful family environments, and showed premorbid signs of social maladjustment" (p. 431). Interestingly, none of the high-risk children who had received "adequate" parenting developed schizophrenia or one of the spectrum disorders. Approximately 60 percent of the schizophrenic parents provided adequate care for their children.

TABLE 15.4 | Diagnoses for Kibbutz and Town Subjects

Group	N	Diagnostic Category						
		Schizo-phrenia	Other Schizo-phrenia Spectrum	Major Affective	Minor Affective	Other Diagnosis	No Diagnosis	Total DSM-III
Kibbutz Index	23	3	3	5	4	1	7	16
Town Index	23	2	1	1	0	3	16	7
Kibbutz Control	23	0	0	0	1	2	20	3
Town Control	21	0	0	0	0	1	20	1
Totals	90	5	4	6	5	7	63	27

SOURCE: Marcus et al., 1987.

What can we conclude from the high-risk studies? First, there is reasonably strong support for the involvement of heredity in schizophrenia and its associated spectrum disorders. Second, childhood and adolescence may be especially vulnerable periods. Third, schizophrenia seems to result from interaction between the predisposition and environmental factors. Fourth, most high-risk children do not develop the disorder.

Studies of high-risk subjects are a promising line of research. However, some methodological problems have already been pointed out. First, it may not be possible to generalize results of a study that takes as subjects the offspring of schizophrenic parents. The majority of diagnosed schizophrenics *do not* have a schizophrenic parent (Zerbin-Rudin, 1972; Lewine, 1986). And differences have been found between patients with familial schizophrenia (those with a schizophrenic first-degree relative) and those patients with no schizophrenia in the family (Kendler & Hays, 1982). Second, the study does not include control groups with other psychopathologies; so it's hard to decide whether the characteristics that are found are specific to schizophrenia. For example, some characteristics listed by Mednick and Schulsinger, such as pregnancy and birth complications, separation from parents, and problems in school, are also reported for other disorders. Third, there is uncertainty about whether the most relevant variables are being measured. Mednick believes that autonomic reactivity is an important factor in schizophrenia and has assessed this variable carefully. But parent-child interaction was not assessed, because the investigators consider it less important. Fourth, the schizophrenic parents in both studies of high risk were diagnosed according to the criteria used at that time; they might not meet DSM-III-R criteria.

PHYSIOLOGICAL FACTORS IN SCHIZOPHRENIA

Two important areas of research into the causes of schizophrenia involve brain chemistry and brain pathology. Logically, either could serve as a vehicle for the genetic transmission of schizophrenia, but no substantive evidence to that effect has yet been found.

Nonetheless, research in these areas has implications for treatment as well as etiology.

Biochemistry: The Dopamine Hypothesis

Biochemical explanations of schizophrenia have a long history. A century ago, for example, Emil Kraepelin suggested that these disorders result from a chemical imbalance caused by abnormal sex gland secretion. Since then, a number of researchers have tried to show that body chemistry is involved in schizophrenia. Most have failed to do so.

What generally happens is that a researcher finds a particular chemical substance in schizophrenic subjects and does not find it in "normal" controls, but other researchers cannot replicate those findings. In addition, schizophrenic patients differ from normals in lifestyle, in food they eat, and in the medication they take, all of which affect body chemistry and tend to confound research results.

One promising line of biochemical research has focused on the neurotransmitter dopamine and on its involvement in schizophrenia (Carlsson, 1978; Snyder, 1974; Bowers, 1981). According to the **dopamine hypothesis** (discussed briefly in Chapter 2), schizophrenia may result from excess dopamine activity at certain synaptic sites. This hyperactivity is caused either by (1) the release of excess dopamine by presynaptic neurons or (2) the oversensitivity of dopamine receptors (Neale & Oltmanns, 1980).

Support for the dopamine hypothesis has come from research with three types of drugs. The first type consists of the *phenothiazines*, which are antipsychotic drugs that decrease the severity of thought disorders, alleviate withdrawal and hallucinations, and improve the mood of schizophrenics. Their effectiveness is not due to a generalized sedating effect (phenobarbital, a depressant with sedative properties, is not nearly as effective against schizophrenic symptoms). Rather, increasing evidence shows that the phenothiazines reduce dopamine activity in the brain by blocking dopamine receptor sites in postsynaptic neurons.

Another drug, *L-dopa*, is generally used to treat such symptoms of Parkinson's disease as muscle and limb rigidity and tremors. The body converts L-dopa to dopamine, and the drug sometimes produces schizophrenic-like symptoms. (By contrast, the phenothiazines, which reduce dopamine activity, can produce side effects that resemble Parkinson's disease.)

Finally, there is research on the effects of the *amphetamines,* stimulants that increase the availability of dopamine and norepinephrine (another neurotransmitter) in the brain. When nonschizophrenic subjects are given continual doses of amphetamines, they show symptoms very much like those of acute paranoid schizophrenia. Continual low dosages of these drugs also produce psychotic-like symptoms in monkeys (Nielsen et al., 1983). And very small doses may increase the severity of symptoms in diagnosed schizophrenics. Other stimulants, such as caffeine, do not produce these effects.

Thus a drug that is believed to block dopamine reception has the effect of reducing the severity of schizophrenic symptoms, whereas two drugs that increase dopamine availability either produce or worsen these symptoms. Such evidence obviously supports the idea that excess dopamine may cause schizophrenic symptoms.

The evidence is not all positive, however. For example, the dopamine hypothesis might lead us to expect that treating schizophrenia with phenothiazines would be effective in almost all cases. Yet about one-fourth of schizophrenic patients responded very little or not at all to antipsychotic medication (Davis et al., 1980). In fact, of sixty-five schizophrenics treated with antipsychotic medications, 25 percent reported *negative* effects (Van Putten et al., 1984). In addition, of a group of schizophrenics who were given amphetamines, one-third did not experience worse symptoms (Angrist et al., 1980). In another study, twenty-eight remitted schizophrenic patients were administered L-dopa. Only five relapsed within four weeks; the others did not meet the criteria for relapse until about three months (Davidson et al., 1987). Such results point to the involvement of something other than excess dopamine.

As noted earlier, schizophrenia may very well be a group of disorders with different causes; that could account for the variable course of the disorders and the uneven responses to phenothiazines. Moreover, researchers may be looking for too simple an explanation by focusing on dopamine alone, without considering the interactive functioning of the brain

and the biochemical system as a whole (Csernansky et al., 1983). Or perhaps dopamine blockers can influence the symptoms of schizophrenia but not the course of the illness. Obviously, much more remains to be discovered.

Neurological Findings

Do the symptoms of schizophrenia indicate neurological impairment? This is certainly a possibility. Anywhere from 20 to 65 percent of schizophrenics show some signs of neurological abnormalities (Heinrichs & Buchanan, 1988; Seidman, 1983). Again, the wide differences in estimates may indicate problems in the reliability of assessment techniques or may reflect the possibility that different subgroups of schizophrenics were assessed.

Some researchers (Carpenter et al., 1988) believe that a group of schizophrenics with predominantly negative symptoms (Type II) such as affect flattening, poverty of speech, and loss of drive, display characteristics associated with neuronal loss or deterioration. These schizophrenics would be expected to show less responsiveness to antipsychotic medication and have a poorer prognosis. In contrast, schizophrenics with positive symptoms (Type I) such as hallucinations and delusions do not show brain deterioration but hyperactive neurological functioning. Some studies have found greater signs of neurological problems in Type II as compared to Type I schizophrenics (Pakkenberg, 1987).

The search for abnormal neurological factors in schizophrenia has intensified as increasingly sophisticated brain-imaging techniques for studying the living brain have been developed. Using these procedures, it has been found that, compared to controls, schizophrenics are more likely to show ventricular enlargement (enlarged spaces in areas of the brain) and cerebral atrophy (neuronal loss) (Berman et al., 1987; Seidman et al., 1987; Shelton et al., 1987). They also show decreased functioning in the frontal lobes and other cerebral areas (Andreasen, 1988). In addition, cerebral glucose metabolism is significantly lower in schizophrenic patients than in control subjects. This is especially true among patients with more negative symptoms—Type II (Volkow et al., 1987; Wolkin et al., 1988).

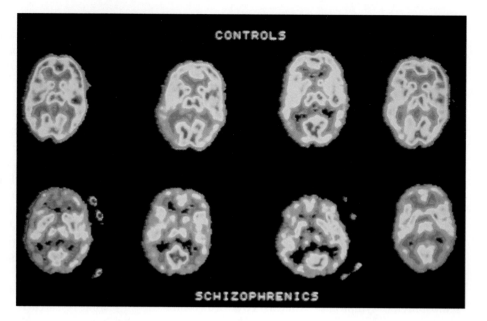

The PET scan measures the metabolic level of different parts of the brain. Orange areas represent greater brain activity; green and blue areas indicate lower activity. Chronic schizophrenics show less activity in the frontal lobes (areas associated with higher intellectual functioning and fluent emotional expression) than normal subjects.

What can we conclude from studies of brain structure and functioning in schizophrenics? It appears that neurological abnormalities are reported more often in schizophrenics than in nonschizophrenics and more in those having Type II characteristics. These observations are intriguing because they highlight the possibility that some subtypes of schizophrenia may be caused by structural brain pathology. Findings that abnormalities in the prefrontal cortex may be a factor are especially interesting, because this area is involved with some of the intellectual symptoms associated with schizophrenia.

Problems in interpreting the findings exist, however. Neurological abnormalities do not seem to be specific to schizophrenia. They are also found in affective disorders, alcohol and substance abuse, and organic impairment (Shelton et al., 1988; Wolkin et al., 1988). Other problems in interpreting the results of neurophysiological studies include small sample sizes, old diagnostic criteria, unreliable assessment techniques, and the potential effects of medication (Heinrichs & Buchanan, 1988). Even more confusing is the report by Feinberg et al. (1988) that pimozide (an antipsychotic drug) specifically relieves negative but not positive symptoms of schizophrenia. If negative symptoms indicate degenerative brain processes,

it is not clear why an antipsychotic medication would be effective. However, the search for neurological abnormalities in schizophrenics is promising.

ENVIRONMENTAL FACTORS IN SCHIZOPHRENIA

Obviously, genetic and biological research has not yet clarified the etiology of the various schizophrenic disorders. If for no other reason, then, psychologists must consider the influence of environmental factors. Here we examine available information and theories concerning the role of family dynamics, social class, and cultural differences in the development of these disorders.

We should first note, however, that environmental factors become involved in psychopathology by acting as stressors. A logical question, then, is "Can stress produce schizophrenia?" Attempts to find an answer have not been successful, primarily because most rely on retrospective reports from people who have sought treatment. Such people do not comprise the entire population of schizophrenics, and their memories of past events may be inaccurate.

In spite of these limitations, studies do show that a substantial minority of patients do experience a greater frequency of stressful events before receiving a diagnosis of schizophrenia. The number of stressful events are also correlated with the probability of relapse after treatment (Dohrenwend & Egri, 1981). In addition, a large number report a single precipitating factor: in a study of 502 schizophrenic individuals, 25 percent reported the death of a spouse or close relative as a precipitating event, 9 percent reported an illness or surgery, and 5 percent had borne a child shortly before diagnosis; the remaining 61 percent reported no precipitating factor (Huber et al., 1980). We do not know whether such stressful events combine with the environmental factors discussed next to precipitate schizophrenia.

Family Influences

In 1978, a researcher in the field of schizophrenia concluded, "No environmental causes have been found that will invariably or even with moderate probability produce genuine schizophrenia in persons who are unrelated to a schizophrenic [individual]" (Gottesman, 1978, p. 67). Another researcher echoed this view: "there are no schizophrenogenic environments . . . environmental contributions have little or no specificity" (Fowler, 1984, p. 82). Both researchers believe that unless a person has a genetic predisposition toward schizophrenia, environmental stress has little impact on the development of the disorder. Others strongly disagree. In this section, we consider theories that are primarily psychological in nature.

Theoretical Constructs Theorists have suggested two ways in which family interaction can contribute to the development of schizophrenia. The first was proposed by psychodynamic theorists who believed that certain behavioral patterns of parents could inhibit appropriate ego development in the child. This, in turn, would make the child vulnerable to the severe regression characteristic of schizophrenia. Attention was focused mainly on the mother, who usually has a great deal of contact with the child; the **schizophrenogenic** (or schizophrenia-producing) mother was characterized as being simultaneously or alternately cold and overprotecting, rejecting and dominating.

The second theory involving family interaction is the communication **double-bind theory** mentioned in Chapter 3 (Bateson et al., 1956). Proponents suggest that the preschizophrenic child has repeated experiences with one or more family members (usually the mother and/or father) in which he or she receives two contradictory messages. The child cannot discern the parent's meaning and cannot escape the situation. This conflict eventually leads the person to develop difficulty in interpreting other people's communications and in accurately and appropriately conveying his or her own thoughts and feelings.

Research indicates that family dynamics may play a role in the development of schizophrenia. Patients returning to a family environment high in negative expressed emotion (i.e., excessive criticism, hostility, or emotional overinvolvement) are more likely to relapse earlier than those returning to a more supportive home situation.

Assume, for example, that a mother harbors hostile feelings toward her daughter and yet wishes to be a good and loving mother. She might send her child to bed, saying, "You're tired and sleep will do you good." The overt message conveys the mother's concern for her child's health. Her tone of voice, however, is such that the child senses anger and the desire to be alone. The child then can interpret the contradictory messages in one of two ways (Bateson, 1978): She may correctly interpret her mother's hostility, in which case she is faced with the awful fact that she is not loved or wanted by her mother. Or she may accept the overt message—that she is tired and that her mother cares for her—and then be forced to deny her real understanding of the message. The child is punished whether she discriminates the message correctly or incorrectly (the double bind). To survive, the child may resort to self-deception, falsely interpreting her own thoughts as well as those communicated by others. She may also withdraw and develop a false concept of reality, an inability to communicate effectively, and other symptoms of schizophrenia.

Problems with Earlier Research   Most studies conducted before the mid-1970s supported the view that communications were less clear and accurate in families with a schizophrenic member than in other families (Jacob, 1975). However, methodological shortcomings kept researchers from generalizing these results to a relationship between schizophrenia and family dynamics. The most common flaws were: (1) a family's interactions were studied only after one of its members had been diagnosed as schizophrenic and (2) the lack of control groups. Thus, even if difficult family interaction was correlated with schizophrenia, researchers could not tell which was the cause and which the effect, or whether the correlation was unique to schizophrenia.

Expressed Emotion   Current research is directed toward a specific behavior pattern called *expressed emotion* (EE) that is found among some relatives of schizophrenics. The expressed emotion index is determined by the number of critical comments by a relative, the number of statements of dislike or resentment toward the patient by family members, and a rating of statements reflecting emotional overinvolvement, overconcern, or overprotec-

tiveness for the patient (Roff & Knight, 1981; Doane et al., 1981). For example, high-EE relatives are likely to make a greater number of statements such as "You have a bad attitude about work, Jim" (Miklowitz et al., 1984). The EE construct strongly predicts the course of the disorder (Mintz et al., 1987; Karno et al., 1987). Patients living with high-EE relatives were three to four times more likely to relapse in the nine months after discharge than those living with low-EE relatives (Miklowitz et al., 1986). In fact, Leff (1976) reported that the amount of contact patients had with their high-EE relatives or spouses was related to relapse rates (see Figure 15.2). Those who had more than thirty-five hours of direct contact were much more likely to suffer a relapse.

Medication seems to be especially important in preventing relapses in patients in high-EE families. Patients not taking medication who spent at least thirty-five hours with high-EE families relapsed at a rate of 92 percent, as opposed to 15 percent for patients on medication who had less than thirty-five hours of direct contact with their high-EE relatives. The importance of expressed emotions was also found among low-income, unacculturated Mexican-Americans. High-EE levels in key relatives increased the risk of relapse among remitted schizophrenic patients who returned home after being discharged (Karno et al., 1987).

These studies are better designed than those discussed earlier. However, they are still correlational in nature. It is possible that living with a more severely ill schizophrenic patient is the cause, not the result, of high-EE communication patterns in relatives. Further research must also determine if this communication pattern is specific to schizophrenia only or to other disorders as well.

Although it appears that environmental factors do not cause schizophrenia, researchers continue to find that the family environment may be involved in the onset and course of the disorder. Several prospective studies have found that high-risk children who develop schizophrenia, as opposed to those who do not, are more likely to have negative family relationships (Burman et al., 1987; Marcus et al., 1987).

The importance of parenting was indicated in the Israeli high-risk study. None who had received "good or adequate parenting" from a schizophrenic parent developed schizophrenia or a spectrum dis-

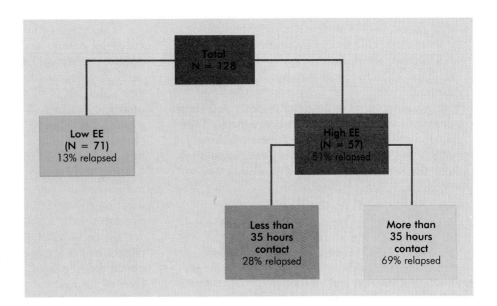

Figure 15.2 Influence of Expressed Emotions on Relapse Rates
SOURCE: Adapted from Leff, 1976.

order. Most investigators now accept the diathesis-stress model in which a predisposition interacts with stressors to produce the onset of schizophrenia.

Effect of Social Class

Schizophrenia is most common at the lower socioeconomic levels, regardless of whether prevalence is measured relative to patient populations or to general populations. According to the Research Task Force of the National Institute of Mental Health (1975), one of the most consistent findings in schizophrenia research is that the disorder is disproportionately concentrated among people in the poorest areas of large cities and in the occupations with the lowest status.

There are two possible explanations for this correlation between social class and schizophrenia. First, low socioeconomic status is itself stressful. Physical and psychological stressors associated with poverty, a lack of education, menial employment, and the like increase the chance that schizophrenia will develop. Second, schizophrenic and preschizophrenic people tend to drift to the poorest urban areas and the lowest socioeconomic levels because they can't function effectively elsewhere in society. This explanation is called the *downward drift theory*.

One way to test downward drift is to determine whether schizophrenics do actually move downward in occupational status. However, the results of such studies have been inconclusive. Some have found evidence of downward mobility, but others have found none (Neale & Oltmanns, 1980).

Another research strategy is to compare the occupations of schizophrenics with their fathers' occupations. If the schizophrenics generally had lower-status jobs than their fathers, a downward drift interpretation would be supported. In several studies, schizophrenics were found to have lower-status occupations than their fathers (Neale & Oltmanns, 1980). Overall, the evidence seems to suggest that both interpretations apply. For some people, the stressors and limitations associated with membership in the lowest socioeconomic class facilitate the development of schizophrenia; for others, low socioeconomic status is a result of the disorders.

Cross-Cultural Comparisons

In the *Report on the International Pilot Study of Schizophrenia* cited in Focus 14.1, no significant differences were found in the prevalence of the disorders in the nine countries studied (World Health Organization, 1973b, 1981). However, a number of studies found various differences in symptomology, and these may result from environmental influences.

Third world countries seem to have a greater percentage of "hysterical psychoses," "possession syndromes," and other brief psychotic disorders. These psychoses tend to be rapid in onset and short in duration. They also have a good prognosis. These cases occur as a reaction to an extreme psychosocial stressor (Wig, 1983). The following case involving a young teacher from Zimbabwe illustrates some of these characteristics.

> A young teacher was brought to the psychiatric hospital by the police after smashing several plate-glass windows in local shops and breaking the windows of cars parked on the street. . . . When captured, he was intensely aggressive, spoke incoherently, and claimed voices were talking to him and directing his actions. Following recovery, which required several weeks of treatment with high dose, high potency neuroleptics, he told the following story.
>
> Approximately one month prior to onset of his running amok, he consulted a local *n'anga* [healer] to determine whether the future of his job was secure. The *n'anga* told him his workmates were jealous of him and might try to harm him. A few weeks later he found a 'flash card' in his office. It read, "To die." He knew at once that his colleagues planned to murder him, probably by bewitchment. This episode would not leave his mind. Hallucinated voices began to echo his thoughts, and his state of wild excitement ensued. (Stevens, 1987, p. 394)

Cases of psychotic reactions after hearing a negative prediction from a witch doctor are not rare in some third world countries.

A comparison of the symptoms of hospitalized schizophrenic Americans of Irish and of Italian descent found that Irish-Americans tended to show less hostility and acting out, but more fixed delusions, than did Italian-Americans. These differences have been attributed to cultural-familial backgrounds: In Irish families, mothers played a very dominant role, were quite strict, and prohibited strong emotional displays; in Italian families, mothers showed the opposite pattern (Opler, 1967). Similarly, Japanese hospitalized for schizophrenia are often described as rigid, compulsive, withdrawn, and passive—symptoms that reflect the Japanese cultural value of conformity within the community and reserve within the family (S. Sue & Morishima, 1982).

The content of delusions also seems to be influenced by culture and society. Since the social and political upheavals of the period known as the Cultural Revolution (during the 1960s), a number of new delusions have appeared among Chinese schizophrenic patients (Yu-Fen & Neng, 1981). These include the delusion of leadership lineage, in which patients insist that their parents are people in authority; the delusion of being tested, in which patients feel that their superiors are assessing them to determine whether they are suitable for promotion; the delusion of impending arrest, in which the patient assumes that he is about to be arrested by authorities; and the delusion of being married, in which a female patient insists she has a husband even though she is unmarried. Each of these is associated with some facet of the new Chinese society.

Racial differences have also been observed. In a study of 273 schizophrenic patients admitted to hospitals and mental health centers in Missouri over a 3½-year period, researchers found that black patients exhibited more severe symptoms than white patients: angry outbursts, impulsiveness, and strongly antisocial behavior. Blacks also showed greater disorientation and confusion and more severe hallucinatory behaviors than whites (Abebimpe et al., 1982). These research findings may be interpreted as real differences in symptomology that may have environmental explanations. According to Abebimpe (1981), however, they may instead be produced by diagnostic errors. He notes that blacks are less likely than whites to be given a diagnosis of mood disorder and more likely to receive a diagnosis of schizophrenia, even when the two racial groups show similar symptoms. Also, cultural differences between patient and clinician tend to result in diagnostic errors—the greater the difference, the greater the likelihood of error. Finally, misdiagnosis can result from racial stereotyping or bias, or from applying diagnostic systems based on white middle-class norms to other racial groups.

THE DIATHESIS-STRESS MODEL OF SCHIZOPHRENIA

The lack of evidence pointing to a single etiology for the schizophrenic disorders has led Bleuler (1984, p. 8) to conclude that

Today, it is certain that in their formation, unfavorable hereditary predispositions interact with unfavorable experiences in life.

Neither a single, inherited predisposition specific only to schizophrenia nor a specific damaging experience in the life course has ever been found.

Instead, there are multitudes of physical and mental, inherited and acquired dispositions that form predispositions for schizophrenia.

Researchers have thus developed a general model emphasizing the interaction between genetics and environmental stressors in schizophrenia (Rosenthal, 1970; Zubin & Spring, 1977; Zubin & Ludwig, 1983). This **diathesis-stress model** involves a vulnerability to the disorder, which may be inherited or acquired, combined with the impact of stressors.

Schizophrenia develops when a vulnerable person encounters stress and lacks access to the resources or social support systems that he or she needs to cope with it.

A particularly elaborate version of the diathesis-stress model has been developed by Nuechterlein and Dawson (1984). As Figure 15.3 shows, these researchers believe that schizophrenics suffer from several "enduring vulnerability characteristics": (1) a predisposition toward poor processing of information and difficulty in sustaining attention brought on by various thought impairments; (2) overreaction to even mildly aversive stimuli; and (3) lack of adequate social competence and coping skills.

The vulnerable person may not experience psychotic episodes if he or she is raised in a supportive

Figure 15.3   The Diathesis-Stress Model of Nuechterlein and Dawson
The vulnerable individual overreacts to environmental stressors that are not buffered by his or her social support system. The feedback loop has the effect of "transforming" such overreaction into added stressors that eventually build up sufficiently to precipitate a schizophrenic episode. SOURCE: Nuechterlein & Dawson, 1984.

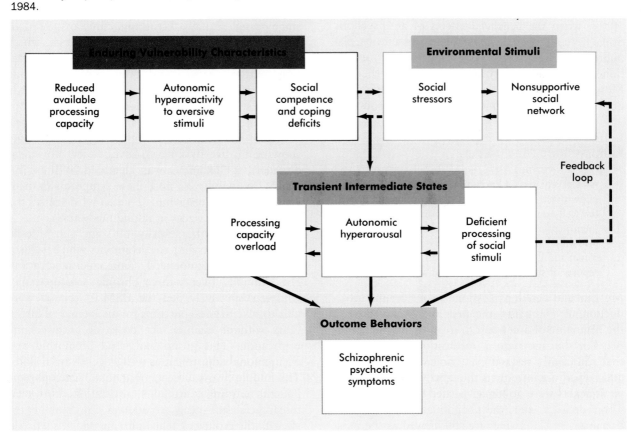

family and encounters only minor stressors. However, in a family that is not sufficiently supportive (overly critical or lacking a parent) stressors are not buffered and the person's reactions to stressors are more severe. When they become severe enough to overload the person's processing capability, a feedback loop is created that continually compounds the stress. Eventually schizophrenic symptoms develop. The diathesis-stress model is useful because it calls attention to the role both biological and psychological factors in schizophrenia.

THE TREATMENT OF SCHIZOPHRENIA

Through the years, schizophrenia has been "treated" by a variety of means ranging from the "warehousing" of severely disturbed patients in overcrowded asylums to prefrontal lobotomy, a surgical procedure in which the frontal lobes are severed from the remainder of the patient's brain (discussed in Chapter 2). Such radical procedures were generally abandoned in the 1950s, when the beneficial effects of antipsychotic drugs were discovered. Today the treatment of schizophrenia typically consists of antipsychotic medication along with some type of psychosocial therapy. More severely disordered patients are still hospitalized until they are able to function adequately in society.

Antipsychotic Medication

> As a psychiatrist, I know that the best way in dealing with the biological basis of schizophrenia is by the well-adjusted intake of psychotropic medication (neuroleptics). I also know that the medication I prescribe has side-effects, at times quite troublesome, and I have to be sensitive to the patient's reports of side effects. (Seeman et al., 1982, p. 120)

Most mental health professionals consider the introduction of *Thorazine*, the first antipsychotic drug, the beginning of a new era in treating of schizophrenia. For the first time, a medication was available that sufficiently relaxed even violent schizophrenics and helped organize their thoughts to the point that straitjackets were no longer needed to contain them. Three decades later, the phenothiazines, which are variations of Thorazine, are still viewed as the most

effective drug treatment for schizophrenia (Donaldson et al., 1983).

The antipsychotic medications (also called **neuroleptics**) are, however, far from perfect and can produce a number of extremely unwelcome side effects because they can produce symptoms that resemble neurological conditions. They quite effectively reduce the severity of the so-called positive symptoms of schizophrenia, such as hallucinations, delusions, bizarre speech, and thought disorders. However, most offer little relief of such "negative" symptoms as social withdrawal, apathy, and impaired personal hygiene (Wahba et al., 1981), and many schizophrenics do not benefit at all from antipsychotic medication (Silverman et al., 1987). (The First Person narrative discusses negative symptoms from an occupational therapist's viewpoint.)

Regulation and monitoring of antipsychotic drugs is especially important. Among 136 newly admitted schizophrenics, Zito et al. (1987) found that many were given doses in "excess of current guidelines." Women received greater doses of antipsychotic medications than men. In addition, medication was seldom reduced to a maintenance level once the acute stage passed. Equally disturbing, clinicians are often unaware of possible reactions to the drugs, which include tremors, motor restlessness, anxiety, agitation, extreme terror, and even impulsive suicide attempts (Drake & Ehrlich, 1985). In one study (Weiden et al., 1987) clinicians did not identify motor symptoms, such as restlessness, rigidity, and tremors, produced by medications. Only one of ten patients showing tardive dyskinesia (involuntary movement disorder), for example, was identified by the clinicians. The inability to note these symptoms in medicated patients is disturbing. Focus 15.1 discusses the issue of patients' rights in taking medication.

Because of the severity of some side effects, researchers are trying to determine which schizophrenic patients do not need maintenance medication. For example, twenty-three chronic schizophrenics who retrospectively met the DSM-III criteria were able to sustain good outcome for an average of fifteen years without maintenance doses or antipsychotic medication. This group had good premorbid and occupational adjustment as well as good social skills. This finding clearly indicates that not all schizophrenic patients require continuous medication. However, researchers still need to address the inability to identify the groups of schizophrenic patients who do

Mary Ann Mayer

FIRST PERSON

Schizophrenia—less a diagnosis than a human condition. Ten years ago I began practicing psychiatric occupational therapy because of my academic interest in the disease. I remain in practice today because of my respect for the people afflicted with it.

A few days after admission to the psychiatric unit, the psychotic storm that engulfs the schizophrenic quiets down and the person emerges, as if from a cocoon. The positive symptoms recede—the command hallucinations, the fear of being stalked or poisoned, hearing one's thoughts whispered by every passerby. But the negative symptoms linger—disturbances in attention, perception, psychomotor behavior, affect, and drive. These are the symptoms that most subtract from the quality of life.

People with schizophrenia are not "crazy"; they have a cognitive disability that robs them of choice and access to the everyday activities you and I take for granted, such as running a household, earning and spending money, and planning for the future. This is why meaningful activity is the treatment method used by occupational therapists; it uses peoples' assets while helping them cope with their limitations. For some, guided involvement in the activities of daily life can restore meaning, purpose, and identity.

I'm expected to help the schizophrenic person and his or her family understand and manage this disability, to reduce environmental barriers to performance, and to restore purpose and place in life. I act as an advocate for the schizophrenic, explaining to others why that person has difficulty doing certain things. I also assess the schizophrenic's environment and try to modify it in ways that optimize that person's performance. Not everything I do works, but anything can work—skills training, simplifying a work site, finding a compatible social group, instilling hope, and showing others alternatives to blaming the schizophrenic person for his or her disability.

The following statements are common misperceptions. One of my responsibilities as an occupational therapist is to interpret a schizophrenic's behavior in a way that can be understood by others, thereby encouraging their understanding and support.

Comment: "He just doesn't apply himself. He's always been lazy."
Response: Daily activities can represent an unachievable challenge. Perhaps he's had more experiences of failure than success. Maybe it's not that he *won't* perform the task, but that he *can't* manage it alone, yet. He might be too afraid to try.

Comment: "She seems so distractible and her work is very disorganized."
Response: Is there a quieter place to work? Is supervision available? Let's analyze the job and work with her to find the easiest methods to perform the assigned tasks.

Comment: "When any medication is prescribed, she takes too much. She can be very uncooperative, you know."
Response: Consistent, familiar routines are important. She may not fully understand the cause and effect of certain actions, such as taking too many pills. A medication daily organizer might help.

Comment: "He has a hard time expressing himself and gets very frustrated when people don't understand. Then he withdraws from everyone, including me. That hurts."
Response: Perhaps he's scared of being rejected, which increases his anxiety, making it more difficult for him to express himself. Encouraging him to take his time when he speaks might help him to relax and feel less self-conscious.

In addition to positive and negative symptoms, social stigma and exclusion have to be grappled with. All these factors contribute to the need for hospitalization, support, and stabilization. Symptoms can be reduced or compensated for. But social barriers are far more difficult to overcome. Fear and misunderstanding need to be replaced with compassion and acceptance. Schizophrenia is not just an illness, it's also a disability, and schizophrenic people deserve the same respect and support we give to other people with disabilities.

Ms. Mary Ann Mayer is a registered occupational therapist at Butler Hospital in Providence, Rhode Island. She evaluates the functional performance of patients, provides rehabilitative activities, and consults to families and caregivers in the community.

FOCUS 15.1   *Side Effects and Patients' Rights*

"There is no known effective treatment for tardive dyskinesia." This warning, contained in the *Physician's Desk Reference* (1989), represents a major source of concern for patients receiving antipsychotic medications. Perhaps even more alarming is the fact that neuroleptics are being prescribed to treat anxiety, hyperactivity in children, aggression, and mood disorders.

Tardive dyskinesia is characterized by involuntary and rhythmic movements of the protruding tongue; chewing, lip smacking, and other facial movements; and jerking movements of the limbs. At risk are elderly patients, women, and people treated with neuroleptics over a long period of time. However, this syndrome is becoming increasingly prevalent in younger patients and nonpsychotic patients. A review of thirty-six studies indicates symptoms of tardive dyskinesia in about 26 percent of chronically ill patients treated with neuroleptics (Jesti & Wyatt, 1981). In the majority of cases, the symptoms persist and cannot be eliminated.

Neuroleptics can produce such Parkinson-like symptoms as loss of facial expression, immobility, shuffling gait, tremors of the hand, rigidity of the body, and poor postural stability. However, these symptoms are usually reversible (Granacher, 1981). *Akathisia* (motor restlessness) and *dystonia* (slow and continued contrasting movements of the limbs and tongue), which are also controllable, may appear as well. Other side effects include drowsiness, skin rashes, blurred vision, dry mouth, nausea, and tachycardia.

Should schizophrenics have the right to refuse antipsychotic medications that produce potentially hazardous side effects? Patients in most state hospitals do not have this right. Groups that support the concept of patients' rights argue that forced administration of drugs vio-

---

not require maintenance medication (Fenton & McGlashan, 1987).

One approach is to reduce medication and watch for a relapse. Those who function well on a lower dosage might later undergo a trial period where medication is totally eliminated. In one study conducted over a twelve-month period, reducing dosage levels by 50 percent tripled the relapse rate (32 percent, as opposed to 10 percent on maintenance medication). There may be a tradeoff, however; reduced-dose patients showed decreased risk of tardive dyskinesia (Johnson et al., 1987). Although a higher relapse rate was associated with a lower level of medication (10 percent of the standard dose), the families of these patients expressed more satisfaction with their adjustment than the families of patients taking a standard dose. On the lower dose, patients showed greater social competence and adjustment. Over 50 percent remained stable. Researchers also found that negative family attitudes toward the patient were associated with relapse. So dosage reduc-

tion, together with careful monitoring, may be useful with some people, but standard dosage levels may be needed in nonsupportive families.

Psychosocial Therapy

Most clinicians today agree that the most beneficial treatment for schizophrenia is some combination of antipsychotic medication and therapy (Feinsilver & Yates, 1984; Falloon & Liberman, 1983). This attitude is fairly new and was resisted for many years by strict advocates of a medical approach. But even as scientists continued to introduce drugs that effectively reduced or eliminated many symptoms of schizophrenia, it became clear that one vital fact was being ignored: medicated and adequately functioning schizophrenics who were discharged from the protective environment of hospitals were being returned to stressful home or work situations (Mosher & Keith, 1980; Donaldson et al., 1983). The typical

lates a person's basic freedoms. Yet hospital staff members fear that violent patients may be dangerous to themselves, other patients, and staff if they are not medicated. One resident care aide said, "Those who refuse drugs may be those who need them most because they are dangerous. We don't have enough staff on the units to deal with that" (*Ann Arbor News*, 1984, p. 4). As the funding of state mental institutions has decreased, the use of medication has increased. According to the director of the Michigan Department of Mental Health, 98 percent of patients in state hospitals are on psychotropic drugs.

The movement for patients' rights seems to be gaining strength. In 1982, relatives of a woman who developed tardive dyskinesia successfully sued the state of Michigan for $1 million. Since that time, a bill has been proposed in the Michigan legislature to grant the following rights to patients residing in state hospitals:

- The approximately 15 percent of all patients who are voluntarily hospitalized should have the right to refuse drugs.

- The remaining 85 percent, who are involuntary patients, should have a limited right to refuse drugs. Such a patient could refuse medication, but then a three-member panel from the hospital would review the case and decide whether it was necessary. The patient could be represented by advocates or an attorney at the review.

Many patients' rights advocates feel that *all* patients should be able to refuse drugs. They expect that increased awareness of the potential harmfulness of neuroleptics will force more careful monitoring of their use and encourage the development of alternative forms of treatment for the psychoses. Patients' rights are discussed more fully in Chapter 21.

---

result was repeated rehospitalization; medication alone was not enough to help schizophrenics function in their natural environment (Caton, 1982; Brown, 1982). Clinicians soon realized that antipsychotic medication had to be supplemented with outpatient therapy. But which therapeutic strategy would yield the best results?

Institutional Approaches Traditional institutional treatments providing custodial care and medication for schizophrenics have yielded poor results, although **milieu therapy** and behavioral therapy were found to be more effective. In milieu therapy, patients exercise a wide range of responsibilities. They are involved in decision making and in managing the wards. This is in sharp contrast to the passive role that they have in traditional settings. Social learning programs focus on increasing appropriate self-care behaviors, conversational skills, and role skills (job training and ward activities). Undesirable behaviors such as "crazy talk" or social isolation are decreased,

Supportive counseling or other forms of psychotherapy can supplement drug therapy for schizophrenic patients. Once the patient's psychotic symptoms are under control, a therapist can try to help the patient improve his or her social and coping skills.

through reinforcement and modeling techniques. These approaches were compared in a carefully controlled study that lasted six years (Paul & Lentz, 1977). Twenty-eight severely ill, chronic schizophrenics were assigned to either a social learning or milieu program. A matched control group of patients received traditional institutional treatment. The results clearly indicated that the experimental programs were more effective. Patients in these two groups showed significant improvements in interpersonal skills and self-care. Nearly 11 percent of the social learning group and 7 percent of the milieu group achieved independent functioning. None of the comparison group achieved this result. Some schizophrenics will always need long-term institutional treatment. But it seems clear that programs in which patients are encouraged to assume responsibility and to develop skills necessary for functioning in the community have the greatest success. Supportive counseling to help the individual deal with the stresses of outside living is also important.

Behavior Therapy In behavior therapy, the therapist concentrates on teaching the patient specific skills. Behavior therapy is a "doing" therapy, whereas supportive counseling is a "talking" therapy.

Because schizophrenics typically lack social skills, a social skills training program is almost always included as part of behavior therapy (Curran & Monti, 1982). In many cases, it is the major part of the therapy. Communication skills in general are emphasized, as is assertiveness training (Bellack et al., 1976). The patient is repeatedly placed in social situations that he or she tends to avoid. Experience with such situations eventually decreases the patient's anxiety concerning them to the point where he or she will seek out, rather than avoid, these situations. This is a crucially important contribution of social skills training, because social withdrawal is a major schizophrenic symptom that is untouched by antipsychotic medication (Wallace et al., 1980).

Interventions Focusing on Expressed Emotions

New psychological interventions had to be developed, especially since over 50 percent of recovering patients return to live with their families (Goldman, 1980). Most of these approaches try to reduce the likelihood of relapse (rather than cure the disorder) and try to improve interaction between the patient and family members. This approach involves a two-pronged strategy (1) disseminating information about the disorder to families of schizophrenics and (2) teaching families and the schizophrenic member how to alter their communication patterns. In one program, high-EE and low-EE family members of schizophrenics meet together in a group to talk about specific themes such as problems faced by families of recovering patients, methods of reducing guilt and responsibility for patients, and healthy ways of dealing with the stress and frustrations of living with a patient. Vaughn and Leff (1981) found that this treatment method successfully reduced EE levels and reduced relapse rates in patients.

A similar approach was developed by Falloon et al. (1984) and outlined in their book *Family Care of Schizophrenia*. Their intervention is much more comprehensive and includes a careful behavioral analysis of communication patterns in family members and patients. Stressful interactions are identified, and training in alternative methods of communicating is implemented. Specific skills such as listening, making requests clear, focusing on positive reinforcement, and reducing criticisms are stressed. These skills are then employed to help increase the individual's problem-solving abilities.

It is also important for the patient to develop social skills that will enable him or her to recognize the emotional responses of family members and learn to respond to them appropriately (Lieberman et al., 1986). Family communication patterns should be combined with skills development in individual patients. The positive gains reported from treatment packages that include family education, altering communication patterns, and the development of social skills and competencies in patients give an impetus to psychosocial treatments.

The combination of medication and psychological interventions has provided hope for many schizophrenic patients; continuing research points to an even more promising future. This optimism is reflected in the words of a young pharmacy student who is also a schizophrenic:

And even now in 1980, in a professional pharmacy school, it would probably shock many people to know that a schizophrenic was in their class, was going to be a pharmacist, and could do a good job. And knowledge of it could cause the loss of many friends and acquaintances. So even now I must write this article anonymously. But I want people to know that I have schizophrenia, that I need medicine and psychotherapy, and at times I have required hospitalization.... When you think about schizophrenia next time, try to remember me; there are more people like me out there trying to overcome a poorly understood disease.... And some of them are making it. (Anonymous, 1983)

SUMMARY

1. Much research and theorizing has focused on the etiology of schizophrenia. Using such research strategies as the analysis of family trees, twin studies, and adoption studies, investigators have shown that heredity does influence this group of disorders. The degree of influence is open to question, however; when methodological problems are taken into account, it appears lower than reported. Obviously, heredity alone is not sufficient to cause schizophrenia; environmental factors are also involved.

2. The process by which genetic influences are transmitted has not been explained. Attempts to find specific biochemical or neurological differences between schizophrenics and nonschizophrenics have not yielded many positive findings. The most promising area of research involves the relationship between dopamine (a neurotransmitter) and schizophrenia.

3. The search for an environmental basis for schizophrenia has met with less success than has the search for genetic influences. Certain negative family patterns, involving parental characteristics or intrafamilial communication processes, seem correlated with schizophrenia. Recent studies have found that high expressed emotions (negative comments) from family members are related to relapse in schizophrenics. The prevalence of these disorders among people in low-status occupations who live in the poorest areas of large cities is highest; differences in symptomology seem to be loosely related to cultural variables. But again, the effects of such sociocultural variables are still open to speculation.

4. The research on the etiology of schizophrenia thus suggests an interaction between genetic and environmental factors. The theoretical diathesis-stress model of schizophrenia includes a personal vulnerability that may be caused by hereditary, biological, or psychological factors. When the vulnerable person is exposed to strong environmental stressors but does not have the resources to cope with them, a schizophrenic episode may result.

5. Schizophrenia seems to involve both biological and psychological factors, and treatment programs that combine drugs with psychotherapy seem to hold the most promise. Drug therapy usually involves a group of antipsychotics called phenothiazines. The accompanying psychosocial therapy consists of either supportive counseling or behavior therapy, with an emphasis on social skills training and changing communication patterns among patients and family members.

KEY TERMS

concordance rate The likelihood that family members will exhibit the disorder that is being studied

diathesis-stress model A theoretical model postulating that a predisposition (diathesis) and the effect of environmental stressors combine in producing mental disorders

dopamine hypothesis The suggestion that schizophrenia results from an excess of dopamine activity at certain brain synapses

double-bind theory The suggestion that schizophrenia develops in a person as a result of the continual reception of contradictory messages from parents during the person's upbringing

milieu therapy A therapy program in which the hospital environment operates as a community and patients have decision-making responsibilities

neuroleptics Antipsychotic medication. Can produce symptoms that mimic neurological disorders

prospective study A long-term study of a group of people, beginning before the onset of a disorder, to allow investigators to see how the disorder develops

schizophrenogenic Causing or producing schizophrenia; generally used to describe a parent who is simultaneously or alternately cold and overprotecting, rejecting and dominating

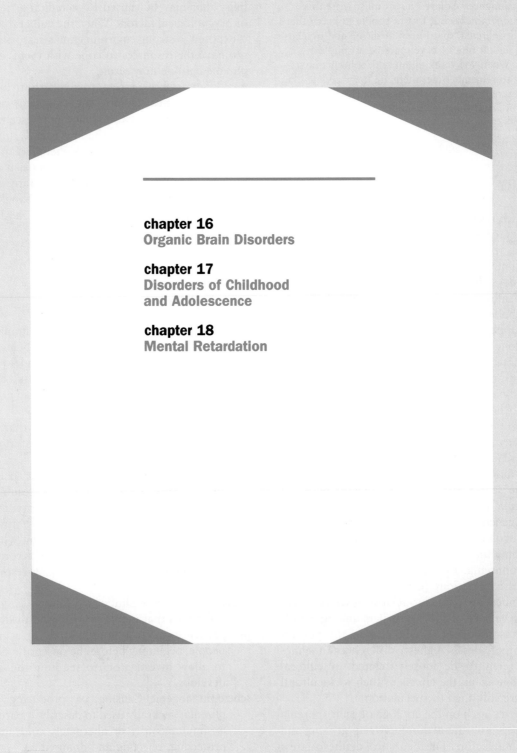

PART 5

Organic and Developmental Problems

chapter 16
Organic Brain Disorders

In the ring, Muhammad Ali was able to "float like a butterfly, sting like a bee" as he won, lost, and twice regained the world heavyweight boxing championship. Outside the ring he was known for his ego, his wit and rapid-fire speech, and his never-ending rhyming. But it was a different Muhammad Ali who, at age forty-two and retired from boxing, entered a New York City hospital for neurological testing. His speech was slurred and sometimes unintelligible, and he tended to shuffle when he walked; he often seemed remote and expressionless, constantly felt tired, and suffered occasional lapses of memory.

Ali's symptoms resembled those of Parkinson's disease, a brain disorder. But are they due to that disorder or to the poundings he must have taken in more than twenty years of boxing? His doctors reported that he did not have Parkinson's disease nor is he "punch-drunk." His disorder was diagnosed as Parkinson's syndrome, meaning that he has many of the symptoms of Parkinson's disease although he does not have the disorder.

Anti-Parkinson's medication has reduced the severity of some of Ali's symptoms, but the prognosis is vague. The former champion has made a few public appearances, but he is far from the old Ali. Five months after his disorder was diagnosed, he was an honored guest at the sixtieth annual Boxing Writers Association dinner. One writer described him thus:

At times, Ali disappeared within himself, as if in a trance. A boxing annual from 1965—the cover headlined "Can Ali Beat Liston a Second Time?"— was deposited in front of him [by a fan]. Ali opened it to a picture of himself and Sonji, his first wife.

"He kept staring at that page," said Schulian [who was sitting next to Ali]. "He put the magazine down in his shrimp and avocado salad and kept staring at it. Finally, José Torres lifted the magazine gently and asked him if he wanted his salad."

Later, while somebody gave an award-acceptance speech, Ali allowed his eyelids to fall, and he slept for 10 minutes. Only then did a faintly quizzical expression replace his usually benign and bemused countenance. (Marantz, 1985, p. 63)

Muhammad Ali's symptoms have not been tied specifically to the head blows he received as a boxer. However, eliminating Parkinson's disease as the cause does seem to indicate that they are due to brain trauma.

As you will see in this chapter, it is often difficult to discern the exact causes of **organic mental disorders,** which are behavioral disturbances that result from organic brain pathology—damage to the brain. Possible causes include aging, trauma, infection, loss of blood supply, and various biochemical imbalances. These may result in cognitive, emotional, and behavioral symptoms that can resemble the symptoms of the functional disorders discussed in preceding chapters. (The **functional disorders** are mental disorders for which no physical basis can be found and that are assumed to be due primarily to psychological factors.) In fact, even highly experienced diagnosticians often have trouble determining whether some mental disorders are organic or functional.

This diagnostic problem stems in part from the fact that the behavioral disturbance of brain pathology is influenced by social and psychological factors as well as by the specific pathology. In other words, people with similar types of brain damage may behave quite differently, depending on their premorbid personalities, their coping skills, and the availability of such resources as family support systems. Furthermore, those with organic brain dysfunctions often are treated insensitively by other people, so they experience a lot of stress. This stress may add to or modify the symptoms that stem from the organic disorder.

Physical, social, and psychological factors thus interact in complicated ways to produce the behaviors of people who have organic brain disturbances (Binder, 1988). Treatment, too, often requires some combination of physical, medicinal, and psychological therapy, behavior modification, and skills training. For some patients who have severe and irreversible brain damage, the only available options may be rehabilitation, modified skills training, and the creation of a supportive environment.

DSM-III-R distinguishes between (1) organic mental syndromes and (2) organic mental disorders, as shown in the disorders chart on p. 424. The term **organic mental syndrome** refers to a pattern of psychological or behavioral signs and symptoms associated with organic causes. An organic mental syndrome in which the etiology is known or presumed, is called an *organic mental disorder.* For example, delirium is a *syndrome* in which someone shows disorganized thinking, inability to maintain attention, and so on. When the delirium results from a known cause (such as alcohol withdrawal) and cannot be attributed to another mental disorder (for example, a mood disorder), it is considered an organic mental *disorder.* Because many syndromes and heterogeneous disorders are listed in DSM-III-R, this chapter focuses primarily on the major causes of organic brain disorders. We begin by discussing the brain structure, and then present ways to assess brain damage, dimensions and syndromes, causes of brain disorders, and treatment.

THE HUMAN BRAIN

The brain is an organ that weighs approximately 3 pounds and is composed of billions of cells. As noted earlier, *neurons* (or nerve cells) transfer information within the brain. Information travels along neurons in the form of electrical impulses; impulse transfer from neuron to neuron is aided by chemical transmitters called *neurotransmitters* or *neuroregulators.*

The brain is separated into two hemispheres. A disturbance in either one (such as by a tumor or by electrical stimulation with electrodes) may produce specific sensory or motor effects. Each hemisphere controls the *opposite* side of the body. For example, paralysis on the left side of the body indicates a dysfunction in the right hemisphere. In addition, the right hemisphere is associated with visual-spatial abilities and emotional behavior. The left hemisphere controls the language functions for nearly all right-handed people *and* for most left-handed ones (Golden & Vincente, 1983).

Viewed in cross section (see Figure 16.1), the brain has three parts: forebrain, midbrain, and hindbrain. Although each part is vital for functioning and survival, the forebrain is probably the most relevant to a discussion of abnormality. Within the forebrain are the thalamus, hypothalamus, reticular activating system, limbic system, and cerebrum. The specific functions of these structures are still being debated, but we can discuss their more general functions with some confidence. The *thalamus,* for example, seems to serve as a "relay station," transmitting nerve impulses to other parts of your brain. The *hypothalamus* ("under the thalamus") regulates bodily drives (such as hunger, thirst, and sex) and body conditions such as temperature and hormone balance. The *reticular activating system* is a network of nerve fibers that controls bodily states such as sleep, alertness, and attention. The *limbic system* seems to be involved in experiencing and expressing emotions and motivation—pleasure, fear, aggressiveness, sexual arousal, and pain.

Figure 16.1 The Internal Structure of the Brain

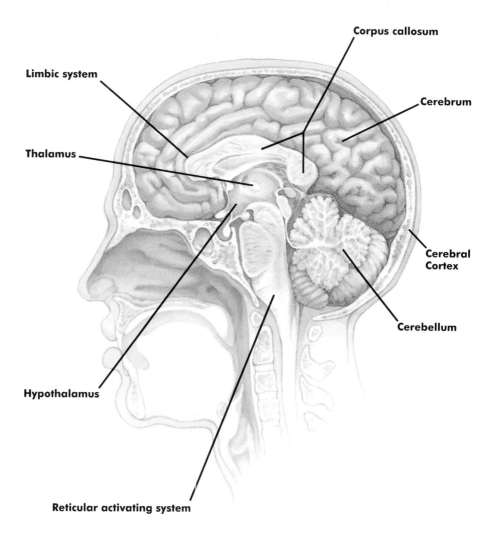

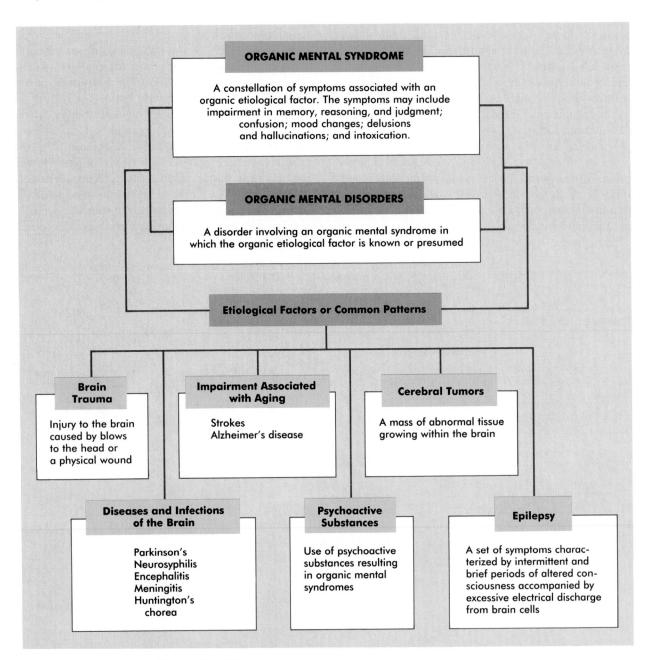

ORGANIC MENTAL SYNDROME

A constellation of symptoms associated with an organic etiological factor. The symptoms may include impairment in memory, reasoning, and judgment; confusion; mood changes; delusions and hallucinations; and intoxication.

ORGANIC MENTAL DISORDERS

A disorder involving an organic mental syndrome in which the organic etiological factor is known or presumed

Etiological Factors or Common Patterns

Brain Trauma

Injury to the brain caused by blows to the head or a physical wound

Impairment Associated with Aging

Strokes
Alzheimer's disease

Cerebral Tumors

A mass of abnormal tissue growing within the brain

Diseases and Infections of the Brain

Parkinson's
Neurosyphilis
Encephalitis
Meningitis
Huntington's chorea

Psychoactive Substances

Use of psychoactive substances resulting in organic mental syndromes

Epilepsy

A set of symptoms characterized by intermittent and brief periods of altered consciousness accompanied by excessive electrical discharge from brain cells

SOURCE: Adapted from DSM-III-R, pp. 97–163.

The largest structure in the brain is the *cerebrum,* whose outermost layer of gray matter is called the *cerebral cortex.* The cerebrum is associated with human consciousness and with learning, speech, thought, and memory. It processes sensory information, controls motor activity, and produces and controls language. The two cerebral hemispheres are connected by a collection of nerve fibers called the *corpus callosum.*

The brain and spinal cord together comprise the **central nervous system.** The spinal cord links the brain to the rest of the body by transmitting sensory and motor information to and from the brain. The spinal cord has some primitive reflex capabilities, but complex behaviors that depend on memory and learning experiences are controlled by the brain. The **autonomic nervous system** (see Figure 16.2), composed of the brain and spinal cord, links the spinal cord with the smooth muscles of various vital organs and with the different glands.

THE ASSESSMENT OF BRAIN DAMAGE

The techniques used in assessing brain damage were discussed in Chapter 4. There are two types: (1) neuropsychological tests that require behavioral responses from the patient and that assess such functions as memory and manual dexterity, and (2) neurological tests that allow one to "look into" the brain. The neurological tests (discussed in Chapter 4) include the **electroencephalograph** (EEG), which measures electrical activity of brain cells, and **computerized axial tomography** (CAT) scanning.

Two additional techniques involve monitoring a radioactive substance as it moves through the brain (Boller et al., 1984). In **cerebral blood flow measurement,** the patient inhales a radioactive gas, which

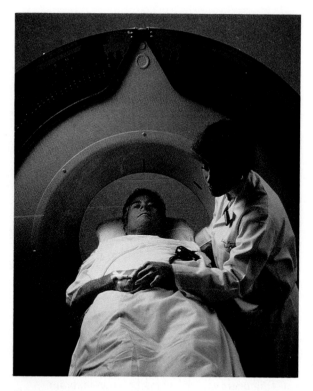

Computerized axial tomography (CAT) scanning uses x-rays to make a three-dimensional representation of the brain. A neurologist can study these computer-enhanced x-rays and locate abnormal tissues within the brain.

Figure 16.2 The Major Areas of the Brain

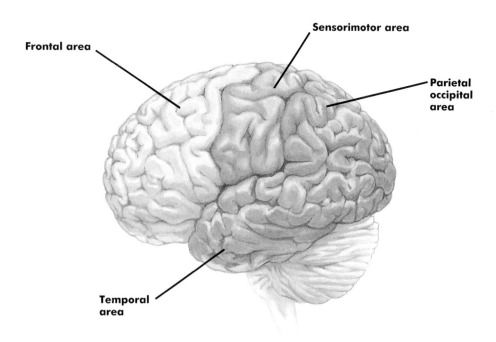

Frontal area

Sensorimotor area

Parietal occipital area

Temporal area

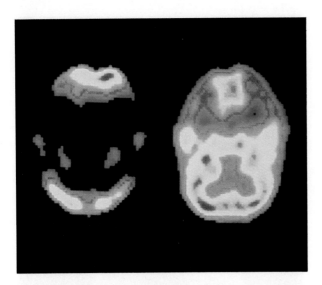

Positron emission tomography (PET) scanning uses a radioactive glucose substance to assess brain activity, which is represented in the photo by different color intensities. Red indicates areas of greatest brain activity. Yellow, blue, and green indicate decreasing levels of brain activity, with black representing the least. The photo on the left is of an Alzheimer's diseased brain, while the photo on the right is of a normal brain.

flows through the brain with the blood. The gas—and thus the flow of blood—is monitored with a gamma ray camera. In **positron emission tomography (PET)**, the patient is injected with a radioactive glucose substance. By monitoring the radioactivity, one can study the metabolism of glucose in the patient's brain, which provides a very accurate means of assessing brain function. A more recent development is **magnetic resonance imaging (MRI)**. MRI uses a magnetic field and radio waves to produce snapshots of brain anatomy that have striking resolution, almost like a photograph—except that this is accomplished without surgery, exposure to x-rays (as in CAT scans), or ingesting radioactive materials (as in PET scans). The procedure involves placing patients in a magnetic field and using radio waves to make pictures of the brain.

These techniques increase diagnostic accuracy in cases of brain damage. Equally important is an assessment of the patient's general cognitive functioning, personality characteristics, and coping skills, as well as his or her behaviors and emotional reactions—particularly when they differ from reported premorbid functioning. Such an assessment can pro-

vide crucial information about brain dysfunction, and is of utmost importance in planning treatment and rehabilitation.

Localization of Brain Damage

Neurological techniques such as CAT and PET scans and MRI help determine the location and extent of brain damage. But can the location of a damaged or disrupted area of the brain be determined from the type of function loss the patient shows? Neuropsychologists have debated this question for a number of years, and have made many attempts to relate functions to specific areas of the brain.

In one study, researchers used CAT scans to examine eighty-seven patients, each of whom had a brain lesion (organic brain damage) that was localized within one of eight areas of the brain (Golden, Graber et al., 1981). Each area was then matched with the particular functions affected. The brain areas (four in each hemisphere) are shown in Figure 16.2; the functions that they seemed to control are listed in Table 16.1.

Note the extensive overlapping of functions, which complicates the assessment of brain damage by determining functional losses. Moreover, "No two human brains are identical in appearance or in distribution of the functional organization of psychological skills. Although there are close approximations in most cases, it is not possible to find one-to-one correspondences for specific physical areas related to specific psychological functions from brain to brain" (Golden et al., 1981).

Two processes that may occur within the brain can further complicate the matching of function (or loss of function) with specific brain areas. The first, documented by many experimental and clinical studies, is *diaschisis*, in which a lesion in a specific area of the brain disrupts other intact areas, sometimes even in the other hemisphere (Smith, 1982).

A possible mechanism for diaschisis is the vast network of neurological pathways connecting the different areas and systems within the brain. These pathways, by which a "message" may be rerouted if it is blocked at a damaged area, may also explain the second process—the recovery of function after an area of the brain has been damaged. Other explanations stress *redundancy*, in which an "unused" portion of the brain takes up the function of the

TABLE 16.1 | **Brain Areas and the Functions They Control**

Left Frontal Area	*Right Frontal Area*
Expression via speech	Motor
Mathematics	Rhythm
Reception of speech	Mathematics
Left Sensorimotor Area	*Right Sensorimotor Area*
Expression via speech	Motor
Mathematics	Tactile
Left Parietal, Occipital Area	*Right Parietal, Occipital Area*
Mathematics	Tactile
Expression via speech	Motor
Writing	
Reading	
Left Temporal Lobe	*Right Temporal Lobe*
Reception of speech	Rhythm
Expression via speech	Motor
Memory	Tactile
Intelligence	

SOURCE: Golden et al., 1981.

damaged area, or *plasticity*, in which an undeveloped portion of the brain substitutes for the damaged portion. This plasticity would account for the development of language in young children who have left-hemisphere damage. For example, a five-year-old boy whose left hemisphere was removed (to stop his seizures) later developed superior language and intellectual abilities. Because the right hemisphere had not yet become fully specialized, it could develop the structure necessary to support language and intellectual ability (Smith & Sugar, 1975).

However, some evidence shows that such a shift of function from one hemisphere to the other may decrease the functional space available for the development of other skills. One person who had left-hemisphere damage at birth did develop normal language ability, but his visual-spatial memory was impaired. The development of language may have required functional space normally devoted to visual-spatial ability (Bullard-Bates & Satz, 1983).

The Dimensions of Brain Damage

Organic brain damage can be evaluated along a continuum of degree, from mild to moderate to severe. In addition, clinicians often distinguish between endogenous and exogenous causes, between (1) diffuse, specific damage and (2) acute, chronic conditions.

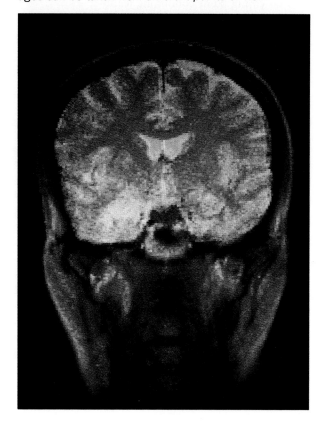

Magnetic resonance imaging (MRI) uses radio waves to produce striking "pictures" of the brain. MRI is more precise than computerized axial tomography, and images can be taken from different points of view.

Endogenous brain damage has been caused by something within the person; for example, insufficient oxygen for neural tissue caused by loss of blood flow to the brain, for any reason. *Exogenous* brain damage is caused by some external factor, such as a severe blow to the head or poisoning.

The diffuse-specific distinction helps indicate the extent of the brain damage. *Diffuse* damage is rather generalized; it typically involves widespread impairment of functioning, including disorientation, poor memory and judgment, and emotional instability. *Specific* brain damage is fairly localized, usually causing impairment or behavioral consequences that correspond only to the psychological or physiological function of the injured area.

An *acute* brain disorder is not accompanied by significant and permanent brain damage. A high fever or a severe bout of alcoholic intoxication can result in acute organic changes that are reversible and thus temporary. (Note, however, that the ability of the central nervous system to repair itself when damaged is extremely limited.) A *chronic* disorder involves permanent and irreversible brain damage—for example, as a result of severe lead poisoning caused by a child eating paint containing lead.

People with chronic organic disorders may display similar symptoms, but impaired memory is usually the first noticeable sign of a chronic condition. Over time, the person may learn to compensate for many of the other symptoms.

Diagnostic Problems

The two major problems in diagnosing brain damage arise because of similarities between the symptoms of organic and functional disorders. Thus people who have not suffered brain damage may be diagnosed as having an organic disorder. Deeply depressed people often show characteristics similar to those of brain-damaged people; in particular, the neuropsychological tests used to assess a wide range of functions (including language, cognition, motor functions, and visual-motor functions) were found to be subject to the effects of depression (Sweet, 1983). It is also difficult to distinguish brain-damaged from schizophrenic patients by using neuropsychological tests (Portnoff et al., 1983).

The elderly are particularly vulnerable to inaccurate diagnosis as being brain-damaged. An aged adult is more likely to perform poorly during assessment testing, because of reduced sensory acuity, performance anxiety, fatigue, or not understanding test instructions. For this reason, tests that differentiate between normal and brain-damaged young adults cannot be assumed to apply to older people. In a study of fifty retired teachers, many scored in the brain-damaged range on the Halstead-Reitan Neuropsychological Test Battery (discussed in Chapter 4), even though they scored in the superior range on the Wechsler Adult Intelligence Scale (WAIS) and functioned very well in their daily lives (Price et al., 1980).

To make sure that a particular set of symptoms stems from an organic brain disorder, clinicians usually try to determine whether the central nervous system has been damaged or whether a causal agent (such as a poison) is responsible for the symptoms. In some cases, support for a diagnosis of organic brain disorder can come from a patient's positive response to a treatment known to be effective against a particular disorder. For example, a diagnosis of Parkinson's disease is supported by the patient's response to treatment with L-dopa.

The second major diagnostic problem is opposite in effect: People who have suffered brain damage may be diagnosed as having a psychological disorder. The following case is an example:

Larry D., age thirty-eight, was an energetic community college teacher and athletic coach and the happily married father of four children. During a particularly busy period, he suffered an apparent seizure while attending a professional conference. Just prior to the seizure, he reported smelling an unusual odor; he then temporarily lost consciousness. Medical evaluations following the episode revealed no obvious cause for Larry's loss of consciousness, and it was assumed to be due to a lack of sleep and general fatigue.

Although he did not pass out again, Larry began to show such symptoms as loss of appetite, difficulty in sleeping, fatigue, and some mental confusion. He became increasingly withdrawn both from his family and from his professional activities, and he mentioned suicide several times. His family and colleagues became extremely concerned about his behavior. A mental health professional was consulted, and psychiatric hospitalization was recommended. But Larry's condition continued to deteriorate.

At this point Larry's wife sought a second opinion from the neuropsychology clinic at a local university.

FOCUS 16.1

FOCUS 16.1 — AIDS and Dementia

It was frightening. It was terrifying. It was terrible headaches, months when I could only stand or lie down. I lost control of one side of my body. I couldn't write. I had lost fine motor control. I also had memory lapses. One time I was in a supermarket and suddenly I couldn't remember how I got there. (Joyce, 1988, p. 38)

The person who made this statement suffered from AIDS, the immunodeficiency disease. Although the general public knows about the disastrous consequences of AIDS—susceptibility to diseases, physical deterioration, and death, often within several years of infection—

relatively few people know that dementia may be the first and sometimes only sign of AIDS. Joyce (1988) has noted that the vast majority of AIDS victims may suffer from some form of dementia. The symptoms involve an inability to concentrate and to perform complex sequential mental tasks. The person may be unable to follow television or movie plots, may miss appointments, and may have hand tremors. Other symptoms involve forgetfulness, impaired judgment, and personality disturbances such as anxiety and depression.

The dementia can be attributed to three factors. First, the AIDS virus itself can infect the brain and lie

dormant for a period of time. When it becomes active, the virus can affect mental as well as physical processes. Second, since AIDS affects the immune system, AIDS-related infections may cause neuropsychological problems. Third, depression, anxiety, and confusion can arise from simply knowing that one has AIDS. Thus, people with AIDS are at high risk for dementia.

The results of neuropsychological testing suggested organic difficulties originating in the right temporal lobe of the brain. A CAT scan was performed, and a brain tumor was located.

In Larry's case, joint neuropsychological and medical assessment was able to pinpoint the cause of the disorder. Naturally, the course of treatment changed significantly once the brain tumor was discovered. In many cases, as here, the initial neuropsychological assessment or even the initial use of techniques such as CAT scanning may not yield information that clearly points to an organic impairment. For this reason, follow-up testing at regular intervals is often recommended. This also allows the monitoring of the patient's performance on succeeding neuropsychological tests, to detect significant patterns of deterioration.

ORGANIC MENTAL SYNDROMES

DSM-III-R outlines ten specific organic mental syndromes or patterns of symptoms that indicate organic mental disorders: dementia, delirium, amnestic syn-

drome, organic delusional syndrome, organic hallucinosis, organic mood syndrome, organic anxiety syndrome, organic personality syndrome, intoxication, and withdrawal. We discuss dementia and delirium in greater detail than the other syndromes, because the two deal with more global cognitive impairment.

Dementia

Dementia is characterized by deteriorating intellectual ability and by impaired judgment, severe enough to hinder social and occupational functioning. (See Focus 16.1 for a discussion of dementia and AIDS.) The most prominent feature appears to be impaired memory. People with dementia may forget to finish tasks, the names of significant others, and past events. In addition, their ability to think abstractly may be impaired. Some people who show this syndrome also display impulse control problems. They may, for example, disrobe in public or make sexual advances to strangers, according to DSM-III-R (American Psychiatric Association, 1987).

Although dementia is most often encountered in the elderly, only a small proportion of elderly people actually develop this syndrome. Only 5 percent of older people are severely demented, and 10 percent are mildly or moderately demented (National Institutes of Health, 1981).

Dementia is, in fact, associated with a range of disorders. Wells (1978) analyzed the records of 222 patients who displayed dementia as the primary sign, rather than a secondary sign, of a diagnosed disorder. The disorders associated with dementia and the percentage of the population suffering from them are listed below. (Data taken from Wells, 1978, p. 2). Note that Alzheimer's disease probably accounts for most cases of dementia among the elderly.

Atrophy of uncertain cause (probably Alzheimer's disease), 51 percent

Vascular disease, 8 percent

Normal pressure hydrocephalus, 6 percent

Dementia in alcoholics, 6 percent

Intracranial masses, 5 percent

Huntington's chorea, 5 percent

Depression, 4 percent

Drug toxicity, 3 percent

Dementia uncertain, 3 percent

Others, 9 percent

These findings have important implications for diagnosis because such problems as depression, drug toxicity, normal pressure hydrocephalus, and benign intracranial masses can be corrected. Identifying noncorrectable causes of dementia is also important, because some may benefit from a specific therapeutic intervention to reduce or limit symptoms.

Delirium

Delirium involves a reduced ability to attend to external stimuli, difficulty in shifting attention, and disorganized patterns of thinking as manifested by rambling, irrelevant, or incoherent speech (Wells, 1985). Often, there is a reduced level of consciousness and disturbances in the cycle of sleep and waking. The following describes a case of a student who was treated for amphetamine-induced delirium:

An 18-year-old high-school senior was brought to the emergency room by police after being picked up wandering in traffic on the Triborough Bridge [in New York City]. He was angry, agitated, and aggressive and talked of various people who were deliberately trying to "confuse" him by giving him misleading directions. His story was rambling and disjointed, but he admitted to the police officer that he had been using "speed." In the emergency room he had difficulty focusing his attention and had to ask that questions be repeated. He was disoriented as to time and place and was unable to repeat the names of three objects after five minutes. The family gave a history of the patient's regular use of "pep pills" over the past two years, during which time he was frequently "high" and did very poorly in school. (Spitzer et al., 1981a, p. 36)

In addition to dementia and delirium, a number of other organic mental syndromes have been listed in DSM-III-R. Unlike dementia and delirium, in which cognitive impairment is global, the other syndromes are relatively more specific in their effects, as shown in Table 16.2.

ORGANIC MENTAL DISORDERS

As mentioned earlier, DSM-III-R notes that when the cause of certain organic mental syndromes is known or presumed, an organic mental disorder is specified. It lists three major types of disorders: (1) senile and presenile dementias, (2) psychoactive substance-induced organic mental disorders, and (3) other organic mental disorders. Because there are many specific disorders within each major type, we focus only on the more common sources of organic brain disorders.

The sources of organic brain damage discussed here are brain trauma, processes associated with aging, disease and infection, tumors, epilepsy, and psychoactive substance-induced disorders. In addition, toxic substances, malnutrition, and even brain surgery may produce organic brain syndromes.

Brain Trauma

On September 13, 1848, at Cavendish, Vermont, Phineas Gage was working as foreman of a railroad

TABLE 16.2 | **Organic Mental Syndromes (Excluding Dementia and Delirium)**

Amnestic syndrome Impairment in short- and long-term memory

Organic delusional syndrome Prominent delusions or false beliefs that defy credibility

Organic hallucinosis Prominent persistent or recurrent hallucinations

Organic mood syndrome Prominent and persistent depressed, elevated, or expansive mood

Organic anxiety syndrome Prominent, recurrent panic attacks or generalized anxiety

Organic personality syndrome A persistent personality disturbance involving mood instability, outbursts of rage, impaired social judgment, apathy, or suspiciousness

Intoxification Maladaptive behavior due to recent ingestion of a psychoactive substance

Withdrawal Development of certain symptoms due to the cessation of, or reduction in, the use of a psychoactive substance that was regularly used

NOTE: In all organic mental syndromes, it is assumed that an organic factor is responsible for the symptoms and cannot be attributed to another (nonorganic) mental disorder such as schizophrenia

excavation crew. A premature explosion of a blast sent a tamping iron—a 3½-foot rod of about an inch in diameter—through the lower side of Gage's face and out of the top of his head. Exhibiting some convulsions and bleeding profusely, Gage soon regained speech. He was taken to his hotel, where he walked up a flight of stairs in order to get to his room. Remarkably, Gage survived the trauma, even though there must have been extensive damage to his brain tissue. Later, he appeared to have completely recovered from the accident with no physical aftereffects. However, Gage began to complain that he had a strange feeling, which he could not describe. Soon, his employers and others noticed a marked personality change in him. Although he had been a very capable employee prior to the accident and was known for his affable disposition, Gage now became moody, irritable, profane, impatient, and obstinate. So radically changed was Gage that his friends said that he was "no longer Gage." (adapted from Harlow, 1868)

A **brain trauma** is a physical wound or injury to the brain, as in the case of Phineas Gage. The severity, duration, and symptoms may differ widely, depending on the person's premorbid personality and on the extent and location of the neural damage. Generally, the greater the tissue damage, the more impaired the functioning. In some cases, however, interactions among various parts of the brain, coupled with brain redundancy, where different parts of the brain may control a specific function, may compensate for some loss of tissue.

Head injuries are usually classified as concussions, or contusions, or lacerations. A **concussion** is a mild brain injury, typically caused by a blow to the head. Blood vessels in the brain are often ruptured, and circulatory and other brain functions may be disrupted temporarily. The person may become dazed or even lose consciousness and, on regaining consciousness, may experience postconcussion headaches, disorientation, confusion, and memory loss. In some cases, symptoms may persist for months or years, for unknown reasons, without neurological signs of impairment (Binder, 1986). The symptoms are usually temporary, lasting no longer than a few weeks.

In a **contusion**, the brain is forced to shift slightly and press against the side of the skull. The cortex of the brain may be bruised (that is, blood vessels may rupture) on impact with the skull. As in concussion, the person may lose consciousness for a few hours

Brain trauma is a physical wound or injury to the brain. Impairment ranges from mild to severe, depending on the extent and location of neural damage. Motorcyclists, especially those who do not wear helmets, are more likely to suffer brain injuries in accidents than people who drive cars.

or even for days. Postcontusion symptoms often include headaches, nausea, an inability to concentrate, and irritability. Although the symptoms are similar to those of concussion, they are generally more severe and last longer.

> Thirteen-year-old Ron G. was catcher for his school baseball team. During a game, one of the players from the other school's team accidentally lost his grip on the bat as he swung at a pitch. The bat hit Ron on the forehead. Although his catcher's mask absorbed some of the blow, the blow knocked Ron out. An hour elapsed before he regained consciousness at a nearby hospital, where he was diagnosed as having a cerebral contusion. Headaches, muscle weakness, and nausea continued for two weeks.

Lacerations are brain traumas in which brain tissue is torn, pierced, or ruptured, usually by an object that has penetrated the skull. When an object also penetrates the brain, death may result. If the person survives and regains consciousness, a variety of temporary or permanent effects may be observed. Symptoms may be quite serious, depending on the extent of damage to the brain tissue and on the amount of hemorrhaging. Cognitive processes are frequently impaired, and the personality may change.

More than eight million Americans suffer head injuries each year, and about 20 percent of these result in serious brain trauma. The majority show deficits in attention and poor concentration, are easily fatigued, and tend to be irritable (Webster & Scott, 1983). Emotional reactions are also displayed. In one study, the subjects were twenty-three patients with severe traumatic brain injuries (seventeen closed-head injuries, three penetrating missile wounds, two cerebral contusions, and one brain stem contusion) who had spent an average of 20 days in a coma. Every one displayed a distress syndrome characterized by depression, anxiety, tension, and nervousness—yet they all denied having these feelings (Sbordone & Jennison, 1983). It is, in fact, common for patients with severe traumatic injuries to deny emotional reactions and physical dysfunctions until they begin to recover from their injuries.

Closed-head injuries are the most common form of brain trauma and the most common reason why physicians refer patients under age forty to neurologists (Golden et al., 1983). They usually result from a blow that causes damage at the site of the impact and at the opposite side of the head. If the victim's head was in motion before the impact (as is generally the case in automobile accidents), the blow produces a forward-and-back movement of the brain, accompanied by tearing and hemorrhaging of brain tissue. Epilepsy develops in about 5 percent of closed-head injuries and in over 30 percent of open-head injuries in which the brain tissue is penetrated. Damage to brain tissues in the left hemisphere often results in intellectual disorders, and affective problems more frequently result from damage to brain tissues in the right hemisphere (Lishman, 1978).

Severe brain trauma has long-term negative consequences. Many young adults who are comatose for at least twenty-four hours later experience residual cognitive deficits that interfere with employment and psychosocial adjustment. Recovery from the trauma often does not ensure a return to the victim's premorbid level of functioning. Along with any physical or mental disabilities produced by the brain damage, motivational and emotional disturbances result from the frustration of coping with these physical or mental deficits. As a consequence, only one-third of patients with severe closed-head injuries can return to gainful employment after traditional rehabilitative therapy (Prigatano et al., 1984).

Newer treatment techniques seem more promising. In one approach, intensive cognitive retraining is combined with psychotherapeutic intervention. This program provides patients with increased awareness and acceptance of their injuries and residual deficits, cognitive retraining to counter selected residual deficits, a repertoire of compensatory skills, and understanding of their emotional and motivational disturbance. When patients in this program were compared with patients in a traditional program, the former showed better neuropsychological functioning, greater improvement in personality traits, and greater success at work (Prigatano et al., 1984).

Aging and Disorders Associated with Aging

Before discussing the organic mental disorders often associated with aging, it seems appropriate to describe the nature of the older population. In a report by the American Association of Retired Persons (1985), a growing proportion of the population is sixty-five years of age or older. This group represented about 12 percent (28 million) of the U.S. population in 1984, and it is expected to climb to 13 percent by the year 2000, and to 21 percent by 2030. The increase is attributable to increased life expectancy and the relatively large numbers of people, who will then be elderly, from the "baby boomer" generation who were born in the 1940s.

Some other characteristics are noteworthy. First, women outlive men; in 1984 there were 148 women for every 100 men in the older population, but the men were twice as likely to be married as were the women. Second, about one-fifth of the older population were poor or near-poor. Fully 89 percent were not working or seeking work. Third, statistics indicated that most older people have at least one chronic health condition and many have multiple conditions. The most frequent were arthritis (50 percent), hypertension (39 percent), hearing impairments (30 percent), heart conditions (26 percent), orthopedic impairments (17 percent), and cataracts and sinusitis (15 percent each). Although the report did not indicate mental disorders, Myers and his colleagues (1984) found that cognitive impairment in people sixty-five years and older was the highest for any age group. Thus, problems of the older population demand greater attention and research.

The organic disorders most common among the elderly are stroke and Alzheimer's disease. Although these conditions are correlated with aging, they also occur among younger people. DSM-III-R classifies certain degenerative dementias associated with aging as senile or presenile dementias, depending on age of onset (over sixty-five or sixty-five years of age and under).

Cerebrovascular Accidents or Strokes Although the brain represents only 2 percent of the body weight, it requires 15 percent of the blood flow and 20 percent of the oxygen used by the body (Oliver et al., 1982). A **stroke** or **cerebrovascular accident** is a sudden stoppage of blood flow to a portion of the brain, which leads to a loss of brain function.

Strokes are the third major cause of death in the United States, afflicting more than 400,000 people annually. Only about 50 to 60 percent of stroke victims survive, and they generally require long-term care while suffering from a variety of mental and sensory-motor disabilities (Oliver et al., 1982). (See Focus 16.2.) Stroke victims are often frustrated and depressed by their handicaps, and they show greater depression and interpersonal sensitivity than other

FOCUS 16.2 › *Aphasia*

Aphasia is the loss of motor or sensory functions that are associated with language. Aphasic people with motor disturbances may have trouble expressing themselves via verbal language (*speech aphasia*), be unable to recall the names of familiar objects (*nominal aphasia*), or have problems in writing words (*manual aphasia*). Sensory aphasias include the inability to understand spoken words (*auditory aphasia*) and the inability to understand written words (*visual aphasia* or *alexia*). Aphasic problems may be extremely specific. For example, people with visual aphasia cannot understand written words, although they can read the words aloud or understand spoken words.

Two primary problems in aphasia are (1) loss of access to words and their meanings and (2) inability to retain words and their meanings (Schuell, 1974). People with aphasia may become quite emotional and frustrated over their deficits, and this, in turn, can hinder rehabilitation.

The following dialogue illustrates some of the problems involved in aphasia. Albert Harris is a sixty-seven-year-old man who suffered a stroke. In addition to physical therapy for his partially paralyzed right side, an effort was made to rehabilitate his speech. Harris could not fully communicate, and expressed himself almost exclusively with the words "Mrs. Harris."

Psychologist: Hello, Mr. Harris.
Harris: (responding to psychologist): Hello, Mrs. Harris. Hello, Mrs. Harris.
Psychologist: You look pretty cheerful today.
Harris: Yes, Mrs. Harris. Ah . . . Ah . . . Ah (apparently trying to elaborate on his response) Yes, Mrs. Harris. Ah . . . Ah (looking disappointed and frustrated).
Psychologist: I know it's hard to say what you want to say.

Harris: Yes, Mrs. Harris, yes. Things will get better, Mrs. Harris.
Psychologist: You've already shown improvement, don't you think?
Harris: Mrs. Harris a little bit better, yes. Slow but sure, Mrs. Harris.

Speech therapy and skills training are frequently used to treat aphasia. Although many patients recover from the problem, the reasons for recovery are not well understood. Perhaps other areas of the brain can be trained to compensate for the damaged areas. A relatively new field, called *neurolinguistics,* is concerned with the relationship between language development and brain functioning and with the interrelationship among brain function, speech and language skills, cognitive capacities, and behavior (Blumstein, 1981).

---

groups of patients. Moreover, in many cases their depression seems to deepen with time (Magni & Schifano, 1984). Their anxiety about their disabilities occasionally leads to further disability.

The bursting of blood vessels (and the attendant intercranial hemorrhaging) causes 25 percent of all strokes and often occurs during exertion. Victims report feeling that something is wrong within the head, along with headaches and nausea. Confusion, paralysis, and loss of consciousness follow rapidly. Mortality rates for this type of stroke are extremely high.

Strokes may also be caused by the narrowing of blood vessels due to a buildup of fatty material on interior walls (*atherosclerosis*) or by the blockage of blood vessels. In either case, the result is *infarction*,

the death of brain tissue due to a decrease in the supply of blood. These strokes often occur during sleep, with the person being paralyzed when he or she awakens. Approximately 20 percent die, 20 percent exhibit full to nearly full recovery, and 60 percent suffer residual disabilities (Lishman, 1978).

The residual loss of function after a stroke usually involves only one side of the body, most often the left. Interestingly, one residual symptom of stroke is a "lack of acknowledgment" of various stimuli to one particular side. For example, a patient who is asked to copy a pattern may draw half the pattern, and may ignore, say, the left side of his or her body (Golden et al., 1983).

Some functional reorganization of the brain may occur after a stroke, to compensate for the loss of function. Three months after suffering a stroke due to cerebral infarction, one patient showed significantly reduced cerebral blood flow in one area. An examination performed one year later showed no abnormalities. However, the pattern of blood flow suggested increased activation in brain areas surrounding the affected area. It is possible that the patient's clinical improvement was due to brain reorganization in which the function of the destroyed area was taken over by other areas.

A series of infarctions may lead to a syndrome known as **multi-infarct dementia,** which is characterized by the uneven deterioration of intellectual abilities (although some mental functions may remain intact). The specific symptoms of this disruption depend on the affected area and the extent of the brain damage. Both physical and intellectual functioning are usually impaired. The patient may show gradual improvement in intellectual functioning, but repeated episodes of infarction can occur and produce additional disability.

Alzheimer's Disease   The disorder perhaps most often associated with aging is **Alzheimer's disease,** which involves the atrophy of cortical tissue within the brain and leads to marked deterioration of intellectual and emotional functioning. Irritability, cognitive impairment, and memory loss are early symptoms that gradually become worse. Social withdrawal,

depression, delusions, impulsive behaviors, neglect of personal hygiene, and other symptoms may eventually appear as well. Death usually occurs within five years of the onset of the disorder.

Autopsies performed on the brains of Alzheimer's victims reveal *neurofibrillary tangles* (abnormal fibers that appear to be tangles of brain tissue filaments) and *senile plaques* (patches of degenerated nerve endings). Both conditions are believed to disrupt the transmission of impulses among brain cells, thereby producing the symptoms of the disorder.

Alzheimer's disease is generally considered a disease of the elderly, and its incidence does increase with increasing age. However, it also can attack people in their forties or fifties. It occurs more frequently in women.

Elizabeth R., a forty-six-year-old woman diagnosed as suffering from Alzheimer's disease, is trying to cope with her increasing problems with memory. She writes notes to herself and tries to compensate for her difficulties by rehearsing conversations with herself, anticipating what might be said. However, she is gradually losing the battle and has had to retire from her job. She quickly forgets what she has just read, and she loses the meaning of an article after reading only a few sentences. She sometimes has to ask where the bathroom is in her own house and is depressed by the realization that she is a burden to her family. (Clark et al., 1984, p. 60).

The increasing deterioration of intellectual and emotional functioning, including memory loss, is perhaps the most debilitating aspect of Alzheimer's disease. Support groups try to help patients maintain their independence, sense of self-worth, and dignity by encouraging them to make personal decisions for themselves and to maintain social contacts.

The deterioration of memory seems to be the most poignant and disturbing symptom of Alzheimer's disease. The person may at first forget appointments, phone numbers, and addresses. As the disorder progresses, he or she may lose track of the time of day, have trouble remembering recent and past events, and forget who he or she is (Reisberg et al., 1982). But even when memory is almost gone, contact with loved ones is still important.

> I believe the emotional memory of relationships is the last to go. You can see daughters or sons come to visit, for example, and the mother will respond. She doesn't know who they are, but you can tell by her expression that she knows they're persons to whom she is devoted. (Materka, 1984, p. 13)

Dorothy Coons, whom Materka quoted in the preceding lines, works at the University of Michigan Institute of Gerontology. She notes that Alzheimer's disease is the fourth leading cause of death in the United States, and she predicts that by the year 2000 as many as 4 million people may be suffering this disorder (Materka, 1984). Yet even then, only about 2 to 3 percent of those in their sixties and seventies, and fewer than 15 percent of those in their nineties, are expected to be victims of Alzheimer's disease (Butler, 1984). Most will be living happy and enjoyable lives, as is indicated in Focus 16.3.

Memory Loss in the Elderly   As we have noted, memory loss is one of the most obvious symptoms of Alzheimer's disease. It is also a major symptom of **senile dementia,** a severe loss of intellectual functioning produced by brain cell deterioration as a result of aging—usually after age seventy-five. Loss of memory may also be shown by elderly people suffering multi-infarct dementia. And finally, occasional loss of memory is part of the normal aging process.

Because memory loss is associated with many disorders as well as normal aging, it is of concern to the elderly and yet difficult for clinicians to assess. Consider, for example, the following letter:

> Dear Dr. Smyer:
>
> I have toyed with the idea of writing you ever since I heard you speak at the Presbyterian Church a couple of years ago. The occasion was one of the series of brown-bag lunches sponsored, I think, by the Area Agency on Aging. You may remember me, since I'm sure you were embarrassed when I substituted one word for another in trying to ask a question about the part inheritance plays in senility. My question made no sense, and you tactfully said, "I don't believe I understand your question," and I repeated it, correctly, saying, "You can see I'm senile already." (I was trying to be funny, but I was not amused.)
>
> The question I asked is one that has haunted me all my adult life (I've just turned 78), and I think I have always known the answer. My father's father, my father, and the three sisters who lived long enough were all senile. I am obviously following in their footsteps, and have discussed the matter with Dr. Klein, who became my physician last year. I have told him that I have never taken much medication and have been opposed to "painkillers," tranquilizers, etc., but that the day may come when I will accept medical help as the lesser of two evils. He assures me that there are new drugs that may help.
>
> My question, Dr. Smyer, is this: Since I'm sure there must be ongoing research into the problem of senility, would it be of any value to such research if I volunteered as a test subject? At this point, my memory is failing so rapidly, and I suffer such frequent agonies of confusion, that I am at the point of calling on Dr. Klein for the help he has promised. But I don't want to do so yet if my experience can be of value to someone else, and particularly to the nine daughters of my sisters, ranging in age from 58 to 70, and to my own daughter, 42, who must be wondering if they too are doomed.
>
> Is there any merit to this proposal? I will be most grateful for any advice you can give me. (Smyer, 1984, p. 20)

From her clear, lucid writing and her recall of events that took place several years ago, it is obvious that the writer is not suffering from senility. Yet her occasional lapses of memory are causing her to become worried. Smyer points out that complaints of memory loss must be examined in light of the person's perception of the event, concurrent factors such as depression or anxiety that might contribute to memory problems, and actual memory behavior. If the Halstead-Reitan Neuropsychological Battery was employed, Gallagher et al. (1980) believe that most normal elderly subjects would be incorrectly identified as brain damaged, because no normative standards are established for their age group.

One of the most common reasons for memory loss and confusion in older patients is therapeutic drug intoxication. People may take several medica-

Is Mental Deterioration the Fate of the Elderly?

Losing cognitive and mental capabilities is the symptom of aging most feared by elderly people. One 82-year-old man commented,

> It's not the physical decline I fear so much. It's becoming a mental vegetable inside of a healthy body. It is a shame that we can rehabilitate or treat so much of the physical ills, but when your mind goes, there's nothing you can do. (Gatz et al., 1980, p. 12)

Reports of intellectual decline in aging have, in fact, been exaggerated. Although tests of intellectual functioning indicate that performance abilities generally start to decline with advancing age, verbal fluency and cognitive skills are usually quite stable over time (Gallagher et al., 1980). About 75 percent of older people retain sharp mental functioning, and an additional 10 to 15 percent experience only mild to moderate memory loss (Butler, 1984).

The vast majority of noninstitutionalized people aged sixty or more can live independently within the community. A statewide sample of 2,146 Virginians, aged sixty to over eighty-five and living in their own communities (rather than in institutions), was studied to determine the prevalence of mental disorders in the elderly population (Romaniuk et al., 1983). Information from questionnaires, self-ratings, and interviews indicated relatively little psychopathology. Only 6.3 percent displayed mild cognitive impairment, and 2.1 percent showed moderate to severe cognitive impairment. Only 15 percent displayed any signs of mental illness.

Most subjects seemed satisfied with their health: 13 percent rated their health as excellent, 46 percent as good, 31 percent as fair, and only 9 percent as poor. About 90 percent of the sample displayed "common sense," "mental alertness," and "coping ability." Over 75 percent said they enjoyed their lives.

---

tions that can interact with one another to produce negative side effects (Butler, 1984). Medication often has a stronger effect on older people and takes longer to be cleared from their bodies, yet dosages are often determined by testing on younger adults only. In addition, cardiac, metabolic, and endocrine disorders and nutritional deficiencies can produce symptoms resembling dementias.

Coping Techniques Like normal aging, the disorders associated with aging are generally irreversible. Nonetheless, there are a variety of means by which people with these disorders may be helped to live comfortably and with dignity while making use of those abilities that remain. The following interventions have been proposed by Butler.

1. To preserve the patient's sense of independence and control over his or her life, the environment must be modified to make it safer. Rails can be installed to allow the patient to move freely in the house. A chair that is easy to get into and out of, a remote-control device for the television set, and guard rails for the bathtub will help the patient do things for himself or herself. The patient should be encouraged to make as many personal decisions as possible—to choose which clothing to wear and which activities to take part in—even if the choices are not always perfect.

2. Continued social contacts are important, but visits by friends and relatives should be kept short so that the patient does not feel pressured to continue the social interaction. Visits should not involve large groups of individuals, which could tend to overwhelm the patient.

3. Diversions, such as going out for a walk, are important. It is better to stroll through a calm and peaceful area than to visit a crowded shopping mall, where the environment tends to be unpredictable.

4. Tasks should be assigned to the patient to increase his or her sense of self-worth. These tasks may not be completed to perfection, but they will provide a very important sense of having contributed. In addition, the elderly can be taught the use of memory aids and other strategies to facilitate remembering. (Butler, 1984, pp. 75–79)

Diseases and Infections of the Brain

A variety of diseases and infections result in brain damage. As a consequence, behavioral, cognitive, and emotional changes occur (including the development of organic brain syndromes).

Parkinson's Disease **Parkinson's disease** is a progressively worsening disorder characterized by muscle tremors, a stiff, shuffling gait, a lack of facial expression, and social withdrawal. Dementia and depression may develop. The disease is usually first diagnosed in people between the ages of fifty and sixty. In some cases the disorder stems from such causes as infections of the brain, cerebrovascular disorders, brain trauma, and poisoning with carbon monoxide; in other cases, a specific origin cannot be determined. Death generally follows within ten years of the onset of Parkinson's disease, although some patients have survived for twenty years or longer.

Parkinson's disease seems to be associated with lesions in the motor area of the brainstem and with a diminished level of dopamine in the brain. Treatment with L-dopa, which increases dopamine levels, relieves most of its symptoms (Lishman, 1978). Mohammad Ali's Parkinson-like condition is being treated with Sinemet and Symmetrel, which have the same effect.

Neurosyphilis (General Paresis) Syphilis is caused by the spirochete *Treponema pallidum,* which enters the body through contact with an infected person. This microorganism is most commonly transmitted from infected to uninfected people through intercourse or oral-genital contact. In addition, a pregnant woman can transmit the disease to the fetus, and the spirochete can enter the body through direct contact with mucous membranes or breaks in the skin. Within a few weeks, the exposed person develops a chancre, a small sore at the point of infection, as well as a copper-colored rash. If it is undetected or untreated, the infection spreads throughout the body. There may be no noticeable symptoms for 10 to 15 years after the initial infection, but eventually the body's organs are permanently damaged. In about 10 percent of untreated cases of syphilis, the spirochete directly damages the brain or nervous system, causing **general paresis.**

The most commonly described form of paresis, which includes approximately 18 percent of all cases, has grandiose characteristics: People display expansive and euphoric symptoms along with delusions of power or wealth. A depressive form has also been described, in which the affected person displays all the classic symptoms of depression.

The most frequent course for the illness begins with simple dementia, including memory impairment and early loss of insight. If the disorder remains untreated, the dementia increases, the occasional delusions fade away, and the patient becomes quiet, apathetic, and incoherent. Paralysis, epileptic seizures, and death usually occur within five years of the onset of symptoms.

If syphilis is treated early, however, clinical remission occurs and the patient often can return to work. After five years of treatment, more than half the patients with disorientation, convulsions, tremors, and euphoria generally lose their symptoms (Golden et al., 1983).

Encephalitis **Encephalitis,** or sleeping sickness, is a brain inflammation caused by a viral infection. It is not known whether the virus enters the central nervous system directly or whether the brain is hypersensitive to a viral infection at some other site in the body. One form, *epidemic encephalitis,* was widespread during World War I, but the disease is now very rare in the United States. It is still a problem, however, in certain areas of Africa and Asia.

Most cases follow a rapidly developing course that begins with headache, prostration (i.e., having to lie down), and diminished consciousness. Epileptic seizures are common in children with encephalitis, and they may be the most obvious symptom. Acute symptoms include lethargy, fever, delirium, and long periods of sleep and stupor. When wakeful, the victim may show markedly different symptoms: hyperactivity, irritability, agitation, and seizures. In contrast to past behaviors, a child may become restless, irritable, cruel, and antisocial. A coma, if there is one, may end abruptly. Usually a long period of physical and mental recuperation is necessary, and the prognosis can vary from no residual effects to profound brain damage (Golden et al., 1983).

Meningitis **Meningitis** is an inflammation of the *meninges,* the membrane that surrounds the brain and spinal cord. Research on meningitis is complicated by the fact that the disorder has three major forms. In the United States, there are approximately 400,000 cases of *bacterial meningitis* annually (Wasserman & Gromisch, 1981). This form generally begins with a localized infection that spreads, via the bloodstream, first to the meninges and then into the cerebrospinal fluid. *Viral meningitis,* which involves symptoms much less serious than those of the bacterial type, is associated with a variety of diseases, including mumps, herpes simplex, toxoplasmosis, syphilis, and rubella. *Fungal meningitis* usually occurs in children with such immunological deficiencies as leukemia.

The symptoms of meningitis vary with the age of the patient. In neonates and young infants, the symptoms are nonspecific (fever, lethargy, poor eating, and irritability), which makes diagnosis difficult (McCracken, 1976). In patients over one year old, symptoms may include stiffness of the neck, headache, and cognitive and sensory impairment. All three forms can produce cerebral infarction and seizures, but their incidence is much greater in the bacterial form than in the others (Edwards & Baker, 1981). The outcome is most serious when meningitis is contracted during the neonatal period.

Residual effects of the disorder may include partial or complete hearing loss as a result of cerebral infarction (Berlow et al., 1981), mental retardation, and seizures (Snyder et al., 1981). Meningitis also seems to attack the abstract thinking ability of some victims (Wright, 1978).

Huntington's Chorea **Huntington's chorea** is a rare, genetically transmitted disorder characterized by involuntary twitching movements and eventual dementia. Because it is transmitted from parent to child through an abnormal gene, approximately 50 percent of the offspring of an affected person develop this disorder. Huntington's chorea can't be treated, so the genetic counseling of afflicted people is extremely important in preventing its transmission.

The first symptoms usually occur as behavioral disturbances when the person is between the ages of twenty-five and fifty, although some are afflicted before age twenty (Brooks et al., 1987). The first physical symptoms are generally twitches in the fingers or facial grimaces. As the disorder progresses, these symptoms become more widespread and abrupt, now involving jerky, rapid, and repetitive movements.

Changes in personality and emotional stability also occur. For example, the person may become moody and quarrelsome (Golden et al., 1983).

Woody Guthrie, a well-known folk singer and the father of Arlo Guthrie, also a well-known singer, was a victim of Huntington's chorea. His first symptoms were increased moodiness and depression. Later he developed a peculiar manner of walking, and he found it difficult to speak normally. His inability to control his movements was often blamed on alcoholism. On one occasion, his apparent disorientation, his walking problems, and his disheveled appearance prompted police to arrest him. When his wife sought his release, she was met by a staff psychiatrist who said, "Your husband is a very disturbed man . . . with many hallucinations. He says that he has written a thousand songs." His wife responded by saying, "It is true." The psychiatrist went on: "He also says he has written a book." Guthrie's wife responded, "That is also true." Then the psychiatrist delivered the *coup de grace:* "He says that a record company has put out nine records of his songs!" The doctor's voice dripped disbelief. "That is also the truth," she replied (Yurchenco, 1970, pp. 147–148).

Huntington's chorea always ends in death, on the average from thirteen to sixteen years after the onset of symptoms. Early misdiagnoses are given in one-third to two-thirds of the cases; schizophrenia is the most common misdiagnosis (Lishman, 1978).

Cerebral Tumors

A **cerebral tumor** is a mass of abnormal tissue growing within the brain. The symptoms depend on which particular area of the brain is affected and on the degree to which the tumor increases intracranial pressure. Fast-growing tumors generally produce severe mental symptoms, whereas slow growth may result in few symptoms. Unfortunately, in the latter case, the tumor is often not discovered until death has occurred in a psychiatric hospital (Lishman, 1978). Tumors that affect the temporal area produce the highest frequency of psychological symptoms (Golden et al., 1983).

The most common symptoms of cerebral tumors are disturbances of consciousness, which can range from diminished attention and drowsiness to coma. People with tumors may also show mild dementia and other problems of thinking. Mood changes may also occur, as a result of either the direct physical impact of the tumor or the patient's reaction to the problem. Removing a cerebral tumor can produce dramatic results.

> The woman was admitted to a mental hospital, exhibiting dementia and confusion. She responded little to questioning by staff, or to attempts at therapy, even after twelve years of hospitalization. She would simply sit blindly, with her tongue protruding to the right, making repetitive movements of her right arm and leg. She also showed partial paralysis of the left side of her face.
>
> This "left-side, right-side" pattern of symptoms suggested that her condition might be due to a physical problem. Surgery was performed, and a massive brain tumor was discovered and removed. After the operation, the patient improved remarkably. She regained her speech and sight and was able to recognize and converse with her relatives for the first time in twelve years. (Hunter et al., 1968)

Epilepsy

Epilepsy is a general term that refers to a set of symptoms rather than to a specific etiology. In particular, **epilepsy** includes any disorder characterized by intermittent and brief periods of altered consciousness, often accompanied by seizures, and excessive electrical discharge from brain cells. It is the most common of the neurological disorders; 1 to 2 percent of the population has epileptic seizures at some time during their lives. It also seems to be one of the earliest recognized organic brain syndromes: Julius Caesar, Napoleon, Dostoevsky, and van Gogh are among those who presumably were epileptic.

Epilepsy is most frequently diagnosed during the first year of life. It can be symptomatic of some primary disorder of the brain without apparent etiology, or it can arise from such causes as brain tumors, injury, degenerative diseases, and drugs (Lishman, 1978). Epileptic seizures and unconsciousness may last anywhere from a few seconds to several hours; they may occur only a few times during the patient's entire life or many times in one day. And they may involve only a momentary disturbance of consciousness or a complete loss of consciousness—in which case they can be accompanied by violent convulsions

and a coma lasting for hours. Alcohol, lack of sleep, fever, a low blood sugar level, hyperventilation, a brain lesion or injury, or general fatigue can all induce an epileptic seizure. Particular musical notes, flickering lights, and emotionally charged situations have also been known to provoke epileptic attacks. Even everyday stress can bring on a seizure (Laidlaw & Rickens, 1976).

Epilepsy can often be controlled but it cannot be cured. Although epileptics usually behave and function quite normally between attacks, their chronic, long-term illness is still regarded with suspicion and repugnance by much of society. An attack can be frightening to the afflicted person and observers alike. Epileptics face fear and anxiety resulting from the unpredictable nature of their seizures. They are embarrassed by their seeming lack of control over their illness, and must deal with society's negative stereotypes concerning epilepsy (University of Minnesota, 1977). Perhaps as a result, approximately 30 to 50 percent of epileptics have accompanying psychological problems (Golden et al., 1983). We shall discuss four types of epilepsy. Each type is associated with a different type of seizure—petit mal, Jacksonian, psychomotor, and grand mal.

Petit Mal Seizures   **Petit mal** ("little illness") **seizures** involve a momentary dimming or loss of consciousness, sometimes with convulsive movements. During an attack, which usually lasts a few seconds, the epileptic displays a blank stare. There may be a fluttering of the eyelids or slight jerking movements, but in general there is little overall movement. After an attack, the epileptic may continue whatever he or she was doing, unaware that a seizure has occurred and that there was a momentary loss of consciousness.

Petit mal seizures are usually seen in children and adolescents; they rarely persist into adulthood. The following description highlights a common problem among petit mal epileptics.

> Jack D. is a sixteen-year-old student who was admitted to the outpatient psychiatric service of a large hospital to receive treatment for petit mal epilepsy. Jack and his parents explained that the seizures lasted only a few seconds each but occurred twenty to thirty times a day. His parents were especially concerned because Jack was very eager to get a driver's license;

driving a car would be quite dangerous if he were subject to momentary losses of consciousness. Jack was interviewed at a case conference where a group of mental health professionals, medical students, and paraprofessionals discussed his symptoms, the etiology of the disorder, the prognosis, and treatment.

During the fifteen-minute interview, Jack experienced two petit mal seizures. The first occurred while he was answering a question. A psychiatrist had asked Jack whether his seizures significantly handicapped him in school. Jack replied, "It really hasn't been that bad. Sometimes I lose track of what the teacher is . . ." At that point, Jack paused. He had a blank stare on his face, and his mouth was slightly opened. After about four seconds, he resumed speaking and said, "Uh, writing on the blackboard." A psychologist then asked Jack if he had noticed that he had paused in midsentence. Jack answered that he was not aware of the pause or the brief seizure. Interestingly, several of those present at the case conference later admitted that they too were unaware that a seizure had occurred at that time. They thought Jack's pause was due to an attempt to find the right words.

Later Jack had another seizure that went unnoticed by most of the interviewers. While the resident psychiatrist was elaborating on a question, Jack appeared to be listening. But when the psychiatrist finished, Jack had a puzzled look on his face. He said, "It [a seizure] happened again. I was listening to what you were saying and suddenly you were all finished. I must have blanked out. Could you repeat the question?"

Epilepsy refers to any disorder that is characterized by intermittent and brief periods of altered consciousness, often accompanied by seizures. It also seems to be one of the earliest recognized organic brain syndromes. Among those who suffered from the disease was Vincent van Gogh shown here in a self-portrait painted sometime after he had cut off his ear.

As you can see, such brief interruptions of consciousness may go unnoticed by people interacting with petit mal epileptics—and sometimes by the epileptics themselves. Fortunately the prognosis for Jack was good. Petit mal seizures usually disappear with age and can be controlled with proper medication and treatment.

Jacksonian Seizures Jacksonian seizures typically begin in one part of the body and then spread to other parts. For example, the hands or feet may first begin to twitch, then the whole arm or leg, and then other parts of the body. Usually the person doesn't completely lose consciousness unless the seizure spreads to the entire body. At this point, the convulsions resemble those of grand mal epilepsy. Jacksonian seizures are frequently due to a localized and specific brain lesion; surgical removal of the affected area can bring about recovery.

Psychomotor Seizures About 25 percent of epileptic seizures are psychomotor (Horowitz, 1970). **Psychomotor seizures** are characterized by a loss of consciousness during which the person engages in well-organized and normal-appearing behavioral sequences. For example, one psychomotor epileptic had an attack and lost consciousness while he was mowing his lawn. During the next hour, he went into his house, changed into swim trunks, and proceeded to take a swim in his pool. An hour later, when he came out of the "trance," he did not recall how he had gotten into the pool. His last memory was of mowing the lawn.

The disturbance in consciousness typically lasts for a brief period of time, usually just a few minutes; occasionally, however, it may affect someone for days. It was originally felt that many people were prone to violence during such seizures. However, violence is actually quite rare. It has been exaggerated because of some case reports in which violence was emphasized. This can be seen in the following report concerning a twenty-nine-year-old female psychomotor epileptic.

> There was a dramatic change in her affect following the onset of spells. The patient developed deepening emotions and reported a marked tendency to become angry about trivial events. Over the past two years sounds of even normal volume had led to angry outbursts in which she had smashed furniture or struck her cat. During a recent examination, this highly intelligent woman had become tearful and anxious while attempting rapid serial seven subtraction. She then turned to the examiner and said in a menacing voice, "You're lucky I didn't punch you in the face for making me do that." (Devinsky & Bear, 1984, p. 651)

Some investigators have suggested that there is a relationship between psychomotor epilepsy and psychotic or schizophrenic behaviors (Glaser et al., 1963; Stevens et al., 1969). The artist Vincent van Gogh is supposed to have cut off his ear during a psychomotor attack. And the defense attorneys for Jack Ruby, the man who killed Lee Harvey Oswald (the alleged assassin of President John F. Kennedy), argued in court that Ruby had epileptic seizures and consequently was not responsible for his actions. But such accounts provide a misleading view of epilepsy. In only a very few cases have acts of violence been related to epileptic seizures (Gunn & Fenton, 1971; Turner & Merlis, 1962).

Grand Mal Seizures   The most common and dramatic type of epileptic seizure is the **grand mal** ("great illness") **seizure.** Although this type usually lasts no longer than a few minutes, it typically consists of four distinct phases. A majority of grand mal epileptics report that they experience an *aura* (an usual sensory experience that provides a warning of an impending convulsion) before the loss of consciousness. The aura lasts only a few seconds and signals the onset of a seizure. During this first phase, the person feels physical or sensory sensations such as headaches, hallucinations, mood changes, dizziness, or feelings of unreality. During the *tonic* phase,

the individual becomes unconscious and falls to the ground. The muscles become rigid and the eyes remain open. During the third or *clonic* phase, jerking movements result from the rapid contraction and relaxation of body muscles. These movements may be so violent that epileptics bruise their heads on the ground, bite their tongues, or vomit. Fourth and finally, the muscles relax and a *coma* ensues, lasting from a few minutes to several hours. When the epileptic awakens, he or she may feel exhausted, confused, and sore. Some people report that they awaken relieved and refreshed.

Grand mal attacks may occur daily or be limited to only once to twice during an entire lifetime. In rare cases, grand mal attacks may occur in rapid succession (a condition known as *status epilepticus*), and result in death if untreated.

Etiological Factors   As we have noted, the epilepsies have been attributed to a wide range of factors. Somehow, these result in excessive neuronal discharge within the brain. Sometimes the discharge appears to be quite localized and to result in focal seizures or twitching in isolated parts of the body. Generalized seizures are presumably caused by general cortical discharge, and the effects involve the whole body.

Some researchers have investigated the hypothesis that genetic or personality factors predispose people to epilepsy. Evidence shows that the concordance rate for epilepsy is greater among identical than among fraternal twins, and that seizures are much more frequent among family members of an epileptic than among unrelated people (DeJong & Sugar, 1972; Jasper et al., 1969; Lennox & Lennox, 1960). However, heredity may not be a necessary or sufficient condition for the onset of epilepsy.

With respect to personality factors, no single type of personality has been associated with epilepsy (Tizard, 1962). Although personality disturbances are correlated with some epileptics, it is unclear whether personality factors predispose people to epilepsy or whether epilepsy influences personality development. Another possibility is that epileptics are under great stress because of their condition and because of the stigma attached to the disorder. This stress, rather than either the disorder or its causes, may affect the personalities of individuals who have epilepsy.

Psychoactive Substance-Induced Organic Mental Disorders

Using psychoactive substances (see Chapter 10) can result in organic mental disorders. Unlike psychoactive substance use disorders, the substance-induced organic mental disorders deal with the effects of the substances on the nervous system rather than with the behaviors associated with taking psychoactive substances. However, most people diagnosed as having an organic mental disorder involving psychoactive substances also have a use disorder. The most common psychoactive substances that can lead to organic mental disorders are alcohol (organic mental disorders associated with alcohol were discussed in Chapter 10), amphetamines, caffeine, marijuana, cocaine, hallucinogens, inhalants, nicotine, opioids, PCP, and sedatives.

Depending on the type of psychoactive substance, certain organic mental syndromes or symptom patterns can occur: intoxication (behavioral, cognitive, and mood changes after ingesting the substance), withdrawal (symptoms occurring when prolonged and heavy use of a substance has stopped), delirium and dementia (disorganized thinking, inability to attend to external stimuli, memory impairment, and confusion), delusions (false beliefs that defy credibility), and mood changes (for example, depression, elation, and anxiety caused by the substance use). The following case illustrates caffeine intoxication:

> Alan was an outgoing athletic, successful, 26-year-old graduate student with no history of anxiety symptoms. He needed to study research materials that were housed at another library. Because he had a tight deadline to meet, he decided to drive through the night in order to be at the library when it opened in the morning. To stay awake over an 8-hour period, he ingested substances such as coffee, cola, and No-Doz tablets for a total of about one gram of caffeine. After his arrival, he had a major panic attack. (Rosenbaum, 1986)

TREATMENT CONSIDERATIONS

Because organic mental disorders can be caused by many different factors, a wide variety of treatment approaches have been used. The major approaches include surgery, medication, skills training, cognitive preparation, psychotherapy, and environmental intervention. Surgical procedures may be used to remove cerebral tumors, relieve the pressure caused by tumors, or restore ruptured blood vessels. Drugs can control or reduce the symptoms of brain disorders. Psychotherapy may help patients deal with the emotional aspects of these disorders. And some patients who have lost motor skills can be retrained to compensate for their deficiencies or can be retaught these skills. Sometimes, patients with organic brain disorders need complete hospital care.

The cognitive therapeutic approaches appear to be particularly promising. As an example, researchers have hypothesized that the impaired attention and concentration shown by head-injured people result from the disruption of *private speech,* which regulates behavior and thought processes (Luria, 1982). One therapeutic program uses self-instructional training to enhance the self-regulation of speech and behavior (Webster & Scott, 1983). The program was used to treat a 24-year-old construction worker who had been in a coma for four days as a result of a car accident. Tests showed him to have poor recall, poor concentration, and attentional difficulties; he couldn't concentrate on any task for a long period of time. He also complained that intrusive nonsexual thoughts kept him from maintaining an erection during intercourse.

The patient was told to repeat the following self-instructions aloud before doing anything:

1. "To really concentrate, I must look at the person speaking to me."

2. "I also must focus on what is being said, not on other thoughts which want to intrude."

3. "I must concentrate on what I am hearing at any moment by repeating each word in my head as the person speaks."

4. "Although it is not horrible if I lose track of conversation, I must tell the person to repeat the information if I have not attended to it." (Webster & Scott, 1983, p. 71)

After he had learned to use these vocalized instructions (actually, he rephrased them in his own words), he was taught to repeat them subvocally before each

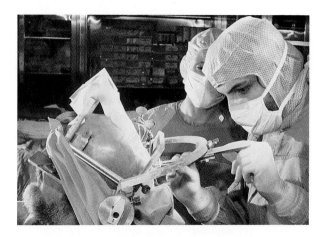

Brain surgery is often necessary to remove cerebral tumors or to restore ruptured blood vessels in the brain. Surgical procedures can be very complicated, requiring a great deal of preparation by the surgical team.

task. He soon improved greatly in concentration and attention and returned to his former job. He also successfully blocked intrusive thoughts during sexual intercourse, by focusing on his partner.

A similar program was developed to eliminate the anger response brain-injured people sometimes display, either as a result of the brain damage or in reaction to their deficits. One 22-year-old patient had suffered a severe head trauma in a motorcycle accident, at age sixteen. After two months of intensive medical treatment, he had returned home to live with his parents. There he showed outbursts of anger toward people and objects, a low frustration level, and impulsiveness. These behaviors led to many failures in a vocational rehabilitation program. Medication didn't help control his outbursts.

A stress inoculation program was developed for this patient. Twelve 30-minute sessions, spread over three weeks, trained him in the following areas:

1. *Cognitive preparation* The function and appropriateness of anger were explained, as were alternatives to being destructive. The situations that produced anger were identified, and appropriate responses were demonstrated.

2. *Skills acquisition* The patient was taught to stop himself from becoming angry, to reevaluate anger-evoking situations, and to use self-verbalizations that were incompatible with the expression of anger.

3. *Application training* A hierarchy of situations evoking anger was developed. The patient role-played and practiced the use of cognitive and behavioral skills to cope with progressively greater anger-evoking stimuli. He also used these techniques in the hospital setting and received feedback about his performance.

Before treatment, the patient had averaged about three outbursts each week. No outbursts at all were recorded immediately after treatment, and a follow-up five months later indicated that the gain had been maintained. He found a part-time job as a clerk and was living independently.

Medication is of the most benefit in controlling some symptoms of organic disorders. For example, about 50 percent of all epileptics can control their seizures with medication; another 30 percent can reduce the frequency of seizures. Only 20 percent of epileptics don't find medications helpful (Epilepsy Foundation of America, 1982).

An interesting seizure prevention program using classical conditioning was reported by Efron (1956, 1957). For example, one woman, suffering from grand mal seizures, learned to prevent the occurrence of the tonic (body extended and stiff) and clonic (rapid alternation of muscle contraction and relaxation) phases by sniffing an unpleasant odor during the initial stage of an attack. The odor was first presented to the woman while she stared at a bracelet. After the smell was paired with the bracelet over a period of several days, the bracelet alone was enough to elicit thoughts of the unpleasant odor. At that point the patient could stop a seizure by staring at her bracelet when she felt the attack starting. Eventually she could cut an attack short by just thinking about the bracelet. Other behavior modification and biofeedback techniques have also been helpful in reducing seizure activity (Mostofsky & Balaschak, 1977).

SUMMARY

1. The left hemisphere of the brain is generally associated with language functions, whereas the right hemisphere is associated with visual-spatial functions. Although each hemisphere shows some specialization,

evidence also shows that lost functions can be regained—especially in a young brain that hasn't yet fully specialized.

2. The effects of organic brain damage vary greatly. The most common symptoms (organic mental syndromes) include impaired consciousness and memory, impaired judgment, orientation difficulties, and personality changes. The effects can be acute (often temporary) or chronic (long term); the causes can be endogenous (internal) or exogenous (external); and the tissue damage can be diffuse or specific (localized). Assessing brain damage is complicated by the fact that its symptoms are often similar to those of functional disorders.

3. Many different agents can cause organic mental syndromes (when the organic cause is known or presumed, it is considered an organic mental disorder); among these are physical wounds or injuries to the brain, processes of aging, diseases that destroy brain tissue (such as neurosyphilis and encephalitis), and brain tumors. Epilepsy, which is an organic mental syndrome, is characterized by intermittent and brief periods of altered consciousness, frequently accompanied by seizures, and excessive electrical discharge by neurons. Psychoactive substances can also cause organic mental syndromes.

4. Treatment strategies include corrective surgery, cognitive training, behavior modification, and psychotherapy. Medication is often used, either alone or with other therapies, to decrease or control the symptoms of the various organic brain disorders.

KEY TERMS

Alzheimer's disease An organic brain disorder that involves the atrophy of brain tissue and leads to marked deterioration of intellectual and emotional functioning

autonomic nervous system The system responsible for regulating the body's internal environment, such as the heart, intestines, and endocrine glands; composed of the sympathetic and parasympathetic systems

brain trauma A physical wound or injury to the brain

central nervous system The brain and spinal cord, which coordinate all activities of the nervous system of vertebrates

cerebral blood flow measurement A technique for assessing brain damage in which the patient inhales radioactive gas and the movement of the substance is followed throughout the brain.

cerebrovascular accident A sudden stoppage of blood flow to a portion of the brain, leading to a loss of brain function; also called *stroke*

computerized axial tomography (CAT) A neurological test for the assessment of brain damage, which uses x-rays and computer technology

delirium A syndrome in which there is a reduced ability to attend to external stimuli, difficulty in shifting attention, and disorganized thinking

dementia A syndrome characterized by the deterioration of brain tissue resulting in decreased intellectual ability and impaired judgment, of sufficient severity to interfere with social and occupational functioning

electroencephalograph (EEG) A neurological test for the assessment of brain damage, which measures electrical activity of brain cells

epilepsy Any disorder characterized by intermittent and brief periods of altered consciousness, often accompanied by seizures, and excessive electrical discharge from brain cells

functional disorder A mental disorder for which no physical basis can be found and that is assumed to be due primarily to psychological factors

magnetic resonance imaging (MRI) A technique to assess brain functioning, using a magnetic field and radio waves to produce pictures of the brain

multi-infarct dementia An organic brain syndrome characterized by uneven deterioration of intellectual abilities and resulting from a number of cerebral infarctions

organic mental disorder Behavioral disturbances that result from organic brain pathology—that is, damage to the brain

organic mental syndrome A pattern of psychological or behavioral signs or symptoms associated with organic causes

Parkinson's disease A progressively worsening organic brain disorder characterized by muscle tremors, a stiff, shuffling gait, a lack of facial expression, and social withdrawal

positron emission tomography (PET) A technique for assessing brain damage in which the patient is injected with radioactive glucose and the metabolism of the glucose is monitored

chapter 17
Disorders of Childhood and Adolescence

The disorders of childhood and adolescence encompass a wide variety of behavioral problems, ranging from the pervasive developmental disorders, which may severely affect many aspects of development and are clearly abnormal, to the less severe developmental disturbances, which are exaggerations of behavior problems shown by most children. Over 11 percent of children in the United States, or about 8 million, have a mental health problem. Under 50 percent receive any form of treatment (Saxe et al., 1988). Children and adolescents are, in fact, subject to many of the "adult" disorders discussed in previous chapters. Here, we discuss only problems that arise primarily during the earlier stages of life. We begin with two severe disturbances that were formerly known as childhood psychoses; then we examine several less disabling disorders of childhood and adolescence. Eating disorders tend to develop during adolescence and are also discussed in this chapter.

PERVASIVE DEVELOPMENTAL DISORDERS

In the past, severe disturbances that led to bizarre behaviors in children were given such labels as childhood schizophrenia and childhood psychosis. However, there are distinct differences between the **pervasive developmental disorders** and the psychotic conditions observed in adolescents and adults. For example, the former do not include such symptoms as hallucinations, delusions, the loosening of associations, and incoherence. A child showing these symptoms would probably be diagnosed as schizophrenic. Other differences between schizophrenia and the pervasive developmental disorders are noted in Table 17.1.

The pervasive developmental disorders are severe childhood disorders that affect psychological functioning in such areas as language, social relationships, attention, perception, and affect. They include both autistic disorder and pervasive developmental disorder not otherwise specified, a category new to DSM-III-R. These impairments are not simply delays in development but rather are distortions that would not be normal at any developmental stage. They are quite rare—about four to seven cases in every 10,000 children. These disorders occur three or four times more frequently in boys than in girls (Wing & Gould, 1979; Gillberg, 1984, 1988).

A diagnosis of *pervasive developmental disorder not otherwise specified* is given to people who do not meet the full criteria for autistic disorder but who are nevertheless impaired in their social interactions and verbal and nonverbal skills. Little research exists on children diagnosed with this disorder. In addition, there is little information on its etiology. Because of this we will direct most of our attention to the causes and treatment of autism.

Autism

At age four, Jerry was diagnosed as suffering from Kanner syndrome (autistic disorder), a severe and pervasive developmental disorder.

As a child, Jerry showed little responsiveness to mothering, refused new foods, cried out at loud noises, and made exaggerated negative responses to certain odors. His speech development was slow and unusual, and his speech didn't seem aimed at communicating. Very early, Jerry showed a fondness for classical music. And, although he didn't seem to understand the meanings of words, he memorized an amazing number of song lyrics.

Jerry was fascinated with spinning things. He would spend hours spinning various objects or watching records spin on his parents' phonograph. When his mother took him to nursery school each day (he didn't acknowledge her leaving), he spent his entire time there spinning objects. Changes in his routine and moving things around in his room provoked strong emotional outbursts. In the third grade, Jerry became very interested in mathematics, and he spent hours writing multiplication tables.

Now thirty-one years old, Jerry describes his childhood as having been filled with confusion and terror. He felt that he was "living in a frightening world that was unpredictable and painful. Noises were unbearably loud and sounds were overpowering. Nothing seemed to be constant." Dogs were especially frightening—he thought they were somehow humanoid and

TABLE 17.1 | **Differences Between Schizophrenia and Pervasive Developmental Disorders**

Schizophrenia (Childhood Onset)	Pervasive Developmental Disorders
Hallucinations	Poor eye contact
Delusions	Disinterest in people
Unusual thought content	Poor playing skills
Loosening of associations	Marked resistance to change
Blunt affect	Gross deficits in language
Family background with schizophrenia	Majority have mental retardation
Equally common in males and females	Four times more common in males than females

SOURCE: Adapted from Lord & Ward, 1984.

yet not really human. Children also scared him, because he could never understand or predict their behavior.

Jerry's growing recognition that he was different from others made his adolescence extremely painful. He wanted social contact but couldn't behave appropriately; as a result, he was usually rejected or ignored. His feelings of isolation are reflected in his responses to the Thematic Apperception Test. For example, shown a picture of a boy staring at a violin, Jerry responded, "He will have to spend the rest of his life alone in agony."

Jerry now has a job completing fiscal efficiency reports. He functions well if he is given explicit instructions, but he can't be relied on to use "common sense." Some verses he wrote when he was fifteen reflect the sense of isolation and confusion that he still feels today at age thirty-six:

I prayed to the Lord
That he show me a path
I waited for his work
He guided me to the subject of math.
The people envy me now and then
As the Lord guided me thru this thunderous world
I like numbers, decimal points and fractions.
Many equations, I learned to create
With multiplications, additions and subtractions
I see mathematics will be my fate. (Bemporad, 1979, p. 188)

In 1943 Leo Kanner, a child psychiatrist, described a group of children who shared certain symptoms with other psychotic children but who also displayed some unique behaviors. Kanner called the syndrome *infantile autism,* from the Greek *autos* ("self"), to reflect the profound aloneness and detachment of these children. A highly unusual symptom of autistic children is their extreme lack of responsiveness to adults: "The child is aware of people . . . but considers them not differently from the way he (or she) considers the desk, bookshelf, or filing cabinet" (Kanner & Lesser, 1958, p. 659).

The puzzling symptoms displayed by the children Kanner described fit the diagnostic criteria for **autistic disorder** in DSM-III-R. Impairment is found in three major areas (American Psychiatric Association, 1987; Maltz, 1982; Rutter, 1983; Weeks & Hobson, 1987):

Social Interactions Autistic children are unaware of other people's feelings. Even when an autistic

Children suffering from autism are profoundly alone. Their unresponsiveness to adults, lack of bonding to parents and others, and language and speech deficits keep them locked in a socially isolated world.

child looks at someone, that looking does not seem to be for the purpose of finding out what the person is feeling. They do not need physical contact with or emotional response from their caretakers. They interact with other people as if people were unimportant objects and show little interest in establishing friendships, imitating behaviors, or playing games. Autistic infants are usually content to be left alone and don't show an anticipatory response to being picked up.

Verbal and Nonverbal Communication About 50 percent of autistic children do not develop speech. Those who do generally show oddities such as *echolalia* (echoing what has previously been said). One child constantly repeated the words "How do you spell relief?" without any apparent reason. In addition, the child may reverse pronouns. For example, "you" might be used for "I," and "I" for "me." Even when they can speak, such children may be unable to, or unwilling to, initiate conversations.

Activities and Interests Autistic children engage in a limited number of activities. They often have unusual repetitive habits such as spinning objects, whirling themselves, or fluttering or flapping their arms. They may show intense interest in symbolic self-induced sounds or in staring at their hands and fingers. They may stare into space and be totally self-absorbed. Minor changes in the environment may produce rages and tantrums. Autistic children show a lack of imaginary activities. They rarely engage in behaviors such as caring for a doll, talking on a "telephone," or drinking from an empty cup (Atlas & Lapidus, 1987).

Jerry, the autistic person described earlier, showed many of these characteristics. During adolescence, for example, he saw that he differed from other people, and he could not understand the viewpoint of others. Once, during a trip to Mexico with his parents, Jerry "took off" by himself for most of a day without saying where he was going. When he returned, he simply could not understand the frantic search that his parents had conducted.

As an adult, Jerry still lacks social awareness. When he is with his parents (his only social contacts), he spends his time silently watching television in their presence. He has no ability whatsoever to make

Even though autistic children often display unusual abilities, their IQs tend to be below average. In addition, their performance on IQ tests is not uniform. Although they might do well on subtests that require drawing, puzzle construction, or rote memory, they tend to do poorly on subtests that require verbal skills, language skills, and symbolic thinking.

"small talk." Jerry's need for sameness also remains, although it has shifted to accommodate adult activities. Taking a shower requires about two hours, because Jerry must first make sure that every item in the bathroom is in its "proper" place, and he has to wash himself in a certain prescribed pattern. Jerry reports having no daydreams, and he does not engage in leisure activities.

Bemporad (1979), who has described Jerry's behaviors in detail, concluded that "He remains an isolated, mechanical being, unable to intuit the social nuances of behavior and therefore forced to retreat from a world that is persistently surprising and lacking in regularity" (p. 195). This lack of social empathy was also evident in another autistic adult who complained that he could not "mind-read." He felt that most people had this capacity because they seemed to know how others would respond. He, however, could never predict how others would react until they actually did so (Rutter, 1983).

Up to three-fourths of autistic children have IQs below 70. High-functioning autistic people such as Jerry or the character played by Dustin Hoffman in the movie, *Rain Man,* account for only a minority of people with this disorder. (See Focus 17.1.) Only about 20 percent have average to above-average intelligence (Maltz, 1982; Gillberg, 1988). In the past, some theorists, including Kanner, believed that these children were unusually bright, primarily because some of them display *splinter skills*—often doing well with drawings, puzzle construction, and rote memory but poorly with verbal tasks and tasks requiring language skills and symbolic thinking. Second, they often display unusual abilities, such as Jerry's memorization of an "amazing" number of song lyrics at the age of three or Rain Man's ability to accurately count toothpicks as they spilled from a box.

Mentally retarded autistic children who score overall in the mentally retarded range on IQ tests but who have specific and unusual abilities have been described as autistic savants. In a survey of over 5,400 autistic children, 10 percent had such special talents. One child who had a talent for arithmetic was asked for the product of 6,427 and 4,234. According·to Rimland (1978 p. 69),

> Arthur turned his head in my direction and said, slowly but without hesitation, "27,211,918." His voice was stilted but precise. His eyes never lost their blank stare, and now he returned to gazing

FOCUS 17.1 The Original "Rain Man"

When screenwriter Barry Morrow first met Kim, his original model for the central character in "Rain Man," Kim already knew Morrow's past and present phone numbers and the number of freeway exits to his house.

They met in Texas where Kim and his father, Fran, were attending a 1984 meeting of the American Association of Retarded Citizens. Kim, 37, is an extremely rare prodigious savant, capable of recalling virtually anything his senses have ever told him.

But while Kim has a seemingly unlimited ability to absorb and recall facts and figures, he has limited reasoning power and his IQ is a below-average 88. He always has lived with Fran in the Salt Lake City area, accompanying him on frequent business trips since Fran and Kim's mother divorced in 1981.

"I am Rain Man," Kim said in an interview. "This is an important time for me. I have many talents now."

Morrow, who calls Kim "an island of genius," believes the movie has changed Kim.

"When I first met him, after he talked to me he dashed across the room and made low moaning sounds," Morrow said. "Now, he would walk into a room and offers you his hand."

Kim's father, who asked for privacy reasons that his and Kim's last name not be used, agrees that his son is changing. After a special screening of "Rain Man" for the Utah Legislature, Kim stood up and stressed the importance of understanding the needs of the handicapped.

"I had no idea he could talk to those guys that way," Fran said. "He is really learning to put his thoughts together."

Coincidentally, Fran and Kim were rolling down the freeway when they heard the news that "Rain Man" had been nominated for eight Academy Awards, including best picture and best actor.

Kim has seen the movie three times, the first seated at the premier between Morrow and Fran. Kim stared at his hands and the floor during most of the movie. When Morrow asked him why, Kim told him he had seen it with his heart.

While there are behavioral similarities between Kim and Hoffman's film character, Kim is far more outgoing. Two years ago he spent an afternoon with Hoffman on a movie set, the actor mimicking his movements and his walk.

When it was over, Kim recalls, Hoffman said, "I may be the star, but you are the heavens."

Daniel Christensen, medical director of the Western Institute of Neuropsychiatry at the University of Utah, has made a thorough study of Kim.

"He has a photographic memory, but no way to minimize stimuli," Christensen said. "He's the closest I've seen to a human computer," unable to filter or forget information, or assign it relative importance.

He can answer untold thousands of questions covering history, sports, maps, literature, mathematics and other subjects.

SOURCE: Abridged from Israelsen, 1987.

into space, without seeing anything, a handsome, impassive eight-year-old.

Another child could tell the day of the week on which any specific date—past or future—would fall. The special abilities most frequently found in autistic children involved music (such as playing a large number of songs), rote memory, drawings, and mathematics.

Diagnosis   Autism might seem to be relatively easy to diagnose, given its relatively unique characteristics. Yet, the opposite is true. One sample of 48 parents of autistic children had difficulty obtaining an accurate diagnosis. Of the many diagnoses received by the children, only two indicated autism. The most frequent diagnoses were mental retardation, hearing impairment, brain damage, and emotional disturbances. In 12 percent of the cases, a correct diagnosis was not given until the child was at least eight years old (Michigan Society for Autistic Citizens, 1979). The diagnosis of autism remains a major problem, primarily because it shares a number of characteristics with other disorders. In addition, symptoms vary widely among autistic children, especially with regard to developmental age and level of functioning (Maltz, 1982).

Because most autistic children are mentally retarded, they are often diagnosed only as retarded. However, there are ways to distinguish children with both autism and mental retardation from children with just mental retardation. For example, the former group exhibits splinter skills much more often than the latter group. Also children with mental retardation are more likely to relate to others and to be socially aware than are autistic children with both autism and mental retardation.

Research on Autism   In this section, we consider some of the recent research investigating social unresponsiveness and the unusual communication patterns of autistic children.

Hobson (1987) was interested in the social unresponsiveness of autistic children and wanted to find out if such children noticed people's age and gender. Even very young infants can distinguish between male and female, and between child and adult, an ability that may indicate responsiveness and attention to social cues. Autistic children, however, have been described as more interested in inanimate objects than in humans. Seventeen autistic and seventeen nonautistic matched control children were exposed to videotapes of nonhuman stimuli (bird, dog, train, and car) and people (boy, girl, man, and woman). The stimuli were presented one at a time. Before, during, and after the videotaped presentations, the children were asked to match the object or person with five schematic drawings. Both the autistic and control children correctly matched videotapes of nonhuman stimuli with the schematic drawings at least 75 percent of the time. However, on the videotapes involving people, autistic children were highly inaccurate in choosing the correct face while control children continued to achieve 75 percent accuracy. Autistic children do appear to be inattentive to human characteristics. They have difficulty responding to people according to qualities such as age or sex. Hobson cites an example of a middle-aged autistic man who talks to babies, children, and elderly people with the same style of speech. This lack of social attentiveness has been demonstrated experimentally but the reason for it has not been determined.

Impaired communication is another characteristic of autistic children. They may have tantrums, engage in self-injurious behaviors, repeat what is said to them (echolalia), or repeat phrases that are out of context. Could these behavior patterns be primitive attempts at communication? Certain patterns were noticed by Carr and Durand (1987); for example,

- A 14-year-old autistic boy has temper tantrums whenever his teacher attempts to give him a lesson. The tantrums are so severe that the teacher must wear gloves and a heavy coat to protect himself. After 10 minutes, the teacher gives up. Then Bob, the autistic boy, begins to hum.

- An autistic child scratches himself badly. This occurs even when he is constantly nagged at by his parents. Interestingly, he stops scratching when his parents pay attention to something else.

Carr and Durand feel that these behaviors can be understood as a need for attention or the desire to avoid a task.

The view that "unusual" behaviors may represent attempts to communicate was suggested by

Durand and Crimmins (1987). A nine-year-old autistic child was referred by his teacher because of his nonsensical speech. Although the child could speak appropriately, he often repeated phrases that were out of context or did not make sense (such as "fried eggs on your head"). Attempts to control this behavior by ignoring and reinforcing appropriate speech were ineffective. The researchers hypothesized that this behavior might represent an attempt to indicate stress from classroom tasks. An alternative means to escape was provided. The child was trained to say, "Help me," whenever the task demands were increased. This response was followed by teacher assistance. With this procedure, psychotic speech was greatly reduced during tasks. Understanding this mode of communication is important for successful treatment. If the misbehavior is a communication to avoid a task, a procedure using time out from a lesson may increase the problem behavior. Also, children can be taught appropriate ways to elicit attention, such as asking, "Am I doing a good job?" or "See what I have done." If the task is difficult, the child can be taught to say, "Help me" or "I don't understand." Such research supports the view that some behavioral patterns in autistic children are attempts to communicate.

Although we are learning more about the symptoms of autism, many questions remain. What causes the bizarre and puzzling abnormalities that are seen in autistic children? Why do they occur so early in life? In the following section, we consider the causes of autism.

Etiology

Autism is a syndrome, and a number of factors cause or contribute to it (Folstein & Rutter, 1988; Gillberg, 1988; Volkmar et al., 1988). Because of the early age of onset, lack of normal development, and distinct cognitive deficits, researchers increasingly acknowledge that autism results from organic rather than psychosocial factors.

Psychoanalytic Theories Psychodynamic theories of autism stress the importance of deviant parent-child interactions in producing withdrawal and rejection. Some theories acknowledge the existence of congenital vulnerabilities that predispose children to develop autism under psychological stress.

According to Bettelheim (1967), an autistic child denies self-identity as a defense against the trauma of parental rejection. When the child experiences such rejection (which is most crucial during the first year of life), withdrawal into an inner fantasy world affords some protection. This withdrawal is so complete that the autistic child seems oblivious to events in the external world. Because of their general lack of responsiveness and their total involvement in a fantasy world, Bettelheim characterizes autistic children as "empty fortresses."

The psychogenic theories of autism are based on case studies and clinical judgments that are subject to error. More carefully controlled studies do not support the view that parents of autistic children are emotional refrigerators; they score in the normal range of the Minnesota Multiphasic Personality Inventory (MMPI) and do not differ from comparison groups of parents with handicapped and normal children (Koegel et al., 1983; Schopler et al., 1979; McAdoo & DeMeyer, 1978). In fact, the evidence supporting the parent-causation hypothesis is so sparse that Koegel and his colleagues suggest that little is to be gained from further study in this area.

Psychological factors are implicated in many disorders, but they do not seem to be involved in autism. Unfortunately, many mental health professionals continue to inflict guilt on parents who already bear the burden of raising an autistic child. In light of current research, no justification exists for allowing parents to think they caused their child's autism.

Family and Genetic Studies Few family or genetic studies have been conducted on autism. This is not surprising because the disorder is so rare. The studies that have been done are methodologically flawed. First let's consider the evidence from family studies.

About 2 percent of siblings of autistic children also are autistic—50 times greater than in the general population (Gottesman & Shields, 1982). Twin studies also support a genetic connection. For example, among forty pairs of twins, the concordance rate for autism was 95.7 percent in MZ twins (twenty-two of twenty-three pairs) and 23.5 percent in DZ twins (four of seventeen) (Ritvo et al., 1985). Such studies strongly support a genetic hypothesis. However, in a review of genetic studies of autism, Folstein and Rutter (1988) say that methodological flaws in the genetic studies tend to inflate concordance figures. For example, there is the possibility of selection bias. In the Ritvo et al. study, for example, a selection factor was probably in operation since more MZ twins than DZ twins were studied. Also, twin pairs in which both twins have the disorder are more likely to be reported than twins who are discordant. Such problems may result in an overestimate of genetic influence.

A well-controlled twin study was performed by Folstein and Rutter (1977). They recruited DZ and MZ twins who were both discordant and concordant; that is, in some pairs both twins were autistic, in others only one twin was. Zygosity was determined through blood analysis, and diagnoses were made without knowing who the twin's siblings were or whether they were DZ or MZ. The concordance rate for twenty-one pairs of twins was 36 percent for MZ twins and 0 percent for DZ twins. Although this concordance rate is lower than reported by Ritvo and his colleagues (1985), the results still support a genetic hypothesis. An interesting finding of the Folstein and Rutter study is that seven of the discordant twins showed some language impairment—one characteristic of autism. The researchers believe that this supports the idea that some type of inherited cognitive impairment is associated with autism. Supporting this view is the finding that 15 percent of the siblings of autistic children have some form of language disorder, learning disability, or mental retardation (August et al., 1981). Folstein and Rutter also say that the diathesis-stress model could account for some of their findings. Among the seventeen disconcordant twin pairs, twelve cases involved a birth complication for the autistic twin. So a predisposition interacting with an environmental stressor may result in the disorder.

Central Nervous System Impairment   As mentioned earlier, autistic disorder seems to be associated with a number of organic conditions. Conditions such as the fragile X chromosome, tuberous sclerosis (a congenital hereditary disease associated with brain tumors), neurofibromatosis (tumors of the peripheral nerves), phenylketonuria (PKU), and intrauterine rubella (measles) have been reported among children with autistic disorder (fragile X and PKU are discussed in Chapter 18). All these diseases affect the central nervous system, but most people with these conditions do not develop autism. Because cognitive and lan-

guage deficits are a major characteristic of autism, attention has been directed to the left hemisphere, which is associated with these functions (Prior, 1984). A plausible hypothesis is that autism only develops when the brain part responsible for the syndrome is affected.

A recent study indicates that in some cases the disorder may result from underdevelopment of the cerebellum region known as the *vermis*. Courchesne et al. (1988) used magnetic resonance imaging (MRI) to study the brains of eighteen autistic children and adults, and compared their scans with those of control subjects. Certain areas of the vermis were significantly smaller. The researchers hypothesize that these brain areas may be associated with the cognitive dysfunctions found in autism. Replication is needed with other autistic samples, but increasing evidence suggests that central nervous system impairment is involved in the etiology of autism.

Biochemical Studies   Interpretations of research on biochemical factors in autism are difficult to make because different intellectual and behavioral measures are often used. In addition, different subgroups of autistic people may be studied. DuVergals et al. (1988) found that some autistic children have elevated serotonin and dopamine levels. Ritvo et al. (1984) also reported elevated serotonin levels in a group of autistic patients they studied. The significance of the role neurotransmitters play in autism is not clear, but it suggests a promising line of research.

Physiological Overarousal   Can such behaviors as avoiding eye contact and withdrawing from social relationships reflect a homeostatic response that helps autistic children avoid overstimulation? Compared to normal and mentally retarded controls, autistic children show greater physiological reaction to novel stimuli and slower habituation to those stimuli (Zentall & Zentall, 1983). Many bizarre symptoms of autism may indicate attempts to block incoming stimulation.

Perceptual Handicaps   The unresponsiveness of autistic children, who often seem to be deaf or blind, has been attributed to *overselective attention* (Lovaas et al., 1979). For example, during imitation training an autistic child may be exposed to both auditory and visual cues. The therapist may ask the child to say "ah" by making this sound and by moving the mouth and lips. Lovaas found that autistic children attended to only one kind of cue—for example, visual cues but not auditory cues. Although a child might reliably learn to say "ah" after seeing the therapist say this word, the child would not repeat this sound if it was presented with the therapist's mouth hidden or if the child was looking away.

In a previous study, investigators had presented a stimulus that contained auditory, visual, and tactile cues to three groups of children: autistic, retarded, and normal (Lovaas et al., 1971). The three dimensions of the stimulus were presented separately to determine which cue (or cues) controlled the children's behavior. The autistic children responded primarily to one stimulus, the retarded children to two; the normal children showed no preference, responding to all three cues. (The investigators also found that they could train autistic children to respond to a cue that they had not initially attended to.)

Autistic children also displayed overselective attention in a study conducted by Schreibman and Lovaas (1973). Although these children learned to discriminate between lifelike boy and girl figures, they did so in response to only one cue. For example, one child could discriminate between the figures only on the basis of their shoes. When these were removed, the child could no longer tell the boy and girl figures apart.

These studies suggest the presence of a perceptual handicap in autistic children that makes it difficult for them to respond to more than one cue at a time. The handicap may be an inability to respond to multiple-cue situations, or it may be a reaction to incidental rather than appropriate cues. The notion of overselectivity could also fit in with findings of unusual abilities in autistic children. That is, their narrow focus of attention could be responsible for both their handicaps and their often-reported special abilities.

Prognosis

The prognosis for children with pervasive developmental disorders is uniformly poor. Of ninety-six people diagnosed as autistic, only 10 percent were employable or had no obvious behavior problems as adults. The only positive prognostic signs were learning to speak before age five and being able to live outside an institution (Kanner et al., 1972). In another study, twenty patients who had been given diagnoses of autism or childhood psychosis, researchers found that their symptomology had not changed. The behaviors of these patients—now adults—resembled those of mild schizophrenics, except that none displayed hallucinations or delusions (Howell & Guirguis, 1984).

Treatment

Because of the symptomatic lack of communication and/or social unresponsiveness, pervasive developmental disorders are very difficult to treat. Therapy with the parents, family therapy, drug therapy, and behavior modification techniques are all currently being used. Although they may improve social adjustment somewhat, overall success has been limited. Intensive behavior modification programs seem the most promising treatment (Maltz, 1982). (The First Person narrative in this chapter relates the experience one teacher had working with an autistic child whose skills improved through a carefully developed behavior modification program.)

Psychodynamic Therapy   As noted, Bruno Bettelheim considers autism to be the result of a rejecting home. His therapeutic program, which is based on this hypothesis, begins with placing autistic children in a residential treatment school where their other emotional needs can be satisfied. To correct their sense of rejection and distrust of the external environment, the staff gives these children total and completely loving acceptance. Once the children learn that they can influence their environment, autonomous and independent growth becomes possible. Although Bettelheim claims a high rate of success, in general, treatment based on psychoanalytic approaches has not been very effective.

Drug Therapy   The drug haldol has reduced symptoms such as withdrawal, stereotyped movements, and fidgetiness. However, long-term use can produce movement problems and other side effects in many children (Gadow, 1986). Recently, fenfluramine has been found to increase attention span and

Susan Safranski

FIRST PERSON

Michigan acknowledges the unique educational needs of autistic children by being one of the few states to recognize autistic impaired as a separate special education category. Specific program options and staffing requirements have been mandated, as has special certification for teachers who serve youngsters with autism.

As a school psychologist who deals with autistic children, I participate in the initial identification and placement of children into special needs programs. I also consult with teachers and work with them to shape educational goals and behavior programs for their students. My role is an ongoing diagnostic one, involving intense observation and analysis of students' skills and behaviors. Among other things, I try to determine how the children process information, how their inappropriate behaviors can be reduced, and what their potential is for growth and learning. Success with these children comes hard, and advances can be short-lived unless they are properly reinforced. One child I know is proof of this.

Annie had been a challenge from the first day she entered our program. She was nine years old at the time. Her parents had been through a painful odyssey, fighting for a school placement for her, struggling

with professionals who had not yet developed the sensitivity or the knowledge of how to treat their child. Although Annie functioned in the trainable mentally impaired range, her behavior had excluded her from classrooms for mentally impaired youngsters. Interestingly, Annie was a twin. Her brother attended regular classes in the same school and had no developmental problems.

Annie's parents and I began our relationship just as federal and state laws made public schools the primary treatment centers for autistic youngsters. Together we began to identify sensible expectations for Annie. We explored various instructional techniques and alternative forms of communication. Jointly, we provided Annie with an integrated communication system, which included speech, sign language, and picture board (a board with pictures of objects and people familiar to Annie). We taught her to sit at a table for half an hour, complete a task, hand it in, and begin another. We also taught her to swim and reduced her fear of using public restrooms. I worked with Annie four days a week for three years until her father was transferred to another state. By that time, she could eat in a restaurant, attend church with her family, and participate in a public school program for autistic children.

In her new school, Annie was placed in a program staffed by people who had no experience with autistic children. They had little understanding of Annie's unusual needs for structure, behavior programming, and alternative communication options. Without the reinforcement provided by a highly structured program, Annie quickly

regressed. When I saw her again a year and a half later, she had reverted to previously extinguished behaviors, including hitting, kicking, and biting people. She was also pulling out her hair and actually had a bald spot on the back of her head. Her parents had come to me to ask my help in developing a program Annie's new teachers could use with her. Annie's former teachers and I described realistic goals and the staffing and classroom requirements that would make the attainment of these goals possible. Unfortunately, this effort was only partially successful.

Not all children are as lucky as Annie. Her parents are her staunchest advocates. They've fought many battles to have their daughter educated in a public school setting, and it is mostly through their efforts that she has achieved her present level of functioning. Although medical research is making some headway into understanding the etiology of autism, I believe at present the best hope for children like Annie lies in effective programs designed to meet their needs and with professionals trained to run them.

Ms. Susan Safranski is a practicing school psychologist with the Birmingham (Michigan) Public School System. For the past ten years, she has worked not only in a program for autistic children but also in regular education programs to help identify children with special needs.

decrease hyperactivity in autistic children. This medication inhibits the uptake of serotonin by nerve terminals and blocks dopamine receptors (Campbell, 1988). Other studies, however, have found few positive effects of fenfluramine, compared to placebos (Campbell et al., 1987). Treatment with medication has produced mixed results.

Behavior Modification Behavior modification procedures have been used effectively to eliminate echolalia, self-mutilation, and self-stimulation. They also have effectively increased attending behaviors, verbalizations, and social play (Phillips & Ray, 1980; Plienis et al., 1987; Schreibman & Koegel, 1975). A three-year follow-up study of 20 autistic children treated by Lovaas and his colleagues indicated that most of the children had improved on intellectual test scores, social adjustment, and use of language (Lovaas et al., 1973). However, Margolies (1977) concluded that, even though these techniques have produced beneficial changes, "these children are not made normal."

Two colleagues of Lovaas reported an astonishingly high success rate in using behavior modification to treat sixteen autistic children. (Six were completely mute, and the other ten seldom spoke; most engaged in self-stimulative and destructive behaviors.) In an intensive training program, both teachers and parents helped the children develop verbalization and social skills (Schreibman & Koegel, 1975).

Within 18 months, ten of the sixteen children were discharged from the program and went on to regular or special-education classes in the public schools. The remaining children also showed progress, but more slowly. Those with lower intelligence and language abilities or who engaged in self-destructive behaviors showed the least gain (Chance, 1987). According to the researchers, the effectiveness of the program stemmed from the training of both teachers and parents to use behavioral techniques. The apparent gains lead them to conclude that autism can be overcome.

OTHER DEVELOPMENTAL DISORDERS

The less severe childhood and adolescent disturbances cover a wide range of problems. In this chapter, we

Behavior modification procedures have been effective in increasing attending behaviors and verbalizations in autistic children. A favorite food or drink is used to reinforce the desired behaviors. The autistic child in this photo must give the proper sign before he can get his drink.

discuss some of the more common disorders, which include disruptive and anxiety disorders, childhood depression, stereotyped movement disorders, and eating disorders. Decisions as to what behaviors constitute a disorder are often based on vague and arbitrary interpretations of the extent to which a given child deviates from some "acceptable" norm.

How do we know whether or not a child has a childhood disorder? The definition of a childhood disorder frequently depends on the tolerance of the referring agent. Kanner (1960) points out that many childhood problems are transient and that "a multitude of early breathholders, nose-pickers, and casual masturbators" develop into normal adults. If a child is brought to a mental health clinic, however, the difficulties will be interpreted as being "far out of proportion to their role as everyday problems of the everyday child."

Problems with Diagnosis

Has DSM-III-R done much to improve the reliability and validity of the diagnosis of childhood disorders?

FOCUS 17.2 *Childhood Disorders: Developmental Problems or Psychiatric Disorders?*

Almost twice as many categories for childhood and adolescent disorders are provided in DSM-III and DSM-III-R than were provided in DSM-II. This expansion is likely to result in a greater tendency to label as mental disorders those troublesome but transient behaviors sometimes described as "problems in living." The American Psychological Association has indicated some concern about the trend, reflected in DSM-III, to "extend the definition of mental illness into areas not previously claimed by psychiatry" (Foltz, 1980). Some of the new diagnostic categories in DSM-III-R include

- *Developmental arithmetic disorder* Significant impairment in the development of arithmetic skills not accounted for by chronological age, mental age, or inadequate schooling.

- *Adjustment disorder with work (or academic inhibition)* Current problems with work or academic performance in a child whose past performance was ad-

equate. The child may be anxious or depressed about taking examinations or may be unable to study or work.

- *Oppositional defiant disorder* "A pattern, for at least six months, of disobedient, negativistic, and provocative opposition to authority figures." The behavior of such children is characterized by excessive argumentativeness, emotional outbursts, and stubbornness.

- *Identity disorder* Severe anxiety over the inability to develop a psychological sense of self. The disturbance is manifested by an inability to establish goals or choose a career and uncertainty about friendship patterns, values, and loyalties. Frequently, this uncertainty is expressed in the question "Who am I?"

The purpose of the expansion is to increase diagnostic accuracy, but new difficulties are created by labeling developmental problems of children and adolescents as mental

disorders. Under the new guidelines, nearly all children and adolescents can, at some point in their lives, be found to be suffering from a "psychiatric condition." The deleterious effects of labeling are well known. One study indicated that normal children who were given a "deviant" label were rated by observers as being significantly more disturbed than the exact same children when they were given a "normal" label (Critchley, 1979). The researcher argued for "decreased reliance on psychiatric labels and greater emphasis on precise descriptive behavioral observations."

Although DSM-III and DSM-III-R are improvements over DSM-II in many areas, they seem to have taken a step backward with regard to child and adolescent disorders, because now many bothersome behaviors can be interpreted as symptomatic of a psychiatric disorder. Fears of low reliability may be justified, at least for the subcategories of childhood disorders.

Unfortunately, criticisms similar to those presented by Kanner remain (see Focus 17.2). Guidelines as to the type of behaviors and the degree of deviation necessary to make diagnostic decisions remain vague and depend on "clinical judgement."

In DSM-III-R, childhood disorder diagnoses involve counting the number of symptoms displayed that belong in a specific category. For example, a diagnosis of overanxious disorder requires endorsement of at least four of seven listed symptoms. An example of a symptom for the disorder is "excessive or unrealistic worry about future events." The clini-

cian must first decide if this behavior is present and then if it is "excessive" or "unrealistic." Because most children show varying amounts of worry, anxiety, rebelliousness, and depression, discrimination between normal concerns and actual childhood disorders is very difficult. Even mental health professionals have difficulty making this judgment. In one study of diagnosticians, interjudge reliability ranged from 0.05 for avoidant disorder, to 0.39 for oppositional disorder, to 0.76 for attention deficit hyperactivity disorder (Werry et al., 1983). Even among mental health professionals, whether or not a problem exists is often "in the eye of the beholder." Ratings of children by parents, teachers, mental health workers, and the subjects themselves, have also produced only low to moderate correlations (Achenbach et al., 1987).

Problems in rating reliability may be partly responsible for the wide differences in the reported prevalence of specific childhood disorders. For example, in one study of 101 preadolescents (six to twelve years old), 55.61 percent of them received a DSM-III-R diagnosis. The diagnoses were based on interviews conducted with the parents and children in this sample. None of the children identified had a prior history of psychological or psychiatric treatment. That such a high percentage of "normal" children would meet the DSM-III-R criteria for a childhood disorders is surprising. The researchers were also taken aback by the results and hypothesize that many of the symptoms of childhood disorders are found among normal children.

Can normal children be distinguished, in terms of severity or frequency of behaviors, from children with childhood disorders? This may be difficult at best. In one study, a number of problems were noted in a group of three-year-old children (Jenkins et al., 1984). Eight percent were "frequently difficult to manage," and up to 46 percent displayed tantrum behaviors. However, in most of the children, the majority of problems were short-lived and depended on such variables as parent-child interaction and environmental stressors. One wonders whether these children would be diagnosed as suffering from a childhood disorder if their parents or teachers were to refer them for psychiatric treatment. The diagnostic reliability and validity of the classification of childhood disorders discussed in this chapter remain in doubt.

DISRUPTIVE BEHAVIOR DISORDERS

The category of disruptive behavior disorders includes disorders whose symptoms are socially disruptive and distressing to others (see the disorders chart on p. 460). These include attention deficit hyperactivity disorder, conduct disorder, and oppositional defiant disorder. These disorders often occur together and have overlapping symptoms.

Attention Deficit Hyperactivity Disorder

Ron, an only child, was always on the go as a toddler and preschooler. He had many accidents as a result of his continual climbing and risk taking. Temper outbursts were frequent.

In kindergarten Ron had a great deal of difficulty staying seated for group work and in completing projects. The quality of his work was poor. In the first grade, Ron was referred to the school psychologist for evaluation. Although his high activity level and lack of concentration were not so pronounced in this one-on-one situation, his impulsive approach to tasks and short attention span were evident throughout the interview. Ron was referred to a local pediatrician who specializes in attention deficit disorders. The pediatrician prescribed Ritalin, which helped reduce Ron's activity level.

Attention deficit hyperactivity disorder (ADHD) is characterized by behaviors such as heightened motor activity (fidgeting and squirming), short attention span, distractibility, impulsiveness, and lack of self-control. ADHD, often referred to as *hyperactivity*, is a confusing term, because it refers to both a diagnostic category and behavioral characteristics. Children who are "overactive" or who have "short attention spans" are often referred to as "hyperactive" even though they may not meet the diagnostic criteria for this disorder (Gadow, 1986). Whether a child is merely overactive or has ADHD must be determined by clinical judgment.

A confusing aspect of ADHD is inconsistency. Attentional deficit or excessive motor activity are not necessarily evident all the time, nor are they displayed in all situations. In one study, ADHD boys showed greater motor activity during academic tasks but did not differ from control boys during lunch, recess, and physical education activities (Porrino et al., 1983). Thus a child might be identified as hyperactive in one situation, but not in others.

ADHD is relatively common. Estimates of its prevalence range from 5 to 10 percent, with boys four times as likely to receive this diagnosis than girls (Shaywitz & Shaywitz, 1984). Some 40 percent of the children display attentional problems at some point in their lives, but in only about 5 percent do these problems persist. (Palfrey et al., 1985). ADHD is associated with a large number of behavioral and

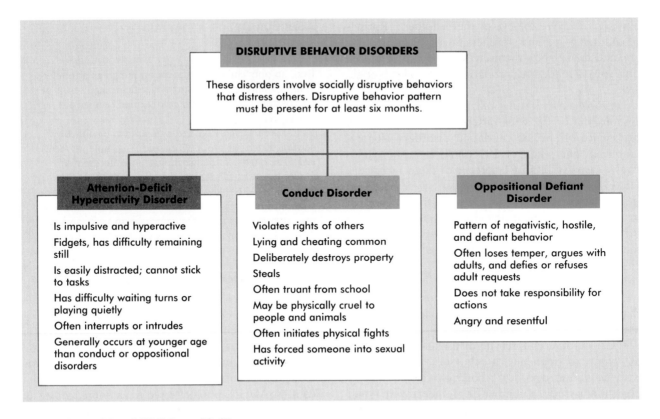

DISRUPTIVE BEHAVIOR DISORDERS

These disorders involve socially disruptive behaviors that distress others. Disruptive behavior pattern must be present for at least six months.

Attention-Deficit Hyperactivity Disorder

Is impulsive and hyperactive

Fidgets, has difficulty remaining still

Is easily distracted; cannot stick to tasks

Has difficulty waiting turns or playing quietly

Often interrupts or intrudes

Generally occurs at younger age than conduct or oppositional disorders

Conduct Disorder

Violates rights of others

Lying and cheating common

Deliberately destroys property

Steals

Often truant from school

May be physically cruel to people and animals

Often initiates physical fights

Has forced someone into sexual activity

Oppositional Defiant Disorder

Pattern of negativistic, hostile, and defiant behavior

Often loses temper, argues with adults, and defies or refuses adult requests

Does not take responsibility for actions

Angry and resentful

SOURCE: Adapted from DSM-III-R, pp. 58–65.

academic problems. Children with this disorder are more likely to need to attend special classes or schools, drop out of school, become delinquent, and have problems with the law (Lambert, 1988; Lambert et al., 1987).

Does ADHD become less severe or disappear with age? The prognosis for this disorder is mixed. When 110 adolescent boys with ADHD were compared with 88 normal boys, researchers found that the delinquency rates for the ADHD boys ranged from 36 to 58 percent and were much higher than those for the comparison group. However, relatively few of the ADHD boys became chronic offenders during their adult years, although most still showed such symptoms as impulsiveness, low educational achievement, poor social skills, and low self-esteem. Only a small percentage continued to have significant antisocial or psychiatric problems as adults (Hechtman & Weiss, 1983). Improvements seem to occur between the ages of sixteen and twenty-one. Those

less likely to improve have a concurrent antisocial disorder (Klein, 1987).

Several conclusions can be reached with regard to the studies just cited. First, improvements do occur; by late adolescence most of those diagnosed with ADHD no longer meet the criteria for the disorder. Second, the prognosis also seems to depend on the presence or absence of antisocial behavior. If conduct disorder occurs concurrently with ADHD, problems in adjustment are more likely. Third, the symptoms of ADHD seem to have the greatest impact on academic performance and peer relationships.

Etiology and Treatment Many researchers feel that the symptoms of overactivity, short attention span, and impulsiveness indicate central nervous system involvement. Satterfield et al. (1984) hypothesize that ADHD children have an abnormal CNS maturation process. It has been proposed that a biological vulnerability combined with environmental and social factors may lead to the development of this disorder (Coleman & Levin, 1988). However, research, including attempts to identify brain impairment, have produced equivocal or negative findings (Langhorne et al., 1976; Knopf, 1984).

Some researchers believe that certain foods or food additives produce physiological changes in the body or brain that result in hyperactive behaviors (Feingold, 1977). Sugar is also suspected as a causal factor in ADHD (Chollar, 1988). Approximately 45 percent of physicians have recommended low-sugar diets for ADHD children (Bennett & Sherman, 1983). Many parents have tried the recommended diets on their children, and many claimed that their children's behavior improved. To determine whether certain chemicals or sugars are implicated in hyperactivity, carefully controlled double-blind studies were conducted. Reviews of such studies indicate that eliminating food additives or certain chemicals from the diets of hyperactive children has little effect on their behavior (Divorky, 1978; Consensus Development Panel, 1982; Milich & Pelham, 1986).

Family variables also seem related to ADHD, although it is not clear whether genetic or environmental factors or a combination are involved. Some evidence supports the hypothesis of genetic transmission, including higher prevalence rates for the disorder in the first- and second-degree relatives of children with ADHD and higher concordance rates among monozygotic twins for this disorder (Knopf, 1984).

Probably ADHD is not produced by a single set of factors. Participants in a panel on ADHD concluded that

> The cluster of symptoms does not represent a single disease, nor is it likely that the etiology is singular; rather, the syndrome may be secondary to (1) organic factors such as trauma, infection, lead intoxication, and significant perinatal hypoxia; (2) predisposing genetic (familial) factors; or (3) psychological factors such as anxiety, inadequate parenting, and environmental stresses. In most cases the etiology is unknown and may be the result of the interaction of several of the predisposing factors listed above. (Consensus Development Panel, 1982, p. 627)

Most children with ADHD have been treated with drug therapy. Stimulants, in particular, increase attention span without significantly affecting academic performance (Ottenbacher & Cooper, 1983).

However, only 70 percent of ADHD respond positively to stimulant medication; 30 percent do not show any response or become worse when taking medication. The drugs seem to treat the symptoms of ADHD rather than the causes, so that drug therapy alone does not produce any long-term benefits (Aman, 1984; Gadow, 1986). In fact, Satterfield et al. (1982) believes that using medication alone may be harmful because problems such as antisocial behavior, poor peer relationships, and learning difficulties are not addressed. Drug therapy may tend to conceal a need for other types of therapies. Perhaps an approach combining counseling and drug therapy is needed (Levine & Jordan, 1987). Other clinicians suggest that both physicians and therapists should pay more attention to family dynamics and child management problems (Prior et al., 1983), rather than relying solely on pharmacological intervention. (Focus 17.3 elaborates on some of the issues surrounding drug therapy.)

Some estimates indicate that as many as 10 percent of all elementary school children suffer from attention deficit hyperactivity disorder (ADHD). These children may show a variety of symptoms such as short attention span, impulsivity, constant activity, and a lack of self-control.

FOCUS 17.3 — Are We Overmedicating Children?

A large number of medications is being prescribed to treat childhood disorders. They include tranquilizers, stimulants, and antipsychotic medication. There has been special concern regarding the use of stimulants for ADHD, attention deficit hyperactivity disorder. Approximately 800,000 children receive Ritalin as treatment for this disorder. Opponents describe the use of medications as a "Band Aid" approach or a "chemical straitjacket" to ensure ease of management (Hutchens & Hynd, 1987).

In Georgia, a mother with an ADHD child filed suit against the Gwinnett County School District and the American Psychiatric Association. She charged that the school had insisted her son be given Ritalin and that the medication made him suicidal and violent. The American Psychiatric Association was included in the charge because the diagnosis was based on DSM-III. The mother's attorney claimed that the diagnostic criteria was too general, resulting in misidentification. In another case, involving a 15-year-

old boy convicted of killing a classmate with a baseball bat, the defense attorney claimed that Ritalin contributed to the boy's act. In addition, five other suits involving medical malpractice for prescribing Ritalin have recently been filed in Massachusetts (Cowart, 1988).

Several questions are raised. Are medications such as Ritalin effective in treating the specific disorders? Are medications being prescribed too freely? Is there adequate assessment or evaluation to determine if medication is appropriate? Is there

---

Self-instructional procedures, modeling, role playing, and self-evaluation have been useful in dealing with the problems involved in ADHD (Kendall, 1984). In one approach, hyperactive children are trained to talk to themselves in a manner that aids self-control. Here is an example of the kind of self-statements that a child learns to make, first overtly and then covertly:

> Okay, what is it I have to do? You want me to copy the picture with the different lines. I have to go slowly and carefully. Okay, draw the line down, down, good; then to the right; that's it; now down some more and to the left. Good, I'm doing fine so far. Remember, go slowly. Now back up again. No, I was supposed to go down. That's okay. Just erase the line carefully. . . . Good. Even if I make an error I can go on slowly and carefully. Okay, I have to go down now. Finished, I did it! (Meichenbaum, 1974, p. 266)

Psychological treatments for ADHD have met with some success. Self-control training was found to be more effective than medication, and a combination of medication and individualized psychological intervention provided both academic gains and better psychological adjustment (Hinshaw et al., 1984).

Oppositional Defiant Disorder

Oppositional defiant disorder (ODD) is characterized by a negativistic, argumentative, and hostile behavior pattern. The child often loses his or her temper, defies rules, refuses to do chores, and blames others for his or her mistakes. The defiant behavior is primarily directed toward parents, teachers, and other people in authority. Although confrontation often occurs, it does not involve the more serious violations of the rights of others that are involved in conduct disorders (American Psychiatric Association, 1987).

Oppositional defiant disorder is a relatively new category and is certainly one of the more controversial childhood disorders. It is not recognized or described as a separate disorder in the mental disorders section of the International Classification of Diseases, Ninth Revision (ICD-9), a classification system used by many other countries.

Diagnostic reliability for ODD is low. The symptoms of ODD can be found in a number of different childhood disorders. One study of preadolescent schoolchildren found that 15.8 percent met the criteria for oppositional defiant disorder (Pfeffer et al., 1987). This percentage in a normal population seems

adequate monitoring of the effects of the drug and identification of possible side effects? A large number of studies indicate that stimulant medication such as Ritalin can help reduce some ADHD symptoms. However, nearly one-third of people with ADHD do not show positive results when given stimulant medication (Gadow, 1986). It is recommended that Ritalin be prescribed only after a comprehensive diagnostic and evaluation procedure. The particular symptom or symptoms to be treated should be identified and the dosage modified if necessary (Shaywitz & Shaywitz, 1984; Garfinkel, 1987). Unfortunately, it is not clear how many physicians or psychiatrists follow these guidelines. In the case of the fifteen-year-old boy convicted of homicide, the pediatrician who prescribed the Ritalin was reported to have monitored the boy only through yearly physical exams.

Using any medication also necessitates the communication of possible side effects and contraindications to the patient and parent. Stimulants, for example, should not be used for children with tics, glaucoma, or seizure disorders (Hutchens & Hynd, 1987). It is estimated that 15 percent of children with Tourette's syndrome (a severe tic disorder) might not have developed this disorder if stimulant medication had not been prescribed. If tics occur, the medication should be discontinued.

Medication has certainly been helpful in treating a variety of childhood disorders such as ADHD. However, medications should be employed only after careful evaluation and monitoring of their effects. Are we overmedicating our children? Barry Garfinkel, M.D., director of Child and Adolescent Psychiatry at the University of Minnesota, answers, "We just don't have a good way to judge that" (Cowart, 1988, p. 2521).

---

high and may reflect the fact that many children and adolescents show some of the signs of oppositional defiant disorder. At this point, there is little information on the course, predisposing factors, or the prevalence of this disorder.

Conduct Disorders

Charles was well known to school officials for his many fights with peers. After a stabbing incident at school, he was put on probation and then transferred to another junior high school. Two months later, at age fourteen, Charles was charged with armed robbery and placed in a juvenile detention facility. He had few positive peer contacts at the juvenile facility and seemed unwilling or unable to form close relationships. Some progress was achieved with a behavioral contract program that involved positive reinforcement from adults and praise for refraining from aggression in handling conflicts. He was transferred to a maximum-security juvenile facility when he seriously injured two of his peers, whose teasing had angered him. Charles completed a vocational training program in this second facility, but he couldn't hold a regular job. He was sent to prison following a conviction for armed robbery. Diagnosis: conduct disorder, solitary aggressive type.

Peter was a high-achieving student during his elementary school years. However, in seventh grade he began to show a pattern of truancy, declining school performance, and frequent lying. Peter had a number of friends, most of whom also skipped school. They spent most of their time taking drugs, playing video games, or "cruising" in an older friend's car. School officials eventually contacted the juvenile court because of Peter's chronic truancy and drug use. Peter was found to have cocaine in his possession, and was placed in a juvenile detention facility by the court. Diagnosis: "conduct disorder, group type."

Conduct disorders involve a persistent pattern of antisocial behaviors that violate the rights of others. Many children and adolescents display isolated instances of antisocial behavior, but this diagnosis is only given when the behavior is repetitive and persistent. Conduct disorders include a wide variety of behaviors such as fighting, temper tantrums, stealing, lying, fire setting, assaults, rape, and truant behavior. The pattern of misconduct must have lasted for at least six months for this diagnosis (DSM-III-R). The

Conduct disorders, such as fighting, stealing, and assault, represent a serious societal problem. Estimates indicate that as many as 10 percent of adolescents (more males than females) have these disorders.

prevalence of conduct disorders is estimated to range from 3 to 10 percent of children and adolescents and is four to five times more prevalent in males than females (Hinshaw, 1987; Kazdin, 1987).

Three subtypes of conduct disorders are recognized in DSM-III-R. Two of these are described in the case studies introducing this section. The *solitary aggressive type* often cannot establish affectionate relationships. Such people tend to be socially isolated. They show aggression against property or other people. The *group type* tends to show normal socialization. These people often establish attachments to significant others and friends. They also may show aggression toward other people or against property. The *undifferentiated type* shows some symptoms of both the solitary and group types.

Conduct disorders in adolescence represent a serious social problem. In the United States, approximately 72,000 juveniles are housed in correctional institutions for antisocial behaviors (Rutherford et al., 1985). Conduct disorders are associated with disciplinary and academic problems and negative interaction with peers (Walker et al., 1987). People with these disorders are more often from lower socioeconomic classes (Hinshaw, 1987). Oppositional defiant disorder often precedes the development of conduct disorders, and often exists concurrently with ADHD. Although many childhood disorders remit over time, people with conduct disorders are unlikely to grow out of their problems. Prognosis is poor; conduct disorders often lead to criminal behavior, antisocial personality, and problems in marital and occupational adjustment during adulthood (Kazdin, 1987). Between 36 and 70 percent of offending delinquent adolescents later become adult criminals (Greenwood & Zimring, 1985). Nearly all adult offenders have a history of repeated antisocial behavior as children. The key factor associated with negative outcome is aggression. Highly aggressive children tend to remain aggressive over time, while other childhood adjustment problems show much less stability (Lerner et al., 1988). People with higher IQs (Kandel et al., 1988) and females (Roff & Wirt, 1984) have a better prognosis.

Etiology Psychoanalysts interpret antisocial and delinquent behaviors in children as symptoms of an underlying anxiety conflict in the child. This conflict results from an inadequate relationship with the parents; the problem behaviors can be produced by either emotional deprivation or overindulgence. In the first case, the parents offer the child little affection or concern, so childhood conflicts are not resolved and the superego does not develop adequately. The lack of a strong conscience increases the likelihood of aggressive and antisocial behaviors. The child becomes unable to form close personal relationships with others.

If the child is overindulged during early childhood, the same pattern may develop. Overindulgence allows the child to display aggression freely, and normal internal controls over aggressive behaviors are never fully developed. Congenital variables may be involved in conduct disorders. Some theorists believe that underarousal causes some people to seek stimulation through antisocial behaviors (Zentall & Zentall, 1983; Farley, 1986).

Genetic factors may also be involved. Boys with conduct disorders have a higher than predicted number of antisocial parents (Hinshaw, 1987). However, this could be the result of either genetic or social factors. Mednick (1985) tried to isolate influences by comparing the adult criminal records of children adopted early in life and their biological and adoptive parents (sample comprised 14,427 adopted children). If genetic factors are most important, the biological parents would have the greatest influence on subsequent criminal behavior in the adoptees. If environmental influences are the most important, the record of adoptive parents should have the greatest impact. As Table 17.2 shows, adopted sons of biological parents with criminal records are more likely to also have criminal records. These results support the view of a genetic predisposition in criminality. However, social factors were also important. Children born to parents from low socioeconomic status had the highest rates of criminality no matter what type of adoptive family they lived with. More convictions were also found among children adopted into lower-versus higher-class families. As Mednick observes, "Regardless of genetic background, improved social conditions seem to reduce criminality" (1985, p. 60).

Patterson (1986) feels that antisocial behaviors are the result of the parental failure to effectively punish misbehavior. In his work with families of conduct-disordered children, he noticed that when a parent requested something from or criticized the child, the child would counterattack. This would result in the parents' withdrawal from the conflict. The child's failure to learn to respect authority generalizes to the school setting, resulting in academic failure and poor peer relations. Patterson has concluded that the specific factors that contribute to the development of antisocial behaviors include (1) a lack of parental monitoring (increases in unsupervised street time were associated with increased rates of antisocial behaviors), (2) inconsistent disciplinary practices, (3) failure to use positive management techniques or to teach social process skills, and (4) failure to teach the skills necessary for academic success (listening, compliance, following directions, and so on). Although Patterson focuses primarily on the learning aspects in the etiology of conduct disorders, he also supports the view that predisposing factors such as difficult child temperament may increase the need for parents to learn and consistently apply appropriate management skills.

Treatment Conduct disorders and group delinquency have resisted traditional forms of psychotherapy. However, cognitive behavioral therapy appears promising. One program, for example, focuses on helping aggressive boys develop self-control. The cognitive element includes using problem-solving skills to identify behavior problems, generate solutions to them, and select alternative behaviors. In addition, the children learn positive social skills through role-playing with teachers, peers, and family members. Researchers studying the effects of this program found that although aggressive behaviors were significantly reduced and social skills improved, the gains had not been maintained until the time of a follow-up six months later. The researchers noted that the ten sessions subjects attended might not have been enough to make change permanent (Dubow et al., 1987). Kazdin (1987) also noted that treatment duration is related to outcome. Durable and significant changes are associated with programs that require up to fifty hours of treatment.

Greater success has been found with the parent management training developed by Patterson (1982, 1986). In this program, specific skills are taught so

TABLE 17.2 | Effect of Parental Criminal Records on Adopted Sons

Parents with Criminal Records		Sons with Criminal Records (Percent)
Biological Parents	Adoptive Parents	
No criminal record	No criminal record	13.5
No criminal record	Criminal record	14.7
Criminal record	No criminal record	20
Criminal record	Criminal record	24.5

SOURCE: Adapted from Mednick (1985).

that the parents learn the appropriate way of establishing rules for the child, implementing consequences, and rewarding positive behaviors. The parents first practice their newly learned skills on simple problems and gradually work on the more difficult problems as they become more proficient in management techniques. Patterson's program has evolved over a period of twenty years of work with problem children. Success has been reported, and treatment changes have been maintained even after periods as long as four years after treatment (Kazdin, 1987).

ANXIETY DISORDERS

Children and adolescents suffer from a variety of problems involving chronic anxiety—fears, nightmares, school phobia, shyness, timidity, and lack of self-confidence. Children with these disturbances display exaggerated autonomic responses and are apprehensive in new situations, preferring to stay at home or in other familiar environments. As opposed to the disruptive behavior disorders, which are socially disruptive and undercontrolled, the anxiety disorders are considered to be overcontrolled. The childhood disorders in which anxiety plays a prominent role include separation anxiety disorder, avoidant disorder of childhood and adolescence, and overanxious disorder (see the disorders chart on p. 468). Some researchers believe that specific personality patterns may predispose a child toward developing anxiety and other childhood disorders (see Focus 17.4).

Separation Anxiety Disorder

Children who suffer from a **separation-anxiety disorder (SAD)** show excessive anxiety when separated from parents or home. They constantly seek their parent's company and may worry too much about losing them. Separation may produce such physical symptoms as vomiting, diarrhea, and headaches (DSM-III-R). This behavior must last at least two weeks to be diagnosed as a disorder. Young children with SAD are the most concerned about separation from their parents. During adolescence, the most frequent symptoms involve physical complaints on school days (Francis et al., 1987).

One type of separation anxiety disorder that has been studied extensively is *school phobia*. The physical symptoms may occur merely at the prospect of having to go to school. About 17 out of each 1,000 children per year display this disorder, which is more common in girls than in boys (Ross, 1982).

Darcy's school phobias were first manifested while riding in the car with her mother on the second day of school. She began to cry and hold on to her mother, scream hysterically, and plead not to be taken to school. Once at school, Darcy screamed and kicked in order to avoid being taken into the building, and then to her classroom. Darcy's mother sat with the child in class and attempted to reassure her that school was pleasant and enjoyable. When the mother got up to leave the room, Darcy immediately began to cry, scream, and grab her mother's arm to prevent her from returning home. (Kolko et al., 1987, p. 251)

Some researchers feel that school phobia can reflect either a fear of separation from a parent or a phobic reaction to the school setting. Last et al. (1987) compared children who met the DSM-III criteria for separation anxiety disorder with those who had a phobia about school. The findings revealed that children with SAD were more likely to be girls, prepubertal, and from lower socioeconomic families. They were also less likely to exhibit school refusal than children with school phobias. Acknowledging this difference is important in designing treatment.

Psychoanalytic explanations of school phobia stress the overdependence of the child on the mother. The reluctance to attend school is not seen as a fear of school but as anxiety over separation from the mother. However, if separation anxiety is the primary etiological factor in this disorder, it should occur in the early school history of the child. But many cases of school phobia do not develop until the third or fourth grade. Also, these children often do not display separation anxiety in other situations that require separation from their mothers.

School phobia has also been explained in terms of learning principles. Parents are important sources of reinforcement during a child's preschool period. Going to school requires a child to develop new skills and encounters with uncertain and anxiety-arousing situations. If a parent reinforces these fears (for example, by continually warning the child not to get lost), the child may seek refuge away from school,

FOCUS 17.4   The Relationship Between Personality and Behavior: The Temperament-Environment Fit Model

For many childhood disorders, there is increasing interest in the temperament-environment fit model. Research continues to support the view that temperament is an important factor in adjustment. In a longitudinal study conducted by Chess and Thomas (1984), about 10 percent of the children studied showed a negative reaction to new situations, and were emotionally reactive. These "difficult" children showed greater adjustment difficulties later in life. Tendencies toward "shyness" also appear early in development. Kagan (1987) found that some children showed behavioral inhibitions such as being cautious around strangers. In addition, they had high heart rates in response to mild mental stress. These early reactions persisted. Other differences in temperament may include characteristics such as depressive mood and need for stimulation.

The child's temperament may predispose that individual to develop a specific disorder. For example, a child with behavioral inhibition may develop an anxiety disorder, or a "difficult" child may develop a disruptive behavior. However, whether or not a child develops a problem also depends on environmental factors and parental skills. If parents are inexperienced, cannot adjust to the child's temperament, have personal difficulties and stress that influence their parenting skills, or are inconsistent with the child, the chances of problem behaviors occurring greatly increase (Chess, 1986; Carey, 1986).

Temperament and the environment can affect one another. Difficult infants elicit more confrontation and conflict with their mothers (Lee & Bates, 1985). Environmental changes can also affect the child's temperament. Kagan (1987) reported that 40 percent of the "inhibited" children became more outgoing. This change was associated with parental encouragement for the child to approach stressful situations.

What are the implications of the temperament-environment fit model? First, more research will be directed toward (1) individual differences in temperament, (2) the neurobiological bases for these differences, and (3) the interaction between temperament and environment. This would allow the identification of children who are at risk for developing a disorder and the type of disorder that they are most likely to develop. Psychotherapeutic interventions and parenting style may have to be altered to "fit" the child's temperament. For example, approaches that might be effective with a difficult child (being firm and consistent) may be inappropriate with an "inhibited" child.

where he or she can get the kind of reinforcement he or she received earlier in life.

For young children treated with most forms of psychotherapy, the prognosis for separation anxiety disorder is very good. But separation anxiety that develops during adolescence may be more resistant to change. In a study of 125 adolescents with school phobia who were treated in a psychiatric inpatient unit, two-thirds showed "appreciable" or "complete" improvement, but the remainder showed little change. School attendance problems remained in about 50 percent of the cases. The researchers feel that "severe school phobia in early adolescence resembled adult mood disorders (six of the children had already developed agoraphobic difficulties) in some clinical features and in outcome" (Berg et al., 1976, p. 80).

Avoidant Disorder

Avoidant disorder of childhood or adolescence is similar to social phobias in adults (see Chapter 6). Children or adolescents with **avoidant disorder** feel severe anxiety in situations that involve contact with peers or strangers. The typical response to this anxiety is withdrawal, which interferes with establishing

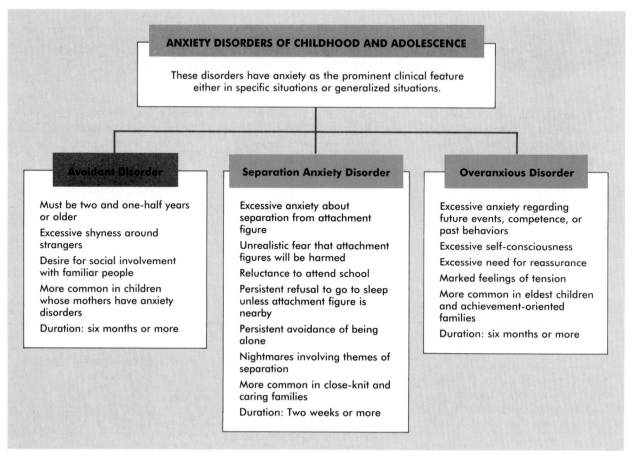

ANXIETY DISORDERS OF CHILDHOOD AND ADOLESCENCE

These disorders have anxiety as the prominent clinical feature either in specific situations or generalized situations.

Avoidant Disorder

- Must be two and one-half years or older
- Excessive shyness around strangers
- Desire for social involvement with familiar people
- More common in children whose mothers have anxiety disorders
- Duration: six months or more

Separation Anxiety Disorder

- Excessive anxiety about separation from attachment figure
- Unrealistic fear that attachment figures will be harmed
- Reluctance to attend school
- Persistent refusal to go to sleep unless attachment figure is nearby
- Persistent avoidance of being alone
- Nightmares involving themes of separation
- More common in close-knit and caring families
- Duration: Two weeks or more

Overanxious Disorder

- Excessive anxiety regarding future events, competence, or past behaviors
- Excessive self-consciousness
- Excessive need for reassurance
- Marked feelings of tension
- More common in eldest children and achievement-oriented families
- Duration: six months or more

SOURCE: From DSM-III-R, pp. 49–58.

Children with avoidant disorder become extremely anxious in situations involving contact with peers or strangers and withdraw from these interactions. These children are very sensitive to rejection and criticism and have a difficult time forming friendships.

friendships. Avoidant disorder is thus characterized by low rates of interaction with peers, few friends, deficits in social skills, anxiety, and unhappiness. Children with the disorder are hypersensitive to rejection or criticism.

Avoidant disorder may occur in children as young as 2½ years of age, but social anxiety is also common among adolescents. Such adolescents experience difficulty when meeting new people, feel depressed or lonely, lack assertiveness, and are excessively self-conscious (Zimbardo, 1977). In its milder forms, the problem dissipates with time and generally does not require treatment. More severe cases may persist because social anxiety hampers the development of the necessary social and interactional skills. Social skills training and desensitization procedures are effective in treating avoidant disorder (Anderson et al., 1987; Wehr & Kaufman, 1987).

Overanxious Disorder

Overanxious disorder is characterized by excessive worry about future or past events, overconcern about performance, and a constant need for reassurance. It is similar to obsessive disorder or generalized anxiety disorder in adults (see Chapter 6). Physical complaints may also be expressed. The disorder is not uncommon. It appears to be more common in eldest children, higher socioeconomic groups, in achievement-oriented families (DSM-III-R). Nearly half of the mothers of such children had overanxious disorder as children (Last et al., 1987). This relationship can be due to modeling or a genetic factor. Most cases don't require treatment, although one that persists may become a generalized anxiety disorder in adulthood.

CHILDHOOD DEPRESSION

> David has had a history of depressive reactions to unpleasant events since infancy, which has become increasingly severe. Two events seemed to have produced affective pain and to have triggered the depressive acting out which led to his referral: one was a cerebral stroke suffered by his maternal grandmother with whom he was very close, and the second was learning of his mother's fourth pregnancy. . . . His parents described him as fearful, socially isolated, and as making self-deprecating statements. His behavior at the time of referral was passive, quiet, and motorically slow, punctuated with occasional hostile outbursts. Suicidal ideation surfaced for several months—twice during the course of therapy (O'Connor, 1987, p. 106).

The five-year-old boy just described displays many symptoms of depression. According to DSM-III-R, major depressive episodes can begin very early in life, even in infancy. Estimates of childhood depression range from 27 to 52 percent in clinical populations and from 1 to 2 percent in nonclinical populations (Winnett et al., 1987). Older children and adolescents have higher rates of depression. Depressive symptoms are also reported more in girls than boys.

In a sample of 1,000 preschool children who were referred to a child development center, only 0.9 percent evidenced a major depression. Symptoms of depression expressed by this group involved feelings of sadness, loss of appetite, sleep difficulties, fatigue, and other somatic complaints. Kashani and Carlson (1987) believe that a pattern of frequent somatic complaints may indicate depression in preschoolers. Environmental factors were also important. All children who were depressed had been abused or seriously neglected, as compared to 22 percent of control children. Depressed children were also more likely to live in a broken home.

Depressed mood appears to be more prevalent during adolescence. Moderate to intense depressive symptoms were reported in 13 percent of adolescent boys and 33.7 percent of adolescent girls (Harris & Howard, 1987). The question of how many adolescents would meet the DSM-III criteria for depressive disorders was examined by Kashani et al. (1987). In a sample of 150 adolescents, 4.7 percent met the criteria for major depression and 3.3 percent met the criteria for dysthymic disorder (mild depression). Of the 12 who had a depressive disorder, 2 were boys and 10 were girls. In addition to depression, the 12 depressives also had a number of other disorders (75 percent had an anxiety disorder, 50 percent had an oppositional disorder, and 33 percent had a conduct disorder).

It is clear that depression does occur in childhood and adolescence. Children are especially vulnerable

Childhood depression can begin in infancy, although it is more common in children and adolescents. Symptoms include feelings of sadness, loss of appetite, sleep difficulties, and fatigue and are reported more by females than males.

to environmental factors because they lack the maturity and skills to deal with various stresses. Conditions such as poor or inconsistent parenting, parental illness, loss of an attachment figure, and neglect or abuse often produce lowered self-esteem and increased vulnerability to depression. Depressed children show many of the same characteristics found in depressed adults. They have more negative self-concepts and are more likely to engage in self-blame and self-criticism (Jaenicke et al., 1987). Programs involving social skills training, cognitive behavioral therapy (Winnett et al., 1987) and supportive therapy (O'Connor, 1987) have been effective in treating childhood depression.

TIC DISORDERS

> Saul Lubaroff, a disc jockey in Iowa City, is able to deliver smooth news reports on the weather, news, and sports. However, whenever he turns off his microphone, an explosive, involuntary stream of obscenities follow. In high school, his classmates would mock and threaten him. Even today, his outbursts are highly embarrassing to him. He has shouted "HEY" and "I MASTURBATE" in a fancy restaurant. However, Saul does have control while he is on the air. He indicates that "I have no problem announcing. I can turn off my 'noises' for 20 to 25 seconds, sometimes up to two minutes." (Dutton, 1986, p. c1)

Saul Lubaroff has a chronic tic disorder. *Tics* are involuntary, repetitive, and nonrhythmic movements or vocalizations. Transient and chronic tic disorders and Tourette's syndrome comprise this group of disorders.

Most tics in children are *transient* and disappear without treatment. If a tic lasts longer than one year, it is diagnosed as a chronic **tic disorder.** Chronic tic disorders may persist into and through adulthood. According to DSM-III-R, a diagnosis of Tourette's syndrome necessitates "both multiple motor and one or more vocal tics have been present at some time during the illness, although not necessarily concurrently" (American Psychiatric Association, 1987, p. 80).

The most common tics are eye blinking and jerking movements of the face and head, although in some cases the extremities and larger muscle groups may be involved. In tic disorders, the movements, which are normally under voluntary control, occur automatically and involuntarily. Examples of tics reported in the literature include eye blinking, facial grimacing, throat clearing, head jerking, hiccoughing, foot tapping, flaring of the nostrils, flexing of the elbows and fingers, and contractions of the shoulders or abdominal muscles. Vocal tics can range from coughing, grunting, and sniffing to repeating words.

Approximately 15 to 23 percent of children have single, transient tics; their occurrence tends to peak at about age seven. Diagnoses of tic disorders can only be made in retrospect, because there is no way of determining if a tic will disappear or develop into a chronic tic disorder or Tourette's syndrome (Gadow, 1986; Golden, 1987).

Tourette's Syndrome

Tourette's syndrome usually begins in childhood, between the ages of two and thirteen. This puzzling disorder is characterized by facial and body tics, which increase in frequency and intensity as the person grows older, and by grunting and barking sounds that generally develop into explosive *coprolalia*, the compulsion to shout obscenities. Stress may increase the severity of these symptoms (Bornstein et al., 1983). Estimates of the number of people with this disorder range from a few thousand up to 3.5 million (Bauer & Shea, 1984; Friel, 1973). It occurs three to six times more frequently in males than in females.

Researchers have not yet determined whether Tourette's syndrome differs from the tic disorders. However, studies seem to indicate that the two are quite similar. For example, Corbett (1971) studied data on groups of children and adults suffering from single or multiple tics, tics with vocalizations, and tics with coprolalia (Tourette's syndrome). These three groups displayed no significant differences in IQ, psychiatric symptoms, or EEG readings. The prognosis was more favorable for those with single or multiple tics (94 percent improved) than for those with Tourette's syndrome (about 60 percent improved). Corbett concluded that the different tic disorders may be different stages of the same syndrome.

Etiology and Treatment

Anxiety and stress seem to be primary factors in producing, maintaining, and exacerbating tic disorders. In the psychodynamic view, tics represent underlying aggressive or sexual conflicts. For example, eye blinking may represent attempts to block out thoughts of the "primal scene" (intercourse between the child's parents) or other anxiety-evoking stimuli. Although tics do appear early in life, when the fixation of sexual or aggressive impulses is most likely to occur, little support has been found for this particular explanation.

According to the learning theorists, tics are conditioned avoidance responses initially evoked by stress. These responses become habit through reinforcement when they reduce anxiety. The therapeutic technique of *negative practice* or *massed practice* is based on this viewpoint. The technique requires that the person perform the tic intentionally, over and over again. This forced practice of the behavior produces fatigue, which inhibits the response. The tic gradually acquires aversive properties, so *not performing the tic* becomes reinforcing. The procedure has had mixed results (Walen et al., 1977).

Only minimal success was reported by researchers who used massed practice and relaxation training to treat three people with Tourette's syndrome (Turpin & Powell, 1984). The patients were required to reproduce their tics as frequently as possible for five minutes; they were also taught to relax on cue. The massed practice failed to reduce tic frequency at all, and the cue-controlled relaxation resulted in only a moderate decrease in one tic in one patient.

Both multiple tics and Tourette's syndrome appear to be transmitted in families. If a parent has a tic disorder, there is an increased risk for the children to also have the disorder (Pauls et al.,1981). This relationship may be due to either genetic or environmental factors—or perhaps to both.

Interestingly, up to 50 percent of children with Tourette's syndrome also meet the DSM-III-R criteria for ADHD, which might reflect a genetic link between the two disorders (Golden, 1987). Treating ADHD with stimulants may precipitate Tourette's syndrome: it should not done if a familial history of tic disorder is present and should be discontinued if tics appear in the patient (Gadow, 1986).

Several investigators feel that Tourette's syndrome may stem from an impairment of the central nervous system (Bauer & Shea, 1984). Reported therapeutic success with the drug haloperidol has supported this view (Gadow, 1986). However, there have also been reports that drug treatment has had unfavorable results (Bauer & Shea, 1984). In addition, haloperidol results in a number of negative side effects in children and could lead to motor dysfunctions such as tardive dyskinesia.

EATING DISORDERS

Eating problems are becoming more prevalent in the United States, especially among younger people. In a survey of over 2,000 high school students, 20 percent indicated that they overeat at least once a week to the extent that their stomachs hurt, 20 percent felt completely out of control over food at least once a week, and 11 percent of the girls ate in response to emotional distress (Kagan & Squires, 1984). Eating problems may be a result of both the availability of a wide variety of attractive high-calorie foods and the American pursuit of thinness. Preoccupation with weight and body dimensions may become so extreme that it develops into one of the eating disorders— anorexia nervosa and bulimia (see the disorders chart on p. 472).

Anorexia Nervosa

Cherry O'Neil dropped from a body weight of 140 pounds to only 80 pounds. She exercised up to six hours a day and wore heavy clothing to hide her condition. To keep her weight down she took diet pills, as well as large amounts of laxatives when she thought she had overeaten (Seligmann et al., March 7, 1983).

Although anorexia has been known for over a hundred years, it is receiving increased attention, owing to greater public knowledge of the disorder and the apparent increase in its incidence.

Anorexia nervosa is a bizarre and puzzling disorder. It occurs primarily in adolescent girls and

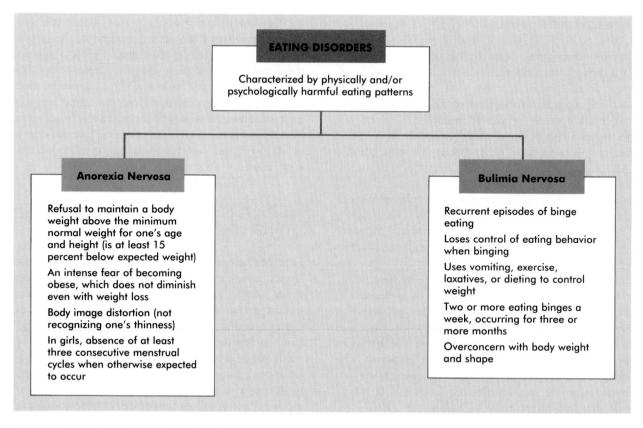

SOURCE: Adapted from DSM-III-R, pp. 65–71.

young women, and only rarely in males. Estimates of its prevalence range from 0.4 to 0.7 percent of the female population (Pope et al., 1984; Hertzog, 1982). A person with the disorder is intensely afraid of becoming fat and literally engages in self-starvation. Even when skeletal in appearance, such patients claim to be overweight. As Bruch (1978, p. 209) notes, anorexics "vigorously defend their often gruesome emaciation as not being too thin ... they identify with the skeleton-like appearance, actively maintain it, and deny its abnormality." The inability to objectively assess one's physical condition is characteristic of this disorder. Because they believe they are overweight, anorexic patients deny that their weight loss is a problem.

Self-starvation produces a variety of physical complications along with weight loss. Anorexic patients often exhibit cardiac arrhythmias as a result of electrolyte imbalance; nine out of ten display bradycardia and hypotension (low blood pressure). One

female patient had a pulse rate of 28 beats per minute and no measurable diastolic blood pressure (Brotman & Stern, 1983). In addition, the heart muscle is often damaged and weakened, because the body may use it as a source of protein during starvation. One result of such complications is a mortality rate of approximately 6 percent (Schwartz & Thompson, 1981).

There appear to be subgroups of patients with anorexia. Of 105 patients hospitalized with this disorder, 53 percent had achieved their weight loss through constant fasting; the remainder had periodically resorted to bulimia (purging or vomiting). Although both groups displayed a vigorous pursuit of thinness, some differences were found. The anorexics who fasted were more introverted and tended to deny that they suffered hunger and psychological distress. The bulimic anorexics were more extroverted; reported more anxiety, depression, and guilt; admitted more frequently to having a strong appetite; and tended to be older. The bulimic anorexics also showed a strong attraction for food, but they did not like to cook because of the temptations involved. On the other hand, the fasting anorexics enjoyed cooking (Casper et al., 1980).

Bulimia Nervosa

> Sandy, a singer-actress who appeared in Broadway musicals such as *Grease* and *Nine,* would secretly gorge herself with enormous amounts of food and then stick her fingers down her throat to induce vomiting. She describes a typical dinner as composed of one large pizza, spaghetti and meat sauce, two veal parmesan sandwiches, two pecan pies, and one cherry pie. Her late night "snack" included a club sandwich, two grilled cheese sandwiches with bacon, an order of onion rings and french fries, three cartons of milk, two root beers and one glazed donut. (Bartlett, 1984)

Bulimia nervosa is an eating disorder characterized by binge eating (the rapid consumption of large quantities of food) at least twice a week. Eating episodes may be terminated when abdominal pain develops or by self-induced vomiting. Bulimics may attempt to lose weight through severe dieting, self-induced vomiting, laxative use, or all three. Frequent weight fluctuations of more than 10 pounds often are caused from alternating binges and fasts. A persistent overconcern with body image and weight also characterizes this disorder.

Bulimic subjects greatly overestimate their body size (Powers et al., 1987) and are afraid to gain weight. When asked to imagine gaining five pounds, a group of bulimic subjects showed pronounced motoric, heart rate, and muscle tension changes (Cutts & Barrios, 1986).

Bulimic people realize that their eating patterns are not normal and are frustrated by that fact. They become disgusted and ashamed of their eating, hide it from others. Some do not eat during the day but lose control and binge in late afternoon or evening. As in Sandy's case, weight is controlled through vomiting or the use of laxatives (Johnson & Berndt, 1983). The vomiting, or purging, produces feelings of relief and, often, a commitment to a severely

Anorexia nervosa is a devastating eating disorder that involves self-starvation. It is most prevalent in adolescent and young adult women. Approximately 6 percent of anorexics die from the disorder.

restrictive diet—one that ultimately fails (Stevens & Salisbury, 1984).

Bulimia is much more prevalent than anorexia, although prevalence estimates depend on the sample being described. These estimates range from 2 to 10 percent of the general population (Fairburn & Cooper, 1983; Pope et al., 1984). However, the prevalence of bulimia nervosa is approximately 3 percent when using strict DSM-III-R criteria. An additional 10 percent of women reported some symptoms but did not meet all the criteria for the diagnosis (Drewnowski et al., 1988). Only a small number of males exhibit the disorder, presumably because there is less cultural pressure for them to remain thin.

The person's weight seems to have little to do with bulimia. Of a sample of 40 women with the disorder, 25 were of normal weight, 2 were overweight, 1 was obese, and 12 were underweight. The average number of binging episodes for these women was twelve per week, and the estimated number of calories consumed in a binge could be as high as 11,500. Typical binge foods included ice cream, candy, bread or toast, and donuts (Mitchell et al., 1981).

A variety of measures are used to control the weight gain accompanying binge eating. These include fasting, self-induced vomiting, diet pills, laxatives, and diuretics (Powers et al., 1987). Side effects and complications occur in bulimics as a result of self-induced vomiting or the excessive use of laxatives. The effects of vomiting include swollen parotid glands, which produces a puffy facial appearance. Vomited stomach acid can erode tooth enamel. Possible gastrointestinal disturbances include esophagitis (inflammation of esophagus) and gastric and rectal irritation. Vomiting also results in a loss of potassium, which can weaken the heart and cause arrhythmia and cardiac arrest (Stevens & Salisbury, 1984).

Some evidence shows that bulimics eat not only out of hunger but also as an emotionally soothing response to distressing thoughts or stress (Casper et al., 1980). Women with this disorder have a negative self-image, feelings of inadequacy, dissatisfaction with their bodies, and a tendency to perceive events as more stressful than most people would (Kagan & Squires, 1984; Wolf & Crowther, 1983; Gray, 1977). Stress and emotional difficulties may lead them to consume food for gratification. Sandy, the bulimic actress-singer, reported that "I would stuff down my feelings with the food. . . . I used the food as a catalyst

to flush my feelings down the toilet and watch them go away. It was numbing" (Bartlett, 1984, p. 1). However, we should note that these characteristics of diagnosed bulimics may be a *result* of their loss of control over eating patterns, rather than causes of the disorder.

Etiology of Eating Disorders

Both social and psychological factors are probably important in the etiology of eating disorders. Yager et al. (1987) believe that the eating disorders result from the sociocultural demand for thinness in females, which produces a preoccupation with weight. However, a disorder involving eating only occurs in combination with intra- or interpersonal problems.

We will first discuss evidence for preoccupation with weight in females and then the social or psychological factors. Many women have a distorted body image. They overestimate the size of their waist, thighs, and hips to a much greater extent than men do (Thompson, 1986). They see themselves as being heavier than they are and have as an ideal body image a picture of a much thinner woman. A study of over 2,000 women found that they wanted to weigh about 9 pounds less than their current weight (Drewnowski et al., 1988). Most men seem to equate their current body shape with their ideal shape (Fallon & Rozin, 1985).

A preoccupation with thinness appears to develop by early adolescence. A study of 288 girls between the ages of 10 and 15 found that girls wanted thinner bodies than they thought boys found attractive. However, they did not consider themselves overweight and displayed less body dissatisfaction than older women (Cohn et al., 1987).

Women in their twenties have a much higher standard of thinness than adolescent girls do. This might indicate that a desire to be increasingly thin begins to develop in adolescence and becomes deeply ingrained by the time the young woman reaches full adulthood. Especially intriguing is the finding by Cohn and his colleagues (1987) that adolescent girls were aware that their desired body shape was thinner than the body shape they thought boys found most attractive.

Variables other than being attractive to men must be involved. An independent standard of thinness might be one factor. Some support for this view was found by Silverstein and Perdue (1988). They found that women equated thinness with attractiveness. In addition, being slim was also associated with professional success and intelligence.

Although preoccupation with weight and evidence of a distorted bodily image appear in most women, other factors must also be involved, because only a small percentage develop eating disorders. Females with eating disorders appear to suffer from poor self-esteem (Mallick et al., 1987). Bulimics and repeating dieters also feel that they have little control over environmental factors (Dyken & Gerrard, 1986). Immaturity, passive-aggression, and a self-defeating behavior pattern was found in patients with anorexia nervosa and bulimia nervosa. They tended to displace their emotional conflicts onto somatic concerns (Scott & Baroffio, 1986).

Weight loss allows anorexics to exert control over some area of their lives and may be used as a means of controlling others (Bruch, 1978; Barker & Webb, 1987; Garner et al., 1984). One recovered anorexic, whose weight had gone down to 70 pounds, commented, "It's such a manipulative disease. . . . You get people wrapped around your little finger. Any time I wanted my father to visit me in the hospital, I knew he'd be there in a second" (Seligman et al., 1983, p. 59).

Treatment of Eating Disorders

First and foremost, the anorexic patient has to gain weight; the goal is to ensure that the body is not endangered by electrolyte imbalance and weakened muscles caused by starvation (Brotman & Stern, 1983). Either a medical or a behavioral inpatient weight gain program can be implemented. The medical approach generally involves complete bed rest and either intravenous or nasogastric (tube through the nose) feeding. The behavioral approach is designed to positively reinforce weight gain. Among the reinforcers that may be earned through weight gain are television or telephone privileges, visits from family and friends, mail, and access to street clothes. The particular reinforcers that are used, of course, depend on the likes and dislikes of the patient. Weight gain plans are generally aimed at increases of up to 1 pound per day.

Once the anorexic patient has gained sufficient weight to become an outpatient, family therapy

Women, especially, are preoccupied with thinness. Diet and weight-loss books regularly appear on best-seller lists, health clubs and athletic wear are growth industries, and everywhere you look people are running or participating in some form of vigorous aerobic activity.

sessions may be implemented. Experience shows that this approach helps to maintain the treatment gains achieved in the hospital (Minuchin et al., 1978; White, 1983). In one case, the struggle over eating served to distract from recognition of conflicts within the family. After issues involving the marital relationship of her parents were worked on, one female patient showed a dramatic weight gain (Lane & Kern, 1987). The patient is still in a weight gain program and may receive additional psychotherapy.

About 50 percent of treated anorexics recover completely (remain within the normal weight range), and another 30 to 40 percent show some weight gain but remain underweight (Schwartz & Thompson, 1981; Anderson et al., 1983). For the most part, these percentages do not include cases in which the family therapy approach was used; expectations are that it will improve overall therapeutic results. There are still two major concerns about recovering anorexics, however. First, although many gain some weight, the majority remain obsessed with the fear of getting fat (Anderson et al. 1983; Mintz, 1983). Second, 14 to 50 percent become bulimics on recovering from anorexia (Hsu, 1980).

Bulimia has been successfully treated through psychotherapy and through antidepressant medication (Bruch, 1982; Pope et al., 1983). One behavioral treatment for bulimia consists of first exposure and then response prevention. Patients are taught to consume enjoyable foods (exposure) without vomiting afterward (response prevention). An important aspect of this approach is that it proves to bulimics that they can control their eating patterns (Rosen & Leitenberg, 1982; Leitenberg et al., 1984).

A somewhat novel treatment is the *psychoeducational group approach,* which combines a number of behavioral and educational techniques. Clients are told that to eliminate binges they must eat regularly. They are taught how to anticipate the urge to binge and how to either prevent or delay binges. Clients also learn to delay purging for as long as possible after an eating binge (in which case they may not require purging at all) and then to go back to eating regularly. Each binge is considered an isolated incident, rather than part of a pattern. Cognitive-behavior approaches have been effective in increasing self-efficacy in bulimics developing a sense of self-control. Bulimics learn to replace urges to binge with exercise, relaxation, or another alternative behavior (Fairburn et al., 1986; Schneider et al., 1987).

SUMMARY

1. Autistic disorder is characterized by an extreme lack of responsiveness and by language and speech deficits. It appears early in life and seems to be inherited. Autistic children may suffer from perceptual handicaps, paying attention to only a small number of cues at any time. Psychological theories of autism emphasize the parent-child relationship. Physiological overarousal and underarousal have also been proposed as explanations. These theories are all highly speculative, and evidence on them is lacking or contradictory. The prognosis for the pervasive development disorders is poor. Behavior modification procedures have yielded promising results, but evidence suggests that long-term (if not lifelong) treatment is needed.

2. Developmental problems are reported in both "normal" children and children who are clinic patients. Attention deficit hyperactivity disorder, or ADHD (characterized by overactivity, restlessness, distractibility, short attention span, and impulsiveness) is a relatively common problem. Although this disorder may be produced by organic problems, many children diagnosed as "hyperactive" do not show pathological neurological signs. Drugs have been used extensively to treat this disorder, but the use of behavior modification and self-control methods is increasing. Oppositional defiant disorders is characterized by a pattern of hostile, defiant behavior toward authority figures.

3. Conduct disorders constitute one of the few childhood conditions that show a clear continuity with adult problems. The behaviors exhibited may be socialized or unsocialized and aggressive or non-aggressive. Unfortunately, the prognosis is poor. Possible causes include understimulation; inadequate superego development; the learning, reinforcement, and modeling of aggression; and the influence of the family.

4. Children may also suffer from a variety of problems related to anxiety. Separation-anxiety disorder involves physical symptoms that appear when the child is separated from parents and home; avoidant disorder involves social situations; and overanxious disorder is similar to generalized anxiety disorder in adults. Children's anxiety reactions are usually transitory and disappear with age.

5. Tics and other stereotyped movements often occur in children and adolescents. In most cases, the disorder is transient, disappearing with or without treatment. Cases that last longer than a year are diagnosed as chronic tic disorders. A more severe problem is Tourette's syndrome, which may involve organic problems, and which may last into adulthood. Drugs and behavior therapy have been only partially successful in treating the movement disorders.

6. The eating disorders, anorexia nervosa and bulimia, are becoming more prevalent in the United States. Anorexia involves a loss of body weight

through self-starvation, body image distortion, and an intense fear of becoming obese that does not diminish with weight loss. Anorexics have poor self-esteem and may use their bizarre behavior as a way to control others. Bulimia is characterized by episodes of binge eating followed by self-induced vomiting or purging. The excessive weight consciousness of bulimics may be a result of societal emphasis on thinness, especially for women. The disorders are treated primarily by reinforcing desirable behaviors.

KEY TERMS

anorexia nervosa An eating disorder in which the person is intensely fearful of becoming obese and engages in self-starvation

attention deficit hyperactivity disorder A disorder of childhood and adolescence characterized by short attention span, impulsiveness, constant activity, and lack of self-control

autistic disorder A severe childhood disorder that is characterized by early onset and an extreme lack of interest in interpersonal relationships, and impairment in verbal and nonverbal communication

avoidant disorder A disorder of childhood and adolescence that involves severe anxiety in situations that demand contact with peers or strangers

bulimia nervosa An eating disorder characterized by the rapid consumption of large quantities of food, usually followed by self-induced vomiting

conduct disorders Disorders of childhood and adolescence that involve a persistent pattern of antisocial behaviors that violate the rights of others

oppositional defiant disorder (ODD) A childhood disorder characterized by negativistic, argumentative, and hostile behavior

overanxious disorder A childhood disorder characterized by excessive worry about past or future events, overconcern about performance, and a constant need for reassurance

pervasive developmental disorders Severe disorders of childhood that affect language, social relationships, attention, perception, and affect; include autistic disorder and pervasive developmental disorder not otherwise specified

separation anxiety disorder A childhood disorder characterized by excessive anxiety concerning separation from parents and home

tics Stereotyped and repetitive but involuntary twitchings or spasms of the voluntary muscles

tic disorders Disorders with onset in childhood and characterized by involuntary and repetitive movements and/or vocalizations, including transient and chronic tic disorders and Tourette's syndrome

Tourette's syndrome A childhood disorder characterized by multiple motor and verbal tics that may develop into coprolalia (compulsion to shout obscenities)

chapter 18
Mental Retardation

A teenager with mental retardation was asked to speak to his fellow students during a high school assembly. He told them how he felt about his handicap:

> My name is Tim Frederick . . . I would like to tell you what it is like to be retarded. . . . I am doing this so that you might be able to understand people like me. I do chores at home. I have to take care of all the animals—12 chickens, three cats, a dog, three goldfish, and a horse. That's a lot of mouths to feed. . . . After I graduate from school, I hope to live in an apartment. . . . The hardest thing is when people make fun of me. I went to a dance a few weeks ago, and no girl would dance with me. Can you guys imagine how you would feel if that happened to you? Well, I feel the same way. (Smith, 1988, pp. 118–119)

A woman with Down syndrome spoke to the Wisconsin legislature on behalf of people with mental handicaps. She wanted people to understand the things people with mental retardation could do, rather than what they cannot do:

> There are a lot of things I can do. I can swim. I can read. I can make friends. I can listen to my records. I can watch television. I can make my own lunch. I can go see a movie. I can take a bus to Chicago and to work. I can count money. I can sing like a bird . . . I can think. I can pray. I know what is right. I know what is wrong. (Turkington, 1987, p. 46)

A man with an IQ of 49 who had been institution-alized at age fifteen now lives in a boardinghouse with four other former residents of institutions. He works as a janitor in a large nursing home and talks about how it feels to be labeled mentally retarded:

> I don't know. Maybe I used to be retarded. That's what they said anyway. I wish they could see me now. I wonder what they'd say if they could see me now. I wonder what they would say if they could see me holding down a job and doing all kinds of things. I bet they would not believe it. (Bogdan & Taylor, 1976, p. 51)

How mental retardation is perceived is undergo-ing a fundamental change. Until recently, it was considered a hopeless condition that required insti-tutionalization. Tim Frederick's mother was told that her son's development would be severely delayed, and he might never be able to walk or talk. We now know that the effects of mental retardation are variable and that with training, even people who are severely handicapped can make intellectual and social gains.

Public Law 94-142 is a major reason why atti-tudes toward mental retardation are changing. This law, enacted in 1975, mandates that education be provided for all handicapped people between the ages of three and twenty-one. The education of handi-capped people is to take place in the "least restrictive environment" (educated with nonhandicapped chil-dren to the maximum extent possible). Before this legislation was passed, schools were allowed to ex-clude people with mental retardation; many were *never* given an opportunity to learn. Integrating the sudden increase in mentally handicapped children into the public schools has created hope for many, but it also has created problems. Schools are only beginning to address the needs of students in inte-grated programs.

The Association for Retarded Citizens, an ad-vocacy organization, estimates that 75 percent of children with mental retardation can become com-pletely self-supporting adults if given appropriate education and training. Another 10 to 15 percent have the potential to be self-supporting. The challenge is to develop appropriate programs to ensure the greatest success. The movement away from institu-tionalization will continue to create greater contact between people with mental retardation and the general population. In 1967, over 200,000 people with mental handicaps lived in public institutions. By 1984, this number had decreased to 110,000 (Landes-man & Butterfield, 1987). It is now widely accepted that mentally retarded people should have the op-portunity to live, work, learn, and develop relation-ships with nonretarded people in integrated settings. The next frontier will be fuller integration of people with mental retardation into the social fabric (Wolf-ensberger, 1988).

In this chapter we discuss what mental retarda-tion is (and what it is not), how it is assessed, its etiology, and some programs that have been devel-oped to help the mentally retarded lead independent and fruitful lives—at least to the extent that their condition permits. We examine several controversies regarding the appropriateness of the tools used to diagnose retardation, the institutionalization of the retarded, and the extremely delicate issue of whether people with mental retardation should have and raise children.

MENTAL RETARDATION AND PEOPLE WHO HAVE IT

In this section, we shall consider misconceptions about people with mental retardation, the way the condition is assessed, and the controversies surround-ing the use of the IQ tests. We will also examine neurological and genetic factors associated with men-tal retardation.

Misconceptions About Individuals with Mental Retardation

An estimated 6 million people in the United States or more are mentally retarded (have an IQ of 70 or less). So a great many people have had either direct or indirect experience with retarded people and with mental retardation. One might expect that miscon-ceptions about the retarded would therefore be short-lived. But attitudes toward mentally retarded people change slowly and unfavorable stereotypes remain. The label "retarded" still impedes communication between retarded and nonretarded people.

The very strong influence of this label was evident in the results of one experiment in which subjects of normal intelligence rated a person either favorably (a success) or unfavorably (a failure) according to transcripts of a bogus interview (Gibbons et al., 1979). This hypothetical person (a female) was labeled either "retarded" by the researchers or given no label at all. When the person was thought to be retarded, the subjects were less likely to express blame for failure, and less likely to give credit for success. She was simply not expected to be able to do much. Even when this person succeeded, her success was seen not as an indication of ability but rather as a piece of luck. The subjects did not believe that as a "retarded" person she had much control over her life, no matter how hard she tried. Obviously, such an attitude can become a self-fulfilling prophecy and reduce motivation.

Along with believing that people with mental retardation have little ability, other misconceptions also exist (Dudley, 1987):

1. *They have little awareness or understanding of the nature and limitations of their handicaps.* In actuality, most mentally retarded people are keenly aware of their condition. The majority admit to having impaired intellectual functioning and use terms such as "slow" or "handicapped" to describe their abilities. They admit that it takes them more time to do things (Gan et al., 1977).

2. *They are all alike.* People with mental retardation differ in intellectual, behavioral, and emotional characteristics. Some have mild mental retardation; others, severe. Some are happy, good-natured, and outgoing; others are withdrawn and anxious. People with mental retardation can experience the full range of emotional and behavioral difficulties displayed by people of normal intelligence (Rodgon, 1984).

3. *They are indifferent to the language used to refer to them.* Most people with mental retardation prefer labels such as "developmentally disabled," or "slow," or no label at all. They feel that being called "retarded" indicates that there is little that they can accomplish.

4. *People with mental retardation cannot meaningfully assess their own situation and capabilities.*

In contrast to common misconceptions about mental retardation, most research shows that people with mental retardation can successfully perform many tasks necessary for daily living. They can control their own lives and have a remarkably clear picture of their own situation and capabilities.

Actually, most do have accurate and realistic information about their capabilities and often ask for information on how to make decisions about family life and employment opportunities and request training.

5. *They are dangerous.* The news media tend to play up possible connections between mental retardation and criminal acts. However, there is only a slight positive correlation between mental retardation and criminality. In addition, the crimes that they commit tend to be associated with poor judgment rather than assaults or homicide. Social factors are much more important than low intelligence in predicting criminality (MacEachron, 1979).

These misconceptions hamper social acceptance of people with mental retardation. However, the more we interact with people who display mental retardation, the more quickly we will move away

FOCUS 18.1   *The Declassification Controversy*

The number of students with mild mental retardation in special education programs has decreased by 13 percent since 1976. To some extent, this reduction is the result of legal challenges to traditional diagnostic methods, such as IQ tests, and the development of assessment procedures (Polloway & Smith, 1983). In two California court cases, one concerning Mexican-American children, (*Diana v. State Board of Education*) and the other concerning black children (*Larry P. v. Riles*) plaintiffs argued that intelligence tests are culturally biased and that the over-representation of minorities in special education programs is a result of discriminatory practices. Decisions for the plaintiffs have resulted in decreases of 11,000 to 14,000 students being removed from classes for the educable mentally retarded

(EMR) in California to date. With these declines, however, the number of students classified as learning disabled has increased dramatically (Reschly, 1988).

Judge Peckham's (1979) decision in the *Larry P. v. Riles* case held that IQ tests were culturally biased and were not to be used in decisions involving the placement of black children in classes for the educable mentally retarded. He broadened his decision in 1986: IQ tests could not be used to determine the educational needs of black children, including whether they were learning disabled, or as part of a comprehensive educational program—even with parental consent.

A challenge to Judge Peckham's decision has come from the mother of a black child. In 1987, Mary Amaya asked that her son, De-

mond, be given an IQ test because she was concerned about his performance at school. The school denied this request because Demond is black. Amaya believes that this is a case of reverse discrimination, because other groups of students can be given IQ tests. In fact, in 1988 Amaya filed a suit (*Crawford et al. v. Honig et al.*) asserting that banning the use of intelligence tests for black children for special education services is discrimination. In California, these tests can be administered to white, Hispanic, Asian-American, and Native American school children for special education services. In addition, IQ tests can be administered to black children who are being considered for gifted and talented programs. Jerome Sattler, who supports the suit, argues that the Peckham decision denies black

---

from stereotypes and develop an attitude of tolerance and acceptance.

Diagnosing Mental Retardation

The definition of **mental retardation** in DSM-III-R is similar to that adopted by the American Association of Mental Deficiency (Grossman, 1983). It includes the following criteria:

1. *Significant subaverage general intellectual functioning* This ordinarily means an IQ of 70 or below on an individually administered IQ test.

2. *Deficiencies in adaptive behavior* (social and daily living skills, degree of independence).

3. *Onset before age eighteen* (subaverage intellectual functioning arising after age eighteen would be categorized as dementia).

DSM-III-R notes that common characteristics that accompany mental retardation are dependency, passivity, low self-esteem, low tolerance to frustration, depression, and behavior that is self-injurious (American Psychiatric Association, 1987). The more severe levels of mental retardation are associated with speech difficulties, neurological disorders, cerebral palsy, and vision and hearing problems (McQueen et al., 1987).

Issues Involved in Diagnosing Mental Retardation Several arguments have been raised against the use of IQ scores to determine mental retardation. First, the validity of IQ scores is questionable, especially when they are used to test members of minority groups (see Focus 18.1). Although IQ tests are increasingly standardized on representative samples, questions regarding their validity remain. IQ tests also may measure familiarity with mainstream

children the opportunity to qualify for programs available to other children (Sattler, 1988).

If IQ tests cannot be used, how can the educational needs of black students be met? Judge Peckham suggested alternative means to IQ testing, such as personal history and development, adaptive behavior, classroom performance, and academic achievement. Unfortunately major questions are raised concerning reliability and validity of these alternatives. Many professionals believe that although IQ tests are less than perfect, they are the most reliable and accurate means of basing educational placement decisions. They also remain good predictors of school performance.

One of the most elaborate alternative assessment programs is the System of Multicultural Pluralistic Assessment (SOMPA) developed by Jane Mercer in 1973 (this was first discussed in Chapter 4). This com-

prehensive package incorporates information about the child's medical history, perceptual and motor skills, adaptive behavior within the home and the community, and sociocultural background. Separate norms are provided for Black, Hispanic, and White children. A child who scores in the retarded range on an IQ measure may not be assessed as retarded when these other variables are considered. According to Mercer and Lewis (1977), it is "a more serious error to underestimate the child's potential than to overestimate it."

Some educators have found fault both with the court decisions and with the use of SOMPA. They note that intelligence tests have received extensive validation and that IQ is measured *after* a child has been referred for evaluation because of academic or behavioral problems. Intellectual measures, they say, are needed to determine whether a child

requires special services (Lambert, 1981). Critics of SOMPA note that its focus on adaptive behavior outside of the school setting "downplays the real difficulties experienced [by some children] within the school" (Polloway & Smith, 1983, p. 151).

Removing the classification of "mentally retarded" may not always be in the best interest of the child, according to some observers. Many children who were declassified from EMR programs were no longer eligible for alternative special education services, even though they continued to show intellectual limitations and learning problems (Reschly, 1981). How do we best identify children with special academic needs?

The controversy over the method to be used is obviously not yet over.

middle-class culture, not intelligence. Jane Mercer (1988) argues that the IQ test has been inappropriately used and that it is unfair to attempt to "measure" the intelligence by using items from one culture in a different cultural group. In addition, IQ tests do not acknowledge the positive coping characteristics of the disadvantaged.

Such objections seem to be supported by research. In one study, researchers obtained individual Wechsler IQ scores and teachers' ratings of social competence, social GPA (grades from school records on social attitudes, work habits, and the like), and academic GPA for 430 White, 201 Black, and 430 Mexican-American children attending public elementary school in Riverside, California. IQ score was found to be a good instrument for predicting scholastic achievement for white children, but it was nearly useless for children from minority-groups (Goldman & Hartig, 1976).

Both DSM-III-R and the American Association on Mental Deficiency acknowledge the danger of depending only on IQ test scores in defining mental retardation. A person must show deficits on IQ tests *and* in the area of adaptive behavior to be classified as retarded. Someone who receives a low score on an IQ test but who functions well socially and in daily activities would not be considered mentally retarded (see Focus 18.1.)

If IQ measures are inadequate for diagnosing mental retardation among members of minority groups, how useful are measures of social competence or of adaptive ability? One widely used instrument is the Vineland Social Maturity Scale (VSMS), developed by Doll (1953) and revised in 1984. Items on this adaptive measure are arranged in order of increasing difficulty and are graded from zero to twenty-five years. The areas assessed are self-help, self-direction, locomotion, occupation, communication, and social relations. Additional information is obtained during interviews with the parents of the child being tested.

To compare the effectiveness of IQ tests and adaptive behavior measures (also known as *social quotients*), researchers examined the records of 50 black children and 59 white children aged four to seventeen who had been classified as mentally retarded. IQ measures indicated that the blacks had greater intellectual impairment than the whites, but the adaptive measures indicated that the two groups were similar. These results show not only that there are differences between measured intelligence and adaptive behavior scores but also that the relative weights given these measures for classification purposes are very important. The researchers concluded, "The decision of how much emphasis to place upon measured intelligence as compared to adaptive behavior in the classification of mentally retarded children is of relatively greater importance in dealing with [black] children" (Adams et al., 1973, p. 2). No doubt their conclusion also applies to children from other minority groups. Current recommended practice is to give equal weight to the two measures, but many practitioners continue to place the most emphasis on IQ scores, (Matson 1987).

What useful information do we obtain from an IQ score? Baumeister (1987) believes the answer is very little, and gives several reasons for his view. First, the correlation between IQ and achievement outside of an academic setting is relatively low. Second, many people are labeled mentally retarded only in, but not outside of, school (the "six-hour retardate"). The prevalence rates for mental retardation seem to support his view. They increase when a child enters school and peak between the ages of twelve to fifteen at about 2 percent. After age fifteen, they decline rapidly, to about 0.5 percent at age thirty. Third, IQ scores yield little information about the condition's cause, nor do they specify the corrective action needed. What is needed is information that would help identify strategies to help children overcome specific deficits and to help them develop skills needed to adjust to their environment. An IQ score does none of this.

The Two-Group Distinction

The names of the two categories of mental retardation are largely self-explanatory. **Cultural-familial retar-** **dation** is thought to be produced by normal genetic variation, by environmental factors (such as poor living conditions), or by a combination of the two. No known organic or physiological condition that is associated with mental retardation is found in this type of retardation. Researchers have suggested that the normal range of intelligence lies between the IQ scores of 50 and 150, and that cultural-familial retardation represents the lower end of this normal range (Zigler, 1967). In any case, it accounts for the majority of people classified as mildly retarded who have normal health, appearance, and physical abilities. It is disproportionately overrepresented in the lower socioeconomic classes.

Organic retardation, which accounts for about 25 percent of all cases of mental deficiency, is the consequence of a physiological or anatomical defect. People with this type of retardation generally have more severe intellectual impairment than is characteristic of cultural-familial retardation, although a small number are only mildly retarded. Many of these people appear "different" from others in both physical appearance and displayed behaviors. The differences can be attributed to the organic disorders associated with impaired intellectual functioning.

Figure 18.1(a) shows the distribution of IQ scores that would be expected if these scores followed the theoretical normal distribution. Figure 18.1(b) shows that the actual distribution follows the theoretical distribution quite closely except at the low end of the scale; that is, more people have IQs below 50 than would be expected. Figure 18.1(c) illustrates one explanation for this phenomenon—that the organic retarded form a distinct group whose physiological defects set them apart from other low-IQ people. When this group is separated from the actual distribution of intelligence, that distribution approaches the theoretical norm through the entire range of IQs.

Levels of Retardation

Both DSM III-R and the American Association on Mental Deficiency (AAMD) specify four different levels of mental retardation, which are based only on IQ scores. The IQ ranges we use in this discussion are those measured on the revised Wechsler scales (WISC-R and WAIS-R). The descriptions are general characterizations of people at each of the levels.

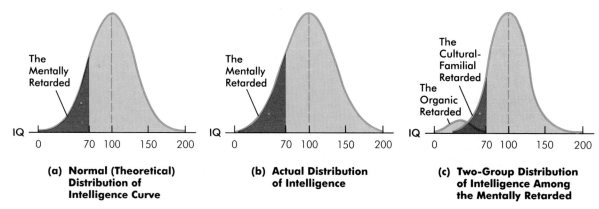

Figure 18.1 *Distribution of Intelligence as Measured by IQ Scores*
SOURCE: Zigler, 1967.

However, social and vocational skills and degree of adaptability may vary greatly for people within each category. Table 18.1 contains estimates of the number of people within each level in the United States.

Mild (IQ 50 to 70)   A disproportionate amount of attention may be devoted to people with more severe deficits. Table 18.1 shows that the majority (85 percent) of people with mental retardation, often referred to as "educable," suffer from only mild intellectual impairment. The majority of these *mildly handicapped* people suffer from cultural-familial retardation, but some organically retarded people with minimal intellectual deficits also score in this range. In some cases, their retardation is not identified until they begin to acquire academic skills; they can acquire up to sixth-grade capabilities. As adults, they may function quite adequately in the community. Many shed the label "retarded" when they enter the work force, although they tend to be employed in unskilled jobs. A large number of these individuals marry and maintain families.

In a study of forty-five mildly retarded adults with a mean IQ of 59, researchers found that seven were currently married and that three had been divorced; twenty-three were unemployed; eleven were living independently. Approximately 60 percent of the subjects perceived themselves as having impaired intellectual functioning, and used such labels as "slow" or "handicapped" to describe their own abilities and disabilities. The others denied having mentally retardation but many participated in programs for the mentally retarded, such as the Special Olympics or sheltered workshops. The majority acknowledged problems with math, reading, writing, self-maintenance, or occupation. The parents of most of these people were aware, even before their children entered school, that they were "handicapped."

TABLE 18.1 | **Estimated Number of Mentally Retarded People by Level**

Level	Range Wechsler IQ	Percentage of All Mentally Retarded	Number
Mild	50–70	85	5,108,500
Moderate	35–49	10	601,000
Severe	20–34	3–4	210,350
Profound	0–19	1–2	90,150

NOTE: Estimates based on percentages from DSM-III-R and applied to the normal probability distribution of intelligence based on a U.S. population of 210 million.

Moderate (IQ 35 to 49) Approximately 10 percent of people with mental retardation are *moderately retarded*. Children in this group have been previously referred to as "trainable"; however, some would like to eliminate this term because they feel it implies that people in this category cannot benefit from educational programs. When other children are beginning school at age six, children with moderate retardation may be functioning at a mental age between 18 months and three years; at adulthood, their intellectual development may peak at a mental age of between six and eight years or up to second grade in academic skills. Most develop self-care skills and can be employed either in sheltered workshops or at unskilled occupations. They can travel independently to familiar places. People with moderate retardation are generally identified during their pre-school years. They can adapt to life in the community, usually in supervised group homes.

Severe (IQ 20 to 34) About 3 to 4 percent of people with mental retardation are *severely retarded*. Most people in this group can be toilet trained and can learn personal care skills related to cleanliness, eating, and dressing. However, their rate of learning is very slow, and constant care and supervision are usually required. Most people with severe retardation can be identified by their physical appearance and evident sensorimotor problems, and the majority suffer organic retardation. In adult life, they may be able to perform simple tasks under close supervision and can adapt to group homes.

Profound (IQ 0 to 19) Only about 1 to 2 percent of people with mental retardation are *profoundly retarded*; these people are so intellectually deficient that constant and total care and supervision are necessary. Many are confined to a bed or wheelchair by the congenital defects that produced the retardation; even with teaching, there is minimal, if any, acquisition of self-help skills. Their mortality rate during childhood is extremely high.

THE ETIOLOGY OF ORGANIC MENTAL RETARDATION

Mental retardation can be caused by genetic abnormalities, metabolic disorders, and environmental conditions such as brain trauma, malnutrition, infection, or prematurity. All these factors result in brain damage.

Genetic Syndromes

As noted, cultural-familial retardation may be caused by the *normal* genetic variation. In contrast, the following conditions involve mental defects caused by genetic anomalies. These conditions are rare and generally result in the more severe forms of mental retardation. People with these genetic syndromes often have unusual physical characteristics as well.

Chromosomal Anomalies The genetic makeup of the human being includes twenty-two pairs of **autosomes** (nonsex chromosomes) and one pair of **sex chromosomes** (XX in the female and XY in the male). Two categories of chromosomal aberrations are associated with mental retardation—those due to autosome abnormalities and those due to sex chromosome abnormalities.

Autosomal Abnormalities **Down syndrome,** which is due to an autosomal abnormality, is one of the most common clinically defined forms of mental retardation; it may occur as often as twice per 1,000 live births. About 10 percent of children with severe or moderate retardation show this genetic anomaly. The condition was first described in 1866 by John Langdon Down, an English physician. The relationship between Down syndrome and chromosomal aberration was discovered in 1959 by a French geneticist, Jerome Lejeune.

Down syndrome is caused by the presence of one more than the normal complement of forty-six chromosomes (twenty-three from the mother and twenty-three from the father). During *meiosis* (cell division), each parent's twenty-three pairs of chromosomes should separate so that the egg and sperm contain only twenty-three chromosomes each. The extra chromosome results from the failure of one parent's number 21 chromosome to separate. When fertilization occurs, the result is a set of three Number 21 chromosomes instead of the normal two. This anomaly is called **trisomy 21** (see Figure 18.2).

The well-known physical characteristics of Down syndrome are short in-curving fingers, short broad hands, slanted eyes, furrowed protruding tongue, flat

Down syndrome is the most common form of mental retardation. It appears in approximately 10 percent of children with moderate to severe retardation. Although these children have below normal intellectual functioning, they can acquire academic skills in highly structured learning environments, geared to their needs.

and broad face, harsh voice, and incomplete or delayed sexual development. Cosmetic surgery (consisting mostly of modifying tongue size) is being used with some Down syndrome children in an effort to make their physical appearance more nearly normal, and to allow them to speak more clearly and to eat more normally. The procedure is intended to allow Down syndrome people to fit in as much as possible with their peers in order to enhance their social interactions and communication abilities.

The average height of people with Down syndrome is 5 feet for males and 4 feet 7 inches for women. Down syndrome people who live past age forty are at high risk for developing Alzheimer's disease (Miniszek, 1983). The gene responsible for *amyloid plaques* (patches of degenerated nerve endings) and *neurofibrillary tangles* (fibers that appear to be tangles of brain tissue filaments), conditions found in Alzheimer's disease, is located on chromosome 21, indicating a possible relationship between Down syndrome and Alzheimer's disease (Clarke & Clarke, 1987; St. Clair, 1987). People who have Down syndrome show a greater intellectual decline with increasing age than do other individuals with mental retardation. However, only 15 to 40 percent develop signs of dementia—deterioration of mental ability (Zigman et al., 1987). Congenital heart ab-

normalities are also common in people with Down syndrome, causing a high mortality rate. Recent surgical procedures have improved the probability of surviving these heart defects but have given rise to legal and ethical issues (see Focus 18.2).

Much has been written about the personality characteristics of children with Down syndrome. Terms such as *good-natured, happy, affectionate,* and *socially well adjusted* have frequently been used (Brink & Grundlingh, 1976). Down syndrome children are more likely than other noninstitutionalized retarded children to be called "clownish," "sociable," and "affectionate," regardless of their race or sex (Gibbs & Thorpe, 1983).

The prevalence of this disorder increases with the age at which the mother gives birth, from 1 in 15,000 live births for mothers under age thirty to 1 in 65 births for mothers over forty-five. One-third of all Down syndrome children are born to mothers over the age of thirty-eight. Although much is made of the fact that older women are more likely than younger women to conceive children with Down syndrome, it must also be remembered that approximately two-thirds of all children with this disorder are born to women under age thirty-seven. There has also been increased interest in the effect of the father's age on the prevalence of Down syndrome.

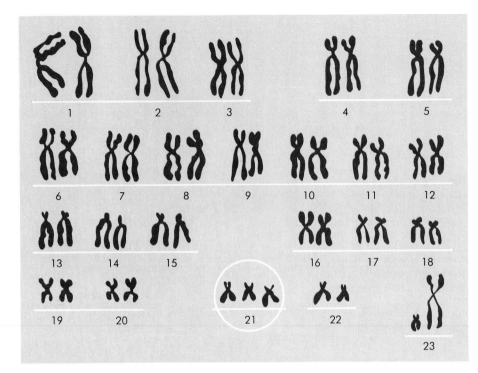

Figure 18.2 Chromosomes of a Down Syndrome Child
The anomaly that causes Down syndrome is the third number 21 chromosome.

Prenatal detection of Down syndrome is possible through **amniocentesis,** which is performed during the fourteenth or fifteenth week of pregnancy. In this procedure, a hollow needle is inserted through the abdominal wall into the amniotic fluid sac. Some of the fluid is withdrawn, and the fetal cells are culti-

Through amniocentesis, it is possible to detect Down syndrome during the fourteenth or fifteenth week of pregnancy. Fetal cells, collected from amniotic fluid, are cultured and tested for the presence of an extra chromosome in pair number 21.

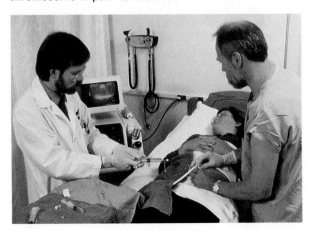

vated. Within three weeks, these cells can be tested to determine whether Down syndrome is present. This procedure involves some risk for both mother and fetus, so it is employed only when the chance of finding Down syndrome is high—as, for example, with women over age thirty-five.

A procedure that allows earlier detection of Down syndrome is *chorionic villus* sampling. Tests are made of cells on the hairlike projections (villi) on the sac that surrounds the fetus and can be performed after the ninth week of pregnancy.

Anomalies of the Sex Chromosomes The normal sex chromosome configuration is XY in males and XX in females. **Turner's syndrome,** or *gonadal dysgenesis,* is caused by the lack of one X chromosome in a female (X0). This condition is rare. The facial appearance remains normal, but some webbing of the neck and retarded growth are typical. Secondary sex characteristics usually fail to appear during puberty. Only about 20 percent of people with Turner's syndrome are mentally retarded but most generally exhibit severe deficits in space-form perception; this finding has prompted an investigation into the relationship between X chromosomes and visual-spatial

FOCUS 18.2   *Rights of Down Syndrome Children and Their Parents*

Phillip is a Down syndrome child who has a life-threatening hole in his heart. His parents denied him an operation that would have repaired the defect, and the California courts supported their decision. Later, however, against the wishes of his parents, guardianship of Phillip was awarded to volunteer workers at the institution where he has lived since birth. Warren and Patricia Becker, Phillip's natural parents, responded that they love their son, took good care of him, and feel that their rights as parents have been violated: "You can lose your loved one solely because you do not meet a level of involvement expected of you by a court of law" (Becker & Becker, 1983, p. 17).

In another case, the parents of an infant with Down syndrome denied him corrective surgery that would have allowed food to reach his stomach. This decision was upheld by the Indiana Supreme Court, and the infant was allowed to die. Columnist George Will, who has a teenage son with Down syndrome, argued that the parents and the court acted as they did solely because the infant was retarded. He characterized their decision as "the right to kill inconvenient life." However, opponents of this viewpoint feel that there is no absolutely right or wrong position and that the quality of life for both the child and the parents must be taken into consideration.

Controversies concerning the rights of the child, the parents, and society in such cases will probably become more heated as advances in medical technology increase survival rates for infants with birth defects.

abilities (Knopf, 1984; McCauley et al., 1987). Women with Turner's syndrome can be treated with female hormones for their lack of sexual development, but they remain sterile.

Klinefelter's syndrome is a disorder in males that is caused by an excessive number of X chromosomes (XXY or XXXY instead of XY). This condition occurs approximately 1.7 times per 1,000 live male births. Mental retardation is found in about 25 percent of the cases; generally, a greater number of X chromosomes is associated with more severe retardation (Knopf, 1984). No specific cognitive deficits are involved, but there is delayed development of secondary sex characteristics, which can be treated with testosterone.

The **fragile X syndrome** is a defect in a particular part of the X chromosome, involving a narrowing or gap near the bottom of the chromosome. This condition may account for an estimated 10 percent of all cases of mental retardation, second only to Down syndrome (Dykens et al., 1988). Some symptoms in this syndrome are similar to those of autistic disorder. A child with the fragile X chromosome was not responsive to the mother, would arch the back when she tried to pick him or her up, and repeat words in a meaningless manner (Murphy, 1987). Interestingly, 10 to 16 percent of autistic children also have the fragile X chromosome. Although the syndrome can occur in either male or females, males are more severely affected. Because females have two X chromosomes, one from each parent, the normal X chromosome mitigates the effects of the chromosome with the fragile X pattern. Studies have found that females with this condition suffer less mental impairment than males. Physical characteristics associated with this condition include a prominent jaw, long thin face, and prominent forehead (Rogers & Simensen, 1987).

Recessive Gene Disorders   These genetic disorders are caused by the pairing of two recessive genes (genes that require pairing with an identical gene for expression) which produces a disturbance or abnormality in the metabolic processes. These disturbances, in turn, produce a variety of physical defects and differing levels of mental retardation. The most common recessive gene disorders are phenylketonuria (PKU), Tay-Sachs disease, and cretinism.

Phenylketonuria (PKU) is a metabolic disorder that is transmitted by a recessive gene that prevents the conversion of *phenylalanine,* one of the amino acids present in many foods, into *tyrosine.* It was discovered in 1934, when a mother brought two children in for an examination because their urine had an unusual musty smell. An analysis revealed that this characteristic was due to the presence of excessive phenylalanine. Both children were mentally retarded. Excessive amounts of phenylalanine result in central nervous system degeneration and brain damage (Stern, 1987). The level of mental retardation in untreated individuals is generally severe to profound; few reach an IQ above 40. One-third of these people cannot walk or control excretion, and two-thirds cannot talk. They are often hyperactive and irritable (Robinson & Robinson, 1976). PKU occurs at a rate of about 1 per 15,000 births in the United States.

Infants with PKU appear normal at birth, but their mental retardation becomes apparent within a year. The accumulation of phenylalanine and the consequent absence of tyrosine also decrease pigmentation; thus people with this condition are often fair-haired and light-skinned.

Early diagnosis of PKU is essential for reducing or preventing mental retardation; mass screening for the disorder is routinely performed in most hospitals. The treatment, which consists of eliminating foods high in phenylalanine from the diet, is usually started during the first six months of life and continued until age four to six; after that, it can be discontinued without harm. The diet must be administered very carefully, because many of the restricted foods contain nutrients necessary for life.

The successful treatment of children with PKU has an unfortunate side effect. In the past, very few PKU women became pregnant because they were severely retarded and were usually institutionalized. Now, many successfully treated and hence intellectually normal women with PKU bear children who suffer birth defects because of their exposure to high levels of phenylalanine in the fetal environment. Dietary treatment during pregnancy has been unsuccessful, and the probability of a treated PKU woman having a child who is retarded and a victim of other defects is very high. Genetic counseling is usually recommended.

Tay-Sachs disease is a recessive gene metabolic disorder in which fatty substances accumulate in the brain and other tissues of the body. More than fifty new cases are reported each year, primarily among Jews. It is estimated that approximately 1 in 33 American Jews of Eastern European ancestry carry this gene, compared to 1 in 300 in other groups (Robinson & Robinson, 1976). Through the use of amniocentesis, scientists have discovered that 25 percent of the fetuses of two carrier parents have this recessive disorder.

Children with Tay-Sachs disease appear normal at birth but soon display progressive muscle weakness (such as an inability to roll over or raise the chest and head), loss of the ability to initiate movements, lack of appetite, and loss of sight and hearing. Death occurs between two and four years of age. There is no known treatment for the disorder. However, detection is possible via blood tests, and mass screening programs are available in many hospitals.

Cretinism, or **hypothyroidism,** can result either from a genetically produced metabolic disorder that prevents the proper synthesis of a hormone of the thyroid gland, or from iodine deficiency in the mother during pregnancy. Cretinism due to the latter cause has been reduced greatly in the United States via the addition of iodine to table salt.

Some diagnostic signs of cretinism appear within the first few weeks of life. The heart rate, respiratory rate, body temperature, and blood temperature are typically low. Other characteristics include poor appetite, a large and protruding tongue, and dry and thick skin. If the problem remains untreated, the child becomes mentally retarded. As adults, people with cretinism are characterized by short stature, listlessness, coarse facial features (puffy eyelids and thick ears and lips), obesity, and a protruding abdomen. Very early treatment with iodine can prevent the appearance of these symptoms. Once irreversible damage occurs, however, this thyroid therapy loses most of its effect.

Until recently it was difficult to diagnose cretinism in an infant before three months of age. Fortunately, a new test for hypothyroidism in the newborn allows routine screening at birth, ensuring prompt treatment.

Nongenetic Organic Factors

Mental retardation may be caused by a variety of environmental mishaps that can occur during the prenatal period (from conception to birth), the perinatal period (during the birth process), and the postnatal period (after birth). During the prenatal period, the developing organism is susceptible to viruses, infections, drugs, radiation, poor nutrition, and other nongenetic influences. During the perinatal period, mental retardation can result from birth trauma, prematurity, or asphyxiation. After birth, head injuries, infections, tumors, malnutrition, and the ingesting toxic substances such as lead can cause brain damage and consequent mental retardation.

Prenatal Factors   A number of viral and bacterial infections can be transmitted to the fetus through the placenta. Many of these can produce inflammation of the fetal brain and subsequent degeneration of brain tissue. For example, mental retardation can follow a case of *rubella*, or German measles. In the mother, the infection is mild, usually causing a low temperature and a slight rash. The danger to the fetus is greatest during the first trimester, when about 50 percent of infected mothers transmit the disease to the fetus. Then birth defects such as sensory handicaps, congenital heart lesions, and mental retardation may result, depending on the severity and location of the brain damage (Carter, 1975).

Increasing attention is being focused on the problem of mental deficits related to alcohol consumption during pregnancy. Some children born to alcoholic mothers show, to varying degrees, a group of congenital physical and mental defects known as **fetal alcohol syndrome** (**FAS**). Children with this syndrome tend to be small and to suffer from **microcephaly**, an anomaly whose most distinguishing feature is an unusually small brain. Usually such children are mildly retarded, but neither moderate retardation nor average intelligence is uncommon (Streissguth et al., 1980). However, those with normal intelligence seem to have significant academic and attentional difficulties, as well as a history of hyperactivity and behavioral deficits (Shaywitz, 1980).

Other common neurological and physical symptoms of FAS include coordination difficulties, shortened eyeslits, impaired development of midfacial tissue, inner epicanthal folds, abnormal creases in the palm of the hand, and cardiac abnormalities (Hanson et al., 1976). Generally, the more pronounced physical abnormalities are associated with greater retardation of intellectual development (Streissguth et al., 1978). Some FAS children show the mental and behavioral deficits of the syndrome but none of the physical abnormalities (Streissguth et al., 1980).

Alcohol is one of the most common causes of retardation. Researchers, however, do not know how much or how little alcohol is necessary to produce fetal alcohol syndrome. Abstention from drinking during pregnancy may be the only certain way to prevent this disorder.

Estimates of FAS incidence in the children of alcoholic women range from 26 to 76 percent, depending on the criteria used to diagnose FAS and on the severity of the alcoholism (Abel, 1984; Streissguth et al., 1980). Smoking and poor nutrition may increase the likelihood that an alcoholic mother will have FAS offspring. Presently available information suggests that one case of FAS occurs in each 750 live births, which places alcohol among the most common causes of retardation for which an etiology can be determined (Streissguth et al., 1980).

Alcohol consumed by a pregnant woman crosses the placental barrier and reaches the fetus in almost full concentration. Researchers assume that the greatest harm to the fetus occurs in the first trimester. Studies seem to indicate only small risk associated with alcohol consumption under one ounce a day.

Between one and two ounces per day increases the risk of significant malformation to 10 percent. Two or more ounces consumed per day increases the risk to 20 percent. Response seems to be related to dose (Cooper, 1987). Efforts to prevent FAS are presently directed toward encouraging pregnant women to abstain from alcohol completely.

Perinatal Factors Prolonged birth, pressure on the head during the birth process, physical trauma, and compression of the umbilical cord can produce brain hemorrhages or other brain damage. Compared with prenatal factors, however, these hazards account for only a small proportion of organically caused mental retardation. The most common birth condition associated with mental retardation is prematurity and low birth weight. Although most premature infants develop normally, approximately 20 percent show signs of neurological problems reflected in learning disabilities and mental retardation (Pound, 1987). In a study of over 53,000 U.S. women and their children, researchers found that low birth weight was generally associated with low IQ scores. The average IQ of children who had birth weights between 26 ounces and 52.5 ounces was 86, whereas those with birth weights between 122 ounces and 140

ounces had an average IQ of 105 (Broman et al., 1975).

Postnatal Factors Relatively few cases of mental impairment are due to damage to the central nervous system after birth. But mental retardation *can* result from asphyxiation, brain tumors, head injury, severe malnutrition, or infectious diseases such as meningitis and encephalitis. These infectious diseases are particularly virulent when they occur during the first years of life, while the brain is still developing rapidly.

Although most types of mental retardation now have decreasing incidence rates, postnatal causes of mental retardation is on the increase. The cause is direct trauma to the head that produces hemorrhaging and tearing of the brain tissue, often as the result of an injury sustained in an automobile accident or from *child abuse*. Depending on the definition of child abuse, estimates of the number of cases of child abuse per year range from 35,000 to 1.9 million. Of this group, a large percentage of children are subjected to violent abuse that could cause serious injury (Gelard & Sanford, 1987). The authors of a British study of child abuse go so far as to argue that violence-induced handicaps should be recognized as

Although most forms of mental retardation now have decreasing prevalence rates, the incidence of postnatal retardation is rising, due to severe brain injury. Some of these injuries are accidental, but many are the result of child abuse, which is a worsening social problem in this country.

a major cause of retardation: "Children rendered mentally handicapped as a result of abuse may account for more cases than PKU. The consequences are frequently more severe than those of Down's syndrome" (Buchanan & Oliver, 1977, p. 465).

Another postnatal cause of retardation is *lead poisoning* from ingesting lead-based paints. Infants may chew on cribs or window sills or eat paint that has flaked off a wall or ceiling. (The public has been alerted to these hazards, and some towns have banned lead-based paint. But if a home has not been painted in the past few years, the old paint probably contains lead.) Recently, there has been concern about the ingestion of lead from water fountains in schools.

Both hereditary and environmental factors contribute to mental retardation. Research shows that poor nutrition, inadequate housing, and substandard school and living environments tend to be associated with lower IQ scores.

THE ETIOLOGY OF CULTURAL-FAMILIAL RETARDATION

As noted earlier, cultural-familial retardation is generally mild intellectual impairment that does not have an identifiable organic cause. This category of retardation has produced many controversies concerning etiology and the cognitive processes. Braginsky and Braginsky (1973) suggest that the "retarded" label should be abandoned entirely because people with cultural-familial retardation fall within the normal range of intelligence. From their observations of institutionalized people, they conclude that people with cultural-familial retardation are "adept, rational, resourceful human beings, capable of protecting their own interests by using complex, subtle interpersonal tactics" (p. 24). The backgrounds of most of these people indicate that they were unwanted and unloved by their families; Braginsky and Braginsky believe that society deals with this problem by labeling them "mentally retarded." This point is well taken. But in fact there are indeed children and adults who display considerable difficulty in learning academic skills. We need to find out why, rather than to discard the category of cultural-familial retardation.

Heredity or Environment?

Certain features of the environment may contribute to retardation. Among these are the absence of stimulating factors or situations, a lack of attention and reinforcement from parents or significant others, and chronic stress and frustration. In addition, poverty, lack of adequate health care, poor nutrition, and inadequate education places children at a disadvantage. A lower socioeconomic status generally implies a lower mean group IQ score (Ardizzone & Scholl, 1985).

Poor nutrition, inadequate housing, and substandard school environments also tend to be associated with lower IQ scores. In one study, higher scores were obtained by children from a family of low socioeconomic status after they were placed in an adequate environment (Scarr & Weinberg, 1976). The investigators predicted that, if the children had been reared by their natural parents, their mean IQ would have been 90. However, after placement these children scored above the national average of 100 on standard IQ tests. This study seems to point up the importance of environmental factors in the full development of intellectual capabilities. But one can also argue that the IQ scores of these children reflect exposure to middle-class values and skills rather than increases in native intellectual ability.

Heredity is also a factor in cultural-familial retardation. One researcher found that the mental retardation associated with slums is not randomly distributed among families living in poverty, but rather is concentrated within individual families and can be identified on the basis of maternal IQ. The data indicated that almost 80 percent of the children with IQs below 80 had mothers with IQs below 80. And the lower the maternal IQ, the greater was the probability that an offspring would score low on an intelligence test (Heber, 1970). This finding can be used to support the belief that innate factors cause cultural-familial retardation, but it is also possible that mothers with mental retardation create a less stimulating social and intellectual environment than by mothers with normal intelligence. Until we can determine whether genetic or environmental factors are more important, the hereditary-environment controversy will continue.

Results of Early Intervention

Programs such as Head Start have not produced dramatic increases in intellectual ability among at-risk children (those from low-income families). But long-term follow-up studies have found that they do produce positive results (Royce et al., 1983; Zigler & Berman, 1983). Children who participated in early intervention programs were found to perform better in school than nonparticipants, and the difference between the two groups continued to widen up to the twelfth grade. In addition, a greater proportion of the participants finished high school, which no doubt helped them obtain and hold better jobs.

The families of participants were also positively influenced by the programs. They rated the programs as personally helpful, spent more time working with their children on school tasks, and perceived their children as becoming happier and healthier. There is continuing optimism about the efficacy of such programs, even though two well-known studies that reported large increases in IQ (the studies of Heber & Garber, 1975 and Skeels, 1966) were found to have severe methodological flaws (Longstreth, 1981; Page, 1972).

Early intervention programs have also been developed for children with mental retardation. Cara, a Down syndrome child, was enrolled in an early intervention program one month after her birth. Her program involved assessment of fine and gross motor skills, eye-hand coordination, and the development of self-help skills. Training in communication skills was also given. She is now fourteen years old and participates in a number of school activities, such as swimming and dancing. Many believe that early intervention techniques, along with training designed to teach parents to exercise and stimulate their child, can decrease the severity of mental handicaps (Jablow, 1988).

In 1986 Public Law 99-457 was enacted. The law broadens Public Law 94-142 by mandating that children from birth to age three be eligible to participate in intervention programs (Public Law 94-142 excluded children younger than three). Such widespread opportunity for intervention may provide the impetus for more early education programs and increased support for parents with developmentally delayed infants and preschoolers (Zantal-Weiner, 1988). As you can see in Focus 18.3, there is cause for both optimism and pessimism regarding mental retardation.

PROGRAMS FOR PEOPLE WITH MENTAL RETARDATION

Most public schools now have special programs for children with mental retardation. This policy contradicts the antiquated view that mentally retarded people were not capable of learning academic skills or holding jobs. The effectiveness of special-education classes for the "educable" retarded can be summarized as follows (Capute, 1985):

◆ Up to 80 percent of the graduates of these programs become self-supporting.

◆ A majority percent marry and maintain a family.

◆ Most are employed in service jobs, but a number have semiskilled jobs or occupations.

Employment Programs

People with mental handicaps can achieve more than was previously thought. The parents of a teenage boy, for example, were told that he would always be childlike and the only job he would ever be fit for was stringing beads. Another person with moderate retardation, who spent most of his time staring at his hands and rubbing his face also appeared to have a dismal future. Both of these men now have paying jobs, one as a janitor and the other as dishwasher.

FOCUS 18.3 *Optimism and Pessimism About the Prevention of Mental Retardation*

In 1972, the President's Committee on Mental Retardation presented a very optimistic view about the prevention of mental retardation. "Using present knowledge and techniques from the biomedical and behavioral sciences, it is possible to reduce the occurrence of mental retardation by 50 percent before the end of the century" (p. 31). To assess possible progress in achieving this goal, Clarke and Clarke (1977, 1987) analyzed epidemiological studies on different degrees of mental retardation. Their analysis re-

vealed that the incidence of the more severe forms of mental retardation had dropped by about one-third from the early 1900s to the 1960s. Advances in immunization against the diseases associated with neurological damage, and better prenatal and postnatal care, have contributed to this reduction. Amniocentesis and the development of other early detection procedures can further reduce the incidence of severe retardation.

Clarke and Clarke are more pessimistic, however, about substantial

reductions in the incidence of milder forms of mental retardation, particularly of the cultural-familial type. Environmental factors such as malnutrition, poor living conditions, and "poverty of culture" are difficult to eradicate, and early and comprehensive intervention would be difficult to apply nationwide. Unless more resources are directed to relieving the conditions that produce cultural-familial retardation, the prospect of reducing its incidence by 50 percent is bleak.

Programs designed to help people with mental handicaps learn occupational skills are largely responsible for the improved outcome of these men and other like them (McLeod, 1985).

One such program is the Structured Training and Employment Transitional Services (STETS) project funded by the U.S. Department of Labor (Kerachsky & Thornton, 1987). The program, designed for people between the ages of eighteen and twenty-four who have moderate to mild levels of mental retardation, has three phases. The first involves initial training and work in a low-stress environment. After a suitable skill level is attained, the second phase begins. This phase involves on-the-job training during which participants are expected to meet the same requirements as nonretarded workers doing the same job. Phase three involves a six-month follow-up of the workers, now employed in unsolicited, competitive jobs.

Participants in this training program were compared to a control group who used other community services, but not STETS services. At the end of the six-month follow-up period, 31 percent of the people in the STETS program were regularly employed in competitive jobs versus 19 percent of the control group. About 45 percent of the people in both groups

had paid employment that involved noncompetitive jobs (sheltered workshops and activity centers). People in the STETS program also received better pay than those in the control group. Interestingly, the most successful participants were those with the lower IQ scores and whose mental handicaps were associated with organic causes. Such training allows people to become self-sufficient members of the community.

Another program is the Electronic Assembly Service (ESA), located in Virginia, people receiving this training have IQs of 35 or below. Participants are taught to assemble circuit boards. Reinforcement principles are used to teach the necessary work skills. Behavioral problems are handled with time out procedures, while appropriate behaviors are reinforced with praise and tangible rewards such as food. Within four months of training, most participants become productive workers, earning a salary (McLeod, 1985). This program and others like it are helping to integrate people with mental retardation into society.

Marriage and Parenting

One researcher investigated the ability of thirty-two married couples with mental retardation to maintain themselves independently in the community. Both partners in each marriage had below-normal intelligence, and most had IQs in the 50s and 60s. The majority of the marriages were described as affectionate and supportive by both husband and wife. The partners accepted their low level of intelligence, and the marriage provided a complementary base in which the skills of each helped to compensate for the other's weaknesses. One wife, for example, said her husband did all the reading for the family while she did all the writing. Resentment toward the spouse was noted in four marriages in which one partner was heavily dependent on the other. However, only three of the marriages were predominantly unsatisfactory relationships (Mattison, 1973).

There are a number of programs designed to develop the capabilities of people with mental retardation. Among the better known is the Special Olympics, which provides the opportunity for special athletes to compete against their peers.

Most people with mental retardation would like to marry and have children. The right of mildly handicapped individuals to do so is generally not questioned. However, some parents with mental retardation do have problems raising their children. Although parents with mental retardation love their children, many of them are unable to provide adequate care, even with the assistance of social service agencies. In one study of parents with moderate levels of mental retardation, half had been reported to authorities for child neglect or abuse (Whitman et al., 1987). Two approaches have been used to deal with this problem: genetic counseling and teaching people with mental retardation how to be better parents. Just as genetic counseling can provide nonretarded parents with the information they need to decide whether to give birth to a child who will be handicapped, counseling can also help to give retarded couples a realistic picture of the responsibilities and economic and psychological burdens of parenthood. However, such counseling must acknowledge the fact that a couple with mental retardation has the right to make its own decision about whether or not to have children.

The second approach is to provide family life education. A group of adolescents with mental retardation clearly indicated a need to know more about marriage and parenting. They also wanted to develop the skills necessary to function in these roles. Marriage, pregnancy, child care, parenthood, and financial management were specific areas of concern (Schultz & Adams, 1987). Developing communication skills and learning about family responsibilities are important for adolescents with mental retardation, especially since many of their parents continue to treat them like children and do little to prepare them for independent living (Flynn & Saleem, 1986). Parents of mentally retarded adolescents and adults are very restrictive in what they teach their children about sex and what they allow them to express (Gami, 1987). Programs that address family issues help to ensure a smooth transition to community living.

Institutionalization

Unfortunately, institutions for the mentally retarded are often substandard and overcrowded, with unfavorable staff-to-resident ratios. In many of these institutions, people with mental retardation are still considered incompetent and incapable of responsible interaction or useful work. The mistreatment and "warehousing" of mentally retarded people have been well documented.

There has been an increase in the deinstitutionalization of people with mental retardation. More of them are being placed in group homes or in situations where they can live independently or semi-independently within the community. The idea is to provide the "least restrictive environment" that is consistent with their condition and that will give them the opportunity to develop more fully. The implication seems to be that institutions are bad places, but the fact is they do not have uniformly negative effects. Nor do group homes always provide positive experiences. What seems to be most important are the goals; programs that promote social interaction and the development of competence have positive effects on the residents of either institutions or group homes (Tjosvold & Tjosvold, 1983).

Nontraditional group arrangements, in which a small number of people live together in a home, sharing meals and chores, do provide more opportunity for social interactions. These "normalized" living arrangements were found to produce such benefits as increased adaptive functioning, improved language development, and socialization (MacEachron, 1983; Kleinberg & Galligan, 1983). However, many of these positive behaviors were already part of the residents' repertoires; what they need are systematic programs that will teach them additional living skills (Kleinberg & Galligan, 1983). Merely moving retarded people from one environment to another does not alone guarantee that they will be taught the skills they need. Nonetheless, properly planned and supported deinstitutionalization does provide the opportunity to experience a more "normal" life (but see also Focus 18.4).

Behavioral therapeutic approaches have also been used to help mentally handicapped people develop basic skills, from bathing and brushing their teeth to living independently (Spiegler, 1983). New programs aimed at developing independent behavior in people with mental retardation are promising. Even though such people often confront difficult obstacles, many face these problems with a positive spirit.

In a study of fifteen people with mild retardation whose mean IQ and mean age were both 62, re-searchers identified such common stressors as poverty, illness, loss of a job or spouse, and lack of social support. Even with these problems, the subjects all appeared to be hopeful, confident, and independent. One woman, who maintained her positive self-esteem in spite of lacking a job, remarked, "Where can I get a job when those knuckleheads there in Washington cut all the plants [factories] and everything?" (Edgerton et al., 1984, p. 347).

SUMMARY

1. Myths and misconceptions about mental retardation still abound, even though 85 percent of those with mental retardation suffer only mild intellectual impairment. Two kinds of retardation are recognized: cultural-familial retardation (produced by normal genetic processes, environmental factors, or a combination of the two) and organic retardation (severe intellectual impairment that is caused by physiological or anatomical defect). The American Association on Mental Deficiency identifies four different levels of retardation, which are based only on IQ scores: mild or "educable" (IQ 50 to 70), moderate or "trainable" (IQ 35 to 49), severe (IQ 20 to 34), and profound (IQ 0 to 19). Research indicates that IQ tests may have differential validity for whites and blacks. As a result, adaptive measures—which include self-help, self-direction, communication, and social skills—are now being used in conjunction with IQ scores to assess intellectual ability.

2. A minority of cases of mental retardation stem from organic factors. These factors include chromosomal anomalies (Down syndrome and fragile X syndrome), disturbances of metabolic processes (PKU and cretinism), prenatal problems (infections and bacteria entering the fetus from the mother), perinatal difficulties (birth trauma), and postnatal influences (severe malnutrition, ingestion of lead, and brain trauma).

3. Cultural-familial retardation does not have an identifiable organic cause and is associated with only mild intellectual impairment. Certain features of the environment may contribute to retardation: absence of stimulating materials, lack of attention and reinforcement from parents, chronic stress and frustration, poor nutrition, and substandard school envi-

FOCUS 18.4 Another View of Institutions

Although there is an increasing movement toward deinstitutionalization, institutions continue to perform a useful function for children with mental retardation and their parents. The need for mental institutions is evident in this quote from an article by Fern Kupfer:

> I watched Phil Donahue recently. He had on mothers of handicapped children who talked about the pain and blessing of having a "special" child. As the mother of a severely handicapped six-year-old boy who cannot sit, who cannot walk, who will be in diapers all of his days, I understand the pain. The blessing part continues to elude me—notwithstanding the kind and caring people we've met through this tragedy. . . .
>
> Our child Zachariah has not lived at home for almost four years. I knew when we placed him, sorry as I was, that this was the right decision, for his care precluded any semblance of normal family life for the rest of us. I do not think that we "gave him up," although he is cared for daily by nurses, caseworkers, teachers and therapists, rather than by his mother and father. When we come to visit him at his "residential facility," a place housing 50 severely physically and mentally handicapped youngsters, we usually see him being held and rocked by a foster grandma who has spent the better part of the afternoon singing him nursery rhymes. I do not feel that we have "put him away." Perhaps it is just a question of language. I told another mother who was going through the difficult decision regarding placement for her retarded child, "Think of it as going to boarding school rather than institutionalization." Maybe euphemisms help ease the pain a little bit. But I've also seen enough to know that institution need not be a dirty word. . . .
>
> This anti-institutional trend has some very frightening ramifications. We force mental patients out into the real world of cheap welfare hotels and call it "community placement." We parole youthful offenders because "jails are such dangerous places to be," making our city streets dangerous places for the law-abiding. We heap enormous guilt on the families that need, for their own survival, to put their no-longer-competent elderly in that dreaded last stop: the nursing home. . . .
>
> Most retarded people do not belong in institutions any more than most people over 65 belong in nursing homes. What we need are options and alternatives for a heterogeneous population. We need group homes and halfway houses and government subsidies to families who choose to care for dependent members at home. We need accessible housing for independent handicapped people; we need to pay enough to foster-care families to show that a good home is worth paying for. We need institutions. And it shouldn't have to be a dirty word.

———
SOURCE: Kupfer, 1982.

ronments. A controversy of major proportions exists between "defect" theorists, who believe that all people with retardation suffer from a specific cognitive defect, and "developmental" theorists, who argue that the cognitive processes of people with cultural-familial retardation are the same as those of people with normal intelligence. Studies have found that there are a variety of motivational and emotional differences between retarded and nonretarded people, but these results are not conclusive.

4. Public schools provide special programs for children and adolescents; even people who are severely retarded are given instruction and training in practical self-help skills. Some communities also provide group care homes. Those who are more profoundly retarded may be institutionalized. Various approaches—behavioral therapy in particular—are being used successfully to help retarded people acquire needed "living" skills.

KEY TERMS

amniocentesis A screening procedure performed during the fourteenth or fifteenth week of pregnancy, used to determine the presence of Down syndrome

cultural-familial retardation Generally mild mental retardation that is thought to be produced by normal genetic processes, environmental factors, or both

cretinism A metabolic disorder that causes mental retardation. It results from iodine deficiency in the mother during pregnancy. Also called hypothyroidism

Down syndrome A condition produced by the presence of an extra chromosome (trisomy 21) and resulting in mental retardation and distinctive physical characteristics

fetal alcohol syndrome (FAS) A group of symptoms, including mental retardation and physical defects, that are produced in the infant by the ingestion of alcohol by a pregnant woman

fragile X syndrome An abnormality in the X chromosome that is associated with mental retardation

mental retardation Substandard intellectual functioning accompanied by deficiencies in adaptive behavior, with onset before age eighteen

Klinefelter's syndrome A disorder in males caused by an excessive number of X chromosomes, sometimes causing mental retardation

organic retardation Generally more severe mental retardation that is a consequence of a physiological or anatomical defect

phenylketonuria (PKU) A metabolic disorder, transmitted by a recessive gene that causes abnormal substances to build up, resulting in central nervous system damage and degeneration

trisomy 21 The existence of an extra chromosome in pair Number 21; the anomaly responsible for Down syndrome

Tay-Sachs disease A recessive gene metabolic disorder in which fatty substances accumulate in the brain and other tissues of the body, resulting in death

Turner's syndrome A rare condition caused by the lack of one X chromosome in a female, resulting in severe space-form perception deficits

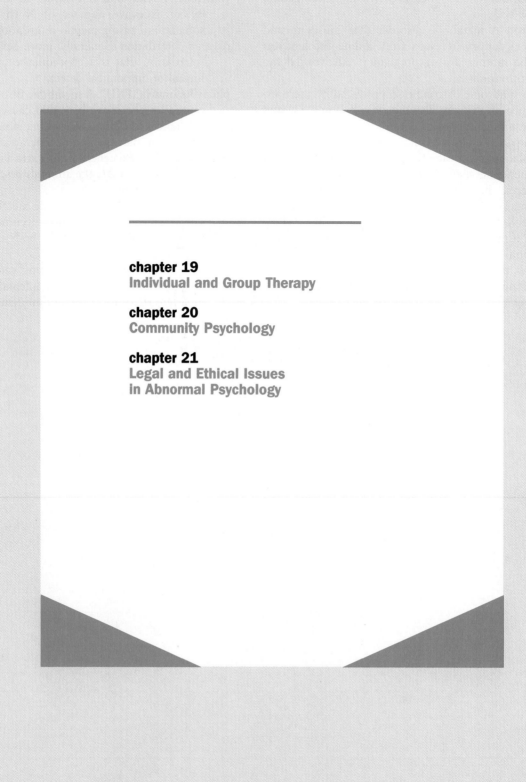

PART 6

Individual, Group, and Community Intervention

chapter 19
Individual and Group Therapy

At some point, nearly everyone has had an emotionally distressing problem, which seemed almost to evaporate after it was discussed with someone who could reassure and advise. People have always relied on friends, relatives, members of the clergy, teachers, and even strangers for advice, emotional and social support, approval, and validation. Recently, however, this function has been increasingly taken over by professionals who practice psychotherapy (Zilbergeld, 1983). In fact, psychotherapists have even been called the "secular priests" of our society (London, 1964a).

In preceding chapters, we have examined a wide variety of disorders, ranging from personality disturbances to schizophrenia. We have also examined the treatment approaches that seem to help people suffering from these disorders. In this chapter, we provide a more rounded view of the various techniques used to treat psychopathology: biological, psychodynamic, behavioral, and group and family therapies. To close the chapter, we examine one possible eclectic (or combined) approach to the treatment of Steven V., whose psychological history was discussed in Part One.

BIOLOGY-BASED TREATMENT TECHNIQUES

Biological or somatic treatment techniques use physical means to alter the patient's physiological state and hence psychological state (Andreasen, 1984). Three biology-based techniques are examined here: electroconvulsive therapy, psychosurgery, and drug therapy.

Electroconvulsive Therapy

Many people consider physically shocking the patient's body an abhorrent form of treatment. But such treatment can be used to successfully treat certain mental disorders. This is especially true for severe depressive reactions in which quite dramatic improvements occur (National Institute of Mental Health, 1985; Fink, 1979; Scovern & Killman, 1980).

The first therapeutic use of shock was *insulin shock treatment,* introduced in the 1930s by psychiatrist Manfred Sakel. Insulin is injected into the patient's body, drastically reducing the blood sugar level, whereon the patient goes into convulsions and then coma. The behavior of some schizophrenic patients is improved after they awaken from this shock treatment.

Also in the 1930s, another psychiatrist, Lazlo von Meduna, hypothesized that schizophrenia and epileptic seizures are antagonistic (seizures seem to prevent schizophrenic symptoms) and that by inducing convulsions in schizophrenics he could eliminate their bizarre behaviors. Meduna injected patients with the drug *metrazol* to induce the seizures. However, neither insulin nor metrazol shock treatment was very effective, and their use declined with the advent of electroconvulsive therapy.

Two Italian psychiatrists, Ugo Cerletti and Lucio Bini, introduced **electroconvulsive therapy** (ECT), or electroshock treatment, in 1938. In ECT, the patient lies on a padded bed or couch and is first injected with a muscle relaxant to minimize the chance of self-injury during the later convulsions. Then 65 to 140 volts of electricity are applied to the temporal region of the patient's skull (refer back to Figure 16.2), through electrodes, for a period of from 0.1 to 0.5 seconds. This treatment induces convulsions, followed by coma. On regaining consciousness, the patient is often confused and suffers a memory loss for events immediately before and after the ECT. Recent findings show that unilateral shock (applying shock to one hemisphere only) causes less confusion and memory loss. Studies indicate that it is just as effective as bilateral shock (Horne et al., 1985; Squire & Slater, 1978; Abrams & Essman, 1982).

ECT is much more useful in treating depression than in treating schizophrenia, against which it provides at most temporary relief (Berkwitz, 1974). But *how* ECT acts to improve depression is still unclear (Alexander & Selesnick, 1966). Some investigators have suggested that ECT is so aversive that some patients get better simply to avoid treatment. Or perhaps shocks stimulate the amines in the brain, leading to increased activity and improved mood. Another possibility is that depressed patients feel better after experiencing ECT because they see the shocks as punishment for perceived sins. Whatever the mechanism, ECT does seem to be effective against severe depression.

For several reasons, the use of ECT declined in the 1960s and 1970s, despite its success. First, there is concern that ECT might cause permanent damage to important parts of the brain. Indeed, animals who have undergone ECT treatment show brain damage. Would it be unreasonable to expect similar damage in humans? Second, a small percentage of patients fracture or dislocate bones during treatment. Although modern techniques have reduced pain and side effects (the convulsions are now almost unnoticeable), many patients anticipate a very unpleasant experience. Third, the abuses and side effects of ECT have been dramatized—often sensationally—in the mass media. In the movie *One Flew Over the Cuckoo's Nest,* for instance, ECT was administered repeatedly to the hero because he would not conform to regulations while in a mental hospital (such use of ECT is now illegal and probably nonexistent). Fourth and most important, recent advances in drug therapy have diminished the need for ECT, except with profoundly depressed patients for whom drugs act too slowly. Objections to ECT were so strong that citizens in Berkeley, California voted to ban its use in the city. This ban was, however, subsequently overturned by the courts. Because the procedure is so controversial and so little is known about how and why it works, ECT should be used only as a last resort.

The 1980s have seen a slight increase in the use of ECT for carefully selected patients. Currently, about 33,000 psychiatric patients undergo ECT each year (National Institute of Mental Health, 1985). Severe depression in old age and the depressed stages of bipolar disorders are most responsive to shock therapy.

Psychosurgery

As noted in Chapter 16, damage to brain tissue can dramatically alter the person's emotional characteristics and intellectual functioning. In the 1930s, the Portuguese neurologist Egas Moniz theorized that destroying certain connections in the brain, particularly in the frontal lobes, could disrupt psychotic thought patterns and behaviors. During the 1940s and 1950s, **psychosurgery** became increasingly popular. The treatment was applied most often to schizophrenic and severely depressed patients, although many patients with personality and anxiety disorders also underwent psychosurgery.

Several procedures or techniques may be used. *Prefrontal lobotomy* involves drilling holes in the skull. A scalpel is inserted through the holes, to cut nerve fibers between the frontal lobes and the thalamus or hypothalamus. In *transorbital lobotomy,* the scalpel is inserted through the eye socket, eliminating the need to drill holes in the skull. In a *lobectomy,* some or all of the frontal lobe is removed (to treat such disorders as brain tumors). Parts of the brain may also be subjected to electrical *cauterization* (searing or burning), which destroys selected brain tissue.

Psychosurgical techniques have been refined to the point where it is possible to operate on extremely small and contained areas of the brain. However, both scientific and ethical objections to these procedures have been raised. Initial reports of results were enthusiastic, but later evaluations seemed to indicate that lobotomies have little therapeutic effect. Whether patients improved or failed to improve was independent of psychosurgical treatment. In addition, serious negative and irreversible side effects were frequently observed. Although postlobotomy patients often became quite manageable, calm, and less anxious, many emerged from surgery with impaired cognitive and intellectual functioning; listless (even vegetative), or showing uninhibitable impulsive behavior. Some such patients were described as "robots"

or "zombies." In rare cases, psychosurgery resulted in death. Finally, because permanent brain damage is always involved, some critics called for a halt to this form of treatment on humanitarian grounds.

Although surgery is widely accepted to treat some organic brain disorders such as tumors, its use to treat functional mental disorders has declined drastically since the late 1960s. Along with the problems cited, increased reliance on drug therapy has contributed to its demise. Nowadays, psychosurgery is considered only as a last resort, in the most intractable cases of dangerous pathological behavior. On the whole, this severe restriction and regulation of its use seems wise. The First Person narrative in this chapter discusses some experiences one therapist had with other treatment methods that are no longer used to combat the effects of mental illness.

Before the 1950s and the development of effective drugs to treat mental illness, a number of seemingly bizarre treatment methods, such as wrapping people in cold wet sheets to offset some of the negative effects of ECT treatment, were routinely used.

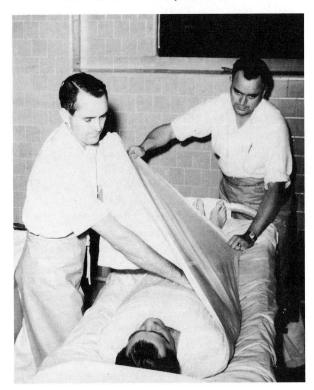

J. Richard Woy

FIRST PERSON

I will never forget my first exposure to people suffering from severe mental disorders, nor will I forget my first involvement in the care and treatment of mental illness. Those first experiences had a strong effect on me, and I was both horrified and fascinated by what I saw.

These experiences occurred just after my graduation from college in 1964. In order to get some firsthand experience in the field before starting a doctoral program in clinical psychology, I worked for several months as a "psychiatric attendant" at a private mental hospital.

The mental health field in 1964 was in the middle of a major transi-
tion. Some mental hospitals were already relying heavily on the recently introduced and powerful new psychotropic medications. Others were more cautious and continued a primary reliance on traditional treatment methods—some of which have disappeared entirely since then.

The mental hospital where I worked was old and very conservative in its practices, and I realized later that I had witnessed a kind of living museum, the last vestiges of an earlier era in the treatment of mental illness. Wearing a starched white jacket and carrying an impressive set of very large keys, I escorted patients from one locked portion of the hospital to another, supervised patients on the ward, and assisted the doctors and nurses in their various treatments.

Three treatment methods made particular impressions on me. The first was the practice of doing "cold wet packs" in conjunction with electroconvulsive shock therapy. "Shock therapy" was done early every Tuesday and Thursday morning. Each patient first was asked to take
off all of his clothes and lie down on a padded rolling cart. We then tightly wrapped each patient from head to foot in wet sheets that had been soaked in cold water. Each patient then lay in the "cold wet pack" for a period of 15 minutes to a half hour. During this time the room looked like it was filled with mummies. Then I and three other attendants rolled each patient individually into the treatment room where we removed the sheets wrapped around the patient's arms and legs. While each of the four of us held one of the patient's limbs, the doctor placed an electrode on each side of the patient's head and then administered the electrical charge, producing an immediate and violent seizure and physical convulsions. We held onto the patient's arms and legs so that the powerful muscular spasms would not cause injury. After the treatment, we rolled patients back to the recovery room, where they gradually returned to a waking condition. The electroconvulsive shock therapy was intended to reduce both manic and

Drug Therapy

As we have said, **drug therapy** has generally replaced shock treatment and psychosurgery for treating serious behavior disorders. Since the 1950s it has been a major factor in allowing the early discharge of hospitalized mental patients and permitting them to function in the community. Drug treatment is now widely used throughout the United States: more mental patients receive medication than receive all other forms of therapy combined (Kovel, 1976).

Four major categories of drugs, already mentioned in previous chapters, are discussed in this section. These are the *antianxiety drugs* (or minor tranquilizers), the *antipsychotic drugs* (or major tranquilizers), the *antidepressant drugs* (which relieve depression by elevating one's mood), and *antimanic drugs* such as lithium. Table 19.1 lists the generic and brand names of the drugs most frequently prescribed to treat psychological disorders.

Antianxiety Drugs (Minor Tranquilizers)   Before the 1950s barbiturates were often prescribed to relieve anxiety. *Barbiturates* are sedatives that have a calming effect, but they are also addictive. Many people who take barbiturates develop a physical tolerance to these drugs and require increasing doses to obtain the same effects. An overdose can result in death, and discon-

depressive symptoms, and the cold wet packs were believed to enhance the effectiveness of the shock treatments.

The second treatment method was called "hydrotherapy." This treatment was administered in a specially constructed room that was tiled from floor to ceiling and looked much like a shower room. However, the only fixtures in the room were sets of metal and leather fasteners on one wall and a powerful adjustable nozzle like those on a fire engine on the opposite wall. Treatment consisted of shackling one or more nude patients spread-eagled on one wall and pummeling them with powerful jets of water from the large nozzle. The physical assault of the water jets was intended to shock depressed patients out of their depression.

I don't recall what the third treatment was called. It also occurred in a specially constructed room that was tiled from floor to ceiling. The only thing in the room was a very large bathtub that was constructed so that warm water would continually circulate through it, much like a jacuzzi. However, the tub had a heavy canvas cover on top of it with a single hole at one end, and the cover could be securely fastened down with straps and buckles. An agitated patient was confined in the tub for several hours at a time with only his head sticking out through the hole in the top. The purpose of the treatment was to reduce the patient's agitation through the soothing effects of immersion in the warm water. I or another attendant remained with the patient to be sure he was safe and was instructed to record everything the patient said and to say nothing.

This hospital was not a backwater or a snake pit. Located in a suburb of a major city, it had an excellent facility on an attractive and spacious campus, had competent and caring staff, was affiliated with a major university medical school, and drew its patients primarily from the wealthy and well to do. Furthermore, in retrospect it is clear to me that the patients I met suffered from the most serious and profound of the mental disorders, including schizophrenia, major depression, manic-depressive disorders, and the like.

Nevertheless, I was disturbed by the methods just described even at the time. The emphasis on physically controlling and constraining patients against their will, even to the extent of tying them up, seemed excessive to me and made me very uncomfortable. These methods seemed to me to be demeaning and to involve a loss of personal dignity that left me feeling guilty and embarrassed. I'm glad that I have never seen those three treatment methods used again in all the years since 1964.

Dr. J. Richard Woy spent ten years as a researcher and administrator at the National Institute of Mental Health. He is currently head of JRW Associates, a management consulting firm in Boston that serves health and human service organizations. In addition, Dr. Woy publishes, teaches, and maintains a clinical practice.

tinuing the drug can produce agonizing withdrawal symptoms. Moreover, physical and mental disturbances such as muscular incoordination and mental confusion can result even from normal dosages. For these reasons, the barbiturates were replaced with antianxiety drugs almost as soon as the latter became available.

During the 1940s and 1950s, researchers first developed *meprobamate* (the generic name of Miltown), for use as a muscle relaxant and anxiety reducer. Within a few years, it was being prescribed for patients who showed neurotic symptoms, complained of anxiety and nervousness, or had psychosomatic problems. Soon other antianxiety drugs, including Librium and Valium, also entered the market. Valium has become the most often-prescribed drug in all medicine.

The antianxiety drugs can be addictive and can impair psychomotor skills; discontinuing these drugs after prolonged usage at high doses can result in withdrawal symptoms (Bassuk et al., 1983; Levenson, 1981). But they are considered safer than barbiturates, and there is little doubt that they effectively reduce anxiety and the behavioral symptoms of anxiety disorder (Rickels, 1966).

The major problem of the minor tranquilizers is the great potential for overuse and overreliance. For example, about one in ten adults uses antianxiety

TABLE 19.1 | The Drugs Most Commonly Used in Drug Therapy

Category	Generic Name	Brand Name
Antianxiety drugs	Meprobamate	Miltown, Equanil
	Chlordiazepoxide	Librium
	Diazepam	Valium
Antipsychotic drugs	Alprozolam	Xanac
	Chlorpromazine	Thorazine
	Trifluoperazine	Stelazine
	Thioxanthene	Haldol
		Prolixin
Antidepressants	Phenelzine	Nardil
	Isocarboxazid	Marplan
	Tranylcypromine	Parnate
	Imipramine	Tofranil
	Doxepin	Sinequan
	Amitriptyline	Elavil
Antimanic drugs	Lithium	Eskalith

drugs at least once a year (Uhlenhuth et al., 1983) and people are becoming more receptive to their use in relieving psychological problems (Clinthorne et al., 1986). Almost everyone feels anxious at one time or another, and the antianxiety drugs are effective, readily available, low in cost, and easy to administer. They are a quick, easy alternative to developing personal coping skills. As a result, people tend to choose the short-term relief offered by these drugs, over the long-term but slower gains of developing the ability to manage stress and solve one's own problems.

Antipsychotic Drugs (Major Tranquilizers)   In 1950 a synthetic sedative was developed in France. This drug, *chlorpromazine* (the generic name of Thorazine), had an unexpected tranquilizing effect, which decreased patients' interest in the events taking place around them. Some two million patients used Thorazine in less than a year after its introduction. Chlorpromazine also seemed to reduce psychotic symptoms (believed to be the biochemical effect of blocking dopamine receptors). Thereafter, a number of other major tranquilizers were developed, mainly for administration to schizophrenics.

Many schizophrenic patients who use these drugs become calm and manageable; show fewer inappropriate behaviors, disturbed associations, and delusional and hallucinatory symptoms; and are more amenable to other forms of treatment, such as psychotherapy. Several experimental studies have demonstrated the efficacy of antipsychotic drugs in treating schizophrenia. A review of many large-scale controlled studies indicated that the beneficial effects of Thorazine, Stelazine, Prolixin, and other antipsychotic drugs have allowed institutions to release of thousands of chronic "incurable" mental patients throughout the country (Wender & Klein, 1981). When hospitalized schizophrenics were given *phenothiazines* (a class of major tranquilizers), they showed more social interaction with others, better self-management, and less agitation and excitement than when they were given placebos (chemically inert or inactive substances). The placebos were used to rule out the possibility that the gains might be due to patients' expectations of improvement or to the attention staff gave patients in administering the drugs (Cole, 1964).

Outcome research on drug treatment (and, for that matter, on psychotherapy) must control **placebo effects.** These are positive responses to a drug that result from the patient's understanding of the drug's action, from faith in the doctor, or from other psychological factors unrelated to the drug's specific physiological action (Korchin, 1976). Similarly, in evaluating any form of treatment or psychotherapy, the patient's expectancy of improvement and the attention received from the doctor may influence improvement rates. A particular treatment is usually considered effective if it results in greater improvement than would result from giving a patient a placebo, as in the Cole (1964) research.

May (1968) assessed the relative effectiveness of phenothiazine treatment, individual psychotherapy, phenothiazine treatment combined with individual psychotherapy, ECT, and milieu therapy (in which a hospital is organized to provide a total *therapeutic community*). The use of phenothiazine alone was as effective as phenothiazine plus individual psychotherapy. And both forms of treatment were superior to individual psychotherapy alone, ECT, and milieu therapy on measures of improvement that included staff ratings of patients and discharge rates from the hospital. All patients in the experimental groups were given some sort of therapy, so placebo effects presumably had no bearing on the results.

Despite their recognized effectiveness, antipsychotic drugs do not always reduce anxiety, and they can produce certain side effects. Patients may develop psychomotor symptoms resembling those of Parkinson's disease, sensitivity to light, dryness of the mouth, drowsiness, or liver disease. After at least six months of continuous treatment with antipsychotic drugs, some patients (usually patients over forty years of age) develop tardive dyskinesia (Kane & Smith, 1982), a side effect that is discussed in Focus 15.3.

Patients discharged from hospitals typically show only marginal adjustment to community life, and psychotic symptoms usually return when the medication is discontinued. As a result, the rehospitalization rate is high. Nevertheless, drug therapy is very important in treating schizophrenia, and nearly all psychiatric institutions use it. Antipsychotic drugs have dramatically increased the proportion of schizophrenic patients who can return and function in the community, even though such patients may show residual symptoms (Lehmann, 1974).

Antidepressants and Antimanic Drugs As in the case of antipsychotic drugs, the development of antidepressants was aided by a fortunate coincidence. During the 1950s, clinicians noticed that patients treated with the antituberculosis drug *iproniazid* became happier and more optimistic. When tested on depressed patients, the drug was found to be effective as an antidepressant. Unfortunately, liver damage and fatalities caused by the drug were relatively high. Continued interest in antidepressants has led to the identification of two large classes of the compounds: the **monoamine oxidase (MAO) inhibitors** and the **tricyclics**. A number of the MAO inhibitors such as *phenelzine* were found to be less dangerous but similar in effect to iproniazid. It is hypothesized that the MAO inhibitors work primarily to correct a deficiency in concentrations of neurotransmitters in the brain. Although this class of compounds did relieve depression (Davis et al., 1967), it produced certain toxic effects and required careful dietary monitoring (certain foods and other drugs when taken with an MAO inhibitor could cause severe illness).

In the 1950s drug therapy began to have a major impact on the prognosis and course of many mental disorders. Many patients with severe psychological problems once thought to be incurable can now live relatively normal lives.

More frequently used in cases of depression are the tricyclics, which seem to work like the MAO inhibitors, but produce fewer of the side effects associated with prolonged drug use. The drug *imipramine*, a tricyclic, has been valuable in relieving the symptoms of depression.

Lithium is another mood-controlling drug (antimanic) that has been very effective in treating bipolar disorders, especially mania (Bassuk et al., 1983; Berger, 1978). It also controls depressive episodes. About 70 to 80 percent of manic states can be controlled by lithium, which has proven a boon in treating bipolar disorders.

Strangely enough, lithium, which is administered as a salt, has no known physiological function (Berger, 1978). Yet, when properly administered, patients' manic and depressive cycles can be modulated and/or prevented by simply taking a single tablet in the morning and in the evening. However, cautions limit the use of lithium in treating bipolar disorders. First, it is largely preventive and must be taken before symptoms appear. Once a manic or depressive state occurs, lithium has minimal effect on these conditions. Second, it is often extremely difficult to determine the appropriate dosage for patients. Often, the effective dosage level borders on toxicity (can cause convulsions, delirium, and so forth). So it is important to carefully and constantly monitor the lithium level in a patient's blood.

Psychopharmacological Considerations   Deciding which drug to use with which kind of patient under what circumstances is a major issue in **psychopharmacology**—the study of the effects of drugs on the mind and on behavior. For example, imipramine is more effective with long-standing depressions without specific situational causes, and is particularly indicated for people over age forty and for people who show psychomotor retardation or psychotic symptoms (Research Task Force of the National Institute of Mental Health, 1975). But antidepressants often do not begin to help patients until two to three weeks after treatment. As a last resort, ECT is used to treat severely depressed or suicidal patients when rapid improvement is necessary.

The use of antidepressants, antianxiety drugs, and antipsychotics has greatly changed therapy. Patients who take them report that they feel better, that symptoms decline, and that overall functioning improves. Long hospitalization is no longer needed in most cases, and patients are more amenable to other forms of treatment, such as psychotherapy. Remember, however, that drugs do not *cure* mental disorders. Medication does not help the patient improve living skills. Many patients discharged from hospitals require continuing medication in order to function even minimally in the community. Unfortunately, many do not go on taking their medication once they leave the mental hospital. For example, many may not realize the importance of continued and timely medication, their ability to obtain medication financially may be impaired, or their lifestyles may not be conducive to taking it. Once this happens, patients may again experience the same disorder that led to their hospitalization.

PSYCHOTHERAPY

In most cases, biological treatments such as drug therapy are used as an adjunct to psychotherapy. But beyond general agreement that psychotherapy is an internal approach to treating psychopathology, involving interaction between one or more clients and a therapist, there is little consensus on exactly what else it is. Psychotherapy has been called "a conversation with a therapeutic purpose" (Korchin, 1976); it has also been called "the talking cure" or the "purchase of friendship" (Schofield 1964). One observer suggests that psychotherapy can be variously defined by goals, procedures and methods, practitioners, or the relationship formed (Reisman, 1971).

For our purposes, **psychotherapy** may be defined as the systematic application of techniques derived from psychological principles by a trained and experienced professional therapist, for the purpose of helping psychologically troubled people. We can't be more succinct or precise without getting involved in specific types of therapy. Depending on their perspective and theoretical orientation, therapists may seek to modify attitudes, thoughts, feelings, or behaviors; to facilitate the patient's self-insight and rational control of his or her own life; to cure mental illness; to enhance mental health and self-actualization; to make clients "feel better"; to remove a cause; to change a self-concept; or to encourage adaptation. Psychotherapy is practiced by many different kinds of people in many different ways—a fact that seems to preclude establishing of a single set of standard therapeutic procedures. And—despite our emphasis on the scientific basis of therapy—in practice it is often more art than science.

We can, however, identify four characteristics of psychotherapy—whether we can define it or not, and whether it is art or science or a combination of the two (Korchin, 1976). First, psychotherapy is a chance for the client to *relearn*. Many people say to their psychotherapists, "I know I shouldn't feel or act this way, but I just can't help it." Psychotherapy provides a chance to unlearn, relearn, develop, or change certain behaviors or levels of functioning.

Second, psychotherapy helps generate the development of new, emotionally important experiences. A person questioning the value of psychotherapy may ask, "If I talk about my problems, how will that cause me to change, even though I may understand myself better? I talk things over now, with friends." But psychotherapy is not merely a "talking cure." It involves the reexperiencing of emotions that clients may have avoided, along with the painful and helpless feelings fostered by these emotions. This *experiencing* allows relearning as well as emotional and intellectual insight into problems and conflicts.

Third, there is *a therapeutic relationship*. Therapists have been trained to listen, show sympathetic concern, be objective, value the client's integrity, communicate understanding, and use their professional knowledge and skills. Therapists may provide reassurance, interpretations, self-disclosures, reflections of the client's feelings, or information, each at appropriate times. As a team, therapist and client are better prepared to venture into frightening areas that the client would not have faced alone.

Finally, clients in psychotherapy have certain *motivations and expectations*. Most people enter therapy with both anxiety and hope. They are frightened by their emotional difficulties and by the prospect of treatment, but they expect or hope that therapy will be helpful.

The goals and general characteristics of psychotherapy as described seem admirable, and most people consider them so. However, psychotherapy itself has been criticized as being biased and inappropriate to the lifestyles of many clients such as members of minority groups. A few of its more specific characteristics, and their potential effects on culturally different clients, are outlined in Focus 19.1.

First we will discuss individual psychotherapy, in which one therapist treats one client at any one

The practice of therapy is both a science and an art. Based upon a conceptual framework, a trained professional must select the appropriate therapy techniques that will be beneficial to a particular client. Moreover, the therapist must establish a rapport with the client in order for the therapeutic process to be successful.

FOCUS 19.1 — *Psychotherapy and Cultural Bias*

Racial and ethnic minorities have frequently criticized psychotherapy as being a "handmaiden of the status quo," a "transmitter of society's values," and an "instrument of oppression." Rather than helping people reach their full potential, critics say, it has often been used to subjugate the very people it was meant to free. The meaning of such statements is clear: the process and goals of psychotherapy are culture bound and thus culturally biased against people whose values differ from those of Western societies. The following "generic characteristics of therapy," which seem to be common to most schools of thought, often conflict with clients' cultural values (Sue, 1981).

1. *Focus on the individual*
Most forms of counseling and psychotherapy stress the importance and uniqueness of the individual, as reflected in the I-thou relationship, the one-to-one encounter, and the belief that the client must take responsibility for him- or herself. In many cultural groups, however, the basic psychosocial unit is not the individual but the family, the group, or the collective society. For example, many Asians and Hispanics define their identities within the family constellation. Whatever a person does reflects not only on that person, but on the entire family as well. Important decisions are thus made by the entire family rather than by the individual.

Therapists who work with people from such cultures may see their clients as "dependent," "lacking in maturity," or "avoiding responsibility." These negative labels do much harm to the self-esteem of minority-group members, especially when they become part of a diagnosis.

2. *Verbal expression of emotions*
The psychotherapeutic process works best for clients who are verbal, articulate, and able to express their feelings and be assertive. The major medium of communication is the spoken word (in standard English). Those who tend to be less verbal, who speak with an accent, or who do not use standard English are placed at a disadvantage. In addition, many cultural groups (including

---

time, and then group and family therapy. We will also distinguish between insight- and action-oriented approaches to individual therapy. This distinction separates (1) approaches that stress awareness, understanding, and consciousness of one's own motivations (that is, insight) from (2) approaches that stress such actions as changing one's behavior or thoughts (London, 1964a). The first set includes the psychoanalytic and humanistic-existential therapies, whereas the second set involves mainly behavioral therapies. Despite this variety of approaches, many therapists use similar treatment strategies (Weiner, 1976). And, as noted in Chapter 1, many therapists choose relevant techniques from all the various "pure" approaches in order to develop the most effective *eclectic* approach for each particular client.

INSIGHT-ORIENTED APPROACHES TO INDIVIDUAL PSYCHOTHERAPY

The theoretical bases of the major insight-oriented psychotherapies were discussed in Chapter 2. Here

we briefly review these theoretical bases, and then discuss most common treatment techniques.

Psychoanalysis

According to Freud's theory of personality, people are born with certain instinctual drives, urges that constantly seek to discharge or express themselves. As the personality structure develops, conflicts occur among the id, ego, and superego. If conflicts remain unresolved, they will resurface during adulthood. The relative importance of such an unresolved conflict depends on the psychosexual stage (oral, anal, phallic, latency, or genital) in which it occurs. The earlier the stage in which an unresolved conflict arises, the greater the conflict's effect on subsequent behaviors. Repressing unacceptable thoughts and impulses (within the unconscious) is the primary way people defend themselves against such thoughts.

Psychoanalytic therapy, or psychoanalysis, seeks to induce ego weakness so that (1) repressed material can be uncovered, (2) the client can achieve insight

Asians and Native Americans) are brought up to conceal rather than verbalize their feelings; therapists often perceived them as "inhibited," "lacking in spontaneity," or "repressed." Thus the therapeutic process, by valuing expressiveness, may not only force minority clients to violate their cultural norms but also label them as having negative personality traits.

3. *Openness and intimacy* Self-disclosure and discussion of the most intimate and personal aspects of one's life are hallmarks of therapy. However, cultural and socio-political factors may make some clients unwilling or unable to engage in such self-disclosure. For example, in Focus 1.1 we discussed the "cultural paranoia" that many black Americans have developed as a defense against discrimination and oppression—a healthy distrust that would make them reluctant to disclose their innermost thoughts and feelings to a white therapist. Unfortunately, therapists who encountered this reluctance might perceive their clients as suspicious, guarded, and paranoid. Likewise, many therapists don't understand the cultural implications of disclosure among Asians, who discuss intimate matters only with close acquaintances, and not with strangers (which therapists may well be).

4. *Insight* Most closely associated with the psychodynamic approach but valued in many theoretical orientations, **insight** is the ability to understand the basis of one's motivations, perceptions, and behavior. But many cultural groups do not value insight. In China, for example, when a person becomes depressed or anxious, he or she may be advised to avoid the thoughts that are causing the distress. This contrasts abruptly with the Western belief that insight is always helpful in therapy.

The solution to this "culture gap" is obvious: Therapists need to (1) become aware of their own cultural values, biases, and assumptions; (2) learn and understand the cultural values of other groups; and (3) develop more appropriate culture-specific intervention strategies for use with minority-group clients (Sue, 1981).

SOURCE: D. W. Sue, 1981.

into his or her inner motivations and desires, and (3) unresolved childhood conflicts can be controlled. Psychoanalysis requires many sessions of therapy over a long period of time. It may not be appropriate for certain types of people, such as nonverbal adults, young children who cannot be verbally articulate or reasonable, schizoid people, those with urgent problems requiring immediate reduction of symptoms, and the mentally retarded (Fenichel, 1945).

Psychoanalysts traditionally use four methods to achieve their therapeutic goals: free association and dream analysis, analysis of resistance, transference, and interpretation.

Free Association and Dream Analysis In **free association** the patient just talks, saying whatever comes to mind, regardless of how illogical or embarrassing it may seem. Psychoanalysts believe the material that surfaces in this process is determined by the patient's psychic makeup and that it can provide some understanding of the patient's conflicts, unconscious processes, and personality dynamics. Simply asking the patient to talk about his or her conflicts is fruitless, because the patient has repressed the really important material from his or her consciousness. Instead, reports of dreams, feelings, thoughts, and fantasies reflect the patient's psychodynamics; the therapist's tasks are to encourage continuous free association of thoughts and to interpret the results.

Similarly, dream analysis is a very important therapeutic tool that depends on psychoanalytic interpretation of hidden meanings in dreams. Freud is often credited with referring to dreams as "the royal road to the unconscious." According to psychoanalytic theory, when you sleep, defenses and inhibitions of your ego weaken, allowing unacceptable motives and feelings to surface. This material comes out in the disguised and symbolic form of a dream. The portion you remember is called the *manifest content*, the deeper, unacceptable impulse is the *latent content*. The therapist's job is to uncover the disguised symbolic meanings and let the patient achieve insight into the anxiety-provoking implications.

Analysis of Resistance Throughout the course of psychoanalytic therapy, the patient's unconscious

Freud often referred to dreams as "the royal road to the unconscious." Dream analysis is based upon the premise that during sleep the ego's defenses weaken, allowing repressed and unacceptable feelings to surface in the form of images and symbols. The therapist's task is to help the client understand the meaning of those images.

may try to block the process—to prevent the exposure of repressed material. In free association, for example, the patient may suddenly change the subject, lose the train of thought, go blank, or become silent. As noted in Chapter 2, such **resistance** may also show up in a patient's late arrival or failure to keep an appointment. A trained analyst is alert to telltale signs of resistance, because they indicate that a sensitive area is being approached. The therapist can make therapeutic use of properly interpreted instances of resistance, to show the patient that repressed material is coming close to the surface and to suggest means of uncovering it.

Transference When a patient begins to perceive, or behave toward, the therapist as though the therapist were an important person in the patient's past, the process of transference is occurring. In **transference** the patient re-enacts early conflicts by carrying over and applying to the therapist feelings and attitudes that the patient had toward significant others—primarily parents—in the past. These feelings and attitudes then become accessible to understanding. They may be positive, involving feelings of love for the analyst, or negative, involving feelings of anger and hostility.

Part of the psychoanalyst's strategy is to remain "unknown" or ambiguous, so that the client can freely develop whatever kind of transference is required. The patient is allowed, even encouraged, to develop unrealistic expectations and attitudes regarding the therapist. These expectations and attitudes are used as a basis for helping the patient deal realistically with painful early experiences. In essence, a miniature neurosis is re-created; its resolution is crucial to the therapy.

At the same time, the therapist must be careful to recognize and control any instances of *counter-transference*. In this process, the therapist—who is also a human being with feelings and fears—transfers those feelings to the patient. This is one reason why Freud believed so strongly that all psychoanalysts need to undergo psychoanalysis themselves.

Interpretation Through **interpretation**—the explanation of a patient's free associations, reports of dreams, and the like—a sensitive analyst can help the patient gain insight (both intellectual and emotional) into his or her repressed conflicts. By pointing out the symbolic attributes of a transference relationship or by noting the peculiar timing of symptoms, the therapist can direct the patient toward conscious control of unconscious conflicts.

The following example shows the timely interpretation of an important instance of transference:

Sandy (the patient): John [her ex-husband] was just like my father. Always condemning me, always making me feel like an idiot! Strange, the two of them—the most important men in my life—they did the most to screw me up. When I would have fun with my friends and come home at night, he would be sitting there—waiting—to disapprove.

Therapist (male): Who would be waiting for you?

Sandy: Huh?

Therapist: Who's the "he" who'd be waiting?

Sandy: John—I mean, my father—you're confusing me now. . . . My father would sit there—smoking his pipe. I knew what he was thinking, though—he didn't have to say it—he was thinking I was a slut! Someone—who, who was a slut! So what if I stayed up late and had some fun? What business was it of his? He never took any interest in any of us. (Begins to weep.) It was my mother—rest her soul—who loved us, not our father. He worked her to death. Lord, I miss her. (Weeps uncontrollably.)—I must sound angry at my father. Don't you think I have a right to be angry?

Therapist: Do you think you have a right to be angry?

Sandy: Of course, I do! Why are you questioning me? You don't believe me, do you?

Therapist: You want me to believe you.

Sandy: I don't care whether you believe me or not. As far as I'm concerned, you're just a wall that I'm talking to—I don't know why I pay for this rotten therapy.—Don't you have any thoughts or feelings at all? I know what you're thinking—you think I'm crazy—you must be laughing at me—I'll probably be a case in your next book! You're just sitting there—smirking—making me feel like a bad person—thinking I'm wrong for being mad, that I have no right to be mad.

Therapist: Just like your father.

Sandy: Yes, you're just like my father.—Oh my God! Just now—I—I—thought I was talking to him.

Therapist: You mean your father.

Sandy: Yes—I'm really scared now—how could I have—can this really be happening to me?

Therapist: I know it must be awfully scary to realize what just happened—but don't run away now, Sandy. Could it be that your relationship with your father has affected many of the relationships you've had with other men? It seems that your reaction to me just now, and your tendency to sometimes refer to your ex-husband as your father—

Sandy: God!—I don't know—what should I do about it?—Is it real?

Modern Psychoanalysis In Chapter 2, we noted the contemporary changes in theoretical formulations of psychoanalytic theory, especially the increased importance of the ego (ego autonomy theorists) and past interpersonal relationships (object relations theorists). Among the former were such people as Anna Freud, Heinz Hartmann, and Erik Erikson, who believed that cognitive processes of the ego were often constructive, creative, and productive (independent from the id). Likewise, object relations theorists such as Melanie Klein, Margaret Mahler, Otto Kernberg, and Heinz Kohut stressed the importance of interpersonal relationships and the child's separation from the mother as important in one's psychological growth. The contributions of these theorists and practitioners expanded and loosened the rigid therapeutic techniques of traditional psychoanalysis. Today, very few psychodynamic therapists practice traditional psychoanalysis. Most are more active in their sessions, restrict the number of sessions they have with clients, place greater emphasis on current rather than past factors, and seem to have adopted a number of client-centered techniques in their practice.

The Effectiveness of Psychoanalysis The theoretical validity of psychoanalysis has come under attack, as have its lack of research support and its methods. The impossibility of providing operational definitions for such constructs as the *unconscious* and the *libido* makes it extremely difficult to confirm the various aspects of the theory. For example, psychoanalytic theory suggests that neurotic symptoms are caused by underlying emotional conflicts. When these symptoms are eliminated without removing the conflict, the person merely expresses the neurosis in other ways and shows other symptoms—a phenomenon known as **symptom substitution**. Many researchers, particularly behavior therapists, assert that it *is* possible to eliminate neurotic symptoms without symptom substitution occurring (Rachman, 1971). Furthermore, they contend that when the symptoms are eliminated the neurosis is cured.

In a classic study, the effectiveness of various treatment approaches was examined, and possible symptom substitution was assessed in a follow-up performed two years later (Paul, 1967). Students who were very afraid of public speaking were assigned to one of four treatment groups:

1. A systematic desensitization group with which a behavior modification approach involving relaxation was used (this technique is discussed later in this chapter)

2. An attention placebo group that was given placebo pills and told that the pills would reduce anxiety

516 Chapter 19 Individual and Group Therapy

3. An insight therapy group conducted by experienced psychotherapists to help the subjects gain insight into their anxieties

4. A control group that received no treatment

Anxiety was measured in several ways, both before and after the treatments, which were conducted over a five-week period. As Table 19.2 shows, the systematic desensitization treatment was the most effective approach, although insight therapy and attention placebo treatment also reduced more anxiety than did no treatment at all. These results persisted over two years; symptom substitution did not occur.

Proponents of psychoanalysis might argue, however, that a five-week treatment is too short to provide full benefit and that the student subjects did not have the kinds of problems typically seen in treatment. Furthermore, in clinical practice it is often evident that *the symptom is not the disorder.* For example, a child who shows antisocial behavior and aggression may really be suffering from neglect. If the symptoms are removed but the neglect remains, symptom substitution may occur. Some behavior therapists acknowledge this potential problem (O'Leary & Wilson, 1975). Meanwhile, psychoanalysis continues to have strong supporters (Silverman, 1976).

Humanistic-Existential Therapies

By contrast to the psychic determinism implicit in psychoanalysis, the humanistic-existential therapies stress the importance of self-actualization, self-concept, free will, responsibility, and the understanding of the client's phenomenological world. The focus is on qualities of "humanness"; human beings cannot be understood without reference to their personal uniqueness and wholeness. Among the several humanistic-existential therapies are client-centered therapy, existential analysis, and gestalt therapy.

Person-Centered Therapy Carl Rogers, the founder of person-centered therapy, believed that people can develop better self-concepts and move toward self-actualization if the therapist provides certain therapeutic conditions. These are the conditions in which clients use their own innate tendencies to grow, to actively negotiate with their environment, and to realize their potential. Thus therapists must accept clients as people, show empathy and respect, and provide unconditional positive regard for clients. A therapist should not control, inhibit, threaten, or interpret a client's behaviors. These actions are manipulative, and they undermine the client's ability to find his or her own direction.

Person-centered therapy thus emphasizes the *kind of person* the therapist should be in the therapeutic relationship rather than the precise techniques to use in therapy. Particular details of this therapeutic approach were discussed in Chapter 2.

Existential Analysis **Existential analysis** follows no single theory or group of therapeutic techniques. Instead, it is concerned with the person's experience and involvement in the world as a being with consciousness and self-consciousness. Existential

| | TABLE 19.2 | Results of Three Treatments for Interpersonal Performance Anxiety |

Treatment	Results Found at 2-Year Follow-up		
	Significantly Improved (%)	No Change (%)	Significantly Worse
Desensitization	85	15	—
Attention-placebo	50	50	—
Insight	50	50	—
Control	22	78	—

SOURCE: Adapted from Paul, 1967.

therapists believe that the inability to accept death or nonbeing as a reality restricts self-actualization. In contemporary society, many people feel lonely and alienated; they lose a sense of the meaning of life, of self-responsibility, and of free will. This state of mind is popularly called "existential crisis." The task of the therapist is to engage clients in an encounter in which they can experience their own existence as being real. The encounter should involve genuine sharing between partners, in which the therapist, too, may grow and be influenced. (The *encounter group*, described in Focus 19.3, owes much to Rogerian and existential analysis.) When clients can experience their existence and nonexistence, then feelings of responsibility, choice, and meaning re-emerge. (Again, see Chapter 2 for additional details.)

Existential approaches to therapy are strongly philosophical in nature. They have not received any research scrutiny because many existential concepts and methods are difficult to define operationally for research purposes. Furthermore, existential therapists point out that therapist and client are engaged in a complex encounter that can't be broken down into components for empirical observation, so research studies are incapable of assessing the impact of therapy. Although impressive case histories indicate its effectiveness, little empirical support exists.

Gestalt Therapy The German word *gestalt* means "whole." As conceptualized by Fritz Perls in 1969, **gestalt therapy** emphasizes the importance of a person's *totality* of experience, which should not be fragmented or separated. Perls felt that when affective and cognitive experiences are isolated, people lack full awareness of their complete experience.

In gestalt therapy, clients are asked to discuss the totality of the here-and-now. Only experiences, feelings, and behaviors occurring in the present are stressed. Past experiences or anticipated future experiences are brought up only in relation to current feelings. Interestingly, Perls was originally trained as a psychoanalyst, but later rejected Freudian theory. He did, however, incorporate dream analysis in his work. Dreams too are interpreted in relation to the here-and-now. As a means of opening clients to their experiences, therapists encourage clients to

1. Make personalized and unqualified statements that help them "act out" their emotions. For

Fritz Perls (1893–1970) developed gestalt therapy to help troubled clients become aware of themselves as whole individuals. He believed this awareness to be therapeutic in and of itself. Experiencing, feeling, and being in the here-and-now were the goals of his therapeutic approach.

example, instead of hedging by saying, "It is sometimes upsetting when *your* boss yells at *you*," a client is encouraged to say "*I* get scared when *my* boss yells at me."

2. Exaggerate the feelings associated with behaviors in order to gain greater awareness of their experiences and to eliminate intellectual explanations for them.

3. Role-play situations and then focus on what was experienced during the role playing.

As in the case of existential analysis, gestalt therapy has generated little research. Thus it is difficult to evaluate its effectiveness. Proponents of gestalt therapy are convinced that clients are helped, but sufficient empirical support has never emerged. (You might be interested in reading Perls's remarkable book *Gestalt Therapy Verbatim* (1969) for a fuller explanation of this approach.)

ACTION-ORIENTED APPROACHES TO INDIVIDUAL PSYCHOTHERAPY

The principles underlying the action-oriented or behaviorist approaches to abnormal behavior were discussed in Chapter 3. Treatment based on classical conditioning, operant conditioning, observational learning, and cognitive-behavioral processes has gained widespread popularity, and behavior therapists typically use a variety of techniques (Kazdin & Wilson, 1978). Many of these techniques have been discussed in preceding chapters; this section presents selected key behavioral techniques.

Classical Conditioning Techniques

Using classical conditioning principles described in Chapter 3, Joseph Wolpe (1973) used systematic desensitization as treatment for anxiety (discussed in Chapter 6). Its objective is to reduce anxiety that is a response to a stimulus situation, by eliciting—in the given situation—a response that is incompatible with anxiety. For example, if a woman is afraid of flying in a jet plane, her anxiety response could be reduced by training her to relax while in airplanes.

Systematic desensitization typically includes training in relaxation, the construction of a fear hierarchy, and the combination of relaxation and imagined scenes from the fear hierarchy. To illustrate the process, we can use the example of the person who wants to overcome her fear of flying. The therapist would first train her to relax, probably employing a progressive relaxation method in which the muscles are alternately tensed and relaxed (Jacobson, 1964). The client would be asked to list situations involved in flying that make her anxious and to rank them from least upsetting to most anxiety producing. For example, making airline reservations might arouse a little anxiety; taking a taxi to the airport could result in more anxiety; entering the plane, fastening the seatbelt, taking off, flying 35,000 feet above sea level, and so on would probably involve increasing anxiety levels.

In systematic desensitization, the client is asked to *imagine* herself in each of these situations. It is obviously more convenient to imagine situations than actually to go through them, and most clients do experience anxiety when they imagine such situations.

(*In vivo* approaches, in which clients are actually present in the fear-provoking situations, have also been used.)

Once the person is able to relax, the therapist asks the client first to imagine a low-anxiety scene (such as making flight reservations) and to relax at the same time. The client then proceeds up the fear hierarchy, imagining each situation in order. If a particular situation elicits too much anxiety, the client is told to return to a less anxiety-provoking one. This procedure is repeated until the client can imagine the entire hierarchy without anxiety.

Behavior therapists believe that systematic desensitization is more effective than psychotherapy; it certainly requires fewer sessions to achieve desired results (Paul, 1967; Wolpe, 1973). Systematic desensitization has stimulated a great deal of research, and its efficacy in reducing fears has been well documented (Rachman & Hodgeson, 1980). Some researchers question the need for certain procedural aspects of the treatment approach. For example, Wolpe's rather rigid format for desensitization may be unnecessary, and alternatives to relaxation, such as the opportunity to talk about the fear or listening to soothing music, may be used in the process (Nathan & Jackson, 1976; Sue, 1972).

Flooding and Implosion   Two other techniques that use the classical conditioning principles of extinction are **flooding** and **implosion** (Levis, 1985; Stampfl & Levis, 1967). The two are very similar to one another: flooding involves placing the client in a real-life anxiety-provoking situation, while implosion relies on the client's ability to imagine the anxiety-arousing scene. The difference between systematic desensitization and flooding and implosion lies in the speed with which the fearful situation is introduced to the client. Systematic desensitization introduces it more slowly. Flooding and implosion require the client to immediately confront the feared situation in its full intensity. The belief is that the client's fears will be extinguished if he or she is not allowed to avoid or escape the situation. In flooding, for example, a client who's afraid of heights may be taken to the top of a tall building, mountain, or bridge and physically prevented from leaving. Some studies indicate that flooding effectively eliminates specific fears such as phobias (Emmelkamp & Wessels, 1975; Foa & Kozak, 1986). In implosion therapy, the client is forced to imagine a feared situation. For example, a therapist might ask a client who is afraid of flying to close her eyes and imagine the following:

> You are flying in an airplane. Suddenly the plane hits an air pocket and begins to shake violently from side to side. Meal trays fly around, and passengers who do not have their seatbelts fastened are thrown from their seats. People start to scream. As you look out the window, the plane's wing is flying by. The pilot's frantic voice over the loudspeaker is shouting: "Prepare to crash, prepare to crash!" Your seatbelt breaks and you must hang on for dear life, while the plane is spinning around and careening. You can tell that the plane is falling rapidly. The ground is coming up toward you. The situation is hopeless—all will die.

Presumably the client would feel intense anxiety, after which she would be told to "wake up." Repeated exposure to such a high level of anxiety would eventually cause the stimulus to lose its power to elicit anxiety and would lead to extinction.

The developers of implosion and flooding believe that they can be effective, though some clients find the procedures too traumatic and discontinue treatment (Emmelkamp & Wessels, 1975). In general, these methods have not been scrutinized as carefully as systematic desensitization, but they have been used successfully with some clients (Barrett, 1969; Baum, 1970).

Aversive Conditioning In **aversive conditioning,** a widely used classical conditioning technique, the undesirable behavior is paired with an unpleasant stimulus. For example, it was used in an attempt to modify the smoking behaviors of heavy smokers (Franks et al., 1966). The smokers were asked to sit in front of an apparatus that delivers either smoke or fresh air to one's face. They were told to smoke their favorite cigarettes; as long as they continued puffing, smoke was blown to their faces. When the smoke became unbearable, they could put out their cigarettes and have fresh air delivered. The program showed limited positive results: Of twenty-three volunteer smokers, fourteen did not complete the four-week program because of low motivation, dislike of the method, or unavailability. Of the remaining nine who completed the project, four stopped smoking, one smoked less, one changed to a pipe, and two showed no change.

Aversive conditioning has also been applied to alcoholics, drug addicts, and people with sexual disorders, again with varying degrees of success. The noxious stimuli have included electric shock, drugs, odors, verbal censure, and reprimands. Some aversive conditioning programs also provide positive reinforcement for alternative behaviors that are deemed appropriate.

Several problems have been encountered in the use of aversive conditioning: First, because noxious stimuli are used, many people in treatment discontinue therapy, as in the smoking-reduction program just described. Second, aversive methods often suppress the undesirable behavior only temporarily, especially when punishment for those behaviors is applied solely in a laboratory situation that bears little resemblance to real life. Third, the client may become anxious and hostile. And some critics argue that punishment is unethical or has potential for misuse and abuse (Silverstein, 1972). Partially as a response to these criticisms, as well as for practical reasons, some therapists advocate the use of *covert sensitization*. Like implosion, it requires imagining the aversive situation along with the behavior one is trying to eliminate (Cautela, 1966, 1967). A person who wants to stop smoking may be asked to imagine a smoke-filled room, becoming nauseous, suffocating, and/or dying of lung cancer and emphysema.

Operant Conditioning Techniques

Behavior modification using operant methods has flourished, and many ingenious programs have been developed. As in the case of classical conditioning, only a few key examples are presented here.

Token Economies Treatment programs that reward patients with tokens for appropriate behaviors are known as **token economies** (Kazdin, 1980). The tokens may be exchanged for hospital privileges, food, or weekend passes. The goal is to modify patient behaviors using a secondary reinforcer (the tokens). In much the same way, money operates as a secondary reinforcer for people who work.

Three elements are necessary to a token economy: (1) the designation by hospital staff of certain patient behaviors as desirable and reinforceable; (2) a medium of exchange, such as coinlike tokens or tallies on a piece of paper; and (3) goods, services, or privileges that the tokens can buy. It is up to the hospital staff to dispense the tokens for desirable patient behaviors (Ullman & Krasner, 1975). In one psychiatric hospital ward, tokens could be exchanged for hospital passes, cigarettes, food, television viewing, and the choice of dining room tablemates. Patients were given tokens for good grooming and neat physical appearance, for washing dishes, and for performing other chores. The program markedly improved the behavior of schizophrenic patients. Moreover, when tokens were no longer given, patient involvement in the previously reinforced activities decreased (Ayllon & Azrin, 1968). This finding supported the conclusion that tokens were responsible for the success. Other studies have also indicated that token economy systems are effective with chronic hospitalized patients who are considered resistant to treatment (Paul, 1982). Token economies also tend to raise staff morale (Ullman & Krasner, 1975).

Token economy programs are used in a variety of settings, with such different types of people as juvenile delinquents, school children, the retarded, and patients in residential community homes. Although such programs have been extremely successful in modifying behaviors in institutional settings, problems remain. Some patients do not respond to token economies; complex behaviors, such as those involving language, are difficult to modify with this technique; and desirable patient behaviors that are exhibited in a hospital may not be continued outside the hospital setting.

Punishment When less drastic methods are ineffective, **punishment** is sometimes used in treating autistic and schizophrenic children (Lovaas, 1977; Lovaas et al., 1965). In an early study, Lovaas and his colleagues attempted to modify the behaviors of two 5-year-old identical twins who were diagnosed as schizophrenics. The children had shown no response to conventional treatment and were largely unresponsive in everyday interpersonal situations. They showed no reaction to speech and did not themselves speak; they did not recognize adults or each other; and they engaged in temper tantrums, self-destructive behaviors, and inappropriate handling of objects. The experimenters decided to use electric shock as a punishment for the purpose of modifying the children's behaviors. A floor gridded with metal tape was constructed so that a painful

but not physically damaging shock could be administered to their bare feet. By turning the shock on and off, the experimenters found it possible to condition approach (social) behaviors in the children. Affectionate responses (kissing and hugging) were developed and tantrum behaviors were eliminated—all via the use of using shock as an aversive stimulus.

Lovaas's work has shown that operant conditioning is a powerful technique for changing the behavior of autistic children who have failed to respond to other forms of treatment. For many years, researchers have stressed that autism and childhood schizophrenia are learned disorders and that autistic behaviors can be modified with behavioral techniques (Ferster, 1961). However, because of the ethical issues raised by the use of electric shocks, this punishment technique has declined in recent years (Harris & Ersner-Hershfield, 1978; Russo et al., 1980).

Observational Learning Techniques

As discussed in Chapter 3, **observational learning** is the acquisition of new behaviors by watching them. The process of demonstrating these behaviors to a person or audiences is called **modeling**. Modeling has been shown to be effective in helping people acquire more appropriate behaviors. In one experiment, young adults who showed an intense fear of snakes were assigned to four groups:

1. The *live modeling with participation* group watched a live model who initiated progressively more fear-evoking activities with the snake. Subjects were then guided to imitate the model and encouraged to touch the snake, first with a gloved hand and then with a bare hand.

2. The *symbolic modeling* group underwent relaxation training and then viewed a film that showed children and adults handling snakes in progressively more fear-evoking circumstances.

3. The *systematic desensitization* group received systematic desensitization treatment for snake phobias.

4. The *control* group received no treatment.

Before treatment, the approach behaviors of all the subjects toward snakes were equally low. After treatment, the ability to approach and touch snakes had increased for all treated subjects (the first three groups), who performed better than the no-treatment group. The *live modeling with participation* group showed the greatest change: Nearly all the subjects voluntarily touched the snake (Bandura et al., 1969).

In a different kind of application, modeling was used to effect changes in institutionalized delinquent boys. The boys were asked to observe the behavior of a model and then to imitate that behavior. The model demonstrated how to behave appropriately in situations that the boys were likely to encounter: job situations, school settings, interactions with parents and authority figures, and such. The results were encouraging. The boys behaved more maturely than an untreated control group, and a follow-up study found them less likely to be institutionalized (Sarason & Ganzer, 1973).

The modeling of behaviors shown in films has been successfully used in medical and dental practices to reduce fears of medical procedures (Wilson & O'Leary, 1980), in teaching social skills (Bellack et al., 1983), and in reducing compulsions and phobias (Rachman & Hodgson, 1980).

Cognitive Behavioral Therapy

In Chapter 3, we discussed in some detail how cognitive-behavioral approaches believe that psychopathology stems from irrational, faulty, negative, and distorted thinking or self-statements a person makes to him- or herself. As a result, most cognitive approaches share several elements. First, cognitive restructuring is used to change a client's irrational, self-defeating, and distorted thoughts and attitudes to more rational, positive, and appropriate ones (Beck, 1976; Meichenbaum, 1977; Ellis, 1973). Second, skills training is used to help clients learn to manage and overcome stress. Third, problem solving provides clients with strategies for dealing with specific problems in living.

Initially, Albert Ellis's rational-emotive therapy, or RET (1962) was not well received by therapists. However, attitudes soon changed when behaviorists became increasingly interested in mediating cognitive processes. In addition, RET and the behavioral strategies are similar in a number of ways. For example, RET incorporates cognitive restructuring, skills training, and problem-solving skills. Cognitive restructuring specifically is used to help clients deal with their irrational thoughts and beliefs. For example, take a

client who believes that he or she should be loved by everyone. This belief is attacked directly by the therapist: "What is so awful about not being loved by everyone? If your father doesn't love you, that's *his* problem!" Once the client begins to restructure his or her thoughts, the therapist then begins to help the client learn new ways to appraise and evaluate situations. Last, homework assignments (behavioral rehearsal) are given to help the client learn new strategies in dealing with situations.

Aaron Beck (1976) has also been a major contributor to cognitive behavioral therapy. Originally using this approach to treat depression, he has extended his treatment to other disorders such as anxiety and phobias (Beck, 1985; Beck & Emery, 1985).

Aaron Beck (b.1921) is probably best known for his cognitive-behavioral approach to the treatment of depression. His theory, however, has wider applications. Believing that many disorders are cognitively produced, Beck attempts to recognize what the client is thinking, help that person recognize faulty or ineffective thinking patterns, and effect change via feedback.

FOCUS 19.2   *Healthy Denial: A Cognitive Means of Coping with Stress*

According to Lazarus (1983) and Lazarus and Launier (1979), denial and illusions may not always be pathological. This line of thought runs counter to the belief that a healthy person accurately recognizes what is real in the world. Lazarus (1979) points out that collective illusions ("Government always deals fairly with citizens") and individual illusions ("I am superior to most people in intelligence") add richness and meaning to our lives. This does not negate the fact that *denial* is often pathological. A woman who finds a lump on her breast and denies that it can be cancer may put off seeing a doctor until too late.

Lazarus distinguishes between two different coping responses to stress: problem-solving responses and emotion-focused responses. A *problem-solving response* is an attempt to change the troublesome situation. For example, a person

trapped in a house that has just collapsed during an earthquake may handle the anxiety by sizing up the situation and deciding to systematically shout at the top of his or her voice while trying to crawl out. A woman who finds a lump on her breast may become anxious but seek additional information through medical examination and advice. In these cases, the circumstances may be changed by means of problem-solving responses. Some realities, however, cannot be changed. In such cases, emotion-focused modes may be used.

Emotion-focused responses do not change the relationship between the person and the environment, but they can make the person feel better. The most common of these are thinking of something else, distancing, minimizing, and making light of the situation. These defenses are frequently referred to as *intra-*

psychic or *cognitive* means of coping.

Traditionally, psychologists have contended that "healthy" people use problem-solving modes, whereas "sick" people use emotion-focused responses. The proponents of "healthy denial" believe that serious sources of stress in life—circumstances for which very little can be done to alleviate the stress—require emotion-focused modes of coping. The healthy person in this case is one who handles his or her feelings through denial. For example, a patient with a terminal illness may choose to deny his or her ultimate fate and sustain hope. According to Lazarus, the competent coper is one who can use problem-solving strategies when something can be done to change the environmental factors that brought on stress, and one who can use denial to soothe feelings when nothing can be done.

Beck holds that emotional disorders are primarily caused by negative patterns of thought, which he labeled the "cognitive triad"—errors in how we think about ourselves (such as "I'm worthless"), our world ("Everything bad happens to me"), and our future ("Nothing is ever going to change"). While RET engages the client in a rational or socratic "debate," Beck's approach emphasizes the client's capacity for self-discovery. Less hurried and confrontive, the therapist and client work as a team to uncover underlying assumptions, to test them out in the client's everyday life situations, and to determine by logical means whether they are valid or not. As in systematic desensitization, smaller challenges are assigned first and more difficult ones are tackled as successes are experienced.

Other variations of cognitive-behavioral methods have been developed, all based on similar assumptions. One of the newer approaches, discussed in Chapter 3, is stress inoculation therapy, developed by Meichenbaum (Meichenbaum, 1985; Meichenbaum & Cameron, 1982). The assumption behind stress inoculation training is that people can be taught to better handle life stresses. Meichenbaum uses cognitive preparation, and skill acquisition, rehearsal, application, and practice. An interesting twist in the use of cognitions is discussed in Focus 19.2.

Cognitive behavioral therapy shows much promise. Studies indicate that RET (Lipsky et al., 1980), Beck's approach (Kovacs et al., 1981), and stress inoculation therapy (Denicola & Sandler, 1980; Meichenbaum, 1986) have been used successfully. Furthermore, some evidence suggests the approaches may be better than drug therapy for certain situational and specific depressions (Simons et al., 1986).

Behavioral Medicine

Behavioral medicine integrates behavioral and biomedical science. The two fields merged because people realized that psychological factors were often related to the etiology and treatment of physical illnesses (Brownell, 1982). The goal of behavioral medicine is to help people change their lifestyles to prevent illness or to enhance the quality of their lives. As discussed in Chapter 8, heart disease, strokes, and cancer have been correlated with lack of exercise, diet, smoking, alcohol consumption, and other behaviors of a particular lifestyle. Behavioral medicine makes people aware of the effects of these behaviors and helps them develop healthier patterns.

One way to do this is through **biofeedback therapy,** which combines physiological and behavioral approaches. A patient receives information, or feedback, regarding particular autonomic functions such as heart rate, blood pressure, and brain wave activity and is rewarded for returning these functions to normal levels. Monitoring devices supply the information; the rewards vary, depending on the patient and the situation. Studies have found that biofeedback therapy can reduce high blood pressure (Benson et al., 1971) and alter brain wave activity (Kamiya, 1962; Nowlis & Kamiya, 1970). The applicability of biofeedback therapy to the treatment of behavioral disorders is still being investigated.

In one particular study, for example, researchers attempted to help patients with essential hypertension (elevated blood pressure) to lower their systolic pressure. They used an operant conditioning feedback system in which patients saw a flash of light and heard a tone whenever their systolic blood pressure decreased. They were told that the light and tone were desirable and were given rewards—slides of pleasant scenes and money—for achieving a certain number of light flashes and tones. The patients did gradually reduce their blood pressure at succeeding biofeedback sessions. When they reached the point where they were unable to reduce their pressure further for five consecutive sessions, the experiment was discontinued (Benson et al., 1971).

Meyer Friedman and his colleagues in 1984 reported a study of 591 coronary patients in which they found that those patients who changed their lifestyles drastically reduced their recurrence of heart attacks. They discovered that 95 percent of patients who suffer heart attacks exhibit what is called Type A behavior (discussed in Chapter 8), which is characterized by time urgency (the compulsion to finish tasks early, be early for appointments, and always race against the clock), attempts to perform several tasks at once, the propensity to anger quickly when others do not perform as expected, and rapid speech and body movements (Friedman & Rosenman, 1974). The patients in Friedman's Recurrent Coronary Prevention Project learned, through counseling and practice drills, to control and change their Type A behaviors.

Most behavioral medicine techniques focus on lifestyle changes. Some of these are listed here:

1. *Establish priorities* It is important for each of us to determine where to put our time and energies. Establishing a daily or weekly priority list, including everything that is to be done, is a helpful strategy. If time is limited, learn to postpone the low-priority items without feeling guilty.

2. *Avoid stressful situations* Do not put yourself in situations that involve unnecessary stress. For example, if you find that a particular traffic route involves constant tie-ups, consider another time for your commuting or take another route. It is good to remember that we can and do have control over much of our lives.

3. *Take time out for yourself* We all need to engage in activities that bring pleasure and gratification. Whether they involve going fishing, playing cards, talking to friends, or taking a vacation, they are necessary for physical and mental health. And they give the body time to recover from the stresses of everyday life.

4. *Exercise regularly* Exercise is effective in reducing anxiety and increasing tolerance for stress. Furthermore, a healthy body gives greater energy to cope with stress and greater ability to recover from a stressful situation.

5. *Eat right* You have heard this advice before, but it happens to be excellent advice: Eat well-balanced meals that are high in fiber and protein but low in fat and cholesterol. Nutritional deficiencies can lower our resistance to stress.

6. *Make friends* Good friends share our problems, accept us as we are, and laugh and cry with us. Their very presence enables us to reduce or eliminate much of the stress we may be experiencing.

7. *Learn to relax* A major finding of stress management research is that tense, "up-tight" people are more likely to react negatively to stress than are relaxed people. Relaxation can do much to combat the autonomic effects of anxiety and stress; thus the various relaxation techniques are helpful in eliminating stress.

Resisting Stress: Guiding Principles

Just as behavioral medicine has given us some helpful suggestions in which to improve our psychological and physical health, some very promising stress research (Lazarus, 1966, 1983; Matheny et al., 1986) has given us ideas on how we can resist the build-up of stress or reduce the severity of stressful situations and events. Stress research and suggestions that arise from it represent a combination of behavioral, cognitive, and social psychology. A review of the literature indicates four major techniques or methods: *practice, preparation*, the *reduction of ambiguity*, and *reliance on social support and reassurance*.

Practice Victims of civilian disasters, combat, and imprisonment are survivors of situations that they have never encountered before and usually don't know how to deal with. Coping behaviors used to mitigate ordinary stress are insufficient to deal with extraordinary stress. Furthermore, considerable confusion and disorientation may occur in a disaster. Unless a coping behavior has been well learned and rehearsed, the victim is likely to be in such a state of shock that he or she can become immobilized.

Practice tends to increase coping skills, to reduce uncertainty, and to enhance a person's confidence that he or she can deal with a situation successfully. For example, fire drills in public schools reflect the importance of practice in reducing panic and stress. The armed forces have also instituted programs that prepare people for survival as prisoners of war. Simulated capture and interrogation prepare the soldier for what to expect and *what to do* if captured.

Preparation Against Harm When people know the type of threat they may encounter and the probability of its occurrence, they can take specific actions to reduce or eliminate the danger. For example, storm shelters can be built against tornadoes, dams can be used against floods, increased studying can guard against the possibility of failing an exam, and so on. About one-third of the residents of San Angelo, Texas, built storm shelters after the first tornado struck. Interviews indicated that these families showed less fear during the subsequent storm.

Reduction of Ambiguity Before people can prepare against harm, they need to know what to expect. Human beings (and animals) prefer predictable aversive events (Seligman, 1975); high anxiety is likely to result when the situation is ambiguous.

People placed in confusing or disorienting situations have a strong need to clarify those situations by actively seeking information about them. Sometimes the unknown is much more frightening than a known threat.

Preparatory information can give people a feeling of cognitive control by allowing them to classify events and situations by expectations. Researchers tested the value of providing surgical patients with preparatory explanations about the expected type and duration of postoperative pain. About half of a large group of patients were given information, while the other half received only minimal information. The fully prepared patients recovered more quickly and experienced less pain and discomfort. Their mental rehearsal of the aftereffects of surgery acted to reduce novelty and surprise (Egbert et al., 1964).

Social Reassurance and Support To a large extent, people depend on others for social support, reassurance, and confirmation. Their resources against a threat are drawn largely from those people on whom they have learned to depend. Reactions to the death of a loved one, for example, vary depending on the supports provided by each culture (Lindemann, 1960). In Italy, severe mourning reactions are less likely because of Italy's extended kinship system. Social reassurance also lets a person know that others have experienced similar difficulties and survived—and thus reduces the perceived magnitude of the crisis.

In short, the easiest way for people to withstand or reduce the stress they feel is to prepare for it. Together, the techniques we have discussed can inoculate individuals against the potentially damaging consequences of excessive stress. They are preventive, not remedial, mental health measures.

EVALUATING INDIVIDUAL PSYCHOTHERAPY

Both insight- and action-oriented approaches have attracted firm followers and loud critics. Behavioral therapists, for example, believe that this approach has solid theoretical support and empirical justification; that it provides a rapid means of changing behaviors; and that (unlike the insight-oriented approaches) it includes specific goals, procedures, and means of assessing its effectiveness. Critics argue that behavioral therapy is dehumanizing, mechanical, and manipulative; that its relationship to learning theory is more apparent than real; and that it is applicable only to a narrow range of problems.

Whether one argues for either insight- or action-oriented therapies depends largely on whether the person believes that human behavior is determined primarily by internal or external factors. There are also psychologists who argue against psychotherapy of every sort.

Over thirty years ago, Hans Eysenck (1952) concluded that there was *no evidence that psychotherapy facilitates recovery* from what were then classified as neurotic disorders. According to the criteria he used, patients receiving no formal psychotherapy recovered at least as well as those who were treated! Since that time, others have also claimed that psychotherapy's success has been oversold and that both practitioners and clients are wasting time, money, and effort in psychotherapy Some opponents feel so strongly that they advocate a "truth in packaging" policy: prospective clients should be warned that "Psychotherapy will probably not help you very much."

Critics of the Eysenck study raise several objections. First, it is not clear that the groups of treated and untreated patients were comparable in demographic variables such as age, socioeconomic class, and race—factors associated with prognosis. Second, the improvement criteria applied to the untreated patients (discharge rate, return to work, lack of complaints) are not the same as those used by many psychotherapists, who aim for far more substantial personality changes. Furthermore, Eysenck's criteria

used to calculate improvement for patients in psychoanalysis were such that he underestimated the rate. In fact, one critic has shown that it is possible to come up with an improvement rate of over 80 percent for psychoanalysis—using Eysenck's data (Bergin, 1971). Finally, was the "untreated" group really untreated? We know that disturbed people often seek help from relatives, friends, or members of the clergy during times of stress. A form of psychotherapy may have been rendered by these other sources. In addition, more recent studies reveal that Eysenck's high spontaneous remission rates have not held up and may be closer to 40–45 percent rather than 70 percent (Bergin & Lambert, 1978).

Reviews of outcome research indicate that psychotherapy *is* effective and that people who are treated show more and larger desirable changes than those who don't receive formal psychotherapy (Bergin, 1971; Meltzoff & Kornreich, 1970; Smith & Glass, 1977; Sloane et al., 1975; Lambert et al., 1986; Smith et al., 1980). One such review examined hundreds of studies on the outcome of psychoanalysis and behavior therapy. The adequacy of research design, outcome measures, and therapist and client factors were all considered, and the investigators systematically weighed and compared variables. They concluded that treated patients show far more improvement than untreated people (Smith & Glass, 1977). In general, the higher the quality of the research, the more the results support psychotherapy.

Controversy over the effectiveness of the various approaches to psychotherapy—and of psychotherapy itself—is likely to continue. We believe that psychotherapy *is* valuable and that it's not productive to unreservedly accept or reject a whole group of treatments, either behavioral or insight-oriented. A more meaningful issue is how best to match therapist, client, and situational variables.

GROUP, FAMILY, AND MARITAL THERAPY

The classic form of psychotherapy involves a one-to-one relationship between one therapist and one client. In **group therapy,** the therapeutic experience always involves more than one client and may involve more than one therapist. The increasing popularity of group therapy stems from certain economic and therapeutic

FOCUS 19.3   *Some Types of Therapy Groups*

1. *Human Relations Training Groups*   The goal of sensitivity training is to help people increase their sensitivity to others and improve their human relations skills so that they can be more efficient and responsive in their relationships with others—particularly in schools or business organizations. The group leader focuses on group processes (such as how members are relating to one another and what is happening in the group) and encourages members to be open, honest, and flexible. Rather than dominating the sessions, the leader helps members develop their own ideas (Korchin, 1976).

2. *Encounter groups*   Drawing on certain principles of sensitivity training, Carl Rogers conceived of encounter groups to facilitate human growth and development (greater effectiveness, openness, spontaneity, and flexibility) through encounter experiences. Freedom of expression and the reduction of defensiveness are encouraged. The group leader acts as a facilitator, refusing to direct the group authoritatively or to manipulate group activities. Merely by providing a climate of respect and freedom, the group helps members develop trust and become less defensive and allows greater freedom to grow and use positive experiences. Although Rogers observed that group members are initially frustrated and anxious over the lack of group structure and direction, they later begin to feel freedom and trust.

3. *Transactional analysis*   Transactional analysis (TA) is a group therapy technique based on the assumption that people play certain "games" that hinder development of genuine and deep interpersonal relationships. These games have disguised goals, which are usually related to the need for recognition. The game of "one-up-manship" is an example: Person A may approach person B to get help with a problem. B sincerely attempts to help A by offering advice and sympathy, taking on the role of therapist. A rejects the advice and points out its flaws. B offers alternative advice, only to have it rejected again. B then feels helpless and perhaps guilty for letting A down. A is "one up" over B, who has been "put

---

advantages: Because the therapist sees several clients at each session, he or she can provide much more mental health service to the community. And, because several clients participate in the sessions, the cost to each is reduced. Saving time and money is important, but the increasing use of group therapy seems to be related to the fact that many psychological difficulties are basically interpersonal in nature; that is, they involve relationships. These problems are best treated within a group rather than individually.

Most of the techniques of individual psychotherapy are also used in group therapy. Rather than repeat them here, we shall first discuss some general features of group therapy and family and marital therapy.

Group Therapy

Group Member 1: What you just said really makes me angry, Frank. You're blaming me for something you should be responsible for.

Frank: I was just pointing out that you never contribute to the decision-making process. I wasn't blaming you! What's your problem anyway?
Group Member 1: There you go again! I don't have a problem with the group exercises. When they go wrong, I try to see what happened and why. If it's my fault, I'll try to correct it—okay?
Frank: If the shoe fits, wear it!
Group Member 1: Damn! It's no use trying to talk to you. Why do you always blame others?
Frank (angrily): Piss on you! It seems like you're the only one who thinks that way. I totally reject your accusations!
Group Member 2 (hesitantly): Frank, you do blame others a lot—
Frank: Shit! Do I have to put up with another conspirator?
Group Member 3: I don't think he's the only one in the group who sees you that way. For the past few times I've been angry at you too. You make me and the others feel incompetent and anxious. Last week you made fun of me when I talked about my problems with Janice.

down" and has become apologetic. A transactional role reversal has been accomplished by Person A.

Underlying TA is the idea that people adopt certain roles (child, adult, and parent) that reflect their ego states (Berne, 1972). "Spoiled brat" behavior or excessive dependency indicates the child role; the adult role is characterized by mature and rational behavior; the parent role is a controlling one, in which the person treats others like children. In many marriages, one spouse often acts as parent (dominating, commanding) while the other adopts the role of child (incapable, immature). Berne felt that such interpersonal transactions hinder the development of authentic relationships. The purpose of TA therapy is first to make the client aware of the games he or she is playing and then to eliminate them

and allow more authentic means of expression, more meaningful relationships with others, and better life adjustment. Transactional analysis may be used for families or for unrelated people in group therapy.

4. Assertiveness training groups Assertiveness training groups use behavior therapy techniques to help people who want to assert or express themselves better. Many people feel unable to express hostility, criticism, or warmth. In assertiveness training, people are constantly reminded of the negative consequences of nonassertive behaviors and are encouraged to act out and practice assertive skills (both in the group sessions and outside of the sessions).

Assertiveness training has been unfairly characterized as a breeding ground for the development of overly critical and hostile people.

The actual intent is to train people to express themselves appropriately.

5. Psychodrama Jacob Moreno (1946) was among the first to use the term *group therapy* in his writings. He developed psychodrama, a form of group therapy in which patients and other people role-play situations. When clients act out current or anticipated situations, they become aware of their feelings, and they can rehearse techniques for working out their problems. Others may play supporting roles, so that the client can fully act out the situation and interact with them. At times the client and another person may exchange roles, so that the client can understand the motives and behaviors of others with whom he or she interacts.

Frank (somewhat bewildered): I wasn't making fun of you. Why are you so defensive?
Therapist: Frank, we have at least three members in this group who are giving you feedback about your behavior and how it affects them. Maybe you should check out how the others feel and think about your behavior.
Frank: Well—I don't want to waste our time—there are more important things—
Therapist: It's important for us to give and ask for feedback from one another. I know it's hard sometimes, but that's one part of learning about ourselves. —If it's OK with you I'd like to start—
Frank (quietly): It's okay.

There are now a great variety of group therapies, reflecting the many dimensions along which a therapeutic group may be characterized. (Focus 19.3 presents several examples.) One obvious dimension is the type of people who comprise the group. In marital and family therapy, they are related; in most other groups, they are initially strangers. Group members may share various characteristics. Groups

may be formed to treat elderly clients, unemployed workers, or pregnant women; to treat clients with similar psychological disturbances; or to treat people with similar therapeutic goals.

Therapeutic groups also differ with regard to psychological orientation and treatment techniques, size, frequency of and duration of meetings and the role of the therapist or group leader. Some groups work without a leader. Others have leaders who play active or passive roles within the group. Moreover, the group may focus on interrelationships and the dynamics of interaction, or on the individual members. And groups may be organized to *prevent* problems as well as to solve them; for example, group therapy has been suggested for divorced people, who are likely to encounter stress (Bloom et al., 1978).

Commonalities of Group Therapy Despite their wide diversity, successful groups and group approaches, share several features that promote beneficial change in clients (Yalom, 1970).

Group therapy is a technique well-suited for treating psychological difficulties that are basically interpersonal in nature. One of the most powerful mechanisms of group therapy is that groups provide an environment in which an individual can develop new communication skills, social skills, and insights.

First, the group experience allows each client to become involved in a social situation and to see how his or her behavior affects others. In the group dialogue that begins this section, Frank is slowly and painfully being asked to examine the impact of his behavior on others. He may easily dismiss unpleasant feedback about his behavior from one member as inaccurate, but it is much more difficult to do so when others reinforce the feedback (agreeing that Frank externalizes his problems and avoids responsibility for his own behavior). Once the group member can view his or her interactions realistically, problems can be identified and then resolved.

Second, in group therapy the therapist can see how clients respond in a real-life social and interpersonal context. In individual therapy, the therapist either must rely on what clients say about their social relationships or must assess those relationships on the basis of client-therapist interactions. But data gathered thus are often unrepresentative or inaccurate. In the group context, response patterns are *observed* rather than communicated or inferred. For example, Frank's therapist could see and hear him try to blame his fellow group members with such statements as

♦   "What's your problem anyway?"

♦   "I totally reject your accusations!"

♦   "Why are you so defensive?"

Third, group members can develop new communication skills, social skills, and insights. (This is one of the most powerful mechanisms of group therapy.) The group provides an environment for imitative learning and practice. Frank's group members can show him that his statements and behaviors indicate defensiveness and that they affect others negatively. He may then be able to change his interpersonal behavior by imitating other group members and practicing better social and communication skills with them.

Fourth, groups often help their members to feel less isolated and fearful about their problems. Many clients enter therapy because they believe that their problems are unique: no one else could possibly be burdened with such awful impulses, evil or frightening thoughts, and unacceptable ways. The fear of having others find out how "sick" they are may be as problematic to clients as their actual disorders. But when they suddenly realize that their problems are common, that others also experience them, and that others have similar fears, their sense of isolation is eased. This allows group members to be more open about their thoughts and feelings.

Finally, groups can provide their members with strong social and emotional support. The feelings of intimacy, belonging, protection, and trust (which members may not be able to experience outside the group) can be a powerful motivation to confront one's problems and actively seek to overcome them. The group can be a safe environment in which to share one's innermost thoughts and to try new adaptive behaviors without fear of ridicule or rejection.

Evaluating Group Therapy Clients are sometimes treated in group and individual psychotherapy simultaneously. There are no simple rules for determining when one or the other, or both, should be employed. The decision is usually based on the therapist's judgment, the client's wishes, and the availability (or unavailability) of one treatment or the other. Of course, people who are likely to be disruptive are generally excluded from group therapy.

As desirable as it would be to base decisions regarding treatment techniques on the observed effectiveness of group therapy, little substantial research has been done on that topic. Review of studies does suggest that group therapy results in improvement, compared to no treatment or placebo treatment (Bednar & Kaul, 1978; Kaul & Bednar, 1986). The problems encountered in evaluating the success of group therapy include all those problems involved in assessing individual therapy, compounded by group variables and the behaviors of group members.

Some disadvantages of group therapy have been pointed out. For example, groups cannot give intensive and sustained attention to the problems of individual clients (Korchin, 1976). Moreover, clients may not want to share some of their problems with a large group, and the sense of intimacy with one's therapist is often lost in a group. Group pressures may prove too strong for some members, or the group may adopt values or behaviors that are themselves deviant. And, in leaderless groups, the group members may not recognize or be able to treat psychotic or potentially suicidal people.

Family Therapy

Johnny is a seven-year-old boy, attractive and energetic, who came to the attention of the school psychologist midway through his third year in grade school. He had been a good student in the first and second grades, but his schoolwork and attention span deteriorated dramatically at the beginning of the third year. Among the symptoms noticed by his teacher were multiple fears, tardiness, and failure to complete school assignments.

Johnny's mother, Mrs. B., was contacted by his teacher several times in the three months before Johnny was referred to the psychologist. Mrs. B. reported that her son had become school-phobic only this year, and that she had tried unsuccessfully to reassure Johnny that there was nothing to fear. Nevertheless, getting Johnny to school was a daily struggle; he overslept, ate breakfast at a snail's pace, and took what seemed like hours to wash and get dressed. When she dropped him off at school, he would cry and beg to be taken back home. Mr. B. noted that Johnny was younger than his classmates and wondered whether his son was simply finding the work too demanding.

Both parents were obviously concerned about their son. They were subsequently referred to a reputable child psychologist, who saw the family together several times. After their third session, both parents reported a marked improvement in Johnny's behavior. The therapist suggested that Johnny be seen individually for a period of time but also recommended marital counseling for the parents. Mr. B. vigorously objected to that suggestion and stated that there was nothing wrong with their marriage; the problem was helping Johnny overcome his school phobia and helping him cope with the pressures of school. At the urging of the wife, however, they did seek marital counseling, attending four sessions before Mr. B. abruptly terminated treatment. His reason was that the counseling was not helping with the family relationships and that, in fact, he and his wife had begun to argue and express anger at one another. In addition, shortly after Mr. and Mrs. B. had sought counseling, Johnny had reverted to his earlier fears and behaviors. The husband felt that the marital therapy had diverted their attention from the real problem—Johnny.

Family therapy may be broadly defined as group therapy that seeks to modify relationships within a family so as to achieve harmony (Foley, 1984). We'll use this definition to include all forms of therapy that involve more than one family member in joint sessions, including marital therapy and parent-child therapy. The important point is that the focus is not on an individual, but rather on the family as a whole. Family therapy is based on three assumptions: (1) it is logical and economical to treat together all those who exist and operate within a system of relationships (here, the primary nuclear family); (2) the problems of the "identified patient" are only symptoms, and

In family therapy the focus is on the family unit, which is considered the client. If one family member has been identified as the patient, family therapy considers his or her problems as symptoms of a deeper problem in the family itself.

the family itself is the client; and (3) the task of the therapist is to modify the relationships within the family system.

These basic tenets have arisen from the repeated observations of therapists who have worked with individuals and families. They are illustrated nicely by Johnny's case. Both parents saw their son as the "identified patient" and the problem. Even the teacher and school psychologist saw the problem as one of adjustment for Johnny. Attempts to treat Johnny individually had to fail, because the problem lay in the family system. For example, marital therapy revealed basic antagonisms and conflicts between Mr. and Mrs. B., but as long as Johnny was the identified patient, the parental problems could be covered up. When Johnny improved with therapy, and the focus shifted to the marital relationship, many of the husband-wife problems were uncovered. To maintain the family's stability, Johnny, who sensed that the relationship was getting worse, became phobic again.

Johnny's return to phobic behavior is typical of family dynamics, and actually serves several functions for the entire family. First, Johnny again becomes the center of attention and helps ward off a possible divorce. Second, the husband and wife can avoid examining their own relationship and its problems. Third, the status quo of the system is maintained.

Obviously, as long as the family members are treated as individuals, little progress will be made. The family is a social system that needs to be treated

as a whole. Mr. and Mrs. B. would probably benefit not only from therapy involving the entire family but from marital therapy as well.

Two general classes of family therapy have been identified: the *communications approach* and the *systems approach* (Foley, 1984). Let us look briefly at each of them.

The Communications Approach The communications approach to family therapy is based on the assumption that family problems are communication difficulties. Many family communication problems are both subtle and complex. Family therapists may have to concentrate on improving not only faulty communications but also interactions and relationships among family members (Satir, 1967). The way in which rules, agreements, and perceptions are communicated among members may also be important (Haley, 1963).

The therapist's role in repairing faulty family communications is active but not dominating. He or she must seek to show family members how they are now communicating with one another; prod them into revealing what they feel and think about themselves and other family members, and what they want from the family relationship; and convince them to practice new ways of responding.

The Systems Approach People who favor the systems approach to family therapy also consider communication important, but they especially emphasize the interlocking roles of family members (Minuchin, 1974). Their basic assumption is that the family system itself contributes to pathological behavior in the family. As in Johnny's case, a family member becomes "sick" because the family system requires a sick member. Treating that person outside the system may result in transitory improvement, but once the client returns to the family system, he or she will be forced into the "sick role" again. Thus, family systems therapy is directed at the organization of the family. It stresses accurate assessment of family roles and dynamics, and intervention strategies to create more flexible or changed roles that foster positive interrelationships.

Marital Therapy

Marital therapy has become increasingly popular for couples who find that the quality of their relationship needs improvement. Typically, the married couple is seen together and the session focuses on communications, role relationships, unfulfilled needs, and unrealistic or unmet expectations. Marital therapists work on the assumption that it is normal for any couple in an intense long-term relationship to experience conflicts. For example, the husband may find it difficult to express affectionate feelings toward his wife, who may have a strong need to be nurtured and loved. Or the couple may be locked in a power struggle involving financial decisions. Or the wife may resent a husband who shows any sign of weakness, because the man she married was supposed to be "strong and invulnerable." In all these cases, marital therapy attempts to clarify and improve the communications, interactions, and role relationships between the couple.

Note that it is not the purpose of marital therapy to "save a marriage," as many couples believe when they first enter treatment. The decision to remain together, separate, or divorce is a decision that must be made by the couple. The role of the therapist is to help the couple understand the nature of their relationship, how it may be contributing to conflicts and unhappiness, the options available for them to choose, and if they want, to work toward a healthier and happier marriage.

Here is an example of how a marital therapy session might run:

Therapist: Betty [the wife], I wonder if the last two sessions have been helpful to you in saying more openly what you think and feel.
Husband: Well, I think she's feeling better about the sessions, but there's been no big change in how she relates to the kids.
Therapist: Is that right, Betty?
Husband: Of course it is. She's always been afraid of—
Therapist (interrupting): I'd like to hear from Betty.
Wife: Well—Leonard [the husband]—he's not exactly right—I have—.
Husband: She tried, but nothing's happened.
Therapist (to Leonard): Do you realize that several times now you've spoken for your wife and cut her off when I've directed questions to her? I wonder if this is something that frequently happens with you and your wife?
Husband: I wasn't doing that. I was just trying to help my wife clarify her thoughts and feelings.
Wife: But—you don't—you only make me feel worse.
Husband: Betty does need a lot of—.
Therapist: What did your wife just say to you?
Husband: Huh! Uh—she said something about—about not feeling well—I think—isn't that right?
Wife: I said you make me feel like a child who can't think or feel for myself.
Therapist (after a long silence): What do you think your wife is saying to you? Can you paraphrase it?
Husband: She's saying that I make her feel incompetent—or dumb.
Therapist: I wonder, Betty, if you could turn to Leonard now, and tell him exactly how you feel. — Did he hear what you said?
Wife: You do make me feel stupid and incompetent, when—when you always speak for me. Don't you realize that I'm my own person with my own feelings and thoughts!
Husband (to therapist): I didn't realize—that my wife or that—I was doing that—I'm sorry if—if—.
Therapist: Don't tell me, tell your wife.
Husband (to wife): I'm sorry—for—for—I didn't know that's what I was doing.

SYSTEMATIC ECLECTICISM

The therapies discussed in this chapter share the common goal of relieving human suffering. Yet, as we have seen, they differ considerably in their basic conception of psychopathology and in the methods used to treat mental disorders. In many cases, various theories and techniques seem almost diametrically opposed to one another. For example, early criticisms of psychoanalysis concentrated on the mystical and unscientific nature of its explanation and treatment of behavioral pathology. Most of these criticisms came from behaviorists, who were likewise attacked by psychoanalysts as being superficial and concerned with "symptom removal" rather than with the cure of "deeper conflicts in the psyche." Recently there have been attempts at rapprochement between psychoanalysis and behavior therapy (Marmor & Woods, 1980; Wachtel, 1982; Davis, 1983; Murray, 1983). But even these sophisticated attempts have come under fire as being empirically and theoretically inconsistent (Yates, 1983).

As we mentioned in Chapter 1, most practicing clinicians consider themselves eclectics. Therapeutic *eclecticism* has been defined as the "process of selecting concepts, methods, and strategies from a variety of current theories which work" (Brammer & Shostrom, 1982, p. 35). An example is the early "technical eclecticism" of Lazarus (1967). This approach has now been refined into a theoretical model called *multimodal behavior therapy* (Lazarus, 1976, 1984). Although behavioral in basis, it embraces many cognitive and affective concepts as well.

Although the eclectic model calls for openness and flexibility, it can also encourage the indiscriminate, haphazard, and inconsistent use of therapeutic techniques and concepts. As a result, therapists who call themselves *eclectic* have been severely criticized as confused, inconsistent, contradictory, lazy, and unsystematic (Patterson, 1980). The resulting negative reception of the term *eclecticism* has led to other terms (including *creative synthesis, masterful integration,* and *systematic eclecticism*) that are more positively associated with attempts to integrate, to be consistent, to validate, and to create a unique and personalized theoretical position.

There is, of course, no single eclectic theory or position. Rather, an eclectic approach recognizes that no one theory or approach is sufficient to explain and treat the complex human organism. All the therapies that we have discussed have both strengths and weaknesses; no one of them can claim to tell "the whole truth." The goal of the eclectic approach is to integrate those therapies that work best with specific clients who show specific problems under specific conditions. Thus, in one sense, all therapists

are eclectics—that is, each has his or her own personal and unique approach to therapy.

In the remainder of this chapter, we present one systematic eclectic approach to the treatment of Steven V. Before you read it, we encourage you to review the discussions of Steve's case in Chapters 1, 2, and 3, to reacquaint yourself with his background and history. And, as you read, remember that what follows represents *one* therapist's integrative attempt to work with Steve as a feeling, thinking, behaving, social, and biological being.

A SYSTEMATIC ECLECTIC APPROACH TO THE CASE OF STEVEN V.

I am the therapist who has worked with Steve throughout his college career. I've been asked to comment on our sessions and to give you insights into Steve's progress, but before I do so, it is important that I explain my therapeutic approach and goals.

I believe strongly that therapy should involve a blend of techniques aimed at recognizing that each client is a whole human being. Many current schools of psychotherapy are one-dimensional; they concentrate only on feelings, or only on cognitions, or only on behaviors. It is important to realize that each of us is comprised of all these and more. I also believe that no single theory or approach to therapy is appropriate for *all* populations and *all* problems. People are similar in many respects, but each is also different and unique. To recognize this difference means to use different strategies and techniques for each individual.

I have tried to organize my comments topically. This may give you the impression that I worked with isolated parts of Steve's makeup, but that impression would be wrong. I try always to work in an integrated fashion and to deal with all aspects of the client's cognitive, affective, and behavioral makeup.

Meeting Steve: The Initial Session   Steven V. first came to my attention during the early part of his junior year. A very "unstable" relationship with Linda, his woman friend, had just ended, and he seemed quite disturbed by it. As I found out later, his own private therapist was on vacation, and he did not like the therapist who was on call. As a result, he contacted the University Psychological Services Center and was assigned to me.

During our initial contact, Steve appeared extremely suspicious, withdrawn, and reluctant to disclose his thoughts or feelings. I can recall the long periods of silence following my questions and his short but sarcastic responses. It was almost as though he were testing me to see what kind of therapist I was, to see whether he could trust me. Usually I try to be less active at first and to encourage the client to tell his or her own story. I employ almost a person-centered approach, listening and mirroring the client's thoughts, feelings, and perceptions. It was obvious, however, that this was not having the desired effect with Steve. It seemed to be alienating him and to be compounding a relationship problem.

Here is a portion of our first conversation.

Therapist: My name is Dr. S., Steve.—I wonder if we could begin by having you tell me what brought you here. (Long silence; Steve looks down, looks up at the therapist, looks down again, crosses his arms in front of his chest, and turns away.)

Therapist: It's hard for you to tell me what's on your mind.

Steve: Yeah (sarcastic tone, but does not change body posture). I'm not sure you can help me. —My therapist is on vacation, otherwise I would be seeing him. He's a psychiatrist, you know.

Therapist: It must be hard to begin a new therapy relationship again—to start all over.

Steve: Great, that's real perceptive.

Therapist: You sound angry right now.—Where is your anger coming from?

(Silence from Steve)

This type of interaction—or lack of interaction—was characteristic of nearly the entire first half of our first session. My attempts to get Steve to open up and to trust me didn't work. It was at this point that I felt a change in approach was necessary. I took on an active and directive manner characteristic of the behavioral therapies.

Therapist: We don't seem to be connecting, Steve; something is blocking us from working together.

Steve: You're the therapist, so you tell me what it is!

Therapist: You want me to tell you what the answer is.

Steve: I don't need a damned *parrot* for a therapist!

Therapist (raising voice): Look, Steve! If you want to waste this session in a tug-of-war, let's just end it now. I'm not going to sit here and be insulted by you. You respect me, and I'll respect you! —I know it must be difficult to trust a stranger. You'd rather be seeing your own therapist, but the fact is, he's not available. You're hurting enough to come for help. If you want to waste the session playing games, go ahead!

Steve (looking up and obviously surprised): I didn't mean to be disrespectful—I was only—only—

Therapist: Testing me—to see if you could trust me, to see where I'm coming from—to see if you could manipulate me.

Steve: Yeah, it was nothing personal.

Therapist: I know. Now suppose we start over again.—What brings you here, Steve?

As I look back, I believe this brief but heated exchange represented the beginning of our relationship. I think Steve realized that I was an authentic person who could get angry but would not let the anger become destructive. Clients like Steve often test the therapist with attempts at manipulation. They are ambivalent about this ploy because they want it to succeed (so they can "win"), but they also want it to fail (which means the therapist is perceptive and competent enough to see through their manipulations and thus to give them the help they need). In any event, this tactic changed the entire tone of our session. Steve became much more cooperative and open, and he lost the conscious antagonism and resistance of the early part of our meeting. It also became much easier for me to use a nondirective approach.

Gathering Information Gathering biographical information is very important to my understanding of clients, and I do much of it during the actual therapy sessions. I needed to know Steven V. Who is he? How does he see things? What are the important events and relationships of his past and present? What type of medical history does he have? Are there any biological conditions that have significant impact on his psychological or social life? What type of therapy has Steve had in the past, and how successful was it? The more information I have about a client, the better I can identify his or her problems and formulate treatment strategies.

In some of our early sessions, Steve briefly mentioned how much he had hated physical education classes in high school. When I asked why, he referred to the "jocks" who were always exhibiting themselves in the shower rooms.

Steve: They strut around like Greek gods, showing off their bodies. —They don't seem to have any shame at all.
Therapist: Shame of what?
Steve: I mean, I don't exactly mean shame.—yes—they're trying to make the others feel ashamed of their own—well, you know.
Therapist: Tell me what you mean.
Steve: Just because they have bigger genitals, they're trying to show off and make the others feel bad.
Therapist: When they did that, how did it make you feel?
Steve: I didn't pay any attention to them. They're not worth it.—Let them strut around, I got *bigger* grades than all of them.
Therapist: But how did that make you feel?
Steve: I know what you're trying to imply. (Raising voice) You're trying to get me to say I felt inadequate!
(Silence)
Steve: The size of a penis is no measure of a man! Those dumb pricks—most of them barely made it out of high school.—I could outthink all of them.
Therapist: You sound very angry at them. What exactly did they do?
Steve: When I had to take a shower, they—they made fun of me.
Therapist: How did they make fun of you?
Steve: Nothing in particular—but I knew what they were thinking.
Therapist: What were they thinking?
Steve: I don't want to talk about it.
Therapist: I know it's difficult to talk about these things, Steve.—Maybe when you feel ready.
Steve: You'd laugh at me.
Therapist: Is that what you really think?

Steve (after a silence): I had this operation when I was young; they removed my left—I mean, I've only got one. And those bastards never let me forget it. They wanted to humiliate me.

When Steve was six years old, his left testicle was surgically removed because of a malignant growth. Apparently this incident and Steve's self-consciousness about it had haunted him throughout his life. I am not particularly psychoanalytic in orientation, but I believe that Steve did relate his sexual potency and his own masculinity to the absence of a testicle. His feelings of inferiority, low self-esteem, and periodic impotence may have evolved from his erroneous interpretation of this relationship. In this discussion Steve also made what might be labeled a Freudian slip (or a slip of the tongue) in describing his grades as *bigger* (unconscious equation of penis size?) when he probably meant *better*. (Steve's Rorschach responses also led the therapist who originally administered the test to infer a severe castration anxiety related to his surgery.)

Our discussions also revealed some potential areas for treatment. For example, cognitive strategies might be used to directly attack Steve's implicit equating of the size and intactness of his genitals with the idea of masculinity. Perhaps strategies aimed at helping Steve get in touch with his feelings would be helpful; he continually avoided "feeling" statements in our conversations.

Using Tests and Formal Assessment   To gather information about my clients, I sometimes resort to more structured, formal assessment means. I may use homework assignments (asking the client to keep a diary of significant events or to write an autobiography) or actual psychological tests. I rarely use projective testing but rely more on objective personality measures. (The use of tests is consistent with the behavioral, the cognitive, and even the psychoanalytic approaches. It is inconsistent, however, with the humanistic-existential school.) When I do use tests, I consider them mainly as a source of corroborating data. I try to demystify testing for the client by explaining what testing is, what its limitations are, and how we will use the results.

The computer interpretation of Steve's MMPI responses, for example, seems to reinforce what I have learned during our interviews. The interpretation suggests that Steve is moderately to severely disturbed. It indicates that he is defensive, is hostile, and has a tendency to blame others. (I saw many of these tendencies in our first interview.) The MMPI suggests that a more confrontive, direct approach might work best with Steve. Other problems that are noted, like Steve's poor perception of his social impact on others, difficulty in getting close to people, confusion of aggression with sexuality, and depression and suicidal tendencies, seem right on target. The MMPI interpretation does note, however, that patients with Steve's profile are typically poor academic achievers. But Steve is an exception to this. He has consistently performed well in school, despite his emotional problems.

Steve keeps a diary, so I asked him to write a brief autobiography, emphasizing important childhood experiences, relationships with peers, relationships with his parents, current struggles, and future goals and aspirations. My intent was, first, to help Steve actively sort out his life experiences, away from our therapy sessions, and second, to help me understand his subjective world. The following portion reveals his reactions to our first therapy session; I believe Steve copied it out of his diary.

My first time with Dr. S. was very confusing. I thought I was in complete control. I'm still not sure what really happened. I know I was angry and resentful the moment I saw him. He was sitting there sipping a cup of coffee without offering me one. When I called the center, they told me I could only come in for an 8 A.M. appointment. I'm not even alive at that time of the morning. Usually Dr. J., the psychiatrist I've been seeing, sees me in the afternoons. I guess I was angry at Dr. J. for going on vacation and making me see another therapist who isn't even a psychiatrist.

I really wanted to talk to somebody about Linda. I guess I was pretty bad with Dr. S. I wasn't sure I could trust him, and I took out my anger on him. I tried to put him down and make him uncomfortable. I tried to make him feel defensive by saying he was *only* a psychologist and not a *psychiatrist*. It scared the shit out of me when he got *angry* back at me. I never had a therapist do that to me. It was like he knew what I was doing. He thinks I do it with other people too. Maybe he's right. He seems to be able to see through me, and I don't like that. I'm afraid to have someone really know what's going on inside. What is going on inside? I don't know! Why should I be afraid? Strange, I really don't like Dr. S. Or do I? Why am I seeing him now instead of *my* therapist? Mom and Dad are angry at me because I won't go back to Dr. J.

There are some very revealing elements in this passage. First, it supports my previous impression that Steve finds it difficult to trust people and behaves so as to push others away. Second, he is beginning to gain some insight into his behaviors—how he attributes his feelings to others and blames them for his troubles. Third, he has a long way to go. There is something within that he is afraid to reveal to himself and others. When he expresses the fear that I can "see through" him, his writing becomes disjointed and fragmented. Obviously, this "dark secret" is deeply frightening to him. It affects not only his emotional state but his cognitive state as well.

What was encouraging was that, despite his discomfort with me, Steve decided to continue in therapy—and with me rather than with his previous therapist. A part of him didn't want to look at himself, but another part seemed to know that this was the only way he could ever get better.

Overall Objectives in Therapy   As I got to know Steve better and better, I was able to identify some treatment objectives that would benefit him. Again, let me emphasize that I saw Steve as I see each of my clients—as a complex individual who feels, thinks, experiences emotions, behaves, and is a social being. I had to deal with each of these aspects during the two years I worked with him. Here, though, I'll discuss only a few facets of Steve's self to illustrate my therapeutic approaches.

Dealing with Steve's Feelings One theme that persisted throughout my work with Steve was his inability to get in touch with his feelings. He found it difficult to experience feelings or to make "feeling" statements. The autobiographical passage suggests that there is something he was afraid to acknowledge. He was ambivalent about therapy because it was forcing him to face frightening parts of his existence; he could no longer be safe and avoid taking risks.

It would have been a mistake to directly reassure Steve that he could trust me and that things would turn out well. Such reassurance would have been transitory at best, unless Steve ventured out on his own to take the risk and to confront his own fears. I saw myself as a guide who would use various strategies to help Steve confront himself. In this respect I relied on existential psychology, which places choice and responsibility clearly in the hands of the client. Here is an example, from one of our sessions.

Steve: My parents are upset with me for terminating with Dr. J. They think I should continue because he's a psychiatrist, and I've been with him for years.—I like him—and he really understands me. I feel comfortable with him.
Therapist: What made you decide to continue seeing me instead of Dr. J.?
Steve: I don't know, I mean—I'm not sure I even like you. Maybe it's just so much more convenient to go to a campus shrink than to travel across town.
Therapist: I don't believe that's the reason. You're hiding from yourself again! When are you finally going to start facing yourself?
Steve (angrily): That's what I mean. I don't know if I like you—you're always picking on me.—Shit!
Therapist: Say it again.
Steve: Shit! (*Pounds the table.*)
Therapist: Again and louder!
Steve: Shit! Shit!
Therapist: What are you feeling?
Steve: I'm pissed off at you!
Therapist: That's not a feeling!
Steve: I'm angry! (*Yells at the top of his lungs.*) Are you satisfied now?
Therapist (after a silence): That was real.
Steve: Yeah. (*Exhales.*) Funny how I felt like an overcooked artichoke crumbling just then.
Therapist: I want you to close your eyes and become that artichoke. What are you feeling now?

Steve: I want to keep all the leaves from falling away so that no one will see my artichoke heart. I want to strike out at whoever tries to peel the leaves off.
Therapist: Imagine the leaves being peeled away—
Steve: No, I can't do it!
Therapist: You *don't want* to do it.—What are you afraid of?
Steve: I'm afraid you'll see me—what's really wrong with me.
Therapist: Become that fear and tell me what's going on now.
Steve: I've got to hide.—All the artichoke leaves help me hide, so others won't see.
Therapist: Can you peel off just a few of the leaves?
Steve: Yes, but it doesn't feel good.
Therapist: For each leaf you peel off, say what it is.
Steve: I'm peeling off my phony self—I'm peeling off my mask—I'm peeling off my rationalizations—I'm peeling off my anger.
Therapist: Okay, open your eyes. What's happening now?
Steve: I feel naked, I feel everyone can see how inadequate I really am. I don't like myself either.—I feel scared—scared you won't like me anymore. I feel ashamed because you saw a part of me that no one else did.
Therapist: I know. It's scary to let others see the real you.—But look at you. Before we began this session you were very uptight and defensive. Your fists were clenched; you were sitting bolt upright on the edge of your chair; you had a strained expression on your face; your voice was tight. Now your body looks more relaxed.—Can you feel it?
Steve: Yeah—
Therapist: Get into your body.—What is it telling you?
Steve: It's funny—I don't like what I see in myself, but—but—I hate myself but I feel relieved. I don't have to always hide from you.
Therapist: You mean you don't have to always hide from yourself.
Steve: Yeah.

Dealing with Irrational Thoughts I had to discover how Steve's feelings and many of his self-defeating behaviors were related to his cognitions. I had enough evidence to indicate that Steve created his own miseries through the thoughts and beliefs he held. My work with him in this vein tended to parallel cognitive behavior modification and rational-emotive therapy: In some way, Steve was feeding himself irrational and unrealistic assumptions. My task was to identify these irrational beliefs, show Steve that he was constantly reindoctrinating himself with these messages, and teach him how to challenge or dispute them.

Some of Steve's irrational beliefs are evident in these words of his, taken from another session:

> I just feel like I'm a miserable failure. I've disappointed my parents. I know Dad wanted someone who was more athletic. I tried, but I'm not a jock. I did well in school and Mom is proud of that—but—I thought when I went to college and could do well at the university, Dad would come around. So far I have a 3.75 GPA, but I should have a 4.0. In several classes I missed an A by just a few points. When I told him [Steve's father] my grade-point average last night, he told me Jeff, my cousin, has a 3.9 GPA. I guess I let him down again. I was so bummed out last night—I couldn't sleep—maybe it's not worth going on. Life just isn't worth it. Why should I keep trying? Maybe I should just take courses I know I'll do well in.

Several themes in this paragraph appear to form the basis for Steve's feelings of worthlessness and his low self-esteem. These absolutist themes are often punctuated with *must, should,* and *ought:*

1. "I *must* do what is necessary to please my parents, especially Dad. I *must* get my parents' approval, love, and recognition. If I fail to do this, I will never be able to value myself or feel I have succeeded. If they don't love me, I can't love myself. And life would not be worth living without their love and approval.

2. "I *must* be at the top of my class. I *must* live up to the expectations of my professors, peers, and parents. I *must* be perfect. If I fail to attain straight A's, it means I've failed again and am basically stupid."

3. "I *must* be thoroughly competent in everything I do. If I can't, I'll avoid trying anything new. I *cannot* make mistakes because they will prove how deficient I really am."

After identifying these themes with Steve, I discussed with him how these thoughts and self-indoctrinations lie at the root of many of his problems. For example, he thinks his parents' lack of approval has caused him to feel unloved and unappreciated. I tried to show Steve that it is *his belief* about a *real or imagined* situation, rather than an actual situation, that is causing his difficulties. In therapy sessions, I confronted his belief system by having him respond to these following questions:

1. Who is telling you that you are worthless unless your parents approve of you?

2. Do you need to be loved and liked by everyone?

3. Do you want to spend the rest of your life in a futile attempt to win over your father?

This line of questioning was helpful in getting Steve to think, to challenge himself, and to decide—for himself—how he would live.

Learning New Behaviors   One thing that I have discovered is that a client's insight into or understanding of a problem doesn't necessarily lead to a behavior change. The understanding that he feared rejection by members of the opposite sex because he equated rejection with his "worthlessness" would not have made it easier for Steve to interact with women. And from my work with Steve, it had become clear that he suffered from immense interpersonal anxiety, especially with women. Not only did he not know how to interact with others or to "make small talk," but he also engaged in inappropriate behaviors that put people off. When Steve was with his friend Linda, he had constantly tried to make her prove she "cared for him." He had accused her of not being faithful to him, of not caring for him, and of not including him in her extracurricular school activities. This continual "prove you love me" testing of their relationship never ended, because no amount of reassurance seemed to be enough. In fact, it pushed Linda away from him.

This mode of interaction was characteristic of nearly all Steve's relationships. While he worked to combat this irrational belief ("I am worthless; therefore no one can like me"), I felt it was important to help Steve become more comfortable in interpersonal and heterosexual relationships. I attempted to help Steve subtract anxiety from his interpersonal encounters by using a behavioral technique: assertiveness training.

Here is Steve talking to me again:

> The truth is I'm always afraid. I panic when I think about being in a group of people and having to talk to them. What am I going to say? Even if I could say something, who would listen? Last month I went to a party with Linda—it was thrown by her friends.—When she introduced me all I could say was "hi." I stuttered when I said anything else. It was like in class—I really felt inadequate. And one of the guys was trying to hustle Linda. He knew Linda came with me, but he ignored me completely. He asked her to dance, and I spent the whole evening sitting in the corner. I was really angry at him and Linda too, but I couldn't do anything about it. Then he came over and asked if I would mind if he took her home. I could only say, "Sure, go ahead." What I really wanted to say was "Go to hell." I feel like I'm a doormat for the world.

Obviously we had to work on Steve's assertive behaviors. What I intended to do was, briefly, the following:

1. Identify Steve's unassertive behaviors that were linked to specific situations (for example, withdrawing and sitting in a corner by himself and not being able to say no).

2. Determine the specific skills he needed for assertion (saying no, introducing himself to strangers, asking Linda to dance, and so on). Then try to grade these skills from least to most assertive.

3. Recreate the problem situations, as vividly as possible, in the consultation room. Engage Steve in role playing and behavioral rehearsal with me or volunteers.

4. Get Steve to practice the assertive behaviors in actual situations, under my guidance and monitoring.

Our first use of the procedure will illustrate how we implemented it. Steve and I identified an upcoming event that was causing him considerable apprehension—a class assignment. He was to give an oral critical analysis of an assigned novel in his English class and then lead a discussion of the novel.

Steve needed to practice the assertive skills related to the oral presentation. First, to desensitize him, I had him practice very low-level assertive skills in front of groups. For example, he practiced *raising his hand* in class in situations where he was sure he would not be called on—for example, when many other students raised their hands or while he was out of sight of the professor. To Steve, this act was an assertive one. After he became comfortable with that, I asked him to *raise his hand* and *ask a simple question* (a safe assertive skill), such as "Could you repeat that last point?" After his anxiety regarding this act was conquered, he proceeded to *paraphrase* what the instructor had said and finally to *state an opinion*. Each succeeding act represented an increase in assertiveness.

While he was practicing these classroom acts, Steve was finishing his book report. I then asked him to do his oral report for me. Next I asked another counselor and the two clerical staff members to be present while he repeated the report. After a second repetition, we simulated a question-and-answer session and then repeated that several times.

This systematic training helped Steve greatly when he finally presented his report to his English class. Although he was anxious throughout the presentation, he felt that he had the anxiety under control.

A similar program, which I developed for his heterosexual anxiety, proved only moderately successful.

Steve's Threat Against Linda "She doesn't deserve to live—I swear, I'm going to kill her." Given the context in which it occurred, Steve's threat to kill Linda placed me in a dilemma. My conflicting feelings and apprehension were, no doubt, similar to those experienced by any therapist whose client threatens to kill someone or to commit suicide. Today more than ever, we as therapists must recognize that our work does not occur in a social vacuum. What we do or don't do in therapy has not only clinical implications but ethical, moral, and legal ramifications as well.

In that particular session Steve was becoming increasingly agitated about his breakup with Linda; his expressions of anger were stronger and stronger. He was quite depressed at the time, and in my therapeutic judgment, his venting of feelings was healthy. I had been working on that with him when he blurted out his threat. The first thoughts that came to my mind were questions: "Does he really mean what he's saying?" "How likely is he to carry out the threat?" "Is this just an empty threat characteristic of his anger and hostility?" "What should I do?" "Should I inform the proper authorities, breaking confidentiality, and risk losing Steve's trust?"

I chose to go along with my clinical judgment to let Steve continue to express his feelings without cutting him off, while constantly assessing the strength of his anger and the likelihood of his acting impulsively. I made that decision for several reasons. First, in the time I had known Steve, he had made several suicide threats. In each case, when he was allowed to express his feelings, the suicidal ideation and threats diminished. I felt that his threat to kill Linda would follow a similar course. Second, despite his often bizarre thoughts and behaviors, I had never considered Steve to be a danger to others. He was more a danger to himself than to anyone else. Third, I felt that some other perspective was needed. There was still time to consult with colleagues about the case and to get their input. And last, I was prepared to cancel other appointments and extend our session if that became necessary. I felt that I could monitor Steve closely, and I even made an appointment for him to return the following day. In other words, after pondering all the issues, including the need to protect myself by informing the proper authorities or even Linda, I decided that the likelihood of his carrying out the threat was very low. Luckily this did prove to be the case.

The dilemma for me as a therapist was not whether I should inform a potential victim or the appropriate authorities about a homicide that I deemed likely. I have no doubt that I would have taken that action if it were necessary. I was disturbed that I lacked the ability to precisely assess dangerousness and—even more—being unable to inform a client about the legal limits of confidentiality without adversely affecting our therapist-client relationship.

An Epilogue to the Case   Several years have passed since my sessions with Steve came to an end. He graduated from the university with a degree in English literature and went to a graduate school in the east. I did get the chance to see some changes in Steve that are definitely for the better. He relates reasonably well to people now, though I still consider him a loner. His bizarre behavior and ideation have eased off, but he still suffers from periodic bouts of depression. Whereas most clients need only brief periodic therapy to help them cope with life's problems, I'm afraid Steve is one of those people who will need some form of therapy for the rest of his life. He has chosen to work toward a doctorate degree and to become a teacher, doing research and writing. I think this is as good a vocational choice as any. Not only does it play to his strengths (writing, reading, and research), but the college environment seems to be one of the few in which Steve has done well and has felt sufficiently secure. Perhaps this is a statement about academic life as well as about Steve. Some perceive it as a protected environment that is structured and, in some ways, undemanding.

I don't know what has happened to Steve since he left this university. I am aware that he signed a release of information form so that his case records could be transferred to the university he now attends. I can only assume that he has chosen to continue therapy, and I wish him well.

SUMMARY

1. A variety of psychotherapeutic or treatment procedures are used to change behaviors, modify attitudes, and facilitate self-insight. Biological (or somatic) treatments use physical means to alter the

bodily and psychological states of patients. The use of electroconvulsive therapy (ECT), or electroshock, has diminished but is still the preferred treatment for some severely depressed patients. Because psychosurgery permanently destroys brain tissue, it too is now rarely used and strictly regulated. One reason for the declining use of ECT and psychosurgery is a correspondingly greater reliance on drug therapy. Antianxiety drugs reduce anxiety, antipsychotic drugs help control or eliminate psychotic symptoms, and antidepressants effectively reduce depression. Drug therapy has enabled very many patients to function in the community and to be more amenable to other forms of treatment, particularly insight-oriented and behavioral therapy.

2. The insight-oriented therapeutic approaches include psychoanalytic therapy, client-centered therapy, existential analysis, and gestalt therapy. These approaches provide the patient with an opportunity to develop better levels of functioning, to undergo new and emotionally important experiences, to develop a therapeutic relationship with a professional, and to relate personal and private thoughts and feelings.

3. Action-oriented or behavior therapies (based on classical conditioning, operant conditioning, modeling, and cognitive restructuring) have been applied to a variety of disorders. Behavioral assessment, procedures, goals, and outcome measures are more clearly defined and more easily subjected to empirical investigation are insight-oriented approaches. Two promising approaches are behavioral medicine and stress resistance training, which combine behavioral, cognitive, medical, and social knowledge.

4. Some critics claim that the effectiveness of psychotherapy—of whatever orientation—has not been demonstrated. Others have refuted that claim. The real issue, however, may be one of finding the best combination of therapies and situational variables for each client.

5. Although critics argue that behavior therapy is dehumanizing, limited to a narrow range of human problems, and mechanical, proponents consider behavior modification both effective and efficient.

6. Group therapy involves the simultaneous treatment of more than one person. Many psychological difficulties are interpersonal in nature, and the group format allows the therapist and clients to work in an interpersonal context. Family and marital therapy consider psychological problems as residing within the family rather than in one individual. The communications approach to family therapy concentrates on improving family communications, whereas the systems approach stresses the understanding and restructuring of family roles and dynamics.

7. Most practicing therapists are eclectic in perspective. They try to select therapeutic methods, concepts, and strategies from a variety of current theories that work. Being eclectic is sometimes criticized as being haphazard and inconsistent, but every therapist who fits the therapy to the client is in fact, eclectic.

KEY TERMS

biofeedback therapy A therapeutic approach in which a patient receives information regarding particular autonomic functions and is rewarded for influencing those functions in a desired direction

drug therapy The treatment of mental disorders with drugs

electroconvulsive therapy (ECT) The application of an electric voltage to the brain to induce convulsions and reduce depression; also called *electroshock therapy*

existential analysis A therapeutic approach that is concerned mainly with the person's experience and involvement in the world and that involves a complex encounter between client and therapist

family therapy Group therapy that seeks to modify relationships within the family in such a way as to achieve harmony

flooding A behavioral treatment aimed at extinguishing fear by having the client confront the real-life feared situation at full intensity

gestalt therapy A humanistic-existential approach to therapy that emphasizes the client's awareness of the "here and now" and his or her totality of experience in the present

group therapy A form of therapy that involves the simultaneous treatment of two or more clients

implosion A behavioral treatment aimed at extinguishing a fear by having the client imagine the feared situation in its full intensity

marital therapy A treatment aimed at helping couples understand and clarify their communications, role relationships, unfulfilled needs, and unrealistic expectations

monoamine oxidase (MAO) inhibitor An antidepressant compound believed to correct balance of neurotransmitters in the brain

person-centered therapy A humanistic therapy that emphasizes the kind of person the therapist should be in the therapeutic process, rather than the techniques that should be used

psychopharmacology The study of the effects of drugs on the mind and on behavior

psychosurgery Brain surgery performed for the purpose of correcting a severe mental disorder

psychotherapy The systematic application, by a trained therapist, of techniques derived from psychological principles, for the purpose of helping psychologically troubled people; includes both insight-oriented and action-oriented therapies

tricyclics Antidepressant compounds that relieve symptoms of depression

chapter 20
Community Psychology

an treatment ever meet the needs of the great numbers of people who are mentally disturbed? According to George Albee, past president of the American Psychological Association, the task is challenging:

> The number and distribution of persons with serious emotional problems in our society were far beyond what our resources, in terms of both personnel and institutions, could deal with on a one-to-one basis. The gap was so wide as to be impossible even to bridge. This reality forced me to look for alternatives to the "early treatment". . . . I became convinced of the logic of the public health dictum that holds that no mass disorder afflicting humankind is ever eliminated or brought under control by attempting to treat affected individuals, or by attempting to train individual practitioners in large numbers. . . . Every assessment of the distribution of disturbance in the society arrives at an estimate of approximately 15 percent of the population. In addition to this number of "hard-core cases," each year there is a much larger number of people experiencing intense life crisis. And when we realize that in any given year only about 7 million separate persons are seen throughout the entire mental health system, both public and private, we can appreciate the hopelessness of our present efforts. (Albee, 1983, p. xi)

In fact, the situation may be worse than Albee suggests: according to a large-scale survey, about 19 percent of adult Americans (more than 29 million people) suffer from a mental disorder or have suffered from one in the previous six months (Myers et al., 1984). The fact that only a small proportion of these people actually seek treatment within the mental health system has caused great concern among many mental health professionals (Shapiro et al., 1984). Other troubled people may seek the help of clergy, teachers, physicians, friends, relatives, or folk or indigenous healers (for example, spiritualists, medicine men, and shamen). But Albee's major concern is that the entire concept—that of treating mental disturbances *after* they have appeared—may not be sufficiently potent. Many psychologists are seeking alternatives to treatment, such as the community psychology approach.

In this chapter we examine some factors that led to the development of community psychology, as well as to the various activities of community psychologists. For the sake of completeness, we discuss a fairly wide range of activities—not everyone considers all these activities to fall within the domain of community psychology.

WHY COMMUNITY PSYCHOLOGY?

Community psychology is an approach to mental health that takes into account the influence of environmental factors and encourages the use of community resources and agencies to eliminate conditions that produce psychological problems. To many, its ecological focus and emphasis on competence and prevention represent a sharp departure from the practices of clinical psychology. This difference is especially apparent in the following three major areas of concentration.

◆ *Social ecological focus* Clinical psychology emphasizes the diagnosis and treatment of individuals; community psychology is interested in **human ecology**—the interaction between human beings and their environments (Kelly, 1966). Clinical psychology seeks to alter clients' behaviors and personality, community psychology seeks to modify social settings, institutions, and ecological systems.

◆ *Emphasis on psychological strengths and competencies* Clinical psychology has tradi-

tionally focused on deviance and disorders. In contrast, community psychology often seeks to foster competencies and to enhance the coping potential of people who may or may not exhibit mental disorders.

◆ *Prevention activities* Rather than treating people with disorders, community psychologists advocate programs to prevent the development of new cases of emotional and behavioral problems (Heller et al., 1984).

Community psychology has evolved primarily in reaction to a growing dissatisfaction with traditional approaches to mental health (Goodstein & Sandler, 1978). A major source of this dissatisfaction is the perceived inability of the one-to-one treatment approach to provide for the mental health needs of the nation. Another is the emphasis of traditional approaches—primarily the medical model but others as well—on the concept that mental problems are *illnesses* that result from *individual dynamics*. Interest in community psychology grew in part because psychologists became more concerned with the role of environmental forces than with the dynamics of the individual's psyche. Klein (1968) suggests that a person's adjustment depends on the nature and extent of environmental stressors, on the person's competencies and skills, and on the kinds of resources available in the community to help people deal with stress. According to this view, one could expect the healthiest people would come from communities in which stressors were minimized and resources were readily available. Klein's notion reflects the focus of community psychologists on promoting prevention programs (to reduce stress) and on increasing the availability of mental health resources.

In the next section we discuss some other problems that have led to the search for new approaches and to the growth of community psychology.

The Ineffectiveness of Mental Institutions

The system of psychiatric hospitals has been another source of dissatisfaction. As early as the eighteenth century, many hospitals freed psychiatric patients from chains and encouraged respect for patients' rights, but hospitalization seemed increasingly unsat-

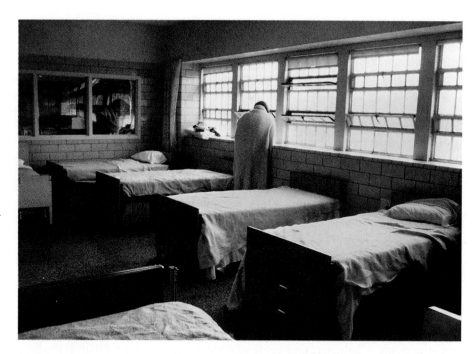

Prolonged hospitalization, while necessary for some patients, often reduces opportunities to learn skills required for living in the community. In addition, many patients receive minimal care and attention from hospital staff, so that hospital treatment often has little value.

isfactory for treating more and more patients. First, it is expensive financially. Second, psychiatric hospitals are frequently understaffed and lack the resources to provide more than custodial care. Third, state mental hospitals tend to be located in rural areas, making them somewhat inaccessible. Fourth, and most important, hospitalization often keeps the patient from developing the coping behaviors needed for life in the community. When institutionalized mental patients are dehumanized and degraded, they learn to adjust to a role that is inconsistent with community demands for responsibility and competence (Goffman, 1961).

Patient Treatment According to one view of institutionalization, hospitalized mental patients are sometimes treated as powerless and irresponsible. Many patients receive only minimal care and attention from hospital staff, so that hospital treatment has little value (Rosenhan, 1973).

An opposing view of the powerlessness just described suggests that patients in mental hospitals often manipulate the image that others have of them in such a way as to control their own fate (Braginsky et al., 1966). In so doing, these patients may regard the hospital as a vacation resort and may see themselves as free of responsibilities and worries. But

again, the problem is that these patients may not learn the skills needed to survive in the community.

In one experiment (Braginsky et al., 1966), hospitalized patients were found to fall into two groups. One group of patients tended to have low discharge rates and presumably wanted to stay hospitalized; the other group was composed of people who tended to be discharged rather early and presumably were motivated to leave the hospital. Patients of both types were given a short version of the Minnesota Multiphasic Personality Inventory (MMPI). Half the patients in each group were told that high scores would increase the likelihood of long hospitalization; the other half were told that high scores would probably mean short hospitalization. Despite the fact that all patients received the same tests, a patient's test performances varied according to the group into which he or she had been placed and the type of instructions given. Among patients motivated to remain hospitalized, higher scores were obtained from those who were told that high scores indicated long hospitalization. Among patients motivated to leave as soon as possible, the reverse was found: lower scores were presented by those who were told that high scores meant long hospitalization. On the basis of these and other findings, the investigators concluded that patients can manage and control their status in hospitals (Braginsky et al., 1966). Whether or not patients are helpless or can manipulate their status, the traditional hospital environment did not seem to help patients to acquire coping skills in communities.

Therapeutic Communities The important issue is whether there is a better way to facilitate the patient's early return to, and functioning in, the community. In the early 1900s, psychiatrist Adolph Meyers suggested that the mental patient's recovery was enhanced when hospital treatment could be integrated into the patient's family and community living situations. Involving the family and community would help smooth the transition between the hospital setting and community life. Along the same lines, Maxwell Jones (1953) conceived of a **therapeutic community,** a hospital environment in which all the hospital activities are structured to have a therapeutic function and in which patients participate to the extent possible. The environment, or *milieu,* would be crucial to the therapy. Patients would be free to interact with staff, who would relinquish much of their traditional authority. Patients would be encouraged to make constructive criticisms during "gripe" sessions and to become more involved in decisions about their own treatment. Patients would receive training in social, recreational, and job skills and would participate in role-playing activities to facilitate the formation of adaptive behaviors. Patient alumni clubs, halfway houses, and day treatment would also be available as bridges to community life. In a halfway house, patients who are discharged from a hospital live together in a house. The halfway house helps the residents make a transition from hospital life to more independent functioning in the community. Residents have an opportunity to help each other to develop social skills, gain emotional support, and learn better ways of coping in the community. Mental health workers may also reside in the house to provide some guidance.

One group of investigators carried the idea of patient autonomy a step further. Noting that adjustment to hospital life often hinders adjustment to community life, they developed an innovative program through which chronic mental patients could be placed in "lodges" located in the community. These lodges were set up so that patients could gain a sense of autonomy, manage their own lives, and

develop a small business (janitorial services). At the same time, patients could also be learning skills necessary to function in the community. Comparing the patients in the lodge program with a matched group of discharged patients who received traditional outpatient mental health care, the investigators found that lodge patients were better able to remain in the community and to work productively. On other measures of adjustment, the two groups showed few differences (Fairweather et al., 1969).

Reviews of such programs, in which patients are given autonomy and an alternative to hospitalization, have been favorable. Alternative programs cost less and result in lower rates of rehospitalization than does treatment in mental institutions (Kiesler, 1982). Given such findings, it is unfortunate that alternative programs have not gained a stronger foothold in the mental health field. Three reasons have been cited for this slow growth: First, the public often resists the idea of housing mental patients in the community rather than in the hospital. Fears about having mental patients in one's neighborhood have caused the public to frown on alternative treatment programs. Second, hospitalization for mental disorders is strongly affected by public and private insurance plans. It is the only treatment for which insurance programs provide full payment, and treatment in alternative programs may not qualify for any payment at all. Third, the mental health staff of a hospital may oppose alternative programs. Accustomed to the roles, procedures, and responsibilities of the hospital system, staff members may be interested in maintaining that system (Kiesler, 1982).

Rising costs and the potential negative side effects of hospitalization have given added impetus to the current trend toward deinstitutionalization. Admissions to hospitals are discouraged, and hospital stays are briefer. The hope has been that community resources (such as halfway houses and outpatient clinics) can be used as alternatives to hospitalization. Deinstitutionalization has reduced the dominance of mental hospitals in long-term mental health care, but some former patients are now living only marginally in communities because alternative resources are not available. (Some effects of deinstitutionalization are more fully discussed in Chapter 21.) There is now an increasingly large population of disturbed people who receive minimal service from the mental health system (Levine & Perkins, 1987).

FOCUS 20.1 — *Culturally Appropriate Mental Health Services*

The United States is one of the most ethnically diverse societies in the world (Comas-Diaz & Griffith, 1988). Although this diversity is enriching, it has also challenged our mental health system. Many ethnic minorities find mainstream mental health services alien to their cultural values and traditions. Consequently, they avoid using services, prematurely terminate services, or find treatment unhelpful. In order to decrease the disparity between the cultural backgrounds of clients and treatment practices, some therapists provide orientation sessions to explain to clients what they can expect from therapy (Acosta, 1984). Another strategy is to tailor treatment to the cultural background of clients, so that the services are less strange or alien to clients.

In San Francisco, which has a large Asian-American population, an effort was made to develop services that would be appropriate to this population. San Francisco General Hospital created a special psychiatric ward for severely disturbed Asian clients (Lee, 1985). Mental health staff who were knowledgeable about Asian cultures and who could speak different Asian languages were hired. The ward had oriental decor, and Asian diets (such as rice and tea) were served. Information was provided in English and Asian languages. The treatment programs were modified, so that they would be more consistent with the cultural backgrounds of clients. For example, because Asian cultural values emphasize the role of family, members of clients' families were encouraged to visit the clients and to participate in treatment. These strategies seem to be successful, at least in terms of service utilization. Whereas Asians represented only 10 percent of the client population in 1981, this figure had increased to 34 percent by 1984.

Culturally consistent forms of treatment were also provided by a mental health program designed to serve a multiethnic population (primarily Afro-Americans, Afro-Caribbeans, Cubans, and Puerto Ricans) in an inner-city area of Miami (Bestman, 1986). Clients were treated by a team of mental health workers that included staff knowledgeable and familiar with the culture of the clients. For those clients who believed in folk or indigenous healers, the mental health team asked such folk healers to collaborate in the treatment process.

In addition to these programs, a variety of other innovative service programs have been created in other cities to more adequately treat the mental health problems of a diverse ethnic population.

Inequities in the Delivery of Services

Another important factor in stimulating the community psychology movement was the highly discriminatory and unresponsive quality of mental health services available to members of minority groups and the poor. An analysis of the community mental health system based on nearly 14,000 patients indicated that minority group patients tend to drop out of therapy after one session at almost twice the rate for white patients (Sue, 1977). A number of studies have indicated the difficulties in establishing trust, rapport, and a working relationship between patients and therapists who differ in race, socioeconomic class, and lifestyle (Jones & Korchin, 1982; Lorion, 1973; Luborsky et al., 1971; White, 1984). Therapists who differ from patients in these characteristics may be insensitive to their clients' needs or may fail to adequately consider the influence of the social environment in which their clients live. As a result, minority or lower-class patients often prematurely terminate therapy at mental health facilities. (See Focus 20.1 for a discussion of innovative treatment programs to serve ethnic minority groups.)

In addition, therapists themselves select clients on the basis of characteristics that place people from low socioeconomic levels at a severe disadvantage. One researcher found that therapists often prefer patients who are young, attractive, verbal, intelligent, and successful—the "YAVIS" syndrome in patient selection (Schofield, 1964). This observation led others to urge that greater attention be given to "HOUND" patients—those who are homely, old, unattractive, nonverbal, and dumb (Goldstein & Simonson, 1971). The problem is twofold: minority and poor patients find therapists unresponsive, and therapists prefer not to work with lower-class or less articulate patients. This problem has led to a call for an appreciation of cultural diversity and the search for mental health practices that respond to different cultural groups (Snowden, 1987).

The search for alternative approaches to mental health care has thus been stimulated by the lack of sufficient professional personnel to meet mental health care needs on a one-to-one basis, by dissatisfaction with the present approach, by the high cost and ineffectiveness of psychiatric hospitalization, and by inequities in the delivery of mental health services. Many mental health professionals have turned to a model in which psychologists draw on community resources to deliver mental health care. Programs based in the community are quite diverse. Several features are, however, particularly characteristic of the community approach to psychology. These include establishing a community mental health center system, emphasizing prevention, training paraprofessionals, becoming socially and politically active, and making increased use of social supports.

COMMUNITY MENTAL HEALTH CENTERS

The community mental health center system, established by Congress in 1963, was created in recognition of the following facts: psychiatric hospitals were overcrowded, short-term treatment appeared to be effective, medication could be used to control grossly bizarre behaviors, and the social stigma attached to the mental patient was declining (Levenson, 1972). The goal of the program was to make services more accessible to the community. **Community mental health centers** were planned to be centrally located and physically harmonious with medium-sized communities (of 75,000 to 200,000 people) and to provide short-term inpatient care, outpatient care, partial hospitalization, emergency services, and community consultation and education (Smith & Hobbs, 1966).

From the beginning of the program, many centers had difficulty fulfilling their goals. First, few centers were opened; only about one-third of the originally planned 2,000 centers received funding (Bellack & Hersen, 1980). More important, many community

mental health centers were criticized for being unresponsive to their communities and for lacking community participation. Critics charged that many centers were structured in a rigid, authoritarian manner and that decisions were made by administrators who took little account of the attitudes and opinions of staff members and consumers. Critics also expressed concern about the system's continued adherence to the biogenic model, which stresses intrapsychic therapy (that is, treatment focusing on the personality dynamics of an individual) rather than on environmental intervention and prevention (Chu & Trotter, 1974; Goldenberg, 1973). Because patients become the passive recipients of treatment, this model discourages the active participation of consumers and of the community.

These criticisms have some validity. Some community mental health centers have failed to form strong enough roots in the communities they serve. And funding problems have indeed limited the system's development (Bloom, 1977). Of necessity, most professional personnel in these centers had been trained traditionally, with emphasis on the biogenic model. The current growth of training programs in community psychology should help alleviate this problem (Heller et al., 1984).

PREVENTION PROGRAMS

Preventing psychopathology is one of the most innovative functions of community psychology. Prevention programs are attempts to maintain health rather than to treat sickness. The main emphasis is on reducing the number of new cases of mental disorders, the duration of disorders among afflicted people, and the disabling effects of disorders. These three areas of prevention have been called *primary*, *secondary*, and *tertiary* prevention (Cowen, 1983).

Primary Prevention

Primary prevention is an effort to lower the incidence of new cases of behavioral disorders by strengthening or adding to resources that promote mental health and by eliminating features of a community that threaten mental health. As an example of the former,

Project Head Start was initiated in 1964, with the goal of setting up a new and massive preschool program to help neglected or deprived children develop social, emotional, and intellectual skills. Examples of the latter are efforts to eliminate discrimination against members of minority groups in order to help them fulfill their potential. Both techniques—introducing new resources and eliminating causal factors—can be directed toward specific groups of people or toward the community as a whole.

In one primary prevention program, researchers demonstrated that mothers can be trained to facilitate the development of interpersonal cognitive problem-solving skills in their children. Children of trained mothers demonstrated greater ability to think of alternative solutions to interpersonal problems and to exhibit less impulsive or inhibited behaviors than a control group of children (Shure & Spivack, 1979). The same researchers also examined the feasibility of having teachers implement an interpersonal, problem-solving, skills-training program with young children. When the children learned coping and problem-solving skills, they showed fewer behavioral disturbances and fewer other problems than a control group of untrained children (Shure & Spivack, 1982).

Emotional Support Marital separation or divorce is a major stressor that is likely to produce emotional distress. One group of investigators reasoned that, by providing emotional support and by enhancing the competencies of separated people, they could reduce the likelihood of disturbance. To test this supposition, they gathered a group of newly separated people, found through media advertisements and by reference from agencies and practitioners, and divided them into an experimental group and a control group. Both groups were given intensive interviews and were reassessed six months later. In addition, the experimental group participated in a prevention program that consisted of one-to-one consultation with a representative who provided emotional support and served as the link between the individual member and the program. People in the experimental group were also offered the chance to participate in study groups that focused on such skills and tasks as job hunting and career planning; legal, financial, and child custody issues; and child-rearing and single-parenting problems; housing and homemaking issues; and socialization and self-esteem

As a primary prevention program, Head Start was designed to help deprived children develop social, emotional, and intellectual skills. By fostering these competencies in children, the program hoped to prevent possible future mental health problems.

building. Results indicated that, after participating in the program, the experimental group (1) favorably evaluated the program, (2) exhibited significantly fewer problems and better adjustment than the control group, and (3) showed a decrease in adjustment problems on a questionnaire of psychological distress and a symptom checklist (Bloom et al., 1982).

Community-Wide Prevention A community-wide project to prevent depression was initiated by Munoz and co-workers (1982). During a two-week period, nine 4-minute programs intended to prevent depression were televised in San Francisco. They showed viewers how to think positively, engage in rewarding activities, deal with depression, and so on. Telephone interviews were conducted with 294 San Francisco residents. Some respondents were interviewed one week before the showing of the television segments; others were interviewed one week after the segments were aired; and still others were interviewed before and after the segments. Information about respondents' depression levels was collected during the interviews (for those who were interviewed before and after the segments, the depression measure was administered twice). Respondents interviewed after the televised segments were also asked to indicate whether they had watched any of the segments. Results indicated that those who saw the segments exhibited a significantly lower level of depression than nonviewers. However, the results held only for respondents who had some depressive symptoms to begin with. Watching the television programs did not change the depression levels of those who initially (before the segments) reported little depression.

The results indicate that a community-wide prevention program can be beneficial. A large proportion (about one-third) of the viewers had some depressive symptoms, and this group showed fewer symptoms. The long-term effects of the programs were not assessed. Another problem in the study was that those who benefited from the television programs exhibited some initial symptoms. If they were clinically diagnosable as being depressed, the intervention might

be considered secondary rather than primary prevention. Nevertheless, the San Francisco study demonstrates the effects of large-scale interventions that may help disorders.

Types of Primary Prevention Programs The goals of primary prevention programs cover an immense range. They include promoting social and intellectual competence in low-income, Mexican-American children (Johnson & Walker, 1987), preventing child abuse (Garbarino, 1980), enhancing competence in older adults (Gatz et al., 1982), and reducing domestic violence (Carlson & Davis, 1980). Such programs can have an enormous impact. Consider, for example, an analogous success in the field of public health: The development of the polio vaccines cost less than $40 million. Since they were first used, these vaccines have prevented 2,000 deaths and 2,500 permanently crippling cases of polio and have saved over $1 billion *each year* in hospital costs and lost income (Jason et al., 1983). Preventing mental disorders can yield similar benefits.

Although interest in primary prevention continues to grow, resistance to prevention is also strong (see Focus 20.2). Problems have been noted by a number of researchers (Cowen, 1983; Felner et al., 1983; Glidewell, 1983). First, primary prevention is future oriented in that the benefits of the effort are not immediately apparent. Second, it competes with traditional programs aimed at treating people who already show emotional disturbances. Third, prevention may require social and environmental changes so that stressors can be reduced or resources can be enhanced. Most mental health workers are either unable or unwilling to initiate such changes; many others doubt that people have the ability to modify social structures. Fourth, the funding for mental health programs has traditionally been earmarked for treatment. Prevention efforts constitute a new demand on the funding system. And fifth, primary prevention requires a great deal of planning, work, and long-term evaluation. This effort alone discourages many from becoming involved.

People in communities need a variety of different social services. Here, a crisis intervention telephone service (help line) is located at a social service center that offers a variety of programs to the community.

Secondary Prevention

Secondary prevention is an attempt to shorten the duration of mental disorders and to reduce their impact. If the presence of a disorder can be detected

FOCUS 20.2 *Prevention Versus Psychotherapy: Who's Wasting the Public's Time and Money?*

With all the lip service paid to prevention these days, it might not sound like it wants for support. But when the bureaucracy doesn't want to do something [prevention programs], including something urgently recommended by the White House, it stalls. . . . Resistance is coming from the mental health industry, from psychotherapists, and from the organicists-geneticists who disparage social causation. . . . Prevention is bad for business. . . . [Mental health] Centers simply can't spare staff for activities that are not reimbursable, and the immediate problems of the mentally distressed leave little time free for prevention efforts that might show results only after many years. (Albee, 1979b, p. 2)

Prevention has remained largely an unrealized hope rather than a technological reality for most health conditions. . . . Albee's assertion . . . that greedy psychotherapists, in collusion with other profit-oriented groups, have conspired to prevent prevention because it is bad

for business is a falsehood. (Wiggins, 1979, p. 2)

I hereby request a debate with Jack Wiggins at a time and place to be chosen by him and his seconds. . . . Anyone with the most elementary knowledge of health care in the Western world knows that practically every significant advance in health maintenance has resulted from primary prevention efforts. (Albee, 1979a, p. 31)

This exchange between advocates of prevention and psychotherapy in the *APA Monitor* set the stage for a debate on the controversy at a meeting of the Division of Psychotherapy of the American Psychological Association at its 1980 convention in San Diego, California. The debate pitted against each other two past presidents of the American Psychological Association as well as two other prominent psychologists.

The prevention advocates acknowledged the importance of psychotherapy in mental health efforts but emphasized the potential bene-

fits of primary prevention. They argued that substantial opposition to primary prevention was based on (1) mental health professionals' lack of training in prevention, (2) the personal satisfaction and economic benefits of conducting psychotherapy, (3) the "newness" of systematic prevention efforts in the mental health field, (4) numerous misconceptions about the concept of primary prevention, and (5) a reluctance to initiate the social reforms that are needed to reduce stress.

The psychotherapy advocates acknowledged the value of prevention but denied that therapists resist prevention because of their own economic interests. They felt that, whereas psychotherapy has demonstrated its value, the field of prevention suffers from disunity and a lack of consensus regarding priorities, goals, and procedures.

Although the debate continues among psychologists, there is growing consensus that prevention programs are valuable, effective, and wise (Price 1987).

---

early and an effective treatment found, it is possible to minimize the impact of the disorder or to prevent its developing into a more serious and debilitating form. For example, classroom teachers can play an important role in secondary prevention by identifying children who are not adjusting to the school environment. Once identified, such children can be helped by teachers, parents, or school counselors.

In practice, secondary prevention has encountered a number of problems. First, traditional diagnostic methods are often unreliable and imply little with regard to treatment procedures. It has been

suggested that more specialized diagnostic techniques be used, perhaps focusing on certain behaviors or on demographic characteristics that may be related to psychopathology (Zax & Spector, 1974). Second, once a disorder is detected, it is often difficult to decide what form of treatment will be most effective with a particular patient. Third, prompt treatment is frequently unavailable because of the shortage of mental health personnel and the inaccessibility of services. Indeed, many mental health facilities have long lists of would-be patients who must wait months before receiving treatment. "Walk-in" clinics, crisis

The goal of secondary prevention programs, such as the alcohol abuse program shown in this photo, is the early detection and prompt treatment of abusers. The idea is to minimize the impact of a disorder or to prevent it from developing into a more serious problem.

intervention facilities, and emergency telephone lines have been established in an attempt to provide immediate treatment.

One of the most elaborate secondary prevention programs focused on first-grade public school children in Rochester, New York. It sought to answer the following questions:

1. Is it possible to identify "high-risk" first-grade children—those who are likely to become emotionally disturbed later on?

2. Can special efforts be made to help high-risk children adjust and to prevent later emotional disturbance?

In the first, or early detection, phase of the study, the investigators used interviews with mothers, teachers' ratings, and psychological tests to determine which children had (or could potentially have) emotional problems; these children were given a "red tag." The remaining children—about 70 percent of the total—were designated "non-red-tag" children. All the students in this school, whether red-tagged or not, were compared with control students from two demographically comparable schools.

The second, or prevention, phase was initiated in the experimental school but not in the control schools. It consisted of special meetings during and after school for teachers, parents, and mental health specialists. These meetings were designed to help teachers understand child development and focus on the needs of individual children. During the prevention phase, teachers gave special after-school attention to particular children who needed it.

In the final, or assessment, phase of the study, the investigators used academic scores and peer and teacher ratings to measure the children's adjustment.

In answer to Question 1, results showed that children given a red tag in the first grade were more likely to show problems in the third and seventh grades than non-red-tag children. Findings about the effectiveness of prevention efforts (Question 2), however, were less consistent. After third grade, children in the experimental group did not do consistently better than control group children on the various adjustment measures. Furthermore, by the seventh grade it was no longer possible to demonstrate positive effects of the prevention program. One benefit of the program was the finding that it resulted in a more positive attitude toward mental health personnel on the part of parents and teachers (Cowen et al., 1963; Zax & Cowen, 1972; Zax & Spector, 1974).

Cowen and his colleagues have continued to modify the program and to increase the number of children in the project. Over 2,000 children have been studied so far. A summary of the overall results suggest that, despite methodological problems (such as the lack of more varied outcome measures and of more comparable, untreated control groups), the findings are quite consistent across a large population (Weissberg et al., 1983). The series of studies showed that intervention reduced problems involving shyness, learning difficulties, and (to some extent) acting out and aggressive behaviors. In addition, adaptive assertiveness, peer sociability, and frustration tolerance improved.

Suicide Prevention   Secondary prevention programs have also been initiated in suicide control. It has been estimated that well over 20,000 self-inflicted deaths occur per year and that there are ten suicide attempts for every suicidal death (Levy, 1988). These alarming statistics have required major efforts to prevent suicide (Farberow & Shneidman, 1961).

Hundreds of suicide prevention centers, functioning autonomously or within mental health centers or hospitals, have been organized. These centers try to identify potentially suicidal people and to prevent suicides. Once a person is identified as running a high risk of committing suicide, attempts can be made to intervene directly.

Suicide prevention centers vary a great deal in complexity, from simple round-the-clock telephone "hot lines" to comprehensive therapeutic services. Many have publicized their availability or have established working relationships with police, hospitals, churches, and other organizations in order to more quickly identify, reach, and serve potentially suicidal people. Although the research evidence for the overall effectiveness of suicide prevention is equivocal (see Chapter 13), these programs represent a major effort in the attempt to prevent suicides. Crisis intervention services are also available for alcoholics, compulsive gamblers, and drug addicts. Some communities have also initiated services to help rape victims handle the emotional trauma and stress of their experience.

Tertiary Prevention

The goal of **tertiary prevention** is to facilitate the readjustment of the person to community life after hospital treatment for a mental disorder. Tertiary prevention focuses on reversing the effects of institutionalization and providing a smooth transition to a productive life in the community. Several programs have been developed to accomplish this goal. One involves the use of "passes," whereby hospitalized patients are encouraged to leave the hospital for short periods of time. By spending gradually increasing periods of time in the community (and then returning each time to the hospital), the patient can slowly readjust to life away from the hospital while still benefiting from therapy.

Psychologists can also ease readjustment to the community by educating the public about mental disorders. Public attitudes toward mental patients are often based on fears and stereotypes. Factual information can help to modify these attitudes so that patients will be more graciously accepted. This help is especially important for the family, friends, and business associates of patients, who must interact frequently with them.

A more difficult problem to deal with is the growing backlash against the discharge of former mental patients into nursing homes or rooming houses in the community. Many community members feel threatened when such patients live in their neighborhoods. Again, education programs may help to dispel the fears and stereotypes held by such members of the community.

Halfway house programs can provide patients with a support system while they learn or redevelop skills they will need if they are to function in the community. In *outpatient* (patients live in the community and visit mental health clinics) and *night hospital* (patients are treated and stay in a hospital at night while working daily in the community) programs, patients can receive therapy and still hold down jobs or spend time with their families. Such programs help smooth the transition from the hospital to the community environment by offering exposure to both settings.

Evaluating Prevention

The concept of prevention has obvious appeal. It adds a proactive component to community psychology. That is, rather than waiting for people to exhibit disorders before treating them, community psychologists actively seek to eliminate the causes or the antecedents of disorders and use community resources to prevent disorders. But the goals of prevention—to reduce the incidence and severity of mental disorders and to foster mental health—are difficult to attain for several reasons. We have noted some of them; others also should be mentioned. First, attempts to identify people at high risk of exhibiting juvenile delinquency or behavioral disorders have come under attack for fear that certain members of political or minority groups may be falsely identified and unwillingly assigned to a prevention program. Second, doubts still remain about whether community psychologists have enough knowledge and power to implement effective programs. Third, prevention programs often require massive funding, and results are difficult to obtain in a short period of time. Because intensive evaluations of program effectiveness are generally rare, people are reluctant to invest in prevention (Bloom, 1972). And, fourth, some people fear that prevention efforts constitute an invasion of personal privacy. Continuing efforts are needed to reorganize priorities and to educate people about the benefits of prevention.

TRAINING PARAPROFESSIONALS

If you had a serious marital problem or a personal adjustment difficulty, where would you seek help? Obviously many factors enter into such a choice. In an analysis of help-seeking behavior, it was found that disturbed people turn first to relatives, friends, and co-workers for assistance. Other helpers within their social networks, such as clergy or teachers, are

A particularly effective form of paraprofessional assistance is to pair therapists and clients with similar backgrounds, problems, or disabilities. Such paraprofessional therapists are a valuable community mental health resource.

also used. Relief agencies and professional mental health services are often used as a last resort (Gourash, 1978).

Clearly, then, a substantial proportion of disturbed individuals are helped by people who are not mental health professionals (Gottlieb, 1981). In an attempt to expand the availability of mental health services and at the same time take advantage of resources outside the mental health profession, community psychologists are training paraprofessional therapists and are themselves becoming more involved in consultation (helping paraprofessionals).

Paraprofessional therapists are people who are taught by professionals to provide some mental health services but do not have formal mental health training. The training of more paraprofessionals would help solve the personnel shortage. In addition, many paraprofessionals have intimate knowledge of and experience in the community, which can help them understand clients and their environment. And paraprofessionals do not typically trigger the reluctance of many patients to enter therapy, a reluctance stemming from distrust or suspicion of mental health professionals.

The role of paraprofessionals in caring for others is not new. For many years Alcoholics Anonymous has used alcoholics, who are no longer drinking, as therapeutic agents for other alcoholics who are trying to stop drinking. The central issue is whether paraprofessionals are as effective as professionals, and there seems to be ample evidence that they *are* effective (Cowen, 1982; Durlak, 1979).

In general, the nature and extent of training of paraprofessionals has varied considerably from program to program. Some programs have selected paraprofessionals on the basis of personality test results (Holzberg et al., 1967), others on the basis of performance in small-group interaction (Goodman, 1972). People from many different groups have also been used as paraprofessionals, including unscreened ghetto youths, many of whom were high-school dropouts (Klein, 1967); college students (Gruver, 1971; Mitchell, 1983); mothers (Shah, 1969); teachers (Harris et al., 1964); grandparents (Johnston, 1967); foster parents (Cobb et al., 1982); and members of minority groups (Sue, 1973). People who are not mental health professionals, yet who frequently offer help in the course of their work, have also been studied; hairdressers, divorce lawyers, industrial supervisors, and bartenders often help others (Cowen,

1982; Toro, 1986). Furthermore, paraprofessionals have acted as therapists (Rioch, 1967), companions (Goodman, 1972), and foster grandparents (Johnston, 1967) and have used a wide variety of therapeutic orientations, including person-centered therapy, behavior modification, and filial therapy (i.e., parents working with their child in person-centered play therapy). One review of forty-two studies of paraprofessional helpers led to the conclusion that paraprofessionals are effective as therapeutic agents (Durlak, 1979). However, little information was presented about the reason for this effectiveness.

The roles of professionals, paraprofessionals, and nonprofessionals have been conceptualized as a "mental health pyramid" (Seidman & Rappaport, 1974). At the narrow top of the pyramid are experienced mental health professionals who serve as teachers, consultants, and supervisors. As one moves down toward the base of the pyramid, one finds more people with less intensive mental health training. For example, in a university setting, psychology faculty (at the pyramid's top) might train graduate students (in the middle of the pyramid), who, in turn, would train undergraduates (near the pyramid's base) to act as therapeutic agents. The influence of this training expands progressively, because a small number of professionals can train a larger number of paraprofessionals, who can train an even larger number of nonprofessionals.

The wide range of programs for training paraprofessionals indicates the growing involvement of lay workers in the mental health field. The community psychology approach gives nonprofessional mental health workers significant responsibility in taking care of others—a role formerly considered exclusively the domain of professionals.

SOCIAL AND POLITICAL ACTION

The development of community psychology has led to a deeper appreciation of the massive influence of environmental forces and resources on mental health. This appreciation, however, has led to a serious conflict among psychologists about the wisdom of political activism: should psychologists become active in the social and political arena, or should they stay out of politics and remain within their traditional professional roles? Advocates of social and political activism argue that, if psychologists are to effect major improvements in mental health, they must be able to influence political decisions and policies regarding environmental resources; that mental health services are already politicized; and that to separate one's professional role from one's social and political concerns is to refuse responsibility for society's future (Altrocchi, 1972). In other words, activists believe that mental health professionals should use their knowledge of human behavior to make positive changes in the policies that affect people. Opponents of this view contend that it is unprofessional for psychologists to become social activists. They fear that politically active psychologists may start imposing their own community-action programs and social policies.

In another sense, it is impossible to avoid social and political implications for creating or changing programs. For example, community psychologists may help to create citizen advisory boards to community agencies, help organize programs for the homeless, advocate changes in mental health programs, act as consultants or experts to the legal system, help powerless groups to gain political clout, and so forth. In all these activities, there are social and political repercussions, because change in one aspect of a social system will have implications for other parts of the social system (Levine & Perkins, 1987). Earlier we mentioned that mental health patients, when given autonomy and alternatives to mental hospitals, seem to have favorable outcomes. Such alternatives to hospitalization affect the entire mental health system: will programs that provide health insurance extend coverage to patients who now enter alternative programs? If alternatives to hospitalization grow, will mental health workers in hospitals feel threatened by the possible loss of jobs in hospital care? In other words, when social change is initiated, many other segments of the system are affected and often these segments are in conflict with each other.

Actually, psychologists within the American Psychological Association have long been addressing four kinds of policy issues. The first deals with Association "housekeeping" concerns, such as devising accreditation criteria for psychology programs. The second issue affects professional interests; for example, seeing that congressional appropriations are sufficient for psychological research and training. The third involves matters of public interest, such as effective programs for children, the elderly, and minority groups. The fourth involves moral and ethical stances concerning such controversial and emotional issues as gun control, abortion, and a nuclear freeze (Kimmel, 1984). The involvement of psychologists in the last two areas has created the greatest controversy.

Is it possible for community psychologists to facilitate social action without directly imposing their own values on others? The answer is "yes and no." Rappaport (1981) has advocated an empowerment model whereby community psychologists enhance the ability of people to control their own lives. Rappaport's model is based on three principles: (1) resources to affect change already exist in communities, (2) people already know what is best for their communities, and (3) no single solution is applicable to all communities. The term *empowerment* implies that the program is aimed at helping people become able to participate in decisions that affect their lives (Rappaport, 1987). The task of psychologists is to help others find better means to use already existing skills and strengths to solve their own problems.

Rappaport's model has value. Advocating the empowerment of people as a preferred model for social action is itself a value decision, and choosing which community groups to empower may also have political implications. The model represents a shift away from the position that mental health professionals are the sole experts, the group that must decide what is best for mental health. It recognizes, appreciates, and makes use of existing competencies in laypeople.

IMPROVING SOCIAL SUPPORTS

As noted, people often turn to others for help and guidance during emotional stress. They first seek support from family members, friends, co-workers, or clergy, and then perhaps from mental health professionals. By **social supports,** we mean the availability and quality of interpersonal resources that people can call on during emotional stress. Social supports can provide guidance, feedback, material aid, behavioral assistance, intimate relationships, and positive social interactions (Barrera & Ainlay, 1983). Community psychologists are particularly interested in social supports as resources that already exist and are available within communities (Rappaport, 1981). Focus 20.3 discusses one form of community support, self-help groups. Of particular interest is their potential for preventing emotional problems.

People with effective support networks tend to show fewer symptoms of both physical and mental

Elderly people often lack social contact with others. Senior citizen programs, such as the one shown in this photo, provide the elderly with social supports and the opportunity to interact with their peers.

FOCUS 20.3

Increasing Social Supports: Use of Community Self-Help Groups

Self-help groups bring people together so that they may help each other to more effectively cope with some personal or life-disrupting problems through the exchange of psychological support, information, and resources. Groups such as these have always existed although perhaps not formally. Alcoholics Anonymous is one self-help group with which most people are familiar.

Community psychologists have been interested in facilitating the development of self-help groups. Indeed, as U.S. Surgeon General C. Everett Koop and others recognize, such groups are a community re-source that can provide immense social supports. The rapid growth of self-help groups reflects the growing belief that people can help themselves and others (Levine & Perkins, 1987). The task of community psychologists is to help organize these groups, facilitate their development, and conduct research on their effectiveness. In California, a self-help center was established to enhance the growth and development of thousands of self-help groups (see Eisman, 1988). Headed by Gerald Goodman, Marion Jacobs, and Mark Mayeda, the center monitors a diverse range of self-help groups such as parents of high-risk infants (those born prematurely), victims of AIDS, single parents, those widowed or divorced men and women, parents of drug abusers, Vietnam War veterans, relatives of people with Alzheimer's disease, survivors of rape or incest, child abusers, and parents of runaway children. People who face common problems because of health or psychological disturbances, and people who are the relatives or friends of those facing such problems, can help each other in these groups.

disorders in the face of stress than do people without such support (Heller et al., 1984). The relationship between social supports, stressors, and psychiatric symptoms was examined in a study in which social supports were measured in terms of interactions and involvement with, as well as feelings toward, friends, neighbors, community organizations, and the like (Lin et al., 1979). Measures of life event stressors and self-reported psychiatric symptoms were also obtained. The results indicated that more severe stressors were related to increased numbers and severity of symptoms, but stronger social supports reduced the number of symptoms. The researchers speculate that social supports mediate the relationship between stress and emotional disturbance. That is, social supports may help decrease the impact of stress on mental health. Other researchers have also recognized the possibility that social supports cushion the impact of stress (Cassel, 1974; Cobb, 1976; Digman et al., 1986).

If social supports *are* important in mental health, then, by improving the number, range, and quality of these supports, we may enable more people to cope better with stress. Many of the studies cited earlier have shown that increasing interpersonal resources can, in fact, reduce or prevent emotional distress. This function is especially important because it would be impossible to eliminate all the stressors that human beings may face.

Although a great deal of research has recently been done on social support, much is still unknown (Gottlieb, 1983). Precisely how do social supports enable one to cope? What aspects of social supports are beneficial? What kinds of people, with what kinds of support, exposed to what kinds of stressors, can adjust and adapt? What are the most effective means for enhancing social supports? These and many more questions have yet to be addressed.

RACISM AND SEXISM: TWO PROBLEMS FOR COMMUNITY PSYCHOLOGISTS

Because of its ecological perspective, community psychology must be involved in modifying or altering social and environmental conditions that give rise to and maintain stress. Such conditions can have a tremendous impact on the mental well-being of large groups of people. One of the most invidious is the personal and institutional practice of prejudice, discrimination, and stereotyping—which has been directed against women, the elderly, ethnic and religious minorities, people with physical handicaps, and homosexuals. Here we examine the psychological consequences of racism and sexism.

Racism

Blacks, Hispanics, Native Americans, and Asian-Americans share many of the experiences of oppression that are manifested through **racism,** discrimination, and prejudice. These attitudes and behaviors are often aimed at specific groups out of hatred, misunderstanding, and fear of people whose values and culture differ in some ways from that of the dominant cultural group. The standard of living of many minority group members is lower than that enjoyed by whites, and rather than identifying this standard as a byproduct of racism, it is often used as "evidence" of the supposed inferiority of minority groups.

There has long been discrimination in housing, employment, income, and education. The results are high unemployment rates, less desirable jobs, and a much lower income for minorities than for whites, as well as higher suicide and juvenile delinquency rates and poorer health. An analysis of census figures reveals that the median income of black families is 57 percent of that of white families, and black males have an unemployment rate nearly two and one-half times that of white males (Moore, 1982). Historically, blacks have suffered from segregated and inferior education—larger class size, lower teacher qualifications, poorer physical facilities, and fewer funds for extracurricular activities.

Beyond such deprivation, extreme acts of racism can come close to wiping out an entire minority group (Wrightsman, 1972). Native Americans have experienced a succession of massacres of genocidal proportions. Time after time, their leadership has been decimated. The Native American population has dropped from 3 million to 600,000, and the Native American's life expectancy is 44 years, compared to 71 for white Americans!

Effects on Self-Esteem The psychological costs of racism for members of minority groups are immense (Sue, 1978; Ruiz & Padilla, 1977; Jones & Korchin, 1982). Constantly bombarded with the belief that whites and their way of life are superior to their lifestyles, many members of minority groups have wondered whether they themselves were not to blame for being different and whether subordination and segregation were not justified. A sense of confused self-identity among black children, to which racism may contribute, was first brought to the attention of social scientists by Clark and Clark (1947). In a study of racial awareness and preference among black and white children, they found that black children preferred to play with a white doll rather than a black one; that the black doll was perceived as being somehow "bad"; and that about a third of the black children, when asked to pick the doll that looked like them, picked the white one.

Malcolm X was a black activist leader who advocated revolutionary change. In the *Autobiography of Malcolm X* (Haley, 1966), he relates how, as a young man, he tried desperately to appear as white as possible. He went to painful lengths to straighten and dye his hair so that he would look more like white males.

The development of a negative self-image and the fostering of racial self-hatred are not unique to blacks. Many minority groups come to accept white standards for physical attractiveness, personality characteristics, and social relationships (Kardiner & Ovesey, 1962). That such an orientation may lead to racial self-hatred is evident in the following clinical description of Janet, a Chinese-American girl:

Janet, a 21-year-old senior majoring in sociology, was born and raised in Portland, Oregon, where she had limited contact with members of her own race. Her father, a second-generation Chinese-American, is a doctor. Her mother is a homemaker. Janet is the middle sibling; she has an older brother in medical school and a younger brother, age 17.

Janet entered therapy suffering from a severe depressive reaction manifested by feelings of worthlessness, by suicidal ideation, and by an inability to concentrate.

She was unable to recognize the cause of her depression throughout the initial interviews. However, much light was shed on the problem when the therapist, also a Chinese-American, noticed an inordinate amount of hostility; it became apparent that Janet really resented being seen by a psychologist of her own race. She suspected that she had been deliberately assigned a Chinese-American therapist. When asked about this, Janet openly expressed scorn for "anything that reminds me of Chinese." She expressed hostility toward Chinese customs and especially Chinese males, whom she described as introverted, passive, and sexually unattractive.

Further exploration revealed that all through school she had associated only with Caucasians. When she was in high school, Janet would frequently bring home white boyfriends, greatly upsetting her parents. It was as though she blamed her parents for having been born Chinese and used this method to hurt them.

During her college years, Janet became involved in two love affairs with Caucasians, both ending unsatisfactorily and abruptly. The last breakup had occurred four months earlier, when the boy's parents had threatened to cut off financial support for their son unless he ended the relationship. Apparently, objections had arisen because of Janet's race.

Although not completely conscious of it, Janet was having increasing difficulty denying her racial heritage. The breakup of her last love affair brought home to her the fact that she was a member of a group that was not fully accepted by all segments of society. At first she vehemently and bitterly denounced the Chinese for her present dilemma. Later, much of her hostility was turned inward against herself. Feeling alienated from her own subculture and not fully accepted by white society, she experienced an identity crisis. This resulted in feelings of worthlessness and depression. It was at this point that Janet had come for therapy. (Sue & Sue, 1971, p. 41)

Racism not only affects housing, employment, income, education, and health care for minority group members, but also affects their self-esteem and self-image. Prejudice and discriminatory behavior may induce negative self-images and even racial self-hatred.

Although some blacks and other ethnic group members show self-hatred, most researchers question how widespread the phenomenon is. First, as pointed out by Banks (1982) and Powell (1983), many studies demonstrating low self-esteem among ethnic minorities contain methodological or conceptual flaws. This may be particularly true of early research studies that were relatively unsophisticated. Second, *some* blacks may exhibit racial self-hatred, and focusing on these individuals may result in overgeneralizations concerning all blacks. Third, being socialized in this country, blacks may adopt some white patterns and standards but not others. Undue emphasis on the former may lead to a misconception that blacks have low self-esteem. (It should also be noted that the adoption of behavioral patterns and standards is a two-way process. For example, many nonblack athletes have adopted handshakes, gestures, mannerisms, and expressions that were initiated by black athletes.) Fourth, times have changed. During the 1960s and 1970s, we witnessed a movement to redefine the minority group's existence by raising consciousness of, and pride in, racial and cultural heritage. Positive aspects of ethnic cultures were emphasized, and many ethnic groups (Blacks, Hispanics, Native Americans, Asian-Americans, and others) joined in the fight against racism. This may have had the effect of changing levels of self-esteem.

Positive aspects of ethnic cultures are emphasized to combat racism and its harmful effects. Raising consciousness and fostering pride in racial and cultural heritages can be used to change prejudicial attitudes and racial stereotypes.

Racism and Mental Health We indicated earlier that oppression, racism, prejudice, and discrimination have deleterious effects. If racism is viewed as a stressor, it would seem reasonable to assume that rates of mental disorders would be greater among oppressed groups. Indeed, the authors of one report on the distribution of mental disorders go so far as to state that "Racist practices undoubtedly are key factors—perhaps the most important ones—in producing mental disorders in blacks and other underprivileged groups" (Kramer et al., 1973, p. 355). But is there any evidence to indicate that blacks, for example, experience higher rates of psychopathology than whites?

Two methods are used to assess the incidence of mental disorders in a population (Dohrenwend & Dohrenwend, 1974). In the first, the rate of disorders in a population is estimated by noting how many people from that population are *treated* for psychological disorders in mental institutions and clinics and by practitioners. (The assumption is that the greater the number of treated cases, the greater the psychological disturbance in that group or population.) In the second method, the rate of disorders is obtained for a *sample* of the population through interviewing, testing, or the like; the rate for the sample is then used to estimate the rate for the whole population.

The results of such assessments have so far been conflicting. Most studies of treated cases support the notion that blacks have higher rates of mental disorders than whites. That is, most studies have found that higher relative proportions of blacks than whites are admitted to mental institutions (Bulhan, 1985). A few investigators have found no difference or have found lower rates among blacks and other ethnic groups (Snowden et al., 1982). These contradictory results may be due to the following conceptual and methodological problems:

1. Treatment rates may not accurately indicate disorder rates, especially in cross-cultural comparisons.

2. Many studies comparing black and white treatment patterns have failed to control for such variables as age, socioeconomic status, or marital status that may confound the effects of race.

3. Because of difficulties in diagnosing people who differ culturally, many blacks may be misdiagnosed by white therapists.

4. Stress may result in increased maladjustment or in adjustment, depending on coping skills, resources, and the ability to learn from negative life experiences (Myers & King, 1983).

The second method of assessing disorder rates—sampling the population—has not been used to any great degree in comparing blacks and whites. This may be due to a lack of adequate data and valid measures of psychopathology for use in comparing ethnic groups. In any case, the question of whether blacks and whites have different rates of psychopathology cannot be fully answered on the basis of the currently available data (Dohrenwend & Dohrenwend, 1974; Jones & Thorne, 1987).

In a survey of psychological distress among 1,000 blacks and whites, blacks were found to be more likely than whites to report psychological symptoms (Neff, 1984). However, after the effects of age and social class were removed, the racial differences were largely negligible. This finding suggests that blacks may not have higher rates of mental disorder. Because blacks are overrepresented among the lower socio-economic classes (which do have higher rates for certain disorders), effects of race and social class may often be confounded. Above and beyond social class, the stress experienced by blacks and other ethnic minority groups may result in problems involving alienation, autonomy, and achievement rather than mental disorders.

Reducing Racism In 1968, the National Advisory Commission on Civil Disorders noted that

> Of the basic causes [of urban riots of the 1960s], the most fundamental is the racial attitude and behavior of white Americans toward black Americans. Race prejudice has shaped our history decisively; it now threatens our future. White racism is essentially responsible for the explosive mixture that has been accumulating in our cities. (p. 10)

The commission recognized that the history of the United States is intertwined with racial prejudice, and that racism is a sickness in our society.

Much has been written about eliminating racism through legislative, judicial, economic, political, and social changes of one kind or another. Various community or national strategies include the following (Katz, 1976):

1. The widespread use of educational programs and the mass media to correct racial stereotypes and to provide accurate information on minority groups
2. Increasing the quality of interpersonal and interracial contacts
3. Changing the way people view violence
4. Rewarding nonaggressive responses
5. Legal remedies

Psychological approaches to the reduction of prejudice have included self-insight, cooperative interactions among various groups, socialization practices that are helpful in rearing unbiased children, and role modeling (see Katz & Taylor, 1988).

The primary goal is to change prejudicial attitudes and eliminate discriminatory behaviors. It is possible to change attitudes and behaviors, but the main problem has been to demonstrate that such changes are long-lasting, meaningful rather than superficial, and comprehensive.

Sexism

Sexism is prejudice and discrimination directed against people of either sex, because of their sex. On the basis of employment, income, and education statistics, women qualify as an oppressed group in our society (Grefe, 1980). (See also Focus 20.4.) In the field of mental health, studies indicate that a significant number of mental health professionals have allowed sex role biases, stereotypes, and a double standard of mental health to influence their practice with female clients (American Psychological Association, 1975). Understanding these biases may be the first step toward eliminating them.

Sex Role Stereotyping The values of this society have traditionally affirmed male supremacy. In an industrial, highly technological society such as ours, great value is placed on a person's role in the labor force. Although there has been a great increase in the number of women in the labor force, especially in the last two decades, this increase has mainly affected the jobs that have customarily been held by women—secretarial, retail sales, and elementary school teaching. Some feel that inborn differences in competencies between men and women justify differential sex roles. Yet substantial evidence shows that sex differences in cognitive abilities are actually quite small (Deaux, 1984) or nonexistent (Caplan et al., 1985). In the Soviet Union, one-third of the engineers and three-fourths of the physicians are women.

Children are usually reared in accordance with sex role stereotypes from birth. A sex role preference can be observed by age three and is well established by age five (Williams, 1977). Boys are socialized to

FOCUS 20.4 *The Status of Women*

1. In 1981, more than half of all adult women in the United States were in the labor force. In 1940, that proportion was only about one-sixth.

2. Even among working couples without children, women spend twice as many hours performing household chores and tasks than do men.

3. The wages of women working at permanent full-time jobs averaged only about 59 percent of the wages paid to men. Women with four or more years of college education received about the same salaries as men with one to three years of high school.

4. In 1982, approximately one in six families was maintained by a woman (41 percent of Black families, 23 percent of Hispanic families, and 13 percent of White families were headed by a woman). The proportion of poor families headed by women was 47 percent in 1981.

SOURCE: Russo & Denmark, 1984.

be aggressive, competitive, and independent; girls are encouraged to be passive and dependent (Russo & Denmark, 1984). Sex-role standards usually stress that women should be nurturing and desirable to men; standards for men emphasize independence and control.

The effectiveness of such socialization practices was illustrated in a national survey in which eight personality characteristics had to be attributed to either males or females. Eighty percent of the respondents said that four of the traits (aggressiveness, independence, objectivity, and mathematical reasoning) were typically male and that the other four traits (nurturance, empathy, monogamy, and emotionality) were typically female (Tavris, 1972). In another study, aging men were seen as becoming more mature, distinguished, and respected. Older women, however, were seen as becoming sexually undesirable, unattractive, powerless, and old (Nutt, 1979).

Men are thought to be more influential than women, and women more easily influenced. In one experiment, subjects were given written scenarios describing two employees (male and female), one of whom was trying to persuade the other on a policy issue. Subjects rated the female as more likely than the male to be influenced by the attempt to persuade. They also inferred that the man in the scenario had a higher-status job than the woman, although no information was provided about job statuses. However, when job titles (a high-status and a low-status title) were assigned to the hypothetical employees,

subjects felt that the low-status person would be more compliant than the high-status person, regardless of sex (Eagly, 1983). This finding emphasizes the importance of status and implies an effect on behavior: The stereotypes that convey a low-status image for women also create expectations about how women should perform. Men and women then may perform in accordance with these expectations. However, such expectations are more likely to affect performance on interactive and interpersonal tasks than on less social and more individualistic tasks (Deaux, 1984).

Like many others, mental health professionals have been found to engage in sex role stereotyping. However, that practice appears to be moderating (Hare-Mustin, 1983). It seems to be due, at least in part, to a lack of knowledge or misinformation that therapists have about women's problems. If this is indeed the case, more accurate information, along with education and training, may eventually eliminate it altogether. Meanwhile, as we are about to see, sex role stereotyping in the mental health professions does have implications for the mental health of women.

Sexism and Mental Health Many studies have shown that most patients in therapy are women (Chesler, 1976; Gove & Tudor, 1973; Kulka, 1982). The role of patient is highly consistent with a female sex role characterized by weakness, dependency, irrationality, and acceptance of care (Williams, 1977).

Relative to the incidence of physical and medical illnesses among women and men, women are more likely to seek medical and psychiatric help (Chesler, 1971; Shapiro et al., 1984). This tendency again may be explained in terms of socialization; a woman's sex role permits her to seek help, whereas males may consider it "unmasculine" to do so. As a group, women are not more prone to mental disorders than men, except for some specific disorders such as depression. They are also less prone to some disorders, including antisocial personality (Myers et al., 1984).

Especially crucial to an understanding of the mental health of women is recognizing the value that society (including mental health professionals) places on the different behaviors that are approved for the sexes. An early study suggests that many clinicians view their patients in a very traditional manner (Broverman & Broverman, 1970). Therapists were asked to complete a questionnaire on sex role stereotypes in which a healthy male, a healthy female, and a healthy adult were rated in terms of 122 antonymous (opposite) pairs of traits. There was high agreement among the clinicians on their ratings, and there were no major differences between male and female clinicians. The results indicated that there is a double standard of mental health for males and females. A healthy male was described and rated in the same terms as a healthy adult. The healthy female was described differently from both, with such terms as *submissive, emotional, easily influenced, sensitive to hurt, excitable, conceited about appearance, dependent, less competitive, unaggressive,* and *unobjective.* This study has powerful implications. When the traits that are said to characterize a healthy woman are considered socially undesirable for a healthy adult, it is not the least bit surprising that women are more likely to seek therapy!

The study by the Brovermans served to alert the mental health profession to the possible sex role bias that therapists may have toward women. However, it is unclear whether the findings from this early study represent the situation today. Furthermore, since the study by the Brovermans focused on therapists, little is known about the perceptions of clients. A recent study by Sesan (1988) examined the attitudes and perceptions of women clients toward their therapists who were male or female. Women who had completed treatment were asked to respond to a survey that was intended to assess sex bias among their therapists. Several interesting results emerged. First, the majority of women clients experienced a sex-fair therapy process. Second, the clients did not perceive differences on the basis of therapist gender. That is, clients with a male therapist reported no more bias than

Women are increasingly assuming roles and positions that were previously limited to men. Thirty years ago, an all-women fire department would have been inconceivable. Today, more and more women are holding key jobs in both the private and public sectors of our society.

those with a female therapist. Third, bias varied somewhat according to educational level and the presence of children, in that women with the least amount of formal education and those with children reported more bias than women with higher levels of education and with no children. If therapist bias did occur, it tended to be when the therapist projected a traditional sex role onto clients and did not accept anger in women clients. The findings suggest that bias exists; however, it is not as pervasive as in 1970, when the Brovermans' study was conducted. Further studies are necessary in order to provide more definitive answers.

The DSM diagnostic system has been criticized as being biased in that females may be diagnosed as being disturbed for acting "out of line"—that is, for not acting "like women" (Kaplan, 1983). Yet DSM also has been defended by others as being unbiased (Williams & Spitzer, 1983). At this point there is no evidence that DSM should be considered a sex-biased system. However, this does not mean that every category within the diagnostic system is unbiased and accurate. As mentioned in Chapter 9, many critics have objected to self-defeating personality disorder proposed in DSM-III-R as a sexist category. The value of criticism is to encourage continuing research into the validity of all the DSM categories and criteria as they apply to both men and women.

Reducing Sexism   As is true for racism, eliminating sexism requires ambitious psychological, educational, and legal efforts—in this case aimed at correcting sex biases, sexual stereotypes, and inequities. To change the image of women conveyed through the mass media alone is a massive undertaking, fortunately already underway. Making the educational system more responsive to the concerns and needs of women is another primary goal. For victims of sexual harassment, legal redress is possible; many employers have now developed guidelines for determining and eliminating harassment (Livingston, 1982). In the mental health field, counselors and therapists have available a publication of the American Psychological Association outlining "Principles Concerning the Counseling and Therapy of Women" (Ad Hoc Committee on Women, 1979). It includes specific recommendations to help therapists confront their own sexism in a way that will enhance their ability to help women clients.

SUMMARY

1. Community psychology is concerned with the influence of community and environmental forces on human behavior and with using these resources to alleviate human problems. The community psychology approach grew out of dissatisfaction with the inability of the treatment approach to care for the large number of disturbed people, with the biogenic or disease model of psychopathology, with the ineffectiveness of psychiatric hospitals, and with inequities in the delivery of mental health services.

2. As a result of this dissatisfaction, community mental health centers were initiated in the 1960s. These centers are located in many communities and are accessible to the surrounding population. They offer a wide range of services including outpatient and short-term inpatient care, consultation, emergency services, and partial hospitalization. Despite the lack of adequate financial support and community involvement in some centers, they are a major mental health resource.

3. One goal of community psychology is to prevent mental disorders. This prevention takes three forms. Primary prevention (reducing the incidence of new cases) seeks to introduce new resources and reduce stressors. Secondary prevention seeks to reduce the duration or severity of a disorder through early detection and prompt treatment. Tertiary prevention seeks to reduce the disabling effects of a disorder by facilitating the adjustment and early return to the community of those who have had mental disorders.

4. To alleviate the shortage of professional mental health personnel, psychologists have begun to train paraprofessionals or laypeople to act as therapeutic agents. Psychologists can thus take advantage of the knowledge and experience of community members and can combat the reluctance of some people to enter therapy with unfamiliar mental health professionals.

5. Some believe that the prevention and treatment of mental disorders in the community requires control or modification of environmental forces and resources. This approach, however, raises the controversial question of whether mental health professionals should become active in the social or political arena in order to effect major changes in mental health. Most psychologists feel that social and political implications of their work cannot be avoided.

6. Social supports, too, have been explored as a tool for fostering adjustment and for preventing disorders. They may act as a buffer against stress.

7. Racism and sexism are community problems that affect mental health. Racism is manifested in a lower standard of living for racial minorities (Asian-Americans, Blacks, Hispanics, and Native Americans). It can cause some people to believe that they are inferior and to feel racial self-hatred. The development of feelings of racial pride and identity is necessary to reverse this negative attitude. Women, like members of racial minorities, represent an oppressed group in our society. Historically, women have been subordinated and controlled through sex role stereotyping. Studies show that some therapists allow sex role biases, stereotypes, and a double standard of mental health to influence their practice with women clients. Eliminating racism and sexism will not be easy. Proposed strategies include using educational programs to correct stereotyping, increasing the quality of interracial contacts, changing perceptual processes, using the mass media for change, using rewards, and instituting legal remedies.

KEY TERMS

community mental health centers Centrally located mental health facilities (for medium-sized communities) that provide a number of services such as short-term inpatient care, outpatient care, partial hospitalization, emergency services, and community consultation and education

community psychology An approach to mental health that takes into account the influence of environmental factors and stresses the use of community resources to eliminate various conditions that produce psychological problems

human ecology The study of the interaction between human beings and their environments

paraprofessional therapists People who are taught by professionals to provide some mental health services but who do not have formal mental health training

primary prevention An effort to lower the incidence of new cases of behavioral disorders by strengthening or adding to resources that promote mental health and by eliminating features of a community that threaten mental health

secondary prevention An attempt to shorten the duration of mental disorders and to reduce their impact

sexism Prejudice and discrimination directed against people of either sex, because of their sex

social supports The availability and quality of interpersonal resources that people can call on during emotional distress

tertiary prevention Efforts to facilitate the readjustment of the person to community life after hospital treatment for a mental disorder

therapeutic community A hospital environment in which all activities are structured to have a therapeutic function and in which patients participate to the extent possible

chapter 21
Legal and Ethical Issues in Abnormal Psychology

For five months between 1977 and 1978 Los Angeles was terrorized by a series of murders of young women whose bodies were left on hillsides. All the women had been raped and strangled; some had been brutally tortured. The public and press dubbed the culprit the Hillside Strangler, and a massive hunt for the killer or killers ensued. A major break occurred one year after the Los Angeles murders when 27-year-old Kenneth Bianchi was arrested for two unrelated murders of college students in Bellingham, Washington. His fingerprints matched those found at the scene of the Hillside murders.

Bianchi was an unlikely murder suspect because many who knew him described him as dependable and conscientious—"the boy next door." Furthermore, despite the strong evidence against Bianchi, he insisted he was innocent. Police noticed he was unable to remember much of his past life. During interviews in which hypnosis was used, a startling development occurred: Bianchi exhibited another personality (Steve). Steve freely admitted to killing the women, called Ken a "turkey," and laughed at Ken's ignorance of his existence.

She was a well-known "bag lady" in the downtown Oakland area who by night slept on any number of park benches and store fronts. By day she could be seen pushing her Safeway shopping cart full of boxes, extra clothing, and garbage, which she collected from numerous trash containers. According to her only surviving sister, the Bag Lady had lived this way for nearly ten years and had been tolerated by local merchants. Over the past six months, however, Bag Lady's behavior had become progressively intolerable. She had always talked to herself, but recently began shouting and screaming at anyone who approached her. Her use of profanity was graphic, and she often urinated and defecated in front of the stores. Bag Lady was occasionally arrested and detained for a short period of time by local law enforcement officials, but she always returned to her familiar haunts. Finally, her sister and several merchants requested that the city take action to commit her to a mental institution.

In 1968, Prosenjit Poddar, a graduate student from India studying at the University of California at Berkeley, sought therapy from the student health services for depression. Apparently, Poddar was upset over what he perceived to be a rebuff from a female student, Tatiana Tarasoff, whom he claimed to love. During the course of treatment, Poddar informed his therapist that he intended to purchase a gun and kill the woman. Judging Poddar to be dangerous, the psychologist breached the confidentiality of the professional relationship by informing the campus police. The police detained Poddar briefly, but freed him because he agreed to stay away from Tarasoff. On October 27, Poddar went to Tarasoff's home, wounded her with a gun, and repeatedly stabbed her to death with a knife. This much-celebrated case elicited the court response that came to be known as the *Tarasoff* decision, regarding the therapist's duty to warn the victim directly and not just the authorities (police).

A male therapist said, "I remember the incident quite clearly. I was seeing a female student for a therapy session at the University Counseling Center. Jennifer, the student, was in extreme distress as she mourned the loss of her younger sister. She was not only grieving about her sister's death, but also attempting to cope with her own feelings of guilt. Jennifer had been the driver when she was broadsided by another car on the passenger side. Both her sister and driver of the other car were killed instantaneously. Jennifer had lost consciousness and had no recollection of the incident. Fault could not be determined definitively, but it was obvious that Jennifer blamed herself (even though police reports suggested the other driver had probably entered the intersection illegally).

"During this particular session, Jennifer's pain seemed especially intense. I could feel the depths of her grief and sorrow. Without thinking about it, I pulled my chair next to her, placed my arms around her, and pulled her to my chest, where she wept uncontrollably."

In Chapter 1, we defined abnormal psychology as the scientific and objective approach to describing, explaining, predicting, and treating behaviors that are considered strange and unusual. All four of the preceding examples of behavior fit this definition well, and we can clearly see their clinical implications. What is less clear to many is that clinical or mental health issues can often become legal and ethical ones as well. This is most evident in the Kenneth Bianchi (Hillside Strangler) case. If his attorneys could prove he was insane, Bianchi could be judged not guilty by reason of insanity. Yet how do we determine whether a person is insane or sane? What criteria do we use? If we call on experts as in the Bianchi case, we find professionals often disagreeing with one another. Might defendants in criminal trials attempt to fake mental disturbances in order to escape guilty verdicts? When defendants are mentally ill and found to be insane, what should the state do with them? These questions lead us into the area of criminal commitment. Furthermore, finding a person insane is a legal ruling that forces mental health practitioners to go beyond clinical concepts defined in DSM-III-R.

The example of the homeless woman raises issues of civil commitment. When should a person who has committed no crime, but appears severely disturbed, be institutionalized? Certainly, defecating and urinating in public is disgusting to most people and truly unusual behavior, but is it enough to deprive someone of her civil liberties? What are the procedures for civil commitment? What happens to people once they are committed?

In the first two examples, the focus of legal and ethical issues tends to be on the individual or defendant. Mental health issues become legal ones (1) when decisions must be made about involuntary commitment to mental hospitals, (2) when competence to stand trial is in doubt, (3) when an accused person bases his or her criminal defense on insanity or diminished mental capacity, and (4) when the rights of mental patients are legally tested.

In the *Tarasoff* case, the focus of legal and ethical concern shifts to the therapist. When is the therapist legally and ethically obligated to breach patient-therapist confidentiality? In this case, had the therapist done enough to prevent a potentially dangerous situation from occurring? According to all previous codes of conduct issued by professional organizations such as the American Psychological Association and according to accepted practice in the field, many would answer yes. Yet in 1976 the California Supreme Court ruled that the therapist should have warned not only the police but also the likely victim.

The ruling has major implications for therapists in the conduct of therapy. One implication is also related to the two earlier cases. How does a therapist predict dangerousness (to self, to others, or to society)? To protect him- or herself from being sued, does the therapist report all threats of homicide or suicide? Should a psychologist warn clients that not everything they say is privileged or confidential? How will this affect the clinical relationship?

Last, but not least, we come to ethical issues related to treatment itself. The male therapist who put his arms around his client, Jennifer, apparently did so as an act of human compassion. Yet although he may have been comforting the client, the act involves some serious controversial questions with respect to the therapeutic value of touching. The incident may appear insignificant, but it has much broader implications. Some people believe that touching is professionally unethical because of its possible erotic implications, especially with opposite-sex clients. Others argue that nonerotic touch is therapeutic for many clients. How does a therapist determine if a touch is erotic or nonerotic? What about hugging or kissing? The point is that therapeutic techniques and strategies have moral and ethical implications. For example, should psychoactive drugs be given to patients against their will? Should painful techniques, such as ECT, be used to treat clients?

We address some of these questions and issues in greater depth in this chapter. First we look at the issues of criminal and civil commitment, and then discuss patient rights and deinstitutionalization. Last, we explore the legal and ethical parameters of the therapist-client relationship.

For five months between 1977 and 1978, Kenneth Bianchi and his cousin Angelo Buono raped, tortured, and murdered a number of young Los Angeles women. To try to escape what would inevitably be a life imprisonment sentence, Bianchi tried to convince pyschiatrists that he was a multiple personality; he thought this would enhance his chances of being found not guilty by reason of insanity. Fortunately, he was unable to pull off his scheme and will now spend the rest of his life in jail.

CRIMINAL COMMITMENT

Basic to the premise of criminal law is the assumption that all of us are responsible beings who exercise free will and are capable of choices (Stone, 1974). If we do something wrong, we are responsible for our actions and should suffer the consequences. **Criminal commitment** is the incarceration of an individual for having committed a crime. Abnormal psychology accepts differing perspectives on free will; criminal law does not. Yet criminal law does recognize that some people lack the ability to discern the ramifications of their actions because they are mentally disturbed. Although they may be technically guilty of a crime, their mental state at the time of the offense exempts them from legal responsibility. Let us explore the landmark cases that have influenced this concept's evolution and application.

The Insanity Defense

The concept of innocence by reason of insanity has provoked much controversy among legal scholars, mental health practitioners, and the general public (Shapiro, 1984). This **insanity defense** is a plea used by defendants who admit they committed a crime but believe they should not be held responsible for the action because they were mentally disturbed at the time it was committed. The insanity plea recognizes that under specific circumstances people may not be held accountable for their behavior. One of the public's greatest fears is that such a plea might be used by a guilty individual to escape criminal responsibility. This fear is further reinforced by findings that people acquitted of crimes because of insanity spend less time in psychiatric hospitals than do convicted people who are sent to prison (Kahn & Raufman, 1981; Pasework et al., 1982). Some point to the Kenneth Bianchi case as a prime example of this tendency. The question confronting the state prosecutors, defense attorney, and mental health experts was whether the defendant was a shrewd, calculating, cold-blooded murderer, or a true multiple personality. It is important to note, however, that any number of psychiatric conditions may be used in an insanity plea.

Psychologist Martin Orne, an internationally recognized expert on hypnosis, was asked by the prosecution to examine Bianchi. Orne knew that Bianchi was either a multiple personality or a clever liar. He reasoned that if Bianchi was pretending, he would be highly motivated to convince others that he was a multiple personality. Orne thought if he told Bianchi that multiple personalities rarely show just two distinct personalities, Bianchi might show still another personality to convince Orne his was a true case. After hinting to Bianchi in the waking state that two personalities are rare, Orne placed Bianchi under hypnosis. Bianchi took the bait. Another personality—Billy—emerged. (Other experts were unable to draw out more than two personalities.)

Orne also noticed that Bianchi's behaviors were unusual for someone under hypnosis. For example, during one session Orne wanted Bianchi to hallucinate the presence of his attorney, so he suggested to Bianchi that his attorney was sitting in the room. Bianchi immediately got up and shook hands with his (hallucinated) attorney. Orne then asked whether his attorney was shaven. Bianchi responded, "Oh, no. Beard. God, you can see him. You must be able to see him" (*Frontline*, "The Mind of a Murderer," Part II, 1984, p. 11). These behaviors are unusual for the following reasons: first, multiple personalities almost never shake hands spontaneously because that requires a tactile hallucination. Bianchi would have to imagine not only seeing his attorney but also feeling the touch of his hand. Second, the statement, "You can see him. You must be able to see him" seemed to be excessive and to be aimed at convincing Orne that Bianchi really saw his attorney. Orne believed Bianchi was faking. His work, coupled with other evidence, forced a change in Bianchi's plea from "not guilty by reason of insanity" to "guilty." Unfortunately, it is the rare but highly publicized cases such as the Hillside Strangler and Hinckley cases that seem to have greatest impact and provoke public outrage and suspicion (Quen, 1978, 1981; Robitscher, 1966; Rogers, 1987).

Legal Precedents In this country, a number of different standards are used as legal tests of insanity. One of the earliest is the *M'Naghten Rule*. In 1843, Daniel M'Naghten, a grossly disturbed woodcutter from Glasgow, Scotland, claimed he was commanded by God to kill the English prime minister, Sir Robert Peel. He killed a lesser minister by mistake and was placed on trial, where it became obvious that M'Naghten was quite delusional. Out of this incident emerged the M'Naghten Rule, which has popularly been referred to as the "right-wrong" test. The ruling held that people could be acquitted of a crime if it could be shown that, at the time of the act they (1) had such defective reasoning that they did not know what they were doing or (2) were unable to comprehend that the act was wrong. The first part of the standard refers to a person being unaware of the *nature* (for example, strangling a person, but believing he or she was squeezing a lemon) or *quality* (a disturbed person's belief that it would be amusing to cut off the head of the person in order to watch him or her search for it in the morning) of the act due to mental impairment (Shapiro, 1984). The M'Naghten Rule has come under tremendous criticisms from some who regard it as being exclusively a cognitive test (knowledge of right or wrong), which does not consider volition, emotion, and other mental activity (Rogers, 1987; Shapiro, 1984). Furthermore, it is not often easy to evaluate the defendant's awareness or comprehension.

The second major precedent that strengthened the insanity defense was the **irresistible impulse test.** In essence, the doctrine says that a defendant is not criminally responsible if he or she lacked the will power to control his or her behavior. Combined with the M'Naghten Rule, this rule broadened the criteria for using the insanity defense. In other words, a verdict of not guilty by reason of insanity could be obtained if it was shown that the defendant was unaware of or did not comprehend the act (M'Naghten Rule), or was irresistibly impelled to commit the act. Criticisms of the irresistible impulse defense revolve around what constitutes an irresistible impulse. Shapiro (1984) asks the question, "What is the difference between an *irresistible* impulse (*unable* to exert control) and an *unresisted* impulse (*choosing* not to exert control)? For example, is a person with a history of antisocial behavior unable to resist his or her impulses, or is he or she choosing not to exert control? Neither the mental health profession nor the legal profession has answered this question in a satisfactory way.

In the case of *Durham v. United States* (1954), the U.S. Court of Appeals broadened the M'Naghten Rule with the so-called *products test.* An accused person was not considered criminally responsible if his or her unlawful act was the *product* of mental disease or defect. It was Judge David Bazelon's intent to (1) give the greatest possible weight to expert evaluation and testimony and (2) allow mental health professionals to define mental illness. The *Durham* standard, unfortunately, also has its drawbacks. The term "product" is vague and difficult to define because almost anything can cause anything (as you have learned by studying the many theoretical viewpoints in this text). Leaving the task of defining mental illness to mental health professionals often results in having to define mental illness in every case. In many situations, relying on psychiatric testimony only serves to confuse the issues because both the prosecution and defense present psychiatric experts, who often present conflicting testimony.

In 1962, the American Law Institute (ALI), in its Model Penal Code, produced guidelines to help jurors determine the validity of the insanity defense on a case-by-case basis. The guidelines combined features from the previous standards.

1. A person is not responsible for criminal conduct if at the time of such conduct as a result of mental disease or defect he lacks substantial capacity either to appreciate the criminality of his conduct or to conform his conduct to the requirements of the law.
2. As used in the Article, the terms "mental disease or defect" do not include an abnormality manifested by repeated criminal or otherwise antisocial conduct. (Sec. 401, p. 66)

It is interesting to note that the second part of this guideline was intended to eliminate the insanity defense for people diagnosed as having antisocial personalities.

With the attempt to be more specific and precise, the ALI guidelines moved the burden of determining criminal responsibility back to the jurors. As we have seen, previous standards, particularly the *Durham* standard, gave great weight to expert testimony, and many feared it would usurp the jury's responsibilities (Simon, 1967; Walker, 1968; Weiner, 1985). By using phrases such as "substantial capacity," "appreciate the criminality of his conduct," and "conform his conduct to the requirements of the law," the ALI standard was intended to allow the jurors the greatest possible flexibility in ascribing criminal responsibility.

The insanity defense has evolved over the last hundred years in recognition of the fact that some people are so mentally disturbed at the time they commit their crimes that under specific circumstances they should not be held responsible for their behavior.

In some jurisdictions, the concept of *diminished capacity* has also been incorporated into the ALI standard. As a result of a mental disease or defect, a person may lack the *specific intent* to commit the offense. For example, a person under the influence of drugs or alcohol may commit a crime without premeditation or intent; a person who is grief-stricken over the death of a loved one may harm the one responsible for the death. Although diminished capacity has been used primarily to guide the sentencing and disposition of the defendant, Shapiro (1984) notes that it is being used more frequently in the trial phase as well.

Guilty, but Mentally Ill   Perhaps no other trial has more greatly challenged the use of the insanity plea than the case of the *United States v. Hinckley* (1982). John W. Hinckley, Jr.'s, attempt to assassinate President Ronald Reagan, and Hinckley's subsequent acquittal by reason of insanity outraged the public as well as legal and mental health professionals (Dix, 1984; Weiner, 1985). The increasingly successful use of the insanity defense had been a growing concern in both legal circles and the public arena. Many had begun to believe that the criteria for the defense were being too broadly interpreted, even though it has been shown that the insanity defense is used in less than 2 percent of cases and that its use is rarely successful (Fersch, 1980; Morse, 1982; Morris, 1968; Steadman, 1979). For some time, the Hinckley case aroused such strong emotional reactions that calls for reform were rampant. The American Psychiatric Association (1983), the American Medical Association (Kerlitz & Fulton, 1984), and the American Bar Association (1984) all advocated a more stringent interpretation of insanity. As a result, Congress passed the Insanity Reform Act of 1984, which based the definition of insanity totally on the individual's ability to understand what he or she did. The American Psychological Association's position on the insanity defense ran counter to these immediate changes (Rogers, 1987). Its position is that even though a given verdict might be wrong, the standard is not necessarily wrong.

Nevertheless, in the wake of the *Hinckley* verdict, some states have begun to adopt alternative pleas such as "culpable and mentally disabled," "mentally disabled, but neither culpable nor innocent," and "guilty, but mentally ill." These pleas are attempts to (1) separate mental illness from insanity and (2) hold people responsible for their acts.

Competency to Stand Trial

The term **competent to stand trial** refers to the defendant's mental state *at the time he or she is being examined* by a practitioner. It has nothing to do with the issue of *criminal responsibility,* which refers to an individual's behavior *at the time of the offense* (insanity defense). Three criteria are usually used to judge whether a person is competent to stand trial. First, does the defendant have a factual understanding of the proceedings? Second, does a client have a rational understanding of the proceedings? Third, can the defendant rationally consult with counsel in presenting his or her own defense (Shapiro, 1984)?

The final criteria for competency involves the ability to consult with counsel. If the defendant is suffering from a paranoid delusion and believes his or her attorney is conspiring with the prosecution, a serious impairment exists.

It is clear that many more people are committed to prison hospitals because of incompetency determinations than are acquitted on insanity pleas (Steadman, 1979). Competency to stand trial is important in ensuring that a person understands the nature of the proceedings and is able to help in his or her own defense. After all, it would be unfair to try a person incapable of self-defense. Although determination of competency is meant to protect mentally disturbed people and to guarantee preservation of criminal and civil rights, being judged incompetent to stand trial may have unfair negative consequences as well. A person may be committed for a long period of time, denied the chance to post bail and isolated from friends and family, without having been guilty of a crime.

Such a miscarriage of justice was the focus of a U.S. Supreme Court ruling in 1972 (*Jackson v. Indiana*). In the Jackson case, a severely retarded, brain-damaged deaf-mute was charged with robbery, but was determined incompetent to stand trial. He was committed indefinitely, which in his case probably meant for life, because it was apparent by the severity of his disorders that he would never be competent. His lawyers filed a petition to have him released on the basis of deprivation of **due process** (legal checks and balances guaranteed to everyone: right to a fair trial, right to face accusers, right to present evidence, right to counsel, and so on). The U.S. Supreme Court ruled that a defendant cannot be confined indefinitely solely on the grounds of incompetency. After a reasonable time, a determination must be made as to whether the person is likely or unlikely to regain competency in the near future. If, in the hospital's opinion, the person is unlikely to do so, the hospital must either release the individual or initiate civil commitment procedures.

CIVIL COMMITMENT

In cases where people are severely disturbed and exhibit bizarre behaviors that can pose a threat to themselves or others, **civil commitment** may be necessary, even though the person has not committed a crime. The commitment of a person in acute distress may be viewed as a form of protective confinement (Ponterotto, 1987) and a concern for the psychological and physical well-being of that person or others (Everstine & Everstine, 1983). Hospitalization is considered in the case of potential suicide or assault, bizarre behavior, destruction of property, and severe anxiety leading to loss of impulse control (Hipple & Hipple, 1983). Involuntary hospitalization, however, should be avoided, if at all possible, because it has many potentially negative consequences. Ponterotto (1987) summarizes these consequences as the lifelong social stigma associated with psychiatric hospitalization, major interruption in the person's life, losing control of his or her life and being dependent on others, and loss of self-esteem and self-concept. To this we would add a possible loss or restriction of civil liberties—a point that becomes even more glaring when we consider that the person has actually committed no crime at all!

Criteria for Commitment

States vary in the criteria used to commit a person, but there do appear to be certain general standards. It is not enough that a person be mentally ill: additional conditions need to exist before hospitalization is considered (Everstine & Everstine, 1983;

In the movie "Nuts" Barbra Streisand plays a woman whose family tries to have her involuntarily committed to a mental hospital after she kills a man in self-defense. She is pictured here at a formal hearing where a judge will decide whether she meets the specific criteria for commitment—being dangerous to herself or to others.

Hipple & Hipple, 1983; Schwitzgebel & Schwitzgebel, 1980; Warren, 1982).

1. *The person presents a clear and imminent danger to self or others.* For example, someone who is displaying suicidal or bizarre behavior that places that person in immediate danger (walking out on a busy freeway or standing on a building ledge). Threats to harm someone or behavior viewed to be assaultive or destructive are also grounds for commitment.

2. *The person is unable to care for him- or herself or does not have the social network to provide for such care.* These criteria vary. This generally involves insufficient (1) food (being malnourished, food is unavailable, and the individual has no feasible plan to obtain it); (2) clothing (not appropriate for climate, dirty or torn, has no plans for obtaining it); and (3) shelter (no permanent residence, insufficient protection from climactic conditions, and no logical plans for obtaining adequate housing).

3. *The person is unable to make responsible decisions about appropriate treatment and hospitalization.* As a result, there is a strong chance for deterioration.

4. *The person is in an unmanageable state of fright or panic.* Such people may believe and feel that they are on the brink of losing control.

Certainly the example of the homeless lady in the beginning of the chapter would seem to fulfill the second and possibly third criteria. In the past, commitments could be obtained solely on the basis of mental illness and a person's need for treatment, which was often determined in an arbitrary manner. Increasingly, the courts have tightened up civil commitment procedures and have begun to rely more on a determination of **dangerousness** to self or others. How do we define dangerousness? Many people would not consider the homeless woman a danger to herself or others. Some, however, might believe that she could be assaultive to others and injurious to herself. Disagreements among the public may be understandable, but are trained mental health professionals more accurate in their predictions? Let's turn to that question.

Assessing Dangerousness   Most studies indicate that mental health professionals have difficulty predicting whether their clients will commit dangerous acts (Stone, 1975; Monahan, 1976) and that they often overpredict violence (Megargee, 1970; Monahan, 1981). The fact that civil commitments are often based on a determination of dangerousness makes this conclusion even more disturbing. The difficulty in predicting dangerousness seems linked to four factors.

1. It is quite apparent that the rarer something is, the more difficult it is to predict. As a group, psychiatric patients are not dangerous! A frequent misconception shared not only by the public, but the courts as well, is that mental illnesses are in and of themselves dangerous. Studies indicate that few psychotic patients are assaultive: estimates range from 10 percent of hospitalized patients to about 3 percent in outpatient clinics (Tardiff, 1984; Tardiff & Sweillam, 1982; Tardiff & Koenigsburg, 1985). Homicide is even rarer, and psychiatric patients are no more likely to commit a homicide than the population at large (Monaham, 1981).

2. It appears that violence is as much a function of the context in which it occurs as it is of the person's characteristics. Although it is theoretically possible for a psychologist to accurately assess an individual's personality, one has little idea about the situations in which people will find themselves. Shapiro (1984) advocates that the mental health professional needs to help the court define the term "dangerous," so testimony can be restricted to a description of the *patient's personality* and *kinds of situations* in which personality may deteriorate and/or lead to assaultive behavior.

3. Probably the best predictor of dangerousness is past criminal conduct or a history of violence or aggression. Such a record, however, is frequently ruled irrelevant or inadmissible by mental health commissions and the courts.

4. The definition of dangerousness is itself unclear. Most of us would agree that murder, rape, torture, and physical assaults are dangerous. Are we confining our definition to physical harm only? What about psychological abuse or even harm to property?

Procedures in Civil Commitment

Despite the difficulties in defining "dangerousness," once someone believes a person is a threat to him- or herself or to others, civil commitment procedures may be instituted. The rationale for this action is that it (1) prevents harm to the person or to others, (2) provides appropriate treatment and care, and (3) ensures due process of law (that is, legal hearing). In most cases, people deemed in need of protective confinement can be convinced to *voluntarily* commit themselves to a period of hospitalization. This process is fairly straightforward, and many believe that it is the preferred one (Ponterotto, 1987). *Involuntary* commitment occurs when the client does not consent to hospitalization. In some instances, though, clients who do not want to be hospitalized, but who realize involuntary commitment is inevitable, will agree to be voluntarily committed and then leave the hospital against hospital advice.

Involuntary commitment can be a temporary emergency action or a longer period of detention that is determined at a formal hearing. All states recognize that cases arise in which a person is so grossly disturbed that immediate detention is required. Because formal hearings may take a long time, delaying commitment might prove adverse to the person or to others.

Formal and civil commitment usually follows a similar process. First, a concerned person such as a family member, therapist, or family physician petitions the court for an examination of the person. If the judge believes there is responsible cause for this action, he or she will order an examination. Second, the judge appoints two professionals with no connection to each other to examine the person. In most cases, the examiners are physicians or mental health professionals. Third, a formal hearing is held in which the examiners testify to the person's mental state and potential danger. Others, such as family members, friends, or therapists, may also testify. The person is also allowed to speak on his or her behalf and is represented by counsel. Last, if it is determined that the person must enter treatment, a finite period (usually six months to one year are common) may be specified. Some states have indefinite periods subject to periodic review and assessment.

Protection Against Involuntary Commitment We have said that involuntary commitment can lead to a violation of civil rights. Some have even argued that criminals have more rights than the mentally ill. For example, a person accused of a crime is considered innocent until proven guilty in a court of law. Usually, he or she is incarcerated only after a jury trial, and only if a crime is committed (not if there is only the possibility or even high probability of crime). Yet, a mentally ill person may be confined without a jury trial and without having committed a crime if it is thought possible that he or she *might* do harm to self or others. In other words, the criminal justice system will not incarcerate a person because he or she might harm someone (they must have done it), yet civil commitment is based on possible future harm. It can be argued that in the former case, confinement is punishment, while in the latter case it is treatment (for the individual's benefit). Stone (1975), for example, argues that mentally ill people may be incapable of determining their own treatment, and that, once treated, will be grateful for the treatment they received! If people resist hospitalization, they are thus being irrational, which is a symptom of their mental disorder.

Critics do not accept this reasoning. They point out that civil commitment is for the benefit of those initiating commitment procedures (society), and not for the individual. Even after treatment, people rarely appreciate it (Ennis & Emery, 1978). These concerns have raised and heightened sensitivity toward patient welfare and rights, resulting in a trend toward restricting the powers of the state over the individual.

Rights of Mental Patients Many people in the United States are concerned about the balance of power among the state, our mental institutions, and our citizens. The U.S. Constitution guarantees certain "inalienable rights" such as trial by jury and legal representation. As indicated in Chapter 1, the mental health profession has great power, which may be used wittingly or unwittingly to abridge individual freedom. In recent decisions, some courts have ruled that commitment for any purpose constitutes a significant deprivation of liberty that requires due process protection.

Until 1979, the level of proof required for civil commitments varied from state to state. In a case that set legal precedent, a Texas man claimed that he was denied due process because the jury that

The Constitution guarantees legal representation and due process to everyone, including mental patients who have often been deprived of their rights. In recent years court decisions have more clearly defined the criteria under which individuals can be committed and how they must be treated once confined to a mental facility.

committed him was instructed to use a lower standard than "beyond a reasonable doubt" (more than 90 percent sure). The appellate court agreed with the man, but when the case finally reached the Supreme Court in April 1979 (*Addington v. Texas*), the court ruled that the state must only provide "clear and convincing evidence" (approximately 75 percent sure) that a person is mentally ill and potentially dangerous before that person can be committed. Although it is important to note that confinement requires a higher standard than advocated by most mental health organizations, this ruling represents the first time the Supreme Court has considered any aspect of the civil commitment process (Shapiro, 1984).

Due to decisions in several other cases (*Lessard v. Schmidt,* 1972, Wisconsin Federal Court; and *Dixon v. Weinberger,* 1975), states must provide the **least restrictive environment** for people. This means that people have a right to the least restrictive alternative to freedom that is appropriate to their condition. Only patients who cannot adequately care for themselves are confined to hospitals. Those who can function acceptably should be given alternative choices, such as boarding homes and other shelter.

Right to Treatment One of the primary justifications for commitment is that treatment will improve a person's mental condition and increase the likelihood that he or she will be able to return to the community. If we confine a person involuntarily and do not provide the means for release (therapy), isn't this deprivation of due process? Several cases have raised this problem as a constitutional issue. In 1966, a suit brought against St. Elizabeth's Hospital in Washington, D.C. (*Rouse v. Cameron*), the court held that (1) **right to treatment** is a constitutional right and (2) failure to provide treatment cannot be justified by lack of resources. In other words, a mental institution or the state could not use lack of funding facilities or labor power as reasons for not providing treatment. Although this decision represented a major advance in patient rights, the ruling provided no guidelines for what constitutes treatment.

This issue was finally addressed in 1972 by U.S. District Court Judge Frank Johnson in the Alabama Federal Court. The case (*Wyatt v. Stickney*) involved a mentally retarded boy who not only did not receive treatment, but had to live in an institution that was unable to meet even minimum standards of care.

Indeed, the living conditions in two of the hospital buildings resembled those found in early asylums of the eighteenth century. Less than 50 cents a day was spent on food for each patient; the toilet facilities were totally inadequate and filthy; patients were crowded in group rooms with minimal or no privacy; and personnel (one physician per 2,000 patients) and patient care were practically nonexistent.

Judge Johnson not only ruled in favor of the right to treatment, but also specified standards of adequate treatment such as staff-patient ratios, therapeutic environment conditions, and professional consensus about appropriate treatment. The court also made it clear that mental patients could not be forced to work (scrub floors, cook, serve food, wash laundry, and so on) or engage in work-related activities aimed at maintaining the institution in which they lived. This practice, widely used in institutions, was declared unconstitutional. Moreover, patients who volunteered to perform these tasks had to be paid at least the minimum wage to do them instead of merely given token allowances or special privileges. This landmark decision ensures treatment beyond custodial care and protection against neglect and abuse (right to humane environment and right to treatment).

Another important case (tried in the U.S. District Court in Florida), *O'Connor v. Donaldson* (1975), has also had major impact on the right-to-treatment issue. It involved Kenneth Donaldson, who at age 49 was committed for twenty years to the Chattahoochee State Hospital on petition by his father. He was found to be mentally ill and dangerous. Throughout his confinement, Donaldson petitioned for release, but Dr. O'Connor, the hospital superintendent, determined that the patient was too dangerous. Finally, Donaldson threatened a lawsuit and was reluctantly discharged by the hospital after 14 years of confinement. He then sued both O'Connor and the hospital, winning an award of $20,000. The monetary award is insignificant compared to the significance of the ruling. Again, the court reaffirmed the client's right to treatment (the court ruled that Donaldson did not receive appropriate treatment), stated that the state cannot constitutionally confine a nondangerous person who is capable of caring for him- or herself outside of an institution or who has willing friends or family to help, and that physicians as well as institutions are liable for improper confinements.

One major dilemma facing the courts in all cases of court-ordered treatment is what constitutes treatment. As discussed in earlier chapters, treatment can range from rest and relaxation to psychosurgery, medication, and aversion therapy. Mental health professionals believe that they are in the best position to evaluate the type and efficacy of treatment, a position supported by the case of *Youngberg v. Romeo* (1982). The court ruled that a mentally-retarded boy, Nicholas Romeo, had a constitutional right to "reasonable care and safety," and it deferred judgment to the mental health professional as to what constitutes therapy. Whether this marks a subtle shift away from patient rights is still to be seen.

Right to Refuse Treatment Patients frequently refuse medical treatment on religious grounds or because the treatment would only prolong a terminal illness. In many cases, physicians are inclined to honor such refusals, especially if they seem based on reasonable grounds. But should mental patients have a right to refuse treatment? At first glance, it may appear that the question does not make sense. After all, patients are committed for treatment, are they not? Why commit them for treatment and allow them to refuse it? Furthermore, isn't it possible that mental patients may be incapable of deciding what is best for themselves? For example, a man with a paranoid delusion may refuse treatment because of his belief that the hospital staff is plotting against him. If he is allowed to refuse medication or other forms of therapy, his condition may deteriorate more. The result is that the client becomes even more dangerous or incapable of caring for himself outside of hospital confinement (Stone, 1975).

Proponents of the right to refuse treatment argue, however, that many forms of treatment, such as medication or electroconvulsive shock may have long-term side effects (discussed in earlier chapters). They also point out that involuntary treatment is generally much less effective than treatment accepted voluntarily (Shapiro, 1984). People forced into treatment seem to resist it, thereby nullifying the beneficial effects.

The case of *Rennie v. Klein* (1978) involved several state hospitals in New Jersey that were forcibly medicating patients in nonemergency situations. The court ruled that people had a constitutional right to refuse treatment (psychotropic medication), and to

be given due process. In another related case, *Rogers v. Okin* (1979) a Massachusetts Court supported these guidelines. Both cases made the point that psychotropic medication was often used only as a means to control behavior or as a substitute for treatment. Furthermore, the decisions noted that drugs might actually inhibit recovery.

In these cases, the courts supported the right to refuse treatment under certain conditions and have extended the least restrictive alternative principle to include *least intrusive forms of treatment*. Generally, psychotherapy is considered less intrusive than somatic or physical therapies (ECT and medication). Although this compromise may appear reasonable, other problems present themselves. First, how do we define an intrusive treatment? Are insight therapies equally intrusive as behavioral techniques (punishment and aversion procedures)? Second, if patients are allowed to refuse certain forms of treatment and if the hospital does not have alternatives for them, can clients sue the institution? These questions are still unanswered.

DEINSTITUTIONALIZATION

Deinstitutionalization is the shifting of responsibility for the care of mental patients from large central institutions to agencies within local communities. When originally formulated in the 1960s and 1970s, the concept excited many mental health professionals. Since its inception, many state-run hospitals have experienced a greater than 50 percent reduction in the hospital population. The impetus behind deinstitutionalization came from several quarters.

First, there has been (and still is) a feeling that large hospitals provide mainly custodial care, produce little benefit for the patient, and may even impede improvement. Court cases discussed earlier (*Wyatt v. Stickney* and *O'Connor v. Donaldson*) exposed that many mental hospitals are being no better than "warehouses for the insane." Institutionalization was accused of fostering dependency, promoting helplessness, and lowering self-sufficiency in patients. The longer patients were hospitalized, the more likely they were to remain hospitalized, even if they had improved (Wing, 1980). Furthermore, symptoms such as flat affect and nonresponsiveness, which were generally thought to be clinical signs of schizophrenia, may actually result from hospitalization.

Second, the issue of patient rights has received increasing attention. As already discussed, recent legal decisions have mandated that patients live in least restrictive environments. Mental health professionals became very concerned about keeping patients confined against their will and began to discharge patients whenever they approached minimal competencies. It was believed that **mainstreaming** (integrating) patients back into the community could be accomplished by providing local outpatient or transitory services (such as board-and-care facilities, halfway houses, and churches). In addition, advances in tranquilizers and other drug treatment techniques made it possible to medicate patients, which made them manageable once discharged.

Deinstitutionalization was originally conceived of as a way to provide better and more effective community-based care to hospitalized patients who were seen to be languishing in state institutions. Unfortunately, due to lack of funds and community support, many patients were released to the streets and were left there to wander, uncared for and homeless.

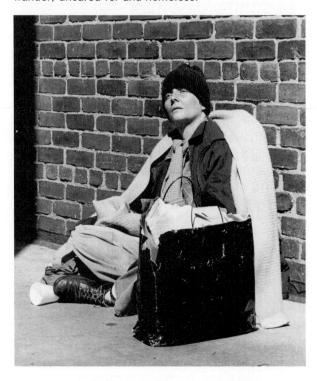

Third, insufficient funds for state hospitals have almost forced these institutions to release patients back into communities. Overcrowded conditions made mental health administrators view the movement favorably; and state legislative branches encouraged the trend, especially since it reduced state costs and funding.

What has been the impact of deinstitutionalization on patients? Critics of deinstitutionalization believe it is a policy that allows states to relinquish their responsibility to care for patients unable to care for themselves. There are alarming indications that deinstitutionalization has been responsible for placing or "dumping" up to one million former patients on the street who should have remained institutionalized (Cordes, 1984a). The majority appear severely disabled, have difficulty coping with daily living, suffer from schizophrenia, and are alcoholic (Goleman, 1986a, 1986b; Jones, 1983; Lamb, 1984). (See Focus 21.1.)

Some criminalization of the mentally ill also seems to be a byproduct of deinstitutionalization. Lamb and Grant (1982, 1983) studied male and female county jail inmates who were referred for psychiatric evaluation. They found that over 85 percent had a history of psychiatric hospitalizations and over 50 percent met the current criteria for involuntary hospitalization (either dangerous to oneself or others or gravely disabled). Over one-third were living on the streets or in missions, and fewer than 12 percent were employed. On the basis of their findings, Lamb and Grant have supported the position that these people should be hospitalized and not imprisoned. In contrast, however, another study produced only modest evidence of such criminalization (Teplin, 1983). Nonetheless, it is becoming apparent that many mentally ill people are not receiving the treatment they need.

Much of the problem with deinstitutionalization appears to be the community's lack of preparation and resources to care for the chronically mentally ill. Many patients lack family or friends who can help them make the transition back into the community; many state hospitals do not provide patients with adequate skills training; many discharged patients have difficulty finding jobs; many find substandard housing worse than the institutions from which they came; many are not adequately monitored and receive

FOCUS 21.1 — *Deinstitutionalization: Treatment or Dumping?*

Mary Jean Willis, founder and president of Families and Friends of the Adult Mentally Ill and the mother of a schizophrenic son, wrote the following comment on current policies regarding the mentally ill:

Now we have deinstitutionalization—release of the mentally ill from hospitals as soon as they are stabilized (and sometimes even sooner).

We think that our son was prematurely discharged from hospitals at least twice. At one time he was sent home on a weekend pass from a state hospital. When the family, including our oldest son, daughter-in-law, and their infant daughter, was gathered around to celebrate his homecoming, he suddenly disappeared into his room, where he proceeded to smash a glass and slash at his throat. Another time, when he was hospitalized in San Francisco after throwing himself in front of a car, he refused med-

ication and demanded to be released. The hospital would not keep him against his will, so he was discharged after a few days, whereupon he jumped in front of a truck and was severely injured.

Deinstitutionalization has meant not only early discharge, but also inaccessibility of hospitals. Because our son is suicidal, we have not had any great difficulty getting him into a hospital. However, I know of a mother who has not been able to gain hospital admission for her son, even though he is violent and a danger to society when he is in his manic phase. . . .

Another common problem for family members is the feeling of being tied down and not able to live one's own life. Families of a chronic mentally ill person find it difficult to travel or to maintain much of a social life.

Our own social life has become practically nonexistent, not necessarily because our friends have deserted us due to the

stigma of mental illness, but because of the unpredictability of our son's illness, and because, after coping with the many problems it causes, we have little energy left over for entertaining.

The financial burden of mental illness is another big problem which families must face. When insurance (if there is any) runs out as it eventually does in most cases, not even well-to-do families can handle the frequent hospitalizations at exorbitant rates. . . .

When all of the above problems are considered, it can be seen that deinstitutionalization has in some ways made life for the families of the chronic mentally ill more difficult than it was for my mother-in-law back in the days when lifelong hospitalization was the fate of most of the mentally ill. (Willis, 1982, pp. 617–619)

---

no psychiatric treatment; and many become homeless (Westermeyer, 1987). It is difficult to estimate how many discharged mental patients comprise the burgeoning ranks of the homeless. We do know that homelessness in the United States, especially in large, urban areas, is increasing at an alarming pace. Certainly, it is not difficult to see the number of people who live in transport terminals, parks, flophouses, homeless shelters, cars, and storefronts. It is hard to determine how many of the homeless, like the woman discussed at the beginning of this chapter, have been deinstitutionalized before adequate support services were present in a community. We do know, however, that the homeless have significantly poorer psychological adjustment, and have higher arrests and con-

viction records (Reiger et al., 1984). The solution is complex but probably does not call for the return to the old institutions of the 1950s, but rather the provision of more and better community-based treatment facilities and alternatives.

For patients involved in alternative community programs, the picture appears somewhat more positive. After reviewing reports of experimental studies on alternative treatment, a group of researchers concluded that such patients fared at least as well as those in institutions. Where differences were found, they favored the alternative programs (Braun et al., 1981). However, such studies are few, and much remains to be done if deinstitutionalized patients are to be provided with the best supportive treatment.

THE THERAPIST-CLIENT RELATIONSHIP

Confidentiality and Privileged Communication

Basic to the therapist-patient relationship is the premise that therapy involves a deeply personal association in which clients have a right to expect whatever they say to be kept private. Therapists believe that genuine therapy cannot occur unless clients trust their therapists and believe they will not divulge confidential communications. Without this guarantee, clients may not be completely open with their thoughts, and may thereby lose the benefits of therapy. This raises several questions. First, what professional ethics and legal statutes govern the therapist-client relationship? Under what conditions can one breach the confidentiality of the relationship? Second, what if, in a conflict between clinical issues (need for trust) and legal ones (need to disclose), the therapist chooses trust? What are the consequences of this choice? Third, if a therapist decides to disclose information to a third party, what effects can the disclosure have on the therapist-client relationship? Last, how can a therapist discuss the limits of confidentiality in a way that would be least likely to disrupt or harm the therapeutic relationship?

Siegel (1979) has defined **confidentiality** as an ethical standard that protects clients from disclosure of information without their consent. Generally, mental health organizations publish codes of ethics endorsing confidentiality in the therapist-client relationship. Confidentiality is an ethical, not a legal obligation. **Privileged communication,** a narrower legal concept, protects privacy and prevents the disclosure of confidential communications without a client's permission (Herlicky & Sheeley, 1988). It must be kept in mind that the "holder of the privilege" is not the therapist, but the client. In other words, if a client waives this privilege, the therapist has no grounds for withholding information. Shapiro (1984) points out that our society recognizes how important certain confidential relationships are, and protects them by law. These relationships are the husband-wife, attorney-client, clergy-congregant, and therapist-client relationships. Psychiatric practices are regulated in all fifty states, including the District of Columbia; and forty-two states have privileged communication statutes (Herlicky & Sheeley, 1988).

Exemptions from Privileged Communication

Although states vary considerably, all states recognize certain situations in which confidential communications can be divulged. Corey et al. (1984) summarizes these conditions:

1. In situations that deal with civil or criminal commitment or competency to stand trial, the client's right to privilege can be waived. For example, a court-appointed therapist who determines that the client needs hospitalization for a psychological disorder, may disclose the results of his examination to an appropriate third party.

2. Disclosure can also be made when a client sues a therapist or in any civil action in which the client introduces mental condition as a claim or defense.

3. When the client is younger than sixteen years of age and information leads the therapist to believe that the child has been a victim of crime (incest, rape, or child abuse), the therapist must provide that information.

4. When criminal action is involved, the therapist is again obligated to disclose related information to that action.

5. When the therapist has reason to believe that a client presents a danger to him- or herself (possible injury or suicide) or may potentially harm someone else, the therapist must act to ward off the danger.

Clearly, privilege in communication is not absolute. It involves the delicate balance between the individual's right to privacy and the public's need to know certain information. Problems arise when we try to determine what the balance should be and how important various events and facts are. Originally, Max Siegel (a former president of the American Psychological Association) argued that under no circumstances should the confidential nature of the therapeutic relationship ever be breached. Clinical concerns are paramount and should be given greatest weight (Siegel, 1979). Others have challenged the position that confidentiality is necessary for effective treatment (Denkowski & Denkowski, 1982). Clearly, the issues are complex. The rights of both clients and the general public must be protected, and the courts must decide when the rights of one group conflict with those of the other.

The Duty-to-Warn Principle

At the beginning of the chapter, we briefly described the case of Prosenjit Poddar (*Tarasoff v. Board of Regents of the University of California*, 1976), a graduate student who killed Tatiana Tarasoff after notifying his therapist that he intended to take her life. Before the homicide, the therapist had decided that Poddar was dangerous and likely to carry out his threat, and had notified the director of the Cowell Psychiatric Clinic that the client was dangerous. He also informed the campus police, hoping they would detain the student. Surely the therapist had done all that could be reasonably expected. Not so, ruled the California Supreme Court. When a therapist determines, according to the standards of the mental health profession, that a patient presents a serious danger to another, that therapist is obligated to warn the intended victim. The court went on to say that the protective privilege ends where the public peril begins.

In another case, *Hedlund v. Superior Court of Orange County*, (1983) the duty-to-warn ruling seems to have been broadened even further. A woman was killed by a shotgun blast while seated in a car next to her seven-year-old son. Advocates for the boy later sued the therapist who had treated the killer (before the shooting) for emotional trauma. The court con-tended that the therapist should have known the child was likely to be with his mother and should have warned him as well.

Criticism of the Duty-to-Warn Principle Siegel (1979) has loudly criticized the *Tarasoff* ruling, stating it was a "day in court for the law and not for the mental health professions." He reasons that if confidentiality had been an absolute policy, Poddar might have been kept in treatment, thus ultimately saving Tarasoff's life. Other mental health professionals have echoed this theme in one form or another. A hostile client with pent-up feelings and emotions may be less likely to act out or become violent when allowed to ventilate his thoughts. The irony, according to critics, is that the duty-to-warn principle may actually be counterproductive to its intent to protect the potential victim.

Another controversial issue surrounding the duty-to-warn principle relates not just to determining danger but to when that determination should be made. Stimulated mainly by the *Tarasoff* ruling, mental health professionals and government and private institutions have begun to develop guidelines to use in dealing with dangerous clients. These guidelines seem to have several common elements. First, there is a recognition that the therapist's principal

Tatiana Tarasoff, a college student at a local community college, was brutally stabbed to death in 1969 by Prosenjit Poddar, a graduate student at the University of California at Berkeley. Although Poddar's therapist notified the university that he thought Poddar was dangerous, the California Supreme Court ruled that the therapist should have warned the victim as well. The duty-to-warn principle is controversial in that it puts the burden on therapists to balance the rights of their clients to privileged communications and the right of society to be protected from violent behavior.

duty is to the client and that confidentiality is a crucial aspect of the therapeutic relationship. Second, therapy necessarily encourages people to engage in open dialogue with the therapist and to share their innermost thoughts and feelings. It is not unusual for clients to voice thoughts about ending their own lives or harming others. Relatively few of these threats are actually carried out, and therapists are not expected to routinely report all of them. Third, only in the most extraordinary circumstances can the duty-to-warn principle be invoked. During the therapy session, however, the therapist should continue to treat the client and, if therapeutically appropriate, attempt to dissuade the client from the threatened violence. Last, somewhere in the therapy process, the therapist must discuss the limits of confidentiality and inform the client about the possible actions he or she must take to protect a third party. In other words, professionals are obligated to inform their clients that they have a duty-to-warn others about the threatened actions of their clients.

SOCIAL AND PERSONAL RELATIONSHIPS

Traditionally, mental health practitioners have emphasized the importance of separating their personal and professional lives. They reasoned that therapists need to be objective and removed from their clients because becoming emotionally involved with them is nontherapeutic. Having a personal relationship with a client may make the therapist less confrontational, allow the therapist to fulfill his or her own needs at the expense of the client, and unintentionally allow the therapist to exploit the client because of his or her position (Corey et al., 1984). Some people question the belief that a social or personal relationship is necessarily antitherapeutic (Burton, 1972). Although it is not within the scope of this section to debate the issue, matters of personal relations with clients are being increasingly raised, especially when they deal with erotic and sexual intimacies.

Touching Clients

At the beginning of the chapter, we presented the case of a male therapist who placed his arms around a young female client as an obvious act of compassion. In this instance, the contact was nonerotic and a spontaneous act of compassion that may have comforted the client in her grief. Some therapists make the point that "touch" as a means of communication is as old as the human species itself. Touch in therapy can enhance communication and be therapeutic (Willison & Masson, 1986).

In therapy, however, touching or any other physical contact is taboo, and many therapists hold back when they feel like touching clients compassionately or affectionately. Many therapists fear that touching a client may be misinterpreted, especially in a male-female relationship (Brodsky, 1985). Research has found that 27 percent of therapists occasionally engaged in nonerotic hugging, kissing, or touching of opposite-sex clients, and 7 percent said they did so frequently (Holroyd & Brodsky, 1977, 1980). Nearly half of the therapists surveyed believed that nonerotic touch could be therapeutic. Whether therapists used nonerotic touch seemed to depend on their theoretical orientation: 25 percent of humanistic therapists did it frequently or always; 10 percent of the eclectics; and fewer than 5 percent of psychoanalytic, behavioral, or rational-cognitive therapists. In addition, therapists who advocated nonerotic touching believed it to be appropriate in the following situations: (1) in relationships with socially or emotionally immature clients (such as those having a history of maternal deprivation), (2) in relationships with people suffering acute distress (grief), (3) in providing emotional support, and (4) in greeting or termination (handshakes).

Opponents of therapeutic touch claim that, at best, it is often misinterpreted by clients, and that, at worst, it represents a clear-cut case of sexual exploitation. This is especially true in male therapist-female client relationships. Their objections are based on the following grounds. First, the definition of erotic and nonerotic touch is vague. *Erotic contact* can be defined as the *intent* to arouse or satisfy sexual desire (Holroyd & Brodsky, 1977). Often the therapist may not be truly aware of his or her intent, and the client is placed in a conflicting situation as well. The patient may wonder what the therapist's intent really is. Female patients often interpret the meaning of a male therapist's touch as sexual. Furthermore, many female clients have reported that many male therapists have stated that the purpose of rubbing, stroking, and touching their female clients was to calm or relax them. Yet such touching frequently progressed to more erotic fondling of their bodies (Brodsky, 1985).

Second, some raise the issue that touch has political implications in the male-female relationship (Alyn, 1988). Sex and status in our society determines who touches whom (women are touched more often) and where (Henley, 1977). Even those who advocate therapeutic touch (Willison & Masson, 1986) admit that touch has power implications. Different touching patterns reflect the different status of men and women in Western culture. The danger, according to critics, is that this power structure is brought into the therapist-client relationship (Alyn, 1988). We have already discussed in a previous chapter how the psychological distress of women in our society is often attributed to their second-class status and sex role stereotypes (Chesler, 1972; Eichenbaum & Orbach, 1983). Critics of physical contact believe that the prevailing power structure in a therapeutic relationship mirrors the power relationships in our society (male-female). Erotic touch in therapy is unethical; nonerotic touch even if ethical may blur the boundaries of the therapeutic relationship.

Physical contact with clients is another controversial issue dividing the therapeutic community. Is it ever appropriate to touch a client or to be sexually intimate with that person? It is difficult not to respond to a person's pain with a simple gesture of compassion—a touched shoulder, a held hand. It is equally difficult to deal with the consequences that any misperception of that gesture might produce. The issue is complex, and a clear consensus on it will be hard to reach. Sexual intimacy is another matter, with most of the therapeutic community opposing any such contact.

Sexual Intimacy with Clients

Unlike the use of "touch" in therapy, for which there is considerable support, sexual relationships with clients is almost universally considered unethical by professional organizations. The American Psychological Association, in no uncertain terms, condemns sexual liaisons with clients:

> Psychologists are continually cognizant of their own needs and of their potential influential position vis-à-vis persons such as clients, students, and subordinates. They avoid exploiting the trust and dependency of such persons. Psychologists make every effort to avoid dual relationships that could impair their professional judgment or increase the risk of exploitation. Examples of such relationships include, but are not limited to, research with and treatment of employees, students, supervisors, close friends, or relatives. Sexual intimacies with clients are unethical. (American Psychological Association, 1981)

But what are the practitioners' thoughts about sexual intimacies with clients? How often does it really occur? Who does what to whom? In one nationwide study of 500 male and 500 female psychologists, Holroyd and Brodsky (1977) report that 5.5 percent

of male therapists and 0.6 percent of female therapists have had sexual intercourse with clients. Sexual intimacy is almost always between male therapists and female clients. Of those who had sexual intercourse with clients, 80 percent were likely to repeat the practice. Of those responding, 88 percent of female and 70 percent of male therapists believed that erotic contact is *never* beneficial to clients. However, 4 percent of the respondents thought that erotic contact with clients was beneficial. Although in the minority, these therapists took the position that sexual intimacy may be beneficial to clients because it validates the clients as sexual beings, frees them from inhibitions and guilt, and allows them to enjoy their sexuality.

Critics of these arguments find them weak and self-serving. First, sexual intimacy represents an abuse of the therapist's power. Clients who discuss the most intimate aspects of their lives (sexual desires and struggles) are very vulnerable, and it is extremely easy for therapists to take advantage of their clients' trust and to exploit it. Second, sexual intimacy fosters dependency in clients, who look toward the therapist as an "ideal" and as someone who has "the answers." An individual's personal therapeutic goals become subordinate to a desire to please the therapist or to live up to his or her standards. Third, objectivity may also be lost. When therapists become sex partners, they cease to be therapists (Corlis & Rabe, 1969). Fourth, clients often feel exploited, used, embittered, and angry. Their self-esteem is also harmed.

Most professional organizations and states have procedures for filing and processing ethical complaints related to sexual intimacies between therapist and client. In the state of California, the Board of Medical Quality Assurance—the parent organization of the Psychology Examining Committee—has power to suspend or revoke the licenses of therapists who engage in sexual misconduct with their clients. Furthermore, clients always have legal recourse to sue their therapists for malpractice. Many cases of misconduct, however, probably go unreported because of the client's shame and guilt over their "complicity." In any case, the consensus is that sexual intimacy with clients is unethical, antitherapeutic, and detrimental.

SUMMARY

1. Legal interpretations of insanity are always changing. Historically, several interpretations have been applied. The M'Naghten Rule holds that people could be acquitted of a crime if it could be shown that their reasoning was so defective that they were unaware of their actions, or if aware of their actions, were unable to comprehend the wrongness of them. The irresistible impulse test holds that people are innocent if they are unable to control their behavior. The *Durham* decision acquits people if their criminal actions were products of mental disease or defects. The American Law Institute guidelines state that people are not responsible for a crime if they lack substantial capacity to appreciate the criminality of their conduct or to conform their conduct to the requirements of the law. Weaknesses in the standards and public outrage with the acquittal of some highly publicized people (such as John Hinckley, Jr.) have resulted in movements to restrict use of the defense. The "guilty, but mentally ill" plea is an attempt to separate mental illness from insanity and to hold people responsible for their actions.

2. The phrase, "competency to stand trial," refers to defendants' mental state at the time they are being examined. It is a separate issue from criminal responsibility, which refers to *past behavior* at the time of the offense. Accused people are considered incompetent if they have difficulty understanding the trial proceedings or cannot rationally consult with attorneys in their defense. Although competency to stand trial is important in ensuring fair trials, being judged incompetent can have negative consequences, such as unfair and prolonged denial of civil liberties.

3. Concern with denial of civil liberties is also present in civil commitment cases. People who have committed no crime can be confined against their will if it can be shown (a) they present a clear and imminent danger to themselves or others, (b) they are unable to care for themselves, (c) they are unable to make responsible decisions about appropriate treatment and hospitalization, and (d) they are in an unmanageable state of fright or panic. Courts have tightened criteria and rely more than ever on the concept of dangerousness. Mental health professionals have great difficulty in predicting dangerousness because dangerous acts depend as much on social situations as personal attributes, and because the definition is unclear.

4. Concern with patient rights has become an issue because many practices and procedures seem to violate constitutional guarantees. As a result, court rulings have established several important precedents. First, the standard of proof for commitment is "clear and convincing evidence." Second, commitment laws are now designed to provide patients with the "least restrictive environment," which does not necessarily involve hospitalization. Third, patients have a right to treatment (as opposed to custodial care) and a right to a humane environment (this latter ruling was a reaction to inhumane and abhorrent conditions that existed in some hospitals). Last, patients also have a right to refuse treatment in certain situations. The courts have used the "less intrusive forms of treatment" concept in applying their rulings.

5. During the 1960s and 1970s, the policy of deinstitutionalization became popular: the shifting of responsibility for the care of mental patients from large central institutions to agencies within the local community. Deinstitutionalization was considered a promising answer to the "least restrictive environment" ruling and to monetary problems experienced by state governments. Critics, however, have accused

the states of "dumping" former patients and avoiding their responsibilities under the guise of mental health innovations.

6. Most mental health professionals believe that confidentiality is crucial to the therapist-client relationship. Exceptions to this privilege include situations that involve (a) civil or criminal commitment and competency to stand trial, (b) a client's initiation of a lawsuit for malpractice or a civil action where the client's mental condition is introduced, (c) the belief child abuse has occurred to a client younger than sixteen, (d) a criminal action, or (e) the danger of a client to him- or herself or to others. Although psychologists have always known that privileged communication is not an absolute right, the *Tarasoff* decision makes therapists responsible for warning a potential victim in order to avoid liability.

7. Mental health professionals are beginning to recognize that ethical and moral values permeate the therapeutic process. The most controversial issues involve erotic and sexual intimacy. Sexual intimacy with clients is almost universally condemned by therapists as immoral, unethical, and antitherapeutic. It is more difficult to make a judgment in the case of "touch." Nonerotic touch as an adjunct to therapy is acceptable to many, but erotic touch is seen as antitherapeutic. It is difficult, however, to determine when a touch is erotic or nonerotic. Furthermore, touch in male-female relationships may reflect status differences in our society and may thus have political implications.

KEY TERMS

civil commitment A form of protective confinement when the person is judged to be a danger to him- or herself or to others even though he or she has not committed a crime

competency to stand trial The defendant's mental state at the time he or she is being examined by a practitioner

confidentiality An ethical standard that protects clients from disclosure of information without their consent

criminal commitment Incarceration of a person on the basis of committing a crime

dangerousness A person's potential for doing harm to him- or herself or to others

deinstitutionalization The shifting of responsibility for the care of mental patients from large central institutions to agencies within local communities

due process Legal checks and balances guaranteed to everyone (right to a fair trial, right to face accusers, right to present own evidence, right to counsel and so on)

insanity defense The legal argument used by defendants who have committed a crime, but plead not guilty because of a mental disturbance

irresistible impulse test One of the tests of insanity, which states that a defendant is not criminally responsible if he or she lacked the will power to control his or her behavior

least restrictive environment A patient's right to the least restrictive alternative to freedom that is appropriate to his or her condition

mainstreaming Integrating mental patients as soon as possible back into the community

privileged communication In therapy, it regulates privacy protection and prevents clients from having their confidential communications disclosed without their permission

right to treatment A mental patient's right to receive therapy that would improve his or her emotional state

Glossary

abnormal behavior Behavior that departs from some norm and is judged harmful to the affected individual, others, or society

abnormal psychology The scientific study whose objectives are to describe, explain, predict, and control behaviors that are considered strange or unusual

action-oriented therapy Therapies that base treatment on classical conditioning, operant conditioning, observational learning, and cognitive-behavioral process

affect Emotion or mood

age regression The hypnotic process in which patients are told that they are reliving their childhood at a specific age and that their thoughts, speech, and actions will reflect this age

agoraphobia An intense fear of being in public places or of being alone where help may not be available; in extreme cases, a fear of leaving one's home

alcohol amnestic disorder (Korsakoff's syndrome) A syndrome sometimes found in chronic alcoholics in which the individual displays a loss of memory of recent events and fills in memory gaps with false or fanciful accounts

alcohol hallucinosis Auditory hallucinations that occur in some alcoholics when they abruptly cease alcohol consumption; similar to delirium tremens

alcoholics People who abuse and depend on alcohol

alcohol idiosyncratic intoxication A condition in which an acute behavior change takes place after the ingestion of a small amount of alcohol

alcoholism Substance dependence in which the substance used is alcohol

altruistic suicide Suicide that is motivated by the need to further group goals or to achieve some greater good

Alzheimer's disease An organic brain disorder that involves the atrophy of brain tissue and leads to marked deterioration of intellectual and emotional functioning

amnesia The partial or total loss of memory due to either organic or psychological causes

amniocentesis A procedure in which a hollow needle is inserted through the abdominal wall and into the amniotic sac to draw out fluid containing fetal cells

amphetamines Drugs that speed up central nervous system activity and produce increased alertness, energy, and euphoria; also called "uppers"

analogue study An investigation that attempts to replicate or simulate, as closely as possible, under controlled conditions, a situation that occurs in real life

anal retentive personality In Freudian theory, a stubborn, stingy, and constantly procrastinating character, caused by childhood conflict with parents over toilet training

anal sadistic phase In Freudian theory, a childhood revolt against authority characterized by the expulsion of feces or gas from the bowels at inappropriate times; fixation at this phase may produce an obsessive-compulsive adult

anal stage In Freudian theory, the stage during the second year of life in which the anal region becomes the focus of pleasurable sensations

anomic suicide Suicide that results when a person's relationship to society is unbalanced in some dramatic fashion

anorexia nervosa An eating disorder in which the person is intensely fearful of becoming obese and engages in self-starvation

antabuse Drug that produces an aversion to alcohol

anterograde amnesia Loss of memory for very recent or immediately preceding events

antidepressant drugs Drugs that relieve depression by elevating mood; include iproniazid, phenelzine, and imipramine

antisocial personality A type of delinquency characterized by impulsivity, inability to delay gratification, inability to profit from punishment or experience, and lack of guilt

antisocial personality disorder A personality disorder characterized by failure to conform to social and legal norms, superficial relationships with others, and lack of guilt feelings for wrongdoing

anxiety Feelings of uneasiness and apprehension

anxiety disorders Disorders (panic disorder, generalized anxiety disorders, phobias, and obsessive-compulsive disorders) whose major characteristic is irrational feelings of fear and apprehension

aphasia The loss of motor or sensory functioning associated with language; results from damage to the brain.

arrythmia Irregular heartbeat

assessment With regard to psychopathology, the process of gathering information and drawing conclusions about the traits, skills, abilities, emotional functioning, and psychological problems of an individual

asthma A respiratory disorder characterized by attacks in which breathing becomes extremely difficult because of constriction of the airways in the lungs

attention deficit hyperactivity disorder A disorder of childhood and adolescence characterized by short attention span, impulsiveness, constant activity, and lack of self-control

autistic disorder A severe childhood disorder that is characterized by early onset and an extreme lack of interest in interpersonal relationships, and impairment in verbal and nonverbal communication

autistic savant autistic child having unusual abilities or special talents

autonomic nervous system The system responsible for regulating the body's internal environment, such as the heart, intestines, and endocrine glands; composed of the sympathetic and parasympathetic systems

autonomic response specificity The concept that each individual has a unique physiological reaction to all types of stressful situations

autosome Nonsex chromosome

aversive behavior rehearsal (ABR) An aversive conditioning treatment for exhibitionism that uses shame or humiliation as the aversive stimulus

aversive conditioning A classical conditioning technique in which an undesirable behavior is paired with a noxious stimulus in order to suppress the undesirable behavior

aversion therapy A conditioning procedure in which the attractiveness of a stimulus is decreased by pairing it with an aversive stimulus

avoidant disorder A disorder of childhood and adolescence that involves severe anxiety in situations involving contact with unfamiliar people, resulting in social withdrawal

avoidant personality disorder A personality disorder characterized by hypersensitivity to rejection and humiliation, and a resultant reluctance to enter into social relationships

barbiturate A substance that is a powerful depressant of the central nervous system; can induce psychological and physical dependency

baseline In behavior therapy, the initial level of responses emitted by the individual

behavioral medicine A number of fields that study social, psychological, and lifestyle influences on health

behavioral models Theories of psychopathology that are concerned with the role of learning in abnormal behavior

behavioral repertoire The range of responses an individual has learned to make in each given situation

being An existential concept referring to the awareness that human beings have of their own existence; this awareness makes people responsible for choosing their own direction in life

being-in-the-world An existential concept referring to the awareness that human beings exist in the context of a "world" of meaningful relationships with other human beings and with nature

Bender-Gestalt Visual-Motor Test A test used to assess visual-motor integration skills; can detect neurological impairment

biofeedback therapy A therapeutic approach in which a patient receives information about particular autonomic functions and is rewarded for influencing those functions in a desired direction

biofeedback training A therapeutic technique in which the person is taught to voluntarily control a particular physiological function, such as heart rate or blood pressure

biogenic model The theory or expectation that every mental disorder has an organic basis and cure

biogenic view The belief or theory that mental disorders have a physical or physiological basis

biological stressors Physical conditions, such as infections, trauma, malnutrition, and fatigue, that can produce stress

bipolar disorder An affective disorder in which both depression and mania are exhibited, or one in which only mania has been exhibited

body dysmorphic disorder A somatoform disorder that involves preoccupation with an imagined physical defect

borderline personality disorder A personality disorder characterized by intense fluctuations in mood, self-image, and interpersonal relationships

bradycardia Slowing down of the heartbeat

brain pathology Dysfunction or disease of the brain

brain trauma A physical wound or injury to the brain

brief reactive psychosis A psychotic disorder due to a stressor that lasts from only a few hours to one month

bulimia An eating disorder characterized by the rapid consumption of large quantities of food, usually followed by self-induced vomiting

caffeine Stimulant found in coffee, tea, and cola drinks

case study Intensive study of one individual that relies on observation, psychological tests, and historical and biographical data

castration anxiety In Freudian theory, the fear in males that they will be punished for their forbidden oedipal desires by suffering the loss of their penis

catatonic schizophrenia A schizophrenic disorder characterized by extreme agitation and excitement or by extreme withdrawal and lack of responsiveness

catecholamines Neurotransmitter substances that are implicated in states of arousal and mood states

cathartic method The therapeutic use of verbal expression to release pent-up unconscious conflicts

central nervous system The brain and the spinal cord, which coordinate all activities of the nervous system of vertebrates

cerebral blood flow measurement A technique for assessing brain damage in which the patient inhales a radioactive gas and the movement of the substance is followed throughout the brain

cerebral cortex The outermost layer of the cerebrum, which is involved in higher mental processes

cerebral tumor A mass of abnormal tissue growing within the brain

cerebrovascular accident A sudden stoppage of blood flow to a portion of the brain, leading to loss of brain function; also called *stroke*

cerebrum The largest structure in the brain; the seat of human consciousness and of all learning, speech, thought, and memory

child abuse Physical or psychological mistreatment of a child, carried out by parents, adult relatives, or other adult caretakers and resulting in physical or psychological trauma that can produce a variety of disorders, among them mental retardation

chromosomal anomaly Abnormality or irregularity that produces inherited defects or vulnerabilities such as Down syndrome or PKU

civil commitment A form of protective confinement when the person is judged to be a danger to him- or herself or to others even when he or she has not committed a crime

classical (respondent) conditioning A theory of learning process, applying to involuntary learning, in which neutral stimuli become able to evoke involuntary responses

classification system With regard to psychopathology, a system of mutually exclusive categories, indicators, and nomenclature for distinct patterns of behavior, thought processes, and emotional disturbances

clinical psychology The professional field concerned with the study, assessment, treatment, and prevention of abnormal behavior in disturbed individuals

cocaine A drug that which induces feelings of euphoria and self-confidence in users; usually inhaled into the nasal cavity

cognition The process of thinking, perceiving, judging, and recognizing

cognitive behavioral model A theory of learning holding that conscious thought mediates, or modifies, an individual's behavior in response to a stimulus

cognitive behavioral therapy A therapy approach directed toward helping clients to restructure their thoughts and to reinterpret environmental inputs and internal stimulation

cognitive restructuring An attempt to alter problematic cognitions by replacing them with more rational and positive thoughts

cognitive slippage The continual shifting of thoughts from topic to topic without any apparent logical or meaningful connection among topics (see also *loosening of associations*)

collective unconscious A term devised by Jung that refers to ancient, primordial memories common to all humanity

community mental health centers Centrally located mental health facilities (for medium-sized communities) that provide a number of services such as short-term inpatient care, outpatient care, partial hospitalization, emergency services, and community consultation and education

community psychology An approach to mental health that takes into account the influence of environmental factors and emphasizes the use of community resources to eliminate various conditions that produce psychological problems

competence to stand trial The defendant's mental state at the time he or she is being examined by a practitioner

compulsion A behavior performed in a stereotyped manner; failure to perform the act results in anxiety

computerized axial tomography (CAT) scanning Neurological test for the assessment of brain damage

concordance rate The likelihood that both of a pair of subjects will exhibit the disorder that is being studied

conduct disorders Disorders of childhood and adolescence that involve a persistent pattern of antisocial behaviors

concussion A mild brain injury often involving the rupture of blood vessels, typically caused by a blow to the head

conditioned response (CR) In classical conditioning, the response made to a previously neutral stimulus

conditioned stimulus (CS) In classical conditioning, a previously neutral stimulus

confabulation Filling memory gaps with false or fanciful accounts that the individual believes are true

confidentiality An ethical standard that protects clients from disclosure of information without their consent

congenital Present from birth but not inherited

conjoint family therapy A type of family therapy in which family members are taught message-sending and message-receiving skills

conscience In Freudian theory, the component of the *superego* that inculcates guilt feelings about engaging in immoral or unethical behavior

consultation Working with and through community institutions such as police, schools, the courts, or corporations to help individuals in the community

contingency Relationship, usually causal, between two events in which one is usually followed by the other

continuous amnesia The inability to recall past and present events; each new event is forgotten after it occurs

control group A group exposed to the same conditions as the experimental group with the exception of the independent variable

controlled drinking A treatment for alcoholism whose goal is to teach alcoholics to control their intake and become social drinkers, rather than to abstain entirely

contusion A brain injury in which the brain shifts slightly and presses against the skull

conversion disorder A somatoform disorder in which there is significant impairment of sensory or motor function without an underlying physical cause (also known as *conversion reaction*)

coping skills training A form of cognitive behavioral therapy aimed at helping clients learn to manage or overcome stress

coping strategies Cognitive and behavioral skills used in stressful situations to reduce the stress

coprolalia A compulsion to shout obscenities; a symptom of Tourette's syndrome

coronary heart disease (CHD) A cardiovascular disease in which the flow of blood and oxygen to the heart is restricted by a narrowing of the arteries in or near the heart

corpus callosum A collection of nerve fibers that connect the two hemispheres of the cerebrum

correlation The degree to which two variables covary or are associated with each other in a population

counseling psychology A professional field similar to clinical psychology, but usually more concerned with the study of life problems in relatively normal people

counterconditioning A therapeutic means of eliminating anxiety by gradually pairing the fear-producing stimulus with a pleasant stimulus

countertransference A process during psychotherapy in which feelings that the therapist had toward significant others (primarily parents) in the past are transferred to the patient; therapist must recognize and control this process

covert sensitization An aversive conditioning procedure in which patients are asked to imagine unpleasant consequences occurring after engaging in undesirable but tempting behavior

cretinism A metabolic disorder that causes mental retardation; it results from iodine deficiency in the mother during pregnancy; also called hypothyroidism

criminal commitment Incarceration of a person on the basis of committing a crime

criminal insanity A legal term referring either to a criminal's unawareness of committing a crime or incomprehension that it was wrong to do so because of a mental disturbance

cultural-familial retardation Generally mild mental retardation thought to be produced through normal genetic processes, by environmental factors, or by both

cultural relativism The belief that lifestyles, cultural values, and world views affect the expression and determination of deviant behavior

cultural universality The belief that many behavior disorders cut across lifestyles, cultural norms, and world views

cyclothymia A mild and chronic mood disorder characterized by nonpsychotic mood swings

dangerousness A person's potential for doing harm to him- or herself or others

death instincts In Freudian theory, the drive for the biological death of the organism, used to explain phenomena such as war and suicide; Thanatos

decompensation Loss of the ability to deal successfully with stress

defense mechanism In psychoanalytic theory, the unconscious and automatic means by which the ego is protected from anxiety-provoking conflicts

deinstitutionalization The shifting of responsibility for the care of mental patients from large central institutions to agencies within local communities

delirium Inability to maintain attention, disorganized thinking, confusion, and disorientation caused by, or presumed to be caused by, an organic factor

delusional disorder A disorder characterized by persistent, nonbizarre delusions that are not accompanied by other unusual or odd behavior

delusions False beliefs steadfastly held by the individual despite contradictory objective evidence

delusion system An internally coherent, systematized pattern of delusions

dementia A syndrome characterized by brain tissue deterioration resulting in decreased intellectual ability and impaired judgment, of sufficient severity to interfere with social and occupational functioning

demonology The belief, commonly held by ancient peoples, that both mental and physical disorders are caused by the influence of supernatural forces

dependent personality disorder A personality disorder characterized by extreme reliance on others and unwillingness to assume responsibility

dependent variable Attitudes or behaviors that are expected to change as a result of the manipulation of the independent variable in a psychological experiment

depersonalization disorder A dissociative disorder in which there are feelings of unreality or distortion concerning the self or the environment

depression An emotional state characterized by intense sadness, feelings of futility and worthlessness, and withdrawal from others

detoxification A treatment aimed at removing all alcohol (or other substance) from a user's body and ensuring that none is ingested

developmental aphasia A childhood speech disorder; children may exhibit *echolalia* or be completely mute

developmental arithmetic disorder A significant impairment in the development of arithmetic skills not accounted for by chronological age or inadequate schooling

diaschisis A condition in which a lesion in one specific area of the brain disrupts other anatomically intact areas

diathesis-stress model A theoretical model which proposes that innate vulnerability (diathesis) and the effect of environmental stressors combine in producing mental disorders

disaster syndrome A hypothesized series of phases an individual goes through when exposed to disaster

discriminative stimulus A cue that is usually present when reinforcement occurs

disorganized schizophrenia A schizophrenic disorder (beginning at an early age) characterized by severe disintegration and absurd and incoherent behaviors beginning at an early age

disorientation Confusion with regard to identity, place, or time

displacement A defense mechanism in which an individual's negative emotions are expressed toward a substitute target

dissociative disorders Mental disorders characterized by alteration or disruption of the individual's identity or consciousness; include psychogenic amnesia, psychogenic fugue, depersonalization disorder, and multiple personality disorder

dizygotic (DZ) twins (fraternal) Twins from two separate eggs; such twins share about 50 percent of the same genes

dopamine A catecholamine neurotransmitter substance

dopamine hypothesis The theory that schizophrenia results from an excess of dopamine activity at certain brain synapses

double-bind theory The suggestion that schizophrenia develops in an individual as a result of the continual reception of contradictory messages from parents during the individual's upbringing

Down syndrome A condition produced by the presence of an extra chromosome (trisomy 21), resulting in mental retardation and distinctive physical characteristics

drug therapy The treatment of mental disorders with drugs

DSM I, II, III, III-R The diagnostic and statistical manuals of mental disorders published by the American Psychiatric Association; contain the diagnostic categories and criteria for differential diagnosis of abnormal behavior

due process Legal checks and balances guaranteed to everyone (right to a fair trial, right to face accusers, right to present own evidence, right to counsel, and so on)

dyspareunia Painful coitus in males or females

dysthymia A mild and chronic mood disorder characterized by nonpsychotic depression

echolalia Echoing what has previously been said; a symptom of autism and other disorders

eclectic approach An openness to all models of abnormal behavior, along with a willingness to borrow and integrate techniques from all approaches and to use them selectively with clients

clecticism In treatment and diagnosis, selection of concepts, methods, and strategies from a variety of current theories in a systematic fashion

ego In Freudian theory, the part of the personality that mediates between the demands of the id, superego, and the environment

ego-dystonic Unacceptable to the ego

ego ideal In Freudian theory, the part of the superego that rewards altruistic or moral behavior with feelings of pride

egoistic suicide Suicide that results from an inability to integrate oneself with society

ego psychologists Followers of Anna Freud and Erik Erikson who accept Freud's three-part division of the personality, but believe the ego is independent of the sexual and aggressive drives

ego weakness In Freudian theory, a state during sleep or times of excessive fatigue when the ego's guard over repressed desires is relaxed and unconscious impulses often seep out

ejaculation In males, the expulsion of semen during orgasm

Electra complex In Freudian theory, a daughter's feelings of possessive love for the father that occur during the phallic stage

electroconvulsive therapy The application of an electrical voltage to the brain to induce convulsions and thereby reduce depression; also called *electroshock treatment*

electroencephalograph (EEG) A neurological test for the assessment of brain damage

encephalitis Inflammation of the brain caused by viral infection that produces symptoms of lethargy, fever, and long periods of stupor and sleep; sleeping sickness

encounter groups Group therapy designed to facilitate

human growth and development by encouraging freedom of expression and reduction of defensiveness

endogenous depression A depression that is caused largely by internal, chemical imbalances

enuresis Bed-wetting

epidemiological research The study of the rate and distribution of mental disorders in a population

epilepsy Any disorder characterized by intermittent and brief periods of altered consciousness, often accompanied by seizures, and excessive electrical discharge from brain cells

erectile dysfunction Inability of a male to attain or maintain a penile erection sufficient for sexual intercourse

essential hypertension High blood pressure, usually with no known organic cause

etiology The causes or origins of a disorder

eustress Any kind of stress that is good for people; a concept developed by Hans Selye

exhibitionism A disorder in which a person gets sexual gratification by exposing his genitals to strangers

existential analysis A therapeutic approach that is concerned with the person's experience and involvement in the world

existential approach The belief that contemporary society has a dehumanizing effect and that mental disorders result from a conflict between the essential human nature and the demands made on people by themselves and others

existential crisis A state in which individuals feel lonely and alienated and lose a sense of the meaning of life, of self-responsibility, and of free will

exogenous depression A depression that is due largely to environmental or external causes

exorcism Ritual in which prayer, noise, emetics, and extreme measures, such as starvation and/or flogging, were used to cast evil spirits out of the body of an afflicted individual

experiment A technique of scientific inquiry in which an independent variable is manipulated, the changes in a dependent variable are measured, and extraneous variables are controlled to the extent possible

experimental hypothesis A prediction that is made concerning how an independent variable affects a dependent variable in an experiment

experimental group In an experiment, a group that is exposed to the independent variable

exposure therapy Gradual or rapid exposure to a feared situation

external validity The degree to which the results of an experiment may be generalized

extinction In classical and operant conditioning, the process by which a response is gradually eliminated by not being reinforced

extraneous variable A variable not being tested or controlled that influences the outcome of a study; a source of error in an experiment

factitious disorders Deliberately self-induced or simulated physical or mental condition

family counseling A professional field of psychology focusing on relationships within the family

family dynamics Everyday patterns of operation in a family system, including communication among its members

family systems model A model of psychopathology that stresses the family's influence on individual behavior

family therapy Group therapy that seeks to modify relationships within the family in such a way as to achieve harmony

fetal alcohol syndrome (FAS) A group of symptoms, including mental retardation and physical defects, that are produced in the infant by the ingestion of alcohol by a pregnant woman

fetishism A disorder characterized by an extremely strong sexual attraction for a particular nongenital part of the anatomy or for an inanimate object

field study An investigative technique in which behaviors are observed and recorded in the natural environment

fixation In Freudian theory, the arresting of emotional development at a particular psychosexual stage due to either overgratification or insufficient gratification at that developmental level

flat affect Abnormal lack of emotional response

flooding A high anxiety exposure treatment aimed at extinguishing a fear by having the client confront the feared situation

folie à deux A condition in which delusional beliefs are shared by two or more individuals

forcible rape An act of sexual intercourse that is accomplished through force or the threat of force

fragile X syndrome An abnormality in the X chromosome that is associated with mental retardation

free association A psychoanalytic method during which the patient says whatever comes to mind, regardless of how illogical or embarrassing it may seem; the material is thought to represent the contents of the patient's unconscious

free-floating anxiety Pervasive anxiety without an identifiable external source

functional disorder A mental disorder for which no physical basis can be found and that is assumed to be due primarily to psychological factors

gender identity disorder A psychological disorder characterized by conflict between an individual's anatomical sex and his or her sexual identity

general adaptation syndrome (GAS) A model for understanding the body's physical and psychological reaction to biological stressors

general paresis Damage to the brain as a result of untreated syphilis

generalization The phenomenon of responding to stimuli that are similar to a conditioned stimulus

generalized amnesia The inability to recall the entire past due to some psychosocial stress

generalized anxiety disorder (GAD) Disorder characterized by persistent high levels of anxiety in situations where no real danger is present

genital stage In Freudian theory, the psychosexual stage beginning at puberty during which true heterosexual rather than narcissistic love can develop

genotype The genetic component of a trait or characteristic

gestalt therapy A humanistic-existential approach to therapy that emphasizes the client's awareness of the "here and now" and his or her totality of experience in the present

graduated exposure Gradual exposure to a feared situation

grand mal seizure The most severe and dramatic form of epilepsy; involves violent contractions, relaxation of body muscles, and loss of consciousness

group therapy A form of therapy that involves the simultaneous treatment of two or more clients

halfway house A program that provides deinstitutionalized patients with a support system while they learn or redevelop skills they will need if they are to function in the community

hallucinations Sensory perceptions not directly attributable to environmental stimuli

hallucinogen A substance that produces hallucinations, more vivid sensory awareness, or increased insight

Halstead-Reitan Neuropsychological Test Battery A series of tests used to differentiate brain-damaged from non-brain-damaged patients, and to locate areas of damage

hardiness A concept developed by Kobasa and Maddi that refers to a person's ability to deal well with stress

historical research The systematic and objective reconstruction of some aspect of the past by use of the evidence available in historical documents

histrionic personality disorder A personality disorder characterized by self-dramatization, the exaggerated expression of emotion, and attention-seeking behaviors

homeostasis A state of physiological, psychological, or emotional equilibrium produced by a balance of functions and chemical composition within the individual

homosexuality Sexual preference for members of one's own sex

human ecology The study of the interaction between human beings and their environments

humanism An emphasis on human welfare and on the worth and uniqueness of the individual

humanistic-existential therapy A therapy that stresses the importance of self-growth, self-concept, free will, and responsibility; includes person-centered therapy, existential analysis, and gestalt therapy

humanistic perspective The optimistic viewpoint that people are born with the ability to reach their full potential, and that abnormal behavior results from disharmony between the person's potential and self-concept

Huntington's chorea A genetically transmitted degenerative disease involving personality changes, depression, delusion, and a loss of control over bodily functions

hyperactive Restless, distractable, and having a short attention span (with reference to a childhood syndrome); sometimes accompanied by attention deficit disorder

hypervigilance Overalertness and arousal; often a characteristic of the anxiety disorders

hypnotherapy The use of hypnosis as an adjunct to psychotherapy to help patients seeking relief from psychological problems and wishing to change

hypnotism An induced state of narrowed perception in which the individual becomes highly suggestible

hypochondriasis A somatoform disorder characterized by persistent and strong preoccupation with one's health and physical condition even in the face of physical evaluations that reveal no organic problems

hypomania Mild form of manic reaction in which affected individuals seem to be high-spirited and are overactive in their behaviors

hypotension Low blood pressure

hypothalamus Part of the brain in the subcortex that regulates bodily activities such as hunger, sex, temperature, and hormone balance

hypothesis A conjectural statement that describes a relationship between variables

hysteria The appearance of physical symptoms that seem to have no organic basis

id In Freudian theory, the part of the personality that is subjective, impulsive, selfish, and pleasure-seeking

identification In Freudian theory, resolution of the Oedipal conflict through adoption of the values or mannerisms of the same-sex parent

implosion therapy A behavioral treatment aimed at extinguishing a fear by having the client imagine the feared situation in its full intensity; often employs unrealistic imagery

incest Sexual relations between close relatives

independent variable The variable or condition that is manipulated to test for its effect on the dependent variable

infarction Death of brain tissue due to a decrease in the blood supply

inhibited male orgasm The inability to ejaculate in the vagina, even with full arousal and penile erection

inhibited orgasm A sexual dysfunction in which the person is unable to achieve orgasm during coitus with adequate stimulation after entering the excitement phase of the sexual response cycle

inhibited sexual excitement A sexual dysfunction characterized by erectile dysfunction in men, or by an inability to attain or sustain arousal in women

insanity defense The legal argument used by the defendant who has committed a crime, but pleads not guilty because of a mental disturbance

insight The ability to understand the basis of one's motivations, perceptions, and behavior

instinct An unlearned behavior pattern

insulin shock treatment An early treatment for schizophrenia in which insulin was injected into the patient, causing convulsions and a coma

intelligence quotient (IQ) A number used to express a person's relative intelligence as assessed by a standardized test, such as the Stanford-Binet or Wechsler scales

intermittent explosive disorder Loss of control over aggressive impulses, resulting in serious assaults or destruction

internal validity In an experiment, the extent to which changes in the dependent variable are actually brought about by the independent variable (rather than extraneously)

introjection In Freudian theory, the process by which a depressed person identifies with the faults of the loved one he or she has lost

introversion-extroversion A personality dimension; introverts are inhibited, less sociable, and quick to learn; extroverts are more sociable, impulsive, and slow to learn

in vivo Taking place in actuality, rather than in the imagination

involuntary commitment Hospitalization, without the person's consent, if he or she is judged to be mentally disturbed and dangerous or incapacitated

irresistible impulse test One of the tests of insanity, which states that a defendant is not criminally responsible if he or she lacked the will power to control his or her behavior

Jacksonian seizures A form of epileptic seizure in which a twitch develops in one part of the body and spreads; loss of consciousness does not usually occur

kleptomania An impulse control disorder in which the person recurrently fails to resist impulses to steal objects

Klinefelter syndrome A disorder in males caused by an excessive number of X chromosomes, sometimes causing mental retardation

Korsakoff's disease See *alcohol amnestic disorder*

lacerations Brain traumas in which brain tissue is torn, pierced, or ruptured, usually by an object that has penetrated the skull

latency stage In Freudian theory, the psychosexual stage that occurs between six and twelve years of age and is generally devoid of sexual motivation

law of effect An increase in behaviors associated with positive consequences, and a reduction when associated with unpleasant consequences

lead poisoning A postnatal cause of retardation produced by an infant's ingestion of lead-based or lead-containing substances

learned helplessness Acquisition of the belief that one is helpless and cannot affect outcomes in one's life

least intrusive form of treatment A concept recognizing that patients may have a right to more benign forms of treatment (psychotherapy) before more severe measures (ECT, medication, etc.) are considered

least restrictive environment A patient's right to the least restrictive situation that is appropriate to his or her condition

libido In Freudian theory, the energy of the id, often associated with the sexual drive

life change model Hypothesis that all life changes can act as stressors

life instincts In Freudian theory, the drives associated with sex and self-preservation; Eros

limbic system The part of the brain involved with experiencing and expressing emotions

lobotomy Severing of the fibers between the frontal lobes and the thalamus or hypothalamus

localized amnesia The most common type of amnesia; the inability to recall all events during a specific period

longitudinal fissure Separation between the left and right hemispheres of the brain

loosening of associations Continual shifting of thoughts from topic to topic without any apparent logical or meaningful connection among topics (see also *cognitive slippage*)

Luria-Nebraska Neuropsychological Battery A relatively inexpensive standardized test used in screening for brain damage and in pinpointing damaged areas

lycanthropy A form of hysteria that historically occurred in rural areas, where individuals believed that they were wolves

lysergic acid diethylamide (LSD) A strong hallucinogen

magnetic resonance imaging (MRI) A technique to assess brain functioning, using a magnetic field end radio waves to produce pictures of the brain

mainstreaming Integrating mental patients back into the community as soon as possible

major depression A major mood disorder in which only depression and not mania has been exhibited (see also *unipolar disorders*)

malingering Faking an illness to obtain a goal

mania An emotional state characterized by great elation, seemingly boundless energy, and irritability

marijuana The mildest and most commonly used hallucinogen; pot

marital schism An antagonistic marital relationship characterized by threats of separation and divorce, mutual distrust, and attempts to coerce the children into siding with one parent or the other

marital skew A marriage in which the serious pathology of one parent dominates the family

marital therapy A treatment aimed at helping couples understand and clarify their communications, role relationships, unfulfilled needs, and unrealistic expectations

marriage counseling A professional field of psychology concerned with improving interaction and communication between husband and wife

masochism A sexual disorder in which erotic or sexual gratification is obtained by receiving pain or humiliation

mass madness Group hysteria

medical model A model of psychopathology that conceptualizes abnormal behavior in the same way as physical disorder

meiosis The process by which the 23 pairs of chromosomes in each parent separate so that the egg and sperm contain only 23 chromosomes each

melancholia Biologically caused depression characterized by loss of pleasure in all activities, weight loss, and guilt

meningitis Inflammation of the membrane surrounding the brain and spinal cord; can produce cerebral infarction and seizures

mental disorder (or mental disturbance) Any of a range of recognizable patterns of abnormal behavior

mental retardation Substandard intellectual functioning accompanied by deficiencies in adaptive behavior, with onset before age eighteen

mesmerism A treatment developed by Anton Mesmer that induced a sleeplike state; considered to be the forerunner of modern hypnotism

methadone A drug prescribed during heroin detoxification to decrease the intensity of withdrawal symptoms

microcephaly An anomaly characterized by an unusually small brain; found in some children with fetal alcohol syndrome

migraine headache Severe headache resulting from constriction and then dilation of the cerebral blood vessels

milieu therapy A therapy program in which the hospital environment operates as a community and patients have decision-making responsibilities

Minnesota Multiphasic Personality Inventory (MMPI) An objective personality inventory used widely in clinical settings to assess psychological disturbances

model An analogy most often used to describe or explain something that cannot be directly observed

modeling The process of learning by observing models' behaviors

modeling therapy A therapeutic approach to phobias in which the phobic individual observes a fearless model coping with the fear-producing situation

monoamine oxidase (MAO) inhibitor An antidepressant compound believed to correct the balance of neurotransmitters in the brain

monozygotic (MZ) twins (identical) Genetically identical twins who developed from a single fertilized egg

mood disorders Severe disturbances of mood in which depression is almost always the primary event

moral treatment movement A shift to more humane treatment of the mentally disturbed; its initiation is generally attributed to Philippe Pinel

moralistic anxiety In Freudian theory, anxiety produced when an individual does not live up to his or her own moral standards

multi-infarct dementia An organic brain syndrome characterized by uneven deterioration of intellectual abilities and resulting from a number of cerebral infarctions

multimodal behavior therapy A model of psychotherapy that advocates using a variety of concepts, methods, and strategies from behavioral as well as cognitive and affective theories

multiple-baseline design A type of single-subject experiment that involves recording multiple behaviors, serially applying the same modification to each behavior, and measuring any changes that occur

multiple personality A disorder in which two or more relatively distinct personalities exist in one individual

narcissistic personality disorder A personality disorder characterized by an exaggerated sense of self-importance

narcotics Opium and its derivatives, which depress the central nervous system, provide relief from pain and anxiety, and are addictive

negative reinforcer In operant conditioning, an aversive event whose removal increases the frequency of a behavior

Neo-Freudians Psychologists whose ideas are strongly influenced by Freud's psychoanalytic model, but who have modified that model in various ways

neologisms New words typically formed by combining commonly used words; often invented by individuals with schizophrenia

neuroleptics Antipsychotic drugs that produce symptoms resembling neurological conditions

neuron Nerve cell

neurosis Formerly a category of mental disorders including the present anxiety, dissociative, and somatoform disorders; now generally a less severe mental disorder; no longer listed as a DSM category

neurotic anxiety In Freudian theory, anxiety produced when the ego loses control over the id's wild impulses

neurotransmitter Substances that contribute to the transmission of nerve impulses from one neuron to another

nicotine A stimulant found in tobacco

night hospital program A program that allows patients to carry on their normal activities during the day while remaining institutionalized at night

nomothetic orientation The scientific approach taken by experimenters who study large groups of individuals to find common laws and principles

nonbeing An existential concept referring to the awareness that human beings have of their impending death; this awareness is the source of *existential anxiety*

norepinephrine A catecholamine neurotransmitter substance

object relations Past interpersonal relations that shape and affect the individual's current interactions with people

objective personality test An inventory of personality attributes in which the test-taker either agrees or disagrees with specific self-descriptive statements

observational learning Acquisition of new behaviors by watching someone else perform them

observational learning theory A theory of learning that proposes that individuals can learn new behaviors by observing other people perform those behaviors and then imitating them

obsession An intrusive, uncontrollable, and persistent thought

obsessive-compulsive disorder An anxiety disorder characterized by intrusive and uncontrollable thoughts, or the need to perform specific acts repeatedly, or both

obsessive-compulsive personality disorder A personality disorder characterized by inability to express warm feelings, perfectionism, indecision, devotion to detail, and a lack of personal warmth

Oedipus complex In Freudian theory, a process during which a male child desires sexual possession of his mother and wants to eliminate his father; eventually resolved by identification with the father

operant behavior A voluntary and controllable behavior that effects a change in the individual's environment

operant conditioning A theory of learning, applying primarily to voluntary behaviors, proposing that these behaviors are controlled by the consequences that follow them, and that new behaviors are learned through reinforcement

operational definition Description of a concept in terms of the operation used to measure it

oppositional defiant disorder (ODD) A childhood disorder characterized by negativistic, argumentative, and hostile behavior toward adults

oral stage In Freudian theory, the stage during the first year of life in which the primary source of pleasure involves the mouth and lips

organicity Brain damage or deterioration

organic mental disorder A behavioral disturbance that results from organic brain pathology—that is, damage to the brain

organic mental syndrome A pattern of psychological or behavioral signs or symptoms associated with organic causes

organic retardation Generally more severe mental retardation that is a consequence of a physiological or anatomical defect

orgasm The pleasurable culmination of sexual arousal that is usually accompanied by ejaculation in males and vaginal contraction in females

orgasmic reconditioning A behavioral technique aimed at increasing appropriate heterosexual arousal

outpatient program A program that allows patients to return to their homes in the community while still receiving therapeutic services from the hospital

overanxious disorder A childhood disorder characterized by excessive worry about past or future events, overconcern about performance, and constant need for reassurance

overselective attention The tendency of an autistic child to focus on only one kind of stimulus or cue, such as either auditory or visual cues but not both

panic disorder An anxiety disorder characterized by severe and frightening episodes of apprehension and feelings of impending doom

paranoid personality disorder A personality disorder characterized by unwarranted suspiciousness, hypersensitivity, lack of emotion, and preoccupation with unfounded beliefs

paranoid pseudocommunity The delusional fantasy world of a paranoid, constructed from subjective interpretations

paranoid schizophrenia A schizophrenic disorder characterized by persistent and systematized delusions

paraphilias Sexual disorders in which unusual or bizarre acts, images, or objects are required for sexual arousal

paraprofessional therapists People who are taught by

professionals to provide some mental health services but who do not have formal mental health training

parasympathetic nervous system The part of the nervous system that controls metabolic function and conserves energy when the organism is at rest

parental management techniques Ways in which a parent can relate to a child, such as a means of supervision or discipline

Parkinson's disease A progressively worsening organic brain disorder characterized by muscle tremors, a stiff shuffling gait, lack of facial expression, and social withdrawal

passive-aggressive personality disorder A personality disorder characterized by the passive expression of aggression through stubbornness, inefficiency, procrastination, andresistance to reasonable demands

pathological gambling An impulse control disorder characterized by an inability to refrain from gambling

pedophilia A disorder in which an adult obtains erotic gratification through sexual contact with children

penis envy In Freudian theory, a condition in which females desire to possess a penis or demonstrate masculine characteristics

peptic ulcer An open sore within the digestive system

personality disorder A behavior pattern characterized by inflexible and maladaptive behaviors

person-centered therapy A humanistic therapy that emphasizes the kind of person the therapist should be in the therapeutic process, rather than the techniques that should be used

pervasive developmental disorders Severe disorders of childhood that affect language, social relationships, attention, perception, and affect; include autistic disorder and pervasive developmental disorder not otherwise specified

petit mal seizure A mild form of epileptic seizure in which there is a momentary dimming or loss of consciousness, sometimes with convulsive movements

phallic stage In Freudian theory, the third stage of life, during which the genital region becomes the focus of pleasurable sensations

phencyclidine (PCP) Hallucinogen that produces perceptual distortions, euphoria, nausea, confusion, delusions, and violent psychotic behavior

phenothiazines Drugs used to control thought disorders, affect, and hallucinations in schizophrenics

phenotype The observable results of the interaction between the genotype and the environment

phenylketonuria (PKU) A metabolic disorder, transmitted by a recessive gene, that causes abnormal substances to build up, and results in central nervous system damage and degeneration

phobia A strong, persistent, and unwarranted fear of a specific object or situation

placebo A chemically inert or inactive substance, administered to a patient who believes it is an active medication

placebo effects Positive responses to a drug that result from the patient's understanding of the drug's effect, faith in the doctor, or other psychological factors unrelated to the specific physiological action of the drug

pleasure principle The impulsive, pleasure-seeking aspect of our being, usually associated with the id, which seeks immediate gratification of instinctual needs regardless of moral or realistic concerns

positive reinforcer In operant conditioning, anything that increases the frequency of the response it follows

positron emission tomography (PET) A technique for assessing brain damage in which the patient is injected with radioactive glucose and the metabolism of the glucose is monitored

posthypnotic amnesia The inability to recall information as the result of a suggestion made to a person while under hypnosis

posttraumatic stress disorders An anxiety disorder that develops in response to an event that is "outside the range of normal" human experience; it is characterized by intrusive memories of the traumatic incident, emotional withdrawal, and increased arousal levels

predisposition An inherited characteristic which favors the development of a certain condition, especially a disease

premature ejaculation Ejaculation before penile entry into the vagina, or so soon after entry that the sexual experience is unsatisfactory

premorbid Existing prior to the onset of mental disorder

preparedness A theory that humans are biologically predisposed to fears that were necessary for the survival of pretechnological man

primal therapy A therapy intended to help patients reexperience early psychological and physical injuries in their original form by encouraging them to express their emotions through violent thrashing, screams, and convulsions

primary prevention An effort to lower the incidence of new cases of behavioral disorders by strengthening resources that promote mental health and eliminating features that threaten mental health

privileged communication In therapy, it regulates privacy protection and prevents clients from having their confidential communications disclosed without their permission

proband In genetic study, an individual with the trait that is under investigation

problem-solving therapy A form of cognitive-behavioral therapy aimed at providing clients with strategies for dealing with specific problems encountered in life

prognosis A prediction of the future course of an untreated disorder

projection A defense mechanism in which a person handles unacceptable impulses by attributing them to others

projective personality test A personality assessment technique in which the test-taker is presented with ambiguous stimuli and is asked to respond to them in some way

prospective study A long-term study of a group of people, beginning before the onset of a disorder, to allow investigators to see how the disorder develops

psychiatric epidemiology The study of the rate and distribution of psychopathological reactions in the population and the relationship of the reactions to the stressors

psychiatric social worker A social worker trained to work with clients who have mental disorders and with their families

psychiatry A medical specialty dealing with the prevention, diagnosis, treatment, and cure of mental disorders

psychoactive substance use disorder Maladaptive behavior associated with the pathological use of a substance over a period of at least one month

psychoanalysis Therapy based on the Freudian view that unconscious conflicts must be aired and understood by the patient if abnormal behavior is to be eliminated

psychoanalytic model The view that adult disorders arise from the unconscious operation of repressed anxieties originally experienced during childhood

psychodiagnosis An attempt to describe, assess, and systematically draw inferences about an individual's psychological disorder

psychodrama A group therapy in which patients and other persons role-play situations

psychogenic amnesia A dissociative disorder characterized by the inability to recall information of personal significance, usually after a traumatic event

psychogenic fugue A dissociative disorder in which psychogenic amnesia is accompanied by flight from familiar surroundings (also called *fugue state*)

psychogenic pain disorder A somatoform disorder characterized by severe pain that has a psychological rather than physical basis; psychalgia

psychogenic view The belief or theory that mental disorders are caused by psychological and emotional factors

psychological autopsy A systematic examination of existing information in order to understand and explain the behavior exhibited by an individual prior to his or her death

psychological test Any test instrument used to assess maladaptive behavior, development of personality, social skills, intellectual abilities, vocational interest, or brain damage

psychometrics Mental measurement, including its study and techniques

psychomotor seizures A form of epilepsy characterized by loss of contact with the environment during which the individual may engage in well-organized and apparently normal behavioral sequences

psychopath An individual with an antisocial personality

psychopathology Abnormal behavior

psychopharmacology The study of the effects of drugs on the mind and on behavior

psychophysiological disorder A physical disorder that has a strong psychological basis or component

psychosexual stages In Freudian theory, the developmental sequence through which all people move; experiences during these stages are responsible for adult personality

psychosis A severe mental disorder in which there is a loss of contact with reality or a significant distortion of reality

psychosurgery Brain surgery performed for the purpose of correcting severe mental disorder

psychotherapy The systematic application of techniques derived from psychological principles, for the purpose of helping psychologically troubled people; includes both insight-oriented and action-oriented therapies

punishment In operant conditioning, either the removal of a positive reinforcer or the presentation of an aversive stimulus to reduce the frequency or probability of a response

pyromania An impulse control disorder characterized by deliberate fire-setting on more than one occasion

racism Discrimination and prejudice aimed at a specific group that is considered inferior in some way

rape An act of intercourse that is accomplished through force or the threat of force

rational-emotive therapy (RET) The system therapy developed by Albert Ellis, which stress cognitive variables as the basis for treating psychological problems; believed to be the result of irrational thought patterns

rationalization A defense mechanism in which individuals justify their behavior through explanation

reaction formation A defense mechanism in which a dangerous impulse is repressed and converted to its direct opposite

reactive disorders Unusual or bizarre behaviors exhibited under stressful conditions

reactivity A situation in which people who know they are being observed or assessed change the way they respond

realistic anxiety In Freudian theory, anxiety arising from a potential danger from the external environment

reality principle That aspect of our being (ego) concerned with the realistic world and with mediating between our instinctual drives and the external environment

recessive gene A gene that produces a physical effect only when it is paired with an identical gene

recessive-gene disorder Genetic disorder caused by the pairing of two recessive genes, producing a disturbance or abnormality in the metabolic processes which, in turn, may produce a physical defect or mental retardation

regression A defense mechanism involving a retreat to an earlier developmental level in the face of stress

reinforcement In operant conditioning, a consequence that increases the frequency or magnitude of the behavior it follows; may be either positive or negative

relaxation training A therapeutic technique in which the person acquires the ability to relax the muscles of the body under almost any circumstances

relearning A characteristic of psychotherapy that refers to the client's opportunity to unlearn, develop, or change certain behaviors or levels of functioning

reliability The degree to which a procedure or test will yield the same result repeatedly, under the same circumstances

replication Repetition of an experiment to ensure that the results obtained in the original experiment are valid

repression A defense mechanism that prevents unacceptable desires from reaching consciousness and expels painful experiences from consciousness

residual schizophrenia A category of schizophrenic disorder reserved for people who have experienced at least one schizophrenic episode but do not now show prominent signs of schizophrenia

resistance The process during psychoanalysis in which the patient unconsciously attempts to impede the psychoanalysis by preventing the exposure of repressed material; tactics include silence, late arrival, or failure to keep an appointment

reticular activating system Bundle of nerve fibers connected to the higher brain centers; controls sleep, attention, and memory

reuptake The process by which a neurotransmitter is reabsorbed by the nerve cells

reversal (ABAB) design An experiment in which behaviors are measured at four times: (A) before the independent variable or treatment is introduced; (B) after the independent variable is introduced; (A) after the independent variable is withdrawn; and (B) after the reintroduction of the independent variable

Rorschach technique A projective technique employing symmetrical inkblots; subjects describe what they see in the blots and what characteristics make them see what they see

sadism A sexual disorder in which erotic gratification is obtained by inflicting pain or humiliation on others

schema A pattern of thinking or a cognitive set that determines (or colors) an individual's reactions and responses

schizoid personality disorder A personality disorder characterized by social isolation and emotional coldness

schizophrenia A group of disorders characterized by severe impairment of cognitive processes, personality disintegration, affective disturbances, and social withdrawal

schizophreniform disorders Disorders similar to the schizophrenic disorders but shorter in duration—lasting no longer than six months

schizophrenogenic Causing or producing schizophrenia; generally used to describe a parent who is simultaneously or alternately cold and overprotecting, rejecting and dominating

schizotypal personality disorder A personality disorder characterized by such oddities of thinking and behavior as recurrent illusions, belief in the possession of magical powers, and digression or vagueness of speech

school phobia A type of separation anxiety whose symptoms may occur merely at the prospect of having to go to school

scientific method A method of inquiry that provides for the systematic collection of data through controlled observation, and the testing of hypotheses based on those data

secondary gain Indirect benefits from neurotic or other symptoms

secondary prevention An attempt to shorten the duration and reduce the impact of mental disorders

selective amnesia The inability to recall only some aspects of a situation due to some psychosocial stress

self The individual's sense of personal identity

self-actualization A humanistic term; one's motivation to actualize the self (realize one's full potential) and advance and grow

self-concept In humanistic thinking, how one views the self, how others relate to the self, and the values attached to it

self-control therapy A therapy approach that assumes people can actively modify their own behaviors by managing behavioral contingencies

senile dementia A severe loss of intellectual functioning that is produced by a deterioration of brain cells

sensitivity training groups (T-groups) A group therapy designed to help individuals increase their sensitivity to others and improve their human relations skills

separation anxiety disorder (SAD) A childhood disorder characterized by excessive anxiety over separating from parents or significant others

serotonin A catecholamine neurotransmitter substance

sex chromosomes Determinants of the sex of an individual; an XX pair of chromosomes produces a female; an XY combination produces a male

sexism Prejudice and discrimination directed against people of either sex, because of their sex

sexual desire disorder A sexual dysfunction involving a lack of sexual interest reflected in low levels of sexual activity and fantasizing

sexual dysfunction A disruption of any part of the normal sexual response cycle, in a male or female

shaping A systematic but incremental method of rewarding similar behavior for the purpose of attaining a desired but more complex behavior

simple phobia An extreme fear of a specific object or situation; a phobia not classed as either agoraphobia or a social phobia

simulation An investigative technique in which a real-life situation is recreated under controlled conditions

single-subject experiment An experiment performed on a single individual in which some aspect of that individual's own behavior is used as the control

socialized, group type conduct disorder A type of conduct disorder characterized by attachments to significant others and friends, and by displays of antisocial behaviors

solitary, aggressive type conduct disorder A type of conduct disorder in which the person is physically violent and is often socially isolated

social phobia An intense fear of being scrutinized

social supports The availability and quality of interpersonal resources that people can call on during emotional distress

somatization disorder A somatoform disorder in which the individual chronically complains of a number of symptoms for which no physiological basis can be found; also called *Briquet's syndrome*

somatoform disorders Mental disorders that involve complaints of physical symptoms that closely mimic authentic medical conditions but have no physiological basis; include somatization disorder, conversion disorder, somatoform pain disorder, and hypochondriasis

somatoform pain disorder A somatoform disorder characterized by pain that has a primarily psychological, rather than physical, basis; also called *psychalgia*

somnambulism Sleepwalking

splinter skills A characteristic of some autistic children that refers to a facility with drawing, puzzle construction, and rote memory but a lack of ability in verbal tasks, language skills, and symbolic thinking

Stanford-Binet Intelligence Scale An individual intelligence test used to assess cognitive development and functioning

statutory rape The seduction of a girl who has not yet reached the legal age of consent

stereotyped movement disorders Disorders that begin in childhood and are characterized by unusual and repetitive movements; include tics and Tourette's syndrome

stimulant A psychoactive substance that is a central nervous system energizer inducing elation, grandiosity, hyperactivity, agitation, and appetite suppression

stimulus control In classical and operant conditioning, the situation in which the occurrence or non-occurrence of a particular behavior is influenced by a preceding stimulus

stimulus discrimination The ability to differentiate between similar stimuli

stress A person's internal reaction to an external stimulus (stressor)

stressor A physical or psychological demand placed on a person by some external event or situation

stroke See *cerebrovascular accident*

structural family therapy A treatment in which the therapist helps clients to restructure the roles and relationships within a pathogenic family system

substance abuse A pathological pattern of excessive use of a substance, in which the person cannot reduce or cease intake despite physical harm or impaired social and occupational functioning

substance dependence A pathological pattern of inability to cut down or control use of a substance, despite knowledge of harmful effects; much time expended in obtaining the substance; frequent intoxication; tolerance or withdrawal symptoms

sudden death syndrome Unexpected abrupt death that may be brought on by stress; in most cases there is an underlying coronary condition

suicidal ideation Thoughts about taking one's own life

suicide The taking of one's own life

superego In Freudian theory, the purely moral facet of the personality, whose goals are idealistic rather than realistic

sympathetic nervous system A division of the nervous system that prepares the body for emergency action

symptom substitution The concept that if neurotic symptoms are eliminated without resolving or removing the underlying conflict, the individual will merely express the neurosis in other ways and exhibit other symptoms

synapse Location where one neuron communicates with another

syndrome A cluster of symptoms that tend to occur together and are believed to indicate a particular disorder

systematic desensitization A therapy in which relaxation is used to eliminate the anxiety associated with phobias and otherfear-evoking situations

tachycardia Speeding up of the heartbeat

tarantism A hysterical reaction in which people raved, danced, and had convulsions; common in the thirteenth century and attributed to the sting of the tarantula

tardive dyskinesia A syndrome characterized by involuntary and rhythmic movements of the protruding tongue, chewing, lip smacking, other facial movements, and sidewise jaw movements; a possible side effect of antipsychotic drugs

Tay-Sachs disease A recessive-gene metabolic disorder resulting in death; fatty substances accumulate in the brain and other tissues of the body

tension headache A headache that is thought to be produced by prolonged contraction of the scalp and neck muscles

tertiary prevention Efforts to facilitate the readjustment of a person to community life after hospital treatment for a mental disorder

thalamus The part of the brain stem that serves as a relay station, transmitting nerve impulses to other regions of the brain

Thematic Apperception Test (TAT) A projective test involving a series of pictures, most portraying scenes of two or more people; subjects make up a story about the pictures

theory A group of principles and hypotheses that together explain some aspect of a particular area of inquiry

therapeutic community A hospital environment in which all activities are structured to have a therapeutic function and in which patients participate to the extent possible

therapeutic relationship The interaction between therapist and client in which the therapist may provide reassurance, interpretations, self-disclosures, reflections of the client's feelings, or information, each at the appropriate time

therapy A program of systematic intervention whose purpose is to modify a client's behavioral, affective, or cognitive state

tic disorders Disorders with onset in childhood and characterized by involuntary and repetitive movements and/or vocalizations, including transient and chronic tic disorders and Tourette's syndrome

token economy A treatment program, based on principles of operant conditioning, that awards tokens for appropriate behaviors; patients can exchange tokens for hospital passes, special privileges, or food

tolerance A condition in which the body requires increasing doses of a substance in order to attain the desired effect, or a markedly diminished effect is experienced with regular use of the same dose

Tourette's syndrome A childhood disorder characterized by multiple motor and verbal tics that generally develop into coprolalia (compulsion to shout obscenities)

transactional analysis (TA) A technique of group therapy based on the assumption that people play certain games that hinder the development of genuine and deep interpersonal relationships

transaction model of stress Hypothesis that a person's perception of a stressor mediates its impact

transference A process during psychotherapy in which the patient reenacts early conflicts by carrying over and applying to the therapist feelings and attitudes that the patient had toward significant others (usually parents) in the past

transsexualism A person's self-identification with the opposite sex

transvestite fetishism A disorder in which the person feels intense sexual interests and urges to cross-dress; the person is highly distressed with these urges or has acted on them

trephining An ancient surgical technique in which part of the skull was chipped away to provide an opening through which evil spirits could escape

trichotillomania An impulse control disorder in which the person cannot resist pulling out his or her own hair

tricyclics Antidepressant compounds that relieve symptoms of depression

trisomy 21 The existence of an extra chromosome in pair Number 21; responsible for Down syndrome

Turner's syndrome A rare condition caused by the lack of one X chromosome in a female, resulting in severe space-form perceptual deficits

unconditional positive regard A humanistic concept referring to love and acceptance of an individual, regardless of his or her behavior

unconditioned response (UCR) In classical conditioning, the response first made to the unconditioned stimulus

unconditioned stimulus (UCS) In classical conditioning, the stimulus that elicits an unconditioned response

unconscious In Freudian theory, an area of unawareness into which repressed desires and memories are forced

undifferentiated schizophrenia A schizophrenic disorder characterized by mixed or undifferentiated symptoms that do not clearly fit the other types of schizophrenia

undoing A defense mechanism involving ritualistic and repetitive behaviors performed in an attempt to atone for misdeeds

unipolar disorder A major mood disorder in which only depression, and no mania, has been exhibited

vaginismus Involuntary contraction of the outer part of the vagina that restricts or prevents penile insertion

validity The degree to which a procedure or test actually performs the function that it was designed to perform

vicarious conditioning The development of an emotional response by observing reactions in others

voyeurism A disorder in which sexual gratification is obtained by surreptitiously observing nude people or couples engaged in coitus

Wechsler Adult Intelligence Scale The most widely used individual intelligence test

withdrawal symptoms Physical or emotional symptoms such as shaking or irritability that appear when the intake of a regularly used substance is reduced or halted

References

Aalpoel, P. N., & Lewis, D. J. (1984). Dissociative disorders. In H. E. Adams & Patricia B. Sutker (Eds.), *Comprehensive handbook of psychopathology*, pp. 223–249. New York: Plenum Press.

Abebimpe, V. R. (1981). Overview: White norms and psychiatric diagnosis of black patients. *American Journal of Psychiatry, 138*, 279–285.

Abebimpe, V. R., Chu, C. C., Klein, H. E., & Lange, M. H. (1982). Racial and geographic differences in the psychopathology of schizophrenia. *American Journal of Psychiatry, 139*, 888–891.

Abel, G. G., Barlow, D. H., Blanchard, E. B., & Guild, D. (1977). The components of rapists' sexual arousal. *Archives of General Psychiatry, 34*, 895–903.

Abel, G. G., Levis, D. J., & Clancy, J. (1970). Aversion therapy applied to taped sequences of deviant behavior in exhibitionism and other sexual deviations: A preliminary report. *Journal of Behavior Therapy and Experimental Psychiatry, 1*, 59–66.

Abels, N. (1986). Proceedings of the American Psychological Association, Incorporated, for the year 1985: Minutes of the Annual Meeting of the Council of Representatives. *American Psychologist, 41*, 631–663.

Abels, G. (1975). *The double bind: Paradox in relationships*. Unpublished doctoral dissertation, Boston University.

Abels, G. (1976). Researching the unresearchable: Experimentation on the double bind. In C. E. Sluzki & D. C. Ransom (Eds.), *Double bind: The foundation of the communication approach to the family*. New York: Grune & Stratton.

Abraham, K. (1948). Notes on psychoanalytic investigation and treatment of manic-depressive insanity and allied conditions. In D. Bryan & A. Strachey (Eds. and Trans.), *Selected papers of Karl Abraham, M.D.* London: Hogarth Press. (Original work published 1911.)

Abrams, R. & Essman, W. B. (1982). *Electroconvulsive therapy*. Jamaica, NY: Medical & Scientific Books.

Abrams, R., & Taylor, M. A. (1983). The genetics of schizophrenia: A reassessment using modern criteria. *American Journal of Psychiatry, 140*, 171–175.

Abramson, L. Y., Seligman, M. E. P., & Teasdale, J. D. (1978). Learned helplessness in humans: Critique and reformulation. *Journal of Abnormal Psychology, 87*, 49–74.

Achenbach, T. M., McConaughty, S. H., & Howell, C. T. (1987). Child/adolescent behavioral and emotional problems: Implications of cross-informant correlations for situational specificity. *Psychological Bulletin, 101*, 213–232.

Acosta, F. X. (1984). Psychotherapy with Mexican Americans: Clinical and empirical gains. In J. L. Martinez & R. H. Mendoza (Eds.), *Chicano psychology* (pp. 163–189). New York: Academic Press.

Ad Hoc Committee on Women. (1979). Principles concerning the counseling and therapy of women. *Counseling Psychologist, 8*, 21.

Adams, J., McIntosh, E., & Weade, B. L. (1973). Ethnic background, measured intelligence, and adaptive behavior scores in mentally retarded children. *American Journal of Mental Deficiency, 78*, 1–6.

Adams, P. R., & Adams, G. R. (1984). Mount St. Helen's Ashfall: Evidence for a disaster stress reaction. *American Psychologist, 39*, 252–260.

Adler, J., Hager, M., Zabarsky, M., Jackson, T., Friendly, D. T., & Abramson, P. (1984, April 23). The fight to conquer fear. *Newsweek*, pp. 66–72.

Ahles, T. A., Cassens, H. L., & Stalling, R. B. (1987). Private body consciousness, anxiety and the perception of pain. *Journal of Behavior Therapy and Experimental Psychiatry, 18*, 215–222.

Albee, G. W. (1979a). Anytime, anyplace. *APA Monitor, 10*, 31.

Albee, G. W. (1979b). Preventing prevention. *APA Monitor, 10*, 2.

Albee, G. W. (1983). Foreword. In R. D. Felner, L. A. Jason, J. N. Moritsugu, & S. S. Farber (Eds.), *Preventive psychology: Theory, research and practice*. New York: Pergamon Press.

Alexander, A. B. (1981). Asthma. In S. N. Haynes & L. Gannon (Eds.), *Psychosomatic disorders*, pp. 320–358. New York: Praeger.

Alexander, F. (1950). *Psychosomatic medicine*. New York: Norton.

Alexander, F. G., & Selesnick, S. T. (1966). *The history of psychiatry*. New York: Harper & Row.

Alexander, F. G., & Selesnick, S. T. (1966). *The history of psychiatry*. New York: Harper & Row.

Alford, G. S., Morin, C., Atkins M., & Schuen, L. (1987). Masturbatory extinction of deviant sexual arousal: A case study. *Behavior Therapy, 18,* 265–271.

Allison, R. B., & Schwartz, T. (1980). *Minds in many pieces: The making of a very special doctor*. New York: Rawson, Wade.

Alloy, L. B., Abramson, L. Y., Metalsky, G. I., & Hartlage, S. (1988). The hopelessness theory of depression: Attributional aspects. *British Journal of Clinical Psychology, 27,* 5–21.

Allport, G. W. (1937). *Personality: A psychological interpretation*. New York: Holt, Rinehart & Winston.

Alter-Reid, K., Gibbs, M. S., Lachenmeyer, J. R., Sigal, J., & Massoth, N. A. (1986). Sexual abuse of children: A review of the empirical findings. *Clinical Psychology Review, 6,* 249–266.

Altman, K., & Krupsaw, R. (1983). Suppressing aggressive-destructive behavior by delayed overcorrection. *Journal of Behavior Therapy and Experimental Psychiatry, 14,* 359–362.

Altrocchi, J. (1972). Mental health consultation. In S. E. Golann & C. Eisdorfer (Eds.), *Handbook of community mental health*. New York: Appleton-Century-Crofts.

Alyn, J. H. (1988). The politics of touch in therapy: A response to Willison and Masson. *Journal of Counseling and Development, 65,* 432–433.

Aman, M. G. (1984). Hyperactivity: Nature of the syndrome and its natural history. *Journal of Autism and Developmental Disorders, 14,* 39–56.

American Association of Retired Persons. (1985). *A profile of older Americans: 1985*. Washington, D.C.: American Association of Retired Persons.

American Bar Association. Standing Committee on Association Standards for Criminal Justice (1984). *Criminal justice and mental health standards*. Chicago: American Bar Association.

American Law Institute. (1962). *American Law Institute Model Penal Code, Section 4.01*. Philadelphia: American Law Institute.

American Psychiatric Association. (1952). *Diagnostic and statistical manual of mental disorders* (1st ed.). [DSM-I]. Washington, D.C.: American Psychiatric Association.

American Psychiatric Association. (1968). *Diagnostic and statistical manual of mental disorders* (2nd ed.). [DSM-II]. Washington, D.C.: American Psychiatric Association.

American Psychiatric Association. (1987). *Diagnostic and statistical manual of mental disorders* (3rd ed.). [DSM-III-R]. Washington, D.C.: American Psychiatric Association.

American Psychological Association. (1981). *Ethical principles of psychologists* (rev. ed.). Washington, D.C.: American Psychological Association.

American Psychological Association. (1985). *Directory*. Baltimore: Port City Press.

American Psychological Association Task Force on Sex Bias and Sex Role Stereotyping in Psychotherapeutic Practice. (1975). *American Psychologist, 30,* 1169–1175.

Ananth, J. (1976). Treatment of obsessive-compulsive neurosis: Pharmacological approach. *Psychosomatics, 17,* 180–184.

Anastasi, A. (1982). *Psychological testing*. New York: Macmillan.

Anderson, A., Hedblom, J., & Hubbard, F. (1983). A multidisciplinary team treatment for patients with anorexia nervosa and their families. *International Journal of Eating Disorders, 2,* 181–192.

Anderson, C. G., Ruth, D., Ayllon, T., & Kandel, H. (1987). Training and generalization of social skills with problem children. *Journal of Child and Adolescent Psychotherapy, 4,* 294–298.

Anderson, N. B., Lane, J. D., Muranaka, M., Williams, L. R. B., & Hoseworth, S. J. (1988). Racial differences in blood pressure and forearm vascular responses to the cold face stimulus. *Psychosomatic Medicine, 50,* 57–63.

Anderson, N. B., Lawrence, P. S., & Olson, T. W. (1981). Within-subject analysis of autogenic training and cognitive training in the treatment of tension headache pain. *Journal of Behavior Therapy and Experimental Psychiatry, 12,* 219–223.

Andreasen, N. C. (1984). *The broken brain*. New York: Harper & Row.

Andreasen, N. C. (1988). Brain imaging: Applications in psychiatry. *Science, 239,* 1381–1388.

Angell, M. (1985). Disease as a reflection of the psyche. *New England Journal of Medicine, 312,* 1570–1572.

Angrist, B., Rotrosen, J., & Gershon, S. (1980). Responses to apomorphine and amphetamine, and neuroleptics in schizophrenia subjects. *Psychopharmacology, 67,* 31–38.

Anonymous. (1983). First person account: Schizophrenia—a pharmacy student's view. *Schizophrenia Bulletin, 9,* 152–155.

Antonovsky, A. (1979). *Health, stress, and coping*. San Francisco: Jossey-Bass.

Aplin, D. Y., & Kane, J. M. (1985). Variables affecting pure tone and speech audiometry in experimentally simulated hearing loss. *British Journal of Audiology, 19,* 219–228.

Ardizzone, J., & Scholl, G. T. (1985). Mental retardation. In G. T. Scholl (Ed.), *The school psychologist and the exceptional child*. Reston, VA: Council for Exceptional Children.

Arkonac, O., & Guze, S. (1963). A family study of hysteria. *New England Journal of Medicine, 268,* 239–242.

Aronson, T. A. (1987). A naturalistic study of imipramine in panic disorder and agoraphobia. *American Journal of Psychiatry, 144,* 1014–1019.

Ash, P. (1949). The reliability of psychiatric diagnosis. *Journal of Abnormal and Social Psychology, 44,* 272–276.

Assalian, P. (1988). Clomipramine in the treatment of premature ejaculation. *Journal of Sex Research, 24,* 213–215.

Atlas, J. A., & Lapidus, L. B. (1987). Patterns of symbolic expression in subgroups of the childhood psychoses. *Journal of Clinical Psychology, 43,* 177–188.

Attorney General's Commission on Pornography. Final reports. (1986). Washington, D.C.: U.S. Department of Justice.

August, G. J., Stewart, M. A., & Tsai, L. (1981). The incidence of cognitive disabilities in the siblings of autistic children. *British Journal of Psychiatry, 138,* 416–422.

Ausubel, D. P. (1961). Causes and types of narcotic addiction: A psychosocial view. *Psychiatric Quarterly, 35,* 523–531.

Ayalon, M., & Mercom, H. (1985). The teacher interview. *Schizophrenia Bulletin, 11,* 117–120.

Ayllon, T., & Azrin, N. H. (1968). *The token economy: A motivational system for therapy and rehabilitation.* New York: Appleton-Century-Crofts.

Bakal, D. A. (1975). Headache: A biopsychological perspective. *Psychological Bulletin, 82,* 369–382.

Bales, J. (1988). New laws limiting duty to protect. *APA Monitor, 19,* 18.

Balon, R., Pohl, R., Yeragani, V. K., Rainey, J. M., & Berchou, R. (1988). Follow-up study of control subjects with lactate- and isoproterenol-induced panic attacks. *American Journal of Psychiatry, 145,* 238–241.

Bancroft, J. (1984). Testosterone therapy for low sexual interest and erectile dysfunctions in men: A controlled study. *British Journal of Psychiatry, 14,* 146–151.

Bandler, R., & Grinder, J. (1979). *The structure of magic.* Palo Alto, CA: Science and Behavior Books.

Bandura, A. (1969). *Principles of behavior modification.* New York: Holt, Rinehart & Winston.

Bandura, A., Blanchard, E., & Ritter, B. (1969). Relative efficacy of desensitization and modeling approaches for inducing behavioral, affective, and attitudinal changes. *Journal of Personality and Social Psychology, 13,* 173–199.

Bandura, A., & Rosenthal, T. L. (1966). Vicarious classical conditioning as a function of arousal level. *Journal of Personality and Social Psychology, 3,* 54–62.

Bandura, A., & Walters, R. H. (1963). Social learning and personality development. New York: Holt, Rinehart & Winston.

Banks, W. C. (1982). Deconstructive falsification: Foundations of a critical method in black psychology. In E. E. Jones & S. J. Korchin (Eds.), *Minority mental health.* New York: Praeger.

Barber, T. X. (1984). Hypnosis, deep relaxation, and active relaxation: Data, theory, and clinical applications. In R. Woolfolk & P. Lehrer (Eds.), *Principles and practice of stress management.* New York: Guilford Press.

Barchas, J., Berger, P., Ciaranello, R., & Elliott, G. (1977). *Psychopharmacology: From theory to practice.* New York: Oxford University Press.

Barker, J., & Webb, W. L. (1987). The difficult-to-treat eating-disordered patient. *Bulletin of the Menninger Clinic, 51,* 383–390.

Barlow, D. H., Abel, G., & Blanchard, E. (1979). Gender identity change in transsexuals. *Archives of General Psychiatry, 36,* 1001–1007.

Barlow, D. H., Cohen, A., Waddell, M., Vermilyea, B., Klosko, J., Blanchard, E., & DiNardo, P. (1984). Panic and generalized anxiety disorders: Nature and treatment. *Behavior Therapy, 15,* 431–449.

Barons, A. P., & Earls, F. (1984). The relation of temperament and social factors to behavior problems in three-year-old children. *Journal of Child Psychology and Psychiatry, 25,* 23–33.

Barraclough, B. M., Nelson, B., Bunch, J., & Sainsbury, P. (1969). *The diagnostic classification and psychiatric treatment of 180 suicides.* Proceedings of the Fifth International Conference for Suicide Prevention, London.

Barrera, M., & Ainlay, S. L. (1983). The structure of social support: A conceptual and empirical analysis. *Journal of Community Psychology, 11,* 133–143.

Barrett, C. L. (1969). Systematic desensitization versus implosive therapy. *Journal of Abnormal Psychology, 74,* 587–592.

Barron, F. (1963). *Creativity and psychological health.* Princeton, NJ: Van Nostrand.

Bartlett, K. (1984, August 26). Bulimia: The secret that becomes a compulsion. *Ann Arbor News,* p. F1.

Bassuk, E. L., Schoonover, S. C., & Gelenberg, A. J. (1983). *The practitioner's guide to psychiatric drugs* (2nd ed.). New York: Plenum.

Bates, J. E., Bentler, P. N., & Thompson, S. K. (1979). Gender-deviant boys compared with normal and clinical control boys. *Journal of Abnormal Child Psychology, 7,* 243–259.

Bateson, G. (1978). The birth of a matrix or double-bind and epistemology. In M. M. Berger (Ed.), *Beyond the double bind.* New York: Brunner/Mazel.

Bateson, G., Jackson, D., Haley, J., & Weakland, J. (1956). Toward a theory of schizophrenia. *Behavioral Science, 1,* 251–264.

Bauer, A. M., & Shea, T. M. (1984). Tourette's syndrome: A review and educational implications. *Journal of Autism and Developmental Disorders, 14,* 69–80.

Baum, M. (1970). Extinction of avoidance responding through response prevention (flooding). *Psychological Bulletin, 74,* 276–284.

Baum, S. K., & Boxley, R. L. (1983). Depression and old age identification. *Journal of Clinical Psychology, 39,* 584–590.

Baumeister, A. A. (1987). Mental retardation. *American Psychologist, 42,* 796–800.

Baumeister, R. F. (1988). Masochism as escape from self. *Journal of Sex Research, 25,* 28–59.

Beck, A. T. (1962). Reliability of psychiatric diagnosis: A critique of systematic studies. *American Journal of Psychiatry, 119,* 210–216.

Beck, A. T. (1963). Thinking and depression. *Archives of General Psychiatry, 9,* 324–333.

Beck, A. T. (1967). *Depression: Causes and treatment.* Philadelphia: University of Pennsylvania Press.

Beck, A. T. (1970). Cognitive therapy: Nature and relationship to behavior therapy. *Behavior Therapy, 1,* 184–200.

Beck, A. T. (1974). The development of depression: A cognitive model. In R. J. Friedman & M. M. Katz (Eds.), *The psychology of depression: Contemporary theory and research.* New York: Wiley.

Beck, A. T. (1976). *Cognitive therapy and emotional disorders.* New York: International Universities Press.

Beck, A. T. (1982). Cognitive therapy of depression: New perspectives. In P. Clayton & J. Barrett (Eds.), *Treatment of depression: Old controversies and new approaches.* New York: Raven.

Beck, A. T. (1985). Cognitive therapy, behavior therapy, psychoanalysis, and pharmacotherapy: A cognitive continuum. In M. Mahoney & A. Freeman (Eds.), *Cognition and psychotherapy.* New York: Plenum Press.

Beck, A. T., Laude, R., & Bohnert, M. (1974). Ideational components of anxiety neurosis. *Archives of General Psychiatry, 31,* 319–325.

Beck, A. T., Rush, A., Shaw, B., & Emery, G. (1979). *Cognitive therapy of depression.* New York: Guilford Press.

Beck, A. T., & Ward, C. H. (1961). Dreams of depressed patients: Characteristic themes in manifest content. *Archives of General Psychiatry, 5,* 462–467.

Beck, A. T., Emery, G., & Greenberg, R. L. (1985). *Anxiety disorders and phobias: A cognitive perspective.* New York: Basic Books.

Beck, S. J. (1953). The science of personality: Nomothetic or idiographic? *Psychological Review, 60,* 353–359.

Becker, J. (1974). *Depression: Theory and research.* Washington, D.C.: Winston-Wiley.

Becker, W. M., & Becker, P. (1983, May 30). Mourning the loss of a son. *Newsweek,* p. 17.

Bednar, R. L., & Kaul, T. J. (1978). Experiential group research: Current perspectives. In S. L. Garfield & A. E. Bergin (Eds.), *Handbook of psychotherapy and behavior change: An empirical analysis* (2nd ed.). New York: Wiley.

Beiser, M., Fleming, J. A. E., Iacono, W. G., Lin, T-Y. (1988). Redefining the diagnosis of schizophreniform disorder. *American Journal of Psychiatry, 145,* 695–700.

Bell, A. P., & Weinberg, M. S. (1978). *Homosexualities: A study of diversity among men and women.* New York: Simon & Schuster.

Bell, A. P., Weinberg, M. S., & Hammersmith, S. K. (1981). *Sexual preference: Its development in men and women.* Bloomington: Indiana University Press.

Bellack, A. S., & Hersen, M. (1980). *Introduction to clinical psychology.* New York: Oxford University Press.

Bellack, A. S., Hersen, M., & Himmelhoch, J. M. (1983). A comparison of social skills training, pharmacotherapy, and psychotherapy for depression. *Behavior Research & Therapy, 21,* 101–108.

Bellack, A. S., Hersen, M., & Turner, S. M. (1976). Generalization effects of social skills training in chronic schizophrenics: An experimental analysis. *Behavior Research and Therapy, 14,* 391–398.

Bemporad, J. R. (1979). Adult recollections of a formerly autistic child. *Journal of Autism and Developmental Disorders, 9,* 179–197.

Bender, L. (1938). A visual-motor Gestalt test and its clinical use. *American Orthopsychiatric Association Research Monographs, No. 3.*

Benjamin, H. (1967). Transvestism and transsexualism in the male and female. *Journal of Sex Research, 3,* 107–127.

Bennett, L. F. C., & Sherman, R. (1983). Management of childhood "hyperactivity" by primary care physicians. *Journal of Developmental and Behavioral Pediatrics, 4,* 88–93.

Bennun, I., & Schindler, L. (1988). Therapist and patient factors in the behavioural treatment of phobic patients. *British Journal of Clinical Psychology, 27,* 145–150.

Benson, H., Shapiro, D., Tursky, B., & Schwartz, G. (1971). Decreased systolic blood pressure through operant conditioning techniques in patients with essential hypertension. *Science, 173,* 740–742.

Berger, P. A. (1978). Medical treatment of mental illness. *Science, 200,* 974–981.

Berger, S. M. (1962). Conditioning through vicarious instigation. *Psychological Review, 69,* 450–466.

Bergin, A. E. (1971). The evaluation of therapeutic outcomes. In A. E. Bergin & S. L. Garfield (Eds.),

Handbook of psychotherapy and behavior change: An empirical analysis. New York: Wiley.

Bergin, A. E. (1980). Psychotherapy and religious values. *Journal of Consulting and Clinical Psychology, 48,* 95–105.

Bergin, A. E. & Lambert, M. J. (1978). The evaluation of therapeutic outcomes. In S. L. Garfield & A. E. Bergin (Eds.), *Handbook of psychotherapy and behavior change: An empirical analysis* (2nd ed.). New York: Wiley.

Berkowitz, A., & Perkins, H. W. (1988). Personality characteristics of children of alcoholics. *Journal of Consulting and Clinical Psychology, 56,* 206–209.

Berkwitz, N. J. (1974). Up-to-date review of theories of shock therapies. *Diseases of the Nervous System, 35,* 523–527.

Berlin, F. S., & Meinecke, C. F. (1981). Treatment of sex offenders with antiandrogenetic medication: Conceptualization, review of treatment modalities, and preliminary findings. *American Journal of Psychiatry, 138,* 601–607.

Berlow, S. J., Caldarelli, D. D., Matz, G. J., Meyer, D. H., & Harsch, G. G. (1981). Bacterial meningitis and SHL. *Laryngoscope, 4,* 1445–1452.

Berman, J., & Bernard, M. L. (1982). Factors related to suicidal behavior. *Journal of College Student Personnel, 23,* 409–413.

Berman, K. F., Weinberger, D. R., Shelton, R. C., Zec, R. F. (1987). A relationship between anatomical and physiological brain pathology in schizophrenia: Lateral cerebral ventricular size predicts cortical blood flow. *American Journal of Psychiatry, 144,* 1277–1282.

Bernard, J. (1976). Homosociality and female depression. *Journal of Social Issues, 32,* 213–238.

Berne, E. (1972). *What do you say after you say hello?* New York: Grove Press.

Bernstein, S. M., Steiner, B. W., Glaisler, J. T. D., & Muir, C. F. (1981). Changes in patients with gender identity problems after parental death. *American Journal of Psychiatry, 138,* 41–45.

Bestman, E. W. (1986). Cross-cultural approaches to service delivery to ethnic minorities: The Miami model. In M. R. Miranda & H. H. Kitano (Eds.), *Mental health research and practice in minority communities: Development of culturally sensitive training programs* (pp. 199–226). Washington, D.C.: U.S. Government Printing Office.

Bettelheim, B. (1967). *The empty fortress.* New York: Free Press.

Bick, P. A., & Kinsbourne, M. (1987). Auditory hallucinations and subvocal speech in schizophrenic patients. *American Journal of Psychiatry, 144,* 222–225.

Bild, R., & Adams, H. E. (1980). Modification of migraine headaches by cephalic blood volume pulse and EMG biofeedback. *Journal of Consulting and Clinical Psychology, 48,* 51–57.

Binder, L. M. (1986). Persisting symptoms after mild head injury: A review of the postconcussive syndrome. *Journal of Clinical and Experimental Neuropsychology, 8,* 323–346.

Blanchard, E. B., & Andrasik, F. (1982). Psychological assessment and treatment of headache: Recent developments and emerging issues. *Journal of Consulting and Clinical Psychology, 50,* 859–879.

Blanchard, R. (1988). Nonhomosexual gender dysphoria. *Journal of Sex Research, 24,* 188–193.

Blanchard, R., Racansky, I. G., & Steiner, B. W. (1986). Phallometric detection of fetishistic arousal in heterosexual male cross-dressers. *Journal of Sex Research, 22,* 452–462.

Blank, R. J. (1981). The partial transsexual. *American Journal of Psychiatry, 35,* 107–112.

Bleecker, E. R., & Engel, B. T. (1973). Application of operant conditioning techniques to the control of cardiac arrhythmias. In P. Obrist, A. Black, J. Brener, & L. DiCara (Eds.), *Contemporary trends in cardiovascular psychophysiology.* Chicago: Aldine-Atherton.

Bliss, E. L. (1980). Multiple personalities: A report of 14 cases with implications for schizophrenia and hysteria. *Archives of General Psychiatry, 39,* 823–825.

Bliss, E. L. (1984). Hysteria and hypnosis. *Journal of Nervous and Mental Disease, 172,* 203–208.

Bliss, E. L., Larson, E. M., & Nakashima, S. R. (1983). Auditory hallucinations and schizophrenia. *Journal of Nervous and Mental Disease, 171,* 30–33.

Bloom, B. L. (1972). Mental health program evaluation. In S. E. Golann & C. Eisdorfer (Eds.), *Handbook of community mental health.* New York: Appleton-Century-Crofts.

Bloom, B. L. (1977). *Community mental health: A general introduction.* Monterey, CA: Brooks/Cole.

Bloom, B. L., Asher, S. J., & White, S. W. (1978). Marital disruption as a stressor: A review and analysis. *Psychological Bulletin, 85,* 867–894.

Bloom, B. L., Hodges, W. F., & Caldwell, R. A. (1982). A preventive program for the newly separated: Initial evaluation. *American Journal of Community Psychology, 10,* 251–264.

Blumstein, S. (1981). Neurolinguistic disorders: Language-brain relationships. In S. Filskov & T. Boll (Eds.), *Handbook of Clinical Neuropsychology.* New York: Wiley.

Bockes, Z. (1987). "Freedom" means knowing you have a choice. In *Schizophrenia: The experiences of patients and families* (pp. 40–42). Rockville, MD: National Institute of Mental Health.

Boersma, K., Den Hengst, S., Dekker, J., & Emmelkamp,

P. M. G. (1976). Exposure and response prevention in the natural environment: A comparison with obsessive-compulsive patients. *Behaviour Research and Therapy, 14,* 12–24.

Bogdan, R., & Taylor, S. (1976). The judged, not the judges: An insider's view of mental retardation. *American Psychologist, 31,* 47–52.

Bohman, M., Cloninger, R., von Knorring, A., & Sigvardsson, S. (1984). An adoption study of somatoform disorders. *Archives of General Psychiatry, 41,* 872–878.

Boll, T. J. (1983). Neuropsychological assessment. In I. B. Weiner (Ed.), *Clinical methods in psychology.* New York: Wiley.

Boller, F., Kim, Y., & Detre, T. (1984). Assessment of temporal lobe disorder. In P. E. Logue & J. M. Schear (Eds.), *Clinical neuropsychology,* Springfield, IL: Thomas.

Booth, G. K. (1988). Disorders of impulse control. In H. H. Goldman (Ed.), *Review of general psychiatry* (pp. 381–390). Norwalk, CT: Appleton & Lange.

Bornstein, R. A., King, G., & Carroll, A. (1983). Neuropsychological abnormalities in Gilles de la Tourette's syndrome. *Journal of Nervous and Mental Disorders, 171,* 497–502.

Bower, B. (1987). Images of obsession. *Science News, 131,* 236–237.

Bowers, M. B. (1981). Biochemical processes in schizophrenia: An update. In S. J. Keith & L. R. Mosher (Eds.), *Special report: Schizophrenia 1981* (pp. 27–37). Washington, D.C.: U.S. Government Printing Office.

Bozzuto, J. C. (1975). Cinematic neurosis following *The Exorcist. Journal of Nervous and Mental Disease, 161,* 43–48.

Bradford, J. W., & Smith, S. M. (1979). Amnesia and homicide: The Padula case and a study of thirty cases. *Bulletin of the American Academy of Psychiatry and Law, 7,* 219–231.

Brady, R. J. (1975). *Emergency psychiatric care: Management of mental health crises.* Bowie, MD: Charles Press.

Braginsky, B. M., & Braginsky, D. D. (1973). The mentally retarded: Society's Hansels and Gretels. *Psychology Today, 7,* 18–20.

Braginsky, B. M., Grosse, M., & Ring, K. (1966). Controlling outcomes through impression management: An experiential study of the manipulative tactics of mental patients. *Journal of Consulting Psychology, 30,* 295–300.

Brammer, L. M., & Shostrom, E. (1984). *Therapeutic psychology.* Englewood Cliffs, NJ: Prentice-Hall.

Brandsma, J. (1979). *Outpatient treatment of alcoholism.* Baltimore: University Park Press.

Bratter, T. (1973). Treating alienated, unmotivated, drug-abusing adolescents. *American Journal of Psychotherapy,* 585–599.

Braucht, G. (1982). Problem drinking among adolescents: A review and analysis of psychosocial research. In National Institute on Alcohol Abuse and Alcoholism, *Alcohol Monograph 4: Special Population Issues.* Washington, D.C.: U.S. Government Printing Office.

Braucht, G., Follingstad, D., Brakarsh, D., & Berry, K. (1973). A review of goals, approaches, and effectiveness, and a paradigm for evaluation. *Quarterly Journal on the Study of Alcoholism, 34,* 1279–1292.

Braun, B. G. (1984). Hypnosis creates multiple personality: Myth or reality? *International Journal of Clinical and Experimental Hypnosis, 32,* 191–197.

Braun, P., Kochonsky, G., Shapiro, R., Greenberg, S., Gudeman, J. E., Johnson, S., & Shore, M. F. (1981). Overview: Deinstitutionalization of psychiatric patients: A critical review of outcome studies. *American Journal of Psychiatry, 138,* 736–749.

Bregman, E. D. (1934). An attempt to modify the emotional attitudes of infants by the conditioned response technique. *Journal of Genetic Psychology, 45,* 169–198.

Breier, A., Albus, M., Pickar, D., Zahn, T. P., Wolkowitz, O. M., & Paul, S. M. (1987). Controllable and uncontrollable stress in humans: Alterations in mood and neuroendocrine and psychophysiological function. *American Journal of Psychiatry, 144,* 1419–1425.

Breier, A., & Strauss, J. S. (1983). Self-control in psychotic disorders. *Archives of General Psychiatry, 40,* 1141–1145.

Brett-Jones, J., Garety, P., & Hemsley, D. (1987). Measuring delusional experiences: A method and its application. *British Journal of Clinical Psychology, 26,* 257–265.

Breuer, J., & Freud, S. (1957). *Studies in hysteria.* New York: Basic Books. (Originally published 1895.)

Brink, M., & Grundlingh, E. M. (1976). Performance of persons with Down's syndrome on two projective techniques. *American Journal of Mental Deficiency, 81,* 265–270.

Brodsky, A. (1985). Sex between therapists and patients: Ethical gray areas. *Psychotherapy in Private Practice, 3,* 57–62.

Broman, S. H., Nichols, P. L., & Kennedy, W. A. (1975). *Preschool IQ: Prenatal and early developmental correlates.* Hillsdale, NJ: Erlbaum.

Bromet, E. J. (1984). Epidemiology. In A. S. Bellack & M. Hersen (Eds.), *Research methods in clinical psychology* (pp. 266–282). New York: Pergamon Press.

Brooks, D. S., Murphy, D., Janota, I., & Lishman, W. A. (1987). Early-onset Huntington's chorea. *British Journal of Psychiatry, 151,* 850–852.

Brotman, A. W., & Stern, T. A. (1983). Case study of

cardiovascular abnormalities in anorexia nervosa. *American Journal of Psychiatry, 140,* 1227–1228.

Broverman, I. K., & Broverman, D. (1970). Sex role stereotypes and clinical judgments of mental health. *Journal of Consulting and Clinical Psychology, 34,* 1–7.

Broverman, I. K., Vogel, S. R., Broverman, D. M., Clarkson, F. E., & Rosenkrantz, P. S. (1972). Sex-role stereotypes: A current reappraisal. *Journal of Social Issues, 28,* 59–78.

Brown, M. (1982). Maintenance and generalization issues in skills training with chronic schizophrenics. In J. Curran & P. Monti (Eds.), *Social skills training.* New York: Guilford Press.

Brownell, K. D. (1982). Behavioral medicine. In C. M. Franks, G. T. Wilson, P. C. Kendall, & K. D. Brownell (Eds.), *Annual Review of Behavior Therapy: Theory and Practice (Vol. 8).* New York: Guilford Press.

Bruch, H. (1978). Obesity and anorexia nervosa. *Psychosomatics, 19,* 208–221.

Bruch, H. (1982). Anorexia nervosa: Therapy and theory. *American Journal of Psychiatry, 139,* 1531–1538.

Buchanan, A., & Oliver, J. E. (1977). Abuse and neglect as a cause of mental retardation. *British Journal of Psychiatry, 131,* 458–467.

Buckner, H. T. (1970). The transvestic career path. *Psychiatry, 33,* 381–389.

Bulhan, H. A. (1985). Black Americans and psychotherapy: The dilemma. *Psychotherapy, 22,* 370–378.

Bullard-Bates, P. C., & Satz, P. (1983). A case of pathological left-handedness. *Clinical Neuropsychology, 5,* 128–135.

Bunney, W. E., Pert, A., Rosenblatt, J., Pert, C. B., & Gallaper, D. (1979). Mode of action of lithium: Some biological considerations. *Archives of General Psychiatry, 36,* 898–901.

Burgess, A. W., Groth, A. N., & McCausland, M. P. (1981). *American Journal of Orthopsychiatry, 51,* 110–119.

Burgess, A. W., Hartman, C. R., McCausland, M. P., Powers, P. (1984). Response pattern in children and adolescents exploited through sex rings and pornography. *American Journal of Psychiatry, 141,* 656–662.

Burgess, A. W., & Holmstrom, L. L. (1979b). Rape: Sex disruption and recovery. *American Journal of Orthopsychiatry, 49,* 648–657.

Burgess, A. W., & Holmstrom, L. L. (1979a). Adaptive strategies and recovery. *American Journal of Orthopsychiatry, 136,* 1278–1282.

Burman, B., Mednick, S. A., Machon, R. A., Parnas, J., & Schulsinger, F. (1987). Children at high risk for schizophrenia: Parents and offspring perceptions of family relationships. *Journal of Abnormal Psychology, 96,* 364–366.

Burton, A. (1972). *Interpersonal psychotherapy.* Englewood Cliffs, NJ: Prentice-Hall.

Buss, A. H. (1966). *Psychopathology.* New York: Wiley.

Butler, G., Cullington, A., Munby, M., Amies, P., & Gelder, M. (1984). Exposure and anxiety management in the treatment of social phobia. *Journal of Consulting and Clinical Psychology, 52,* 642–650.

Butler, G., Gelder, M., Hibbert, G., Cullington, A., & Klimes, I. (1987). Anxiety management: Developing effective strategies. *Behaviour Research and Therapy, 25,* 517–522.

Butler, G., & Mathews, A. (1983). Cognitive processes in anxiety. *Advances in Behavior Research and Therapy, 5,* 51–62.

Butler, R. N. (1984). Senile dementia: Reversible and irreversible. *Counseling Psychologist, 12,* 75–79.

Cadoret, R. J., & Cain, C. (1981). Environmental and genetic factors in predicting adolescent antisocial behavior in adoptees. *Psychiatric Journal of the University of Ottawa, 6,* 220–225.

Calhoun, K. S., Atkeson, B. M., & Resick, P. A. (1982). A longitudinal examination of fear reactions in victims of rape. *Journal of Counseling Psychology, 29,* 655–661.

Calhoun, L. G., Selby, J. W., & Selby, L. E. (1982). The psychological aftermath of suicide: An analysis of current evidence. *Clinical Psychology Review, 2,* 409–420.

Cameron, N. A. (1959). Paranoid conditions and paranoia. In S. Arieti (Ed.), *American handbook of psychiatry.* New York: Basic Books.

Campbell, D., Sanderson, R. E., & Laveny, S. G. (1964). Characteristics of a conditioned response in human subjects during extinction trials following a single traumatic conditioning trial. *Journal of Abnormal and Social Psychology, 68,* 627–639.

Campbell, M. K. (1988). Fenfluramine treatment of autism. *Journal of Child Psychology and Psychiatry, 29,* 1–10.

Campbell, M. K., Small, A. M., Palij, M., Perry, R., Polonsky, B. B., Lukashok, D., & Anderson, L. T. (1987). The efficacy and safety of fenfluramine in autistic children: Preliminary analysis of a double-blind study. *Psychopharmacology Bulletin, 23,* 123–127.

Campbell, R. J. (1981). *Psychiatric dictionary* (5th ed.). New York: Oxford University Press.

Camus, A. (1946). *The stranger.* New York: Random House.

Caplan, P. J. (1984). The myth of a woman's masochism. *American Psychologist, 39,* 130–139.

Caplan, P. J., MacPherson, G. M., & Tobin, P. (1985). Do sex-related differences in spatial abilities exist? A multilevel critique with new data. *American Psychologist, 40,* 786–799.

Cappell, H., & Pliner, P. (1973). Volitional control of marijuana intoxication: A study of the ability to "come down" on command. *Journal of Abnormal Psychology, 82,* 428–434.

Capute, A. J. (1985). Mental retardation. In R. H. A. Haslam & P. J. Valletuti (Eds.), *Medical problems in the classroom* (pp. 199–220). Austin, TX: Pro-Ed.

Carey, W. B. (1986). The difficult child. *Pediatrics in Review, 9,* 287–298.

Carey, W. B. (1986). Interactions of temperament and clinical conditions. In M. Wolraich & D. Routh (Eds.), *Advances in developmental and behavioral pediatrics.* Greenwich, CT: JAI Press.

Carlson, B. E., & Davis, L. V. (1980). Prevention of domestic violence. In R. H. Price, R. F. Ketterer, B. C. Bader, & J. Monahan (Eds.), *Prevention in mental health: Research, policy, and practice.* Beverly Hills, CA: Sage.

Carlsson, A. (1978). Antipsychotic drugs, neurotransmitters, and schizophrenia. *American Journal of Psychiatry, 135,* 164–173.

Carpenter, L. W., Straus, J. S., & Mulch, S. (1973). Are there parthognomic symptoms in schizophrenia? *Archives of General Psychiatry, 28,* 847–852.

Carpenter, W. T., Jr., Heinrichs, D. W., Wagman, A. M. I. (1988). Deficit and nondeficit forms of schizophrenia: The concept. *American Journal of Psychiatry, 145,* 578–583.

Carr, A. T. (1974). Compulsive neurosis: A review of the literature. *Psychological Bulletin, 81,* 311–318.

Carr, E. G. (1977). The motivation of self-injurious behavior: A review of some hypotheses. *Psychological Bulletin, 84,* 800–816.

Carr, E. G., & Durand, V. M. (1987). See me, help me. *Psychology Today, 21,* 62–64.

Carter, C. H. (Ed.). (1975). *Handbook of mental retardation syndromes.* Springfield, IL: Thomas.

Casper, R. C., Eckert, E. D., Halmi, K. A., Goldberg, S. C., & Davis, J. M. (1980). Bulimia: Its incidence and clinical importance in patients with anorexia nervosa. *Archives of General Psychiatry, 37,* 1030–1035.

Cassel, J. (1974). Psychosocial processes and "stress": Theoretical formulations. *International Journal of Health Services, 4,* 471–482.

Cassileth, B. R., Lusk, E. J., Miller, D. S., Brown, L. L., & Miller, C. (1985). Psychosocial correlates of survival in advanced malignant disease? *New England Journal of Medicine, 312,* 1551–1555.

Caton, C. (1982). Effect of length of inpatient treatment for chronic schizophrenia. *American Journal of Psychiatry, 139,* 856–861.

Cautela, J. R. (1966). Treatment of compulsive behavior by covert sensitization. *Psychological Record, 16,* 33–41.

Cautela, J. R. (1967). Covert sensitization. *Psychological Reports, 20,* 459–468.

Chaika, E. (1985). Crazy talk. *Psychology Today, 30–35.*

Chance, P. (1987). *Saving grace. Psychology Today, 21,* 42–44.

Chapman, L. J., & Chapman, J. P. (1967). Genesis of popular but erroneous psychodiagnostic observations. *Journal of Abnormal Psychology, 72,* 193–204.

Chemtob, C. M., Hamada, R. S., Bauer, G., Torrigue, R. Y., & Kinney, B. (1988). Patient suicide: Frequency and impact on psychologists. *Professional Psychology: Research and practice, 19,* (4), 416–420.

Chesler, P. (1971). Men drive women crazy. *Psychology Today, 5,* 22–28.

Chesler, P. (1972). *Women and madness.* Garden City, NY: Doubleday.

Chesler, P. (1976). Patient and patriarch: Women in the psychotherapeutic relationship. In S. Cox (Ed.), *Female psychology: The emerging self.* Chicago: Science Research Associates.

Chess, S. (1986). Commentary on the difficult child. *Pediatrics in Review, 8,* 35–37.

Chess, S., & Thomas, A. (1984). *Origins and evolution of behavior disorders.* New York: Brunner/Mazel.

Chess, S., & Thomas, A. (1986). *Temperament in clinical practice.* New York: Guilford Press.

Chodorow, N. (1978). *The reproduction of mothering: Psychoanalysis and the sociology of gender.* Berkeley: University of California Press.

Chollar, S. (1988). Food for thought. *Psychology Today, 22,* 30–34.

Chu, F. D., & Trotter, S. (1974). *The madness establishment.* New York: Grossman.

Ciompi, L. (1980). Long-term study on the course of life and aging of schizophrenics. *Schizophrenia Bulletin, 6,* 606–618.

Clarizio, H. F., & McCoy, G. F. (1976). *Behavior disorders in children* (2nd ed.). New York: Crowell.

Clark, D., Salkovskis, P., & Chalkley, A. (1985). Respiratory control as a treatment for panic attacks. *Journal of Behavior Therapy and Experimental Psychiatry, 16,* 23–30.

Clark, D. M. (1986). A cognitive approach to panic. *Behaviour Research and Therapy, 24,* 461–476.

Clark, K. B., & Clark, M. K. (1947). Racial identification and preference in Negro children. In T. M. Newcomb & E. L. Hartley (Eds.), *Readings in social psychology.* New York: Holt, Rinehart & Winston.

Clark, M., Gosnell, M., Witherspoon, Huck, J., Hager, M., Junkin, D., King, P., Wallace, A., & Robinson, T. (1984, December 3). A slow death of the mind. *Newsweek,* pp. 56–62.

Clark, M., Gosnell, M., Hager, M., Shapiro, D., Norris, E., & Gordon, J. (1988, Spring). Headaches: How to ease the pain. *Newsweek on Health*, pp. 12–21.

Clarke, A. D. B., & Clarke, A. M. (1977). Prospects for prevention and amelioration of mental retardation: A quest editorial. *American Journal of Mental Deficiency, 81*, 523–533.

Clarke, A. D. B., & Clarke, A. M. (1987). Research on mental handicap, 1957–1958: A selective review. *Journal of Mental Deficiency Research, 31*, 317–328.

Cleckley, J. (1976). *The mask of sanity* (5th ed.). St. Louis, MO: Mosby.

Clinthorne, J. K., Cisin, I. H., Balter, M. B., Mellinger, G. D., Uhlenhuth, E. H. (1986). Changes in popular attitudes and beliefs about tranquilizers: 1970–1979. *Archives of General Psychiatry, 43*, 527–532.

Cloninger, C. R., Reich, T., Sigvardsson, S., Von Knorring, A. L., & Bohman, M. (1986). The effects of changes in alcohol use between generations or the inheritance of alcohol abuse. In American Psychological Association (Ed.) *Alcoholism: A medical disorder.* Proceedings of the 76th Annual Meeting of the American Psychological Association.

Coates, J. (1980, March 26). Pot more perilous than we thought. *Chicago Tribune*, pp. 1, 14.

Cobb, E. J., Leitenberg, H., & Burchard, J. D. (1982). Foster parents teaching foster parents: Communication and conflict resolution skills training. *Journal of Community Psychology, 10*, 240–249.

Cobb, S. (1976). Support as a moderator of life stress. *Psychosomatic Medicine, 38*, 300–314.

Coelho, G. V., Hamburg, D. A., & Murphy, E. G. (1963). Coping strategies in a new learning environment: A study of American college freshman. *Archives of General Psychiatry, 9*, 433–443.

Cohen, M. J., Rickles, W. H., & McArthur, D. L. (1978). Evidence for physiological response stereotypy in migraine headaches. *Psychosomatic Medicine, 40*, 344–354.

Cohen, S. L., & Fiedler, J. E. (1974). Content analyses of multiple messages in suicide notes. *Life-Threatening Behavior, 4*, 75–95.

Cohen, S. M., Allen, M. G., Pollen, W., & Hrubec, Z. (1972). Relationships of schizo-affective psychosis to manic depressive psychoses and schizophrenia. *Archives of General Psychology, 26*, 539–546.

Cohn, L. D., Adler, N. E., Irwin, C. E. Jr., Millstein, S. G., Kegeles, S. M., & Stone, G. (1987). Body-figure preferences in male and female adolescents. *Journal of Abnormal Psychology, 96*, 276–279.

Cole, J. O. (1964). Phenothiazine treatment in acute schizophrenia: Effectiveness. *Archives of General Psychiatry, 10*, 246–261.

Coleman, W. L., & Levine, M. D. (1988). Attention deficits in adolescence: Description, evaluation, and management. *Pediatrics in Review, 9*, 287–298.

Collins, B. E. (1970). *Social psychology.* Reading, MA: Addison-Wesley.

Comas-Diaz, L., & Griffith, E. E. (Eds.). (1988). *Clinical guidelines in cross-cultural mental health.* New York: Wiley.

Comings, D. E., & Comings, B. G. (1987). Hereditary agoraphobia and obsessive-compulsive behaviour in relatives of patients with Gilles de la Tourette's syndrome. *British Journal of Psychiatry, 151*, 195–199.

Commission on Obscenity and Pornography. (1970). *The report of the commission on obscenity and pornography.* New York: Bantam.

Committee on Drug Abuse of the Council on Psychiatric Services. (1987). Position statement on psychoactive substance use and dependence: Update on marijuana and cocaine. *American Journal of Psychiatry, 144*, 698–702.

Committee on the Review of Medicines (1980). Systematic review of the benzodiazepines. *British Medical Journal, 280*, 910–912.

Conant, J., Gordon, J., & Donovan, J. B. (1988). Scalpel slaves just can't quit. In *Newsweek on Health* (pp. 10–11). Livingston, NJ: Newsweek, Inc.

Conger, J. J. (1951). The effects of alcohol on conflict behavior in the albino rat. *Quarterly Journal of Studies on Alcohol, 12*, 1–30.

Consensus Development Panel. (1982). Defined diets and childhood hyperactivity. *Clinical Pediatrics, 21*, 627–630.

Cook, E. W. III, Hodes, R. L., & Lang, P. J. (1986). Preparedness and phobia: Effects of stimulus content on human visceral conditioning. *Journal of Abnormal Psychology, 95*, 195–207.

Coons, P. M. (1986). Treatment progress in 20 patients with multiple personality disorder. *Journal of Nervous Mental Disease, 174*, 715–721.

Coons, P. M., & Bradley, K. (1985). Group psychotherapy with multiple personality patients. *Journal of Nervous and Mental Diseases, 173*, 515–521.

Coons, P. M., Milstein, V., & Marley, C. (1982). EEG studies of two multiple personalities and a control. *Archives of General Psychiatry, 39*, 823–825.

Cooper, A. J. (1969). A clinical study of coital anxiety in male potency disorders. *Journal of Psychosomatic Research, 13*, 143–147.

Cooper, J. R., Bloom, F. E., & Roth, R. H. (1986). *The biochemical basis of neuropharmacology.* 5th ed. New York: Oxford University Press.

Cooper, M. L., Russell, M., & George, W. H. (1988). Coping, expectancies, and alcohol abuse: A test of social learning formulations. *Journal of Abnormal Psychology, 97*, 218–230.

Cooper, S. (1987). The fetal alcohol syndrome. *Journal of Child Psychology and Psychiatry, 28,* 223–227.

Corbett, J. A. (1971). The nature of tics and Gilles de la Tourette's syndrome. *Journal of Psychosomatic Research, 15,* 32.

Cordes, C. (1984). The plight of the homeless mentally ill. *APA Monitor, 15* (1), 13.

Corey, G., Corey, M. S., & Callahan, P. (1984). *Issues and ethics in the helping professions.* Monterey, CA: Brooks/Cole.

Corlis, R., & Rabe, P. (1969). *Psychotherapy from the center: A humanistic view of change and of growth.* Scranton, PA: International Textbook.

Coryell, W., Endicott, J., Andreasan, N. C., Keller, M. B., Clayton, P. J., Hirschfeld, R. M. A., Scheftner, W. A., & Winokur, G. (1988). Depression and panic attacks: The significance of overlap as reflected in follow-up and family study data. *American Journal of Psychiatry, 145,* 293–300.

Cosand, B. J., Bourque, L. B., & Kraus, J. F. (1982). Suicide among adolescents in Sacramento County, California 1950–1979. *Adolescence, 17,* 917–930.

Costello, C. G. (1982). Fears and phobias in women: A community study. *Journal of Abnormal Psychology, 91,* 280–286.

Courchesne, I., Yeung-Courchaesne, R., Press, G. A., Hesselink, J. R., & Jernigan, T. L. (1988). Hypoplasia of cerebellar vermal lobules VI and VII in autism. *New England Journal of Medicine, 318,* 1349–1354.

Cowart, V. S. (1988). The ritalin controversy: What made this drug's opponents hyperactive. *Journal of the American Medical Association, 259,* 2521–2523.

Cowen, E. L. (1982). Help is where you find it: Four informal helping groups. *American Psychologist, 37,* 385–395.

Cowen, E. L. (1983). Primary prevention in mental health: Past, present, and future. In R. D. Felner, L. A. Jason, J. N. Moritsugu, & S. S. Farber (Eds.), *Preventive psychology: Theory research and practice.* New York: Pergamon Press.

Cowen, E. L., Izzo, L. D., Miles, H. C., Teleschow, E. F., Trost, M. A., & Zax, M. (1963). A preventive mental health program in the school setting: Description and evaluation. *Journal of Psychology, 56,* 307–356.

Cox, D. J., & McMahon, B. (1978). Incidence of male exhibitionism in the United States as reported by victimized college students. *International Journal of Law and Psychiatry, 1,* 453–457.

Cox, W. M., & Klinger, E. (1988). A motivational model of alcohol use. *Journal of Abnormal Psychology, 97,* 168–180.

Coyne, J. C. (1976). Depression and the response of others. *Journal of Abnormal Psychology, 85,* 186–193.

Creer, T. L. (1982). Asthma. *Journal of Consulting and Clinical Psychology, 50,* 912–921.

Critchley, D. L. (1979). The adverse influence of psychiatric diagnostic labels on the observation of child behavior. *American Journal of Orthopsychiatry, 49,* 157–160.

Crowe, R. R., Noyes, R. Jr., Pauls, D. L., & Slymen, D. (1983). A family study of panic disorder. *Archives of General Psychiatry, 40,* 1065–1069.

Crowley, C., Crowley, D., & Clodfelter, C. (1986). Effects of a self-coping cognitive treatment for test anxiety. *Journal of Counseling Psychology, 33,* 84–86.

Csernansky, J. G., Holman, C. A., & Hollister, L. E. (1983). Variability and the dopamine hypothesis of schizophrenia. *Schizophrenia Bulletin, 9,* 325–328.

Cummings, N. A. (1984). The future of clinical psychology in the United States. *Clinical Psychologist, 37,* 19–20.

Curran, J., & Monti, P. (1982). *Social skills training: A practical handbook for assessment and treatment.* New York: Guilford Press.

Curtis, G. C. (1981). Sensory experiences during treatment of phobias by *in vivo* exposure. *American Journal of Psychiatry, 138,* 1095–1097.

Cutting, J. (1987). The phenomenology of acute organic psychosis. *British Journal of Psychiatry, 151,* 324–332.

Cutts, T. F., & Barrios, B. A. (1986). Fear of weight gain among bulimic and nondisturbed females. *Behavior Therapy 17,* 626–636.

Dahlstrom, W. G., & Welch, G. S. (1965). *An MMPI handbook.* Minneapolis: University of Minnesota Press.

Danto, B. L. (1971, Fall). Assessment of the suicidal person in the telephone interview. *Bulletin of Suicidology,* pp. 48–56.

Darrach, D. (1976, March 8). Poetry and poison. *Time.*

Darwin, C. (1859). *On the origin of the species by means of natural selection.* London: Murray.

Davidson, J., Allen, J. G., & Smith W. H. (1987). Complexities in the hospital treatment of a patient with multiple personality disorder. *Bulletin of the Menninger Clinic, 51,* 561–568.

Davidson, M., Keefe, R. S. E., Mohls, R. C., Siever, L. J., Losonczy, M. D., Horvath, T. B., & Davis, K. L. (1987). L-dopa challenge and relapse in schizophrenia. *American Journal of Psychiatry, 144,* 934–938.

Davis, J. D. (1983). Slaying the psychoanalytic dragon: An integrationist's commentary on Yates. *British Journal of Clinical Psychology, 22,* 133–134.

Davis, J. M., Klerman, G., & Schildkraut, J. (1967). Drugs used in the treatment of depression. In L. Efron, J. O. Cole, D. Levine, & J. R. Wittenborn (Eds.), *Psychopharmacology: A review of progress.* Washington, D.C.: U.S. Clearinghouse of Mental Health Information.

Davis, J. M. (1985). Suicidal crisis in schools. *School Psychology Review, 14,* 313–324.

Davis, J. M., Schaffer, C. B., Killian, G. A., Kinard, C., & Chan, C. (1980). Important issues in the drug treatment of schizophrenia. In S. J. Keith and L. R. Mosher (Eds.), *Special report: Schizophrenia 1981* (pp. 109–126). Washington, D.C.: U.S. Government Printing Office.

Davison, G. (1968). Elimination of a sadistic fantasy by a client-controlled counterconditioning technique: A case study. *Journal of Abnormal Psychology, 73,* 84–90.

Davison, G. (1974). *Homosexuality: The ethical challenge.* Presidential address at the meeting of the Association for the Advancement of Behavior Therapy, Chicago.

de Calazaro, D. (1981). *Suicide and self-damaging behavior: A sociobiologic perspective.* New York: Academic Press.

de Gobineau, A. (1915). *The inequality of human races.* New York: Putnam.

Deaux, K. (1984). From individual differences to social categories: Analysis of a decade's research on gender. *American Psychologist, 39,* 105–116.

Deffenbacher, J. L., & Hahnloser, R. M. (1981). Cognitive and relaxation coping skills in stress inoculation. *Cognitive Therapy and Research, 10,* 635–644.

DeJong, R. N., & Sugar, O. (1972). *The yearbook of neurology and neurosurgery.* Chicago: Year Book Medical Publishers.

Denicola, J., & Sandler, J. (1980). Training abusive parents in child management and self-control skills. *Behavior Therapy, 11,* 263–270.

Denkowski, K. M., & Denkowski, G. C. (1982). Client-counselor confidentiality: An update of rationale, legal status, and implications. *Personnel and Guidance Journal, 60,* 371–375.

DeSilva, P. (1988). Phobias and preparedness: Replication and extension. *Behaviour Research and Therapy, 26,* 97–98.

Deutsch, A. (1949). *The mentally ill in America.* 2nd ed. New York: Columbia University Press.

Devinsky, O., & Bear, D. (1984). Varieties of aggressive behavior in temporal lobe epilepsy. *American Journal of Psychiatry, 141,* 651–656.

Dick-Barnes, M., Nelson, R. O., & Aine, C. J. (1987). Behavioral measure of multiple personality: The case of Margaret. *Journal of Behavior Therapy and Experimental Psychiatry, 18,* 229–239.

Digman, J. T., Barrera, M., & West, S. G. (1986). Occupational stress, social support, and burnout among correctional officers. *American Journal of Community Psychology, 14,* 177–194.

Dimsdale, J. E., Pierce, C., Shoenfeld, D., Brown, A., Zusman, R., & Graham, R. (1986). Suppressed anger and blood pressure: The effects of race, sex, social class, obesity, and age. *Psychosomatic Medicine, 48,* 430–436.

Divorky, D. (1978, December). Behavior and food coloring: Lessons of a diet fad. *Psychology Today,* pp. 145–148.

Dix, G. E. (1984). Criminal responsibility and mental impairment in American criminal law: Response to the Hinckley acquittal in historical perspective. In D. N. Weisstub (Ed.), *Law and mental health: International perspectives* (pp. 1–44). New York: Pergamon Press.

Doane, J. A., West, M. J., Goldstein, M. J., & Rodnick, E. H. (1981). Parental communication deviance and affective style: Predictions of subsequent schizophrenia spectrum disorders in vulnerable adolescents. *Archives of General Psychiatry, 38,* 679–685.

Dohrenwend, B. P., & Dohrenwend, B. S. (1974). Social and cultural influences on psychopathology. *Annual Review of Psychology, 25,* 417–452.

Dohrenwend, B. P., & Dohrenwend, B. S. (1982). Perspectives on the past and future of psychiatric epidemiology: The 1981 Rema Lapouse Lecture. *American Journal of Public Health, 72,* 1271–1279.

Dohrenwend, B. S., & Dohrenwend, B. P. (1974). An approach to the problem of valid comparison of psychiatric disorders in contrasting class and ethnic groups from the general population. In M. Hammer, K. Salzinger, & S. Sutton (Eds.), *Psychopathology: Contributions from social, behavioral, and biological sciences.* New York: Wiley.

Dohrenwend, B. P., Dohrenwend, B. S., Gould, M. S., Link, B., Neugebauer, R., & Wunsch-Hitzig, R. (1980). *Mental illness in the United States: Epidemiological estimates.* New York: Praeger.

Dohrenwend, B. P., & Egri, G. (1981). Recent stressful life events and episodes of schizophrenia. *Schizophrenia Bulletin, 7,* 12–23.

Doll, E. A. (1953). *Measurement of social competence: A manual for the Vineland Social Maturity Scale.* Circle Pines, MN: American Guidance Service.

Dollinger, S. J. (1983). A case of dissociative neurosis (depersonalization disorder) in an adolescent treated with family therapy and behavior modification. *Journal of Consulting and Clinical Psychology, 15,* 479–484.

Donaldson, S., Gelenberg, A., & Baldessarini, R. (1983). The pharmacologic treatment of schizophrenia: A progress report. *Schizophrenia Bulletin, 9,* 504–527.

Donnerstein, E., Berkowitz, L., & Linz, D. (1986). Role of aggressive and sexual images in violent pornography. Unpublished manuscript, University of Wisconsin—Madison.

Donnerstein, E., & Linz, D. (1986). Mass media sexual

violence and male viewers. *American Behavioral Scientist, 29,* 601–618.

Draguns, J. G. (1985). Psychological disorders across cultures. In P. Pedersen (Ed.), *Handbook of cross-cultural counseling and therapy.* Westport, CT: Greenwood Press.

Drake, R. E., Ehrlich, J. (1985). Suicide attempts associated with akathisia. *American Journal of Psychiatry, 142,* 499–501.

Dressler, W. W., Dos Santos, J. E., & Viteri, F. E. (1986). Blood pressure, ethnicity, and psychosocial resources. *Psychosomatic Medicine, 48,* 509–519.

Drewnowski, A., Yee, D. K., & Krahn, D. D. (1988). Bulimia in college women: Incidence and recovery rates. *American Journal of Psychiatry, 145,* 753–755.

Dublin, L. I. (1963). *Suicide: A sociological and statistical study.* New York: Ronald Press.

Dubovsky, S., Franks, R., Lifschitz, M., & Coen, R. (1982). Effectiveness of verapamil in the treatment of a manic patient. *American Journal of Psychiatry, 139,* 502–504.

Dubow, E. F., Huesmann, L. R., & Eron, L. D. (1987). Mitigating aggression and promoting prosocial behavior in aggressive elementary school boys. *Behavior Research and Therapy, 25,* 527–531.

Dudley, J. R. (1987). Speaking for themselves: People who are labeled as mentally retarded. *Social Work, 32,* 80–82.

Durand, V. M., & Crimmins, D. B. (1987). Assessment and treatment of psychotic speech in an autistic child. *Journal of Autism and Developmental Disorders, 17,* 17–28.

Durand, V. M., & Crimmins, D. B. (1988). Identifying the variables maintaining self-injurious behavior. *Journal of Autism and Developmental Disorders, 18,* 99–117.

Durkheim, E. (1951). *Suicide.* New York: Free Press. (Originally published 1897.)

Durlak, J. A. (1979). Comparative effectiveness of paraprofessional and professional helpers. *Psychological Bulletin, 86,* 80–92.

Dutton, J. (1986). Doctors seek reason for bizarre syndrome. *Bellingham Herald,* C1, September 30, 1986.

Du Verglas, G., Banks, S. R., & Guyer, K. E. (1988). Clinical effects of fenfluramine on children with autism: A review of the research. *Journal of Autism and Developmental Disorders, 18,* 297–308.

Dykens, E. M., & Gerrard, M. (1986). Psychological profiles of purging bulimics, repeat dieters, and controls. *Journal of Consulting and Clinical Psychology, 54,* 283–288.

Dykens, E., Leckman, J., Paul, R., & Watson, M. (1988). Cognitive, behavioral and adaptive functioning in fragile X and non-fragile X retarded men. *Journal of Autism and Developmental Disorders, 18,* 41–52.

Eagly, A. H. (1983). Gender and social influence: A social psychological analysis. *American Psychologist, 38,* 971–981.

East-West. June 16, 1976.

Eaton, W. W., Holzer, C. E. III, Von Korff, M., Anthony, J. C., Helzer, J. E., George, L., Brunam, A., Boyd, J. H., Kessler, L. G., & Locker, B. Z. (1984). The design of the Epidemiologic Catchment Area surveys. *Archives of General Psychiatry, 41,* 942–948.

Edgerton, R. B., Bollinger, M., & Herr, B. (1984). The cloak of competence: After two decades. *American Journal of Mental Deficiency, 88,* 345–351.

Edman, G., Asberg, M., Levander, S., & Schalling, D. (1986). Skin conductance habituation and cerebrospinal fluid 5-hydroxyindoleactic acid in suicidal patients. *Archives of General Psychiatry, 43,* 586–592.

Edwards, M. S., & Baker, C. J. (1981). Meningitis infections in children. *Journal of Pediatrics, 99,* 540–545.

Edwards, S. & Kickerson, M. (1987). On the similarity of positive and negative intrusions. *Behaviour Research and Therapy, 25,* 207–211.

Efron, R. (1956). The effect of olfactory stimuli in arresting uncinate fits. *Brain, 79,* 267–281.

Efron, R. (1957). The conditioned inhibitions of uncinate fits. *Brain, 80,* 251–262.

Egbert, L., Battit, G., Welch, C., & Bartlett, M. (1964). Reduction of postoperative pain. *New England Journal of Medicine, 270,* 835–837.

Egeland, J. A., Berhard, D. S., Pauls, D. L., Sussex, J. N., Kidd, K. K., Allen, C. R., Hostetter, A. M., & Housman, D. E. (1987). Bipolar affective disorders linked to DNA markers on chromosome 11. *Nature, 325,* 783–787.

Egeland, J. A., & Hostetter, A. M. (1983). Amish study, I: Affective disorders among the Amish. *American Journal of Psychiatry, 140,* 56–61.

Ehlers, A., Margraf, J., Roth, W. T., Taylor, C. G., & Birbaumer, N. (1988). Anxiety induced by false heart rate feedback in patients with panic disorder. *Behaviour Research and Therapy, 26,* 1–11.

Ehrardt, A. A., Grisanti, G., & McCauley, E. A. (1979). Female-to-male transsexuals compared to lesbians: Behavioral patterns of childhood and adolescent development. *Archives of Sexual Behavior, 8,* 481–490.

Eichenbaum, L., & Orbach, S. (1983). *Understanding women: A feminist psychoanalytic approach.* New York: Basic Books.

Eisenberg, M. M. (1978). *Ulcers.* New York: Random House

Eisman, C. (1988). *California self-helper.* Los Angeles: California Self-Help Center.

Ellenberger, H. F. (1972). The Story of "Anna O.": A critical review with new data. *Journal of the History of the Behavior Sciences, 8,* 267–279.

Ellingson, R. (1954). Incidence of EEG abnormality among patients with mental disorders of apparently nonorganic origin: A critical review. *American Journal of Psychiatry, 111*, 363–375.

Elliott, C. H., & Jay, S. M. (1987). Chronic pain in children. *Behaviour Research and Therapy, 25*, 263–271.

Ellis, A. (1957). Outcome of employing three techniques of psychotherapy. *Journal of Clinical Psychology, 13*, 344–350.

Ellis, A. (1962). *Reason and emotion in psychotherapy.* New York: Stuart.

Ellis, A. (1971). *Growth through reason.* Palo Alto, CA: Science and Behavior Books.

Ellis, A. (1973). Are cognitive behavior therapy and rational therapy synonymous? *Rational Living, 8*, 8–11.

Ellis, L., & Ames, M. A. (1987). Neurohormonal functioning and sexual orientation: A theory of homosexuality-heterosexuality. *Psychological Bulletin, 101*, 233–258.

Ely, D. L., & Mostardi, R. A. (1986). The effects of recent life events stress, life assets, and temperament pattern on cardiovascular risk factors for Akron city police officers. *Journal of Human Stress, 12*, 77–91.

Emmel Kamp, P. M. G., & Wessels, H. (1975). Flooding in imagination vs. flooding in vivo: A comparison with agoraphobics. *Behavior Research & Therapy, 13*, 7–15.

Emslie, G. J., & Rosenfeld, A. (1983). Incest reported by children and adolescents hospitalized for severe psychiatric problems. *American Journal of Psychiatry, 140*, 108–111.

Endler, N. S. (1982). *Holiday of darkness.* New York: Wiley.

Engel, G. (1971). Sudden and rapid death during psychological stress. *Annals of Internal Medicine, 74*, 771.

English, H. B. (1929). Three cases of the conditioned fear response. *Journal of Abnormal and Social Psychology, 24*, 221–225.

Ennis, B., & Emery, R. (1978). *The rights of mental patients: An American Civil Liberties Union Handbook.* New York: Avon.

Epstein, S. (1972). The nature of anxiety with emphasis upon its relationship to expectancy. In C. D. Spielberger (Ed.), *Anxiety: Current trends in theory and research* (Vol. 2). New York: Academic Press.

Erickson, W. D., Luxenberg, M. G., Walbek, N. H., & Seely, R. K. (1987). Frequency of MMPI two-point code types among sex offenders. *Journal of Consulting and Clinical Psychology, 55*, 566–570.

Erickson, W. D., Walbek, N. H., & Seely, R. K. (1988). Behavior patterns of child molesters. *Archives of Sexual Behavior, 17*, 77–86.

Erikson, E. H. (1968). *Identity: Youth and crisis.* New York: Norton.

Eron, L. D., Lefkowitz, M. M., Huesmann, L. R., & Walder, L. O. (1972). Does television violence cause aggression? *American Psychologist, 27*, 253–263.

Essau, C. A., & Jamieson, J. L. (1987). Heart rate perception in the type A personality. *Health Psychology, 6*, 43–54.

Eth, S., & Pynoos, R. S. (1985). Developmental perspective on psychic trauma in childhood. In C. R. Figley (Ed.), *Trauma and its wake* (pp. 36–52). New York: Brunner/Mazel.

Everstine, D. S., & Everstine, L. (1983). *People in crisis: Strategic therapeutic interventions.* New York: Brunner/Mazel.

Exner, J. E. (1983). Rorschach assessment. In I. B. Weiner (Ed.), *Clinical methods in psychology.* New York: Wiley.

Eysenck, H. J. (1952). The effects of psychotherapy: An evaluation. *Journal of Consulting Psychology, 16*, 319–324.

Eysenck, H. J. (1954). The science of personality: Nomothetic vs. idiographic. *Psychological Review, 61*, 339–342.

Eysenck, H. J. (1988). *Health's character. Psychology Today, 22*, 28–35.

Eysenck, H. J., & Rachman, S. (1965). *The causes and cures of neurosis.* San Diego: Knapp.

Fagan, J., & McMahon, P. P. (1984). Incipient multiple personality in children: Four cases. *Journal of Nervous and Mental Disease, 172*, 26–36.

Fairburn, C., & Cooper, P. (1983). The epidemiology of bulimia nervosa. *International Journal of Eating Disorders, 2*, 61–67.

Fairburn, C. G., Kirk, J., O'Connor, M. O., & Cooper, P. J. (1986). A comparison of two psychological treatments for bulimia nervosa. *Behavior Research and Therapy, 24*, 629–643.

Fairweather, G. W., Sanders, D. H., Cressler, D. L., & Maynard, H. (1969). *Community life for the mentally ill: An alternative to institutional care.* Chicago: Aldine.

Fallon, A. E., & Rozin, P. (1985). Sex differences in perceptions of desirable body shape. *Journal of Abnormal Psychology, 94*, 102–105.

Falloon, I. R. J., Boyd, J. L., & McGill, C. W. (1984). *Family care of schizophrenia.* New York: Guilford Press.

Falloon, I. R. J., & Liberman, R. (1983). Interactions between drug and psychosocial therapy in schizophrenia. *Schizophrenia Bulletin, 9*, 555–562.

Farberow, N. L. (1970). Ten years of suicide prevention—past and future. *Bulletin of Suicidology, 6*, 5–11.

Farberow, N. L., & Shneidman, E. S. (Eds.). (1961). *The cry for help.* New York: McGraw-Hill.

Farberow, N. L., & Simon, M. D. (1975). Suicide in Los Angeles and Vienna. In N. L. Farberow (Ed.), *Suicide in different cultures*, pp. 185–204. Baltimore: University Park Press.

Farley, F. (1986). World of the Type T personality. *Psychology Today, 20*, 45–52.

Farrell, A. D., Stiles-Camplair, P., & McCullough, L. (1987). Identification of target complaints by computer interview: Evaluation of the computerized assessment system for psychotherapy evaluation research. *Journal of Consulting and Clinical Psychology, 55*, 691–700.

Fedora, O., Reddon, J. R., & Yeudall, L. T. (1986). Stimuli eliciting sexual arousal in genital exhibitionists as possible clinical application. *Archives of Sexual Behavior, 15*, 417–427.

Feingold, B. F. (1977). Behavioral disturbances linked to the ingestion of food additives. *Delaware Medical Journal, 49*, 89–94.

Feinberg, S. S., Kay, S. R., Elijovich, L. R., Fiszbein, A., & Opler, L. A. (1988). Pimozide treatment of the negative schizophrenic syndrome: An open trial. *Journal of Clinical Psychiatry, 49*, 235–238.

Feinsilver, D., & Yates, B. (1984). Combined use of psychotherapy and drugs in chronic, treatment-resistant schizophrenic patients. *Journal of Nervous and Mental Disease, 172*, 133–139.

Feldman-Summers, S., Gordon, P. E., & Meagher, J. R. (1979). The impact of rape on sexual satisfaction. *Journal of Abnormal Psychology, 88*, 101–105.

Felner, R. D., Jason, L. A., Moritsugu, J., & Farber, S. S. (1983). Preventive psychology: Evolution and current status. In R. D. Felner & L. A. Jason (Eds.), *Preventive psychology: Theory, research and practice*. New York: Pergamon Press.

Fenichel, O. (1945). *The psychoanalytic theory of neuroses*. New York: Norton.

Fenton, W. S., & McGlashan, T. H. (1987). Sustained remission in drug-free schizophrenic patients. *American Journal of Psychiatry, 144*, 1306–1309.

Fersch, E. A., Jr. (1980). *Psychology and psychiatry in courts and corrections*. New York: Wiley.

Ferster, C. B. (1961). Positive reinforcement and behavior deficits of autistic children. *Child Development, 32*, 437–456.

Ferster, C. B. (1965). Classification of behavior pathology. In L. Krasner & L. P. Ullmann (Eds.), *Research in behavior modification*. New York: Holt, Rinehart & Winston.

Festinger, L., Riecken, H. W., & Schachter, S. (1957). *When prophecy fails*. Minneapolis: University of Minnesota Press.

Fichter, M. M., Wallace, C. J., Liberman, R. P., & Davis, J. R. (1976). Improving social interaction in a chronic psychotic using discriminated avoidance ("nagging"): Experimental analysis and discrimination. *Journal of Applied Behavioral Analysis, 9*, 377–386.

Fieve, R., Dunner, D., Kumbaraci, et al. (1976). Lithium carbonate prophylaxis in three subtypes of primary affective disorder. *Pharmakopsychiatri Neuropsychopharmakol, 9*, 100–107.

Figley, C. R. (Ed.), *Trauma and its wake* (pp. 53–69). New York: Brunner/Mazel.

Fink, M. (1979). *Convulsive therapy: Theory and practice*. New York: Raven Press.

Finkelhor, D. (1980). Sex among siblings: A survey on prevalence, variety, and effects. *Archives of Sexual Behavior, 9*, 171–194.

Finkelhor, D., & Araji, S. (1986). Explanations of pedophilia: A four-factor model. *Journal of Sex Research, 22*, 145–161.

Fishman, S. M. & Sheehan, D. V. (1985). Anxiety and panic: Their cause and treatment. *Psychology Today, 19*, 26–32.

Fleming, I., Baum, A., Davidson, L. M., Rectanus, E., & McArdle, S. (1987). Chronic stress as a factor in physiologic reactivity to challenge. *Health Psychology, 6*, 221–237.

Fleming, M. Z., MacGowan, B. R., Robinson, L., Spitz, J., & Salt, P. (1982). The body image of the post-operative female-to-male transsexual. *Journal of Consulting and Clinical Psychology, 50*, 461–462.

Flynn, M. C., & Saleem, J. K. (1986). Adults who are mentally handicapped and living with their parents: Satisfaction and perceptions regarding their lives and circumstances. *Journal of Mental Deficiency, 30*, 379–387.

Foa, E., Steketee, G., Turner, R., & Fischer, S. (1980). Effects of imaginal exposure to feared disasters in obsessive compulsive checkers. *Behaviour Research and Therapy, 18*, 449–455.

Foa, E., & Tillmanns, A. (1980). The treatment of obsessive-compulsive neurosis. In A. Goldstein & E. Foa (Eds.), *Handbook of behavioral interventions*. New York: Wiley.

Foa, E. B. & Kozak, M. J. (1986). Emotional processing of fear: Exposure to corrective information. *Psychological Bulletin, 99*, 20–35.

Foley, V. D. (1984). Family therapy. In R. Coisine, *Current psychotherapies*, Itasca, IL: Peacock.

Folstein, S., & Rutter, M. (1977). Infantile autism: A genetic study of 21 twin pairs. *Journal of Child Psychology, 18*, 297–321.

Folstein, S., & Rutter, M. (1988). Autism: Familial aggregation and genetic implications. *Journal of Autism and Developmental Disorders, 18*, 3–30.

Foltz, D. (1980). Judgment withheld on DSM-III, new child classification pushed. *APA Monitor, 11*, 33.

Ford, M., Stroebel, C., Strong, P., & Szarek, B. (1982). Quieting response training: Treatment of psychophysiological disorders in psychiatric inpatients. *Biofeedback and Self-Regulation, 7,* 331–339.

Fordyce, W. E. (1982). A behavioral perspective on chronic pain. *British Journal of Clinical Psychiatry, 21,* 313–320.

Fordyce, W. E. (1988). Pain and suffering: A reappraisal. *American Psychologist, 43,* 276–283.

Foreyt, J. P. (1987). Behavioral medicine. In G. T. Wilson, C. M. Franks, P. C. Kendall, & J. P. Foreyt (Eds.), *Review of behavior therapy: Theory and practice* (Vol. 2) (pp. 154–176). New York: Guilford Press.

Forgac, G. E., Cassel, C. A., & Michaels, E. J. (1984). Chronicity of criminal behavior and psychopathology in male exhibitionists. *Journal of Clinical Psychology, 40,* 827–832.

Forgac, G. E., & Michaels, E. J. (1982). Personality characteristics of two types of male exhibitionism. *Journal of Abnormal Psychology, 91,* 287–293.

Fowles, D. C. (1984). Biological variables in psychopathology. In H. E. Adams & P. B. Sutker (Eds.), *Comprehensive handbook of psychopathology* (pp. 77–110). New York: Plenum Press.

Foxx, R., & Brown, R. (1979). Nicotine fading and self-monitoring for cigarette abstinence or controlled smoking. *Journal of Applied Behavior Analysis, 12,* 111–125.

Francis, G., Last, C. G., Strauss, C. C. (1987). Expression of separation anxiety disorder: The roles of age and gender. *Child Psychiatry and Human Development, 18,* 82–89.

Frank, E., Anderson, C., & Rubenstein, D. (1978). Frequency of sexual dysfunction in "normal" couples. *New England Journal of Medicine, 299,* 111–115.

Franklin, D. (1987). The politics of masochism. *Psychology Today, 21,* 51–57.

Franklin, J. A. (1987). The changing nature of agoraphobic fears. *British Journal of Clinical Psychology, 26,* 127–133.

Franks, C., Fried, R., & Ashem, B. (1966). An improved apparatus for the aversive conditioning of cigarette smokers. *Behaviour Research and Therapy, 4,* 301–308.

Freedman, D. X. (1984). Psychiatric epidemiology counts. *Archives of General Psychiatry, 41,* 931–933.

Freud, S. (1905). Psychical (or mental) treatment. In J. Strachey (Ed. and Trans.), *The complete psychological works (Vol. 7).* New York: Norton.

Freud, S. (1962). Analysis of a phobia in a five-year-old boy, 1909. In *Collected Works of Sigmund Freud* (Vol. 10). London: Hogarth Press, 1962.

Freud, S. (1924). Mourning and melancholia. In J. Riviere (Trans.), *Collected papers* (Vol. 4). London: Hogarth Press. (Original work published 1917.)

Freud, S. (1938). The psychopathology of everyday life. In A. B. Brill (Ed.), *The basic writings of Sigmund Freud.* New York: Modern Library.

Freud, S. (1949). *An outline of psychoanalysis.* New York: Norton.

Freud, S. (1959). *Beyond the pleasure principle.* New York: Bantam.

Freud, S. (1895). *Studies on hysteria.* In J. Strachey (Ed.). *The Standard Edition of the Complete Psychological Works of Sigmund Freud,* Vol. II. London: The Hogarth Press, 1962.

Friedman, A. P. (1979). Characteristics of tension headache: Profile of 1,420 cases. *Psychosomatics, 20,* 451–461.

Friedman, M., & Rosenman, R. H. (1974). *Type A Behavior.* New York: Knopf.

Friedrich, J. (1985, January 7). Seven who have succeeded. *Time,* pp. 41–45.

Friel, P. B. (1973). Familial incidence of Gilles de la Tourette's disease with observations on etiology and treatment. *British Journal of Psychiatry, 122,* 655–658.

Fritz, G. K., Rubenstein, S., & Lewiston, N. J. (1987). Psychological factors in fatal childhood asthma. *American Journal of Orthopsychiatry, 57,* 253–257.

Fromm, E. (1941). *Escape from freedom.* New York: Holt, Rinehart & Winston.

Fyer, A. J., Liebowitz, M. R., Gorman, J. M., Campeas, R., Levin, A., Davies, S. O., Goetz, D., & Klein, D. (1987). Discontinuation of Alprazolam treatment in panic patients. *American Journal of Psychiatry, 144,* 303–308.

Gadow, K. D. (1986). *Children on medication* (Vol. 1). San Diego: College-Hill Press.

Gallagher, D., & Frankel, A. S. (1980). Depression in (an) older adult(s): A moderate structuralist viewpoint. *Psychotherapy: Theory, Research, and Practice, 17,* 101–104.

Gallahorn, G. E. (1981). Borderline personality disorders. In J. R. Lion (Ed.), *Personality disorders: Diagnosis and management.* Baltimore: Williams & Wilkins.

Galton, F. (1869). *Hereditary genius: An inquiry into its laws and consequences.* London: Macmillan.

Gamble, E., & Elder, S. (1983). Multimodal biofeedback in the treatment of migraine. *Biofeedback and Self-Regulation, 8,* 383–392.

Gami, A. (1987). Coping with the sexuality of the disabled: A comparison of the physically disabled and the mentally retarded. *International Journal of Rehabilitation Research, 10,* 41–48.

Gan, S., Tymchuk, A. J., & Nishihara, A. (1977). Mentally retarded adults: Their attitudes toward retardation. *Mental Retardation, 15,* 5–9.

Ganellen, R. J. (1988). Specificity of attributions and

overgeneralization in depression and anxiety. *Journal of Abnormal Psychology, 97,* 83–86.

Gangadhar, B., Kapur, R., & Kalyanasundaram, S. (1982). Comparison of electroconvulsive therapy with imipramine in endogenous depression: A double blind study. *British Journal of Psychiatry, 141,* 367–371.

Gannon, L. R., Haynes, S. N., Cuevas, V., & Chavez, R. (1987). Psychophysical correlates of induced headaches. *Journal of Behavioral Medicine, 10,* 411–423.

Garakani, H., Zitrin, C. M., & Klein, D. F. (1984). Treatment of panic disorder with imipramine alone. *American Journal of Psychiatry, 141,* 446–448.

Garbarino, J. (1980). Preventing child maltreatment. In R. H. Price, R. F. Ketterer, B. C. Bader, & J. Monahan (Eds.), *Prevention in mental health: Research, policy, and practice.* Beverly Hills, CA: Sage.

Garcia, J. (1981). The logic and limits of mental aptitude testing. *American Psychologist, 36,* 1172–1180.

Garfield, S. L. (1974). *Clinical psychology: The study of personality and behavior.* Chicago: Aldine.

Garfield, S. L., & Kurtz, R. (1976). Clinical psychologists in the 1970s. *American Psychologist, 31,* 1–9.

Garfinkel, B., Froese, M., & Hood, J. (1982). Suicide attempts in children and adolescents. *American Journal of Psychiatry, 139,* 1257–1261.

Garmezy, N. (1987). Stress, competence, and development: Continuities in the study of schizophrenic adults, children vulnerable to psychopathology, and the search for stress-resistant children. *American Journal of Orthopsychiatry, 57,* 159–173.

Garner, D. M., Olmstead, M. P., Polivy, J., & Garfinkel, P. E. (1984). Comparison between weight-preoccupied women and anorexia nervosa. *Psychosomatic Medicine, 46,* 255–266.

Gartner, A. F., & Gartner, J. (1988). Borderline pathology in post-incest female adolescents. *Bulletin of the Menninger Clinic, 52,* 101–113.

Gatz, M., Barbarin, 0. A., Tyler, F. B., Mitchell, R. E., Moran, J. A., Wirzbicki, P. J., Crawford, J., & Engelman, A. (1982). Enhancement of individual and community competence: The older adult as community worker. *American Journal of Community Psychology, 10,* 291–304.

Gatz, M., Smyer, M. A., & Lawton, M. P. (1980). The mental health system and the older adult. In L. W. Poon (Ed.), *Aging in the 1980s.* Washington, D.C.: American Psychological Association.

Gelard, M. S., & Sanford, E. E. (1987). Child abuse and neglect: A review of the literature. *School Psychology Review, 16,* 137–155.

Gentry, W. D. (Ed.) (1984). *Handbook of behavioral medicine.* New York: Guilford Press.

George, D. T., Ladenheim, J. A., & Nutt, D. J. (1987).

Effect of pregnancy on panic attacks. *American Journal of Psychiatry, 144,* 1078–1079.

Georgotas, A. (1985). Affective disorders: Pharmacotherapy. In H. I. Kaplan & B. J. Sadock (Eds.), *Comprehensive textbook of psychiatry.* (4th ed., pp. 821–833). Baltimore: Williams & Wilkins.

Ghosh, A., & Marks, I. M. (1987). Self-treatment of agoraphobia by exposure. *Behavior Therapy, 18,* 3–16.

Gibbons, F. Y., Sawin, L. G., & Gibbons, B. N. (1979). Evaluations of mentally retarded persons: "sympathy" or patronization? *American Journal of Mental Deficiency, 84,* 124–131.

Gibbs, J. P., & Martin, W. T. (1964). *Status integration and suicide.* Eugene: University of Oregon Press.

Gibbs, M. V., & Thorpe, J. G. (1983). Personality stereotype of non-institutionalized Down's syndrome children. *American Journal of Mental Deficiency, 87,* 601–605.

Gilberg, C. (1984). Infantile autism and other childhood psychoses in a Swedish urban region: Epidemiological aspects. *Journal of Child Psychology and Psychiatry, 25,* 35–43.

Gilbert, B., & Cunningham, J. (1986). Women's post-rape sexual functioning: Review and implications for counseling. *Journal of Counseling and Development, 65,* 71–73.

Gillberg, C. (1988). The neurobiology of infantile autism. *Journal of Child Psychology and Psychiatry, 29,* 257–266.

Ginsburg, H. (1972). *The myth of the deprived child.* Englewood Cliffs, NJ: Prentice-Hall.

Girard, F. (1984, August 5). State crime data called flawed, late. *Detroit News,* pp. 1, 12.

Glaser, G. H., Newman, R. J., & Schafer, R. (1963). Interictal psychosis in psychomotor-temporal lobe epilepsy: An EEG psychological study. In G. H. Glaser (Ed.), *EEG and behavior.* New York: Basic Books.

Glasgow, M., Gaarder, K., & Engel, B. (1982). Behavioral treatment of high blood pressure 11. Acute and sustained effects of relaxation and systolic blood pressure biofeedback. *Psychosomatic Medicine, 44,* 155–170.

Glassman, J. N. S., Magulac, M., & Darko, D. F. (1987). *Folie à famille:* Shared paranoid disorder in a Vietnam veteran and his family. *American Journal of Psychiatry, 144,* 658–660.

Glidewell, J. C. (1983). Prevention: The threat and the promise. In R. D. Felner, L. A. Jason, J. Moritsugu, & S. S. Farber (Eds.), *Preventive psychology: Theory, research, and practice.* New York: Pergamon Press.

Goffman, E. (1961). *Asylums.* Garden City, NY: Doubleday.

Golden, C. J. (1981). A standardized version of Luria's

neuropsychological tests: A quantitative and qualitative approach to neuropsychological evaluation. In S. Filskov & T. J. Boll (Eds.), *Handbook of clinical neuropsychology*. New York: Wiley.

Golden, C. J., Graber, B., Blose, I., Berg, R., Coffman, J., & Bloch, S. (1981). Differences in brain densities between chronic alcoholic and normal control patients. *Science, 211*, 508–510.

Golden, C. J., Moses, J. A., Coffman, J. A., Miller, W. R., & Strider, F. D. (1983). *Clinical neuropsychology*. New York: Grune & Stratton.

Golden, C. J., Moses, J. A., Fishburne, F. J., Engum, E., Lewis, G. P., Wisniewski, A. M., Conley, F. K., Berg, R. A., & Graber, B. (1981). Cross-validation of the Luria-Nebraska Neuropsychological Battery for the presence, lateralization, and location of brain damage. *Journal of Consulting and Clinical Psychology, 49*, 491–507.

Golden, C. J., & Vincente, P. J. (Eds.) (1983). *Foundation of clinical neuropsychology*. New York: Plenum Press.

Golden, G. S. (1987). Tic disorders in childhood. *Pediatrics in Revies, 8*, 229–234.

Golden, J. (1988). A second look at a case of inhibited sexual desire. *Journal of Sex Research, 25*, 304–306.

Goldenberg, H. (1973). *Contemporary clinical psychology*. Monterey, CA: Brooks/Cole.

Goldfried, M. R., & Davison, G. C. (1976). *Clinical behavior therapy*. San Francisco: Holt, Rinehart & Winston.

Goldman, H. H. (1980). The post-hospital mental patient and family therapy: Prospects and populations. *Journal of Marriage and Family Therapy, 6*, 447–452.

Goldman, H. H. (1988). Psychiatric epidemiology and mental health services research. In H. H. Goldman (Ed.), *Review of general psychiatry* (pp. 143–156). Norwalk, CT: Appleton & Lange.

Goldman, H. H., & Foreman, S. A. (1988). Psychiatric diagnosis and psychosocial formulation. In H. H. Goldman (Ed.), *Review of general psychiatry* (pp. 136–142). Norwalk, CT: Appleton & Lange.

Goldman, R. D., & Hartig, L. K. (1976). The WISC may not be a valid predictor of school performance for primary grade minority children. *American Journal of Mental Deficiency, 80*, 583–587.

Goldstein, A. P., & Simonson, N. (1971). Social psychological approaches to psychotherapy research. In A. Bergin & S. Garfield (Eds.), *Psychotherapy and behavior change*. New York: Wiley.

Goleman, D. (1976). Why your temples pound. *Psychology Today, 10*, 41–47.

Goleman, D. (1986a, November 4). To expert eyes, city streets are open mental wards. *New York Times*, pp. C1, C3.

Goleman, D. (1986b, November 11). For mentally ill on the street, a new approach shines. *New York Times*, pp. C1, C3.

Goodman, G. (1972). Systematic selection of psychotherapeutic talent: Group assessment of interpersonal traits. In S. E. Golann & C. Eisdorfer (Eds.), *Handbook of community mental health*. New York: Appleton-Century-Crofts.

Goodstein, L. D., & Sandler, I. (1978). Using psychology to promote human welfare: A conceptual analysis of the role of community psychology. *American Psychologist, 33*, 882–892.

Goodstein, R. K. (1981). Inextricable interaction: Social, psychologic and biologic stresses facing the elderly. *American Journal of Orthopsychiatry, 51*, 219–229.

Goodwin, D. W. (1979). Alcoholism and heredity. *Archives of General Psychiatry, 36*, 57–61.

Goodwin, D. W. (1985). Alcoholism and alcoholic psychoses. In H. I. Kaplan & B. J. Sadock (Eds.), *Comprehensive textbook of psychiatry/IV* (pp. 1016–1025). Baltimore: Williams & Wilkins.

Goodwin, D. W., & Guze, S. B. (1984). *Psychiatric diagnosis* (3rd ed.). New York: Oxford University Press.

Goodwin, D. W., Schulsinger, F., Knop, J., Mednick, S., & Goodwin, F. (1974). On the biology of depression. In R. J. Friedman & M. M. Katz (Eds.), *The psychology of depression: Contemporary theory and research*. New York: Wiley.

Goodwin, F. K. (1977). Diagnosis of affective disorders. In M. Jarvik (Ed.), *Psychopharmacology in the practice of medicine*. New York: Appleton-Century-Crofts.

Gordon, E., Kraiuhin, C., Meares, R., & Howson, A. (1986). Auditory evoked response potentials in somatization disorder. *Journal of Psychiatric Research, 20*, 237–248.

Gossett, T. F. (1963). *The history of an idea in America*. Dallas: Southern Methodist University Press.

Gottesman, I. I. (1978). Schizophrenia and genetics: Where are we? Are you sure? In L. C. Wynne, R. L. Cromwell, & S. Matthysse (Eds.), *The nature of schizophrenia: New approaches to research and treatment* (pp. 59–69). New York: Wiley.

Gottesman, I. I., & Shields, J. (1972). *Schizophrenia and genetics: A twin study vantage point*. New York: Academic Press.

Gottesman, I. I., & Shields, J. (1982). *Schizophrenia: The epigenetic puzzle*. New York: Cambridge University Press.

Gottlieb, B. H. (Ed.). (1981). *Social networks and social support*. Beverly Hills, CA: Sage.

Gottlieb, B. H. (1983). Social support as a focus for integrative research in psychology. *American Psychologist, 38*, 278–287.

Gould, M. S., & Schaffer, D. (1986). The impact of suicide in television movies: Evidence of imitation. *New England Journal of Medicine, 315,* 690–693.

Gourash, N. (1978). Help-seeking: A review of the literature. *American Journal of Community Psychology, 6,* 413–424.

Gove, W. R., & Tudor, J. F. (1973). Adult sex roles and mental illness. *American Journal of Sociology, 78,* 812–835.

Granacher, R. P. (1981). Differential diagnosis of tardive dyskinesia: An overview. *American Journal of Psychiatry, 138,* 1288–1297.

Gray, S. H. (1977). Social aspects of body image: Perception of normalcy of weight and affect on college undergraduates. *Perceptual and Motor Skills, 45,* 1035–1040.

Green, B. L., Wilson, J. P., & Lindy, J. D. (1985). Conceptualizing PTSD: A psychosocial framework. In C. R. Figley (Ed.), *Trauma and its wake* (pp. 53–69). New York: Brunner/Mazel.

Green, L. E., Green, A. M., & Walters, E. D. (1970). *Self-regulation of internal stress in progress of cybernetics: Proceedings of the International Congress of Cybernetics.* London: Gordon & Breech.

Green, R. (1968). Childhood cross-gender identification. *Journal of Nervous and Mental Disease, 147,* 500–509.

Green, R. (1974). A profile of boyhood femininity. *Psychology Today, 7,* 51–54.

Green, R. (1978). Sexual identity of 37 children raised by homosexual or transsexual parents. *American Journal of Psychiatry, 135,* 692–697.

Greenwood, P. W., & Zimring, F. E. (1985). One more chance: The pursuit of promising intervention strategies for chronic juvenile offenders. Santa Monica, CA: Rand.

Greer, S., & Morris, T. (1975). Psychological attributes of women who develop breast cancer: A controlled study. *Journal of Psychosomatic Research, 19,* 147–153.

Grefe, M. A. (1980, March/April). Equity—a cause for every woman. *Graduate Woman,* pp. 11–17.

Grinker, R. R., & Robbins, F. P. (1954). *Psychosomatic case book.* New York: Blakiston.

Grossman, H. J. (Ed.). (1983). *Classification in mental retardation.* Washington, D.C.: American Association on Mental Deficiency.

Groth, A. N., Burgess, A. W., & Holstrom, L. (1977). Rape: Power, anger, and sexuality. *American Journal of Psychiatry, 134,* 1239–1243.

Gruver, G. G. (1971). College students as therapeutic agents. *Psychological Bulletin, 76,* 111–127.

Gunn, J., & Fenton, G. (1971, June 5). Epilepsy, automatism, and crime. *Lancet,* pp. 1173–1176.

Guntrip, H. (1968). *Schizoid phenomena, object relations, and the self.* New York: International Universities Press.

Guttmacher, L. B., & Nelles, C. (1984). In vivo desensitization alteration of lactate-induced panic: A case study. *Behavior Therapy, 15,* 369–372.

Guze, S. B., Cloninger, C. R., Martin, R. L., & Clayton, P. J. (1983). A follow-up and family study of schizophrenia. *Archives of General Psychiatry, 40,* 1273–1276.

Haier, R. J., Rosenthal, D., & Wendler, P. H. (1978). MMPI assessment of psychopathology in the adopted-away off-spring of schizophrenics. *Archives of General Psychiatry, 35,* 171–175.

Haley, A. (1966). *The autobiography of Malcolm X.* New York: Grove.

Haley, J. (1963). *Strategies of psychotherapy.* New York: Grune & Stratton.

Haley, J. (1977). *Problems-solving therapy.* San Francisco: Jossey-Bass.

Haley, J. (1980). *Leaving home.* New York: McGraw-Hill.

Hall, C. S., & Lindzey, G. (1970). *Theories of personality.* New York: Wiley.

Hall, G. S. (1904). *Adolescence: Its psychology and its relation to physiology, anthropology, sociology, sex, crime, religion and education.* New York: Appleton.

Hall, J. C., Bliss, M., Smith, K., & Bradley, A. (1970). Suicide gestures, attempts found high among poor. *Psychiatric News,* July 1, 1970, p. 20.

Hall, S. M., Tunstall, C. D., Ginsberg, D., Benowitz, N. L., & Jones, R. T. (1987). Nicotine gum and behavioral treatment: A placebo controlled trial. *Journal of Consulting and Clinical Psychology, 55,* 603–605.

Hammen, C., & Peters, S. (1978). Interpersonal consequences of depression: Responses to men and women enacting a depressed role. *Journal of Abnormal Psychology, 87,* 322–332.

Hammen, C. L. (1985). Predicting depression: A cognitive-behavioral perspective. In P. Kendall (Ed.), *Advances in cognitive-behavioral research and therapy* (Vol. 4). New York: Academic Press.

Hanback, J. W., & Revelle, W. (1978). Arousal and perceptual sensitivity in hypochondriacs. *Journal of Abnormal Psychology, 87,* 523–530.

Harburg, E., Blackelock, E. H., & Roeper, P. J. (1979). Resentful and reflective coping with arbitrary authority and blood pressure: Detroit. *Psychosomatics, 41,* 189–202.

Harding, C. M., Brooks, G. W., Ashikaga, T., Strauss, J. S., Breier, A. (1987). The Vermont longitudinal study of persons with severe mental illness. II: Long-term outcome of subjects who retrospectively met DSM-III criteria for schizophrenia. *American Journal of Psychiatry, 144,* 727–735.

Hare, R. D. (1968). Psychopathy, autonomic functioning and the orienting responses. *Journal of Abnormal Psychology, 73,* 1–24.

Hare, R. D. (1970). *Psychopathy: Theory and research.* New York: Wiley.

Hare, R. D. (1975). Anxiety, stress, and psychopathy. In I Sarason & C. Spielberger (Eds.), *Stress and anxiety* (Vol. 2). Washington, D.C.: Hemisphere Publishing.

Hare-Mustin, R. T. (1983). An appraisal of the relationship between women and psychotherapy: 80 years after the case of Dora. *American Psychologist, 38,* 593–601.

Harlow, J. M. (1868). Recovery from the passage of an iron bar through the head. *Publication of the Massachusetts Medical Society, 2,* 327.

Harris, B. (1979). Whatever happened to little Albert? *American Psychologist, 34,* 151–160.

Harris, E. L., Noyes, R., Crowe, R. R., & Chaudhry, D. R. (1983). Family study of agoraphobia. *Archives of General Psychiatry, 40,* 1061–1064.

Harris, I. D., & Howard, K. I. (1987). Correlates of depression and anger in adolescence. *Journal of Child and Adolescent Psychotherapy, 4,* 199–203.

Harris, R. R., Wolf, M. M., & Baer, D. M. (1964). Effects of adult social reinforcement of child behavior. *Young Children, 20,* 8–17.

Harris, S. L., & Ersner-Hershfield, R. (1978). Behavioral suppression of seriously disruptive behavior in psychotic and retarded patients: A review of punishment and its alternatives. *Psychological Bulletin, 85,* 1352–1375.

Harrow, M., Grossman, L. S., Silverstein, M. L., & Meltzer, H. Y. (1982). Thought pathology in manic and schizophrenic patients. *Archives of General Psychiatry, 39,* 665–671.

Hartmann, H. (1958). *Ego psychology and the problem of adaptation.* New York: International Universities Press.

Hathaway, S. R., & McKinley, J. C. (1943). *Manual for the Minnesota Multiphasic Personality Inventory.* New York: Psychological Corporation.

Hawton, K. (1987). Assessment of suicide risk. *British Journal of Psychiatry, 150,* 145–153.

Hawton, K., Catalan, J., Martin, P., & Fagg, J. (1986). Long-term outcome of sex therapy. *Behavior Research and Therapy, 24,* 665–675.

Hayes, S. C., Brownell, K. D., & Barlow, D. H. (1983). Heterosexual skills training and covert sensitization: Effects on social skills and sexual arousal in sexual deviants. *Behaviour Research and Therapy, 21,* 383–392.

Hayes, S. C., & Zettle, R. D. (1979). The mythology of behavioral training. *Behavior Therapist, 2,* 5–6.

Heber, R. (1970). *Epidemiology of mental retardation.* Springfield, IL: Thomas.

Heber, R., Garber, H., & Falender, C. (1973). *The Milwaukee project: An experiment in the prevention of cultural-familial retardation.* Unpublished manuscript.

Heber, R., & Garber, H. (1975). The Milwaukee project: A study of the use of familial retardation to prevent cultural-familial retardation. In B. Z. Friedlander, G. M. Sterrit, G. E. Kirk (Eds.), *Exceptional Infant,* Vol. 3: *Assessment and intervention.* New York: Brunner/Mazel.

Hechtman, L., & Weiss, G. (1983). Long-term outcome of hyperactive children. *American Journal of Orthopsychiatry, 53,* 532–541.

Heckler, M. H. L., Chesney, M. A., Black, G. W., & Frautschi, N. (1988). Coronary-prone behavior in the Western Collaborative Group study. *Psychosomatic Medicine, 50,* 53–164.

Heiby, E. M. (1983). Depression as a function of the interaction of self- and environmentally controlled reinforcement. *Behavior Therapy, 14,* 430–433.

Heilbrun, A. B., Jr., & Loftus, M. P. (1986). The role of sadism and peer pressure in the sexual aggression of male college students. *Journal of Sex Research, 22,* 320–332.

Heilig, S. M. (1970). Training in suicide prevention. *Bulletin of Suicidology, 6,* 41–44.

Heim, N. (1981). Sexual behavior of castrated sex offenders. *Archives of Sexual Behavior, 10,* 11–19.

Heinrich, D. W., & Buchanann, R. W. (1988). Significance and meaning of neurological signs in schizophrenia. *American Journal of Psychiatry, 145,* 11–18.

Hekmat, H., Lubitz, R., & Deal, R. (1984). Semantic desensitization: A paradigmatic intervention approach to anxiety disorders. *Journal of Clinical Psychology, 40,* 463–466.

Heller, K., Price, R. H., Reinharz, S., Riger, S., & Wandersman, A. (1984). *Psychology and community change: Challenge of the future.* Homewood, IL: Dorsey.

Hendin, H., Pollenger, A., Singer, P., & Ulman, R. (1981). Meanings of combat and the development of posttraumatic stress disorder. *American Journal of Psychiatry, 131,* 1490–1493.

Henley, N. (1977). *Body politics.* Englewood Cliffs, NJ: Prentice-Hall.

Henryk-Gutt, R., & Rees, L. W. (1973). Psychological aspects of migraine. *Journal of Psychosomatic Research, 17,* 141–153.

Herlicky, B., & Sheeley, V. L. (1988). Privileged communication in selected helping professions: A comparison among statutes. *Journal of Counseling & Development, 65,* 479–483.

Herman, J., & Hirschman, L. (1981). Families at risk for father-daughter incest. *American Journal of Psychiatry, 38,* 967–970.

Herman, S., Russell, D., & Trocki, K. (1986). Long-term effects of incestuous abuse in childhood. *American Journal of Psychiatry, 154,* 1293–1296.

Herschkowitz, S., & Dickes, R. (1978). Suicide attempts in a female-to-male transsexual. *American Journal of Psychiatry, 135,* 368–369.

Hersen, M., & Bellack, A. S. (1984). Research in clinical psychology. In A. S. Bellack & M. Hersen (Eds.), *Research methods in clinical psychology* (pp. 1–23). New York: Pergamon Press.

Hersen, M., Bellack, A., & Himmelhoch, J. (1980). Treatment for unipolar depression with social skills training. *Behavior Modification, 4,* 547–556.

Hertzog, D. B. (1982). Anorexia nervosa: A treatment challenge. *Drug Therapy, 7,* 3.

Heston, L. L. (1966). Psychiatric disorders in foster-home-reared children of schizophrenic mothers. *British Journal of Psychiatry, 122,* 819–825.

Heston, L. L., & Denny, D. (1968). Interactions between early life experience and biological factors in schizophrenia. In D. Rosenthal & S. Kety (Eds.), *The transmission of schizophrenia.* New York: Pergamon Press.

Hibbert, G. (1984). Ideational components of anxiety: Their origin and content. *British Journal of Psychiatry, 144,* 618–624.

Hill, D., & Watterson, D. (1942). Electroencephalographic studies of the psychopathic personality. *Journal of Neurology and Psychiatry, 5,* 47–64.

Hillyer, J. (1964). Reluctantly told. In B. Kaplan (Ed.), *The inner world of mental illness.* New York: Harper & Row.

Hingtgen, J. N., & Trost, F. C. (1966). Shaping cooperative responses in early childhood schizophrenics: Reinforcement of mutual physical contact and vocal responses. In R. Ulrich, T. Stachnik, & J. Mabry (Eds.), *Control of human behavior.* Glenview, IL: Scott, Foresman.

Hinshaw, S. (1987). On the distinction between attentional deficits/hyperactivity and conduct problems/aggression in child psychopathology. *Psychological Bulletin, 101,* 443–463.

Hinshaw, S., Henker, B., & Whalen, C. K. (1984). Self-control in hyperactive boys in anger-inducing situations: Effects of cognitive-behavioral training and methyl-phenidate. *Journal of Abnormal Child Psychology, 12,* 55–77.

Hipple, J. L., & Hipple, L. B. (1983). *Diagnosis and management of psychological emergencies.* Springfield, IL: Thomas.

Hiroto, D. S. (1974). Locus of control and learned helplessness. *Journal of Experimental Psychology, 102,* 187–193.

Hirschfeld, R. M., & Shea, T. (1985). Affective disorders: Psychosocial treatment. In H. I. Kaplan & B. J. Sadock (Eds.), *Comprehensive textbook of psychiatry* (4th ed., pp. 786–810). Baltimore: Williams & Wilkins.

Hite, S. (1976). *The Hite report.* Chicago: Dell.

Hobson, R. P. (1987). The autistic child's recognition of age- and sex-related characteristics of people. *Journal of Autism and Developmental Disorders, 17,* 63–79.

Hoch, Z., Safir, M. P., Peres, Y., & Stepler, J. (1981). An evaluation of sexual performance—comparison between sexually dysfunctional and functional couples. *Journal of Sex and Marital Therapy, 7,* 195–206.

Hodgson, R. J., & Rachman, S. (1972). The effects of contamination and washing in obsessional patients. *Behavior Research amd Therapy, 10,* 111–117.

Hoffman, R. E., Stopek, S., & Andreasen, N. C. (1986). A comparative study of manic vs. schizophrenic speech disorganization. *Archives of General Psychiatry, 43,* 831–838.

Holden, C. (1986). Proposed new psychiatric diagnoses raise charges of gender bias. *Science, 231,* 327–328.

Holden, N. L. (1987). Late paraphrenia or the paraphrenias? A descriptive study with a 10–year follow-up. *British Journal of Psychiatry, 150,* 635–639.

Hollender, M. H. (1980). The case of Anna O.: A reformulation. *American Journal of Psychiatry, 137,* 797–800.

Holmes, T. S., & Holmes, T. H. (1970). Short-term intrusion into the life style routine. *Journal of Psychosomatic Research, 14,* 121–132.

Holmes, T. H., & Rahe, R. H. (1967). The social readjustment rating scale. *Journal of Psychosomatic Research, 11,* 213–218.

Holroyd, J. (1980). Psychotherapy and women's liberation. *Counseling Psychologist, 6,* 22–28.

Holroyd, J., & Brodsky, A. (1977). Psychologists' attitudes and practices regarding erotic and nonerotic physical contact with patients. *American Psychologist, 32,* 839–843.

Holroyd, J., & Brodsky, A. (1980). Does touching patients lead to sexual intercourse? *Professional Psychology, 11,* 807–811.

Holt, R. R. (1962). The logic of the romantic point of view in personology. *Journal of Psychoanalysis, 38,* 377–402.

Holzberg, J. D., Knapp, R. H., & Turner, J. L. (1967). College students as companions to the mentally ill. In E. L. Cowen, E. A. Gardner, & M. Zax (Eds.), *Emergent approaches to mental health problems.* New York: Appleton-Century-Crofts.

Horne, R. L., Pettinati, H. M., Sugerman, A. A., & Varga, E. (1985). Comparing bilateral to unilateral electroconvulsive therapy in randomized study with EEG monitoring. *Archives of General Psychiatry, 42,* 1087–1092.

Horney, K. (1965). *Feminine psychology.* New York: Norton.

Horowitz, M. J. (1970). *Psychosocial function in epilepsy.* Springfield, IL: Thomas.

Howells, J. G., & Guirgis, W. R. (1984). Childhood schizophrenia 20 years later. *Archives of General Psychiatry, 41,* 123–128.

Hsu, L. (1980). Outcome of anorexia nervosa: A review of the literature (1954–1978). *Archives of General Psychiatry, 37,* 1041–1046.

Huber, G., Gross, G., Schuttler, R., & Linz, M. (1980). Longitudinal studies of schizophrenic patients. *Schizophrenia Bulletin, 6,* 592–605.

Hudgens, A. (1979). Family-oriented treatment of chronic pain. *Journal of Marital and Family Therapy, 5,* 67–78.

Hugdahl, K., Fredrickson, M., & Ohman, A. (1977). Preparedness and arousability determinants of electrodermal conditioning. *Behaviour Research and Therapy, 15,* 345–353.

Hunt, M. M. (1974). *Sexual behavior in the 1970s.* Chicago: Playboy Press.

Hunter, R., Blackwood, W., & Bull, J. (1968). Three cases of frontal meningiomas presenting psychiatrically. *British Medical Journal, 3,* 9–16.

Hunter, R., & Macalpine, I. (1963). *Three hundred years of psychiatry, 1535–1860.* London: Oxford University Press.

Hurtig, A. L., & Rosenthal, I. M. (1987). Psychological findings in early treated cases of female pseudohermaphroditism caused by virilizing congenital adrenal hyperplasia. *Archives of Sexual Behavior, 16,* 209–223.

Hutchens, T. A., & Hynd, G. W. (1987). Medications and the school-age chile and adolescent: A review. *School Psychology Bulletin, 16,* 527–542.

Hutchings, B., & Mednick, S. A. (1977). Criminality in adoptees and their adoptive and biological parents: A pilot study. In S. A. Mednick & K. L. Christianson (Eds.), *Biosocial bases of criminal behavior.* New York: Garden Press.

Hyler, S. E., & Spitzer, R. L. (1978). Hysteria split asunder. *American Journal of Psychiatry, 135,* 1500–1504.

Irwin, M., Daniels, M., Smith, T. L., Bloom, E., & Weiner, H. (1987). Impaired natural killer cell activity during bereavement. *Brain, Behavior, and Immunity, 1,* 98–104.

Israelson, Hilary. 1989 (February 19). "Original 'Rain Man' proud to be movie's inspiration." *Bellingham Herald.*

Jablow, M. M. (1988, April). Caran: Breaking all the rules. *Parents,* pp. 126–128.

Jackson, H. J., & King, N. J. (1981). The emotive imagery treatment of a child's trauma-induced phobia. *Journal of Behavior Therapy and Experimental Psychiatry, 14,* 343–347.

Jacob, T. (1975). Family interaction in disturbed and normal families: A methodological and substantive review. *Psychological Bulletin, 18,* 35–65.

Jacobson, E. (1938). *Progressive relaxation.* Chicago: University of Chicago Press.

Jacobson, E. (1964). *Self-operations control.* New York: Lippincott.

Jacobson, E. (1967). *Tension in medicine.* Springfield, IL: Thomas.

Jacobson, N. S., & Anderson, E. A. (1982). Interpersonal skill and depression in college students: An analysis of the timing of self-disclosures. *Behavior Therapy, 13,* 271–282.

Jaenicke, C., Hammen, C., Zupan, B., Hiroto, D., Gordon, D., Adrian, C., & Burge, D. (1987). Cognitive vulnerability in children at risk for depression. *Journal of Abnormal Child Psychology, 15,* 559–572.

Jahoda, M. (1958). *Current concepts of positive mental health.* New York: Basic Books.

James, G. D., Yee, L. S., Harshfield, G. A., Blank, S. G., & Pickering, T. G. (1986). The influence of happiness, anger, and anxiety on the blood pressure of borderline hypertensives. *Psychosomatic Medicine, 48,* 502–508.

Janis, I. (1971). *Stress and frustration.* New York: Harcourt, Brace, & World.

Janssen, K. (1983). Treatment of sinus tachycardia with heart-rate feedback. *Psychiatry and Human Development, 17,* 166–176.

Janoff-Bulman, R. (1985). Aftermath of victimization: Rebuilding shattered assumptions (pp. 15–31). In C. R. Figley (Ed.), *Trauma and its wake.* New York: Brunner/Mazel.

Jason, L. A., Felner, R. D., Moritsugu, J., & Farber, S. S. (1983). Future directions for preventive psychology. In R. D. Felner, L. A. Jason, J. Moritsugu, & S. S. Farber (Eds.), *Preventive psychology: Theory, research, and practice.* New York: Pergamon Press.

Jasper, H. H., Ward, A., & Pope, A. (Eds.) (1969). *Basic mechanisms of the epilepsies.* Boston: Little, Brown.

Jellinek, E. M. (1971). Phases of alcohol addiction. In G. Shean (Ed.), *Studies in abnormal behavior.* Chicago: Rand McNally.

Jemmott, III, J. B., & Locke, S. E. (1984). Psychosocial factors, immunologic mediation, and human susceptibility to infectious diseases: How much do we know? *Psychological Bulletin, 95,* 78–108.

Jenkins, S., Owen, C., Bax, M., & Hart, H. (1984). Continuities of common behavior problems in pre-school children. *Journal of Child Psychology and Psychiatry, 25,* 75–89.

Jenner, F. A., Gjessing, L. R., Cox, J. R., Davies-Jones, A., Hullin, R. R., & Hanna, S. M. (1967). A manic-depressive psychotic with a persistent forty-eight-hour cycle. *British Journal of Psychiatry, 113,* 895–910.

Jensen, A. (1969). How much can we boost IQ and school achievements? *Harvard Educational Review, 39,* 1–123.

Jessor, R., & Jessor, S. L. (1977). *Problem behavior and psycho-social development: A longitudinal study of youth.* New York: Academic Press.

Jesti, D. V., & Wyatt, R. J. (1981). Changing epidemiology of tardive dyskinesia: An overview. *American Journal of Psychiatry, 138,* 297–309.

Johnson, C., & Berndt, D. J. (1983). Preliminary investigation of bulimia and life adjustment. *American Journal of Psychiatry, 140,* 774–777.

Johnson, D. A. W., Ludlow, J. M., Street, K., & Taylor, R. D. W. (1987). Double-blind comparison of half-dose and standard-dose flupenthixol decanoate in the maintenance treatment of stabilized out-patients with schizophrenia. *British Journal of Psychiatry, 151,* 634–638.

Johnson, D. L., & Walker, T. (1987). Primary prevention of behavior problems in Mexican-American children. *American Journal of Community Psychology, 15,* 375–385.

Johnston, L. D., O'Malley, P. M., & Bachman, J. G. (1987). *National trends in drug use and related factors among American high school students and young adults, 1975–1986.* Washington, D.C.: U.S. Government Printing Office.

Johnston, R. (1967). Some casework aspects of using foster grandparents for emotionally disturbed children. *Children, 14,* 46–52.

Jones, E. E., & Korchin, S. J. (Eds.) (1982). *Minority mental health.* New York: Praeger.

Jones, E. E., & Thorne, A. (1987). Rediscovery of the subject: Intercultural approaches to clinical assessment. *Journal of Consulting and Clinical Psychology, 55,* 488–496.

Jones, K. L., Shainberg, L. W., & Byer, C. O. (1977). *Sex and people.* New York: Harper & Row.

Jones, M. (1953). *The therapeutic community: A new treatment method in psychiatry.* New York: Basic Books.

Jones, M. C. (1924). A laboratory study of fear: The case of Peter. *Pedagogical Seminary, 31,* 308–315.

Jones, M. C. (1968). Personality correlates and antecedents of drinking patterns in adult males. *Journal of Consulting and Clinical Psychology, 32,* 2–12.

Jones, M. C. (1971). Personality antecedents and correlates of drinking patterns in women. *Journal of Consulting and Clinical Psychology, 36,* 61–69.

Jones, N. F., Kahn, N. W., & Langsley, D. G. (1965). Prediction of admission to a psychiatric hospital. *Archives of General Psychiatry, 12,* 607–610.

Jones, R. E. (1983). Street people and psychiatry: An introduction. *Hospital Community Psychiatry, 34,* 899–907.

Joyce, C. (1988). Assault on the brain. *Psychology Today, 22,* 38–44.

Junginger, J. & Turner, S. M. (1987). Spontaneous exposure and "self-control" in the treatment of obsessive checking. *Journal of Behavior Therapy and Experimental Psychiatry, 18,* 115–119.

Kagan, D. M., & Squires, R. L. (1984). Eating disorders among adolescents: Patterns and prevalence. *Adolescence, 19,* 15–29.

Kagan, J., Reznick, J. S., & Snidman, N. (1987). The physiology and psychology of behavioral inhibition in children. *Child Development, 58,* 1459–1473.

Kahn, A. U., Staerk, M., & Bonk, C. (1974). Role of counterconditioning in the treatment of asthma. *Journal of Psychosomatic Research, 18,* 88–92.

Kahn, M. W., & Raufman, L. (1981). Hospitalization versus imprisonment and the insanity plea. *Criminal Justice and Behavior, 8(4),* 483–490.

Kallman, W. M., Hersen, M., & O'Toole, D. H. (1975). The use of social reinforcement in a case of conversion reaction. *Behavior Therapy, 6,* 411–413.

Kamiya, J. (1962, April). *Conditioning discrimination of the EEG alpha rhythm in humans.* Paper presented at the meeting of the Western Psychological Association.

Kanas, N. (1988). Psychoactive substance use disorders: Alcohol. In H. H. Goldman (Ed.), *Review of general psychiatry* (pp. 286–298). Norwalk, CT: Appleton & Lange.

Kandel, E., Mednick, S. A., Kirkegaard-Sorenson, L., Hutchings, B., Knop, J., Rosenberg, R., & Schulsinger, F. (1988). IQ as a protective factor for subjects at high risk for antisocial behavior. *Journal of Consulting and Clinical Psychology, 56,* 224–226.

Kane, J. M., & Smith, J. M. (1982). Tardive dyskinesia: prevalence and risk factors, 1959–1979. *Archives of General Psychiatry, 39,* 473–481.

Kanfer, F. H., & Phillips, J. S. (1969). A survey of current behavior therapies and a proposal for classification. In C. M. Franks (Ed.), *Behavior therapy: Appraisal and status.* New York: Wiley.

Kanner, L. (1960). Do behavior symptoms always indicate psychopathology? *Journal of Child Psychological Psychiatry, 1,* 17–25.

Kanner, L., & Lesser, L. I. (1958). Early infantile autism. *Pediatrics Clinic of North America, 5,* 711–730.

Kanner, L., Rodriguez, A., & Ashendeau, B. (1972). How far can autistic children go into matters of social adaptation? *Journal of Autism and Childhood Schizophrenia, 2,* 9–33.

Kaplan, H. I., & Sadock, B. J. (1981). *Modern synopsis of comprehensive textbook of psychiatry* (3rd ed.). Baltimore: Williams & Wilkins.

Kaplan, H. S. (1974). No nonsense therapy for six sexual malfunctions. *Psychology Today, 8,* 76–80, 83, 86.

Kaplan, M. (1983). A woman's view of DSM-III. *American Psychologist, 38,* 786–792.

Kardiner, A., & Ovesey, L. (1962). *The mark of oppression.* New York: Norton.

Kashani, J. H., & Carlson, G. A. (1987). Seriously depressed preschoolers. *American Journal of Psychiatry, 144,* 348–350.

Karno, M., Jenkins, J. H., De la Selva, A., Santana, F., Telles, C., Lopez, S., & Mintz, J. (1987). Expressed emotion and schizophrenic outcome among Mexican-American families. *Journal of Nervous and Mental Disease, 175,* 143–151.

Kaszniak, A. W., Nussbaum, P. D., Berren, M. R., & Santiago, J. (1988). Amnesia as a consequence of male rape: A case report. *Journal of Abnormal Psychology, 97,* 100–104.

Katchadourian, H. A., & Lunde, D. T. (1975). *Fundamentals of human sexuality* (2nd ed.). New York: Holt, Rinehart & Winston.

Katon, W., Vitaliano, P. P., Russo, J., Jones, M., & Anderson, K. (1987). Panic disorder: Spectrum of severity and somatization. *Journal of Nervous and Mental Disease, 175,* 12–19.

Katz, P. A. (Ed.) (1976). *Toward the elimination of racism.* New York: Pergamon Press.

Katz, P. A., & Taylor, D. A. (Eds.). (1988). *Eliminating racism: Profiles in controversy.* New York: Plenum.

Kaufman, A. S., Kamphaus, R. W., & Kaufman, N. L. (1985). The Kaufman Assessment Battery for Children (K-ABC). In C. S. Newmark (Ed.), *Major psychological assessment instruments* (pp. 249–276). Boston: Allyn & Bacon.

Kaufman, A. S., & Kaufman, N. L. (1983). *Kaufman Assessment Battery for Children.* Circle Pines, MN: American Guidance Services.

Kaul, T. J., & Bednar, R. L. (1986). Experiential group research: Results, questions, and suggestions. In S. L. Garfield and A. E. Bergin (Eds.), *Handbook of psychotherapy and behavior change: An evaluative analysis.* New York: Wiley.

Kayton, W., Bitaliano, P. P., Russo, J., Jones, M., & Anderson, K. (1987). Panic disorder. *Journal of Nervous and Mental Disease, 175,* 12–19.

Kazdin, A. E. (1980). *Behavior modification in applied settings* (2d ed.). Homewood, IL: Dorsey.

Kazdin, A. E. (1987). Treatment of antisocial behavior in children: Current status and future directions. *Psychological Bulletin, 102,* 187–203.

Kazdin, A. E., & Wilson, G. T. (1978). *Evaluation of behavior therapy: Issues, evidence and research strategies.* Cambridge, MA: Ballinger.

Keane, T. M., Fairbank, J. A., Caddell, J. M., Zimering, R. T., & Bender, M. E. (1985). A behavioral approach to assessing and treatment of posttraumatic stress disorder in Vietnam veterans (pp. 257–294). In C. R. Figley (Ed.), *Trauma and its wake.* New York: Brunner/Mazel.

Kellner, R. (1982). Psychotherapeutic strategies in hypochondriasis: A clinical study. *American Journal of Psychotherapy, 36,* 146–157.

Kellner, R. (1985). Functional somatic symptoms and hypochondriasis. *Archives of General Psychiatry, 42,* 821–833.

Kelly, G. A. (1955). *The psychology of personal constructs.* New York: Norton.

Kelly, J. G. (1966). Ecological constraints on mental health services. *American Psychologist, 21,* 535–539.

Kendall, P. C. (1984). Cognitive-behavioral self-control therapy for children. *Journal of Child Psychology and Psychiatry, 25,* 173–179.

Kendler, K. S. (1983). A current perspective on twin studies of schizophrenia. *American Journal of Psychiatry, 140,* 1413–1425.

Kendler, K. S. (1988). Familial aggregation of schizophrenia and schizophrenic spectrum disorders. *Archives of General Psychiatry, 45,* 377–383.

Kendler, K. S., Glaser, W. M., & Morgenstern, H. (1983). Dimensions of delusional experience. *American Journal of Psychiatry, 140,* 466–469.

Kendler, K. S., Gruenberg, A. M., & Tsuang, M. T. (1988). A family study of the subtypes of schizophrenia. *American Journal of Psychiatry, 145,* 57–62.

Kendler, K. S., & Hays, P. (1982). Familial and sporadic schizophrenia: A symptomatic, prognostic, and EEG comparison. *American Journal of Psychiatry, 139,* 1557–1562.

Kerachsky, S., & Thornton, C. (1987). Findings from the STETs transitional employment demonstration. *Exceptional Children, 53,* 515–521.

Kerlinger, F. N. (1971). *Foundations of behavioral research.* New York: Holt, Rinehart & Winston.

Kerlitz, I., & Fulton, J. P. (1984). *The insanity defense and its alternatives: A guide to policy makers.* Williamsburg, VA: National Center for State Courts.

Kernberg, O. F. (1975). *Borderline conditions and pathological narcissism.* New York: Jason Aronson.

Kernberg, O. (1976). Technical considerations in the treatment of borderline personality organization. *Journal of the American Psychoanalytic Association, 24,* 795–829.

Kernberg, O. (1980). Developmental theory, structural organization, and psychoanalytic technique. In *Reapproachment.* New York: Aronson.

Kety, S. S. (1979). Disorders of the human brain. *Scientific American, 241,* 202–214.

Kety, S. [S.], Rosenthal, D., Wender, P. H., & Schulsinger, F. (1968). The types and prevalence of mental illness in the biologic and adoptive families of adopted schizophrenics. In D. Rosenthal & S. Kety (Eds.), *The transmission of schizophrenia.* New York: Pergamon Press.

Kety, S. S., Rosenthal, D., Wender, P. H., Schulsinger, F., & Jacobsen, B. (1975). Mental illness in the biological and adoptive families of adopted individuals who have become schizophrenic: A preliminary report based on psychiatric interviews. In R. R. Fieve, D. Rosenthal, & H. Brill (Eds.), *Genetic research in psychiatry.* Baltimore: Johns Hopkins University Press.

Keyes, D. (1981). *The minds of Billy Milligan.* New York: Bantam.

Khanna, S., Desai, N. G., & Channabasavanna, S. M. (1987). A treatment package for transsexualism. *Behavior Therapy, 2,* 193–199.

Kiecolt-Glaser, J. K., & Glaser, R. (1988). Psychological influences on immunity: Implications for AIDS. *American Psychologist, 43,* 892–898.

Kiecolt-Glaser, J. K., Glaser, R., Dyer, C., Shuttleworth, E. C., Ogrocki, P., & Speicher, C. E. (1987). Chronic stress and immune function in family care-givers of Alzheimer's disease victims. *Psychosomatic Medicine, 49,* 523–535.

Kiesler, C. A. (1982). Mental hospitals and alternative care: Noninstitutionalization as potential public policy for mental patients. *American Psychologist, 37,* 349–360.

Kilbourne, B., & Richardson, J. T. (1984). Psychotherapy and new religions in a pluralistic society. *American Psychologist, 39,* 237–251.

Kilmann, P., Sabalis, R., Gearing, M., Bukstel, L., & Scovern, A. (1982). The treatment of sexual paraphilias: A review of theoutcome research. *Journal of Sex Research, 18,* 193–252.

Kilmann, P. R., & Auerbach, R. (1979). Treatments of premature ejaculation and psychogenic impotence: A critical review of the literature. *Archives of Sexual Behavior, 8,* 81–100.

Kilmann, P. R., Mills, K. H., Caid, C., Davidson, E., Bella, B., Milan, R., Drose, G., Boland, J., Follingstad, D., Montgomery, B., & Wanlass, R. (1986). Treatment of secondary orgasmic dysfunction: An outcome study. *Archives of Sexual Behavior, 15,* 211–229.

Kilpatrick, D. G., Veronen, L. J., & Best, C. L. (1985). Factors predicting psychological distress among rape victims (pp. 113–141). In C. R. Figley (Ed.), *Trauma and its wake.* New York: Brunner/Mazel.

Kilpatrick, D. G., Veronen, L. J., & Resick, P. A. (1979). The aftermath of rape: Recent empirical findings. *American Journal of Orthopsychiatry, 49,* 658–669.

Kimmel, P. (1984). Information and action. *Division of Community Psychology Newsletter, 18,* 13.

Kinsey, A. C., Pomeroy, W. G., & Martin, C. E. (1948). *Sexual behavior in the human male.* Philadelphia: Saunders.

Kinsey, A. C., Pomeroy, W. B., Martin, C. E., & Gebhard, P. H. (1953). *Sexual behavior in the human female.* Philadelphia: Saunders.

Kinzie, J. D., Frederickson, R. H., Ben, R., Fleck, J., & Karls, W. (1984). Posttraumatic stress disorder. *American Journal of Psychiatry, 141,* 645–650.

Kirkpatrick, D. R. (1984). Age, gender and patterns of common intense fears among adults. *Behavior Research and Therapy, 22,* 141–150.

Kirkpatrick, J. S. (1975). Guidelines for counseling young people with sexual concerns. *Personnel and Guidance Journal, 54,* 145–148.

Kirkpatrick, M., Smith, D., & Roy, R. (1981). Lesbian mothers and their children: A comparative survey. *American Journal of Orthopsychiatry, 5,* 545–551.

Klagsbrun, F. (1976). *Too young to die: Youth and suicide.* Boston: Houghton Mifflin.

Klein, D., Gittelman, R., & Quitkin, F., et al. (1980). *Diagnosis and drug treatment of psychiatric disorders: Adults and children* (pp. 268–404). Baltimore: Williams & Wilkins.

Klein, D. C. (1968). *Community dynamics and mental health.* New York: Wiley.

Klein, D. F. (1981). Anxiety reconceptualized. In D. F. Klein & J. G. Rabkin (Eds.), *Anxiety: New research and changing concepts* (pp. 235–262). New York: Raven Press.

Klein, D. F. (1984). Psychopharmacologic treatment of panic disorder. *Psychosomatics, 25,* 32–36.

Klein, E., & Uhde, T. W. (1988). Controlled study of Verapamil for treatment of panic disorder. *American Journal of Psychiatry, 145,* 431–434.

Klein, M. (1975). *Envy and gratitude and other works, 1946–1963.* London: Hogarth.

Klein, R. G. (1987). Prognosis of attention deficit disorder and its management in adolescence. *Pediatrics in Review, 8,* 216–222.

Klein, W. L. (1967). The training of human service aides. In E. L. Cowen, E. A. Gardner, & M. Zax (Eds.), *Emergent approaches to mental health problems.* New York: Appleton-Century-Crofts.

Kleinberg, J., & Galligan, B. (1983). Effects of deinstitutionalization on adaptive behavior of mentally retarded adults. *American Journal of Mental Deficiency, 88,* 21–27.

Kleinmutz, B. (1967). Personality measurement: An introduction. Homewood, IL: Dorsey.

Klerman, G. L. (1982). Practical issues in the treatment of depression and mania. In E. S. Paykel (Ed.), *Handbook of affective disorders.* New York: Guilford Press.

Klopfer, B., & Davidson, H. (1962). *The Rorschach technique.* New York: Harcourt, Brace, & World.

Kluft, R. P. (1982). Varieties of hypnotic interventions in the treatment of multiple personality. *American Journal of Clinical Hypnosis, 24,* 230–240.

Kluft, R. P. (1985). Using hypnotic inquiry protocols to monitor treatment progress and stability in multiple personality disorder. *American Journal of Clinical Hypnosis, 28,* 63–74.

Kluft, R. P. (1987). First-rank symptoms as a diagnostic clue to multiple personality disorder. *American Journal of Psychiatry, 144,* 293–298.

Kneisel, P. J., & Richards, G. P. (1988). Crisis intervention after the suicide of a teacher. *Professional psychology: Research and practice, 19,* 165–169.

Knopf, I. J. (1984). *Childhood Psychopathology* (2nd ed.). Englewood Cliffs, NJ: Prentice-Hall.

Knott, J., Platt, E., Ashley, M., & Gottlieb, J. (1953). A familial evaluation of the electroencephalogram of patients with primary behavior disorder and psychopathic personality. *EEG and Clinical Neurophysiology, 5,* 363–370.

Kobasa, S. C., Hilker, R. J., & Maddi, S. R. (1979). Psychological hardiness. *Journal of Occupational Medicine, 21,* 595–598.

Kockott, G., & Fahrner, E.- M. (1987). Transsexuals who have not undergone surgery: A follow-up study. *Archives of Sexual Behavior, 16,* 511–522.

Koegel, R. L., Schreibman, L., O'Neill, R. E., & Burke, J. C. (1983). The personality and family-interaction characteristics of parents of autistic children. *Journal of Consulting and Clinical Psychology, 51,* 683–692.

Kohlenberg, R. J. (1973). Behavioristic approach to multiple personality: A case study. *Behavior Therapy, 4,* 137–140.

Kohlenberg, R. J. (1974). Directed masturbation and the treatment of primary orgasmic dysfunction. *Archives of Sexual Behavior, 3,* 349–356.

Kohon, G. (1987). Fetishism revisited. *International Journal of Psycho-Analysis, 68,* 213–228.

Kohut, H., & Wolf, E. S. (1978). The disorders of the self and then treatment: An outline. *International Journal of Psychoanalysis, 59,* 413–425.

Kolarsky, A., & Madlatfousek, J. (1983). The inverse rule of preparatory erotic stimulation in exhibitionists: Phallometric studies. *Archives of Sexual Behavior, 12,* 123–148.

Kolb, L. C. (1987). A neuropsychological hypothesis explaining posttraumatic stress disorder. *American Journal of Psychiatry, 144,* 989–995.

Kolko, D. J., Ayllon, T., & Torrance, C. (1987). Positive practice routines in overcoming resistance to the treatment of school phobia: A case study with follow-up. *Journal of Behavior Therapy and Experimental Psychiatry, 18,* 249–257.

Koop, C. E. (1987). Report of the Surgeon General's Workshop on pornography and public health. *American Psychologist, 42,* 944–945.

Kopelman, M. D. (1987). Amnesia: Organic and psychogenic. *British Journal of Psychiatry, 144,* 293–298.

Korchin, S. J. (1976). *Modern clinical psychology.* New York: Basic Books.

Korchin, S. J., & Ruff, G. E. (1964). Personality characteristics of the Mercury astronauts. In G. H. Grosser, H. Wechsler, & M. Greenblatt (Eds.), *The threat of impending disaster.* Cambridge, MA: M.I.T. Press.

Kosky, R. (1983). Childhood suicidal behavior. *Journal of Child Psychology and Psychiatry, 24,* 3, 457–468.

Koss, M. P., Gidycz, C. A., & Wisniewski, N. (1987). The scope of rape: Incidence and prevalence of sexual aggression and victimization in a national sample of higher education students. *Journal of Consulting and Clinical Psychology, 55,* 162–170.

Kourany, R. F. C., & Williams, B. V. (1984). Capgras' syndrome with dysmorphic delusion in an adolescent. *Psychosomatics, 25,* 715–717.

Kovacs, M. (1980). The efficacy of cognitive and behavior therapies for depression. *American Journal of Psychiatry, 137,* 1495–1501.

Kovacs, M., Rush, A., Beck, A., & Hollon, S. (1981). Depressed outpatients treated with cognitive therapy or pharmacotherapy. *Archives of General Psychiatry, 38,* 33–39.

Kovel, J. (1976). *A complete guide to therapy.* New York: Crown.

Kraemer, G. W., & McKinney, W. T. (1979). Interactions of pharmacological agents which alter biogenic amine metabolism and depression: An analysis of contributing factors within a primate model of depression. *Journal of Affective Disorders, 1,* 33–54.

Kraepelin, E. (1923). *Textbook of psychiatry* (8th ed.). New York: Macmillan. (Originally published 1883.)

Kramer, B. (1973, November 16). Mass hysteria: An age-old illness still crops up in modern times. *Wall Street Journal,* p. 36b.

Kramer, M., Rosen, B. M., & Willis, E. M. (1973). Definitions and distributions of mental disorders in a racist society. In C. V. Willie, B. M. Kramer, & B. S. Brown (Eds.), *Racism and mental health*. Pittsburgh: University of Pittsburgh Press.

Kratochwill, T. R., Mott, S. E., & Dodson, C. L. (1984). Case study and single-case research in clinical and applied psychology. In A. S.Bellack & M. Hersen (Eds.), *Research methods in clinical psychology* (pp. 55–99). New York: Pergamon Press.

Kringlen, E. (1964). *Schizophrenia in male MZ twins*. Copenhagen: Scandinavia University Books.

Kringlen, E. (1980). Schizophrenia: Research in Nordic countries. *Schizophrenia Bulletin, 6*, 566–578.

Kroll, P., Chamberlain, K. R., & Halpern, J. (1979). The diagnosis of Briquet's syndrome in a male population: The Veteran's Administration revisited. *Journal of Nervous and Mental Disorders, 167*, 171–174.

Kulka, R. A. (1982). Monitoring social change via survey replication: Prospects and pitfalls from a replication survey of social roles and mental health. *Journal of Social Issues, 38*, 17–38.

Kupfer, F. (1982, December 13). My turn. *Newsweek*, p. 17.

Kushner, M. (1965). The reduction of a long-standing fetish by means of aversive conditioning. In L. P. Ullmann & L. Krasner (Eds.), *Case studies in behavior modification*. New York: Holt, Rhinehart & Winston.

Lacey, J. I., Bateman, D. E., & Van Lehn, R. (1953). Autonomic response specificity. *Psychosomatic Medicine, 15*, 8–21.

Lader, M. H., & Wing, L. (1964). Habituation of the psychogalvanic reflex in patients with anxiety states and in normal subjects. *Journal of Neurology, Neurosurgery, and Psychiatry, 27*, 210–218.

LaGreca, A. M., & Stringer, S. A. (1985). The Wechsler Intelligence Scale for Children—Revised. In C. S. Newmark (Ed.), *Major psychological assessment instruments* (pp. 277–322). Boston: Allyn & Bacon.

Laidlaw, J., & Rickens, A. (Eds.) (1976). *A textbook of epilepsy*. Edinburgh, Scotland: Churchill & Livingston.

Laing, R. D. (1965). Mystification, confusion and conflict. In I. Boszormenyi-Nagy & J. Framo (Eds.), *Intensive family therapy*. New York: Harper & Row.

Lam, T. (1984, June 6). Mental patients may get right to refuse psychotropic drugs. *Ann Arbor News*, pp. 1–4.

Lamb, H. R. (1984). Deinstitutionalization and the homeless mentally ill. *Hospital Community Psychiatry, 35*, 899–907.

Lamb, H. R., & Grant, R. W. (1982). The mentally ill in an urban county jail. *Archives of General Psychiatry, 39*, 17–22.

Lamb, H. R., & Grant, R. W. (1983). Mentally ill women in a county jail. *Archives of General Psychiatry, 40*, 363–368.

Lambert, M. J., Shapiro, D. A., & Bergin, A. E. (1986). The effectiveness of psychotherapy. In S. L. Garfield & A. E. Bergin (Eds.), *Handbook of psychotherapy and behavior change* (3rd ed., pp. 157–212. New York: Wiley.

Lambert, N. (1981). Psychological evidence in Larry P. vs. Wilson Riles: An evaluation by a witness for the defense. *American Psychologist, 36*, 937–952.

Lambert, N. M. (1988). Adolescent outcomes for hyperactive children. *American Psychologist, 43*, 786–799.

Lambert, N. M., Hartsough, C. S., Sassone, D., & Sandoval, J. (1987). Persistence of hyperactivity symptoms from childhood to adolescence and associated outcomes. *American Journal of Orthopsychiatry, 57*, 22–23.

Lambley, P. (1974). Treatment of transvestism and subsequent coital problems. *Journal of Behavior Therapy and Experimental Psychiatry, 5*, 101–102.

Landesman S., & Butterfield, E. C. (1987). Normalization and deinstitutionalization of mentally retarded individuals. *American Psychologist, 42*, 809–816.

Lane, W. D., & Kern, R. M. (1987). Multidimensional treatment of a 14-year-old anorexia nervosa patient. *Journal of Child and Adolescent Psychotherapy, 4*, 211–215.

Lane, R. D., & Schwartz, G. E. (1987). Induction of lateralized sympathetic input to the heart by the CNS during emotional arousal: A possible neurophysiologic trigger of sudden cardiac death. *Psychosomatic Medicine, 49*, 274–284.

Lang, P. J. (1968). Fear reduction and fear behavior: Problems in treating a construct. In J. M. Shlien (Ed.), *Research in psychotherapy* (Vol. 3, pp. 90–102). Washington, D.C.: American Psychological Association.

Langer, E. J., & Rodin, J. (1976). The effects of choice and enhanced personal responsibility for the aged: A field experiment in an institutional setting. *Journal of Personality and Social Psychology, 34*, 191–198.

Langevin, R., Paitich, D., Ramsay, G., Anderson, C., Kamrad, J., Pope, S., Geller, G., Pearl, L., & Newman, S. (1979). Experimental studies of exhibitionism. *Archives of Sexual Behavior, 8*, 307–331.

Langhorne, J. E., Loney, J., Paternite, C. E., & Bechtoldt, H. P. (1976). Childhood hyperkinesis: A return to the source. *Journal of Abnormal Psychology, 85*, 201–209.

Larkin, A. R. (1979). The form and content of schizophrenic hallucinations. *American Journal of Psychiatry, 136*, 940–943.

Last, C. G., Francis, G., Hersen, M., Kazdin, A. E., & Strauss, C. C. (1987). Separation anxiety and school phobia: A comparison using DSM-III criteria. *American Journal of Psychiatry, 144*, 653–657.

Last, C. G., Phillips, J. E., & Statfeld, A. (1987). Childhood anxiety disorders in mothers and their children. *Child Psychiatry and Human Development, 18,* 103–109.

Laughlin, H. P. (1967). *The neuroses.* Washington, D.C.: Butterworth.

Lazarus, A. A. (1967). In support of technical eclecticism. *Psychological Reports, 21,* 415–416.

Lazarus, A. A. (1968). Learning theory and the treatment of depression. *Behavior Research and Therapy, 6,* 83–90.

Lazarus, A. A. (Ed.) (1976). *Multimodel behavior therapy.* New York: Springer.

Lazarus, A. A. (1977). Has behavior therapy outlived its usefulness? *American Psychologist, 32,* 550–554.

Lazarus, A. A. (1984). Multimodel therapy. In R. J. Corsini (Ed.), *Current psychotherapies.* Itasca, IL: Peacock.

Lazarus, R. S. (1966). *Patterns of adjustment and human effectiveness.* New York: McGraw-Hill.

Lazarus, R. S. (1969). *Psychological stress and the coping process.* New York: McGraw-Hill.

Lazarus, R. S. (1979, November). Positive denial: The case for not facing reality. *Psychology Today,* pp. 44–60.

Lazarus, R. S. (1983). *Psychological stress.* New York: McGraw-Hill.

Lazarus, R. S., & Launier, R. (1979). Stress-related transactions between person and environment. In L. A. Pervin & M. Lewis (Eds.), *Internal and external determinants.* New York: Plenum.

Leach, B. (1987). How to retain black students on predominantly white campuses. *Black Issues in Higher Education, 4,* 36.

LeDoux, J. C., & Hazelwood, R. R. (1985). Police attitude and beliefs toward rape. *Journal of Police Science Administration, 13,* 211–220.

Lee, C. L., & Bates, J. E. (1985). Mother-child interaction at age two years and perceived difficult temperament. *Child Development, 56,* 1314–1325.

Lee, E. (1985). Inpatient psychiatric services for Southeast Asian refugees. In T. C. Owan (Ed.), *Southeast Asian mental health: Treatment, prevention, services, training, and research* (pp. 307–328). Washington, D.C.: U.S. Government Printing Office.

Leff, J. P. (1976). Schizophrenia amd sensitivity to the family environment. *Schizophrenia Bulletin, 2,* 566–574.

Leff, M. J., Roach, J. F., & Bunney, W. E. (1970). Environmental factors preceding the onset of severe depressions. *Psychiatry, 33,* 298–311.

Lehmann, H. E. (1974). Physical therapies of schizophrenia. In S. Arieti (Ed.), *American handbook of psychiatry* (2nd ed., Vol. 2). New York: Basic Books.

Lehmann, H. E. (1985). Affective disorders: Clinical features. In H. I. Kaplan & B. J. Sadock (Eds.), *Comprehensive textbook of psychiatry/IV.* (pp. 786–810). Baltimore: Williams & Wilkins.

Leitenberg, H., Gross, J., Peterson, J., & Rosen, J. (1984). Analysis of an anxiety model and the process of change during exposure plus response prevention treatment of bulimia nervosa. *Behavior Therapy, 15,* 3–20.

Lelliott, P. T., Marks, I. M., Monteiro, W. O., Tsakiris, L. F., & Noshirvani, H. (1987). Agoraphobics 5 years after imipramine and exposure. *Journal of Nervous and Mental Disease, 175,* 599–605.

Lennox, W. J., & Lennox, M. A. (1960). *Epilepsy and related disorders.* Boston: Little, Brown.

Leonard, S. R., & Hayes, S. C. (1983). Sexual fantasy alternation. *Journal of Behavior Therapy and Experimental Psychiatry, 14,* 241–249.

Leong, F. (1986). Counseling and psychotherapy with Asian-Americans: Review of the literature. *Journal of Counseling Psychology, 33,* 196–206.

Lerner, J. V., Hertzog, C., Hooker, K. A., Hassibi, M., & Thomas, A. (1988). A longitudinal study of negative emotional states.

Levenkron, J. C., Cohen, J. D., Mueller, H. S., & Fisher, E. B. (1983). Modifying the type A coronary-prone behavior pattern. *Journal of Consulting and Clinical Psychology, 51,* 192–204.

Levenson, A. I. (1972). The community mental health centers program. In S. E. Golann & C. Eisdorfer (Eds.), *Handbook of community mental health.* New York: Appleton-Century-Crofts.

Levine, D. S., & Willner, S. G. (1976, February). *The cost of mental illness, 1974. Mental Health Statistical Note No. 125,* pp. 1–7. Washington, D.C.: National Institute of Mental Health.

Levine, M. D., & Jordan, N. C. (1987). Learning disorders: The neurodevelopmental underpinnings. *Contemporary Pediatrics, 4,* 16–43.

Levine, M., & Perkins, D. V. (1987). *Principles of community psychology: Perspectives and applications.* New York: Oxford University Press.

Levine, S. V. (1984). *Radical departures: Desperate detours to growing up.* New York: Harcourt, Brace, Jovanovich.

Levis, D. J. (1985). Implosive therapy: A comprehensive extension of conditioning theory of fear/anxiety to psychology. In S. Reiss & R. R. Bootzin (Eds.), *Theoretical issues in behavior therapy.* New York: Academic Press.

Levy, R. (1988). Suicide, homicide, amd psychiatric emergencies. In H. H. Goldman (Ed.), *Review of General Psychiatry* (pp. 651–657). Norwalk, CT: Appleton & Lange.

Lewine, R. (1986). Familial and nonfamilial schizophrenia? *American Journal of Psychiatry, 143,* 1064–1065.

Lewinsohn, P. M. (1974a). A behavioral approach to depression. In R. J. Friedman & M. M. Katz (Eds.), *The psychology of depression: Contemporary theory and research*. New York: Wiley.

Lewinsohn, P. M. (1974b). Clinical and theoretical aspects of depression. In K. S. Calhoun, H. C. Adams, & K. M. Mitchell (Eds.), *Innovative treatment methods of psychopathology*. New York: Wiley.

Lewinsohn, P. M. (1977). The behavioral study and treatment of depression. In M. Hersen, R. M. Eisler, & P. M. Miller (Eds.), *Progress in behavior modification*. New York: Academic Press.

Lewinsohn, P. M., & Graf, M. (1973). Pleasant activities and depression. *Journal of Consulting and Clinical Psychology, 41*, 261–268.

Lewinsohn, P. M., Hoberman, H. M., & Rosenbaum, M. (1988). A prospective study of risk factors for unipolar depression. *Journal of Abnormal Psychology, 97*, 251–264.

Lewinsohn, P. M., & Libet, J. (1972). Pleasant events, activity schedules, and depression. *Journal of Abnormal Psychology, 79*, 291–295.

Lewinsohn, P. M., Weinstein, M. S., & Alper, T. (1970). A behavioral approach to the group treatment of depressed persons: A methodological contribution. *Journal of Chemical Psychology, 26*, 525–532.

Lichtenstein, E. (1982). The smoking problem: A behavioral perspective. *Journal of Consulting and Clinical Psychology, 50*, 804–819.

Lichtenstein, E., & Danaher, B. (1976). Modification of smoking behavior: A critical analysis of theory, research, and practice. In M. Hersen, R. Eisler, & P. Miller (Eds.), *Progress in behavior modification: 3*. New York: Academic Press.

Lichtenstein, E., & Glasgow, R. (1977). Rapid smoking: Side effects and safeguards. *Journal of Consulting and Clinical Psychology, 45*, 815–821.

Lichtenstein, E., & Rodrigues, M. (1977). Long-term effects of rapid smoking treatment for dependent cigarette smokers. *Addictive Behaviors, 2*, 109–112.

Lieberman R. P., Mueser, K. T., & Wallace, C. J. (1986). Social skills training for schizophrenic individuals at risk for relapse. *American Journal of Psychiatry, 143*, 523–526.

Liebert, R. M., & Baron, R. A. (1972). Some immediate effects of television violence on children's behavior. *Developmental Psychology, 6*, 469–475.

Lin, N., Simeone, R. S., Ensel, W. M., & Kuo, W. (1979). Social support, stressful life events, and illness: A model and an empirical test. *Journal of Health and Social Behavior, 20*, 108–119.

Lindemann, E. (1960). Psychosocial factors as stressor agents. In I. H. Tanner (Ed.), *Stress and psychiatric disorder*. Oxford, England: Basil, Blockwell & Mott.

Lindsay, W. R., Gamisu, C. V., McLaughlin, E., Hood, E. M., & Espie, C. A. (1987). A controlled trial of treatments for generalized anxiety. *British Journal of Clinical Psychology, 26*, 3–15.

Lipkowitz, M. H., & Idupuganti, S. (1983). Diagnosing schizophrenia in 1980: A survey of U.S. psychiatrists. *American Journal of Psychiatry, 140*, 52–55.

Lipsitt, D. R. (1974). Psychodynamic considerations of hypochrondriasis. *Psychosomatic Medicine, 23*, 132–141.

Lipsitt, D. R. (1983). The Munchausen mystery. *Psychology Today, 17*, 78–79.

Lipsky, M. J., Kassinove, H., & Miller, N. J. (1980). Effects of rational-emotive therapy, rational role reversal and rational-emotive imagery on the emotional adjustment of community mental health center patients. *Journal of Consulting & Clinical Psychology, 48*, 366–374.

Lishman, W. A. (1978). *The psychological consequences of cerebral disorder*. Oxford, England: Blackwell.

Livingston, J. A. (1982). Responses to sexual harassment on the job: Legal, organizational, and individual actions. *Journal of Social Issues, 38*, 5–22.

Livnat, S., & Felton, D. L. (1985). To the editor. *New England Journal of Medicine, 313*, 1357.

London, P. (1964a). *Modes and morals of psychotherapy*. New York: Holt, Rinehart & Winston.

London, P. (1964b). Subject characteristics in hypnosis research: Part 1. A survey of experience, interest, and opinion. *International Journal of Experimental Hypnosis, 9*, 151–161.

Longstreth, L. E. (1981). Revisiting Skeels's final study: A critique. *Developmental Psychology, 17*, 620–625.

LoPiccolo, L. (1980). Low sexual desire. In S. R. Leiblum & L. A. Pervin (Eds.), *Principles and practice of sex therapy*. New York: Guilford Press.

LoPiccolo, J., Heiman, J. R., Hogan, D. R., & Roberts, C. W. (1985). Effectiveness of single therapists versus cotherapy teams in sex therapy. *Journal of Consulting and Clinical Psychology, 53*, 287–294.

LoPiccolo, J., & Stock, W. E. (1986). Treatment of sexual dysfunction. *Journal of Consulting and Clinical Psychology, 54*, 158–167.

Lord, C., & Ward, M. J. (1984). Autism and childhood psychosis. In H. E. Adams & P. B. Sutker (Eds.), *Comprehensive handbook of psychopathology* (pp. 973–1000). New York: Plenum Press.

Lorion, R. P. (1973). Socioeconomic status and traditional treatment approaches reconsidered. *Psychological Bulletin, 79*, 262–270.

Lothstein, L. (1977). Psychotherapy with patients with gender dysphoria syndromes. *Bulletin of Menninger Clinic, 41*, 563–582.

Lothstein, L. M. (1982). Sex reassignment surgery: Historical, bioethical, and theoretical issues. *American Journal of Psychiatry, 139,* 417–426.

Lovaas, O. I. (1977). *The autistic child: Language development through behavior modification.* New York: Halsted Press.

Lovaas, O. I., Koegel, R. L., & Schreibman, L. (1979). Stimulus over selectivity in autism: A review of research. *Psychological Bulletin, 86,* 1236–1254.

Lovaas, O. I., Koegel, R., Simmons, J. Q., & Long, J. S. (1973). Some generalization and follow-up measures on autistic children in behavior therapy. *Journal of Applied Behavior Analysis, 6,* 131–166.

Lovaas, O. I., Schaeffer, B., & Simmons, J. Q. (1965). Building social behavior in autistic children by use of electric shock. *Journal of Experimental Research in Personality, 1,* 99–109.

Lovaas, O. I., Schreibman, L., Koegel, R., & Rehm, R. (1971). Selective responding by autistic children to multiple sensory input. *Journal of Abnormal Psychology, 77,* 211–222.

Luborsky, L., Chandler, M., Averbach, A. H., Cohen, J., & Bachrach, H. (1971). Factors influencing the outcome of psychotherapy: A review of quantitative research. *Psychological Bulletin, 75,* 145–185.

Ludwig, A. M., Brandsma, J. M., Wilbur, C. B., Bendfeldt, F., & Jameson, D. H. (1972). The objective study of multiple personality. *Archivesof General Psychiatry, 26,* 298–310.

Luiselli, J. K., & Slocumb, P. R. (1983). Management of multiple aggression behaviors by differential reinforcement. *Journal of Behavior Therapy and Experimental Psychiatry, 14,* 343–347.

Luparello, T., Lyons, H. A., Bleecker, E. R., & McFadden, E. R. (1968). Influences of suggestion on airway reactivity in asthmatic subjects. *Psychosomatic Medicine, 30,* 819–825.

Luria, A. R. (1982). *Language and cognition.* New York: Oxford University Press.

Lykken, D. F. (1957). A study of anxiety in the sociopathic personality. *Journal of Abnormal and Social Psychology, 55,* 6–10.

Lykken, D. T. (1982). Fearlessness: Its carefree charm and deadly risks. *Psychology Today, 16,* 20–28.

Macaskill, N. D. (1986). Delusion and parasitosis: Successful nonpharmacological treatment of Folie-á-deux. *British Journal of Psychiatry, 150,* 261–263.

MacEachron, A. E. (1979). Mentally retarded offenders; Prevalence and characteristics. *American Journal of Mental Deficiency, 84,* 165–176.

MacEachron, A. E. (1983). Institutional reform and adaptive functioning of mentally retarded persons: A field experiment. *American Journal of Mental Deficiency, 88,* 2–12.

Machover, K. (1949). *Personality projection in the drawing of the human figure: A method of personality investigation.* Springfield, IL: Thomas.

Maddi, S. R. (1972). *Personality theories.* Homewood, IL: Dorsey.

Madsen, C. H., Becker, W. C., Thomas, D. R., Koser, L., & Plager, E. (1970). An analysis of the reinforcing function of "sit-down" commands. In R. K. Parker (Ed.), *Readings in educational psychology.* Boston: Allyn & Bacon.

Magni, G., DiMario, F., Rizzardo, R., Pulin, S., & Naccarato, R. (1986). Personality profiles of patients with duodenal ulcer. *American Journal of Psychiatry, 143,* 1297–1300.

Magni, G., & Schifano, F. (1984). Psychological distress after stroke. *Journal of Neurology, Neurosurgery and Psychiatry, 47,* 567–568.

Maher, B. A. (1966). *Principles of psychopathology.* New York: McGraw-Hill.

Maher, W. B., & Maher, B. A. (1985). Psychopathology: I. From ancient times to the eighteenth century. In G. A. Kimble & K. Schlesinger (Eds.), *Topics in the history of psychology* (Vol. 2). Hillsdale, NJ: Erlbaum.

Mahler, M. S. (1979). *The selected papers of Margaret S. Mahler. Vol. 2.* New York: Aronson.

Mahler, M. S., Pine, F., & Bergman, A. (1975). *The psychological birth of the human infant.* New York: Basic Books.

Mahoney, M. J. (1977). Reflections on the cognitive-learning trend in psychotherapy. *American Psychologist, 32,* 5–13.

Mahoney, M. J., & Lyddon, W. J. (1988). Recent developments in cognitive approaches to counseling and psychotherapy. *Counseling Psychologist, 16,* 190–234.

Maier, S. F., & Laudenslager, M. (1985). Stress and health: Exploring the link. *Psychology Today, 19,* 44–49.

Malamuth, N. M., & Briere, J. (1986). Sexual violence in the media: Indirect effects on aggression against women. *Journal of Social Issues, 42,* 75–92.

Malamuth, N. M., & Check, J. V. P. (1981). The effects of mass media exposure on acceptance of violence against women: A field experiment. *Journal of Research in Personality, 15,* 436–446.

Malamuth, N. M., & Check, J. V. P. (1983). Sexual arousal to rape depictions: Individual differences. *Journal of Abnormal Psychology, 92,* 55–67.

Malatesta, V. J., & Adams, H. E. (1984). The sexual dysfunctions. In H. E. Adams & P. B. Sutker (Eds.). *Comprehensive handbook of psychopathology,* pp. 725–776. New York: Plenum Press.

Malatesta, V. J., Pollack, R. H., Wilbanks, W. A., & Adams, H. E. (1979). Alcohol effects on the orgasmic-ejaculatory response in human males. *Journal of Sex Research, 15,* 101–107.

Malinow, K. L. (1981). Passive-aggressive personality. In J. R. Lion (Ed.), *Personality disorders: Diagnosis and management*. Baltimore: Williams & Wilkins.

Mallick, M. J., Whipple, T. W., & Huerta, E. (1987). Behavioral and psychological traits of weight conscious teenagers: A comparison of eating disordered patients and high- and low-risk groups. *Adolescence, 22,* 157–168.

Malloy, P. F., Fairbank, J. A., & Keane, T. M. (1983). Validation of a multi-method assessment of posttraumatic stress disorders in Vietnam veterans. *Journal of Consulting and Clinical Psychology, 51,* 488–494.

Maltz, A. (1982). *Autism: Diagnostic and placement consideration*. Michigan State Planning Council for Developmental Disabilities.

Mann, J. J., Stanley, J. M., McBride, P. A., & McEwen, B. S. (1986). Increased serotonin Z and B-adrenergic receptor binding in the frontal cortices of suicide victims. *Archives of General Psychiatry, 43,* 954–956.

Marantz, S. (1985, May 12). In the eyes of his public Ali is still the greatest. *Boston Globe,* p. 63.

Marchione, K., Michelson, L., Greenwald, M., & Dancu, C. (1987). Cognitive behavioral treatment of agoraphobia. *Behaviour Research and Therapy, 25,* 319–328.

Margolies, P. J. (1977). Behavioral approaches to the treatment of early infantile autism: A review. *Psychological Bulletin, 84,* 359–365.

Marcus, J., Hans, S. L., Nagler, S., Auerbach, J. G., Mirsky, A. F., & Aubrey, A. (1987). Review of the NIMH Israeli kibbutz-city study and the Jerusalem Infant Developmental study. *Schizophrenia Bulletin, 13,* 425–437.

Margraf, J., Ehlers, A., & Roth, W. T. (1986). Biological models of panic disorder and agoraphobia—A review. *Behaviour Research and Therapy, 24,* 553–567.

Margraf, J., Ehlers, A., & Roth, W. T. (1987). Panic attacks associated with perceived heart rate acceleration: A case report. *Behavior Therapy, 18,* 84–89.

Marks, I. M. (1976). The current status of behavioral psychotherapy: Theory and practice. *American Journal of Psychiatry, 133,* 253–261.

Marks, I. M. (1983). Are there anticompulsive or antiphobic drugs? Review of the evidence. *British Journal of Psychiatry, 143,* 338–347.

Marks, I. M. (1987). *Fears, phobias, and rituals*. New York: Oxford University Press.

Marks, I. M., Gray, S., Cohen, D., Hill, R., Mawson, D., Rammn E., and Stern, R. S. (1983). Imipramine and brief therapist-aided exposure in agoraphobics having self-improvement homework. *Archives of General Psychiatry, 40,* 153–162.

Marlatt, G. A. (1978). Craving for alcohol, loss of control and relapse: A cognitive-behavioral analysis. In P. E. Nathan & G. A. Marlatt (Eds.), *Experimental and behavioral approaches to alcoholism*. New York: Plenum.

Marlatt, G. A. (1983). The controlled-drinking controversy: A commentary. *American Psychologist, 38,* 1097–1110.

Marlatt, G. A., Demming, B., & Reid, J. (1973). Loss-of-control drinking in alcoholics: An experimental analogue. *Journal of Abnormal Psychology, 81,* 233–241.

Marmar, C. R. (1988). Personality disorders. In H. H. Goldman (Ed.), *Review of General Psychiatry* (pp. 401–424). Norwalk, CT: Appleton & Lange.

Marmor, J., & Woods, S. M. (1980). *The interface between the psychodynamic and behavioral therapies*. New York: Plenum Medical.

Marmot, M. G., & Syme, S. L. (1976). Acculturation and coronary heart disease in Japanese-Americans. *American Journal of Epidemiology, 104,* 225–247.

Marshall, W. L. (1988a). Behavioral indices of habituation and sensitization during exposure to phobic stimuli. *Behaviour Research and Therapy, 26,* 67–77.

Marshall, W. L. (1988b). The use of sexually explicit stimuli by rapists, child molesters, and non offenders. *Journal of Sex Research, 25,* 267–288.

Marshall, W. L., Earls, C. M., Segal, Z., & Durke, J. (1983). A behavioral program for the assessment and treatment of sexual aggressors. In K. D. Craig & R. J. McMahon (Eds.), *Advances in clinical behavior therapy,* pp. 148–174. New York: Brunner/Mazel.

Martin, C. E. (1981). Factors affecting sexual functioning in 60-79-year-old married males. *Archives of Sexual Behavior, 10,* 399–420.

Maslow, A. H. (1954). *Motivation and personality*. New York: Harper & Row.

Masserman, J., Yum, K., Nicholson, J., & Lee, S. (1944). Neurosis and alcohol: An experimental study. *American Journal of Psychiatry, 101,* 389–395.

Masters, W. H., & Johnson, V. E. (1966). *Human sexual response*. Boston: Little, Brown.

Masters, W. H., & Johnson, V. E. (1970). *Human sexual inadequacy*. London: Churchill.

Masters, W. H., & Johnson, V. E. (1979). *Homosexuality in perspective*. Boston: Little, Brown.

Masterson, J. F. (1981). *The narcissistic and borderline disorders: An integrated developmental approach*. New York: Brunner/Mazel.

Mastropieri, M. A. (1987). Age at start as correlate of intervention effectiveness. *Psychology in the Schools, 24,* 59–62.

Masuda, M., & Holmes, T. H. (1976). The social readjustment rating scale: A cross-cultural study of Japanese and Americans. *Journal of Psychosomatic Research, 11,* 227–237.

Matarazzo, J. D. (1984). Behavioral health: A 1990 challenge for the health profession. In J. D. Matarazzo, S. M. Weiss, J. A. Herd, N. E. Miller, & S. M. Weiss (Eds.), *Behavioral health: A handbook of health enhancement and disease prevention* (pp. 3–40). New York: Wiley.

Matheny, K. B., Aycock, D. W., Pugh, J. L., Curlette, W. L., & Silva Cannella, K. P. (1986). Stress coping. *Counseling Psychologist, 14*, 499–549.

Matson, J. L. (1987). Trends and developments in behavioral assessment and treatment of mentally retarded persons. *School Psychology Review, 16*, 566–581.

Mattick, R. P., & Peters, L. (1988). Treatment of severe social phobia: Effects of guided exposure with and without cognitive restructuring. *Journal of Consulting and Clinical Psychology, 56*, 251–260.

Mattison, J. (1973). Marriage and mental handicap. In F. F. De la Crux & G. D. Laveck (Eds.), *Human sexuality and the mentally retarded*. New York: Brunner/Mazel.

Mavissakalian, M. (1987a). Initial depression and response to imipramine in agoraphobia. *Journal of Nervous and Mental Disease, 175*, 358–361.

Mavissakalian, M. (1987b). The placebo effect in agoraphobia. *Journal of Nervous and Mental Disease, 175*, 95–99.

Mavissakalian, M., Michelson, L., & Dealy, R. S. (1983). Pharmacological treatment of agoraphobia: Imipramine with programmed practice. *British Journal of Psychiatry, 143*, 348–355.

May, P. R. (1968). *Treatment of schizophrenia: A comparative study of five treatment methods*. New York: Science House.

May, R. (1958). *Existence: A new dimension in psychiatry and psychology*. New York: Basic Books.

May, R. (Ed.) (1961). *Existential psychology*. New York: Random House.

May, R. (1967). *Psychology and the human dilemma*. New York: Van Nostrand.

May, R., Angel, E., & Ellenberger, H. F. (Eds.). (1958). *Existence*. New York: Basic Books.

McAdoo, W. G., & DeMeyer, M. K. (1978). Personality characteristics of parents. In M. Rutter & E. Schopler (Eds.), *Autism: A reappraisal of concepts and treatment*. New York: Plenum Press.

McBride, M. C., & Ender, K. L. (1977). Sexual attitudes and behavior among college students. *Journal of College Student Personnel, 18*, 183–187.

McCann, B. S., Woofolk, R. L., & Lehrer, P. M. (1987). Specificity in response to treatment: A study of interpersonal anxiety. *Behaviour Research and Therapy, 25*, 129–136.

McCary, J. L. (1973). *Human sexuality*. New York: Van Nostrand.

McCauley, E., & Ehrhardt, A. A. (1984). Follow-up of females with gender identity disorders. *Journal of Nervous and Mental Disease, 172*, 353–358.

McCauley, E., Kay, T., Ito, J., & Treder, R. (1987). The Turner Syndrome: Cognitive deficits, affective discrimination, and behavior problems. *Child Development, 58*, 464–473.

McClelland, D., Davis, W., Kalin, R., & Wanner, E. (1972). *The drinking man*. New York: Free Press.

McConaghy, N. (1983). Agoraphobia, compulsive behaviours, and behaviour completion mechanisms. *Australian and New England Journal of Psychiatry, 17*, 170–179.

McCord, W., & McCord, J. (1964). *The psychopath: An essay on the criminal mind*. Princeton, NJ: Van Nostrand.

McCracken, G. H. (1976). Neonatal septicemia and meningitis. *Hospital Practice, 11*, 89–97.

McEwan, K. L., & Devins, G. M. (1983). Is increased arousal in social anxiety noticed by others? *Journal of Abnormal Psychology, 92*, 417–421.

McGeer, P. L., & McGeer, E. G. (1980). Chemistry of mood and emotions. *Annual Review of Psychology, 31*, 273–307.

McGrath, M. E. (1987). *Where did I go? Schizophrenia: The experiences of patients and families*. Rockville, MD: National Institutes of Health.

McGuire, R. J., Carlisle, J. M., & Young, B. G. (1965). Sexual deviations as conditioned behavior: A hypothesis. *Behavior Research and Therapy, 2*, 185–190.

McIntosh, J. L., & Santos, J. F. (1981). Suicide among Native Americans: A compilation of findings. *Omega: Journal of Death and Dying, 11*, 303–316.

McKeon, P., & Murray, R. (1987). Familial aspects of obsessive-compulsive neurosis. *British Journal of Psychiatry, 151*, 528–534.

McLarnon, L. D., & Kaloupek, D. G. (1988). Psychological investigation of genital herpes recurrence: Prospective assessment and cognitive-behavioral intervention for a chronic physical disorder. *Health Psychology, 1*, 231–249.

McLeod, B. (1985). Real work for real pay. *Psychology Today, 19*, 42–50.

McNally, R. J., & Lorenz, M. (1987). Anxiety sensitivity in agoraphobics. *Journal of Behavior Therapy and Experimental Psychiatry, 18*, 3–11.

McNamee, H. B., Mello, N. K., & Mendelson, J. H. (1968). Experimental analysis of drinking patterns of alcoholics: Concurrent psychiatric observations. *American Journal of Psychiatry, 124*, 1063–1069.

McNeil, E. B. (1974). *The psychology of being human*. San Francisco: Canfield Press.

McQueen, P. C., Spence, M. W., Garner, J. B., Pereira, L. H., & Winson, E. J. T. (1987). Prevalence of major mental retardation and associated disabilities in the

Canadian Maritime Provinces. *American Journal of Mental Deficiency, 91,* 460–466.

Mead, M. (1949). *Male and female.* New York: Morrow.

Meares, A. (1979). Mind and cancer. *Lancet, 22,* 978.

Mechanic, D. (1974). Discussion of research programs on relations between stressful life events and episodes of physical illness. In B. S. Dohrenwend & B. P. Dohrenwend (Eds.), *Stressful life events.* New York: Wiley.

Mechanic, D. (Coordinator). (1978). Report of the task panel on the nature and scope of the problems. In *President's Commission on Mental Health* (Vol. 2, pp. 1–138). Washington, D.C.: U.S. Government Printing Office.

Mednick, S. A. (1970). Breakdown in individuals at high risk for schizophrenia: Possible predispositional perinatal factors. *Mental Hygiene, 54,* 50–63.

Mednick, S. A. (1985). Crime in the family tree. *Psychology Today, 19,* 58–61.

Mednick, S. A., & Christiansen, K. O. (Eds.). (1977). *Biosocial bases of criminal behavior.* New York: Gardner Press.

Mednick, S. A., & Schulsinger, F. (1968). Some premorbid characteristics related to breakdown in children with schizophrenic mothers. In D. Rosenthal & S. Kety (Eds.), *The transmission of schizophrenia.* New York: Pergamon Press.

Meehl, P. E. (1962). Schizotaxia, schizotypia, schizophrenia. *American Psychologist, 17,* 827–838.

Megargee, E. I. (1970). The prediction of violence with psychological tests. In C. D. Speilberger (Ed.), *Current topics in clinical and community psychology* (Vol. 2). New York: Academic Press.

Meichenbaum, D. H. (1972). Cognitive modification of test-anxious college students. *Journal of Consulting and Clinical Psychology, 39,* 370–380.

Meichenbaum, D. H. (1974). The clinical potential of modifying what clients say to themselves. In M. J. Mahoney & C. E. Thoresen (Eds.), *Self-Control: Power to the person.* Monterey, CA: Brooks/Cole.

Meichenbaum, D. H. (1976). Cognitive behavior modification. In J. T. Spence, R. C. Carson, & J. W. Thibaut (Eds.), *Behavioral approaches to therapy.* Morristown, NJ: General Learning Press.

Meichenbaum, D. H. (1977). *Cognitive-behavior modification: An integrative approach.* New York: Plenum.

Meichenbaum, D. H. (1985). *Stress-innoculation training.* New York: Pergamon Press.

Meichenbaum, D. H., & Cameron, R. (1982). Cognitive behavior therapy. In G. T. Wilson & C. M. Franks (Eds.), *Contemporary behavior therapy: Conceptual and empirical foundations.* New York: Guilford Press.

Meichenbaum, D. H., Gilmore, J., & Fedoravicius, A.

(1971). Group insight versus group desensitization in treating speech anxiety. *Journal of Consulting and Clinical Psychology, 36,* 410–421.

Melges, F., & Bowlby, J. (1969). Types of hopelessness in psychopathological process. *Archives of General Psychiatry, 20,* 690–699.

Meltzoff, J., & Kornreich, M. (1970). *Research in psychotherapy.* New York: Atherton.

Mendels, J. (1970). *Concepts of depression* (p. 6). New York: Wiley.

Mercer, J. R. (1979). *System of Multicultural Pluralistic Assessment (SOMPA): Technical manual.* New York: Psychological Corporation.

Mercer, J. R. (1988). *Death of the IQ paradigm: Where do we go from here?* In W. J. Lonner & V. O. Tyler (Eds.). *Cultural and ethnic factors in learning and motivation: Implications for education.* Bellingham, WA: Western Washington University.

Mercer, J. R., & Lewis, J. F. (1977). *SOMPA: For the meaningful assessment of culturally different children.* New York: Psychological Corporation.

Methodology and data analysis of epidemiological investigation on mental disordered in twelve regions of China. (1986). *Chinese Journal of Neurology and Psychology, 19,* 36–79. (Translated into English)

Meyer, J., & Peter, D. (1979). Sex reassignment: Follow-up. *Archives of General Psychiatry, 36,* 1010–1015.

Meyer, R. G., & Osborne, Y. V. H. (1982). *Case studies in abnormal behavior.* Boston: Allyn & Bacon.

Meyer, V., Levey, R., & Schnurer, A. (1974). The behavioral treatment of obsessive compulsive disorders. In H. Beech (Ed.), *Obsessional states.* London: Methuen.

Michelson, L. (1987). Cognitive-behavioral assessment and treatment of agoraphobia. In L. Michelson & M. Ascher (Eds.), *Anxiety and stress disorders: Cognitive behavioral assessment and treatment.* New York: Guilford Press.

Michelson, L., Mavissakalian, M., & Marchione, K. (1988). Cognitive, behavioral, and psychophysiological treatment of agoraphobia: A comparative outcome investigation. *Behavior Therapy, 19,* 97–120.

Michigan Society for Autistic Citizens. (1979). *Autism: Parent survey of early identification and interaction services.* William P. Walsh, M. S. W.

Miklowitz, D. J., Goldstein, M. J., Falloon, I. R. H., & Doaner, J. A. (1984). Interactional correlates of expressed emotion in the families of schizophrenics. *British Journal of Psychiatry, 144,* 482–487.

Miklowitz, D. J., Strachan, A. M., Goldstein, M. J., Doane, J. A., Snyder, K. S., Hogarty, G. E., & Falloon, I. R. H. (1986). Expressed emotion and communication deviance in the families of schizophrenics. *Journal of Abnormal Psychology, 95,* 60–66.

Milich, R., & Pelham, W. E. (1986). Effects of sugar ingestion on the classroom and playground behavior of attention deficit disordered boys. *Journal of Consulting and Clinical Psychology, 54,* 714–718.

Miller, N. (1983). Behavioral medicine: Symbiosis between laboratory and clinic. *Annual Review of Psychology, 34,* 1–31.

Miller, N. E. (1974). Applications of learning and biofeedback to psychiatry and medicine. In A. M. Freedman, H. I. Kaplan, & B. J. Sadock (Eds.), *Comprehensive textbook of psychiatry* (2nd ed.). Baltimore: Williams & Wilkins.

Millon, T. (1973). *Theories of psychopathology and personality.* Philadelphia: Saunders.

Millon, T. (1975). Reflections on Rosenhan's "On being sane in insane places." *Journal of Abnormal Psychology, 84,* 456–461.

Millon, T. (1983). The DSM-III: An insider's perspective. *American Psychologist, 38,* 804–814.

Millon, T., & Diesenhaus, H. I. (1972). *Research methods in psychopathology.* New York: Wiley.

Millon, T., & Everly, G. S. (1985). *Personality and its disorders.* New York: Wiley.

Mills, C. J., & Noyes, H. L. (1984). Patterns and correlates of initial and subsequent drug use among adolescents. *Journal of Consulting and Clinical Psychology, 52,* 231–243.

The mind of a murderer. *Frontline:* Part I (1984).

Miniszek, N. A. (1983). Development of Alzheimer's disease in Down syndrome individuals. *American Journal of Mental Deficiency, 87,* 377–385.

Mintz, I. (1983). Psychoanalytic description: The clinical picture of anorexia nervosa and bulimia. In C. Wilson (Ed.), *Fear of being fat.* New York: Aronson.

Mintz, J., Mintz, L., & Goldstein, M. (1987). Expressed emotion and relapse in first episodes of schizophrenia. *British Journal of Psychiatry, 151,* 314–320.

Minuchin, S. (1974). *Families and family therapy.* Cambridge, MA: Harvard University Press.

Minuchin, S., Rosman, B., & Baker, L. (1978). *Psychosomatic families: Anorexia nervosa in context.* Cambridge, MA: Harvard University Press.

Mischel, W. (1968). *Personality and assessment.* New York: Wiley.

Mitchell, C. M. (1983). The dissemination of a social intervention: Process and effectiveness of two types of paraprofessional change agents. *American Journal of Community Psychology, 11,* 723–740.

Mitchell, J. E., Pyle, R. L., & Eckert, E. D. (1981). Frequency and duration of binge-eating episodes in patients with bulimia. *American Journal of Psychiatry, 138,* 835–836.

Moergen, S., Maier, M., Brown, S., & Pollard, C. A.

(1987). Habituation to fear stimuli in a case of obsessive-compulsive disorder: Examining the generalization process. *Journal of Behavior Therapy and Experimental Psychiatry, 18,* 65–70.

Monahan, J. (1976). The prevention of violence. In J. Monahan (Ed.), *Community mental health and the criminal justice system.* Elmsford, NY: Pergamon Press.

Monahan, J. (1981). *The clinical prediction of violent behavior.* Rockville, MD: National Institute of Mental Health.

Monday, J., Montplaisir, J., & Malo, J-L. (1987). Dream process in asthmatic subjects with nocturnal attacks. *American Journal of Psychiatry, 144,* 638–640.

Money, J. (1987). Masochism: On the childhood origin of paraphilia, opponent-process theory, and antiandrogen therapy. *Journal of Sex Research, 23,* 273–275.

Money, J., & Brennan, J. G. (1968). Sexual dimorphism in the psychology of female transsexuals. *Journal of Nervous and Mental Diseases, 247,* 487–499.

Money, J., Hampson, J. G., & Hampson, J. L. (1957). Imprinting and establishing gender role. *Archives of Neurological Psychiatry, 77,* 333–336.

Mooney, J. (1988, November 18). A flight from pain for Vietnam veterans. *Seattle Post-Intelligencer,* p. B2.

Moore, T. (1982). Blacks: Rethinking service. In L. R. Snowden (Ed.), *Reaching the underserved: Mental health needs of neglected populations.* Beverly Hills, CA: Sage.

Moos, R. H., & Finney, J. W. (1983). The expanding scope of alcoholism treatment evaluation. *American Psychologist, 38,* 1036–1044.

Moreno, J. L. (1946). *Psychodrama.* New York: Beacon.

Morey, L. C. (1988). Personality disorders in *DSM-III* and *DSM-III-R*: Convergence, coverage, and internal consistency. *American Journal of Psychiatry, 145,* 573–577.

Morgan, S. B., & Brown, T. L. (1988). Luria-Nebraska Neuropsychological Battery—Children's Revision: Concurrent validity with three learning disability subtypes. *Journal of Consulting and Clinical Psychology, 56,* 463–466.

Morris, N. (1968). Psychiatry and the dangerous criminal. *Southern California Law Review, 41,* 514–547.

Morse, S. J. (1982). Failed explanation and criminal responsibility: Experts and the unconscious. *Virginia Law Review, 68,* 971–1084.

Moser, C., & Levitt, E. E. (1987). An exploratory-descriptive study of a sadomasochistically oriented sample. *Journal of Sex Research, 23,* 322–337.

Moses, A. N., & Hollandsworth, J. G. (1985). Relative effectiveness of education alone versus stress innoculation training in treatment of dental phobia. *Behavior Therapy, 16,* 531–537.

Mosher, L. R., & Keith, S. J. (1979). Research on the psychosocial treatment of schizophrenia: A summary report. *American Journal of Psychiatry, 136,* 623–631.

Moss, R. A. (1986). The role of learning history in current sick-role behavior and assertion. *Behaviour Research and Therapy, 24,* 681–683.

Mostofsky, D. I., & Balaschak, B. A. (1979). Psychological control of seizures. *Psychological Bulletin, 84,* 723–750.

Mowrer, O. H., & Mowrer, W. M. (1938). Enuresis—a method for its study and treatment. *American Journal of Orthopsychiatry, 8,* 436–459.

Munford, P. R., & Pally, R. (1979). Outpatient contingency management of operant vomiting. *Journal of Behavior Therapy and Experimental Psychiatry, 10,* 135–137.

Munoz, R. F., Glish, M., Soo-Hoo, T., & Robertson, J. (1982). The San Francisco mood survey project: Preliminary work toward the prevention of depression. *American Journal of Community Psychology, 10,* 317–330.

Murdock, C. W. (1973). Civil rights of the mentally retarded—some critical issues. *Family Law Quarterly, 7,* 1–74.

Murphree, O. D., & Dykman, R. A. (1965). Litter patterns in the offspring of nervous and stable dogs: I. Behavioral tests. *Journal of Nervous and Mental Disorders, 141,* 321–332.

Murphy, C. E. (1973). Suicide and the right to die. *American Journal of Psychiatry, 130,* 472–473.

Murphy, J. (1987, March 16). Tracing fragile X syndrome. *Time,* p. 78.

Murray, E. J. (1983). Beyond behavioral and dynamic therapy. *British Journal of Clinical Psychology, 22,* 127–128.

Murray, H. A., & Morgan, H. (1938). *Explorations in personality.* New York: Oxford University Press.

Myers, H. F., & King, L. M. (1983). Mental health issues in the development of the black American child. In G. J. Powell (Ed.), *The psychosocial development of minority group children.* New York: Brunner/Mazel.

Myers, J. K., Weissman, M. M., Tischler, G. L., Holzer, C. E., Leaf, P. J., Orvaschel, H., Anthony, J. C., Boyd, J. H., Burke, J. D., Kramer, M., & Stoltzman, R. (1984). Six-month prevalence of psychiatric disorders in three communities. *Archives of General Psychiatry, 41,* 959–967.

Nagler, S., Marcus, J., Sohlberg, S. C., Lifshitz, M., & Silberman, E. K. (1985). Clinical observation of high-risk children. *Schizophrenia Bulletin, 11,* 107–111.

Nash, M. R., Drake, S. D., Wiley, S., & Khalsa, S. (1986). Accuracy of recall by hypnotically age-regressed subjects. *Journal of Abnormal Psychology, 95,* 298–300.

Nathan, P., & Jackson, A. (1976). Behavior modification. In I. Weiner (Ed.), *Clinical methods in psychology.* New York: Wiley.

Nathan, P. E. (1976). Alcoholism. In H. Leitenberg (Ed.), *Handbook of behavior modification and behavior therapy.* Englewood Cliffs, NJ: Prentice-Hall.

Nathan, P. E. (1988). The addictive personality is the behavior of the addict. *Journal of Consulting and Clinical Psychology, 56,* 183–188.

Nathan, P. E., & Wiens, A. N. (1983). Alcoholism: Introduction and overview. *American Psychologist, 38,* 1035.

National Academy of Sciences. (1982). *Marijuana and health.* Washington, D.C.: National Academy Press.

National Institute of Mental Health. (1970). *Biological correlates of mental health.* U.S. Department of Health, Education, and Welfare. Mental Health Publication No. 5027. Washington, D.C.: U.S. Government Printing Office.

National Institute of Mental Health. (1975). *Report of research task force: Research in the service of mental health.* DHEW Pub. 75-236. Rockville, MD: National Institute of Mental Health.

National Institute of Mental Health. (1985). *Mental Health: United States, 1985.* Washington, D.C.: U.S. Government Printing Office.

National Institute of Mental Health. (1986). *Phobias and panic.* Rockville, MD: U.S. Department of Health and Human Services.

National Institutes of Health. (1981). *The dementias: Hope through research.* Bethesda, MD: National Institutes of Health.

Neale, J. M., & Oltmanns, T. F. (1980). *Schizophrenia.* New York: Wiley.

Neff, J. A. (1984). Race differences in psychological distress: The effects of SES, urbanicity, and measurement strategy. *American Journal of Community Psychology, 12,* 337–352.

Nettlebladt, P., & Uddenberg, N. (1979). Sexual dysfunction and sexual satisfaction in 58 married Swedish men. *Journal of Psychosomatic Research, 23,* 141–148.

Neugebauer, R. (1979). Medieval and early modern theories of mental illness. *Archives of General Psychiatry, 36,* 477–483.

Newman, L. E., & Stoller, R. J. (1974). Nontranssexual men who seek sex reassignment. *American Journal of Psychiatry, 131,* 437–441.

Newmark, C. S. (1985). The MMPI. In C. S. Newmark (Ed.), *Major psychological assessment instruments* (pp. 11–64). Boston: Allyn & Bacon.

Niaura, R. S., Rohsenow, D. J., Binkoff, J. A., Monti, P.

M., Pedraza, M., & Abrams, D. B. (1988). Relevance of cue reactivity to understanding alcohol and smoking relapse. *Journal of Abnormal Psychology, 97,* 133–152.

Nichols, M. (1984). *Family therapy.* New York: Gardner Press.

Nielsen, E. B., Lyon, M., & Ellison, G. (1983). Apparent hallucinations in monkeys during the around-the-clock amphetamine for seven to fourteen days. *Journal of Nervous and Mental Disease, 171,* 222–233.

Nolen-Hoeksema, S. (1987). Sex differences in unipolar depression: Evidence and theory. *Psychological Bulletin, 101,* 259–282.

Norcross, J. C., & Prochaska, J. O. (1988). A study of eclectic (and integrative) views revisited. *Professional Psychology, 19*(2), 170–174.

Norton, G. R., Harrison, B., Hauch, J., & Rhodes, L. (1985). Characteristics of people with infrequent panic attacks. *Abnormal Psychiatry, 94,* 216–221.

Nowlis, D., & Kamiya, J. (1970). The control of EEG algorithm through auditory feedback and the associated mental activity. *Psychophysiology, 6,* 476–484.

Nuechterlein, K. H., & Dawson, M. E. (1984). A heuristic vulnerability/stress model of schizophrenic episodes. *Schizophrenic Bulletin, 10,* 300–311.

Nutt, R. L. (1979). Review and preview of attitudes and values of counselors of women. *Counseling Psychologist, 8,* 18–20.

O'Connor, K. (1986). The interaction of hostile and depressive behaviors: A case study of a depressed boy. *Journal of Child and Adolescence Psychotherapy, 3,* 105–108.

Office of Technical Assessment. (1983). *The effectiveness of costs of alcoholism treatment.* Washington, D.C.: U.S. Congress.

O'Leary, K. D., & Wilson, G. T. (1975). *Behavior therapy: Application and outcome.* Englewood Cliffs, NJ: Prentice-Hall.

Oliver, J., Shaller, C. A., Majovski, L. V., & Jacques, S. (1982). Stroke mechanisms: Neuropsychological implications. *Clinical Neuropsychology, 4,* 81–84.

Ollendick, T. H., Matson, J. L., & Helsel, W. J. (1985). Fears in children and adolescents: Normative data. *Behaviour Research and Therapy, 23,* 465–467.

Opler, M. K. (1967). *Culture and social psychiatry.* New York: Atherton Press.

Ornstein, R., & Sobel, D. (1987). The healing brain. *Psychology Today, 21,* 48–52.

Ost, L. G. (1987a). Age of onset in different phobias. *Journal of Abnormal Psychology, 96,* 223–229.

Ost, L. G. (1987b). Applied relaxation: Description of a coping technique and review of controlled studies. *Behavior Research and Therapy, 25,* 397–409.

Ost, L. G., & Hugdahl, K. (1981). Acquisition of phobias and anxiety response patterns in clinical patients. *Behaviour Research and Therapy, 19,* 439–447.

Ottenbacher, K. H., & Cooper, H. M. (1983). Drug treatment of hyperactivity in children. *Developmental Medicine in Child Neurology, 25,* 358–366.

Overholser, J. C., & Beck, S. (1986). Multimethod assessment of rapists, child molesters, and three control groups in behavioral and psychological measures. *Journal of Consulting and Clinical Psychology, 54,* 682–687.

Overmier, J. B., & Seligman, M. E. P. (1967). Effects of inescapable shock upon subsequent escape and avoidance learning. *Journal of Comparative and Physiological Psychology, 63,* 23–33.

Page, E. B. (1972). Miracle in Milwaukee: Raising the IQ. *Educational Researcher, 1,* 3–16.

Pakkenberg, B. (1987). Post-mortem study of chronic schizophrenic brains. *British Journal of Psychiatry, 151,* 744–752.

Paley, A-M., N. (1988). Growing up in chaos: The dissociative response. *American Journal of Psychoanalysis, 48,* 72–83.

Palfrey, J. S., Levine, M. D., Walker, D. K., & Sullivan, M. (1985). The emergence of attention deficits in early childhood: A prospective study. *Developmental and Behavioral Pediatrics, 6,* 339–348.

Pardine, P., & Napoli, A. (1983). Physiological reactivity and recent life-stress experience. *Journal of Consulting and Clinical Psychology, 51,* 467–469.

Parnas, J. (1987). Assortative mating in schizophrenia: Results from the Copenhagen high-risk study. *Psychiatry, 50,* 58–64.

Pasework, R. A., Pantel, M. L., & Steadman, H. J. (1982). Detention and rearrest rates of persons found not guilty by reason of insanity and convicted felons. *American Journal of Psychiatry, 139*(7), 892–897.

Pasnau, R. O. (1984). Clinical presentations of panic and anxiety. *Psychosomatics, 25,* 4–9.

Patterson, C. H. (1980). *Theories of counseling and psychotherapy.* New York: Harper & Row.

Patterson, G. (1982). Coercive family process. Eugene, OR: Cascalia Press.

Patterson, G. R. (1986). Performance models for antisocial boys. *American Psychologist, 41,* 432–444.

Paul, G. L. (1967). Insight versus desensitization in psychotherapy two years after termination. *Journal of Consulting Psychology, 31,* 333–348.

Paul, G. L., & Lentz, R. J. (1977). *Psychosocial treatment of chronic mental patients: Milieu versus social-learning programs.* Cambridge, MA: Harvard University Press.

Pauls, D. L., Cohen, D. J., Heimbuch, R., Dettor, J., &

Kidd, K. K. (1981). Familial pattern and transmission of Gilles de la Tourette's syndrome and multiple tics. *Archives of General Psychiatry, 38,* 1091–1093.

Pauly, I. B. (1968). The current status of the change of sex operation. *Journal of Nervous and Mental Diseases, 147,* 460–471.

Paykel, E. S. (Ed.) (1982). *Handbook of affective disorders.* New York: Oxford University Press.

Pearl, D., Bouthilet, L., & Lazar, J. (Eds.) (1982). *Television and behavior: Ten years of scientific progress and implications for the eighties* (Vols. 1 and 2). Washington, D.C.: U.S. Government Printing Office.

Peck, M. A., & Schrut, A. (1971). Suicidal behavior among college students. *HSMHA Health Reports, 86,* 149–156.

Pendery, M. L., Maltzman, I. M., & West, L. J. (1982). Controlled drinking by alcoholics? New findings and a reevaluation of a major affirmative study. *Science, 217,* 169–175.

Perodeau, G. M. (1984). Married alcoholic women: A review. *Journal of Drug Issues, 14,* 703–720.

Perris, C. (1966). A study of bipolar (manic-depressive) and unipolar recurrent depressive psychosis. *Acta Psychiatrica Scandinavica* (Suppl. 194).

Perse, T. L., Greist, J. H., Jefferson, J. W., Rosenfeld, R., & Dar, R. (1987). Fluvoxamine treatment of obsessive-compulsive disorder. *American Journal of Psychiatry, 144,* 1543–1548.

Persky, V. W., Kempthorne-Rawson, J., & Shekelle, R. B. (1987). Personality and the risk of cancer: 20 years follow-up of the Western Electric Company. *Psychosomatic Medicine, 49,* 435–449.

Persons, J. B. (1986). The advantages of studying psychological phenomena rather than psychiatric diagnosis. *American Psychologist, 41,* 1252–1261.

Pfeffer, C. R., Zuckerman, S., & Plutchik, R., & Mizruchi, M. S. (1987). Assaultive behavior in normal school children. *Child Psychiatry and Human Development, 17,* 166–176.

Pfeiffer, E. (1977). Psychopathology and social pathology. In J. E. Birren & K. W. Schaie (Eds.), *Handbook of psychology and aging.* New York: Van Nostrand Reinhold.

Phares, E. J. (1984). *Clinical psychology: Concepts, methods, and professions.* Homewood, IL: Dorsey.

Philips, H. C. (1983). Assessment of chronic tension headache behavior. In R. Melzack (Ed.), *Pain measurement and assessment* (pp. 155–165). New York: Raven Press.

Philips H. C. (1987). Avoidance behavior and its role in sustaining chronic pain. *Behavior Research and Therapy, 25,* 273–279.

Phillips, D. P., & Carstensen, L. L. (1986). Clustering of teenage suicides after television news stories about suicide. *New England Journal of Medicine, 315,* 685–689.

Phillips, J. S., & Ray, R. S. (1980). Behavioral approaches to childhood disorders. *Behavior Modification, 4,* 3–34.

Physician's Desk Reference. (1988). Oradell, NJ: Medical Economics Company.

Pickering, P. G., Harshfield, G. A., Kleinert, H. D., Blank, S., & Laragh, J. L. (1982). Blood pressure during normal daily activities, sleep, and exercise: Comparison of values in normal and hypertensive subjects. *Journal of the American Medical Association, 247,* 992–996.

Pilisuk, M. (1975). The legacy of the Vietnam veteran. *Journal of Social Issues, 31*(4), 3–12.

Pines, M. (1983, October). *Science,* pp. 55–58.

Platt, J. J. (1986). *Heroin addiction: Theory, research, and treatment.* New York: Wiley.

Plienis, A. J., Hansen, D. J., Ford, F., Smith, S., Jr., Stark, L. J., & Kelly, J. A. (1987). Behavioral small group training to improve the social skills of emotionally-disordered adolescents. *Behavior Therapy, 18,* 17–32.

Pogue-Geile, M. F., & Rose, R. J. (1985). Developmental genetic studies of adult personality. *Developmental Psychology, 21,* 547–557.

Pohl, R., Rainey, J., & Gershon, S. (1984). Changes in the drug treatment of anxiety disorders. *Psychopathology, 17,* 6–14.

Polivy, J., Schueneman, A. L., & Carlson, K. (1976). Alcohol and tension reduction; Cognitive and physiological effects. *Journal of Abnormal Psychology, 85,* 595–600.

Polloway, E. A., & Smith, J. D. (1983). Changes in mild mental retardation: Population, programs, and perspectives. *Exceptional Children, 50,* 149–159.

Ponterotto, J. G. (1987). Client hospitalization: Issues and considerations for the counselor. *Journal of Counseling and Development, 65,* 542–546.

Pope, H. G., Hudson, J. I., Jonas, J., & Yurgelun-Todd, D. (1983). Bulimia treated with imipramine: A placebo-controlled, double-blind study. *American Journal of Psychiatry, 140,* 554–558.

Pope, H. G., Hudson, J. I., & Yurgelun-Todd, D. (1984). Anorexia nervosa and bulimia among 300 suburban women shoppers. *American Journal of Psychiatry, 141,* 292–294.

Pope, H. G., Jonas, J. M., & Cohen, B. M. (1982). Failure to find evidence of schizophrenic probands. *American Journal of Psychiatry, 139,* 826–828.

Pope, H. G., & Lipinski, J. F. (1978). Diagnosis in schizophrenia and manic-depression illness: A reassessment of the specificity of "schizophrenic" symptoms in light of current research. *Archives of General Psychiatry, 35,* 811–828.

Porrino, L. J., Rapoport, J. L., Behar, D., Sceery, W., Ismond, D. R., & Bunney, W. E. (1983). A naturalistic assessment of the motor activity of hyperactive boys. *Archives of General Psychiatry, 40,* 681–687.

Portnoff, L. A., Golden, C. J., Wood, R. E., & Gustavson, J. L. (1983). Discrimination between schizophrenic and parietal lesion patients with neurological tests of parietal involvement. *Clinical Neuropsychology, 5,* 175–178.

Portwood, D. (1978, January). A right to suicide. *Psychology Today, 2,* pp. 66–74.

Pound, E. J. (1987). Children and prematurity. In A. Thomas & J. Grimes (Eds.), *Children's needs: Psychological perspectives* (pp. 441–450). Washington, D.C.: National Association of School Psychologists.

Powell, C. J. (1982, August). *Adolescence and the right to die: Issues of autonomy, competence, and paternalism.* Paper presented at the meeting of the American Psychological Association, Washington, D.C.

Powell, G. J. (1983). Coping with adversity: The psychosocial development of Afro-American children. In G. J. Powell (Ed.), *The psychosocial development of minority group children.* New York: Brunner/Mazel.

Powers, P. S., Schulman, R. G., Gleghorn, A. A., & Prange, M. E. (1987). Perceptual and cognitive abnormalities in bulimia. *American Journal of Psychiatry, 144,* 1456–1460.

Praeger, S. G., & Bernhardt, G. R. (1985). Survivors of suicide: A community in need. *Family and Community Health, 3,* 62–72.

Price, L. H., Goodman, W. K., Charney, D. S., Rasmussen, S. A., & Heninger, G. R. (1987). Treatment of severe obsessive-compulsive disorder with fluvoxamine. *American Journal of Psychiatry, 144,* 1059–1061.

Price, L. J., Fein, G., & Feinberg, I. (1980). Neurological assessment of cognitive function in the elderly. In L. W. Poon (Ed.), *Aging in the 1980's.* Washington, D.C.: American Psychological Association.

Price, R. (1987). Series Editor's preface. In J. Hermalin & J. A. Morell (Eds.), *Prevention planning in mental health.* Beverly Hills, CA: Sage.

Prichard, J. C. (1837). *Treatise on insanity and other disorders affecting the mind.* Philadelphia: Haswell, Barrington, & Haswell.

Prigatano, G. P., Fordyce, D. J., Zeiner, H. K., Roueche, J. R., Pepping, M., & Wood, B. C. (1984). Neuropsychological rehabilitation after closed head injury in young adults. *Journal of Neurology and Neuropsychology, 47,* 505–513.

Prior, M. (1984). Developing concepts of childhood autism: The influence of experimental cognitive research. *Journal of Consulting and Clinical Psychology, 52,* 4–16.

Prior, M., Leonard, A., & Wood, G. (1983). A comparison study of preschool children diagnosed as hyperactive. *Journal of Pediatric Psychology, 8,* 191–207.

Putnam, F. W., Guroff, J. J., & Silberman, E. K. (1986). The clinical phenomenology of multiple personality disorder: Review of 100 recent cases. *Journal of Clinical Psychiatry, 47,* 285–293.

Quay, H. C. (1965). Psychopathic personality as pathological stimulation seeking. *American Journal of Psychiatry, 122,* 180–183.

Quen, J. M. (1978). Isaac Ray and Charles Doe: Responsibility and justice. In W. E. Barton & C. J. Sanborn (Eds.), *Law and the mental health professions* (pp. 235–250). New York: International Universities Press.

Quen, J. M. (1981). Anglo American concepts of criminal responsibility. In S. J. Hucker, C. D. Webster, & M. H. Ben-Aron (Eds.), *Mental disorder and criminal responsibility* (pp. 1–10). Toronto, Canada: Butterworths.

Rabkin, J. G. (1979). The epidemiology of forcible rape. *American Journal of Orthopsychiatry, 49,* 634–647.

Rachman, S. (1966). Sexual fetishism: An experimental analogue. *Psychological Record, 16,* 293–296.

Rachman, S. (1971). *The effects of psychotherapy.* New York: Pergamon.

Rachman, S. (1974). *The meaning of fear.* Middlesex, England: Penguin Books.

Rachman, S. (1984). Agoraphobia—A safety-signal perspective. *Behaviour Research and Therapy, 22,* 59–70.

Rachman, S., & DeSilva, P. (1987). Abnormal and normal obsessions. *Behaviour Research and Therapy, 16,* 233–248.

Rachman, S., & Hodgson, R. (1980). *Obsessions and compulsions.* Englewood Cliffs, NJ: Prentice-Hall.

Rachman, S., Lopatka, C., & Levitt, K. (1987). Panic: The link between cognitions and bodily symptoms—I. *Behavior Research and Therapy, 25,* 411–423.

Rachman, S., Lopatka, C., & Levitt, K. (1988). Experimental analysis of panic—II. Panic patients. *Behaviour Research and Therapy, 26,* 33–40.

Rachman, S., Marks, I. M., & Hodgson, R. (1973). The treatment of obsessive-compulsive neurotics by modeling and flooding in vivo. *Behaviour Research and Therapy, 13,* 271–279.

Rachman, S. J., & Wilson, G. I. (1980). *The effects of psychological therapy* (2nd ed.). New York: Pergamon Press.

Radloff, L. S., & Rae, D. S. (1981). The components of the sex difference in depression. In R. G. Simmons (Ed.), *Research in community and mental health* (Vol. 2). Greenwood, CT: JAI Press.

Rahe, R. H. (1968). Life change measurement as a predictor of illness. *Proceedings of the Royal Society of Medicine, 61,* 1124–1126.

Rahe, R. H., & Arthur, R. J. (1978). Life change and illness studies: Past history and future directions. *Journal of Human Stress, 4,* 3–15.

Rapaport, K., & Burkhart, B. R. (1984). Personality attitudinal characteristics of sexually coercive college males. *Journal of Abnormal Psychology, 93,* 216–221.

Rappaport, J. (1981). In praise of paradox: A social policy of empowerment over prevention. *American Journal of Community Psychology, 9,* 1–26.

Rappaport, J. (1987). Terms of empowerment/exemplars of prevention: Toward a theory for community psychology. *American Journal of Community Psychology, 15,* 121–148.

Rappaport, J., & Cleary, C. P. (1980). Labeling theory and the social psychology of experts and helpers. In M. S. Gibbs, J. R. Lachenmyer, & J. Sigal (Eds.), *Community psychology: Theoretical and empirical approaches.* New York: Gardner Press.

Raps, C. S., Peterson, C., Reinhard, K. E., Abramson, L. Y., & Seligman, M. E. P. (1982). Attributional styles among depressed patients. *Journal of Abnormal Psychology, 91,* 102–108.

Raskin, M., Pecke, H. V. S., Dickman, W., & Pinsker, H. (1982). Panic and generalized anxiety disorders. *Archives of General Psychiatry, 39,* 687–689.

Reading, C., & Mohr, P. (1976). Biofeedback control of migraine: A pilot study. *British Journal of Social and Clinical Psychology, 15,* 429–433.

Redestam, K. E. (1977). Physical and psychological response to suicide in the family. *Journal of Consulting and Clinical Psychology, 45,* 162–170.

Redlich, R. C., & Freedman, D. X. (1966). *The theory and practice of psychiatry.* New York: Basic Books.

Rees, L. (1964). The importance of psychological, allergic, and infective factors in childhood asthma. *Journal of Psychosomatic Research, 1,* 253–262.

Rees, L. (1983). The development of psychosomatic medicine during the past 25 years. *Journal of Psychosomatic Research, 27,* 157–164.

Regan, J., & LaBarbera, J. D. (1984). Lateralization of conversion symptoms. *American Journal of Psychiatry, 141,* 1279–1280.

Regier, D. A., Goldberg, I. O., & Taube, C. A. (1978). The de facto U.S. mental health services systems: A public health perspective. *Archives of General Psychiatry, 35,* 685–693.

Reich, J. (1987). Sex distribution of *DSM-III* personality disorders in psychiatric outpatients. *American Journal of Psychiatry, 144,* 485–488.

Reid, W. H. (1981). The antisocial personality and related symptoms. In J. R. Lion (Ed.), *Personality disorders:*

Diagnosis and management. Baltimore: Williams & Wilkins.

Reiger, D. A. et al. (1984). The NIMH epidemiologic catchment area program: Historical context, major objectives, and study population characteristics. *Archives of General Psychiatry, 41,* 934–941.

Reilly, D. (1984). Family therapy with adolescent drug abusers and their families: Defying gravity and achieving escape velocity. *Journal of Drug Issues, 14,* 381–389.

Reisberg, B., Ferris, S. H., Crook, T. (1982). Signs, symptoms, and course of age-associated cognitive decline. In S. Corkin, K. L. Davis, J. H. Growdon, E. Usdin, & R. J. Wurtman (Eds.), *Alzheimer's disease: A report of progress.* New York: Raven Press.

Reiser, D. E. (1988). The psychiatric interview. In H. H. Goldman (Ed.), *Review of general psychiatry* (pp. 184–192). Norwalk, CT: Appleton & Lange.

Reisman, J. (1971). *Toward the integration of psychotherapy.* New York: Wiley.

Reiss, S., Peterson, R. A., Gursky, D. M., & McNally, R. J. (1986). Anxiety sensitivity, anxiety frequency, and the prediction of fearfulness. *Behaviour Research and Therapy, 24,* 1–8.

Rekers, G. A., & Varni, J. W. (1977a). Self-monitoring and self-reinforcement processes in a pre-transsexual boy. *Behaviour Research and Therapy, 15,* 177–180.

Rekers, G. A., & Varni, J. W. (1977b). Self-regulation of gender-role behaviors: A case study. *Journal of Behavior Therapy and Experimental Psychiatry, 8,* 427–432.

Rekers, G. A., & Yates, C. E. (1976). Sex-typed play in feminoid boys versus normal boys and girls. *Journal of Abnormal Child Psychology, 4,* 1–8.

Reschly, D. (1981). Psychological testing in educational classification and placement. *American Psychologist, 36,* 1094–1102.

Reschly, D. J. (1988). Minority MMR overrepresentation and special education reform. *Exceptional children, 54,* 316–323.

Research Task Force of the National Institute of Mental Health. (1975). *Research in the service of mental health* (DHEW Publication No. ADM 75–236). Washington, D.C.: U.S. Government Printing Office.

Resick, P. A. (1983). The rape reaction: Research findings and implications for intervention. *Behavior Therapist, 6,* 129–132.

Reus, V. I. (1988). Affective disorders. In H. H. Goldman (Ed.), *Review of general psychiatry* (pp. 332–348). Norwalk, CT: Appleton & Lange.

Rickels, K. (1966). Drugs in the treatment of neurotic anxiety. In P. Solomon (Ed.), *Psychiatric drugs.* New York: Grune & Stratton.

Rimland, B. (1978). Inside the mind of the autistic savant. *Psychology Today, 12,* 69–80.

Rimm, D. C., Janda, L. H., Lancaster, D. W., Nahl, M., & Dittmar, K. (1977). An exploratory investigation of the origin and maintenance of phobias. *Behaviour Research and Therapy, 15,* 231–238.

Rimm, D. C., & Lefebvre, R. C. (1981). Phobic disorders. In S. M. Turner, K. S. Calhoun, & H. E. Adams (Eds.), *Handbook of clinical behavior therapy.* New York: Wiley.

Rimm, D. C., & Litvak, S. B. (1969). Self-verbalization and emotional arousal. *Journal of Abnormal Psychology, 74,* 181–187.

Rimm, D. C., & Masters, J. C. (1979). *Behavior therapy: Techniques and empirical findings* (2nd ed.). New York: Academic Press.

Rioch, M. J. (1967). Pilot projects in training mental health counselors. In E. L. Cowen, E. A. Gardner, & M. Zax (Eds.), *Emergent approaches to mental health problems.* New York: Appleton-Century-Crofts.

Risley, T. R., & Baer, D. M. (1970). Operant conditioning: "Develop" is a transitive verb. In B. Caldwell & H. Ricciuti (Eds.), *Review of child development research: Vol. 3. Social influences and social action.* Chicago: University of Chicago Press.

Rist, K. (1979). Incest: Theoretical and clinical views. *American Journal of Orthopsychiatry, 49,* 680–691.

Ritro, E. R., Freeman, B. J., Yuwiler, A., Geller, E., Yokota, A., Schroth, P., & Novak, P. (1984). Study of fenfluramine in outpatients with the syndrome of autism. *Journal of Pediatrics, 105,* 823–828.

Roberto, L. (1983). Issues in diagnosis and treatment of transsexualism. *Archives of Sexual Behavior, 12,* 445–473.

Robertson, J., Wendiggensen, P., & Kaplan, I. (1983). Toward a comprehensive treatment for obsessional thoughts. *Behaviour Research and Therapy, 21,* 347–356.

Robins, L. N. (1966). *Deviant children growing up: A sociological and psychiatric study of sociopathic personality.* Baltimore: Williams & Wilkins.

Robins, L. N., Helzer, J. E., Weisinann, M. M., Orvaschel, H., Gruenberg, E., Burke, J. D., & Regier, D. A. (1984). Lifetime prevalence of specific psychiatric disorders in three sites. *Archives of General Psychiatry, 41,* 949–958.

Robinson, L. R. (1975). Basic concepts in family therapy: A differential comparison with individual treatment. *American Journal of Psychiatry, 132(10),* 1045–1048.

Robinson, N. M., & Robinson, H. B. (1976). *The mentally retarded child.* New York: McGraw-Hill.

Robitscher, J. B. (1966). *Pursuit of agreement: Psychiatry and the law.* Philadelphia: Lippincott.

Rodgon, M. M. (1984). Emotional and behavioral pathology in mentally retarded individuals. In H. E. Adams and P. B. Sutker (Eds.), *Comprehensive handbook of psychopathology* (pp. 1001–1022). New York: Plenum Press.

Rodin, J., & Langer, E. J. (1977). Long-term effects of a control-relevant intervention with the institutionalized aged. *Journal of Personality and Social Psychology, 35,* 897–902.

Roff, J. D., & Knight, R. (1981). Family characteristics, childhood symptoms, and adult outcome in schizophrenia. *Journal of Abnormal Psychology, 90,* 510–520.

Roff, J. D., & Wirt, R. D. (1984). Childhood aggression and social adjustment as antecedents of delinquency. *Journal of Abnormal Child Psychology, 12,* 111–126.

Rogers, C. R. (1951). *Client-centered therapy.* Boston: Houghton Mifflin.

Rogers, C. R. (1959). A theory of therapy, personality, and interpersonal relationships, as developed in client-centered framework. In S. Koch (Ed.), *Psychology: A study of science* (Vol. 3). New York: McGraw-Hill.

Rogers, C. R. (1961). *On becoming a person.* Boston: Houghton Mifflin.

Rogers, R. (1987). APA's position on the insanity defense. *American Psychologist, 42,* 840–848.

Rogers, R. C., & Simensen, L. R. J. (1987). Fragile X syndrome: A common etiology of mental retardation. *American Journal of Mental Deficiency, 91,* 445–449.

Rolider, A., & Van Houten, R. V. (1985). Suppressing tantrum behavior in public places through the use of delayed punishment mediated by audio recordings. *Behavior Therapy, 16,* 181–194.

Romaniuk, M., McAuley, W. J., & Arling, G. (1983). An examination of the prevalence of mental disorders among the elderly in the community. *Journal of Abnormal Psychology, 92,* 458–467.

Roper, G., & Rachman, S. (1976). Obsessive-compulsive checking: Experimental replication and development. *Behavior Research and Therapy, 14,* 25–32.

Roper, G., Rachman, S., & Marks, I. M. (1975). Passive and participant treatment of obsessive-compulsive neurotics. *Behaviour Research and Therapy, 13,* 271–279.

Rosen, J., & Leitenberg, H. (1982). Bulimia nervosa: Treatment with exposure and response prevention. *Behavior Therapy, 13,* 117–124.

Rosen, R. C., & Leiblum, S. R. (1987). Current approaches to the evaluation of sexual desire disorders. *Journal of Sex Research, 23,* 141–162.

Rosen, R. C., Kostis, J. B., & Jekelis, A. W. (1988). Beta-blocker effects on sexual function in normal males. *Archives of Sexual Behavior, 17,* 241–255.

Rosenbaum, J. F. (1986). Cocaine and panic disorder. *American Journal of Psychiatry, 143,* 1320.

Rosenbaum, M., & Weaver, G. M. (1980). Dissociated state: Status of a case after 38 years. *Journal of Nervous and Mental Disease, 168,* 597–603.

Rosenfield, A. H. (1985). Discovering and dealing with deviant sex. *Psychology Today, 19,* 8–10.

Rosenhan, D. L. (1973). On being sane in insane places. *Science, 179,* 250–258.

Rosenthal, D. (1970). *Genetic theory and abnormal behavior.* New York: McGraw-Hill.

Rosenthal, D. (1971). *Genetics of psychopathology.* New York: McGraw-Hill.

Rosenthal, J., & Jacobson, L. (1968). *Pygmalion in the classroom.* New York: Holt, Rinehart & Winston.

Rosenthal, P., & Rosenthal, S. (1984). Suicidal behavior by preschool children. *American Journal of Psychiatry, 141,* 520–525.

Ross, A. O. (1982). *Psychological Disorders of Children.* New York: McGraw-Hill.

Roth, D., Bielski, R., Jones, M., Parker, W., & Osborn, G. (1982). A comparison of self-control therapy and combined self-control therapy and antidepressant medication in the treatment of depression. *Behavior Therapy, 13,* 133–144.

Rotter, J. B., & Rafferty, J. E. (1950). *Manual for the Rotter Incomplete Sentences Blank, college form.* New York: Psychological Corporation.

Roy, A., Adinoff, B., Roehrich, L., Lamparski, D., Custer, R., Lorenz, V., Barbaccia, M., Guidotti, A., Cost, E., & Linnoila, M. (1988). Pathological gambling: A psychobiological study. *Archives of General Psychiatry, 45,* 369–373.

Roy-Byrne, P. P., Geraci, M., & Uhde, T. W. (1986). Life events and course of illness in patients with panic disorder. *American Journal of Psychiatry, 143,* 1033–1035.

Royce, J. M., Lazar, I., & Darlington, R. B. (1983). Minority families, early education, and later life changes. *American Journal of Orthopsychiatry, 53,* 706–720.

Rubinstein, E. A. (1983). Television and behavior. *American Psychologist, 38,* 7.

Ruch, F. L., & Zimbardo, P. G. (1971). *Psychology and life.* Glenview, IL: Scott, Foresman.

Rueger, D., & Liberman, R. (1984). Behavioral family therapy for delinquent and substance-abusing adolescents. *Journal of Drug Issues, 14,* 403–417.

Ruff, G. E., & Korchin, S. J. (1964). Psychological responses of Mercury astronauts to stress. In G. H. Grosser, H. Wechsler, & M. Greenblatt (Eds.), *The threat of impending disaster.* Cambridge, MA: M.I.T. Press.

Ruiz, R. A., & Padilla, A. M. (1977). Counseling Latinos. *Personnel and Guidance Journal, 55,* 401–408.

Russo, D. C., Carr, E. G., & Lovaas, O. I. (1980). Self injury in pediatric populations. In J. Ferguson & C. R. Taylor (Eds.), *Comprehensive handbook of behav-ioral medicine.* Vol. 3: Extended applications and issues. Holliswood, NY: Spectrum Publications.

Russo, N. F., & Denmark, F. L. (1984). Women, psychology, and public policy: Selected issues. *American Psychologist, 39,* 1161–1165.

Rutter, M. (1983). Cognitive deficits in the pathogenesis of autism. *Journal of Child Psychology and Psychiatry, 24,* 513–531.

Sabalis, R. F., Frances, A., Appenzeller, S. N., & Moseley, W. B. (1974). The three sisters: Transsexual male siblings. *American Journal of Psychiatry, 131,* 907–909.

Sabalis, R. F., Staton, M. A., & Appenzeller, S. N. (1977). Transsexualism: Alternative diagnostic etiological considerations. *American Journal of Psychoanalysis, 37,* 223–228.

Sackeim, H. A., Nordlie, J. W., & Gur, R. C. (1979). A model of hysterical and hypnotic blindness: Cognition, motivation, and awareness. *Journal of Abnormal Psychology, 88,* 474–489.

Sackeim, H. A., & Vingiano, W. (1984). Dissociative disorders. In S. Turner & M. Hersen (Eds.), *Adult psychopathology and diagnosis.* New York: Wiley.

Sahakian, W. S. (1979). *Psychopathology today.* Itasca, IL: Peacock.

Saigh, P. A. (1987). In vivo flooding of an adolescent's posttraumatic stress disorder. *Journal of Clinical Child Psychology, 16,* 147–150.

Sakheim, D. K., Barlow, D. H. Abrahamson, D. J., & Beck, J. G. (1987). Distinguishing between or genogenic and psychogenic erectile dysfunction. *Behavior Research and Therapy, 25,* 379–390.

Sakheim, D. K., Barlow, D. H., Beck, J. G., & Abrahamson, D. J. (1984). The effects of an increased awareness of erectile cues on sexual arousal. *Behaviour Research and Therapy, 22,* 151–158.

Sakheim, D. K., Hess, E. P., & Chivas, A. (1988). General principles for short-term inpatient work with multiple personality disorder patients. *Psychotherapy, 25,* 117–124.

Salim, A. S. (1987). Stress, the adrenergic hypothalamovagal pathway, and the aetiology of chronic duodenal ulceration. *Journal of Psychosomatic Research, 31,* 231–237.

Salkovskis, P. M., & Harrison, J. (1984). Abnormal and normal obsessions—A replication. *Behaviour Research and Therapy, 22,* 549–552.

Salkovskis, P., Jones, D., & Clark, D. (in press). Respiratory control in the treatment of panic attacks: Replication and extension with concurrent measurement of behaviour and pCO_2.

Salkovskis, P. M., & Warwick, H. M. C. (1986). Morbid preoccupations, health anxiety and reassurance: A cognitive-behavioral approach to hypochondriasis. *Behavior Research and Therapy, 24,* 597–602.

Salley, R. D. (1988). Subpersonalities with dreaming functions in a patient with multiple personalities. *Journal of Nervous and Mental Disease, 176,* 112–115.

Sanavio, E. (1988). Obsessions and compulsions: The Padua Inventory. *Behaviour Research and Therapy, 26,* 169–177.

Sarason, I. G., & Ganzer, V. (1973). Modeling and group discussion in the rehabilitation of delinquents. *Journal of Counseling Psychology, 20,* 442–449.

Sarason, I. G., Johnson, J. H., & Siegel, J. M. (1978). Assessing the impact of life changes: Development of the Life Experiences Survey. *Journal of Consulting and Clinical Psychology, 46,* 932–946.

Sarason, S. B. (1984). If it can be studied or developed, should it be? *American Psychologist, 39,* 477–485.

Sarbin, P. R., & Cole, W. C. (1979). Hypnosis and psychopathology: Replacing old myths with fresh metaphors. *Journal of Abnormal Psychology, 88,* 506–526.

Sartorius, N., Jablensky, A., & Shapiro, R. (1978). Cross-cultural differences in the short-term prognosis of schizophrenic psychoses. *Schizophrenia Bulletin, 4,* 102–112.

Satir, V. (1967). A family of angels. In J. Haley & L. Hoffman (Eds.), *Techniques of family therapy.* New York: Basic Books.

Satow, R. (1979). Where has all the hysteria gone? *The Psychoanalytic Review, 66,* 463–477.

Satterfield, J. H., Hoppe, C. M., & Schell, A. M. (1982). A prospective study of delinquency in 110 adolescent boys with attention deficit disorder and 88 normal adolescent boys. *American Journal of Psychiatry, 139,* 795–798.

Satterfield, J. H., Schell, A. M., Backs, R. W., & Hidaka, K. C. (1984). A cross-sectional and longitudinal study of age effects of electrophysiological measures in hyperactive and normal children. *Biological Psychiatry, 19,* 973–989.

Sattler, J. M. (1988, September). Larry P. Extension challenged in court. *Communique,* pp. 10–11.

Saxe, L., Cross, T., & Silverman, N. (1988). Children's mental health. *American Psychologist, 43,* 800–807.

Sbordone, R. J., & Jennison, J. H. (1983). A comparison of the OBD-168 and MMPI to assess the emotional adjustment of traumatic brain-injured inpatients to their cognitive deficits. *Clinical Neuropsychology, 5,* 87–88.

Scarr, S., & Weinberg, R. A. (1976). IQ test performance of black children adopted by white families. *American Psychologist, 31,* 726–739.

Schacht, T. E. (1985). DSM-III and the politics of truth. *American Psychologist, 40,* 513–521.

Schacht, T. E., & Nathan, P. E. (1977). But is it good for the psychologists? Appraisal and status of DSM-III. *American Psychologist, 32,* 1017–1025.

Schachter, S. (1977). Nicotine regulation in heavy and light smokers. *Journal of Experimental Psychology (General), 106,* 5–12.

Schachter, S., & Latane, B. (1964). Crime, cognition, and the autonomic nervous system. *Nebraska Symposium on Motivation, 12,* 221–274.

Schacter, D. L. (1986). Amnesia and crime. *American Psychologist, 41,* 186–295.

Schaefer, H. H. (1970). Self-injurious behavior: Shaping "head banging" in monkeys. *Journal of Applied Behavior Analysis, 3,* 111–116.

Schaefer, H. H., & Martin, P. L. (1969). *Behavioral therapy.* New York: McGraw-Hill.

Scheppele, K. L., & Bart, P. B. (1983). Through women's eyes: Defining danger in the wake of sexual assault. *Journal of Social Issues, 39,* 63–80.

Schiavi, R. C., Fisher, C., White, D., & Thornton, J. (1986). Plasma prolactin and estradiol during sleep in impotent men and normal controls. *Archives of Sexual Behavior, 15,* 285–291.

Schildkraut, J. J. (1965). The catecholamine hypothesis of affective disorders: A review of supporting evidence. *American Journal of Psychiatry, 122,* 509–522.

Schleifer, S. J., Keller, S. E., Camerino, M., Thornton, J. C., & Stein, M. (1983). Suppression of lymphocyte stimulation following bereavement. *Journal of the American Medical Association, 250,* 374–377.

Schmauk, F. J. (1970). Punishment, arousal, and avoidance learning. *Journal of Abnormal Psychology, 76,* 325–335.

Schmidt, J. A. (1974). Research techniques for counselors: The multiple baseline. *Personnel and Guidance Journal, 53,* 200–206.

Schmidt, H. O., & Fonda, C. P. (1956). The reliability of psychiatric diagnosis: A new look. *Journal of Abnormal and Social Psychology, 52,* 262–267.

Schneider, J. A., O'Leary, A., & Agras, W. S. (1987). The role of perceived self-efficacy in recovery from bulimia: A preliminary examination. *Behaviour Research and Therapy, 25,* 429–432.

Schneidman, B., & McGuire, L. (1976). Group therapy for nonorgasmic women: Two age levels. *Archives of Sexual Behavior, 5,* 239–247.

Schofield, W. (1964). *Psychotherapy: The purchase of friendship.* Englewood Cliffs, NJ: Prentice-Hall.

Schopler, E., Rutter, M., & Chess, S. (1979). Editorial: Change of journal scope and title. *Journal of Autism and Developmental Disorders, 9,* 1–10.

Schover, L. R., Friedman, J. M., Weiler, S. J., Heiman, J. R., & LoPiccolo, J. (1982). Multiaxial problem-oriented system for sexual dysfunctions. *Archives of General Psychiatry, 39,* 614–619.

Schreiber, F. R. (1973). *Sybil*. Chicago: Regnery.

Schreibman, L., & Koegel, R. L. (1975). Autism: A defeatable horror. *Psychology Today, 8*, 61–67.

Schroth, M. L., & Sue, D. W. (1975). *Introductory psychology*. Homewood, IL: Dorsey.

Schuell, H. (1974). Aphasia theory and therapy: Selected lectures and papers of Hildred Schuell. Baltimore: University Park Press.

Schulsinger, F. (1972). Psychopathy: Heredity and environment. *International Journal of Mental Health, 1*, 190–206.

Schultz, B. (1982). *Legal liability and psychotherapy*. San Francisco: Jossey-Bass.

Schultz, J. B., & Adams, D. U. (1987). Family life education needs of mentally disabled adolescents. *Adolescence, 22*, 221–230.

Schwartz, D. M., & Thompson, M. G. (1981). Do anorectics get well? Future research and current needs. *American Journal of Psychiatry, 138*, 319–323.

Schwartz, R., & Geyer, S. (1984). Social and psychological differences between cancer and noncancer patients: Cause or consequence of the disease? *Psychotherapy and Psychomatics, 41*, 195–199.

Schwitzgebel, R. L., & Schwitzgebel, R. K. (1980). *Law and psychological practice*. New York: Wiley.

Scott, R. L., & Baroffio, J. R. (1986). An MMPI analysis of similarities and differences in three classifications of eating disorders: Anorexia nervosa, bulimia, and morbid obesity. *Journal of Clinical Psychology, 42*, 708–713.

Scovern, A. W., & Kilmann, P. R. (1980). *Status of electroconvulsive therapy: A review of the outcome literature. Psychological Bulletin, 87*, 260–303.

Seeman, M. V., Littman, S. K., Thornton, J. F., Jeffries, J. J., & Plummer, E. (1982). *Living and Working with Schizophrenia*. Toronto: University of Toronto Press.

Segraves, R. T., Schoenberg, H. W., & Ivanoff, J. (1983). Serum testosterone and prolactin levels in erectile dysfunction. *Journal of Sex and Marital Therapy, 9*, 19–26.

Seiden, R. H. (1966). Campus tragedy: A study of student suicide. *Journal of Abnormal and Social Psychology, 71*, 389–399.

Seiden, R. H. (1984a). Death in the West—a regional analysis of the youthful suicide rate. *Western Journal of Medicine, 140*, 969–973.

Seiden, R. H. (1984b). The youthful suicide epidemic. *Public Affairs Report, 25*, 1.

Seidman, E., & Rappaport, J. (1974). The educational pyramid: A paradigm for research, training, and manpower utilization in community psychology. *American Journal of Community Psychology, 2*, 119–130.

Seidman, L. J. (1983). Schizophrenia and brain dysfunction: An integration of recent neurodiagnostic findings. *Psychological Bulletin, 94*, 195–238.

Seidman, L. J., Sokolove, R. L., McElroy, C., Knapp, P. H., & Sabin, T. (1987). Lateral ventricular size and social network differentiation in young, nonchronic schizophrenic patients. *American Journal of Psychiatry, 144*, 512–514.

Seligman, J., Huck, J., Joseph, N., Namuth, T., Prout, L. R., Robinson, T. L., & McDaniel, A. L. (1984, April 9). The date who rapes. *Newsweek*, pp. 91–92.

Seligman, M. E. P. (1971). Phobias and preparedness. *Behavior Therapy, 2*, 307–320.

Seligman, M. E. P. (1975). *Helplessness*. San Francisco: Freeman.

Seligman, M. E. P. (1987). Stop blaming yourself. *Psychology Today, 21*, 30–32, 34, 36–39.

Seligman, M. E. P., & Maier, S. F. (1967). Failure to escape traumatic shock. *Journal of Experimental Psychology, 74*, 1–9.

Seligmann, J., Zabarsky, M., Witherspoon, D., Rotenberk, L., & Schmidt, M. (1983, March 7). A deadly feast and famine. *Newsweek*, pp. 59–60.

Selye, H. (1956). *The stress of life*. New York: McGraw-Hill.

Selye, H. (1982). Stress: Eustress, distress, and human perspectives. In S. B. Day (Ed.), *Life stress* (pp. 3–13). New York: Van Nostrand Reinhold.

Semans, J. H. (1956). Premature ejaculation: A new approach. *Southern Medical Journal, 49*, 353–357.

Sesan, R. (1988). Sex bias and sex-role stereotyping in psychotherapy with women: Survey results. *Psychotherapy, 25*, 107–116.

Shah, S. (1969). Training and utilizing a mother as a therapist for her child. In B. G. Guemey (Ed.), *Psychotherapeutic agents: New roles for nonprofessionals, parents, and teachers*. New York: Holt, Rinehart & Winston.

Shahar, A., & Marks, I. (1980). Habituation during exposure treatment of compulsive rituals. *Behavior Therapy, 11*, 397–401.

Shapiro, D. L. (1984). *Psychological evaluation and expert testimony*. New York: Van Nostrand Reinhold.

Shapiro, S., Skinner, E. A., Kessler, L. G., Von Korff, M., German, P. S., Tischler, G. L., Leaf, P. J., Benham, L., Cottler, L., & Regier, D. A. (1984). Utilization of health and mental health services. *Archives of General Psychiatry, 41*, 971–978.

Sharp, J. J., & Forman, S. G. (1985). A comparison of two approaches to anxiety management for teachers. *Behavior Therapy, 16*, 370–383.

Shave, D. (1976). Transsexualism as a manifestation of orality. *American Journal of Psychoanalysis, 36*, 57–66.

Shaywitz, S. E., Cohen, D. J., & Shaywitz, B. A. (1980). Behavior and learning difficulties in children of normal intelligence born to alcoholic mothers. *Journal of Pediatrics, 96,* 363–367.

Shaywitz, S. E., & Shaywitz, B. A. (1984). Evaluation and treatment of children with attention deficit disorders. *Pediatrics in Review, 6,* 99–109.

Shean, G. (1987) *Schizophrenia.* Cambridge, MA: Winthrop Publishers.

Sheehan, P. W., Grigg, L., & McCann, T. (1984). Memory distortion following exposure to false information in hypnosis. *Journal of Abnormal Psychology, 93,* 259–265.

Shelton, R. C., Karson, C. N., Doran, A. R., Pickar, D., Bigelow, L. B., & Weinberger, D. R. (1988). Cerebral structural pathology in schizophrenia: Evidence for a selective prefrontal cortical defect. *American Journal of Psychiatry, 145,* 154–163.

Shine, K. I. (1984). Anxiety in patients with heart disease. *Psychosomatics, 25,* 27–31.

Shneidman, E. S. (Ed.) (1957). The logic of suicide. In E. S. Shneidman & N. L. Farberow (Eds.), *Clues to suicide.* New York: McGraw-Hill.

Shneidman, E. S. (1968). *Classifications of suicide phenomena: Bulletin of suicidology.* For the National Institute of Mental Health, Alcohol, Drug Abuse, and Mental Retardation, U.S. Department of Health, Education, and Welfare. Washington, D.C.: U.S. Government Printing Office.

Shneidman, E. S. (1976). Introduction: Contemporary overview of suicide. In E. S. Shneidman (Ed.), *Suicidology: Contemporary developments.* New York: Grune & Stratton.

Shneidman, E. S., & Farberow, N. L. (Eds.). (1957). *Clues to suicide.* New York: McGraw-Hill.

Shneidman, E. S., Farberow, N. L., & Litman, R. E. (Eds.). (1970). *The psychology of suicide.* New York: Aronson.

Shockley, W. (1972). *Journal of Criminal Law and Criminology, 7,* 530–543.

Shotten, J. H. (1985). The family interview. *Schizophrenia Bulletin, 11,* 112–116.

Shuey, A. (1966). *The testing of Negro intelligence.* New York: Social Science.

Shure, M. B., & Spivack, G. (1979). Interpersonal problem-solving thinking and adjustment in the mother-child dyad. In M. W. Kent & J. E. Rolf (Eds.), *Primary prevention of psychopathology* (Vol. 3). Hanover, NH: University Press of New England.

Shure, M. B., & Spivack, G. (1982). Interpersonal problem-solving in young children: A cognitive approach to prevention. *American Journal of Community Psychology, 10,* 341–356.

Sibler, E., Hamburg, D. A., Coelho, G. V., Murphy, E. B., Rosenberg, M., & Perle, L. I. (1961). Adaptive be-

havior in competent adolescents. *Archives of General Psychiatry, 5,* 354–365.

Siegel, M. (1979). Privacy, ethics, and confidentiality. *Professional Psychology, 10,* 249–258.

Siegel, R. A. (1978). Probability of punishment and suppression of behavior in psychopathic and nonpsychopathic offenders. *Journal of Abnormal Psychology, 87,* 514–522.

Siegelman, M. (1972). Adjustment of homosexual and heterosexual women. *American Journal of Psychiatry, 120,* 477–481.

Siever, L. J. (1981). Schizoid and schizotypal personality disorders. In J. R. Lion (Ed.), *Personality disorders: Diagnosis and management.* Baltimore: Williams & Wilkins.

Silver, M. A., Bohnert, M., Beck, A. T., & Marcus, D. (1971). Relation of depression of attempted suicide and seriousness of intent. *Archives of General Psychiatry, 25,* 573–576.

Silverman, J. M., Mohs, R. C., Davidson, M., Losonczy, M. F., Keefe, R. S. E., Breitner, J. C. S., Sorokin, J. E., & Davis, K. L. (1987). Familial schizophrenia and treatment response. *American Journal of Psychiatry, 144,* 1271–1276.

Silverman, L. H. (1976). Psychoanalytic theory: "The reports of my death are greatly exaggerated." *American Psychologist, 31,* 621–637.

Silverstein, B., & Perdue, L. (1988). The relationship between role concerns, preference of slimness, and symptons of eating problems among college women. *Sex Roles, 18,* 101–160.

Silverstein, C. (1972). *Behavior modification and the gay community.* Paper presented at the annual convention of the Association for Advancement of Behavior Therapy, New York.

Simon, R. A. (1967). *The jury and the defense of insanity.* Boston: Little, Brown.

Simons, A. D., Murphy, G. E., Levine, J. L., & Wetzel, R. D. (1986). Cognitive therapy and pharmacotherapy for depression: Sustained improvement over one year. *Archives of General Psychiatry, 43,* 43–48.

Simonton, O. C., Mathews-Simonton, S., & Creighton, J. (1978). Getting well again: A step-by-step, self-help guide to overcoming cancer for patients and their families. Los Angeles: Tarcher.

Singer, J. L., & Singer, D. G. (1983). Psychologists look at television: Cognitive developmental, personality, and social policy implications. *American Psychologist, 38,* 826–834.

Sizemore, C., & Pittillo, E. (1977). *I'm Eve.* New York: Doubleday.

Skeels, H. M. (1966). Adult status of children with contrasting early life experiences. *Monographs of the Society for Research in Child Development, 31.*

Slag, M. F., Morlem, J. E., Elson, M. K., Trence, O. L., Nuttall, F. Q., & Shafer, R. B. (1983). Impotence in medical clinic outpatients. *Journal of the American Medical Association, 294,* 1736–1749.

Slater, E. (1975). The diagnosis of "hysteria." *British Medical Journal, 1,* 1395–1399.

Slater, E., & Shields, J. (1969). Genetic aspects of anxiety. In M. H. Lader (Ed.), *Studies of anxiety.* Ashford, Kent, England: Headley Brothers.

Slater, J., & Depue, R. A. (1981). The contribution of environmental events and social support to serious suicide attempts in primary depressive disorder. *Journal of Abnormal Psychology, 90,* 275–285.

Sloane, R. B., Staples, F. R., Cristol, A. H., Yorkston, N. J., & Whipple, K. (1975). *Psychotherapy versus behavior therapy.* Cambridge, MA: Harvard University Press.

Smith, A., & Sugar, 0. (1975). Development of above normal language and intelligence 21 years after left hemispherectomy. *Neurology, 25,* 813–818.

Smith, D. (1982). Trends in counseling and psychotherapy. *American Psychologist, 37,* 802–809.

Smith, D., & Kraft, W. A. (1983). DSM-III: Do psychologists really want an alternative? *American Psychologist, 38,* 777–785.

Smith, D. E., & Landry, M. J. (1988). Psychoactive substance use disorders: Drugs and alcohol. In H. H. Goldman (Ed.), *Review of general psychiatry* (pp. 266–285). Norwalk, CT: Appleton & Lange.

Smith, E. K. (1972). *The effect of double-bind communications upon the state of anxiety of normals.* Unpublished doctoral dissertation, University of New Mexico, Albuquerque.

Smith, K. (1988, May). Loving him was easy. *Reader's Digest,* pp. 115–119.

Smith, M. B. (1949). Combat motivations among ground troops. In S. A. Stouffer (Ed.), *The American soldier.* Princeton, NJ: Princeton University Press.

Smith, M. B. (1950). The phenomenological approach in personality theory: Some critical remarks. *Journal of Abnormal and Social Psychology, 45,* 516–522.

Smith, M. B., & Hobbs, N. (1966). The community and the community mental health center. *American Psychologist, 21,* 299–309.

Smith, M. L., & Glass, G. V. (1977). Meta-analysis of psychotherapy outcome studies. *American Psychologist, 32,* 752–760.

Smith, T. W., Turner, C. W., Ford, M. H., Hunt, S. C., Barlow, G. K., Stults, B. M., & Williams, R. R. (1987). Blood pressure reactivity in adult male twins. *Health Psychology, 6,* 209–220.

Smyer, M. A. (1984). Life transitions and aging: Implications for counseling older adults. *Counseling Psychologist, 12,* 17–28.

Snowden, L. R. (1987). The peculiar successes of community psychology: Service delivery to ethnic minorities and the poor. *American Journal of Community Psychology, 15,* 575–586.

Snowden, L. R., Collinge, W. B., & Runkle, M. C. (1982). Help seeking and underservice. In L. R. Snowden (Ed.), *Reaching the underserved: Mental health needs of neglected populations* (pp. 281–298). Beverly Hills: Sage Publications.

Snyder, R. D., Stovring, J., Cushing, A. H., Davis, L. E., & Hardy, T. L. (1981). Cerebral infarction in childhood bacterial meningitis. *Journal of Neurology, Neurosurgery, and Psychiatry, 44,* 581–585.

Snyder, S. H. (1974). *Madness and the brain.* New York: McGraw-Hill.

Snyder, S. H. (1976). The dopamine hypothesis of schizophrenia. *American Journal of Psychiatry, 133,* 197–202.

Snyder, S. H. (1980). *Biological aspects of mental disorder.* New York: Oxford University Press.

Snyder, S. H., Baneyee, S. P., Yamamura, H. I., & Greenberg, D. (1974). Drugs, neurotransmitters and schizophrenia. *Science, 184,* 1243–1253.

Sobell, M. B., & Sobell, L. C. (1978). *Behavioral treatment of alcohol problems.* New York: Plenum.

Sohlberg, S. C. (1985). Personality and neuropsychological performance of high-risk children. *Schizophrenia Bulletin, 11,* 48–65.

Solkoff, N., Gray, P., & Keill, S. (1986). Which Vietnam veterans develop posttraumatic stress disorders? *Journal of Clinical Psychology, 42,* 687–698.

Solomon, R. L. (1977). An opponent-process theory of motivation: The affective dynamics of drug addiction. In J. D. Maser & M. E. Seligman (Eds.), *Psychopathology: Experimental models.* San Francisco: Freeman.

Solomon, R. L. (1980). The opponent-process theory of acquired motivation: The costs of pleasure and the benefits of pain. *American Psychologist, 35,* 691–712.

Southern, S., & Gayle, R. (1982). A cognitive behavioral model of hypoactive sexual desire. *Behavioral Counselor, 2,* 31–48.

Spanos, N. P. (1978). Witchcraft in histories of psychiatry: A critical analysis and an alternative conceptualization. *Psychological Bulletin, 85,* 417–439.

Spanos, N. P., Weekes, J. R., & Bertrand, L. D. (1985). Multiple personality: A social psychological perspective. *Journal of Abnormal Psychology, 94,* 362–376.

Sparr, L., & Pankratz, L. D. (1983). Factitious posttraumatic stress disorder. *American Journal of Psychiatry, 140,* 1016–1019.

Speer, D. C. (1971). Rate of caller re-use of a telephone crisis service. *Crisis Intervention, 3,* 83–86.

Speer, D. C. (1972). *An evaluation of a telephone crisis service.* Paper presented at the meeting of the Midwestern Psychological Association, Cleveland, Ohio.

Speltz, M. L., & Bernstein, D. A. (1979). The use of participant modeling for claustrophobia. *Journal of Behavior Therapy and Experimental Psychology, 10,* 251–255.

Spencer, S. L., & Zeiss, A. M. (1987). Sex roles and sexual dysfunction in college students. *Journal of Sex Research, 23,* 338–347.

Spiegler, M. D. (1983). *Contemporary behavioral therapy.* Palo Alto, CA: Mayfield Publishing.

Spiess, W. F., Geer, J. H., & O'Donohue, W. T. (1984). Premature ejaculation: Investigation of factors in ejaculatory latency. *Journal of Abnormal Psychology, 93,* 242–245.

Spitzer, R. L. (1975). On pseudoscience in science, logic in remission, and psychiatric diagnosis: A critique of Rosenhan's "On being sane in insane places." *Journal of Abnormal Psychology, 84,* 442–452.

Spitzer, R. L., & Forman, J. B. (1979). DSM-III field trials: 2. Initial experience with the multiaxial system. *American Journal of Psychiatry, 136,* 818–820.

Spitzer, R. L. (1981a). The diagnostic status of homosexuality in DSM-III: A reformation of the issues. *American Journal of Psychiatry, 138,* 210–215.

Spitzer, R. L. (1981b). Nonmedical myths and the DSM-III. *APA Monitor, 12*(3), 33.

Spitzer, R. L., Skodol, A. E., Gibbon, M., & Williams, J. B. W. (1981). *DSM-III casebook.* Washington, D.C.: American Psychiatric Association.

Spitzer, R. L., & Williams, J. B. (1987). Introduction. In American Psychiatric Association *Diagnostic and statistical manual of mental disorders* (3rd ed. [DSM-III]). Washington, D.C.: American Psychiatric Association.

Spotnitz, H. (1963). The toxoid response. *Psychoanalytic Review, 50*(4), 81–94.

Spotnitz, H. (1968). *Modern psychoanalysis and the schizophrenic patient.* New York: Grune & Stratton.

Spotnitz, H. (1976). *Psychotherapy of preoedipal conditions.* New York: Aronson.

Squire, L. R., & Slater, P. C. (1978). Bilateral and unilateral ECT: Effects on verbal and nonverbal memory. *American Journal of Psychiatry, 135,* 89–95.

Srole, L., Langer, T. S., Michael, S. T., Opler, M. K., & Rennie, T. A. (1962). *Mental health in the metropolis: The midtown Manhattan study.* New York: McGraw-Hill.

Srole, L., & Fischer, A. K. (1980). The midtown Manhattan longitudinal study vs. "the mental paradise lost" doctrine: A controversy joined. *Archives of General Psychiatry 37*(2), 209–221.

St. Clair, D. (1987). Chromosome 21, Down's syndrome and Alzheimer's disease. *Journal of Mental Deficiency Research, 31,* 213–214.

Stampfl, T., & Levis, D. (1967). Essentials of implosive therapy: A learning-theory-based psychodynamic behavioral therapy. *Journal of Abnormal Psychology, 72,* 496–503.

Stanley, M., & Mann, J. J. (1983). Increased serotonin-z binding sites in frontal cortex of suicide victims. *Lancet, 2,* 214–216.

Stark, E. (1984). The unspeakable family secret. *Psychology Today, 18,* 38–46.

Steadman, H. J. (1979). *Beating a rap: Defendants found incompetent to stand trial.* Chicago: University of Chicago Press.

Steege, J. F., Stout, A. L., & Carson, C. C. (1986). Patient satisfaction in Scott and Small-Carrion penile implant recipients: A study of 52 patients. *Archives of Sexual Behavior, 15,* 393–399.

Steele, C. M., & Josephs, R. A. (1988). Drinking your troubles away II: An attention-allocation model of alcohol's effect on psychological stress. *Journal of Abnormal Psychology, 97,* 196–205.

Steffen, J. J., Nathan, P. E., & Taylor, H. A. (1974). Tension-reducing effects of alcohol: Further evidence and methodological considerations. *Journal of Abnormal Psychology, 83,* 542–547.

Stern, J. (1987). The biochemical approach to mental handicap: 30 years of achievements and disappointments. *Journal of Mental Deficiency Research, 31,* 357–364.

Stern, R. S., & Cobb, J. P. (1978). Phenomenology of obsessive-compulsive neuroses. *British Journal of Psychiatry, 182,* 233–239.

Stern, R. S., Lipsedge, M. A., & Marks, I. M. (1973). Thought-stopping of neutral and obsessive thoughts: A controlled trial. *Behavior Research and Therapy, 11,* 659–662.

Stevens, E. V., & Salisbury, J. D. (1984). Group therapy for bulimic adults. *Archives of Orthopsychiatry, 54,* 156–161.

Stevens, J. (1987). Brief psychoses: Do they contribute to the good prognosis and equal prevalence of schizophrenia in developing countries. *British Journal of Psychiatry, 151,* 393–396.

Stevens, J., Mark, B., Erwin, F., Pacheco, P., & Suematsu, K. (1969). Deep temporal stimulation in man. *Archives of Neurology, 21,* 157–169.

Stevens, J. H., Turner, C. W., Rhodewalt, F., & Talbot, S. (1984). The type A behavior pattern and carotid artery atherosclerosis. *Psychosomatic Medicine, 46,* 105–113.

Stewart, R. S., Devous, M. D., Rush, A. J., Lane, L. & Bonte, F. J. (1988). Cerebral blood flow changes during sodium-lactate-induced panic attacks. *American Journal of Psychiatry, 145,* 442–449.

Stoller, R. J. (1969). Parental influences on male transsexualism. In R. Green & J. Money (Eds.), *Transsexualism and sex reassignment*. Baltimore: Johns Hopkins University Press.

Stoller, R. J., Marmor, J., Bieber, I., Gold, R., Socarides, C. W., Green, R., & Spitzer, R. I. (1973). A symposium: Should homosexuality be in the APA nomenclature? *American Journal of Psychiatry, 130*, 1207–1216.

Stone, A. A. (1975). *Mental health and law: A system in transition*. Rockville, MD: National Institute of Mental Health.

Strassberg, D. S., Kelly, M. P., Carroll, C., & Kirchner, J. C. (1987). The psychophysiological nature of premature ejaculation. *Archives of Sexual Behavior, 16*, 327–336.

Strassberg, D. S., Roback, H., Cunningham, J., McKee, E., & Larson, P. (1979). Psychopathology in self-identified female-to-male transsexuals, homosexuals, and heterosexuals. *Archives of Sexual Behavior, 8*, 491–496.

Stravynski, A. (1986). Indirect behavioral treatment of erectile failure and premature ejaculation in a man without a partner. *Archives of Sexual Behavior, 15*, 355–360.

Streissguth, A. P., Herman, C. S., & Smith, D. W. (1978). Intelligence, behavior and dysmorphogenesis in the fetal alcohol syndrome: A report on 20 patients. *Journal of Pediatrics, 92*, 363–368.

Streissguth, A. P., Landesman-Dwyer, S., Martin, J. C., & Smith, D. W. (1980). Teratogenic effects of alcohol in humans and laboratory animals. *Science, 209*, 353–361.

Stripling, S. (1986). Crossing over. *Seattle Post Intelligencer*, August 3, 1986, pp. K1–K2.

Stuart, F. M., Hammond, D. C., & Pett, M. A. (1987). Inhibited sexual desire in women. *Archives of Sexual Behavior, 16*, 91–106.

Sue, D. (1972). The role of relaxation in systematic desensitization. *Behaviour Research and Therapy, 10*, 153–158.

Sue, D. (1978). The use of masturbation in the in vivo treatment of impotence. *Journal of Behavior Therapy and Experimental Psychiatry, 9*, 75–76.

Sue, D. (1979). Erotic fantasies of college students during coitus. *Journal of Sex Research, 15*, 299–305.

Sue, D. W. (1975). Asian-Americans: Social-psychological forces affecting their lifestyles. In J. S. Picon & R. E. Campbell (Eds.), *Career behavior of special groups*. Columbus, OH: Merrill.

Sue, D. W. (1978). Eliminating cultural oppression in counseling: Toward a general theory. *Journal of Counseling Psychology, 25*, 419–428.

Sue, D. W. (1981). Counseling the culturally different: Theory and practice. New York: Wiley.

Sue, D. W., & Sue, D. (In press). *Counseling the culturally different: Theory and practice*. New York: Wiley.

Sue, S. (1973). The training of third world students to function as counselors. *Journal of Counseling Psychology, 20*, 73–78.

Sue, S. (1977). Community mental health services to minority groups: Some optimism, some pessimism. *American Psychologist, 32*, 616–624.

Sue, S., & Morishima, J. K. (1982). *The mental health of Asian Americans*. San Francisco: Jossey-Bass.

Sue, S., & Nakamura, C. Y. (1984). An integrative model of physiological and social/psychological factors in alcohol consumption among Chinese and Japanese Americans. *Journal of Drug Issues, 14*, 349–364.

Sue, S., & Sue, D. W. (1971). Chinese-American personality and mental health. *Amerasia Journal, 1*, 36–49.

Suicide belt. (1986, February 24). *Time, 116(9)*, 56.

Suinn, R. (1977). Anxiety management training for general anxiety. In R. Suinn & R. Weigel (Eds.), *The innovative psychological therapies: Critical and creative contributions*. San Francisco: Harper & Row.

Suinn, R. M. (1984). *Fundamentals of abnormal psychology*. Chicago: Nelson-Hall.

Sullivan, H. S. (1953). In H. S. Perry & M. L. Gawel (Eds.), *The interpersonal theory of psychiatry*. New York: Norton.

Sulser, F. (1979). Pharmacology: New cellular mechanisms of antidepressant drugs. In S. Fielding & R. C. Effland (Eds.), *New frontiers in psychotropic drug research*. Mount Kisco, NY: Futura.

Sundberg, N. D., Taplin, J. R., & Tyler, L. E. (1983). *Introduction to clinical psychology*. Englewood Cliffs, NJ: Prentice-Hall.

Surwit, R. S., Williams, R. B., & Shapiro, D. (Eds.). (1982). *Behavioral approaches to cardiovascular disease*. New York: Academic Press.

Sutker, P. B., & Allain, A. N. (1988). Issues in personality conceptualizations of addictive behaviors. *Journal of Consulting and Clinical Psychology, 56*, 172–182.

Swartz, M., Hughes, D., George, L., Blazer, D., Landerman, R., & Bucholz, K. (1986). Developing a screening index for community studies of somatization disorder. *Journal of Consulting and Clinical Psychology, 56*, 233–238.

Sweet, J. J. (1983). Confounding effects of depression on neuropsychological testing: Five illustrative cases. *Clinical Neuropsychology, 5*, 103–108.

Tal, A., & Miklich, D. R. (1976). Emotionally induced decreases in pulmonary flow rates in asthmatic children. *Psychosomatic Medicine, 38*, 190–200.

Tardiff, K. (1984). Characteristics of assaultive patients in private psychiatric hospitals. *American Journal of Psychiatry, 141*, 1232–1235.

Tardiff, K., & Koenigsberg, H. W. (1985). Assaultive behavior among psychiatric outpatients. *American Journal of Psychiatry, 142,* 960–963.

Tardiff, K., & Sweillam, A. (1982). Assaultive behavior among chronic inpatients. *American Journal of Psychiatry, 139,* 212–215.

Tarasoff vs. The Regents of the University of California, 17 Cal. 3d 435, 551 P.2d, 334, 131 Cal. Rptr. 14, 83 Ad. L. 3d 1166 (1976).

Tarrier, N. (1987). An investigation of residual psychotic symptoms in discharged schizophrenic patients. *British Journal of Clinical Psychology, 26,* 141–143.

Tavris, C. (1972, March). Woman and man. *Psychology Today,* pp. 57–64.

Taylor, S. E. (1983). Adjustments to threatening events: A theory of cognitive adaptation. *American Psychologist, 38,* 1161–1173.

Teen gets 30 years in Howard Beach case. (1988, January 23). *Oakland Tribune,* p. A4.

Telch, M. J., Tearnan, B. H., & Taylor, C. B. (1983). Antidepressant medication in the treatment of agoraphobia: A critical review. *Behaviour Research and Therapy, 21,* 505–517.

Teplin, L. A. (1983). The criminalization of the mentally ill: Speculation in search of data. *Psychological Bulletin, 94,* 54–67.

Terman, L. M. (1916). *The measurement of intelligence.* Boston: Houghton Mifflin.

Thiers, N. (1988, August 1). Murder rampant in America: Professionals respond. *Guidepost, 51,* pp. 1, 4, 5.

Thigpen, C. H., & Cleckley, H. (1957). *The three faces of Eve.* Kingsport, TN: Kingsport Press.

Thomas, A., Chess, S., & Birch, H. G. (1968). *Temperament and behavior disorders in children.* New York: New York University Press.

Thomas, A., & Sillen, S. (1972). *Racism and psychiatry.* New York: Brunner/Mazel.

Thompson, J. K. (1986). Larger than life. *Psychology Today, 20,* 39–44.

Thompson, N. L., McCandless, B. R., & Strickland, B. R. (1971). Personal adjustment of male and female homosexuals and heterosexuals. *Journal of American Psychology, 78,* 237–240.

Thorpe, G., & Burns, L. (1983). *The agoraphobic syndrome.* Chichester, England: Wiley.

Thyer, B. A. (1981). Prolonged in vivo exposure therapy with a 70-year-old woman. *Journal of Behavior Therapy and Experimental Psychiatry, 12,* 69–71.

Tienari, P. (1963). Psychiatric illness in identical twins. *Acta Psychiatrica Scandinavica, 39* (Suppl. 171).

Tierney, J. (1988, July 3). Research finds lower-level workers bear brunt of workplace stress. *Seattle Post Intelligencer,* pp. K1–K3.

Tizard, B. (1962). The personality of epileptics: A discussion of the evidence. *Psychological Bulletin, 59,* 1906–2010.

Tjosvold, D., & Tjosvold, M. M. (1983). Social psychological analysis of residences for mentally retarded persons. *American Journal of Mental Deficiency, 88,* 28–40.

Tobin, J. J., & Friedman, J. (1983). Spirits, shamans, and nightmare death: Survivor stress in a Hmong refugee. *American Journal of Orthopsychiatry, 53,* 439–448.

Torgersen, S. (1983). Genetic factors in anxiety disorders. *Archives of General Psychiatry, 40,* 1085–1089.

Toro, P. A. (1986). A comparison of natural and professional help. *American Journal of Community Psychology, 14,* 147–160.

Toufexis, A. (January 23, 1989). A not-so-happy anniversary. *Time,* p. 54.

Triandis, H. C. (1983). Essentials of studying cultures. In D. Landis & R. W. Brislin (Eds.), *Handbook of intercultural training.* New York: Pergamon Press.

Tsuang, M. T., Winokur, G., & Crowe, R. (1980). Morbidity risks of schizophrenia and affective disorders among first degree relatives of patients with schizophrenia, mania, depression, and surgical conditions. *British Journal of Psychiatry, 137,* 497–504.

Tuckman, J., Kleiner, R., & Lavell, M. (1959). Emotional content of suicide notes. *American Journal of Psychiatry, 16,* 59–63.

Turkington, C. (1987). Special talents. *Psychology Today,* pp. 42–46.

Turner, J. A. (1982). Comparison of group progressive-relaxation training and cognitive-behavioral therapy for chronic low back pain. *Journal of Consulting and Clinical Psychology, 50,* 757–765.

Turner, J. A., & Clancy, S. (1988). Comparison of operant behavioral and cognitive-behavioral group treatment for chronic low back pain. *Journal of Consulting and Clinical Psychology, 56,* 261–266.

Turner, S. M., Beidel, D. C., Nathan, R. S. (1985). Biological factors in obsessive-compulsive disorders. *Psychological Bulletin, 97,* 430–450.

Turner, S. M., Jacob, R. G., & Morrison, R. (1984). Somatoform and factitious disorders. In H. E. Adams and P. B. Sutker (Eds.), *Comprehensive handbook of psychiatry* (pp. 307–348). New York: Plenum Press.

Turner, W. J., & Merlis, A. (1962). Clinical correlations between electroencephalography and antisocial behavior. *Medical Times, 90,* 505–511.

Tyrer, P., Lee, I., & Alexander, J. (1980). Awareness of cardiac function in anxious, phobic, and hypochondriacal patients. *Psychological Medicine, 10,* 171–174.

Uhlenhuth, E. H., Balter, M. B., Mellinger, G. D., Cisin, I. H., & Clinthorne, J. (1983). Symptom checklist syndromes in the general population. *Archives of General Psychiatry, 40,* 1167–1173.

Ullmann, L. P., & Krasner, L. (1965). Introduction. In L. P. Ullmann & L. Krasner (Eds.), *Case studies in behavior modification*. New York: Holt, Rinehart and Winston.

Ullmann, L. P. & Krasner, L. (1975). *A psychological approach to abnormal behavior* (2nd ed.). Englewood Cliffs, NJ: Prentice-Hall.

University of Minnesota. (1977). *Epilepsy and the school age child*. Minneapolis, MN: State of Minnesota.

Vaillant, G. E. (1975). Sociopathy as a human process: A viewpoint. *Archives of General Psychiatry, 32*, 178–183.

Vaillant, G. E., & Milofsky, E. S. (1982). The etiology of alcoholism. *American Psychologist, 37*, 494–503.

Vaillant, G. E., & Perry, J. C. (1985). Personality disorders. In H. I. Kaplan & B. J. Sadock (Eds.), *Comprehensive textbook of psychiatry* (4th ed.) (pp. 958–986). Baltimore: Williams & Wilkins.

Van Der Molen, G. M., Van Den Hout, M. A., Vroemen, J., Lousberg, H., & Griez, E. (1986). Cognitive determinants of lactate-induced anxiety. *Behaviour Research and Therapy, 24*, 677–680.

Van Evra, J. P. (1983). *Psychological disorders of children and adolescents*. Boston: Little, Brown.

Van Pragg, H. M. (1983). CSF 5–H1AA and suicide in non-depressed schizophrenics, *Lancet, 2*, 977–978.

Van Putten, T., Philip, R. A., May, M. D., & Marder, S. R. (1984). Response to antipsychotic medication: The doctor's and the consumer's view. *American Journal of Psychiatry, 141*, 16–19.

Varni, J. W., Russo, D. C., & Cataldo, M. F. (1978). Assessment in modification of delusional speech in an 11–year-old child: A comparative analysis of behavior therapy and stimulant drug effect. *Journal of Behavior Therapy and Experimental Psychiatry, 9*, 377–380.

Vaughn, C., & Leff, J. (1981). Patterns of emotional response in relatives of schizophrenic patients. *Schizophrenia Bulletin, 7*, 43–45.

Velten, E. (1968). A laboratory task for induction of mood states. *Behaviour Research and Therapy, 6*, 473–482.

Visintainer, M. A., Volpicelli, J. R., & Seligman, M. E. P. (1982). Tumor rejection in rats after inescapable or escapable shock. *Science, 216*, 437–439.

Vogel, G., Vogel, F., McAbee, R., & Thurmond, A. (1980). Improvement of depression by REM sleep deprivation. *Archives of General Psychiatry, 37*, 247–253.

Vogler, R. E., & Bartz, W. R. (1983). *The better way to drink*. New York: Simon & Schuster.

Volkmar, F. R., Cicchetti, D. V., Dykens, E., Sparrow, S. S., Leckman, J. F., & Cohen, D. J. (1988). An evaluation of the Autism Behavior checklist. *Journal of Autism and Developmental Disorders, 18*, 81–97.

Volkow, N. D., Wolf, A. P., Van Gelder, P., Brodie, J. D., Overall, J. E., Camcro, R., & Gomez-Mont, F. (1987). Phenomenological correlates of metabolic activity in 18 patients with chronic schizophrenia. *American Journal of Psychiatry, 144*, 151–158.

Wachtel, P. L. (1977). *Psychoanalysis and behavior therapy*. New York: Basic Books.

Wachtel, P. L. (1982). Vicious circles: The self and the rhetoric of emerging and unfolding. *Contemporary Psychoanalysis, 18*, 280–282.

Wahba, M., Donlon, P. T., & Mendow, A. (1981). Cognitive changes in acute schizophrenia with brief neuroleptic treatment. *American Journal of Psychiatry, 138*, 1307–1310.

Wakefield, J. (1988). Female primary orgasmic dysfunctions: Masters and Johnson versus DSM-III-R on diagnosis and incidence. *Journal of Sex Research, 24*, 363–377.

Walder, C. P., McCraken, J. S., Herbert, M., James, P. T., & Brewitt, N. (1987). Psychological intervention in civilian flying phobia. *British Journal of Psychiatry, 151*, 494–498.

Walen, S., Hauserman, N. M., & Lavin, P. J. (1977). *Clinical guide to behavior therapy*. Baltimore: Williams & Wilkins.

Walker, H. M., Shinn, M. R., O'Neill, R. E., & Ramsey, E. (1987). A longitudinal assessment of the development of antisocial behavior in boys: Rationale, methodology, and first-year results. *Remedial and special education, 8*, 7–16.

Walker, N. (1968). *Crime and insanity in England: The historical perspective*. Edinburgh, Scotland: Edinburgh University Press.

Wallace, C., Nelson, C., Liberman, R., Aitchison, R., Lukoff, D., Elder, J., & Ferris, C. (1980). A review and critique of social skills training with schizophrenic patients. *Schizophrenia Bulletin, 6*, 42–64.

Ward, C. H., Beck, A. T., Mendelson, M., Mock, J. E., & Erbaught, J. K. (1962). The psychiatric nomenclature: Reasons for diagnostic disagreement. *Archives of General Psychiatry, 7*, 198–205.

Warner, R. (1986). Hard times and schizophrenia. *Psychology Today, 50–51*.

Warren, C. A. B. (1982). *The court as a last resort: Mental illness and the law*. Chicago: University of Chicago Press.

Warwick, H. M. C., & Marks, I. M. (1988). Behavioural treatment for illness phobia and hypochondriasis. *British Journal of Psychiatry, 152*, 239–241.

Wasserman, E., & Gromisch, D. (1981). *Survey of clinical pediatrics*. New York: McGraw-Hill.

Watkins, E. C., & Peterson, P. (1986). Psychiatric epidemiology: Its relevance for counselors. *Journal of Counseling and Development, 65,* 57–59.

Watson, C. G., & Buranen, C. (1979). The frequencies of conversion reaction symptoms. *Journal of Abnormal Psychology, 88,* 209–211.

Watson, J. B., & Rayner, R. (1920). Conditioned emotional responses. *Journal of Experimental Psychology, 3,* 1–14.

Weakland, J. H. (1960). The "double-bind" hypothesis of schizophrenia and three-party interaction. In D. D. Jackson (Ed.), *The etiology of schizophrenia.* New York: Basic Books.

Webster, J. S., & Scott, R. P. (1983). The effects of self-instruction training in attention deficit following head injury. *Clinical Neuropsychology, 5,* 69–74.

Wechsler, D. (1981a). Manual for the Wechsler Adult Intelligence Scale-Revised (WAIS-R). New York: Psychological Corporation.

Wechsler, D. (1981b). Wechsler Adult Intelligence Scale. New York: Harcourt, Brace, Jovanovich.

Weddington, W. W. (1979). Single case study: Conversion reaction in an 82-year-old man. *Journal of Nervous and Mental Diseases, 167,* 368–369.

Weeks, S. J., & Hobson, R. P. (1987). The salience for facial expression for autistic children. *Journal of Child Psychology and Psychiatry, 28,* 137–152.

Wehr, S. H., & Kaufman, M. E. (1987). The effects of assertive training on performance in highly anxious adolescents. *Adolescence, 22,* 195–205.

Weiden, P. J., Mann, J. J., Haas, G., Mattson, M., & Frances, A. (1987). Clinical nonrecognition of neuroleptic-induced movement disorders: A cautionary study. *American Journal of Psychiatry, 144,* 1148–1553.

Weile, E. F. (1960). On social psychological questions in suicidal personalities. *Psychological Research, 11,* 37–44.

Weiner, B. (1975). On being sane in insane places: A process (attributional) analysis and critique. *Journal of Abnormal Psychology, 84,* 433–441.

Weinberg, T. S. (1987). Sadomasochism in the United States: A review of recent sociological literature. *Journal of Sex Research, 23,* 50–69.

Weiner, B. A. (1985). Insanity evaluation. In S. J. Brakel, J. Parry, & B. A. Weiner (Eds.), *Mental disability and criminal law* (pp. 693–801). Chicago: American Bar Association.

Weiner, H., Thaler, M., Reisner, M. F., & Mirsky, I. A. (1957). Etiology of duodenal ulcer: 1. Relation of specific psychological characteristics to rate of gastric secretion. *Psychosomatic Medicine, 19,* 1–10.

Weiner, I. B. (Ed.) (1976). Individual psychotherapy. *Clinical Methods in Psychology.* New York: Wiley.

Weintraub, W. (1981). Compulsive and paranoid personalities. In J. R. Lion (Ed.), *Personality disorders: Diagnosis and management.* Baltimore: Williams & Wilkins.

Weiss, D. S. (1988). Personality assessment. In H. H. Goldman (Ed.), *Review of general psychiatry* (pp. 221–232). Norwalk, CT: Appleton and Lange.

Weiss, J. M., Glazer, H. I., & Pohorecky, L. A. (1975). Coping behavior and neurochemical changes: Alternative explanation for the original "learned helplessness" experiments. In G. Serban & A. Ling (Eds.), *Relevance of the animal model to the human.* New York: Plenum.

Weissberg, R. P., Cowen, E. L., Lotyczewski, B. S., & Gesten, E. L. (1983). The primary mental health project: Seven consecutive years of program outcome research. *Journal of Consulting and Clinical Psychology, 51,* 100–107.

Weissman, M. M., & Klerman, G. L. (1977). Sex differences and the epidemiology of depression. *Archives of General Psychiatry, 34,* 98–111.

Weitz, S. (1977). *Sex roles: Biological, psychological, and social foundations.* New York: Oxford University Press.

Welgan, P. R. (1974). Learned control of gastric acid secretions in ulcer patients. *Psychosomatic Medicine, 36,* 411–419.

Wells, C. E. (1978). Role of stroke in dementia. *Stroke, 9,* 1–3.

Wells, C. E. (1985). Organic syndromes: Delirium. In H. I. Kaplan & B. J. Sadock (Eds.), *Comprehensive textbook of psychiatry/IV* (pp. 838–851). Baltimore: Williams & Wilkins.

Wender, P. H., & Klein, D. F. (1981, February). The promise of biological psychiatry. *Psychology Today,* pp. 25–41.

Wender, P. H., Rosenthal, D., Rainer, J. D., Greenbill, L., & Sarlan, M. B. (1977). Schizophrenics' adopting parents. *Archives of General Psychiatry, 34,* pp. 777–784.

Werner, A. (1975). Sexual dysfunction in college men and women. *American Journal of Psychiatry, 132,* 164–168.

Werry, J. S., Methuen, R. J., & Fitzpatrick, J. (1983). The interrater reliability of DSM-III in children. *Journal of Abnormal Child Psychology, 11,* 341–354.

Westermeyer, J. (1987). Public health and chronic mental illness. *American Journal of Public Health, 77,* 667–668.

Wexler, L., Weissman, M. M., & Kasl, S. V. (1978). Suicide attempts 1970–1975: Updating a United States study and comparison with international trends. *British Journal of Psychiatry, 132,* 180–185.

Wheat, W. D. (1960). Motivational aspects of suicide in patients during and after psychiatric treatment. *Southern Medical Journal, 53,* 273.

White, J. L. (1984). *The psychology of blacks.* Englewood Cliffs, NJ: Prentice-Hall.

White, M. (1983). Anorexia nervosa: A transgenerational system perspective. *Family Process, 22,* 255–273.

Whitehead, W. E., Winget, C., Fedoravicius, A. S., Wooley, S., & Blackwell, B. (1982). Learned illness behavior in patients with irritable bowel syndrome and peptic ulcer. *Digestive Diseases and Sciences, 27,* 202–208.

Whitehill, M., DeMeyer-Gapin, S., & Scott, T. J. (1976). Stimulus seeking in antisocial preadolescent children. *Journal of Abnormal Psychology, 85,* 101–104.

Whitman, B. Y., Graves, B., & Accardo, P. (1987). Mentally retarded parents in the community: Identification method and needs assessment survey. *American Journal of Mental Deficiency, 91,* 636–638.

Wickramasekera, I. (1976). Aversive behavior rehearsal for sexual exhibitionism. *Behavioral Therapy, 7,* 167–176.

Widom, C. S. (1976). Interpersonal and personal construct systems in psychopaths. *Journal of Consulting and Clinical Psychology, 44,* 614–623.

Wiens, A. N. (1983). The assessment interview. In I. B. Weiner (Ed.), *Clinical methods in psychology.* New York: John Wiley.

Wiggins, J. (1979). Attractive notion. *APA Monitor, 10,* 2.

Wild, C. (1965). Creativity and adaptive regression. *Journal of Personality and Social Psychology, 2,* 161–169.

Wilding, T. (1984). Is stress making you sick? *American Health, 6,* 2–5.

Williams, J. B., & Spitzer, R. L. (1983). The issue of sex bias in DSM-III: A critique of "A woman's view of DSM-III" by Marcie Kaplan. *American Psychologist, 38,* 793–799.

Williams, J. H. (1977). *Psychology of women: Behavior in a biosocial context.* New York: Norton.

Williams, J. M. (1984). Cognitive-behaviour therapy for depression: Problems and perspectives. *British Journal of Psychiatry, 145,* 254–262.

Williams, R. (1974). The problem of match and mismatch. In L. Miller (Ed.), *The testing of black children.* Englewood Cliffs, NJ: Prentice-Hall.

Williams, R. B., Benson, H., & Follick, M. J. (1985). To the editor. *New England Journal of Medicine, 312,* 1356–1357.

Williams, R. B., Jr., Barefoot, J. C., Haney, T. L., Harrell, F. E., Jr., Blumenthal, J. A., Pryor, D. B., & Peterson, B. (1988). Type A behavior and angiographically documented coronary atherosclerosis in a sample of 2,289 patients. *Psychosomatic Medicine, 50,* 139–152.

Willis, M. J. (1982). The impact of schizophrenia on families: One mother's point of view. *Schizophrenia Bulletin, 8,* 617–619.

Willison, G., & Masson, R. (1986). The role of touch in therapy: An adjunct to communications. *Journal of Counseling and Development, 65,* 497–500.

Wilson, G. T., & O'Leary, K. D. (1980). *Principles of behavior therapy.* Englewood Cliffs, NJ: Prentice-Hall.

Wilson, M. S., & Meyer, E. (1962). Diagnostic consistency in a psychiatric liaison service. *American Journal of Psychiatry, 19,* 207–209.

Wilson, P. (1982). Combined pharmacological and behavioural treatment of depression. *Behaviour Research and Therapy, 20,* 173–184.

Wincze, J. P., Bansal, S., & Malamud, M. (1986). Effects of medrox progesterone acetate on subjective arousal, arousal to erotic stimulation, and nocturnal penile tumescence in male sex offenders. *Archives of Sexual Behavior, 15,* 293–305.

Wincze, J. P., Hoon, E. F., & Hoon, P. W. (1978). Multiple measure analysis of women experiencing low sexual arousal. *Behaviour Research and Therapy, 16,* 43–49.

Wing, J. K. (1980). Social psychiatry in the United Kingdom: The approach to schizophrenia. *Schizophrenia Bulletin, 6,* 557–565.

Wing, L., & Gould, J. (1979). Severe impairment of social interaction and associated abnormalities in children: Epidemiology and classification. *Journal of Autism and Developmental Disorders, 9,* 11–29.

Winnett, R. L., Bornstein, P. H., Cogsuell, K. A., & Paris, A. E. (1987). Cognitive-behavioral therapy for childhood depression: A levels-of-treatment approach. *Journal of Child and Adolescent Psychotherapy, 4,* 283–286.

Winokur, G., Clayton, P. J., & Reich, T. (1969). *Manic depressive illness.* St. Louis: Mosby.

Winokur, G., Reich, T., Rimmer, J., & Pitts, F. (1970). Alcoholism III: Diagnosis and familial psychiatric illness in 259 alcoholic probands. *Archives of General Psychiatry, 23,* 104–111.

Wittkower, E. C., & Rin, H. (1965). Cultural psychiatric research. In W. Caudell & T. Lin (Eds.), *Mental health research in Asia and the Pacific.* Honolulu: East-West Center Press.

Wolf, L. E. M., & Crowther, J. H. (1983). Personality and eating habit variables as predictors of severity of binge eating and weight. *Addictive Behavior, 8,* 335–344.

Wolfensberger, W. (1988). Common assets of mentally retarded people that are commonly not acknowledged. *Mental Retardation, 26,* 63–70.

Wolkin, A., Angrist, B., Wolf, A., Brodie, J. D., Wolkin, B., Jaeger, J., Camcro, R., & Retrosen, J. (1988). Low frontal glucose utilization in chronic schizophrenia: A replication study. *American Journal of Psychiatry, 145,* 251–253.

Wolpe, J. (1958). *Psychotherapy by reciprocal inhibition.* Stanford, CA: Stanford University Press.

Wolpe, J. (1973). *The practice of behavior therapy.* New York: Pergamon.

Wolpe, J. (1982). *The practice of behavior therapy* (3rd ed.). Elmsford, NY: Pergamon Press.

Wood, C. (1986). The hostile heart. *Psychology Today, 20,* 10–12.

World Health Organization. (1973a). *Manual of the international statistical classification of diseases, injuries and causes of death* (Vol. 1). Geneva: World Health Organization.

World Health Organization. (1973b). *Report on the international pilot study of schizophrenia* (Vol. 1). Geneva: World Health Organization.

World Health Organization. (1981). *Current state of diagnosis and classification in the mental health field.* Geneva: World Health Organization.

World Health Organization. (1987). The Dexamethasone Suppression Test in depression. *British Journal of Psychiatry, 150,* 459–462.

Wright, L. (1978). A method for predicting sequelae to meningitis. *American Psychologist, 33,* 1037–1039.

Wrightsman, L. S. (1972). *Social psychology in the seventies.* Monterey, CA: Brooks/Cole.

Wyler, A. R., Masuda, M., & Holmes, T. H. (1971). Magnitude of the life events and seriousness of illness. *Journal of Psychosomatic Medicine, 33,* 115–122.

Yager, J., Landsverk, J., & Edelstein, C. K. (1987). A 20-month follow-up of 628 women with eating disorders, I: Course and severity. *American Journal of Psychiatry, 144,* 1172–1177.

Yalom, I. D. (1970). *The theory and practice of group psychotherapy.* New York: Basic Books.

Yarnold, P. R., & Grimm, L. G. (1982). Time urgency among coronary-prone individuals. *Journal of Abnormal Psychology, 91,* 175–177.

Yates, A. J. (1970). Behavior Therapy. New York: Wiley & Sons.

Yates, A. (1983). Behavior therapy and psychodynamic psychotherapy: Basic conflict or reconciliation and integration? *British Journal of Clinical Psychology, 22,* 107–125.

Yates, A. J. (1958). The application of learning theory to the treatment of tics. *Journal of Abnormal and Social Psychology, 56,* 175–182.

York, D., Borkovec, T. D., Lasey, M., & Stern, R. (1987). Effects of worry and somatic anxiety induction on thoughts, emotion, and physiological activity. *Behaviour Research and Therapy, 25,* 523–526.

Young, M. (1980). Attitudes and behavior of college students relative to oral-genital sexuality. *Archives of Sexual Behavior, 9,* 61–67.

Youngren, M., & Lewinsohn, P. M. (1978). The functional relationship between depression and problematic interpersonal behavior. *Journal of Abnormal Psychology, 89,* 333–341.

Yu-Fen, H., & Neng, T. (1981). Transcultural investigation of recent symptomatology of schizophrenia in China. *American Journal of Psychiatry, 138,* 1484–1486.

Yurchenco, H. (1970). *A mighty hard road: The Woody Guthrie story.* New York: McGraw-Hill.

Zajonc, R. B. (1975). Birth order and intelligence: Dumber by the dozen. *Psychology Today, 8,* 37–43.

Zantal-Weiner, K. (1988). Early intervention services for pre-school children. *Teaching Exceptional Children,* pp. 61–62.

Zax, M., & Cowen, E. L. (1972). *Abnormal psychology.* New York: Holt, Rinehart & Winston.

Zax, M., & Spector, G. A. (1974). *An introduction to community psychology.* New York: Wiley.

Zeiss, A. M., Rosen, G. M., & Zeiss, R. A. (1977). Orgasm during intercourse: A treatment strategy for women. *Journal of Consulting and Clinical Psychology, 45,* 891–895.

Zeiss, R. A. (1977). Self-directed treatment for premature ejaculation: Preliminary case reports. *Journal of Behavior Therapy and Experimental Psychiatry, 8,* 87–91.

Zelt, D. (1981). First person account: The messiah quest. *Schizophrenia Bulletin, 7,* 527–531.

Zentall, S. S., & Zentall, T. R. (1983). Optimal stimulation: A model of disordered activity and performance in normal and deviant children. *Psychological Bulletin, 94,* 446–471.

Zerbin-Rudin, E. Genetic research and the theory of schizophrenia. *International Journal of Mental Health, 1,* 42–62.

Zigler, E. (1967). Familial mental retardation: A continuing dilemma. *Science, 155,* 292–298.

Zigler, E., & Bergman, W. (1983). Discerning the future of early childhood intervention. *American Psychologist, 38,* 893–905.

Zigman, W. B., Schupf, N., Lubin, R. A., & Silverman, W. P. (1987). Premature regression of adults with Down syndrome. *American Journal of Mental Deficiency, 92,* 161–168.

Zilbergeld, B. (1983). *The shrinking of America.* Boston: Little, Brown.

Zilboorg, G., & Henry, G. W. (1941). *A history of medical psychology.* New York: Norton.

Zimbardo, P. (1977). *Shyness: What is it, what to do about it*. Reading, MA: Addison-Wesley.

Zito, J. M., Craig, T. J., Wanderling, J., & Siegel, C. (1987). Pharmaco-epidemiology in 136 hospitalized schizophrenic patients. *American Journal of Psychiatry, 144,* 778–782.

Zubin, J. (1978). But is it good for science? *Clinical Psychologist, 31*(1), 5–7.

Zubin, J., & Ludwig, A. M. (1983). What is schizophrenia? *Schizophrenia Bulletin, 9,* 331–334.

Zubin, J., & Spring, B. (1977). Vulnerability—a new view of schizophrenia. *Journal of Abnormal Psychology, 86,* 103–126.

Zuger, B. (1984). Early effeminate behavior in boys: Outcome and significance for homosexuality. *Journal of Nervous and Mental Disease, 172,* 90–97.

Zuger, B. (1987). Childhood cross-gender behavior and adult homosexuality. *Archives of Sexual Behavior, 16,* 85–87.

Zullow, H. M., Oettingen, G., Peterson, C., & Seligman, M. E. (1988). Pessimistic explanatory style in the historical record: Caving LBJ, presidential candidates, and East versus West Berlin. *American Psychologist, 43,* 673–682.

Zverina, J., Lachman, M., Pondelickova, J., & Vanek, J. (1987). The occurrence of atypical sexual experience among various female patient groups. *Archives of Sexual Behavior, 16,* 321–326.

Credits

CHAPTER 8

p. 205 © The Stock Market/Chris Sorensen   p. 207 (*left*) Cliff Peulner/The Image Bank; (*right*) © The Stock Market/Jon Reis   **Figure 8.1** Adapted from Rahe, R. H., & Arthur, R. J. (1978). Life change and illness studies: Past history and future directions. *Journal of Human Stress, 4,* 3–15. Reprinted by permission.   p. 210 Beth Ullman/Taurus Photos, Inc. p. 213 Stuart Cohen/Stock, Boston   p. 216 © The Stock Market/R. B. Sanchez   **Table 8.1** Adapted from *Ulcers* by Michael M. Eisenberg, M. D. Copyright © 1968 by Michael M. Eisenberg, M. D. Reprinted by permission of Random House, Inc.   **Figure 8.2** From Newsweek on Health, Spring 1988. © 1988 Newsweek, Inc. All rights reserved. Reprinted by permission.   **Table 8.2** Adapted from Alexander, F. (1950). *Psychosomatic medicine.* New York: Norton.   p. 223 Eric Knoll/Taurus Photos, Inc.

CHAPTER 9

p. 233 Susan Rosenberg/Photo Researchers, Inc. p. 235 © Andrew Brilliant   p. 239 © Dan McCoy/Rainbow   p. 245 Esaias Bartel/Rapho/Photo Researchers, Inc.   p. 248 Guy Savage/Photo Researchers, Inc. **Figure 9.1** Reprinted from *1964 Nebraska Symposium on Motivation,* by permission of University of Nebraska Press. Copyright © 1964 by The University of Nebraska Press.   **Figure 9.2** Schmauk, F. J. (1970). Punishment, arousal, and avoidance learning. *Journal of Abnormal Psychology, 76,* 325–335. Copyright © 1970 by the American Psychological Association. Reprinted by permission of the author.   p. 253 George A. Dillon/Stock, Boston p. 254 Michael Weisbrot and Family/Stock, Boston

CHAPTER 10

p. 262 Mieke Maas/The Image Bank   **Table 10.1** Adapted from Vogler, R. E., and Bartz, W. R. (1983). *A better way to drink.* New York: Simon & Schuster. Copyright © 1983 by Robert E. Vogler and Wayne R. Bartz. Reprinted by permission of Simon & Schuster, Inc.   p. 265 Martin Rogers/Stock, Boston   p. 270 Robert Pacheco/EKM-Nepenthe p. 272 Excerpts from "The Expanding Scope of Alcoholism Treatment Evaluation," by Moos and Finney, *American Psychologist, 38,* 1036–1044. Copyright 1983 by the American Psychological Association. Reprinted by permission. p. 277 Jon Feingersh/Stock, Boston   **Focus 10.3** Lichtenstein, "The Smoking Problem." *Journal of Consulting and Clinical Psychology, 50,* 804–819. Copyright 1982 by the American Psychological Association. Adapted by permission of the author.   **Table 10.4** Milla and Noyes, "Initial and Subsequent Drug Use Among Adolescents." *Journal of Consulting and Clinical Psychology, 52,* 231–243 (1984). Copyright 1984 by the American Psychological Association. Adapted by permission of the authors.   **Table 10.5** Solomon, "The Opponent Process Theory of Acquired Motivation." *American Psychologist,* vol. 35, pp. 691–718. Copyright 1980 by the American Psychological Association. Reprinted by permission of the author. p. 285 © The Stock Market/Palmer/Kane, Inc., 1977

CHAPTER 11

p. 291 (*left*) AP/Wide World Photos; (*right*) AP/Wide World Photos   **Table 11.1** Bernard Zuger, "Early Effeminate Behavior in Boys: Outcome and Significance for Homosexuality." *Journal of Nervous and Mental Disease,* February 1984, vol.

172, p. 93. © 1984 The Williams & Wilkins Co., Baltimore. Used by permission.   p. 297 Brian Drake/EKM-Nepenthe   p. 298 Miro Vintoniv/The Picture Cube p. 299 Jim Pickerell/Stock, Boston   p. 305 Bettye Lane/Photo Researchers, Inc.   p. 309 Ed Lettau Studio, Inc./Photo Researchers, Inc.   p. 313 UPI/Bettmann Newsphotos p. 317 Summer Productions/Taurus Photos, Inc.

CHAPTER 12

Table 12.1 Adapted from Mendels, J. (1970). *Concepts of depression.* New York: Wiley. Reprinted by permission. p. 328 © The Stock Market/Richard Dunoff p. 331 Giraudon/Art Resource   p. 337 © Dan McCoy/Rainbow   **Table 12.2** Adapted from Seligman, Martin E. P. (1975). *Helplessness: On depression, development, and death.* San Francisco: W. H. Freeman, p. 106. Used by permission of the publisher.   p. 340 Peter Bates/The Picture Cube p. 345 Will McIntyre/Photo Researchers, Inc. **Focus 12.3** From *Holiday of Darkness* by Norman S. Endler. Reprinted by permission of John Wiley & Sons, Inc. Copyright 1982 by John Wiley & Sons, Inc.   **Figure 12.1** After A. T. Beck, R. Laude, and M. Bohnert, "Ideational components of anxiety neurosis," *Archives of General Psychiatry, 31* (1974), 319–325. Copyright 1974, American Medical Association.

CHAPTER 13

p. 356 Topham/The Image Works, Inc.   p. 359 UPI/Bettmann Newsphotos   p. 360 Carroll Seghers II/Photo Researchers, Inc.   p. 361 Oscar Palmquist/Lightwave p. 364 UPI/Bettmann Newsphotos   p. 367 © Linda Moore/Rainbow   p. 369 George W. Gardner/Stock, Boston

CHAPTER 14

p. 375 Prinzhorn-Sammlung/Foto:Klinger   **Focus 14.1** From *International Pilot Study of Schizophrenia,* World Health Organization 1973, 1981. Reprinted by permission. p. 380 Prinzhorn-Sammlung/Foto:Klinger   p. 381 Prinzhorn-Sammlung/Foto:Klinger   p. 382 Michael Weisbrot and Family   p. 383 E. S. Beckwith/Taurus Photos, Inc. p. 385 Giraudon/Art Resource, © ARS N.Y./SPADEM, 1989   p. 386 Prinzhorn-Sammlung/Foto:Klinger p. 387 Prinzhorn-Sammlung/Foto:Klinger p. 392 Prinzhorn-Sammlung/Foto:Klinger

CHAPTER 15

Table 15.1 "Risk of Schizophrenia Among Blood Relatives of Schizophrenics." From *The Nature of Schizophrenia: New Approaches to Research and Treatment,* L. C. Wynne, R. L. Cromwell, S. Matthysse (Eds.). Copyright © 1978 by John Wiley & Sons, Inc. Reprinted by permission of John Wiley & Sons, Inc.   p. 398 Alan Becker/The Image Bank   p. 400 AP/Wide World Photos   **Table 15.3** From Heston, *British Journal of Psychiatry,* vol. 112, 819–825 (1966). Reprinted by permission.   **Figure 15.1** Mednick (1970). *Mental Hygiene, 54,* National Mental Health Association. Reprinted by permission.   p. 406 University of California, Irvine/Peter Arnold, Inc.   p. 407 © James Carroll   p. 410 Excerpts from "Brief Psychoses: Do They Contribute to the Good Prognosis and Equal Prevalence of Schizophrenia in Developing Countries?" by J. Stevens. *British Journal of Psychiatry, 151,* pp. 393–396 (1987). Reprinted by permission.   p. 415 James Prince/Photo Researchers, Inc.

CHAPTER 16

p. 425 © Steve Chenn/West Light   p. 426 NIH/Science Source/Photo Researchers, Inc.   p. 427 (top) Table 16.1 Golden, C. J., et al. Difference in brain densities between chronic alcoholic and normal control patients. *Science, 211*, 508–510, Table 30, January 1981. Copyright © 1981 by the American Association for the Advancement of Science. Used by permission. (bottom) © Dan McCoy/Rainbow p. 432 Frank Siteman/The Picture Cube p. 435 Marianne Gontarz/The Picture Cube p. 436 Smyer, M. A. (1984). Life transitions and aging: Implications for older adults. *The Counseling Psychologist, 12*, 17–28. Copyright © 1984 by Sage Publications, Inc. Reprinted by permission of Sage Publications, Inc.   p. 437 Butler, R. N. (1984). Senile dementia: Reversible and irreversible. *The Counseling Psychologist, 12*, 75–79. Copyright © 1984 by Sage Publications, Inc. Reprinted by permission of Sage Publications, Inc.   p. 441 Giraudon/Art Resource   p. 444 Peter Menzel/Stock, Boston

CHAPTER 17

p. 448 Reprinted from "Adult Recollections of a Formerly Autistic Child" by J. R. Bemporad, *Journal of Autism and Developmental Disorders*, Vol. 9. By permission of Plenum Publishing Corporation.   Table 17.1 From "Autism and Childhood Psychosis" by C. Lord and M. J. Ward in *Comprehensive Handbook of Psychopathology* (1984), H. E. Adams and P. B. Sutker (Eds.), pp. 973–1000. Reprinted by permission of Plenum Publishing Corporation and the author.   p. 449 Alan Carey/The Image Works, Inc.   p. 450 Michael Weisbrot and Family/Stock, Boston   p. 451 AP/Wide World Photos Focus 17.1 Abridged from "Original 'Rain Man' Proud to Be Movie's Inspiration" by Hilary Israelsen. Reprinted by permission of Associated Press Newsfeatures.   p. 457 Alan Carey/The Image Works, Inc.   p. 461 Michael Weisbrot and Family   p. 464 Adolahe/Southern Light   Table 17.2 From "Crime in the Family Tree" by S. A. Mednick (1985). Reprinted with permission from *Psychology Today* Magazine. Copyright © 1985 (PT Partners, L. P.)   p. 468 Bob Daemmrich/Stock, Boston   p. 469 Steve Weber/Stock, Boston   p. 473 Susan Rosenberg/Photo Researchers, Inc.   p. 475 Miro Vintoniv/The Picture Cube

CHAPTER 18

p. 481 Alan Carey/The Image Works, Inc.
Figure 18.1 Zigler, E. (1967). Familial mental retardation: A continuing dilemma. *Science, 155*, 292–298, Fig. 20. Copyright © 1967 by the American Association for the Advancement of Science. Reprinted by permission.   p. 487 Mel Diagiacomo/The Image Bank   p. 488 SIU/Peter Arnold, Inc. p. 491 Michael Siluk/EKM-Nepenthe   p. 492 © Carol Palmer   p. 493 John Pennington/The Picture Cube p. 496 Mark M. Walker/The Picture Cube Focus 18.4 From Kupfer, F. (1982, December 13). My turn: Institution is not a dirty word. *Newsweek*, p. 13. Copyright © 1982 by Newsweek, Inc. All rights reserved. Reprinted by permission of the author.

CHAPTER 19

p. 505 Culver Pictures   p. 509 Michael Weisbrot and Family   p. 511 SIU/Peter Arnold, Inc.   Focus 19.1 From *Counseling the Culturally Different* by D. W. Sue. Copyright © 1981 by D. W. Sue. Reprinted by permission of John Wiley & Sons, Inc.   p. 514 Nimatallah/Art Resource, © C. Herscovici/ARS N.Y., 1989   Table 19.2 Adapted from Paul, G. L. (1967). Insight versus Desensitization in Psychotherapy Two Years after Termination. *Journal of Consulting Psychology, 31*, 333–348. Copyright © 1967 by American Psychological Association. Reprinted with permission.   p. 517 Photo by Deke Simon   p. 521 © Jerry Bauer   p. 528 Stacy Pick/Stock, Boston   p. 530 Bob Daemmrich/Stock, Boston

CHAPTER 20

p. 545 Eric Roth/The Picture Cube   p. 549 Elizabeth Crews/The Image Works, Inc.   p. 550 Alec Duncan/Taurus Photos, Inc.   p. 552 Michael Weisbrot and Family/Stock, Boston   p. 554 Judy Canty/Stock, Boston   p. 556 James H. Karales/Peter Arnold, Inc.   p. 559 Laurie Cameron/Stock, Boston   p. 560 Bohdan Hrynewych/Southern Light p. 563 © Charles O'Rear/West Light

CHAPTER 21

p. 569 UPI/Bettmann Newsphotos   p. 571 © The Stock Market/John Maher   p. 573 Photofest   p. 575 John Bunyea/Southern Light   p. 578 Will & Deni McIntyre/Photo Researchers, Inc.   p. 580 Adapted from *Issues and Ethics in the Helping Professions*, 2nd. Ed., by G. Corey, M. Morey and P. Callahan. Copyright © 1984, 1979 by Wadsworth, Inc. Reprinted by permission of Brooks/Cole Publishing Company, Pacific Grove, CA 93950.   p. 581 AP/Wide World Photos   p. 583 Louis Fernandez/Black Star

Name Index

Subject Index

STUDENT EVALUATION OF **UNDERSTANDING ABNORMAL BEHAVIOR**, THIRD EDITION, BY SUE, SUE, AND SUE

Your comments on this book will help us in developing other new textbooks and future editions of this book. Please answer the following questions and mail this page to:

College Marketing Services
Houghton Mifflin Company
One Beacon Street
Boston, MA 02108

1. What was your overall impression of the text? _____

_____

2. Did you find the book easy to read and understand? ☐ Yes ☐ No

   If not, what problems did you have? _____

_____

3. Did the tables, graphs, and figures clarify the text in a useful way?

_____

4. How would you rate the following features of the text?

	Excellent	Very good	Good	Fair	Poor
Interest level	☐	☐	☐	☐	☐
Definitions of terms	☐	☐	☐	☐	☐
Explanations of psychological concepts	☐	☐	☐	☐	☐
Descriptions of theories and research	☐	☐	☐	☐	☐
Discussion of symptoms of disorders	☐	☐	☐	☐	☐
Descriptions of the etiology of abnormal behavior	☐	☐	☐	☐	☐
Descriptions of the treatment of abnormal behavior	☐	☐	☐	☐	☐
Clinical cases	☐	☐	☐	☐	☐
Extended Steven V. case	☐	☐	☐	☐	☐
Focus boxes	☐	☐	☐	☐	☐
"First Person" mini-essays	☐	☐	☐	☐	☐
Disorder charts	☐	☐	☐	☐	☐

Feel free to comment on any of the above items. _____

_____

5. Which chapters were required reading for your class? _____

_____

6. Did you read any chapters on your own that were not required reading?

_____

7. Did your instructor assign any additional books for this course? □ Yes □ No

If so, what were they? _____

8. Did you find the key terms and glossary useful? _____

_____

9. Do you have any suggestions that might help make this a better textbook?

_____

Name of your school: _____

Course title: _____

Number of students in the class: _____

Your age: _____

Your major: _____

Thank You!